Principles of
BUSINESS LAW
and the
LEGAL ENVIRONMENT

Principles of
BUSINESS LAW
and the
LEGAL ENVIRONMENT

Joseph L. Frascona, J.D.
University of Colorado, Professor Emeritus

Contributing Authors

Edward J. Conry, J.D.
University of Colorado at Denver

Gerald R. Ferrera, J.D.
Bentley College

Terry L. Lantry, J.D.
Colorado State University

Bill M. Shaw, J.D., LL.M.
The University of Texas at Austin

George J. Siedel, J.D., D.C.L.S.
The University of Michigan

George W. Spiro, J.D.
University of Massachusetts at Amherst

Arthur D. Wolfe, J.D.
Michigan State University

Allyn and Bacon, Inc.
Boston · London · Sydney · Toronto

Copyright © 1988 by Allyn and Bacon, Inc.
A Division of Simon & Schuster
160 Gould Street
Needham Heights, Massachusetts 02194–2310

All rights reserved. No part of the material protected by this copyright notice may be reproduced or utilized in any form or by any means, electronic or mechanical, including photocopying, recording, or by any information storage and retrieval system, without the written permission of the copyright owner.

Library of Congress Cataloging-in-Publication Data

Principles of business law and legal environment.

    Includes index.
    1. Commercial law—United States.   I. Frascona,
Joseph Lohengrin.
KF889.P75 1988   346.73′07   87-71347
ISBN 0-205-11568-3   347.3067

Printed in the United States of America
10 9 8 7 6 5 4 3 2 1 92 91 90 89 88 87

to Students

The Authors

Joseph L. Frascona, J.D.
Professor Emeritus of Business Law at the University of Colorado, formerly a member of its faculty teaching Legal Issues for Executives in its Executive M.B.A. Program, and the past Director of the Graduate School of Banking at Colorado. He is a member of the New York, Colorado, and Federal Bars; a past president of the American Business Law Association; a member of the Rocky Mountain Business Law Association; and is on the Commercial Arbitration Panel of the American Arbitration Association. Professor Frascona was formerly an Associate Attorney in the Office of the Attorney General of the United States and General Counsel to the Office of the Foreign Liquidation Commission, U.S. Department of State, in England. He is the author of numerous books and articles on business law and international law; many articles are in the current edition of *Encyclopedia Americana*. Presently, he is a legal consultant to business and industry, and is Of Counsel to the law firm of Frascona, McClow & Joiner. He earned a B.S. from City College, City University of New York, and a J.D. from Harvard University.

Edward J. Conry, J.D.
Associate Professor of Business Law and Ethics, University of Colorado at Denver. He has both worked in and served as a consultant to business, and he has written extensively on consumerism and real estate topics. Professor Conry is a past president of the Rocky Mountain Business Law Association, a former member of the governing body of the American Business Law Association, has served as a reviewer for the *American Business Law Journal,* and is the author of numerous books and articles. During 1981–1982 he was the Research Fellow in Business Ethics at Yale University. He has a B.A. from California State University at Fullerton, an M.B.A. from the University of California, Berkeley, and a J.D. from the University of California, Davis.

Gerald R. Ferrera, J.D.
Professor of Business Law and Chairman of the Law Department, Bentley College. He is a past president of the North Atlantic Regional Business Law Association and was Editor-in-Chief of the *North Atlantic Regional Business Law Review*. He is a co-author of a book on business law and the author of numerous articles on business law. Under a grant from the National Endowment for the Humanities, Professor Ferrera developed an interdisciplinary course on "Law and Philosophy." He is a legal consultant to professional and business associations and is a member of the Massachusetts and Federal Bars. Professor Ferrera earned his B.S. from Boston College, an M.S. in Taxation from Bentley College, and a J.D. from the New England School of Law.

Terry L. Lantry, J.D.
Professor of Accounting and Business Law at Colorado State University. He is a member of the Colorado and Indiana State Societies of Certified Public Accountants and of the Colorado, Indiana, and Federal Bars. He is a past president of the American Business Law Association. Professor Lantry is the author or co-author of numerous articles, monographs, and textbooks. He has a B.A. and J.D. from Valparaiso University and an M.B.A. from Indiana University.

Bill Shaw, J.D., LL.M.
Professor of Business Law at The University of Texas at Austin. He is particularly interested in environmental law and corporate social responsibility and has written extensively on these topics. Professor Shaw is a staff editor of the *American Business Law Journal*, former president of the Southern Business Law Association, and on the Arbitration Panel of the American Arbitration Association, among other professional associations. He is a member of the Texas and Louisiana Bars. He earned a B.S. and M.B.A. at Louisiana Tech University, a J.D. at Tulane University, and an LL.M. at the University of Texas at Austin.

George J. Siedel, J.D., D.C.L.S.
Professor of Business Law at The University of Michigan. He is Chief Editor of the *Michigan Real Property Review* and has served as a staff editor of the *American Business Law Journal*. The author of numerous books and articles, Professor Siedel has received the Award of Excellence for the best paper presented at the Midwest Business Law Association Annual Meeting, and the 1981 University of Michigan Faculty Recognition Award for teaching and research. He has served as Visiting Professor of Business Law at Stanford University and has been elected a Visiting Fellow of Wolfson College, Cambridge University, England. Professor Siedel has a B.A. from The College of Wooster, a J.D. from The University of Michigan, and a Diploma in Comparative Legal Studies from Cambridge University, England.

George W. Spiro, J.D.
Acting Dean of the School of Management, and Professor of Business Law and Management at the University of Massachusetts at Amherst. He specializes in labor relations and labor studies and has written primarily on the interfaces of law, management theory, jurisprudence, and labor studies. Professor Spiro has a B.S. in Personnel and Industrial Relations and an M.S. in Labor Studies from the University of Massachusetts at Amherst, and a J.D. from Syracuse University.

Arthur D. Wolfe, J.D.
Professor of Business Law at Michigan State University. He is past president of the Tri-State Regional Business Law Association and has served on the Editorial Board of the American Business Law Journal for 10 years and was Editor-In-Chief in 1984–85. Together with Professor Bill Shaw, he received the 1981 Holmes-Cardozo Award given by the American Business Law Association for scholarly presentation at its annual meeting. He is a member of the Indiana, Ohio, and U.S. Virgin Islands Bars. He is the author of several books on business law and has published articles on law, business and ethics. In 1985–86 he was a "Visiting Scholar" in the Business and Public Policy Group at the University of California-Berkeley. Professor Wolfe earned a B.A. in history and a J.D. from Ohio State University, and an M.A. in Economics from the University of Illinois.

Contents

Illustrations xii
Preface xiii
Introduction: To the Student xvii

Part 1
The Foundations of Legal Systems
2

1. The Nature of Legal Systems and Law 4
2. Organization of the United States Legal System 14
3. Criminal Law 31
4. The Law of Torts 42

Ethics and Business Law in Part 1 58

Part 2
Contracts
70

5. Concept of Contractual Agreement 72
6. Formation of a Contract 87
7. Relief from Contractual Obligations 104
8. Consideration/Value Given for a Promise 115
9. Capacity/Ability to Create a Contract 128
10. Public Policy and Contractual Purpose 139
11. Contractual Form: Requirement of a Writing for Enforceability, Statute of Frauds 151
12. Contractual Duties of Performance, Nonperformance, and Discharge 166
13. Contractual Rights, Third Parties, and Remedies for Breach of Contract 180

Ethics and Business Law in Part 2 199

Part 3
Personal Property and Bailments
204

14. Personal Property 206
15. Bailments 216
16. Carriers, Documents of Title, and Innkeepers 225

Ethics and Business Law in Part 3 234

Part 4
Sales and Consumer Law
238

17. Introduction to the Uniform Commercial Code   240
18. Formation and Interpretation of the Sales Contract   253
19. Performance of the Sales Contract   273
20. Breach of the Sales Contract, Courses of Action, and Remedies   289
21. Consumer Law: A. A Seller's Warranties, Their Waiver, Modification, and Breach   308
22. Consumer Law: B. A Manufacturer's Liability for Defective and Unreasonably Dangerous Products, and Recent Consumer Protection Legislation   322

Ethics and Business Law in Part 4   339

Part 5
Commercial Paper
344

23. Introduction to Commercial Paper and Banking Operations   346
24. Transfer and Negotiation   372
25. Holder, Holder in Due Course, and Defenses   393
26. Banks, Checks, and Customer Relations   408
27. Deadlines and Discharge   421

Ethics and Business Law in Part 5   433

Part 6
Secured Transactions, Bankruptcy, and Insurance
438

28. Creation of Security Interests in Personal Property   440
29. Enforcement of Personal Property Security Interests; and Suretyship   452
30. Bankruptcy under the Bankruptcy Reform Act of 1978   464
31. General Principles of Insurance Law   475
32. Life, Fire, and Automobile Insurance Law   485

Ethics and Business Law in Part 6   494

Part 7
Agency and Employment
498

33. Nature and Creation of Agency   500
34. Duties of Principal and Agent to Each Other   516
35. Agency and the Law of Contracts and Torts   528
36. Termination of Agency   541
37. Employment   551

Ethics and Business Law in Part 7   571

Part 8 — Business Organizations
A. General Partnerships and Special Ventures — 576

38. Creation and Termination of General Partnerships   578
39. Partnership Management and the Authority of Partners   595
40. Rights, Duties, and Remedies of Partners among Themselves   603
41. Special Ventures   613

Part 8 — Business Organizations
B. Corporations — 624

42. Nature and Classes   626
43. Creation and Termination   639
44. Corporate Powers   652
45. Corporate Stock and Shareholders   662
46. Corporate Management   684

Ethics and Business Law in Parts 8 A and B   695

Part 9 — Government Regulation of Business — 700

47. Antitrust Law   702
48. Administrative Law   713
49. Labor Law   723
50. Environmental Law   734

Ethics and Business Law in Part 9   750

Part 10 — Real Property — 756

51. Real Property and Its Ownership   758
52. Transferring Ownership of Realty   772
53. Renting Realty   783

Ethics and Business Law in Part 10   795

Part 11 — Wills and Decedents' Estates, and Trusts — 800

54. Wills and Decedents' Estates   802
55. Trusts   819

Ethics and Business Law in Part 11   839

Part 12 — Business Law in the International Marketplace — 844

56. Business Law in the International Marketplace   846

Ethics and Business Law in Part 12   871

Appendices

A. An Explanation of the Civil Trial Process   A1
B. Uniform Partnership Act (1914)   A8
C. Uniform Limited Partnership Act (1916)   A15
D. (Revised) Uniform Limited Partnership Act (1976)   A19
E. Uniform Commercial Code (1978 Text)   A26
F. Excerpts from the United States Constitution, As Amended   A99

Table of Cases   T1
Glossary of Legal Terms and Definitions   G1
Index   I1

Illustrations

1.1	The Law-Government Continuum 9	16.1	Negotiable Bill of Lading (Front) 230	24.14	Overlap of Indorsement Liability and Warranty Liability 385
2.1	State Court System 18	17.1	Diagram of UCC 2-201—Statute of Frauds 247	28.1	Financing Statement 446
2.2	Federal Court System 18	23.1	Check Flow Chart 349	33.1	Relationships among Principal-Agent-Third Party 503
2.3	Example of a Complaint/Pleading 22	23.2	Sample Check 349	33.2	Limited Power of Attorney 506
2.4	Example of a Summons 23	23.3	Deposit Stamp on Back of Check 349	33.3	Full Power of Attorney 507
4.1	The Concept of Wrongs 44	23.4	Certificate of Deposit 350	38.1	General Partnership Agreement (Short Form) 582
5.1	Law Governing Contracts 74	23.5	Promissory Note 351	41.1	Comparison of Business Organizations 619
5.2	A Check 76	23.6	Envelope Draft 352	42.1	Structure of the Corporation 627
5.3	A Simple Contract 76	23.7	Letter of Credit 354	43.1	Statutory Merger 646
6.1	Stated Time Periods Measuring Duration of Offer 92	23.8	Diagram of Check Collection Process 358	43.2	Statutory Consolidation 647
7.1	Invalidating Table 107	23.9	"Handmade" Instrument 370	45.1	Example of Certificate of Stock (Front) 664
8.1	The Basics of Consideration 124	24.1	Check 374	45.2	Form 10-Q 676
9.1	Incapacity Table 130	24.2	Indorsements on Check 374	46.1	Corporate Management 690
10.1	Contracts—Public Policy Violations 140	24.3	Blank (and Qualified) Indorsement 375	47.1	Diagrammatic Representation of Stop Time, Inc.'s Competitive Situation 707
11.1, 11.2	Promises Within and Without the Statute of Frauds 155	24.4	Special (and Restrictive) Indorsement 375	51.1	Characteristics of Co-ownership
12.1	Performance 168	24.5	Qualified Indorsement 378	51.2	Easement Appurtenant for the Benefit of Property A 766
12.2	Discharge of Contracts 175	24.6	Irregular Indorsement 378	52.1	Warranty Deed 774
13.1	Assignment 182	24.7	Reacquired Instrument by Arturo 380	53.1	Creation and Termination of a One Year Leasehold Estate 784
13.2	Third-Party Creditor or Donee Beneficiary Contract 188	24.8	Instrument Renegotiated to Arturo 380	56.1	RESTATEMENT (SECOND) CONFLICT OF LAWS SECTION 187 853
13.3	Novation 189	24.9	Forged Instrument 382	56.2	EEC Treaty Article 85 860
13.4	Rights of Third Parties 191	24.10	Forged Indorsement 383	56.3	EEC Treaty Article 86 861
14.1	Bill of Sale 209	24.11	Impersonator Receives an Instrument 383		
15.1	Types of Ordinary (Private) Bailments and Bailee's Duty of Care 219	24.12	Indorsement by Impersonator 383		
15.2	Parking Ticket with Disclaimer 220	24.13	Negotiable Promissory Note Indorsed in Blank by P, Payee, and Delivered to A, to B, to H 384		

Preface

This first edition of a new book on business law is a *shortened version* of the large third edition of BUSINESS LAW, TEXT AND CASES, THE LEGAL ENVIRONMENT. There is no compromise with the outstanding quality of that third edition. Reorganization, deletion, and addition of material has been very carefully done, and the constructive comments and suggestions of reviewers of the manuscript have been very helpful.

This book has a three-fold thrust. *First,* it pushes back the frontiers of the law of business, reflecting not only what the law is but also where it is developing and expanding. A good illustration is the excellent enlarged text and case material on Consumer Law in chapters 21 and 22. *Second,* this book takes the position that law is a limitation on freedom to act, particularly in freedom of contract, as reflected by current common law, case law, statute, and judicial decision. *Third,* this is a *teaching* book, written specifically *for,* and not at, students. All writing has been primarily with the student in mind for interest, readability, and enjoyment.

Users of this short book will find: the text has been thoroughly updated and made more readable for student comprehension; terms and definitions have been checked for accuracy and clarity; and new helpful explanatory charts have been added. Many terms are defined in the margins of the text, and some are included in more than one Part for completeness of understanding of each individual Part.

A few of the many major items may be of interest. There are 263 short cases, and 56 long cases (one at the end of each chapter). Each of the case opinions has been edited to show the "essential" facts and the judge's reasoning. There are forms, charts, and diagrams. There is extensive material on women's rights, constitutional law, the status and liability of auditors, and the law of corporations, bankruptcy, and sales, including "lemon" laws. Also, there is distinctively new ethics material, unlike the typical listing of quasi-ethical issues so common today, based on the findings in the field of moral psychology and on the work of Professor Conry as the Research Fellow in Business Ethics at Yale University 1981–82. *The unique feature of this material is that it is designed to help students form their own beliefs, now and in later life, about what is right and wrong conduct in business.* The material in the first Part gives students the analytic tools needed to engage in mature ethical analysis. Subsequent Parts ask students to apply these tools to a variety of ethical issues. *Each* of these following Parts begins with a survey of the range of ethical issues related to the legal topics covered in that Part, followed by an in-depth discussion of a single *basic* business ethics issue, and concludes with four problems for student and class consideration and discussion.

Appendices include: An Explanation of the Civil Trial Process; the Uniform Partnership Act (1914); Uniform Limited Partnership Act (1916); (Revised) Uniform Limited Partnership Act (1976); Uniform Commercial Code (1978 Text); and excerpts from the United States Constitution, As Amended.

A note on sexism. The text was previously thoroughly reviewed by an editor skilled in the use of gender-inclusive language to eliminate gender from the text wherever practicable. There is no generic singular for "they" or "them." One solution to this problem is to use "he or she," "his or her." However, such wording can become awkward, especially when repeated frequently. To avoid cumbersome structures, sentences have been worded, as much as possible, to avoid gender references. In cases where it is not feasible to solve the problem in this way, the singular pronoun "he" or the adjective "his" has been used. This usage is also true in legal definitions, case opinions, and statutes where the language cannot be changed. We have done our best in this regard.

The seven professors who are the contributing authors have written the following portions of this book: Conry, Part 10, and the Part portions on Ethics and Business Law; Ferrera, Parts 7 and 8, except for chapter 37; Lantry, Part 2; Shaw, Part 5 and chapter 50; Siedel, Parts 3 and 6; Spiro, Parts 1 and 9, except for chapter 50; Wolfe, Part 4 and Appendix A. Professor Frascona has written chapter 37 and Parts 11 and 12; and as the author responsible for the overall book, he has edited and rewritten some portions of the other Parts.

The design of the text, Instructor's Manual, and Student Study Guide/Workbook as an integrated unit is an innovation not available in any other business law textbook. This has been accomplished by the use of a matrix analysis which allows the instructor to integrate case materials from the text and application questions from the Student Study Guide/Workbook into the lecture formats provided in the Instructor's Manual.

A comprehensive student study guide programmed learning format is available. It provides for self-paced instruction and contains practice examinations. Included in the student study guide are exercises with answers covering terminology, concepts, and applications of law. A Student Study Guide/Workbook for *Principles of Business Law and The Legal Environment* is available either at your bookstore or by special order through your bookstore.

The total educational package makes *Principles of Business Law and The Legal Environment* a true *short* teaching text, the only one available on the market.

Acknowledgments

As in all research and writing, there are always those persons—silent and unsung—whose efforts, patience, and sacrifices are quietly intertwined into the final product. The authors are deeply grateful for help afforded to them by their families in this process. Also, the authors wish to acknowledge with thanks the excellent assistance of Professor Oscar J. Miller, Librarian of the School of Law, University of Colorado, and the library staffs of both the various Schools of Law and the various Colleges and Schools of Business.

Helpful reviewers and faculty have contributed to the excellence of the first edition of this short book with their constructive comments and perceptive suggestions for this book and for its longer third edition *Business Law, Text and Cases, The Legal Environment*. Some of them include the following. Thank you all very much: John J. Balek, Morton College; Caryn Beck-Dudley, Utah State University; Earl W. Coblyn, University of the District of Columbia; Wallace Conard, Columbus Technical Institute; Renee D. Culverhouse, Auburn University at Montgomery; Robert Ek, Seminole Community College; James C. Fetterman, St. Louis University; Sally Genson, Milwaukee Area Technical College, North Campus; Christopher L. Hamilton, Golden West College; Nancy Hauserman, University of Iowa; J. Roland Kelley, Tarrant County Junior College, Northeast Campus; Mike R. LaFrance, Kirkwood Community College; William F. Lynch, Niagra University; James E. Macdonald, Weber State College; Peter J. Musante III, Milwaukee Area Technical College; Gregory Naples, William Rainy Harper College; Michael Noonan, Frostburg State College; Gena Ousley, Chaffey College; William Parks, Orange Coast College-Costa Mesa; Paul Peckosh, Loras College; George N. Plavac, Cuyahoga Community College; Hank Ramp, Merced College; Roger Reinsch, Emporia State University; William E. Ringle, Queensborough Community College; Gabe Sanders, Jersey City State College; Gary R. Schwartz, Harrisburg Area Community College; J. Gregory Service, Broward Community College; Arthur F. Stelley, Hankamer School of Business, Baylor University; William S. Vanderpool, Appalachian State University; Lamont Walton, Michigan State University; Edd Welsh, Phoenix College.

The authors also wish to acknowledge with appreciation the permissions to reprint the following material: the 1978 text of the Uniform Commercial Code and some Official Comments to various sections therein copyrighted 1978 by The American Law Institute and the National Conference of Commissioners on Uniform State Laws and reprinted with permission of the Permanent Editorial Board for the Uniform Commercial Code; various sections from the RESTATEMENTS (SECOND) OF AGENCY, copyrighted 1958, CONFLICT OF LAWS, copyrighted 1969, TORTS, copyrighted 1965, and TRUSTS, copyrighted 1959, by and reprinted herein with the permission of The American Law Institute; the texts of the Uniform Partnership Act, copyrighted 1914, the Uniform Limited Partnership Act, copyrighted 1916, and the (Revised) Uniform Limited Partnership Act, copyrighted 1976 by and reprinted herein with the permission of the National Conference of Commissioners on Uniform State Laws; various sections from the 1984 Revised Model Business Corporation Act, copyrighted 1984 by and reprinted with the permission of the American Bar Foundation; two forms, General Partnership Agreement (Short Form) and Limited Partnership Certificate (Short Form), reprinted herein with permission from Edmund O. Belsheim's "Modern Legal Forms," copyrighted 1971 by West Publishing Company; two forms, Form 10-K and Form 10-Q in SEC Compliance—Financial Reporting and Forms, reprinted herein with permission of Stanley Weinstein, Daniel Schechtman and Michael A. Walker, copyrighted 1983 by Mann Judd Landau, published by Prentice-Hall, Inc.; two forms, Franchisor's Agreement—Sale of Franchisor's Products—Use of Franchisor's Trademark, and (full) Power of Attorney, reprinted herein by permission from Basic Legal Forms with Commentary, copyrighted 1981 by Warren, Gorham and Lamont, Inc.

Joseph L. Frascona

Introduction
To the Student

Congratulations *to you* as a student for wishing to learn about the law of business! You and other students have motivated us authors to write this book for you to enjoy, find interesting and stimulating, and serve you well both in and outside the classroom.

This book is not designed to make you a lawyer but, rather, to help you recognize and understand the legal significance of the business transactions occurring around you and in which you will participate, and to know when to call a lawyer. It is so written as to cause you to *want* to read it and to hold your attention and interest as you proceed through the book, building on what you have read as you go along.

This text has not been "leveled down," but has been authoritatively written to "lift up" the subject in a very innovative, current, and useful manner. The book is continually addressed to you, involving you in the text discussion. It will challenge you, as well as the instructor, by its smooth and deceptively easy style. Everything has been done to be helpful to you, as a student. Easily understandable language is used throughout the text, which is thoroughly up to date.

Each of the book's twelve Parts begins with a very brief overview statement of the chapters in that Part and a summary paragraph covering the whole Part. Each chapter begins with a list of the learning objectives for that chapter. Then comes an introduction leading you into the subject of that chapter. The text reads easily and logically as the subject is developed progressively. Many legal forms, charts, and diagrams are used at points in the book where they will be helpful. As you read through the text, guides and definitions of important legal terms appear in the margins highlighting topics discussed in the text.

Important legal terms are clearly defined and printed in bold type *as soon as they appear* in the text so that you can quickly understand their meaning and how they are used. They are included in the Glossary at the end of the book. Many factual examples appear in the text as you read along, illustrating how the legal principles apply.

A great many condensed court cases occur throughout the text showing how the courts use these principles in live situations. There is an introductory sentence leading into each case indicating the point of that case and tying the case into the text. First the "Facts" are presented, then the "Decision," and finally the "Reasoning" of the court for its decision. These cases (with their citations) are carefully selected so as to be interesting to you and are *not* a lot of legal verbiage. Most of them are recent cases.

At the end of each chapter is a Summary Statement, briefly pointing up some of the high points that you should have learned from the chapter. This is helpful in your review of what you have read. Following the summary is a carefully selected *long* interesting case that will give you the "feel" of a court's thinking as the court analyzes the facts and moves toward its decision. The case illustrates the application of an important legal principle that you have learned as you read through the chapter. Like the first famous long case in the book, all these long cases should be very interesting to you. Many of these are *the* outstanding cases on the subject, guiding the courts and followed by the courts as new cases are later considered.

In this text we have presented four different kinds of material. *First,* there is textual material which presents a statement of the general rules of law applicable to most of the important areas of business activity. These rules are both legislative and judicial in origin.

However, presenting the written rules is only a starting point. A *second* type of information illustrates how some of the important rules are applied by those in charge of rule application, either the state or federal governments or private individuals. This rule application is illustrated by presenting both short and long excerpts from mostly appellate case opinions. These case opinions demonstrate how the abstract statements presented by the written rules of law are applied to reality. The cases literally breathe life into the rules and are absolutely necessary to an understanding of how the laws "work." Therefore, you are encouraged to read them carefully.

Third, we have presented at the end of the chapters review questions and case problems and also a long important case. Most of these review case problems are actual cases; others, created by us, should not be viewed as portraying an actual occurrence.

Fourth, at the end of each Part is a discussion of business ethics as it is applicable in the context of business law. The portion at the end of Part 1 introduces you to the ethics material as it applies in each of the following Parts.

At the back of the book are six appendices to provide you ready access to source material. Appendix A is "An Explanation of the Civil Trial Process." This explains in detail how a civil case proceeds and how the judgment is appealed. Appendix B is the "Uniform Partnership Act (1914)," Appendix C is the "Uniform Limited Partnership Act (1916)," Appendix D is the "(Revised) Uniform Limited Partnership Act (1976)," Appendix E is the "Uniform Commercial Code (1978 Text)." Throughout the book many footnote references are made to the Code, which is here in its complete up-to-date form. Appendix F is "Excerpts from the United States Constitution, As Amended."

This is followed by a "Table of Cases" listing the cases (with page references) that have occurred throughout the book. Next is an extensive "Glossary of Legal Terms and Definitions," followed finally by an Index to the book.

After the Contents at the beginning of the book there is a list of the many helpful illustrations that occur in the book (by figure number, title, and page reference).

Principles of
BUSINESS LAW
and the
LEGAL ENVIRONMENT

PART **1** The Foundations of Legal Systems

1. **The Nature of Legal Systems and Law**
   The concept of jurisprudence and its relationship to the role of law in society.
2. **Organization of the United States Legal System**
   Why the United States system of jurisprudence exists and how it operates.
3. **Criminal Law**
   The role of criminal law in society and legal rights and duties as they appear in a relationship between an individual and society.
4. **The Law of Torts**
   The role of tort law in society and legal rights and duties as they involve individual relationships.

Summary
Part 1 of this text introduces you to the subject matter of law and the nature and functions of law in our nation. You will learn as you progress through this text how law is used to improve our society.

Part 1 opens with an attempt to provide a workable definition of law. Next we move to an outline of the workings of the United States legal system. Finally we turn to two subject areas which are of increasing importance to managers—criminal law and the law of torts.

Business ethics as it relates to the text material in this Part is considered at the end of the Part.

1 The Nature of Legal Systems and Law

After you have read this chapter, you should be able to:

1. Define "legal system."
2. Identify the various concepts of law proposed by Aristotle, St. Thomas Aquinas, and Friedrich Karl von Savigny.
3. Explain natural law.
4. Explain the historical school of jurisprudence.
5. Explain why contemporary social scientists study our legal system.
6. Define "norm."
7. Distinguish between formal and informal norms.
8. Explain the meaning of the word "sanctions" and how it applies.
9. Define "law."
10. Explain social engineering.

Introduction

You are about to embark on a study of the subject of law. You may be surprised to discover that the search for an accurate, all-encompassing definition of law has gone on for thousands of years and will not end as long as people continue to think about the subject. Today researchers are studying legal systems throughout the world to make them work better for all of us. While you may not have an exact definition of law in mind as you pick up this textbook, you certainly are affected by law each and every day. Think about the incident described below.

In Dubuque, Iowa a farmer closes a deal to sell a portion of his land to some investors from Boston, Massachusetts. The investors plan to build condominiums to house the city's projected increase in population. The farmer thinks about all the other dwellings in town and wonders what the difference is between an apartment and a condominium. His daughter, a legal secretary, says that a condominium is an individually-*owned* apartment in a multiunit facility, whereas a typical apartment is merely a *rented* unit.

In this case and in thousands like it each day, individuals or groups of people try to understand or work with a little piece of something we call "law." Every nation in the world has a **legal system,** and law touches each of us as we go about the business of participating in society. If we are to be effective citizens and participate fully in society, it becomes important for each of us to have a *knowledge* about and a concern for law.

legal system
a set of laws adopted by a society or group of people

What Is Law?

Anthropologists, philosophers, historians, sociologists, and political scientists are only a few of the kinds of scholar who have tried to give an accurate definition of the term "law."[1] A practicing lawyer would probably give yet another definition. Your own idea of law might include legal craftsmen, such as judges, police, bailiffs, and lawyers; the places where these craftsmen work, such as courts and jails; and the endless stream of books they refer to, such as *Black's Law Dictionary,* the criminal codes, and the *Uniform Commercial Code.* Indeed, each of these is a part of the legal system in the United States. But this is not the whole picture. The historical background of law plays a large part in our understanding.

Aristotle built upon the Greek notion that the world was ordered by cosmic law, or, to use his term, **natural law**. He simply meant that there is a law higher than that which is made by mortals—a kind of ideal law. Aristotle tried to connect moral principles and legal principles.

natural law
an ideal or cosmic law

As part of their philosophies of law, Aristotle and St. Thomas Aquinas shared a belief in a transcendent law given to man. Both men saw a relationship between moral justice and law. Others also have worked with the concept of natural law. To pursue this perspective on the law somewhat further, you might examine the works of Emmanuel Kant or John Locke. But if this perspective is unsatisfactory, your thoughts may be closer to those of Friedrich Karl von Savigny.

Savigny was instrumental in developing the **historical school of jurisprudence.** This school of thought suggests that law evolves as a result of a particular nation's entire history; that lawyers or judges simply interpret the historical direction of the nation. Even legislators, Savigny would suggest, merely put into words that which is embedded in the larger web of a given nation's history. The name that Savigny gave this expression of the

historical school of jurisprudence
a school of thought that holds that law evolves from a nation's history

---

[1] For a more complete picture of the various perspectives on law, see the original works by any of these philosophers or one of the many fine texts on jurisprudence, such as J. Feinberg and H. Gross, *Law in Philosophical Perspective* (Encino, California: Dickenson Publishing Co., 1977); or C. Morris, *The Great Legal Philosophers* (Philadelphia: University of Pennsylvania, 1959).

spirit of the people is *Volksgeist*. Critics of the historical school of jurisprudence in general and of Savigny in particular ask whether law simply reflects the common consciousness of the nation, as he suggests, or helps to mold the future.

The most important feature of Savigny's work for our purposes is that it marked a move away from traditional generalizations about law toward a more careful pattern of study of society. Indeed, contemporary social scientists are indebted to Savigny for his work. Students interested in learning more about the historical school of jurisprudence might look into the writings of Sir Henry Maine, another legal philosopher of similar persuasion.

Why Is Law Investigated?

It should be clear by now that there are a number of different ways of viewing law, each of which has a particular strength or weakness. Yet contemporary legal scholars are always searching for new and workable models of law which would be useful in organizing and analyzing the information that they are continually uncovering. Why are social scientists dissatisfied with the traditional models?

> Social scientists.

Today's rapidly changing world presents us with issues which were rare or unheard of only a short while ago. This is particularly true in the world of work. In our society, people are calling upon business to have a heightened sense of social responsibility, and law is ever more frequently the vehicle used to move business people in the desired direction. Products liability[2] cases reflect this trend.

We have all been disappointed by products at some time in our lives. Some people have found unusual substances in soft drink bottles, and others have been hurt by machines that contained defective parts. For many years consumers had little recourse against companies that put defective or harmful products on the market. For example, in the case of *MacPherson v. Buick Motor Co.*,[3] a person was injured when a wheel on an automobile collapsed because of a defect and thus caused an accident. In order to recover damages caused by such an incident, the court said, the driver had to prove that the company failed to use reasonable care (the same care an ordinary prudent person would use in these circumstances) in assembling the car or, to use the legal terms, that the company was **negligent** in manufacturing the car. The driver also had to defend against the company's assertion that he was **contributorily negligent**—that he failed to exercise reasonable care as a driver and so could not blame the motor company for his misfortune.[4]

> **negligence** (conduct) failure to use the degree of care demanded by the circumstances; (tort) negligent conduct proximately causing injury to another person's interest
>
> **contributory negligence** plaintiff's conduct which falls below the standard to which he should conform for his own protection and which is a legally contributing cause with the defendant's negligence causing the plaintiff's harm

Needless to say, it was difficult to establish that the company did not use reasonable care in assembling the car. The problem of defending against the company's assertion of contributory negligence merely complicated the situation. In recent years, the buying public has demanded that this burden be lifted in instances where a particular product is unreasonably dangerous to the consumer, so people have turned to law to resolve this difficulty. The legal system has responded to this social pressure by increasing business responsibility. In more than 60 percent of our states, those who sell products that will reach the consumer virtually unchanged are responsible for injury if the product is defective, even if due care was used in putting together the item.

You can expect to see changes in this and almost every other area of law discussed in this text. Clearly, law is not a set of unchanging rules; rather, it changes to reflect movements in our society and, at times, even leads the way for change. The following case illustrates a change in the common law awarding damages for emotional trauma and upset from witnessing an automobile accident.

---

[2] Products liability is discussed below, pp. 53–54, 323–33.

[3] 111 N.E. 1050 (N.Y. 1916). For a short abstract of this case, see pp. 53–54.

[4] For a full discussion of the tort of Negligence, see pp. 48–52.

Facts
Defendant drove his automobile in a southerly direction on Bluegrass Road, and at that time plaintiff mother's infant daughter, Erin, lawfully crossed Bluegrass Road. Defendant's negligent operation of his vehicle caused the death of Erin. Erin's sister, also a **plaintiff,** and the mother both witnessed the accident from different distances. The surviving mother and daughter join in an action for damages for their emotional trauma. Defendant contends that, since there was no physical impact on the plaintiffs, there is no **common law** basis for recovery for emotional trauma.

Decision
Judgment for the plaintiffs.

Reasoning
Damages may be had for emotional trauma and physical injury resulting from plaintiffs' witnessing of an accident in which a closely related person is injured or killed if an ordinary person should have foreseen injury to the plaintiff. The possibility that the witnesses may feign trauma to collect damages does not justify a different result. The court recognizes that it is creating a *new* concept of duty by including a right to recovery for injury experienced within an *emotional* impact zone, where before one could only recover for injury experienced within a *physical* impact zone.

Dillon v. Legg, 441 P.2d 912 (Cal. 1968).

defendant
the party against whom a civil suit (or criminal action) is brought

plaintiff
the party who initiates a civil suit by filing a complaint in the proper court

common law
principles of nonstatutory law reflecting the customs and usages of society and found in judicial decisions.

Concepts.

Because the range of disputes that are considered amenable to solution through legal systems continues to grow, and because the complexity of the issues within the range increases all the time, we need to study our legal machinery constantly to make sure that it is functioning at its best. Social scientists who study the legal system perform that task. They seek new models of law because the older models do not enable them to study how law and legal systems really function.

How Is Law Perceived?

As was suggested several times above, there are a number of different ways of understanding what is meant by the term "law." In this section we present a view shared by a significant number of contemporary writers about the subject. We begin by learning certain fundamental concepts.

Norm
A **norm** is a standard shared by members of a group about how they should behave. We all adhere to standards of behavior that we learned as members of a family, a town, and our society as a whole. Many of us have learned these standards so well that we do not even consciously think about them unless we deviate from the norm.

Several years ago a music group called the Beatles created quite a stir when they violated a norm. Until then most men had worn their hair rather short. The Beatles violated the norm by growing their hair so that it covered their ears. Many people considered their action outrageous and looked upon these young men with scorn. Other simple examples of norms are that people should have three meals a day, that dogs in fire stations should be dalmations, and that nurses should wear white uniforms while working in hospitals.

The kind of norms just mentioned are largely "informal." That means that although they define how a person should behave, they are really casual in that enforcement is not usually strict and punishment for deviation is minor. The norm which dictates that forks be placed on the left side of a plate is another informal norm. Although you might raise some eyebrows or be chastised for failing to follow the correct procedure, you probably would receive, at worst, nothing more than a serious reprimand.

Norms may be very "formal," and deviation may be punished severely. Any number of standards for performance fit into this category. As a society we do not approve of one person taking another's life, nor do we approve of embezzlement, forgery, and arson. In each case society has defined the norm in legal words, in something we call the "criminal code." Violations of the code bring punishments ranging from fines to loss of one's own life.

norm
a group's standard of behavior

sanction
a group's technique for controlling its members

Norms and Freedom of Choice

The term **sanction** may be used to describe the techniques for maintaining social control over the members of a group. As was suggested above, a violation of a society's criminal code can bring a sanction ranging from a fine to loss of one's own life. In the following case the court upheld a state's habitual criminal statute.

Facts
Jimmy F. Freeman was convicted of third degree burglary with punishment fixed at not less than 3 years nor more than 6 years confinement in a state penitentiary. He was also found to be a habitual criminal which increased the punishment for burglary to life imprisonment. Tennessee has a habitual criminal statute. Freeman appeals, arguing that the Tennessee statute violates the 8th Amendment to the U.S. Constitution.

Decision
This statute does not violate the U.S. Constitution.

Reasoning
The Tennessee legislature has selected crimes it obviously deems to be the most serious [and] likely to be repeated. [The U.S. Supreme Court] recognizes that a state may impose harsher or milder penalties for a given crime than its sister states according to its own notions of severity.

State of Tennessee v. Freeman, 669 S.W.2d 688 (Tenn. Cr. App., 1983).

In the above case failure to adhere to the norm brought punishment to the individual. Sanctions are often used by our legal systems. We punish our wrongdoers.

Psychologists tell us that there are also rewards. When a person does something particularly good, he or she is rewarded. Children know that if they do some chores they will be rewarded by their mother or father. A sales employee knows that achieving a certain level of sales in a month will mean receiving a bonus, which is a reward. An employee who works hard all year long may expect a reward in the form of a raise in pay or a promotion.

Basically, people are free to choose how they behave. Whether you wear a sport jacket and tie to school or a sweat shirt and blue jeans is a matter of your own choice. Not all people choose to follow the norms prescribed by their peer group or by the larger society. A course in psychology would probably help you begin to understand the reasons for that kind of decision. Here it is important to note that all of us have a range of choices from which we may choose our behavior. If we choose within the norms, we are rewarded; a choice outside the norms results in a sanction.

Conflict between Norms

Difficult choices arise when the norms of one group of people come into conflict with society's formal norms. In certain groups—particularly among young people—individuals are pressured to conform to norms that advocate drinking or the use of drugs. The larger society has norms which severely punish such behavior; hence, there is a potential for conflict. In the following case the norm of a school was upheld by the court as superior to the norm as perceived by a dental student.

Facts
Plaintiff was a student at the Indiana University School of Dentistry. Plaintiff was dismissed by the Dental School. His greatest deficiency was in his consistent record of absences. The Dental School sent him a letter stating that he was dismissed effective immediately, the stated bases for his dismissal were his unsatisfactory grades, his deficiency in clinical achievement, and a "lack of responsibility in the management of [his] clinical practice." Plaintiff contends that his termination was in violation of due process in that the School failed to comply with the Student Rights & Responsibilities handbook.

Decision
Plaintiff was given adequate due process.

Reasoning
The clinical deficiencies and absences were discussed with him a number of times. In the case of an academic dismissal, due process does not require a formal hearing; the Dental School was within the bounds of any constitutionally required due process.

Neel v. Indiana University Board of Trustees, 435 N.E.2d 607 (Ind. App. 1982).

Figure 1.1   The Law-Government Continuum

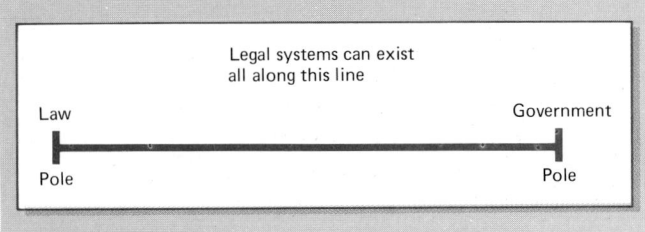

The strains can be great in business as well. A company may be able to maximize profits by polluting the atmosphere instead of purchasing expensive pollution control equipment, and many firms have a norm which dictates that managers should try to maximize the company's profits. Even so, in the United States today, many norms have developed which apply powerful sanctions to firms that destroy the environment. Managers may find themselves in a terrible bind, torn between competing norms.

Law As a Form of Norm

Some social scientists could argue persuasively that law can exist in any number of situations. For example, in a family, parents "make laws" that children must obey; in a company, the personnel director makes rules that employees must obey. In fact, whenever a group gets together, law may appear. These laws, which are not supported by the official sanctions of the government, are called "private laws" and are generated in "private legal systems."

This text, however, takes the position that law is one type of norm or, more specifically, that *norms established by the official leaders of society may be characterized as law*. We will limit our discussion to the study of the United States' legal system—those norms established by any part of our government—and we will not discuss private legal systems, except to note that they are actively studied by people interested in the sociology of law.

law
norms established by the official leaders of society; also those interests recognized and secured by society

Legal Systems

Once you understand the concept of law, you can imagine a number of different *ways* of putting together the laws of a particular society. Lawmakers can put together laws to create a very democratic or a very autocratic society. For example, the American system of government allows individual citizens to participate extensively in creating laws. On the other hand, for decades Spain's legal system was dominated by the whims of its dictator, General Franco. In fact, there are an enormous number of different ways to construct a legal system.

The late Karl Llewellyn (1893–1962) developed what he called the **law-government continuum** to illustrate the point that legal systems can be constructed in an infinite number of ways. He suggested that, in a legal system at the government end of the continuum, decisions would be made according to the arbitrary whim of a leader. Laws would exist or disappear depending on the leader's mood. Llewellyn called this extreme situation the *government pole,* while the other end of the continuum is the *law pole,* as diagrammed in figure 1.1. At the law pole, the rules of law would be so complete that there would be no need for human judgment. Whim would play no role in such a system.

law-government continuum
a method of showing the numerous ways of constructing legal systems

Both ends of the continuum are extreme systems, and it is difficult to imagine any modern legal system at either extreme. It is possible, however, to place nations closer to one pole than the other. For example, countries controlled by a dictator are closer to the government pole than to the law pole. The United States and Great Britain are closer to the law pole.

Our text will focus on the legal system of the United States. However, students should remember that the laws of other nations may vary significantly from ours. For students interested in legal history, some legal systems predate the United States' legal system—for example, the Code of Hammurabi (2000 B.C.) and the Mosaic Code (1200 B.C.). The laws of other nations are very important for future business managers. Many firms in the United States actively do business all over the world. The laws governing business transactions vary from nation to nation. Managers should be very careful not to assume that rules of law and interpretation of them are the same worldwide. In the following early case the English court reflected upon the laws of other nations in deciding the law of liability for negligence in England in connection with impure food.

privity
a mutuality of relationship between persons or between persons and a particular transaction

Facts
Plaintiff is a woman who became ill while drinking some carbonated beverages. She traced the illness to the fact that she had swallowed a bit of decomposed snail which was found in the bottle of soda. She did not see the impurity at first because of the dark color of the bottle. Will she be allowed to recover from the manufacturer, defendant, who contended that, since there was no **privity** between the plaintiff and the defendant, the plaintiff should not recover.

Decision
Yes, there is a sufficient degree of privity between the consumer and the manufacturer.

Reasoning
After looking at the laws of several nations and the laws of Great Britain, the court announced that "a manufacturer of products . . . who sells those products in the form intended for the consumption of the ultimate consumer, and with the knowledge that the absence of reasonable care in the preparation will result in an injury to the consumer's life or property, owes a duty to the consumer to take that reasonable care."

Donoghue v. Stevenson, (1932) L.R., A.C. 562.

Summary Statement

1. It is important for every citizen to have a knowledge of, and a concern for, law.
2. Our society relies upon law as society becomes more complex.
3. An all-encompassing definition of law has not yet been agreed upon.
4. Different theories of jurisprudence exist.
5. Law changes, and it is a fertile field of research for determining why it changes.
6. Norms are behavior standards shared by members of a group. Sanctions are techniques for maintaining social control over group members.
7. Law is a form of a norm, and is defined as norms established by the official leaders of society; also law is those interests recognized and secured by society.
8. In our system of government, the individual participates extensively in creating laws.
9. Our legal system is close to the "law pole continuum."
10. Our legal system deserves our support.

The point made in this chapter that there is a difference among morals, norms, and law is illustrated in the following famous English case. The idea that what one might consider morally right does not necessarily protect one in a criminal action is shown by this case.

Regina v. Dudley and Stephens
[1884] L.R., Q.B. 61*

Lord Coleridge, C.J. The . . . verdict . . . [for the crime of murder] as it is finally settled before us is as follows:

On July 5, 1884, . . . Thomas Dudley and Edward [sic] Stephens, with one Brooks, . . . English seamen, and the deceased also an English boy, between seventeen and eighteen years of age, . . . were cast away in a storm on the high seas 1,600 miles from the Cape of Good Hope, and were compelled to put into an open boat belonging to the said yacht. That in this boat they had no supply of water and no supply of food, except two 1 lb. tins of turnips . . . [and a small turtle which they caught]. That on the twelfth day the remains of the turtle were entirely consumed, and for the next *eight days* they had nothing to eat. That they had no fresh water. . . . That the boat was drifting on the ocean, and was probably more than 1,000 miles away from land. That on the eighteenth day, when they had been seven days without food and five without water, the prisoners spoke to Brooks as to what should be done if no succour came, and suggested that some one be sacrificed to save the rest, but Brooks dissented, and the boy to whom they were understood to refer, was not consulted. That on the 24th of July, the day before the act now in question, the prisoner Dudley proposed to Stephens and Brooks that lots should be cast who should be put to death to save the rest, but Brooks refused to consent, and it was not put to the boy. . . . Dudley proposed that if there was no vessel in sight by the morrow morning the boy should be killed. That next day, the 25th of July, no vessel appearing, . . . the prisoner Stephens agreed to the act, but Brooks dissented from it. That the boy was then lying at the bottom of the boat quite helpless and extremely weakened by famine and by drinking sea water, and unable to make any resistance, nor did he ever assent to his being killed. . . . That Dudley, with the assent of Stephens, went to the boy, and telling him that his time was come, put a knife into his throat and killed him then and there; that the three men fed upon the body . . . of the boy . . . ; that on the fourth day after the act had been committed the boat was picked up by a passing vessel, and the prisoners rescued. . . . That they were carried to the port of Falmouth, and committed for trial at Exeter. That if the men had not fed upon the body of the boy they would probably not have survived to be so picked up and rescued, but would within the four days have died of famine. . . . That at the time of the act in question there was no sail in sight, nor any reasonable prospect of relief. That under these circumstances there appeared to the prisoners every probability that unless they then fed or very soon fed upon the boy or one of themselves they would die of starvation. That there was no appreciable chance of saving life except by killing some one for the others to eat. . . . [If] upon the whole matter the Court shall be of opinion that the killing of Richard Parker be felony and murder, then the jurors say that Dudley and Stephens were each guilty of felony and murder as alleged in the indictment.

. . . [This case differs from killing done] in the service of . . . [the] Sovereign and in the defense of . . . [the] country. Now it is admitted that the deliberate killing of this unoffending and unresisting boy was clearly murder, unless the killing can be justified by some well-recognized excuse admitted by the law. It is further admitted that there was in this case no such excuse, unless the killing was justified by what has been called "necessity." But the temptation to the act which existed here was not what the law has ever called necessity. Nor is this to be regretted. Though law and morality are not the same, the many things may be immoral which are not necessarily illegal, yet the absolute divorce of law from morality would be of fatal consequence; and such divorce would follow if the temptation to murder in this case were to be held by law an absolute defense of it. It is not so. . . .

It must not be supposed that in refusing to admit temptation to be an excuse for crime it is forgotten how terrible the temptation was; how awful the suffering; how hard in such trials to keep the judgment straight and the conduct pure. We are often compelled to set up standards

① Case Title
② Citation
③ Judge
④ Body of Case

---
*Author note: This series of numbers and letters is a case citation (English Law Reports, Queen's Bench). It is the information you need to look up this case in a law library.

we cannot reach ourselves. . . . A man has no right to . . . allow compassion for the criminal to change or weaken in any manner the legal definition of the crime. It is therefore our duty to declare that the prisoners' act in this case was willful murder, that the facts as stated in the verdict are no legal justification of the homicide; and to say that in our unanimous opinion the prisoners are upon this special verdict guilty of murder.

Questions and Case Problems

1. Alan Bakke applied to the Medical School at the University of California at Davis under the regular admissions program for one of 100 seats. He was rejected. Under a special admissions procedure, certain minority group members with lesser academic credentials were admitted. Does this represent reverse discrimination? Does this illustrate conflict between norms? [*Regents of the University of California v. Alan Bakke,* 438 U.S. 265 (1978).]

2. Read the following statute: "When any person shall be convicted of two or more offenses, before sentence shall have been pronounced upon him for either offense, the imprisonment to which he shall be sentenced upon the second or other subsequent conviction shall commence at the termination of the term of imprisonment to which he shall be adjudged upon the prior conviction." It is clear that the purpose of this statute is to ensure that *some* multiple criminal offenders are to be punished more severely than others by having criminal sentences run consecutively rather than concurrently. However, it is also clear that the section does not apply to *all* convicted multiple offenders. It applies if, but only if, a defendant at the same time in one trial is convicted of at least two offenses before he is sentenced for either offense. Is this a reasonable way to punish people? [*State of Missouri v. Baker,* 524 S.W.2d 122 (Mo. 1975).]

3. Esop, a native of Bagdad, is aboard a ship docked in Great Britain. While in port he was indicted for committing an unnatural act which from his background he did not know was wrongful or illegal. Should he be punished? [*Rex v. Esop,* 7 Car. & P. 456 (1836).]

4. A passenger runs to catch a train which is leaving a railroad station. In an attempt to help the potential passenger, a trainman pulled the man aboard and dislodged a package from his arms. The package, which contained fireworks, exploded and overturned some distant scales which fell upon plaintiff and injured her. The courts have for years argued the question of to what extent one person should be liable to another where the injury is not clearly foreseeable. What practical norm might you create which would allow you to answer the question posed? Would you hold the Long Island Railroad responsible for the injury to the woman hurt by the scales? [*Palsgraf v. Long Island R. Co.,* 162 N.E. 99 (N.Y. 1928).]

5. "In each of the cases before us, minors of the Negro race, through their legal representatives, seek the aid of the courts in obtaining admission to the public schools of their community on a nonsegregated basis. In each instance, they had been denied admission to the schools attended by white children under laws requiring or permitting segregation according to race. This segregation was alleged to deprive the plaintiffs of equal protection." Does segregation of children on the basis of race, even though physical and other factors may be equal, represent discriminatory and illegal treatment? [*Brown v. Board of Education,* 347 U.S. 483 (1954).]

6. The following comment was made by a radio talk show host on the air: ". . . and it kills me to say this because I would like to dump on their restaurant. I keep going there hoping it will decline and it doesn't. The food is fine, the people who run it are PIGS." Would you stop the commentator from using such language? What norm is illustrated? [*Pritsker,* et al. *v. Brudnoy,* et al., 452 N.E.2d 227 (Mass. 1983).]

7. Musicians are being interviewed on a radio station. During the interview the musicians used the words "fooling around with his wife." Some of the listeners think that the words mean that the plaintiff was engaged in an affair with a defendant. The plaintiff thinks that the use of these words should be punished. If you were designing a legal system, would this kind of action be punishable? Would this be a violation of a norm? Explain. [*Matherson,* et al. *v. Marchello,* et al., 473 N.Y.S. 2d 998 (N.Y. 1984).]

8. A television commercial attempting to illustrate the moisturizing capacity of a shaving cream is demonstrated to be capable of making it possible to shave sandpaper. In fact, sandpaper is not used. Rather, Plexiglass with sand sprinkled on it is used. What rule would you establish as head of the Federal Trade Commission (FTC)? What norm is illustrated? [*Colgate-Palmolive Co. v. FTC,* 310 F.2d 89 (1962).]

9. Several people filed income tax returns for 1982 but did not enter on the returns any information about their incomes, the sources of their incomes, exemptions, or even their social security numbers. They explained that supplying the missing information would violate the protection to which they are entitled under the Fifth Amendment to the U.S. Constitution. Does the law do itself a disservice by allowing people to plead the Fifth Amendment privilege against self-incrimination? Explain. [*Aune, Beeker,* et al. *v. United States,* 582 F.Supp. 1132 (1984).]

10. The case of *Regina v. Dudley and Stephens,* Queen's Bench Division, 1884 [1881–85] All England Law Reports 61,[5] illustrates a case in which a judge is trying to apply the law without allowing his personal reaction to the facts to enter into his judgment. Is this always appropriate?

---

[5] See pp. 11–12.

2 Organization of the United States Legal System

After you have read this chapter, you should be able to:

1. Identify and explain several techniques for resolving disputes.
2. Explain the advantages and disadvantages of arbitration, mediation, and conciliation.
3. Explain the roles of lawyers and paralegals.
4. Identify the different kinds of state and federal courts.
5. Explain the process of beginning a lawsuit.
6. Distinguish between statutory law, common law, administrative law, case law, and constitutional law.

Introduction

In the preceding chapter of this Part we discussed basic notions about law and the nature of legal systems. In this chapter we will discuss the United States legal system, its operation, and alternatives to the use of the legal system in order to resolve civil disputes.

In a society as large as our own, people are bound to have conflicting ideas about how things ought to be done. Indeed, even in a relatively small group such as a family or business organization, it is likely that from time to time individuals will disagree. Fortunately, most of the time these disagreements can be settled promptly and with no formal proceeding necessary. But what happens when the problem is complex or difficult to resolve? For example, what happens when a truck owned by Kross Kuntrie Freight, Inc. collides with another truck owned by One Way, Inc. and both drivers deny that they are the cause of the accident?

Suppose that in the situation just mentioned one of the drivers decides that the best way to resolve the dispute is to start a fight with the other driver and the fight results in serious injury to that other driver. Further, what happens if some of the cargo is damaged as a result of the accident? Who should be held responsible—the trucking firm, the individual drivers, the seller, the purchaser? As we will see, these perplexing issues can be resolved in a number of ways.

Response of the Law

In the next few pages we will first examine the nonjudicial procedures that people use to resolve grievances among themselves. Then we will look at the legal forums available for resolving disputes. This material is preparation for treatment in later chapters of the substantive rules applied to particular cases. We will focus primarily on a branch of the U.S. legal system known as civil procedure, although we will first look at alternatives to using law, such as compromise, arbitration, or mediation.

Forums.

No time will be spent in this chapter on the U.S. criminal law. But students should bear in mind that the procedures used for resolving criminal cases are markedly different from those described here, as illustrated by the following case, which discusses the burden of proof of the prosecution in a criminal case.

Facts
In June 1966 a jury found respondent Stillman E. Wilbur, Jr. guilty of murder. However, on appeal, Mr. Wilbur's attorney argued that the charge should be reduced to manslaughter. The State of Maine requires a *defendant* to establish by a preponderance of the evidence that he acted in the heat of passion on sudden provocation in order to have a murder charge reduced to manslaughter. Is this violative of due process?

Decision
Yes.

Reasoning
Under this statutory burden of proof a defendant can be given a life sentence when the evidence indicates that he could deserve a lesser sentence. The due process clause of the United States Constitution requires the *prosecution* to prove beyond a reasonable doubt the absence of heat of passion on sudden provocation when the issue is presented in a homicide case.

Mullaney v. Wilbur, 421 U.S. 684 (1975).

Most of the events mentioned in the introductory statement for this chapter would be handled in the civil courts of the United States. *Civil* courts deal with disputes between parties which are not concerned with offenses against society and are not punishable by society. *Criminal* courts deal with individuals who have wronged *society* by committing a crime defined by one of the various criminal codes. In our truck driver incident the fight might result in criminal charges of assault and/or battery being filed. All the other disputes would involve interpreting contracts between the parties or ascribing the fault to one of the drivers for causing the accident or deciding who bears the burden for damaged cargo. They would all lie within the purview of a *civil* court of law, and will be resolved by the parties either nonjudicially or by the use of the legal procedures discussed later.[1]

Alternative Mechanisms— Nonjudicial, or Use of the Legal System

Suppose you purchase a stereo system from a reputable store in your community and the system simply does not live up to your expectations. What do you do? It is highly unlikely that your first response would be to sue the department store. Rather, you would probably begin by taking the set back to the store and asking for a refund or a replacement. You have a grievance and you are looking for the simplest, most direct route toward a solution. Most reliable stores would be happy to replace the set or refund your money if the cause of the difficulty could not be traced to something you had done. That is the simple case. But let's make the problem more difficult. Suppose you discovered a large scratch on the speaker cabinet. You know you did not cause the scratch. But what if the retail dealer thinks that the scratch looks like something you might have done through your carelessness in unpacking the speaker and, thus, the dealer is unwilling to take it back or refund your money? What can you do without resorting to the courts?

Nonjudicial Mechanisms

compromise
an agreement resolving a dispute outside of court reached through concessions offered by the aggrieved parties

arbitration
a method for deciding disputes outside of court by persons called arbitrators, appointed by the disputing parties

mediation
the process of using a third party to bring disputants closer to resolution of their differences

lawyer
a person who is licensed to practice law by advising and representing clients in legal matters

The chances are you would still not run off to your lawyer in preparation for a lawsuit. Even if you did, a responsible attorney would not instantly file a suit. Rather, a more logical step would be to seek a **compromise** solution. A compromise is an agreement resolving a dispute outside of court reached through concessions offered by the aggrieved parties. Compromise is an alternative to litigation and so are **arbitration** and **mediation.** Arbitration is the process of resolving a dispute by using a third party chosen for his or her neutrality to decide the disputed issue. The key to arbitration is that the parties agree to be bound by the decision of the arbitrator. Sometimes the disputing parties would like the help of a third individual but would not like to feel bound by the proposed solution. In that case, the parties would hire a mediator for mediation. All of these alternatives are faster and less costly than litigation and each of them generates goodwill between the disputing parties as decisions are made.

Using the Legal System: Lawyers

If compromise, arbitration, or mediation should fail to result in a solution, the next step might be to turn to the law. For most people this means turning to a lawyer.

A **lawyer** is an individual trained as an advocate to represent clients in the legal process. The training involved normally amounts to four years of college followed by three years of law school. Students come to law from all college majors—from business to fine arts. Law schools look for inquisitive, thoughtful students in their admissions process. Even after this rather lengthy period of time, almost all of the states require that potential lawyers pass a bar examination which tests their understanding of basic legal concepts and special understanding of particular states' laws. Although most people imagine that

---

[1] See pp. A1–8.

lawyers spend the majority of their time in court, this is not true. In the following case the court indicated that discussion giving legal advice is practicing law, which occurs outside the courtroom, but that the activities of the defendants, nonlawyers, were not of that character and did not constitute practicing law.

Facts
The defendants maintained an office in Portland and advertised in the Portland papers. One sample ad read as follows: "Divorce. Join the thousands of people who have been successful in securing their own non-contested divorce. Oregon Divorce Council."
The plaintiff, Oregon State Bar, brought suit to enjoin the defendants from practicing law through advertising and sale of do-it-yourself divorce kits. None of the defendants is a lawyer. May they be enjoined?

Decision
Some of their activities may continue.

Reasoning
The defendants did not actually practice law by publishing and advertising and selling such kits. But any *discussion* they might have with the parties is a violation of the law.

Oregon State Bar v. Gilchrist, 538 P.2d 913 (Or. 1975).

Lawyers enter into a relationship with their clients based upon the client's trust that the lawyer will help to resolve the client's concerns in an expeditious manner. This trust is called a **fiduciary** relationship. In the following case the court points out that an attorney must be very careful how he or she handles a client's money.

In the following case the court points out that the conduct of the attorney with respect to his client's funds violated their trust in him as a lawyer.

fiduciary
a person with a duty to act primarily for the benefit of another

Facts
The lawyer admits that he (1) failed to obtain written directions for disbursement of $18,000 of his client's funds, (2) delivered the $18,000 to another without obtaining a receipt, and (3) received $2,000 in reimbursement for expenses for which he maintained no substantiating records. He maintains that he acted in good faith in accordance with his client's oral directions and neither injured his client nor violated any rules or statutes governing professional conduct. Did the attorney breach the trust?

Decision
The attorney's failure to maintain adequate records warrants discipline (and) Petitioner is publicly reproved.

Reasoning
The rules of Professional conduct specify "Unless the client otherwise directs in writing, [the attorney] shall promptly deposit his client's funds. It is largely irrelevant that an attorney may have violated the rule in good faith and without damage to his client.

Fitzsimmons v. State Bar of California, 667 P.2d 700 (Cal. 1983).

Using the Legal System: The Courts

It was mentioned above that the United States has a dual system of **courts.** What this means is that each state has a court structure and the federal government also has a court structure. The courts may be diagrammed as in figures 2.1 and 2.2.

court
a judicial tribunal

State Courts

State Inferior Courts. **State inferior courts** are the lowest order of state courts and they are sharply limited in **jurisdiction.** Jurisdiction is the power of a court to hear and to decide a case involving a person or subject matter properly brought before the court. Every state decides what configuration of courts it needs to deal with the case load which it faces. Therefore it would be difficult to list every kind of inferior court. However, typically, states have *probate courts* designed to work on the estates of the deceased. They also have *small claims courts,* which can hear cases involving relatively small amounts of money, the amount varying from state to state. *Traffic courts, criminal courts, police courts, mayor's courts, magistrate's courts, municipal* or *city courts, justice of the peace courts,* and *county courts* are other relatively common inferior courts. Note that the word

state inferior court
the lowest order state trial court

jurisdiction
the power of a court to hear and decide a case involving a person or subject matter properly brought before the court

Figure 2.1 State Court System

Figure 2.2 Federal Court System

"inferior" refers to the fact that these courts are the lowest in the state system, not that they are of lesser quality. These inferior courts are *trial* courts, but they may not hear cases outside their jurisdiction. For example, a traffic court may not hear a case involving the probate (proof) of a will, nor may a small claims court hear controversies which exceed a certain dollar limit.

state court of general jurisdiction
the highest order state *trial* court

State Courts of General Jurisdiction. **State courts of general jurisdiction** have many different names, such as *circuit court, superior court, district court,* or *court of common pleas.* In all states these represent the highest *trial* level court. Since all cases begin in a trial level court, they begin at an inferior court which can hear the case or, if appropriate, a court of general jurisdiction. Also, if a lawyer gets an unsatisfactory result in the inferior court and wishes to further argue a point of law, he or she may appeal to the court of general jurisdiction. These courts are called general jurisdiction courts because they may hear any type of case. However, if there is an inferior court which can hear the case, they will allow it to hear the case first. Technically, its only limitation is territorial. For example, a Texas court of general jurisdiction would not hear a case involving an incident that took place in New York and that involved disputants also from New York.

State (Intermediate) Appellate Courts. **Questions of fact** (e.g., did the person sign the paper?) are settled in trial courts and many cannot be appealed. But lawyers and judges often disagree on the meaning of particular points of law, and these **questions of law** (e.g., should the witness have been required to answer a question?) may be appealed to the next higher level court—(intermediate) appellate courts. They are intermediate, or in between, the trial court and the court above the intermediate court, e.g., the supreme court. Since (intermediate) appellate courts are not involved in disputes over factual issues, a jury is not required. Lawyers argue points of law in front of a panel of judges (usually three). Just as with inferior courts, the need for intermediate appellate courts varies from state to state depending on case load requirements.

question of fact
a dispute over what happened

question of law
a dispute over the legal effect of what happened

State Supreme Court. If a question of law is particularly troublesome, lawyers may appeal to the highest level court—the supreme court of the state. Students should note that the highest state court does not always have the name "Supreme Court," but sometimes has a different name. The supreme court, again, is not involved in disputes over questions of fact and so does not require a jury. Rather, a panel of between five and nine judges, depending upon the state, listens to the lawyers argue their points of law. If there is no federal issue involved in a case (such as a federal constitutional question), the determination of law by the state supreme court would terminate a case. There then could be no appeal to the federal court system. However, in certain limited instances (e.g., the validity of a federal statute is questioned in the state court proceedings), the United States Supreme Court may certify for review a decision by the state supreme court.

Federal Courts
The United States Constitution authorizes the creation of the federal court system. Article III, section 1 of the Constitution says: "The Judicial Power of the United States shall be vested in one Supreme Court and in such inferior courts as the Congress may from time to time ordain and establish." This has resulted in the formation of the U.S. Supreme Court, which derives its power from the U.S. Constitution, and, over the years, the formation by Congress of all the lower federal courts.

Federal District Courts. The **federal district court** is the *trial* level court of the federal system. At this point you may wonder how one decides whether to use the state or federal trial level court. The answer is found in the procedural law. In order for a federal district court to hear a case, the case must fall into one of the following categories. (1) One category is that it may be a federal question (that is, it must be a question arising out of a federal law, treaty, or the federal Constitution). (2) Another way of getting into federal court is to have a question that deals with a federal law that has no dollar requirements, such as civil rights issues or copyrights. (3) A final way of getting into federal court requires that the disputants be from different states or from a state and a foreign nation *and* the amount in controversy must be *over* $10,000. If there are more than two disputants, no plaintiff (the person bringing the case to court) and no defendant (the person against whom the case is brought) can be from the same state. These requirements are known as subject matter requirements, because they literally define which subjects the federal courts will hear and which will be heard by state courts. In addition to subject matter jurisdiction, courts must also have jurisdiction over the person (**in personam**) or property (**in rem**) in dispute, and there are additional rules of civil procedure which define these requirements.

federal district court
the *trial* level court of the federal legal system

in personam
against the person

in rem
against the thing

U.S. Court of Appeals. There are thirteen courts of appeals in the federal system, often called the federal "circuit courts of appeals." Just as with intermediate appellate courts in the state system, the court of appeals does not have "original" jurisdiction over cases.

That is, it is not the first court to hear a particular federal case. Rather, the district court or some other federal inferior court holds the trial and the appellate court hears appeals on questions of law. Each of the cases brought before it is heard by a panel of three judges.

U.S. Supreme Court. Of course, the highest court within the federal system is the Supreme Court of the United States. In rare cases it has original jurisdiction, such as in cases involving ambassadors and in controversies between two or more states or between a state and citizens of another state. But the vast majority of its time is spent on appeals made to it from other courts. The Supreme Court is established by the federal Constitution and is composed of nine justices, one being the chief justice, each of whom has lifetime tenure in the job. These justices hear certain appeals to it and also decide which limited number of cases they will certify for review by it during the upcoming year. The term used to denote a review by the Supreme Court, and indeed by any appellate courts, is "certiorari."

The Supreme Court considers not only cases from the federal District Courts and Courts of Appeal, but also those cases where a state's highest court has rendered a final judgment in a case in which the validity of a state statute has been drawn into question on the ground of its being repugnant to the U.S. Constitution. In a recent case the U.S. Supreme Court considered the validity of a Minnesota statute which allowed state taxpayers, in computing their state income tax, to deduct expenses incurred in providing "tuition, textbooks, and transportation" for their children attending an elementary or secondary school. Petitioners were Minnesota taxpayers who claimed that the statute violated the Establishment Clauses of the First and Fourteenth Amendments of the United States Constitution prohibiting Congress from making any law "respecting an establishment of religion." They claimed that parents had taken the tax deduction for expenses incurred in sending their children to parochial schools, and that the statute thereby violated the Establishment Clause by providing financial assistance to sectarian institutions. The U.S. Supreme Court held that the Minnesota statute was valid and constitutional. The tax deduction has as its secular purpose ensuring that the state's citizenry is well educated. The deduction does not have the primary effect of advancing the sectarian aims of nonpublic schools. It is only one of many deductions available under Minnesota laws for educational expenses incurred by all parents, whether their children attend public schools or private sectarian or nonsectarian schools. (*Mueller and Noyes v. Allen, Jr.*, et al., 463 U.S. 388 (1983).)

Other Federal Courts and Administrative Tribunals. There are several additional federal courts, each with limited subject matter jurisdiction. The U.S. Tax Court is a specialized federal court which deals with questions that arise concerning federal taxation. Before using the tax court, individuals must first exhaust their administrative remedies through the Internal Revenue Service. The U.S. Claims Court hears cases which deal with claims made by individuals against the U.S. government. As mentioned previously, many administrative agencies are also administrative tribunals which are also part of this federal system. Examples are the National Labor Relations Board and the Federal Trade Commission. Appeals from these special courts (except the claims court) and administrative tribunals are heard first by the U.S. Court of Appeals and later, if further litigation is needed, by the U.S. Supreme Court. The U.S. Court of Military Appeals is worth noting here as a separate federal court. It is important to note that the U.S. Supreme Court can review decisions of the U.S. Court of Military Appeals.

Using the Legal System: The Lawsuit

Once the proper court is chosen by your attorney, he or she must begin the case by notification of the grievance to the court and the person or group you wish to proceed against. Instituting a lawsuit is a complex branch of a discipline known as civil (or criminal) procedure. In the next few pages we will sketch an outline of the proceedings in a civil lawsuit. Later in the book there is a detailed outline of the civil trial process.[2]

Parties to the Suit

In a lawsuit there are two primary parties, the **plaintiff** and the **defendant.** The plaintiff is the person who has a grievance and begins a civil lawsuit. The defendant is the party against whom the lawsuit (or criminal action) is brought and who must be notified of the case.

Complaint and Response

The plaintiff must notify both the court and the defendant that he or she wishes to begin a lawsuit. In order to do this the plaintiff prepares papers known as **pleadings.** The initial paper prepared is called the **complaint** (see figure 2.3), which sets forth in detail the cause of action that the plaintiff has against the defendant. It states the position of the plaintiff in clear and concise language. The plaintiff's attorney or **paralegal** assistant then takes the papers to the appropriate court. The plaintiff's attorney usually also prepares a **summons** (see figure 2.4) which, usually along with a copy of the complaint, is served (delivered) upon the defendant.

The summons sets forth the place for the trial as determined by the court, and the complaint tells the defendant why he or she is being sued. Service of the summons upon the defendant is necessary for the court to have jurisdiction over the defendant and to try the case. Obviously care must be taken to ensure that the defendant is actually notified, so ideally a court officer or other proper person must personally serve the summons upon the defendant or, in a proper case, mail it to the defendant via registered mail.

Upon receiving the summons and complaint, the defendant then has several alternatives. The simplest thing to do, although probably the least wise, would be to disregard the summons. This would result in a *default* judgment being filed against the defendant. A default means that the defendant has automatically lost the case.

A wiser course of action would be for the defendant to choose a lawyer and turn over the summons and complaint to the lawyer. Lawyers can be located through friends or through the state or local bar associations. If the defendant cannot afford a lawyer, there are a number of organizations which may provide assistance. In criminal cases the court would appoint a lawyer to ensure that the defendant receives competent legal assistance in protecting his rights. In civil cases organizations, such as legal aid societies, legal service corporations, the American Civil Liberties Union, and special interest groups such as public interest research groups, might wish to assist.

The defendant's lawyer would then choose from a number of options. Often the lawyer will file an *answer* to the complaint by agreeing with, or denying, each of the points raised in the plaintiff's pleading. The defendant may add some additional points or may even choose to **counterclaim,** which means a cause of action asserted by the defendant against the plaintiff. The entire process is designed to focus attention on those points about which there is disagreement.

---

[2] See pp. A1–8.

---

plaintiff
the party who initiates a civil suit by filing a complaint in the proper court

defendant
the party against whom a civil suit (or criminal action) is brought

pleadings
the formal documents filed with a court that usually include the complaint, answer, and motions regarding them

complaint
the first pleading in a civil action

paralegal
an individual trained to assist lawyers in their practice

summons
a writ or process served on the defendant in a civil action notifying him of the action and summoning him to appear and plead

counterclaim
a claim asserted by the defendant against the plaintiff's claim in a civil action

Figure 2.3 Example of a Complaint/Pleading

```
            IN THE DISTRICT COURT IN AND FOR THE
                 COUNTY OF BOULDER AND
                    STATE OF COLORADO
              Civil Action No._____
```

QUICK COMMERCIAL LOANS,   )
INC. A Colorado Corporation,)
)
            Plaintiff,   )   COMPLAINT ON
)
v.   )   PROMISSORY NOTE
)
GERALD K. JONES,   )
)
            Defendant.   )

COMES NOW the Plaintiff, by and through its counsel, FISH, FISH, and LAKE, and complains and alleges as follows:

1. That the amount involved herein is in excess of $1,000.00.

2. That venue is proper in this Court because Defendant resided at 621 Pine Street, Boulder, Colorado (Boulder County) as of the commencement of this action.

3. That the Defendant, on or about March 30, 1983 executed and delivered to Plaintiff a Promissory Note, a copy of which is attached hereto and hereby made a part of this Complaint.

4. That the Defendant on or about March 30, 1983 received $5,000.00 as a loan under the terms of the Promissory Note above referenced.

5. That the Defendant has refused to make payments when due and there remains yet due and payable the sum of $3,652.19.

WHEREFORE, Plaintiff demands Judgment against the Defendant in the amount of $3,652.19 together with interest and legal fees as provided in said note, for the costs of suit and collection of the Judgment, interest on the entire amount due at the legal rate from date of Judgment and such other relief as the Court may deem just and proper.

                                    FISH, FISH and LAKE
                                    Attorneys at Law

Plaintiff's Address   By: Frank R. Fish, Jr. #2232
                                    1909 Pearl Street, Suite 1300
828 Arapahoe Street   Boulder, Colorado 80302
Boulder, Colorado 80302   Telephone: (303) 499-1058

Figure 2.4 Example of a Summons

```
                Court Filing Stamp
    ┌──────────────────────┐          IN THE...DISTRICT........COURT
    │                      │                    IN AND FOR
    │                      │          ..............COUNTY OF....BOULDER................
    │                      │                ·AND STATE OF COLORADO
    │                      │
    │                      │          Civil Action No. ..................... Div. ..............
    └──────────────────────┘
```

QUICK COMMERCIAL LOANS, INC.
A Colorado Corporation

              Plaintiff..........,   SUMMONS

                vs.

GERALD K. JONES

              Defendant............

THE PEOPLE OF THE STATE OF COLORADO
TO THE ABOVE NAMED DEFENDANT.........., GREETINGS:

  You are hereby summoned and required to file with the clerk an answer to the complaint within 20 days after service of this summons upon you. If you fail so to do, judgment by default will be taken against you for the relief demanded in the complaint.

  If service upon you is made outside the State of Colorado, or by publication, or if a copy of the complaint be not served upon you with this summons, you are required to file your answer to the complaint within 30 days after service of this summons upon you.

  Warning: If this summons does not contain the docket number of the civil action, then the complaint may not now be on file with the clerk of the court. The complaint must be filed within ten days after the summons is served, or the court will be without jurisdiction to proceed further and the action will be deemed dismissed without prejudice and without further notice. Information from the court concerning this civil action may not be available until ten days after the summons is served.

  This is an action* in debt, as set forth more fully in the Complaint.

Dated......January 20......................, 19..87..   FISH, FISH and LAKE
                                                          Attorneys at Law

    ....
         Clerk of said Court   Attorney for Plaintiff
                                                          Frank R. Fish, Jr. #2232
    By..   1909 Pearl Street, Suite 1300
              Deputy Clerk   Boulder, Colorado 80302
                                                          Address of Attorney 499-1058

(Seal of Court)

*This summons is issued pursuant to Rule 4, C.R.C.P., as amended. If the summons is published or served without a copy of the complaint, after the word "action" state the relief demanded. If body execution is sought the summons must state, "This is an action founded upon tort."

Of course, lawyers should make every effort to resolve cases before they come to trial. It may be clear from the pleadings that a ground for compromise exists, and lawyers often negotiate with each other compromise solutions which are in the best interests of all the parties to the dispute. Compromise solutions to civil disputes are encouraged by the courts, and it is possible to compromise at any time prior to the trial.

Appearing in Court

If the lawyers cannot settle out of court and if the pleadings have been finalized, it is time to prepare for trial. Each of the lawyers marshals as much **evidence** as possible in anticipation of the courtroom appearance. If there are both questions of law (e.g., was the writing a contract?) *and* questions of fact (e.g., was the defendant negligent?) to be decided, then there is a need to have a **jury.** Either party may demand a jury; but if both parties decide not to have a jury, the judge alone will decide the questions of fact. If no dispute exists as to the facts of a case (i.e., what happened), then there is no need for a jury and the case can be tried in front of a judge. Choosing a jury must be done with the utmost care to avoid bias.

In a very recent important criminal case shattering precedent, *Batson v. Kentucky,* 106 S.Ct. 1712 (1986), the U.S. Supreme Court, in reversing and remanding for further proceedings the conviction by an all white jury of a black defendant, held that purposeful racial discrimination in the selection of a jury denies a defendant the "protection that a trial by jury is intended to secure," namely a jury of one's peers. The prosecutor had exercised its **peremptory challenges** to exclude four blacks from the jury. Prior to this case, a black defendant who alleged discriminatory exclusion of black jurors had the burden of showing that the prosecution invariably used peremptory challenges to exclude blacks *in case after case*—"a crippling burden of proof." In this case the court held that, if the defendant can show a pattern of discriminatory challenges *in that defendant's trial alone,* then the prosecutor has the burden of demonstrating a nonracial motive for making such challenges.

Once the jury is chosen the trial may begin. Each side presents its evidence to the judge and jury. Lawyers must be careful that they present their views without violating the rules of evidence for the admission of materials to the court. Lawyers not only present their best evidence, but they try to find flaws in their opponents' evidence. For example, oral evidence which is presented by a witness for the plaintiff may be rebutted through skillful **cross-examination** by the defendant's lawyer—the process of questioning an opposing witness following his or her original testimony.

When both sides have concluded their presentation, including their summations, the judge makes a statement to the jury explaining what law they must consider in coming to a verdict. These explanations to the jury are called the jury instructions.

The jury then retires to a private room in the courthouse or elsewhere to deliberate the **verdict.** When this is done they return to the court and announce their decision. The judge then renders **judgment.**

The losing side then has a set period of time within which it must decide whether or not to appeal to a higher court. Again, the appeal must be based upon a disagreement about a point of *law,* either substantive or some procedural violation. Generally, there can be no appeal of questions of *fact.* For example, if we go back to the case of the scratched stereo, a question of *fact* would be: Who scratched the speaker cabinet? A question of *law* might be centered around the interpretation of some aspect of contract law, such as determination of the meaning of unconscionable contracts, or whether the conduct of the parties created a contract.

On appeal, the case is heard by a panel of judges. Normally a party has the right to one appeal. Prior to the hearing date, each lawyer submits a written report outlining his or her position on the disputed point of law. This document is called a *brief.* On the day

---

evidence
a fact from which an inference can be drawn of another fact

jury (trial)
a group of people selected to decide the facts in a trial

challenge
(in a jury trial) objection by a party to an action to persons chosen for service on a jury to try a case who have not been selected properly, or who are not qualified or impartial

peremptory challenge
a challenge to an individual juror for which no cause need be stated. Only a limited number of peremptory challenges are allowed in each case

cross-examination
a party's initial examination of a witness other than his own in a trial

verdict
a jury's finding of fact

judgment
the final decision of a case by a court

of the hearing, each lawyer argues the points of law before the panel of judges, and the panel at some later time files a written decision. This decision may in certain instances be appealed to the next highest court in the particular system. Sooner or later final resolutions of the dispute occur either because the parties are satisfied or because there are no additional grounds or opportunities for appeal.

The Law Relevant to the Situation

Statutory Law

The form of law that most people think of when asked to answer the question "What is a law?" is **statutory law.** Federal statutory laws are bills passed by the United States House of Representatives and Senate, signed by the President, and not declared unconstitutional by the court system. Each of the states also has statutory laws, passed through their equivalents of the House and Senate and signed by the governor and allowed to stand by the courts. Further, cities, towns, and other municipalities have the authority to pass *ordinances,* which are forms of statutory law. One simple example of a statute is the law which requires some businesses to close on Sunday. But statutory law is not the only source of law.

statutory law
bills passed by a legislature and signed into law by the president or governor

Common Law

In the previous chapter we discussed how norms of a society can become translated into law. When settlers came to America, there obviously were no American laws for them to follow; but they did have norms for behavior based on the laws of their native lands. Many of these norms, mostly from England, have been incorporated by reference into the laws of the United States, both federal and state. This happens when courts of law refer to these norms and use them in deciding cases. Norms may not be in statutory form but are reflected in the principles of law made by courts in their decisions. Judges often refer to these principles as **common law,** the common concept of justice *not in statutory form.* And the principles are just as binding as statutory law. The early colonies in America had the common law of England, much of which continues as a part of the law in the states today, except for Louisiana, where the civil code or Roman law influence continues.

common law
principles of nonstatutory law reflecting the customs and usages of society and found in judicial decisions

Society has left to the courts the power to make law in certain areas without statutory help. Examples of such legal areas of law are torts, contracts, and agency. Society can change the common law by legislation. For example, the common law age of majority was twenty-one years; today in almost all states by legislation the age of majority generally has been changed to eighteen years.

A second great system of law is the Roman or Civil Law. Roman Law is legislative, in the form of a written code, and the judge has the function of applying the pertinent code provision of rule or principle to the particular facts in the case before him. In contrast, the common law is nonlegislative, consisting of those principles of nonstatutory law reflecting the customs and usages of society and found in judicial decisions.

Administrative Law

Chapter 48, on **administrative law,** is devoted to discussion of the administrative rules and regulations that implement constitutional and statutory law. For the time being it is important to realize that both state and federal administrative agencies have the power to make such rules, all of which have the strength of law. There are a number of reasons for granting administrative bodies the power to make rules which have the force of law. One of the most important reasons is that administrative agencies have expertise which goes far beyond the expertise of the legislative bodies who would otherwise have to create the rules. There are literally hundreds of administrative agencies, including the Federal Trade Commission (FTC) and the National Labor Relations Board (NLRB).

administrative law
rules and regulations created by an administrative agency, thereby becoming law

Case Law

Every time a case is heard, a judge is asked to interpret the law in the light of a new set of facts and apply case precedent if it is still applicable—a doctrine called **stare decisis.** When a judge is called upon to interpret the meaning of a word in a statute or administrative rule, or even interpret what a previous judge has said, the judge is in a position to "make law." All the decisions judges write are filed in court reports by court reporters, and their interpretations become binding on lower courts in the same jurisdiction as the lower courts consider future cases on the same point of law. In effect, the legislatures and administrative agencies leave to the judges the task of making more meaningful and clear these pronouncements, which need such attention when they create law. Judges, in doing their job, make law which we call **case law.**

stare decisis
a principle of law which says that earlier cases which are similar should, if possible, be followed to decide current issues before the court

case law
the law that comes from decided cases

Constitutional Law

Each of the states that comprise the United States of America has its own state constitution. These constitutions describe the structure of state government. In a similar fashion, the federal government is structured in accordance with the model described in the U.S. Constitution.

The federal Constitution describes the structure of the three major components of our government. The components are the legislative, executive and judicial branches. In addition, the Constitution contains a series of amendments. The first ten amendments are known as the Bill of Rights. The balance of the amendments describe the various changes we have made to our governance structure over time.

Legislative Branch. The Legislative Branch of our federal government, the Congress, has the power to make laws. There are two branches of the Congress. They are the House of Representatives and the Senate. As most students are aware, a major step in the creation of law is to introduce a bill to either the House or the Senate. In some cases the Constitution specifies which branch should act on a bill first. For example, Article I, Section 7 of the federal Constitution states: "All bills for raising revenue shall originate in the House of Representatives."

Congress has many important powers which are enumerated in the Constitution. In Article I, Section 8 of the Constitution, some of these powers are listed. Many of these powers have a profound effect on business. For example, Congress has the power to establish taxes to pay the debts of the United States and to promote the general welfare and provide for our defense needs. Congress has the power to establish post offices. Congress has the power to grant patents and copyrights, and has the right to establish uniform laws on the subject of bankruptcies.

Executive Branch. Article II of the Constitution defines the Executive Branch of the government. Of course, the executive power is vested in the office of the President of the United States. The Constitution defines how a president is elected. For example, while most of you are aware of the fact that a president is elected for a four year term, you may not recall that only a natural born citizen of the United States is eligible to serve as president. Furthermore, that a person must be at least 35 years old in order to hold the office of president.

The President today is also Commander in Chief of the Army, Navy, and Air Force. The President has the power to make treaties, provided the President gets the concurrence of two-thirds of the Senate. Further, the President has, with the concurrence of the Senate, the right to appoint ambassadors.

Judicial Branch. The federal judiciary consists of the federal judges. Perhaps at this point it would be well to add that all cases involving ambassadors, or other public ministers and consuls as well as those cases in which a state is a party come under the original jurisdiction of the Supreme Court.

The Bill of Rights. The first ten amendments to the Constitution are known as The Bill of Rights. This text cannot provide a detailed analysis of each of the Constitutional Amendments. The First Amendment has particular importance for business. It declares that Congress shall make no law abridging the freedom of speech, or of the press, or of the right of the people peaceably to assemble. The following case is illustrative of the importance of the First Amendment for business.

Facts
On October 13, 1983, plaintiffs Janet Lawson and Sherry Evans purchased personalized license plates from the Indiana Bureau of Motor Vehicles, paying the $30 political contribution "not willingly and voluntarily, but because it was the only means whereby they could obtain a personalized license plate." In Indiana a portion of the fee for a personalized license plate is distributed in equal amounts to the two political parties that cast the largest and next largest number of votes at the most recent election for governor. The individual plaintiffs, and the Libertarian Party on behalf of its members, alleged that the Indiana scheme violated their rights under the First and Fourteenth Amendments of the U.S. Constitution by conditioning the availability of a government benefit on the surrender of their First Amendment rights of free association and free expression. The plaintiffs ask for an injunction to restrain implementation of the distribution of the money to the political parties. Should an injunction be granted?

Decision
No.

Reasoning
The reason that government constitutionally may be allowed to use public funds to finance political parties is that the funds are not considered to be contributing to the spreading of a political message, but rather are advancing an important public interest, the facilitation of "public discussion and participation in the electoral process, goals vital to a self governing people."

Given that public financing of qualifying political parties does not offend the First Amendment, it should make no constitutional difference that the money for such financing is raised through what in effect is a sales tax on personalized license plates.

Libertarian Party of Indiana v. Packard, 741 F.2d 981 (1984).

The Amendments. There are 26 amendments to the Constitution, including The Bill of Rights. These amendments deal with matters such as succession to the presidency in the event of the president's death or resignation, the age at which people can vote, and the right to vote without reference to the sex of the voter.

Summary Statement

1. There are alternatives to the legal system for resolving disputes. Not all problems need to be brought to a lawyer. Compromise, arbitration, and mediation are natural alternatives. If the dispute cannot be settled in any other way, the legal system presents the forum for grievance resolution.
2. Lawyers and judges are necessary for the federal and state legal systems to function.
3. The basic design of all state legal systems is the same, and in both the federal and state systems we have courts of general and special jurisdictions and courts of trial and review.

4. The legal process is a series of interrelated actions that are normally taken in an attempt to resolve controversies over the applicability of law in a given situation.
5. Law that can be applied to a dispute varies. The law of any one state consists of the U.S. Constitution, the public Acts of Congress, its own state constitution, the public Acts of its own legislature, case decisions of the Supreme Court of the United States on a constitutional question, case decisions of its own courts, federal and state administrative law, and the private law of individuals within its boundaries.
6. The structure of the federal Constitution consists of three components—legislative, executive, and judicial branches. The first ten amendments to the Constitution are known as The Bill of Rights.

The following is a classic case illustrating the purpose of pleadings and the need for a lawyer, and how the United States legal system works. It also shows how the law is concerned with justice rather than pure procedure. However, in most instances failure to follow the rules of procedure is fatal to a case.

Dioguardi v. Durning
139 F.2d 774 (1944)

Clark, Circuit Judge. In his complaint, obviously home drawn, plaintiff attempts to assert a series of grievances against the Collector of Customs . . . of New York growing out of his endeavors to import . . . bottles of "tonics." We may pass certain of his claims as either inadequate or inadequately stated and consider only these two: (1) that on the auction day, October 9, 1940, when defendant sold the merchandise at "public custom," "he sold my merchandise to another bidder with my price of $110, and not of his price of $120," and (2) "that three weeks before the sale, two cases, of 19 bottles each case, disappeared." Plaintiff does not make . . . clear how these goods came into the collector's hands . . . but he does say he made a claim for "refund of merchandise which was two-thirds paid in Milano, Italy," and that the collector denied the claim. These and other circumstances alleged indicate . . . that his original dispute was with his consignor. . . . *This complaint was dismissed by the District Court . . . [because] it "fails to state facts sufficient to constitute a cause of action."*

. . . [P]laintiff filed an amended complaint, wherein, with an obviously heightened conviction that he was being unjustly treated, he vigorously reiterates his claims, including those quoted above and now stated as that his "medicinal extracts" were given to the Springdale Distilling Company "with my betting [bidding?] price of $110: and not their price of $120," and "It isn't so easy to do away with two cases with 37 bottles of one quart. Being protected, they can take this chance." . . . [D]efendant . . . explained the loss of the two cases by "saying that they had leaked, which could never be true in the manner they were bottled." *On defendant's motion for dismissal on the same ground as before, the court made a final judgment dismissing* the complaint, and plaintiff now comes to us with increased volubility, if not clarity.

. . . [H]owever, . . . he has stated enough to withstand a mere formal motion, directed only to the face of the complaint, and . . . here is another instance of judicial haste which in the long run makes waste.

We think that . . . the plaintiff has disclosed his claims; as it stands, we do not see how the plaintiff may properly be deprived of his day in court to show what he obviously so firmly believes and what for present purposes defendant must be taken as admitting. . . . The record indicates that he refused further help from a lawyer . . . ,and his brief (which was a recital of facts, rather than an argument of law) shows distrust of a lawyer of standing at this bar. . . . [This] is the plaintiff's privilege . . .; but we fear that he will be indeed ill advised to attempt to meet a motion for summary judgment or other similar presentation of the merits without competent advice and assistance.

Judgment is reversed and the action is remanded for further proceedings not inconsistent with this opinion.

Questions and Case Problems

1. What is the difference between arbitration and mediation?

2. What is the difference between statutory law and common law?

3. Just before leaving office, John Adams, President of the United States, appointed 42 Federalists. The Senate confirmed these appointments, but the new President told his Secretary of State, Madison, not to deliver 17 of these commissions. William Marbury was to have received one of the commissions. Marbury appealed to the Supreme Court of the United States for his appointment under legislation passed by Congress which was contrary to the United States Constitution. Must legislation which is contrary to a constitution give way to the constitution under our system of law? [*Marbury v. Madison*, 1 Cranch 137 (1803).]

4. Dr. Sabates, on behalf of his professional association, contracted with International Medical Centers, Inc., (IMC) to provide ophthalmologic services for IMC patients. A condition of Sabates' employment was that he was to meet the qualifications and standards for staff membership at International Hospital. Although IMC assured Sabates' application for permanent staff privileges at the hospital would be promptly processed, his temporary privileges were allowed to expire resulting in IMC terminating its contract with Sabates. Sabates objected to this breach of contract. What mechanisms might be used by the parties to resolve their dispute? [*Sabates, M.D. v. International Medical Centers, Inc.*, 450 So.2d 514 (Fla. 1984).]

5. Standard Oil Company of New Jersey and thirty-three other corporations, John D. Rockefeller, William Rockefeller, and five other individuals decided to seek a reversal of a decree in a lower court which attempted to dissolve a holding company which was believed to be a violation of a certain federal antitrust law because its actions were in restraint of trade. The statute did not define "in restraint of trade." The court developed a rule of reason which gave meaning to the words "restraint of trade." This rule of reason is an example of what type of law? [*Standard Oil Company of New Jersey v. United States*, 221 U.S. 1 (1910).]

6. Robbins had transported construction and road building materials for at least 30 years, but had never before sought an ICC (Interstate Commerce Commission) authorization. Lacking this authorization in the past Robbins often had to pay "civil forfeitures" for unlawful operations.

    In March 1982, Robbins applied for an ICC certificate authorizing him to operate as a motor common carrier. According to the Department of Commerce, ICC had to consider the nature and extent of past violations, whether Robbins had made sincere efforts to correct his past mistakes, etc. In considering the matter, is the court dealing with a question of fact or law? Explain. [*Department of Transportation Federal Highway Administration v. Interstate Commerce Commission*, 733 F.2d 105 (1984).]

7. Tompkins, a citizen of Pennsylvania, was injured on a dark night by a passing train of the Erie Railroad. He claimed the accident occurred through the train company's negligence. The action was brought in the U.S. District Court, for the Southern District of New York. The case resulted in a battle over the appropriate law to apply since there was a diversity of citizenship. It was held in the case that the federal court had to apply state law to determine whether Tompkins' complaint contained a cause of action, and it could not create by case decision a federal right for Tompkins. This means there is one type of law which the federal system does not have. What is this law? [*Erie Railroad v. Tompkins*, 304 U.S. 64 (1938).]

8. Alleging negligence, appellant filed in the county court at law an original petition seeking $4,750 in damages for personal injuries. In her pleading she filed a supplemental petition, a deceptive trade practice claim, and prayed for treble damages. Appellee's argument is based upon the premises that plaintiff's petition should be contained in one instrument in writing and that a party may not adopt by reference in an amended pleading a statement

from a prior pleading. The appellee did not specially *plead* in writing the appellant's impropriety, and now seeks to assert the impropriety in an oral motion to dismiss appellant's petition. Based on this information, should the appellant's pleading fail? [*Hawkins v. Anderson,* 672 S.W.2d 293 (Tex. 1984).]

9. In order to make the law in certain legal areas uniform among the various states, each state appoints lawyer "Commissioners" to a national body called the National Conference of Commissioners on Uniform State Laws which drafts proposed uniform laws for consideration by each state. One of the uniform laws presented to the states for adoption is the Uniform Commercial Code. When a state legislature adopts the Code making it the law of the state, is this law an example of common law, statutory law, administrative law, or some other form of law? Explain the difference between the form of law you chose and these other forms of law.

10. One of the most basic rights of our legal system is that every individual is entitled to his or her day in court. It has also been said that a lawyer who represents himself or herself has a fool for a client. Evaluate these statements in the light of *Dioguardi v. Durning,* 139 F.2d 774 (1944).[3] Notice that Mr. Dioguardi was unable to communicate his claim very clearly. Should this make any difference in proceeding with a legal case?

---

[3] See p. 28.

Criminal Law 3

After you have read this chapter, you should be able to:

1. Distinguish between criminal law and tort law.
2. Identify the different categories of crime: felony, misdemeanor, violation, treason.
3. Explain the difference between legality and morality.
4. Describe the requisites for crime.
5. Explain several defenses to criminal acts.
6. Explain several different business crimes: arson, forgery, bad checks, embezzlement, burglary.

Introduction

In the preceding chapters of this Part, we discussed legal systems and utilization of those systems and alternatives in order to resolve *civil* disputes. In this chapter we will discuss the nature of criminal law as a wrong to the *public* interest and, in the next chapter, discuss the law of torts concerned with wrongs to *private interests*.

Unfortunately, the number of crimes committed in the United States provides convincing evidence of the necessity for spending some time discussing criminal law. The FBI reported that in 1940 there were approximately 100 crimes committed per 100,000 population; 118 crimes per 100,000 in 1950; 145 in 1960, and 180 in 1965. Subsequent figures available from the FBI indicate that in 1975 over 11 million serious crimes were committed (approximately 5,000 per 100,000 population). The number of crimes continues to be a problem. By 1983 approximately one violent crime was being committed every 6 *seconds* somewhere in the United States and one property crime (e.g., theft of another's goods) was being committed every three *seconds*.[1]

Alarming as these figures are, they tell only part of the story. Increasingly, business organizations have had to face the reality that the number of "white-collar" crimes is also increasing. These are offenses such as embezzlement or larceny.

The substantive law of crime is concerned with defining what duties we owe to society and what rights we have as members of society. Thus, a study of criminal law is important to us so that we may know our legal rights and duties.

Moreover, because crime has a significant impact upon us as individuals and has an impact upon business, it is important for us to have an exposure to this area of law.

Concern of the Law

Society is concerned not only with disputes among persons for wrongs committed by them on each other for which they seek *relief against each other,* but also with wrongs to society and its members for which *punishment should be imposed.*

The greater part of this book discusses civil law and civil procedure. In this chapter we will examine briefly "the other half of the law" known as criminal law. A **crime** is an act, committed or omitted, in violation of a public law governing it[2] (e.g., robbery, traffic violation). The major difference between a crime and a **tort** is that a crime is an offense against the state (a public wrong) in which the *state prosecutes* the individual; whereas a tort is a civil (private) wrong to a person other than breach of contract and the *injured party must be the one to bring the civil lawsuit* (e.g., negligence). For example, one who negligently drives a car is civilly liable to the pedestrian injured by such negligence.

In a criminal offense, the society as a whole takes action against a person who has violated a formalized norm. Most of society dislikes murder, burglary, arson, and other such criminal offenses, and collectively we have delegated the responsibility of dealing with accused criminals to various governmental prosecutors. If an individual is found to be guilty of an offense, he or she is punished by the government. We are saying that society as a whole found the act reprehensible. Some acts are reprehensible to both society as a whole *and* to private individuals who are hurt. Therefore, certain acts are considered both torts and crimes. For example, A shoots and wounds B. A can be prosecuted for *criminal* assault and battery, and B can sue A civilly for damages for the torts of *civil* assault and battery.

crime
an act, committed or omitted, in violation of a public law governing it

tort
a civil (private) noncontractual wrong for which a court will give a remedy

---

[1] See FBI statistics, *Uniform Crime Reports,* 1975, 1980, and 1984 (Washington, D.C., U.S. Government Printing Office), as well as *New York Times,* June 10, 1971, p. 22, col. 3, and June 9, 1972, p. 1, col. 2.

[2] *Shick v. United States,* 195 U.S. 65 (1904).

Categories of Crime

Felony
A **felony** is the most serious category of crime. It is a crime for which, usually, the punishment can be more than one year in prison. Some states have an alternative definition for felony: any crime punishable by death or imprisonment in the state prison. Examples of felonies include murder, robbery, and rape. In some states a convicted felon loses certain citizenship rights, such as the right to vote and to hold public office.

felony
a serious crime for which, usually, the punishment can be more than one year in prison

Misdemeanor
Another kind of criminal act is a **misdemeanor.** It is a crime for which the punishment is imprisonment for less than one year, usually in a city or county jail, and the possibility of a fine. Examples of misdemeanors include shoplifting and petty larceny.

misdemeanor
a crime for which the punishment is less than one year in prison and the possibility of a fine

Violation or Infraction
Some jurisdictions have an additional classification for offenses of lesser importance, such as parking or traffic citations. These are called *violations* or *infractions* and are generally distinguished by the minimal nature of the punishment, such as a fine. Usually they are classified as misdemeanors.

Treason
Treason is a felony which is specifically defined in the U.S. Constitution as "levying war against them [the states], or in adhering to their enemies, giving them aid and comfort."[3]

treason
a felony specifically defined by the U.S. Constitution

Requisites for Crime

Morality versus Criminality
Just as in the law of torts, certain acts may seem reprehensible to you, but they may be only morally wrong and not criminal in nature. You will not be treated as a criminal if you do not yield your seat in a crowded bus to an elderly individual, or if you fail to remember an engagement (even if it's a promise to witness your best friend's wedding). Similarly, commission of certain infractions generally is insufficient to label someone a moral bankrupt. For example, few would argue that overtime parking at a meter is an indication of immorality.

Act and Intent
Every crime requires either an act or an omission (failure to act) when action is required by law. This very simple statement is an extremely important base of criminal law. If people could be punished without having committed an act required by law, we would be liable to punishment just for our thoughts. In addition, all people are charged with the responsibility of knowing the law. The following case illustrates that ignorance of the law is no excuse.

Facts
Students were involved in a long-standing dispute. They agreed to meet in a parking lot. When the victim arrived at the designated spot, he encountered his adversary and several other individuals. The victim was forced into a van, then taken to a selected spot and severely beaten. The defendants claimed that they thought that they might be charged with assault, but did not know that they could be charged with kidnapping. Is ignorance of the law an excuse?

Decision
No.

Reasoning
One is obliged to discover whether a contemplated activity is criminal. And if he acts without such knowledge, he runs the risk of violation and consequent criminal prosecution.

State of Iowa v. Clark, 346 N.W.2d 510 (Ia. 1984).

---
[3] U.S. Constitution, Art. III, sec. 3.

mens rea
the mental element required for a crime

This mental element of intent stated by the court in the decision is sometimes given the name **mens rea.** However, students should not confuse *mens rea* with *motive*. You do not have to prove a motive to prove a crime. Different kinds of intent are required for different crimes. Some crimes require *specific intent,* which means they require the proof that the accused intended to commit the particular wrongful act proscribed by law. For example, a general definition of forgery is the false making or materially altering, with intent to defraud, of any writing which, if genuine, might apparently be of legal efficacy. To be guilty of forgery you must have the intent to defraud. If you are merely reproducing an item with the honest belief that you have permission, you will not be held criminally responsible.

Some crimes require only *general intent* but not *specific intent*. This means that you do not have to have the particular intent to commit a certain crime, but only an intent to be doing what you did. An example of a crime usually involving simply general intent is robbery. Robbery often is defined as "taking property from the person or presence of another by use of force or threatening the imminent use of force." Note that no specific intent is spelled out in such statutory language.

Sometimes the mere agreement to commit an offensive act is regarded as violative of the law. For example, if two individuals communicate to each other the desire to commit embezzlement, they have committed a crime. That crime is known as *conspiracy*. Notice that the act of communicating this desire is enough to warrant a criminal charge. Some states require also an overt act.

Defenses.

Ability to Commit Crime—Defenses

Insanity

The classic defense to crime is that the actor was insane *at the time the actor* committed the offense. There are a number of definitions of legal insanity. Traditionally two tests were employed to prove insanity. The first is the *McNaghten test*. Under this older rule, the persons accused would have to prove that either they did not know the nature of the act, or if they did know the nature of the act they did not know that it was wrong. A second traditional test is the *irresistible impulse test*. This requires that defendants prove that they were suffering from a mental disease which caused them to act in the criminal way (irresistible impulse) even though they knew right from wrong.

More recently, two additional tests have been added. According to the *Durham test,* insanity is demonstrated by proof that the actor was suffering from a mental condition and that the act was a result of that condition. The *American Law Institute Model Code test* suggests that a person is not responsible if, as a result of his mental disease, he lacked substantial capacity "to appreciate the criminality of his conduct or to conform his conduct to the requirements of the law." The ALI Model Code test was used in the judge's instructions to the jury in the 1982 criminal trial of John W. Hinckley, Jr. for the alleged attempted assassination of President Reagan in 1981. Additionally the term "mental disease" does "not include an abnormality manifested only by repeated criminal or otherwise anti-social conduct."[4] In the following case the court held that the trial judge did not instruct the jury that the necessary relationship between the defendant's mental disease and the criminal act must be established beyond a reasonable doubt.

Facts
Defendant was convicted of murder. He was mentally ill at the time that the alleged murder was accomplished. Four doctors testified at the trial as experts. Fifteen witnesses testified concerning Carter's life history, his personality and habits. The jury was not instructed to find the defendant not guilty if, at the time of the killing, his insanity caused the act of taking human life. On conviction, the defendant appealed.

Decision
Reversed and remanded for a new trial.

---

[4] American Law Institute Model Penal Code Proposed Official Draft, May 4, 1962, sec. 4.01.

Reasoning
There must be a relationship between the disease and the criminal act; and the relationship must be such as to justify a reasonable inference that the act would not have been committed if the person had not been suffering from the disease. The relationship must be established beyond a reasonable doubt.

Carter v. United States, 252 F.2d 608 (1957).

Minors
At common law there existed a sliding scale for determining the responsibility of children (minors) for the commission of a crime. Under seven years old a child is conclusively presumed not to have the ability to commit a crime. Between seven and fourteen the child is presumed incompetent to commit a crime, but the state may rebut the presumption. Finally, between fourteen and adulthood the child is presumed to have the ability, but he or she may rebut that presumption. The trend in many states is to treat some minors as adults if they are charged with serious crimes.

Duress
If a defendant commits a wrongful act because he or she was induced to do so by the use of, or threat to use, unlawful force against the defendant or another, which a reasonable person would have been unable to resist, the defendant can assert the defense of **duress**. For example, if someone orders you to rob a bank while holding a gun at you and threatening your life if you do not cooperate, you can later use the defense of duress to charges of robbery leveled at you by the state.

duress
wrongful inducement to do that which a reasonable person would have been unable to resist

Corporate Responsibility
For years, a perplexing problem facing criminal lawyers was whether to hold corporations liable for criminal acts. The answer today is generally yes. Although corporations obviously cannot be imprisoned, they can be fined for offenses. An officer of the corporation will be held criminally liable only if he or she actually committed the wrongful act or directed that the act be done.

Other Defenses
Intoxication or *drug use* is often used as a defense to criminal culpability. However, voluntary drunkenness will not help you avoid liability. For example, if Carol, a student, voluntarily indulges her drug habit and then commits a crime, most courts would still find her guilty of the crime she committed. *Consent*—that is, voluntary agreement to do what would otherwise be the commission of a crime—may sometimes be a defense. For example, bodily harm which might otherwise be criminal in nature is consented to by the participants in a boxing match.

Select Crimes Relevant to Business

For a more complete treatment of any of the following business crimes,[5] see one of the many excellent legal encyclopedias such as *Corpus Juris Secundum* or *American Jurisprudence*.

Arson
Arson may be defined as the willful and malicious burning of the dwelling house of another. This is a common law definition, which today has been extended to include one's own house and the buildings of another, depending on the particular state statute. Recall that common law consisted of those norms of behavior which became embodied in the case law over time. Each state has its own statutory definition of arson. For example: West Virginia Code 61–31–1: "Any person who willfully and maliciously sets fire to or

arson
the willful and malicious burning of the dwelling house of another (at common law); today, by statute, arson includes one's own house and the buildings of another

---
[5] The definitions that follow are useful *for teaching purposes only*. Students with legal problems are reminded that the best source of advice for their particular problems is an attorney.

burns or causes to be burned or aids, counsels or procures the burning of any dwelling house whether occupied, unoccupied or vacant, or any kitchen, shop, barn, stable or other outhouse that is parcel thereof, or belonging to or adjoining thereto, whether the property of himself or another shall be guilty of arson in the first degree."

Crimes Involving Computer Use
All business students are aware of the growing importance of computers in the world of management. Because computers contain many different kinds of information, it is possible for an adventurous individual to commit a host of different crimes. If a person steals a particular program that the computer can use, he or she has stolen property of value, that is, committed "theft." If this program is a trade secret and the individual uses the program for personal advantage, he or she may have committed the crime of "misappropriation of a trade secret." Of course, stealing competitors' lists from a computer file might also qualify as a misappropriation of a trade secret.

Embezzlement is another crime that increasingly involves the use of a computer. Employees with access to computers in banks, for example, may learn how to transfer money from one account to another. If the employee abuses this understanding and trust and takes the money owed by the bank to its customers, the employee may have committed "embezzlement." In the following case two individuals used a computer to commit a crime.

Facts
Paladino and Giovengo were convicted for transgressing the Federal Wire Fraud Statute, and Paladino appealed. Paladino devised and executed a scheme to defraud TWA of money paid by passengers who purchased one-way airline tickets with cash. When a passenger approaches the TWA agent at an airport with a request to purchase a ticket, the agent enters ticket information into a TWA computer terminal. The terminal transfers the information through interstate telephone circuits and then to the main TWA computer. Through careful planning the two men were able to obtain airline tickets which they would mark void and send to the TWA accounting office for cash. Is this a computer crime?

Decision
Yes.

Reasoning
The Federal Wire Fraud Statute of 1976 provides: whoever, having devised or intending to devise any scheme or artifice to defraud or for obtaining money or property by means of false or fraudulent pretenses or promises, transmits or causes to be transmitted by means of wire, radio or television communication in interstate or foreign commerce, any writings, scheme or artifice, shall be fined not more than a thousand dollars or imprisoned for not more than five years or both. Paladino maintained that this law does not apply to all interstate wire communications but only to those regulated by the Federal Communications Commission. He contends that TWA is not a common carrier regulated by the FCC. However, we find no merit in this argument. Nothing in the language of the statute suggests that its scope is limited to fraud committed by use of interstate wires subject to FCC regulation. Instead, the terms of the statute indicate that it applies to anyone who commits fraud. The legislative history of the statute also fails to confirm Paladino's theory. Therefore, a crime was committed.

United States v. Giovengo, 637 F.2d 941 (1980).

The increasing unauthorized and improper use of counterfeit electronic devices in computer and electronic fund transfer systems in or affecting interstate commerce has resulted in federal legislation making such conduct a federal crime. Under the Electronic Fund Transfers Act, it is a crime to: knowingly use, or attempt or conspire to use, counterfeit, fictitious, altered, forged, lost, stolen, or a fraudulently obtained debit instrument (electric control device) to obtain money, goods, services or anything else of value above a specified amount; or, with unlawful or fraudulent intent, sell or transport such counterfeit devices; or knowingly to obtain money, goods, or services by the use of such counterfeit devices. Under the Counterfeit Access Device and Computer Fraud and Abuse Act, unauthorized access to a computer, and unauthorized use when access is authorized, is a federal crime.

Misappropriation of Trade Secrets

Recently a number of cases have come to the courts that involve an employee or some other individual copying a company secret and using that secret for personal advantage and without permission. This is a particularly troublesome problem when the secret "involves a formula, pattern device, or bit of information critical to the success of the business involved."[6] These kinds of secrets are called "trade secrets," and the crime of copying and using these trade secrets without permission is called "misappropriation of trade secrets." In the following case the court held that there was no trade secret and, therefore, the alleged crime of misappropriation of trade secrets had not occurred.

Facts
Robinson, defendant, on the pretext of becoming a dealer for Energy Management, Inc. gained access to a partial list of Energy's customers. He then formed a competing company and used this list to his advantage. Energy never took precautions to secure or preserve the secrecy of the list. The defendant was tried for committing the crime of misappropriation of a trade secret. Is this a misappropriation of a trade secret?

Decision
No.

Reasoning
In deciding whether a secret is a trade secret, one must examine (1) the extent to which the information is known outside the business, (2) the extent to which it is known by employees and others involved in the business, and (3) the extent of measures taken by the employer to guard the secrecy of the information. Here, no attempt was made to guard the secrecy of the list, so there is no trade secret here. Therefore, the defendant is not guilty of the alleged crime.

Commonwealth v. Robinson, 388 N.E.2d 705 (Mass. 1979).

Forgery

The false making or altering, with intent to defraud, of any writing which, if genuine, might be of legal efficacy is known as common law **forgery**. In a business setting, forgery might include altering public records, issuing false certificates, or falsifying a doctor's prescription. Altering of checks is also considered forgery and is a particularly common form of forgery.

forgery
the unauthorized act of imitating or altering a writing with the intent to defraud and impose liability

Issuing a Bad Check

As stated in the consolidated laws of New York, a person is guilty of issuing a bad **check** when: (a) as a **drawer** or representative drawer, he utters a check knowing that he or his principal, as the case may be, does not then have sufficient funds with the **drawee** to cover it, and (b) he intends or believes at the time of utterance that payment will be refused by the drawee upon presentation, and (c) payment is refused by the drawee upon presentation.

check
a negotiable "draft drawn on a bank payable on demand" UCC 3-104(2)(b)

drawer
the person who initially draws or creates and signs a draft

drawee
the person on whom a draft is drawn and ordered to pay

Embezzlement and Larceny

Embezzlement and larceny are two closely related crimes. **Embezzlement** involves depriving someone of his or her property through breach of a trust relationship.[7] Note that the property is generally obtained lawfully but later converted to the embezzler's own use. **Larceny** is a common law crime which involves the taking and carrying away of the personal property of another by someone who does not have the right to do so. Notice that there is no relationship of trust between the parties to larceny. In the following case an employee had a position of authority and violated his employer's trust.

embezzlement
depriving someone of his property through breach of a trust relationship

larceny
the taking and carrying away of the personal property of another without the right to do so

---

[6] Restatement (Second) of Torts sec. 757 (1965).

[7] 26 Am. Jur. 2d *Embezzlement*, secs. 1–7 (1966).

Facts
Boueri was a Vice President of Caesar's Palace in charge of hosting affluent guests. As part of his job, he would arrange complimentary air fare and other services for such people. At the grand jury hearing, evidence was presented that Boueri had authorized tickets for several people who neither received tickets nor money, and Boueri kept the refund money received from the travel agency for unused tickets. Boueri sought dismissal of the grand jury's indictment for embezzlement claiming the tickets were not the property of Caesar's Palace, thereby making embezzlement impossible.

Decision
The Court decided embezzlement was possible.

Reasoning
Although Caesar's Palace did not furnish Boueri with a cash box from which to embezzle funds, Caesar's Palace did entrust Boueri with power and authority through which he could possess his employer's funds. Therefore, embezzlement was possible.

State of Nevada v. Boueri, 672 P.2d 33 (Nev. 1983).

It is interesting to note that the Supreme Court of the United States recently held that, where a state legislature specifically authorizes cumulative punishment under two statutes, regardless of whether those two statutes proscribe the same conduct, under the Blockburger case (*Blockburger v. United States,* 284 U.S. 299 (1932)) cumulative punishments may be imposed in a single trial under such statutes. (*Missouri v. Hunter,* 459 U.S. 359 (1983).)

Burglary versus Robbery

Two crimes which are often confused by lay persons but which are actually quite different are burglary and robbery. Both are common law crimes. **Robbery** is the taking of money or goods of value from the person of another or in his or her presence, against that person's will, by force or fear. In effect, it is an aggravated larceny. **Burglary,** however, is the breaking and entering in the night of the home of another with the intent to commit *any* felony therein. Many states have amended the burglary statute or have alternative laws to deal with burglary-type offenses during the daylight hours. Most states now say burglary can involve any structure, not just a home.

Commercial Bribing

All states have laws regulating *bribery*. Some have special statutes which regulate bribery in a business setting. For example: New York sec. 180.00 ". . . guilty of commercial bribing when he confers, or offers or agrees to confer, any benefit upon any employee, agent or fiduciary without the consent of the latter's employer or principal, with intent to influence his conduct in relation to his employer's or principal's affairs." The federal Foreign Corrupt Practices Act of 1977[8] condemns foreign corrupt payments as a form of bribery.

Preparatory Crimes

Sometimes merely preparing to commit a crime results in a criminal offense being committed. *Solicitation* involves inciting someone else to commit a felony. It is a common law crime. Contemporary laws would include inciting to commit misdemeanors as solicitation. **Attempt** is a preparatory crime. Here an actor has the specific intent to commit a crime; makes some act toward accomplishing the crime which goes beyond mere preparation; and has the apparent ability to complete the crime but is stopped by something beyond the actor's control.

Violation of the Antitrust Laws

Violation of the antitrust laws can be a crime. Antitrust laws are discussed in chapter 47.

robbery
the taking of money or goods of value from the person of another or in his presence, against his will, by force or fear

burglary
the breaking and entering in the night of the structure (e.g., building) of another with the intent to commit a felony therein

attempt
(in criminal law) a preparatory crime

---

[8] For a discussion of this Act, see pp. 678–79.

Summary Statement

1. Crime has a significant impact on society, and an individual will want to know his legal rights and duties as defined by criminal law.
2. There is a difference in rights and duties as defined by the substantive areas of crime, tort, and contract law.
3. Crimes have been categorized according to the seriousness of the end result of the crime—a felony being the most serious, followed by misdemeanor and violation.
4. In criminal law, act plus intent (mens rea) determine whether or not a crime was committed; motive is not a requisite element.
5. Society has certain rights shown in its statutory criminal law, but these rights are limited by defenses to crimes. Some defenses are insanity, minority, consent, duress.
6. Certain crimes have special significance for business. These include arson, larceny, forgery, embezzlement, burglary, computer crimes, and misappropriation of trade secrets. Statutory definitions of the various crimes differ from state to state.

The following case illustrates corporate and corporate executives' responsibility for criminal wrongdoing.

United States v. Park
421 U.S. 658 (1975)

Burger, C. J. Acme Markets Inc. is a national retail food chain with approximately 36,000 employees, 874 retail outlets, and four specialty warehouses. Its headquarters is located in Philadelphia, Pennsylvania. In a five count information filed in the U.S. District Court . . . the government charged Acme and respondent, its president, with violations of the Food, Drug, and Cosmetic Act. Each count of the information alleged that the defendants had received food that had been shipped in interstate commerce and that, while the food was being held for sale in Acme's Baltimore warehouse following shipment in interstate commerce, they caused it to be held in the building accessible to rodents and to be exposed to contamination by rodents. These acts were alleged to have resulted in the food being adulterated (in violation of the law). . . . Acme pleaded guilty to each of the counts of the information. Respondent pleaded not guilty.

Respondent was the only defense witness. He testified that, although all of Acme's employees were in a sense under his general direction, the company had an organizational structure for responsibilities for certain functions according to which different phases of its operation were assigned to individuals who, in turn, have staff and departments under them. He identified those individuals responsible for sanitation, and related that upon receipt of the January 1972 FDA letter he had conferred with the Vice President for Legal Affairs, who informed him that the Baltimore division vice president was investigating the situation immediately and would be taking corrective action and would be preparing a summary of the corrective action through reply to the letter. Respondent stated that he did not believe there was anything he could have done more constructively than what he found was being done.

The jury found respondent guilty on all counts of the information . . . the Court of Appeals reversed the conviction and remanded for a new trial.

We granted *certiorari* because of an apparent conflict among the Courts of Appeals with respect to the standard of liability of corporate officers under the federal Food, Drug, and Cosmetic Act. We reverse.

We cannot agree with the Court of Appeals that it was incumbent upon the District Court to instruct the jury that the government had the burden of establishing "wrongful action" in the sense in which the Court of Appeals used that phrase. The concept of a "responsible relationship" to or a "responsible share in a violation of" the Act indeed imports some measure of blameworthiness; but it is equally clear that the government establishes a *prima facie* case when it introduces evidence sufficient to warrant a finding by the trier of the facts that the defendant had, by reason of his position in the corporation, responsibility and authority either to prevent in the first instance, or promptly correct, the violation complained of, and that he failed to do so. The failure thus to fulfill the duty imposed by the interaction of the corporate agent's authority and the statute furnishes a sufficient causal link. The considerations which prompted the imposition of this duty, and the scope of the duty, provide the measure of culpability.

Therefore, we reverse.

Questions and Case Problems

1. William Doucette can clearly remember that he stabbed and killed Ronald Landry after they arrived at their motel room together. However, he does not seem to be consistent in his explanation of why he killed the victim. Doucette had been drinking rather heavily and states that he was incoherent at the time of the stabbing. Do you think he can successfully use the defense of intoxication? Explain your answer. [*Commonwealth v. Doucette,* 462 N.E.2d 1084 (Mass. 1983).]

2. Burns, whose house was insured against fire, decided that it would cost him less to rebuild his house rather than repair the old one. A cheap way of getting rid of the old house would be to burn it to the ground, which was exactly what Burns did. Under which circumstances would this be an act of arson and when would it not be? Explain your answers. [*Burns v. The State of Georgia,* 305 S.E.2d 398 (Ga. 1983).]

3. One afternoon, at 4 P.M., Patricia DeWall and her cousin looked over some used cars on Russ DeVine's car lot. On DeWall's request, DeVine gave her permission to take a car for a test drive to a motel nearby. However, DeWall and her cousin also stopped at some other local businesses and failed to be back before DeVine's closing hours. They decided to take a spin and took a three hundred mile drive. When they arrived back in the early morning hours, they left the car in DeVine's lot with the keys locked in it. Was this a crime? Explain. [*State of South Dakota v. DeWall,* 343 N.W.2d 790 (S.D. 1984).]

4. Howard Babits was working as a store clerk in a store when he one day accepted a credit card from a person who he knew was not the person named on the card. Was this an offense? Explain. [*People of the State of New York v. Babits,* 469 N.Y.S.2d 537 (N.Y. 1983).]

5. Luther Butler was observed breaking the vent window of a parked automobile on a public street, entering the car, and kneeling on the front passenger's seat facing the dashboard when he was interrupted and fled. He was later caught possessing a pair of pliers. The only damage to the car was the broken vent window. Did Butler commit the crime of larceny? Why or why not? [*People of the State of New York v. Butler,* 465 N.Y.S.2d 477 (N.Y. 1983).]

6. Dianne and Earline occasionally let Montrae and Ricky stay in their apartment overnight. Ricky even kept some clothes and personal effects in the apartment, and T. S. J. often visited when Ricky was there. One morning after Dianne and Earline had left the apartment the night before, someone had broken through the lock in the back door and taken a sweater, two cameras, etc. It was proved that Ricky, Montrae and T. S. J. were responsible for the break-in. The two roommates testified that neither T. S. J., Ricky nor Montrae had permission to enter the apartment that night, although T. S. J. was not aware of this. In addition, T. S. J. did not know that the property taken did not belong to Ricky or Montrae and he did not see how the back door was opened by Ricky. Given these facts, did T. S. J. commit a crime? Explain your answer. [*T. S. J. v. State of Florida,* 439 So.2d 966 (Fla. 1983).]

7. Defendant was the president of the union which represented the Wellston firefighters, and he strongly supported a proposed tax increase for the districts they were serving. On March 26, City of Pagedale and others filed suit against the Wellston Fire Protection District seeking to eliminate this tax proposition due to an illegal election.

William Speiser, Mayor of Pagedale, was the principal witness against defendant. On March 31 and April 1 defendant offered him money and other benefits in return for which the City of Pagedale would withdraw from the lawsuit. Assuming no money or benefits were passed, has a crime been committed? Explain. [*State of Missouri v. Walker,* 657 S.W.2d 704 (Mo. 1983).]

8. Defendants were charged with purchasing and "aiding" in the concealment of certain intellectual property contained in and on two video cassettes of a movie entitled "Star Wars." Note that no charge was made that the video cassettes themselves were stolen property. Is the taping of a movie in this manner a criminal taking of property? [*Commonwealth v. Yourawski,* 425 N.E.2d 298 (Mass. 1981).]

9. Jones and Smith are employed by a large computer company. They worked on a project whose aim was to develop a system for computerizing the generation of sheet music. Using their employer's equipment and time, Jones and Smith decided to market the program through the mails claiming it as their own. Their employer did not know of this activity. Is this a crime?

10. Consider the case of *United States v. Park*, 421 U.S. 658 (1975).[9] Do you think that a corporation and its corporate president should be held criminally liable for acts of the corporation's employees?

---

[9] See pp. 39–40.

4 The Law of Torts

After you have read this chapter, you should be able to:

1. Identify and explain the concept of tort.
2. Distinguish between a tort and a crime.
3. Distinguish between an intentional tort and a negligent tort.
4. Explain the torts of assault and battery.
5. Define at least an additional kind of intentional tort.
6. Explain defenses to intentional torts.
7. Define negligent torts.
8. Explain proximate cause as a legal concept.
9. Explain the concept of immunity from tort liability.

Introduction

In chapter 3 of this Part we discussed criminal law which is concerned with wrongs to the *public* interest. In chapters 1 and 2 of this Part we discussed legal systems and utilization of those systems and alternatives in order to resolve *civil* disputes. In this chapter we will discuss the law of torts, which is one of the areas concerned with civil disputes and wrongs to the interests of *persons* (individuals, or legal entities such as corporations). Another area concerned with civil disputes is the law of contracts, discussed in Part 2.

The word **tort** is not a part of the vocabulary of most people. Yet, torts are committed every day in almost every community in the United States. In fact, the chances of you or a member of your family having committed a tort or being otherwise involved in a tort action at one time or another are reasonably high. The reason is that the number of different kinds of torts is very large. The next few paragraphs will give you some examples of the kind of problem included within the subject matter of torts.

tort
a civil (private) noncontractual wrong for which a court will give a remedy

The most common kind of tort action in the United States is the typical automobile accident. It happens in every large city every single day. Driver X drives his car in a careless manner and dents the fender of driver Y's car. Add passengers to either car or more automobiles or trucks to the accident and you have made the tort more complex—but it is still a tort action.

If the drivers of the cars involved in the accident get out of their cars and exchange more than driver's licenses and ultimately end up in a fight, this too can result in a tort action. If the driver of car X is hurt very badly and is rushed to a hospital, where the doctor in charge carelessly administers the wrong drug or performs the wrong operation, this can result in a tort.

If driver X begins to recuperate in the hospital and is served food with an unwanted foreign object (such as a cigarette butt in his milk) or becomes sick from being carelessly served spoiled food, there is a chance for a tort action. If, in reconstructing the accident, the police discover that the incident was caused by a poorly constructed steering column rather than the driver's carelessness, once again there is a possible tort action.

Torts exist in the business world in the form of trademark infringement, copyright abuse, products liability, and more. Almost any time a person acts below a generally accepted standard of behavior, he or she is risking becoming involved in a tort action.

Response of the Law

All of us are involved in incidents at one time or another for which we are at fault. These incidents may be as simple as accidentally tripping someone in a hallway or as severe as an automobile accident involving damages which might exceed a million dollars. In the vast majority of these cases nobody accused you of being a criminal although you may have angered others or even cost them large sums of money. However, both a tort *and* a crime may arise from the same act or facts.

Assuming that a **wrong** has been committed, and there is neither a crime involved nor a contractual arrangement existing, our legal system has developed a body of rules for redressing these wrongs. The late William L. Prosser (1898–1971) was the foremost scholar of his time concerning the law of torts. He said that a precise definition of tort was difficult if not impossible to provide but suggested that, "broadly speaking, a tort is a civil wrong, other than breach of contract, for which the court will provide a remedy in the form of an action for **damages**." It is an area that is at once exciting and rapidly changing. We will look at the three major subdivisions of tort law and see how it is evolving. The three major subdivisions are intentional torts, negligent torts, and strict liability torts. (See figure 4.1.)

wrong
the illegal invasion of another person's interest

damages
the money judicially awarded to an injured party for another's wrongful conduct

Figure 4.1 The Concept of Wrongs

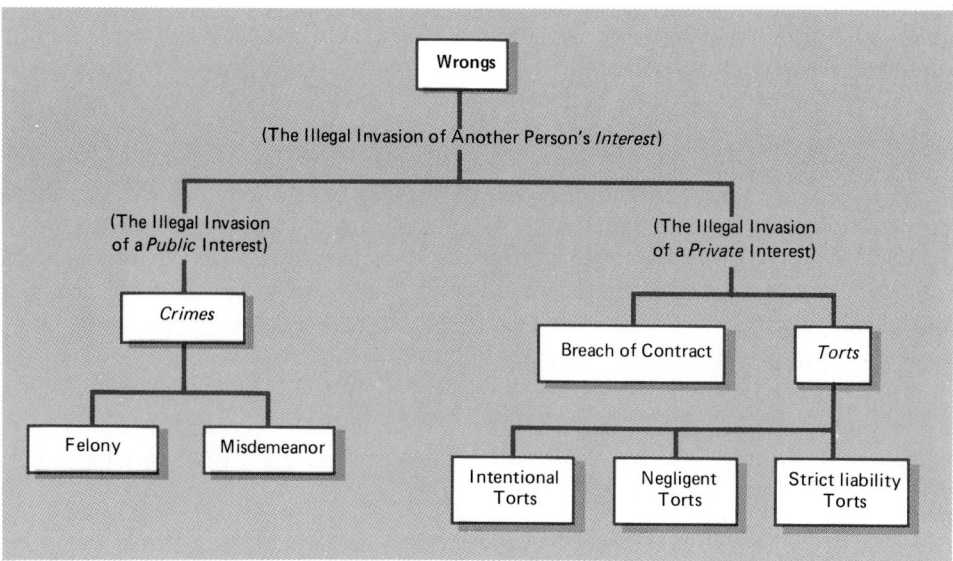

Intentional Torts

While we are free to do as we please in the United States, if we *intentionally* hurt others in the process, we can be held responsible. Certain acts are so repulsive that all members of our society agree to punish the wrongdoer through the vehicle of criminal law. But, for example, assume X punches you in the nose and society demands that X spend some time in jail for violating the criminal law. The problem of paying your doctor's bills remains even if society is satisfied that X is behind bars. You, as the individual damaged, still are personally unsatisfied even though society as a whole has achieved relief. For this reason there are several *intentional* torts which parallel criminal acts. However, the causes of action are different, and students should not confuse criminal actions with their parallel intentional tort actions. If an intentional tort has been committed, an individual may collect an amount of money beyond that which merely "repairs the wrongdoing." The injured party may collect **punitive damages.** Punitive damages are designed to punish the wrongdoer *civilly*.

punitive (exemplary) damages
the money judicially awarded to an injured party in excess of compensatory damages to punish for malicious, wanton, or intentional wrongful conduct

Battery and Assault

One of the incidents cited in the first part of this chapter was a fist fight between two individuals. This is an example of a battery. A **battery** is committed when an individual acts *intentionally* to cause a harmful or offensive bodily contact with another and a harmful or offensive bodily *contact* directly or indirectly results.[1] The following case illustrates that, without the intent to cause harmful bodily contact, there cannot be a battery.

battery
an act by a person intentionally causing harmful or offensive bodily contact with another

Facts
Perkins, plaintiff, alleged that the defendant, Stein and Co., was the owner of a large brewery and numerous brewery wagons; that while delivering company beer the defendant's drivers carelessly, negligently, and recklessly ran into, over, and upon the plaintiff. Suit brought for battery.

Decision
Judgment for defendant.

Reasoning
This is not a battery. The intent to do harm is not present. A battery is more than an attempt to do corporal (bodily) hurt to another; but any intentional injury whatsoever, be it ever so small, is a battery.

Perkins v. Stein, et al., 22 S.W. 649 (Ky. 1893).

---

[1] See, generally, RESTATEMENT (SECOND) OF TORTS sec. 13 (1965).

Note that the court is not concerned with the fact that a small injury or a large injury resulted. It is concerned with *intentional* harm and the factual issue of *bodily contact*, which is what differentiates battery from assault. An **assault** is an unprivileged act by a person intentionally causing another to *apprehend* that an immediate harmful or offensive bodily contact will occur to the other. In order for an assault to exist, it is not necessary that the actor have the ability to carry out the intended threat, as long as the actor has the *apparent* ability to do so. It is necessary only that the receiver of the threat believes that the actor has the ability to carry out the threat. Battery and assault are separate torts which may occur separately or at the same time. It should be noted that civil battery and assault can also be separate crimes of criminal assault and battery, because the wrong is also to a member of society and, therefore, a wrong to the public interest.

assault
an unprivileged act by a person intentionally causing another to apprehend an immediate harmful or offensive bodily contact to the other

False Imprisonment

False imprisonment, often called *false arrest,* is another intentional tort which may be of concern to business people. False imprisonment may be defined as the unprivileged act of intentionally restraining the movement of another who is aware of such restraint. As with other intentional torts, the actor must have the requisite intent to confine another. Further, the confined party must know he or she is restrained. For example, if you were working with a friend taking inventory of goods in a warehouse and accidentally locked your friend in the warehouse, this would not be false imprisonment. You simply do not have the requisite intent. If your friend had continued to work while you left on an errand and had been unaware of having been locked up, this also would not be false imprisonment. In the following case locking a person in a room was not false imprisonment.

false imprisonment (false arrest)
an unprivileged act intentionally restraining the movement of another who is aware of such restraint

Facts
Plaintiff employee was asked to come down to the donut shop. She was not told why. Upon arrival she was asked by her employer to accompany him into the baking room, which was located at the rear of the store. A Mr. Ralph Bell was also present in the room. Her employer asked the plaintiff to sit down. She indicated that they closed the door and locked it by putting a "little latch on." She stated that the two men told her that they had proof that spotters going from store to store had purchased two dozen donuts from her, but that her register had not shown the sale. Based on these facts, is there a case for false imprisonment?

Decision
No.

Reasoning
In the tort of false imprisonment, it is not enough for the plaintiff to have felt "compelled" to remain in the baking room in order to protect her reputation. The evidence must establish a restraint against the plaintiff's will, as where she yields to force, to the threat of force or to the assertion of authority. In the present case, our search of the record reveals no evidence that plaintiff yielded to constraint of a physical threat, express or applied, or to physical force of any kind.

Lopez v. Winchell's Donut House, 466 N.E.2d 1309 (Ill. 1984).

Invasion of Privacy

There are a number of additional intentional torts. However, brief mention should be made of one other intentional tort which may occur in a business setting. A tort that has increased in importance in recent years is the *intentional invasion of one's privacy*. Here, the cause of action often arises in a business situation when a company unauthorizedly uses an individual's name or likeness for profit.[2] One example might be using your picture in an advertisement without your permission. Another type of invasion occurs when objectionable, highly private information about an individual is made public without the individual's permission. Still another type of invasion occurs when there is unwarranted intrusion into one's private life, as is illustrated by the following case.

---

[2] *Carlisle v. Fawcett Publications, Inc.,* 201 Cal. App.2d 733 (1962).

Facts
Ralph Nader, plaintiff, is a well-known advocate for automobile safety and consumer protection. Nader sued General Motors Corporation, defendant, claiming that the defendant through its agents was invading his privacy by, among other things, (1) wiretapping his telephone and eavesdropping on private conversations, as well as (2) conducting ongoing and harassing investigations. The defendant's actions arose because of Nader's decision to publish a book entitled "Unsafe At Any Speed." Did these activities by the defendant constitute the tort of invasion of privacy?

Decision
Yes. Judgment for the plaintiff, Nader.

Reasoning
In order for there to be a cause of action for invasion of the plaintiff's privacy, the plaintiff must show that the actions of General Motors Corporation were intrusive and for the purpose of gathering information not normally available on inquiry. This occurred here.

Nader v. General Motors Corporation, 255 N.E.2d 765 (N.Y. 1970).

In an effort to control invasions of privacy, the federal government has passed a number of new laws. The Fair Credit Reporting Act gives people the right to examine files compiled about them pertaining to their credit record. Incorrect files must be changed. Later the Privacy Act was passed which placed severe restrictions on the use of private records by federal agencies.

Some Other Intentional Torts

A few other intentional torts should be mentioned here briefly.

1. *Malicious prosecution* is concerned with a person's initiation or procurement of criminal proceedings against an innocent person, done without probable cause and with malice, the proceedings terminating in favor of the accused person.
2. *Mental and emotional disturbance* is a relatively new and developing tort consisting of outrageous conduct interfering with another person's mental and emotional tranquility.
3. *Deceit* occurs when a person knowingly misrepresents a material fact, intending to mislead another person by inducing him to rely on the misrepresentation and to act in a particular business transaction, causing financial damage to him.
4. *Trespass to chattels* is concerned with a person's wrongful interference with another person's possession of **chattels** (e.g., automobile, furniture) causing damage to the other person's interest in the chattels.
5. *Conversion* is a more serious type of wrongful interference with another person's possession of chattels by wrongfully exercising control and dominion over them.
6. *Trespass to land* is concerned with a person's wrongful interference with another person's possession of land.
7. *Public nuisance* and *private nuisance* are concerned with a person's unreasonable, substantial interference with either the *public's* use and enjoyment of *public* land (e.g., blocking a public highway), or with a *private* person's use and enjoyment of his or her *private* land (e.g., excessive and continuous loud noise or offensive odors from a neighbor).
8. Miscellaneous torts concerned with unfair trade practices, such as: *fraudulent marketing* of goods or services (e.g., S markets and sells goods or services to P, misrepresenting that they are made or provided by R when, instead, they are from Z); and wrongful *imitation of physical appearance* of goods.

chattel
a tangible, movable thing

Defenses to Intentional Torts

Occasionally there exists a legally justifiable *reason* for committing what would otherwise be an intentional tort. Some of these reasons provide enough protection for the actor so that he or she is shielded from what would otherwise be wrongful with resulting liability. These reasons create a *privilege* so to act.

Privilege. A **privilege** is that which exempts a person from liability for his or her conduct which, but for the exemption, would subject the person to liability for such conduct. A privilege may be in the form of *consent* to such conduct by the person affected or by operation of law.

1. Consent. A person's **consent** to the illegal invasion of his interest by another person privileges such invasion. The person consenting must have had full capacity to consent and have acted freely, without fraud or mistake, in assenting to the invasion. For example, in all body contact sports the participants consent to body contact by each other, thus precluding the commission of the tort of battery. It should be clear that consent is not present if assent was induced through fraudulent means. For example, if a person **assents** to eat a tablet which he or she believes to be an aspirin and which was intentionally misrepresented to be such when in fact it was actually LSD, the victim has not *consented* to the negative consequences and has a valid cause of action for tort. Finally, consent may be expressly stated or may be implied from the situation.
2. By Operation of Law. There are various privileges given by operation of law and without the consent of the person whose interest is threatened with invasion or has been invaded.
    a. Self-Defense. If there is an *assault,* the person assaulted has the privilege of *self-defense,* which includes the right to self-help by that person by the use of such physical force as is reasonably required under the circumstances to protect that person from *the threatened battery.* If the threat is danger of substantial bodily harm or danger to life itself, the person assaulted may use force amounting to substantial bodily harm or death to the assaulting party.[3] The privilege of self-defense extends to one person protecting a second person from a third person.
    b. Possessory Interests in Property. A person whose *possessory interest in property is superior* to that of a person *threatening to interfere with such property interest* has the privilege to use such physical force as is reasonably required under the circumstances as protection against *such interference,* but the force may not amount to substantial bodily harm or death. An example is a person threatening to commit a trespass to land or chattels of another who has a superior right to possession of such land or chattels. However, if the threatening person also threatens *assault,* then the privilege of *self-defense* becomes available to the person assaulted.
    A person with a *superior right to possess* land or chattels *which are in another person's possession* has a privilege of *recapturing* such property. Whether the first person may use physical force to recapture depends upon whether or not the person in possession *initially* obtained possession rightfully or wrongfully. If the person in possession was *initially rightfully in possession,* then physical force cannot be used to recapture. For example, if you defaulted in making an installment payment on your automobile and your creditor, with the right to repossess the automobile on your default, seeks to repossess it, the creditor cannot use physical force on you to do so if you refuse to consent to the creditor's repossession. You were initially rightfully in possession. However, if the person in possession *initially obtained possession wrongfully,* and the person with a superior right to possession seeking to recapture the property acts *promptly* to repossess after wrongful dispossession has occurred, then reasonable force may be used, but not amounting to substantial bodily harm or

privilege
that which exempts a person from liability for his or her conduct which, but for the exemption, would subject the person to liability for such conduct

consent
a person's approval of something, made with full capacity, freely and without fraud or mistake; (in torts) such approval permitting what would otherwise be an intentional tort

assent
a person's *manifestation* of approval of something

---
[3] See, generally, RESTATEMENT (SECOND) OF TORTS secs. 63–76 (1965).

death. For example, if you see a thief running off with your tires, you can chase the thief and use reasonable physical force on the thief to recapture your tires.

Another illustration of this privilege to recapture chattels is in the area of merchandising. Some states allow shopkeepers the privilege of detaining an individual suspected of shoplifting.

Negligent Torts

In this section we turn to the largest subdivision of the law of torts, in terms of the number of cases litigated each year. It is the branch of the law which uses *fault* rather than *intent* for imposing liability. However, not all incidents for which a person is at fault result in legal liability. There are a number of issues to consider before legal liability may be established.[4]

The person found responsible for committing a negligent tort will not have to pay punitive damages as does the wrongdoer in the case of an intentional tort. Instead, the responsible party will probably have to pay only an amount of money which will rectify the negligent act. It is often said that the object of damages is to make the injured party "whole again."

Negligent Torts and Morality

As small children, our parents direct us in our activities. When we make a mistake, we are punished and taught the correct behavior. As we grow older, we discover that the community in which we live has standards of behavior to which we must adhere. However, no one ever can or does tell us the precise behavior deemed acceptable for every conceivable situation. Nonetheless, a certain standard of conduct prevails in all situations, and if we fail to live up to the prevalent standard of conduct, we will be held responsible either morally or legally.

On occasion, certain behavior will fail to meet the community's standard of care but will not be a legal wrong. For example, assume that Franklin Moneypockets is a multimillionaire. Years ago Franklin had his life saved by Ben Pennyless, an extremely poor individual. If Franklin knows of Ben's financial plight, many of us would expect that Franklin would come to Ben's aid. However, there is no legal responsibility to do so. This is because there is *no legal duty* which extends from Franklin to Ben no matter how strong the moral obligation seems to be. The elements involved in suing for the tort of negligence are: a duty of care and its breach; causation, called *proximate cause;* and damage, or loss or harm.

Legal Duty

This leads us to the *first step* of establishing tort liability through *negligence*. There can be an established case of negligence only where there is a *legal duty which extends between the parties*. The question of whether such a legal duty *exists* is strictly a question of law and not a question of fact subject to jury interpretation.

Standard of Care

On the assumption that a legal duty exists, the *next step* would be to establish that the person committing the *tort* of negligence *acted below the prevailing standard of care*. The term we use to describe such *conduct* is **negligence.** Negligence (careless conduct) is the failure to use the degree of care demanded by the circumstances[5] at the time of the act or failure to act. Another definition for negligence is the failure to use the care which an ordinary, prudent person would use under the same or similar circumstances to avoid

negligence (conduct) failure to use the degree of care demanded by the circumstances

---

[4] See pp. 48–52. [5] *Fort Smith Gas Co. v. Cloud,* 75 F.2d 413 (1935).

causing injury to another or to protect another from injury.[6] Negligence (careless conduct) should be distinguished from the **tort of negligence,** which occurs when (1) a person's negligent conduct (2) proximately causes (3) injury to another person's interest. Until negligence proximately causes such injury, the tort does not exist. In the following case failure to exercise reasonable care was not shown; therefore, there being no negligence, no tort of negligence had occurred.

negligence (tort) negligent conduct proximately causing injury to another person's interest

Facts
Appellant testified during his deposition that he descended the steps in a shopping mall, engaged in a telephone conversation at a telephone approximately 1 and ½ to 2 feet from the bottom step, and slipped on a melted or partially melted ice cream cone within several inches of the bottom step immediately upon completing his telephone call. The melted ice cream extended out from the base of the bottom step to approximately 6 to 8 inches beyond the base and extended nearly the entire length of the step. The appellant testified that he did not see the ice cream prior to his telephone call. The complaint alleges negligent maintenance and inspection of the area in which appellant fell, and negligent use of floor materials. Were the defendant-appellees shopping mall proprietors negligent?

Decision
No.

Reasoning
Appellant produced no admissible evidence whatsoever showing that appellees knew or should have known of the substance. While the affidavit and deposition testimony in this case demonstrate the absence of knowledge of the substance on the part of the appellees, appellant has failed to produce any admissible evidence to demonstrate that the substance was on the floor for a length of time sufficient for knowledge of it to be imputed to the appellees. Thus, the trial court correctly ruled that appellees had pierced the allegations of appellant's complaint, and that appellant had failed to produce the responsive evidence creating an issue of fact as to defendant-appellees' liability for negligent maintenance.

Pritchard v. Wilson, et al., 316 S.E.2d 604 (Ga. App. 1984).

A question which must naturally arise is: How do you determine if a person is acting as an ordinary, prudent person would act under the same or similar circumstances? The answer to that question lies within the province of the jury. In each case that comes before it, the jury listens to the fact pattern as shown by the evidence and as explained by the lawyers and decides whether the parties were acting above or below the standard. If the actor was below the standard, he or she is negligent.

Not only is the standard of care a difficult thing to measure for the reason noted above, but the standard varies for other reasons as well. For example, if an individual has certain special skills which he or she is using (usually those licensed), such as a physician or beautician, then that individual must adopt as a personal standard of conduct the standard of care of the reasonable person within that profession or specialty. The question faced by the jury would be, What would the reasonable and prudent doctor have done under the same or similar circumstances? This is called the "reasonable person test."

Obviously, the standard is not a precise line, and that is one of the major issues of debate in a negligence trial. Lawyers may present *expert witnesses* to testify on the issue of negligence in the particular situation. For example, the lawyer may get a physician to testify before the jury about the standard of conduct among doctors. Lawyers may also be able to put together a fact pattern in which the facts speak for themselves, which is called **res ipsa loquitur.** This involves inferring negligence from the fact pattern. For example, a tack in a can of beans bought at a store implies negligence by the manufacturer. Yet another way of building a case of negligence is by illustrating that trade rules were not adhered to, or in select cases that a statute was violated. Once again, it is for the jury to decide if a person was acting as he or she should. It may well be that the jury will decide that, even if a person followed trade standards or adhered to a statute, the person's conduct was still negligent.

res ipsa loquitur the thing speaks for itself

---
[6] *Hewlett v. Schadel,* 68 F.2d 502 (1934).

Condition and Use of Land. Chapter 51, Real Property and Its Ownership, discusses the duty and standard of care and liability for the condition and use of land.

Proximate Cause of Injury by Negligence

After negligence is proved, the *third step* is to prove that the negligent conduct in question was the **proximate cause** of the injury. Proximate cause refers to the *legal cause* of the injury. The definition of proximate cause most often quoted is "that cause which in natural and continuous sequence, unbroken by an intervening cause, produces the injury, and without which the result would not have occurred." The courts often discuss the issue of the *foreseeability* of the incident when determining proximate cause. However, the terms "proximate cause" and "foreseeability" are not interchangeable. Foreseeability of injury from negligence is an element in proximate cause. The following well-reasoned case makes this distinction.

> **proximate cause**
> the cause of an injury without which the injury would not have occurred

Facts
Plaintiff, a longshoreman, employee of the defendant vessel owner, was injured while working aboard ship. The defendant failed to provide adequate flooring to support the weight of a loaded handtruck used by the plaintiff. The flooring collapsed and the plaintiff and the loaded handtruck fell into the hole. The plaintiff, in trying to get the truck and load out of the hole, strained the muscles in his rib cage. He sued for this injury, claiming that the *inadequate flooring* was the proximate cause of his injury. Defendant claimed that he could not reasonably *foresee* that plaintiff would go into the hole and, therefore, he should not be liable because the inadequate flooring was not the proximate cause of plaintiff's injury; his going into the hole was the nonforeseeable proximate cause.

In a suit for negligence against the defendant, the court found that the flooring was insufficient and the proximate cause of plaintiff's injury. Defendant appealed.

Decision
Affirmed for plaintiff.

Reasoning
In this case for the tort of negligence, there was no error in finding that the insufficient flooring was the *proximate cause* of plaintiff's injury. Foreseeability was an element of proximate cause. The court held that the failure to furnish adequate flooring prompted the plaintiff, when he fell, to act as he did. Plaintiff's attempt to lift the truck out of the hole was a normal response of a worker under the circumstances and, therefore, foreseeable. It was part of the flooring collapse, which was the proximate cause of plaintiff's injury.

Dewey v. A. R. Klaveness & Co., 379 P.2d 560 (Or. 1963).

Defenses to the Tort of Negligence

In an accident it is often the case that each party blames the other for the occurrence. Sometimes only one party is at fault, but at other times each party's fault may contribute to the incident. At still other times one party or the other may assume a risk as part of the activity in which they are participating. These points lead us to a discussion of the defenses to the charge of negligence.

Contributory Negligence. Suppose you were involved in a minor car accident and that you were at fault. Suppose, further, that you knew that the driver of the other car was not driving very carefully either. Would you willingly agree to pay for all the damage done? Probably not! **Contributory negligence** may be the doctrine you use to protect yourself. It is "conduct on the part of the plaintiff which falls below the standard to which he should conform for his own protection, and which is a legally contributing cause cooperating with the negligence of the defendant in bringing about the plaintiff's harm."[7] In the following case the plaintiff's contributory negligence prevented him from obtaining a judgment against the defendant who was negligent.

> **contributory negligence**
> plaintiff's conduct which falls below the standard to which he should conform for his own protection and which is a legally contributing cause with the defendant's negligence causing the plaintiff's harm

---

[7] Restatement (Second) of Torts sec. 464 (1965).

Facts
Defendant put a pole across the road while making repairs to his home. Plaintiff was riding a horse at top speed and it tripped over the pole. Plaintiff sued defendant for negligence.

Decision
Judgment for defendant.

Reasoning
Contributory negligence was present. One is not to cast oneself upon an obstruction which had been made by the fault of another, and avail oneself of it, if one does not use common and ordinary caution to be in the right.

Butterfield v. Forester, K.B. 11 E 60 (1809).

Last Clear Chance and Comparative Negligence. As we have seen, in the simplest of *negligence* cases there is merely one argument:

1. X accuses and proves Y negligent.

In the case of *contributory negligence*, the problem becomes slightly more difficult:

1. X accuses and proves Y negligent, but
2. Y claims X was negligent also (i.e., contributory negligence).

In yet another possible ripple, we can add a *third* stage which would look like this:

1. X accuses and proves Y negligent.
2. Y claims X was negligent also (contributory negligence).
3. X says "I may have been contributorily negligent, but you (Y) had the *last clear chance* to avoid the incident."

Indeed, *last clear chance* is a well established line of defense to a charge of contributory negligence. Along with each of these charges comes the difficulty of proof. Each claim of negligence, contributory negligence, or last clear chance must be substantiated using the patterns of proof we have been discussing throughout this chapter. This is why even seemingly simple automobile accidents can result in large, elaborate, and costly trials. It is almost an endless cycle with each of the participants claiming the other is at fault.

Some jurisdictions have established a system of *comparative negligence*. Under this system the jury is not required to determine ultimate responsibility, as it must in a system using negligence, contributory negligence, and last clear chance. Rather, comparative negligence merely asks the jury to apportion the percentage of fault among the parties to the case. Thus, driver X may be 30 percent at fault and must pay 30 percent of the cost, while driver Y is 70 percent at fault and pays 70 percent of the cost. In contrast, in many jurisdictions *any* amount of contributory negligence will preclude recovery by the contributorily negligent party.

Assumption of Risk. One final defense which is frequently used by attorneys is **assumption of risk.** This involves a situation in which a person *knowing* of the risk of harm agrees to voluntarily assume the risk of harm. The effect of this defense is that the defendant may claim that the plaintiff agreed to subject himself or herself to potential danger, and therefore plaintiff, if injured, may not be successful in collecting damages. In the following case the injured plaintiff did not assume any risk because he was not aware of the specific danger.

assumption of risk
voluntarily assuming a known risk of harm

Facts
Plaintiff, Vierra, was injured when a piece of *steel* dislodged from a broken tool being used by the defendant and flew several feet striking him in the eye. Plaintiff knew only of the danger from flying particles of *concrete* within a range of seven feet. However, he was standing more than nine feet from the tool. In the trial court judgment was rendered for the defendant. Plaintiff appealed, claiming error in that the court should not have instructed the jury on the doctrine of assumption of risk.

Decision
The lower court was not correct in its instructions; reversed, for plaintiff.

Reasoning
"The basic question in this case is whether the trial court was justified, under the facts, in instructing on the doctrine of assumption of risk. We have concluded that it was in error . . . and therefore reversible to have instructed on this doctrine. To warrant the application of the doctrine of assumption of the risk, the evidence must show that the victim appreciated the *specific* danger involved. He does not assume any risk he does not know or appreciate." Here, the plaintiff appreciated the *specific* danger from flying concrete but not from flying steel.

Vierra v. Fifth Avenue Rental Service, 383 P.2d 777 (Cal. 1963).

immunity
exemption from liability

Immunities. On occasion, certain categories of persons are granted an **immunity** from tort liability. There must be a very special underlying policy reason for granting such an immunity, and these immunities are greatly limited in number and scope. Historically, both *charitable organizations* and *governmental organizations* were granted such a shield. Over the years these two immunities have come under severe attack. Indeed, under the Federal Tort Claims Act the federal government can be held liable for *negligent* torts. Even under the Federal Tort Claims Act the government cannot be sued for intentional or strict liability torts. Further, most high-ranking government officials are immune provided they do not act with malice.

There is also an *intra-family immunity.* In order to promote family harmony, there was a common law immunity between *parent and child.* However, today this immunity is limited to negligent torts. Thus, children can sue their parents for intentional torts.

Liability Without Regard to Negligence or Fault: Strict Liability

In the first part of this chapter we spoke of torts which were intentional in nature. Next we turned to torts which were caused through someone's negligence. In this section we turn to those instances in which courts are not concerned with negligence at all. Rather, they believe that the particular action was of such a nature that the defendant should accept responsibility without reference to their standard of conduct.

Hazardous Activities

The courts state that if you are engaged in activity involving danger of serious harm to another person or property— a danger which cannot be eliminated even using due care and which is not a matter of common usage—you may be held **strictly liable** without reference to your standard of care. This is illustrated in the following famous English case.

strict liability
absolute liability irrespective of the absence of negligence or fault

prima facie
at first sight

Facts
Defendants owned a mill and, in order to supply it with water, constructed a reservoir on some nearby land. Plaintiff owned a nearby coal mine which was inundated by water that escaped from the reservoir. There is proof that the defendant used a great deal of care in building the reservoir. Plaintiff sued for damage caused to his land.

Decision
Judgment for plaintiff.

Reasoning
"We think . . . that the person who for his own purpose brings on his lands . . . anything likely to do mischief if it escapes must keep it at his peril, and if he does not do so, is **prima facie** answerable for all the damage which is a natural consequence of its escape."

Rylands v. Fletcher, [1868] L.R., 3 H.L. 330.

Animals
Another area in which there is strict liability without reference to negligence is in the keeping of wild animals. Thus, people who want to keep exotic pets such as snakes or tigers are in most cases responsible for their pets' activity even if they use due care in keeping them restrained. This rule does not apply to animals kept in a zoo, used for the entertainment or education of the public.[8]

---

[8] See 4 *Am. Jur.* 2d, Animals p. 80.

Workmen's Compensation

State Workmen's Compensation laws impose upon an employer strict liability to most employees for personal injury in the course of and arising out of employment, except for self-inflicted injury and intoxication. This subject is discussed in chapter 37, Employment.

Products Liability

This is one of the most rapidly growing fields of tort liability in the United States today.[9] Until recently, people injured while using a product had to demonstrate that the producer was negligent in manufacturing the product. The plaintiff had the difficult task of proving that the manufacturer had fallen below the standard of care required. As you can imagine, this was a difficult task. For example, if you were hurt because of a defect in your car, you would have to collect evidence that the person who put together your particular automobile was negligent at the particular time that person was working on your car.

Even if you could accomplish that task, you still had to avoid the defenses to a charge of negligence, such as contributory negligence. You had to prove that you did not contribute to the carelessness of the situation resulting in the accident. These problems are being resolved today through the application of the doctrine of *strict liability* in tort to those who put products on the market. That is, *in certain areas,* the courts will impose liability on the manufacturer without reference to negligence.

At first, the scope of products liability was sharply limited to a select number and kinds of products. The first cases demanded that there had to be direct contact between the manufacturer and purchaser, called **privity**. This meant that, if you purchased a defective product from a middleman or retailer, you could not sue the manufacturer. You lacked privity with the manufacturer. Gradually, the privity doctrine gave way in select cases, such as those involving drugs or poisoned foods.

Soon even this requirement gave way, and you now can sue a manufacturer in some instances without having privity of contract with the manufacturer. Today manufacturers of a chattel which they know or reasonably should believe to be *inherently dangerous* for the use supplied are strictly liable for harm caused by the chattel unless they give adequate warning of the danger. An example is an explanatory label on a container of poison. Also, manufacturers are held liable for manufacturing a chattel which, they should realize, *if negligently manufactured,* would create an *unreasonable risk of substantial bodily harm* when used for the purpose for which it was manufactured. In this case, what is important is the risk of harm from the *imperfect manufacture* of the chattel rather than the *inherently dangerous character* of the chattel. For example, a glass coffee urn is not inherently dangerous, but its negligent manufacture could cause it to be an unreasonable risk of substantial bodily harm to a consumer. This trend in the case law has caused concern to many manufacturers since they are increasingly subject to lawsuits brought by injured consumers. In the following famous case the court made new law by extending the duty to manufacture carefully to the remote consumer, thereby hurdling the privity of contract rule.

privity
a mutuality of relationship between persons or between persons and a particular transaction

Facts

The defendant, Buick Motor Company, purchased automobile wheels from a wheel manufacturer. A wheel was defective and the defendant could, by reasonable care, have discovered the defect. However, the defendant did not exercise such care and overlooked the defect. The defendant attached the wheel to one of its automobiles, which was sold to a retailer who, in turn, resold the car to the plaintiff consumer, who was unaware of the defective wheel. The wheel collapsed because of the defect, causing the car to collapse, and the plaintiff was injured. Plaintiff sued the defendant for such injury.

Decision

Judgment for plaintiff.

---

[9] See pp. 323–33.

Reasoning
The defendant manufacturer owed a duty of care to the remote plaintiff consumer. "We hold that when the nature of a thing is such that it is reasonably certain to place life and limb in peril when negligently made, it is then a thing of danger. [If] . . . its nature gives warning of the consequences to be expected [then] . . . the manufacturer is under a duty to make it carefully." The court extended the manufacturer's duty under the facts to the remote consumer, plaintiff, even though there was no privity of contract between the plaintiff and the defendant.

MacPherson v. Buick Motor Company, 111 N.E. 1050 (N.Y. 1916).

Protection of Inventions, Authorship, Identification of Products, Certain Contractual Business Relationships, and Reputation through Tort Law

At the beginning of this chapter it was suggested that tort law provided a wide range of protection to persons. Before we close this chapter, brief mention should be made of the use of tort law to protect personal and business creations, certain contractual business relationships, and reputation.

Certain Contractual Business Relationships

People have a right to deal and contract with whom they please, and also to refuse to do so if they please, unless their conduct is wrongful because it breaches a duty to another person or is contrary to law. It is wrongful intentionally to induce other persons to breach their contracts with third persons or to induce other persons to refuse to deal or to continue a business relationship with third persons, thereby causing damage to such third persons. These are the torts of *inducing breach of contract* and *inducing refusal to deal*.

Reputation

Persons have an interest in their reputations, and they have a right to freedom from false disparagement of their reputations. It is wrongful intentionally, without privilege, to publish matter which is false and disparages another person's reputation, thereby causing damage to that person's reputation. Published matter is disparaging if it tends to belittle or diminish the esteem in which the defamed person is held by third persons or by the community. *Slander* is an oral disparagement, while *libel* generally is a written disparagement or any form other than oral. The tort is called *defamation*. In the following case the plaintiff could not prove libel by the defendant's *oral* statement.

Facts
Plaintiff was a physician and a candidate for political office. Defendant, his opponent, called out, "Here comes Doctor E. (Plaintiff), the spick and span practitioner. . . . Sufficient be it that we do not look to a quack to set us right in the matter." Plaintiff sued for libel. Judgment was rendered for the plaintiff. Defendant appealed contending that, since his statement was oral, it could not be libel.

Decision
Reversed, judgment for the defendant.

Reasoning
Without more, this is not libel. "That the court erred in submitting the primary question of respondent's liability to the jury, we regard so clear that we are not justified in saying more." The defendant's statement was *oral*.

Elmergreen v. Horn, 91 N.W. 973 (Wis. 1902).

Summary Statement

1. Tort law has a significant impact on our society, and an individual will want to know his or her legal rights and duties as defined by tort law.
2. There is a difference between rights and duties as defined by the legal areas of tort, crime, and contract.
3. There are three major subdivisions of tort liability, namely, intentional torts, negligent torts, and strict liability.
4. Intentional torts include assault and battery, false imprisonment, invasion of privacy, and others.

5. There are defenses to the commission of intentional torts, among which are consent, self-defense, and privilege.
6. Negligent torts involve careless behavior and require that a complainant prove three things: a legal duty of care, a breach of a standard of care, and proximate cause of damage or harm.
7. There are defenses to liability for negligent torts, among which are contributory negligence, last clear chance, comparative negligence, assumption of risk, and immunities.
8. Society has imposed strict liability in certain instances upon suppliers of chattels irrespective of any lack of privity with the injured user.
9. Protection is extended to the rights of persons in their contractual relationships and in their reputations.

The following case deals with strict liability for asbestos related injury. The corporation attempted to use a defense called "state of the art."

Beshada et al. v. Johns-Manville Products Corporation
447 A.2d 207 (N.J. 1982)

Pashman, J. The sole question here is whether defendants in a products liability case based on strict liability for failure to warn may raise a "state of the art" defense. Defendants assert that the danger of which they failed to warn was undiscovered at the time the product was marketed and that it was undiscoverable given the state of scientific knowledge at that time.

These 6 consolidated cases are personal injury and wrongful death actions brought against manufacturers and distributors of asbestos products. Plaintiffs are workers, or the survivors of deceased workers, who claim to have been exposed to asbestos for varying periods of time. They allege that as a result of that exposure, they contracted asbestosis and other asbestos related illnesses.

These cases involve asbestos exposure dating back to perhaps as far as the 1930s. The suits are first arising now because of the long latent period between exposure and the discernible symptoms of asbestosis. Plaintiffs have raised a variety of legal theories to support their claims for damages. The important claim, for purposes of this appeal, is strict liability for failure to warn. Prior to the 1960s, defendants' products allegedly contain no warning of their hazardous nature. Defendants responded by asserting the state of the art defense. They allege that no one knew or could have known that asbestos was dangerous when it was marketed.

We conclude that plaintiffs' position is consistent with our holding in *Freund* and prior cases and will achieve the various policies underlying strict liability. The burden of illness from dangerous products such as asbestos should be placed upon those who profit from its production and, more generally, upon society at large, which reaps the benefits of the various products our economy manufactures. That burden should not be imposed exclusively on the innocent victim. Although victims must in any case suffer the pain involved, they should be spared the burdensome financial consequences of unfit products. At the same time, we believe this position will serve the salutary goals of increasing product safety research and simplifying tort trials.

Defendants have argued that it is unreasonable to impose a duty on them to warn of the unknowable. Failure to warn of a risk which one could not have known existed is not unreasonable conduct. But this argument is based on negligence principles. We are not saying what defendants should have done. That is negligence. . . . We impose strict liability because it is unfair for the distributors of a defective product not to compensate its victims. As between those innocent victims and the distributors, it is the distributors—and the public who consumes their product—who should bear the unforeseen costs of the product.

The judgment of the trial court is reversed; the plaintiffs' motion to strike the state of the art defense is granted.

Questions and Case Problems

1. Plaintiff was a welfare applicant. Defendant, Easton Publishing Co., published an article concerning the private lives of the plaintiff and her family based on information supplied by the Department of Public Welfare. From this article, 17 people identified the plaintiff and her family. Assume that the facts in the article were collected without the plaintiff's knowledge. Is this an invasion of privacy? [*Harris by Harris v. Easton Publishing Co.*, 483 A.2d 1377 (Pa. 1984).]

2. Comprecare was a Colorado Corporation and health maintenance organization where plaintiff, Paula Rederscheid, had an insurance policy that should cover her corrective oral surgery. When defendant, Comprecare, failed to pay for this surgery, plaintiff experienced distress and anxiety. Does plaintiff have any recourse? Explain. [*Rederscheid v. Comprecare Inc.*, 667 P.2d 766 (Colo. 1983).]

3. Isaacs, M.D., was working at Huntington Memorial Hospital. One day when leaving work, he was shot at and injured in the hospital's parking garage. This had never happened to Isaacs before, neither had the hospital ever been involved in such an incident. However, since Isaacs was injured, what result if he sues the hospital for negligence? Explain. [*Isaacs, M.D. v. Huntington Memorial Hospital,* 204 Cal. Rptr. 765 (Cal. 1984).]

4. 12-year-old Kenneth A. Demeri was running his unregistered, uninsured motor cycle in Lynn Park. He did not have a license and his father did not allow him to ride the bike alone. When crossing the public road on his way home, Kenneth did not see the automobile before it was too late. As a result of the collision, Kenneth suffered severe and permanent injuries. Who is in this case liable for negligence—if anyone? Explain. [*Demeri v. Morris,* 477 A.2d 426 (N.J. 1983).]

5. Mr. Tate, a farmer, was delivering eggs to defendant the day after a heavy snowfall. After the delivery, he fell on the defendant's private, unshoveled driveway and fractured his wrist. The defendant said it was their practice to let snow and ice melt away naturally, which was the reason for the state of the driveway. Even though Mr. Tate frequently used this driveway, what result in a suit against defendant for negligence? Explain. [*Tate v. Rice,* et al., 315 S.E.2d 385 (Va. 1984).]

6. Linda Lee was a part-time medical assistant working in Dr. Morales' office. One day, she was called into his office in the presence of a co-worker and the doctor's son. A small amount of money was missing and Dr. Morales asked if she took the money. Lee replied "no." The doctor got all mad and was accusing and threatening Lee. He said: "If you leave, I'll call the police, and the police will be here in a minute." Lee was scared and remained in his office. May Lee sue Dr. Morales for false imprisonment? Explain. [*Morales v. Lee,* 668 S.W.2d 867 (Tex. 1984).]

7. Plaintiff Douglas A. Campbell was a passenger in a car owned by defendant Carla M. Hundley and driven by defendant Tammye S. Van Roekel, 17 years old. Even though they all knew that Van Roekel was intoxicated they let her drive, and the predictable had to happen—they struck a utility pole causing injuries to Campbell's nose. Since Van Roekel's intoxication was the proximate cause of the accident, may Campbell recover damages? Explain. [*Campbell v. Van Roekel,* 347 N.W.2d 406 (Iowa. 1984).]

8. A young lady orders baked beans in Boston. "I started to eat [them] and there were two or three dark pieces which I thought were hard beans; that is, baked more than the others, and I put it in my mouth [and bit down and hurt myself]." If there was no evidence of negligence on the part of the dining hall which baked the food, may she recover damages? [*Friend v. Childs Dining Hall, Co.,* 120 N.E. 407 (Mass. 1918).]

9. Joe Smith, a toothpaste manufacturer, knows that Jim Goodheart has a contract with Great Toothpaste Company to deliver fifty boxes of a chemical needed to manufacture Crest. Smith induced Goodheart to deliver the chemical to him instead of to Crest. Is this a violation of the law?

10. In the case of *Beshada*, et al. *v. Johns-Manville Products Corporation*, 447 A.2d 207 (N.J. 1982),[10] the court indicated that products liability could be imposed by law without reference to negligence. It could even be argued that tort law is being used as a tool for social change. The case also would seem to suggest that the law should place the burden of payment on those who are best able to prevent the loss. Does this standard satisfy you? Assume that you are a member of top management of a major manufacturing firm. Would your answer be the same?

---

[10] See p. 55.

Ethics and Business Law in Part 1
Ethical Concepts

Introduction

Now that you have completed studying the material on The Foundations of the Legal System, we want to introduce you to the subject of *ethics,* particularly the *business ethics* which underpins business law.

Organization

At the end of each Part of this book there is a short discussion of business ethics as it relates to the business law discussed in that particular Part. This end-of-Part discussion is the longest and is the foundation for all the others. Subsequent end-of-Part materials are organized in a different, but uniform, way. They first present an overview of a variety of ethical issues, next, an in-depth discussion of a particular issue, and last, business ethics dilemmas to be resolved by students.

Ethics and Morality Defined

Philosophy is the study of the basic issues of life; it is characterized by the clarity and logical consistency of the assumptions and reasoning used. One branch of philosophy is *ethics*. It examines the *rightness or wrongness of conduct.* Business ethics is, of course, concerned with examining the rightness or wrongness of *business* conduct. While some thinkers attach different meanings to the words ethics and morals, we will use them interchangeably in this and the other end-of-Part materials.

The Goals of These Materials

All the end-of-Part materials are designed to help students study business law in ways which increase their ability to make ethical decisions. Specifically, the materials try to equip students to do the following:

1. Spot ethical issues in business,
2. Analyze ethical problems rigorously,
3. Define personal (i.e., one's own) standards of ethical behavior in business, and
4. Act in conformity with these personal ethical standards.

The following section describes in detail the way the critical study of business law and the study of these materials can move students closer to personal ethical competence.

Ethical Competence and the Critical Study of Business Law

Ability to Spot Ethical Issues

One of the objectives of this course is to equip you to spot the *legal* problems which typically arise in the conduct of business. By studying legal topics you learn to spot the business situations which raise legal problems. Since laws have been created to handle situations where ethical issues are significant, the study of business law is also the study of situations where ethics is important. Since law and ethics overlap extensively, and both are vitally concerned with *what is right and wrong,* the study of business law topics will increase your ability to spot ethical issues in business.

In addition, each of the other end-of-Part discussions also seeks to build this skill; they do this by giving an *overview* of the principal ethical issues related to the law discussed in that Part. By comparing the ethics overview with the legal topics, you should quickly begin to see the strong relationship between situations raising legal issues and situations raising ethical issues.

Ability to Analyze Ethical Problems Rigorously

The skills which you use in analyzing the law, particularly appellate cases and the end of chapter problems, are the same skills which are required for ethical analysis. In particular, the ability to *reason* about facts, and about rules of conduct, are skills common to both legal analysis and ethical analysis. Thus, when you increase your ability to engage in legal reasoning, you also increase your ability to analyze ethical problems rigorously.

The material presented later in this first end-of-Part discussion is designed to help you engage in the type of ethical reasoning used by philosophers. In many ways it is similar to legal reasoning.

Develop Individual Ethical Standards

A major problem in business is that many people do not have personal beliefs about what is ethical or unethical conduct in business. Since business law is a very sophisticated statement of *society's ethical standards for business,* studying it can help individuals form personal beliefs about what is ethical in business.

We call the evaluation of business law to develop personal ethical beliefs "critical study". This requires that students *try to understand the ethical issues which particular laws seek to advance.* Critical study also asks students to assess the law's ethical strengths and weaknesses, its alternatives and its consequences. This approach contrasts with studying the law with the single objective of learning the rules. Critical study can give you the ethical experience and insight needed to develop mature personal beliefs about what is right and wrong in business.

In addition, other end-of-Part materials present *in-depth discussions of a few, pivotal, ethical issues.* These issues were very carefully selected. Most were picked because they greatly influence large numbers of business ethics decisions. Other in-depth discussions help students see more clearly the ethical content of the law. Further, each end-of-Part contains problems related to the in-depth issue. These in-depth discussions and the related problems encourage students to begin articulating their own beliefs.

Actions Consistent with Ethical Beliefs

Even when persons *know* what they believe is right or wrong conduct in business, their *actions* are often not consistent with their ethical beliefs. Philosophers sometimes call the ability to act on our ethical beliefs "will," or "integrity," or "moral character." Moral psychologists have studied this problem and found that people who casually state as their beliefs the "views of their peer group" or "what they think most people believe" are easily pressured into violating such beliefs. Beliefs, like these, which are not carefully thought out are called *conventional wisdom.* In contrast, those who cautiously adopt a belief *after* critically examining its strengths and weaknesses, its alternatives and its consequences, are much more likely to act in ways consistent with their ethical beliefs.

Research in moral psychology indicates that age and education also are major factors contributing to the "moral maturity" required to act consistently with one's ethical beliefs. Education which stresses *differing* styles of reasoning generally produces the most maturity. However, courses in business usually focus on a single style of reasoning. Thus, courses in economics, finance, marketing, and management typically share the common objective of identifying that conduct which is economically most *profitable.* In contrast, business law is a course rich with differing *styles of reasoning.* Thus, this course may be the best in the business curriculum for promoting *moral* maturity and thus the ability to act in ways consistent with one's ethical beliefs.

The end-of-Part materials foster moral maturity by explicitly articulating different, and frequently conflicting, styles of *moral* reasoning. Students are then asked to apply these differing styles to the problems at the end of each Part. Repetition of this activity is intended to encourage the development of moral maturity.

Perhaps you can see that society very much needs individuals who can manage business in ways which are ethical. As a manager, you will undoubtedly confront situations where, acting alone, you must decide whether an action is morally right or wrong. But unless you deliberately try to develop mature ethical beliefs in advance, you are likely to find it difficult both to decide and to act on your decisions. We are convinced that the critical study of business law and the careful study of the end-of-Part materials are the best ways for you to develop the ethical competence essential for professional management.

Business Law and Markets in Critical Study

The context of *managerial* decision making is what distinguishes *business* ethics from other types of ethics. Managers try to decide what is right and wrong in an environment shaped in large part by the free market and by business law. They must therefore have a firm grasp of the ethical attributes both of the market and of the law as they attempt to control business behavior. Both of these social systems seek to compel, or at least encourage, ethical conduct in business.

Often, it is difficult to discern the ethical goals behind particular market transactions or business laws. In large part this is because students do not clearly understand the general ethical goals of the market and of business law. Since critical study of business law focuses on understanding the ethical goals behind laws, it is essential to understand the ethical grounding of markets and the law. The following two sections describe *first* the ethical attributes of the market, *then* the ethical attributes of the law.

The Ethical Character of the Free Market

How the Market Works

In the view of Adam Smith, a Scottish moralist, the theory of the free market assumes that consumers select from the range of goods and services offered in the marketplace those which each desires most. All of these choices tell producers (business) by the dollars that consumers spend what consumers want.

Producers who are not sensitive to the needs and desires of consumers are likely to lose business to more sensitive competitors and perhaps even be driven out of business. On the other hand, those businesses which are highly skilled at serving consumer needs are likely to grow and generate significant profits.

Rivalry—competition for the consumer's dollars—is the driving force of the market. When there are lots of producers, the rivalry is more intense; it often causes price reductions, or product innovations, in attempts to win or keep customers. Rivalry may be substantially reduced if there are few producers.

Often, the marketplace controls business behavior by making unethical conduct unprofitable. If, for example, a tire manufacturer sold dangerous tires, its reputation among consumers would decline and sales would probably fall. Similarly, if Sears sold power lawnmowers which lasted only a single season, consumers would become upset and future sales of Sears lawnmowers, and perhaps other items, would decline.

The free-market process is a very potent force in directing business conduct in ethically desirable directions. The following are some of the ethical attributes of profits earned in the free market:

1. Profits are the product of a system that, because of its efficiency, advances the ethical objective of increasing the *material well-being of society*. It does this by

offering rewards (wealth) to those who efficiently satisfy society's needs. This profit incentive fosters innovation and tends to place society's resources in the hands of the most talented individuals.
2. Profits are the product of a system which has the effect of maximizing *personal liberty*. Because the free market places economic decision making in the hands of many consumers and many producers, few have very great economic power over individuals.
3. These profits are justified by *merit*. That is, because rewards are in proportion to social contribution, the profits are morally justified by the extent to which the individual or firm has contributed to society.

Imperfections in the Free Market System
While the market mechanism is quite powerful, it is widely acknowledged to be seriously imperfect. When the economic system is imperfect, some or all of its ethical attributes may not be achieved. Thus, an imperfect market may not advance society's material well-being or it may reduce personal liberty, or it may cause the profits earned not to be proportional to one's social contribution. Some of these market imperfections with their adverse ethical effect are described below:

1. Either *too few sellers or too few buyers* can lead to *market power*. Market power is the ability to be *insensitive* to customers or suppliers without a reduction in profits. For example, if there were only a single seller of heating fuel in the country, it might become insensitive to consumer desires and yet not lose business. Consumers would not have other heating fuel businesses to turn to for better service. Thus, a solitary seller (one not subject to rivalry) has the effect of reducing the personal liberty of consumers.
2. *Barriers to entry into business* can cause either few sellers or few buyers. A barrier to entry is an artificial condition which prohibits or discourages new entrants into a field of business. Often the law creates barriers to entry. For example, in Utah, you must pay a fee and pass a test before you can install lawn sprinkling systems in residential yards. This law discourages entrants into this business and thus reduces rivalry. Perhaps it allows the fewer persons in the business to increase the price for their services. Thus, the profits earned in this line of business may not fairly reflect the social contribution of this business.
3. If either of the participants in the marketplace transaction operates with *imperfect knowledge* about the market or the transaction, this can create an imperfection. For example, if you bought a new car from your local Ford dealer when another dealer ten miles away would have sold you the same car for $2,000 less, but you didn't know it, an imperfection would exist. You would suffer a $2,000 injury, the local dealer would have an inappropriately high profit, and the other dealer would have inappropriately low revenues. This imperfection keeps the economic system from placing resources in the hands of those who use them most efficiently. Thus, the material well-being of society is less.
4. Market imperfections called *externalities* may exist when *costs or benefits go to the wrong party*. The most widely used example is pollution. If a factory dumps its waste into a local river, it *benefits* by saving money over what it would cost if the factory paid to have the waste trucked to a nonpolluting waste disposal site. The *cost* of this pollution is borne, not by the manufacturer, but by the other users of the river.

While there are some other widely recognized imperfections, these examples of market power, barriers to entry, imperfect knowledge and externalities, illustrate the point that the marketplace is sometimes flawed. When flaws are serious, then it is likely that one or several of the ethical objectives in the marketplace may not be advanced in particular transactions.

The Ethical Character of the Law

Jurisprudence is the study of the *philosophy of law* as opposed to the study of only the rules of law. An understanding of jurisprudence is essential to the critical study of business law because it illuminates the ethical ideas which underpin our business law. Jurisprudence is characterized by fairly well-defined schools of thought. Although these schools agree on many points they conflict on others. Following are three schools of jurisprudential thought.

Natural Law Jurisprudence

As we discussed in chapter 1, natural law jurisprudence was articulated by Aristotle and Aquinas. The core idea of this school of thought is that *there are truths about right law that humankind can come to know, usually by the use of the reasoning mind.* The following are some examples of natural law conclusions:

1. Do good and avoid evil. (Aquinas)
2. Keep your promises. (Grotius)
3. Apply the law equally to all persons. (The Constitution of the United States)
4. Do not lie. (The Bible)
5. Repay those whom you've carelessly injured. (Grotius)

Natural law is not necessarily written law; it exists independent of laws made by people and is in fact superior to them. For example, there were in Nazi Germany many laws designed to persecute the Jews. Some persons who obeyed these laws were, after the Allied victory in World War II, convicted at the Nuremburg trials of violating natural law even though they obeyed the written laws of their country. *Natural law seeks justice as its most fundamental goal.*

Historical School of Jurisprudence

Also as indicated in chapter 1, the core idea of historical jurisprudence is that law is an expression of the historical "spirit of the people." That is, the unique history of each nation produces something similar to a consensus of the population, or *Volksgeist,* on *what the law ought to be.* Legislators and judges then simply give their voice to this *Volksgeist* by creating law. The philosophical justification of historical law is that *it reflects the will of those governed.* Thus this law is sometimes viewed as being justified by consent.

Positive Law Jurisprudence

The core idea of positive law jurisprudence is simply that, in order to be legitimate, a law need only be the end product of the authorized process of the government in power. *Order is the primary goal* underlying positive law jurisprudence.

The Law and the Market-Mechanism

Business law is concerned with *both* traditional jurisprudential objectives and also with facilitating the operation of the marketplace. Thus, as the legal system regulates business, its chief purposes are (1) to achieve the traditional jurisprudential objectives of *justice, order,* and *advancing the popular will,* and also (2) to achieve the market-related objectives of *efficiency, liberty,* and *merit.*

The Law as a Cure for Market Imperfections. One common response to market imperfections is to enact laws to cure them. Indeed, your study of business law will focus on many laws designed to minimize the impact of market imperfections. For example, labor law in large part attempts to redress the market power that a single employer has when there are very many persons willing to do the work. Laws responding to the problem of imperfect information given to consumers are described in chapter 21 on consumer rights; in many instances these laws require *full disclosure* as a cure for imperfect information. Thus, the Truth-In-Lending Act requires disclosure of the actual interest rate on certain consumer loans. Externalities are, of course, a major focus of chapter 50 on environmental law. Products liability law can also be viewed as addressing the issue of human injury as an externality. It is clear that the law is a powerful resource for minimizing the imperfections in the market process.

Imperfections in the Legal System. The legal system has its imperfections, and, because of this, business law sometimes fails to compel ethical conduct. The following are some of the principal reasons for such failure:

1. Often it is quite profitable to violate the law. The potential for illegal profits can create great pressures which many are unable to resist, so they violate the law.
2. Frequently, the penalties for violating laws regulating business are weak deterrents. Some studies have shown that, generally, fines are too small to motivate businesses to comply. And some observers note that, for large businesses, the decision makers (corporate executives) are seldom the ones subject to punishment. More commonly, any fine merely reduces the money available for shareholders.
3. Enforcement of laws regulating business is often haphazard. In some areas, such as civil law, enforcement by injured private parties may be too time-consuming or expensive. Administrative laws may not be adequately enforced because the governmental agency's budget is too small. Also, when a new political party takes office, enforcement policies for administrative laws may change.
4. Laws regulating business conduct are often much more complex than other laws and this makes it difficult for some, particularly small, businesses to know what the law is.
5. The process of creating new laws or modifying existing laws can be influenced through political campaign contributions and lobbying so that the law may not accomplish society's real objectives.
6. Laws regulating business often appear to lack the *legitimacy* of many other areas of the law. In contrast, laws regulating crimes, torts, adoption, and inheritance seem to most persons clearly worthy of their support. Such laws have such a strong natural law component that the desired conduct might occur even in the absence of written laws. But many business laws appear to unsophisticated persons as lacking visible legitimacy. For example, people often see nothing wrong when competing merchants agree to charge the same price. Business law condemns this, and often other, conduct which is not, in the minds of the legally uneducated, obviously wrong.

Because of the growing awareness of the flaws in the legal system, many persons now argue that something more than just obeying the law is expected from business; many assert that business managers must better evaluate the ethical character of their decisions.

Traditional Ethical Thinking

You will be able to better engage in the critical study of business law if you develop the ability to think and reason the way some philosophers do. This thinking has two fundamental attributes. First, it is directed toward a goal, often called "the good". Second, it uses a *consistent* "style of reasoning".

The Good

The *good* is the principal object toward which moral life is directed. It is the *principal ethical standard for evaluating ethical reasoning and business conduct*. While philosophers disagree about what the good ought to be, their varying conclusions and thinking can be quite useful to persons trying to sort out their own ethical values. If you can learn to perceive which good is implicit in a particular law or economic activity, your powers of ethical analysis will greatly increase. More significantly, if you can begin seeing the *conflicts* among goods, and the ways in which legal and economic systems weigh and choose between the conflicting goods, you will become skilled in the critical analysis of business law.

We have described the principal goods of the marketplace—material well being, liberty, and merit. In addition we have identified some traditional goods implicit in the legal system—justice, order, and consent. There are many other goods such as respect for human dignity, love, pleasure, power and status.

One attribute of any good is its perspective. Perspective answers the question, whose good—that of the decision maker or that of others? If you were to conclude that pleasure were the good, then you would need to decide whose pleasure you would want to maximize. One perspective is the *self*. This perspective would cause you to maximize a good for your own benefit. The second perspective is *others*. The other may be a *group*, perhaps a majority of the membership of a particular group, or a minority, or it may be God, or anyone (or thing) other than the decision maker. Thus, the good of pleasure would have an "other" perspective if you sought to maximize the pleasure of the other employees in your firm.

The Roots of Ethical Reasoning
While there are a variety of ethical theories and categories, two are most fundamental. The first judges the rightness or wrongness of conduct by weighing the *consequences* of the conduct. The second rejects the importance of consequences and focuses on *duty*. It holds that there is an ethical character to acts themselves that determines whether one has a duty to do them.

You would evaluate lying differently using these categories for ethical analysis. The *consequentialist* views lying as morally neutral. If the consequences of a particular lie are good, then the act of lying is good. In contrast, an analysis based on *duty* is likely to conclude that lying is inherently evil and cannot be justified by good consequences. This conflict between consequences and duty is captured by the question, "Can the ends ever justify the means?" Duty says no, while consequences sometimes say yes.

An Illustrative Law and Business Problem
It will help you to better understand the styles of ethical reasoning if we are able to use them to assess a particular business law and apply them to a concrete business decision. The process of critical study of business law will also become clearer as you see the way a law is evaluated for its ethical content. The following fact pattern illustrates a business ethics problem which we can use in discussing the principal ethical concepts.

Assume you are the manager of production for the swing shift of a small firm. You supervise ten production line workers but you have been told one must be laid off. Nine of your workers are college women and men who are earning extra spending money while attending school. Three drive brand new cars: two Corvettes and one BMW. Several are saving money for trips to Europe and Asia. All the college students achieve between 105 and 115 percent of their individual production goals. The other worker is a 38-year-old divorced mother of 4 children. All of her salary is used to purchase such basic necessities as food, housing, and clothing for her family. She achieves only 85 percent of her production goal because she isn't as physically coordinated as the younger workers. If the mother is fired, you forecast that she will be able to collect welfare support equal to about one half her salary, and it will take her up to two years to find another job. If any of the college students are fired, you forecast that they will be able to find similar employment immediately. Whom should you fire? We will refer to this dilemma as "the mother of four" problem.

The business law we assess is described in the case on strict liability for products at the end of chapter 4, *Beshada, et al. v. Johns-Manville Products Corporation.* Recall that the case held Johns-Manville liable to those injured by asbestos even though it was not proven that Johns-Manville was at fault. This will be referred to as the "strict liability law." *We will examine this law* using the differing styles of ethical analysis in the same way you might critically examine other business laws. *After evaluating the law we will evaluate the problem of the divorced mother of four.* One of our objectives is to help you see how the critical examination of the law can increase your ability to deal with business ethics problems which may not involve the law.

In discussing the application of different ethical concepts to the business problem and the law, we will try to communicate only a basic flavor rather than present an exhaustive analysis. Sometimes this may mean making assumptions with which you do not agree. But once you see the rough outlines of the analysis associated with a particular ethical concept, you should be able to forecast the outcome of an analysis based on differing assumptions.

Styles of Ethical Reasoning

Egoism. One type of *consequential* thinking with a large business following is called *egoism*. Its perspective is self-centered. Egoists generally judge conduct against *the good of their self-interested pleasure*. Often they engage in cost/benefit analysis to identify which alternative generates the most pleasure for them. Egoists claim that people are selfish, and that philosophy, economics, and law must take this into account. It is a *consequential* type of thinking which judges the rightness or wrongness of conduct by weighing the consequences of the conduct. If the consequences of particular conduct will further the egoist's pleasure, then the conduct is ethically right and fair. It is a philosophy where "the end justifies the means".

The ethical nature of the *strict liability law* with respect to manufacturers of products is dependent on the position occupied by the egoist. If the egoist is a Johns-Manville Company shareholder, the law can be judged *unethical* because the Company's liability reduces the egoist's income. If the egoist is a person injured by asbestos, the law is *ethical* because it allows the egoist to recover money for the injury. If the egoist is not involved in the litigation, the law is probably good because it promotes order by specifying who pays when chance causes injury. Order benefits everyone, including egoists.

For the egoist, *the problem of the mother of four* is easily resolved by *ignoring the plight of the mother and her family and applying the standard of self-interested pleasure*. Since firing the mother will increase the department's productivity, this is the path most likely to result in a pay raise for the egoist head of the department. This pay raise can then be used to purchase material things and services which increase the pleasure of the decision maker egoist.

Utilitarianism. Utilitarian theory is another form of *consequential ethics*. It has been important in philosophy since the nineteenth century, when one of its greatest proponents, John Stuart Mill, lived and wrote. Utilitarianism says an action is morally right if it produces *the greatest amount of good for the greatest number of people affected by the act*. Conversely, an action is wrong if it affects the majority adversely. Note that this focus is more on *whose* good rather than on *which* good. Utilitarian theory, like egoism, uses cost/benefit analysis. However, utilitarian analysis is based on a calculation of how an action will affect *others* in the long run. A variety of "goods" can be the object of utilitarianism. For example, Jeremy Bentham argued that the greatest pleasure for the greatest number is the best standard. Personal liberty is another good which might be sought by some utilitarians.

Capitalism is to a very large extent utilitarian. In Adam Smith's view of capitalism, the self-interested behavior (egoism) causes producers in the marketplace to allocate scarce resources in ways which produce a utilitarian good—the greatest material benefit for the greatest number of consumers. Thus, capitalism is a distinctive system which, at least in Smith's theory, links the "self"-interest and "other"-interested views.

In assessing the *strict liability law,* the utilitarian would again look at what produces the greatest good for the greatest number. On the benefit side, the law helps the party injured. On the cost side, the law increases costs for many consumers. If there were no such law, the loss would be borne by the injured party—just one person. With this law, many must bear the burden of higher prices for asbestos. Therefore, it is quite arguable that *the greatest good for the greatest number occurs when there is no law of strict liability.*

A utilitarian who analyses *the problem of the mother of four* children might try to separately assess costs and benefits, reasoning as follows. There is a *cost* to society in firing the mother. But there is little cost in firing one of the college students because the student will easily find another job. Therefore, on the cost side, the greatest good for the greatest number probably occurs when a college student is dismissed. In reasoning about the *benefits* side, a utilitarian might conclude that the more productive workers will make the department and the company more profitable. The efficiency associated with keeping the most productive persons active in the workplace is likely to support economic growth, and perhaps lower prices. Thus, the benefit side of the analysis suggests dismissing the mother may be the best strategy. In balancing the costs against the benefits, many utilitarians would be likely to conclude that *dismissing the mother generates the best consequences for society.*

Egoism and utilitarianism are two major *consequential* systems often motivating business behavior. There are also major systems of *duty based ethics* with great influence in business. Two are discussed next.

Kant's Philosophy. Immanuel Kant's system of ethics is based on *duty,* all persons have a duty to obey the moral law established by their practical reasoning. The conduct to be ethical must be capable of being *universally* followed. Basically:

1. One ought never to act unless one is willing to have one's act, or the principle on which it is based, become *universal.*
2. One is obligated to treat every individual as an *end* and never as a *means;* meaning that humans as moral beings must be treated with moral dignity.
3. One must act as though one were *both* a person who makes the law and one who is bound by the law, that is, one must act in ways consistent with the way one desires others to act.

A Kantian analysis of the *strict liability law* would ask several questions but the one yielding the most clear-cut answer is the means/ends question. It is clear that allowing some to benefit without compensating the party injured is a way by which the injured party is used exclusively as a means (to lower prices) and not as an end. *A Kantian would support the strict liability law.*

A Kantian might analyze *the problem of the mother of four* children along the following lines. Is dismissing any of the workers treating them as means and not as ends? Would it be appropriate to make as a universal law that the lowest producing employee ought to be the one dismissed when layoffs are required? Since this law is likely to make the organization more efficient, it may therefore reduce the risks that additional layoffs will be required. Making a universal law of laying off the most productive worker probably is self-defeating, since that would make the firm more inefficient, thereby increasing the need for further layoffs, and eventually probably destroying and eliminating the firm. Since this is self-defeating, it fails Kant's test of universality. Accordingly, a Kantian may conclude that *laying off the mother of four is ethical,* consistent with duty.

Religious Ethics. For *many business persons* their *religious views* are the primary source of standards for judging rightness or wrongness. For this reason it is useful to consider the attributes of religious ethics. Judeo-Christian ethics is certainly the dominant ethic of this country, and many of its conclusions about business ethics overlap those of the other major religions of the world such as Islam, Hinduism, and Buddhism. You can see the ethics content, rather than the religious content, of Judeo-Christian ethics more clearly if you focus on those aspects that describe people's relationships with one another as opposed to those which describe their relationship with God. For example, the first three of the Christian Ten Commandments deal with people's relationship with God while the last seven deal with relations among persons.

The character of this ethic is largely based on *duty*. It consistently imposes duties on believers that must be followed simply because of the source and inherent correctness of the duty. The command, "Thou shalt not steal" is an example. On the other hand, many religious denominations interpret religious duties in a utilitarian way, as almost exclusively means—that is, steps on a path leading to eternal salvation.

The perspective of this ethic is primarily, but not exclusively, "other" oriented. Exhortations to "Honor thy father and mother"; "Do unto others as you would have them do unto you"; and the central command from Jesus to "Love one another as I have loved you" all display the "other" orientation. Again, however, in some denominations the focus on salvation evokes a self-oriented perspective.

Some of the Judeo-Christian precepts have *direct* application to business. For example, the commandment against lying has pervasive implications for nearly all business activities and particular importance for such functions as advertising.

Other Judeo-Christian concepts influence business behavior *indirectly*. For example, special concern for the weakest members of society is a part of this ethic. Many business decisions by persons who embrace this ethic reflect this special concern for the poor.

To a large degree the Judeo-Christian ethic rejects materialism, particularly material excesses such as conspicuous consumption. This ethic encourages participation in the market economy when the motivating impulse is other-oriented service rather than egoistic greed. Even when profits are earned honestly and thus reflect the amount of service rendered, this ethic speaks to the *use* of this earned profit.

When evaluating the strict liability law, it is likely that someone applying the Judeo-Christian ethic would conclude that the injured person ought to be compensated. Selling products can generally be viewed as Judeo-Christian service to humanity. This definition of service however would probably not be met if a product, such as asbestos, seriously injured others. Thus, the activity of selling products which cause serious injury violates the Judeo-Christian ethic. If you sold a product which, unknown to you, caused injury to another, the "other" orientation, implicit in the command to love others, would probably require that, at the least, you compensate them for their injury. In another line of analysis, the injured party might be viewed as one of society's disadvantaged members who is entitled to special treatment and therefore the injured party ought to be compensated. These two lines of analysis lead to the same conclusion—*the strict liability law is ethical.*

In applying the Judeo-Christian ethic to *the problem of the mother of four* children, we minimize injury—and therefore maximize love—by *dismissing one of the college students* who will find other work quite soon. Also, the disadvantaged status of the mother argues for special treatment. So again two lines of analysis lead to the same Judeo-Christian conclusion.

The ethical theories we have described cannot give you "the" answer to every moral dilemma that you or other people in business face; mature persons must ultimately decide for themselves. However, ethical theory can prove quite helpful in defining the exact *nature* of the moral problems. And it offers insight into the *manner* in which philosophers who have given great thought to moral systems might *solve* a problem. Together with an understanding of the ethics of the law and of markets, this ethical theory equips students to engage in the critical study of business law.

Solving Ethics Problems

Like the other end-of-Part discussions in this book, this one presents four problems for you to consider and discuss. The problems present the kinds of ethical issues frequently confronted by today's managers. Unless you are unusually mature or have substantial work experience, you may not be able to reach firm conclusions about what you ought to do in considering these problems.

The following suggestions may help as you first try to analyze business ethics issues. After you've analyzed a variety of ethics problems using these procedures, you may find it more comfortable to use a different approach. But as you start out, try to follow this procedure.

1. After reading the problem, determine whether the *marketplace* plays an important role in the problem. If it does, decide what goals the market tries to advance and whether you think market imperfections are present.
2. Determine whether *a law* plays an important role in the problem. If it does, try to decide what jurisprudential goal, or "good", the law seeks to advance and whether, based on your standards, the legal system is working appropriately.
3. Ask if there are *philosophic goods other than* those associated with the *market* or the *law* which are important in the problem. Once you have identified the relevant philosophic goods present in the problem, decide whether there are conflicts among the goods. That is, does the achievement of one good, such as egoistic pleasure, eliminate the possibility of achieving another good, such as order?
4. If you conclude that *goods* are *in conflict* you must decide which good is more important. You will find your judgment improved if you assess the alternative goods using the four *styles* of *ethical reasoning* (egoism, utilitarianism, Kant's philosophy, religious ethics) discussed previously. After you have used the four styles of reasoning, decide what you personally believe is ethical (fair or right) conduct in response to the problem.

An Illustration of Ethics Problem Analysis

The following paragraphs depict one person's attempt to follow this process in evaluating the *divorced mother of four problem*.

THE MARKET'S ROLE: The marketplace plays a critical role in this problem. The market here tries to advance the material well-being of society by creating incentives to keep employed only the most talented members of the work force, *so the divorced mother should be fired*.

THE LAW'S ROLE: This problem does not involve the law directly.

AN EGOISTIC ANALYSIS: Self-interest for the manager requires that the *divorced mother be fired*. This alternative increases the output per dollar spent. Thus, the manager looks more effective and is therefore more likely to win pay raises and promotions.

A UTILITARIAN ANALYSIS: The greatest good for the greatest number occurs when the *divorced mother is let go*. This is because the total wealth of society is increased when the most talented are employed. This wealth benefits those who work and it also pays for the welfare system.

A KANTIAN ANALYSIS: There is a duty to the organization to act in its best interest. Also, since firing the most productive worker is self-defeating if made universal, there is a duty to fire the divorced mother. Both these lines of analysis suggest the same conclusion, *fire the divorced mother*.

RELIGIOUS ANALYSIS: Since the divorced mother is poor she's entitled to special status and, therefore, if no one else is significantly injured, she ought *not to be fired*.

PERSONAL BELIEF: As the manager of production, I believe that the way this society generates the greatest total material well-being is by hiring only the most productive people. Hiring the least productive people is self-defeating for firms and society because this reduces the size of society's pie of wealth. In general, we ought to hire the most productive people.

However, I think this case represents an exception to the general rule. The way we cut the pie may be more important than the reduction in the size of the pie. I weigh two factors in coming to this conclusion. First, our Judeo-Christian heritage asks us to be particularly sensitive to the weakest members of society. I think the mother qualifies for this treatment. Second, the four children involved here mean that society's welfare system may not be able to adequately provide for them in this case. Therefore, I think we ought to *keep the divorced mother.*

Additionally, as the manager, I must realize that the authority to fire anyone is coupled with the understanding that I will act in the best interest of the company. Since in keeping the mother I will *not* be doing that, I am obligated to obtain consent from the organization. *I would meet with my boss* and try to persuade my boss that the company ought *to keep the divorced mother.*

Ethical Problems for Discussion

The following problems give you the opportunity to engage in ethical reasoning using the four Styles of Reasoning—Egoism, Utilitarianism, Kant's Philosophy, Religious Ethics.

1. Suppose you were the owner of a company and needed to hire a production line worker. Also suppose the two best applicants included an old high school friend, but the other applicant was clearly better qualified for the job. You and your friend are the same sex, while the other applicant is a member of the opposite sex. Assume that you would rather have the good company of your friend than any increased profits created by selecting the best qualified applicant. You also know that hiring your friend would violate the federal law which prohibits discrimination on the basis of sex. Should you violate this law in these circumstances? Why or why not?

2. Suppose you owned one of three gasoline stations in a small rural town located more than fifty miles away from the nearest competition. Further, assume that the other two station owners had agreed to raise prices fifteen cents per gallon. They approached you and asked you to join them. You know that this conduct is illegal. After a very careful analysis, you concluded that if you participated your income would double. You and your family definitely need the money. Assume that there is absolutely no risk that you would be caught. If you believe that such conduct is unfair or wrong, would you be willing to give up the additional income? If you do believe the conduct unfair and wrong, do you think the greater wrong is violating the law or causing someone an economic injury?

3. Assume that you are the personnel manager of a firm. Your new employees are instructed not to discuss their salaries with other employees. ("Pay secrecy" is, in fact, a reality of organizational life.) Assume you have interviewed a great candidate for the unique position of sales representative. The market salary for this position is $20,000. However, this applicant, when asked about her salary expectations, said, "I'd feel good if I could land a job at $17,500." You know you could pay her this amount without violating any equal employment opportunity or equal pay laws because there is only one position like this in the organization. Also, you have been instructed to hire people at the lowest possible salary. What will you do and why?

4. Assume that you are the northeastern regional sales manager for a company. Suppose your boss, the national sales manager, quit recently. His boss, the president, has announced that he will pick one of the six regional sales managers for promotion. You judge that it will be a close race, but only between you and the southwestern regional manager, Kirk. You are aware that the president has very strict sexual standards. You know that Kirk has been living with three girlfriends at different periods over the last year. Will you weave this information into your conversation with the president if you think it will help you win the promotion?

PART 2 Contracts

5. Concept of Contractual Agreement
The concept of freedom of contract. Every contract requires the existence of an agreement based on a proper promise.

6. Formation of a Contract
The freedom to contract is not without limits. The promise necessary to the formation of a contract is contained in an offer which, when accepted, can spring a contract into existence.

7. Relief from Contractual Obligations
The law's concern is that the promise made in the offer be made fairly and voluntarily.

8. Consideration/Value Given for a Promise
A contract is a serious matter. The promise contained in an offer must be the result of a bargain; something of legal value called "consideration" is usually required for a promise to become a contract.

9. Capacity/Ability to Create a Contract
Individuals need protection in the marketplace when faced with the reality of a contract. Persons vary in their capacity (ability) to contract, and the law considers this in determining what contractual obligations have been incurred by these persons.

10. Public Policy and Contractual Purpose
Further development of the concept of freedom of contract. The interests of persons other than the immediate parties to the contract must be considered before a contract will be enforced by law. The concerns of society also are important and must be considered by the law.

11. Contractual Form: Requirement of a Writing for Enforceability, Statute of Frauds
The law's concern is with proof and form of a contract so that the courts not be misled into enforcing alleged contracts which never existed. Without a required writing, a contract is usually unenforceable.

12. Contractual Duties of Performance, Nonperformance, and Discharge
How a contractual obligation is performed and ended.

13. Contractual Rights, Third Parties, and Remedies for Breach of Contract
A contract is property involving the interests, rights, and duties which are acquired by the contracting parties and also, in certain situations, by third parties who were not parties to the contract. A party's breach of contract (wrongful nonperformance of a promissory duty to perform) creates new rights in the remedies available to the non-breaching party.

Summary
While a contract can be simply stated as "a promise which the law recognizes as creating a legal obligation of performance," *the finding of a contract* requires that a proper contractual purpose be manifested by genuineness of assent, by parties with capacity to contract, who have exchanged consideration. A contract will be *enforced* if its contractual purpose is not in conflict with public policy and, in certain instances, only if the contract is in writing or there is a proper written note or memorandum of the oral contract. Legal obligations to perform a contract end by performance or by other methods of discharge. A contract is property which, in certain instances, can be transferred to third parties. The property interest in the contract is protected by law.

Business ethics as it relates to the text material in this Part is considered at the end of the Part.

5 Concept of Contractual Agreement

After you have read this chapter, you should be able to:

1. Discuss the concept of "freedom of contract" and its current applications.
2. Understand the distinction between the terms "promise" and "agreement."
3. Explain why every contract requires the existence of an agreement based on a proper promise.
4. Become familiar with those words and phrases which are currently used in the law of contracts.
5. Be able to identify what concepts of contract law are summarized in legal terms or phrases.

Introduction

The Constitution of the United States of America guarantees to each of us the *freedom to contract*.[1] Such a guaranty ensures that you and I may become personally involved in the legal environment in which we all reside. We do this every day by creating *rights and duties* for ourselves and others. This direct participation by us in our legal environment takes place when we buy groceries at the store, rent an apartment, buy a car, enroll in a course at a university, or do many other activities.

Generally, a right is that which one is legally entitled to have, or to do, or to receive from others within limits prescribed by law. Generally, a duty is a legal obligation owing from one person to another.

Without freedom to contract, called "freedom of contract," business in the United States as we know it would cease to exist and our ability to maintain our standard of living would be reduced.

It is important, therefore, that every person understand, use wisely, and preserve such a basic freedom so necessary to our way of life.

The important point you should note in this chapter and throughout Part 2 is that *the concept of freedom to contract has legal limitations*. It is not an absolute freedom.

The Agreement—A Prerequisite to a Contract

The law specifies what promises can form the basis of a contract. Some promises create only an "agreement," while some create a "contract" in which the promises create legal obligations to perform them. Thus there is a difference between the words "agreement" and "contract." To have a contract, there must be (1) mutual assent with a promise or promises, (2) consideration, (3) capacity to contract, and (4) legality. Obviously, if a person does not have the capacity to make a promise creating a legal obligation, there is no contract. Also, if a promise is to do that which society condemns as illegal, such a promise does not create a contract because there is no legal obligation to perform the promise. These four elements will be discussed in separate chapters.

How You Might View It
"We agreed." "We shook hands." "You said you would do it!" "But Mom, Dad said I could have the car tonight." To the casual observer these statements imply the existence of an **agreement**. Each statement suggests that some accord or understanding might exist. In a nonlegal sense we might have an agreement or understanding.

agreement
a manifestation of mutual assent between parties by offer and acceptance

What the Dictionary Says
The dictionary defines an "agreement" as an "arrangement" and notes certain equivalent words—namely, "bargain," "compact," and "contract."[2]

What the Law Says
Two bodies of law are applicable here: the **Uniform Commercial Code** (statutory law) and the common law (the nonstatutory law common to the people and to society). The Code defines an agreement as a "bargain in fact" between parties. It also defines a contract in Article 1 section 201(11) resulting from the agreement of the parties. Whether an agreement has *legal consequences* is determined by the Code, when applicable, or by the *common*

Uniform Commercial Code
a body of statutory law governing commercial transactions concerning personal property (movable things)

---

[1] U.S. Constitution, Art. I, sec. 10: "No State shall . . . pass any . . . law impairing the obligation of contracts. . . ."

[2] *The Random House College Dictionary* (New York: Random House, 1982), p. 28.

Figure 5.1 Law Governing Contracts[3]

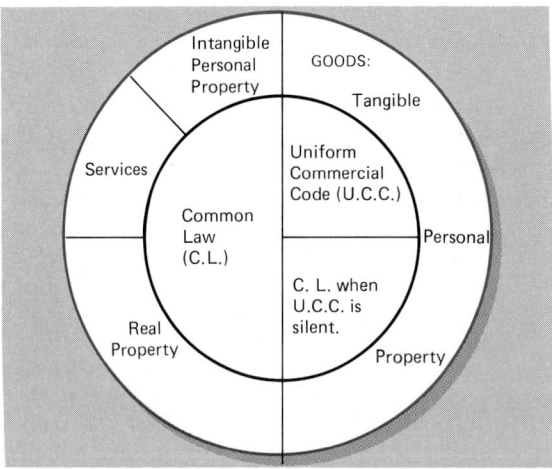

law of contracts.[4] Whether an agreement will result in a *contract*, which imposes *legal obligations on the parties*, is also determined by the Code and the common law of contracts.[5] (See figure 5.1.)

The Uniform Commercial Code. An application of the Uniform Commercial Code definition of an agreement is found in UCC 2–106. In that Article, an agreement must be for the present or future *sale* of **goods** to result in a contract. This Code Article limits the subject matter of a sales contract to goods and excludes land and services. Another application is found in UCC 2–204. There the Code requires that an agreement exist before a contract can be formed. Both definitions and applications under the Code lead one to the conclusion that the words "agreement" and "contract" have different meanings under the Code—that agreement is a part of, and necessary to, a contract.

The Common Law. Under the **common law,** certain arrangements or understandings with regard to social obligations or illegal activities might be recognized as agreements but not as contracts. This is done because the purpose of the understanding is considered to be of minor importance, or it conflicts with what law seeks to prevent others from doing because society has determined such conduct to be undesirable. Thus, under the common law, a contract and an agreement have different meanings—again, agreement being a part of, and necessary to, a contract.

Definition of Contract

A **contract** is *a promise which the law recognizes as creating a legal obligation of performance. A promise* creates such a legal obligation and thereby becomes a contract *when the four elements previously stated have occurred*. A minimum of two persons, called *parties,* are required in order to have a contract. The definition of contract requires a *promise. Thus, we have the rule that a contract can be formed only if we have at least one promise and at least two parties*. In the following case the court found that, since the defendant had not made a promise, he had not made a contract.

goods
tangible, movable things

common law
principles of nonstatutory law reflecting the customs and usages of society and found in judicial decisions

contract
a promise which the law recognizes as creating a legal obligation of performance

---

[3] When the Uniform Commercial Code does not specifically modify the common law, the common law is determinative of the legal result accorded to the transaction.

[4] UCC 1–201(3). This means Article 1, Part 2, Section 1(3).

[5] UCC 1–201(11).

Facts
This is an action for damages. Plaintiff, Stanley Smith & Sons, contracted with defendant, Limestone College, to construct a gymnasium on campus. The building was completed on or before October 1, 1976, at a cost to the College of $655,178. On October 1, 1976, the campus experienced extraordinary heavy rainfall which caused damage to the gymnasium. Plaintiff repaired the damage at a cost of $37,255.24 and seeks recovery under an express contract.

Decision
Judgment for defendant.

Reasoning
A contract is an obligation which arises from actual agreement of the parties manifested by words, oral or written, or by conduct. If agreement is manifested by words, the contract is said to be express. If it is manifested by conduct, it is said to be implied. In either case, the parties must manifest a mutual intent to be bound. Without the actual agreement of the parties, there is no contract. The Board (Limestone College) never expressly promised to pay for the repairs and therefore there is no express contract upon which plaintiff can achieve recovery.

Stanley Smith & Sons v. Limestone College, 322 S.E.2d 474 (S.C.1984).

Certain promises will not be *enforced* by law as legal obligations. Social obligations, promises which violate a strongly felt public policy, and usually promises to do illegal acts or promises that will produce **unconscionable** results are not enforced by law as contracts. Except for these types of promise, all other promises normally can form the basis for a contract. In the following case the court held that the contract was unconscionable and against public policy.

unconscionable
offends the conscience; immoderate, too one-sided

Facts
Plaintiffs, Clifton and Cora Jones, welfare recipients, agreed to buy a home freezer for $900 from the defendant, Star Credit Corp., through a salesman representing Your Shop At Home Service, Inc. After adding time credit charges, credit life insurance, credit property insurance and sales tax, the purchase price came to a total of $1,234.80. So far the plaintiffs have paid $619.88 toward the purchase. The defendant claims that with added credit charges paid for an extension of time the plaintiffs still owe a balance of $819.81. The freezer unit, when purchased, had a maximum retail value of approximately $300. Plaintiffs sued to have the sales contract reformed on the ground that the contract was unconscionable as a matter of law. The question is whether this transaction and the resulting contract could be considered unconscionable within the meaning of section 2–302 of the Uniform Commercial Code.

Decision
The Court held that selling a freezer for $900 ($1,439.69 including credit charges and $18 sales tax) that had an actual retail value of $300 was unconscionable as a matter of law under the Uniform Commercial Code.

Reasoning
Section 2–302 of the Uniform Commercial Code enacts the moral sense of the community into the law of commercial transactions. It authorizes the court to find that a contract or a clause of a contract was "unconscionable at the time it was made," and upon so finding the court may refuse to enforce the contract, remove the objectionable clause, or limit the application of the clause to avoid an unconscionable result. The prevention of oppression and unfair surprise is the principle embodied in this section. It is apparent that the defendant has been adequately and amply compensated, already having been paid more than $600 for a $300 freezer unit. In accordance with the statute, the application of the payment provision should be limited to amounts already paid by the plaintiffs and the contract should be rewritten to change the payments called for to equal the amount of payment actually so paid by the plaintiffs.

Jones v. Star Credit Corp., 59 Misc.2d 189 (N.Y. 1969).

formal contract
a contract which must be in a certain form

recognzance
an obligation acknowledged by a person in a court to do something (e.g., to appear in court at a later time), i.e., personal bond

check
a negotiable "draft drawn on a bank payable on demand" UCC 3–104(2) (b)

promissory note
a written promise to pay money

Types of Contract

Formal and Informal Contracts
A written promise which the law will enforce because it is in a certain required form is called a **formal contract.** Examples of formal contracts would be a contract under seal, a **recognizance,** and various types of negotiable commercial paper such as a **check** and a negotiable **promissory note.**

Figure 5.2 A Check

```
Anywhere,                (d)  October 1    19 XX         No.  1
Colorado
                              FIRST BANK
(b) Pay to the
(e) order of    John Doe                              $  10.01  (c)

              Ten----------------and-------------.01/100      Dollars (c)

                              (a)  Harvey Smith
```

Figure 5.3 A Simple Contract

```
                                Sale

Agreement (a) between (c) Barnes and Smith whereby this day Smith has sold and
Barnes has bought the (b) entire crop of Niagra grapes, same to be (d) clean and free
of mildew and fungi diseases, now growing on the ranch of Smith, situate at Fort
Collins, Colorado, consisting of 50 acres, more or less, and the crop estimated as 1,000
tons. Above grapes to be packed and delivered by seller to buyer's packing house at
Loveland, Colorado, at such times as may be desired by buyer. Terms (b) $1,000 cash,
payment as follows: Net 30.

      June 1, 19XX      Date      Signature    Barnes        buyer
                                  Signature    Smith         seller
```

Required Form for a Negotiable Instrument. As figure 5.2 illustrates, a negotiable instrument must (a) be in writing and signed by the drawer. It must (b) contain an unconditional order or promise (c) to pay a sum certain in money. It must (d) be payable on demand or at a definite time. It must (e) be payable to order or bearer. Several chapters are devoted to the concept of a negotiable instrument as a *formal* contract in a later part of this book.[6]

simple contract
a contract which need not be in any particular form

An *informal* or **simple contract** contains a promise which the law does not require to be in any particular form—e.g., a promise to employ a person. It may or may not be in writing; if in writing, it may be long or short. Figure 5.3 is an example of a simple contract, with identification of (a) mutual assent, (b) the consideration, (c) the parties, and (d) legality. In this section of the text, our discussion of contracts will be limited to the informal or simple contract.

Elements of a Simple Contract

As was previously mentioned, the elements necessary for a *promise* to become a simple contract are: (a) mutual assent, (b) consideration, (c) capacity to contract, and (d) legality. Accordingly, we will first examine the promise which leads to mutual assent and an agreement.

---
[6] See chapters 23–27.

The Promise

The Character of a Promise. The expression of a **promise** necessary to the formation of a contract looks to the future and is one person's assurance to another or others that something in the future shall happen or not happen. "I'll build the bridge" or "the can will not leak" are examples. The word "promise" need not occur.

The Number of Promises. While we must have at least one promise to create a contract, the contract can contain any number of promises. If the promise seeks the performance of an act (e.g., dig a ditch), or a forbearance (refraining from doing something), the contract, if it comes into being, will be called a **unilateral contract** because there is only *one* promise. For example, X promises to pay Y $3,000 if Y *will paint* X's house by the end of August, or C promises to pay D $10,000 if D *will not* sue E. If the promise seeks a return promise which is given and the contract comes into existence, the contract will be called a **bilateral contract** because there is *more than one* promise. For example, A promises to pay B $200 for certain services to be rendered by B, and B promises to render such services.

Communication of the Promise. The promise necessary to the formation of a contract must be *communicated* to another party before it can act as an effective basis for forming a contract. The person who initiates the process for formation of a contract by making the original promise is called the **promisor.** The person to whom a promise has been made is called the **promisee.**

The person who has the duty to carry out the promise is called the **obligor.** The person who has the right to the benefit of the promise is called the **obligee.** (In a contract, A promises to pay B $100. A is the promisor and obligor. B is the promisee and obligee.)

An agreement which manifests by oral or written words the terms of a promise in a unilateral contract situation, and the return promise in a bilateral contract situation, is called an *express contract,* provided that the other requirements of a contract are present.

An agreement which can be *inferred* only from the conduct of persons and which has the other requirements of a contract is called a *contract implied in fact.* For example, J enters D's drugstore, picks up a magazine for sale, waves it in the air to get D's attention, and D nods his head. Upon leaving the store, J will have communicated to D a promise to pay for the magazine and D will have accepted the promise—all by action.

In alimony cases a live-in partner failing to qualify for a division of property by divorce or **common law marriage** seeks to be compensated for lawful services rendered by alleging an express or implied in fact contract. In the following case the plaintiff won the right to go to trial to prove express and implied *contracts* for support, but in a subsequent trial of this case plaintiff was unable to prove the existence of any *contract.*

promise
an assurance or undertaking that something shall or shall not happen

unilateral contract
a contract in which the consideration for a promise is an act or a forbearance

bilateral contract
a contract in which the consideration is mutual promises

promisor
the person who makes a promise

promisee
the person to whom a promise is made

obligor
the person who owes a legal obligation

obligee
the person to whom a legal obligation is owed

common law marriage
a status of marriage not solemnized in the ordinary way, but created by an agreement of marriage, followed by cohabitation

Facts
Plaintiff, Michelle Marvin, who had lived with defendant Lee Marvin, the actor, for seven years without marriage, brought suit to enforce an alleged oral contract under which she had claimed she was entitled to half the property which had been acquired during that period and taken in the name of Lee Marvin and for support payments. Upon stipulation that Lee Marvin was married to one Betty Marvin during his cohabitation with Michelle Marvin, defendant's motion to dismiss was granted. The case is before the court to hear the appeal of Michelle Marvin.

Decision
Judgment for appellant, Michelle Marvin. Reversed and remanded to lower court for trial.

quantum meruit
an action for services rendered based on an implied promise to pay plaintiff as much as plaintiff reasonably deserved to have for the plaintiff's services

unjust enrichment
a legal doctrine that prevents persons from profiting or enriching themselves inequitably at the expense of others

quasi
as if

Reasoning
Provisions of the Family Law Act of the State of California do not govern the distribution of property during a nonmarital relationship. The court should enforce express contracts between nonmarital partners except to the extent the contract is explicitly founded on consideration of meretricious sexual services, despite a contention that such contracts violate public policy. In the absence of an express contract, the court should inquire into the conduct of the parties to determine whether that conduct demonstrates an implied contract, agreement or joint venture, or some other tacit understanding between the parties. The court may also employ the doctrine of **quantum meruit** or equitable remedies such as constructive or resulting trust, when warranted by the facts of the case. In the instant case, Michelle Marvin's complaint states a cause of action for breach of an express contract and the complaint also can be amended to state a cause of action founded on a theory of implied contract or equitable relief.

Marvin v. Marvin, 557 P.2d 106 (Cal. 1976).

The Implied Promise. When no promise was intended, yet one is *implied* in law to prevent **unjust enrichment,** and an agreement is found by law, we have a *contract implied in law,* or **quasi** *contract.* The implied contract is not expressed in words but is inferred or implied from the circumstances. This is illustrated by the following case.

Facts
Plaintiff, Hertz, a former tenant of Ficus, defendant, brought this action based on *unjust enrichment* to Ficus for expenditures Hertz made in remodeling a restaurant-lounge business owned by Ficus. While the *lease contract* was being negotiated, Hertz remodeled the premises with the knowledge and consent of the owner, Ficus. Because of failure to pay the rent, Hertz was evicted. The defendant contended that there was no contract and, therefore, there was no liability to the plaintiff. The plaintiff contended that there was a contract implied in law.

Decision
Judgment for Hertz for his expenditures to remodel the restaurant.

Reasoning
The court noted that, under a theory of quasi contract, recovery does not require the existence of a contract. The defendant had received a benefit which it would be inequitable to allow him to retain without compensating Hertz. A contract implied in law is not a contract at all but an obligation imposed by law for the purpose of bringing about justice.

Hertz v. Ficus, 567 P.2d 1 (Ida. 1977).

Joint and Several Promises. We can have any number of parties in a contract. Also we can have any number of promises in a contract. When we relate parties to promises, we have three basic relationships present.

When more than one party appears on either side of a contract, depending upon their intentions, their promises will be considered *joint, several,* or *joint and several.*

If there is only *one promise* and more than one party *together* obligate themselves to perform the *same* promise, the parties' obligation is *joint;* their obligation is to perform together, **jointly.** They are collectively **liable** and can be sued only together. A and B contract with C "We promise to purchase from C." A and B are jointly liable to C.

If the *same* performance is *separately promised* by each party, the obligation is **several,** performable by each of the several parties. They are individually **liable** and can be sued individually. A and B contract with C "Each of us promises to buy from C." A and B are severally liable to C.

If the promise is in terms of "I promise" rather than "we promise," and is undertaken by more than one party, the obligation assumed is *joint and several,* so that the parties are liable and can be sued together or individually. This is illustrated in the following case where the court held that where two or more parties to a contract promise the same performance to the same promisee, each is collectively bound for the whole performance.

joint liability
occurs when parties together obligate themselves to perform the same promise

several liability
occurs when the same performance is separately promised by each party

Facts
Defendants, Chang Nim Barnes and Wiley Barnes, III, wife and husband, held title to certain property as joint tenants. They entered into a contract to sell this property to plaintiff, John Neal Anderson. This contract contained a clause requiring that "the seller shall execute and deliver a good and sufficient general warranty deed" conveying the property free and clear of all liens and encumbrances except for a first deed of trust which Anderson agreed to assume. Plaintiff Billy S. King is an assignee of certain of Anderson's rights. Prior to closing, a **judgment lien** was recorded against the interests of Wiley Barnes, III. Plaintiff King paid off the **lien** and brought this suit for breach of the contractual promise "free and clear of all liens" against both Chang Nim and Wiley Barnes, III, arguing that Chang Nim had warranted that *both* Barnes' interests were free and clear and that Chang Nim had breached her contract.

Decision
Judgment for plaintiff.

Reasoning
Chang Nim Barnes' warranty in contract extended to her husband's interest in the property. Unless a contrary manifestation is shown, where two or more parties to a contract promise the same performance to the same promisee, each is bound to the performance thereof. Thus, the promise creates a joint and several duty to perform the entire contract. Here, because the Barnes signed one contract and the contract contained but one warranty, each was bound by the warranty for the entire interest subject to the contract.

Anderson v. Barnes, 671 P.2d 1327 (Colo. 1983).

> **judgment lien**
> a lien binding the real estate of a judgment debtor and giving the holder of the judgment lien a right to levy on the real estate for satisfaction to the exclusion of other adverse interests subsequent to the judgment
>
> **lien**
> a legal right in another's property as security for the performance of an obligation

Objective Test

In express and implied-*in-fact* contracts, the law looks to the *objective evidence* that parties normally *manifest* in a *bargain* situation in order to determine whether a contract has been formed and then whether it is express or implied in fact.

If I **subjectively** (personally) do not want a contract but my actions or words, oral or written, would lead a reasonable person to understand or presume that I do intend a contract, that presumption will control. A promise communicated in a bargain setting raises a strong presumption that a contractual intent is present. The following case so holds.

> **subjectively**
> existing only in one's mind

Facts
The sole issue presented by the defendant, appellant, Thomas E. Green, is as follows:
> Whether the trial court erred in holding that the Guaranty signed by Thomas E. Green was an individual Guaranty and therefore making him personally liable for the debts of Safety Signal of Tennessee, Inc. up to the aggregate sum of $2,500.00 for which amount the court entered judgment against the defendant.

At the end of the continuing guaranty document the following appeared:
> s/s Thomas E. Green
> President, Safety Signal of Tenn.

The form contains two lines for signatures of guarantors. On the first line, the signature of Thomas E. Green was signed in script. On the second line, the words "President, Safety Signal of Tenn., In(c)" are printed by hand with an ink pen. Appellant relies upon his testimony that his intention was to sign for the corporation and not as an individual. No other evidence was offered as to the mutual intent of the parties.

Decision
Judgment for plaintiff, appellee.

Reasoning
It is possible for an officer of a corporation to avoid personal liability by signing his name and adding his title and the name of the corporation. However, such a signature does not produce the presumptive effect of a signature in which the name of the corporation appears first followed by the word "by" or "per." In the former case, additional evidence, such as text of the instrument or evidence of the joint intent of the parties, would be required to establish that only the corporation was to be bound. In the latter case, the intention of the parties is self-evident from the form of the signature. Since no additional evidence of intent was offered, the court held that a secret, unexpressed intent of one party to the contract cannot bind the other party who has no notice of the secret intent.

Cone Oil Co., Inc. v. Green, 669 S.W.2d 662 (Tenn. 1983).

Risk

When one makes a promise, one assumes all the risks associated with its performance. Where the promise cannot be fulfilled because of **factual impossibility** of carrying it out, one is excused from the consequence of the promise. *Subsequent illegality* of the contractual obligation contained in the promise (a later event making performance illegal) and *destruction of the subject matter* of the promise (the building to be painted burns) will in proper cases *excuse* the promisor from the risk consequence involved in making the promise. In the following case insurance agents and managers assume the risk that a loss ratio would prevent them from receiving a bonus.

factual impossibility
the facts prevent performance of the promise

Facts
In consolidated actions, insurance agents and agency managers brought suit against an insurance company, contending they were entitled to certain bonus renewal commissions pursuant to their employment agreements. In their employment agreements, the following clause appears:
"10. Company shall pay to Agent a bonus of 2% of all his premiums, (excluding Crop, Hail and Tobacco Floater) in his territory, if a production quota assigned by the Company is reached and if the Company loss ratio (annual statement to Insurance Department) for the year in question does not exceed 63%."
Losses reported exceeded 63% so the insurance company did not pay the bonus. The agents contend that if recoupments were included in the calculation of the loss ratio it would be below 63% and they would be entitled to a bonus.

Decision
Judgment for insurance company, defendant.

Reasoning
In the present case, the loss ratio precondition was bargained for and understood. By entering into their respective agreements plaintiffs *accepted the risk* that the loss ratio might exceed 63% for a given year and that their bonus renewal commissions would not be paid.

Fraver v. North Carolina Farm Bureau Mutual Insurance Company, 318 S.E.2d 340 (N.C. 1984).

Classification of Agreements

Void Agreement. A void *agreement* is one which the law will not enforce as a legal obligation, nor does the law recognize its performance as a duty. It is not a contract because the promise or promises do not create a legal obligation of performance. An example is an agreement to commit a crime or to perpetrate a fraud. In the following case the court held that the agreement to support a live-in mate was void because its enforcement would be in violation of a public policy found in a state statute.

Facts
Plaintiff appealed the order of a trial court dismissing her complaint which asked that the court grant her a just, fair share of the property, earnings, and profits of the defendant, order a proper provision for support and maintenance of plaintiff and their minor children, or, in the alternative, divide the joint property of the parties and impress a trust on other properties acquired through the joint efforts of plaintiff and defendant. The complaint alleges that plaintiff became pregnant by defendant out of wedlock, that defendant told plaintiff they would live together as husband and wife and that no formal marriage ceremony was necessary, that defendant stated that he would share his life, future earnings and property with plaintiff, that the parties announced their marriage to their respective parents and thereafter lived together as husband and wife in the community for 17 years during which plaintiff helped defendant complete his professional education and helped him in his professional practice, bore him children and performed other motherly and wifely duties. The appellate court reversed the trial court and held for the plaintiff. The case is now before the Supreme Court to hear the appeal of the defendant.

Decision
Judgment for defendant. Plaintiff's complaint dismissed.

Reasoning
The view in *Marvin v. Marvin* was that the issue before the court is governed solely by contract law. In the court's view, however, the situation alleged here was not the kind of arm's length bargain envisioned by traditional contract principles, but an intimate arrangement of a fundamentally different kind. The issue, realistically, is whether it is appropriate for this court to grant a legal status to a private arrangement substituting for the institution of marriage sanctioned by the State. The question whether change is needed in the law governing the rights of parties in this delicate area of marriage-like relationships involves evaluation of sociological data and alternatives the court believes best suited to the superior investigative and fact-finding facilities of the legislative branch in the exercise of its traditional authority to declare public policy in the domestic relations field. That belief is reinforced by the fact that judicial recognition of mutual property rights between unmarried cohabitants would, in this court's opinion, clearly violate the policy of the recently enacted Illinois Marriage and Dissolution of Marriage Act. The court, therefore, holds that plaintiff's agreement with defendant is void and unenforceable.

Hewitt, et al. *v. Hewitt,* 394 N.E.2d 1204 (Ill. 1979).

Voidable Agreement. A voidable agreement can result in a **voidable contract.** However, it gives one or more of the parties to a contract the alternative of avoiding it or of enforcing it. (A fraudulently induced B to enter into a contract. It is voidable by B.) In the following case the court held that there were sufficient facts on the basis of which the contract could be found to be voidable.

voidable contract
a contract which can be avoided by one or more of the parties

Facts
Defendants are Arthur Murray, Inc., a national **franchisor** of dancing schools, and J. P. Davenport, a franchisee in Florida. Davenport made various contracts with plaintiff, a widow without family and sold to her 2302 hours of dance lessons for a total cash outlay of $31,090.45 over a period of less than sixteen months. Plaintiff alleges the sales contracts were entered into by her because of means and methods of Davenport, defendant, and his associates which, though legally permissible, went beyond the unsavory perimeter of "sales puffing" and went well into the forbidden area of undue influence, the suggestion of falsehood, the suppression of truth, and the free exercise of rational judgment, if what the plaintiff alleged was true. From the time of her first contact with the dancing school, she was influenced unwittingly by a constant and continuous barrage of flattery, false praise, excessive compliments, to such extent that, in her estimation, it would be not only inequitable, but unconscionable, for a Court to allow such contracts to stand. Plaintiff asked the court to declare the contracts null and void. Her complaint was dismissed for failure to state a cause of action, and plaintiff appealed.

Reasoning
Although it is true that generally a misrepresentation, to be actionable, must be one of fact rather than opinion, there are significant qualifications to this rule and they are applicable in this case. It does not apply where there is a fiduciary relationship between the parties or where there has been some artifice or trick employed by the representor, or where the parties do not in general deal at arm's length, or where the representee does not have equal opportunity to become apprised of the truth or falsity of the fact represented. It is reasonable to suppose that the defendants had "superior knowledge" as to whether plaintiff had the potential to become a good dancer and whether she was noticeably improving as the lessons progressed. One could infer from the undenied statements of the complaint that the flowery compliments heaped upon her by the defendants proceeded as much or more from the urge to "ring the cash register" as from any honest or realistic appraisal of her dancing ability or a factual representation of her progress. In the court's view, plaintiff is entitled to her day in Court and the order dismissing plaintiff's complaint with prejudice should be and is reversed.

Vokes v. Arthur Murray, Inc., and J. P. Davenport, 212 So.2d 906 (Fla. 1968).

franchise
a business relationship between a franchisor, who markets goods or services through a franchisee, who has the right to use the franchisor's trade name, trademark, and methods of operation

Decision
Judgment reversed, for plaintiff, the widow.

Unenforceable Agreement. An unenforceable agreement is an agreement which cannot be successfully sued upon or proved. It cannot be enforced in the courts. If it is a contract, it is called an **unenforceable contract.**

Executed Agreement. An **executed contract** is a contract which has been completely performed by all the parties to it.

unenforceable contract
a contract which the courts will not enforce

executed contract
a contract which has been performed by all the parties to it

Chapter 5: Concept of Contractual Agreement

executory contract
a contract which has not been performed by all the parties to it

unconscionable contract
a contract in which one of the parties is in too unequal or one-sided a bargaining position

Executory Agreement. In an **executory contract** something has not been accomplished. The contract can be completely executory, i.e., all of the parties to it have not performed their respective duties. A contract can also be partially executory—i.e., one party has performed but the other party has not performed.

Unconscionable Agreement. An **unconscionable contract** for the *sale of goods* under the Uniform Commercial Code is a contract which the court may refuse to enforce or which the court may modify because one of the parties is in too unequal a bargaining position. The crucial test is whether the bargain is so one-sided in its benefit to one party as to strike the conscience of the court.[7]

While freedom of contract is basic to our way of life, we see a number of developments in our law, perhaps best represented by the Uniform Commercial Code, which temper the results of an application of freedom of contract contained in the words "buyer beware." Certainly the concept of the unconscionable contract is designed to soften the harshness of the marketplace.

A total concept of freedom, it could be argued, would allow each state to develop its own law of contracts. The purpose of the statutory Uniform Commercial Code is, because of the needs of commerce and the economy, to bring uniformity in all states to the law of commercial transactions concerning personal property, such as in sales of goods, which is a part of contract law.

Other statutes which have as their purpose the protection of the consumer make inroads on the concept of freedom of contract. Some of them are the Consumer Product Safety Act and the Truth-in-Packaging Act, discussed in chapter 22; the Federal Trade Commission Act, discussed in chapter 47; the Securities Acts, discussed in chapter 45, and other Acts discussed in the chapters of Part 9, Government Regulation of Business.

The labor relations Acts—i.e., the Wagner Act, the Taft-Hartley Act, and the Landrum-Griffin Act, discussed in chapter 49, Labor Law—have their impact on the freedom of labor and management to contract.

caveat emptor
let the buyer beware

The conclusions to be drawn from observation of the evolutionary process of contract law are that the concept of *freedom* of contract has been questioned and found wanting, that the concept of **caveat emptor** (let the buyer beware) continues to erode and is being replaced by the concept of *caveat venditor* (let the seller beware).

Summary Statement

1. The concept of freedom to contract is not unlimited. The understandings we reach with others in our daily lives are not always contracts. The law does not give importance to social obligations.
2. In law, the word "contract" has a very special meaning separate from what we find in the dictionary.
3. In application, the definition of a contract as a promise which creates a legal obligation of performance becomes quite complex.
4. The promise creates a legal obligation and becomes a contract when four things are present: (1) mutual assent, (2) consideration, (3) capacity to contract, and (4) legality.
5. While we require at least one promise and two parties as a minimum for a contract, any number of parties, relationships, and promises can become part of a contract.
6. The importance of the need to communicate the promise by language and/or action before a contract is formed has been illustrated. The objective analysis of the actions of the parties was developed as a critical concept to determine if there is a manifested meeting of the minds.

---

[7] UCC 2–302.

7. The importance of terminology as a way of expressing conceptual ideas about contracts has also been illustrated.
8. This chapter has evaluated the concept and evolution of contract law and indicated the path of its future development.

The following case has been chosen for you to read because it represents current thinking on what *freedom of contract* should really mean. The implications of the case are far-reaching, and no doubt you will have a strong feeling for or against the court's decision. The case highlights the importance of contract law both to an individual and to business organizations.

Johnson v. Mobil Oil Corporation
415 F.Supp. 264 (1976)

Feikens, J. Plaintiff, Johnson, brought this action against defendant, Mobil Oil Corporation, to recover for losses suffered when the service station he operated was destroyed by fire. Plaintiff alleges that the fire was caused by events following the defendant's delivery of gasoline containing water, and seeks to recover for the loss of inventory and other **consequential damages.** Defendant moves for a partial summary judgment dismissing plaintiff's claim for consequential damages. Defendant seeks to limit any recovery to the difference of the value of the gasoline as gasoline and its value as watered gasoline.

Defendant relies on a clause contained in a contract between itself and the plaintiff which reads as follows: *"In no event shall seller be liable for prospective profits or special, indirect or consequential damages."*

Plaintiff opposes the motion on the ground that the clause excluding consequential damages is unconscionable.

The court noted that the law in Michigan was such that unreasonable terms in a contract for goods and services used by a significant segment of the public and obtainable from limited sources would not be enforced as a matter of public policy. In the eyes of the court this *might* represent a departure from the majority view in a direction away from the freedom to contract but was the law in Michigan.

Since gasoline is used by a significant body of consumers and is available from limited sources, the court felt the question of unconscionability was properly before it.

The court noted that unconscionability can be shown in two ways: by proving either **substantive unconscionability** or **procedural unconscionability.**

The court noted that under the Uniform Commercial Code the clause of the contract in question would not be **prima facie** unconscionable in a commercial setting. Thus a finding of substantive unconscionability might not be present.

On the other hand, the court found procedural unconscionability present. The court noted that the plaintiff could not read, except perhaps for certain items in the sports section of the newspaper, and therefore could not understand the significance of the clause in question. Moreover, the court found that neither was the clause brought to plaintiff's attention nor was its legal significance explained to him.

The court found the clause to be unconscionable and not binding on the plaintiff.

In the court's words:

However, before a contracting party with the immense bargaining power of the Mobil Oil Corporation may limit its liability vis-à-vis an uncounseled layman, as it seeks to do in this case, to 'difference money damages,' it has an affirmative duty to obtain the voluntary, knowing assent of the other party. This could easily have been done in this case by explaining to plaintiff in layman's terms the meaning and possible consequences of the disputed clause. Such a requirement does not detract from the freedom to contract, unless that phrase denotes the freedom to impose the onerous terms of one's carefully drawn printed document on an unsuspecting contractual partner. Rather, freedom of contract is enhanced by a requirement that both parties be aware of the burdens they are assuming. The notion of free will has little meaning as applied to one who is ignorant of the consequences of his acts.

Motion of defendant Mobil Oil Corporation denied.

---

consequential (or special) damages
the money judicially awarded to an injured party for loss which the breaching party reasonably could foresee would be a result of his breach

substantive unconscionability
contract terms which cause one of the parties to be in too unequal or one-sided a bargaining position

procedural unconscionability
circumstances, other than the contract terms, which cause the enforcement of the contract to be unreasonably excessive

prima facie
at first sight

Questions and Case Problems

1. The plaintiff, Crosby, a construction contractor, is seeking compensation from a company named APL for the use or rental of his equipment. Crosby originally had a contract for the rental of his drag line with Mr. Smith. Mr. Smith had a contract with APL, where he was using Crosby's equipment. APL terminated its contract with Mr. Smith and hired another general contractor to complete certain work.

    APL received a monthly billing from Mr. Crosby for the rental of his drag line. APL promptly responded to this billing by a letter informing Mr. Crosby that the new general contractor was making a survey of its equipment needs and, until it was determined whether the drag line was needed, there would be no responsibility for rental payments. Included in the letter was a statement that, until Mr. Crosby was advised by the new general contractor that the drag line was needed, any rental charges were the obligation of Mr. Smith. Mr. Crosby charged that an implied-in-fact contract came into existence because he was not informed until some period of time had passed that his equipment would not be used on the job. What result? [*Crosby v. Paul Hardeman, Inc.*, 414 F.2d 1 (1969).]

2. Plaintiff, Kennedy, a general contractor, obtained a quotation from defendant, Moore-Handley, a distributor for Westinghouse products, to provide various electrical equipment called for by specifications. Kennedy negotiated with Moore-Handley as to price, achieved a price reduction in quoted price and then issued a purchase order to Moore-Handley. This purchase order called for Moore-Handley to provide equipment "per the attached bill of materials," and the attached bill of materials was a complete copy of the Moore-Handley written quotation. On the back of the first page of the quotation sent with the purchase order were certain provisions, printed in red, limiting Moore-Handley's liability for consequential and delay damages. Kennedy's contention is that the court should not have found the limiting conditions on the back of the front page of the quotation to be part of the overall contract. Is Kennedy correct? [*Kennedy Electric Co. v. Moore-Handley Inc.*, 437 So.2d 76 (Ala. 1983).]

3. A lease contained the following paragraph:
    "At the expiration of this Second Supplemental Lease Extension Agreement on May 1, 1983, the second party [lessee] shall have the privilege of an option for the further extension of this lease for an additional period of 10 years from and after May 1, 1983. Both parties agree that the rental terms and conditions for this lease shall be renegotiated as of May 1, 1983 for the 10 year term beginning on that date. The rental terms and conditions shall be negotiated upon a basis which is satisfactory and acceptable to both parties. Both parties agree to negotiate such terms consistent with conditions existing on May 1, 1983, to provide rental terms and conditions substantially the same as those now existing, with appropriate adjustments, however, satisfactory to both parties and covering the ten year term beginning May 1, 1983."
    The parties could not agree as to rent in the renewed lease. Plaintiff, lessee, seeks specific performance of the clause. Defendant alleges the clause is not sufficient to create a contract. Who should prevail? [*R.A.S., Inc. v. Crowley*, 351 N.W.2d 414 (Neb. 1984).]

4. Knack, a cook, and plaintiff in this case, is suing under an Arizona workmen's compensation statute for injuries sustained on a job. The defendant, State Industrial Commission, contends that the plaintiff was hired to perform a series of unilateral contracts to act as cook in various states for an employer who provided services to railroad track-laying crews. Both parties agree that the terms of the agreement were communicated in Arizona. The defendant contends that the contract was not formed until the acts were performed in the other states. The defendant maintains that the plaintiff is not entitled to the protection of the workmen's compensation statutes of Arizona since the contract was not formed in Arizona. On the other hand, Knack contends that a bilateral contract, in which he promised to act as a cook and his employer promised to pay for his services as a cook, was formed in Arizona, one of the conditions of the contract being that the performance of his services as a cook was to take place in various other states. What result? [*Knack v. Industrial Commission of Arizona*, 503 P.2d 373 (Ariz. 1972).]

5. The parties were close personal friends while residents in St. Joseph, Missouri. In 1972, defendants moved to a mobile home located on 23 acres owned by their uncle. Two years later, defendants discussed with plaintiffs the possibility of plaintiffs moving on the same acreage so that their personal association could continue and plaintiffs could aid defendants in taking care of the partially disabled uncle. Defendants agreed to deed three acres to plaintiffs if they came, conditioned upon defendants inheriting the 23 acres. The plaintiffs sold their home and purchased a mobile home which they put on the three acres after making substantial improvements such as putting in a foundation and driveway. The uncle died. The defendants inherited the 23 acres. The plaintiffs were evicted. Are the plaintiffs entitled to three acres of land? [*Leeson v. Etchison,* 650 S.W.2d 681 (Mo. 1983).]

6. Lon Lucas (appellant) and Perry Lucas (appellee) were brothers and partners in a business venture in which Perry Lucas was to finance the construction and operation of a dinner club while Lon Lucas was to manage the business. Lon also supervised the extensive renovation of a structure purchased by appellee to house the dinner club. Perry Lucas was initially hired by his brother to do minor work on the project. After Perry had worked for a short time he claimed he entered into a contract with Lon through Lon's agent, Constantini, to perform certain remodeling tasks. The following oral conversation between Constantini and Perry became part of the court record:
    A. "Constantini asked me if I could build the kitchen, lay tiles on the floor, lay tiles around the bar, do some minor repairs, lay tiles in the bathroom, fix the ceilings in the dining room, bathrooms, and kitchen, and work for half the bid (made by one Larcomb) and I told her yes. And that, she asked me if it would include the work that I had already done, and I told her yes.
    Q. Then, under your new contract, did you proceed to do work?
    A. Yes, sir.
    Q. What did you do?
    A. Exactly what we talked about.
    Q. You did all those things?
    A. Yes, sir."
    The judge instructed the jury that there was no express building contract. Was the judge correct? [*Lucas v. Constantini,* 469 N.E.2d 927 (Ohio 1983).]

7. The plaintiff, Clayton, sold his radio station. Suit is being brought against the purchasers upon a promissory note given by a now-bankrupt corporation formed by the purchasers. The contract of sale stipulated that the balance of the purchase price was to be paid by a note of either the buyers or a corporation formed by them. The defendants, purchasers, contend that the contract was executed and that they were discharged when the note was issued to the plaintiff upon formation of the corporation. What result? [*Clayton v. Communications Capital Corporation,* 440 P.2d 330 (Ariz. 1968).]

8. Strickland set out to bribe a judge named Woods to throw a case. The judge contacted the State's Attorney and told him of the bribe offer. The judge was advised to play along with Strickland. A $2,500 bribe was delivered to the judge by Strickland. Strickland was subsequently indicted for bribery, pled guilty, and was sentenced to imprisonment for a term of 4 years. Three months after the criminal trial, Strickland seeks return of the $2,500. Is he entitled to the return of his money? [*State of Maryland v. Strickland,* 400 A.2d 451 (Md. 1979).]

9. Premier Electrical Construction Company, defendant, is a prime contractor about to bid on a construction project for the Atomic Energy Commission, a large part of that project being electrical work. Miller-Davis Company, plaintiff, is an electrical subcontractor about to submit its electrical bid to the various competing prime contractors who were going to bid on the project. However, Miller-Davis and Premier agreed that: if Miller-Davis would submit an electrical bid to the other prime contractors much higher than the bid it would submit to Premier, this would help Premier submit the low bid on the project; and, in return, Premier would give the electrical subcontract to Miller-Davis for the fixed price of Miller-Davis' bid to Premier. Miller-Davis performed its part of the agreement, Premier got

the project as the low bidder, but Premier gave the electrical subcontract to another electrical subcontractor. Miller-Davis sued Premier for breach of contract between them. Judgment for whom? Explain. [*Premier Electrical Constr. Co. v. Miller-Davis Company*, 291 F.Supp. 295 (1968).]

10. In *Johnson v. Mobil Oil Corporation*, 415 F.Supp. 264 (1976),[8] the court held that a contracting party having immense bargaining power has an affirmative duty to explain in layperson's terms the meaning and possible consequences of a contractual obligation to be assumed by another contracting party who is an uncounseled layperson. Evaluate this holding by the court.

---

[8] See p. 83.

Formation of a Contract 6

After you have read this chapter, you should be able to:
1. Discuss the law of offer and acceptance, recognizing that it acts as a limitation on the freedom to contract.
2. Recognize that the law of offer and acceptance is evolving and moving to facilitate broad social objectives.
3. Appreciate how the promise necessary to the formation of a contract is absorbed into an offer.
4. Understand the complexity of the creation of an offer which places a power in another.
5. Note how the law of offer and acceptance can create rights and duties not previously recognized by law.
6. Note the critical importance of the agency authorized to communicate the acceptance.
7. Realize the critical impact the Uniform Commercial Code has had upon the law of offer and acceptance.

Introduction

The preceding chapter discussed the importance of a promise and the necessity of having an agreement between the parties in order to have a contract. We saw that an agreement is a manifestation of mutual assent between parties by their offer and acceptance. This chapter will discuss the offer which contains the promise, the acceptance, what they are, how they work, and how they create an agreement and a resulting contract with its rights and duties.

The *offer and acceptance* is critical to the formation of a simple express, or implied-in-fact, contract. One reason is that the offer normally contains the promise required for the formation of a contract. Another reason is that by offer and acceptance there is an apparent meeting of the minds of the parties resulting in an agreement. Before we can have a contract, except for the implied-in-law (quasi) contract, *we need an offer.*

The importance of offer and acceptance to the formation of a contract is apparent from the role the concept is designed to play in the law of contracts. (A *offers* to sell a house to B for $100,000, and B *accepts*. A is *promising* to sell and B is *promising* to buy the house.)

Necessary to the finding of an offer is the satisfaction of *two tests: a certainty of terms test* and *an intention test.* The law, having given us the *freedom to contract* and the ability to create *rights and duties,* is concerned that we truly *want* to assume certain duties which would not otherwise be imposed upon us by law, and that we truly *want* to gain rights which we would not otherwise be entitled to by law. To satisfy its concerns, the law limits *our freedom to contract* until the two tests necessary for the existence of an offer are satisfied—the certainty of terms and intention tests. These two tests will be examined later.

The important point in this chapter is the concern of the law for determining *from the parties' conduct whether or not the minds of the parties have apparently met in order to have a contract.* The need to determine this factor *objectively* has resulted in the law of offer and acceptance.

The Offer

Terms of an offer must be communicated to an offeree before we place in the offeree the power to accept and to create a contract—to spring a contract into existence.

Once the terms of an offer are communicated to an offeree, the power to spring a contract into existence does not last forever. It ends with the passage of time, or it can end prematurely through acts of the parties to the proposed contract.

The Uniform Commercial Code has brought major changes to the common law of *offer* and of *acceptance* where the subject matter of the offer is *goods.* These changes will be discussed later in this chapter.

An important point to watch for in this chapter is how the law of offer and acceptance is *evolving* to accomplish social objectives.

Offer Contains a Promise

offer
a promise proposed in exchange for another's act, forbearance, or return promise

offeror
the promisor making an offer

offeree
the promisee to whom an offer is made

An **offer** is a promise proposed with the expectation that it will provoke an exchange of another's act, forbearance, or return promise. The offer gives the offeree the legal power to accept the offer and to spring a contract into existence. Except for the *inverted unilateral contract* in which there is an act in search of a promise, the offer will contain the promise necessary to the formation of a contract. The promisor, the one who makes the promise contained in the offer, becomes an **offeror.** The promisee, to whom the promise is made, becomes the **offeree** when the promisee receives the offer. It should be recognized that in the law of contracts the promise is merged into the concept of offer. The following case dealt with an inverted unilateral contract. It involved an idea for a film for which a promise to pay was enforced as a contract.

Facts
Plaintiff, Blaustein, is suing Richard and Elizabeth Burton for breach of contract, unjust enrichment, breach of confidential relationship, services rendered, and benefits conferred on the grounds that the defendants had used plaintiff's idea for filming "The Taming of the Shrew" without compensating plaintiff. Blaustein had come to the Burtons and had explained to them his ideas about making the film.

Decision
Judgment for plaintiff.

Reasoning
The court held the Burtons liable for breach of contract on the basis that they had breached an inverted unilateral contract. The court noted that a contract for the conveyance of, and payment for, an idea may be either express or implied where an idea has been conveyed with the expectation that compensation will be paid by the recipient if the idea is used. The recipient may thereafter gratuitously promise to pay a reasonable compensation for the idea and create a valid obligation. This is what happened in this case when an inverted unilateral contract was created. The conveyance of the idea was the act in search of a promise to compensate.

Blaustein v. Burton, 88 Cal.Rptr. 319 (Cal. 1970).

Certainty of Terms Test

Before a *proper promise*[1] can result in an offer, it must have *certainty of terms*. A promise can *undertake only two things:* an *act,* or a *forbearance* (refraining from doing something). The promise *can ask from the offeree only three things in exchange:* an act, a forbearance, *or* the offeree's return promise. The promise must tell the offeree what the offeree is to do (an act) or refrain from doing (a forbearance), and what the offeror will do or not do. (I'll pay you $100 for digging the ditch. The offeror's *promise* is to do an act—*to pay $100;* and the offeree is to do an act—*to dig the ditch.*) If the offer does not objectively manifest the promise, it will fail for uncertainty of terms and no contract can be formed. There are a number of combinations of statements which satisfy the certainty of terms test.

One can understand why advertisements are not intended to be offers. Advertisements normally state what the promisee is required to do, but they do not normally state what the promisor/offeror will do because no limit is placed upon what the promisor will be required to do. Is the promisor willing to sell one item, two hundred, or an infinite quantity? This question is not answered in the typical advertisement; therefore, it is not an offer. Normally an advertisement is construed as *soliciting or inviting offers.* (A reads an advertisement in the local newspaper for frying chickens at 59 cents per pound. When A takes a chicken to the checkout counter, A is making an offer to the store through its clerk to buy the chicken for 59 cents per pound.) However, advertisements can be offers when it is obvious from the way they are phrased that this is the intent of the advertiser and when the advertisement leaves nothing open to negotiation. (A advertises in a large Chicago newspaper that A will pay a specified reward to anyone who gives A certain information within one year. B sees a copy of the advertisement one month later and immediately sends the requested information to A. The advertisement is an offer by A. There is a contract between A and B. A will have to pay the reward to B.) Under a rule promulgated by the Federal Trade Commission, goods advertised as *specials* must be available for purchase at the advertised price unless a specific quantity is indicated in the advertisement. A raincheck must be provided for later purchase if the item is unavailable for a reason beyond the control of the store. The following case illustrates how the consumer is entitled to a *statutory remedy* when the requirements of the rule are not observed by the seller.

certainty of terms test
the promise must have certainty of terms in what it promises and what it asks for

---

[1] See p. 74. In chapter 5 we noted that social obligations, illegal objectives, and objectives violative of public policy contained in promises would not be enforced as contracts.

Facts

J. C. Penney, Inc., appellee, ran an advertisement in a newspaper which stated that it had a number of small appliances including a waffle baker for sale at $9.99. The sale was advertised as a closeout with limited quantities available. The specific number of items for sale did not appear in the advertisement. Plaintiff, Weaver, appellant, sought to purchase a waffle baker and was told that they had all been sold. Mr. Weaver asked for a raincheck giving him the right to purchase a waffle baker for $9.99 in the future, but since Penney was not going to stock the item in the future they refused his request. Mr. Weaver sued Penney claiming a violation of a substantive rule of the Ohio Department of Commerce pursuant to the Ohio Consumer Sales Practice Act. The lower court held for J. C. Penney, Inc. and the case is before the court on appeal.

Decision

Reversed, judgment for Weaver for $100.

Reasoning

The court held that a failure to state a specific quantity of waffle bakers available for sale and a refusal to issue a raincheck or place an order for the waffle baker at $9.99 constituted a deceptive sales practice under rule 3–01.03(A)(2)(d) which provides: it is a deceptive act or practice to (d) fail to give rainchecks to consumers after the original quantity of goods is exhausted or to refuse to take orders for the advertised goods or services at the advertised price to be delivered within a reasonable period of time, unless the supplier has clearly and adequately disclosed the specific quantity of advertised goods or services available. The court noted that for a deceptive act or practice the statute provided that the consumer could rescind the transaction or recover actual damages or $100.

Weaver v. J. C. Penney Company, 372 N.E.2d 633 (Ohio 1977).

---

auction
a public sale of property by public outcry to the highest bidder

Similar points can be raised regarding catalogs or requests for bids to be made by contractors on jobs. These are not offers but invitations to make offers. Generally, a bid is an offer; but special rules apply to **auctions** of property. In an auction "with reserve," the auctioneer reserves the right to accept or reject any bid and a bid is an offer. In an auction "without reserve," the auctioneer does not reserve such right and a bid is an acceptance of the auctioneer's offer to sell. In both auctions a bid may be withdrawn until the auctioneer announces completion of the sale.[2]

cost-plus contract
a contract in which the price is the cost of production or performance (whatever it turns out to be) plus an agreed-upon profit

Under the common law, if the promise contained in the offer includes a formula which will in the future provide the terms of the certainty of terms test, the offer will not fail for uncertainty of terms. An example of a contract which contains a formula that provides certainty of terms is a **cost-plus contract.**

Intention Test

One must intend to make an offer before an offer legally exists. Whatever form the certainty of terms statement takes, it must be done with the *intent* to make an offer. The certainty of terms statement taken alone is *not* enough to be construed as an offer.

intention test
the promise must cause the offeree reasonably to believe that the promise was intended to be an offer

The **intention test** is concerned with a person's expression and its interpretation by a reasonable person to whom it was made that the expression was intended to be an offer. The person making the expression may not have intended it to be an offer; but if the expression is interpreted as an offer by the reasonable person to whom it was made, then it is an offer. The intention test will not result in an offer without certainty of terms being satisfied. *Both* the certainty of terms test and the intention test must be satisfied before an offer will exist. In the following case the court found an expression to be reasonably understood as manifesting an intent to make an offer and not to be a joke.

Facts

Plaintiff, Barnes, sued Treece, vice president of a punch board corporation, who publicly stated before the State Gambling Commission that he would pay $100,000 to anyone who could find a crooked punch board. The statement brought laughter from an audience in attendance at the hearing. Plaintiff, who read about the statement, telephoned Treece and asked if he was serious. Treece said he was, so Barnes presented two rigged punch boards to the defendant but was denied payment. Treece contended that he made the public statement in jest and had no serious contractual intent. Barnes contended that he reasonably understood that Treece intended his public statement to be an offer.

---

[2] See RESTATEMENT (SECOND) OF CONTRACTS sec. 28 (1982) and UCC 2–328.

Decision
Judgment for plaintiff, Barnes.

Reasoning
The court found that, there was a sufficient manifestation of mutual assent to form a contract. The court stated that when expressions are intended as a joke and are understood or would be understood by a reasonable person as being so intended, they cannot be construed as an offer and acceptance to form a contract. But if the jest is not apparent, and a reasonable hearer would believe that an offer was being made, then the speaker risks formation of a contract which he has not intended. It is the objective manifestations of the offeror which are important and not the secret unexpressed subjective intentions of the offeror.

Barnes v. Treece, 549 P.2d 1152 (Wash. 1976).

The Power Concept

If certainty of terms and intention tests of an offer are satisfied, and if the offer has been communicated to the offeree, the offeror has given the offeree the *power* to spring a contract into existence by the offeree's *acceptance* of the offer. In the *unilateral contractual* situation, this power is exercised by the offeree's *acceptance* in performing, or refraining from doing, the *requested act*. In the *bilateral contractual* situation, this power is exercised by the offeree's *acceptance* in giving the *requested return promise,* to the offeror. (A asks B to *paint* A's fence. B paints A's fence. A asks B to *promise* to pay the selling price A is asking for A's used car and B so promises. In each case B, by doing what was requested in the offer, created a contract.)

> **power concept**
> the offeree has the power to create a contract by making an acceptance knowingly complying with the offer

Communicating the Offer: Express and Implied Terms

In order for the offeree to spring a contract into existence the offeree must have notice of the offer. This requires that the offer be communicated to the offeree in some fashion. The offeror may *communicate* the offer to the offeree directly or through some third party or other *agency*. If the offeree does what the offeror requests without notice of the offer, no contract results because, since the offeree did not rely on any offer, there is no acceptance.

Terms of an offer can be distributed to the general public at large by announcements, such as for rewards, or to particular members of the public by use of tickets or stubs, such as terms on the back of airline tickets or claim tickets. In the following case the court held that a **bailee**[3] could not limit its liability by a ticket unless its terms are called to the attention of the **bailor.**

> In an **ordinary bailment,** goods are *delivered* by a bailor to a bailee, who is liable for damage to the bailed goods caused by the bailee's negligence, unless the bailment contract provides otherwise
>
> **bailment**
> a delivery of goods by a bailor to a bailee which are to be returned to the bailor or as the bailor directs in accordance with the bailment agreement
>
> **bailee**
> the person to whom goods are bailed
>
> **bailor**
> the person who bails goods

Facts
Plaintiffs alleged that they sustained damage to their couch and chair pillow covers left with defendant for cleaning. The trial court found that the items were damaged because of improper drycleaning by defendant. Defendant contends relief from liability by the inclusion of a disclaimer of responsibility to warrant work contained on the reverse side of the cleaning ticket.

Decision
Judgment for plaintiff.

Reasoning
No notice was given to plaintiff that there was a risk attendant to drycleaning the covers and that defendant intended to disclaim responsibility for defendant's own negligence. Under such circumstances, the disclaimer is ineffective.

Brooks, et al. *v. Angelo's Cleaners,* 477 N.Y.S.2d 922 (N.Y. 1984).

Duration of the Offer

In the absence of a time period stated in the offer, an offer *expires* after the passage of a *reasonable time.* The reasonable time period can be short or long, depending upon whether the subject matter of the offer is perishable or fluctuating greatly in value over short periods of time. Also, the offer expires and ceases to exist if the offeror or offeree becomes mentally ill (insane) or dies. If *performance* of the contemplated contract to be formed in the future *becomes* illegal—normally because of enactment of a criminal statute—the

---
[3] The subject of bailments is considered in chapter 15.

Figure 6.1 Stated Time Periods Measuring Duration of Offer

Dated Offer	Undated Offer	Delayed Undated Offer
May 1. Stated time period 10 days. Offer ends on May 11.	Received June 6. Stated time period 20 days. Offer ends on June 26.	Received June 9, should have been received June 6. Stated time period 20 days. With notice of delay, offer ends on June 26. Without notice of delay, offer ends June 29.

offer which looks to the formation of the future contract expires because of the subsequent illegality. Destruction of the specific subject matter of an offer *before* acceptance occurs by performance causes the offer to expire, and since there is no offer to accept there cannot be a contract. (See figure 6.1.) In the following case an offer ends by the expiration of a stated period of time.

Facts
Plaintiff, Sullivan, became interested in purchasing a tract of land owned by defendant, Economic Research Properties. Sullivan, through his agent Hone, mailed a written offer to defendant for acceptance through February 4, 1980. Defendant made several changes to the offer including extending the time for acceptance through February 14, 1980 so as to allow sufficient time for the counteroffer to reach Sullivan via the mails and for him to execute it. On February 19, 1980 defendant called plaintiff and advised plaintiff that negotiations were terminated. This oral conversation was confirmed by telegram on February 25, 1980. The trial court specifically found that no contract for sale existed because the "Plaintiff failed to accept timely, within the time specified, the counteroffer for a contract submitted by defendant." The case is before this court on appeal.

Decision
Affirmed, judgment for defendant.

Reasoning
The court recognized the general principle that the acceptance of an offer, to result in a contract, must be absolute and unconditional, identical with the terms of the offer and in the mode, at the place and within the time expressly or impliedly required by the offer. The court stated that there can be no question that when an offer is made for a time limited in the offer itself, no acceptance afterwards will make it binding. Any offer without consideration may be withdrawn at any time before acceptance; and an offer which in its terms limits the time of acceptance is withdrawn by the expiration of the time.

Sullivan v. Economic Research Properties, 455 So.2d 630 (Fla. 1984).

The offer can end also by *revocation, rejection* and *counteroffer*. These means of ending an offer are equally applicable to the potential bilateral or unilateral contract.

revocation
the offeror's recalling of the offeree's power to accept as contained in the offer

Revocation of an offer occurs when the offeror recalls the power to accept the offer, which is contained in the offer. Revocation takes place when notice is *received* by the *offeree* that the offer no longer exists. *Actual notice* of the ending of the offer need not be received by the offeree *from the offeror* to cause the offer to end. For example, if the offeree finds out that the subject matter of the offer has been disposed of by the offeror, the offer is revoked. Revocation also occurs when the offeror *delivers* a notice of revocation to the offeree's place of business, personal residence, or **agent** with authority or apparent authority to receive notices for the offeree. The notice of revocation is effective whether or not it is read by the offeree. However, a public offer, as in reward situations, is revoked when a revocation is distributed using the same means which were used to communicate the offer.

agent
a person authorized to act on behalf of another and subject to the other's control

rejection
the offeree's expression refusing the offer

Rejection of an offer occurs by the offeree's act refusing the offer. Rejection takes effect when a rejection or counteroffer to an original offer is received by an offeror. The same requirements for notice discussed for revocation are applicable for rejection and counteroffer. A **rejection** is some expression by the offeree which indicates that the offeree is not interested in the offer. A **counteroffer** is an offer made by the offeree which changes the terms of the original offer and, therefore, under the common law is a rejection of the original offer. A type of counteroffer is the "conditional acceptance"—there is a purported acceptance of the offer but the acceptance is conditioned upon the assent of the offeror to additional or different terms.

Two kinds of *irrevocable* offers which are of great importance in business are the "option" and the "firm offer."

Option, under the Common Law. Under the common law, an *option contract* is a contract to keep an offer stated therein open for a definite time. The offer is irrevocable and is called an **option.** The option offer looks to the formation of a future contract. The effect of an option contract is to prevent the offeror from withdrawing the option offer for a stated period of time or until a specified date, unless the offeror wishes to take the risk of being sued for breach of the option contract. The offeree must pay (give consideration) for the option in order to have an option contract. (I'll sell you this land for $30,000, and I'll keep my offer open for 90 days if you will pay me $1,000—which the offeree then pays. There is a contract to keep the offer to sell open for 90 days.)

In the situation where the offer requests solely an act (and not a return promise) in order to create a *unilateral* contract, the offeror can revoke the offer only *before* the offeree starts to perform. Once the offeree has *started to perform* the requested act an option contract[4] has been created, and the offeror is required to allow the passage of a reasonable amount of time in which the offeree may *complete* performance of the act necessary to *spring the unilateral contract into existence.* The offeror cannot revoke the offer prior to the expiration of that time, because to do so would be unfair to the offeree who has started to perform the requested act. (A offers to pay B $150 for painting a tall pipe. When B has started to paint the pipe, A cannot revoke the offer. B's beginning to paint created an option contract.) In the following case the employer could not revoke its offer for a unilateral contract pension plan once the employee had begun to comply with the offer.

counteroffer
an offer which rejects a previous offer

option
the irrevocable offer in an option contract

Facts
Plaintiff, a retired employee, brought suit against his employer, the defendant, for breach of contract with regard to an employee pension plan. Originally plaintiff had agreed to enter into the pension plan and allow deductions from his pay. He had worked for some seven months before he received notice from his employer of the potential change in benefits. The employer informed the employee that he would not be covered by the pension plan. The plaintiff contended that the defendant could not revoke its unilateral contract offer to include the plaintiff in the pension plan. The defendant contended it could revoke its offer.

Decision
Judgment for plaintiff, employee.

Reasoning
The court held that the signing of the plan and the employee's engaging in work for the employer constituted substantial performance, after which the employer's unilateral contract offer, embodied in the original announcement for enrollment in the pension plan, could not be revoked. The court held that an offer for a unilateral contract may not be revoked after substantial performance has taken place.

Miller v. Dictaphone Corporation, 334 F.Supp. 840 (1971).

Firm Offer, under the Code. The Uniform Commercial Code governs commercial transactions concerning personal property, for example a sale of goods. To the extent that the Code conflicts with the common law, the Code governs. The common law supplements the Code and applies if the Code does not provide to the contrary. For example, the Code does not define an offer and, therefore, the common law of contracts applies.

---

[4] See RESTATEMENT (SECOND) OF CONTRACTS sec. 45 (1982).

We have just discussed the common law of option for which consideration is required. The Uniform Commercial Code[5] has its version of the common law option when the transaction involves the sale of goods. The Code provides that a *written* offer signed by a **merchant** to buy or sell *goods* which gives assurance that it will be held open is not revocable for a stated time or, if no time is stated, for a reasonable time. The maximum amount of time that the offer will not be revocable is three months. Such an offer is called a **firm offer**. (I'll sell you this machine for $900, and I'll keep my offer open for 60 days—which is in writing and signed by the merchant offeror.)

The offeree need not pay (give consideration) for the firm offer to make it binding upon the offeror, as is necessary to the creation of the option contract under the common law. But if consideration is given, there will be an option as well as a firm offer. However, the offeror will not be bound to the firm offer if it is contained in a form supplied by the offeree and the offeror has not **signed** the *clause* containing the firm offer provision.[6]

Under the Uniform Commercial Code

As under the common law of contracts, the Uniform Commercial Code Article on Sales of goods places a heavy reliance upon the *intention test*—that is, the *intent* of the parties to make an offer.[7] This can be seen in the Code's reliance upon conduct of the parties in determining whether an offer was made[8] and the Code's lack of concern with regard to the moment when the offer effectively formed the basis for springing a contract into existence.[9]

The Code deemphasizes the certainty of terms test and is willing to rely heavily upon flexible terms like "reasonable" and "seasonable" in the determination of *what the offeror has stated will be done or not done and what the offeree must do or not do*.[10] The Code also relies heavily upon "course of dealing" and "usage of trade" in interpreting terminology used in an offer.[11]

The approach used in the Uniform Commercial Code provides significant differences from the common law of offer. *The changes are limited to offers which have goods as their subject matter.*

Code Offer. Under the Uniform Commercial Code an offer will not fail for *uncertainty of terms* if price is not stated[12] if the parties intend a contract for sale with price to be established in the future.

Nor will a contract of purchase fail though no quantity is specified if the contract provides for a portion of the seller's "output" or for the buyer's "needs" or "requirements."

In each case the Code establishes and relies upon formulae external to the offer to establish the terms of price and quantity. In the case of price, the market itself establishes the terms. The controlling price will always be a reasonable price for like goods as the goods would have sold for at the time and place of delivery. In the case of quantity, past ability to produce (an output contract) or consume (a requirements contract) the items in question provides the formula which will determine quantity.[13]

In the following case a requirements contract was deemed *not* to fail because of indefiniteness.

---

merchant
a person who deals in goods or, by occupation, holds himself out as having knowledge or skill in a transaction concerning goods, or who uses someone who holds himself out as having such knowledge or skill in a transaction concerning goods

firm offer
a merchant's signed irrevocable offer to buy or sell goods, giving assurance that it will be kept open; consideration is not required, and its maximum time is three months

signed
"includes any symbol executed or adopted by a party with present intention to authenticate a writing" UCC 1–201(39)

---

[5] UCC 2–205.

[6] Offers irrevocable by statute: bids for State, municipality or other governmental body; preincorporation stock subscription agreements. See Revised Model Business Corporation Act sec. 6.20(a) (1984).

[7] UCC 2–204(3).   [8] UCC 2–204(1), 1–201(3).   [9] UCC 2–204(2).

[10] UCC 1–204.   [11] UCC 1–205.   [12] UCC 2–305.   [13] UCC 2–306.

Facts
The legal controversy centers on the following agreement:

March 9, 1977

Mr. John B. Stacks
Route 1
Damacus, Arkansas
Dear Mr. Stacks:
With further reference to our conversations in regard to our supplying you with motor gasoline at your gasoline outlet which is now under construction in Bee Branch, I have listed below the points which we discussed Sunday, February 20, 1977:

1. We agree to furnish you fuel in an amount up to 50,000 gallons per month. We will withhold this amount from our various allotments. The amounts will be subject to allocation adjustments by the Federal Energy Administration.
2. We will be your exclusive supplier upon the following terms.
   a. Costs will be laid-in costs per gallon plus $.01 per gallon.
   b. Gallons will be temperature corrected.
   c. Billing terms will be net 4 days from invoice.
3. If the Federal Energy Administration allocation falls below 96% terms in "a" will be negotiated and revised upward.

The above is, in substance, the terms upon which we agreed in our meeting. Please sign below after our signatures and return the original to me.
F & S Petroleum Company, Inc.
/s/ Dee Francy, President
/s/ John B. Stacks

Stacks contends the foregoing agreement is indefinite and fails to obligate Stacks for gasoline subsequently supplied to Stacks' outlet.

F & S Petroleum (plaintiff) sued Stacks (defendant) for gasoline supplied at the sales price stipulated in the agreement. Judgment was rendered for the plaintiff, and defendant appeals.

Decision
For F& S Petroleum Co., Inc., appellee.

Reasoning
Under the Uniform Commercial Code, a requirements contract is simply an agreement by the buyer to buy the buyer's good faith requirements exclusively from the seller. The buyer, who will determine quantity, is required to operate the buyer's plant or conduct business in good faith according to commercial standards of fair dealing in the trade so that the buyer's requirements will approximate a reasonably foreseeable figure and not be indefinite. The fact that the agreement left open the number of gallons to be purchased monthly does not support invalidation of the agreement.

Stacks v. F & S Petroleum Co., Inc., 641 S.W.2d 726 (Ark. 1982).

The end result of this approach is to use reliable formulae to ensure commercial honesty and restrict sharp business practices and yet facilitate the transaction of business.

The Acceptance

The Power Concept
An **acceptance** is the offeree's exercise of the power given by an offer to assent to the offer by performing the act or forbearance, or by giving a return promise, in reliance on and in compliance with the offer. By accepting an offer, the offeree has exercised the power given in the offer to spring a contract into existence.

In the *bilateral* contractual situation, the contract comes into existence the moment the return promise requested is *effectively* communicated to the offeror.

In the *unilateral* contractual situation, the contract comes into existence the moment the requested act or forbearance has been performed. If the offer requires notice of performance by the offeree, then such notice must be given. However, on performance of the act or forbearance, there *is an acceptance* and the contract immediately comes into existence irrespective of whether or not notice has been given. While the offer may not *expressly* require notice, it may *impliedly* require notice if the offeree reasonably can believe that the offeror will not learn of his performance within a reasonable time in the ordinary course of affairs. Failure to give such notice causes the offeror to be **discharged** from his contract. It should be noted that, once performance is begun by the offeree, the offer is irrevocable by the offeror and can be accepted only by *full* performance. In the following case full performance of the act did not occur; so, without an acceptance, there was no unilateral contract.

acceptance
the offeree's expressed assent to the offer in reliance on and in compliance with the offer

discharge
termination of a contractual duty to perform a promise

Facts
This breach of contract action is based on a series of communications by U.S. Steel Corp., defendant, to the workers, plaintiffs, at its Mahoning Valley plants. Plaintiffs allege these communications constitute a promise by the company to keep the mills operating if and so long as the workers made the mills profitable. U.S. Steel Corp. closed the mills and the workers seek damages.

Decision
For defendant, U.S. Steel Corp.

Reasoning
The alleged contract must either be unilateral or bilateral—that is, parties must either exchange a promise for a promise or a promise for an act. In this action, plaintiffs' allegation can be simplified as follows: the company promised to keep the plants operational as long as they remained profitable, and the workers in fact made the plants profitable. Therefore, the contract must be of the unilateral type. At the time the alleged promise was made by the company, the workers did not immediately execute the contract in full—profitability would have to be achieved over a long period of hard work. This means that the contract would not come into existance until the workers had *fully performed* their side of the contract making the plant profitable. A unilateral contract does not come into existence until one party to it has done all that is necessary on that party's part. In this case, that did not happen.

United Steel Workers of America, Local No. 1330, et al. v. U.S. Steel Corp., 492 F.Supp. 1 (1980).

To be effective, the acceptance must be unqualified or unconditional (no new terms added) *under the common law* and made by the offeree. An attempt to accept an offer by someone other than the offeree will not cause a contract to come into existence. Only the intended offeree can accept the offer.

The offeree usually has the choice of accepting or rejecting the offer. Inaction on the part of the offeree normally results in the offer *expiring* because of the passage of time. Unless otherwise indicated by language or circumstances, an offer by *mail* is not **seasonably** accepted if an acceptance is mailed anytime after midnight on the day on which the offer is received.

Unless otherwise agreed, normally silence is not a manifestation of assent and is not an acceptance. If, however, past **course of dealing** has made silence an acceptance, *active* rejection of the offer by the offeree will be necessary to prevent the silence from being an acceptance and resulting in the formation of a contract. *Silence* plus the offeree's *use* of the subject matter of the offer normally results in an implied acceptance of the offer under the common law. However, by statute, unsolicited items received through the mail can be used without creating a contract. Silence or inaction of a manufacturing or merchandise distributing company soliciting offers by salespersons for acceptance at the home office will be treated as an acceptance if rejection of the offer is not given to the offeror within a reasonable period of time. In the following case the defendant's silence in not objecting to the renewal of an insurance policy did not constitute an acceptance of such policy contract.

seasonably
"an action is taken seasonably when it is taken at or within the time agreed or if no time is agreed at or within a reasonable time" (UCC 1–204(3))

course of dealing
"a sequence of previous conduct between the parties to a particular transaction which is fairly to be regarded as establishing a common basis of understanding for interpreting their expressions and other conduct" (UCC 1–205(1))

Facts
This is an appeal from a judgment awarding to the plaintiff insurance company premiums allegedly due on an insurance contract sold by plaintiff to the defendant. The defendant's apartment building was insured against fire loss under a policy sold by plaintiff which had expired and contained no provisions for automatic renewal. Some two months before the expiration date, plaintiff wrote the defendant recommending increasing coverage for the building. Defendant telephoned plaintiff and told him that if he could not obtain insurance for just $24,000, which was the outstanding balance on his mortgage, he would be forced to obtain insurance elsewhere. Plaintiff sent the defendant a new policy with a face amount of $48,000. This policy contained the provision that the defendant could "cancel the new policy by returning the policy itself or the last policy receipt. Absent that, the policy would be automatically accepted through the inaction of the defendant." The defendant did not respond and was sued for nonpayment of premiums which had fallen due under the purported insurance contract.

The plaintiff contends that defendant's silence was an acceptance of plaintiff's offer to reinsure creating a new contract, and that defendant was liable for premiums under it. The defendant contends that his silence was not an acceptance.

Decision
Judgment for defendant.

Reasoning
An offeror cannot force the offeree to speak or be bound by his silence. Silence gives consent only where there is a duty to speak. There is no such duty here. The past dealings of the parties establish no course of conduct, and the record is silent as to custom within the industry, or the defendant's familiarity therewith. Under these circumstances there was no acceptance, hence no contract and no premiums.

J. C. Durick Insurance v. Andrus, 424 A.2d 249 (Vt. 1980).

There are exceptional instances where the offeree cannot refuse to accept the offer. These instances arise primarily because of statutory law, the typical example of which would be antidiscrimination laws which prevent an individual who has solicited offers from the public to refuse to accept the tendered offer because of color, religion, sex, race or nationality. This is a further inroad on the freedom to contract but an inroad approved of by legislative bodies for some more important, usually public, purpose.

Communication of the Acceptance
Expressly Authorized Medium. If the offeree uses the expressly authorized **medium** for accepting the offer, the acceptance becomes *effective* when sent. The contract is formed the moment the message is delivered to the indicated medium. For example, the acceptance would be *effective* the moment the letter was mailed, the telegram handed to the telegraph clerk, or the acceptance spoken into the phone. The acceptance is *effective* though it might never be received by the offeror. However, if the offeror specifies or makes the use of a particular medium for communicating the acceptance a *condition* of acceptance, then the use of any other medium will result in a counteroffer. (A's letter to B states "reply only by telephone." B replies by letter. There is no acceptance.)

The offeror can require actual receipt of the acceptance as necessary to the formation of a contract. In this circumstance a contract can result only if the acceptance is actually received while the offer continues in existence.

Both the common law and the Uniform Commercial Code are in agreement on the above points.[14] In the following case the company's offer required receipt of acceptance at its home office to be effective as an acceptance, and, since the offeree died before his acceptance was received by the company, there was no acceptance. The offer had expired by the offeree's death.

medium
an agency, instrument, means, or channel

Facts
Plaintiff, representative of Winney, deceased, sought to recover death benefits under a life insurance policy issued to Winney by Franklin Life Insurance Co., defendant. The policy contained an offer which allowed the owner of a policy to terminate the policy and receive its cash value. The company required that a written request for termination and cash value of a policy be received at the home office per the policy before a policyholder could cancel the insurance contract and be entitled to the cash value of the insurance policy. A letter of termination by the owner, Winney, requesting cash value was sent in the mail but was not received at the insurance company's office until after Winney's death. The insurance company contends its offer to terminate contained in the insurance policy was accepted when Winney's letter was mailed to the insurance company. The plaintiff, representative of the deceased owner, Winney, contends that the company's offer was never effectively accepted by Winney because he died before the company received his letter. Therefore, the decedent's estate is entitled to death benefits under the life insurance policy.

Decision
Judgment for plaintiff representative.

Reasoning
The court reasoned that the acceptance never became effective since the owner-insured died before his letter was received by the insurance company. An offeror can specify any mode of acceptance he pleases and can require that the acceptance of his offer not be operative until received by him. In this case, this was the impact of the clause requiring written request to be filed at the home office. It was not to be effective until received.

Franklin Life Insurance Company v. Winney, 469 S.W.2d 21 (Tex. 1971).

---

[14] UCC 2–206(1).

Impliedly Authorized Medium. If the offeror does not require actual receipt of the acceptance and does not indicate the communication medium, the medium used by the offeror to send the offer becomes impliedly authorized as a medium for acceptance. Also, impliedly authorized is any medium customarily used for transactions of that nature at the place where the offer was received.

Deposit Rule. The use of the expressly or impliedly authorized means by the offeree to communicate the acceptance will cause the acceptance to become *effective* and springs the contract into existence the moment the acceptance is delivered to the medium of communication. Again, the acceptance is *effective* though it might never be received by the offeror.

deposit rule
an acceptance is effective when sent, though never received, if an authorized medium is timely used by the offeree

Unauthorized Medium. Any medium not expressly nor impliedly authorized is unauthorized. If the offer *requires* the use *exclusively* of a specific medium for acceptance, the offeree's use of an unauthorized medium is not an acceptance but, instead, is a rejection and a counteroffer. If the offer *does not require* such an *exclusive* medium but *suggests* or *invites* a medium, then the offeree's use of an unauthorized medium is an acceptance *when sent,* not when received by the offeror. *Such receipt, however, must be within the time expectations that the offeror had for receipt from the impliedly authorized agency.* (A uses the mail asking for an acceptance by mail. It takes three days for the letter to get to B without delay. A's expectation, at the outside, for the receipt of the acceptance by mail is probably six days. If B uses a telegram and the telegraphed acceptance arrives within six days after the offer was sent by A, under the *common law* the telegram is treated as an acceptance. However, if the telegram arrives ten days after the offer was sent by A, under the *common law* the telegram will be treated as a counteroffer.)

Timeliness. In order for the acceptance to be *timely* in the expressly and impliedly *authorized* medium situations, it should be *capable of being received* within the stated time required by the offeror, and in the absence of a stated time, then within a reasonable time. If the acceptance is not timely, then the offer expires, and the offeree's late-attempted acceptance is a new offer.

The only difference in the *unauthorized* situation is that the acceptance *must be received* within the stated time required by the offer or, in the absence of a stated time, within a reasonable time.

Under the Uniform Commercial Code

Under UCC 2–206, unless the offeror *clearly requires* otherwise, if the offeree uses a *medium reasonable in the circumstances* to communicate an acceptance, such use will spring a contract into existence immediately when the acceptance is *sent* even though it is never *received* by the offeror.

A medium reasonable in the circumstances is one which the offeree calculates will enable the timely receipt of the acceptance by the offeror—e.g., mail, telegram, telephone, depending on the circumstances.

A Code change in the common law is that an offer to buy goods to be shipped may be accepted either *by shipment,* creating a *unilateral* contract, or by a *prompt promise to ship,* creating a *bilateral* contract. Under the common law, such a *promise* to ship would have been construed as a counteroffer.

In addition, the seller's shipment of *non-conforming* goods will be an acceptance and result in a contract unless the seller clearly indicates that such shipment is a counteroffer being made for the accommodation of the buyer. Under the common law such a shipment would always have resulted in a counteroffer.

Confirmation, and Additional Terms in Acceptance. Under UCC 2–207, the offeree's written confirmation of an offer is an acceptance. This is not so under the common law, because a confirmation merely acknowledges receipt of the offer and does not assent to the offer.

Also under the Code, a definite and reasonable expression of acceptance can act as an acceptance though it states terms additional to or different from those offered, unless the offeree clearly indicates that the offeree is making a counteroffer. In such a case, *there is a contract to the extent* that the terms of the offer are accepted, and the additional terms stated by the offeree are a counteroffer by the offeree. Under the common law the result is always a counteroffer in the described situation. (S offers to sell B 1,000 raincoats at $20 each. B replies that he'll take 500 at $20 and 500 at $18 each. Under the common law of contracts, there is no acceptance and no contract. Under the Code, there is an acceptance and a contract for 500 at $20 each and a counteroffer for 500 at $18 each.)

The Code provides formulae to determine what the terms of the contract will be. Between the parties, the changes must be consented to by the offeror before they become part of the contract.

Between merchants, the additional terms automatically become part of the contract unless (a) the offer expressly limits acceptance to the terms of the offer, (b) the changes materially alter the offer, or (c) notification of objection to changes in the terms of the offer has already been given or is given within a reasonable time after notice of them is received. In the above raincoats example, B's counteroffer of $18 materially alters the offer.[15]

If parties by their conduct recognize the existence of a contract, then there is a contract. The terms of the contract will be established by the writings of the parties where agreement exists and also by supplementary terms incorporated under any other provision of the Code such as has been illustrated in this chapter for open quantity and price terms.[16] In the following case the court recognized that a contract existed by the conduct of the parties, the offeree's oral notification constituting an acceptance.

Facts
Maryland Supreme Corporation, a general contractor, filed a counterclaim against the Blake Co., a subcontractor, for its breach of contract to supply concrete at a set price. The general contractor received a letter from the subcontractor which stated a quotation on readimix for a project to be built by the general contractor, asserting that the price will be guaranteed to hold throughout the job period. Upon successfully being awarded the contract, the general contractor orally notified the subcontractor that the subcontractor had the job and that they were to supply the concrete. As the job progressed, the subcontractor began to raise the price. The subcontractor now contends that the general contractor's oral notification was not an acceptance of the subcontractor's original offer and higher prices can now be charged.

Decision
Judgment for Maryland Supreme Corporation.

Reasoning
The court held that, under the Uniform Commercial Code, any reasonable manner of acceptance is intended to be regarded as available to the offeree unless the offeror has made it quite clear that it will not be acceptable. Former technical rules as to acceptance are rejected in favor of a substitute criterion that the acceptance be in any manner and by any medium reasonable under the circumstances. The general contractor's oral acceptance of the subcontractor's written offer was reasonable under the circumstances in this case. (Note: the court applied the Uniform Commercial Code because the contract was for the *sale of goods*.)

Maryland Supreme Corporation v. Blake Co., 369 A.2d 1017 (Md. 1977).

---

[15] For a detailed discussion of additional terms in the acceptance under the Code, see pp. 258–61.

[16] See p. 94.

Summary Statement

1. The offer contains the required promise necessary for the formation of a contract.
2. To be effective, an offer must be communicated to the offeree, be intended to be an offer, and in addition must contain certainty of terms (intentions test and certainty of terms test).
3. Offers do not last forever. Some expire after the passage of a stated period of time; some end after the passage of a reasonable time; and others end by the death or mental incompetence (insanity) of the offeror or offeree.
4. Offers can also end by revocation, rejection and counteroffer, and subsequent illegality.
5. The concepts of option and of firm offer limit the ability of the offeror to revoke the offer without being responsible to the offeree for damages for breach of contract on the offeree's acceptance.
6. The Uniform Commercial Code has vastly changed the impact of the common law on offers which have goods as their subject matter. The purpose of these changes is to facilitate commercial transactions and promote commercial honesty.
7. The act of acceptance springs a contract into existence.
8. The acceptance must be unqualified and made with the intent to accept.
9. An authorized means for communicating an acceptance must be used in order for the deposit rule to be applicable.
10. The use of an unauthorized means for communicating the acceptance can result in a counteroffer.
11. The Uniform Commercial Code significantly changes the common law of acceptance when the subject matter of the contract is goods.
12. In addition to the Uniform Commercial Code, other statutes have an impact on the law of offer and acceptance in order to accomplish other goals.
13. The law of offer and acceptance conceptually sets a limit on the freedom of contract by the requirements needed to be fulfilled before a contract can come into existence.
14. This area of contract law is still evolving.

The point made in chapter 5 that it may be unlawful *not* to contract is illustrated by the following case. Because of a right guaranteed to one party by statute, another party loses the right *not to contract*. The point being made by this case is that the freedom to contract does not necessarily include the freedom *not* to contract.

McDonald v. Verble
622 F.2d 1227 (1980)

Edwards, C.J. Plaintiffs, (the McDonalds) husband and wife, are black citizens of the United States. Defendants, (the Verbles), are white citizens of the United States, who were owners of property located in McArthur Park, Sandusky, Ohio (hereinafter McArthur Park property).

On or about July 3, 1975, in response to an advertisement plaintiffs called the Verbles and inquired about the property. The plaintiffs were informed that the purchase price was $26,500.

On the evening of July 3, 1975 the plaintiffs met the Verbles at the McArthur Park property and observed the exterior of the residence and the inside of two apartments. Later that evening plaintiffs called the Verble residence and informed Mrs. Verble that they had called about buying the McArthur Park property. The plaintiffs did not receive a return phone call from the Verbles.

On Sunday, July 6, 1975, plaintiffs called the Verble residence to inquire as to the status of the property and were informed by Mr. Verble that two men were going to purchase the property. Plaintiffs informed Verble that they were interested in purchasing the property. The plaintiffs did not hear again from the Verbles.

The plaintiffs observed that the newspaper advertisement for the sale of the property continued to appear on July 8 and 9, 1975. Thereafter plaintiffs contacted Owens, a longtime white friend of plaintiffs to seek his help in purchasing the McArthur Park property and to ascertain whether or not the Verbles were discriminating against them on the basis of color or race. Plaintiffs asked Owens to call the Verbles, make an appointment to see the property and submit an offer to purchase the property.

On July 15, 1975 the Verbles listed the property for sale with a broker for $29,500. During the conversation between Verble and the broker on July 15, 1975, Mr. Verble told the broker that he preferred not to sell the property to blacks.

At a later date, Owens, the friend of the plaintiffs, was shown the McArthur Park property by the broker. After Owens had contact with the broker, plaintiffs visited the broker's office and inquired about property for sale in the McArthur Park area and, after much evasion, the broker indicated that the McArthur Park property was for sale, but that he was interested in purchasing the property for himself. Plaintiffs then told the broker that they wanted to purchase the property. The broker informed plaintiffs that the purchase price of the McArthur Park property was $29,500. In a written offer to purchase dated July 24, 1975, plaintiffs offered to purchase the McArthur Park property for $26,500 effective until July 28, 1975.

Owens testified that the broker called him and told him that the owners had a buyer, but that the owners did not want to sell to that party and that the owners might take an offer of $27,500. Owens conferred with plaintiffs who told him not to offer more than $27,500. Owens executed an offer to purchase the property for $27,500 on July 28, 1975, and the broker informed him the same day that the offer had been accepted by the Verbles. On that same day the Verbles rejected plaintiffs' offer to purchase the property for $26,500. The broker thereafter called plaintiffs and told them that their offer had been rejected. The broker admitted that after Owens placed his offer for $27,500, he did not contact plaintiffs to inform them of the offer or encourage them to "up" their own bid.

After plaintiffs were informed that their offer had been rejected, they contacted the NAACP (National Association for the Advancement of Colored People) who indicated their lawyer would look into the matter. The NAACP lawyer contacted the defendants concerning the plaintiffs' claims of discrimination on August 1, 1975. In a letter dated August 4, 1975, the broker informed the NAACP that if the present purchaser of the property was unable to complete the transaction, the Verbles were willing to sell the property to the plaintiffs for $27,500.

On August 11, 1975 Owens informed the broker that he was withdrawing his offer to purchase the property. The broker informed plaintiffs that the other offer had fallen through so on August 12, 1975 plaintiffs submitted an offer to purchase the McArthur Park property for $26,500. The Verbles rejected the plaintiffs' offer, as well as a subsequent offer for $27,500 submitted by the plaintiffs on August 15, 1975. The Verbles said they would take nothing less than $29,500. Mr. Verble admitted at the trial that the only offers he ever got for the property were those of Owens and the plaintiffs.

Plaintiffs alleged in their action that the defendants had refused to sell them the McArthur Park property for racially discriminatory reasons. The Court entered a restraining order preventing the defendants from selling the property to anyone other than the plaintiffs. The defendants subsequently withdrew their rejection of plaintiffs' offer and accepted their $27,500 offer. The plaintiffs took possession of the property after executing a purchase agreement with the defendants. Plaintiffs testified that they were upset, embarrassed and humiliated by the actions of the defendants, which they perceived to be based on race.

Since 1866, when Congress sought to spell out the civil rights of the newly freed slaves, federal law has recognized the right to purchase and own a house as a fundamental part of American citizenship. Since 1968 the federal law has provided that it is unlawful to refuse to sell or rent after a bona fide offer is made, or to refuse to negotiate for the sale or rental of, or otherwise make unavailable or deny, a dwelling to any person because of race, color, religion, sex, or national origin.

Black citizens, who saw a promise of freedom in the Thirteenth Amendment to the United States Constitution, must be assured by Congress that their dollars will purchase the same thing as a white citizen's dollars. The court held that the defendants, the Verbles, had effectively implemented their initial indication "they preferred not to sell the property to blacks" when they rejected the plaintiffs' offer of $27,500 on August 15, 1975, although the defendants had previously wanted to sell to a white buyer at the same price.

The defendants' prior discriminatory conduct was not altered by the subsequent sale of the property by the defendants to the plaintiffs, nor did the sale wipe out the need for consideration of damages. The case is sent back to the District Court for determination of damages, costs, and attorney fees in favor of plaintiffs.

Questions and Case Problems

emancipated minor
a minor whose parents have given up their rights to take care of the minor and to have custody of and to claim the minor's earnings

1. The defendant, a widow, and her 18 year old son lived together until 1976. The son began associating and staying overnight with people his mother did not like and of whom she did not approve. Arguments over his associations and conduct resulted in mother and son agreeing that he should move out and support himself. Shortly after moving the son was shot and was taken to a hospital where expenses were incurred. At the time of admission to the hospital his mother signed a consent to an operation, anesthetics, and other medical services form. The document contained no language of a promise, express or implied, to pay for services. At that time, in Nebraska a person 18 years of age was a minor. The hospital, plaintiff, seeks to recover from the mother, defendant, the cost of medical services rendered to the son. Should the hospital recover from the mother? [*Accent Service Company, Inc. v. Ebsen,* 306 N.W.2d 575 (Neb. 1981).]

2. Plaintiff, Lefkowitz, is suing the Great Minneapolis Surplus Store, Inc. for refusal to sell to the plaintiff a fur piece which it had offered for sale in a newspaper advertisement that read as follows: "Saturday 9 a.m. sharp, three brand new fur coats worth $139.50, first come, first serve. $1 each." The defendant's contention is that a newspaper advertisement offering items of merchandise for sale at a named price is not an offer and may be withdrawn without notice. Plaintiff was first in line but was refused when he offered $1 for the fur coat advertised. Is the contention of the defendant correct, or does the plaintiff have a contract to buy the fur coat for $1? [*Lefkowitz v. Great Minneapolis Surplus Store, Inc.,* 86 N.W.2d 689 (Minn. 1957).]

3. The plaintiff, a fabricator of steel and wire products, brought this action against the defendant, a steel broker, and the defendant filed a contractual counterclaim claiming there was a contract. The plaintiff orally offered the defendant a specified quantity of two different sizes of steel rods at specified prices. The defendant responded that he thought he wanted the rods but he wanted to check with his customers. Some five weeks later the defendant called the plaintiff and agreed to buy one size of rods and then two days later agreed to purchase the other size at the price originally discussed. The defendant contended that the plaintiff replied, "Fine, thank you," to both telephone calls. The trial court nonsuited the defendant's counterclaim (dismissed the case) and the defendant appealed claiming that, if the case had been submitted to the jury, it could have found for the defendant on the counterclaim. Was there a timely acceptance of the offer of the plaintiff? Was there a contract? You decide. [*Textron, Inc. v. Froelich,* 302 A.2d 426 (Pa. 1973).]

4. Plaintiffs sued defendant for the negligent design and construction of plaintiffs' residence. On July 21, 1982 plaintiffs mailed defendant an offer to accept $10,000 in compromise of plaintiffs' claim. On August 16, 1982 defendant made a counteroffer of $7,000 on the condition it be accepted that day. The counteroffer was rejected by plaintiffs. On August 21, 1982 plaintiffs wrote the defendant of the fact that they were revoking their offer of July 21, 1982. Defendant received the letter the following day but nevertheless on August 25, 1982 sent plaintiffs a letter accepting their offer of July 21, 1982. Did the defendant create a valid contract by its acceptance or was the offer revoked? [*T. M. Cobb Co., Inc. v. Superior Court of Marin County,* 682 P.2d 338 (Cal. 1984).]

5. Plaintiff, Ivey's Plumbing & Electric Company, Inc., brought this action against defendant, a material supplier, for refusal to supply materials at a price originally quoted on an "Estimate Sheet." Defendant knew that plaintiff would rely on the "Estimate Sheet" in bidding for a job with a general contractor. Is the quotation by the seller defendant irrevocable for a reasonable time or simply an offer to sell subject to revocation by the seller at any time prior to the buyer's acceptance? [*Ivey's Plumbing & Electric Company, Inc. v. Petrochem Maintenance, Inc.,* 463 F.Supp. 543 (Miss. 1978).]

6. Defendant operates a woodpulp mill and produces a by-product known as rayon rejects. Plaintiff's sole business was purchasing rayon rejects from defendant for resale. Deliveries of rayon rejects were scheduled throughout the year but no annual price was set. Prices were negotiated each quarter depending upon current market conditions. Defendant refused to continue to make deliveries of rayon rejects to plaintiff. Is a failure by the parties to set a firm price fatal to the finding of a contract? [*Pulprint Inc. v. Louisiana-Pacific Corporation,* 477 N.Y.S.2d 540 (N.Y. 1984).]

7. Plaintiff, Roberts, insurance agent, sent defendant a policy which was a renewal of one which defendant's father previously held. Defendant had not ordered or requested issuance of this policy, but he accepted it and paid the premium. At a later date, just prior to the expiration date of the renewed policy, a second unsolicited renewal was sent by the plaintiff to the defendant and attached to it was a printed notice stating that, if defendant did not wish to accept it, he must return it or be liable for the premium. Defendant made no response. The plaintiff inquired about the premium by telephone with the defendant. Defendant informed him that he had purchased another policy elsewhere. Plaintiff sues on the second renewal. What result? [*Roberts v. Buske*, 298 N.E.2d 795 (Ill. 1973).]

8. The plaintiff brought an action to recover damages for the defendant's breach of an alleged contract to appoint the plaintiff as an authorized dealer for the defendant's photocopy products. The issue is whether a contract exists between the parties notwithstanding that the writing which was to be the contract was signed by the plaintiff *but not by the defendant,* and contained a provision requiring approval by the defendant's executive office. What result? [*Pacific Photocopy v. Canon U.S.A., Inc.*, 646 P.2d 647 (Or. 1982), petition for review denied, 652 P.2d 810 (Or. 1982).]

9. Plaintiff, CIC, sought to enforce a reorganization plan tendered by defendant, CAC, wherein money loaned by the defendant would be converted into other long-term debts and stock. A proposal for the reorganization was delivered to the plaintiff on September 27. By the terms of the proposal, the entire plan of reorganization was to be completed by November 1. Contained in this proposal were the following words: "Will you kindly examine this proposal and let us know your reaction to it at the earliest possible time. We wish to point out that it is not an inflexible proposal, but we also point out that a recapitalization along these lines is imperative." CIC prepared a written acceptance of the offer, dated it October 8, but deliberately withheld mailing the letter until October 19; it was not received by the offeror defendant until October 21. The offeror contends that the offer expired before it was accepted due to the passage of a reasonable amount of time. What result? You decide. [*Central Invest. Corp. of Denver v. Container Advertising Co.,* 471 P.2d 647 (Colo. 1970).]

10. In *McDonald v. Verble,* 622 F.2d 1227 (1980),[17] the court held that one could lose one's right not to contract in order to further a legislative purpose contained in a statute. It is quite appropriate to use business law as a tool for social change. Evaluate the above statement of the court's holding.

---

[17] See pp. 100–102.

7 Relief from Contractual Obligations

After you have read this chapter, you should be able to:

1. Discuss the law associated with the law of relief from contractual obligation and recognize that it acts as a legal safeguard on the freedom to contract.
2. Recognize that the law of genuineness of assent is a strongly felt force in society.
3. Understand the philosophical importance of the fact that the promise forming the basis of a contract must be fairly and voluntarily given.
4. Realize how the concept of unconscionability has given new importance to the exercise of free will in the contractual setting.
5. Recognize that this area of law is still evolving.

Introduction

In the formative stage of a simple express or implied-in-fact contract, the concern of the law is to determine whether or not the parties to the contract *truly intended to create rights and duties not otherwise imposed by law*. The preceding chapter developed an *objective* test to determine the existence of a contract. The law also approaches the parties through a *subjective* test to ascertain *whether they are acting with free will or* **genuineness of assent** in their manifestations of mutual assent, i.e., offer and acceptance.

It is not the intent of the law to protect the fool from folly. The intent of the law is to protect the freedom of voluntary action of the individual.

As it provides *relief from contractual obligations,* the law looks at the parties as individuals and applies a subjective test which considers the traits and characteristics of the individual.

The importance of this chapter to the concept of *freedom to contract* is with regard to what the law means by a promise *voluntarily made* as being basic to the formation of a contract. A proper promise *voluntarily and fairly made* is necessary to the formation of an *enforceable* contract.

genuineness of assent
reality of consent to an offer or acceptance

Concern of the Law

After it has been determined that the requirements of offer and acceptance have been satisfied, the concern of the law is to see whether or not the **manifestations of mutual assent** to a contract were freely given. In the requirements necessary to satisfy offer and acceptance, parties who choose to contract must pass an *objective* test (certainty of terms and intention tests). (A, evidencing a serious contractual intent, offers to sell her car to B for $2,000. B accepts the offer with the intent to buy the car.)

Genuineness of assent presents parties to a contract with a second test which must be passed before a contract at its formative stage becomes enforceable. Was the offer and/or acceptance an act of free will? The answer to the question necessarily is very *subjective* (personal). Each individual has a different strength of will.

Both the *objective* and *subjective* tests must be satisfied in order to successfully form an *enforceable* contract.

manifestation of mutual assent
offer and acceptance

Result

If genuineness of assent is not present (the manifestation of mutual assent was not an act of free will), then the party to the *contract* not exercising free will has the right to avoid, **rescind,** or set aside what objectively appears to be a contract.

The act of *avoidance* must be timely or it is lost. Conduct which is inconsistent with avoidance will reaffirm the contract. This is illustrated by the following case.

rescind
to cancel, annul

Facts

Plaintiff, Tidwell, and defendant, Critz, are medical doctors who allegedly entered into an oral agreement to form a medical association to practice radiotherapy in Atlanta, Georgia. Shortly after the purported agreement Tidwell began to work with Critz. Later Critz presented Tidwell with a second agreement prepared by Critz's attorney which created an employer-employee relationship between Tidwell and Critz and provided that Tidwell would be compensated for his association with Critz in the amount of $1,000 per month, "plus such bonus amounts" as Critz approved. The agreement further provided that either party could terminate his association by giving 30 days notice. Tidwell objected to this agreement contending it did not reflect their previous "partnership" understanding. Tidwell contends he signed it three months after review by his lawyer because Critz threatened to end his association with Tidwell and have his privilege to practice at Georgia Baptist Hospital taken away. Tidwell continued to work for Critz for some nine months until Critz terminated his association with Tidwell because of Tidwell's poor work performance and his inability to cooperate with other hospital employees. Tidwell seeks to avoid the written agreement on the grounds of duress and seeks an accounting for profits under the purported partnership association. Critz contended that he did not use duress.

Chapter 7: Relief from Contractual Obligations

Decision
Judgment for the defendant, Critz.

Reasoning
Tidwell waived any claimed duress, which would have allowed him to avoid the contract, surrounding the signing of the agreement with Critz to be his employee when Tidwell ratified the contract by accepting compensation under the agreement without apparent complaint until termination of employment. Contracts made under duress are not ordinarily void, but merely voidable, and may be ratified. Once ratified such contracts cannot be avoided.

Tidwell v. Critz, 282 S.E.2d 104 (Ga. 1981).

In the case of fraud[1] (intentional misrepresentation), one can rescind *or* waive one's power to avoid the contract and, instead, seek damages for the tort of deceit.[2] (S sold a twelve-year-old tractor to B intentionally misrepresenting it to be ten years old. B kept the tractor and sued S for deceit for the difference in value between a ten-year-old tractor and a twelve-year-old tractor.) Under the Code,[3] a party can rescind *and* seek damages. A mistake in drafting a contract will be corrected by **reformation**.[4]

reformation
an action to correct a writing so as to reflect correctly the intentions of the parties which mistakenly were not properly expressed in the writing

Mistake

In certain situations one can avoid the consequences of the offer or acceptance by proving a **mistake**. A mistake of *law* does not allow one to avoid a contract; we are all presumed to know the law. A mistake of *fact* may justify avoidance of a contract. If only one party is mistaken without the other party knowing of the mistake, avoidance of the contract *is not allowed*. (A contracts to sell certain goods to B, forgetting that he had already sold them to C. A cannot avoid for his mistake of fact.) If the other party knows a mistake is being made by a party to a contract, avoidance by the mistaken party *is usually allowed*. This is the situation of *unilateral mistake*—one party making the mistake. The law seeks to prevent one from knowingly taking advantage of the mistake of another.

Figure 7.1 should be helpful as a summary chart of invalidations.

In the *mutual* or *bilateral mistake* situation, *both* parties to the contract are mistaken and either party can avoid the contract. It is most commonly said that *the minds of the parties never met*. Most often this occurs in a situation of *ambiguity*. In an ambiguous fact situation, the fact is capable of two meanings. Each of the contracting parties associates with a different fact meaning. *Objectively* their minds seem to have met but *subjectively* no meeting of the minds has taken place. Additionally, if both parties assume a fact to be in existence when it is not in existence, or not to be in existence when it is in existence, mutual mistake occurs. The following case illustrates how an insurance company was not allowed to escape liability on a malpractice policy because of a mistake of the insured.

mistake
believing a fact to exist when it does not exist, or believing a fact not to exist when it does exist

Facts
Plaintiffs established an architecture and engineering business and contracted for malpractice insurance with defendant. The policy required continuous coverage in order that claims made in a policy year for prior years' negligent acts be covered. While the policy was in effect, plaintiffs contracted for work on a construction project. Due to lack of business, the plaintiffs were unable to maintain their insurance and cancelled the policy. Three years later they renewed their policy with the defendant but were not informed that they could have purchased a "prior acts" endorsement. Defendant also had never informed them of the effect of the continuous coverage requirement. After renewal of their insurance policy plaintiffs were sued for negligence on the previous construction project. The insurance company refuses to defend the plaintiffs citing absence of continuous coverage or prior acts endorsement as justification for its inaction. Plaintiffs seek an order requiring the insurance company to defend them.

---

[1] For a discussion of fraud, see pp. 108, 400–401.

[2] For the tort of deceit, see p. 46.

[3] UCC 2–720, 2–721.

[4] For a discussion of reformation, see p. 194.

Figure 7.1 Invalidating Table

Category of Invalidation	Result		Reason for Determination of Invalidation
	Void	Voidable	
Unilateral mistake with notice		x	Unfairness to party mistaken
Bilateral mistake		x	No meeting of the minds
Misrepresentation of a material fact *Innocent* *Negligent*		x	No assurance that the misled party would have manifested assent if reality were known
Fraud in the *inducement*		x	Same as above
Fraud in the *procurement* (factum, execution, or essence)	x		No free manifestation of assent
Concealment		x	No assurance that party would have manifested assent if reality were known
Duress - *knowing* character of transaction		x	No free manifestation of assent, but knowledge of reality
Duress - *not knowing* character of transaction	x		No free manifestation of assent
Undue Influence		x	Unfair persuasion
Unconscionable		x	Unfair result: one-sided

Decision
Judgment for plaintiffs in the architecture and engineering firm.

Reasoning
Where there is a mistake by one party and inequitable conduct by the other, an insurance contract can be reformed. Plaintiffs were mistaken in their assumption that they were covered for malpractice for past acts at the time they were insured and at the time they renewed their insurance policy. The defendants, having handled plaintiffs' insurance needs for ten years, owed a duty to inform them as to what coverage they actually had and how they could obtain complete coverage. Defendant's silence justifies this court in reforming the current insurance contract so that plaintiffs are insured for the suit by the construction company.

Stein, Hinkle, Dawe, and Associates, Inc., v. Continental Casualty Co., 313 N.W.2d 299 (Mich. 1981).

The area of mistake reflects the concern of the law that the parties contract knowing the reality of the situation. Without this assurance, the law cannot ascertain if the parties to the contract would have entered into it voluntarily. On the other hand, as between two innocent parties, the one causing his or her own distortion of reality and the other party contracting in reality, the court will hold for the latter and against the former. Thus, if a person negligently signs a contract misinterpreting its impact or terms, or mistakenly assumes that he or she is contracting with a named party but is actually contracting with someone else, the person, nevertheless, will be bound to the contract.

Misrepresentation

misrepresentation
an assertion of what is not true

When one *unintentionally* misrepresents a *material* fact and this induces another to enter into a contract, the misled party can avoid the contract if the party reasonably relied upon the **misrepresentation.** This is so because the law cannot assure itself that, if the true state of affairs had been known, the misled party would have freely entered into the contract. In the following case the plaintiff sought to avoid the contract alleging that the defendant knew, or should have known, that its representation was false. The court held that the complaint sufficiently stated a cause of action justifying avoidance.

Facts

franchise
a business relationship between a franchisor, who markets goods or services through a franchisee, who has the right to use the franchisor's trade name, trademark, and methods of operation

Plaintiff purchased an automobile business from defendant believing the business included the Oldsmobile agency and **franchise.** Plaintiff alleged that the defendant knew, or should have known, that the franchise was not saleable as part of the business. General Motors refused to transfer the franchise to plaintiff, who then returned the business to defendant and demanded rescission of the purchase contract. Defendant **demurred** to the complaint on the basis that it failed to allege that defendant intentionally made false representations that the plaintiff would receive the franchise.

demurrer
a pleading which states that a preceding pleading does not state a cause of action

Decision
Demurrer overruled, for plaintiff.

Reasoning
The court noted that, in an action for deceit, the basis for responsibility is the intent to deceive, proved by the fact that the speaker believes the statement to be false or the representation is made without any belief in its truth. Recovery in damages is also allowed for fraud not amounting to deceit where there was a representation of fact or the speaker is supposed to possess complete knowledge of the facts. In negligence actions, defendant need only fail to exercise ordinary care in making a representation or in ascertaining facts, but, like other cases of negligence, it requires a duty of care or an assumption of a duty. Recovery is allowed even though representations are innocently made, because it would be unjust to allow one making false representations to retain the fruits of a bargain induced by them. A misrepresentation may be innocent, negligent, or known to be false. If innocently made, the contract is still voidable. Since the defendant here was alleged to know or should have known that the franchise was not saleable as part of the business, the order overruling the demurrer was sustained.

Whipp v. Iverson, 168 N.W.2d 201 (Wis. 1969).

Fraud

fraud
(in contracts) a misrepresentation of fact, known to be false, intentionally made to induce another person to make or to refrain from making a contract, and reasonably relied on by the other person

An *intentional* misrepresentation of a fact inducing a *contractual mistake* is called **fraud.** If the intentional misrepresentation of fact is to *induce* the *formation of a contract,* it is called "fraud in the inducement." Fraud in the inducement causes the resulting *contract* to be *voidable* at the election of the party defrauded who innocently reasonably relied on the fraud. Alternatively, the party defrauded may sue to recover damages under the common law. The statement of an opinion by a person who does not profess to be an expert normally is not a statement of a material fact and cannot be reasonably relied on. (A says, "This is the best car on the market." The statement is puffing one's wares and is an opinion.)

However, if the *intentional* misrepresentation of fact is of the *nature of what is to be done* and the defrauded party innocently relied on the fraud without negligence on his or her part, it is called "fraud in the procurement" (or fraud in the "factum", "execution", or in the "essence") and *no contract* is made. This result is because the defrauded party did not manifest assent to the misrepresented transaction, but was assenting to another transaction. (A misrepresents to B that the form to be signed by B is a receipt, when in fact it is a promissory note. If B reasonably believes the paper is a receipt, and B is not negligent in B's exercise of reasonable care to acertain what the paper is, there is fraud in the procurement and no contract nor note of any legal effect comes into being.) In this illustration the *transaction* is *void,* rather than voidable as when one is fraudulently induced to make a contract. If the defrauded party is negligent (e.g., the misrepresentation could have been discovered on a reasonable examination by the defrauded party), it is fraud in the inducement causing *the contract* to be *voidable* by the defrauded party.

Concealment

Both in misrepresentation and in fraud there is action which distorts reality. In concealment normally there is passive *inaction,* a failure to disclose. Concealment may also occur by *actively* hiding the facts, e.g., the owner of a house covers a wall damaged by termites so that a prospective buyer of the house will not see the damage. In the following case of passive inaction, a failure to disclose was deemed to be fraud in the inducement.

Facts
A seller of a water conditioning business appealed the judgment of the lower court in favor of the buyers granting rescission (avoidance) of a contract for sale of the business. The buyers alleged fraud by seller's failure to disclose a security arrangement and an agreement with a manufacturer of the water conditioner's subsidiary. Said agreement provided that leases of water conditioners through the business could not be sold or assigned or given as security other than to the subsidiary. Upon taking control of the business, the buyers converted 34 leases to sales. Learning of this, the subsidiary took over the business. The buyers immediately sought rescission of the purchase contract for the business. Judgment was rendered for the buyers and the seller appealed.

Decision
Affirmed, judgment for buyers.

Reasoning
An inadvertant failure to disclose the security interest and agreement which posed restraints on the free conduct of the business amounts to fraud. The sellers owed an express duty to inform the buyers of these provisions which made the conduct of the business impossible without the consent of the manufacturer's subsidiary.

Cady v. Pitts, 625 P.2d 1089 (Ida. 1981).

A growing body of law is accumulating which requires parties to disclose facts whenever justice, equity, and fair dealing demand it so that the law can be assured that the parties are exercising *free will* in the contractual setting.[5] This is especially true under the Uniform Commercial Code, as illustrated by the following case.

Facts
This is a suit by a buyer, Wells, against the dealer, seller, for revocation of his acceptance of a new Volvo automobile, which he had purchased from the defendant, on the ground of breach of warranty. The dealer defends on the basis of a **disclaimer** which was contained in a warranty manual. The disclaimer was in slightly different print than other provisions in print in the warranty manual. Judgment was rendered for the plaintiff, and defendant appeals.

Decision
Judgment affirmed for the buyer.

Reasoning
This disclaimer of warranties was not sufficiently revealed to be binding upon the buyer. The court held that, under the requirements of the Uniform Commercial Code, section 2–316, the disclaimer had been concealed. In order to be an effective disclaimer, it had to be in bold print or in enlarged print such that it would be conspicuous in order to come to the attention of the buyer. (Note: the court applied the Uniform Commercial Code because the contract was for the *sale of goods.*)

Volvo of America Corp. v. Wells, 551 S.W.2d 826 (Ky. 1977).

disclaimer
denial of an obligation or a claim

Duress

Duress is wrongful pressure by threat which induces one to enter into a contract, without freedom of choice, because of fear that the threatened, *wrongful* act will be carried out. Its effect is to make a contract *voidable* by the injured party if he or she *knew* the character of the transaction. If the injured party *did not know* the character of the transaction, there is *no contract.* (X is wrongfully induced to sign a paper evidencing a contract. If X knew the contents of the paper, the contract is voidable by him. If he did not know, there is no contract.) The most crude form of duress which prevents the exercise of *free will* is when one is threatened with criminal or tortious *conduct* if a contract is not formed. More

duress
wrongful inducement to do that which a reasonable person would have been unable to resist

---

[5] See chapter 21, Consumer Law A, for a discussion of the Magnuson-Moss Warranty-Federal Trade Commission Improvements Act.

abuse of civil legal process
to make excessive and improper use of the right to sue in an attempt to exhaust someone into submission

subtle forms of duress are recognized where free will is controlled by threat to *bring criminal action,* or by **abuse of civil legal process,** or by threat to *withhold goods.* The key to understanding duress is to recognize that the law is identifying conduct of one party which is wrongful and calculated to control the will of another in the contractual setting. The threat of a civil *justifiable* suit does not constitute duress nor prevent the other party's free exercise of will. In the following case a threat of criminal sanction did not constitute duress nor prevent the other party's exercise of freedom.

Facts

Plaintiff, Willig, failed to observe an agreement made between himself and the 150 Crown Street Tenants' Association to place money in **escrow** to make repairs to a building necessitated by his prior gross mismanagement. Thereafter, the Housing and Development Administration (HDA) commenced an action against Willig for correction of 300 building violations. An order by the court to make repairs was ignored by Willig, so HDA brought contempt proceedings. Willig agreed to turn over the deteriorating buildings to a court-appointed trustee and to pay a $20,000 fine to be used for repair of the building. A stay of a 30-day jail sentence was entered when Willig made this agreement. Approximately six months later, the agreement not having been carried out, the HDA moved for judgment on the agreement and vacation of the stay of the 30-day jail sentence. During this latter proceeding, Willig was asked to sign a new agreement which the judge said if not signed would result in Willig serving 30 days in jail. Willig signed the new agreement but failed to comply with it and brings this suit against HDA and several of the trustees of the Tenants' Association to have it set aside on the basis that he entered into the new agreement under duress.

escrow
the conditional delivery of property to a person who is to deal with it on the occurrence of specified conditions

Decision
Judgment for defendant.

Reasoning
The law is well settled that threats of arrest or imprisonment may constitute such duress as will render a contract entered into voidable at the election of the person threatened. It is immaterial whether such person was guilty or innocent of the act for which arrest or imprisonment was threatened in order for there to be duress. On the other hand, it does not constitute duress to do what one has the legal right to do. All that the judge did was to inform Willig that, if he did not enter into the agreement, the judge would grant the motion to vacate a prior stay of the 30-day jail sentence. This is not a situation of duress which will avoid a contract.

Willig v. Rapaport, et al. 438 N.Y.S.2d 872 (N.Y. 1981).

Undue Influence

The law recognizes that, because of closeness of relationship (e.g., fiduciary, close friend, confidant), age, physical or mental condition, the will of a person can be manipulated—called **undue influence.** If, because of the unique relationship, contemplated undue contractual advantage is taken of the manipulated party by *unfair* persuasion, the contract can be avoided. Mere persuasion is proper and does not cause the contract to be voidable. In the following case the court held that there was a **fiduciary** relationship between the parties which was violated by the undue influence of the party with the fiduciary duty to act for the benefit of the others.

undue influence
unfair persuasion by one who, because of his relationship with another, dominates the other

fiduciary
a person with a duty to act primarily for the benefit of another

Facts
This is an action by the conservator of the estate of the decedent, Conrad Schaneman, Sr., to set aside and cancel a deed of real estate excuted by Conrad Schaneman, Sr. in favor of his eldest son, defendant in this action. Schaneman, Sr. was born in Russia and could neither read nor write the English language. He was the father of eight sons and five daughters, all living heirs. Over the years the family had been close-knit, especially the father and the sons. In 1974, defendant advised his brothers and sisters that he would henceforth manage his father's business matters and that they no longer need be concerned in that regard. Thereafter, the defendant was the primary person who advised his father on business matters and handled his father's business matters. On March 18, 1975 Schaneman, Sr. was for all intents and purposes an invalid. Schaneman, Sr.'s children testified that during 1975 their father seemed mentally confused. In 1977, one of the children discovered that defendant's name was on Schaneman, Sr.'s bank account as a joint tenant with right of survivorship. It was also discovered that defendant was listed as a joint tenant with right of survivorship on a certificate of deposit purchased with Schaneman, Sr.'s money.

Schaneman, Sr. had also executed a power of attorney in favor of defendant. Before his death, Schaneman, Sr. testified at a **conservatorship proceeding** that he never agreed to sell the farm to defendant but decided to give defendant the farm since he had asked for it several times out of the presence of his other children and that he could not refuse anything to the defendant since the defendant was his best boy. Schaneman, Sr. also testified that defendant had told him not to tell the other children about the gift, but to keep it quiet. Schaneman, Sr. said the defendant dictated everything and told him what to do. The lower court held in favor of the plaintiff, finding that the execution of the deed was a result of fraud and undue influence, and set aside the deed. Defendant appealed.

conservatorship proceeding
a court hearing to determine whether or not a guardian, protector or preserver should be appointed to have charge of the person and estate of a person incapable of managing his or her own affairs

Decision
Affirmed, judgment for plaintiff.

Reasoning
The court held that evidence indicating that, due to age and physical infirmities, Schaneman, Sr. was, for all intents and purposes, an invalid at the time of the conveyance of the farm, that Schaneman, Sr.'s mental acuity was impaired at times and that he sometimes suffered from disorientation and lapse of memory, that Schaneman, Sr. was subject to the influence of defendant who was acting in a confidential relationship, that opportunity to exercise undue influence existed, that there was a disposition on the part of the son to exercise undue influence, and that the conveyance of the farm appeared to be the effect of such influence, was sufficient to establish a prima facie case of undue influence and to cast upon defendant the burden of going forward with the evidence which he did not do.

Schaneman v. Schaneman, 291 N.W.2d 412 (Neb. 1980).

The Uniform Commercial Code

Under the Uniform Commercial Code,[6] the court is allowed to test the subjective question of the exercise of free will in the commercial setting. The question the court answers is whether or not the contract is **unconscionable.** The test is whether, in light of the general commercial background and the commercial needs of the particular trade or case, the clauses are so *one-sided* as to be unconscionable under the circumstances *existing at the time of the making of the contract.* If the conclusion is yes, the contract can be avoided. In the area of genuineness of assent, the law's concern is to give relief from contractual obligations not fairly and voluntarily assumed.

unconscionable
offends the conscience, immoderate, too one-sided

Summary Statement

1. Not only must we satisfy the requirements of manifestation of mutual assent before there is an *enforceable* contract, but genuineness of assent must also exist.
2. In the absence of genuineness of assent, a contract can be avoided through rescission, and in some instances damages will be given.
3. The traditional areas wherein problems of exercise of free will may result are mistake, misrepresentation, fraud, concealment, duress, and undue influence.
4. The Uniform Commercial Code in its development of the concept of unconscionability has given renewed importance to problems involving the exercise of free will in a contractual setting.

The most modern form of relief from contractual obligation can be found in the application of avoidance of contractual responsibility found in UCC 2–302. The following case is included in depth to illustrate how the concept of unconscionability is applied in a commercial setting.

---
[6] UCC 2–302.

Wille v. Southwestern Bell Telephone Company
549 P.2d 903 (Kan. 1976)

Harman, Commissioner. The question before the court is whether an advertiser can recover damages for breach of contract from a telephone company for an omission in the yellow pages of its telephone directory when the contract entered into by the parties limits the company's liability for errors and omissions to an amount equal to the cost of advertisement. The trial court granted summary judgment for the telephone company, and the advertiser has appealed.

The facts of the case are that the plaintiff has operated a heating and air conditioning business in Wichita for some thirteen years and has had some listing in the yellow pages of the phone directory for his business over this period of time.

In the year involved in this case plaintiff was in the process of expanding his business and sought additional telephone listings. Additional listings were given by the defendant but one of the telephone numbers was inadvertently omitted from the directory. Upon learning of the omission plaintiff began advertising the omitted number on television, incurring expenditures of some $5,000.

The written contract contained a *conspicuous* clause which limited defendant's damages in case of breach of contract:

The applicant agrees that the Telephone Company shall not be liable for errors in/or omissions of the directory advertising beyond the amount paid for the directory advertising omitted, or in which errors occur, for the issue life of the directory involved.

exculpatory clause
a clause which relieves one from liability

Plaintiff contends the **exculpatory clause** is contrary to public policy and should not be enforced. He asserts unconscionability of contract in two respects: the party's unequal bargaining position, and the form of the contract and the circumstances of its execution.

The court noted that the traditional view is that competent adults may make contracts on their own terms, provided they are neither illegal nor contrary to public policy. *Absent fraud, mistake, or duress,* a party who has fairly and voluntarily entered into such a contract is bound thereby, notwithstanding that it is unwise or disadvantageous to him. However, *such a rule is tempered by the principle of unconscionability.*

The UCC neither defines the concept of unconscionability nor provides the elements or perimeters of the doctrine. To define the doctrine is to limit its application, and to limit its application is to defeat its purpose.

Aids to a determination of whether a contract is unconscionable include:

1. Use of printed form or boilerplate contracts drawn skillfully by the party in the strongest economic position, which establish industrywide standards offered on a take-it-or-leave-it basis to the party in the weaker economic position.
2. A significant cost-price disparity or excessive price.
3. A denial of basic rights and remedies to a buyer of consumer goods.
4. Inclusion of penalty clauses.
5. Circumstances surrounding execution of the agreement including its commercial setting, purpose, and effect.
6. Hiding of disadvantageous clauses in a mass of fine print trivia or in places which are inconspicuous.
7. Phrasing clauses in language that is incomprehensible to a layman or that divert his attention from the problems raised by them or the rights given up through them.
8. Overall imbalance in the obligations and rights imposed by the bargain.
9. Exploitation of the underprivileged, unsophisticated, uneducated, and illiterate.
10. Inequality of bargaining or economic power.

The doctrine of unconscionability is used to police the excesses of certain parties who abuse their right to contract freely. It is directed against one-sided, oppressive, unfairly surprising contracts and not against the consequences per se of uneven bargaining power or even a simple old-fashioned bad bargain.

In this case the contract was not unconscionable because the form of the agreement directed the reader's attention to the clause limiting damages. The clause was clearly legible and was phrased in common words and was not one-sided. Moreover, the advertiser was an experienced businessman, and the omission arose from a clerical error which in its commercial setting was reasonably contemplated as falling within the purview of and purpose of the clause.

Judgment for defendant telephone company was affirmed.

Questions and Case Problems

1. The plaintiff entered into a contract with defendant whereby the defendant agreed to supply alumina (aluminum ore) to the plaintiff who agreed to convert it into molten aluminum requiring intensive use of oil fuel. This molten aluminum would then be repossessed by the defendant for further processing. The plaintiff sought reformation or modification of the contract in the face of a potential $60 million dollar loss brought about by an unforeseeable rise in nonlabor production costs due to an unexpected rise in OPEC's pricing system. Plaintiff contends that unforeseeable rise in costs constituted a mutual mistake of fact justifying reformation or modification in the face of both parties contemplating a risk variance of only three cents per pound. Is plaintiff correct? [*Aluminum Co. of America v. Essex Group, Inc.,* 499 F.Supp. 53 (1980).]

2. Two ships both named *Peerless* were leaving Bombay, India, one in October and the other in December. An offer was made to sell 125 bales of a commodity to be shipped from Bombay, India, to arrive on the ship *Peerless.* The buyer accepted the offer and had in mind the ship that sailed in October. The seller, on the other hand, believed that the agreement referred to the ship *Peerless* which was sailing in December. Each party, seller and buyer, believed in good faith that a different ship was intended in the contract. What result? [*Raffles v. Wichelhaus,* (English) 2 Hurlstone & Coltman 906 (1864).]

3. Plaintiff, a franchisor of motor inns, brought suit against defendant franchisee on a franchise agreement for nonpayment of fees and other charges. Defendant terminated (exercised avoidance) the franchise after experiencing extremely poor occupancy rates when referrals promised by the franchisor did not materialize. A statute provides
    > "it is unlawful when selling or establishing a franchise—for any person (1) intentionally to misrepresent the prospects or chances for success of a proposed or existing franchise."

    Defendant alleged that plaintiff made false and fraudulent representations of future profit in negotiations and discussions leading to defendant's purchase of the franchise. Assuming defendant can prove his allegation, is he entitled to avoid the franchise agreement? [*Travelodge International, Inc. v. Eastern Inns, Inc.,* 382 So.2d 789 (Fla. 1980).]

4. Plaintiffs negotiated with the defendants to purchase the defendants' tavern. During the negotiations, the defendants did not permit the plaintiffs to inspect their business records, but assured them that the business was profitable and that the earnings received during the winter months would cover their expenses. The defendants also made representations concerning the quality of the condition of the building. The plaintiffs then agreed to purchase the tavern. However, the plaintiffs did not earn enough during the winter to meet expenses. They were forced to close the business at one point because of the activities of motorcycle gangs and they had to make extensive repairs to the property. Therefore, nine months after the purchase, the plaintiffs stopped making payments to defendants and sued to **rescind** the contract. Should plaintiffs be allowed to rescind the contract? [*Moschelle v. Hulse,* 622 P.2d 155 (Mont. 1980).]

    rescind
    cancel, annul

5. The defendants, who were convicted of offenses arising out of a jailbreak, appealed the conviction on the grounds that certain agreements had not been enforced. The first alleged agreement was with the Commissioner of Corrections, made while the Commissioner was a hostage. It was that the inmates would not be punished for crimes arising out of the jailbreak attempt. The second alleged agreement was an order issued by a federal judge, in the presence of the inmates and their hostage, that no action be taken against the inmates for their participation in the jailbreak. Can the agreements be avoided? [*United States v. Gorham,* 523 F.2d 1088 (1975).]

6. In 1971, Sambo's Restaurants, Inc. petitioned the City of Ann Arbor, Michigan, for site plan approval for construction of a Sambo's Restaurant. When the City Council balked at accepting the proposal, Sambo's agreed not to use the name in connection with the restaurant. Approval by the City Council followed quickly. After six years of small profits operating under the name of "Jolly Tiger," the restaurant applied to the City for sign permits to display the name "Sambo's." Those permits were granted and the signs erected. The permits were subsequently revoked by the City as in contravention of the earlier "agreement". Sambo's refuses to take down the signs. Can Sambo's avoid the earlier "agreement" because of duress? [*Sambo's Restaurants, Inc. v. City of Ann Arbor,* 663 F.2d 686 (1981).]

7. After a 99-year-old aunt executed a deed conveying certain property to her nephew and his wife, the aunt commenced an action seeking a determination that the deed was null and void and a judgment directing reconveyance of the property. The aunt initiated the conveyance and selected the price and was not dependent upon the nephew or his wife in personal or business affairs, although the aunt had respect for the nephew's judgment and trust in his character. The property was worth more than the $5,000 she asked for from the nephew. Does this case present a fiduciary relationship which would allow the contract to be avoided because of the differences in value exchanged? [*Bruno v. Bruno,* et al., 422 N.E.2d 1369 (Mass. 1981).]

8. Religious counselor appealed a judgment of the lower court rescinding a partnership agreement between the counselor and the devotee with regard to the financial purchase of apartments. Evidence was introduced to show that the devotee had fallen in love with the counselor and that several times a week she received treatment from the counselor which involved intense spiritual and emotional pressure. The devotee advanced $13,000 for the purchase of the building and the counselor only $2,987.50. Originally the devotee did not want to enter into the partnership but the counselor changed her mind by noting that she was ungrateful for all he had done for her and that her refusal violated the tenets of her faith. Can the partnership be rescinded? [*Ferguson v. Jeanes,* 619 P.2d 369 (Wash. 1981).]

9. Patient's father brought action against hospital and radiological association for a declaratory judgment that he did not owe the association for the expense of interpretation of X rays of his son's wrist. Plaintiff's son was injured in a motorcycle accident and taken to a hospital for treatment of his injuries. Upon admittance to the hospital, plaintiff signed a form containing the following language: "I hereby authorize and direct the above-named surgeon and/or his associates to provide such additional services for me as he or they may deem reasonable and necessary, including, but not limited to, the administration and maintenance of the anesthesia, and the performance of services involving pathology and radiology, and I hereby consent thereto. I understand that the above mentioned . . . are independent contractors and as such are the agents, servants or employees of myself." Plaintiff alleges that the consent form is a **contract** of **adhesion** and thus is void. He states that the form is a standardized form which was presented to him by a party with greater bargaining power. He contends there was no bargaining between the parties as to its contents; rather, if he wanted medical treatment for his son, then he had to sign the form presented. This lack of negotiation, he contends, makes the contract unenforceable, and he cites *Weaver v. American Oil Co.,* 276 N.E.2nd 144 (Ind. 1972)—see text p. 144— as authority. What result? [*Rumple v. Bloomington Hospital,* 422 N.E.2d 1309 (Ind. 1981).]

adhesion contract
a standard form contract in which the weaker party has no realistic choice or opportunity to bargain

10. In *Johnson v. Mobil Oil Corporation,* 415 F.Supp. 264 (1976),[7] the court held that a contracting party having immense bargaining power has an affirmative duty to explain in layman's terms the meaning and possible consequences of a contractual obligation to be assumed by another contracting party who is an uncounseled layman. Because this was not done, a clause limiting liability was declared null and void. In *Wille v. Southwestern Bell Telephone Company,* 549 P.2d 903 (Kan. 1976),[8] a clause limiting liability was deemed valid and binding. Reconcile the two cases. Why in one instance deny the freedom to contract and in the next instance enforce it? Are the cases inconsistent?

---

[7] See p. 83.   [8] See pp. 112–13.

Consideration/Value Given for a Promise 8

After you have read this chapter, you should be able to:

1. Discuss the law of consideration, recognizing that it acts as a limitation on the freedom to contract.
2. Recognize that the law is moving in the direction of not requiring consideration in more and more instances so as to achieve a better sense of fairness to the parties involved and a better understanding of their intentions about assuming legal obligations.
3. Appreciate the differences among the requirements of consideration, manifestation of mutual assent, and genuineness of assent.
4. Note the exceptions to the requirement of consideration in both the common law and the Uniform Commercial Code.
5. Apply the objective tests used to determine whether consideration exists.

Introduction

In the preceding chapters of this Part, we discussed the promise and one of the four elements required for a contract, namely mutual assent of the parties. We now consider the second of the four elements, consideration. **Consideration** as *value* and as the *price for a promise* is a basic requirement for a contract. The concept of consideration is: What did the promisor request and receive for his or her promise to which the promisor was not already legally entitled? (A promises B $5 for mowing A's lawn. Mowing the lawn is the consideration/value for A's promise, which, stated legally, says "In consideration of your mowing my lawn, I'll pay you $5.")

However, the law, by case decision and by statute, is reflecting a trend in public policy of making more and more exceptions to this requirement in order to achieve a better sense of fairness to the parties in particular transactions and a better understanding of their intentions about assuming legal obligations.

The fact that the requirement of consideration must be satisfied to have a *simple contract* can be better understood by learning how the concept of consideration developed and how it relates to the *freedom to contract*.

A type of formal contract, a *contract under* **seal,** did not require consideration to prove its validity or enforceability. It was presumed that a person who pressed a signet ring into wax on a contractual document became committed to the obligation evidenced by the document, truly intending to be so bound.

A signet ring bearing some symbol normally was restricted in use to nobles. Merchants wishing to engage in trade and commerce found it necessary to prove to the court that they truly wanted and intended to be bound to a contractual obligation. In most cases merchants were not nobles and therefore could not resort to the use of a seal to satisfy the concerns of the law. Thus, the concept of consideration developed to substitute for the necessity of a seal to show that a common person intended to be bound to a contractual obligation.

Historically, then, it is easily seen why the requirement of consideration is important to the freedom to contract. It is a *further limitation on our ability to create a contract*. By requiring that consideration be present, as well as manifestation of mutual assent and genuineness of assent, the law can be more satisfied that the parties to a contract *want to be bound to the obligation*. Otherwise, consideration as value would not be requested and given for a promise.

By case development and under the Uniform Commercial Code numerous exceptions to the requirement of consideration are being discovered.

Consideration—A Third Test to Determine Intent to Contract

In previous chapters we discussed the concern of the law to determine *whether the parties to a contract truly wanted and intended to be bound to an obligation*. There are three tests to make this determination, all of which are necessary elements in order to have a *contract*. They are: (1) manifestation of mutual assent by offer and acceptance, (2) genuineness of assent, and (3) consideration. We have already discussed the first two, and now we will consider the third, *consideration*.

Unlike the concept of *genuineness of assent,* wherein a *subjective test* was applied to determine whether the parties' manifestation of mutual assent was an act of free will, consideration requires the satisfaction of two *objective* requisites. One is that **detriment** be given for the return obligation by both parties to the contract under the assumption that detriment to one party is normally of benefit to another party. The other requisite is that the detriment be bargained for. (A contracted with B to dig a ditch for B. A's digging is a detriment to A given by A in return for B's promissory obligation to pay A. A's digging is a benefit to B, and B's payment is a benefit to A. A and B bargained for the digging and payment.)

---

consideration
the legal price bargained for a promise and inducing a party to enter into a contract

seal
a symbol attached to a writing attesting that it is a legal document

detriment
the doing, or forbearing from doing, something by a party who had no previous legal obligation so to do or refrain from doing

The detriment by one party is the price, value, or consideration for the promise of the other party justifying enforcement of the promise. The detriment also indicates the intent to contract, as does the promise requesting the detriment.

The Bargain Theory

Under the common law, the basic theory of consideration was the *bargain* theory with one major exception, *promissory estoppel*. Only the bargain theory demands the satisfaction of the requirements of *detriment bargained for,* next to be explained. When applicable, the exception requires something different to show that consideration is present. The concern of the promissory estoppel is different from that which is traditional to the concept of consideration. The concern is that *equity and justice be done* in the contractual setting rather than the concern about whether the parties intended to commit themselves to a contractual obligation.

Detriment Bargained For

Detriment is *the giving up of a legal right one has by law to do or not do something (forbearance), or the assumption of a legal duty to do or not do something not otherwise imposed by law.* In the following case the plaintiff mother gave up a legal right which she honestly believed she had, even though its exercise would not have produced a result in her favor. Her forbearance constituted a detriment to her and consideration for the defendant's promise, making it a contract.

Facts
Plaintiff, mother, brought suit against the defendant, a claimed putative father, to recover for breach of an oral agreement under which he was to pay birth expenses and to support a child upon condition that the plaintiff would refrain from instituting bastardy proceedings. The putative father did not carry out his part of the oral agreement and, in a subsequent bastardy proceeding, upon medical proof in the form of blood tests, it was shown that he could not have fathered the child.
    The plaintiff contends that her forbearance was a detriment to her and consideration for the defendant's promise to pay. The defendant contends that, since he was not the father, there was no detriment to the plaintiff and, therefore, no contract.

Decision
Judgment for the mother. The court enforced the agreement.

Reasoning
Forbearance to sue for a lawful claim or demand is sufficient consideration where the promise to pay is for a forbearance. The party forbearing must have an honest intention to prosecute litigation which is not frivolous, vexatious, or unlawful and which he or she believes to be well founded. The court found in this case that the mother believed the putative father to actually be the father of the child, and therefore her forbearance to sue was valid, good, and sufficient consideration.

Fiege v. Boehm, 123 A.2d 316 (Md. 1956).

Forms of Detriment

The certainty of terms test[1] illustrates some forms that detriment can take. Consideration is unique in that it requires that the offer and acceptance contain bargained-for legal rights and duties. Detriment need not have economic value. In the following case the court held that detriment can consist of an implied promise to forbear from repossessing a car.

Facts
The evidence showed that a grandson of defendant entered into a retail installment sales contract with plaintiff to purchase an automobile and that he forged his grandmother's (defendant) signature as a co-signer on the contract to purchase the car. Thereafter, plaintiff obtained a replacement contract with the real signature of defendant.

Defendant, grandmother, testified that she knew her signature was forged on the first contract and that she knew her grandson would not be able to keep the car unless she signed the replacement contract. Defendant now contends she received no consideration to support her promise to pay the pre-existing debt of her grandson.

---
[1] See pp. 89–90.

Decision
Judgment for plaintiff.

Reasoning
The court found sufficient evidence of mutual consideration consisting of plaintiff's implied promise to forbear from repossessing the car in exchange for defendant's promise to pay if the grandson did not. An agreement to forbear need not be in express terms or for an exact period of time; the terms may be gathered from the surrounding circumstances from which forbearance for a reasonable time may be implied.

Zimmerman Ford, Inc. v. Cheney, 271 N.E.2d 682 (Ill. 1971).

Bargained For. Whether or not detriment has been *bargained for* is decided by whether it *was mutually requested. This determination will be made objectively by looking at the facts of the contractual setting and deciding as a reasonable person whether the request has been made*. This is illustrated by the following case.

Facts
This is an admiralty action concerning the sinking of plaintiff's harbor tug, the result of the negligence of a pilot hired by the defendant, said negligence being imputed to the defendant. Immediately after the harbor tug sank and defendant's vessel had docked, the pilot presented the captain of defendant's vessel with a pilotage agreement, the pertinent part of which read:

> "It is agreed between Pilot and the Vessel, her owners . . . etc. that the Pilot . . . will not be held personally liable for any damage whatsoever . . . caused by Vessel . . . [due] to Pilot's negligence. . . ."

The captain signed the agreement without reading it as was his custom. At the time the agreement was entered into, the pilot's association to which the pilot belonged offered a 15% discount on pilot fees to any vessel using an association pilot and a 15% discount on billing was given to defendant. Defendant contends that it is not an agreement since it never received consideration for the right it purportedly gave up not to sue the pilot for damage experienced due to his negligence.

exculpatory clause
a clause which relieves one from liability

Decision
Judgment for defendant.

Reasoning
The court said it is black letter law that consideration must be bargained for by the promisor and given by the promisee in exchange for the promise. In this case the pilotage discount was not bargained for by defendant as consideration for its agreement to accept the **exculpatory clause** and the discount was not given in exchange for the exculpatory agreement. Such discounts were given to any vessel using an association pilot, regardless of a vessel's acceptance of the exculpatory clause. Furthermore, the signing of the pilotage agreement after the services had been rendered was intended to be a receipt for services rendered and not a contract. The court stated that it was not likely that *after* the grounding took place the captain would have agreed without consideration to an exculpatory clause which would have left the ship *solely responsible* for *heavy damage*.

Gulf Towing Co., Inc. v. Steam Tanker, Amoco, et al., N.Y., 648 F.2d 242 (1981).

Adequacy and Mutuality of Obligations

If only one party to a proposed contract has been requested to give detriment, no binding contractual obligation will be formed, under the general principle that if one party is not bound to a contract (did not give consideration), the other is not bound.

Adequacy of consideration does not deal with a problem of economic value directly. However, where the detriment exchanged is economically worthless or *greatly* disproportionate in value, it will not be adequate consideration if it can be shown it was *not intended* to be consideration. *Adequacy questions* for the most part limit themselves to questions of *whether consideration was intended or whether a contract was intended at all*. (For example, perhaps a gift was intended and the purpose of the gift was not meant to be consideration for any promise.) This is illustrated by the following case where the consideration exchanged is of disproportionate value yet the court finds a contract to exist.

Facts

Ruby Trump Ruffner died **testate** leaving the residue of her estate to St. Andrews Episcopal Church. Twenty-one months before her death, she executed a contract transferring stock representing a controlling interest in High Lawn Memorial Park Co. to an escrow agent retaining the income from the stock for her life and upon her death to transfer the stock to one Ballard, defendant, should he survive. The stated consideration for the transfer was that Ballard "covenants and agrees to immediately assume the full management of High Lawn Memorial Park Co. corporation as may be necessary in and about its proper operation and with a full effort towards its profitable operation." Plaintiff, trustee of the church, brings this action to have the alleged contract set aside on the ground that it lacks consideration, and that, the friendship between Ruby and Ballard was the basis for undue influence by Ballard on Ruby in causing Ruby to make the transaction. The lower court rendered judgment for the plaintiff, and the defendant appeals.

Decision

Judgment reversed, for the defendant, Ballard.

Reasoning

The doctrine of failure of consideration in the law of contracts is certainly a nebulous one. Cases can be found where the slightest consideration is adequate to support a contract while others can be found in which substantial consideration has been held insufficient. In this case, it was held that, though Ballard was a friend of Ruby and already employed by defendant corporation, he could have withdrawn from management at any time but contracted with Ruby not to do so. Such is the nature of consideration. Though Ruby may have given disproportionately more than she got, she did receive consideration of some value for the contract. There is insufficient evidence of undue influence here.

Newell v. High Lawn Memorial Park Co., 264 S.E.2d 454 (W. Va. 1980).

testate
a decedent who executed a will

Applications

Past Consideration. Under the bargain theory, "past consideration" is no consideration. Thus, detriment given to support a *prior* contract cannot be used or brought forward to support a new contract. (A promises to pay B an additional $1,000 if B will perform the contract previously made by them. B's obligation to perform the *previous* contract is not a detriment for A's new promise. A's promise is not a contract.) Nor can one already under a *legal duty* offer the performance of that duty as consideration for a contract. The right already exists for the other contracting party. Therefore, a promise not to commit a tort or crime, or a promise by a public official to perform a public duty, cannot act as consideration for a contract. In the following case giving incriminating evidence to stop a crime was not deemed to be performance of a pre-existing duty.

Facts

In 1982, executives of Gulf Oil Corporation received a letter announcing that one of its plant facilities would be sabotaged by explosive charges unless $15,000,000 was paid, whereupon the bombs would be deactivated. The executives were told not to inform the authorities and were sent a sample bomb. The letter closed with "Gentlemen, THE CLOCK IS RUNNING." The FBI investigated the extortion attempt and arrested defendant and others. Shortly after defendant's arrest, he stated he would give the government everything it needed in exchange for his girlfriend's release and non-prosecution. An assistant United States Attorney drafted an agreement which gave defendant's girlfriend statutory immunity. This agreement was accepted by defendant and he gave all requested information to the authorities. Subsequent to these events, defendant's girlfriend was indicted and now the defendant's girlfriend moves to dismiss her indictment on the grounds that it is in violation of the Government's agreement not to prosecute her. The Government argued that the agreement fails as a contract because of lack of consideration.

Decision

Judgment for defendant on the consideration issue.

Chapter 8: Consideration/Value Given for a Promise

Reasoning

The court said that the argument that defendant, in promising to locate and describe explosives, was not furnishing consideration but merely fulfilling a pre-existing duty to refrain from criminal activity could not be upheld. Defendant, the court said, had no duty to provide the Government incriminating evidence. In doing so, he relinquished his rights under the Fifth Amendment to the United States Constitution and thereby suffered a detriment. He was induced to suffer that detriment by the Government's promise not to prosecute his girlfriend. The court held that defendant's promise clearly fits the well-established definition of consideration: a promise to act or forbear that is bargained for and exchanged for a return promise.

United States v. McBride, 571 F.Supp. 596 (1983).

Liquidated and Unliquidated Debt. In a *liquidated debt,* the *amount* of the debt has been agreed to by the parties or is ascertainable by a standard. For example, a five-cent deposit on a beverage bottle is the amount agreed to by the buyer and the retailer as the liquidated debt for not returning the bottle. In an *unliquidated debt,* the amount of the debt is unascertained. (Pursuant to the contract, A performed services for B. The contract did not state what amount B was to pay A.) In a *disputed debt* or claim, the person against whom the debt is asserted *honestly and reasonably believes it not to be valid,* but the claimant disagrees. (A performs a service for B and claims $150 as its value, but B honestly and reasonably believes and contends that she never requested the service.)

An attempt to discharge a *liquidated* debt by doing something *less* than what is required by the contract (even though accepted) is ineffective, unless a *gift* is made by the creditor of the remaining legal duty not performed. The doing of something *more* than what was initially bargained for will discharge the debt. Thus, when a creditor promises to discharge the debtor if the debtor will pay a *lesser* amount *at an earlier date,* this is something *more* than the debtor was obligated to do, and, therefore, if the debtor does this, the debtor is discharged from the debt.

A **composition** (agreement) outside of bankruptcy will discharge *liquidated* debts. The agreement by some or all of the creditors with their **insolvent** or *financially embarrassed* debtor, each to take something less than what is owed to him, is sufficient new legal detriment bargained for to bind the creditors to the new agreement which, *when performed,* will discharge the previous liquidated debts. The mutual promises of the creditors provide the consideration for each other. This reflects public policy.

An acceptance of something *less* than what is demanded satisfies and discharges an *unliquidated debt* because each of the parties to the contract has suffered detriment by foregoing the opportunity to have a court determination of what is owed. This type of discharge is a form of compromise which is technically called an **accord and satisfaction.** The parties are in "accord" with their new contract, which the parties *intend of itself* to "satisfy" the obligation of the old contract and thus discharge the old contract.[2]

Payment by the debtor of a *disputed debt* is consideration for the creditor's promise of discharge on such payment. The debtor is experiencing a forbearance in that the debtor is giving up the defense of not being liable for the agreed upon larger amount, which the debtor *honestly and reasonably believes* is not owing. (C and D disagree on what D owes C. C claims it is $100 and D honestly and reasonably believes it is $50. C promises to discharge D from D's debt if D will pay C $75, which D does. C's promise is supported by D's forbearance to refuse to pay more than $50 and D's payment of $75 as consideration and is a contract binding on C.) It is irrelevant whether C's claim or D's defense was correct. Payment by the debtor of a disputed claim results in an accord and satisfaction and a discharge of the debtor's obligation to the creditor.

However, in an **account stated** the balance due is *later* agreed to by the parties.

---

composition
(outside of bankruptcy) an agreement among some or all of the creditors with their insolvent or financially embarrassed debtor, each to take something less than what is owed to him and, on the debtor's performance, the debtor is discharged fully as to those creditors who are parties to the agreement

insolvency
(in bankruptcy) when the debtor's assets are less than his liabilities; when the debtor "either has ceased to pay his debts in the ordinary course of business or cannot pay his debts as they become due or is insolvent within the meaning of the federal bankruptcy law" UCC 1–201(23) and Restatement (Second) of Contracts, sec. 252(2)

accord and satisfaction
a new contract (accord) which discharges a party from a previous contractual obligation; the old contract is discharged (satisfied)

account stated
an account which has been settled and the matured items and balance expressly or impliedly agreed to by the parties

---

[2] For a discussion of accord and of accord and satisfaction, see p. 173.

Promissory Estoppel

The concept of **promissory estoppel** is an exception to the bargain theory of consideration. It requires that certain elements exist: (1) an existing promise (2) made with the expectation that it will be relied upon (3) and justifiably relied upon substantially (4) to the injury of the promisee should the promise not be enforced. In the typical situation, no detriment or benefit is given by one of the parties to the contract. Under the *bargain theory of consideration* there would be no contract because of lack of mutuality of obligation. However, *in limited circumstances,* a contract will be found on the ground of promissory estoppel because of the need to promote strongly felt public policy, justice, and equity. In the following case a promise was enforced to avoid injustice.

promissory estoppel
an equitable principle of preventing injustice by enforcing a gratuitous promise as a contract, without consideration and agreement, the promisor reasonably expecting that his promise would be justifiably relied upon substantially by the promisee

Facts
Defendants, a county in the state of Florida, advertised for bids for a road resurfacing. The bid instructions provided that all bidders were to submit bids for both of two alternatives, A and B. One bidder bid only on alternative A because the county inadvertently failed to include in the bidder's information the instruction to bid for both alternatives. The county awarded the project to this bidder who submitted the low bid only on alternative A. Plaintiff, the lowest bidder on alternatives A and B, sought an injunction against the awarding of the bid. While the injunction action was pending, the county allowed the project to be completed by the low bidder on only alternative A. The injunction, issued too late, ordered the bid process to be readvertised. Plaintiff now sues under promissory estoppel for damages.

Decision
Judgment for plaintiff.

Reasoning
The court found that where the government solicited bids promising the contract to the lowest bidder, the lowest bidder could reasonably rely on the government's promise. Whereas here the lowest bidder for *alternatives A and B* did rely to its detriment, it was entitled to reliance damages to include the costs of preparing its bid and the legal costs associated with defending its interest, but not alleged loss of profits, said loss being speculative.

Baxter's Asphalt & Concrete, Inc., v. Liberty County, 421 So.2d 505 (Fla. 1982).

The evidence of the need to do **equity** and fair dealing is causing the courts to apply the concept to the *business* promise in limited circumstances. The following case illustrates the application of promissory estoppel in enforcing a business promise.

equity
principles of justice and fairness which developed when the relief at common law was inadequate

Facts
The plaintiffs, a married couple, bought a used home in Mississippi from another married couple. The plaintiff husband desired a warranty against defects, and as part of the negotiated transaction, the sellers paid for and delivered to the buyers a document entitled Home Buyers Protection Plan issued by defendant insurance company. The defendant published a brochure that stated that the policyholder would be protected against major repair bills resulting from hidden defects. Plaintiff read the brochure and relied upon it in his decision to purchase the home. The actual insurance policy contained limited warranties for repairs. Nine months after taking possession of the home, major repairs became necessary due to hidden defects. The insurance company refused to pay for the repairs under the limited warranty. To determine whether the terms of the brochure could constitute covenants between plaintiffs and defendant, the court turned to the Restatement's definition of promissory estoppel.

Decision
Judgment for plaintiffs.

Reasoning
The court concluded that a Mississippi state court would hold an insurer **estopped** to deny that an insurance contract contained a clause that the insurer represented (in its brochure) to be among its terms after the insured relied on that representation.

Vogel v. American Warranty Home Service Corp., 695 F.2d 877 (1983).

estop
prohibit, bar

In limited situations, promises between closely related parties have been enforced under the concept of promissory estoppel because of the need of justice.

Pledge of a Gift

eleemosynary
charitable, benevolent

A pledge to an **eleemosynary** institution (e.g., church, United Way) is not enforceable under the bargain theory of consideration because the one making the promise to give a gift has not bargained for anything (detriment) in return. For example, A promises to contribute $100 toward the cost of a new organ for a church. A promise has been made. It is calculated to be relied upon. It may be justifiably relied upon. If relied on, the institution will suffer loss if it is not carried out, and there is a strongly felt public policy to assist such organizations by enforcing the promise as an obligation by promissory estoppel.

Moral Obligation

A person may be motivated to do, or to refrain from doing, something and thereby experience an "obligation" to cause this to happen or not to happen. The obligation may be a "legal obligation" or a "moral obligation." When a promise is made to perform, it becomes important to determine whether there is a legal or a moral obligation to perform under the law of contracts. We have seen that, under the bargain theory of contracts, a promise *requesting* and *receiving* a detriment or benefit creates a *legal obligation* to perform the promise and the promise is then called a contract. A *previous moral obligation* does *not* involve a detriment or benefit and, not being consideration, it is *not* sufficient to cause a promise to perform the moral obligation to become a contract. Examples are: A's promise to B to pay $100 to B for B's previous love and affection; D's promise to E to pay E for F's previous injury to E; X's promise to Y to pay Z's previous debt to Y. All of these promises do not create legal obligations to perform and, therefore, are not binding as contracts.

Statutes

statute of limitations
a statute limiting the time in which a claim may be asserted in court; expiration bars enforcement of the claim

In situations where contractual obligations have been discharged by the passage of a **statute of limitations** or a proceeding in bankruptcy, a promise to pay a debt due under the discharged contract will reinstate the debt even though this runs counter to the rule that "past consideration" is no consideration. The new promise is enforceable *in accordance with its terms*. (A owes B three debts of $600 each. All of the debts are barred by the statute of limitations. A writes B, "I promise to pay you one of those $600 debts which I owe; the other two I shall not pay." A's promise of $600 is binding.)

In most cases the new promise must be in writing. There is some justification for this holding when one recognizes that good and adequate consideration was given in the previous contract, and that the court is merely requiring a promisor to abide by the new promise and to carry out what the promisor was obligated to carry out previously before having been discharged by operation of law. However, the new promise may be implied from the debtor's conduct, such as the debtor's part payment of the debt. (For example, A owes B a debt of $1,000, barred by the statute of limitations. A orally promises to pay the debt in monthly installments of $10, and subsequently *pays* $5 on account of the first installment. The part payment, though excepted from a statute requiring a writing, binds A only to pay in monthly installments.) The same is true by the debtor's issuance of new collateral security for the debt, or acknowledgement of the debt. (A owes B $400 and sends B a post-dated check for $200, stating that it is sent as part payment of the debt. The delivery of the check operates as a new promise to pay the debt and payment of the check by the drawee bank on the subsequent date shown on the check operates as a second new promise by A. The bank's authority to pay was revocable, and A could have stopped payment.)

If the debtor has several debts with the same creditor, the effect of the debtor's unqualified part payment depends upon whether or not the debtor has *specified the particular debt to which the payment is to be applied*. If the debtor has so specified, the creditor must apply the payment to that debt, and if the statute has run on that debt the part payment reinstates the barred debt and the statute starts running anew. If the debtor has not so specified, then the creditor may apply the payment to any of the debts; but the creditor's application of the payment to a debt on which the statute has run does not reinstate the barred debt nor halt the statute.

The new federal Bankruptcy Reform Act of 1978, sec. 524(c)(d), as amended in 1984, makes new special provision for a debtor who wishes to reinstate, wholly or partially, the debtor's obligation discharged in **bankruptcy.** The subject is discussed in chapter 30, Bankruptcy under the Bankruptcy Reform Act of 1978,[3] to which reference should be made at this time. Bankruptcy is solely a federal matter; there are no state bankruptcy laws.

bankruptcy
a federal procedure whereby a debtor's nonexempt assets are gathered together and used to discharge the debtor from most of his debts

The Uniform Commercial Code

Under the Uniform Commercial Code, consideration no longer is required in the following instances: to support a "firm offer"[4] (UCC 2–205); to support an agreement which modified a contract for the sale of goods (UCC 2–209(1)); to discharge a claim arising out of an alleged breach of contract if the aggrieved party has signed and delivered a written waiver or renunciation (UCC 1–107). In other sections of the Code, consideration has been dispensed with for other purposes.[5]

In the following case under the Code, the court held that a subcontractor's bid was not a firm offer.

Facts
Coronis, a subcontractor firm, bid on a subcontract for Gordon, a general contractor firm, who used the bid for its own bid on a job, which was awarded to Gordon. Coronis' bid was contained in a letter which stated in part "We are pleased to offer" [structural steel and two buildings to be erected for a price], and closed "Thank you very much for the opportunity to quote." Coronis telegraphed Gordon withdrawing its offer, and Gordon then telegraphed Coronis its acceptance. Gordon claimed breach on contract. The lower court dismissed the case and Gordon appealed.

Reasoning
The firm offer provision in the Code reverses the common law rule that an offer for a period of time which is not supported by *consideration* can be revoked any time prior to acceptance. The bid did not meet the requirements of a writing under UCC 2–205 which by its terms gives assurance that it will be held open for a stated *or reasonable time*, and there being no firm offer Coronis' offer was effectively revoked. Also, no consideration was given to support Coronis' promise contained in the bid.

E. A. Coronis Assocs. v. M. Gordon Constr. Co., 216 A.2d 246 (N.J. 1966).

Decision
Reversed and remanded to determine if the elements of promissory estoppel are present.

See figure 8.1 on the basics of consideration.

---

[3] See "reaffirmation," p. 470.

[4] See p. 94.

[5] See Commercial Paper, UCC 3–605; Letters of Credit, UCC 5–105.

Figure 8.1 The Basics of Consideration

Theory	Exception	Contracts without Consideration	
Bargain	Promissory Estoppel	Moral Obligation	U.C.C.
1. Detriment	1. Promise	1. Waiver of Statute of Limitations	1. Firm Offer
2. Bargained for	2. Induce Reliance	2. Waiver of Bankruptcy Discharge	2. Modification of Sales Contract
	3. Justified Reliance	3. Extreme Moral Obligation	3. Discharge by Written Waiver or Renunciation
	4. Injury		4. Other

Summary Statement

1. Consideration is a necessary element to the existence of a contract, though there are numerous exceptions.
2. Under the bargain theory of consideration, two objective tests must be satisfied before consideration will be found. These are (a) detriment and (b) bargained for.
3. Detriment bargained for requires that the giving of a detriment be a condition for bringing the contract into existence.
4. Detriment can be recited as a formula: doing or refraining from doing something which one was under no previous legal obligation to do or not do.
5. Mutuality of obligation requires that if one is not bound to a contract, the other party to the contract is not bound.
6. Adequacy of consideration deals with a question of intention.
7. Past consideration is no consideration, with exceptions.
8. An unliquidated debt can be discharged by compromise.
9. Promissory estoppel is applied in situations where the doing of equity is required.
10. Moral obligation is not consideration for a subsequent promise to perform the previous moral obligation.
11. The Uniform Commercial Code in many instances has dispensed with requiring that consideration be present in order to have a contract.

The following case is included in depth to illustrate why consideration exists in contract law.

Baehr v. Penn-O-Tex Oil Corporation
104 N.W.2d 661 (Minn. 1960)

Loevinger, J. Plaintiff, Baehr, sued the defendant, Penn-O-Tex Oil Corporation, for rent because of an alleged breach of contract. Baehr leased gasoline filling stations to one Kemp, who was heavily in debt to the defendant. The plaintiff received a letter from Kemp stating that his (Kemp's) assets were all tied up by the defendant and this was why he had not paid the rent due on the leased stations.

A short time after receiving Kemp's letter, Baehr called the agent of the *defendant* and asked about payment of the filling station rents. Defendant told Baehr "that Mr. Kemp's affairs were in a very mixed up form but that he would get them straightened out and mail *Baehr . . .* checks for the rents."

Hearing nothing further, plaintiff wrote a letter to defendant asking what he had to do to get his rent checks and added "or will I have to give it to an attorney to sue?"

Defendant wrote the plaintiff indicating that they were trying to help Kemp "but in no way *were* they operating the business." The letter denied knowledge of or responsibility for any rent due the plaintiff.

After receiving the letter, the plaintiff called the defendant demanding payment of the rent.

The defendant's agent said the defendant would pay the rent. He would take it up with the home office.

The rent was never paid by defendant, and the communications described took place over an eighteen-month period of time.

The court reasoned that if it accepted the plaintiff's version of the statements made by the agent of the defendant as recorded, there was an unequivocal assurance given that the rents would be paid—a promise.

But the court noted "the fact that a promise is given does not necessarily mean a contract was made." Not every promise is legally enforceable. It is not practical nor reasonable to expect full performance of every assurance given whether it be thoughtless, casual, and gratuitous, or deliberately and seriously made.

The test, the court stated, that has been developed by the *common law* for determining the enforceability of promises is the *doctrine of consideration.* Consideration requires that a contractual promise be the product of a bargain. It means a negotiation resulting in the voluntary assumption of an obligation by one party upon condition of an act or forbearance by the other *(legal value)* [detriment]. *Consideration thus ensures that the promise enforced as a contract is not accidental, casual, or gratuitous but has been uttered intentionally as the result of some deliberation, manifested by reciprocal bargaining or negotiation.* In this view, the requirement of *consideration is no mere technicality, historic anachronism, or arbitrary formality.* It is an attempt to be as reasonable as we can in deciding which promises constitute contracts.

Consideration, as essential evidence of the parties' intent to create a legal obligation, must be something adopted and regarded by the parties as such. In substance, a contractual promise must be of logical form: "If . . . [consideration] is given . . . then I promise. . . ."

In this case, though a promise was made by the defendant, a contract was not created. While plaintiff suffered detriment by forbearing to sue Kemp, such detriment was not bargained for by the defendant. Hence the plaintiff did not give consideration for the defendant's promise. The voluntary relinquishment of a legal right is not consideration. Nor did the court find factually that there was evidence that either party took the defendant's assurances seriously or acted upon them in any way. Judgment for defendant.

Questions and Case Problems

1. A foreman for a subcontractor brought a breach of contract action against the subcontractor based on an alleged oral contract which provided that the foreman would receive a bonus of one-half of the difference between the estimated and actual cost of a construction project. At the time the promise was made, a collective bargaining agreement with a union existed which set forth the foreman's salary. The subcontractor denies the oral promise is enforceable because of lack of consideration. Does the promise of a bonus lack consideration? [*Leone v. Precision Plumbing and Heating of Southern Arizona,* 591 P.2d 1002 (Ar. 1979).]

2. An agreement was made between prisoners, plaintiffs, and a director of a department of correction who was a hostage of a prisoner which gave the prisoners absolute immunity from prosecution if they would cease engaging in further violence in a prison uprising. The prisoners subsequently were tried and convicted for the criminal acts, and they then sued the U.S. Government, defendant, for breach of contract. Judgment for plaintiffs and the defendant appealed. What result? [*United States v. Bridgeman,* 523 F.2d 1099 (1975).]

3. Plaintiff instituted suit against defendant seeking $2,673.26 for labor performed pursuant to an oral contract. The trial court sustained defendant's motion to strike plaintiff's evidence of the oral contract on the basis that the labor price plaintiff claimed was "exorbitant" and, hence, contrary to public policy. Did the trial court err in substituting its judgment for what should be consideration when it feels the underlying bargain is foolish or exorbitant? [*Jessee v. Smith,* 278 S.E.2d 793 (Va. 1981).]

4. Upon receipt of a certified check from a bank, subcontractors on a construction project signed the following receipt:

   "RECEIVED of The Omaha National Bank the sum of _____ Dollars _____ in payment of the above order. In consideration of said payment the undersigned hereby acknowledges that the mortgage in favor of The Omaha National Bank in the above property constitutes a prior lien, superior to any lien which the undersigned may now have or hereafter may acquire. . . ."

   The bank had the right to pay the general contractor first and for the general contractor to pay the subcontractors. Subcontractors contend there was no consideration for the agreement to subordinate their liens. Are they correct? [*The Omaha National Bank v. Goddard Realty, Inc.*, 316 N.W.2d 306 (Neb. 1982).]

5. The plaintiff, an 83-year-old married woman, contended that she was enticed and induced to leave her apartment and move in with the defendant, a 79-year-old widower, in a house on land which at the time he owned in **fee simple.** At a later date the defendant deeded to the plaintiff a fee simple interest in the house and land, reserving a life estate to himself. Shortly thereafter relationships became strained and an agreement was entered into. The agreement stated, "It is mutually agreed by and between the parties hereto that during the remainder of their life-times, they shall live together in harmony in the above-described residential premises. Neither shall have the right to dispossess the other from these premises." Shortly after the signing of this agreement, the defendant changed the locks on the doors of the house and refused to allow the plaintiff to reenter. The plaintiff claims that she has a right to reside in the house and brings this suit to enforce the contract. What result? [*Maszewski v. Piskadlo,* 318 So.2d 226 (Fla. 1975).]

fee simple absolute
the greatest bundle of ownership rights in, and powers over, realty

6. The following provision appeared in an agreement:

   "The Contractor [plaintiff] shall transport in contractor's truck *such tonnage of beets as may be loaded by the Company* [defendant] from piles at receiving stations of the Company, and unload said beets at such factory or factories as may be designated by the Company. The term of this contract shall be from October 1, 1980 until February 15, 1981."

   The plaintiff had been transporting beets under the agreement for approximately two months when in early December 1980 the defendant informed the plaintiff that his services were no longer needed. The plaintiff sues for lost profits that would have been earned had he been allowed to continue to haul beets. Does the plaintiff have a contract that the plaintiff can enforce against the defendant? [*De Los Santos v. Great Western Sugar Co.,* 348 N.W.2d 842 (Neb. 1984).]

7. The lower court ruled that an agreement was not a contract because it lacked mutuality of obligation. The case has been appealed. The written agreement provided that Amoco was to maintain facilities capable of providing Laclede Gas Company with commercial propane gas suitable for delivery to Laclede's customers as required. Laclede agreed in the written agreement to provide distribution facilities and to pay Amoco four cents per gallon for gas provided. A clause in the agreement which raises the issue of mutuality provides:

   "This agreement shall remain in effect for one (1) year following the first delivery of gas by Amoco to Laclede hereunder. Subject to termination as provided in paragraph II hereof dealing with conversions to natural gas, this Agreement shall automatically continue in effect for additional periods of one (1) year each unless Laclede shall, not less than 30 days prior to the expiration of the initial one (1) year period or any subsequent one (1) year period, give Amoco written notice of termination."

   There was no provision under which Amoco could cancel the agreement. Does the agreement lack mutuality of obligation? [*Laclede Gas Company v. Amoco Oil Company,* 522 F.2d 33 (1975).]

8. A retired union officer brought suit to compel a union retirement committee to pay the retired officer an increased pension. A compromise, arising from a disagreement between the retirement committee and the retired officer as to the salary on which the pension was to be based, was reached after the retired officer agreed to accept a pension based on a certain salary, waiving his right to a pension based on a higher salary. Over a period of time the union officer accepted retirement benefits based upon this compromise. Approximately two and a half years later the retired officer argued that his pension should be increased, alleging that it should have been based upon a higher salary. The request was denied. The officer filed a complaint in equity seeking to compel the retirement committee to pay him the requested higher pension. What result? [*Cohen v. Sabin*, 307 A.2d 845 (Pa. 1973).]

9. In an action to foreclose a mortgage, defendant, Virgie E. Tinsley's Enterprises Inc., appeals from an order of the Supreme Court, Suffolk County, dated August 18, 1983, which denied its motion to dismiss the complaint against it on the ground that the action was barred by the statute of limitations. The mortgage in question was executed on April 1, 1974 and provided for the payment of any unpaid balance of the $10,000 principal on or before April 1, 1976. On April 15, 1978, some two years after the note remained unpaid, defendant signed a written memorandum promising to pay the mortgage debt. Action was brought by plaintiff in April 1982. In New York the applicable statute of limitations on mortgage debt is six years. On appeal, should the court bar the action by the running of the statute of limitations? [*Aleci v. Virgie E. Tinsley's Enterprises, Inc.*, 476 N.Y.S.2d 595 (N.Y. 1984).]

10. In *Baehr v. Penn-O-Tex Oil Corporation,* 104 N.W.2d 661 (Minn. 1960),[6] the court said "the requirement of consideration is no mere technicality, historic anachronism, or arbitrary formality. It is an attempt to be as reasonable as we can in deciding which promises constitute contracts." Evaluate this statement.

---

[6] See pp. 124–25.

9 Capacity/Ability to Create a Contract

After you have read this chapter, you should be able to:

1. Discuss the concept of capacity to make a contract and explain what purpose it serves in the law of contracts.
2. Recognize that there are individuals (a) who have no capacity to contract, (b) who have a limited capacity to contract, and (c) who can avoid the consequences of contract.
3. Be aware of the similarities and differences in the way classes of individuals avoid and ratify contracts.
4. Understand that necessaries occupy a unique position with regard to avoidance of contracts.
5. Perceive the current movement of the law to expand contractual capacity.

Introduction

In the preceding chapters of this Part we discussed two of the four elements required for a contract: mutual assent and consideration. We now consider the third element, a party's capacity to contract. The existence of the necessary *contractual capacity* of the parties is *an element* necessary to the formation of *a contract*. It is important to note that the capacity to create a contract provides yet *another barrier to our freedom* to create, through a contract, rights and duties not otherwise imposed by law.

The law associated with the capacity to create a contract recognizes that there are certain situations in which one should *not* be *allowed* to contract. Moreover, there is a recognition that certain persons should be given a chance to *escape* the consequences of a contract because they need protection. These are the important *value judgments* which have resulted in the law which determines one's capacity to create a contract.

A study of the law relating to the capacity to create a contract is a study of who has no capacity to contract, who has limited capacity to contract, and who can avoid the consequences of a contract.

Protection—Limited or No Capacity

When one is **adjudged** mentally incompetent (insane), any attempt to contract is **void**. The party has no *capacity* to contract. A **trust** will normally give a trustee a *limited power* to contract to further the purpose of the trust. A corporation, which contracts through agents, can enter into contracts that only further the purpose contained in the corporate charter. Convicted felons in some states have a limited capacity to contract. In some states, as a protective public policy, a married woman cannot act as a **surety** for her husband's debts. Enemy aliens cannot contract or sue on contracts. Minors, often called infants, who are so young that they *cannot understand* the significance of a contract have no capacity to contract.

These various situations, which run the full spectrum from no ability to contract to partial inability to contract, exist for various purposes—mainly protection and punishment. (See figure 9.1.)

Protection—Right to Avoid

A **voidable contract** is one which is subject to being avoided by a party or the parties and, on avoidance, is discharged. (A fraudulently induces B to contract with A. B has a power of avoidance, so the contract is voidable by B.) It *is* a good contract until it is avoided.

Those persons who are minors under the law (below the age of 18 in most states, below 21 in a few states)[1] can *avoid* (rescind) their contracts. Avoidance of the contractual obligation is possible by those who are induced to enter into a contract because of insane delusions or by those who are so under the influence of drugs or alcoholic beverages that they *do not know* they are entering into a contract. Only the party with the power of avoidance can avoid the contract, e.g., the minor, not the adult; the insane person after becoming sane, but not the other contracting party. (See figure 9.1.)

The purpose for giving the right to avoid a contract is the value judgment of the law that these classes of people need protection from what might turn out to be an improvident act. This principle of law is in a state of evolution. In the following case a contract was set aside (avoided) because of a party's limited mental capacity and business competence.

adjudged
the result of a formal legal process

void
of no legal effect

trust
a legal device whereby legal title to property is held by one person (a trustee) for the benefit of a beneficiary

surety
a person who promises the creditor to pay the principal's debt or to perform his obligation

voidable contract
a contract which can be avoided by one or more of the parties

---

[1] The law disregards fractions of a day. Thus, a person born at 1:00 P.M. on November 11, 1970 becomes 18 at the *beginning* of the day of November 10, 1988.

Figure 9.1 Incapacity Table

Category of Person	Incapacity		Reason for Determination of Incapacity
	Total	Limited	
Adjudged mentally incompetent (insane)	Yes		Inability to protect oneself
Mentally incompetent (insane)		Yes	Inability to protect oneself
Trustee		Yes	To ensure that the purpose of a trust is carried out
Corporation		Yes	To ensure that the purpose of a corporation is carried out
Convicted felons		Yes	Punishment
Married women in special situations		Yes	Protection from undue influence
Minors of a tender age	Yes		Inability to protect oneself
Minors not of a tender age		Yes	Inability to protect oneself
Intoxicated	Yes	Yes	The degree of intoxication determines whether incapacity is total or limited
Enemy alien	Yes		Punishment
Felon in jail		Yes in some states	Public policy

Facts
This is an action by the plaintiff to set aside certain business transacted by one deemed to be limited in mental capacity and business competence. The court found that the defendant ingratiated himself into the confidence of the plaintiff and fraudulently took advantage of the plaintiff's mental and physical infirmities and incompetency to induce the business which has been transacted. Both plaintiff and defendant immigrated to the United States from Austria, had known each other for many years, had common tastes and interests, and both spoke the Croatian language. Plaintiff was unable to read or write English, and because of his injuries it was extremely difficult for him to understand matters read or related to him; he relied upon the defendant for explanations. The eyesight of the plaintiff was also impaired due to an unsuccessful operation on cataracts. He was also quite hard of hearing.

Decision
Judgment for plaintiff.

Reasoning
The court set aside the contract. The court stated that, where it is established that the mind of a party to a transaction has become infirm or his comprehension weakened by age, accident, or illness, the usual presumption of normality and capacity to contract is dissipated. The weakness of mind may not amount to absolute incapacity to transact any business at all, and the mental infirmity need not have been established judicially in order to require the person who has received benefits from dealings with one so afflicted to prove that they were not affected thereby. If one does not have sufficient understanding to protect one's own interests and mental strength to compete in the marketplace, he lacks capacity to transact ordinary business, and dealings with him may be viewed with caution.

Paskvan v. Mesich, 227 F.2d 646 (1955).

disaffirm
to nullify one's previous consent

Avoidance is the **disaffirming** of a contract. This is done by a party to the contract manifesting that he or she no longer intends to be bound by a contract previously made by him or her. The following case illustrates how conduct was held to manifest an intent to avoid a contract.

Facts
The plaintiff obtained a **confession of judgment** against defendant on a note, and defendant sought to have the judgment set aside, arguing that he had timely disaffirmed the note. The defendant as a minor had used the proceeds of the note for the purchase of an automobile. He had made two payments on the car and was then drafted by the armed forces. He contacted the bank and told them to pick up the car, which they did and sold it for salvage for $30.

Decision
Judgment for defendant.

Reasoning
The court held that the contract had been disaffirmed. The court reasoned that, as a general rule, a contract of a minor may be avoided by any act showing unequivocally his renunciation of, or a disposition not to abide or be bound by, the contract made during minority. The court noted that disaffirmance or renunciation is a question of intent, and it seemed to the court that when the minor called the bank to pick up the car it was his manifestation of intent to disaffirm the note. There is no requirement for the nth degree of unequivocalness. To impose specificity and formality in the act of disaffirmance is to disregard the basis for the policy of law that protects minors from their improvident actions and which accords to them the right to disaffirm.

Logan County Bank v. Taylor, 295 N.E.2d 743 (Ill. 1973).

confession of judgment
a party's consent to jurisdiction and judgment of a court without a trial in a civil case

Avoidance (Disaffirmance) by Minors

When disaffirming a contract, a minor must return the consideration received by the minor if the minor still has it. Disaffirmance by a minor for contracts concerning **personal property** can occur anytime during minority and within a *reasonable time* after reaching majority. For **real property** contracts, most states require minors to wait until reaching **majority** and then give to them as new adults a *reasonable time* thereafter in which to disaffirm. Statutes usually specify what is a reasonable time. Unless a statute provides otherwise, an individual is a minor until the beginning of the day of the individual's eighteenth birthday. In the following case a minor was able to disaffirm a contract seven years after it was made for her by her parents.

Facts
An internationally known model and actress, Brooke Shields, brought action against a photographer revoking her parents' consent granting a photographer unrestricted right to use, reuse and/or publish or republish photographs taken by him of her when she was 10 years old in a series of photographs of her unclothed in a bathtub. In a lower court action, the court held that the plaintiff, Shields, could not disaffirm the contract made on her behalf by her mother. Defendant informed plaintiff that he intended to publish the pictures in Playboy magazine. Plaintiff appealed.

Decision
Reversed, judgment for plaintiff.

Reasoning
The court noted that, absent a specific provision in a statute denying a minor a right to disaffirm, the general rule is that a minor has a right to disaffirm a contract even when the contract has been entered into on behalf of the minor by a parent or guardian. In this case, the statutes cited by defendant which require consent of a parent or guardian in the making of a contract by a minor with an adult did not specifically take away a minor's right to disaffirm the contract and, therefore, did not prevent plaintiff from disaffirming the contract.

Shields v. Gross, 451 N.Y.S.2d 419 (N.Y. 1982).

personal property
a movable thing, along with interests and rights in the thing

real property
land and immovable things attached to land, along with interests and rights in the land; also a freehold interest in land

majority
the legal age at which a minor becomes an adult

The minor is entitled to get back all that was given by the minor as consideration for the contract, unless what was given was tangible personal property which was sold to another for value without notice that the property once belonged to a minor. This result is based upon section 2–403 of the Uniform Commercial Code. (I, a minor, sold his skis to A, an adult, in exchange for A's typewriter. A then sold the skis to P, a good faith purchaser for value unaware of I's infancy. I disaffirmed the transaction. P keeps the skis.)

Avoidance by Others

Mentally incompetent (insane) persons, alcoholics, or drug addicts, *if they qualify for the right to avoid a contract,* must exercise the right within a *reasonable time* and must give back to the other party the consideration received or its equivalent value if they still have it, except as otherwise provided by case law or statute.

If the other party *knew and took advantage of the disabled party,* the disabled party, like the minor, can avoid the contract and must return only that portion of the consideration the disabled party received and still has, and the disabled party, in turn, *has the right to receive back what the disabled party gave as consideration.* This is illustrated by the following case involving a mentally incompetent person.

status quo
the state of things at any given time

Facts
A committee for an incompetent party to a land sale contract brought an action attempting to set aside a conveyance of property to a purchaser. In an earlier proceeding the circuit court had confirmed the sale of the children's interest in the land as being fair and held that the incompetency of the mother in making the contract of sale was adequately protected in the court's review of the sales price of the land with regard to the children.

Decision
Judgment for plaintiff, committee for the incompetent party.

Reasoning
The court erred in not hearing evidence on the issue of whether the purchaser knew of the incompetency in order to determine whether the incompetent party would be entitled to have the contract set aside without placing the purchaser in **status quo.** When the consideration is fair, the contract has been executed and the other party acts in good faith without knowledge of the incompetency, the contract will be set aside only if the incompetent party can be placed in status quo. However, where the competent party has knowledge of the incompetency and overreaches the incompetent party, the contract will be set aside and the competent party will not be entitled to reimbursement.

Upton v. Hall, 300 S.E.2d 777 (Va. 1983).

Necessaries

Minors are responsible for their contracts for necessaries. What is a "necessary" is a question of fact. All authorities agree that those things *actually needed* for survival (food, clothing, shelter, and medical care) are necessaries. The following case illustrates this point.

Facts
A duly licensed optometrist, plaintiff, was requested by defendant, Carol Ann White, 19 years of age and a minor under New York law at that time, to furnish her with contact lenses. She advised plaintiff that she urgently desired them as soon as possible. She agreed to pay $225 for the lenses and gave the doctor her personal check for $100. After examining Ms. White's eyes, plaintiff immediately ordered the lenses from his laboratory and incurred an indebtedness of $110. The examination was held on Thursday evening, the lenses were ordered on Friday and received by the doctor on Saturday. On Monday morning, Carol called and disaffirmed her contract on advice of her father and stopped payment on her check. The contact lenses could be used by no one but Carol. Ms. White contends the contact lenses are not a necessary.

Decision
Judgment for plaintiff.

Reasoning
The term "necessaries" as used in the law relating to the liability of minors is a relative term, somewhat flexible, except when applied to such things as are obviously requisite for the maintenance of existence, and also depends on the social position and situation in life of the minor. The contact lenses are a necessary for Carol White.

Cidis v. White, 336 N.Y.S.2d 362 (N.Y. 1972).

Generally, for the *minor* those things needed to maintain a social status equal to the station in life of one's peers are deemed to be necessaries. The flexibility of the concept as it has been applied to minors has resulted in contracts which indirectly provide survival needs (e.g., employment agency services, tools) and tuition fees for an undergraduate college education being considered necessaries. Something is not a necessary for a minor if the parents are willing and able to provide, or have already provided, what would otherwise be necessaries. A contract by a minor for these items is considered not to be for a necessary. However, if a minor is not emancipated and his or her parents have not provided the minor with necessaries, the parents may become liable under agency law for necessaries purchased by the minor. In the following case the court held that vinyl siding on a house was not a necessary.

Facts
Plaintiff seeks a personal money judgment against the defendant, Janet Bundy, for $3,380 for siding placed on a house owned by her and acquired from her parents. The plaintiff placed the vinyl siding on the house in question under a written contract with Janet's parents, not knowing that twelve year old Janet was the owner of the house. Janet's parents have declared bankruptcy and plaintiff says he is entitled to recover against Janet under the doctrine of "necessaries."

Decision
Judgment for defendant, Janet.

Reasoning
The doctrine of "necessaries" gets around the defense of minority when a person has provided necessaries to a minor in reliance upon the minor's credit and not upon the credit of another. Here plaintiff relied upon the credit of the parents, not the minor child. Furthermore, there is no showing that these house improvements were "necessaries." While housing is in general a necessary, that is not to say that adding additional siding to a house falls into that category.

Dalton v. Bundy, as Guardian, 666 S.W.2d 443 (Mo. 1984).

While those who have the right to avoid a contract can avoid a contract for *necessaries,* they must *keep* the necessaries; and they remain liable to the other party to pay a *reasonable value* for the items or services provided. Reasonable value will normally be something less than the usual contract price.

Ratification

Ratification is the opposite of avoidance. In the law of contracts, it is a party's manifestation of intent to continue to be bound by a contract which the party could have avoided. The ratifying party waives his or her power of avoidance.

Ratification by a minor can occur immediately upon the minor reaching the age of majority. For mentally ill persons or those under the disability of alcohol or drugs, ratification can take place only *after the disability is removed, or* through the action of a **guardian** or other legal representative. Ratification may be made by conduct, as is illustrated by the following case in which a minor's conduct after majority ratified his contract made during minority.

Facts
On November 17, 1973, the plaintiff, who was then seventeen years old, signed a contract with defendant. The contract allowed the plaintiff to use defendant's recreational skydiving facilities, which included use of an airplane to ferry skydivers to the parachute jumping site. A **covenant not to sue** and a clause exempting defendant from liability were included in the contract. On December 28, 1973, plaintiff attained the age of eighteen. Ten months later, on October 19, 1974, he suffered serious personal injuries in an airplane crash shortly after the takeoff of an airplane provided by defendant for skydiving purposes. On November 21, 1975, nearly two years after attaining his majority, plaintiff sues defendant in negligence for injuries experienced in the crash. Based upon the exculpatory agreement, **summary judgment** was granted. Plaintiff contends he disaffirmed the contract with defendant by filing suit a reasonable time after he attained his majority.

Decision
Judgment for defendant.

ratification
(in contracts) a person's waiver of his power of avoidance

guardian
a person legally entrusted with the custody and/or the property of another

covenant not to sue
a promise not to sue as part of a contract

summary judgment
a judgment rendered on a motion by a party in a civil action that, solely on the basis of the pleadings, with affidavits, if any, there is no genuine issue as to any material fact and the moving party is entitled to judgment as a matter of law without the necessity of a trial on the facts

Chapter 9: Capacity/Ability to Create a Contract

Reasoning

A minor may disaffirm a contract made during his minority within a reasonable time after attaining his majority or he may, after becoming of legal age, by acts recognizing the contract, ratify it. Affirmance is not merely a matter of intent. It may be determined by the actions of minors who accept the benefits of a contract after reaching the age of majority, or who are silent or acquiesce in the contract for a considerable length of time. What constitutes ratification or disaffirmance is a question of law. Plaintiff ratified the contract, as a matter of law, by accepting the benefits of the contract when he used defendant's facilities on October 19, 1974. Since the contract was ratified, the factual issue of whether the suit for personal injuries was filed within a reasonable time after attaining his majority and constituted disaffirmance of the contract, is not relevant. Plaintiff, therefore, cannot sue for negligence because the exculpatory clause is enforceable.

Jones v. Dressel, 623 P.2d 370 (Colo. 1981).

Minor's Misrepresentation of Age

It has been said that the right of a minor to disaffirm a contract, while shielding the minor, could be used by the minor as a sword against an adult. Thus, if the minor misrepresented his or her age and induced the adult to enter into a contract thinking the minor was an adult, the minor would have the possibility of avoidance but the adult would be bound to the contract.

In earlier common law, the court did not allow adults to sue minors (who generally are responsible for their own crimes and torts) for the damage caused by misrepresentation. The principle was that one could not do indirectly what one could not do directly. Allowing the suit in tort would have the indirect effect of holding minors to the contract which they were capable of avoiding.

Today in misrepresentation cases a compromise—known as **restitution**—seems to be developed by case law which retains the right of the minor to avoid the contract but requires the minor to return the *total* consideration given by the adult for the contract. However, restitution is not allowed in some states. Also, in some cases the minor's misrepresentation causes the contract to be *voidable by the adult party* to the contract. This is illustrated by the following case.

restitution
a legal remedy restoring one to his original position prior to the particular transaction

foreclosure
the cutting off of an owner's interest in realty by sale pursuant to court decree

Facts
Plaintiff sued to recover on a loan of $22,000 made to defendant and her husband on a real estate mortgage to build a home. The defendant, who was nineteen and a minor at the time of taking out the loan, recited in an affidavit of title in three places that she was of the age of majority in seeking a loan. After the loan was made, she and her husband built the home, separated, abandoned the property, and defaulted on the mortgage payments. In a subsequent **foreclosure** suit on the mortgage, the defendant counterclaimed, asserting her infancy and disaffirmance of the mortgage agreement, and she demanded a return from the plaintiff of personal funds used by her in making the mortgage payments and improving the premises.

Decision
Judgment for plaintiff.

Reasoning
The court held for the plaintiff because the defendant misrepresented her age. Infancy is no defense to an action to recover money advanced to an infant on the basis of misrepresentation of majority reasonably relied upon by a lender. While the defendant here tenders her entire interest in the real estate to the plaintiff for the return of her advances, the difficulty is that the plaintiff cannot be made whole. It is entitled to be made whole, and the plaintiff is entitled to complete foreclosure free of any claim of the defendant except that she may have an interest in surplus funds.

Manasquan Savings and Loan Ass'n. v. Mayer, 236 A.2d 407 (N.J. 1967).

Special Cases

In some cases a minor cannot disaffirm a contract completely or can only partially disaffirm it. A minor's contracts which, by statute, cannot be disaffirmed include purchases of corporate investments, insurance policy purchases, contract of marriage, and enlistment in the armed forces. In a few states a married minor cannot disaffirm his or her contracts. A minor's contracts that can be only partially disaffirmed would be partnership contracts. While the contract creating the partnership can be avoided, the capital committed by the minor to the partnership must remain available to the creditors of the partnership.

Emancipation of a Minor

Emancipation means freedom from something. An **emancipated minor** is a minor whose parents have given up their rights to take care of the minor and to have custody of and claim to the minor's earnings. The minor has now become self-supporting. The minor may declare emancipation either expressly, or impliedly as by marriage or voluntary enlistment in military service. An emancipated minor has capacity to contract and, in the absence of statute to the contrary, still has the power of avoidance.

emancipated minor
a minor whose parents have given up their rights to take care of the minor and to have custody of and to claim the minor's earnings

Summary Statement

1. Certain classes of persons have no capacity to contract, others have limited capacity to contract, and still others can escape the consequence of a contract.
2. The right to avoid a contract is in a process of evolving in two directions: one, contract law is becoming more specific about who can avoid a contract; and two, it is limiting the right to avoid a contract.
3. Avoidance requires the avoiding party's express or implied manifestation of intent no longer to be bound by the contract which must be made within a reasonable time.
4. A minor may disaffirm during minority or within a reasonable time after attaining majority, except that for real property contracts disaffirmance can occur only within a reasonable time after attaining majority.
5. Generally, the minor must return what the minor has received or its equivalent value if the minor still has it in order to disaffirm and to get restitution (except for UCC 2–403). This is also true for a disadvantaged party with limited capacity to contract.
6. In cases of a minor's misrepresentation of age, or of contracts by those not known to be incapacitated, *all* consideration must be returned by such persons in order to avoid their contracts. For contracts where the subject matter is necessaries, such persons must keep what they have received and pay for their reasonable value.
7. An emancipated minor still has the power to disaffirm a contract.
8. Ratification is the waiver of a power to avoid a contract. A minor can ratify only after attaining majority; others within a reasonable time after their disability has been removed.

The following case is included in depth to illustrate the value judgment that the law needs to protect people in the legal area of capacity. The case also illustrates the current trend in this area of law making limitations on who and what will be protected and how protection will be afforded. At the time of this case, a minor was a person below twenty-one years of age.

Gastonia Personnel Corporation v. Rogers
172 S.E.2d 19 (N.C. 1970)

Bobbitt, C.J. The defendant was graduated from high school when he was seventeen. By the time he was nineteen years old he was emancipated and married. He needed only "one quarter, or 22 hours" for completion of the course requirements at Gaston Tech for an A.S. degree in civil engineering. His wife was employed as a computer programmer at First Federal Savings and Loan. He and she were living in a rented apartment. They were expecting a baby in September. Defendant had to quit school and go to work.

For assistance in obtaining suitable employment, defendant went to the office of the plaintiff, an employment agency. Defendant signed a contract which contained the following: "If I ACCEPT employment offered me by an employer as a result of a lead . . . from you within twelve (12) months of such lead . . . I will be obligated to pay you as per the terms of (this) contract."

After making several phone calls, the employment agency was successful in obtaining an interview for the defendant for a draftsman job. Defendant was interviewed and hired.

The plaintiff has sued for its service charge, and the defense of the defendant was infancy (below twenty-one years of age at that time).

The court held the infant liable for the service charge. The court noted that the early common law recognized that "*an infant may bind himself to pay for his necessary meat, drinks, apparell, necessary physicke, and* such other necessaries, *and likewise for his good teaching or instruction whereby he may profit himself afterwards.*" The court continued by recognizing the ancient rule of the common law that an infant's contract, unless for "necessaries" or unless authorized by statute, is voidable by the infant, at his election.

Such other necessaries, the court noted, traditionally meant those articles suitable to the infant's degree and estate. The court also stated that today such other necessaries has become a very flexible concept.

The dominant purpose of the law in permitting infants to disaffirm their contracts is to protect children and those of tender years from their own improvidence, or want of discretion, and from the wiles of designing men.

Society, the court said, has a moral obligation to protect the interest of infants from overreaching adults. But this protection must not become a straightjacket, stifling the economic and social advancement of infants who have the need and maturity to contract. Nor should infants be allowed to turn that protective legal shield into a weapon to wield against fair-dealing adults. It is in the interest of society to have its members contribute actively to the general economic and social welfare, *if this can be accomplished consistently with the protection of those persons unable to protect themselves in the marketplace.*

The court concluded that the common law rule by judges centuries ago was in need of modification. One of the great virtues of the common law is its dynamic nature that makes it adaptable to the requirements of society at the time of its application in court.

While the court noted that prior decisions were to the effect that the "necessaries" of an infant, his wife, and child include only such necessities of life as food, clothing, shelter, medical attention, etc., its view is that the concept of "necessaries" *should be enlarged* to include such articles of property and such services as are reasonably necessary to enable an infant to earn money required to provide the necessities of life for himself and those legally dependent upon him.

Questions and Case Problems

1. Defendant, McCoy, was discharged from the U.S. Army in 1960 because of his mental condition and has been, and still is, receiving psychiatric treatment and medication ever since at a V.A. hospital. It was generally known in the community where McCoy resided that he was mentally incapable of handling his affairs. Plaintiff, Fidelity Financial Services, Inc., entered into negotiations with defendant for an automobile loan to the defendant in the presence of a car dealer who wanted to sell McCoy a car. The car was sold to the defendant, who borrowed the purchase money from the plaintiff giving the plaintiff the defendant's promissory note and a chattel mortgage (a nonpossessory security interest) on the car as security for the loan. The transaction took about forty-five minutes and

plaintiff stated that McCoy acted and appeared normal. The note was not paid and the plaintiff sued defendant on the note and to enforce the chattel mortgage. Defendant asserted his insanity at the time the note and mortgage were executed by him. Plaintiff never called the car dealer to testify. In the lower court, the note was annulled and the chattel mortgage cancelled because of the defendant's insanity. Plaintiff appealed. What result? [*Fidelity Financial Services, Inc. v. McCoy,* 392 So.2d 118 (La. 1980).]

2. A provision in a **testamentary trust** provided that no extension of promissory notes due to the trust fund from a land development corporation would be made after a specified date. It was decided by the trustee to collect the notes as rapidly as possible without insisting on immediate payment in full as they came due. Beneficiary of the trust objected, insisting that this is an extension beyond the power of the trustee. What result? [In re *Estate of Gilliland,* 140 Cal.Rptr. 795 (1977).]

testamentary trust
a trust created by the will of a decedent

3. From 1920 to July 1965, Iota Chapter of Kappa Alpha Theta, Inc., a nonprofit corporation, owned real property in Ithaca, New York. In 1965, because of the national sorority's discriminatory membership policies which excluded those of certain religious and ethnic groups, the chapter's active membership voted to end its affiliation with the national, surrender its charter, and sell its principal asset, the real property. In 1966, the board of directors entered into a trust agreement with defendant, Cornell University, whereby $115,000, the proceeds of the sale, was transferred to Cornell University to hold as trustee in a scholarship fund provided that if IOTA was reactivated, the balance of the funds in trust would be returned to the sorority. In January 1967, IOTA changed its name to IOTA Alumnae, Inc., plaintiff herein. In January 1980, IOTA was reincorporated for purposes of re-establishing Kappa Alpha Theta at Cornell. Plaintiff argued that the 1966 trust agreement was ***ultra vires*** and hence invalid. The bylaws in 1965 read "the board of directors shall have entire charge and control of the corporation and its affairs, funds and property." Was the action of the board *ultra vires*? [*IOTA Alumnae, Inc. v. Cornell University,* 453 N.Y.S.2d 879 (1982).]

ultra vires
beyond the powers

4. The plaintiff, a prisoner for life, brought this action against the state penal institution seeking an order to allow him to appear in court to sue on several contracts made by him through his attorney while in prison. What result? [*Courtney v. Bishop,* 409 F.2d 1185, cert. denied 396 U.S. 915 (1969).]

5. Husband, owner of a corporation, obtained a $30,000 loan from plaintiff bank to the corporation to finance his business. When the note came due, he sought an extension. The bank determined that neither the corporation nor its owner personally qualified for an extension. Wife of the husband had considerable assets of her own. The bank agreed to an extension on the loan to the corporation if both the husband and wife as sureties guaranteed its payment, which they did. The state in which the transaction took place has a Married Women's Act which protects married women from the improvidence or predatory conduct of their husbands and from the husbands' creditors. Was the guaranty of the corporation debt beyond the wife's capacity to contract? [*National Bank of Rochester v. Meadowbrook Heights, Inc.,* 265 N.W.2d 43 (Mich. 1978).]

6. The plaintiff was refused employment as fruit picker when he could not prove to the owner of a farm that he was an alien *lawfully* in the United States to work as a farm laborer during the harvest season. Is this a violation of a freedom to contract? [*Alonso v. State of California,* 123 Cal.Rptr. 536, cert. denied 425 U.S. 903 (1976).]

7. On August 21, 1981, William Todd Wallace, then sixteen years old, purchased a 1977 Datsun automobile from Whitley's Discount Auto Sales for $3,080. Wallace paid $1,200 in cash from Social Security benefits and financed the remaining $1,880 with a car loan from Richmond County Bank. According to the credit application, Wallace's age was eighteen which was untrue. Whitley's indorsed the credit application. After Wallace and the Datsun had been involved in two car accidents while Wallace was still under eighteen, Wallace returned the Datsun to Whitley's and demanded payment of all monies paid. Can Wallace, through Gillis his **guardian ad litem,** disaffirm the contract and, if so, what money must be returned to Wallace? [*Gillis v. Whitley's Discount Auto Sales, Inc.,* 319 S.E.2d 661 (N.C. 1984).]

guardian ad litem
guardian for the legal action, appointed by a court

Chapter 9: Capacity/Ability to Create a Contract

8. In July the plaintiff, a minor, contracted to buy a 1968 Oldsmobile for $1,250 from the defendant. The plaintiff paid $1,000 to the defendant and the remainder was to be paid at $25 per week. In September, after the plaintiff had paid a total of $1,100, a connecting rod on the car's engine snapped. The plaintiff had the car repaired but never paid the bill. In October, plaintiff disaffirmed the contract on the grounds that plaintiff was a minor. The repair garage repossessed the engine. The car, without engine, sitting in front of the house of the father of the minor, was repeatedly vandalized and became unsalvageable. Plaintiff sued to recover his payments on the car and defendant counterclaimed for the amount still owed on the purchase price. Who wins? [*Halbman, Jr. v. Lemke,* 298 N.W.2d 562 (Wis. 1980).]

9. This action against a mentally incompetent widow, through her guardian, was based upon a contract which she entered into with plaintiff for the conduct of her deceased husband's funeral services. At the time of the contract, the estate of the husband was insolvent, and the funeral director could not observe any mental impairment on the part of the widow. Are funeral services a necessary? What is the measure of recovery if they are found to be necessaries? [*Charles Melbourne & Sons, Inc. v. Jesset,* 163 N.E.2d 773 (Ohio 1960).]

10. In the case of *Gastonia Personnel Corporation v. Rogers,* 172 S.E.2d 19 (N.C. 1970),[2] the court implied that traditional cases of incapacity should be viewed on individual merits. What implications does this have for the law governing one's ability to make a contract?

---

[2] See p. 136.

Public Policy and Contractual Purpose 10

After you have read this chapter, you should be able to:

1. Ascertain that the subject matter reflects a value judgment that the courts should scrutinize contractual purposes for the good of society.
2. Recognize that there are both traditional and nontraditional contractual purposes that do not further the interests of society.
3. Note how the concept of public policy and contractual purpose limits the freedom of individuals to contract.
4. Discuss the most recent development of importance in the area of contractual purpose and public policy, namely, "unconscionability."
5. Recognize that the law of public policy and contractual purpose is evolving to facilitate a broad social objective—greatest good.

Figure 10.1 Contracts—Public Policy Violations

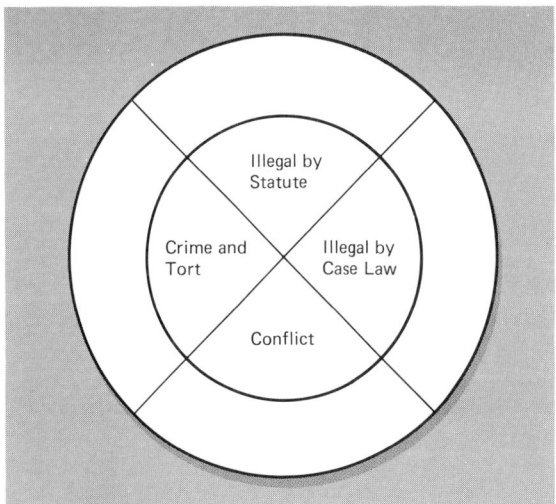

Introduction

In the preceding chapters of this Part we discussed three of the four elements required for a contract: mutual assent, consideration, and capacity to contract. We will now consider the fourth element, legality.

public policy
the concept of law under which the freedom to act is limited for the good of the community

The importance of **public policy** and contractual purpose is evident in that this area of contract law requires that the interests of society or the *community* be *balanced* against the interests of *individuals* in the contractual setting. The end result of this balancing or weighing process directed toward the *greatest good* is that an *agreement* between individuals may be held to be unenforceable *as a contract* because it works against the good of the community. (See figure 10.1)

The study of public policy and contractual purpose reveals a *further restriction upon an individual's freedom to contract.* The rights of a "third party" must be considered—society's rights.

What Is Illegal?

illegal
contrary to law

enforce
to compel performance

It can be said that if a contractual purpose looks to the doing of something which is **illegal**, then that agreement *violates public policy* and will not be **enforced** *as a contract* by the courts. It is a void *agreement;* there is no contract because there is no legal duty to perform a promise.

What is illegal in the contractual setting is a contractual *purpose* which is directed toward the commission of a tort or a crime.

Crime and Tort

crime
an act, committed or omitted, in violation of a public law governing it

tort
a civil (private) noncontractual wrong for which a court will give a remedy

The definition of a **crime** can be found in criminal codes. Generally it is a wrong *against society*. A **tort** is normally defined by the common law—by case decision. Generally it is a *civil* (private), noncontractual wrong *against person or property*. In the following case the court refused to enforce the agreement because it was an agreement to insure against the results of criminal acts.

Facts
In 1977, plaintiff became a member of the United States Taxpayers Union (USTU), defendant. In the "Declaration of Client Membership Agreement," USTU promised that, in the event a client member should be incarcerated for a time, USTU would meet all necessary, personal and family obligations of the member plus all costs incurred in the defense of the member. In 1979, following plaintiff's conviction for violation of the Federal tax laws, plaintiff was incarcerated for a period of four months. USTU failed to fulfill its promises and plaintiff sued for breach of contract.

Decision
Judgment for defendant.

Reasoning
The court noted that generally an agreement which contravenes some recognized public policy is void. USTU's promise amounted to an agreement to insure against the results of criminal acts. Such a bargain contravenes public policy and is unenforceable.

McBrearty v. United States Taxpayers Union, 668 F.2d 450 (1982).

Illegality by Statute

Something declared by **statute** not to be a proper contractual purpose is deemed to be in violation of public policy and *unenforceable.*

statute
law created by a legislative body and approved by the executive

Revenue Versus Regulatory Licenses
If licensing is required by statute *to protect the public,* such as licensing of medical doctors or lawyers to practice a profession or real estate brokers or beauticians to engage in a business, the absence of such a license will cause the objective of the *agreement* to be *violative of public policy,* and the *agreement* will not become a contract. However, if the sole purpose of the license is *to raise revenue* for the state, the agreement is enforceable as a *contract.* Examples are sales licenses to sell merchandise.

In the following case a condominium association was prevented from making real estate contracts because it did not have a broker's license.

Facts
A realtor brought an action to enjoin the defendant, a condominium association—which did not possess a license to act as a real estate broker—from assisting its unit owners in the sale or rental of their units by soliciting prospective purchasers or renters through advertisement and by negotiating such transactions. The defendant association employs at a salary a manager who in part performs the above services. The association receives a commission for these activities. Defendant contends the injunction should not be issued because, since its membership consists solely of unit owners, it is in essence the owner of the property to be sold or leased and thus is not subject to license requirements.

Decision
Injunction issued preventing defendant from continuing to make contracts on behalf of its membership.

Reasoning
The argument of the defendant is without merit and contrary to the public policy behind the statute designed to protect the public from "fraud, incompetence, misrepresentation and sharp or unconscionable practice." The licensing Act is a regulatory measure and any exception must be strictly construed. The law allows real property to be sold only by a licensed broker or salesperson or by the owner. An unlicensed condominium association is none of these and, therefore, cannot sell or lease units for a unit owner.

Zaid v. Island House Condominium Association, 406 A.2d 196 (N.J. 1979).

Sunday Agreements
In certain states, by statute, any attempt to *form a contract* on Sunday is a **nullity.** *Negotiations* of contracts on Sunday are allowed. Exceptions exist in these statutes for contracts directed toward humanitarian purposes, e.g., the sale of a life-saving drug, acts of charity or necessity. Normally, however, these statutes prohibit the formation on Sunday of those *ordinary* contracts that allow one to earn a living. This is an illustration of a state reasonably exercising its police power in order to promote the public comfort, health, safety, morals, and welfare of society.

nullity
of no legal effect

usury
charging a rate of interest on a loan higher than that permitted by statute

legal rate of interest
the maximum rate of interest fixed by statute where no rate of interest is fixed by the contract

Usury Law

Most states have declared by statute a *maximum rate* of interest which it is unlawful to exceed in a contract to lend money. Various penalties exist for violation of this statutory provision, ranging from loss of interest to loss of interest and principal. In some states, corporations can borrow money at any rate of interest. If no rate of interest has been stated in a contract, then the **legal rate of interest** will apply. The declared legal rate of interest by statute may be less than the maximum rate.

Discounting loans, service charges, points, requiring insurance, and other charges must all be taken into account to determine whether the maximum rate has been exceeded. In the following case the court held that usury had occurred.

Facts
The appellant, Strawn Furniture Company, Inc., compounded interest (charged interest on the unpaid interest) by using the following formula: the amount of the indebtedness was multiplied by 10% to obtain the yearly amount of interest; that amount was then divided by 360 and then multiplied by 30 to obtain the amount of unpaid interest for the month which was added to the principal. Each succeeding month the interest was compounded using the same formula. The evidence is uncontradicted that the compounding of interest in this case resulted in an annual percentage rate of 10.76%. The usurious rate of interest in Arkansas is an annual rate of interest above ten percent.

Decision
Affirmed, judgment for appellee, debtor, Austin.

Reasoning
It is well settled that compounding interest will render a contract usurious if it effectively raises the annual rate of interest above 10%.

Strawn Furniture Company, Inc. v. L. K. Austin, 655 S.W.2d 397 (Ark. 1983).

Revolving charge account[1] plans are in the nature of credit sales on a *revolving* basis. In most states, and under the 1974 Uniform Consumer Credit Code,[2] such plans are not considered to involve the lending of money but, rather, the revolving extension of credit over *time* in a sales transaction for a *price*. There is a *difference* between a sale for cash and for credit in the revolving charge account. This concept is called the "time-price differential" theory. Any amount may be charged; it is immaterial whether the enhanced price be ascertained by the simple addition of a lump sum to the cash price, or by a percentage thereon. The transaction is not usurious.

Exceptions. Lending by certain financial institutions such as small loan companies in some states can be at a rate of interest which would exceed the normal maximum rate.

Discrimination

It is interesting that there are statutes which *require* a contracting party *to contract* with another party on a *nondiscriminatory* basis. The primary impact areas are employment, housing, and the service industry, e.g., businesses providing food, drink, lodging. What is violative of public policy in these areas is not in doing something but in *having not done something*. One is required *not* to discriminate on the basis of color, race, national origin, religion, sex, or age. In the following case the court held that the plaintiff was entitled to back pay, interest, and attorney's fees because of the failure of the defendant to enter into a contract of employment with her.

---

[1] " 'Revolving charge account' means an arrangement between a seller and a buyer pursuant to which (1) the seller may permit the buyer to purchase goods or services on credit either from the seller or pursuant to a seller credit card, (2) the unpaid balances of amounts financed arising from purchases and the credit service and other appropriate charges are debited to an account, (3) a credit service charge if made is not precomputed but is computed on the outstanding unpaid balances of the buyer's account from time to time, and (4) the buyer has the privilege of paying the balances in installments." Uniform Consumer Credit Code, sec. 2.108 (1974).

[2] Ibid. sec. 2.201(1).

Facts
A former employee, plaintiff, brought this action against the defendant, her former employer, alleging discrimination against her on the basis of gender in violation of the federal Civil Rights Act of 1964 and the antidiscrimination statutes of Massachusetts. Plaintiff was originally employed as a waitress with the understanding that she had bartending experience and would be interested in applying for any bartending positions which became available. Several times she asked to be promoted to a bartender's position which became available periodically. Despite defendant's knowledge of her desire to be employed as a bartender, her previous work experience in that capacity, and her job seniority, the defendant refused to promote her to the position of bartender trainee and consistently hired males for these positions. Plaintiff seeks damages for failure to employ her as a bartender trainee.

Decision
Judgment for plaintiff for back pay.

Reasoning
The facts of this case show that defendant intentionally discriminated against the plaintiff on the basis of gender (sex). Under the Civil Rights Act of 1964, failure to promote (employ) on the basis of sex discrimination entitles the one discriminated against to attorney's fees, interest on damages award, and back pay, here based on the higher compensation of a bartender trainee.

Thurber v. Jack Reilly's, Inc., 521 F.Supp. 238 (1981).

It may be statutorily unlawful *not* to contract, as is illustrated by the case of *Faraca v. Clements*[3] involving discrimination in which the court held the defendant liable for damages for *refusal to employ* because of the plaintiff's color.

"Contracts" of Chance

What is called a "contract of chance" is really an *agreement* creating a risk of loss rather than the legal shifting of an existing risk of loss from a possible future event (e.g., insurance against loss of property by fire). The parties do not have any legal interest in the subject matter at the time the agreement is made. Gambling or wagering agreements meet the criteria of a contract of chance. Insurance contracts are nothing more than contracts which share *existing* risks. Buying stock, hedging contracts, and transactions in futures are speculative but valid business contracts. In the great majority of states, contracts of chance are against public policy and are *void agreements*. In the following case trading in commodity futures were not wagering agreements and were lawful.

Facts
Appellant is an attorney who invested in commodities futures. Respondent is a futures commission merchant. On September 10, 1980, appellant executed a Risk Disclosure statement, a Customer's Agreement, an Authorization to Transfer Funds, and a Non-Hedge Commodity Accountant Information letter. Respondent opened the account to invest in strategic metals. When appellant discovered he could not presently invest in strategic metals, he chose to trade commodities futures contracts. The trading began in October 1980 and ended in July 1981. On July 22, 1981, the last trading day in contracts for July delivery, appellant held open oats contracts for July delivery. Appellant had either to buy the commodity with $60,000 cash or enter off-the-board transactions at prices above market prices. Appellant liquidated his position resulting in losses of $4,171.50 for which respondent sues as a debt owed to respondent. Appellant contends there was no intent to deliver the oats, thus the agreement was illegal and unenforceable. Judgment was rendered for the respondent and the attorney appealed.

Decision
Affirmed, judgment for respondent.

Reasoning
The court held that trading commodities futures does not constitute gambling. The customer's agreement stated "Orders are to be received and executed with the understanding that actual delivery is contemplated." If appellant subjectively rejected the prospect of delivery, contrary to the written contract, his own uncommunicated intentions cannot render the actions of the respondent unlawful, the court said. An agreement is illegal only if parties intend *at the time of the agreement* that no delivery of the commodity shall be made.

ACLI International Commodity Services, Inc. v. Lindwall, 347 N.W.2d 522 (Minn. 1984).

---
[3] 506 F.2d 956 (1975).

The Uniform Commercial Code

The broad and general concept of *unconscionability,* as it appears in UCC 2–302, has allowed for a *flexible* determination of what contractual purpose is a violation of public policy.

Likewise, in Section 208 of the Restatement (Second) of Contracts the general concept of unconscionability is stated. In both the Restatement and UCC 2–302, provision is made for rendering the agreement void or unenforceable as a contract or for enforcing the remainder of the contract without its unconscionable clauses or terms.

In the following case an **exculpatory clause** in a contract was held to be unconscionable and against public policy and, therefore, void.

exculpatory clause
a clause which relieves one from liability

Facts
This was an action on behalf of the plaintiff, Weaver, to set aside an exculpatory clause in a lease on the ground that the clause was unconscionable. The plaintiff leased a service station from the defendant, American Oil Company. The lease contained a clause relieving the lessor oil company from liability for any and all negligence on its part. The court found it a matter of fact that the clause in question had not been explained to Weaver, who had left high school after 1-1/2 years and had worked in unskilled jobs.

Decision
Judgment for plaintiff.

Reasoning
The court held that the clause in question was violative of public policy and on this basis unenforceable. The court found as a matter of fact that the take-it-or-leave-it basis of the contract and the ignorance of the plaintiff in business matters met the definition of an unconscionable contract.

Weaver v. American Oil Company, 276 N.E.2d 144 (Ind. 1972).

Other Statutes

Under federal legislation, antitrust Acts prohibit contracts which reduce competition, such as contracts in unreasonable restraint of trade.[4] Various consumer protection legislation, such as labeling requirements promulgated by the Federal Trade Commission, make sales of mislabeled products unlawful.

Illegality by Case Law—Reflection of Community Standards

What is *violative of public policy* has also developed by *case law* (common law). Contractual purposes which violate community standards of morals and ethics is a very *flexible concept*. The court will look to the values of the community, and that community may be the nation or it may be the block you live on. There are some well established concepts of what is a violation of public policy in this area.

Restraint of Trade

A *national value judgment* is presumed to exist which suggests that competition is good and that any contract which has the elimination of competition as its purpose is bad. Thus, any contract whose sole purpose is the elimination of competition violates public policy.

If the agreement not to compete exists to protect some other worthwhile purpose, such as the goodwill in the sale of a business, then it is deemed to be *not in violation of public policy* if it is *reasonable for the benefit of the person to be protected.*

Thus, if a business and its goodwill are being sold, whether or not the restraint provision in the contract for sale is in *reasonable* restraint of trade is tested by what is reasonable in time, geographical area, and subject matter *for the benefit and protection of the buyer.* (S sells his drugstore to B, who would not want S to open (1) another competing drugstore (2) across the street (3) within the next six months. A restraint provision to this effect in the contract for sale would be reasonable in (1) subject matter, (2) geographical area, and (3) time.)

---

[4] See chapter 47, Antitrust Law.

If the restraint provision is in an employment contract, it must be reasonable only to the extent of the *protection needed by the person to be benefited*. It must not be unduly harsh and burdensome *on the employee*. In the following case the court held there was no substantial right that could qualify for a restraint of trade.

Facts
The plaintiff employer brought an action to enjoin a former employee, defendant, from competing with it. The parties had entered into a contract which sought to prevent the employee from competing for a five year period following termination of employment. In the course of employment, the defendant was taught how to install vinyl tops and became proficient in that craft. Subsequently, the defendant voluntarily terminated employment and became employed by a competing vinyl top shop. The trial court granted the injunction and defendant appeals.

Decision
Reversed, judgment for defendant.

Reasoning
The court said it would not enforce a negative covenant unless (1) the employer had a protected interest, (2) the restriction was reasonably related to that interest, (3) the restriction was reasonable in time and place, and (4) the restriction imposed no undue hardship. In this case the court concluded that the employer had no protected interest. In order to have such an interest, the employer must possess a substantial right in its business sufficiently unique to warrant the type of protection contemplated by a noncompetition agreement. Here defendant learned no more than the normal skills of the vinyl top installation trade. A simple labor skill, without more, was simply not enough to give an employer a substantial protectable right unique in his business.

DeVoe v. Cheatham, et al., 413 So.2d 1141 (Ala. 1982).

Corruption
Agreements which cause a fiduciary to ignore duties owed to others and agreements that have a tendency to corrupt a public official are against public policy. This judgment seeks to prevent self-dealing on the part of fiduciaries and partiality in treatment by public officials.

Promise Detrimental to Marital Relationship
A promise by a person contemplating marriage or by a married person, other than as part of an enforceable separation agreement, is unenforceable on grounds of public policy if it would change some essential incident of the marital relationship in a way detrimental to the public interest in the marriage relationship. For example, the following agreement is deemed detrimental to the public interest because A may have to be supported by the State should the agreement be enforced. A and B, who are about to marry, make an antenuptial agreement in which A promises to leave their home at any time on notice by B and to make no further claims against B, and B promises thereupon to pay A $100,000. Also, a promise that tends unreasonably to encourage divorce or separation is unenforceable on grounds of public policy. For example, X, who is married to Y, promises to pay Y $50,000 in return for Y's promise to obtain a divorce. Such promises of X and Y will be deemed to encourage divorce and will be unenforceable on grounds of public policy.

Conflict

Areas of **substantive law** usually complement each other. If areas of substantive law were in conflict with each other, the logic of the law would be impaired. It follows, therefore, that *contract law should complement the law of crime and tort.*

substantive law
that part of the law which creates, defines, and regulates rights

Contract Against Liability for Illegality

It would be against public policy to allow a contracting party, by the contract, to relieve himself from liability for the consequences of *criminal* action. However, it is lawful to limit one's liability for *negligent* acts by contract, but not for acts of gross negligence, as illustrated by the following case in which a waiver of liability for *negligence* was upheld but was deemed inadequate as a shield against an action for *gross negligence*.

Facts
On September 9, 1978, Mr. Gillespie, plaintiff, and a friend went to Westboro Speedway to race the friend's midget racing car. In order to gain access to the track area, Mr. Gillespie signed a form purporting to release certain parties, defendants, from any injuries he sustained while at the track. While driving around the track the car spun out on a curve, flipped over, and came to rest upside down upon one of the vertical posts. As a result of that accident, Mr. Gillespie was rendered a permanent quadriplegic. Plaintiff sues for damages and defendant offers the release in defense.

Decision
Judgment for plaintiff.

Reasoning
The court granted summary judgment for some of the defendants on the issue of ordinary negligence. Under pertinent state law, the release executed by the plaintiff was sufficient to prevent any suit for ordinary negligence. However, this court ruled that such a release was inadequate to shield against an action for gross negligence. Accordingly, the court permitted the plaintiff to amend his complaint to allege gross negligence.

Gillespie v. Papale, 541 F.Supp. 1042 (1982).

Exculpatory clauses, like the one illustrated in the *Gillespie* case, generally are not enforced in contracts when a party to the contract has imposed the clause because of a superior bargaining position or where a public service or a specific legal duty is the subject matter of the contract.

Legality of Purpose

The *law* always *presumes* that parties to a contract intend a *lawful result*. If the purpose of the contract can be interpreted either as lawful or unlawful, the lawful result will be preferred. If the contractual purpose is unlawful (e.g., violative of public policy), the general rule is that the court will leave the parties where it finds them. The court will not lend its aid to enforce the agreement.

Divisible Contract. A contract can consist of more than one promise or more than one act. If the contractual promises and/or acts can be *divided* into lawful contractual purposes and unlawful contractual purposes without destroying the substance of the agreement, the lawful contractual purposes will be enforced.

Exceptions

There are certain exceptions to the general principle that the court will not aid the parties to an illegal agreement and will leave them where the court finds them. A party to an *illegal* agreement may enforce it if the person is one of the class of individuals *for whose protection the agreement was made illegal.* For example, a bank can enforce an agreement for an investment made illegal by banking regulation in order to protect a depositor's assets. Additionally, a party who *withdraws* from an illegal agreement before its purpose is carried out is entitled to return of the consideration given by him or her for the agreement. A party who was misled or pressured into an illegal agreement may rescind it. Normally, parties in **pari delicto** will not be aided, and, while ignorance of law is generally no excuse, a party who is ignorant of facts making a bargain illegal will be given relief as justice (equity) requires relief to be given. For instance, an innocent party agreeing to take part in what would be a bigamous marriage will be able to sue the party with guilty knowledge for breach of contract based upon mutual promises to marry. In the following case the court reformed a note to reflect a lawful rate of interest because justice and equity required it.

pari delicto
equal in legal fault or guilt

Facts
Plaintiff borrowers brought an action requesting that a judge declare void a loan which they had obtained from defendant lenders. The defendants extended the loan at a rate of interest which turned out to be usurious. Before the loan was advanced, defendants were advised in writing by a Massachusetts attorney that the mortgage note and the mortgage to secure it were not in violation of Massachusetts' usury statutes. The judge declined to void the loan and entered a judgment reforming the mortgage note by reducing the stated interest rate to the maximum permissible limit. The plaintiff argues that the loan was void and that the judge was powerless to reform the mortgage note.

Decision
Judgment for defendant.

Reasoning
Reformation is available to parties where there has been mutual mistake which is material to an instrument and where no rights of third parties are affected. It is of no critical importance whether the mutual mistake is one of fact or law; it is sufficient that it is material and that it is of a type which can be remedied in equity. In this case, the parties freely entered into the transaction at arms length in the mistaken belief that the interest rate provided in the note was proper and legal and, under these circumstances, the judge is allowed to exercise discretion in granting relief.

Beach Associates, Inc. v. Fauser et al., 401 N.E.2d 858 (Mass. 1980).

Summary Statement

1. The rights of society, as they are impacted by a contract, are given due consideration by the law.
2. There are three aspects of identified contractual purposes that work against the greatest good—namely, torts and crimes, those declared so by statutes, and those deemed unconscionable at common law by case decision.
3. The traditional areas that have been identified as having contractual purposes which violate public policy are licensing, Sunday agreements, usury, contracts of chance, unreasonable restraint of trade, corruption, and conflict.
4. Nontraditional areas having contractual purposes violative of public policy which are growing in importance are governmental regulation, discrimination, and unconscionability.
5. Exceptions exist to defined areas of public policy violations such as in lending institutions and usury, speculative business contracts, and exculpatory clauses.
6. Exceptions exist to the normal result that the court leaves the parties in "illegal" agreement where it finds them. This occurs when the one who seeks to enforce it was the one to be protected or when one withdraws or when one was "forced" into the agreement.
7. The end of what is necessary to protect society is not yet in sight.

The following case, *although overruled by the U.S. Supreme Court subsequently in another case,* is included in depth as an illustration of how the interests of society, here represented by a child's welfare, can restrict the ability of individuals to contract.

In re Adoption of Brousal
66 Misc.2d 711 (N.Y. 1971)

Sobel, Surrogate. The husband of the natural mother seeks to adopt her son, James, born out of wedlock. The birth certificate bore the surname of the child's natural father. There is no issue as to paternity.

Despite the fact that neither notice of nor consent to the adoption was required of the father of a child born out of wedlock, the natural father was joined in the action for adoption.

He appeared and filed an answer. He set up a written contract entered into between the natural mother and himself. Under the contract the father has been paying for the support of the child until the commencement of this adoption proceeding. In more pertinent part the contract provides: "The partial relinquishment of the custody by the father to the mother, as in this paragraph provided, shall not be construed to be a consent on the part of the father to the adoption of the child by another person."

In their submission of the issue to the court, the parties treat this provision as an agreement by the mother that the child will not be offered for adoption. On its face, the court said it is nothing of the kind. It is merely a declaration that the agreement shall not be considered as a consent to such an adoption.

No "consent" is required of the father of a child born out of wedlock. The statute is explicit. It states that only the consent of the mother of a child born out of wedlock is required. The natural father simply has no standing before the court to object to the adoption by the husband of the natural mother.[5]

Even if this were, however, a contract not to offer the child for adoption, it would be against public policy.

The welfare of a child simply cannot be the subject of barter. Adoption is a status created by statute. The statutes vest in courts the determination of the child's welfare. The rights of unoffending natural parents must of course be considered and their wishes will rarely be disregarded. However, even natural married parents may not contract between themselves or with others concerning the welfare of the child. A court, and a court alone, must make each and every determination affecting the child's status.

As noted, the statutes give the father of a child born out of wedlock no rights in such determination. This has always been so. It represents a legislative determination that only by marriage to the mother may the father attain status.

The answer to the petition for adoption is stricken. The adoption by the husband of the natural mother of the child is approved.

Questions and Case Problems

1. Plaintiff sued the estate of deceased for unpaid salary and other compensation for personal services rendered the deceased for two years prior to his death. Plaintiff had left her husband to live with the deceased, a married man. Deceased's gross estate was valued at over several hundred thousand dollars and plaintiff seeks $29,200. Plaintiff rendered housekeeping, farming, and nursing services to the deceased. Plaintiff also engaged in an adulterous relationship with the deceased. Can she recover for her services? [Matter of *Estate of Steffes,* 290 N.W.2d 697 (Wis. 1980).]

2. Baron & Company, Inc. entered into an agreement with a Corporation whose assets were placed in a trust administered by The Bank of New Jersey as a liquidating trustee. The agreement provided that Baron would attempt to secure a ready, willing, and able buyer for real property owned by the Corporation for a finder's fee. Baron found a qualified buyer and claims its finder's fee. Defendant, The Bank of New Jersey, claims that Baron is not entitled to a finder's fee because Baron was not licensed as a broker in New Jersey where the real property is located. Baron claims that it is still entitled to a finder's fee because it used a broker licensed in New Jersey as an independent consultant. Is Baron & Company, Inc. entitled to a finder's fee? [*Baron & Company, Inc. v. The Bank of New Jersey,* 504 F.Supp. 1199 (1981).]

---

[5] See *Caban v. Mohammed,* et ux. 441 U.S. 380 (1979) in which the U.S. Supreme Court, by a five to four decision, held that the Equal Protection Clause of the Fourteenth Amendment to the U.S. Constitution was violated by the sex-based distinction between unmarried mothers and unmarried fathers in the New York Domestic Relations Law provision. The provision permits an unwed mother but not an unwed father to block the adoption of their child simply by withholding consent. Since such distinction bears no substantial relation to any important state interest, that provision in the New York Law was held unconstitutional and void, thereby in effect reversing the decision in the *Brousal* case, which is here to show the impact of conflicting societal interests on freedom to contract.

3. Defendant, Jim Edgar, Secretary of State, appeals from a judgment of a circuit court which held the following state statute unconstitutional:

   "No person . . . may keep open, operate or assist in keeping open or operating any established place of business for the purpose of buying, selling, bartering or exchanging, or offering for sale, barter or exchange, any motor vehicle, whether new or used, on the First day of the week, commonly called Sunday. . . ."

   Plaintiffs, Fireside Chrysler-Plymouth Mazda, contend the statute denies them equal protection of the law in violation of the Fourteenth Amendment of the Constitution of the United States. They argue there is no reasonable basis to single out auto dealers for a Sunday closing law. Defendant argues that the law does not create an unreasonable classification and the law is a reasonable restriction in a compendium of rules which specifically governs a class licensee to engage in the sale of automobiles. Who should prevail? [*Fireside Chrysler-Plymouth Mazda, Inc. v. Edgar, Secretary of State*, 464 N.E.2d 275 (Ill. 1984).]

4. Defendant made a loan commitment to plaintiff to loan plaintiff $400,000 for one year, at 9% interest with a 1% point or "service fee." The $4,000 service fee was shown on a closing statement as a "discount." The $4,000 service fee was deducted in full from the loan proceeds. During the year plaintiff was charged and paid $36,347.78 in interest. Plaintiff therefore paid more than $40,000 or 10% of his $400,000 loan. By statute, the maximum rate of interest that could be charged was 10%. Was the loan usurious? [*Abramowitz v. Barnett Bank of West Orlando*, 394 So.2d 1033 (Fla. 1981).]

5. Plaintiff filed a suit against defendant for failure to make required payments as provided in a retail installment contract. Defendant counterclaimed alleging a usurious rate of interest in the contract. The subject matter of the contract was a mobile home. The contract provided for a cash price of $15,000 or a deferred payment price of $24,225.12. Defendant bought the mobile home for the deferred payment price and the seller sold the contract to the plaintiff. Is the contract usurious? [*First National Bank of Ottawa v. Larkins*, 444 N.E.2d 818 (Ill. 1983).]

6. An insurance company brought an action for an injunction against its former employee alleging that the employee breached the employment contract by engaging in the insurance business in the same area as the employer within ten years after termination of employment. Defendant had agreed at the outset of employment not to compete for the ten year period. Should the injunction be issued? [*1st American Systems, Inc. v. Rezatto*, 311 N.W.2d 51 (S.D. 1981).]

7. The plaintiffs, directing and managing officers of a corporation, brought this action for an alleged breach of contract by the defendant. The plaintiffs had a contract with the defendant which provided for the exchange of stock in the plaintiffs' corporation for the stock in the defendant's corporation; for the plaintiffs' promise to continue as management; and for a loan by the defendant to the plaintiffs so they could buy out the other shareholders of the plaintiffs' corporation. Said shareholders were not given notice by the officers that negotiations for resale to third parties were in progress. These acts and promises were not carried out by the defendant. Will the plaintiffs succeed in their suit? [*Childs v. RIC Group, Inc.*, 331 F.Supp. 1078 (1970), aff'd 447 F.2d 1407 (1970).]

8. Burne, as beneficiary under an insurance policy, sued for double indemnity accidental death benefits because of the death of the **insured.** The insured had been struck by an automobile and was kept alive in a vegetative state for four and a half years before he died. The policy provided that the accidental death benefits would be paid only if death occurred within ninety days of the accident, and that such benefits would not be paid if death occurred during a time when premiums were being waived due to the insured's disability. Will the beneficiary be allowed to recover the insurance? [*Burne v. Franklin Life Ins. Co.*, 301 A.2d 799 (Pa. 1973).]

insured
the person whose risk has been assumed by another

escrow.
the conditional delivery of property to a person who is to deal with it on the occurrence of specified conditions

9. In 1979, the Arizona Department of Transportation gave notice that it would sell a parcel of property at public auction. The notice stated that the successful bidder would be required to pay $500 as an initial deposit and also pay 20% of the purchase price as a down payment before the close of **escrow.** The notice further stated that the buyer would have thirty days from notice of approval of sale to close escrow. Defendant was the successful bidder at public auction and subsequently received 120 days extension to close the escrow from plaintiff bank who was the escrow agent in return for a $15,000 earnest money deposit. This deposit was returned by plaintiff to defendant because of a dispute by the defendant with the Department, and when the defendant did not close the transaction, plaintiff paid the $15,000 to the Arizona Department of Transportation as earnest money forfeited for breach of contract, and by this suit plaintiff seeks to recover the $15,000 from the defendant. Plaintiff's agreement with defendant for the 120 day extension was in violation of Arizona's competitive bidding statutes. The trial court found in favor of the defendant. Plaintiff appeals. Should plaintiff be allowed to recover the $15,000? [*Chicago Title Insurance Co. v. Renaissance Homes, Ltd.*, 679 P.2d 517 (Ariz. 1983).]

10. Discuss the merits and demerits of the legal system acting as the final judge on what is for the greatest good of society in the contractual setting. Consider the implications of the statement in In re *Adoption of Brousal,* 66 Misc.2d 711 (N.Y. 1971):[6] "However, even natural married parents may not contract between themselves or with others concerning the welfare of the child. *A court, and a court alone, must make each and every determination affecting the child's status.*" (See footnote 5.) What do you think of the Supreme Court's decision that preventing sex discrimination is more important than promoting the best interests of a child through adoption, recognizing that today, as a result of this decision, the natural father could have prevented the adoption by withholding consent rather than seeking enforcement of the contract?

---

[6] See pp. 147–48.

Contractual Form
Requirement of a Writing for Enforceability, Statute of Frauds

After you have read this chapter, you should be able to:

1. Recognize that the law tries to assure itself that it is not being misled when it enforces a contract.
2. Understand that the law has developed many exceptions to the rule that certain contracts must be in writing or that there must be a written memorandum of an oral contract in order for the contract to be enforced.
3. Note how the concept of contractual form limits the freedom of individuals to contract.
4. Appreciate the interrelationships among the statute of frauds, the parol evidence rule, and rules of interpretation.
5. Discuss how the evolution of the law associated with the concept of the statute of frauds may be leading to a substantial limitation in its application.

In the preceding chapters of this Part we discussed the four elements required for a contract: mutual assent, consideration, capacity to contract, and legality. In order to prevent fraud by persons who assert that certain contracts were made when, in fact, they were not made, certain contracts must be proved by a proper writing before the courts will recognize and enforce them. Accordingly, we will now consider the contractual form and proof necessary for the enforcement of certain contracts.

Jim claims that he had a contract with Mary, who denies this. Was there a contract, and if so what were its terms? Would this kind of problem be solved if the law required that, for the purpose of proving a contract and its terms, *all* contracts must be in writing or that there be a written memorandum of an oral contract? Obviously it would be very inconvenient, and all transactions would be much slowed down if such a writing were required for *all* contracts. Also, the opportunity to escape from being bound by a contract that had been made is present by showing that there is no writing. Or should only selected kinds of contract be required to be proved by a writing?

The Statute of Frauds

statute of frauds
a statute requiring that certain kinds of contract be proved only by a proper writing

enforceable contract
a contract which can be proved and enforced by the courts

Any statutory provision in the law which requires that a contract be *proved only by a proper writing* is called a **statute of frauds**. Its purpose is to prevent fraud by perjured testimony in proving the *existence* of a contract. The statute applies only to certain selected kinds of alleged contract which, over many years, have been the subject of much fraud in proving their existence.

Compliance with the statute's requirement of proof by a writing is necessary for a contract to be *enforced*. Failure to comply with the statute does *not* affect a contract's validity, only its **enforceability.** The courts will not *enforce* the contract if it cannot be proved by a proper writing.

Often when a contract does exist but cannot be proved because a required writing does not exist, fraud has been perpetrated upon a contracting party and fraud has not been prevented. Therefore, to be safe, one is well advised to have all contracts in writing, to the extent possible, and not be caught in the pitfall of the statute of frauds requirements.

While there are contracts for which there must be a writing to be proved, numerous exceptions exist that allow many of these *kinds* of contract to be proved orally. Even if the writing does not exist to support these contracts, the party who cannot enforce the contract is not always without a remedy.

If the *subject matter* of a contract does *not* fall within the statute of frauds, the contract can be proved orally. Such oral proof of a contract must be sufficiently definite that a court can ascertain that the elements necessary for the formation of a contract are present.

There is a distinction between a contract to *sell land,* and a collateral (additional) contract which *refers* to the sales contract. The first contract is within the statute of frauds and must be proved by a writing to be enforceable. The second contract is not within the statute of frauds and need not be proved by a writing to be enforceable. In the following case note how the court sought to achieve justice by treating the case as one of tort for **fraud** rather than as a contract case.

fraud
(in contracts) a misrepresentation of fact, known to be false, intentionally made to induce another person to make or to refrain from making a contract, and reasonably relied on by the other person

Facts

Kett, plaintiffs, purchasers of real property, brought this action against the sellers, defendants, on an oral promise allegedly made by the sellers, collateral to the sales contract, to make certain specific repairs to the real property sold. Kett alleged they were induced to buy the home when the sellers orally agreed to repair a leaky shower, splits in the cement driveway, split bricks in the fireplace, and split kitchen walls. The defendants raised the statute of frauds as a defense, contending that the alleged collateral oral promise was under that part of the statute of frauds concerning the sale of real property and, therefore, was unenforceable because the alleged oral promise could not be proved by a proper writing. The defendants referred to a deposit receipt, signed by the sellers, which stated "This [sales] agreement contains the entire agreement and all representations not herein set forth are deemed waived." In the lower court, the defendants' motion for summary judgment was granted, and the plaintiffs appealed.

Decision
Reversed, for the plaintiffs, and sent back to the lower court for trial.

Reasoning
The court reasoned that the written sales contract was the final expression of the parties and the alleged oral collateral promise was not a part of it. However, this is not an action to enforce a contract for the sale of real property and, therefore, the statute of frauds does not apply. Nor is this an action for damages for breach of the sales contract. The property has been sold and paid for. This is an action in tort for fraud by the alleged sellers' collateral oral promise made to induce Kett to buy, and made without any intention to perform—a promissory fraud.

Kett v. Graeser, 50 Cal.Rptr. 727 (1966).

Contracts Within the Statute

Traditionally, and *under the law of contracts,* the following kinds of contract cannot be proved unless there is a proper writing: (1) contracts which cannot be performed within one year; (2) contracts concerning the sale of real property; (3) a promise given in consideration of marriage but not between the parties to be married; (4) a promise to answer for the duty (debt, default, or miscarriage); (5) a promise by an **executor** or **administrator** to answer personally for the debt of a **decedent's** estate; and *now, under the Uniform Commercial Code,* (6) a contract for the *sale of goods for $500 or more.*[1]

One Year Plus

For a *bilateral* contract that will require more than one year to perform from the date of its *formation,* there must be a writing for the contract to be enforceable. When computing time, the day upon which the contract is *formed* is not counted. Thus, a contract made on the first day of the month to start on the third day of the month and to run for one year would require a writing to render it enforceable. The contract runs for one year and one day. The extra day is the second day of the month. A writing will not be required when it is *possible* that the consideration promised can be given within one year. A promise to work for one's lifetime is capable of performance in one year because one might die within a year.

If the contract is *unilateral* and the act *has been performed,* though the promise for the act will take more than one year to perform, no writing will be required to prove its existence. In the following case the oral contract was provable because the defendant was unable to show that the promise could not be performed within one year.

executor (executrix)
a court-appointed man (woman) designated in a decedent's will as the decedent's personal representative

administrator (administratrix)
a court-appointed man (woman) as an intestate's personal representative

decedent
one who is dead

Facts
The plaintiff orally contracted with the defendant to level *four thousand* acres of the defendant's land. The defendant never paid the plaintiff for the performed work and the plaintiff brought an action for breach of contract. The defendant contended that because the plaintiff had estimated that it would take a year to level *two thousand* acres, the project to level four thousand acres could not be completed within one year. The defendant therefore argued that the Statute of Frauds applied making the oral contract unenforceable.

Decision
Judgment for plaintiff.

Reasoning
The court rejected this argument noting that it was not established that performance could not possibly have been completed within one year; thus, the contract did not fall within the Statute of Frauds.

Augusta Bank & Trust v. Broomfield, 643 P.2d 100 (Kan. 1982).

---

[1] UCC 2–201. Other Code sections requiring a writing are UCC 8–319, sale of securities; 9–203 (1)(a), security agreement; and 1–206, sale of other personal property.

Real Property

A writing is needed to prove a contract which concerns itself with the *sale of land* or of an *interest in land*. A lease of land, **easement,** and real property mortgage are illustrations of interests in land. However, by statute, often leases for not more than one year are not included within the statute and are enforceable without a writing.

Contractual purposes which touch, or are collateral to, an interest in land need not be in writing to be enforced. Thus, a commission agreement with a broker who is to produce a purchaser of real property (absent a statutory requirement for a writing), or a contract to paint or repair a house on land, touch an interest in land but are not concerned with the *sale* of an *interest in land* and, therefore, *need not be in writing to be enforceable*.[2]

However, if there is an oral contract for the sale of land and the seller *conveys the title to the land to the buyer,* who is to pay the purchase price to the seller later, the contract is no longer within the statute of frauds. The reason is that the purpose for protecting the seller against a fraudulent charge that he made a contract is no longer applicable since the seller has conveyed the title to the buyer. Therefore, the seller can enforce the oral contract against the buyer for the purchase price without proof by any writing.

Also, while there is a difference of view, in many states if the seller *delivers possession* to the buyer and the buyer either makes payment or, with the seller's consent, makes substantial improvements on the land, the contract is no longer within the statute of frauds.

easement
irrevocable right to the limited use of another's land

Marriage

The exchange of promises to marry are enforceable and can be proved without a writing. However, a writing is required to prove a promise containing additional consideration other than to marry. For example, A orally promises B, a divorcee, to pay for the education of B's son if B will marry A, which B then does. A's oral promise is unenforceable.

Debt, Default, and Miscarriage

A promise to answer for (be responsible for) the duty (debt, **default,** or miscarriage) *of another* is unenforceable unless proved by a writing. S orally promises C that, if C will extend credit to D and if D does not pay, then S will pay C. Or X orally promises Y that, if Z does not build the building pursuant to his contract with Y, then X will be liable for Z's default in not performing his contract. In both of these examples the promises of S and X must be proved by a writing for them to be enforceable.

However, for a promise to come within this part of the statute of frauds, *all* of the following three things must occur.

default
a failure to perform a legal duty

1. The promise must be made to the obligee, the person to whom the obligation is owing. Thus, C and Y are the obligees—C the creditor, and Y the person for whom the building was to be built. If S had made the promise to D, or X had made the promise to Z, their promises would *not* be made to the obligees and would *not* be within the statute and, therefore, would be enforceable without a writing. (See figure 11.1.)
2. The promise must not *assume* the obligation of performance but, rather, must be to perform if *another* did not perform. Thus, S and X promised to perform if D and Z did not perform. If, instead, S had promised to be liable with D as a co-debtor, or X had promised to build the building with Z, the promises of S and X would *not* be to answer for the debt or default *of another* (D and Z), and their promises would *not* be within the statute. They would have *assumed* the obligations, and their promises would be enforceable without a writing. (See figure 11.2.)

---

[2] For more detail on what is an interest in land, see pp. 765–68.

Figure 11.1 Promises within and without the Statute of Frauds (the promise must be made *to the obligee*)

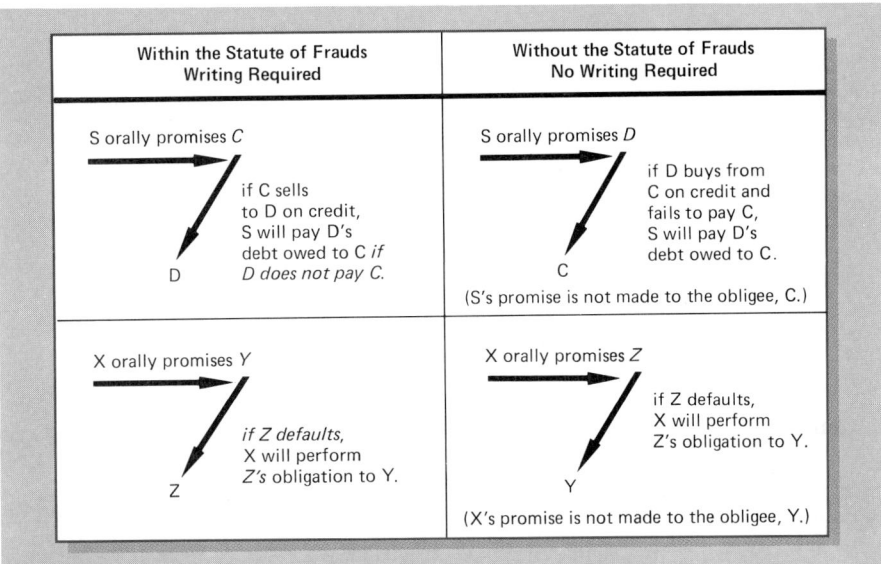

Figure 11.2 Promises within and without the Statute of Frauds (the promise must *not be to assume* another's obligation of performance)

3. The promise must be made *primarily* for the *benefit of another,* namely the obligor, and not for the promisor. Thus, if S's promise was made primarily so that D could buy goods from C and supply them to S, or if X's promise was made primarily so that X could lease and occupy the building from Y, the promises of S and X would *not* be *primarily for the benefit of D and Z,* and their promises would *not* be within the statute. They would be enforceable without a writing. This is illustrated by the following case.

Facts
From February 19, 1974 through June 13, 1974, plaintiff delivered gravel to defendant's construction site. Defendant's subcontractor had run up a bill with plaintiff for $13,332.60. At this point, plaintiff stopped delivering gravel. A responsible officer of defendant told plaintiff orally to continue delivering gravel to the construction site and they would pay the $13,332.60 owed by the subcontractor. Evidence during trial showed (1) defendant needed plaintiff's gravel badly (2) plaintiff's gravel was the right grade for the job (3) the job was behind schedule when the promise was made. Defendant seeks a directed verdict.

Decision
Judgment for plaintiff.

Reasoning
To the extent defendant's promise was an undertaking to pay the debt of another it was, unless committed to writing, unenforceable under the Statute of Frauds. If, however, defendant's undertaking fell into a class of cases in which the essence of the transaction is to obtain some benefit for the promisor from the promisee, the Statute of Frauds would not apply. A contract that all or part of a duty of a third person to the promisee shall be satisfied is not within the Statute of Frauds as a promise to answer for the duty of another if the consideration for the promise is in fact, or apparently desired by the promisee, mainly for the promisor's own economic advantage, rather than in order to benefit the third person. The directed verdict is denied and the question of fact should go to the jury.

Barboza, et al. *v. Liberty Contractors Co., Inc.,* 469 N.E.2d 1303 (Mass. 1984).

By "miscarriage" is meant misdoing, a miscarriage of justice. An example is a bonding or insurance company promising to an employer that, if an employee cashier embezzles the employer's money, the company will pay the employer its loss. There must be a writing to prove the company's promise.

Decedent's Estate
A special application of answering for the duty (debt, default, or miscarriage) of another is recognized—namely, for the obligations of a deceased person. The process of winding up the affairs of a decedent are normally handled by an executor or an administrator, who pays the decedent's debts out of the money in the decedent's estate. If this personal representative promises to become personally responsible for a debt of the decedent's estate, there must be a writing proving the promise.

Effect of the Parol Evidence Rule
Common Law. Under the common law, when there *is a written contract,* it cannot be *contradicted* (added to or varied) by any prior or contemporaneous oral (**parol**) agreement or by a prior written agreement. This is called the **parol evidence rule.** All the terms and conditions should have been included in (integrated into) the writing.

The parol evidence rule should not be confused with the statute of frauds, just discussed. Each has a different purpose. The statute of frauds is concerned with requiring *written proof that a contract exists.* The parol evidence rule is concerned with preventing contradiction of a written contract which *has been already proven to exist.*

---

parol
oral

parol evidence rule
a rule of law which provides that, when there is a written contract, it cannot be *contradicted* (added to or varied) by any prior or contemporaneous oral agreement, or by a prior written agreement

However, there are exceptions when certain *oral evidence* can be introduced in a legal action seeking to enforce a written contract. Under the common law, oral evidence could be introduced to prove the nonexistence of a contract. This is done most often by proving the *absence* of one of the elements necessary to the formation of a contract—namely, *genuineness of assent*.[3] Oral evidence can also be introduced (1) to show that the written contract *violates public policy*;[4] (2) to show that a condition which was to occur before the contract was to be enforced failed to happen; (3) to show that the contract is voidable; (4) to show that the contract was discharged by a subsequent oral or written agreement; and (5) to show the meaning of ambiguous language in a contract or to fill in obvious gaps in an *incomplete* written contract.

In the following case the court permitted oral proof of fraud even though a written contract existed that stated (an integration clause) it contained the entire agreement.

Facts
The plaintiff purchased a building and subsequently brought suit against the defendant seller to recover some $80,000 spent repairing the floor of the building. Plaintiff made known to defendant a particular need for the floor of the building to be able to bear a loading capacity of at least 750 pounds per square foot. Defendant orally stated that the floor would meet plaintiff's needs. A written contract was signed by plaintiff and defendant which contained the following language: "This agreement contains the whole agreement between the Seller and Buyer and there are no other terms, obligations, covenants, representations, statements or conditions, oral or otherwise, of any kind whatsoever." Subsequently plaintiff found the floor unfit for its purposes and alleged fraud in the inducement in the making of the contract in its suit to recover the cost of repairs. Defendant objects to oral evidence being introduced with regard to its statement to plaintiff in the face of the written contract.

Decision
Evidence of fraud in the inducement is outside the parol evidence rule and, therefore, admissible.

Reasoning
It is always competent to aver and prove that an engagement in writing was induced by fraudulent oral representations of material facts that affect the consideration. The purpose in such case is not to alter or vary the terms of the writing by parol evidence but to strike the writing down, just as though it had never been in existence, or to strike down such part of it as is dependent on the fraud, if the balance of the contract can be sustained as enforceable. To give effect to an integration clause permits language to shield a party from the consequences of fraud, contrary to public policy.

Betz Laboratories, Inc. v. Hines, 647 F.2d 402 (1981).

course of dealing
"a sequence of previous conduct between the parties to a particular transaction which is fairly to be regarded as establishing a common basis of understanding for interpreting their expressions and other conduct" (UCC 1–205(1))

usage of trade
"any practice or method of dealing having such regularity of observance in a place, vocation, or trade as to justify an expectation that it will be observed with respect to the transaction in question" (UCC 1–205(2))

The Uniform Commercial Code. UCC 2–202 broadens the traditional parol evidence rule by permitting the introduction of **course of dealing** and **usage of trade** orally to *explain* terms in a written contract where the subject matter is goods. A course of dealing is a sequence of previous conduct between parties to an agreement which is fairly to be regarded as establishing a common basis of understanding for interpreting their expressions. Usage of trade is a usage having such regularity of observance in a place, vocation, or trade as to justify an expectation that it will be observed with respect to a particular agreement. Additional terms can be introduced orally despite the writing when the court is not convinced that the writing was intended to be the *complete* and *exclusive* agreement of the parties to the contract.

---

[3] See chapter 7, Relief from Contractual Obligations.

[4] *Ibid.*

The Required Writing

The best writing to prove a contract is the *written contract!* However, if the contract is oral, what kind of a writing or written memorandum of the oral contract will be sufficient to prove the oral contract?

The Common Law of Contracts

A writing which will satisfy the requirements of the statute of frauds can be in *any form* (need not be labeled a "contract"). It can be pieced together if one document *refers* to another (e.g., one letter refers to another letter). To be complete, however, the memorandum of an *oral contract* must (1) identify the parties to the contract and their relationship (e.g., seller and buyer); (2) identify the subject matter of the contract; (3) indicate that a contract was made; and (4) state all the terms and conditions of each promise and to whom made (e.g., price and credit terms). The writing must be signed by the party charged with having made the contract—namely, the party *against whom* the enforcement of the contract is sought. For example, if A orally contracts with B and A wishes to enforce the contract against B, A must prove that a memorandum was signed by B or by B's lawfully authorized agent. B is the party charged by A with having made the contract. In the following case an advertisement failed as a writing because it lacked an essential term.

Facts
Plaintiff, a former employee of a municipality, defendant, brought this action against the municipality to recover damages for breach of an oral contract of employment. The employee had been employed for a little over five months when the employment was terminated despite the employee's insistence that the employment period was to be for 18 months. The employee had learned of the position through a newspaper advertisement placed by the municipality. The advertisement did not mention the salary to be paid the person hired. No formal written employment contract was entered into by the parties. The municipality asserted that the employment contract, to be performed in 18 months, and not being in writing, was within the Statute of Frauds and thus unenforceable.

Decision
Judgment for defendant.

Reasoning
Since the alleged contract by its terms was not to be performed within one year from the making thereof, it was subject to the Statute of Frauds and would be unenforceable unless some sufficient memorandum existed to prove it. A classified advertisement published in the McCook Daily Gazette not containing the essential term of salary is not a sufficient memorandum.

McBride v. City of McCook, 321 N.W.2d 905 (Neb. 1982).

The Uniform Commercial Code

Under UCC 2–201, a writing is necessary to prove a contract for the sale of goods for $500 or more. However, such a writing is not required if: (1) *part payment* for or *part delivery* of the goods has been accepted; (2) the goods are to be specially manufactured for the buyer, are not suitable for sale to others in the ordinary course of the seller's business, and the seller has either substantially begun their manufacture or made commitments to procure them; or (3) the oral contract has been *admitted in court proceedings.*[5] Under (1) and (3) above, the contract is enforceable without a writing only to the extent of goods for such part payment or goods delivered, and to the extent of such court admission. In the following case the question was whether part payment by the buyer of goods had been made causing the oral contract for sale to be enforceable.

---

[5] For a more detailed discussion of these exceptions, see pp. 245–46.

Facts

Plaintiff, an automobile enthusiast, orally contracted with defendant, automobile retailer, for a specific optioned Corvette to be manufactured by Chevrolet in limited quantities to commemorate the selection of Corvette as the Indianapolis 500 Pace Car. Plaintiff made a $500 deposit with defendants for purchase of the car. Defendants refused to deliver the car to plaintiff and offered plaintiff a chance to bid on it. Plaintiff filed this suit for **specific performance.**

Decision

Judgment for plaintiff.

Reasoning

Some courts take the position that under the 'Code' part payment takes the case out of the Statute of Frauds only to the extent for which payment has been made, thereby denying enforcement of an oral contract where in the case of a single object the payment made is less than the full amount. This court does not. This court holds that where, as here, there is no dispute as to quantity, part payment for a single indivisible commercial unit validates an oral contract. The purpose of the Statute of Frauds is to prevent the enforcement of alleged promises that were never made; it is not and never has been to justify contractors in repudiating promises that were in fact made. Enforcement of the oral contract here carries out the purpose of the Statute of Frauds.

Sedmak III v. Charlie's Chevrolet, Inc., 622 S.W.2d 694 (Mo. 1981).

specific performance
the exact performance of a contract by a party as ordered by a court

All that the writing needs are: (1) an overall expression of an intent to contract; (2) the statement of some quantity of goods; and (3) the signature of the party (or his agent) against whom the contract is to be enforced. Any symbol may be used or adopted by a party as a signature if done with the intention of authenticating the writing. However, *as between merchants,* if a *merchant* does not object *seasonably* (within ten days) to a sufficient writing from the other merchant after receipt, he will be deemed to have authenticated it as his own, causing the contract to be proved and enforceable against him. In the following case all three of these items were present, and the court held that the plaintiff's letter was sufficient to comply with the Code's requirement of a proper writing.

Facts

Defendant buyer, Fortune Furn. Mfg. Co., and plaintiff seller, Mid-South Plastic Fab. Co., agreed orally, respectively, to purchase and to supply plastic products. The president of Fortune told the sales representative of Mid-South to send him a letter containing the terms of the oral contract. The following letter was sent: "Mr. Sidney Widcock, President, Fortune Furn. Mfg. Co., Inc., Okolona, Mississippi 38860, Dear Sid: This is to confirm the agreement entered into this date between Phil on behalf of Mid-South Plastic Co., Inc. and you on behalf of Fortune Furn. Mfg. Co., Inc. We agree to maintain expanded and 21-ounce plastic in the warehouse of Mid-South Furniture Suppliers, Inc. in sufficient amounts to supply all the plastics for your plant's use, and if for any reason we do not have the necessary plastic you will be at liberty to purchase the plastic from any other source and we will pay the difference in price between the other source and our current price. We also agree to pay Fortune a 2 percent rebate on the gross sales price of our plastic as an advertisement aid to your company, which rebate to be paid at your request. We assure that all fabrics you need will be in our warehouse at all times and we appreciate your agreeing to buy all of your plastics from us. Very truly yours, /s/ W. E. Walker, President." In a suit by the plaintiff for the balance of the purchase price, defendant entered a **counterclaim** based on Walker's letter. The plaintiff's contention to the defendant's counterclaim is that the letter does not satisfy the statute of frauds. Judgment was entered in favor of the plaintiff regarding the counterclaim in that the letter did not satisfy the statute of frauds. Defendant appealed.

Decision

Judgment reversed, for the defendant, Fortune, on its counterclaim.

Reasoning

The court noted there are only three requirements to make a memorandum sufficient to take the case outside of the statute of frauds provision of the Uniform Commercial Code. Those requirements are (1) the memorandum must evidence a contract for sale of goods, (2) it must be signed by the party against whom enforcement is sought, and (3) it must specify a quantity. The court held that the letter in question satisfied all three requirements.

Fortune Furn. Mfg. Co., Inc. v. Mid-South Plastic Fabric Co., 310 So.2d 725 (Miss. 1975).

counterclaim
a claim asserted by the defendant against the plaintiff's claim in a civil action

Interpretation

In interpreting a written contract, usually ordinary words are given their ordinary meaning and technical words their technical meaning. Each part (i.e., paragraph in the contract) will be interpreted so that it is compatible with the primary purpose of the contract. Special terms will prevail over general terms, and written terms will prevail over printed terms in a form contract. In the following case typewritten provisions of a contract prevail over printed portions which were inconsistent.

Facts
A dispute over the payment for additional electrical usage came about as the result of certain provisions in a lease. Paragraph 10A(4) of the printed form lease provided:

10. Utilities and Services. A. Lessor agrees to furnish or cause to be furnished to the Demised Premises, in common with other lessees where appropriate, the following services. . . .
    (4) Electricity for normal office usage, it being agreed that all additional electricity costs stemming from such causes as, but not limited to, Lessee's operation of special equipment from Lessee's extraordinary usage of heating and air conditioning shall be paid by Lessee. . . .

Two typewritten paragraphs appear at the end of the lease which read as follows:

37. Lessor agrees rent shall be inclusive of hot water, *electricity and air conditioning charges.*

38. In event *electrical charges* are determined to be less than Lessor has projected, an appropriate credit will be applied to the Lease.

Plaintiff lessee contends that the lease rental includes all electricity and air conditioning charges. Defendant landlord claims that such charges are not included in the rental.

Decision
Judgment for plaintiff lessee.

Reasoning
These typewritten paragraphs reflect a clear intent that the stated rental should include all electricity and air conditioning charges. The typewritten provisions of a contract ordinarily prevail over printed portions which are inconsistent. Such is the case here.

The Natural Kitchen, Inc. v. American Transworld Corp., 449 So.2d 855 (Fla. 1984).

All writings making up the contract are interpreted together as a whole agreement.

As was stated and explained in chapter 10, Public Policy and Contractual Purpose, a legal rather than an illegal result will be presumed.

Conduct with regard to terminology and circumstances surrounding the creation of the contract will be considered in interpreting words.

Usage of trade, or custom, is used to explain ambiguous terms, and such terminology is construed when needed against the interest of the party who wrote the contract.

Result If No Writing, in General

A *defendant* who raises the defense of the lack of a writing where required by the *statute of frauds* renders the contract *unenforceable* because it cannot be proved by a writing. It should be remembered that an oral contract *not* within the statute of frauds is enforceable if proved without any writing.

Quasi Contract
In many instances where performance has been rendered under an oral agreement which is not provable, recovery can be obtained for unjust enrichment under the theory of a contract implied in law, namely quasi contract.[6]

---
[6] See p. 78.

Partial Performance

Partial performance, as we have seen in the sale of goods under the Code,[7] can be proved. Under the common law of contracts, when, with the permission of the owner (seller), one (buyer) has taken possession of land under an oral contract and either pays part or all of the purchase price or vastly improves the property, the court, if convinced of the existence of an oral contract, will enforce it without a writing.

Full Performance

Full performance of all duties by both parties to the contract prevents the introduction of the plea of the statute of frauds. The defense of the statute of frauds applies only to **executory contracts;** it does not apply to executed contracts because there is no longer any contract to enforce.

executory contract a contract which has not been performed by all the parties to it

Equity

To promote justice and fairness should the situation demand it, a court can employ equity and thereby waive the requirement of compliance with the statute of frauds. An example is promissory estoppel, discussed previously.[8]

Summary Statement

1. As a practical matter, all contracts should be in writing.
2. Most oral contracts can be proved orally.
3. If the writing is the contract, *previous* oral or written evidence or *contemporaneous* oral evidence should not be heard that would *contradict* its terms.
4. There are the following *six* types of contract (the first five being under the law of contracts), which must be proved by a writing: (a) cannot be performed within one year; (b) sale of real property; (c) marriage consideration; (d) debt, default, or miscarriage of another; (e) executor's or administrator's promise; and (under the Uniform Commercial Code) (f) sale of goods for $500 or more.
5. Under the common law, oral evidence can be introduced irrespective of the content of a writing in *five* general instances: (a) violation of public policy; (b) failure of conditions; (c) voidable contracts; (d) discharge by subsequent oral or written agreement; and (e) ambiguity and incompleteness.
6. The parol evidence rule under the Code is more liberal than the common law in allowing oral testimony to explain terms in a *written* contract where the subject matter is goods.
7. Under the common law, there are *four* requirements for a writing which will satisfy the requirements of the statute of frauds if the contract is oral. The writing must: (a) identify the parties and their relationship, (b) describe the subject matter, (c) indicate that a contract was made, and (d) state all the terms and conditions of each promise and to whom made. The writing becomes effective when it is signed by the party to be charged with its performance.
8. There are *three* exceptions under the Code to the necessity for a writing to prove an oral contract for the sale or purchase of goods for $500 or more: (a) part performance; (b) specially manufactured goods; and (c) admitting the contract in court proceedings.

---

[7] See p. 158.

[8] See pp. 122–23.

9. Under the Code, if the contract for the sale of goods is oral, for a writing to be sufficient there are only *three* requirements: (a) quantity of goods; (b) a writing showing intent to contract; and (c) signature. Between merchants, the writing of one may become that of the other. The signature on a writing must be that of the party sought to be charged with the contract.
10. There are a limited number of rules of interpretation of a writing.
11. There are numerous exceptions which allow enforcement of contracts normally not provable because of the lack of a writing.
12. Equity—through the concept of part performance, quasi contract, and promissory estoppel—has provided remedies when parties can prove contracts at law in the absence of a writing.

The following case illustrates how the court applied promissory estoppel.

Kiely v. St. Germain
670 P.2d 764 (Colo. 1983)

Kirshbaum, J. In October 1978, St. Germain and the Boshouwers began discussing the possibility of St. Germain joining the color film processing business then operated by Boshouwers and his wife. At that time St. Germain had been employed by the Public Service Company of Colorado for approximately 12 years.

On December 8, 1978, St. Germain and Boshouwers visited the office of St. Germain's lawyer. In response to questions by the attorney, both parties stated that they had reached an agreement on all major terms of a new business venture. Those terms included payment of a monthly salary to St. Germain of $1,500 and an agreement by Boshouwers to sell stock to St. Germain in the corporation that ran the film processing business and which was to guarantee the salary to be paid to St. Germain.

St. Germain's attorney then drafted a document containing these provisions and both parties assured him that a "firm deal" was in existence. *Neither party executed the document* [Emphasis added]; however, at the conclusion of the meeting Boshouwers made the following statements: "Well, now we have a deal and you can tell your employer . . . that you are leaving." St. Germain terminated his employment with the Public Service Company later that same day.

St. Germain then obtained a second mortgage on his house to finance the purchase of the stock, took a prearranged vacation with his family and, on January 17, 1979, tendered a document containing the terms of the December 8, 1978 *oral agreement* to Boshouwers for signature. At this point, Boshouwers denied that the parties had an *oral agreement*.

St. Germain sued and sought damages on claims of breach of an oral contract or, alternatively, promissory estoppel. Defendants raised an affirmative defense asserting the Colorado Statute of Frauds which provides that "a contract for the sale of securities is not enforceable" unless proved by a proper writing.

The trial court concluded that St. Germain was entitled to lost wages and legal service costs based on promissory estoppel, but barred his claim for lost profits relating to the purchase of the corporate stock. The appeals court found for St. Germain on all issues and the Supreme Court of Colorado granted **certiorari** to consider the assertion that the doctrine of promissory estoppel may not be invoked to enforce an alleged oral agreement in the face of a statute of frauds defense.

The court noted that the doctrine of promissory estoppel is part of the common law of Colorado and that it has been given most recent expression in section (90)(1) of the *Restatement (Second) of Contracts*, as follows:

"A promise which the promisor should reasonably expect to induce action or forbearance on the part of the promisee or a third person and which does induce such action or forbearance is *binding* if injustice can be avoided only by enforcement of the promise. *The remedy granted for breach may be limited as justice requires."* [Emphasis added]

certiorari, writ of
an appellate court's certification to an inferior court that a case will be reviewed by the appellate court

The court pointed out that the doctrine of promissory estoppel encourages fair dealing and discourages conduct which unreasonably causes foreseeable economic loss because of action or inaction induced by a specific promise. The doctrine represents in part a modest extension of the basic contract principle that one who makes promises must be required to keep them. The doctrine is grounded upon principles of fair dealing. Fraudulent conduct by the promisor is not an element of promissory estoppel. When *injustice* to a promisee who reasonably and justifiably relies on a promise can be prevented only by recognizing a right of recovery from the promisor, *neither the lack of a written contract* nor the absence of fraudulent conduct *can defeat the claim for recompense.*

The policies furthered by the statute of frauds were to represent a forceful effort to prevent the perpetration of fraud by the device of perjury. However laudable this goal, courts, when faced with inequity by its strict application, have found ways to circumvent it. The doctrine of promissory estoppel is but one principle developed by the courts to prevent parties from employing the statute of frauds to defeat just claims. [The Colorado Statute, reflecting the Uniform Commercial Code, provides] ". . . the principles of law and equity, including . . . the law relative to . . . estoppel shall supplement its provisions."

Section 139 of the *Restatement (Second) of Contracts,* the court noted, states as follows:

"(1) A promise which the promisor should reasonably expect to induce action or forbearance on the part of the promisee or a third person and which does induce the action or forbearance is *enforceable* not withstanding the Statute of Frauds if injustice can be avoided only by enforcement of the promise. The remedy granted for breach is to be limited as justice requires. [Emphasis added]
(2) In determining whether injustice can be avoided only by enforcement of the promise, the following circumstances are significant:
   (a) the availability and adequacy of other remedies, particularly cancellation and restitution;
   (b) the definite and substantial character of the action or forbearance in relation to the remedy sought;
   (c) the extent to which the action or forbearance corroborates evidence of the making and terms of the promise, or the making and terms are otherwise established by clear and convincing evidence;
   (d) the reasonableness of the action or forbearance;
   (e) the extent to which the action or forbearance was foreseeable by the promisor."

By this rationale the court held that it affirmed the trial court's award of lost wages and legal service costs and remanded the case to the trial court for a determination of an award of lost profits under section 139 of the *Restatement (Second) of Contracts* in the circumstances of this case.

Questions and Case Problems

1. After submitting a low bid of $239,975, Construction Company was awarded a contract to build an apartment project for Sellers and Win. Upon completion of the project, Construction Company was paid $239,975 plus $8,275.30 for charge orders. Construction Company now sues Sellers and Win for fraud claiming that if the Construction Company rebated Sellers and Win the $25,000 they had paid for the construction site, Sellers and Win promised orally to pay Construction Company $260,000 for the project despite the $239,975 term written in the contract. Sellers and Win assert that the trial court erroneously admitted into evidence conversations between the parties concerning and leading up to the oral construction contract and indicating fraudulent misrepresentations. Did the court err? [*Sellers v. West-Ark Const. Co.,* 676 S.W.2d 726 (Ark. 1984).]

2. Manning, plaintiff, brought the action against the defendant, Metal Stamping Corporation, under a written contract for commissions related to a successful bid by the defendant for the manufacture of Illinois license plates. The defendant offered to prove orally that part of the agreement with the plaintiff was that the plaintiff was to bribe, and did bribe, the late Secretary of State to obtain the contract. The plaintiff objects to the introduction of the oral evidence as a violation of the parol evidence rule. What result? [*Manning v. Metal Stamping Corporation,* 396 F.Supp. 1376, aff'd 530 F.2d 980 (1975).]

3. Plaintiff, a purchaser of land, brought action for specific performance of a contract for the sale of land and introduced the following memorandum dated 4-20-72:

   Contract of sale of property known as George Nusbaum tract and Percy Burns property located between old Balto Pike and Route 140. Bounded on the north side by Ethel Williams property and on the south side by old Sam Sulser property for $28,000. Terms $7,000 pd. at time of signing of contract on June 1 and $7,000 to be paid each three months until amt. of sale satisfied. Mr. George Nusbaum to receive no interest for the unpaid balance and he be allowed to live rent free in his house until the money is paid in full. Deposit pd. 4-20-72 in the amount of $500 to bind the agreement. Signed James G. Saffell, George A. Nusbaum. Witness Earl H. Younger.

   The court noted the following issue in this case: whether the written memorandum of April 20, 1972 is sufficiently definite and certain to permit specific performance. What conclusion? [*Nusbaum v. Saffell,* 313 A.2d 837 (Md. 1974).]

4. Defendant, through its agent, orally placed orders for fuel for three buildings located in New York City. As of December 26, 1977, unpaid fuel bills amounted to $18,105.38. As of December 27, 1977, defendant delivered a letter to plaintiff indicating that defendant would no longer pay for contracts previously entered into by its agent. Upon suit by plaintiff, defendant asserted the statute of frauds as a defense. Is plaintiff entitled to be paid? [*Plymouth Rock Fuel Corp. v. Leucadia, Inc.,* 474 N.Y.S.2d 79 (N.Y. 1984).]

5. Landowners brought action against lessees of adjoining land seeking to enjoin lessees from discharging irrigation waste water upon their land. Adjoining landowners intervened, seeking to quiet title to alleged oral **easement** over land for purpose of discharging water and to enjoin landowners from interfering with its discharge. Can the "oral" easement be upheld? [*Darsaklis,* et al. *v. Schildt,* et al., 358 N.W.2d 186 (Neb. 1984).]

6. The plaintiff, a husband, brought a suit for divorce. The wife in her answer prayed that, if he should be granted the divorce, she be awarded custody of their minor child, her husband be required to perform specifically an alleged oral contract made prior to their marriage to adopt her daughter of a previous marriage, and that she be awarded temporary and permanent alimony in support of their minor child. The wife's daughter filed a petition to intervene to require the husband to specifically perform the alleged oral agreement to adopt her as his child. Can the oral agreement be proved? [*Maddox v. Maddox,* 161 S.E.2d 870 (Ga. 1968).]

7. Thomas was awarded a finder's fee of $25,000 to be paid to Thomas for procuring a buyer for the sale of controlling stock of a company. The stock was held by executors in trust for themselves as beneficiaries of the trust for various decedents. Hill, representing the executors, was the one who made the oral promise to Thomas to pay him $25,000 if he could find a desirable buyer. The executors asserted the defense of the statute of frauds when Thomas sued them for the commission. Hill and others are appealing the award to Thomas. What result? [*Hill v. Thomas,* 462 S.W.2d 922 (Ky. 1970).]

8. This case arises from a family dispute over the ownership of a well. Plaintiffs are the son and daughter-in-law of defendant. In 1977, plaintiffs and defendant, together with the now deceased husband of defendant, purchased adjoining one-acre parcels of property near Pendleton. In that year, a water well was drilled on defendant's property. Plaintiff, Mr. Mund, and defendant's husband shared the installation cost of the well and water system and worked together installing the system. Plaintiffs secured a $40,000 commercial loan in 1977 and constructed a residence on their property. There was, and is, no other source of water for plaintiffs. In less than a year after installation, the parties began to quarrel about the well and water. Do plaintiffs gain an irrevocable license in the well and water? [*Mund v. English,* 684 P.2d 1248 (Or. 1984).]

---

easement
an irrevocable right to the limited use of another's land

9. Plaintiff had contacted the defendants to see if they were interested in his becoming a part owner in their business. After a period of negotiations, the parties met to draw up a final agreement. At the meeting's end, the defendants stated they had a final agreement wherein the plaintiff was to receive a certain salary for six months and was to buy 49% of the corporation's outstanding stock. The parties were to sign the agreement when the plaintiff started work. The plaintiff took out a second mortgage on his house to raise the money for the stock purchase and terminated his employment. The defendants then told the plaintiff they were no longer interested in the agreement but they would hire plaintiff at a smaller salary. In this state, sale of securities is covered by a statute of frauds. Can plaintiff enforce the contract? [*St. Germain v. Boshouwers*, 646 P.2d 952 (Colo. 1982).]

10. It has been said that the statute of frauds has perpetrated as much fraud (inequity) as it has prevented. *Kiely v. St. Germain*, 670 P.2d 764 (Colo. 1983),[9] is a case example illustrating how the court attempted to prevent fraud (inequity). Evaluate the pros and cons of the court's action.

---

[9] See pp. 162–63.

12 Contractual Duties of Performance, Nonperformance, and Discharge

After you have read this chapter, you should be able to:

1. Discuss the law of contractual duties, recognizing that it is directed at ending a contract.
2. Recognize that the law of contractual duties is evolving and is constantly balancing the rights of society and the rights of the immediate parties to the contract.
3. Understand the complexity of determining when one should be allowed to be discharged of a contractual obligation when in breach of contract.
4. Note the role of conditions in contract law.
5. List the methods of discharge.
6. Appreciate the thrust of the Uniform Commercial Code in this area of law.

Introduction

In the preceding chapters of this Part we discussed the creation and enforceability of contracts and found that a contract created duties of performance. We will now consider what these duties are, when performance of such duties occurs, and how these duties are ended or discharged.

The duties assumed when a contract is created do not last forever. The law, as it has provided for the creation of a contract, also provides for its ending. As it was important for an individual to know how to create a right, it is equally important to know how to *discharge* (end) an obligation assumed under a contract.

Society has a concern that contractual duties be performed. To bring assurance to the community that contractual obligations will be carried out, the law cannot lightly discharge an individual from duties assumed by contract.

There is, however, a line of reasonableness between an individual's need to be discharged from a specific contractual obligation and society's interest in seeing that all contractual obligations be enforced. This line constantly shifts as law reflects the collective judgment of the community.

The important point in this chapter is the concern of the law for providing means and ways whereby contractual obligations are terminated.

The Concept of Performance

The expectations of parties when they contract is that they will receive what was promised in a contract. A substitute performance provided by a remedy or something less than complete **performance** was not thought of by the parties when the contract was made. We are, however, human beings and as such not always reliable. The law has taken this into account when it determines what will be required when complete performance of a contractual obligation is not forthcoming.

performance
the fulfillment of a contractual obligation

Performance

Performance means complete performance. If one party to a contract has *completely performed* his obligation under the contract, *he* is **discharged.** He has met the original expectation, and the law will not hold him to any further obligation. As far as he is concerned, *his part* of the contract is **executed** (performed). If all parties to the contract have completely performed, the contract is *executed* and all the parties are discharged.

If the parties have not performed, the contract is **executory;** if only one party has not performed, as to that party's *obligation* the contract is *executory*. Only when the contract is *executory* and there is *wrongful* nonperformance of a promise is there a **breach of contract** by the nonperforming party. In the following case the contract of the debtor on a promissory note was executory and he would be liable only as he failed to pay each installment.

discharge
termination of a contractual duty to perform a promise

executed contract
a contract which has been performed by all the parties to it

executory contract
a contract which has not been performed by all the parties to it

breach of contract
wrongful nonperformance of a contractual promise

Facts
Debtor signed four promissory notes. There were no installments due on three of the four notes and the fourth note was at most in default as to only one or two installments. None of the notes contained a clause specifically stating that each note was dependent upon the others and that the default in the payment of an installment under one note permitted acceleration for all other notes. Creditor sought judgment for all notes.

Decision
Judgment for debtor.

Reasoning
The majority rule is that a unilateral contract for the payment of money is not subject to the rule of anticipatory breach particularly when the suit is upon a promissory note. The rationale for such a rule is to avoid what would, in effect, be a rewriting of the terms of the note to permit recovery prior to the date on which it is due. At most, the debtor is responsible only for the installments not paid on one note.

Parliament Industries Inc. v. William H. Vaughan & Co., 430 A.2d 981 (Pa. 1981).

Figure 12.1 Performance

Type of Performance Rendered	Resulting in Type of Nonperformance	Time of Occurrence Relative to the Contract	Resulting in Type of Breach of Contract
None ▶	Material ▶	At formation ▶	Anticipatory
Partial ▶	Material ▶	Beginning of performance ▶	Threshold
Substantial ▶	Not material ▶	Midpoint plus ▶	Breach
Complete ▶	None ▶	At end ▶	None

Tender of Performance

tender
an unconditional offer by one contracting party to perform, with present ability to do so

A contracting party's **tender** of performance has the effect of performance. A tender is an unconditional offer by one contracting party to perform, with present ability to do so. (A, pursuant to the contract, tenders the goods to B, who is to pay A.) A party's improper refusal to accept a valid tender of performance causes the tendering party to be discharged of his or her contract to perform (B's refusal to receive the goods in the above example); except that when the refused tender is of payment of money, then the debt continues but interest on the debt stops running.

It should be mentioned that, if the debtor has several debts with the same creditor and tenders a payment which the creditor accepts, the creditor must apply the payment to the particular debt specified by the debtor or, if the debtor does not so specify, then the creditor can apply it to any of the debts due or past due.[1]

Substantial Performance

Performance means *complete* performance. Sometimes the expectations of the parties are not met in that they receive only *substantial* or *partial* performance. The test of whether there is substantial performance or partial performance is often called the "main purpose" rule—*has the main purpose* of the contract been performed or not defeated? If the answer is yes, then there is substantial performance; if no, then there is partial performance. The answer is determined by the facts in each case.

substantial performance
incomplete performance which is sufficient to accomplish, and does not defeat, the main purpose of a contract

Substantial performance is some performance *slightly less than complete performance. The main purpose of the contract has been performed or not defeated.* The nonperformance is *not material* and there is a *nonmaterial breach* of contract. *When substantial performance has been rendered* but it cannot be returned to the performing party and the breach of contract is not intentional, the law will allow both parties to be discharged by giving to the party in breach what he was originally entitled to less what it will cost the non-breaching party to get complete performance elsewhere. For example, B substantially performs his contract to build a building for C. B painted the front door brown instead of yellow. There is substantial performance and a nonmaterial breach by B. C must pay to B the contract price less what it will cost to repaint the door yellow. This prevents a **forfeiture** and is considered a just result in law. The expectations of the parties have been *approximately* met.

forfeiture
to lose a legal right as a penalty

Partial Performance

partial performance
incomplete performance which is insufficient to accomplish, or which defeats, the main purpose of a contract

Partial performance is *only slight performance*. The nonperformance is *material* and there is a *material breach* of contract. The expectations of the non-breaching party have *not even approximately* been met. *The main purpose of the contract has not been performed or has been defeated.* A material breach normally happens at the *threshold* or beginning

---

[1] To see how this applies with respect to the statute of limitations, see pp. 122–23.

stages for *time* of performance under the contract. Since the expectation of future performance is dim and will not be forthcoming, the non-breaching party can discharge himself from the obligation and seek **damages**.[2] In the following case of partial performance the plaintiff was not allowed to recover for building just the shell of an office addition.

damages
the money judicially awarded to an injured party for another's wrongful conduct

Facts
In a complaint for breach of payment of a construction contract of a warehouse, plaintiff included a claim for work partially performed on an office addition pursuant to a separate oral agreement. Plaintiff abandoned work before installing a floor and roof.

Decision
Judgment for defendant.

Reasoning
A party who has partially performed a contract and who has materially defaulted in completing it is not entitled to recover for part performance unless a legal excuse can be established for not completing the work.

Waters v. Glasheen, 478 N.Y.S. 2d 437 (N.Y. 1984).

Nonperformance

If *no performance* is given as of the date of expected performance under the contract, the non-breaching party is discharged. The non-breaching party also can **cover** his or her lost performance, and also can seek damages. (See figure 12.1.)

cover
to seek a substitute performance of a contract

Threat of No Performance. A threatened nonperformance of a *bilateral* contract is an *anticipatory repudiation* resulting in an **anticipatory breach.** However, the party not in breach is not discharged unless the non-breaching party *materially changes his or her position in reliance* on the anticipatory repudiation. The non-breaching party may immediately bring a suit for damages for such breach. (On September 1, A hires B as a secretary to begin work on September 10. On September 5, A tells B he will not need B. B immediately gets a job with C. A cannot withdraw his anticipatory repudiation, which he could have done *before* B obtained employment elsewhere. A is liable to B for his anticipatory breach.) There cannot be an anticipatory breach of a proposed *unilateral* contract because, until performance of the act or forbearance occurs, there is no acceptance and no contract. For example, a promissory note is a *unilateral* contract by the maker to pay the money at the maturity date, and, therefore, the maker cannot anticipatorily repudiate and breach his or her contract prior to the maturity date.

anticipatory breach
a party's material breach of contract made by his repudiation before his performance is due

Failure Midway

If a *failure* to *perform* happens *midway* through the contract but before substantial performance occurs, the party not in breach is not automatically discharged. For example, A contracts with B for twenty tons of coal to be delivered by B to A over twenty months at one ton per month. A is not automatically discharged if B misses the eleventh delivery. A must wait until, perhaps, the time for delivery of the twelfth installment and its nondelivery before the breach will be material. After the passage of a reasonable time such that a reasonable person would assume that the remainder of performance was not forthcoming, the non-breaching party's discharge will then take place.

Personal Satisfaction

If one has agreed to perform an obligation to the *personal* satisfaction, judgment, or taste of the other contracting party, he or she will not have *performed* the obligation nor be discharged from the contract until the other party has acknowledged that the *personal* standard has been met.

If, however, the obligation involves a matter of *mechanical fitness or suitability* for a particular purpose, a *reasonable person* test will be applied to determine whether satisfactory performance had been rendered resulting in discharge of the performing party. The following case is one of personal satisfaction as determined by interpreting the word "opinion."

---

[2] See pp. 192–93 for damages.

Facts
In May 1976, MMA and Action entered into a written agreement for the construction of a lime storage facility. Paragraph 7 of the contract provided that if in MMA's *opinion* Action fails to carry on the work diligently and on schedule . . . MMA shall have the right . . . to terminate the contract forthwith. Under the original progress schedule, work was to be completed by November 1, 1976. Delays required a revised completion date of December 25, 1976. On December 1, 1976, without advance notice, MMA terminated the contract based on its opinion that the job could not be completed by the revised deadline. Action sued MMA for wrongful termination. The lower court judged MMA's termination under an objective standard of reasonableness. The court found that Action could have had the job 89% complete by December 25, 1976 and since this performance would have been substantial, MMA's termination was unreasonable. MMA appeals.

Decision
Reversed, judgment for defendant, MMA.

Reasoning
Section 228 of the *Restatement (Second) of Contracts* provides

"When it is a condition of an obligor's duty that he be satisfied with respect to the obligee's performance or with respect to something else, and it is practicable to determine whether a reasonable person in the position of the obligor would be satisfied, an interpretation is preferred under which the condition occurs if such a reasonable person in the position of the obligor would be satisfied."

The court noted that section 228 states only a preference for interpreting an ambiguous contractual provision and that Comment (a) to the section indicates that if it is clear that the contract intends to leave a decision to one party subject only to the requirement of good faith, then the court should not imply an additional requirement of reasonableness. Here, the court said, the contract did not use the usual terminology of "satisfaction" clauses, but used the term opinion. The term "opinion" implies a personal subjective determination made in good faith. The case, therefore, is remanded back to the trial court to determine if MMA terminated the contract in good faith.

Action Engineering v. Martin Marietta Aluminum, 670 F.2d 456 (1983).

Time of the Essence

The time for performance of a contract is normally a *reasonable time* under the circumstances *if* no time is stated in the contract.

If time is of the essence because it is *expressly* made so by the contract or because a nontimely performance will be *valueless,* any performance other than on time results in a *material breach* and a *discharge* of the non-breaching party. In the following case the court held that time is of the essence in exercising a simple option.

Facts
On December 19, 1964, plaintiffs, lessees, entered into a primary lease for eight years with defendant, lessor. The lease contained the following provision:

Five years after the start of lease, Lessee has the option to request Lessor to expand the building. . . . *If the option to expand is exercised, it is understood that this lease inclusive of all options, shall be beginning anew.*

On February 20, 1980, plaintiffs wrote defendant as follows:

As per the lease . . . I choose to expand the building. . . .

On March 5, 1980, defendant wrote plaintiffs:

This is to advise you that your letter of February 20, 1980 is not acceptable. . . . Unless a new lease containing terms acceptable to us has been negotiated . . . we will expect you to surrender quiet and peaceable possession to us on August 31, 1980.

Lessees, plaintiffs, seek a declaration that they are entitled to an extension of their lease.

Decision
Judgment for the defendant.

Reasoning
The chancellor noted that the request for extension was made February 20, 1980, some fifteen years and five months after the start of the lease, whereas the option stated "Five years after the start of lease. . . ." The chancellor concluded it was manifestly unreasonable for plaintiffs to exercise the option some ten plus years beyond its terms. In a simple option, given without additional consideration, the optionee (the one who has the option) is free to exercise or ignore it whereas until the option expires the optionor (the one who gave the option) is bound. For this reason time is of the essence in exercising a simple option.

Frazier v. Northeast Mississippi Shopping Center, Inc., 458 So.2d 1051 (Miss. 1984).

Impossibility of Performance

Concept
Impossibility of performance discharges one's obligation assumed by contract. Impossibility means *"it cannot factually be done"* as opposed to "it is more difficult or less profitable for me to do it." This is often called "prospective failure of consideration" meaning prospective material nonperformance of the contract because of impossibility of performance.

impossibility
performance cannot factually be done

When Impossible
There are four situations where the law deems that factually something cannot be done:

1. where the *personal services of the obligor* are so necessary to the performance of the contract that the *death* or *incapacitation* of the obligor can make a *personal service obligation* impossible of performance. (X, a famous painter, agrees to paint Y's portrait. X dies. X's estate is not liable to Y for X's failure to paint Y's portrait);
2. where **commercial frustration** is experienced and the contract is deemed "commercially impracticable" (see *Transatlantic Financing Corp. v. U.S.*),[3]
3. where the subject matter essential to the performance of the contract is destroyed. (A and B enter into a contract for the sale by A to B of a famous oil painting by an old master. The painting is destroyed by fire before delivery to B. A is excused from performing the obligation under the contract because it is impossible for A to perform); and
4. where the performance of the obligation is deemed, after the formation of the contract but before the date of performance, to violate public policy.

commercial frustration
an excuse offered by a party to a contract justifying nonperformance of an obligation, usually because performance has been made impossible in fact

The following case illustrates impossibility of performance by supervening, later illegality resulting in a discharge of the contract.

Facts
Pursuant to the terms of a contract for supply of military aircraft parts to Iran which excuses performance arising out of causes beyond the control of the supplier, in the face of the political upheaval in Iran and of the U.S. Department of Treasury promulgating the following Iranian Assets Control Regulation

"No property subject to the jurisdiction of the United States or which is in its possession or control of persons subject to the jurisdiction of the United States in which . . . Iran has any interest of any nature whatsoever, may be transferred, paid, exported, withdrawn or otherwise dealt in except as authorized."

McDonnell Douglas Corporation found it impractical to perform its contract. Plaintiff seeks a declaratory judgment that it is not liable to Iran for breach of contract.

Decision
Judgment for plaintiff.

Reasoning
Because the contract relating to the sale or export of military aircraft parts requires an export license and these licenses were refused by the United States State Department, plaintiff *could not legally* export military aircraft parts and is thereby *excused from* performance because of supervening legal impossibility.

McDonnell Douglas Corp. v. Islamic Republic of Iran, 591 F.Supp. 293 (1984).

The Concept of Conditions

The *duty to perform* a promise arises when the contract is created. The *time for performance* is normally at a later time. If a **condition** must happen *before* one is *required to perform*, the *promise* forming the basis of the contract is deemed *dependent* for its *performance* upon the *occurrence of the condition*. For example, A's promise to pay B for digging a ditch is an offer for a unilateral contract and is performable when the condition

condition
an uncertain event on the occurrence of which a contractual obligation is made contingent or dependent

---
[3] See pp. 177–78.

dependent promise
a promise the performance of which is dependent upon the occurrence of a condition

independent promise
a promise the performance of which is not dependent upon the occurrence of a condition

(the act) occurs, namely when B has dug the ditch. A's promise is a **dependent promise,** dependent for its performance on condition of B's digging the ditch. A promise which forms the basis of a contract and renders the promisor *unconditionally* responsible to carry out the obligation contained in the promise is an **independent promise.** In the above example, if A's promise asked for and received *B's promise* to dig the ditch, B's promise is not dependent upon any condition. B's promise is an *independent promise.* A *dependent promise* can be *discharged* by the *happening or nonhappening* of a *condition.* An independent promise is *discharged by its performance.* In the above examples: in the unilateral contract situation, if B never dug the ditch, A's dependent promise has never been accepted and is no longer binding on A; in the bilateral contract situation, when B dug the ditch B's independent promise to perform is discharged, and A's dependent promise is to pay B. In the following case the defendant husband was discharged from performing his dependent promise because the condition did not occur.

Facts
The defendants owned property that the plaintiffs were interested in buying as a homesite. The parties met twice and signed a document by which the defendant husband agreed to sell the property to the plaintiffs for $15,000 with a $4,000 downpayment. The plaintiffs were told before they entered into the contract that the defendant wife's approval was necessary. The defendant's wife did not give approval and said to plaintiffs, "If it was the Lord's will that plaintiffs moved up there, it would be so."

Decision
Judgment for defendants.

Reasoning
The event on which the defendant husband's performance was conditioned, the giving of his wife's consent, did not occur. Failure of this condition to happen meant no contract came into existence that could be specifically enforced.

Hill v. Oland, 655 P.2d 1088 (Or. 1982).

Kinds of Condition

Conditions are either express, implied in fact, or implied in law and are classified as *precedent, concurrent,* or *subsequent.*

An *express* condition becomes part of a contract by words, written or oral. It is expressly stated. ("I'll repair your watch *if* you deliver it to me." Delivery is an express condition.) *Implied in fact* conditions are part of the contract though not expressed. They are inferred by the promisee because they are necessary for performance of the promisor's promise. (If A wants her watch fixed by B as B promised to do, A has to deliver her watch to B. Delivery is the condition implied in fact. If A cannot deliver her watch to B, B has no duty to perform his promise to repair.) *Implied in law* conditions exist to ensure fairness between parties. (A and B enter into a contract for the sale of goods to B; nothing is said about the time for payment of price. Payment upon delivery is implied in law. Delivery is the condition implied in law.) Implied in law conditions need only be substantially performed.

Conditions are normally introduced by words like "if," "when," "after," "as soon as," "provided that," "on condition that."

condition precedent
a condition which must occur or not occur before a dependent promise becomes performable

condition concurrent
a condition which must occur at the same time as another condition

condition subsequent
a condition, on the occurrence or nonoccurrence of which, after a promise becomes performable, excuses the duty of performance

A **condition precedent** requires something to occur or not to occur *before* the performance of a promissory duty is required (e.g., "dig the ditch and then I'll pay you"). **Concurrent conditions** are mutual conditions which are required to happen theoretically simultaneously (e.g., unpaid seller is to deliver the goods at the same time that payment is made). On the other hand, a duty to perform will be excused upon the occurrence or nonoccurrence of a **condition subsequent.** For example, a contract for transportation of goods provides that, after delivery, any claim for damage to the goods must be made within thirty days. The carrier's promissory duty to pay for any such damage will be excused if the condition subsequent, namely thirty days, expires before any claim is made.

The Concept of Discharge

As we have seen, discharge takes place by performance or by the occurrence or nonoccurrence of a condition. Discharge can also take place *by acts of the parties* or *by operation of law*.

Discharge by Acts of the Parties

Novation. Novation will be discussed fully later.[4] This is an act by the parties to a contract who mutually discharge their obligations under their contract so that a new contract with a new party can replace it. It is (1) a *new contract* with (2) a *new party* (3) *immediately discharging the old contract*. It is also an *accord and satisfaction*.

Accord, and Accord and Satisfaction. When a subsequent new contract is made *between the same parties,* it is called an **accord**. The old contract still exists and will be discharged only by performance of the new contract. For example, M defaults on his promissory note held by the bank and he gives the bank his renewal note, the bank keeping both notes. M is still obligated on the original note, as well as on the new note which is an accord with the bank. However, if *at the time of its formation the new contract satisfies* the old contract and thereby causes its discharge, the new contract is called an **accord and satisfaction.** In the above example, if the bank returned the old note to M, the old note is discharged and the renewal note is an accord and satisfaction.

Account Stated. One person may have a right against another person for payment under their contract. Such a right is called an **account.** When they have settled their account and the matured items have been expressly or impliedly agreed to, the account is called an **account stated** discharging each of the matured items in the account. (At various times during one month, A ordered and received goods from B, seller. When B has totaled the monthly amount owing by A, the total is the account. When A assents to the total either expressly or by A's silence, the balance becomes an account stated causing A's contract debts to B for *each* of the contracted items to be discharged, the account stated replacing them.)

Mutual Rescission, Waiver, and Release. Some other acts of the parties may cause a discharge. If the parties mutually agree to discharge each other from obligations assumed by a contract, *mutual* **rescission** occurs.

An *oral agreement* for mutual rescission is enforceable and will discharge an enforceable, executory *written contract* even if the written contract is within the statute of frauds and even if the written contract provides that it can be mutually rescinded or modified only in writing. (Jones and Smith enter into a *written* employment contract for two years, which is within the statute of frauds and is enforceable being in writing. Four months later they *orally* agree to rescind the contract. The oral agreement of rescission is enforceable discharging the written contract.)

However, if an *oral* agreement for mutual rescission of a *written* contract involves a *retransfer of the subject matter* which *brings* the oral rescission agreement *within* the statute of frauds, the oral rescission agreement would be *unenforceable* and the written contract will *not* be discharged. (Solomon and Brown contract in writing for the sale of a desk to Brown for $600, the contract being within the statute of frauds under the Uniform Commercial Code but enforceable because the contract is in writing. Delivery of the desk and payment are made. Ten days later they *orally* agree that, if Brown is not satisfied with the desk, the contract for sale is rescinded. No redelivery or repayment is made. If Brown becomes dissatisfied, since the oral agreement for rescission involves the *retransfer of the $600 desk* it is within the statute of frauds and, being oral, it is unenforceable.)

accord
a new contract which provides that, on its performance, a previous contract as well as the new contract are discharged

accord and satisfaction
a new contract (accord) which discharges a party from a previous contractual obligation; the old contract is discharged (satisfied)

account
a right to payment under a contract

account stated
an account which has been settled and the matured items and balance expressly or impliedly agreed to by the parties

rescission
cancellation

---
[4] See pp. 188–89.

If one party knowingly accepts a defective performance, this is a waiver of the nonperformance and is a discharge of the other party's duty to perform. One party can also extinguish a claim to performance by *releasing* the other party.

Intentional Material Alteration of a Written Contract. A written contract which is *intentionally* and *materially altered* by a party to a contract without the consent of the other contracting party *discharges* the other party.

Destruction of a Sealed Contract. The intentional physical destruction of a contract under seal by the person entitled to its performance discharges the person obligated to perform under the contract.

Substituted Contract. A substituted contract is a contract that is itself accepted by the obligee in satisfaction of the obligor's existing duty. The substituted contract discharges the original duty, and breach of the substituted contract does not give rise to a right to enforce the original duty.

Discharge by Operation of Law

Statute of Limitations. By statute in each state, the law gives a specific limited time period for the bringing of a suit for breach of contract. The time varies from three to ten years, depending upon whether the contract was oral or written. These time periods are contained in what is called a *statute of limitations*. The time period starts from the moment of breach of the contract, but it is suspended for periods when the breaching party is not within the jurisdiction of the court. If the *statute of limitations runs,* this acts as a barrier to suit for the nonperformance of a contract which is now *unenforceable* and thus, *in effect, discharges* the party who is in breach of contract.

Bankruptcy Discharge. A discharge in *bankruptcy* acts as a barrier to the enforcement of a contract. It terminates the bankrupt debtor's duty to perform and, therefore, is a discharge of such duty.[5]

judgment
the final decision of a case by a court

Judgment. Contracts are also discharged by mergers into **judgments** of claims for performance of a contractual duty. (A sues B for nonperformance and obtains a judgment. The contract is discharged and is merged into the judgment.)

arbitration
a method for deciding disputes outside of court by persons called arbitrators, appointed by the disputing parties

Arbitration Award. Contracts are also discharged by an **arbitration** award by an arbitrator on the existence and violation of a contractual duty which merges the duty into the award and discharges the duty.[6]

See figure 12.2, a summary chart on discharge of contracts.

The Uniform Commercial Code

Performance under the Code

The Code does not require performance to one's personal satisfaction but, rather, requires a *good faith performance*[7] in all applicable cases, thus requiring that the *reasonable expectations* of a contracting party be met. Nonperformance is excused if performance as agreed has been made impractical by either the occurrence of a contingency the nonoccurrence of which was a basic assumption on which the contract was made, or by compliance in good faith with any applicable foreign or domestic governmental regulation or order.[8] If a contingency affects only part of the capacity of the seller to perform, an allocation of production and deliveries among customers must be made and notification of delay or any limited allocation of goods must be given to customers. This is illustrated by the following case.

---

[5] For a discussion of bankruptcy, see chapter 30.

[6] For a brief discussion of arbitration, see p. 16.

[7] UCC 1–203.

[8] UCC 2–615(a).

Figure 12.2 Discharge of Contracts

By Act of the Parties	Reason	By Operation of Law	Reason
Complete Performance	Nothing remains to be done	Death	Impossibility
Substantial Performance	Avoidance of forfeiture	Commercial Frustration	Impossibility
Material Breach of Contract	Nonperformance of Contract's Main Purpose at Non-breaching Party's Election	Destruction of Subject Matter	Impossibility
Novation	Substitution of a new party	Subsequent Illegality of the Contract	Violation of public policy
Accord and Satisfaction	New contract discharging old contract		
Account Stated	Matured items in the account are discharged	Failure of Condition	No duty to perform
Mutual Rescission	Mutual agreement of cancellation	Statute of Limitation	Unenforceable contract
Waiver	Acceptance of defective performance	Bankruptcy	Public policy
Release	Giving up right		
Intentional Material Alteration of a Written Contract	Fraud	Judgment	Merger of contractual duty
Destruction of a Sealed Contract	Fraud	Arbitration Award	Merger of contractual duty
Substitute Contract	Mutual agreement		

Facts
Terry, a gasoline dealer, sued the defendant for breach of contract. Defendant, in a time of gasoline shortage, was required to allocate gasoline supplies among its dealers, including Terry. The defendant found it *impossible* to fully meet its contractual commitments to its dealers due to the energy crisis. The defendant allocated its supplies among its customers on a quota-percentage basis based upon the previous year's gallon usage.

Decision
Judgment for the defendant.

Reasoning
The court noted that under the Uniform Commercial Code as it is enacted in California, partial performance will discharge one from his obligation to multiple customers when suppliers *inadvertently* become short, making full performance impossible. What is required is that the party allocating scarce supplies act *in good faith* and proceed in *a fair and reasonable manner*. The court concluded that the quota system met the criteria for discharging the contractual obligation of the defendant.

Terry v. Atlantic Richfield Co., 140 Cal.Rptr. 510 (1977).

Discharge under the Code
In the case of a *material breach,* meaning a failure to provide perfect tender by any deviation from the promised performance,[9] the Code provides that the non-breaching party may *cancel* a contract reserving, however, remedies for nonperformance.[10] The following case discusses the requirement of perfect tender.

---

[9] UCC 2–703(f), 711(i).

[10] UCC 2–106(3).

Facts

Following a mobile home show, plaintiffs agreed to buy from defendant a new camper. Defendant required two weeks to prepare the new van. The contract provided for delivery on or about August 3, 1978. On that date, plaintiffs arrived to pick up their van but found it was not quite ready. On August 14 the plaintiffs arrived to accept delivery of the van but found defendant touching up with paint scratch marks and that cushions in the van were wet because the windows had been left open. Plaintiffs agreed to accept the van if they could withhold $2,000 of the purchase price. Defendant said "no" but agreed to replace the cushions. On October 5, the van still was not ready and plaintiffs rejected it. On November 20, plaintiffs sought rescission of the contract and defendant counterclaimed for breach of contract.

Decision

Judgment for plaintiffs.

Reasoning

Underlying the Uniform Commercial Code is the recognition of the revolutionary change in business practices in this century. The purchase of goods is no longer a simple transaction in which a buyer purchases individually-made goods from a seller in a face-to-face transaction. Our economy depends on a complex system for the manufacture, distribution and sale of goods, a system in which manufacturers and consumers rarely meet. Faceless manufacturers mass produce goods for unknown consumers who purchase these goods from merchants exercising little or no control over the quality of production. In an age of assembly lines, we are accustomed to cars with scratches, television sets without knobs and other products with all kinds of defects. Buyers no longer expect a "perfect tender." If a merchant sells defective goods, the reasonable expectation of the parties is that the buyer will return the goods and the seller will repair or replace them. Recognizing the commercial reality, the Code permits a seller to cure imperfect tenders. Should the seller fail to cure the defects, whether substantial or not, the balance shifts again in favor of the buyer, who has the right *to cancel* or seek damages. Such is the case here and plaintiffs may cancel the contract.

Ramirez v. Autosport, 440 A.2d 1345 (N.J. 1981).

In the case of a party's repudiation by anticipatory breach, nevertheless the Code seeks to encourage performance by the repudiating party. Therefore, the Code permits the repudiating party to retract the repudiation before the performance is due if, meanwhile, the party not in breach has not *cancelled* the contract or *materially changed his or her position in reliance* on the repudiation.[11] However, the party not in breach, upon such repudiation, can ask for *additional assurances*—e.g., a bond.[12] If such assurances are not forthcoming, the non-breaching party can *discharge* himself or herself by **cancellation.**

cancellation
the nullification of a contractual obligation

Termination of a contract occurs *without a breach* but, rather, by one party exercising a power (e.g., exercising a power of avoidance caused by a contract fraudulently induced). Termination acts as a discharge of all parties to a contract, reserving, however, to the party not in breach any remedies for a *prior* breach or defective performance.[13]

The Code provides for a four-year statute of limitations for a sales contract which, in effect, can discharge the contract by its running.[14] Moreover, unlike the common law of contracts, a *written* waiver or renunciation of an obligation owed under a sales contract acts as a discharge even though it is not supported by consideration.[15] But if a written contract provides that it cannot be modified or rescinded except by a signed writing, an oral agreement to mutually rescind will not act as a discharge of the contract.[16]

Summary Statement

1. Normally parties to a contract expect complete performance, but the law recognizes other types of performance—namely, substantial and partial. Partial performance when coupled with a damage award will discharge contracts.

---

[11] UCC 2–611.

[12] UCC 2–609.

[13] UCC 2–106(4).

[14] UCC 2–725.

[15] UCC 1–107.

[16] UCC 2–209(2).

2. In special cases, such as anticipatory breach, personal satisfaction, and time of the essence, a party can be discharged from performing his or her side of the contractual commitment.
3. Four situations exist in law which are deemed factual situations of impossibility which will discharge one's duty assumed by contract.
4. There are conditions precedent, concurrent, subsequent, and also express, implied in fact, and implied in law. The failure of a condition may cause a contract obligation to cease to exist or never to come into existence.
5. Discharge of obligations assumed by contract can happen by acts of the parties through novation, an accord and satisfaction, mutual rescission, waiver, release, intentional material alteration of a written contract, and destruction of a sealed contract.
6. By operation of law, a contract can be discharged by (in effect) the running of the statute of limitations, discharge in bankruptcy, judgment, and arbitration award.
7. The primary interest of the Code is to encourage a good-faith performance of contractual obligations.

The following case illustrates how the interest of society in seeing that contracts are performed is balanced against impossibility of performance.

Transatlantic Financing Corp. v. United States
363 F.2d 312 (1966)

Wright, Circuit Judge. This case involves an appeal from a judgment entered in favor of the United States. Transatlantic sued the United States for additional cost of carriage pursuant to a contract for the shipment of wheat on the vessel *S.S.Christos* from Texas to Iran.

The carriage cost of $43,972 above and beyond the contract price of $305,842.92 resulted from an extension of a 10,000 mile voyage by about 3,000 miles around the Cape of [Good Hope] Africa after the closing of the Suez Canal by the Egyptian government through obstruction by sunken vessels. This action by the Egyptian government took place on November 2, 1956, shortly after the invasion of Egypt by Israel on October 29, 1956 and the invasion of the canal zone by Britain and France on October 31, 1956. The canal had been nationalized by Egypt on July 26, 1956.

It was on October 2, 1956 that the contract was made by the plaintiff and defendant in an atmosphere of international tension. On October 27, 1956 the *S.S. Christos* sailed from Galveston, Texas for Bandar Shapur, Iran on a course which would have taken her through Gibraltar and the Suez Canal.

On November 7, 1956 a representative of Transatlantic contacted the United States government, requesting instructions concerning the disposition of the cargo and an agreement for payment of additional compensation for a voyage around the Cape of Good Hope. The United States informed Transatlantic that *they were expected to perform their obligation assumed by contract without additional compensation.* The *Christos* changed course following this discussion and delivered the wheat in December at Bandar Shapur, Iran.

Plaintiff seeks additional compensation denied to them by the United States District Court.

This court affirmed the judgment of the district court denying relief to the plaintiff.

The court recognized the plaintiff's argument that implicit in the contract was the contemplation that the *Christos* would use the "usual and customary" route to deliver the wheat (a constructive condition); such route would normally include passage through the Suez Canal; and when that route was closed, the contract was impossible to perform as originally contemplated; and because of the need for altered performance, additional compensation was owed.

The court rejected the plaintiff's argument, holding that "*a thing is impossible in legal contemplation when it is not practicable, and a thing is impracticable when it can only be done at an excessive and unreasonable cost.*" The court noted that this approach ultimately represents the ever-shifting line drawn by courts hopefully responsive to commercial practices and mores, at which the community's interest in having contracts enforced according to their terms is outweighed only by the commercial senselessness of requiring performance.

In order to apply the ever-shifting line to excuse one from performance of obligations assumed by contract by applying the doctrine of impossibility the court noted the need to satisfy three reasonably definable steps. First, a contingency, something unexpected, must have occurred. Second, the risk of the unexpected occurrence must not have been allocated either by agreement or custom. Finally, occurrence of the contingency must have rendered performance commercially impracticable.

The court held the timing of the closing of the canal met the first requirement of an unexpected event. The contingency of foreclosure of the route was to a certain extent, in the eyes of the court, somewhat foreseen by Transatlantic (international tension) and, since the continued passage of the canal was not made an *express condition* of the contract, it could be argued to have been assumed by them. Thus, requirement two *could* be interpreted adversely against Transatlantic.

The court, however, decided the case based upon the third element, of commercial impracticability. The court pointed out that (any) *increased cost and difficulty of performance never constitutes impracticability.* Justification for relief in this case would require more of a variation between expected cost and the actual cost of performing by the available alternative route.

Questions and Case Problems

1. A contract of sale of a broadcasting corporation provided that a certain purchase price was to be paid by the buyer by executing a personal note *or* by executing a note by a corporation formed by the buyer. The corporation was formed and it issued the note. The corporation was unable to pay the note, and the seller sued the buyer for payment. What result? [*Clayton v. Communications Capital Corp.*, 440 P.2d 330 (Ariz. 1968).]

2. On October 5, 1976, the parties signed a written contract for the plaintiffs to construct a three-family house on land owned by defendants. The contract price was $91,000, to be paid in five installments as various stages of the work were finished. The house was to be completed within 150 days from the date of the execution of the contract, which would make the projected completion date March 4, 1977. Except for $2,000 withheld for incomplete items, the first four scheduled payments were made. Defendants refused to make the final installment payment because the house was not substantially completed until November 9, 1977 and $2,060.40 was needed to repair stress cracks in foundation walls as well as $1,527 and $533.40 for five minor items. Defendants contend that the doctrine of substantial performance is inapplicable because plaintiffs were guilty of willful or intentional breach of contract by failing to complete all the work required. Is defendant correct? [*Vincenzi* et al. *v. Cerro* et al., 442 A.2d 1352 (Conn. 1982).]

3. This is a Uniform Commercial Code case involving repossession of collateral (a car) by a bank which subsequently disposed of the collateral by private sale and seeks to recover a deficiency in an amount owed on a note by defendant. Defendant had borrowed from the bank to purchase a car and signed a note. On November 15, 1979 the first payment on the note was due. Defendant was in the process of getting a divorce from his wife and closed his checking account with the bank so his wife could not withdraw funds. The account was closed on October 17, 1979. The bank repossessed the car on October 23, 1979. Defendant contends he does not owe the bank a deficiency because the bank wrongfully repossessed the car. Is defendant correct? [*Bank of Cabot v. Bledsoe*, 653 S.W.2d 144 (Ark. 1983).]

4. Plaintiff signed a contract for $25,000 worth of dancing lessons from the defendant. A clause in the contract read "NONCANCELLABLE NEGOTIABLE CONTRACT" and "I UNDERSTAND THAT NO REFUNDS WILL BE MADE." Plaintiff had some lessons, and then he was involved in an automobile accident and suffered injuries which prevent him from dancing. Plaintiff sued for a refund of his money less the cost of completed lessons. Can the defendant enforce the contract? [*Parker v. Arthur Murray, Inc.*, 295 N.E.2d 487 (Ill. 1973).]

5. The plaintiffs leased a specific piece of property from one defendant (landlord) and then subleased it to another defendant (subtenant). The plaintiffs failed to give the landlord timely notice of intent to renew and the landlord began negotiations directly with the subtenant. The plaintiffs brought suit seeking a declaratory judgment that they should be able to renew their lease, and seeking to enjoin the landlord from terminating the lease and dealing with the subtenant. Should the plaintiff prevail? [*Lemay* et al. *v. Rouse* et al., 444 A.2d 553 (N.H. 1982).]

6. The appellant had obtained a judgment by confession against the appellee in the amount of $26,544.37. To collect its judgment, the appellant caused various items of appellee's property to be attached. Before any of the property was attached, the appellee had delivered to the appellant's attorney a cashier's check, marked "paid in full in settlement of all claims." The appellant informed the appellee that the cashier's check had been negotiated (transferred), but that the appellant considered it only partial payment. If the balance was not forthcoming, the attached property would be sold. Appellee seeks an injunction to prevent the sale of the attached property. Should the injunction be given? [*Air Power, Inc. v. Omega Equipment Corp.*, 459 A.2d 1120 (Md. 1983).]

7. The defendant, homeowner, paid a general contractor and in return received from the plaintiff, subcontractor, a promise not to sue on a **mechanic's lien.** When the subcontractor did not receive payment from the general contractor, the subcontractor sued the defendant homeowner for the money due him for his work. The defendant claimed that the plaintiff had breached his contract with the defendant not to assert his mechanic's lien and not to sue the defendant. Plaintiff asserts that the homeowner could not set off a breach of contract not to sue under a statute which provided that claims arising out of the same transaction cannot be offered as a counterclaim to a mechanic's lien. What result? [*Malin v. Nuss*, 338 A.2d 676 (Pa. 1975).]

mechanic's lien
a statutory lien on real property given to a person who, pursuant to contract, has rendered labor or services, or supplied materials for the improvement of the property and who has not been paid

8. Husband and wife opened a joint checking account which became overdrawn. Husband gave two notes totaling $181,000 to the bank to cover some loans and the overdraft. When activity in the account ceased, there remained an overdraft of $75,983.06. The wife had written checks on the account totaling $82,252.31. Deposits made to the account while it was active were applied to the overdrafts of husband by the bank. The wife contends she should not owe $16,811.43 since her overdrafts should have been reduced proportionately by the deposits. Must the bank apply part of the deposits to the wife's overdrafts? [*United States Trust Company of New York v. McSweeney III*, 457 N.Y.S. 2d 276 (N.Y. 1982).]

9. After having been employed by defendant for over ten years, plaintiffs were required to sign new employment contracts with more restrictive non-competition clauses or be discharged. The plaintiffs refused to sign, and their employment was terminated. A master found plaintiffs had performed their obligations under their original contract of employment "fully, faithfully, and competently," and that defendant had discharged them in violation of their employment contract. After discharge, the master found that plaintiffs had violated the original contract non-competition clause. The master concluded this barred plaintiffs from recovery for breach of contract. Is the master correct? [*Ward v. American Mutual Liability Insurance Co.*, 433 N.E.2d 1342 (Mass. 1983).]

10. In *Transatlantic Financing Corp. v. United States*, 363 F.2d 312 (1966),[17] the court held that the concept of impossibility ultimately represents an ever-shifting line drawn by courts responsive to commercial practices and mores which shows that the community's interest in having contracts enforced according to their terms is outweighed only by commercial senselessness of requiring performance. Discuss the significance of this statement.

---

[17] See pp. 177–78.

13 Contractual Rights, Third Parties, and Remedies for Breach of Contract

After you have read this chapter, you should be able to:

1. Discuss the law associated with contractual rights, recognizing that the concern of the law in this area is to enhance and protect contract rights gained by exercising the freedom of contract.
2. Appreciate that exercising one's freedom of contract and assuming duties is not viewed lightly by the law.
3. Understand how third parties become associated with a contract.
4. Realize that a remedy is normally a substitute for the right acquired by contract.
5. Note that the Uniform Commercial Code does not differ substantially from the common law in this area of contractual rights.

Introduction

In the last chapter we discussed the contracting parties' contractual duties of performance. We will now consider their contractual rights, how contractual rights and duties may be transferred to or otherwise acquired by third persons, and the legal effect, and remedies for breach of contract.

The creation of a simple contract creates property, rights, and duties.

Property usually refers to a *thing*, which may be either *tangible* (e.g., that house, that bag, that typewriter is my property) or *intangible* (e.g., that account receivable, that copyright, that patent, that idea is my property). It belongs to me; I have an interest in it, a right to it, and other persons have a duty not to interfere with my property. Legally, then, *property* is a thing, and also an interest or a right in a thing, recognized by law.

My *desire* to enjoy a thing exclusively has been recognized as proper by society. An **interest** is a person's *desire* which has been legally recognized as *dominant* over a similar desire of another person. For example, an owner's title to a house is a legal interest in that house recognized by law.

I have the right to *claim* that others will not interfere with my legal interest. So a **right** is a legal claim by the owner of an interest that others shall not interfere with that interest. For example, the owner of a house has the right to claim that others are not to interfere with the owner's enjoyment of the house.

Other persons have a legal obligation to respect my legal interest and not to interfere with it. So a **duty** is a legal obligation not to interfere with another person's legal interest. For example, other persons have a duty not to interfere with my enjoyment of my house.

Thus, the creation of a simple contract gives to each of the immediate parties to the contract: (1) an *interest* in the other party's performance of what he contracted to do; (2) a *right* to have the other party not violate that interest by his failure to perform; and (3) a *duty* to perform the contract and not fail to perform.

These interests, rights, and duties can be transferred to third persons who are not immediate parties to the original contract. Often interests in things are transferred for the purpose of security. For example, I borrow $100 from you and deliver my ring to you as security, and you now have a security interest in the ring which includes the right to sell it if I don't pay you. A contract right can be transferred or *assigned* and a contract duty can be transferred or *delegated* to a third person. Also, the contract may provide for a benefit to a third person who, as a third-party beneficiary of the contract, thereby obtains a right to enforce the contract to which he or she is not a party. For example, a husband contracts with an insurance company and obtains a policy of life insurance in which his wife is named as the beneficiary on his death.

The important point in this chapter is the concern of the law with enhancing and protecting the rights which parties gained by exercising the *freedom of contract*.

The Concept of Parties

As was discussed previously,[1] there can be any number of parties to a contract. The obligations of the immediate parties to the contract may be *joint, several,* or *joint and several.*

Unless the contracting parties otherwise agree, if two or more parties *together* are obligated to perform the *same* duty to the *same* person, the obligation is *joint* (collective). They can sue and be sued only together. If each of the several parties *separately* promises to perform the *same* obligation, the obligation is *several* (independent). Each of them can sue and be sued separately. The obligation to perform a duty can be both *joint and several.*

Only the parties to a contract have the *right* to enforce it, called **privity of contract,** with two exceptions to be discussed, namely, *assignments* and *third-party creditor or donee beneficiary contracts.*

---

[1] See p. 78.

property
a thing; also an interest or right in a thing

interest
a person's desire which has been legally recognized as dominant over a similar desire of another person

right
a legal claim by the owner of an interest that others shall not interfere with his interest

duty
a legal obligation not to interfere with another person's interest

privity of contract
a legal relationship between two or more parties created by their contract

Figure 13.1 Assignment

Rights

assignment
the transfer of a contract right

assignor
the transferor of a contract right

assignee
the person to whom a contract right is transferred

Rights *under a contract* are normally capable of transfer by the process of **assignment.** The party to a contract who assigns the right under a contract is called an **assignor,** and the person who receives the right is called an **assignee.** For example, B owes S $10, and S assigns to E his right against B for the $10. S is the assignor and E is the assignee.

An assignment can take any form as long as the original party to the contract indicates a present intent to transfer a contract right to another. In the following case the court found that the purported assignment failed because the debtor attempting to assign retained control over the subject matter of the assignment.

inter alia
among other things

Facts
On March 22, 1974, a debtor made to plaintiff a demand promissory note. On April 8, 1974, in order to secure payment of the note, the debtor granted plaintiff a security interest in, **inter alia,** "accounts receivable . . . now owned or hereafter acquired." A financing statement evidencing plaintiff's security interest was filed with the Minnesota Secretary of State on April 29, 1974. The debtor established with plaintiff a "collateral account" into which all payments on accounts receivable made to the debtor would be deposited. Without the debtor's consent, plaintiff could not use the funds in the collateral account for any purpose other than to satisfy the debtor's liability to plaintiff in the event of default on the loan. Notice was given by the debtor, to a debtor of the debtor, to make future payments on contracts to the plaintiff. Accordingly, the debtor of the debtor made the plaintiff the payee on its checks and the plaintiff deposited the proceeds of the checks to the "collateral account". The United States filed a tax lien on the collateral account for taxes owed by the debtor. Plaintiff claims it has priority over the United States to the funds in the collateral account.

Decision
Judgment for United States Internal Revenue Service.

Reasoning
Although under Minnesota law "no particular form or words are required" for an assignment, an intent to transfer must be manifested and the assignor must not retain control over the fund or any power of revocation. In the present case, the letter from the debtor to its debtor would have been sufficient to establish an assignment of the accounts receivable had there been manifested the necessary intent to transfer the accounts receivable and relinquishment of all control over them and their proceeds. Since the debtor retained some control over the collateral account, all things necessary to perfect the assignment were not accomplished.

Guaranty State Bank of St. Paul v. Lindquist, 304 N.W.2d 278 (Minn. 1981).

When an effective assignment has been accomplished, the assignee has the assignor's right to enforce the contract against the party who had contracted with the assignor. In the above example of S's assignment to E, E has S's right to enforce the contract against B. (See figure 13.1.)

Duties

While contract *rights* are *assignable,* contract *duties* are only **delegable.**

A contractual mechanical or ministerial duty requiring no special factor or person with special abilities necessary to performance is normally freely delegable. Examples of persons with special abilities are lawyers, doctors, certified public accountants, and famous artists. When a party to a contract delegates a contractual duty to another, that party, as the original **obligor,** remains responsible for seeing that the *duty* is performed. The **obligee,** the one holding the *right* to performance, can hold responsible either the obligor or the obligor's consenting delegate for nonperformance of the owed duty. In this way a *third party* (the delegate) not originally a party to "the contract" can become responsible for its performance. In the above example of S and B, if B delegates to C his duty to pay S $10 and C agrees to pay S, B is still liable to S (and now C is also liable to S).[2]

delegation
the transfer of one's duty to another, the transferor still being responsible for the duty

obligor
the person who owes a legal obligation

obligee
the person to whom a legal obligation is owed

Special Rules for Assignment and Delegation

Notice to Obligor of Assignment

Notice of an assignment of a right *not for the purpose of security* is normally given by an assignee to the obligor who owes a duty under the contract in order to cut off *defenses* of the obligor which may occur subsequently. Notice is also given to prevent the *discharge* of the obligor by the obligor's *innocent* performance of the obligor's contractual duty for the benefit of the obligee. For example, D owes money to C, who assigns his or her right to the money to E. D is unaware of the assignment and D pays C. D is discharged from the debt, and E has no right against D, but only against C. If E had notified D of the assignment, then D must pay only E. The following case illustrates this point.

Facts
On October 31, 1973, plaintiff leased seven trucks to a lessee and secured the lease by taking delivery of six savings certificates issued by defendant to the lessee. The lessee subsequently encountered financial straits and notified defendant that it had lost the certificates and desired to effect an early withdrawal of the funds. Without notice of the lessee's pledge of the certificates to plaintiff, the defendant disbursed the funds to the lessee. Plaintiff contends as true owner of the certificates by pledge (assignment) defendant should have to pay the value of the certificates to the plaintiff.

Decision
Judgment for defendant.

Reasoning
The general rule applicable to this case is that an assignee must notify a debtor prior to the debtor's payment to the assignor in order to bind the debtor to the obligation asserted by the assignee, otherwise the debtor is discharged of the debt by its innocent payment to the assignor.

Equilease Corporation v. State Federal Savings and Loan Association, 647 F.2d 1069 (1981).

Obligor's Defense against the Assignee

Since the assignee takes rights under the contract through the assignor, any defenses *arising from the contract itself* are *not* cut off by the assignee giving notice to the obligor of the assignment to the assignee of the contract right. *The assignee gets only what the assignor has.* For example, A fraudulently induced B to contract with him. Thus the contract is voidable by B against A. Later, A assigns to C his right against B for $100 owing by B to A under the contract. B can avoid the contract and assert the fraud as a defense to C's claim against B.

---

[2] C is now liable to S who becomes a "third-party creditor beneficiary." See p. 187, for a discussion of third-party creditor beneficiary contracts.

If a defense *separate from the contract* arises between the obligor and the obligee-assignor *after* notice is given by the assignee to the obligor, such defense is cut off. This is not the result if the "separate defense" came into being *before* notice of the assignment was given to the obligor.

Discharge

If the obligor performs the duty owing to the assignor *before the obligor receives notice* from the assignee of the assignment of the right, the assignee has no claim against the obligor. The obligor having performed his or her contractual obligation innocent of the assignment is discharged of the obligation. The assignee's claim is directed at the *assignor* for breach of the assignor's warranty not to defeat or impair the value of the assignment. When a person claims he is the assignee, the obligor has the right to request such person to furnish the obligor reasonable proof of assignment to him.

Since most assignments are made *for the purpose of security for a debt,* when this occurs the Uniform Commercial Code then *governs* and provides in Article 9 on Secured Transactions that, if the assignee of an account receivable wishes the obligor *to pay directly to the assignee,* the assignee must not only give the obligor notice of the assignment but he must also *demand payment* from the obligor. If this is done, then the obligor *must* pay only the assignee. Notice of assignment alone is not enough to prevent the obligor from paying the assignor and thereby being discharged. In the following case notice was given and demand made by the assignee and the debtor's subsequent payment to the assignor did not discharge the debtor's obligation to pay the assignee.

Facts
Employee of a claims service settled an uninsured motorist's claim for an Insurance Company, defendant, with the insured. A memo was delivered to the insured addressed "to whom it may concern, a $4,300 settlement draft will be issued by the insurance company in the first week in May 1982." Insured obtained a loan from plaintiff bank and assigned to the bank the settlement payment as security for the loan payment. Plaintiff called the employee of the claim service and asked the employee to inform the insurance company of the assignment. The employee of the claim service sent a letter to the insurance company informing them of the assignment. On May 3, the plaintiff called the insurance company and relayed the request that the insurance company should send the insured's check to the bank. On May 12, the mother of the insured called the insurance company and asked that they stop payment on the insured's check sent to the bank. The insurance company stopped payment on the check, and issued a second check to the insured which was cashed by the insured. No funds have been paid by the insured to the plaintiff to pay off the loan. Plaintiff sues the insurance company to recover the proceeds of the first check.

Decision
Judgment for plaintiff.

Reasoning
An obligor is liable to an assignee for the debt assigned if the obligor pays that debt to the obligee-assignor after either actual or constructive notice of the assignment *and the assignee's demand of payment* by the obligor. Both by letter and by telephone call, the insurance company obligor had constructive notice of the assignment and of the assignee-bank's demand of payment. Therefore the company's payment to the insured does not relieve it from liability to the assignee–bank for the proceeds of the settlement claim.

Security State Bank of Aitkin v. Morlock, 355 N.W.2d 441 (Minn. 1984).

Warranty

warranty
an express or implied assurance that certain facts exist

The **warranty** an assignor makes to his assignee is that the contract is valid and that the right exists which the assignor can assign. The assignor also warrants there will be no interference with the assignee's perfection of the right. By the assignor later accepting performance from the obligor of the duty owed under a contract, the assignor has interfered with the assignee's right. An assignor does not warrant that the obligor is solvent (pays his or her debts), nor that the obligor will perform the obligation due under the contract.

Priority among Successive Assignees when the Assignment Is Not Made for the Purpose of Security

If an assignor *wrongfully* assigns a right *for value* to several successive assignees who are *innocent* of a prior assignment, there exist several claimants. *As among the claimants,* only one is entitled to performance of the duty owed by the obligor. Under the American rule in the majority of the states and the Restatement (Second) of Contracts, sec. 174, *generally* the first assignee in time has the best claim. Under the English rule, the first assignee to give notice to the obligor of the assignment to him or her has the best claim to the right. However, irrespective of the rights of several assignees among themselves, performance by the *innocent* obligor to *any* assignee discharges the obligor of the obligation.

Nonassignability

Certain *rights acquired* under a contract are nonassignable. Assignment may be prohibited by law. For example, in some states the assignment of *future* wages and personal injury claims is prohibited. Also, if the contract expressly or impliedly precludes assignment, it is personal in character, and the contract rights are *not assignable* by the obligee without the consent of the obligor. The contract is personal to the *obligor.*

A contract is impliedly personal in character and *nonassignable* when either (1) it involves the personal taste, skill, judgment, character, credit, or fancy of the obligor or (2) assignment would materially change the duties of the obligor or impose additional material risks or burdens upon the obligor or change the obligor's duty.

For example, the contracts of lawyers and public accountants with their clients are personal in character and nonassignable by the clients as obligees of such professional services because of the skill and judgment of the lawyer and the accountant obligors. The clients *cannot assign* their rights to such legal and accounting services without the consent of the lawyer and the accountant.

Basically, *assignment* by the obligee here is *not* allowed because it violates the *obligor's freedom of contract.*

However, a right as to *what is due* under an *executed nonassignable* contract is enforceable by the assignee. For example, the fire insurance contract on O's house prohibited assignment of the contract. A fire occurred and O assigned to E O's *right to the insurance proceeds* due O under the policy. E can enforce O's right to the proceeds. The *contract* had not been assigned, only the *right to the proceeds* had been assigned.

Nondelegability

Certain *duties imposed by the contract* cannot be delegated. Delegation may be prohibited by law. Also, if the contract expressly or impliedly precludes delegation, it is personal in character, and the contract duties are not delegable by the obligor without the consent of the obligee. The contract is personal to the *obligee.*

A contract is impliedly personal in character and *nondelegable* when either (1) it involves the personal taste, skill, judgment, character, credit, or fancy of the obligor or (2) delegation would materially alter the performance due to the obligee.

In the lawyer and accountant example given above, their contracts are impliedly personal and nondelegable for the same reason. The lawyer and the accountant are obligors with contractual duties to render professional services, and they *cannot delegate* their duties without the consent of their clients, obligees.

Basically, *delegation* here is *not* allowed because it violates the *obligee's freedom to contract.* In the following case the court held that, since the contract was not for personal service, contract duties were delegable.

Facts
Defendant is the owner of a tree farm. One Mooney had been performing management services on the farm for defendant. Mooney requested that defendant enter into a contract for management services and harvesting trees with a corporation for which Mooney worked and in which Mooney owned stock. The contract was entered into and subsequently assigned by the defendant to plaintiff, a successor corporation. Defendant wishes to avoid the contract with the successor corporation on the basis that the duties were nondelegable because of defendant's personal reliance on the services of Mooney.

Decision
Judgment for plaintiff.

Reasoning
The contract defendant made was not with Mooney personally but with the corporation for which Mooney worked. In fact, defendant was shown to have talked with one Santiago about the contract and knew that Santiago was also maintaining and harvesting trees for the corporation and would later take charge of the operation. Such evidence is sufficient to support a finding that the contract was not for personal services and, therefore, was delegable.

Emerald Christmas Tree Company v. Bedortha, 674 P.2d 76 (Or. 1984).

Some Code Provisions

Assignment. We have already seen that the Uniform Commercial Code requires that, when an assignment is made *for the purpose of security,* the assignee is to give *notice* to the obligor of the assignment and to *demand performance directly to the assignee* to assure that the obligor must perform only to the assignee. If the obligor, not knowing of any assignee prior to the demanding assignee, performs to the latter, the obligor is discharged.[3]

While the Code permits a buyer in a contract to agree that the buyer will not assert against an assignee who takes an assignment for value and in good faith any claim or defense which the buyer may have against the seller, such provisions have been invalidated in consumer credit transactions.[4] In the following case the court held that the contract granted the buyer the right to assert against the seller as well as the seller's assignee-holder of the retail installment contract all the buyer's claims and defenses arising out of the sale.

Facts
Plaintiff purchased a new pickup truck from defendant and signed a retail installment contract providing that the purchase price would be paid in 36 monthly payments and that other terms and conditions would apply. The contract was assigned by the defendant to General Motors Acceptance Corporation (G.M.A.C.). The vehicle was purchased for personal use and not for resale. It is undisputed that this transaction was a retail installment transaction subject to the provisions of the Texas Credit Code. Plaintiff contends that the retail installment contract violates the Credit Code. Above plaintiff's signature appeared the following in bold print:

NOTICE
ANY HOLDER OF THIS CONSUMER CREDIT CONTRACT IS SUBJECT TO ALL CLAIMS AND DEFENSES WHICH THE DEBTOR COULD ASSERT AGAINST THE SELLER OF GOODS OR SERVICES OBTAINED PURSUANT HERETO OR WITH THE PROCEEDS HEREOF

On the back of the contract in paragraph 7(c) the following was provided:

7. It is mutually understood and agreed that
   (c) except where the seller is also the manufacturer of said property, buyer will not assert against any subsequent holder as assignee of this contract any claim or defense which the buyer may have against the manufacturer or a seller other than the seller of said property obtained pursuant hereto.

TEX. REV. CIV. STAT. ANN. art 5069–7.07(6) (Vernon Supp. 1984) reads:

No retail installment contract . . . shall
(6) Provide that the buyer agrees not to assert against the seller or holder of . . . any claim or defense arising out of the sale. . . .

---

[3] See p. 184. Also, see p. 185 for priorities among successive assignees.

[4] UCC 9–201. Also see pp. 403–4 for Federal Trade Commission Rule.

Decision
Judgment for plaintiff.

Reasoning
The court found that a reasonable construction of the contract requires that the buyer have the right to assert against the seller, as well as any holder (assignee) of the retail sales contract, all claims and defenses arising out of the sale. The provision on the back of the contract, being in violation of a Texas statute, does not limit the buyer in this right.

Hinojosa v. Castellow Chevrolet Oldsmobile Inc. and G.M.A.C., 678 S.W.2d 707 (Tex. 1984).

Also under the Code,[5] a *right* as to what is due under an *executed* contract is assignable, and *its* assignment cannot be prohibited by the contract. (A contracts with B to supply goods to B, who is to pay A $1,000. The contract provides that *neither* the contract nor A's right to the $1,000 is assignable. A supplies the goods to B. The *contract* is nonassignable; nevertheless, A's *right* [account receivable] to the $1,000 is assignable by A to C, A's creditor.)

Delegation. The common law of delegation is changed by the Uniform Commercial Code,[6] which provides that, in the absence of anything to the contrary, an assignment *in general terms* is also a delegation of the assignor's duties, *and* the assignee's acceptance is a promise to perform them. When both contractual right and duty are simultaneously assigned and delegated to a third party by one of the parties to the contract, the other original party to the contract affected thereby may demand additional assurances, such as a bond or deposit, from the *third party* that the contractual duty assumed by the third party will be performed.

Other Third Parties

Third-Party Donee and Creditor Beneficiaries—Intended Beneficiaries

There are three types of **beneficiaries** to a contract: donee, creditor, and incidental. The first two are *intended beneficiaries;* that is, *the contract provides* that they are to receive certain contract rights. This is not true of the incidental beneficiary.

A **donee** *beneficiary* of a contract is a third person who has been given the right *under the contract* as a *gift* by a contracting party. For example, the life insurance policy of a husband designates his wife as the beneficiary with the right to receive the policy proceeds on the husband's death.

A **creditor** *beneficiary* is a third person (C) who is given the right *under the contract* (between S and B) to obtain performance by one of the contracting parties (B) of *an obligation owing to* the other contracting party (S) in discharge of the latter's (S) duty to the third person (C). For example, S contracts with B to sell his house to B, who agrees to pay S's mortgage (real property security) debt to C, the mortgagee (secured creditor). C is a third-party creditor beneficiary of the contract between B and S, and B is now liable to C for S's *duty* to pay C on the mortgage debt. S is still liable to C on S's mortgage contract with C; but when B fully pays C on the debt, S is then discharged of S's debt to C. (See figure 13.2.)

A third-party *incidental* beneficiary has *no* enforceable claim to any right under contract to which the beneficiary is not a party but *anticipates a benefit* if the contract is performed. Beneficiaries can enforce the contracts naming them as beneficiaries and to which they are not parties only *when the contract right is created for their benefit as creditors or donees.* In the following case the court held that the plaintiff was an incidental beneficiary because the contract was devoid of any contemplation of a third party.

beneficiary
a person who is to receive a benefit

donee
the recipient of a gift

donor
the person who makes a gift

creditor
one to whom money is owed

---

[5] UCC 2–210 and 9–318(4).

[6] *Ibid.*

Figure 13.2 Third-Party Creditor or Donee Beneficiary Contract

Facts
Plaintiff leased UNIVAC computer system and supporting equipment to Sci-Tek and TDC. One of the requirements of the lease was that Sci-Tek and TDC were required to enter into a maintenance contract for the leased equipment. Sci-Tek contracted with the defendant to maintain and repair the leased computers. Thereafter, Sci-Tek and TDC ran into financial difficulties and eventually became insolvent. Plaintiff seeks recovery from defendant contending it breached its maintenance contract with Sci-Tek/TDC thereby causing damage to the computer system.

Decision
Judgment for the defendant.

Reasoning
There are three theories to prove a third party beneficiary. One theory requires that the third party beneficiary must be *wholly* disclosed within the "four corners" of the contract. Another theory suggests that the third party beneficiary status can be ascertained wholly from extrinsic evidence. In this state, extrinsic facts and circumstances surrounding the execution of the contract can be examined for purposes of ascertaining third-party beneficiary status only when the language of the contract shows that it was entered into for the benefit of a third party, even though it may not specifically identify the party. Such is not the case here. The rationale for this court's theory is premised on the following:

To allow the unilateral intent of one party, without safeguards, to determine the existence of a third-party beneficiary would thwart the power that contracting parties should have to control their legal relations, particularly in a commercial setting.

American Financial Corporation v. Computer Sciences Corporation, 558 F.Supp. 1182 (1983).

Novation

novation
a new contract in which one of the parties was not a party to the old contract and which immediately discharges the old contract

In a **novation** (novo—new), (1) a *new* contract is made in which (2) one of the parties was *not a party to the old contract,* and (3) the new contract immediately *discharges the old contract.* A new party is substituted for one of the parties under the former contract. The new party may be a new debtor or a new creditor, usually a new debtor. For example, the bank creditor holds the debtor's land as security for the debt; the bank discharges the debtor's contract; and the bank takes in its place the new contract of the buyer of the land, who contracts with the bank to pay the bank on the new debt, the bank holding the same land as security for the buyer's debt. (See figure 13.3.)

The *consideration* given by one of the original parties to the contract (the bank in the example) for the substitution of a *new third party* (the buyer in the example) who assumes the duty to perform the obligations of the original contract is the discharge of the other original contracting party (the debtor in the example). In the following case the court held that there was a new contract of novation which bound the new party to the terms of the old contract.

Figure 13.3 Novation

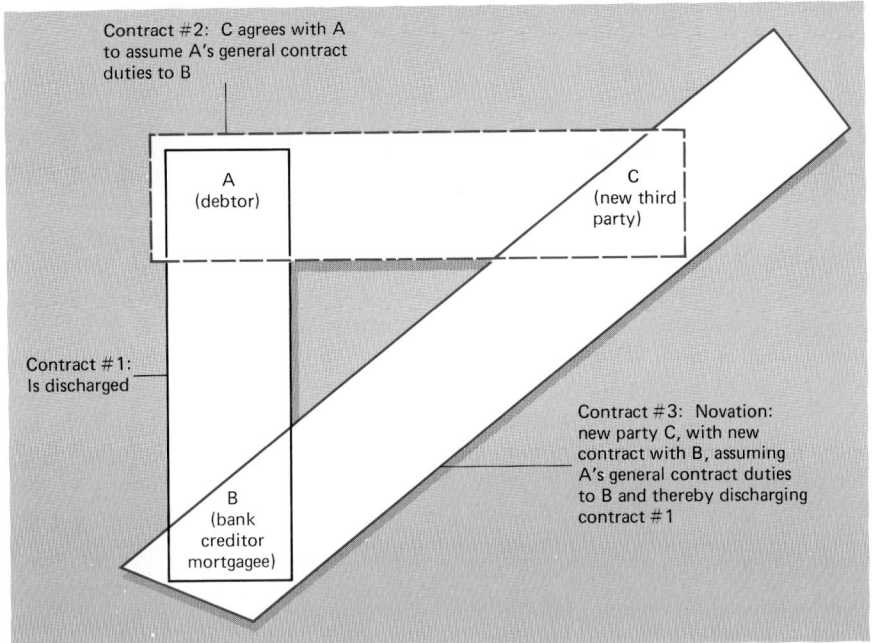

Facts
Plaintiff seeks to recover the purchase price of a refrigerated semi-trailer unit sold to defendant at an auction conducted by plaintiff. Defendant registered to bid at plaintiff's auction but was outbid on a five unit lot of Hobbs refrigerated semi-trailers. After the lot was "struck off" defendant approached the successful bidder and arranged to purchase four of the units. Both the successful bidder and defendant went to one of plaintiff's employees and had her mark through the successful bidder's bidding number on the auction memorandum and substitute defendant's bidding number. One of the terms of the auction sales contract was that a buyer of a sales item assumes "full responsibility" for the item at the time it is sold. In the process of transporting the trucks, defendant discovered that one of the trucks had been stolen off the auction lot after the auction sale. Defendant refuses to pay for this stolen truck.

Decision
Judgment for plaintiff.

Reasoning
In order to constitute a contract of novation subjecting the new party to the terms of the old contract, there must be (1) a previous contractual obligation (2) extinguished by a new contract, *effected by substitution of parties* or of undertaking; (3) with the consent of all the parties, the debtor, the creditor, and the third party. Assent to the terms of a novation need not be shown by express words, but may be inferred from the facts and circumstances attending the transaction and the conduct of the parties thereafter. Further, a person substituted as a party to a contract who agrees to perform the original obligation becomes bound by all the terms of the contract to the same extent as the original party. Here we have a sale when the auctioneer announced it by the fall of the hammer. The mark through the auction memo indicates the substitution of a new party for the obligation of the old contract. All parties consent to the novation. Under the terms of the contract, defendant bore the risk of loss upon sale and must pay for the stolen unit.

Taylor & Martin, Inc. v. Hiland Dairy, Inc., 676 S.W.2d 859 (Mo. 1984).

Creation of Third-Party Intended Relationships

At the Time the Contract Is Formed

The rights of a *third-party beneficiary* in the contract in which the beneficiary is named are created *at the time the contract is formed*. A *donee* beneficiary's rights arise the moment the contracting party who owns the right acknowledges that the right is being held for the beneficiary. If the contracting party reserves the right to change beneficiaries, the beneficiary's right is subject to divestment (termination) should the contracting party change the beneficiary. For example, H takes out a life insurance policy naming W, his wife, as a donee beneficiary, H reserving the right to change the beneficiary. H can inform the insurance company to change the beneficiary. If the contracting party does not reserve this right in a life insurance policy, the interest of the beneficiary is vested (fixed and irrevocable), and change cannot be made without the beneficiary's consent.

The interests of *creditor* beneficiaries normally vest in the contract after they have knowledge of it and move in reliance upon the right given. The beneficiary must be a creditor of the party (promisee) to whom the assuming party's (promisor) contract obligation is owed. For example, D takes out a policy of car collision insurance with I company, naming B bank as beneficiary, from whom D had borrowed the money to buy the car. B is the third-party creditor beneficiary of the policy, the insurance company is the assuming party promisor, and D is the debtor promisee. In summary, the assuming party's promise is made to the debtor promisee to perform the debtor's duty to the creditor third party.

In the following case the court held that a creditor of a corporation could be a third-party creditor beneficiary of individual shareholders' binding promises to a corporation to pay its debts.

Facts

Plaintiff alleges in substance as follows: Before February 3, 1967, she was an employee of General Aviation and had loaned it $4,602.50 and that the corporation also owed her $800 for back salary plus interest on both debts. Defendants, Freeman and Croom, were, at the time these debts were owed, officers, directors and sole shareholders of the corporation. On February 3, 1967, Freeman and Croom contracted in writing on behalf of General Aviation with defendant Colucci that the latter would pay General Aviation the sum of $10,000 for a 50% interest in the corporation. Part of the agreement reads as follows:

"Out of monies coming to the corporation . . ., the corporation shall pay accrued salary to Mrs. Snyder, [Plaintiff] of approximately $800, . . . and to Mrs. Snyder [Plaintiff] notes payable in the amount of $4,602.50 plus interest; . . ."

Plaintiff further alleges that, after the execution of the agreement and pursuant thereto, Colucci paid $10,000 to Freeman and Croom for General Aviation, but defendants failed to pay the plaintiff the funds owed her. Plaintiff seeks payment from the defendants.

Decision

Judgment for plaintiff.

Reasoning

Unless otherwise agreed between promisor and promisee, the beneficiary (plaintiff, Snyder) of a promise (made by Colucci) is an intended beneficiary if recognition of a right to performance in the beneficiary is appropriate to effectuate the intention of the parties (Colucci and General Aviation) and the performance of the promise will satisfy an obligation of the promisee (General Aviation) to pay money to the beneficiary (Snyder). This type of promise is referred to as a creditor beneficiary promise. In such a case, the promisee (General Aviation) is surety for the promisor (Colucci), the promise is an asset of the promisee, and a direct action by the beneficiary (Snyder) against the promisor is appropriate to carry out the intention of promisor and promisee. The agreement here is tantamount to a promise by the signatories, to *cause the corporation* to receive the capital and to pay plaintiff.

Snyder v. Freeman, 266 S.E.2d 593 (N.C. 1980).

Figure 13.4 Rights of Third Parties

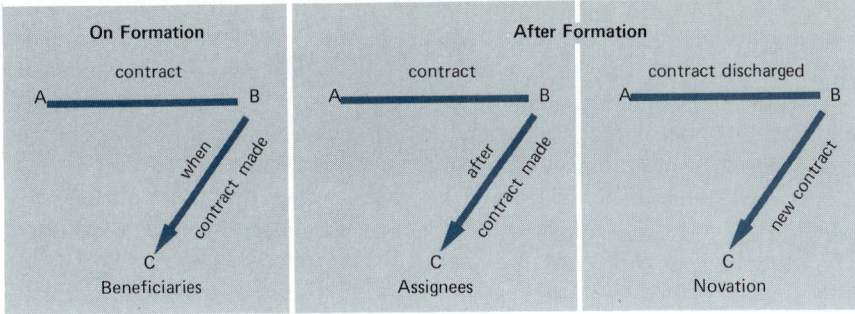

Since beneficiaries take their rights through a contracting party, they are subject to all the terms of the contract. If the contract provides that only the original parties to the contract may enforce it, then, although the right is created in the beneficiary *as of the time of the formation of the contract,* such right cannot be directly enforced by the beneficiary.

After the Contract Is Formed
Rights taken under a contract by novation or assignment occur *after* a contract is formed. (See figure 13.4.)

A contract may prohibit assignment by the creditor obligee of the obligee's *right to payment of money* from the debtor, or the contract may prohibit assignment of one party's *right to performance other than to pay money* by the other party. With respect to the prohibition of assignment of the *right to payment of money,* some courts hold that such a prohibition is contrary to public policy and of *no legal effect* because it limits the *assignor's freedom to contract* with third persons. Other courts hold that the prohibition is *valid.*

With respect to the prohibition of assignment of the *right to performance other than to pay money,* such a provision is valid and will cause the contract to be "personal in character" and nonassignable without the consent of the other party obligor.

A contractual promise *to* assign *future* contract rights in an *existing contract* gives only an expectation to an assignee which can be enforced in the future.

Remedies

The Concept of Remedy
We are still considering rights, but these are *new* rights contained *in remedies* for breach of contract. When a right is acquired by contract, the legal system will seek to protect it. If the one who owes the duty wrongfully does not perform, a **breach of contract** exists for which the law provides relief by giving a **remedy.** The various remedies available are money *damages, specific performance* by order or **injunction,** and *restitution. Reformation* is briefly discussed. These will be considered in turn.

Since the party enforcing the *remedy* may in all probability not get the *original right* due him or her under the contract, it should be recognized that the *right* which the remedy affords is a *second* type of *right* with its corresponding duty. For example, S contracts to dig a ditch for B. B has a *right* to have the ditch dug by S. On S's wrongful refusal to dig the ditch, B now has a *remedy* for S's breach of contract and, thus, a *new right* against S for one of the three remedies.

breach of contract
wrongful nonperformance of a contractual promise

remedy
the means by which a right is enforced or protected

injunction
a court order requiring a person to do or not to do something

Margin Glossary

damage
loss or harm

damages
the money judicially awarded to an injured party for another's wrongful conduct

injury
the wrongful invasion of another person's interest

nominal damages
the money judicially awarded to an injured party when no damage has occurred from another's wrongful conduct

anticipatory repudiation
a party's manifestation of an intent not to perform his contractual obligation, made before his performance is due

compensatory damages
the money judicially awarded to an injured party to compensate for damage caused by another's wrongful conduct

consequential (special) damages
the money judicially awarded to an injured party for loss which the breaching party reasonably could foresee would be a consequence of his breach

incidental damages
the money judicially awarded to a non-breaching party for expenses reasonably incurred by the non-breaching party on the other party's breach

quantum meruit
an action for services rendered based on an implied promise to pay plaintiff as much as plaintiff reasonably deserved for the plaintiff's services

Damages

A breach of contract is a *wrongful* nonperformance of a contractual duty. The word **damage** means loss or harm. **Damages** means the money judicially awarded (by the court) to an **injured** party for another's wrongful conduct. If a breach of contract has occurred but the injured party cannot show that he actually suffered damage, a symbolic award of **nominal damages** can be obtained. Usually the money award is $1. (A unauthorizedly walks over B's land without damaging the land. B's possessory interest in the land has been wrongfully invaded, and B can obtain nominal damages against A.)

Damages are determined as of the time of the breach, except that for an **anticipatory repudiation** and breach, damages are determined as of the time performance was to have occurred. For example, E employs X on Wednesday, X to report for work on the following Monday. On Thursday E tells X not to report for work. E has committed an anticipatory repudiation and breach of the contract. If X sues E on Friday, damages will be fixed as of Monday when X was to have begun work.

When loss due to breach of contract is something other than nominal, one is entitled to recover **compensatory damages,** compensating for damage actually sustained. One measure of compensatory damages is the difference between fair market value (the cost of a substitute performance) and the contract price. Another measure of compensatory damages (for a defective performance rather than no performance) is the difference between the value of a performance as promised or warranted and the actual value received. Compensatory damages could also be lost profits on lost sales or the cost necessary to make a defective performance whole.

Consequential (special) damages for loss *foreseeable* from a breach of contract are recoverable. For example, if A *knows* B's plant will be shut down if a promised machine is not delivered by a promised date by A, A can be held liable for B's loss of profit from lost production as a consequence of A's nonperformance and breach of contract. Consequential damages, when applicable, are given in addition to compensatory damages.

Incidental damages are another form of consequential damages and are usually incurred in a reasonable effort by the injured party, whether successful or not, to avoid loss. For example, an injured contracting party pays brokerage fees in arranging or attempting to arrange a substitute transaction for the one which the other contracting party failed to perform.

The following case shows that no matter what we call damages it is the purpose of the court to redress the wrong suffered by the party who has not breached the contract.

Facts
The plaintiff, a skilled baker, immigrated to this country from Greece and met an uncle, the decedent. The plaintiff moved in with the decedent and rendered personal services to him for many years. The decedent orally promised to leave the plaintiff one-half of his estate in his will. When the decedent was in poor health, he persuaded the plaintiff to give up his plans for acquiring his own bakery by again stating that he would leave plaintiff one-half of his estate. The decedent died but did not mention plaintiff in his will. The trial judge held that justice and equity required that judgment be rendered for plaintiff on a theory of **quantum meruit.** The dollar value of the judgment amounted to $375,000. Defendant, the representative of the decedent's estate, appealed.

Decision
Affirmed, judgment for plaintiff.

Reasoning
The measure of damages for the reasonable value of the plaintiff's services is premised on principles of restitution, that is, the party liable in restitution for monetary damages must pay an amount equal to the benefits conferred upon him. The promisee possesses a protected restitution interest because the promisor (the decedent), who is treated for purposes of the analysis as the contract breaker, has been unjustly enriched. The ascertainment of the fair market value of services so unusual in nature and so uncommon in ordinary experience is doubtless a matter of some difficulty, but the problem lies primarily in the domain of fact and its solution to a large extent is left to the good sense, practical wisdom and sound judgment of the trier of fact, mindful of the evidence and guided by the correct principles of law.

Hastoupis v. Gargas, Executor, 398 N.E.2d 745 (Mass. 1980).

Punitive (exemplary) damages are given in certain *tort* actions, but not for *contract* loss. Punitive damages seek to punish a wrongdoer and they need bear no relationship to *actual damages (compensatory and/or consequential)*. Victims of *intentional torts* can receive punitive damages awards. Under the common law, if one is defrauded into making a contract, one can either (1) avoid the contract; or (2) affirm the contract, sue for the tort of **deceit,** and obtain punitive damages. In the following case punitive damages were not awarded, both because the action was for *breach of contract,* and because the defendant had not *intentionally* committed a tort.

> **punitive (exemplary) damages**
> the money judicially awarded to an injured party in excess of compensatory damages to punish for malicious, wanton, or intentional wrongful conduct
>
> **deceit**
> briefly, a tort consisting of contractual fraud causing loss (for a full definition see the Glossary)

Facts
The plaintiff and defendant entered into an agreement providing that, in return for the plaintiff's assistance in the development, acquisition, marketing, production and distribution of the defendant's educational materials, the defendant would reserve an annual fee of $35,000 for three years on the plaintiff's behalf and provide the option of purchasing 25 percent of the defendant's authorized stock in lieu of payment of fees. The plaintiff alleged that plaintiff had performed all obligations but the defendant refused to perform. Among the counts of the plaintiff's complaint was one seeking punitive damages.

Decision
Judgment for defendant as not liable for punitive damages.

Reasoning
The court noted that as a general rule, courts would not award punitive damages for actions grounded solely in contract, only when the breach itself constituted an independent and willful tort accompanied by fraud, malice, wantonness or oppression, would recovery of punitive damages be permitted for a breach of contract. Here, the court was unable to identify any independent cause of action sounding in tort arising simply from the defendant's breach of contract.

McIntosh v. Magna Systems, Inc., 539 F.Supp. 1185 (1982).

Triple damages, a form of punitive damages, are assessed against violators of the federal Sherman Antitrust Act.[7]

Liquidated damages is the judicial award of the money *agreed upon by the contracting parties* as compensation for a breach of contract *before* the breach is experienced. For example, a contract for the sale of real estate may provide that, if the buyer does not pay the purchase price at the time of the closing of the deal, the buyer's money deposit shall be the liquidated damages. If the liquidated damages provision bears some reasonable relationship to the *actual damage,* it will be awarded for breach of the contract. If the liquidated damages provision is excessive, it will be denied. Such excessive damages agreements are considered penalties which are not enforced by law.

> **liquidated damages**
> the money judicially awarded in the amount as agreed to by the parties in their contract at the time it was made as reasonable compensation for damage which may be caused by the wrongful conduct of one of the parties in the future

Mitigation. If the non-breaching party to the contract can lessen the damage caused by a breaching party, the non-breaching party will be required by law so to act as to minimize the damage. For example, if an employer wrongfully discharged an employee under a contract with three months remaining, the employee has a duty to seek employment elsewhere for the three months period and thereby reduce the employee's loss of wages under the first contract. In the following case the defendant could not prove that the plaintiff had failed to minimize the damage.

Facts
In 1974, plaintiff, by virtue of having taught in the school district since 1959, was a permanent tenured teacher. In June 1974, it was found that the defendant Board of Education had wrongfully terminated plaintiff's teaching contract. Plaintiff was awarded damages of back pay plus six percent interest. Plaintiff made no effort to secure a teaching position in the community during the five years she had been unemployed. Defendant introduced evidence that teaching jobs in plaintiff's subject matter were available in the community, but it was shown that applicants outnumbered the jobs available and that none of the jobs filled were hires in plaintiff's age bracket. Defendant contends that plaintiff's damage award should be reduced because of plaintiff's failure to mitigate damages.

---

[7] For a discussion of the Sherman Antitrust Act, see pp. 704–5.

Decision
Judgment for plaintiff.

Reasoning
The employer has the burden to prove the employee's failure to mitigate damages. This burden is met when the employer proves that (a) one or more discoverable opportunities for comparable employment were available in a location as, or more convenient than, the place of former employment, (b) the improperly discharged employee unreasonably made no attempt to apply for any such job, and (c) it was reasonably likely that the former employee would obtain one of those comparable jobs. What the evidence showed was that there was not a reasonable likelihood that plaintiff could have received a job. Plaintiff's age and higher starting salary requirements made the finding of a teaching job slim at best. The defendant employer has failed to meet its burden of proof.

Stewart v. Board of Education of Ritenour Consolidated School District, 630 S.W.2d 130 (Mo. 1982).

Specific Performance
If damages will adequately compensate one for a breach of contract, an order from a court with equity power to specifically perform the contract will not be given. If the subject matter of the contract is *land* or a *unique item of personal property,* an order to specifically perform the contract will be given by a court with equity powers. Normally, before one is entitled to an equitable remedy, one must show that: (1) *his or her remedy at law for damages is inadequate;* (2) such equitable relief will *not* work an extreme hardship on the party in breach; (3) there is an enforceable contract; and (4) the court can grant such an *effective remedy.*

In contracts for *personal services,* a mandatory injunction ordering specific performance by a party will not be issued. Such an injunction would be in violation of the U.S. Constitution prohibition of "involuntary servitude" and also would be difficult to enforce. Also, a prohibitory injunction ordering that an act *not* be done will not be issued unless there is a threat of *irreparable harm* to the wronged party. Failure to comply with an injunction invites punishment for contempt of court.

Restitution

restitution
a legal remedy restoring one to his original position prior to the particular transaction

Restitution is a remedy which is an alternative to damages for material breach of contract. One cannot have both restitution and damages, nor restitution and specific performance. It is available against a party in default, for a party who may not enforce the contract because of the statute of frauds, and to a party upon his avoidance of a voidable contract. In restitution, the parties to the breached contract return what they have received, or the value of what was given if what was given cannot be returned. The objective is to restore the contracting parties to the positions they occupied before the contract was formed.

Reformation

reformation
an action to correct a writing so as to reflect correctly the intentions of the parties that mistakenly were not properly expressed in the writing

The remedy of **reformation** is not concerned with breach of contract, but it should be mentioned here. A written contract which, because of the parties' mutual mistake, does not state the parties' real agreement, generally will be reformed to reflect their real agreement by an action in a court with equity powers. For the purpose of reformation (changing the writing to reflect the real agreement) resort can be made to parol evidence as an exception to the parol evidence rule.[8] The result is that the contract can be reformed and enforced based upon the real agreement of the parties.

Election of Remedies
A party suing for breach of contract will be required to select a remedy. If one seeks damages, one is not entitled to restitution. If one seeks restitution, one is not entitled to specific performance. One can join an action for specific performance with a request for damages.

---

[8] For a discussion of the parol evidence rule, see pp. 156–57.

In the following case the court held that when one seeks restitution one is entitled to restorative restitutive damages.

Facts
The defendant, Gregg, fraudulently induced the plaintiff, Head & Seemann, Inc., to sell to the defendant a home which the defendant occupied for five months before being ejected by a court order. Plaintiff sought damages for the five months lost use of the property. At issue was whether a defrauded party who obtains rescission and restitution of real estate may also recover the rental value and out-of-pocket expenses for the period of lost possession. The trial court held that the election of remedies doctrine barred an additional action for rental value and out-of-pocket expenses. Plaintiff appealed.

Decision
Rescission and an action for restorative damages are not inconsistent remedies. Reversed, judgment for the plaintiff, seller.

Reasoning
The election of remedies doctrine is an equitable principle barring one from maintaining inconsistent theories or forms of relief. The classic application of the election of remedies doctrine is that a defrauded party has the election of either rescission or affirming the contract and seeking damages. Thus, it appears superficially that, if a claimant chooses to seek rescission, the claimant may not sue for incidental expenses. Rescission is always coupled with restitution. Restitution to a rescinding fraud victim includes everything the victim has reasonably paid out or given up in the transaction—here the rental value of the premises.

Head & Seemann, Inc. v. Gregg, 311 N.W.2d 667 (Wis. 1981).

Under the Uniform Commercial Code

Generally. Special damages under the Uniform Commercial Code are called consequential damages and can be recovered.[9] Under the Code, an action by the seller for the price of goods sold can be maintained when the goods are damaged or destroyed and risk of loss has passed to the buyer.[10]

Specifically. The remedies of an unpaid *seller* under the Code are: (1) actions directed toward the goods for security for payment of price; (2) mitigation of damage by reselling the goods; (3) suit for price and incidental damages; (4) damages; and (5) cancellation of the contract.

Under the Code, the remedies of a *buyer* are: (1) damages; (2) specific performance; (3) obtaining a security interest in goods and sale of the goods; and (4) cancellation of the contract.[11]

Summary Statement

1. The creation of a simple contract creates property, rights, and duties.
2. An obligation assumed by contract may be joint, several, or joint and several. Each of the contracting parties has rights and duties.
3. Rights are normally freely assignable unless the contract is personal in character. Duties are normally freely delegable if mechanical or ministerial in nature, but they are not delegable if the contract is personal in character.
4. A contract is personal in character if it expressly or impliedly precludes assignment or delegation.
5. The assignee gets only what the assignor has.
6. There are three types of third-party beneficiaries: donee, creditor, and incidental.
7. Rights of a third-party beneficiary arise at the moment the contract is created.
8. Rights taken by contract through the process of novation or assignment occur after the contract is formed.

---

[9] UCC 2–714 and 2–715.
[10] UCC 2–509 and 2–510.
[11] For detailed information on Code remedies in sales of goods, see pp. 290–302.

9. When an assignment of a contract right is *not made for the purpose of security,* if the assignee *notifies* the obligor of the assignment, the obligor must pay only to the assignee. If no such notice is given and the obligor innocently pays the obligee assignor, the obligor is discharged.
10. When the assignment is made *for the purpose of security,* under the *Code* the assignee must *notify* the obligor of the assignment *and demand* payment so that the obligor must pay only the assignee. If no such demand is made, the obligor may pay the obligee assignor and be discharged.
11. Under the Uniform Commercial Code, rights for what is due under an executed contract remain assignable; and the right to payment cannot be made nonassignable.
12. The remedies available for breach of a sales contract are numerous and varied under the Uniform Commercial Code. Under the common law of contracts, remedies for breach of contract are damages, specific performance, and restitution.
13. There are five types of damages: nominal, compensatory, consequential, punitive, and liquidated. Restitution is a remedy which is an alternative to damages and to specific performance.
14. One must mitigate damage.
15. The remedy of specific performance is given in limited circumstances.
16. The law associated with contractual rights seeks to enhance and protect rights created by one's exercise of the freedom to contract.

This chapter has made the point that the creation of a contract creates rights which can be transferred to or acquired by third parties and which the law will protect.

The following case is presented to illustrate how personal service contracts not normally considered assignable can, *in certain instances,* be assigned and how the law protects rights.

Munchak Corporation v. Cunningham
457 F.2d 721 (1972)

Winter, Circuit Judge. This is a suit by owners and operators of a professional basketball club to enjoin one of its players from performing services as a player for any other basketball club.

Cunningham, a basketball player of special, exceptional and unique knowledge, skills and ability, was under contract to play basketball for the Philadelphia 76ers. Cunningham's contract was about to run out with the 76ers, although they had a right under the contract to prevent him from playing basketball with any club for one year if he did not renew his contract with them.

A team called the Cougars entered into contract negotiations by intermediaries with Cunningham whereby they agreed to compensate Cunningham if he sat out a year under the "penalty" clause in the Philadelphia contract and, if he agreed for a stipulated compensation, to play for them for an extended period of time after the one-year suspension was over.

Cunningham entered into a contract with the Cougars, then owned by Southern Sports Corporation, on the terms previously indicated, but required in his contract with Southern Sports Corporation that it be prohibited from assigning its contractual right to his services to another "club" without his consent. *This contract contained no prohibition against its assignment to another owner of the same club.*

Subsequent to the contract, Southern Sports Corporation assigned its franchise to the plaintiffs, Munchak Corporation. Cunningham was not asked to consent, nor has he consented to this assignment. *The club "Cougars" still remains the same, only the ownership has changed.*

Cunningham wishes now to remain with the 76ers. His contention is that his contract with the Cougars was not assignable and that, by reason of a purported assignment, he is excused from performance of the previous contract with the Cougars.

The court recognized that, generally, the right to performance of a personal service contract requiring special skills and based upon the personal relationship between parties cannot normally be assigned without the consent of the parties rendering those services. However, the court held that such contracts may be assigned when the character of the performance and the obligation will not be changed. Change of ownership of a franchise does not change the character of the performance or obligation assumed by contract. The right is assignable and will be enforced by granting the injunction.

Questions and Case Problems

1. Charles and Linda Austin executed a promissory note in favor of plaintiff on January 27, 1981. On February 26, 1981, Charles Austin signed a document entitled "Assignment" wherein he purportedly assigned to plaintiff any proceeds which may result from settlement of an automobile accident between Charles Austin and Hazel Snyder, who was insured by defendant. Could Charles Austin assign this right to plaintiff? [*Town & Country Bank of Springfield v. Country Mutual Life Insurance Co.,* 459 N.E.2d 639 (Ill. 1984).]

2. Potential buyers had contracted to buy a house with a specific condition precedent that the contract was subject to the buyer receiving a conventional real estate mortgage loan. The bank involved subsequently withdrew its loan commitment and the potential buyer of the house rescinded the contract. The seller sued the bank for money damages. Is the seller a third party beneficiary of the bank's original loan commitment to the potential buyer? [*Khabbaz v. Swartz,* 319 N.W.2d 279 (Iowa 1982).]

3. The husband of a woman killed in an automobile accident involving another car brought suit against the manufacturer of the wife's automobile for the fatal injuries. Following the accident and in exchange for valuable consideration, the husband executed releases in favor of the driver of the other car and his insurance company. The releases also contained language releasing all other possible parties in the action for damages arising from the accident. The language was:

    "*any and all other persons, associations and corporations, whether herein named or referred to or not. . . .*"

    The husband was represented by counsel and freely executed the releases in consideration for the sum paid. The automobile manufacturer moved for summary judgment asserting that the releases acted to prevent the husband from bringing suit against it. What type of beneficiary is the manufacturer, if any? [*White v. General Motors Corporation,* 541 F.Supp. 190 (1982).]

4. Plaintiff, Boulevard National Bank of Miami, lent money to Air Metal Industries, Inc., defendant. To secure the loans, Air Metal purported to assign to the Bank certain accounts receivable it had with a contractor. At a later date Air Metal assigned as security to a surety company all its accounts receivable to reimburse the surety company in the event the defendant defaulted on certain contracts and the surety company had to pay damages on its performance bond. In July 1963 the surety company notified the contractor of the assignment of his account, the surety having had to pay on its performance bond. In August 1963 the Bank notified the contractor of the assignment and its claim thereunder. The contractor paid remaining funds owed to Air Metal Industries, Inc. to the surety company and the Bank sues the contractor on the basis that it had the preferred and prior right to payment. What result? Will the Bank win? [*Boulevard National Bank of Miami v. Air Metal Industries, Inc.,* 176 So.2d 94 (Fla. 1965).]

5. American Air Filter Company, Inc., is suing McNichol, a former employee, for an alleged breach of a restrictive covenant and employment contract not to compete. American Air Filter Company, Inc., claimed that McNichol in his new sales position had been competing with them in violation of the covenant. What is the compensatory measure of damages for a salesman's breach of a covenant not to compete? [*American Air Filter Company, Inc. v. McNichol,* 527 F.2d 1297 (1975).]

6. Plaintiffs engaged the defendants, a lawyer and the law firm, to examine title to unimproved property which they had contracted to purchase, and to effect a conveyance if title proved marketable. The defendants were attorneys engaging in real estate transactions and were aware of the inflationary trends in interest rates and construction costs. Defendants failed to discover that there was no recorded access to the property and this delayed obtaining a bank loan commitment until an easement of necessity was awarded in a judicial action. In a subsequent suit by plaintiffs, defendants were required to pay as damages the increase in construction and financing costs arising from the delay in obtaining bank financing. Defendants appeal. Who wins, defendants or plaintiffs? [*Myerberg, Sawyer & Rue, P.A.* et al. *v. Agee*, 446 A.2d 69 (Md. 1982).]

7. The plaintiff, the United States Government, entered into a contract with the defendant, Bubble Up Delaware, Inc., whereby the plaintiff would provide the defendant with $1,000,000, and in turn the defendant agreed to employ 300 hard core unemployed persons for a period of nine months. The contract contained a damages clause which obligated the defendants to refund $2,500 to the plaintiff for every employment opportunity short of 300. Is the clause a valid liquidated damages clause or an invalid penalty clause? [In re *Bubble Up Delaware, Inc.*, 684 F.2d 1259 (1982).]

8. Richter decided to purchase a used 1971 Ferrari Daytona Coupe automobile for $17,500 from Tatum, a dealer in foreign cars. Tatum did not have a car in stock but purported to locate one in the hands of another dealer which he described in some detail, giving serial number and other pertinent information on an order form and a bill of sale. These documents were used to support a bank loan for purchase of the car by Richter. Richter placed a deposit of $7,500 for purchase of the car with Tatum. Within a day or two after the cashing of the check, a car was delivered to Tatum which was a European version of a 1971 Ferrari Daytona Coupe intended for racing and not for operation on highways. Tatum took the position that it was not the car which Richter had ordered and refused to deliver the car, saying that he would try to locate another car. Tatum failed to produce another car. Richter brings this action for specific performance of the contract for the sale of the car. What result? [*Tatum v. Richter*, 373 A.2d 923 (Md. 1977).]

9. Under date of February 12, 1962, Blethen, an assignee of Howard Manor, executed instructions addressed to Prudential Escrows of Palm Springs:

escrow
the conditional delivery of property to a person who is to deal with it on the occurrence of specified conditions

"You are . . . authorized and instructed to advise American Express, Diners Club and Carte Blanc that all sums due Howard Manor, Palm Springs, California, are to be paid direct to this **escrow,** commencing April 1, 1962 to apply on final payment of a Note owed to me."

On April 5, 1962, Continental Bank entered into a written agreement with "Howard Manor," which set forth the terms under which "Howard Manor" would sell to the bank "such assets belonging to Assignor as may be acceptable to the bank." Notice of assignment of accounts receivable by Howard Manor, assignor, to Continental Bank, assignee, was filed with the County Recorder of Riverside County on April 9, 1962. $14,506.06 of Diners Club accounts were assigned to the bank. Diners Club was not aware of the assignment by Howard Manor to the bank. Diners Club paid Prudential Escrows on its accounts who then disbursed the money to Blethen. Who had priority as to the accounts—Blethen or Continental Bank? [*Continental Bank v. Blethen*, 86 Cal.Rptr. 485 (Cal. 1970).]

10. In *Munchak Corporation v. Cunningham*, 457 F.2d 721 (1972),[12] the court perfected the assigned right to personal services by preventing the basketball player from playing basketball for any club but the Cougars. Evaluate the action by the court.

---

[12] See pp. 196–97.

Ethics and Business Law in Part 2
Contracts

Introduction

This end-of-Part discussion, like the others in this book, is designed to encourage students to begin forming personal beliefs about what is right or wrong conduct in business. The discussion here builds on the material in the first end-of-Part discussion on pages 58 to 69; you may find it helpful to review that.

This material has several goals. The overview section is designed to help you see the range of ethical issues associated with this area of the law. The in-depth discussion is intended to provide you with a background for forming your own beliefs about a single very important ethical issue in business. The problems at the end of this Part are designed to build your skill in ethical analysis while exploring further the in-depth issue.

Overview of Ethical Issues in Contract Law

Promises are the heart of contract law. But is it ethical to break a promise just because it does not constitute a contract? This opportunity arises in a variety of ways. For example, a promise is affected by the statute of frauds, or the statute of limitations. This alters its *legal and enforceable* character; but do you think this changes its *moral* character? Similarly, a promise not supported by consideration may not be legally enforceable but may still constitute an *ethical* obligation. Business persons are frequently called on to decide whether or not they are justified in breaking a promise which is not enforceable in court.

In contract law, a promise is enforceable if consideration is present, but it need not be adequate or fair. Stated another way, courts will enforce contracts even if the items exchanged are unequal in economic value. This doctrine compels persons to look out for their own self-interests. Both the legal doctrine and its consequences (making people more careful in looking out for their own self-interests) keep people out of court. But some are injured when they contract on terms which are very unfavorable. Is it ethical to enforce contract rights if this causes financial injury to one party?

Another ethical issue is associated with contractual capacity. Is it ethical for a minor to disaffirm a fair contract for the purchase of non-necessaries? This law is designed to protect those who have limited capacity, yet disaffirmance can do very serious injury to an innocent party on the other side of the contract. This presents knowledgeable persons who lack capacity with a dilemma: ought they to assert their legal rights when it benefits them, yet injures others?

The law of remedies can be viewed as a system for defining liability for breaking your promise. In business, situations frequently arise where it is more profitable to breach and pay damages than to fulfill a contractual duty. For example, assume you contracted to deliver 10 box cars of frozen chickens at $1.75 per chicken. Then a nearby soup company encountered an emergency which caused it to offer you $2.00 per chicken. If the market value was still at $1.75, you could, assuming there were no consequential damages, breach without being liable for damages and still earn an extra 25 cents per chicken. But would this be ethical? Do additional profits justify violating your promise?

199

In-Depth Discussion of a Basic Issue: Truth Telling

Your study of the law of contracts has also been the study of the way the courts view truth telling in the context of contract law. Fraud, concealment, and other types of misrepresentation are legal ideas which confront the ethical issue of truth telling.

When Does Deception Constitute Lying?
Exactly when is it that we have failed to tell the truth? Obviously, when we state as true something which is untrue, we have lied. Suppose you say to me, "Please sign this lease document right now because I'm in a hurry to get home; the rental amount in the lease is $295 per month." If the rental amount stated in the lease is actually $395 and you know it and intend to deceive, then clearly you have lied (and probably committed fraud). However, once we depart from this type of clear-cut situation, truth telling and/or lying become more difficult for most of us to define.

Material Omissions. Would it be lying for you to ask the prospective tenant to sign the lease after stating the true monthly rent, but without disclosing that the lease agreement gave you, the landlord, the right to keep the cleaning deposit even if the apartment were left spotless at the end of the lease? In other words, is it a lie if you leave out of your description important information about the transaction?

Would it matter to you that the party injured by your material omission is someone with whom you have a relationship of trust, such as an elderly relative? Notice that the law imposes greater obligations on fiduciaries—those who occupy positions of trust. Can you ethically justify treating strangers differently from those you know better?

Concealment. Do you think your obligation to tell the whole story is increased because someone has asked a question about a particular issue such as the cleaning deposit? Can you justify not telling the tenant about the cleaning deposit clause in the lease on the grounds that the tenant failed to ask?

Fraudulent Misrepresentation. Suppose I ask you, "How much will the utilities for the apartment cost?" If you do not know, would it be a lie for you to say, "They are about average for an apartment this size"?

Puffing. There are truth-telling issues associated with the use of broad, flowery language such as, "It is a *wonderful* place for you to live!" "Wonderful" is a very vague term. Courts call such terms puffing. Generally, people are not liable for false puffing. If you knew the noise, distractions, price, and distance from campus made your apartment a bad place for this tenant to live, would the vagueness of the term "wonderful" make it ethical for you to use it?

Affirmative Non-Disclosure. If someone clearly misunderstands reality, and you are doing business with them, are you obligated to correct their perception? Suppose I said to you, "I like the apartment because it is only 25 minutes from campus." If you knew that during most times of the day the actual travel time in congested traffic was 65 minutes, would you be lying if you remained silent?

Asserted Justifications for Lying
A Right to the Truth. Many people believe that they are not obligated to give information to everyone. Thus, if the owner of a competing apartment building asked you for information about the rental rates in your building, do you think you have a duty to disclose that information? Most people would say, no. Some of these people conclude that since there is not a right to the information, we can also deceive the competitor, perhaps by giving him wrong information about our rental rates. Do you think this is ethical?

Protecting Others. Sometimes people lie to others to protect their feelings. Suppose I say, "I am sure I will meet lots of members of the opposite sex in this apartment complex whom I can date, don't you think so?" If you think I will not because I am an unappealing person, should you tell me so? Would it be ethically wrong to lie to me by agreeing with my statement? Do you think it makes any difference if your reason, or motive, for lying to me were to rent the apartment rather than to protect my feelings?

Profits. In business, the most frequent justification for lying is profits. When there is money to be made by legal lying, many will do it. Will you?

Ethical Reasoning about Truth Telling

Markets
The market assumes that the parties to business transactions have complete information about both the market and the particular transaction. If one party lacks this information, it is called a market imperfection. When a market imperfection is present, the market may not achieve all of its moral goals. It is clear that markets are based upon the assumption of truth telling.

The Law
The legal system generally seeks the same objectives as the market when it regulates business conduct. Legislative and judicial penalties for fraud, concealment, and other types of misrepresentation promote truth telling in business transactions. But the legal and market systems are imperfect. They do not always *compel* the conduct which they were intended to foster. Thus it is often profitable to lie.

Consequential Ethical Reasoning
For many persons, whether or not one may lie is based on the *results* of the lying. If these people are purely self-interested, they are *egoists* who may lie only if there is a benefit to them. Additional rental income would be such a benefit. Of course many sophisticated egoists would refuse to lie because they fear a reputation for lying will cause them injury resulting in loss of benefits.

Others who look at consequences judge the impact of lying on all the people affected. These people are *utilitarians*. Thus, a utilitarian might decline to lie if it would injure the tenant and his family of five. That is because only one landlord is benefited while five tenants are injured.

Kantian Philosophy and Religious Ethics
Some people embrace certain things as "good" in and of themselves, without regard for the consequences. Truth telling is one of the things these people usually consider a "good" irrespective of its consequences. The Kantian is always under a duty to tell the truth without regard for the consequences.

Similarly, those who hold religious beliefs judge truth telling to be fundamentally good. Religious writings from the Bible, to the Koran, to the Gita all condemn lying.

Solving Ethics Problems

Like the other end-of-Part discussions in this book, this one presents problems for *you* to consider. These problems have three goals. The first is to give you the opportunity to further explore the in-depth issue. The second goal is to give you experience in ethical reasoning about the law and about related management problems. The third goal is to let you see how thinking critically about the law can increase your ability to make ethical decisions. To facilitate this, the problems begin by asking you to analyze the law for its ethical content and then shift to looking at related problems in managerial ethics.

For a discussion of the ethical roles of markets and the law and examples of the four styles of ethical reasoning—egoism, utilitarianism, Kant's philosophy, and religious ethics—read the business ethics material at the end of Part 1.

Problems

1. Recall the case of *Dalton v. Bundy* in chapter 9 on page 133. There, the Bundy parents placed the title of their home in the name of their 12-year-old daughter, Janet Bundy. Later they contracted for the purchase of vinyl siding for $3,380 for the house. After the siding was installed they declared bankruptcy. The seller of the vinyl siding sued Janet for the value of the siding. Janet defended by asserting her minority and prevailed. Assess the conduct of Janet's parents using the four styles of ethical reasoning. Do you think the conduct of the Bundy parents was a form of lying? If you conclude they engaged in deception, how do you reconcile that ethical conclusion with the outcome of this case? Is the law here attempting to balance another ethical good against the ethical good of truth telling? Can you articulate what that other "good" is?
2. In May of 1978, the St. George, Staten Island Branch of Citibank, conducted a "Fire Sale Promotion" offering free checking to new customers opening a Citibank Checking and Savings account along with a Checking Plus line of credit. The only advertisements of this promotional campaign were signs in windows and on counters of the Staten Island branch. In August of 1979, the bank decided to terminate the free checking privileges of selected depositors. Did the bank's signs misrepresent the nature of its offer by failing to disclose its reserved right to terminate free checking at its own discretion? Is the bank's conduct ethical?
3. Recall the case of *McBride v. City of McCook* in chapter 11 on page 158. There the city advertised a job in the local newspaper, purportedly for a period of 18 months. McBride took the job, but was terminated after just 5 months. When McBride sued for the loss of income for the other 13 months, the city asserted the statute of frauds, stating that since the contract required more than one year to complete and there was no writing, the purported 18 month contract was unenforceable. Who won the lawsuit? Assume that there was an oral agreement for a job for 18 months, then assess the conduct of the city using the four styles of ethical reasoning. Do *you* think the city acted ethically? If you conclude that the city acted unethically, how do you reconcile this with the outcome of the case? Do you think the law is sometimes compelled to have arbitrary rules even if they lead to unfair results?
4. Joe is the owner of a small manufacturing firm. A retailer is interested in purchasing 100 air compressors from Joe for immediate delivery. The retailer is pressed for time and asks Joe about prior safety testing, price, terms of credit, the tank's capacity, and the delivery schedule. Joe responds truthfully to nearly all the inquiries, but he intentionally omits discussing safety testing because there has *not* been any. The retailer is in such a hurry that he does not notice the omission. Assess Joe's conduct using the four styles of ethical reasoning.

PART **3** Personal Property and Bailments

14. **Personal Property**
    Description of personal property, how it is distinguished from real property, how it is acquired, and the various kinds of ownership of property.

15. **Bailments**
    The meaning of bailment, how the law of bailments applies in business and other transactions, and the rights and duties of the parties to a bailment. Lost, misplaced, and abandoned personal property are also discussed.

16. **Carriers, Documents of Title, and Innkeepers**
    The use of carriers of goods—particularly the common carrier—their liability, and the documents of title (e.g., bills of lading and warehouse receipts) issued by carriers and warehousemen. Innkeepers (e.g., hotel and motel operators) are also considered.

Summary

Property is something that is the subject of ownership. Personal property consists of movable things and interests in those things. A good (chattel) is a tangible, movable thing (e.g., a typewriter) and, as such, it can be transferred from one person to another in many types of business transactions.

One method of transfer is to deliver only *possession* of the goods, with the goods to be returned to the owner later. This creates a "bailment" of the goods. *Title* to the goods may be transferred in various ways, as by gift or sale, and there may be various forms of ownership.

The goods may be added to, as when a muffler is placed on an automobile. Or the goods may produce something, as when an animal produces offspring. This is a form of "accession." The goods may also be permanently affixed to land, in which case they become a part of the realty and are called "fixtures."

Warehousemen and carriers as "bailees" issue paper, called "documents of title," which acknowledge receipt of goods and contain the contract terms. This paper is personal property and capable of transfer by sale, as security, or in other ways. All bailees have duties of care with respect to the bailed goods and have varying levels of liability.

Business ethics as it relates to the text material in this Part is considered at the end of the Part.

14 Personal Property

After you have read this chapter, you should be able to:

1. Define real property, personal property, and fixtures.
2. Explain why property distinctions are legally important.
3. List the methods by which property is acquired.
4. Define and distinguish accession and confusion.
5. Define gifts inter vivos and gifts causa mortis.
6. List and define the different types of common ownership of property.

Introduction

In this chapter we will discuss what is meant by property, the different kinds of property, the methods of acquiring property, and the various forms of property ownership.

Let us assume, for example, that Susan, a recent college graduate, made a list of the property she owned. The property included: (1) ten shares of corporate stock in Widgets International Corporation; (2) an antique dresser; (3) a valuable bookcase which Susan had attached to the wall in her apartment; and (4) an acre of farmland which Susan used for organic farming. Susan now wonders how this property would be legally classified and whether the classification would affect her rights to use or transfer the property.

If Susan acquires additional property, with her husband or with another person, additional questions will be raised. Susan might question the different methods of acquiring property. For example, is it safe to purchase goods from a merchant who might not own them? May Susan transfer property to her sister, who is a minor? What are the tax consequences of making a gift? Susan also might question the form of ownership. What is the nature of joint ownership of property? What are the special joint ownership rules in southwestern states such as California? Is joint ownership a good substitute for a will?

The Meaning of Property

Property is difficult to classify because the concept of property has a number of meanings. Property is a concept that is the cornerstone of law, for the law developed to protect property rights. **Property** means a thing or any interest or right in a thing that is capable of being owned. The owner of an interest or right in a thing is entitled to use, enjoy, or dispose of such interest or right, subject only to governmental regulations. The owner has "property."

property
a thing; also an interest or right in a thing

Property Classifications

Real and Personal Property

Real property is land or an interest or right in land and other immovable things fixed to the land, including structures on the land. Land is a tangible, immovable thing. The owner of the surface of land owns the soil beneath the surface and the air above the surface, subject to reasonable use by aircraft. Susan's acre of land is classified as real property.

Personal property is a movable thing or an interest or right in the thing. It moves with the person, thus "personal" property. Personal property is considered to be *tangible* if it can be touched. The word **chattel** means tangible personal property. Intangible property is property which cannot be touched. Susan's antique dresser would be considered tangible personal property. Her *shares* of stock would be intangible personal property because, while the certificate is tangible, the shares are interests in the corporation and cannot be touched. Another illustration of intangible personal property is an account receivable. (Dan owes Charlie $100. Charlie has an account receivable—an intangible claim—against Dan for $100.)

real property (realty)
land and immovable things attached to land, along with interests and rights in the land; also a freehold interest in land

personal property (personalty)
a movable thing, along with interests and rights in the thing

chattel
a tangible, movable thing

Fixtures

The remaining item on Susan's list, the bookcase, is difficult to classify as real or personal property because it once was movable but now it is immovable, having been attached to the wall. The bookcase is considered to be a **fixture,** which is defined as a chattel which has become attached to real estate in such a way that it is considered to be real property, but is still available for chattel financing.[1]

fixture
a chattel which, under real estate law, has become permanently attached to realty and thus ceases to be a chattel and becomes part of the realty; it still can be used as collateral for a **security interest**

---

[1] The fixture still retains sufficient character as a chattel. For example, a bathtub fixed in a house can be used as security for a loan. However, the brick, lumber, tile, and glass in a building are not fixtures; they are a part of the structure. Fixture financing is discussed on page 454.

Three tests are used to decide whether a chattel has become a fixture. *First,* is the chattel annexed to the real estate by nails, screws, glue, or other methods? It is possible that even where the property is not physically annexed, the *annexation test* will be met because of the weight of the object, as is illustrated by the following very early case.

Facts
A statue weighing three to four tons was erected in a courtyard in front of a house. The statue was not fastened to the real estate with clamps, cement, or by any other device. The plaintiffs bought the owner's personal property; the defendant bought the owner's real property. Plaintiffs sued defendant for the value of the statue contending that it was not a fixture.

Decision
Judgment for defendant as the owner.

Reasoning
The statue is a fixture and therefore part of the real estate. A chattel may be annexed to real estate as much by weight as by any other device.

Snedeker v. Warring, 12 N.Y. 170 (2 Kernan) (1854).

The *second* fixture test is *adaptation*—is the article adapted to, and necessary for, the use of the real estate? A furnace installed in a house is necessary for the use of the house and would meet this test. In some cases, where the article is closely adapted to the use of the real estate, it will be considered a fixture even though there is no physical annexation. Examples include garage door openers and television antenna dials.

The *third* and most important test used by courts is *intention*—do the actions, words, purposes, and relationships of the parties show that they intended to make the property fixtures? In determining intention, the courts are not interested in the hidden or secret intention of the parties.

Reasons for Property Distinctions

Now that Susan has classified her property, she faces the question of why the classification is important. There are four reasons why property distinctions are legally important.

Transfer During Life. If Susan wants to transfer her *real property* and fixtures attached to the real property during her lifetime, she will use a deed. A **deed** is a written document which must be in a form required by law. When Susan transfers her *personal property,* however, it is unlikely that she will use a document to transfer title; although in cases involving a substantial transfer of personal property, a document called a **bill of sale** is often used. A bill of sale is somewhat similar in form to a deed. (See figure 14.1.)

Transfer at Death. The distinction between real and personal property is important in determining the transfer of property at death. Susan might have a **will,** a document which governs the transfer of her property at her death. A will has no legal significance until a person's death and can be revoked at any time before death. If Susan dies without a will, she is said to have died **intestate.** In such cases, state law determines the disposal of her property, and the law usually distinguishes between real and personal property.

Source of the Law. The source of the law will vary, depending on whether property is classified as real or personal. For instance, when personal property is sold, the sale is governed by the provisions of the Uniform Commercial Code, a statute which has been enacted in all states except Louisiana, where parts of it have been enacted. The law relating to the sale of real property, on the other hand, will usually be found in case decisions or in statutes other than the Uniform Commercial Code.

Taxation. The taxation of property varies, depending on whether the property is real or personal. Real property is normally taxed by a local governmental body, such as a city or township. Personal property is often not subject to taxation, or is taxed locally or by the state at a different rate than real property.

---

security interest
"an interest in personal property or fixtures which secures payment or performance of an obligation" UCC 1–201(37)

deed
a formal document used to transfer title to real estate

bill of sale
a formal document used to transfer title to personal property

will
a formal document which governs the transfer of property at death

intestate
(noun) a person who died without a will

Figure 14.1 Bill of Sale

BILL OF SALE

I, John H. Doe, in consideration of the sum of $5000 paid by Tom J. Smith, the receipt whereof is hereby acknowledged, do grant and convey to Tom J. Smith, his executors, administrators or assigns, my Eversharp Riding Lawn Mower, serial #1007, to have and to hold forever.

In witness whereof, I have set my hand and seal this 12th day of April, 1987.

WITNESSES:

_____

_____   _____
                                     John H. Doe

State of _____ ⎤
                          ⎬ ss
County of _____ ⎦

John H. Doe, being duly sworn, deposes and says that he is the vendor named in the within Bill of Sale, that he has knowledge of the facts, and that the consideration of said instrument was actual and adequate, and that the same was given in good faith for the purpose therein set forth, and not for the purpose of security, or for defrauding creditors of the vendor or subsequent purchasers.

_____

Subscribed and sworn to before me this 12th day of
_____April_____ 1987.
Notary Public, County of _____
State of _____
My commission expires _____ 19__

Methods of Acquiring Ownership

A number of methods may be used to acquire personal property. For example, an artist may acquire personal property by creating it—through painting or sculpture. A creditor may acquire personal property by obtaining a court judgment against a debtor. A person may acquire personal property by finding it, as discussed in the following chapter. And the state may acquire personal property through **escheat,** whereby property passes to the state when a person dies leaving no one to inherit the property. Four methods of acquisition, however, have special legal significance—accession, confusion, gifts, purchase.

escheat
the transfer of property to the state when a person dies without heirs

Accession

Susan has decided to replace the shelving in her antique dresser. She takes the dresser to a furniture repair shop, where the new shelving is built into the dresser. This is an example of **accession**—the increase in property by what it produces or by the addition of other property to it. Examples are adding a muffler to an automobile or a mare producing a foal. Here, the shelving as property is added to other property in the form of the dresser. In such cases, Susan, as owner of the dresser, becomes owner of the shelving as well.

The situation becomes more complicated when the new shelving is installed by an innocent third party to whom the shopowner has wrongfully sold Susan's dresser or by a thief who steals the dresser from Susan. If the shelving cannot be removed without damaging the dresser, the general rule is that Susan may recover from the thief either the

accession
the increase in property by what it produces or by the addition of other property to it

dresser or damages based on the value of the dresser as repaired. The result would be the same if Susan sued the innocent third party, with two major qualifications. First, Susan would not be allowed to recover the dresser if the innocent purchaser substantially altered the dresser to such an extent that it is in reality a different and more valuable dresser than the one which Susan originally owned. Second, in a suit for damages against the innocent purchaser, value would be based upon the value of the dresser when Susan owned it rather than its value with the new shelves, as is illustrated by the following early case.

Facts
On Christmas Eve, 1918, Ochoa's Studebaker truck was stolen. Eventually it was sold to Rogers, defendant, as "junk"—a pile of broken parts—for $85. Rogers used the parts to construct a delivery truck at an expense of $800. In 1920 Ochoa, plaintiff, spotted the truck and recognized the parts. Ochoa sued Rogers for return of the truck or for the present value of the truck, $1,000.

Decision
Judgment for plaintiff, Ochoa, for only $85.

Reasoning
Rogers was an innocent party who made improvements to the property which exceeded the value when Rogers acquired the property. In such cases, the innocent purchaser is liable only for the market value at the time he acquired possession.

Ochoa v. Rogers, 234 S.W. 693 (Tex. 1921).

Confusion

Confusion occurs when chattels of different persons are mixed so that the chattels of one person cannot be distinguished from the chattels of the other persons. Fungible goods are like units of goods (e.g., wheat), and are the most common kind of goods confused. Confusion is different from accession.

In most cases, confusion of personal property is not complicated in legal terms. For instance, assume that Susan grows wheat on her real estate and stores her wheat at a local grain elevator, where it is mixed with the wheat of the elevator operator. If the wheat is of the same quality, it can easily be divided when Susan decides to sell her share of the wheat.

Gifts

Gift Inter Vivos. While a gift may be made of personal or real property, here we are concerned with only personal property, particularly chattels. Accordingly, a **gift** is a voluntary transfer of a chattel by a **donor** who is not to receive anything in exchange from the person receiving the chattel, the **donee**. A gift after the death of a person is accomplished by the use of a will. A gift during life, an **inter vivos** gift, is somewhat more complicated than after-death gifts because two requirements must be met: (1) the donor must have intended to make a gift, and (2) there must be delivery of the chattel to the donee.

The *intent* requirement means that the donee needs to prove more than mere possession of the chattel to prove a gift. In many cases, the intent of the donor is clearly spelled out in a letter or other writing. In other cases, courts will infer intent to make a gift because of factors such as the relationship between the parties and the size of the gift.

The *delivery* requirement is met when the donor transfers the chattel to the donee in such a manner that the donor relinquishes all right to and control over the chattel. Delivery may be *actual,* as when the donor delivers a new automobile to the donee, or *symbolic,* as when the donor delivers the keys to the car to the donee instead of delivering the car itself. Additionally, the delivery may be made to a third party who is to hold the property for the donee, or to a person already in possession of the chattel who is to keep it as a gift.

Acceptance by the donee is frequently mentioned as an additional requirement for a valid inter vivos gift. However, this requirement is rarely important to the outcome of a case because courts presume that acceptance is present when the gift benefits the donee.

The requirements of donor intent, delivery, and donee's acceptance for a valid gift to occur are illustrated by the following case:

---

confusion
the mixing of chattels of like kind of different persons so that the chattels of one person cannot be distinguished from the chattels of the other persons

gift
a voluntary transfer of personal or real property by someone who is not to receive anything in return

donor
the person who makes a gift

donee
the recipient of a gift

inter vivos
among living persons

Facts
Alfred opened a joint savings account in his name and in the name of a friend, Mary. He later delivered the account passbook to Mary. After Alfred's death, his executor claimed that Alfred had not made a gift because, when he opened the account, he signed Mary's name on the signature card. Mary claimed that a gift had been made to her.

Decision
Judgment for Mary.

Reasoning
This was a valid gift. Alfred clearly intended to make a gift when he opened the account, even though he signed Mary's name. Delivery occurred when Alfred delivered the passbook to Mary, and the acceptance requirement was met when Mary received the passbook, although acceptance is also presumed.

In re the *Estate of Alfred V. Sipe, Deceased,* 422 A.2d 826 (Pa. 1980).

Gift Causa Mortis. Gift cases are not difficult to resolve when the required intent and delivery exist and when the donor makes an *unconditional* gift to the donee. The cases are more difficult when the donor places a condition on the gift, such as, "This stereo is yours if I do not return from my trip to Boulder." In this case there is not a valid gift because it is not a *present* gift but, instead, an attempted future gift. This is true even if the condition is met.

The major exception to the conditional gift rule is the case where a donor facing imminent death from a present illness or impending peril makes a conditional gift to a donee which is to be *effective immediately.* The donor may revoke the conditional gift anytime before the donor's death from that illness or peril, and revocation occurs automatically if either the donor recovers or the donee predeceases the donor. However, the gift is valid if not revoked. This is a **gift causa mortis**.

gift causa mortis
a conditional, revocable gift by someone facing imminent death from a present illness or impending peril

Gift to a Minor. Susan wants to make a gift of $100 and a share of stock to her sister Sally, aged ten, but feels that Sally is too young to manage the property. How should Susan make the gift? The answer is found in the Uniform Gifts to Minors Act which has been adopted in 48 states.

Gift Tax. The federal government imposes a gift tax on a donor and an estate tax on an estate at death. Gifts are popular because, under the Tax Reform Act of 1976, no tax is levied for gifts which do not exceed $10,000 per year for each donee. Thus, by combining their gift tax exclusions, a husband and wife could jointly give a child $20,000 per year tax free.

Purchase
The last method of acquiring property is by purchase. The sale and purchase of *goods* under the Uniform Commercial Code is the subject of Part 4, Sales. The most troublesome area in the purchase and sale of chattels in general is the case where a nonowner sells the chattel.

Assume, for example, that a thief, Clyde, steals Susan's bookcase and sells it to an innocent third party, Rudolph. If Susan sues Rudolph to recover the dresser, the difficult question the law faces is deciding which innocent party, Susan or Rudolph, must suffer the loss. The cases generally fall into one of the following four categories.

Void Title. If the person selling property had *void title,* which is no title at all, the purchaser acquires no title. Thus, in our example, Susan would win the case because the thief, Clyde, having no title of his own, had no title to transfer to Rudolph.

Voidable Title. In many cases a person will acquire title to goods that may be avoided by the seller. For instance, if Susan were fraudulently induced by Clyde to sell the bookcase to Clyde, Clyde would have *voidable title. Susan* could avoid her contract *with Clyde.* In such cases, however, *Rudolph* would win if sued by Susan because, under sec. 2–403(1) of the Uniform Commerical Code, a person with a *voidable title* to goods, such as Clyde, has the *power* to transfer a good title to a good faith purchaser who pays value.

damages
the money judicially awarded to the injured party for another's wrongful conduct

conversion
the tort of intentional interference with another's right to possession, control, and dominion of a chattel

estoppel
a principle of law that when one person "holds out" (represents) a material fact to another person, who changes his position materially to his prejudice in reasonable reliance on the holding out, the first person is "estopped" (prohibited) to deny what he asserted previously

joint tenancy
a form of ownership of property by more than one person with the right of survivorship

Entrustment. Whenever an owner entrusts goods to a merchant who deals in similar goods, under the Code the merchant has the power to sell the goods to a "buyer in the ordinary course of business." If Susan delivered a valuable antique necklace to a dealer in jewelry for repairs, and the jeweler sold the necklace to Rudolph, Rudolph would be the owner of the necklace. Susan's only recourse would be to sue the jeweler either for **damages** for breach of the bailment contract, or for the tort of **conversion** for the value of the necklace.

Estoppel. If the owner of goods indicates to a third party that someone else owns the goods, and the third party, in reliance on the statement, buys the goods from the nonowner, the third party may keep the goods under the principle of law called **estoppel.** This principle prevents a person from denying what he or she had represented (held out) previously to another person if, meanwhile, the other person had changed his or her position materially in reasonable reliance on the representation.

Forms of Ownership

Ralph and Betty are engaged to be married. Before the marriage they decide to purchase personal property (a car) and real property (a summer cottage on a lake). If either Ralph or Betty purchases the property as individuals, the form of ownership would not be complicated in legal terms because the title would be in the name of only one of the two. However, whenever two or more persons join together to purchase property, they must decide whether to purchase the property as joint tenants, tenants by entirety (or the entireties), or tenants in common. Each of these methods will result in different legal consequences.

Joint Tenancy

Ownership in **joint tenancy** is ownership of property by more than one person with the right of survivorship. When one person dies, the other surviving person or persons automatically becomes the *sole* owner or owners because this is what the parties intended in using joint tenancy. If Ralph and Betty purchased the car and cottage as *joint tenants,* on Betty's death the property would be owned by Ralph *alone* without the necessity of probate (proof of a will) court proceedings, which are usually necessary when a person dies.

Four requirements must be met if there is to be a joint tenancy between two or more persons such as Ralph and Betty. First, Ralph and Betty must acquire their interests at the *same time.* Second, they must acquire their interests in the *same conveyance;* that is, their title must be the same. Third, they must have an *equal interest* in the property. And fourth, they must have the right to *equal possession* of the property.

Severance. A joint tenancy will be *severed,* that is, the interest of the parties will be separated, whenever one of the four requirements is destroyed. A joint tenancy interest, however, cannot be severed or transferred by a will. There are four common methods of severance: conveyance, divorce or dissolution of marriage, partition, or murder.

Conveyance. A conveyance by one of the joint tenants will sever the joint tenancy. For instance, if Ralph and Betty own the cottage as joint tenants and Betty sells her interest to Steve, Ralph and Steve would own the property as tenants in common, not as joint tenants. The same result is reached in cases of involuntary conveyance where a sheriff sells Betty's interest in order to pay her creditors. If *three* persons, A, B, and C, own as joint tenants and C sells his interest to D, the relationship between A and B is still a joint tenancy but, with respect to D, they are tenants in common. As the following case shows, severance also occurs when one joint tenant deeds her interest to herself.

Facts
Agnes and Ida, who were sisters, owned property as joint tenants. Ida deeded her interest in the property to herself as a tenant in common. When Agnes died, Ida claimed that the conveyance was invalid and that she was the sole owner of the property as the surviving joint tenant.

Decision
The deed is valid and therefore Ida owns only a half interest in the property as a tenant in common.

Reasoning
A joint tenant can sever by conveying her interest to herself as a tenant in common. Conveyance to a third party is not necessary to create a joint tenancy and should not be required for severance.

Minonk State Bank v. Grassman, 432 N.E.2d 386 (Ill. 1982).

Divorce/Dissolution of Marriage. If Ralph and Betty own property as joint tenants as a married couple, severance occurs when they are divorced. In some states, however, the divorce judgment must specifically order severance; and, if the property is not specifically mentioned in the divorce judgment, the joint tenancy continues after the divorce.

Partition. A **partition** takes place when Ralph and Betty divide their property either voluntarily or by court order. If a court handles the partition, a physical division of the property is preferred. It is not possible, however, to physically divide a cottage or a car, and in such cases a court will order that the property be sold and the proceeds divided between Ralph and Betty.

partition
a division of property between joint owners

Murder. Assume that Ralph murders Betty while they hold property as joint tenants. Should Ralph be allowed to take the property as the survivor? This has been a difficult question for the courts, and three different approaches have developed. The first approach is to decide that Ralph receives the property as survivor despite the murder. The second approach would be that the property passes to Betty's estate, with Ralph receiving nothing. The third approach would be to give Ralph half the property and Betty's estate the other half.

Tenancy by Entirety

A **tenancy by entirety** (or by the entireties) is identical to a joint tenancy except that it can be created only between a husband and wife, and the couple must have been husband and wife at the time the property was acquired. Furthermore, a tenancy by entirety can be terminated only when *both* husband and wife agree to the sale.

tenancy by entirety
a form of co-ownership between husband and wife with the right of survivorship

Control. In most states both the husband and the wife have equal right to control and possess the property held as tenants by entirety. However, in some states, following an older view of the marriage relationship, the husband has the exclusive right to control and possession.

Tenancy in Common

A **tenancy in common** is distinguished from the joint tenancy and tenancy by entirety by the fact that in a tenancy in common, when one person dies, the decedent's interest passes to the decedent's estate rather than to the surviving tenant. A tenant in common is free to convey his or her interest or seek a partition by agreement or by court proceedings.

tenancy in common
a form of ownership of property by more than one person without survivorship

Community Property

If Ralph and Betty settle in one of nine states in the Midwest, Southwest and West, much of their property would be considered **community property.** These states are Arizona, California, Idaho, Louisiana, New Mexico, Nevada, Texas, Washington, and Wisconsin.[2]

community property
a form of ownership by husband and wife of property acquired by their efforts during their marriage

Although community property laws often vary from state to state, the law generally provides that all property acquired through the efforts of the husband and wife during

---

[2] For further discussion of community property, see p. 763. The "sharing" concept in community property law is now embodied in the new Uniform Marital Property Act (UMPA) of 1983, which is a community property act being presently considered by a number of state legislatures.

their marriage is considered to be community property. All other property—property acquired either before marriage, by gift, or by inheritance during marriage—is the separate property of the husband or wife.

Summary Statement

1. The distinctions of real property, personal property, and fixtures are important in matters such as transfer of property and taxation.
2. Accession involves the addition of property; confusion involves the mixing of chattels of different owners.
3. Gifts may be made during life if there is intention and delivery. A conditional gift may be made during life, such as a gift causa mortis.
4. In making a gift to a minor, the donor must meet the requirements of the Uniform Gifts to Minors Act.
5. A good faith purchaser for value will acquire good title from a nonowner if the nonowner: (1) has voidable title; (2) is a merchant dealer of goods to whom similar goods have been entrusted; or (3) has been held out as the owner by the real owner under the principle of estoppel.
6. When property is acquired by more than one person, it may be held in (1) tenancy in common, (2) joint tenancy, or (3) tenancy by entirety. In the Midwest, Southwest and West, community property represents another form of ownership of property.

The following older but well-known case has been chosen because it illustrates the difficult decision courts face when one joint tenant murders another.

Bradley v. Fox
129 N.E.2d 699 (Ill. 1955)

Lawrence Fox murdered his wife, Matilda, with whom he owned property in joint tenancy. After the murder a question arose concerning ownership of the property.

    Davis, Justice. In this category of cases the courts have differed as to whether the murderer should be allowed his survivorship rights. Those courts which hold that he is entitled to the entire property as surviving joint tenant predicate their conclusion on the legal fiction incident to the concept of joint tenancy, whereby each tenant is deemed to hold the entire estate from the time of the original investiture, and reason that the murderer acquired no additional interest by virtue of the felonious destruction of his joint tenant, of which he can be deprived. . . . Other courts, however, concerned with the equitable principles prohibiting a person from profiting from his own wrong, and with the realities of the situation, have abandoned the Common Law fictions, and have either divested the killer of the entire estate . . . or have deprived him of half the property . . . or have imposed a constructive trust on the entire estate held by the murderer for the benefit of the heirs of the victim . . . or a constructive trust modified by a life interest in half the property.

    In joint tenancy the contract that the survivors will take the whole necessarily presupposes that the death of either will be in the natural course of events and that it will not be generated by either tenant murdering the other. One of the implied conditions of the contract is that neither party will acquire the interest of the other by murder. It is fundamental that four coexisting unities are necessary and requisite to the creation and continuance of a joint tenancy; namely, unity of interest, unity of title, unity of time, and unity of possession. Any act of a joint tenant which destroys any of these unities operates as a severance of the joint tenancy and extinguishes the right of survivorship. . . . It is our opinion, therefore, that it would be unconscionable for defendant Fox, as murderer of his joint tenant, and for defendant Downey, as transferee [of the property from Fox] with full knowledge of how Fox acquired the sole legal title to the property and of the fact that the conveyance was in fraud of creditors' claims, to retain and enjoy the beneficial interest in the property. It is our conclusion that Fox, by his felonious act, destroyed all rights of survivorship and lawfully retained only the title to his undivided one-half interest in the property in dispute as a tenant in common with the heir-at-law of Matilda Fox, deceased.

Questions and Case Problems

1. The Premonstratensian Fathers purchased a supermarket and leased it back to the prior owners. The building contained five coolers, valued at over $23,000. The cooler walls constituted the walls of other rooms, and the coolers were attached to a hardwood floor which was attached to concrete. When the coolers were destroyed by fire, the insurance company refused to pay on the grounds that they were not fixtures and therefore were not covered by fire insurance on the building. Is the company correct? [*The Premonstratensian Fathers v. Badger Mutual Insurance Co.,* 175 N.W.2d 237 (Wis. 1970).]

2. Emma decided to assign certain property rights to her children. .Her attorney prepared an assignment and his secretary took it to Emma's house. After the secretary read the assignment, Emma signed it and gave it to the secretary with the intent that it be delivered to her children. Three days later, Emma changed her mind and asked the attorney to return the assignment. Did Emma make a valid gift? [*Estate of Leo G. Saathoff,* 295 N.W.2d 290 (Neb. 1980).]

3. Sligo Furnace Co. owned timberland. Hobart-Lee Tie Co. trespassed on the land, cut down timber and used it to make railroad ties. Sligo sues Hobart-Lee to recover the value of the ties, claiming that, under the law of accession, a willful trespasser is liable for the value of the timber as improved. Decision? [*Sligo Furnace Co. v. Hobart-Lee Tie Co.,* 134 S.W. 585 (Mo. 1911).]

4. A mother, using her own money, purchased securities in her name and the name of her daughter as joint tenants with the right of survivorship. The mother retained possession of the certificates. A dispute arose regarding dividends, and the mother brought suit against the daughter claiming that the daughter had no interest in the securities. Decision? [*Kinney v. Ewing,* 492 P.2d 636 (N.M. 1972).]

5. Closter lived in the same rooming house with his friend Schutz. Closter owned a note for a debt owed him by a third party. One day Closter went to his room, indorsed the note to Schutz, placed the note on a table and shot himself. Schutz entered the room and took the note while Closter was unconscious but before death. Did Closter make a valid gift to Schutz? [*Liebe v. Battman,* 54 P. 179 (Or. 1898).]

6. Montgomery, a career soldier, had a savings account in a bank. Before going to Germany, he delivered the savings account passbook to his first cousin, Mrs. Stone, and stated: "If I happen to crap out, it is all yours." Montgomery died in Germany. Does Mrs. Stone own the savings account? [*Guest v. Stone,* 56 S.E.2d 247 (Ga. 1949).]

7. Green sold his house to Strain but, after the sale, Green removed a chandelier from the dining room. The chandelier had been in Green's family for fifteen years and he had moved it from house to house whenever he moved. Strain sued Green for the chandelier contending that it was a fixture. Decision? [*Strain v. Green,* 172 P.2d 216 (Wash. 1946).]

8. A husband and wife own a home as tenants by entirety. After thirty-five years of marriage, they become estranged and the husband refuses to allow the wife into the home. May the husband exclude his wife from the home? [*D'Ercole v. D'Ercole,* 407 F.Supp. 1377 (Mass. 1976).]

9. A husband and wife lived in a community property state. Husband owned two restaurants as separate property. Through the husband's efforts during the marriage, the restaurants were income-producing. Is this income community property? [*Steward v. Torrey,* 95 P.2d 990 (Ariz. 1939).]

10. In *Bradley v. Fox,* 129 N.E.2d 699 (Ill. 1955),[3] the court held that it would be unconscionable for Fox to profit from his criminal conduct by taking, as a joint tenant, property by surviving his victim. How does this decision evidence the complementary nature of the various areas of the law and a limit to the concept of property?

---

[3] See p. 214.

15 Bailments

After you have read this chapter, you should be able to:

1. List at least five situations where bailment law personally affects you.
2. Define a bailment.
3. Discuss some of the applications of bailment principles.
4. Describe the duties of a bailee in the three types of bailment.
5. Decide whether a bailee may disclaim liability.
6. Describe the rights of a person who finds lost or mislaid goods.

Introduction

In the preceding chapter of this Part, we discussed the concept of property and its *ownership*. In this chapter we will discuss the subject of "bailments," which is concerned with the transfer of *possession* of *goods,* the goods to be returned on the accomplishment of a particular purpose.

Bailment Defined

A **bailment** may be defined generally as the delivery of goods (or chattels) by one person, the **bailor,** to another person, the **bailee,** for a particular purpose, with the understanding that at a future time the goods are to be redelivered to the bailor or delivered to a third person as directed by the bailor in accordance with the bailment agreement. For example, a seller (bailor) delivers goods to a railroad (bailee) for delivery to a buyer. Another example is the commercial bailment (for hire)—e.g., the rental of office furniture, equipment, or machines, which are to be returned at the end of the rental period.

The word bailment is derived from the French word *bailler* meaning "to deliver." The key to the creation of any bailment is *delivery* of *goods* and their *return*. The courts interpret *delivery* as a combination of a voluntary transfer of *physical possession* coupled with the bailee's *intention to control* the property. This combination will be further explored in the applications which follow.

Using the general definition of a bailment, two related transactions may be distinguished, a **lease** of space and a sale. When a person leases a locker or a parking space and deposits goods in the locker or parks a car in the space, a bailment is not created because the *goods* have *not been delivered* to the lessor. Instead, the owner of the goods has retained possession and control of the goods. However, a *lease of goods* creates a bailment.

A **sale** is distinguished from a bailment in that the purchaser acquires *title* to the goods and is under no duty to return the goods, although it is possible that the purchaser will deliver other goods to the seller as payment.

Applications

To illustrate the application of bailment principles, we will examine three situations where bailment law has been especially troublesome to courts.

The Cloakroom

A common bailment issue arises when a person hangs his or her coat in a cloakroom in a theater, restaurant, or store. To illustrate the application of bailment law to the cloakroom setting, we might assume that three students—Tom, Dick, and Harry—visit a clothing store to shop for sweaters. Tom takes off his coat, lays it across a clothes rack, and begins to try on sweaters. A clerk helps Dick remove his coat and lays it next to Tom's coat. Harry leaves his coat on a hook in a changing room before trying on the sweaters. A thief steals all three coats, and the question arises whether the store is liable for the coats as a bailee.

In all three cases the coats were left on the store's property, and consequently the store potentially had the power to physically control the coats. But was the other requirement met? Did the store show an *intention to control* the coats? Most courts would agree that there was no intention to control Tom's coat. There is no proof that the store even knew that Tom had laid down his coat. A clerk physically removed Dick's coat, however, and this act implies an intention to control. Thus the store would be a bailee of Dick's coat but not of Tom's coat.

---

bailment
a delivery of goods by a bailor to a bailee which are to be returned to the bailor or as the bailor directs in accordance with the bailment agreement

bailor
the person who bails goods

bailee
the person to whom goods are bailed

lease
(of goods) a form of contract giving one person, the lessee, the exclusive right to use or possess for a period the goods of another, the lessor

sale
the transfer of title from seller to purchaser for a price

Harry's coat presents the greatest legal difficulty. On the one hand, it is generally held that a store does not become a bailee merely because there are hooks on the wall for customers' garments, for the reason that the store offers this as a service to the public and makes no attempt to supervise the clothing. On the other hand, a bailment would exist if a coat is *checked* with a person in a restaurant cloakroom, or if the coat is left in a *private* room or office, as is illustrated in the following case concerning a clothes closet in a doctor's office used for patients' clothing.

Facts
A woman visited her psychiatrist wearing a fur coat worth $1,725. Upon entering the office, she deposited her coat in a clothes closet in the reception room. After her consultation with the psychiatrist she discovered that her coat was missing, and she sued the psychiatrist, claiming that he was liable as a bailee. Is the psychiatrist a bailee?

Decision
The psychiatrist is a bailee.

Reasoning
By maintaining the closet, the psychiatrist was impliedly inviting his patients to leave their coats there under his control. He also should know that patients normally must remove their coats before their consultation.

Laval v. Leopold, 47 Misc.2d 624 (N.Y. 1965).

The Parking Lot
Let us assume that, upon leaving the store without their coats, Tom, Dick, and Harry proceeded to their respective cars. Tom had parked his car in an unfenced, unguarded lot. He had paid the attendant upon entering the lot, kept the keys to the car, and was free to pick up his car and to leave at any time. Dick had parked his car in a lot where an attendant had taken the key to his car, had parked it for him, and had retained the key. Harry parked his car in the type of lot commonly found at airports. He entered the lot by removing a ticket from a machine and, in order to leave the lot, he must produce the ticket and pay an attendant. Upon arriving at the three lots from the store, Tom, Dick, and Harry discover that thieves have stolen their cars and, once more, they question whether a bailment has been created.

In Tom's case, clearly a bailment has not resulted, because Tom has retained control of the car. Dick clearly has created a bailment because, in delivering the key to the attendant, he also delivered physical possession, and the attendant, by taking the key, showed the required intent to control the car. In other words, in many cases the key to determining whether a bailment exists is the possession of the key!

Harry's case is more difficult. In cases involving airport lots, most courts hold that a bailment relationship is not created because the parking lot owner does not control vehicles parked in the lot.

If we assume that Dick can recover the value of his car because of the bailment relationship, can he also recover the value of a CB radio which he had installed in the car and the value of his tennis racket which was in the trunk of the car? Under the **closed container rule,** the bailment of the automobile includes only those items of which the parking lot attendant has actual notice or which the parking lot attendant should have known were in the car. Thus, if Dick did not give the attendant actual notice that the CB and the racket were in the car, the bailment would cover only the CB, because the attendant should have seen the CB when he parked the car. The bailment would not include items in the "closed container," the trunk, such as the tennis racket, but would include the spare tire, the jack, and other ordinary accessories, because people generally are aware of their presence in a car trunk.

closed container rule a bailee is not responsible for the contents of a closed container unless the bailee knows or should know the contents

Safe Deposit Box
Courts have decided that the bank is the bailee of the box and generally also bailee of the contents of the box because banks should know that customers use the boxes to store valuable possessions. In many states court decisions have been overturned by statutes which provide that the rental of the box is a lease of the box but not a bailment of its contents, and which allow a bank to limit its liability to a certain amount.

Figure 15.1 Types of Ordinary (Private) Bailments and Bailee's Duty of Care

Type of Ordinary Bailments	Bailee's Degree of Care
Sole benefit of bailor	Minimal
Mutual benefit	Reasonable, ordinary
Sole benefit of bailee	Extraordinary

Rights and Duties

Bailee's Duty to Return Identical Property to Bailor

At the conclusion of the bailment, the bailee must return the identical property to the bailor—even if the bailor is not the owner—or to a third person, as directed by the bailor or as previously agreed. If there is no duty to return identical property, the transaction is a sale rather than a bailment.

Bailee's Duty of Care

A bailee is not liable as an insurer of the goods. That is, a bailee is not liable in all cases when goods within the bailee's control are damaged or destroyed. Instead, the bailee is responsible only when he is *negligent* by failing to exercise the proper degree of care, which will vary depending on the facts of each case. However, in all cases the burden of proving that the requisite degree of care was met is on the bailee since, because of his possession and control of the goods, he is in the best position to explain why they were damaged or destroyed.[1]

To illustrate the different degrees of care required of a bailee, we might assume that Jimmy owns a pair of tennis shoes, a tennis racket, and a can of tennis balls. In preparation for a trip, Jimmy asks his good friend Able to do him a favor and keep his tennis shoes for him, which Jimmy then delivers to Able. Jimmy then delivers his tennis racket to Susan who is to restring the racket for $10. And Chance borrows Jimmy's tennis balls for use in a local tournament. Three different types of bailment have been created. The bailment of the tennis shoes is a *bailment for the sole benefit of the bailor,* Jimmy, and the bailee owes only a duty of *minimal care* in looking after the shoes. The bailment of the tennis racket is a *bailment for mutual benefit* in that Jimmy benefits by having his racket restrung and Susan benefits by being paid. In such cases the bailee owes a duty of *ordinary care*. The bailment of the tennis balls is for the *sole benefit of the bailee,* Chance, who must exercise *extraordinary care* in looking after them. See figure 15.1.

A bailee who uses the goods for his own purposes without the permission of the bailor is liable for any loss. For example, if Susan, after stringing Jimmy's racket, had used it in a tournament and, during the tournament, an armed robber stole the racket, Susan would be liable for the loss even though she exercised reasonable care under the circumstances.

---

[1] There is an additional reason for the element of the bailee's negligence in bailments. A bailee has the duty to return the goods in proper condition to the bailor. The bailee's failure to do this subjects him to liability for breach of their agreement, usually a contract, unless the bailee can prove that such failure was *not* due to his negligence. If the bailee is not negligent, then his failure is excused. If the bailee is negligent, his failure is not excused.

Figure 15.2 Parking Ticket with Disclaimer

> **FAIL-SAFE PARKING LOT**
>
> TICKET #10567
>
> Company is not responsible for any loss or damage to the automobile or its contents.

Contractual Modification of the Duty

The bailor and the bailee may decide to modify the legal duty of care of the bailee when they negotiate the bailment contract. In some cases the bailee will assume a greater duty. For example, the contract might provide that the bailee is an insurer of the goods, or that the bailee has a duty either to return or to pay for the goods. This agreement is legally valid.

A more common type of contractual modification is a **disclaimer** of liability by the bailee. For example, when you deliver a car to a garage for repairs, a sign on the wall might provide: "The garage is not responsible for loss or damage to cars"; or when you deliver your coat to a restaurant cloakroom attendant, there might be a provision on the back of the claim check: "The restaurant is not responsible for any loss or damage to articles."

A bailee using these disclaimers faces two major legal problems. *First,* since the disclaimer involves a contractual agreement, the bailee must prove that the bailor agreed to the terms of the contract. A bailor who was unaware of the sign or the language on the *back* of the claim check will not be bound by the disclaimer. Furthermore, courts generally do not favor disclaimers and will not uphold them unless the language is clear. In the following case the disclaimer did not specifically cover negligence.

disclaimer
denial of an obligation or a claim

Facts
A corporation, plaintiff, which was engaged in commercial photography, purchased several rolls of Kodak film which it used to shoot movies in Alaska. After the movies were taken, the film was sent to Eastman Kodak Co., defendant, for processing. However, as a result of Kodak's negligence, a substantial portion of the film was damaged. The corporation sued Kodak for over $1,500, expenses incurred in refilming. Kodak's defense was that the box containing the film noted that, except for replacement of film, the sale "is without warranty or other liability of any kind."

Decision
Kodak is liable. Judgment for plaintiff.

Reasoning
The law disfavors disclaimers of liability especially when, as in this case, the disclaimer does not specifically cover negligence.

Willard Van Dyke Productions v. Eastman Kodak Co., 189 N.E.2d 693 (N.Y. 1963).

The *second* problem is that many courts have decided that, on the grounds of public policy, a bailee may not disclaim liability for his own negligence. The public policy reasons are especially strong when the person receiving the goods is in the bailment business and when the bailor has little bargaining power. For instance, Waldo wanted to park his car in a major city, and all of the parking lots had signs disclaiming liability for damage to cars. (See figure 15.2.) When Waldo tried to negotiate with the lots by offering to pay more if they would remove the disclaimer, they all refused and, in effect, told him, "Take it or leave it." Most courts would hold that Waldo would not be bound by the disclaimer because it was forced on him by the party offering an essential service. However, the result would be different when the bailor is a large corporation with strong bargaining power of its own or when Waldo is negotiating with a friend who wants to rent his stereo. In such cases the disclaimer will probably be upheld because the bargaining power is equal.

Part 3: Personal Property and Bailments

Lost, Mislaid, and Abandoned Personal Property

Finder's Rights

In leaving class one day Ray discovered someone's business law book. Ray is legally considered a *finder,* and his rights depend upon the legal status of the book.

The book might be considered **abandoned property,** discarded goods in which the owner has voluntarily relinquished all interest. If the book was found in a wastebasket, it is likely that the book would be considered *abandoned,* and Ray, the finder, would now own the book.

But the book might also be classified as **lost property,** goods in a place where they were not intentionally put by the owner, who does not know where they are. If the book were accidentally dropped in the hall by the owner, it would be considered *lost* property. The book might also be considered **mislaid property,** goods which the owner has voluntarily laid down and forgotten where they were laid. If the owner laid the book on a windowsill and then forgot where it was laid, it would be considered *mislaid* property. With both *lost* and *mislaid* property, the owner retains the right to the goods.

However, the finder, as an *involuntary* bailee,[2] has a right to the goods which is superior to everyone in the world except that of the owner. If the owner never reclaims the goods, the finder may keep them. In other words, the rule is "finders keepers," although the losers are not weepers if the losers reclaim the goods! In the following early, classic case, the finder of jewelry prevailed over a person to whom the finder bailed the goods and who refused to return the goods to the finder.

abandoned property
discarded goods in which the owner has voluntarily relinquished all interest

lost property
goods in a place where they were not put by the owner who does not know where they are

mislaid property
goods which the owner has voluntarily laid down and forgotten where they were laid

Facts
A chimney sweep, plaintiff, found a piece of jewelry. He delivered it to a jeweler, defendant, to have it appraised. The jeweler's apprentice removed the jewels and refused to return them to the chimney sweep. The chimney sweep sued the jeweler for the value of the jewels.

Decision
Judgment for the plaintiff, chimney sweep.

Reasoning
A finder has superior rights of ownership against everyone but the real owner.

Armory v. Delamire, 1 Strange 505, 93 Eng. Rep. 664 (1722).

Owner of the Locus in Quo

Although as a general rule the finder's rights to the goods are superior to all but the owner, the rule often has no effect when the goods are discovered on *private* property. The owner of the private property is called the owner of the **locus in quo,** which means the "place in which" the goods are found. If the owner of the *locus* can prove any one of five tests, he or she will be considered the *involuntary* bailee and, if the owner never appears, will keep the goods.

First, the owner of the *locus* will prevail if the goods are found in a *private area* on the property. The reason for this rule is that the owner of the *locus* is considered to have taken constructive possession of the goods in the private area. For example, if goods are found in a bank in a private room used to open safe deposit boxes, the bank has the better right to possession of the goods. But if the goods are found in an area open to the public, such as the bank lobby, the finder has the better right to possession.

Second, if the finder is an *employee* with a duty to turn goods over to the employer, the employer will have the superior right to possession.

Third, courts generally hold for the owner of the *locus* if the goods are *mislaid.* The reason for this rule is that the owner of the goods is likely to remember where the mislaid property was left and to return to that spot. If the true owner does, the owner of the *locus* would be holding it for the true owner.

locus in quo
the place in which

---

[2] While a finder is not a bailee because the goods have not been delivered to the finder and there is no understanding with the owner, nevertheless, the law imposes a duty upon the finder involuntarily to exercise the care of a bailee. This is called an "involuntary bailment."

treasure trove
found buried treasure

Fourth, courts will hold for the owner of the *locus* if the property has been buried in the ground. In some states, however, if the property is **treasure trove,** the finder will have the superior right to possession. *Treasure trove* is defined as found buried treasure such as gold, silver, or money. The following case involving buried property was decided in favor of the owner of the *locus.*

Facts
Plaintiffs, while swimming in the Chariton River, discovered a twenty-seven-foot prehistoric Indian canoe, one-third of which was embedded in the soil. They sued the owner of the *locus in quo* to recover possession of the canoe.

Decision
Judgment for the owner of the *locus in quo.*

Reasoning
The canoe is considered to be property embedded in the soil. In such cases the finder has no rights in the property; it belongs to the owner of the *locus in quo.*

Allred v. Biegel, 219 S.W.2d 665 (Mo. 1949).

Fifth, courts will hold for the owner of the *locus* if the finders are *trespassers.* In the following well-reasoned case the court discussed this and other issues relating to lost or mislaid property.

Summary Statement

1. Bailment law is important both to business and the consumer. Bailment questions often arise when you park a car in a parking lot, leave goods in a safe deposit box, or hang your coat in a store or restaurant.
2. A bailment is a delivery of goods by one person, bailor, to another person, bailee, with the understanding that the bailee is to return the goods to the bailor or deliver them to a third person, as directed by the bailor or as previously agreed.
3. If a bailment is for the sole benefit of the bailor, the bailee owes a duty of minimal care of the goods. A bailee in a bailment for mutual benefit owes a duty of ordinary care. In a bailment for the sole benefit of the bailee, the bailee must exercise extraordinary care.
4. A bailee may disclaim liability only if the bailor agreed to the disclaimer, the language of the disclaimer is clear, and the disclaimer does not violate public policy.
5. The finder of lost or mislaid goods has superior right to the goods against everyone but the true owner. However, if the goods are found on someone else's property, the owner of the property will usually have rights superior to the finder.

Bishop v. Ellsworth
234 N.E.2d 49 (Ill. 1968)

Stouder, Presiding Justice. Dwayne Bishop, plaintiff, filed a complaint alleging that on July 21, 1965, defendants, Mark and Jeff Ellsworth and David Gibson, three small boys, entered his salvage yard premises at 427 Mulberry Street in Canton, without his permission, and while there, happened upon a bottle partially imbedded in the loose earth on top of a landfill, wherein they discovered the sum of $12,590.00 in United States currency. It is further alleged that said boys delivered the money to the municipal chief of police, who deposited it with defendant, Canton State Bank. . . . In the trial court the defendants' motion for summary judgment was granted, and plaintiff appeals.

There is a presumption that the owner or occupant of land or premises has custody of property found on it or actually embedded in the land. . . . The ownership or possession of the locus in quo is related to the right to possession of property discovered thereon or embedded therein in two respects. First, if the premises on which the property is discovered are private, it is deemed that the property discovered thereon is and always has been in the constructive possession of the owner of said premises, and in a legal sense the property can be neither mislaid nor lost. . . . Second, the question of whether the property is mislaid or lost in a legal sense depends upon the intent of the true owner. The ownership or possession of the premises is an important factor in determining such intent. If the property be determined to be mislaid, the owner of the premises is entitled to the possession thereof against the discoverer. It would also appear that if the discoverer is a trespasser, such trespasser can have no claim to possession of such property even if it might otherwise be considered lost. . . .

. . . The facts as alleged in substance are that the plaintiff was the owner and in possession of real estate, that the money was discovered in a private area of said premises in a bottle partially embedded in the soil, and that such property was removed from the premises by the finders without any right or authority and in effect as trespassers. We believe the averment of facts in the complaint substantially informs the defendants of the nature of and basis for the claim and is sufficient to state a cause of action.

The judgment of the Circuit Court of Fulton County is reversed and the cause is remanded with directions to proceed in accordance with this opinion.

Judgment reversed and remanded with directions.

Questions and Case Problems

1. The plaintiff left his car with the defendant parking lot, a bailee. The plaintiff's golf clubs were in the trunk of the car but plaintiff did not tell defendant of their presence. The car was stolen and later recovered but the golf clubs were missing. Is the defendant bailee liable for the clubs? [*Allen v. Houserman,* 250 A.2d 389 (Del. 1969).]

2. Baer shipped merchandise to Slater, a salesperson, who was to sell the merchandise. Baer later directed Slater to return the merchandise to Baer. Slater delivered the merchandise to a person dressed in an American Railway Express uniform who gave Slater a receipt and who was to deliver the goods to Baer. The person was an imposter who left with the goods and has not been seen again. Is Slater liable to Baer for the goods? [*Baer v. Slater,* 158 N.E. 328 (Mass. 1927).]

3. The Freeds delivered their household furniture to Barrett for storage at 618 I. Street, Washington, D.C. Barrett later moved the goods to another address, where they were destroyed by fire. Barrett was in no way negligent. The warehouse receipt which Barrett gave the Freeds stated that he would not be liable for loss by fire. Is he liable for the loss? [*Barrett v. Freed,* 35 A.2d 180 (D.C. 1943).]

4. The plaintiff delivered his registered Tennessee Walking mare, a show horse, to the defendant's stables for breeding. The defendant was warned that the mare was skittish and would kick. The defendant placed the mare in a stall next to a stall which held defendant's stallion. After she was left unattended for eighteen minutes, the mare was found with a broken leg and had to be destroyed. No one knew how the injury occurred. If we assume that the defendant exercised minimal care but failed to exercise ordinary care, would he be liable? [*David v. Lose,* 218 N.E.2d 442 (Ohio 1966).]

5. Healy checked his handbag in the parcel room of a railroad company. He was given a receipt which stated that the company would not be liable for any loss or damage in excess of $10. The wording on the receipt was not pointed out to Healy, and he put the receipt in his pocket without reading it. The clerk later mistakenly gave Healy's handbag, which was worth $70, to another person and it was not recovered. Is the railroad liable for $70? [*Healy v. New York Cent. & H.R.R.,* 138 N.Y.S. 287 (1912), aff'd 105 N.E. 1086 (1914).]

6. A motorist parked her car in a parking lot and was instructed by an attendant to leave her keys in the car so that it could be moved. The motorist was given a ticket which stated that the parking lot company would not be liable for any loss, regardless of the cause. The motorist was not warned of the printed condition on the parking ticket. The car was stolen and was later recovered in a damaged condition. Is the parking lot company liable for the damages? [*Agricultural Insurance Co. v. Constantine,* 58 N.E.2d 658 (Ohio 1944).]

7. A chambermaid, plaintiff, in a hotel discovered eight $100 bills hidden beneath the paper lining of a dresser drawer. She turned the bills over to the owner of the hotel, defendant. When the owner of the money could not be located, the chambermaid asked the hotel owner to return the bills to her and, when he refused, she sued him. Decision? [*Jackson v. Steinberg,* 200 P.2d 376 (Or. 1948).]

8. Mr. and Mrs. Smiley delivered household goods to a bailee. Later, when they became involved in divorce proceedings, Mrs. Smiley notified the bailee that the goods were not to be delivered to either her or her husband until further instructions were given. Despite the notice, the bailee delivered the goods to Mr. Smiley. Is the bailee liable? [*Bishop v. Allied Van Lines, Inc.*, 399 N.E.2d 698 (Ill. 1980).]

9. Singer stored air conditioning units in Stoda warehouses. A fire in one of the warehouses totally destroyed Singer's units. Singer sued Stoda for damages and at trial showed that the sprinkler system in the warehouse did not operate (which Stoda knew), the fire alarm would not automatically activate and no watchmen were present. Should Stoda be held liable? [*Singer Company v. Stoda Corporation*, 436 N.Y.S.2d 508 (N.Y. 1981).]

10. In *Bishop v. Ellsworth*, 234 N.E.2d 49 (Ill. 1968),[3] the court refused to give ownership of found property to trespassers. How does this result illustrate the complementary nature of substantive areas of law?

---

[3] See pp. 222–23.

Carriers, Documents of Title, and Innkeepers 16

After you have read this chapter, you should be able to:

1. Distinguish a common carrier from a private carrier, and discuss the liability of each.
2. List five exceptions to the general rule governing liability of the common carrier.
3. Determine when the exceptional liability of the common carrier begins.
4. Define the term "document of title."
5. Discuss the rights of a purchaser of a document of title after due negotiation.
6. Summarize the liability of a common carrier to passengers.
7. Compare the liability of a common carrier to that of an innkeeper.

Introduction

The general principles of bailment law were discussed in chapter 15. While bailment law affects each of us personally, certain bailment situations are especially important to the person in business.

In this chapter, three of these business bailments are examined: those involving delivery of goods to a common carrier, to a warehouseman, and to an innkeeper. These bailments are unique for two major reasons. *First,* under the common law, the common carrier and the innkeeper were absolutely or strictly liable as insurers for lost or damaged property. Exceptions to this rule and statutory modification will be explored below.

Second, it is usual for common carriers and warehousemen to issue receipts, called *documents of title,* when they receive goods. These receipts are of special legal importance because they represent the contract between the bailor and bailee, and often the purchaser of the document acquires greater rights than the seller. Two documents of title, the bill of lading and the warehouse receipt, are discussed in this chapter.

These bailments are a necessary part of everyday business experience, and the law covering them is, therefore, important. For a discussion of the rights and remedies of buyers and sellers *with respect to each other* concerning shipped goods that do not conform to their contract, see chapter 20 in Sales.

Common Carrier of Goods

Defined

After graduating from college, Rollo accepted a job in Chicago and began to make arrangements for moving his personal belongings. Eventually Rollo discovered that he had two options for moving his goods: (1) he could hire a professional moving company, or (2) his friend Sam could move the goods in his pickup truck free.

In legal terms, Rollo must choose between a **common carrier** and a **private carrier,** and his choice will become important if the goods are lost or destroyed enroute. A common carrier is a carrier which offers its services to the public and charges a fee; if either of those two elements is missing, the carrier is considered to be a private carrier. Thus, Rollo's friend would be classified as a private carrier, while the moving company would be considered a common carrier.

Liability

There are two reasons why the distinction between common and private carriers is important. *First,* a *common carrier must* accept and deliver goods of the type it normally ships from any member of the public, while a *private carrier is free* to pick and choose its customers. *Second,* and more important, a *private carrier* is liable only for loss caused by its *negligence,* as an *ordinary bailee.* The *common carrier,* however, is said to be absolutely liable as an *insurer* of the goods and will be held liable for *any* loss unless it can prove one of the following five exceptions to absolute liability: act of God, act of public enemy, act of the shipper, inherent nature of the goods, and act of public authorities.

Act of God. If the goods are destroyed by an act of God, the carrier will not be liable. An **act of God** is generally defined as an unexpected force of nature, such as an earthquake or lightning which cannot be prevented or avoided. However, if the loss resulted from a combination of an act of God and *human* error, the carrier remains liable as an insurer.

Act of Public Enemy. A carrier is not liable for the acts of a public enemy. The term *public enemy* is defined narrowly to include only a foreign nation at war with the United States, pirates on the high seas, and in some cases rebels in insurrection against the government. Today piracy would probably include piracy by aircraft. The following case held that domestic criminals are not public enemies.

---

common carrier
a carrier which offers its services to the general public for a fee

private carrier
a carrier which does not offer its services to the general public

act of God
an unexpected force of nature

Facts
A shipper, plaintiff, delivered goods to a common carrier, defendant. While the goods were being shipped, the truck on which they were loaded was hijacked on the streets of New York City. The shipper sued the carrier claiming that the carrier is liable for the loss. The carrier's defense is that the loss resulted from the act of a public enemy.

Decision
Judgment for the plaintiff, shipper.

Reasoning
Domestic criminals are not public enemies under the exception to common carrier liability, even when they have been designated "public enemies" by the F.B.I.

David Crystal Inc. v. Ehrlich-Newmark Trucking Co., 64 Misc.2d 325 (N.Y. 1970).

Act of the Shipper. Widget Corporation has just received an order for 1000 crystal widgets, which are to be shipped by railroad. An employee of Widget carelessly packs the crystal widgets so that they all are shattered while being shipped by the railroad. Widget Corporation now claims that the railroad is liable as an insurer on the **consignment**.

As a general rule a common carrier, the railroad, is not liable for losses caused by the acts of the shipper—the **consignor**. However, there are two long-recognized exceptions to this rule. *First,* if the loss was caused in part by the negligence of the common carrier, the carrier must bear the full loss. The fact that the shipper was contributorily negligent is irrelevant because the carrier is not being sued for committing the tort of negligence but, instead, as an insurer. In our case, if the engineer accidentally stopped the train too quickly and, as a result, the poorly packed widgets were damaged, the carrier would be liable. *A common carrier is liable for loss caused by its negligence as well as for loss as an insurer.*

Second, common carriers are liable as insurers in cases when they *know* that the shipper has been careless in packing or loading the goods. Thus, if the railroad has inspected the boxes and knew that they were packed defectively or if the railroad knew that Widget Corporation was careless in loading the boxes, the carrier would be absolutely liable for resulting losses.

Inherent Nature of the Goods. In many cases the inherent nature of the goods will result in damage or destruction while the goods are being shipped. For instance, goods such as molasses will be damaged through natural fermentation, certain metals will become rusted or corroded, perishable fruits will deteriorate, and animals will die during shipment. In each of these cases the common carrier will not be liable unless the carrier's own negligence was a contributing factor. In the following case the damage to goods was not caused by the inherent nature of the goods.

consignment
the shipment of goods from one person to another

consignor
one who ships goods to another

Facts
A shipper, plaintiff, shipped crates of honeydew melons from Rio Grande City, Texas to Chicago, Illinois. The melons were in good condition when they were delivered to the common carrier, defendant, but 640 crates of melons were damaged upon arrival in Chicago even though the carrier was not negligent. The shipper now sued the carrier claiming that the carrier is liable for the loss.

Decision
Judgment for the plaintiff, shipper.

Reasoning
The carrier bears the burden of proving the cause of the loss. In this case, the carrier did not prove that the loss resulted from the inherent nature of the goods.

Missouri Pacific R.R. v. Elmore & Stahl, 377 U.S. 134 (1964).

Act of Public Authorities. A common carrier is not liable for failure to deliver the goods because of the act of a public authority. For example, a **writ of execution** is a court order which authorizes a sheriff or other proper legal officer to seize tangible property in order to satisfy a court judgment. If a sheriff seizes property from the carrier because the shipper has failed to pay a court judgment, the carrier would not be liable. However, the carrier should notify the shipper of the execution so that the shipper may take appropriate legal action to defend itself.

writ of execution
a court order authorizing a sheriff or other proper legal officer to seize tangible property to satisfy a court judgment

Scope of Carriage

Beginning of Carriage. A **warehouseman** is a person who stores goods in a warehouse in return for compensation. When goods are stored in a warehouse, a bailment for mutual benefit is created and the warehouseman has a duty of ordinary care. In many cases a common carrier will act as a warehouseman in storing goods either before or after shipment and, as such, will be liable as a bailee rather than as an insurer.

To illustrate, Mary works for a banana company and wants to ship 1000 crates of bananas from Tampa to a buyer, Tom, in Phoenix. She delivers 600 crates to the common carrier, a railroad, and asks the carrier to delay shipment until she delivers the other 400 crates. Before she completes the delivery, the 600 crates are stolen by thieves. If the railroad proves that it exercised ordinary care, is it still liable as an insurer?

The test to be applied in such cases is: Must the shipper do something else before the goods can be shipped? If so, the carrier is liable only as a bailee. But if the shipper has done everything necessary for shipment, the carrier is liable as an insurer. Thus, where the shipper has not yet told the carrier where the goods are to be shipped or, as in Mary's case, the shipper has not yet completed delivery of the goods to the carrier, the carrier is a warehouseman-bailee and is liable only for not exercising ordinary care. When goods are delivered to a common carrier for *immediate shipment,* there is a **shipper-carrier** relationship between the shipper and the carrier, who is now liable as an insurer.

Termination of Carriage. A similar problem exists after the goods have arrived at the destination point. If the 1000 crates of bananas arrived in Phoenix but, before the buyer, Tom, could pick them up, they were stolen from the carrier by thieves, would the railroad be considered an insurer or a warehouseman-bailee?

The answer usually depends on the contract in each case. If the contract is silent, or if the contract specifies that delivery is to be made *to Tom's company,* the railroad would be liable as a carrier until the goods are delivered to Tom or, at least, until the carrier has made reasonable efforts to deliver the bananas to Tom.

However, if the contract or the local business custom dictates that Tom is *to pick up* the goods at the station, the carrier must unload the crates in the depot so that they are ready to be picked up by Tom. In a few states, once this has been done, the railroad's liability is that of a bailee. However, most state courts have decided that the railroad does not achieve bailee status until the **consignee** has had a reasonable chance to pick them up or until the railroad notifies the consignee that the goods have arrived and the consignee has had an opportunity to pick them up.

Limitation of Liability

If goods are shipped *interstate,* the *federal* Interstate Commerce Act governs attempts by the common carrier to limit its liability. Under this Act, carriers may not limit their liability, with two exceptions: (1) liability may be limited for damage to *baggage* carried on passenger trains and boats; and (2) a carrier may establish *rates* which are dependent upon the value of the goods being shipped. The second exception has the effect of limiting liability because the shipper will be allowed to recover only *up to* the value *declared* by the shipper if the goods are lost or damaged. For example, if the declared value is $1000 and the loss or damage is $600, the carrier will be liable only for $600.

If the goods are not shipped interstate, the *state* rule in most cases is found in section 7–309 of the Uniform Commercial Code. Under this section, a common or private carrier who issues a bill of lading—which will be discussed below under Documents of Title—must at least act with reasonable care. However, as under federal law, the carrier may limit damages by providing that its liability is limited to the value stated by the shipper, provided that rates are dependent on value and that the shipper is given the chance to declare a higher value. In the following case the shipper did not declare any value and could recover only for the common carrier's maximum fixed rate for goods which were stolen from the carrier.

---

warehouseman
a person in the business of storing goods for a fee

shipper-carrier
a legal relationship between the shipper and the common carrier when goods have been delivered to the carrier for immediate shipment

consignee
one to whom goods are shipped

Facts
A suitcase was delivered to a common carrier, defendant, in New York City for delivery in Jacksonville, Florida. The shipper, plaintiff, selected the lowest freight rate available, with a maximum carrier liability of $10. The contents of the suitcase were stolen enroute. The shipper sued the carrier to recover the actual value of the property.

Decision
Judgment for the plaintiff, shipper, for only $10.

Reasoning
Carriers may limit their liability by establishing rates based on valuations. Classifications and tariffs filed by carriers with the Interstate Commerce Commission have the force of law, and, therefore, shippers are presumed to know the relation between the values and the rates charged.

Kaufman v. Penn. R.R., 47 N.Y.S.2d 639 (1944).

Documents of Title

Definition
If Herman delivers his furniture to a warehouseman for storage, the warehouseman will give him a receipt for the furniture called a **warehouse receipt.** If Herman delivered the goods to a carrier for shipment, he would receive a receipt called a **bill of lading** (see figure 16.1). Both the warehouse receipt and the bill of lading are **documents of title** and, as such, are more than mere receipts. Documents of title normally spell out the terms of the contract between Herman and the bailee. In many cases, a person who has possession of the document is the only one entitled to recover the goods from the bailee.

warehouse receipt
a document issued to the bailor by a warehouseman

bill of lading
a document issued to the shipper by a carrier

document of title
a document evidencing that the person possessing it "is entitled to receive, hold, and dispose of the document and the goods it covers" UCC 4–104(f)

Source of Law
State law governing documents of title is found in Article 7 of the Uniform Commercial Code. If goods are shipped interstate, federal treaties and statutes take precedence over state law. The Uniform Commercial Code also provides that Article 7 is subject to the provisions of state regulatory statutes.

Negotiation
In Part 5, chapter 23, we discuss commercial paper generally and the distinction between negotiable and non-negotiable commercial paper. A document of title is a type of commercial paper which is referred to as "commodity paper" in order to distinguish it from the "money paper" (for example, checks and notes) discussed in Part 5. The tests to determine whether a document of title is negotiable differ from the "money paper" tests to be discussed in chapter 23.

A **document** of title is considered to be **negotiable** if it states that the goods are to be delivered either to *bearer,* meaning any person in possession of the document, or to the *order* of someone. If neither of these requirements is met, the document is non-negotiable. Thus, if the warehouse receipt stated that the goods are to be delivered "to the order of Herman," it is negotiable. If it states that the goods are to be delivered "to Herman," it is non-negotiable.

The difference between a negotiable and a non-negotiable document of title has an important consequence for the bailee. If the document is negotiable, the goods must be delivered to the *holder* of the document—namely, the person who has *possession* of the document which *flows to that person either originally or by indorsement*. If the document is non-negotiable, the goods must usually be delivered to the person named in the document.

Furthermore, if Herman's document of title is negotiable, Herman must follow certain procedures to *duly negotiate* it to his friend Fred. If the document is **bearer** paper, it is negotiated by simple delivery to Fred. If the document is order paper, Herman must first indorse the document and then deliver it to Fred. In either case, Fred must purchase the document as a holder in good faith without notice of any claim or defense to the

negotiable document
a document of title which states that the goods covered by the document are to be delivered to bearer or to the order of someone

bearer
the person in possession of an instrument, document of title, or certificated security payable or deliverable to bearer or indorsed in blank (a signature without additional words)

Figure 16.1 Negotiable Bill of Lading (Front)

[Figure: Union Pacific Railroad Company Uniform Order Bill of Lading, Original, Form 1585]

due negotiation
delivery of a negotiable document of title to a holder who purchases it for value, in good faith, and without notice of any claim or defense to the document

document and must pay value in order to claim **due negotiation.** If Fred were to purchase the document as payment for a *past money debt* owing to him by Herman, Fred would not be giving value. *Fred must also purchase the document in the regular course of business or financing.* If there is due negotiation, the holder usually takes the document, and the goods, free of claims and defenses raised by the bailee or third persons, with two exceptions not discussed here.

Common Carrier of Passengers

The common carrier of passengers faces two main legal concerns. *First,* the carrier faces possible liability for injuries to passengers during the course of the journey. The general rule is that the carrier is not liable as an insurer for every injury suffered by passengers, but the carrier does owe the highest degree of care to passengers. In the following case the court held that a woman was a "passenger" while walking on the station platform to the train.

Facts
A woman, plaintiff, waited on an elevated platform for a train. As the train arrived, she walked toward the train but fell when the heels of her shoes caught in spaces between the wooden planks of the platform. The woman sued the railroad defendant, claiming that the railroad is liable for damages of $27,500. The railroad defends by claiming that it owed only a duty of ordinary care, which was met here since the railroad had no knowledge of the condition which caused the injury.

Decision
Judgment for the plaintiff, woman.

Reasoning
The railroad owed the highest degree of care to the woman, who was a passenger. A person does not have to be in physical contact with a vehicle in order to be a passenger. The purpose of the law is to increase the duty of care as the danger increases.

Katamay v. Chicago Transit Authority, 289 N.E.2d 623 (Ill. 1972).

Second, the common carrier faces liability as an insurer in cases where a passenger's baggage is lost or damaged. However, in order to recover, the passenger must prove that there was a *bailment* of the baggage. If the passenger retained possession of the baggage during the trip, there would be *no bailment* because the *delivery* requirement is missing. Furthermore, even when there is delivery to the carrier, the carrier is normally not liable for the contents of the baggage unless the contents were for the personal use and convenience of the passenger. This rule prevents unexpected liability on the part of the carrier when a passenger attempts to ship valuables, such as paintings or rare china, as baggage without paying the customary rates for goods of higher value and greater risk to the carrier.

Innkeepers

An **innkeeper** is an operator of a hotel, inn, motel, or any other establishment engaged in making lodging accommodations available to transients.

At common law, the liability of an innkeeper for lost or damaged goods was similar to that of the common carrier: the innkeeper was liable as an insurer of the goods, unless an exception applied, such as loss resulting from an act of God, an act of a public enemy, an act of a public authority, or the inherent nature of the goods. In most states the common law rule has been changed by statute.

innkeeper
operator of an establishment engaged in making lodging accommodations available to transients

Summary Statement

1. The liability of a common carrier is unique in bailment law in that the carrier is liable in most cases as an insurer of the goods.
2. A common carrier is not liable for (a) an act of God, (b) an act of a public enemy, (c) an act of the shipper, (d) a loss resulting from the inherent nature of the goods, and (e) an act of public authorities.
3. A common carrier is liable as an ordinary bailee until the shipper has done everything necessary to make the goods ready for shipment (thereby creating a *shipper-carrier relationship*), the carrier then becoming liable as an insurer.
4. A document of title is a receipt given by a warehouseman or common carrier which also serves as the contract between the bailor and the bailee.
5. In most cases, when a document of title has been duly negotiated, the purchaser takes the document free and clear of defenses which could have been raised by the bailee against the bailor, and also free and clear of claims to the document and to the goods by third persons.

6. A common carrier is not liable as an insurer of the safety of passengers; however, the carrier does owe passengers the highest degree of care.
7. Under the common law, an innkeeper was liable as an insurer for guests' belongings which were damaged or destroyed. This liability has been changed by statute in most states.

In the following case the court discussed the common law liability of the innkeeper and problems which arise in interpreting modern statutes.

Federal Insurance Co. v. Waldorf-Astoria Hotel
60 Misc.2d 996 (N.Y. 1969)

Hilda G. Schwartz, Judge. Defendant hotel moves for summary judgment under Section 200 of the General Business Law which provides that the proprietor of a hotel is relieved from liability for loss to a guest of his money, jewels, ornaments, bank notes, bonds, negotiable securities or precious stones, if the hotel provides a place of safekeeping and patrons do not avail themselves of it. Defendant argues that the gold cuff-links lost by plaintiff's subrogors [the original complainants whose claim the plaintiff insurance company acquired by **subrogation**] satisfied the definition of "jewels" under Sec. 200.

Both parties agree that . . . the sole question to be determined is whether the missing cuff-links come within the meaning of the words "jewels," "ornaments" or "precious stones" in the statute.

It is not disputed that plaintiff's subrogors were guests of the hotel on May 18 and 19, 1968 and that, at some time between the evening of May 18 and the morning of May 19, they discovered that a nightcase in their hotel room had been opened and a pair of gold cuff-links with a 9 mm. pearl in each, valued at $175, were missing.

At common law, an innkeeper was liable as an insurer of the property of his guests unless the loss was occasioned by the negligence or fault of the guest. . . .

The purpose of Sec. 200, in providing that the hotelkeeper shall not be liable for money, jewels, ornaments, and precious stones if they are not deposited in the hotel safe provided, is to protect the hotel from an undisclosed excessive liability. . . .

The cuff-links in suit, even though fashioned of gold and ornamented with a pearl in each, cannot be considered as jewels or ornaments, as these terms are used and understood in common parlance. Black's Law Dictionary defines "jewels" as "an ornament of the person, such as earrings, pearls, diamonds, etc. prepared to be worn . . . , an ornament made of precious metal or a precious stone." Cuff-links are not used as jewels or ornaments but to close the cuffs, otherwise buttonless, of shirts. They are articles of utilitarian and ordinary wear in daily use, on all occasions, with business clothes as well as clothes designed for leisure, in the daytime as well as the evening. They are carried principally for use and convenience and not for ornament. Cuff-links, as with watches and other articles of ordinary wear, may be made of precious metals, and even made more elaborate with precious stones, but these do not change their essential description as articles of ordinary wear.

Section 200 of the General Business Law has modified the hotelkeeper's liability only as to the articles named. Cuff-links, even though made of gold and decorated with a pearl, are articles of use and are not jewels or ornaments within the meaning of Section 200. The defendant hotel is therefore not relieved of liability for their loss despite the failure of the guests to deposit them in the hotel safe provided.

subrogation the substitution of one person for another with reference to a claim or a right

Questions and Case Problems

1. A shipper shipped packaged jewelry from Dallas to New York City on Delta Air Lines. The shipper told Delta that the package contained "printed matter," and the package was not wrapped in accordance with Delta's regulations covering jewelry shipments. The jewelry was lost during shipment, but Delta claims it is not liable because of the shipper's misdescription and improper packaging. Is Delta liable? [*Travelers Insurance Co. v. Delta Air Lines, Inc.*, 498 S.W.2d 443 (Tex. 1973).]

2. A shipper delivered pine seed to a common carrier in Birmingham, Alabama for transport to New Orleans, Louisiana. However, the shipment was delayed when Hurricane Betsey struck New Orleans and later the shipment could not be located. The seed finally turned up at the carrier's home office in Hattiesburg, Mississippi. As a result of the delay, the seed was commercially worthless. Is the carrier liable? [*West Bros. Inc. v. Resource Management Serv., Inc.*, 214 So.2d 431 (Ala. 1968).]

3. A common carrier contracted with a shipper to ship 100 bales of cotton. The shipper delivered 29 bales to the shipping platform and advised the carrier that the remaining 71 bales would be delivered within a few days. A fire destroyed the 29 bales on the platform. Is the carrier absolutely liable for the cotton? [*Rio Grande City Ry. Co. v. Guerra*, 26 S.W.2d 360 (Tex. 1930).]

4. A seventeen-year-old desk clerk gave a pass key to all rooms in the motel where he worked to two strangers. The strangers unlocked a room, broke the chain, entered the room, and assaulted and robbed a husband and wife staying in the room. A statute provides that innkeepers are not responsible for property stolen by force or extraordinary violence. Is the motel liable for damages to the couple? [*Kraaz v. La Quinta Motor Inns, Inc.* 410 So.2d 1048 (La. 1982).]

5. A passenger checked a bag and contents worth $2,190 at a room in the railroad station at Portland, Oregon. A railroad employee gave him a receipt which limited the railroad's liability to $25, unless the passenger paid a higher rate. The passenger was unaware of the limitation. When the passenger returned, the bag could not be found. The railroad claimed that the limitation of liability was valid because the rules and regulations governing carriers allowed such contracts. Is the carrier correct? [*Allen v. Southern Pacific Co.*, 213 P.2d 667 (Utah 1950).]

6. A construction company entered into a contract with a railroad to build a section of track. The railroad agreed to ship materials needed for construction to the company at a special rate, but their contract also provided that the common carrier would not be liable for any losses. Is the exemption from liability valid? [*Santa Fe, P. & P. Ry. Co. v. Grant Bros. Const. Co.*, 228 U.S. 177 (1913).]

7. A seventy-year-old passenger was riding on a streetcar. The motorman of the streetcar, in driving through an intersection, had to stop quickly because of an approaching vehicle. The passenger fell to the floor and fractured two vertebrae. Is the streetcar owner liable? [*Dolan v. New Orleans Public Service Inc.*, 317 So.2d 688 (La. 1975).]

8. A seaman was riding on a bus. Four drunken youths entered the bus and sat behind the seaman. They tried to pick his pocket and asked him for money. When he refused, they began to punch and kick him. The driver then stopped the bus, called the police, and ordered the youths off the bus. Is the bus company liable for the seaman's injuries? [*Orr v. New Orleans Public Service Inc.*, 349 So.2d 417 (La. 1977).]

9. The wife of an army general who had no permanent home was residing with him at a hotel. She expected to stay at the hotel from November until the next spring or summer, and they were given a special rate for room rent. The wife's belongings were stolen from her room, and she claimed that, under the common law rule, the innkeeper was liable. Is the innkeeper liable? [*Hancock v. Rand*, 94 N.Y. 1 (1883).]

10. In *Federal Insurance Co. v. Waldorf-Astoria Hotel*, 60 Misc.2d 996 (N.Y. 1969),[1] the court indicated that the statute is in derogation of the common law and must be strictly construed. How does this approach provide flexibility to meet the needs of commerce?

---

[1] See p. 232.

Ethics and Business Law in Part 3
Personal Property and Bailments

Introduction

This end-of-Part discussion, like the others in this book, is designed to encourage students to begin forming personal beliefs about what is right or wrong conduct in business. The discussion here builds on the material in the first end-of-Part discussion on pages 58 to 69; you may find it helpful to review that.

This material has several goals. The overview section is designed to help you see the range of ethical issues associated with this area of the law. The in-depth discussion is intended to provide you with a background for forming your own beliefs about a single very important ethical issue in business. The problems at the end of this Part are designed to build your skill in ethical analysis while exploring further the in-depth issue.

Overview of Ethical Issues in Personal Property and Bailments

The remarkable and rapid development of technology in recent years has raised many ethical issues related to infringing and pirating of intangible industrial property interests, such as patents, copyrights, trademarks, computer programs, and video cassette recordings. Such conduct occurs not only in the U.S. but also worldwide in national and international trade. Creative innovation of original works is encouraged, protected, and rewarded by the law. But often these laws are difficult to enforce. Society depends to a large extent on the personal ethics of individuals to make this law work.

In reading about the liability of hotels for the loss of guests' property, you were learning about how our legal system resolves the conflict between the guests and the hotels. Recall that at common law the innkeeper acted as the insurer of a guest's goods. However, most states have, by statute, changed the common law. Now, even if the innkeeper is negligent, the innkeeper's liability is generally limited to $100.

Most likely, the hotel industry lobbied their state legislatures to get the common law modified. They did this probably because they suffered repeated financial losses, so lobbying was an understandable worthwhile effort. Guests, however, were not highly motivated; it wasn't worth their time to lobby. In this instance the more numerous hotel lobbyist prevailed over the less numerous guest. Thus the law makes the individual's interest secondary to the interests of the hotels.

The legislative process is the law-making mechanism which most often reflects the desires of a group—usually a majority on an issue. On the other hand, constitutions and the courts most often protect the desires of a minority such as a solitary individual. Notice that the courts fashioned the protection for the guests while the legislatures took that protection away.

In-Depth Discussion of a Basic Issue: Private Ownership of Property.

The ethical basis for the law of personal property and bailments is the right of ownership of property by private parties. Because this is such a basic attribute of our society and our legal system, as well as an essential element of personal and economic liberty, it is important for you to develop mature beliefs about it.

Groups and Individuals

Generally, when you, as an individual, join a *group,* it is because your desires coincide with those of the group. Occasions often arise, however, when the desires of the individual differ from, or conflict with, those of the group.

This conflict between the individual and the group occurs frequently on several levels in all societies. The way it is resolved accounts for basic differences between economic systems such as capitalism and socialism, between political systems such as democracy and communism, between philosophical systems such as egoism and utilitarianism, and between styles of managing and interacting with others.

Alternative Paths to the Common Good

Nearly all societies try to advance "the common good"; that is, they try to improve the welfare of the society. While most societies share this goal, they differ dramatically on the extent to which they emphasize the individual good and the collective good as a means for achieving the common good. In some societies, most decisions are made by asking whether the decision will directly advance the interests of the group or collective. In other societies, there is more of a willingness to see the individual as a *vehicle* for improving the welfare of the group. Thus, each society has a different conception of the relative rights of the individual and the rights of the group.

A nation's *property law* usually reflects its basic attitude about individual and group rights. For example, the property law of socialist countries is based on the idea that property should be held for the benefit of *all* citizens rather than for the benefit of particular individuals. In these countries, only the government can own the "means of production." In capitalist societies, however, the means of production are owned by individuals. Capitalists generally believe that the common good is advanced when individual self-interest is channeled, perhaps somewhat indirectly, toward the common good.

In some socialist societies, property cannot be willed from one private party to another, it must go to the state on death. In contrast, our property law goes to great length to benefit the individual. Our law of intestacy causes your property to go to your relatives even if you die without a will. Only if you die both without a will and without surviving relatives will the property escheat, that is go to the state.

Philosophic Views

Karl Marx articulates the strongest opposition to the institution of private property and the role of the individual versus that of the group. His view is that working for others undermines our humanity and that private property stimulates greed. He writes:

Private property has made us so stupid and partial that an object is only *ours* when we have it, when it exists for us as capital or when it is directly eaten, drunk, worn, inhabited, etc., in short, *utilized* in some way.

****

The suppression of private property is, therefore, the complete *emancipation* of all the human qualities and senses.

The most widely recognized justification for private ownership of property was articulated by John Locke. Locke makes an argument grounded largely on natural law and religion. He wrote:

Whether we consider natural reasons . . . or revelation . . . it is very clear that God . . . 'has given the earth to the children of men,' given it to mankind in common. Though the earth and all inferior creatures be common to all men, yet every man has a property in his own person; this nobody has any right to but himself. Whatsoever then he removes out of the state that nature has provided . . . , he has mixed his labor with, and joined to it, something that is his own, and thereby makes it his property.

A more modern—and clearly utilitarian—justification for private ownership has been articulated by Richard Posner, who writes:

Imagine a society in which all property rights have been abolished. A farmer plants corn, fertilizes it, and erects scarecrows, but when the corn is ripe his neighbor reaps and sells it. The farmer has no legal remedy against his neighbor's conduct since he owns neither the land that he sowed nor the crop. After a few such incidents the cultivation of land will be abandoned and the society will shift to methods of subsistence (such as hunting) that involve less preparatory investment.

This example suggests that the legal protection of property rights has an important economic function: to create incentives to use resources efficiently. . . .

The creation of exclusive rights is a necessary rather than sufficient condition for the efficient use of resources. The rights must be transferable. Suppose the farmer in our example owns the land that he sows but is a bad farmer; his land would be more productive in someone else's hands. The maximization of value requires a mechanism by which the farmer can be induced to transfer rights in the property to someone who can work it more productively. A transferable right is such a mechanism. . . .

The foregoing discussion suggests three criteria of an efficient system of property rights. The first is universality. Ideally, all resources should be owned, or ownable, by someone, except resources so plentiful that everybody can consume as much of them as he wants without reducing consumption by anyone else.

The second criterion—is exclusivity. We have assumed so far that either the farmer can exclude no one or he can exclude everyone, but of course there are intermediate stages: the farmer may be entitled to exclude private individuals from reaping his crop, but not the government in time of war. It might appear that the more exclusive the property right, the greater the incentive to invest the right amount of resources in the development of the property.

The third criterion of an efficient system of property rights is transferability. If a property right cannot be transferred, there is no way of shifting a resource from a less productive to a more productive use through voluntary exchange. The costs of transfer may be high to begin with; a legal prohibition against transferring may, depending on the penalties for violation, make the costs utterly prohibitive.

In 1864, Abraham Lincoln addressed the issue of *unequal* distribution of property in the following words:

Property is the fruit of labor; property is desirable; it is a positive good in the world. That some should be rich shows that others may become rich, and hence is just encouragement to industry and enterprise.

Let not him who is houseless pull down the house of another, but let him work diligently and build one for himself, thus by example assuring that his own shall be safe from violence when built.

As you can see, the views of these thinkers vary dramatically. In order to function effectively in the business world, and make high-quality ethical decisions, you need to develop your own views on private ownership of property. Is Marx right, or are Locke, Posner, and Lincoln correct?

Solving Ethics Problems

Like the other end-of-Part discussions in this book, this one presents problems for you to consider. These problems have three goals. The first is to give you the opportunity to further explore the in-depth issue. The second goal is to give you experience in ethical reasoning about the law and about related management problems. The third goal is to let you see how thinking critically about the law can increase your ability to make ethical decisions. To facilitate this, the problems begin by asking you to analyze the law for its ethical content and then shift to looking at related problems in managerial ethics.

For a discussion of the ethical roles of markets and the law, and examples of the four styles of ethical reasoning—egoism, utilitarianism, Kant's philosophy, and religious ethics—read the business ethics material at the end of Part 1.

Problems
1. In *Bishop v. Ellsworth,* on page 222, you read about a dispute over lost property (money in a bottle) which had been found. The case tried to resolve the claims of the finders and the claims of the party on whose property the bottle had been found. In a moral sense, neither has a very strong claim to ownership. These claims are morally quite weak, especially when compared to the claims of the party who owned the money but lost it. Isn't it possible to assume that society has a stronger claim to the found money than either the finder or owner of the land? Do you think the laws of communist countries would differ in their approach to this problem? Try to make persuasive arguments which justify allowing one of the private parties to keep the money. Do you believe this law is the best law?
2. In the chapter on personal property you learned about the concept of *escheat*. This is the legal requirement that when someone dies without heirs, his or her property goes to the state. Can you make a persuasive argument justifying the transfer of property to heirs, when they exist? Do you think property should escheat even when there *are* heirs? *Or* do you think property should be passed on death from one individual to another?
3. Frequently in business discussions, people toss out ideas to be evaluated by a group. Suppose you are brainstorming a problem with a group of your subordinates and one of them comes up with an idea that you judge to be quite useful to your company. Further assume that you could appropriate this idea as your own, in your discussions with your boss, without any risk of adverse consequences to yourself. If you think there might be a substantial benefit to you, perhaps a significant raise, should you do so? Why or why not? Do you think you would?
4. Suppose you were the manager of a programming group for a software firm. One of your star programmers has approached you with a request for 15 percent release time and tuition reimbursement of $4,000 for attending evening classes reading the "Great Books" of western literature. He believes this will broaden his perspective and allow him to generate more creative ideas for the firm. Do you think that such an investment in him (an individual) can be justified by its indirect benefit to the firm (the group)? Why or why not?

PART 4 **Sales and Consumer Law**

17. **Introduction to the Uniform Commercial Code**
    The history and application of the Code, reflecting current commercial practice with flexible terminology for an expanding future and ease of use. Article 2 applies only to transactions in goods.

18. **Formation and Interpretation of the Sales Contract**
    The rules established by the Code when the parties have not expressed their intent concerning risk of loss and passage of title to goods. Many changes from the common law reflect current methods of doing business and assist merchants and consumers in their dealings with each other.

19. **Performance of the Sales Contract**
    The obligations of the seller and the buyer in performing their contractual duties. Sales terms are examined to understand their meaning and to determine the intentions of the parties about performance of the agreement. Bulk transfers of the seller's inventory are defined.

20. **Breach of the Sales Contract, Courses of Action, and Remedies**
    What the seller and the buyer may do when the other has breached the contract. The various Code remedies are explained.

21. **Consumer Law: A. A Seller's Warranties, Their Waiver, Modification, and Breach**
    The consumer's protection given by the Code consists of warranties made by the seller to the buyer. How are these warranties modified, excluded or waived? The doctrine of unconscionability is explained.

22. **Consumer Law: B. A Manufacturer's Liability for Defective and Unreasonably Dangerous Products, and Recent Consumer Protection Legislation.**
    The tort liability of manufacturers and sellers for negligent manufacture and design of a product, and strict liability, which is a rather new development by the courts, are examined together with federal and state consumer protection legislation.

Summary

The Uniform Commercial Code, Article 2, establishes guidelines and rules of interpretation for merchants and consumers in their sales transactions in the absence of their agreement to the contrary. In some instances the Code does not permit variation and establishes fixed rules. The first four chapters discuss the history and objectives of the Code, and the formation, performance, breach, and remedies in connection with the sales contract for goods. Many changes in the common law of contracts are made by the Code.

However, Article 2 is not enough to reflect the protection needed by the consumer when dealing with merchants, and particularly in establishing manufacturer liability for defective products. A whole new body of consumer law has exploded making a startling change in consumer/retailer/manufacturer relations. Chapters 21 and 22 on Consumer Law, discuss this breakthrough in consumer protection, particularly with respect to the area called "products liability."

Business ethics as it relates to the text material in this Part is considered at the end of the Part.

17 Introduction to the Uniform Commercial Code

After you have read this chapter, you should be able to:

1. Give the reasons for having a uniform commercial code.
2. Define a code.
3. State the purposes of the UCC.
4. Define the term "merchant."
5. In a short paragraph describe:
    a. the contributions of Professor Karl Llewellyn to the formulation of the UCC.
    b. "goods" and distinguish goods from items or commercial circumstances not covered by Article 2.
    c. the standard of conduct required by Article 2 and explain how this standard of conduct is to be "found" in many cases.
6. Define the statute of frauds and the parol evidence rule under Article 2, and then explain how they apply in real-life situations.

Introduction

Most American automobiles are manufactured in Michigan from parts made in Pennsylvania, Ohio, Minnesota, and other states and then shipped to all states, where they are sold to consumers. If each state had its own different set of commercial rules applicable to the sale of **goods** within its borders, then the thousands of transactions required to produce an automobile would be governed by at least fifty sets of state rules. If this were the case, then our economy and standard of living would not be what they are today. The numerous transactions required to produce an automobile and other complex goods demand that only one set of commercial rules applies to most of the transactions. Such a single set of commercial rules has been formulated and is entitled the Uniform Commercial Code. The Code has been adopted by all the states except Louisiana.[1] It is a response to a business need.

goods
tangible, movable things

The Uniform Commercial Code (UCC) is concerned with certain commercial transactions in, or regarding, **personal property,** and contracts and other documents concerning them. It has nine substantive Articles. Part 4 of this book will focus primarily upon Article 2, Sales, and will include some explanation of Article 1, General Provisions, and Article 6, Bulk Transfers.

personal property (personalty)
a movable thing, along with interests and rights in a thing

The Concept of a Code

There is a distinct difference between a code and other statutory enactments. A **code** is a comprehensive, systematic collection of statutes in a particular legal area. The Uniform Commercial Code contains and governs much of the law applicable to ordinary commercial transactions. The purposes of the Uniform Commercial Code are set out in one of its initial passages. These purposes are as follows:

code
a comprehensive, systematic collection of statutes in a particular legal area

(a) to simplify, clarify and modernize the law governing commercial transactions;
(b) to permit the continued expansion of commercial practices through custom, usage and agreement of the parties; [and]
(c) to make uniform the law among the various jurisdictions.[2]

The Legal Philosophy of Karl Llewellyn

Perhaps the single most influential person in the drafting of the UCC was its "chief reporter," Karl Llewellyn, a law professor at the University of Chicago Law School. He determined which subjects the UCC would cover and in what order. He was the principal draftsman of Articles 1 and 2. Of greater importance, however, was the fact that much of the language of Articles 1 and 2 reflected notions Professor Llewellyn held as a result of his commitment to "legal realism." Legal realism is a phrase used to designate a school of jurisprudential thought which maintains that the "law" is embedded fundamentally in situations or the everyday transactions of life. *The rules should reflect what is socially desirable in "reality."* No rule should be made for its own sake or merely because it is a logical extension of another rule. Thus, when one applies this notion to the development of a commercial code for the sale of goods as Professor Llewellyn did, one should appreciate the fact that the rules are an attempt to *state simply* and *make uniform* much of the changing *current* commercial practices. Llewellyn believed commercial law is to reflect the most desirable practices of business people.[3]

Legal realism.

---

[1] Louisiana has adopted only Articles 1, 3, 4, and 5 of the UCC.

[2] UCC 1–102(2).

[3] See Danzig, "A Comment on the Jurisprudence of the Uniform Commercial Code," 27 Stan. L. Rev. 621–35 (1975).

In our study of Articles 1 and 2, be mindful of the fact that the *words* of these Articles are but a *starting point* for our study. In many key instances the words direct us to current commercial practice to establish the standards for a transaction. No better example of this manifestation of Llewellyn's legal philosophy can be found than section 1–204(2), which provides:

> What is a reasonable time for taking any action depends on the nature, purpose and circumstances of such action.

unconscionable
offends the conscience; immoderate, too one-sided

In addition, the official comments to section 2–302 on **unconscionable** contracts, one of the most important sections of Article 2, provides in part:

> The basic test is whether, *in the light of the general commercial background and the commercial needs of the particular trade or case,* the clauses involved are so one-sided as to be unconscionable under the circumstances . . . [Emphasis added]

The genius of this approach to law accommodates the seemingly inconsistent needs of our commercial society. On the one hand, our commercial society demands consistency, regularity, and stability in its rules. On the other hand, because our commercial society is very dynamic, we must provide for change and development of the rules. The required measure of stability is provided by the fact that so many state legislatures have adopted the UCC and the fact that these state legislatures are discouraged from amending the UCC. However, a means for growth is provided by the fact that in interpreting and applying the words of the UCC, especially Articles 1 and 2, attorneys and courts are directed to current commercial standards of performance.[4] As the standards change, so do the meanings of some of the key words of the Sales Article.

Introduction to Article 2: Transactions Covered

sale
the transfer "of title from seller to purchaser for a price" UCC 2–106(1)

security interest
"an interest in personal property or fixtures which secures payment or performance of an obligation" UCC 1–201(37)

gift
a voluntary transfer of real or personal property by someone who is not to receive anything in return

lease (of goods)
a form of contract giving one person, the lessee, the exclusive right to use or possess the goods of another, the lessor, for a stated period

Article 2 applies (1) to *commercial transactions* (2) *in goods*. A commercial transaction is usually interpreted to mean a **sale** of goods and does not include transactions where only a **security interest** is transferred or where a **gift** or a **lease** of goods is involved. In the following case the court distinguished a sale from a lease.

Facts
Plaintiff was a passenger in a truck rented by his employer from Hertz. It was alleged that the truck had defective brakes and the plaintiff was injured as a result. Should the plaintiff's claim against the defendant, Hertz, be determined by Article 2?

Decision
No.

Reasoning
The court held that no "sale" was involved, so Article 2 was not to be applied directly.

However, the appellate court did find in the plaintiff's favor by relying both on the common law and the general policy embedded in the warranty provisions of the UCC. It held that the offering to the public of trucks and pleasure vehicles for hire necessarily carries with it a representation or implied warranty that they are fit for operation.

Cintrone v. Hertz Truck Leasing & Rental Service, 212 A.2d 769 (N.J. 1965).

You will notice that the case above makes two important points. The first is that the UCC does not apply to leases of goods. The second is that just because the UCC is not directly applicable does not mean it cannot be used as a general reference to shape the rights and duties of parties to nonsales transactions. A central point of this chapter is that

---

[4] The words "reasonable" and "unreasonable" appear at least 97 times in Article 2. See Bonsignore, *Existentialism, The Rule of Law and Article 2 of the Uniform Commercial Code,* 8 AM. BUS. L. J. 133 at 147 (1970).

the UCC and Article 2 are more than an isolated grouping of statutes; they are a comprehensive treatment of commercial law enacted by almost all the states and represent the major policy statements regarding commercial transactions. The impact of the UCC in shaping commercial law may go far beyond its "technical" applications.[5]

Goods are those things which must be dealt with *uniformly* by the states, or the value they have because they can be shipped and used elsewhere will be impaired. **Services**—such as those rendered by an accountant, a doctor, an architect, or a plumber—are peculiarly local in nature, and the necessity for uniform treatment by states is not as apparent. The same is true for land and things so fastened to the land that they cannot be moved.

service
usually labor rendered by one person for another

Growing crops and timber are goods (2–105); and so are minerals (including oil and gas) and other substances or structures *in* the land if they are to be mined, extracted, or severed by the *seller*.[6] If minerals or structures in the land (not crops or timber) are to be mined or severed by the *buyer,* then the contract is viewed as a sale of an interest in *land* and is not covered by Article 2. The reason that minerals, etc. to be severed by the *buyer* are not covered by Article 2 is not explained clearly in the Code, but it seems that this is the traditional distinction recognized by the common law. That is, a lease of land to an oil company to extract oil and gas has always been treated as a lease of real property; and a sale of coal to be mined by the seller has always been treated as a sale of goods and not a sale of an interest in land. The UCC maintains this distinction.

The most difficult distinction to make, however, is whether Article 2 applies to transactions involving *both* the sale of goods and the sale of services or labor. The "test" used to determine the applicability of Article 2 in this circumstance is clearly defined in the following case.

Facts
The defendants, the Cox brothers, had operated a bowling alley for twenty years in Missouri Valley, Iowa. In February 1968 it was gutted by fire and they contracted with the plaintiff, Simek, to "rebuild" the bowling alley with "used" equipment. Some of the used equipment furnished did not operate properly, and, before the job was completed and the liabilities for the faulty equipment established, Simek died. The defendants hired someone else to complete the work, and the representative of Simek's estate sued the Cox brothers for breach of contract. Should the obligations of the parties be determined by Article 2 of the UCC?

Decision
Yes.

Reasoning
The court held that Article 2 did apply even though the contract involved "substantial amounts" of labor. The test, it held, is not whether the contract involves a service too, but, granting that it does, "whether the predominant factor, the thrust, the purpose, reasonably stated, is the rendition of service with goods incidentally involved (e.g., contract with an artist for a painting . . .) or is a transaction of sale, with labor incidentally involved (e.g., installation of a water heater in a bathroom . . . .)"

Bonebrake v. Cox, 499 F.2d 951 (1974).

By applying the test in the above *Bonebrake v. Cox* case in other cases, courts have held that an operation requiring the transfusion of blood and a beauty parlor treatment requiring the sale of hair dye did not involve the sale of goods. These transactions involved a *service* as the *predominant* factor with the sale of goods incidental to the service.

If a transaction in goods exists, then Article 2 applies whether the goods are in existence at the time the contract is made. In a later chapter we will discuss the consequences of distinguishing between "existing" and **"future" goods.** For the present, it is important just to note that, if the predominant factor in a transaction is the sale of goods, then Article 2 applies even though the goods are to be made in the future.[7]

future goods
"goods which are not both existing and identified" to the contract UCC 2–105(2)

---

[5] R. J. Nordstrom, *Handbook of the Law of Sales* (St. Paul: West Pub. Co., 1970), pp. 43–44.

[6] UCC 2–107.

[7] UCC 2–105(2), 2–106(1).

Standard of Conduct under Article 2

Good Faith

Article 2 preserves our fundamental American notions about freedom of contract by allowing the parties to vary the effect of Code provisions or determine standards of performance by their agreement. These standards of performance will be upheld as long as they are not "manifestly unreasonable."[8] One standard of performance which may not be waived or altered by agreement because it would be unreasonable is the requirement that "every contract" covered by the Code must be entered into and conducted in good faith.[9] *Good faith* is defined as "honesty in fact in the conduct or transaction concerned."[10] In addition to the "honesty" requirement of section 1–201(19), section 2–103(b) says that when *merchants* are involved, good faith also means "the observance of reasonable commercial standards of fair dealing in the trade." Almost every contract involves the exercise of some discretion. It is these discretionary elements which must be governed by the concept of good faith. The court found the lack of good faith in the following case.

Facts
The plaintiff, seller, contracted to plant and cultivate 28 acres of beans. The defendant, buyer, was to use its own judgment as to when the beans would be ripe and was then to send its crew in to pick the beans. A severe drought in the area made the time for picking the beans very critical. The plaintiff notified the defendant that they should be picked by Tuesday, July 1. An agent for the buyer inspected the crops on June 30 and indicated they would be picked after Ennis's crop, which had been planted earlier than plaintiff's. The pickers finished Ennis's crop on July 2 but were directed by defendant to go elsewhere because the crops were of better quality. Defendant began picking plaintiff's crops on July 4, but stopped after a short while because the beans were of "unacceptable" quality. Did the defendant fail to meet its standard of performance?

Decision
Yes.

Reasoning
The trial court found for the plaintiff, and the appellate court affirmed this. The court held that matters of judgment in contractual understandings must be exercised honestly and in good faith. In this case, there was evidence which could demonstrate that the buyer's decision to delay harvesting the crop was not made in good faith. "To begin with there was testimony that the effect of hot temperatures and drought on any snap beans is not only to accelerate the maturing process but also to dehydrate the crop. . . . Since this type of crop, even under normal weather conditions, must be harvested within a few days of when it ripens, a three-day delay during a drought is evidence from which a jury may conclude bad faith was exhibited."

Dorsey Bros., Inc. v. H. Anderson, 287 A.2d 270, at 272 (Md. 1972).

Merchants

merchant
"a person who deals in goods of the kind or otherwise by his occupation holds himself out as having knowledge or skill peculiar to the practices or goods involved in the transaction. . . ."
UCC 2–104(1)

In the following chapters of Part 5 we will see that in some instances Article 2 imposes on **merchants** more rigid standards of performance than on nonmerchants. The common law of contracts did not recognize a difference between someone who sells goods only occasionally (e.g., selling a lawnmower at a garage sale) and someone who sells goods of a particular kind for a living (e.g., retailer). However, it seems obvious that someone who holds himself or herself out as a seller of goods of a particular kind should have a certain "expertise" in the sale of those items. Thus, a "professional" seller or merchant should be held to a higher standard of care in some instances. This is a "realistic" view of some sales transactions.

---

[8] UCC 1–102(3).

[9] UCC 1–203.

[10] UCC 1–201(19).

Article 2 and the Common Law of Contracts

The fact that Article 2 imposes more rigid standards of performance on merchants than on nonmerchants when the **common law** did not do this highlights the fact that *Article 2 does change some of the contract law you studied in Part 2*. In general, the purpose of the Code changes was to recognize circumstances of current commercial practice not recognized by the common law of contracts. More specifically, *Article 2 differs from "contract" law and embodies notions of current commercial practice* in the following important areas (in addition to the distinction made for merchants noted above):

1. statute of frauds;
2. firm offers;
3. additional terms in acceptance;
4. modification;
5. unconscionable contracts.

> **common law**
> principles of non-statutory law reflecting the customs and usages of society and found in judicial decisions

Some of these changes were noted in chapters 5–13, on contract law. However, here in Part 4 we will go into greater detail on these changes. Of course, in those areas of commercial law not covered by Article 2 (lease of goods, sale of an interest in land, contracts for services, etc.), the common law of contracts still controls.

Statute of Frauds

In chapter 11, on the common law of contracts, we observed that an enactment by the English Parliament in 1677 called the Statute of Frauds stated which promises had to be evidenced by a writing before they would be *enforced* by a court. Both the present-day law of contracts and the UCC retain the use of the phrase "statute of frauds" to designate those enforceable promises which must be evidenced by a writing.

> Enforceability of sales contracts.

Article 2 adds to the list of transactions under the law of contracts, to which the statute of frauds applies. It provides that a contract for the sale of goods for the *price* of $500 or more is not enforceable unless there is some *writing* (1) *recognizing the contract,* (2) *stating the quantity of goods involved,* and (3) *signed by the party against whom enforcement is sought.*[11] There is a distinction between saying *the contract must be in writing* and stating that the promises must *be evidenced* by a writing. Article 2 requires only the latter. For example, S orally agrees to sell his car to P for $1,000 and S then refers to this fact in his letter to Q, P's sister. S may not assert the statute of frauds as a defense if P should sue S for breach of S's promise because the letter, if signed by S, is sufficient evidence of S's promise to sell. This would be true even if the letter incorrectly stated one of the terms, but the promise would not be enforceable beyond the *quantity* of the goods referred to in the letter. Office memos, minutes of a board of directors' meeting, and the like may also be used.

Purpose of the Statute of Frauds

The purpose of the statute of frauds is to protect an innocent party against others who might *fraudulently* assert that the innocent party had promised to perform. The opportunity for fraud is minimized when there is some evidence that a party who made an oral promise has begun to perform. Article 2 recognizes this and provides that an *oral promise is enforceable without a writing* when: (1) goods are to be specially manufactured for the buyer, and they are not suitable for sale to others in the ordinary course of the seller's business, and the seller has made either a substantial beginning of their manufacture or commitments for their procurement;[12] or, (2) if the party being charged admits in its

---

[11] UCC 2–201(1).

[12] UCC 2–201(3)(a).

pleadings or testimony in court that a contract was made;[13] or, (3) if the party being charged has either paid for the goods in question or accepted the goods.[14] It should be obvious that, in these three circumstances, the *actions* of the party being charged with having made a contract have themselves minimized the chance for fraud: the party has either begun work on the goods requested, admitted the contract, or paid for or accepted the goods.

Merchants and the Statute of Frauds

Finally, Article 2's version of the statute of frauds recognizes a different standard of performance for merchants and in so doing substantially changes the older common law interpretations. It provides that, if a *written* **confirmation** of the contract is sent by one *merchant* to another *merchant* within a reasonable time of the exchange of oral promises and the receiver has reason to know its contents, it satisfies the writing requirement for both the sender *and* the receiver even though not signed by the receiver, unless the receiver objects to its contents within ten days of receipt.[15] Since much of today's business is conducted by one merchant's merely filling in a few blanks on a form and sending it off to another merchant, this section of the statute puts a duty on merchants to read their mail! If the merchant receiving the form or confirmation has no intent to contract with the sending merchant and has reason to know the contents of the form, then the receiving merchant must reject the form within ten days. If this is not done, the receiving merchant may be bound by the terms on the form of the sending party.

confirmation
an assuring expression of understanding

Contents of the Writing

In general, Article 2 is fairly liberal in allowing evidence of an oral contract. The Code Comments to the statute of frauds section make it clear that, when a writing is required, it need not state the price, time, or place of payment or delivery, nor the general quality of the goods. Business people frequently base their agreement as to price on a price list or catalogue known to both of them. Therefore, the only three essential ingredients of the required writing are that (1) it must refer to a contract for the *sale of goods* between the parties, (2) it must specify the *quantity* of goods, and (3) it must be *signed by the party* to be charged with performance of the contract.

A diagram of Article 2's statute of frauds (2–201) might appear as in figure 17.1.

Applying the Statute of Frauds

In applying section 2–201 to a factual situation, we must keep the position of the parties in mind. In a case where the plaintiff alleges that the defendant orally promised to sell or buy goods, it is unlikely that the plaintiff's claim is untrue. *Usually* the plaintiff is asserting the existence of an agreement with the defendant and the fact that the defendant did not perform in some respect. The plaintiff, then, is met with a defense. It is a defense which does not go to the merits of the case but which is intended to clarify preliminary matters about precisely what was agreed upon, if anything, and to minimize the chances of fraud.[16] The defense asserts that the statute of frauds requires a signed writing (unless the parties are merchants) sufficient to allow the plaintiff to continue with the proof, and no such writing exists. At this point the court focuses upon the sufficiency of the writings, if any, or other facts required by the statute of frauds. If these requirements are not met, the court will hold that a good defense exists and dismiss the case for lack of proof that a required signed writing was made by the defendant. However, if the requirements are met, then this simply means the plaintiff must proceed with proof of the contents of the

---

[13] UCC 2–201(3)(b).

[14] UCC 2–201(3)(c).

[15] UCC 2–201(2).

[16] R. J. Nordstrom, *supra* note 10, at 54.

Figure 17.1 Diagram of UCC 2-201—Statute of Frauds

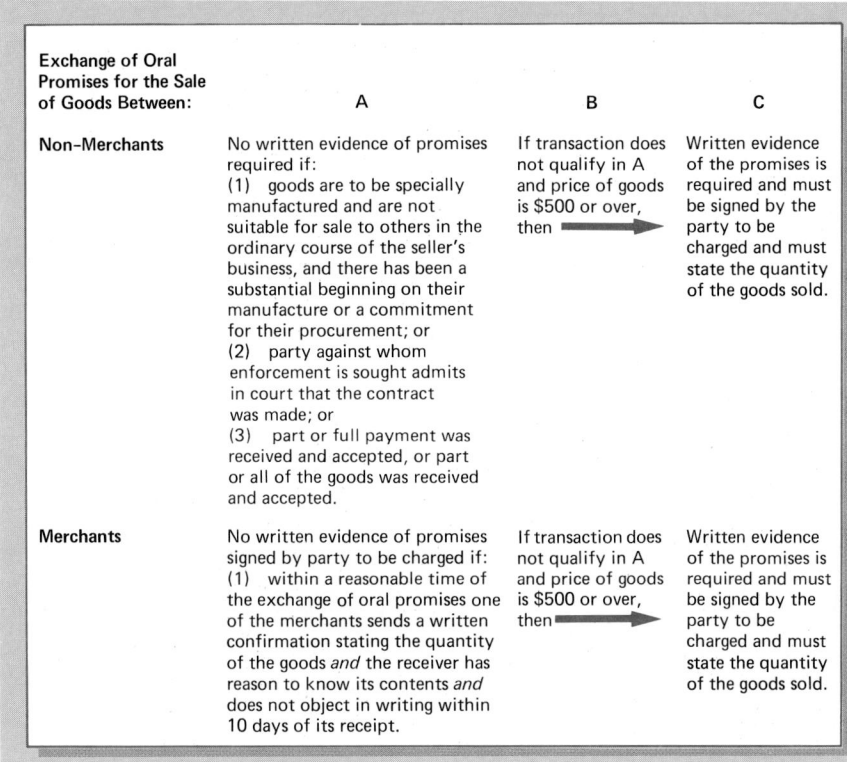

contract, its breach, and loss. Because the defense of the statute of frauds is overcome, do not assume that the plaintiff has won. Substantial problems of proof may remain. The plaintiff must still prove that there was an offer and acceptance, consideration, breach, damage, etc.

Parol or Extrinsic Evidence

An issue often perceived as closely related to the application of the statute of frauds—but, in reality, quite different—is the use of oral testimony (**parol evidence**) or written evidence to clarify a *written* understanding. The usual position of the parties when we see the **parol evidence rule** asserted is that the plaintiff has introduced as evidence a *writing* which purports to be "the understanding" between the parties. The defendant admits the existence and signing of the document but counters with an assertion that one of the terms of the writing was varied or modified by a *prior* oral understanding or other evidence.

Article 2 attempts to resolve this rather common situation by providing:

> Terms with respect to which confirmatory memoranda of the parties agree or which are otherwise set forth in writing intended by the parties as a final expression of their agreement with respect to such terms . . . may not be contradicted by evidence of any prior agreement or of a contemporaneous oral agreement but may be explained or supplemented:
> (a) by course of dealing or usage of trade . . . or by course of performance . . .; and
> (b) by evidence of consistent additional terms unless the court finds the writing to have been intended also as a complete and exclusive statement of the terms of the agreement.[17]

parol evidence
oral testimony

parol evidence rule
a rule of law which provides that, when there is a written contract, it cannot be contradicted (added to or varied) by any prior or contemporaneous oral agreement, or by a prior written agreement

---
[17] UCC 2-202.

Application of the Parol Evidence Rule

The key features of this section direct a court first to find whether the parties intended their *writing,* namely the memoranda in question, to be a "final" expression of their agreement with respect to the "term" in question. If a court so finds, then any oral (parol) or other evidence of an agreement between the parties which occurred *before,* and any oral agreement which occurred *contemporaneously* with, the writing will not be admitted if it *contradicts* the writing. Please note that oral agreements made *after* the confirmatory memoranda will be admissible as evidence unless the statute of frauds requires their exclusion. Evidence which *explains* and does not contradict will be admissible. The parol evidence rule will not be applied in situations where one of the parties is alleging that contractual capacity was lacking, or that the agreement was procured through fraud, duress, or illegality.

The case below is a recent example of the application of the parol evidence rule, section 2–202 of Article 2.

Facts

Philipp Brothers Division of Engelhard Minerals and Chemical Corporation, buyer, plaintiff, agreed to buy sugar from the defendant, El Salto, S. A., seller, in five written contracts made in the months of September, October and November, 1979. The contracts were expressed on a standard written form. From September 1979, through March 1980, there were extensive communications between the parties by letter, telephone and personal visits. The defendant seller contends that during this period (after some of the contracts in question had been made) the parties had orally agreed that Philipp would furnish $750,000 in cash advances on the contract so that the El Salto could purchase sugar cane for processing. Philipp, buyer, did not make such advances and the defendant declared the contracts void as of February 19, 1980. The buyer sues the seller for breach of contract. The defendant argued that oral evidence about the cash advance should be admitted. The trial court held for the plaintiff and excluded the oral testimony. The defendant appeals arguing it was error to exclude this oral testimony. Should the oral testimony about the cash advances be admitted?

Decision

No. The appellate court affirmed a decision for the plaintiff, buyer.

Reasoning

The defendant argues that the oral evidence of the cash advance should be admitted because the parties did not intend the written form contracts to be a final expression of their agreement. The court said that this issue is to be resolved by measuring the completeness of the written instrument itself and not on the basis of evidence of the subjective beliefs of the parties. The language relating to payment makes no provision for advance payments. "We thus conclude that the law of New York (section 2–202 of Article 2) forbids the admissibility of oral evidence to prove the alleged requirement for a cash advance. Admissibility of such evidence would altogether vary the complete and clear terms of the contract.

Philipp Brothers Division of Engelhard Minerals & Chemicals Corp. v. El Salto, S. A., 487 F.Supp. 91 (1980).

We can see from our study of both the statute of frauds and the parol evidence sections how Article 2 attempts to achieve the main objectives of the UCC. Both sections require merchants and others to meet certain minimum standards in the statement and modification of their agreement for the sale of goods. Yet, in defining these standards, the parties are allowed a large measure of flexibility. This flexibility is intended to reflect changes in custom and commercial usage of documents dictated by an ever-changing commercial world.

Summary Statement

1. The purposes of the Uniform Commercial Code are to simplify, clarify, and modernize the law governing commercial transactions; to permit the growth of commercial law; and to make uniform the commercial law of the various states.

2. Article 2 of the UCC was drafted by Professor Karl Llewellyn, who believed that the best commercial rules were those that reflected the best parts of current commercial practice. Article 2 uses such words as "reasonable" and "good faith" so that courts may update the Article by continuing to focus on the best commercial conduct as defining what is "reasonable" and so forth.
3. Article 2 applies to transactions in *goods* and does not apply to leases, gifts, the sale of an interest in land (and other nonmovables), investment securities, and services.
4. Every transaction for the sale of goods covered by Article 2 must be conducted in good faith.
5. Even though Article 2 changes some of the rules of the common law of contracts, the latter still supplements the UCC and is applicable in cases where Article 2 or the UCC do not provide the answer to a legal question.
6. Article 2's statute of frauds provision provides that a contract for the sale of goods for the price of $500 or more is not enforceable unless there is some writing recognizing the contract and stating the quantity of goods involved, and it is signed by the party against whom enforcement of the contract is sought. No writing is needed when:
   a. the goods are to be specially manufactured for the buyer, they are not suitable for sale to others in the ordinary course of the seller's business, and the seller has made either a substantial beginning of their manufacture or commitments for their procurement; or
   b. the party being charged admits in court a contract was made; or
   c. the party being charged with performance of the contract has paid for or accepted the goods.
7. If a written confirmation of the contract is sent by one *merchant* to another *merchant* within a reasonable time of the exchange of oral promises, and the receiver has reason to know its contents, it satisfies the writing requirement for both the sender and receiver even though not signed by the receiver, unless the receiver objects to its contents within ten days of receipt.
8. The parol evidence rule is a rule of evidence which excludes testimony of an oral agreement made prior to, or contemporaneously with, a written agreement, or a prior written agreement, which would contradict the written agreement.

The following case is a good example of how the Code's statute of frauds is applied to merchants.

Campbell v. Yokel
313 N.E.2d 628 (Ill. 1974)

Crebs, J. The plaintiffs, owners and operators of the Campbell Grain and Seed Company, alleged that they had reached an oral agreement on February 7, 1973 with the defendant group of farmers to purchase 6,800 to 7,200 bushels of yellow soybeans at a price of $5.30 per bushel. After the conversation between the plaintiffs and the defendants on February 7, the plaintiffs signed and mailed a written confirmation of the oral agreement. Defendants received the written confirmation but did not sign it or give any notice of objection to its contents to the plaintiffs. The defendants refused to deliver any soybeans to the plaintiffs and, on April 30, 1973, informed the plaintiffs that, since the defendants did not sign the written confirmation, they were not bound by it. They also stated that it was their understanding that the agreement was tentative and was not to be binding unless a written contract was signed.

The plaintiffs rely on UCC 2-201(2), the Statute of Frauds, which provides that there is no writing required if:

> Between merchants if within a reasonable time a writing in confirmation of the contract and sufficient against the sender is received and the party receiving it has reason to know its contents, it satisfies the requirements of subsection (1) against such parties unless notice of objection to its contents is given within 10 days after it is received.

The first issue the court had to decide was whether the defendants were merchants. The court noted that some state courts have held that farmers were not merchants but that the better reasoned opinions held that farmers were merchants, especially with regard to an agreement to sell growing crops. UCC 2-104(1) defines a merchant as

> . . . a person who deals in goods of the kind or otherwise by his occupation holds himself out as having knowledge or skill peculiar to the practices or goods involved in the transaction or to whom such knowledge or skill may be attributed by his employment. . . .

The defendants admitted in discovery depositions that they had grown and sold soybeans and other grains for several years. The court concluded that "we believe that a farmer who regularly sells his crops is a person who 'deals in goods of that kind.' " Holding that farmers are merchants and applying Section 2-201(2) of the Statute of Frauds to these defendants lessens the possibility that the Statute of Frauds would be used as an instrument of fraud. For example, assuming that an oral agreement had been reached, . . . that the farmers had received written confirmation signed by the plaintiffs, and that the farmers were not "merchants," the farmers would be in a position to speculate on a contract to which the grain company was bound. If the market price fell after the agreement had been reached, the farmers could produce the written confirmation and enforce the contract. If the market price rose, the farmers could claim the protection of the Statute of Frauds and sell their crops on the open market.

The court concluded, "Our decision is not tantamount to a finding that a contract did exist between plaintiffs and defendants. We hold merely that since the defendants were merchants Section 2-201(2) operates to bar the defendants from asserting the defense of the Statute of Frauds. The burden of persuading the trier of fact that an oral contract was in fact made prior to the written confirmation is unaffected."

Questions and Case Problems

1. In your own words, write a short but complete paragraph describing the need for a uniform commercial code, the purposes of the UCC, and the basic philosophy underlying many of Article 2's key provisions.

2. Make up an example of a sales transaction involving both goods and services. Then state the "standard" or "test" a court would use in determining whether or not Article 2 would apply. Finally, state your conclusion as to whether or not Article 2 would apply. In reaching this conclusion, be sure to integrate the proper facts from your example with the stated standard or test used.

3. The plaintiff, a manufacturer of textiles, contracted with the defendant, a large processor of textiles, to "finish" and dye a large quantity of unfinished textiles. The defendant accepted a large shipment of textiles from the plaintiff and "finished" and dyed the material and then sent it on to the plaintiff's customer. The defendant billed the plaintiff, but the plaintiff refuses to pay because it maintains that the defendant improperly performed the finishing and dyeing and this was a breach of warranty. The plaintiff sues the defendant for breach of implied warranty; but, before the parties can reach the issue of the breach of warranty, the defendant moves to dismiss the case because it is not governed by the UCC. The plaintiff maintains that the UCC applies. How would a court decide this issue? Is the defendant right? [*The Manes Organization, Inc. v. Standard Dyeing and Finishing Co.*, 472 F.Supp. 687 (D.C.S.D.N.Y., 1979).]

4. The plaintiffs allege that they entered into a contract with the defendants for the purchase of a Falcon Jet, Model 50, for a total consideration of $9.4 million. The defendants allege that the series of meetings held with the plaintiffs did include discussions of the sale of the aircraft but no final terms were agreed to and no written agreement existed that could satisfy the statute of frauds. The plaintiffs counter and prove that a check for $250,000

had been accepted by the defendants as a deposit on the aircraft. The defendants allege that the check was payment as an option and all defendants were obligated to do was hold the plane off the market. With regard to the defendant's claim that the statute of frauds applied in this case, since there was no writing should a court enter judgment for them on these facts? [*Songbird Jet Ltd., Inc. v. Amax Inc.,* 581 F.Supp. 912 (1984).]

5. A printing company, the plaintiff, accepted typed and edited pages and other material from the defendant, publisher of a magazine, sufficient for the printing company to print the magazine. Fifteen thousand copies of the magazine were printed based on the publisher's original copy as submitted to the printer. After the printing, the printer submits a bill for more than the publisher says they agreed upon. The printer argues that under the UCC no new consideration is needed for a modification of the original agreement. The defendant argues that the UCC is not applicable. Make this argument for the publisher. Do you think a court would agree? State why or why not. [*Gross Valentino Printing Co. v. Clarke,* 458 N.E.2d 1027 (Ill., 1983).]

6. Indicate which, if any, of the following transactions and legal disputes arising therefrom would be governed by sections of Articles 1 and 2 of the UCC:
   a. a written contract in which S agrees to manufacture special parts for P which are not currently in existence;
   b. an oral contract for the sale of a used car from one neighbor to another for $450;
   c. an oral contract to paint your neighbor's house for $800;
   d. a contract to sell an **easement** over your farm so a neighbor may water his cattle in your stream;
   e. an agreement made with an oil drilling company to drill for oil on your land;
   f. a written agreement to sell your fall crop of apples, which will be picked by you;
   g. an agreement to lease your sailboat to a friend for the summer.

easement
an irrevocable right to the limited use of another's land

7. The plaintiff bought a used car from the defendant, a car dealer. The plaintiff signed a contract which clearly stated there were no warranties made by the seller beyond the manufacturer's new car warranty insofar as it may be applicable. Several weeks after the purchase, the plaintiff alleges, the paint on the car developed "defects." The plaintiff sues the defendant for the value of a new paint job and attempts to state at the trial that the defendant's agent made certain oral representations about the condition of the car (and paint) at the time of the sale. Should oral testimony of the representations or warranties of the seller's agent be admissible? [*Tracy v. Vinton Motors, Inc.,* 296 A.2d 269 (Vt. 1972).]

8. The plaintiff, Lipschutz, a large New York wholesaler of diamonds, sends a **consignment** of diamonds to the defendant, Linz, retailer of diamonds. The defendant acknowledges receipt of the diamonds by sending the following "all risk" memorandum to the wholesaler:

consignment
the shipment of goods from one person to another

Received on consignment from Lipschutz & Gartwirth Co., 630 Fifth Avenue, New York City, the following goods pursuant to the following agreement:
The goods described and valued as below are delivered to undersigned Linz Bros. for examination, . . . and shall be at once returned to you on demand. The undersigned assumes full and unqualified responsibility for the absolute return of the said property, or the cash proceeds to you on demand, without any excuse or defense whatsoever. . . .

After receipt of the diamonds there was a robbery at Linz in which merchandise valued at $1.5 million (retail value) was taken; of this amount, Lipschutz owned $700,000. The insurance policy of Linz did not cover the entire *retail* value of the loss. The plaintiff asserts the defendant Linz is liable for the full *retail* market value of its diamonds, $700,000. The defense argues that custom and trade usage in the diamond business establish that, where the loss is the result of a robbery and there is insufficient insurance, the consignee is liable not for the *retail value* of the diamonds, but the consignor's *actual cost* plus a small percentage to cover the costs of handling the diamonds. Should oral and other evidence be admitted to substantiate the defendant's arguments? [*Lipschutz v. Gordon Jewelry Corp.,* 373 F.Supp. 375 (1974).]

9. P, a store owner, entered into a written contract with S, an air conditioning company, to purchase an air conditioning system and to have it installed in the store. The contract referred to a sale and installation of an "air conditioning apparatus." The total contract price was $1,200. The contract contained this statement: "This contract contains the entire agreement of the parties, and no representations or promises or warranties of any kind and no other agreements written or oral exist except as contained in this written agreement."

    In a dispute between P and S which centers on the sufficiency of the "air conditioning apparatus," will S be allowed to introduce oral or extrinsic testimony to prove that it was the parties' intent to have installed a G.E. air conditioning unit #L.B. 4 and not a larger model as P argues? How will this dispute be resolved?

10. In the case of *Campbell v. Yokel*, 313 N.E.2d 628 (Ill. 1974),[18] a farmer was held to be a merchant. Why are farmers merchants?

---

[18] See pp. 249–50.

Formation and Interpretation of the Sales Contract 18

After you have read this chapter, you should be able to:

1. Describe the general circumstances in which merchants contract.
2. State how the UCC altered the common law of offer and acceptance in the creation of a sales contract.
3. Describe how section 2–207 resolves some of the problems created by the fact that most merchants do business by exchanging forms.
4. Define "course of performance," "course of dealing," and "usage of trade" and then clearly state how these terms are used by courts to help them ascertain the parties' intended meanings of words used by them.
5. State how the UCC allows merchants to modify a contractual agreement.
6. Define an insurable interest; describe when an insurable interest is created in a buyer; then define when the "risk of loss" for damage to or destruction of goods passes to the buyer; and, finally, be able to differentiate between the creation of an insurable interest and passage of the risk of loss.
7. Describe the significance of "title" under Article 2 of the UCC and determine how and when title is transferred.

Introduction—How to Think about Commercial Transactions

In the preceding chapter of this Part, we discussed the concept, history, and thrust of the UCC, compared Article 2 of the Code with the common law of contracts, and discussed the Statute of Frauds and the Parol Evidence Rule. In this chapter, we will discuss the business environment in which sales transactions occur, the formation of the sales contract by offer and acceptance, and the problems of interpreting the sales contract to determine the intentions of the parties.

Let us first think about the concepts and ideas involved in making a sales contract. The conventional wisdom about the law, its rules, its functions, and its value lags behind the fast-moving sociological and economic events of our day. A good illustration of this can be found by pointing out that it is a common belief (the conventional wisdom) that consumers "contract" in the traditional sense when they purchase consumer goods from a merchant. At the heart of our conventional wisdom about "contracting" is the notion that the parties **bargain** or **negotiate.** This implies that they are each aware of all unfavorable and favorable terms, and they consciously select those that best serve their interests.

> **bargain** or **negotiate** terms used to indicate that both parties to a sales contract are aware of all the terms of the contract and that both parties exchanged value to establish the terms

Yet this image does not reflect reality, and it misleads us in our study of the law. When was the last time you made a "bargain" or "negotiated" the terms of a sale as a consumer? The belief that one "bargains" with Standard Oil, Sears, General Motors, a McDonald's restaurant, the Adidas sports shop, or a utility such as your local electric or gas company and almost all merchant-sellers of goods persists today despite the fact that many of the notions you have learned about "contracting" are not applicable. You may shop around and choose from several alternatives, but when the "bargain" is struck, you as a consumer take what is *given!*

In short, despite the conventional wisdom of the central place of contract law and the value of a "bargain" in our economy, you as a consumer usually do business on the *seller's terms* or not at all! Have you ever tried to vary so much as one word in the written, contractual language found on your Standard Oil, Sears, or other charge card?

The disparity between how one *imagines* contracting is done and how it *is,* in fact, done is greatest with regard to the sale of goods from a merchant to a consumer. The standardized contract produced by the thousands or, in the case of very large merchants, by the millions, is the rule of the day. Moreover, it is reasonable to expect that such contracts are more favorable to their authors than to the other party to the transaction.

Highlighting this disparity between how one imagines commercial contracting is done and how it is done in reality serves as a basis for understanding *why* the "consumer movement" developed. Simply put, the conventional wisdom was that our commercial law, and particularly the UCC, is a *neutral* body of legal principles protecting equally the interests of merchants and consumers. However, this view failed to account for a political reality. As merchants have become larger and larger economic units, their impact on state legislatures has grown proportionately. When the UCC was adopted, the interests of merchants vis-à-vis consumers were predominant. This predominance and the resulting bias in the UCC has only recently been perceived, and the response has been a piecemeal effort to redress the imbalance.

> The inadequacy of commercial law and the pressure of consumer groups resulted in legislation providing further consumer relief in sales transactions.

The remedy has not been to change the UCC, since the merchants want to maintain uniformity of the UCC. Rather, the remedy has been for both the federal government and state legislatures to pass laws giving consumers remedies *outside* the UCC. It is very difficult in such a short space to assess adequately the reasons for the "consumer" movement. Some of the reasons and a more general inquiry into "consumer" law can be found in chapters 21 and 22 on Consumer Law.

We only wish to emphasize at this point that it is useful to imagine at least two general patterns of commercial conduct (with numerous variations) and, consequently, two broad categories of commercial law. On the one hand, we have commercial activity in large economically concentrated markets in which, generally, *merchants deal with merchants.* On the other hand, we have the retail level of markets for goods in which large, *powerful merchants contract with consumers.*

Since the reality is that we have at least these two general commercial patterns and two categories of legal principles, we have separated the remaining material in this Part on the UCC into two broad categories. This chapter and the two that follow, chapters 19 and 20, are largely based on an image of the parties involved *both* being merchants. Chapters 21 and 22 are on consumer law and the image there should be one of a consumer contracting with a merchant.

A General Pattern of Commercial Conduct

Today, dealings between merchants, especially the large corporate merchants, are often conducted by employees at a low level in the corporate organization who use standardized forms provided by their legal departments or management. These employees do not think of themselves as "contracting," but they do realize that they place and receive "orders" or "confirmations," using "order forms," "quotation forms," or any of a series of forms provided for use.

Very often a supplier will provide a catalogue with prices and descriptions of goods, and the first response from a merchant purchaser may be by telephone, asking for clarifications of price or credit terms. If the response is satisfactory, the purchaser's employee will take a form from a drawer and, in the blank spaces, either write or type the price, description of the goods, quantity, delivery time and means of transportation, and credit terms. When the seller receives the form, an employee will usually transfer the crucial information from the filled-in blanks (after perhaps varying some terms) to the seller company's "confirmation" form and send it back to the purchaser. If the "contract" is a complex one, as for the construction of a large machine or the sale of complex goods over a period of years, it is highly likely that the exchange of forms was preceded by "negotiations" at several levels within the two corporate organizations.

Moreover, after the exchange of forms, there may be numerous further changes or modifications as the economic, technological, or political environment changes. In addition to the forms, there may be telephone calls, letters, resolutions from the board of directors, intracorporate communications, standard operating procedures, and other similar pieces of evidence, *all of which* reflect the understanding of the parties.

If one were to attempt to apply the common law contract rules of offer and acceptance to this typical situation, then a court would be compelled to hold that *no* contract existed because a few essential terms in the offer or acceptance varied. Under the common law, an acceptance was effective only if it "mirrored" the offer by *completely* complying with the offer, the terms of the acceptance being identical to the terms of the offer. Given the common actual pattern of commercial activity as sketched above, this result would be absurd, especially when one considers that it was the *terms* and not the *general intent* which had been varied. The authors of the UCC recognized this and drafted Article 2 to reflect reality.

The remaining portion of this chapter will focus upon contract formation and interpretation and the various ways that both large and small merchants may protect themselves from loss caused by damage or destruction to the goods.

Making the contract by offer and acceptance.

Contract Formation—Offer and Acceptance

How is a sales contract made? Article 2 substantially changes the common law doctrines of contract formation. It provides that *a contract for the sale of goods* may be made in *any* manner sufficient to show *agreement* by the parties.[1] This includes *conduct* by both parties that recognizes the existence of a contract. Moreover, it states that a contract for the sale of goods may be found to exist even though the moment of its making is undetermined or one or more terms are left open, so long as a court could find the general *intent to contract* and there is a reasonably certain basis for giving an appropriate remedy for its breach.[2] In the following case the court found that a contract existed even though some terms were left open.

Facts
The plaintiff, Admiral Plastics Corp., ordered three specially designed machines from the defendant, Trueblood, Inc. The chief engineer for the plaintiff, Paul Marcus, was told by the defendant at the time of the initial contact that the defendant had never made machines of the type ordered but would consider doing so if Admiral would provide the specifications. Based upon preliminary specifications and Marcus' oral discussions with the defendant, the defendant quoted a price to the plaintiff on May 24, 1966 of $39,750 per machine. At this point Marcus orally ordered three machines and promised that a down payment, a written order form, and the specifications would be sent.

Not until July 20, 1966 did the defendant receive from Admiral a check for $29,812.50 as a partial payment as well as a set of specifications and a purchase order. The purchase order provided that the delivery dates for the three machines were to be November 1, November 15, and December 1, 1966. In late August, Marcus visited the defendant's plant and expressed concern that the construction had not started. Marcus was informed that there were discrepancies between the specifications as submitted and Marcus' earlier discussions and that revised specifications were needed. On September 9, 1966 revised specifications were received by the defendant, but they were inadequate in some respects. On November 11, 1966 and again on December 1, 1966 an agent of Admiral visited the defendant's plant to observe the machines in operation and found that the basic welding on only one machine had been done. The defendant never did sign the purchase order form. On December 8, 1966 the plaintiff informed the defendant that there was a default and the plaintiff was initiating suit. No machines were ever delivered, and the defendant did not return the $29,812.50 paid, stating that this did not even cover its expenses. Was there a contract?

Decision
Yes. The court rendered a partial judgment for the plaintiff.

Reasoning
The trial court found that there was a contract followed by mutual rescission. The appellate court affirmed this. The court relied upon UCC 2-204 and said, in part, that "a contract for sale of goods may be made in any manner sufficient to show agreement, including conduct by both parties which recognizes the existence of such a contract [and] . . . a contract for sale does not fail for indefiniteness if the parties have intended to make a contract and there is a reasonably certain basis for giving an appropriate remedy." In the designing and producing of special machines, it is understandable that certain terms were to be left unspecified and that difficulties would be encountered.

The court emphasized that the nature of the contract made it imperative that both parties cooperate to the fullest extent in order for the machines to be successfully designed and built. Both parties failed to act in good faith and failed to cooperate. There was evidence that Admiral was delinquent in furnishing the specifications, as was the defendant in failing to pursue its obligations.

The court concludes by noting that the UCC does not provide a remedy for the specific situation of a *mutual* breaching of contract, so it turns to "other . . . principles of law and equity." The court dismissed the defendant's counterclaim and ordered the return of the plaintiff's down payment.

Admiral Plastics Corp. v. Trueblood, Inc., 436 F.2d 1335 (1971).

---

[1] UCC 2-204(1).

[2] UCC 2-204(3).

The above case reveals that in complex commercial transactions not all details of the transaction can be spelled out at the time the parties become bound. Article 2 clearly accounts for this reality and rejects many of the technical requirements of contract formation developed by the common law. However, while such common law formalities as the effect of a seal on a document today have no legal effect under Article 2 (2–203), the *method of analysis* for finding the existence of an agreement that courts will enforce remains intact. That is, courts still *search for an offer and a response thereto, indicating an intent to be bound, called an acceptance*. Also, the promise of the parties must *manifest a desired exchange of value*. This exchange of value was defined as "consideration" in the chapters on the common law of contracts, and this concept retains its vitality in Article 2 with some notable exceptions. We will discuss one exception here and another one when discussing modification, rescission, and waiver.

At common law, if an offeree wanted to be sure that an offeror would hold his offer open for a given length of time, the offeree was bound to give something of value (consideration) to the offeror. As you read in Part 2, Contracts, when such value was given, a contract was formed to keep the main offer open for a time, which became an **option**. While Article 2 does not eliminate the option in a transaction for the sale of goods, it adds a new term, **firm offer**, which has the same effect as an option, but value is *not required* to keep an offer open for a limited time. Article 2 provides that when a *merchant* gives a *signed written assurance* in an offer that it will be held open for a stated time, then it is not revocable for lack of consideration.[3] If no time is stated, then the courts will infer that a reasonable time was intended, but in no event shall the period of the open or "firm" offer exceed *three months*.

option
the irrevocable offer in an option contract

firm offer
a merchant's signed irrevocable offer to buy or sell goods, giving assurance that it will be kept open; consideration is not required, and its maximum time is three months

At What Moment Are The Parties Bound by Their Promises?
Generally, offers may be made in any way that reveals an intent to be bound by the promises contained in the offer, and an acceptance shall be made in any manner and by any medium reasonable in the circumstances.[4] What did the drafters of Article 2 do to the famous **"mail box rule"**?[5] At what point does an acceptance become effective? This very question was not of great importance to the drafters. In one sense they minimized its importance by providing that a court could find that a contract existed even though the time of its "making" was uncertain, and by adding that acceptance could be by any reasonable means.

mail box rule
the rule in *Adams v. Lindsell:* an acceptance is effective when it is sent if the means of sending it were impliedly authorized by, for example, the offeror's use of the mails to send the offer

Bilateral and Unilateral Promises
Article 2 recognizes the distinction between bilateral promises and unilateral promises by providing that an order or other offer to buy goods for prompt shipment shall be construed as inviting acceptance either by a prompt promise to ship (forming a bilateral contract) or by the prompt shipment of conforming goods (forming a unilateral contract). If the offer requests prompt shipment, then a contract for sale is formed upon the prompt shipment by the seller even though the goods shipped are non-conforming.[6] The drafters thought it would expedite commerce by recognizing that the shipment of non-conforming goods was an acceptance. In this case, although technically a contract exists upon shipment of non-conforming goods, the contract has been breached, and the purchaser has a remedy for the breach (paradoxically, the act of shipping non-conforming goods may be both an acceptance and a breach).

---

[3] UCC 2–205.   [4] UCC 2–206(1)(a) and (b).

[5] Under the common law of contracts, if A mailed an offer to B and B received it on September 15 and then sent an acceptance by mail the same day, a contract was formed as of the time B posted the letter of acceptance. A later attempt by A to revoke his offer and a later attempt by B to revoke his acceptance are not effective.

[6] UCC 2–206(1)(b).

"Accommodating" the Buyer

If a seller realizes that the goods shipped are non-conforming and ships them anyway to "accommodate" the buyer, then the act of shipment may not be an acceptance so long as the seller notifies the buyer that the goods are being shipped only as an "accommodation." For example, assume that P Co. orders for prompt shipment a large quantity of #10 *aluminum* wood screws from S Co. Upon receiving the order, the agent for S Co. realizes that it has no #10 aluminum wood screws but can ship immediately #10 *steel* wood screws. If S Co. ships the steel wood screws, there is an acceptance of the offer and a contract results, but P Co. may have a remedy for breach of the contract. However, the proper response here would have been for S Co. to notify P Co. that it was out of the aluminum screws and, if the steel screws would suffice, they would be sent as an accommodation to P Co.[7] In this case, no contract for the sale of aluminum wood screws would result and, therefore, there could be no breach of contract. If P Co. assents, there would be a contract for the sale of #10 steel wood screws.

Performance As Acceptance

Finally, section 2–206 protects the offeror by adding that where the beginning of a requested performance is a reasonable mode of acceptance, the offeree must notify the offeror that performance has begun. If the offeror is not notified within a reasonable time, the offeror may treat the offer as having lapsed before acceptance.[8] This section of the Code recognizes a basic fact of commercial life: both buyers and sellers are looking forward to performance, and usually the sooner the better. If an "offer" form or "order" form requests prompt shipment, then, to protect the offeree, an acceptance occurs when the requested performance begins so long as some notification is sent to the offeror. This notice must be sent within a reasonable time or the offeror may treat the offer as having lapsed. What is a reasonable time? When a merchant makes such an offer, it is usually to some other merchant from whom goods have been received in the past. It is the past conduct or, in the absence of this conduct, current commercial practice which will establish whether the notice of the beginning of performance was sent within a reasonable time.

The Battle of the Forms and Section 2–207

Recall now the fact pattern we discussed at the beginning of this chapter to show how many commercial contracts are formed. We have an exchange of forms together with prior and subsequent agreements. What is "the contract"?

The difficulty of interpreting the terms in the forms used by seller and buyer in order to determine their intentions as to whether they have agreed, creating a sales contract.

Section 2–207 provides:

(1) A definite and seasonable expression of acceptance or a written confirmation which is sent within a reasonable time operates as an acceptance even though it states terms additional to or different from those offered or agreed upon, unless acceptance is expressly made conditional on assent to the additional or different terms.

(2) The additional terms are to be construed as proposals for addition to the contract. Between merchants such terms become part of the contract unless:
(a) the offer expressly limits acceptance to the terms of the offer;
(b) they materially alter it; or
(c) notification of the objection to them has already been given or is given within a reasonable time after notice of them is received.

---

[7] R. J. Nordstrom, *Handbook of the Law of Sales* (St. Paul: West Pub. Co., 1970), p. 88.

[8] UCC 2–206(2).

(3) Conduct by both parties which recognizes the existence of a contract is sufficient to establish a contract for sale although the writings of the parties do not otherwise establish a contract. In such case the terms of the particular contract consist of those terms on which the writings of the parties agree, together with any supplementary terms incorporated under any other provisions of this Act.

It should be obvious from the first paragraph above that section 2–207 shatters the mirror-image requirement of an acceptance that prevails at common law, so long as the acceptance is *definite* and timely *and* the acceptance was not made *expressly* conditional on assent to the additional terms.

Section 2–207 reflects this approach of the Code: *Is there a bargain between the parties;* do their forms agree on *anything?* If they do, then there is a contract on what they agree upon, unless the offer clearly indicates that acceptance can be *only* in compliance with the offer's terms. The Code is saying: speak up clearly to indicate your intent, for if you do not do so, this is how the UCC will interpret your expression or silence or conduct in order to determine your intent and its legal effect. The search for a bargain from the forms of the parties.

In the battle of forms context, then, the starting point is that there is a contract that consists of the *terms on which the forms agree,* unless it is expressly stated in the acceptance that the acceptance is a counteroffer. When the terms in the forms agree.

With regard to terms in the forms that *vary,* section 2–207 provides two lines for analysis depending upon the character of the parties. *If one or both of the parties are not merchants,* then the additional terms are to be construed as *proposals for additions to the contract.* This means they are *not* part of the contract unless the offeror agrees to them. This provision protects the offeror by allowing courts to find that a contract exists but essentially on the offeror's terms. However, the offeree is also not without protection. If the *offeree* intends to be bound *only* if *all* of its conditions are met, then it must conspicuously state this, in which case the offeree's form will not appear as a definite and seasonable expression of acceptance. It will be a *counteroffer,* and no contract will result until the offeror accepts the offeree's terms. When the terms in the forms vary. If one or both parties are not merchants.

However, section 2–207 contemplates our given factual pattern involving *merchants* and provides a second and more significant line of analysis. *If both the parties are merchants* and the acceptance does not expressly state it is a counteroffer, then the added terms of the offeree in the acceptance *become part of the contract* unless (1) the offer form expressly limits acceptance to *its* terms, or (2) the added terms materially alter the offeror's form, or (3) notification of objection to the added terms is given within a reasonable time after notice of them is received. If both parties are merchants.

Although neither of the merchants in our factual pattern may have read the other's form, the law properly assumes that they should. Again, section 2–207 seems to favor the merchant offeror by making its document controlling if it limits acceptance to its terms only. If the offering form does not so limit acceptance, then the offeree's additions become part of the contract (again, on the assumption that the acceptance cannot be termed a counteroffer) unless the offeror objects to them within a reasonable time after notice of them is received *or* they materially alter the offeror's form.

This brings us to the crucial question of what is a material alteration? The Comments to section 2–207 state that *a material alteration is one that would result in unreasonable surprise or hardship to the other party.* Comment 4 gives (in part) the following general examples of additions that would materially alter an offer: Offeree's terms materially altering offeror's terms.

1. "a clause negating . . . standard warranties"; and
2. "a clause reserving to the seller the power to cancel upon the buyer's failure to meet any invoice when due."

Another example is a clause requiring one of the parties to meet a much higher standard of performance than is accepted in the trade generally.

Chapter 18: Formation and Interpretation of the Sales Contract

Comment 5 suggests alterations that would not materially alter an offer. They are (in part):

1. "a clause setting forth and perhaps enlarging slightly upon the seller's exemption [from liability] due to supervening causes beyond his control";
2. "a clause fixing a reasonable time for complaints within customary limits";
3. "a clause providing for interest on overdue invoices . . . where they are within the range of trade practice."

By comparing the above suggestions on defining materiality, one may discern the central policy of this section. It is, stated briefly: *Where either of the parties attempts to vary standard or accepted commercial usage, they should bring this to the attention of the other party and make it a subject of negotiation.* If such a variation is not negotiated, then a court may find that such a provision is not part of the contract.

In the following case there was no express consent to a disclaimer of **consequential damages,** so the disclaimer did not become part of the contract.

consequential damages
the money judicially awarded to an injured party for loss which the breaching party reasonably could foresee would be a result of his breach

Facts
The plaintiff, Air Products and Chemicals, Inc., purchased from the defendant, Fairbanks Morse, Inc., ten large electric motors ranging from 800 to 1700 horsepower. The negotiations formally began on April 15, 1964 when the plaintiff orally ordered some of the motors which were to become the subject of this controversy. On April 21, 1964 the plaintiff sent its "purchase order" confirming its verbal order of April 15. On April 30, 1964 the defendant returned an executed copy of the plaintiff's purchase order together with the defendant's "Acknowledgment of Order" form. After the motors were constructed, shipped, and installed, the plaintiff alleged that they failed to perform as promised and sued the defendant for more than $31,000.

In this case there were numerous issues of law and fact to be decided, and just one of them was whether the plaintiff could sue for damages beyond what it cost to have the motors repaired to perform properly. These damages, called consequential damages, may be awarded if they are a foreseeable event at the time the contract is made and the other party is aware of them. In this case the plaintiff was asking for consequential damages because of work stoppage and lost profits.

The plaintiff's purchase order form stated, in part:

Seller recognizes that failure to make delivery of . . . equipment conforming to the requirements of this purchase order . . . will subject buyer to substantial damages due to delay and disruption of work schedules, inefficient use of manpower and other reasons. . . .

In response to the purchase order, the defendant sent its "Acknowledgment of Order" form, which read, in part:

We thank you for your order as copied hereon, which will receive prompt attention and shall be governed by the provisions on the reverse side hereof unless you notify us to the contrary within 10 days or before shipment whichever is earlier. . . .

On the reverse side of the acknowledgment form it stated, in part:

The Company nowise assumes any responsibility or liability with respect to use, purpose, or suitability, and shall not be liable for damages of any character, whether direct or consequential, for defect, delay, or otherwise. . . .

Was there a "contract"? If so, which contract provision controls the question of whether the plaintiff may seek damages for the delay caused by the improper performance of the motors?

Decision
There was a contract. Judgment for the plaintiff, who can sue for consequential damages.

Reasoning
The appellate court held that the plaintiff could sue for consequential damages caused by the delay. The court held that a contract existed because the "Acknowledgment of Order" form stated that the provisions contained there "form part of the order acknowledged and accepted on the face hereof," and, this form contained no express provision making assent to its different or additional terms necessary. The remaining issue was whether the additional or different terms of the "Acknowledgment of Order" form were material. On this point the court held that a disclaimer for consequential loss that has the effect of eliminating millions of dollars in damages is sufficiently material to require that a waiver or alteration of it be expressly consented to by the party affected, which did not occur here, so plaintiff may sue for consequential damages.

Air Products & Chemicals, Inc., v. Fairbanks Morse, Inc., 206 N.W.2d 414 (Wis. 1973).

Section 2–207 makes another important change in the common law of contracts. Under that law, a confirmation is not an acceptance because it does not assent to the offer; it only confirms receipt of the offer. Section 2–207 provides that a *written* confirmation is an acceptance, the above discussion being applicable to it. Of course, if the confirmation specifies that it is not an acceptance, then it is not an acceptance.

The confirmation as an acceptance.

Finally, section 2–207 should not be viewed as a rigid mechanistic legal rule. It cannot be understood in isolation. This section must be thought of as part of a general effort in Article 2 to free up the courts to search for an agreement in fact between the parties. If the intention of the parties is ambiguous, courts are to refer to current commercial usage to reach a resolution of the conflict. Again we see the impact of Article 2—let us fit the law to business rather than fit business to the law.

Interpretation of the Sales Contract

The Significance of "Course of Performance," "Course of Dealing," and "Usage of Trade"

We have just completed an analysis of the Article 2 sections that tell us which *words* should be controlling when forms are exchanged. The UCC provides us with another line of analysis to help us in arriving at a fair interpretation of the parties' contractual intent. Comment 1 to section 1–205 sets out the general rule that "the meaning of the agreement of the parties is to be determined by the language used by them and by their action, read and interpreted in the light of commercial practices and other surrounding circumstances." Of course, the terms of the agreement and any **course of performance, course of dealing** and **usage of trade** are to be construed as consistent with each other whenever reasonable.[9]

When there is conflict between events such as those just mentioned, the UCC provides this order of priority of controlling events:

1. express terms of an agreement;[10]
2. course of performance;[11]
3. course of dealing;
4. usage of trade.

The distinction between course of performance and course of dealing is directly related to the *time* in the transaction when the conduct occurs. Conduct *after* the particular agreement is made and which is a result of the agreement is a "course of performance"; conduct of the parties *prior* to the particular agreement is a "course of dealing."[12]

Usage of trade is defined by the conduct of "the great majority of decent dealers, even though dissidents ready to cut corners do not agree" and is not defined solely by the parties themselves.[13] The following case is concerned with an industry-wide practice as a usage of trade.

course of performance
"where the contract for sale involves repeated occasions for performance by either party with knowledge of the nature of the performance and opportunity for objection to it by the other, any course of performance accepted or acquiesced in without objection shall be relevant to determine the meaning of the agreement" UCC 2–208(1)

course of dealing
"a sequence of previous conduct between the parties to a particular transaction which is fairly to be regarded as establishing a common basis of understanding for interpreting their expressions and other conduct" UCC 1–205(1)

usage of trade
"any practice or method of dealing having such regularity of observance in a place, vocation or trade as to justify an expectation that it will be observed with respect to the transaction in question" UCC 1–205(2)

Facts
During February 1973 a general contractor, defendant, telephoned a supplier of concrete, plaintiff, and inquired about the price and terms for the sale of concrete. The supplier said that the stated price would be "adhered to for the year." The supplier provided concrete for the general contractor from February 1973 through March 1974. The price remained the same from February 1973 until December 30, 1973. These deliveries were paid for by the general contractor. The general contractor was notified of a price increase effective January 1, 1974 but believed that since "the contract" was for "the year" they would not be effective regarding him until the end of February 1974. Deliveries were made by the supplier to the general contractor during January and February 1974. When billed for these at the

---

[9] UCC 1–205(4), 2–208(2).   [10] UCC 1–205(4).   [11] UCC 2–208(2).

[12] R. J. Nordstrom, p. 152.   [13] UCC 1–205, comment 5.

increased price, the general contractor offered to pay only at the 1973 price. Plaintiff sued defendant for the additional amount under the new price contending that the contract price was only for the 1973 calendar year. Was the initial oral contract, neither of which the parties deny, for the delivery of concrete at a stated price for "the year" to run for one year from the date of its making or to run until the end of the calendar year?

Decision
The contract price was only for the 1973 calendar year. Judgment for the supplier, plaintiff.

Reasoning
The court pointed out that the words used, the course of performance, and course of dealing were not helpful in giving meaning to the words "the year." The court relied on three other reasons. The first is that both parties agreed the words were "the" year and not "a" year. Seeing no circumstances surrounding the contract formation or the subsequent conduct of the parties which would lead it to believe the parties intended anything other than the normal and natural meaning, the court concluded that when one uses the words "the year," the calendar year is contemplated.

Secondly, the court noted that it was an industry-wide practice to make price increases effective on January 1, and the general contractor could be charged with notice of this.

Finally, the court said that, in fact, the general contractor had actual notice of the price increase.

Loizeaux Builders Supply Co. v. Donald B. Ludwig Co., 366 A.2d 721 (N.J. 1976).

Contract Modification

The UCC recognizes that merchants often modify their agreements. So, it provides that modifications are binding and need no added consideration to support them so long as they are done in good faith.

<small>Modification and the statute of frauds.</small>

A problem may involve the application of the statute of frauds. If the contract as modified (a change of price from $600 to $550, for example) is the type which originally had to be evidenced by a signed writing, then a signed writing by the party to be charged is needed for the modification to be effective.

The Exchange of Property Interests in a Sales Transaction

The nature of property merits our attention as another dimension to our image of a typical sales transaction between merchants. **Property,** as the word is conventionally used, refers to things, such as goods or land, which are tangible, and rights of action (e.g., accounts receivable) which are intangible. However, the law and the UCC in particular recognize numerous different legal rights in property often called **property interests.** This accumulation of property interests, usually likened to a bundle of sticks, should be the object of our attention together with the physical item that is the object of the contract. In other words, we are talking about a thing and an interest in that thing. For example, if you own a typewriter, the typewriter is the thing and your title is the interest in the thing. The contract of sale is merely the legal device by which these property interests are shifted—sometimes one at a time, sometimes in bunches—from one party to another.

<small>**property**
a thing; also an interest or right in a thing

property interest
a legally recognized and protected right in property</small>

The UCC recognizes many different property interests. Article 3, for example, sets out the law on commercial paper, the use of which, among other things, shifts property interests in checking accounts. Also, all of Article 9 is devoted to the creation, transfer, enforcement, and destruction of a property interest called a "security interest." This property interest allows the holder of it to claim possession of goods under certain circumstances—usually when a buyer defaults in payment of the purchase price to the holder of the interest.

In this part of the chapter we analyze a very important property interest recognized by Article 2, the "insurable interest." Following this we analyze a related notion, risk of loss of the goods. And finally, we discuss the concept of title under Article 2.

Part 4: Sales and Consumer Law

Insurable Interest

One of the most important things in the minds of contracting merchants is how to protect themselves from some unforeseeable event which might cause damage or destruction to goods that are the subject of the contract. Section 2–501 was drafted specifically to cover this concern of the parties. It is one of the least complicated sections of Article 2, so spelling it out is the best way to begin our analysis of it. It provides:

> (1) The buyer obtains a special property and an insurable interest in goods by identification of existing goods as goods to which the contract refers. . . . Such identification can be made at any time and in any manner explicitly agreed to by the parties. In the absence of explicit agreement identification occurs
>
>   (a) when the contract is made if it is for the sale of goods already existing and identified;
>
>   (b) if the contract is for the sale of future goods . . . when goods are shipped, marked or otherwise designated by the seller as goods to which the contract refers. . .

insurable interest (in sales) a person's interest in property which can be insured against loss

Possession of an insurable interest in goods *enables the possessor to obtain insurance on the goods* to cover the risks of damage to, or loss of his interest in, the goods. *An insurable interest exists independently of which party has title, and of which party has the risk of loss; and, it may exist in duplicate so that both the seller and buyer may have insurable interests in the same goods.*[14] For example, when a seller identifies goods as those which will fill a specific contractual obligation, then an insurable interest passes to the buyer (unless the contract provides otherwise). If the goods are destroyed while still in the possession of the seller, the buyer, if it had insurance, could recover the value it lost (usually the downpayment) and the seller, assuming it still had an insurable interest and in fact had insurance, could recover the value of its loss.

The crucial inquiry is: when is the earliest possible moment that a buyer can acquire an insurable property interest in goods for which the buyer may have already made a substantial payment? The answer is: as soon as the seller (or in some cases the buyer) *identifies* the goods—designates those goods for that contract. *The act of identification* may be defined by the agreement of the parties and, if it is not, then it occurs according to subsections (a) and (b) above. The following case illustrates that an insurable interest passed to the purchaser when the contract was made since the goods were existing and could be identified then.

Facts
The Missouri Pacific Railroad sold to the firm of Carrow and McGee all of its equipment located in five buildings in DeSoto, Missouri, on April 21, 1966. Carrow and McGee were to remove all of the equipment, and the best reading of the contract for sale was that title to the equipment was to pass when the equipment was removed. Before removal of the equipment, Carrow and McGee sold a large compressor on the property to Davis, who some weeks later sold it to the National Compressor Corporation for $12,000, which was paid. A fire destroyed the compressor before its removal.

The National Compressor Corporation sued numerous parties alleging that *its* compressor was destroyed by the fire which was negligently caused by the various parties involved in cleaning up the property. The defendants moved to have the plaintiff, National Compressor Corporation, dismissed from the suit because it had no property interest in the compressor because title was to pass upon removal.

Decision
Judgment for the plaintiff.

Reasoning
The court held that the passage of title to the compressor was *not* controlling because the plaintiff had a "special property" or insurable interest in the compressor. This property interest passed at the time the contract for sale was made because the compressor was existing and had been identified at that time.

National Compressor Corporation v. Carrow and McGee, 417 F.2d 97 (1969).

---

[14] R. J. Nordstrom, pp. 383, 387.

Risk of Loss

Article 2 has two sections directly applicable in determining which party has the risk of loss. The underlying theory of both of these sections is that the risk of loss should shift according to the *agreement* of the parties. If the agreement is *silent,* then the point at which the risk shifts depends upon *whether the seller has completed its performance and whether the seller breaches the agreement by tendering non-conforming goods*. That is, the drafters of Article 2 did not think it fair that the seller, who is assumed to have the risk of loss, could shift the risk to the buyer by tendering goods that failed to conform to the contract. So, two sections were devised: one to operate in the absence of a breach, the other to operate when there has been a breach by either party.

First, in the absence of a breach by the seller and in the absence of a contractual provision to the contrary, the *risk of loss shifts, generally speaking, when the seller completes its performance with regard to the goods*. So, where the contract requires the seller *to ship the goods by carrier,* the risk of loss passes to the buyer when the goods are duly delivered[15] to the carrier[16] or, if the contract requires *delivery at a particular destination,* the risk of loss passes at the destination when the goods are so tendered to enable the buyer to take delivery.[17] In the following case the seller was to ship the goods by carrier and so the risk of loss shifted to the buyer when the seller completed its performance with regard to the goods.

Risk of loss without breach of contract.

Facts
The plaintiff, Pestana, is the personal representative of Amar, deceased. Amar contracted to buy some watches from the defendant, Karinol Corporation. The watches were to be shipped to Amar in Chetumal, Mexico. The contract contained no specific terms such as F.O.B. destination for allocation of loss while the goods were in transit. Amar made a deposit and the watches were shipped but were lost in transit. Amar asked for a refund of the deposit. The defendant claimed that the risk of loss was on the purchaser and that the balance of the purchase price should be paid. The plaintiff, acting for the purchaser decedent, sues for the deposit and the trial court held for the defendant seller. The plaintiff was ordered to pay the balance of the purchase price. The plaintiff appeals.

Decision
The appellate court affirmed the decision for the defendant seller. Since Amar, the purchaser, had to pay the balance owed on the purchase of the watches, Amar's estate would be liable for this balance.

Reasoning
The appellate court held that where the contract has no explicit provisions allocating the risk of loss while the goods are in the possession of the carrier and when no delivery terms such as F.O.B. place of destination are in the contract, then such a contract constitutes a shipment contract wherein the risk of loss passes to the buyer when the seller duly delivers the goods to the carrier. Thus, where the risk of loss falls on the buyer at the time the goods are lost or destroyed, the purchaser is liable to the seller for the purchase price of the goods sold if payment has not been made in full.

Pestana v. Karinol Corporation, et al., 367 So.2d 1096 (Fla. 1979).

Risk of loss on breach of contract.

cure
a seller's correction of his failure to deliver conforming goods under a contract for sale before the due date has expired

Second, obviously, the seller should not be able to shift the risk of loss to the buyer *when the seller has breached the contract,* as by tendering non-conforming goods or otherwise failing to fulfill its obligations. This result is reached by section 2–510, which provides that the risk does not shift when the goods fail to conform until the seller **cures** the defect or the buyer accepts the goods. If the goods have been accepted by the buyer and then the buyer discovers a defect that would be a breach of contract by the *seller,* or if

---

[15] The words "duly delivered" are meant to incorporate the tender requirements of a shipment contract (set out in 2–504) which are that the seller must (1) put the goods in the possession of such a carrier as is reasonable; (2) make a reasonable contract for their transportation; and (3) obtain and promptly deliver the necessary documents and notify the buyer of shipment. See section 2–509, comment 2.

[16] UCC 2–509(1)(a).   [17] UCC 2–509(1)(b).

the *buyer* breaches the contract while the goods are still in the possession of the seller and the goods are damaged or loss occurs, then the one suffering the loss may recover any amounts not covered by its insurance from the other party. The UCC comments state this rule this way: "In cases where there has been a breach of the contract, if the one in control of the goods is the aggrieved party, whatever loss . . . may prove to be uncovered by his insurance falls upon the contract breaker. . . ."[18] For example, if the buyer repudiates the contract *after* the seller has identified conforming goods to the contract but *before* shipment, and the goods are damaged through no fault of its own, the seller may collect the loss not covered by its insurance from the buyer. In short, the wrongdoer suffers the loss.

In conclusion, insurable interests and the risk of loss, are special property interests which may exist independently, although there are circumstances in which both will pass to the buyer at the same time. One example of an insurable interest in the buyer being significant—without risk of loss passing—exists when the buyer contracts for the construction and delivery of a large, complex machine. After the machine has been *identified* to the contract in the seller's plant, it is destroyed by fire that consumed the entire plant. The buyer, let us assume, had paid $10,000 at the time the contract was formed on a total price of $50,000. Further, let us assume the seller is now insolvent and had not carried sufficient insurance to cover the loss of the machine. The *risk of loss* may still be on the seller because it has *not delivered* the machine; but if the buyer had been prudent, it should have *insured its interest* in the machine, which would have been at least $10,000. The buyer could have done so because an *insurable interest* (its contract right to the machine) passed to the buyer when the machine was *identified* to the contract.

Basically, the party with an insurable interest can obtain insurance against damage or destruction to the goods, *while the party with the risk of loss will suffer such loss as between the contracting parties.* The creation and recognition of these two property interests is a major contribution of Article 2.

Transfer of Title under Article 2

In pre-UCC law, the predominant property interests in goods were all linked to the concept of title to the goods. Title to goods was and is today often represented by a piece of paper identifying the goods, e.g., bill of lading, warehouse receipt. Possession of the piece of paper usually gave the possessor the legally enforceable right to get the goods, if the paper flowed to the possessor either originally or by indorsement as a "holder." But the abstract notion of who had title became confusing as merchants entered into increasingly complex commercial transactions. The drafters of the UCC realized that what the parties were essentially interested in when they referred to title, was who could get insurance on the goods and who would suffer damage due to loss if the goods were destroyed. Therefore they drafted Article 2 to deal specifically with these circumstances, which were discussed above.

When Title Can Pass under Article 2. Title to goods cannot pass prior to the time *goods exist and are identified to the contract*. If the goods exist and are identified to the contract *at the time the contract is made,* then the passage of title will depend upon the express or implied intention of the parties. If the agreement *expresses* when title is to pass, it will pass at that time. However, if the agreement contains no expression of intent, then title will pass at the moment the seller *commits* those goods to the contract.[19] Under the Code,

Existing and identified goods at the time the contract is made.

---

[18] UCC 2–510(2)(3), comment 3.

[19] UCC 2–401.

Delivery without movement of the goods.

committing goods to the contract depends on whether *delivery* is to be made by moving the goods. When delivery is to be made *without moving the goods* (seller says, pick up the goods at my warehouse or from a third party), then:

(a) if the seller is to deliver a document of title, title passes at the time when and the place where he delivers such documents; or
(b) if the goods are at the time of contracting already identified and no documents are to be delivered, title passes at the time and place of contracting.[20]

Delivery by movement of the goods.

When delivery is to be made *by moving the goods,* title passes at the time and place at which the seller completes *its performance* with reference to the physical delivery of the goods.[21] Determining when this performance has been completed is aided by using certain shipment abbreviations.

If the seller is *to ship* the goods, then when the title passes depends on whether the seller is to "send" the goods—namely, "**F.O.B.** shipping point"—or the seller is to "deliver" the goods at a destination—namely, "F.O.B. destination." If "F.O.B. shipping point," then there is no expense to the buyer until the goods are delivered to the carrier. If "F.O.B. destination," then there is no expense to the buyer until the goods are tendered at the destination point. *If F.O.B. shipping point, title passes at the time and place the goods are delivered to the carrier. If F.O.B. destination, title passes when the goods are tendered at the destination.* Delivery may be of the actual goods, or of a negotiable bill of lading covering them. The form of the bill of lading, whether negotiable or non-negotiable, and irrespective of who the consignee is, has no effect on the transfer of title.

F.O.B.
free on board

C.O.D.
collect on delivery

When, pursuant to the contract, goods are shipped **C.O.D.**, meaning "collect on delivery," the carrier is to collect the purchase price before delivering the goods. C.O.D. has no effect on the transfer of title. It defers the buyer's right to inspect the goods before accepting them.

In a "sale on approval," neither title nor risk of loss passes until the buyer approves. However, in a "sale or return," title and risk of loss pass to the buyer subject to the buyer's right to return the goods instead of paying the purchase price. If the intention of the parties is unclear as to which of these it is, the following applies: if the goods are acquired *primarily for use,* it is a sale on approval; if *primarily for resale,* it is a sale or return.[22]

Future goods at the time the contract is made.

The above discussion of *when* title could pass under Article 2 was premised on the fact that the goods existed and were identified at the time the contract was made. If the goods do not exist and are therefore not identified to the contract (for example, a contract to sell a machine to be built), they are "future goods." A contract for future goods is enforceable, but title cannot pass until the goods are identified to the contract in accordance with the intention of the parties.

How Title Can Be Transferred under Article 2. The general rule is that *a person can transfer only what he or she has.* So a seller cannot pass to a buyer a "better" title than the seller had. (T steals O's goods and sells them to B, a **good faith** purchaser for value. B got what T had and, since T got nothing from O, then O still owns the goods.) Section 2–403 recognizes this rule, but adds to it that in three instances the seller has a "power" to transfer a better title than the seller has. These three instances are the result of conduct by the original owner which is unfair to the buyer. This conduct results in the buyer obtaining the owner's title.

good faith
"honesty in fact in the conduct or transaction concerned"
UCC 1–201(19)

The transferee gets only what the transferor has or has power to transfer.

1. *Estoppel.* When one person *holds out* (manifests) to another person that something is or is not so, and the other person *materially changes his or her position in reasonable reliance on the holding out,* the first person is "estopped" (precluded, stopped,

---

[20] UCC 2–401(3)(a) and (b).   [21] UCC 2–401(2).

[22] UCC 2–326(1). But, with one exception, if the goods are delivered to a person for sale who has a place of business under a name other than that of the person selling him the goods, then, solely with respect to the buyer's creditors, the transaction can be only a sale or return and not a sale on approval irrespective of the intentions of the parties. UCC 2–326(3).

prevented) from asserting the reverse of what was held out. (T steals your goods and tells B that he, T, owns the goods and will sell them to B. B then telephones you, describes the goods, tells you that he, B, is about to buy the goods from T, and asks you if they are your goods. You say they are not your goods. B then, for value and innocent of the theft, buys the goods from T. Later you demand the goods from B. You are estopped to assert that the goods belong to you because you had held out to B that they did not belong to you and B then materially changed his position in reasonable reliance on your statement when he bought the goods from T. T had the "power" to transfer your title to B because of your conduct creating **estoppel,** and B gets your title to the goods.)

2. *Voidable title transfer.* If the seller has a voidable title, the seller has the "power" to transfer a good title, free of the power of avoidance, to a "good faith purchaser for value." (S fraudulently induced you to sell your goods to S, thereby creating a voidable contract voidable by you. S has a voidable title to the goods. S sells the goods to B, a good faith purchaser for value. You could have exercised your power of avoidance *before* S's sale to B and, since S would no longer have title to the goods, S could not later pass any title to B. Since you did not do this before B's innocent purchase, your power to avoid as to B ceases to exist, T now has the "power" to transfer your title to B, and B gets the title.)

3. *Entrusting goods to a merchant who deals in goods of that kind.* UCC 2–403(2) provides:

Any entrusting of possession of goods to a *merchant* who deals in goods of that kind gives him power to transfer all rights of the entruster to a buyer in ordinary course of business. [Emphasis added.]

When the owner of goods "entrusts" (delivers) them to a merchant who deals in goods of that kind, the owner clothes the merchant with the appearance of being the owner of the goods. The merchant's unauthorized sale of the goods to a buyer in ordinary course of business transfers a good title to such buyer. (You deliver your watch for repair to a jeweler, J, who *sells* watches. J sells your watch for $100 to B, who believes J owns the watch. B gets title to your watch. You may recover the reasonable value of the watch from J because of his tort of **conversion** by his unauthorizedly exercising control and dominion over your watch as the owner without authority to do so, but B will have title to the watch.)

A problem of "value" arises under the "entrusting" rule above. You have learned in Part 2, Contracts, that under contract law a past debt is not consideration for a promise so that such a promise is not a contract. However, under the Code, which reflects the law merchant, "value" for a promise is a past debt as well as consideration. In the watch example above, if B had previously loaned money to J and J now promised to deliver the watch to B in satisfaction of that debt, J's promise under the law of contracts would not be a contract. However, since J is *selling goods* (a watch) to B, J's promise comes under Article 2 of the Code and *ordinarily* is "value" and enforceable. *But there are two exceptions under the Code, which are of particular importance here, when a past debt is not value.* One is in the case of a "duly negotiated holder" of a negotiable document of title, previously discussed in chapter 16, Carriers, Documents of Title, and Innkeepers. The other is for the "entrusting" rule above. Since B paid $100 as consideration for the watch, B is called a **buyer in ordinary course of business,** signifying that B is a good faith purchaser *who paid consideration* and not a past debt for that watch. If B had taken the watch for a past debt, B would not have paid value and you would have the right to regain the watch from B.

The reason for these three exceptions to the general rule of transfer of title is to protect and encourage the free flow of commerce. However one may rationalize these exceptions, it does appear that they represent an assertion on behalf of our collective society at the expense of individual property rights.

---

estoppel
(UCC Sales) a holding out by the owner and a material change of position by the buyer in reasonable reliance on the owner's holding out

Voidable title transfer, and a "good faith purchaser for value."

Entrusting goods to a merchant who deals in goods of that kind, and a "buyer in ordinary course of business."

conversion
the tort of intentional interference with another's right to possession, control, and dominion of a chattel

buyer in ordinary course of business
"a person who, in good faith and without knowledge that the sale to him is in violation of the ownership rights or security interest of a third party in the goods, buys in ordinary course from a person in the business of selling goods of that kind but does not include a pawnbroker"; buying does not include a transfer for a past debt UCC 1–201(9)

Under the Code, but not under the common law of contracts, a past debt is value, with two exceptions.

Summary Statement

1. In your study of this chapter and the next two chapters, imagine two corporate merchants doing business; usually they "contract" by exchanging various form documents.
2. A contract for the sale of goods may be made in any manner sufficient to show agreement.
3. When a merchant gives a signed, written assurance in an offer that it will be held open for a stated time, it is not revocable for lack of consideration.
4. Generally, offers may be made in any way that reveals an intent to be bound, and an acceptance shall be made in any manner and by any medium reasonable in the circumstances.
5. A shipment of non-conforming goods may be an acceptance, and so may the beginning of a requested performance if it is a reasonable mode of acceptance.
6. An acceptance sent within a reasonable time is effective even though it includes additional or different terms from those offered unless the acceptance is expressly made conditional on assent to the additional or different terms. Additional terms are to be construed as proposals for additions to the contract and, as between merchants, they become part of the contract unless:
   a. the offer expressly limits acceptance to the terms of the offer;
   b. the added terms materially alter the offer; or
   c. notification of the objection to the added terms has been given or is given within a reasonable time after notice of them is received.
7. Express terms of an agreement together with course of performance, course of dealing, and usage of trade are all used to ascertain the parties' contractual intent.
8. The parties to a sales contract may modify their contractual understanding without consideration.
9. An insurable interest in the goods may pass to the buyer independently of the passage of the risk of loss or title to the goods; it passes when goods are identified to the contract. If the goods are existing, then identification occurs when the contract is made; if the contract is for the sale of future goods, then they are identified when they are shipped or otherwise designated by the seller as goods to which the contract refers.
10. The risk of loss for the goods passes from seller to buyer when the parties agree it will pass. If they have not so agreed, then the risk of loss shifts when the seller completes its performance with regard to the goods. But if the seller tenders non-conforming goods, then the risk shifts when the seller cures the defect or the buyer accepts the goods.
11. Goods must exist and be identified to the contract before title can pass, depending on the intention of the parties. If no intent is expressed, then the Code establishes the rules for the implied intent.
12. Generally, a seller cannot pass to a buyer a better title than the seller itself has. However, the doctrines of estoppel, voidable title, and the entrusting of goods section of Article 2 make it possible for a seller to have the power to transfer a better title than the seller has.

The following very long appellate case presents a typical, complex commercial dispute and its resolution by Article 2. The court's opinion is very clear and educational, tying together the common law of contracts concerning offer and acceptance and the need for Article 2, particularly section 2–207. The case is well worth reading, even though it is long.

Dorton & Castle, d/b/a The Carpet Mart v. Collins & Aikman Corp.
453 F.2d 1161 (1972)

d/b/a
doing business as

Celebrezze, Circuit J. The plaintiff, a carpet dealer doing business under the name of The Carpet Mart, sued the defendant, Collins & Aikman, a carpet manufacturer. Between 1968 and 1970 the plaintiff and defendant entered into more than 55 transactions involving the purchase and sale, respectively, of substantial quantities of carpeting. In 1970 the plaintiff learned that some of the carpeting purchased from the defendant was not 100 percent Kodel polyester fiber, as ordered, but was made of cheaper carpet fiber. The plaintiff sued for $450,000 based upon fraud and misrepresentation. Before the trial court could reach the merits of the case, the defendant moved to stay [stop] the proceedings based upon the allegation that its printed "sales acknowledgment" form *compelled* the parties to arbitrate their agreement if a dispute should arise. Before proceeding to an account of how the court resolved the issue about whether the parties were compelled to arbitrate, it is instructive to consider this factual background recounted by the court because it serves as an excellent explanation of the pattern of much merchant-to-merchant contracting today.

> In each of the more than 55 transactions, one of the partners in The Carpet Mart, or on some occasions, Collins & Aikman's visiting salesman, telephoned Collins & Aikman's order department in Dalton, Georgia, and ordered certain quantities of carpets listed in Collins & Aikman's catalog. There is some dispute as to what, if any, agreements were reached through the telephone calls and through the visits by Collins & Aikman's salesman. After each oral order was placed, the price, if any, quoted by the buyer was checked against Collins & Aikman's price list, and the credit department was consulted to determine if The Carpet Mart had paid for all previous shipments. After it was found that everything was in order, Collins & Aikman's order department typed the information concerning the particular order on one of its printed acknowledgment forms. Each acknowledgment form bore one of three legends: "Acknowledgment," "Customer Acknowledgment," or "Sales Contract." The following provision was printed on the face of the forms bearing the "Acknowledgment" legend: "The acceptance of your order is subject to all of the terms and conditions on the face and reverse side hereof, including arbitration, all of which are accepted by buyer; it supersedes buyer's order form, if any. . . ."

The small print on the reverse side of the forms provided, among other things, that all claims arising out of the contract would be submitted to arbitration in New York City. Each acknowledgment form was signed by an employee of Collins & Aikman's order department and mailed to The Carpet Mart on the day the telephone order was received or, at the latest, on the following day. The carpets were thereafter shipped to The Carpet Mart, with the interval between the mailing of the acknowledgment form and shipment of the carpets varying from a brief interval to a period of several weeks or months. Absent a delay in the mails, however, The Carpet Mart always received the acknowledgment forms prior to receiving the carpets. In all cases The Carpet Mart took delivery of and paid for the carpets without objecting to any terms contained in the acknowledgment form.

Before the court reached the application of section 2–207 to these facts, it stated the following about the intended purpose of section 2–207:

> . . . [I]t is clear that section 2–207, and specifically subsection 2–207(1), was intended to alter the . . . "mirror" rule of common law, under which the terms of an acceptance or confirmation were required to be identical to the terms of the offer or oral agreement. . . . Under the common law, an acceptance or a confirmation that contained terms additional to or different from those of the offer or oral agreement constituted a rejection of the offer or agreement and thus became a counteroffer. The terms of the counteroffer were said to have been accepted by the original offeror when he proceeded to perform under the contract without objecting to the counteroffer. Thus, a buyer was deemed to have accepted the seller's counteroffer if he took receipt of the goods and paid for them without objection.
>
> Under section 2–207 the result is different. This section of the Code recognizes that in current commercial transactions, the terms of the offer and those of the acceptance will seldom be identical. Rather, under the current "battle of the forms," each party typically has a printed form drafted by his attorney, containing as many terms as could be envisioned to favor that party in his sales transactions. Whereas under common law the disparity between the fineprint terms in the parties' forms would have prevented the consummation of a contract when these forms are exchanged, section 2–207 recognizes that in many, but not all, cases the parties do not impart such significance to the terms on the printed forms. . . . [U]nder subsection (1), a contract is recognized notwithstanding the fact that an acceptance or confirmation contains terms additional to or different from those of the offer or prior agreement, provided

that the offeree's intent to accept the offer is definitely expressed . . . and provided that the offeree's acceptance is not expressly conditioned on the offeror's assent to the additional or different terms. When a contract is recognized under subsection (1), the additional terms are treated as "proposals for addition to the contract," under subsection (2), which contains special provisions . . . such additional terms are deemed to have been accepted when the transaction is between merchants. Conversely, when no contract is recognized under subsection 2-207(1)—either because no definite expression of acceptance exists or, more specifically, because the offeree's acceptance is expressly conditioned on the offeror's assent to the additional or different terms—the entire transaction aborts (stops) at this point. If, however, the subsequent conduct of the parties—particularly, performance by both parties under what they apparently believe to be a contract—recognizes the existence of a contract, under subsection 2-207(3) such conduct by both parties is sufficient to establish a contract, notwithstanding the fact that no contract would have been recognized on the basis of their writings alone. . . .

The appellate court remanded this case back to the trial court for further findings of fact and suggested a method for resolving the issue of whether the parties had "agreed" to arbitrate the dispute. First, it said the court should find if the agreement was composed of the plaintiff's oral order and the defendant's acknowledgment. Second, if it was, was the arbitration provision an addition to or a term different from the offer? Third, if the arbitration provision was additional or different from the offer, was the acceptance expressly made conditional on assent to the additional terms so that 2-207(1) would be applicable? On this point the court advised that merely stating that the acceptance was "subject to all of the terms and conditions on the face and reverse side hereof including arbitration, all of which are accepted by the buyer," might not be sufficient to meet the requirement of 2-207(1). It suggested: "In order to fall within this proviso (2-207(1)), it is not enough that an acceptance is expressly conditional on additional or different terms; rather an acceptance must be *expressly* conditional on the offeror's assent to those terms."

Fourth, if on remand the trial court were to find that the acceptance was not expressly made conditional on assent to the additional terms, then the court must find there was a contract and, finally, the term compelling arbitration would bind both of the parties unless it materially altered the parties' understanding. This finding of materiality was the final point demanding the trial court's opinion.

[Authors' note: in most cases, a provision requiring arbitration would be a material alteration, unless requiring arbitration was a well established practice in that particular business.]

Questions and Case Problems

1. The plaintiff, general contractor, relied on a bid from a subcontractor to build over 400 wardrobes, to be used in refurbishing a state institution for the mentally retarded in New York. The plaintiff was awarded the bid and then it began correspondence with the defendant subcontractor about some of the details of the work. In one exchange of letters, the general contractor said the wardrobes must meet state standards and the general contractor agreed to pay an extra $17,375 to cover extra work done by the subcontractor. The subcontractor replied by letter 3 days later that the $17,375 was for "additional costs for amending specifications, method of assembly and construction of wardrobes to meet (state) requirements." The subcontractor failed to perform and the general contractor sued. The subcontractor argues that it never (subjectively) intended to accept the offer for additional work and $17,375, and the letter in response to the general contractor's offer to pay the extra money was a mere acknowledgement of receipt of that letter. Should the court allow evidence of the subjective intent of the subcontractor and do you believe there was an acceptance based on the language used? [*J. Baranello & Sons v. Hausman Industries, Inc.* 571 F.Supp. 333 (E.D.N.Y. 1983).]

2. In April of 1968, Litton Industries wrote a letter that was not quite 2 pages long to Bethlehem Steel Corporation stating that it was "extending to (Bethlehem) an option to purchase . . . 'vessels' " . . . of 1,000 feet in length. In the letter the prices of 5 vessels were set out and these ranged from $22.4 million to $18.4 million each. If all 5 vessels were to be built, the total value of the contract would exceed $100 million. No ship construction contracts setting out all the specifications of design and the like were ever finalized and when Bethlehem attempted to order the first vessel mentioned in the letter, Litton refused. Litton argued that the two page letter was merely an agreement to agree on the construction of from 1 to 5 vessels. The letters exchanged showed only the price of

each vessel and its length. Is such a writing sufficient for a court to conclude that the parties manifested an intent to contract? [*Bethlehem Steel Corp. v. Litton Industries, Inc.*, 468 A.2d 748 (Pa. 1983).]

3. Courts often must go beyond the terms of a written contract to give the words used some meaning. Clearly state what items of evidence or circumstance they may use in this inquiry and state the relative weights that must be given to each; that is, which bits of evidence are to control over others when there is a conflict?

4. An item of great importance to any sales contract is the question of which party is to bear the risk of loss for damage or destruction of the goods. Describe the point at which the risk of loss passes from the seller to the buyer, and how and when a buyer can protect itself from suffering a loss due to damage or destruction of the goods.

5. Roto-Lith, Ltd. is a corporation engaged in manufacturing cellophane bags for packaging vegetables. It ordered a drum of N-132-C emulsion from F.P. Bartlett & Co. on October 23, 1969 for the stated purpose of making wet pack spinach bags. In response to Roto-Lith's order form, the seller sent its "acknowledgment" form and the goods were shipped. The acknowledgment form and the invoice accompanying the goods both stated in conspicuous language, "all goods sold without warranties, express or implied. . . ." Further, on the back of the acknowledgment there was this statement, "If these terms are not acceptable, buyer must so notify seller at once."

    Roto-Lith did not protest the waiver of the warranties; it received, paid for, and used the emulsion. The emulsion was defective and Roto-Lith sued F.P. Bartlett for breach of contract (warranties). Article 2 states that, in every contract for the sale of goods, the seller makes a warranty that the goods sold were fit for the use for which the goods were sold. These "implied" warranties exist unless *the contract* between the parties waives these warranties. What was the contractual understanding between these parties with regard to the warranties? [*Roto-Lith Ltd. v. F.P. Bartlett & Co.*, 297 F.2d 497 (1962).]

6. Blue Rock Industries, a seller of sand, contracted with Raymond International to deliver large quantities of sand for road construction in Maine. The initial contract between the two stated that Blue Rock's price was to be as follows:

    . . . for truck measured sand delivered to the job site as you require:
    $2.75 per cubic yard delivered to the north side of the project;
    $2.60 per cubic yard delivered to the south side of the project.

    Assume that the sand delivered may be measured in at least two ways. One way is to fill a five-yard dump truck up to the top; another is to figure what one yard of sand weighs, then weigh the sand (in the truck) and compute the price on this basis. That is, one method is to price the sand by volume, and one by weight.
    a. Looking at the contract, which method was contemplated?
    b. If a dispute arose between the two parties over these two varying methods of measuring sand, how would a court resolve it?

7. The firm of Bowman Hydro-Vat owned an airplane which they agreed to sell to Hemmer on December 12, 1970 for a price of $18,500. On that date $15,000 was paid down and the balance of $3,500 was to be paid later. Both parties agreed that title was to pass when "the necessary paperwork" was completed. A formal document of title was requested from the Federal Aviation Administration (FAA), and meanwhile Hemmer began using the airplane. The formal document was received by the seller on December 18, 1970 and was put in the mail on that date to Hemmer. On that same day, while Hemmer was piloting the aircraft, the tip of the wing caught a snow bank on takeoff, resulting in extensive damage. According to FAA regulations, the purchaser of an aircraft had to sign the title document received from the seller and then send it to the FAA, which would issue a title to the purchaser.
    a. Can the seller, Bowman Hydro-Vat, recover for the damage from its insurance company, provided that premiums were paid and the policy had not been cancelled?
    b. Could the purchaser have purchased insurance on the aircraft on December 12, 1970? [*Bowman v. American Home Assurance Company*, 213 N.W.2d 446 (Neb. 1973).]

8. Purchaser orders $10,000 worth of goods from seller and pays $5,000 down. The contract said that the seller was "to ship" the goods to the purchaser's plant. The parties did not otherwise agree on who was to bear the risk of loss, and the contract did not state that the shipment was to be F.O.B.
   a. When does the purchaser have an insurable interest?
   b. If the goods are placed on board a carrier by the seller and the goods conform to the contract and a reasonable contract for their shipment is made and the goods are destroyed in transit, which party bears the loss?
   c. Would the result in "b" above change if the goods placed on board the carrier by the seller were non-conforming? If so, how?

9. F fraudulently induced O, the owner of goods, to sell and deliver certain goods to F. F then sold and delivered the goods to G, a good faith purchaser for value without notice of the fraud. G made a gift of the goods to D, who also is innocent of the fraud. O now discovers the fraud and demands the goods from D. Who gets the goods?

10. In the case of *Dorton & Castle, d/b/a The Carpet Mart v. Collins & Aikman Corp.*, 453 F.2d 1161 (1972),[23] the court discussed the impact of UCC 2-207 on that part of the law of contracts concerned with offer and acceptance. How would you explain that impact?

---

[23] See pp. 269–70.

Performance of the Sales Contract 19

After you have read this chapter, you should be able to:

1. Define how performance obligations of the parties are determined.
2. List and define the performance obligations of the seller and buyer in a typical sales transaction and be able to define the terms "F.O.B.," "F.A.S.," "C.I.F.," "C.F.," and "C. & F." and state the legal consequences of using them.
3. State what is meant by "perfect tender" of goods and documents and then state two circumstances in which the requirement of perfect tender is lessened.
4. Define what is meant by payment and state when and under what circumstances it is due.
5. Describe two special circumstances in which both the seller and buyer have performance obligations to one another and, in one case, obligations to creditors of the seller.
6. Define and explain three exceptions to the general rule that the parties must perform as promised.

Introduction

When you enter into a contract you expect performance by the other contracting party who, in turn, expects performance by you. This chapter presents the key sections of Article 2 governing performance by the parties to a sales contract. As you study this chapter, imagine two *merchants* in cities some distance apart doing business. The "contract" between these parties is evidenced by one or more pieces of paper or one or more conversations exchanged by the parties. Based upon the material in chapters 17 and 18, you should be able to determine *the parties' contractual intent* when several documents or conversations or a mixture of both are present.

The express and implied contractual intent of the parties under the Code regarding their performance of the sales contract.

Generally, *it is this manifested intent that will determine the performance of the parties to the agreement.* That is, in almost all cases in which the *parties have reached* agreement about performance, this agreement will control. Where the parties *have not* reached agreement, because nothing was said or clearly understood about a particular performance obligation, then *Article 2 and the sections discussed* in this chapter *will control* the parties' performance.

Performance Obligations of the Seller

Tender Obligations of the Seller

The general obligations of both parties to a sales contract are set out clearly in section 2–301. It provides:

tender (verb) proffer, make available

> The obligation of the seller is to transfer and deliver and that of the buyer is to accept and pay in accordance with the contract.

This section creates a set of **concurrent conditions**—**conditions** which must occur at the same time unless otherwise agreed. The seller must duly tender the goods as a condition to the buyer's duty to accept and pay,[1] and the buyer must offer payment as a condition to the seller's duty to tender and complete delivery of the goods.[2] One of the parties must manifest an intent to perform (by either tendering the goods or payment) before the other party can be put in default. To put a buyer in default, *the seller must tender the goods in accordance with the contract,* and, if the buyer does not respond with payment, then a breach exists. Conversely, to put the seller in default, *the buyer must tender payment.* Remember that both parties are under a fundamental duty to *perform in good faith.* We must proceed then on the assumption that, unless otherwise agreed, the parties will *begin* their performance after the agreement is made, by the seller making plans for delivery of goods and the buyer making plans for payment.

condition an uncertain event on the occurrence of which a contractual obligation is made contingent or dependent

condition concurrent a condition which must occur at the same time as another condition

Let us first examine what is meant by the seller's performance and start with the seller's *obligation to tender.* This is expressed in section 2–503 which provides that the seller is to "put and hold conforming goods at the buyer's disposition," but it does not state *where* this is to take place. If the seller is to *ship* the goods, there are at least *three* possible places, depending on the circumstances. Usually the contract of the parties will *state* either where the *seller* is to ship the goods or where tender is to take place.

Methods of seller's tender of delivery.

"Destination" Sales Contracts. The *first common circumstance concerned with tender* is where the contract provides that the goods are to be shipped **F.O.B.** or **F.A.S.** destination. If, for example, a seller in Chicago agrees to tender the goods in Los Angeles, or at *any particular destination not in the seller's town,* then the seller must make all shipment arrangements and tender, through an agent of some sort, *at that destination.* This obligation is *usually* imposed upon the seller by the use of the term "F.O.B." (e.g., "F.O.B. Los Angeles" and the seller is in Chicago), or "F.A.S." followed by the name of a vessel and a port.

F.O.B. free on board

F.A.S. free alongside

---

[1] UCC 2–507(1).   [2] UCC 2–511.

In the first instance (F.O.B. Los Angeles), tender is to take place in Los Angeles and the seller must, at its own expense and risk, transport the goods there to an address provided by the purchaser and there tender the goods.[3] If the term used is "F.O.B. Los Angeles" and the *port* and a *vessel* are named, then the *seller* must, again at its own expense and risk, transport the goods to Los Angeles and *load* the goods on board the vessel.[4]

If the term "F.A.S." followed by a named port and vessel is used, the seller must deliver the goods at its own expense and risk *alongside* the vessel and there tender documents to an agent of the buyer.[5]

"Delivery" Sales Contracts. A *second common circumstance concerned with tender* is that the contract will state F.O.B. "place of shipment," "seller's town," or "seller's factory" (e.g., "F.O.B. Chicago" if the seller is in Chicago), or will merely state that the seller is "to ship" the goods. In this case the seller must, in *its town or place of business,* put the goods in the possession of such a carrier and make such a contract for their shipment as may be reasonable, having regard for the nature of the goods, and then promptly notify the buyer of the shipment.[6] The seller will obtain from the carrier a document, e.g., **bill of lading**, which is sufficient to enable the buyer to obtain possession of the goods, and the seller must then deliver or tender this document to the buyer.[7]

Pricing Terms. The terms "F.O.B." and "F.A.S." are not intended to be used in pricing goods, but are intended to be used to determine *performance with regard to delivery and tender.* However, merchants often use the term "**C.I.F.**" when they do not use the terms F.O.B. or F.A.S. When they use this term they intend that the price quoted is a lump sum which includes the cost, insurance, and freight to a named destination. If they use the term "**C. & F.**" or "C.F.," it means that the price includes the cost of the goods plus freight to the named destination. The obligations imposed on the seller when the term "C.I.F. *destination*" is used are to load the goods onto a carrier, make a contract for their shipment, and pay for the freight and insurance. (The insurance is purchased for the benefit of the buyer since the risk of loss passes upon the loading of the goods.) Finally, the seller must obtain a document enabling the buyer to obtain possession of the goods from the carrier and must deliver it or tender it to the buyer.[8] Under the terms C. & F. or C.F., the seller is obligated to do the same except that insurance is not purchased.

The main distinction between using F.O.B. or F.A.S., on the one hand, and C.I.F. or C. & F. or C.F., on the other, will be discussed later in this chapter. The important point to remember here is that the terms F.O.B., or "F.A.S. vessel," followed by either the town of the point of shipment or the town of destination *indicate where the seller is to tender the goods* and, consequently, where the risk of loss passes from the seller to the buyer.

Sales Contracts with No Delivery or Pricing Terms. A *third circumstance establishing the seller's obligation to tender* at a specific place occurs when the agreement states nothing about delivery—the terms F.O.B., F.A.S., C.I.F., etc. are not used. When this occurs, the place for delivery is the seller's place of business,[9] if that is where the goods are located. If the goods are located at some other place at the time of the contract and if the goods are identified, then the delivery is presumed to be wherever the goods are located.[10]

Moving the goods—or not, as the case may be—is not the final event of tendering. When the goods are to be shipped from the seller's town or when the goods are in the possession of a bailee, *the seller must send to the buyer the proper documents* enabling it legally to gain possession of the goods.[11] But is the seller required to tender the goods *and* send the documents entitling the other party to possession without first being paid?

---

bill of lading
a document issued to the shipper by a carrier of goods

C.I.F.
cost, insurance, freight

C. & F.
cost plus freight

Place of tender in the absence of express agreement.

---

[3] UCC 2–319(1)(b). [4] UCC 2–319(1)(c). [5] UCC 2–319(2)(a).
[6] UCC 2–504(a)(c). [7] UCC 2–504(b). [8] UCC 2–320.
[9] UCC 2–308(a). [10] UCC 2–308(b). [11] UCC 2–503(3)(4)(5).

The answer is yes! Unless the agreement provides otherwise, payment must be made when the obligations of tender are met. But does this not put the seller at a slight disadvantage? The seller does not want to give up possession of the goods until it is paid, nor, really, does the buyer want to pay until the goods have been properly shipped and tendered. How is this difficulty of both parties dealt with in practice?

A Typical Sales Transaction—Tendering the Goods and Payment. Although there are many ways of dealing with this circumstance, a usual one might be as follows. Let us assume that a manufacturer of steel desks near Chicago, Illinois, contracts to sell 100 of them "F.O.B. Los Angeles, California" for a total price of $10,000. The seller has the duty to deliver them to Los Angeles, California, and, unless the agreement specifies otherwise, the seller is to tender, usually at the carrier's terminal in Los Angeles, in accordance with the terms set out in section 2–503, already discussed. The seller crates the desks and delivers them to the railroad and receives a bill of lading from the railroad. For purposes of this discussion, a bill of lading is a document issued by the carrier entitling the holder of it to the physical possession of the goods. The seller takes the bill of lading to its bank in Chicago and there signs a money instrument called a "draft." A draft is simply an instrument drawn by the seller ordering the buyer to pay the sum of $10,000 to the Chicago bank. The seller then usually indorses (signs) the bill of lading over to the buyer and asks his Chicago bank to send the bill of lading and the draft to a Los Angeles bank which the Chicago bank knows and trusts. The Chicago bank then indorses the draft, stating thereon, "Pay to the order of any bank." What has happened so far is that the seller has asked its bank to be a collecting agent, and the bank has, by its indorsement, empowered a bank in Los Angeles to be its (the bank's) collecting agent. Both the draft and the bill of lading are then mailed to a Los Angeles bank. The two items together are called a **documentary draft**.

documentary draft
"any negotiable or non-negotiable draft with accompanying documents, securities or other papers to be delivered against honor of the draft"
UCC 4–104 (f)

When the documentary draft arrives in Los Angeles (before, we assume, the goods arrive), the buyer is notified and an employee of the buyer will go to the Los Angeles bank and make arrangements for payment. Before the actual payment is made, the buyer has a right to inspect the goods. After the goods arrive and while they are still in the possession of the carrier, they are inspected, and then the employee goes to the bank to complete the transaction. The employee pays at the bank and then receives the bill of lading. The employee delivers the indorsed bill of lading to the carrier and receives the desks. The $10,000, through various bank transfers, will be credited to the seller's account in the Chicago bank. This use of banks as agents enables both the seller and buyer to be more comfortable with the transaction. The seller was able to retain control of the goods until the price was paid (its agents had the bill of lading), and the buyer was not required to pay until it was assured that the goods were on the carrier, shipped to it, and inspection had been completed.[12]

The mechanics of tender, then, usually involve two separate events. One is the tendering of the goods, and a second is tendering the proper documents to the buyer. These mechanics are greatly simplified if tender is to be at the seller's plant.

Standard of Performance by the Seller

We have just discussed the mechanics of *where* and *how* the seller is to tender. *What* the seller is obligated to tender are the *exact goods* required by the agreement of the parties.

Under the common law of contracts, the seller was required "substantially" to perform its obligations before triggering the buyer's obligation to pay. Article 2 has changed this and now requires that the seller perform in *every respect*. More particularly, Article 2 provides that if either *the goods* or the *tender of delivery* fail in *any respect* to conform to the contract, then the buyer may: reject the whole; accept the whole; or accept

---
[12] See R. J. Nordstrom, *Handbook of the Law of Sales* (St. Paul: West Pub. Co., 1970).

any **commercial unit** or units and reject the rest.[13] This section imposes on the seller the requirement of a perfect tender[14] of both the goods and any documents needed to make the mechanics of tender good.[15] At first, this requirement may seem burdensome. Certainly it would have been burdensome in the late 19th and early 20th centuries before our manufacturing processes could produce uniform quality of a single line of products. Today, however, when a large merchant seller represents that goods will be exactly as they appear in either a catalog or a sales presentation where models are used, the seller is not unduly burdened by a requirement that the goods tendered be exactly like those originally represented to the buyer. In the following case the court held that the buyer could reject non-conforming goods.

commercial unit
"such a unit of goods as by commercial usage is a single whole for purposes of sale and division of which materially impairs its character or value on the market or in use" UCC 2–105 (6)

Facts
Maas, a large commercial grower of wheat and corn, agreed to purchase a large silo and other needed equipment for the storage of grain. The contract stated that there was a "one year warranty of customer satisfaction." The silo was constructed on Maas property in October of 1966. There was some evidence that the equipment and the construction of the silo were not exactly as they should be. From time to time the equipment would fail and, it was alleged, several hundred bushels of corn out of 3,000-plus spoiled. In August of 1967 Maas wrote the seller saying it was rejecting the silo and the equipment. Rather than ask for damages, Maas requested the seller simply to remove all of the items provided from his property. Did Maas accept the goods sold, or could he still reject them because they failed to conform? Also, to what standard of performance should the seller be held in this case?

Decision
The appellate court found in favor of Maas.

Reasoning
The court held that the one-year warranty of customer satisfaction gave the buyer, Maas, the right to reject the goods one year from the date of installation. With regard to the standard of performance, the court recognized that courts follow one of two rules. The first is that the test of the buyer's satisfaction is his own personal judgment (which must be exercised in good faith). The second is that the purchaser is bound to be satisfied with the goods if a reasonable person would be satisfied with them. Since section 2–601 states, "If the goods or the tender of delivery fail in *any respect* to conform to the contract. . .", the first standard must be used. The court concluded that so long as the rejection was done in good faith and not capriciously, the jury in the trial court could have properly found for Maas. The seller was required to remove all of the equipment and the silo.

Maas v. Scoboda, 195 N.W.2d 491 (Neb. 1972).

Exceptions to the Perfect Tender Rule. There are two important instances in which the impact of this requirement of a perfect tender on the seller's obligations may be *lessened*.

The first instance gives the seller, following an initial defective tender, an opportunity to tender again, or to **cure** the original defective tender of goods or documents *when there is time* or when the seller believed the original defective tender would be accepted (section 2–508).

cure
a seller's correction of his failure to deliver conforming goods under a contract for sale before the due date has expired

Assume that a contract calls for delivery on September 1. If there is a tender *before* that date and it is rightfully rejected, and there is time remaining in which to perform, the seller is given the opportunity to do so as long as reasonable notice is given to the buyer. In the case just described, Maas did give the seller of the equipment an opportunity to make it perform properly, but apparently this was not sufficient to meet Maas' satisfaction.

---

[13] UCC 2–601.

[14] R. J. Nordstrom, p. 308; and see comment 2, section 2–106, defining "conforming goods" wherein it is stated it is the policy of Article 2 to require "exact performance" by the seller.

[15] This discussion assumes that the goods sold are *new* and not used. When used goods are sold, the term "as is" is usually used to describe them, and the use of such a term requires the seller to deliver the goods in the used condition as they exist.

installment contract
"one which requires or authorizes the delivery of goods in separate lots to be separately accepted"
UCC 2–612 (1)

The *second instance* in which the impact of perfect tender on the seller's obligations is *lessened* occurs when the parties have agreed to an **installment contract.** If the goods are to arrive in separate lots, then the buyer may reject any such lot only if it *substantially impairs* the value of that installment *and cannot be cured.*[16] The Uniform Commercial Code generally favors any reasonable legal standard that attempts to keep goods moving in commerce. When parties contract for a one-time sale, the standard of the seller's performance, as we have seen, is that it must tender precisely what the contract calls for. When, however, the parties have contracted for a series of deliveries over a period of some months or years, Article 2 lessens the perfect tender requirement and allows the buyer to reject the goods only if the non-conformity *substantially impairs* the value of that installment and cannot be cured.

We assume that if the tender of an installment did not *exactly* meet the standards of the contract but the defect *did not substantially* impair its value, there would be some adjustment in price. If the defect in tender does substantially impair the value of that installment, the seller is given the opportunity to cure. If the seller cannot cure within a reasonable time and if the defect would substantially impair the value of the *whole* contract, there may then be a breach of the *whole* contract.[17] This is illustrated by the following case.

Facts
Hans Holterbosch, Inc., was an American importer and distributor of Lowenbrau beer. It applied for and received permission to operate a Lowenbrau Pavilion at the 1964 New York World's Fair. It contracted with Graulich Caterer, Inc. to provide quality food for the pavilion. The quality of the food was to be equal to that presented to the agents of Holterbosch at a meeting on March 17, 1964 in which eight different platters of food were displayed and sampled. The initial contract was for about 1,000,000 units of food to be delivered over a one-year period. The first delivery of food on April 23, 1964 did not, according to Holterbosch's employees, in any way match the contract samples presented on March 17. The first 955 unit installment was rejected as unacceptable. Holterbosch agreed that it would allow Graulich to tender another batch of food. On April 25, 1964, 2520 units were delivered. Out of this number, between 500 and 700 were distributed among employees of Holterbosch and patrons at the exhibit. The complaints in response to this food were numerous. Generally, Holterbosch complained that the food was not German in character and was of such inferior quality that it could not be served. Holterbosch cancelled the contract.

Graulich sued Holterbosch for out-of-pocket loss of $29,937 spent on platters, trays, and doilies, and for the amount of profit lost, $35,950. Was Holterbosch liable for cancelling the entire contract?

Decision
No! The appellate court found in favor of Holterbosch.

Reasoning
The appellate court relied on the trial court's conclusion that the tenders of food on April 23 and 25 did not conform to the samples provided on March 17. This conclusion was reached by the jury, who observed the testimony and demeanor of the witnesses for both sides.

The key question was, however, did the non-conforming tenders substantially impair the value of the whole contract? The court said that the failure of the second delivery to be acceptable left Holterbosch without food for one week. Time was critical, and Graulich knew that platters of maximum quality German food were required on a daily basis. So, because of Holterbosch's immediate need for quality food and the failure of Graulich to cure and the non-conformity of the second delivery, the court found a substantial impairment of the value of the whole contract and allowed the buyer, Holterbosch, to cancel.

Graulich Caterer, Inc. v. Hans Holterbosch, Inc., 243 A.2d 253 (N.J. 1968).

Do the Goods in Fact Conform to the Contract? Ascertaining whether a carload of construction lumber is in accordance with the contract is easy compared to ascertaining whether a Boeing 747, a supertanker, or a new model computer is in accordance with the contract. In many instances, issues involving the failure of such complex goods are re-

---

[16] UCC 2–612(2).   [17] UCC 2–612(3).

solved by a breach of warranty analysis. We point this out here simply to illustrate that the seller's performance obligations to tender goods exactly as they were promised are subject to at least two methods of analysis. The *first*—whether the goods conformed to the contract *at the time of delivery*—is relatively easy. Only obvious defects will be revealed at this point. However, failure of goods *during the time of its use* requires a second method of analyzing a seller's obligation to provide the *quality* of goods promised. This *second* method relies on a breach of warranty analysis and will be found in chapter 21.

Performance Obligations of the Buyer

The performance obligations of the buyer, not as complex as those of the seller, may be divided into two classifications. Unless the agreement provides another order of performance, and if the buyer wishes to put the seller in default, the buyer must perform *first* by tendering payment.[18] This, then, is the first classification of performance obligations for the buyer.

Tender of payment by the buyer.

Payment by the Buyer

Obviously the buyer is to pay, but what are the specifics of this obligation? What is payment? When and where must it (usually) be made? Tender of payment is sufficient when it is made by any means current in the ordinary course of business.[19] Unless the agreement provides otherwise, this means that the full price must be tendered in cash or check. If the payment tendered is by check and the seller demands cash, the buyer will be allowed an extension of time reasonably necessary to procure the cash.[20] Credit or a delay in payment is available only if the parties have agreed to it.

Tender of payment by cash, check, or other property.

Also, the parties may agree to exchange something other than cash for goods. Goods, for example, may be exchanged for goods,[21] and such a "barter" transaction is a sale for purposes of Article 2. The parties need not have agreed upon a price or payment, but as long as there is evidence that *the parties intend to be bound,* a court may find that an enforceable agreement exists. In this case the amount of the price is to be a reasonable one.[22]

When and where must the tender of payment be made? Generally, the buyer is to tender payment at the time and place at which the buyer is *to receive* the goods.[23] This clearly means that the *seller must complete all obligations of shipment and delivery* and must wait until the buyer has received the goods before it can expect payment. In the absence of the need for the buyer to establish a breach of the agreement, the delivery and receipt of the goods is a precondition and not a concurrent condition.[24]

Tender of payment, when and where.

Inspection by the Buyer

A second significant precondition to payment is the buyer's right to inspect the goods. The buyer has a right to inspect the goods after they have been identified to the contract for sale or after tender or delivery (or whenever the seller completes its performance) and *before* payment.[25] The time, place, and manner of inspection must be reasonable, and the expenses of inspection must be borne by the buyer but may be recovered from the seller if the goods do not conform and are rejected.[26]

The buyer's right to inspect the goods before tendering payment, unless otherwise agreed.

---

[18] UCC 2-511(1).   [19] UCC 2-511(2).   [20] UCC 2-511(2).

[21] UCC 2-304(1).   [22] UCC 2-305(1).   [23] UCC 2-310(a).

[24] J. White and R. Summers, *Handbook of the Law Under the Uniform Commercial Code* (St. Paul: West Pub. Co., 1972).

[25] UCC 2-513(1).   [26] UCC 2-513(2).

> The buyer must accept conforming goods tendered pursuant to the contract.

Acceptance by the Buyer

Finally, Article 2 requires that the buyer accept the goods. This is a technical performance obligation and occurs when the buyer

(a) after a reasonable opportunity to inspect the goods signifies to the seller that the goods are conforming or that he will take or retain them in spite of their non-conformity; or

(b) fails to make an effective rejection . . . but such acceptance does not occur until the buyer has had a reasonable opportunity to inspect them; or

(c) does any act inconsistent with the seller's ownership. . . .[27]

Acceptance is important because, once it occurs, the *seller* is given an additional remedy in the case of a breach of the sales contract. Generally, before acceptance the seller's chief remedy upon the breach by a buyer is to stop shipment, recover the goods, or sue for lost profit. *After acceptance,* the buyer may not reject the goods[28] and the seller has the additional remedy of suing for the entire purchase price.[29]

In summary, the buyer's obligations, generally speaking, follow those of the seller to ship or deliver the goods. Upon receipt of the goods, the buyer is to inspect, pay, and accept them.

Performance Obligations in Special Circumstances

Article 2 has more performance obligations of the parties than we present here. However, this text on commercial law is intended to be as thorough as possible given space constraints. Of necessity, some of the provisions of Article 2 must be left for explanation and analysis in later courses on commercial law. Two sets of performance obligations are so important, however, that they merit special attention. The first set arises from Article 2 itself. The second arises from Article 6, Bulk Transfers. First we present the additional performance obligations of Article 2.

> Impairment of one party's expectation of another party's performance, and the right to additional adequate assurance from the other party that the expected performance from the other party will occur.

The Obligation to Provide Adequate Assurance of Performance when Demanded

The parties to a contract for the sale of goods contemplate *performance* and not breach or the right to sue. So, "if either the willingness or the ability of a party to perform declines materially between the time of contracting and the time for performance, the other party is threatened with the loss of a substantial part of what has been bargained for."[30] Article 2, section 2–609(1) attempts to protect both parties by providing these additional obligations of the parties:

> (1) A contract for sale imposes an obligation on each party that the other's expectation of receiving due performance will not be impaired. When *reasonable grounds* for insecurity arise with respect to the performance of *either* party the other may in writing demand *adequate assurance* of *due performance* and until he receives such assurance may, if *commercially reasonable,* suspend *any performance* for which *he has not already received the agreed return.* [Emphasis added.]

> **insolvency**
> when the debtor "either has ceased to pay his debts in the ordinary course of business or cannot pay his debts as they become due or is insolvent within the meaning of the federal bankruptcy law" (assets are less than liabilities) UCC 1–201(23)

The italicized words in the section above are the key ones. Between merchants, they are defined according to current commercial standards[31] and the general obligation of acting in good faith. From the seller's point of view—and this is especially true if it is selling on credit—any information that the buyer is **insolvent** or in financial difficulty should cause the seller to demand in writing that the buyer clarify its financial condition.

---

[27] UCC 2–606.   [28] UCC 2–607(2).   [29] UCC 2–709.

[30] UCC 2–609, comment 1.   [31] UCC 2–609(2).

A mere rumor of insolvency is not sufficient grounds upon which the seller may refuse to perform;[32] however, if the rumor is true, or if the seller learns by inquiring from the buyer that there are reasonable grounds to believe that the buyer may be insolvent, the seller may refuse to deliver except for cash.[33]

If either party receives a written demand reasonable under the circumstances for adequate assurance of performance and does not respond with an adequate assurance within a reasonable time—in any event, not longer than thirty days—then the demanding party may treat this as a repudiation of the contract.[34] In short, if reasonable grounds for insecurity exist, the party owing the obligation to perform may: (1) suspend performance; (2) demand in writing an adequate assurance of performance from the other party; (3) await a reply for a reasonable time, which is not over thirty days; and (4) if there is not an adequate reply, view the contract as repudiated by the other party. In the following case since adequate assurance was demanded by the seller and not given, there was justifiable ground for the seller's suspended performance.

Facts
Gestetner, defendant, sold goods on credit to Turntables, Inc., plaintiff. After delivery of some of the goods, Gestetner found out that Turntables' "Fifth Avenue Showroom" address was a telephone answering service, that its "Island Park factory" was someone else's premises and Turntables had no leased space, and that they had a "bad" reputation for performance. Gestetner demanded adequate assurance for future performance (payment on delivery, we assume) even though the sales were to be on credit. Turntables was not insolvent at the time even though Gestetner believed it to be so. Adequate assurance was not given, so Gestetner refused to make more deliveries required by the contract. Turntables, Inc. sued Gestetner for failure to perform.

Decision
The appellate court entered judgment for Gestetner, defendant.

Reasoning
The facts of the case, not disputed by Turntables, do reveal reasonable grounds for insecurity, and section 2–609 allows such a party having reasonable grounds for insecurity to suspend performance for which he has not already received an agreed exchange.

Turntables, Inc. v. Gestetner, 382 N.Y.S.2d 798 (1976).

Performance Obligations Imposed when Bulk Sales Are the Subject of the Contract

Article 2 is premised on the notion that a seller is offering goods in the *ordinary course of its business*. When a seller of goods decides either to change the nature of its business or to sell out completely by selling a major part of all of its materials, supplies, or other inventory, then there is a potential for commercial injury to those who normally rely on the fact that the seller will continue in operation. Those persons who could be commercially injured by a "bulk sale" are the creditors of the seller.

Article 6 defines a **bulk transfer** as one that is a transfer, not in the ordinary course of the **transferor's** business, of *a major part* of the materials, supplies, merchandise, or other inventory. The Article does not clearly define what a "*major part*" of the materials, supplies, etc. is. It has been suggested by prominent authorities that a "major part" refers to *value* and not *quantity* of the materials or inventory, and that certainly a transfer of *45 percent* of the total *value* should be a "major part."[35] Some courts have recognized a sale of 25 percent of a merchant's *inventory* as a major part.[36]

Generally, there are four performance obligations required of the transferor (seller) and the transferee (buyer). The *first* is that, before the actual transfer takes place, the intended **transferee** must demand and receive a sworn list of creditors of the transferor

bulk
a great part or number

bulk transfer
"any transfer in bulk and not in the ordinary course of the transferor's business of a major part of the materials, supplies, merchandise or other inventory of an enterprise subject to Article 6" UCC 6–102(1)

transferor
one who has transferred some thing to another

transferee
one to whom another has transferred some thing

---

[32] R. J. Nordstrom, p. 495. [33] Ibid. [34] UCC 2–609(4).
[35] J. White and R. Summers, p. 646. [36] See *Danning v. Daylin, Inc.,* 488 F.2d 185 (1973).

together with a schedule of the property sufficient to identify it. The transferee must preserve the schedule for six months after the transfer and permit inspection of it by any creditor of the transferor during this period.[37]

Second, at least ten days before the *transferee* is to take possession of the goods or is to pay for them (whichever happens first), *it* must give notice of the transfer to creditors of the transferor.[38]

Third, this notice must state, among other things the names of the parties and a description of the property.[39]

Finally, this notice must be either delivered personally or sent by registered or certified mail to all persons shown on the list provided by the transferor, and to all other persons who, the transferee knows, hold or assert claims against the transferor.[40]

The failure to comply with the above four obligations renders the bulk transfer ineffective as against any creditor.[41] In such cases, the creditor of the seller will be able to assert whatever legal rights it has in the goods. In the following case the buyer did not comply with the notice requirements, and the bulk sale was declared ineffective.

Facts
Pastimes Publishing Co. was a publisher of books and on August 23, 1968 sold its entire inventory of books to Saalfield for $27,000. At this time Pastimes owed Midland Paper Company $34,000 and owed other unsecured creditors substantial sums. No notice of the sale was sent to the creditors of Pastimes. The entire proceeds of the sale were credited to Midland. The other creditors of Pastimes objected, and litigation resulted. What are the remedies of the unsecured creditors of Pastimes against Saalfield and Midland?

Decision
The appellate court declared the sale ineffective and affirmed a judgment in favor of the unsecured creditors of Pastimes on a **pro rata** basis.

Reasoning
The court held that a bulk sale was made and that the failure to meet the notice requirements of Article 6 resulted in a violation. Article 6 itself provides no specific remedies for unsecured creditors of bulk-sale sellers except to provide that the sale is ineffective. Under Illinois law, the unsecured creditors of Pastimes could recover the inventory sold or, at their option, divide the proceeds of the sale. The creditors opted to divide the proceeds, and this had to be done on a pro rata basis. The credit of the entire proceeds to Midland was inappropriate since the amount credited arose from an ineffective transfer.

Pastimes Publishing Co. v. Advertising Displays, 286 N.E.2d 19 (Ill. 1972).

pro rata distribution distribution in proportion to one's contribution, loan or advance

When nonperformance is excused.

Circumstances Excusing Performance of the Parties

Almost the entire body of our commercial law is built upon the assumption that parties to a commercial agreement intended and contemplated *performance.* In a sense, the commercial law is weakened in each instance in which the law recognizes an exception to the general rule that parties *must* perform when they have promised to do so. In some circumstances, however, there are good reasons for such exceptions. Generally, the reasons for excusing one or both of the parties from their agreement are based upon *the occurrence of events which neither party could reasonably foresee, given the current commercial realities.*

Article 2 recognizes four important circumstances in which a court will excuse performance. Three of these will now be considered. A fourth, involving "unconscionable contracts," will be discussed in chapter 21, Consumer Law A. As you read this final part of the present chapter, remember that, generally speaking, exceptions to the fundamental obligations of performance are narrowly defined and are recognized only where our *notions of fairness override the necessary emphasis on performance.* Note also that, since the seller usually has the first obligation to perform, it is generally the seller who is excused from performance.

---

[37] UCC 6–104.   [38] UCC 6–105.   [39] UCC 6–107.

[40] UCC 6–107(3).   [41] UCC 6–105.

First: Excuse by Casualty to Identified Goods

A contract for the sale of goods contemplates the delivery of specific, identifiable goods, so their *total* destruction through no fault of either party will excuse *both* parties from their performance obligations.

Excused nonperformance by reason of total destruction of the identified goods.

There are four important conditions that must be satisfied before the seller is excused from performance because of casualty to the goods.

1. The first condition is that the goods must be "identified when the contract is made." The term "identified" means that *they could be reasonably specified* or *described* at the time of the contract.
2. The goods must be *totally* destroyed. If the goods are only partially damaged, the seller should notify the buyer and, if the buyer desires, the buyer may demand tender and inspection and may accept the goods with an allowance in price for the diminution of value. If the buyer chooses this option, however, it may not sue the seller for failure to deliver conforming goods.
3. The casualty must not have been caused by either party.
4. The risk of loss must not have passed to the buyer.

While these four conditions are necessary to excuse the seller *and* buyer *from their performance obligations,* which one will suffer the *loss*? If the casualty to the goods occurs *before* the risk of loss passes to the buyer, although the seller is excused from its performance obligation, it will suffer the loss. The seller is excused from having to tender new goods or a set of goods. If the casualty occurs *after* the risk passes to the buyer, the parties are not excused from their performance obligations, and the buyer suffers the loss.

Second: Excuse by Failure of the Manner of Delivery, or Failure of the Means or Manner of Payment

Excused nonperformance by reason of failure of the manner of delivery, or failure of the means or manner of payment.

Failure of the Manner of Delivery. When neither party is at fault and the agreed *manner of delivery becomes commercially impracticable,* if there is a reasonable *substitute,* it must be tendered and accepted.[42] The "excuse" provided by this section is not a total one. From the *seller's* point of view, the excuse is from the *agreed* manner of delivery. *Delivery is still required,* but a reasonable substitute for the agreed manner of delivery may be used. Generally, "commercially impracticable" means something more than simply "more expensive." If the agreed means of delivery becomes tremendously more expensive, then the seller will probably seek application of the next section below for "excuse by failure of presupposed conditions."

Failure of the Means or Manner of Payment. The *buyer* is also protected by this section. If the agreed means or manner of payment *fails* because of a domestic or foreign governmental regulation, then the buyer may provide payment by a means which is a substantial equivalent.[43]

Third: Excuse by Failure of Presupposed Conditions

Excused failure of presupposed conditions.

At a very basic level, the law of contracts and Article 2 of the UCC are intended to protect and enforce the intention of parties to an agreement when they consciously allocate business risks. The general rule is that *the law will not excuse performance merely because a transaction may have become unprofitable because a foreseeable risk has occurred.* A rise or a collapse in the market for goods is not in itself a justification for excuse of performance; that is exactly the type of business risk that business contracts made at set prices are intended to cover.[44] There are thousands, perhaps millions, of transactions each day that result in losses to one or both parties. There is no excuse from such performance unless a court can be convinced that the parties *did not consciously allocate the risk of an event that occurred.*

---

[42] UCC 2-614 (1).   [43] UCC 2-614(2).   [44] See UCC 2-615, comment 4.

When unforeseeable catastrophic storms, crop failures, bankruptcies of major suppliers, embargoes or wars, and so forth occur, causing a *drastic* or *unusual* change in price, then the seller must first give notice to the buyer that there will be a delay or nondelivery[45] and may then attempt to "renegotiate" the contract with the buyer. However, if the parties cannot agree, the final arbiter will be a court. Whether the court will classify the event as a normal business risk, or a totally unforeseen contingency altering the essential nature of the performance obligation, is not certain. In the following case the court found a normal business risk and imposed liability for nonperformance by the seller.

Facts
Wegematic Corporation, defendant, designed and produced a small computer known as the ALWAC III-E, which enjoyed considerable success. Wegematic designed in a preliminary way the ALWAC 800, which was characterized as a "truly revolutionary system," and submitted a proposal to the Federal Reserve Board for the production of the ALWAC 800 computer. The proposal was submitted as a competitive bid and was selected by the Federal Reserve Board. The parties agreed that the ALWAC 800 would be delivered on June 30, 1957 at a cost of $231,000. The board emphasized the importance of delivery on time, and the parties agreed that Wegematic would pay the board $100 per day for each day the delivery was late.

In March of 1957 Wegematic requested a postponement of the delivery date to late summer. In April they requested an October 30 delivery date because of design difficulties. And in mid-October Wegematic announced that it had become impracticable to deliver the ALWAC 800 due to engineering difficulties. They requested a cancellation of the contract with the board and a waiver of damage claims.

In October, 1957 the Federal Reserve Board set out to purchase comparable equipment and then the United States sued Wegematic for a total of $235,806, which included damages for delay and the increased price they had to pay another computer firm for substantially similar goods. Wegematic argued that to produce the ALWAC 800 would have taken an additional $1 million to $1.5 million and between one or two years full-time research. It argued that the agreement had become commercially impracticable because of the occurrence of events it could not predict in the fields of electronic engineering and rapidly developing computer technology.

Should the seller be excused from performance and the payment of damages because it was involved in a high risk field where developing new products was uncertain and hazardous?

Decision
No! The court awarded judgment to the government for $235,806 plus interest.

Reasoning
The court acknowledged that UCC section 2–615 is the controlling section and lamented the "somewhat complicated" way it states the rule. If one of the parties expressly assumed the risk attendant to some promised performance, then it must suffer the consequences. The court stated, "We see no basis for thinking that when an electronics system is promoted by its manufacturers as a revolutionary breakthrough, the risk of the revolution's occurrence falls on the purchaser." Even in fields of new and rapidly developing technology, a seller of a product should not be able to transfer the risks accompanying development to the purchaser. Sellers should not be free to gamble on mere probabilities of development without any risk of liability.

United States v. Wegematic Corporation, 360 F.2d 674 (1966).

Concluding Ideas about Risk Allocation
The best method for determining which of the parties assumed which risks is to read the agreement, or, where there is no written agreement, ascertain the oral understanding of the parties. Course of performance, course of dealing, and usage of trade are also important in ascertaining which risks the parties allocated in the absence of an express statement in the agreement.

---

[45] UCC 2–615(c).

Mistake by One of the Parties

There are no specific Article 2 sections directly applicable to circumstances in which one or both of the parties makes a mistake of calculation, typing, or the like. However, the common law rules on mistake are to supplement Article 2 (1–103), so the rules you learned in Part 2, Contracts, on mistake are applicable in appropriate circumstances and may be argued using the language of section 2–615.[46]

Summary Statement

1. Generally, it is the parties' intent as expressed in their contractual documents that will determine the performance obligations of the parties.
2. The obligation of the seller is to transfer and deliver the goods and that of the buyer is to accept and pay for them in accordance with the contract.
3. The seller must tender the goods to the buyer in a manner and at the time and place as set in the agreement. The use of the terms F.O.B. or F.A.S. followed by a destination (e.g., the name of a distant town) require the seller at its own expense and risk to transport the goods *there* and tender them. If the terms used are F.O.B. or F.A.S. seller's town, or if the seller is "to ship" the goods, then the seller must put the goods in the possession of a carrier in *its* town and make a reasonable contract for their shipment and then notify the buyer.
4. If the term C.I.F. is used (e.g., C.I.F. Austin, Texas, when the seller is in Lansing, Michigan), the seller is to load the goods onto a carrier, make a contract for their shipment, and pay for the freight and insurance.
5. Where the agreement states nothing about the place for delivery, the place for delivery is the seller's place of business, but if the goods are somewhere else, then delivery is where the goods are located.
6. The goods tendered by the seller must conform to the contract in every respect; if they do not, the buyer may reject them but the seller may cure its tender if there is time or if the seller reasonably thought the goods would be accepted.
7. The obligations of the buyer are to inspect, pay for, and accept the goods. The buyer is to tender payment at the time and place at which the buyer is to receive the goods.
8. A party has an obligation to provide an adequate assurance of performance when demanded if there are reasonable grounds for insecurity with respect to the party's performance.
9. In some states the sellers and buyers involved in bulk transfers have performance obligations to inform the creditors of the seller of the transfer.
10. The parties to a sales agreement may be excused from their performance obligations when:
    a. the goods are totally destroyed through no fault of either party before the risk of loss passes to the buyer;
    b. the manner of delivery or the manner of payment fails; however, a reasonable substitute must be tendered;
    c. an event occurs which neither party could foresee and the risk for which was not allocated between the parties.

In the following case the question of who was to bear the risk of loss was determined by the seller's typing-in certain words on its form.

---

[46] R. J. Nordstrom, p. 334. See pp. 106–7.

National Heater Company, Inc. v. Corrigan Co. Mechanical Contractors, Inc.
482 F.2d 87 (1973)

Stephenson, Circuit J. National Heater, the seller, offered on March 1, 1969 to sell certain heating units to be used in the construction of the Chrysler automobile plant in Fenton, Missouri. The original offer of the seller stated that the price quoted was for the merchandise "F.O.B., St. Paul, Minnesota." The buyer, Corrigan Company, sent its "purchase order" back to the seller with the statement that the price was "$275,640—Delivered." The seller then mailed to the buyer an "Acknowledgment of Purchase Order" bearing the printed words "Sale Price Total" followed by typed-in wording "$275,640, Total Delivered to Rail Siding." In another of the seller's acknowledgment forms were the printed words "delivery of equipment hereunder shall be made F.O.B. point of shipment unless otherwise stated."

The heating units were shipped by the seller but were damaged in transit. The buyer received the goods and accepted them subject to a reduction in the sales price. The full contract price was not paid and the seller sued the buyer for the balance. The buyer counterclaimed, arguing that the risk of loss due to shipment damage was on the seller until delivery to the construction site in Missouri. The seller argued that the risk of loss was on the buyer once a reasonable contract for the delivery of the heaters was made in St. Paul. At the trial it was shown that both parties contemplated a Fenton, Missouri "rail siding" when the words "rail siding" were used.

When did the agreement of the parties state that the risk of loss was to pass? Judgment for the buyer, Corrigan Company. Seller appeals.

The intention of the parties is to control in determining the allocation of the risk of loss. When a written contract is partly written or typewritten and partly printed, any conflict between the printed portion and the typewritten portion will be resolved in favor of the latter. Also, any ambiguity in a party's form will be construed against that party since they drafted it and should not be allowed to take advantage of their own ambiguous draftsmanship. The seller's form stated in print that delivery was to be F.O.B., point of shipment, unless otherwise stated. It was "otherwise stated." The seller had typed in the words "$275,640, Total Delivered to Rail Siding." There was uncontradicted evidence that the rail siding referred to was the one at the construction site in Fenton, Missouri. The seller's obligations were to deliver to that point, and there the risk of loss would pass to the buyer.

Affirmed for the buyer, Corrigan Company.

Questions and Case Problems

1. Explain how banks are sometimes used in commercial transactions to facilitate the surrendering of possession of goods, the inspection of the goods by the buyer, and payment.

2. The plaintiff, Joc Oil USA, Inc., contracted to sell fuel oil to the defendant, Consolidated Edison, Inc. The contract described the oil as .50% maximum sulfur content. The contract included a clause which provided for a price adjustment between the parties under certain circumstances. The refinery certificate indicated a sulfur content of .52% and another test measured the sulfur content at .92%. The defendant rejected the shipment. Plaintiff then offered to reduce its price but this offer was rejected. Then the plaintiff made an offer to cure by providing oil to arrive 7 days after the contract date. Time was not a factor. The defendant rejected this offer. In addition, the evidence showed the defendant was legally authorized to burn oil with up to 1.0% sulfur content, was in fact using and mixing oils with up to between .6% and .8% sulfur content with a few of the oils burned in excess of 1.0%. Did the defendant act reasonably in rejecting the plaintiff's shipment and the plaintiff's offer to cure? [*Joc Oil USA, Inc. v. Consoldated Edison Co. of New York*, 434 N.Y.S.2d 623 (N.Y. 1980).]

3. S, seller, has just sold $14,000 worth of chains, sprockets, and steel tubing to B, buyer, on credit. B has a business in which it manufactures bicycles for the retail market. You are interested in starting a bicycle manufacturing operation and agree with B to buy 40 percent of B's inventory of parts. Explain the performance obligations imposed on your transaction with B by Article 6 of the UCC (Bulk Transfers). If these obligations are not met, what are the remedies available to S if S is not paid?

4. The seller, plaintiff, agreed to custom-manufacture metal siding for the buyer, defendant. The exact shipping date was not agreed upon but, through correspondence, it was clear that the defendant needed the siding by May 1. It appeared from the evidence that this was a commercially reasonable time and that the defendant was relying on delivery on or before this date. The doors had not arrived by June and the buyer cancelled the contract. The seller alleges that this was a breach of contract and had it not been for strikes and faulty material received from its suppliers it would have performed on time. Do the strikes and faulty material excuse the seller from its failure to deliver on time so that it may now maintain an action against the buyer? [*Morin Building Products, Co., Inc. v. Volk Construction, Inc.,* 500 F.Supp. 82 (Mont. 1980).]

5. S agreed to sell to B 50 crates of machine parts for $300 per crate. The agreement stated nothing about the place of delivery nor the place or manner of payment. Several months after the agreement, B demanded that S deliver the machine parts to B's place of business in a town 150 miles from S's place of business. S countered by demanding that B pay for and pick up the crates of machine parts which had been identified and were at S's warehouse. How is this dispute resolved by Article 2? Where is delivery and tender to take place? What must both parties do to place the other in default?

6. S contracted to sell to B 1,000 bushels of apples at $6 per bushel, "to be shipped in September" to B in B's city. On September 20, 850 bushels were shipped to B and they arrived on September 25, when the price of apples in B's city was $5 per bushel. The usual time of shipment was three to seven days. B refused the delivery after inspection because it found there were only 850 bushels. On September 26, S was notified and on that date shipped the remaining 150 bushels. What are the rights and obligations of the parties?

7. A agreed to sell and B agreed to purchase 1,000 small electric motors for $85 each, "F.O.B., Lansing, Michigan," the buyer's place of business. Nothing else in the agreement defined the delivery or payment obligations. The seller's place of business is Mobile, Alabama. What are the performance obligations of A and B?

8. In the fact pattern of question 7 above, assume that after B took possession of the motors, it is discovered that 20 percent of the motors would not perform according to the specifications supplied to A by B. What should B do? If there is sufficient time, what course should A follow? How would the performance obligations differ if the parties had negotiated an "installment contract?"

9. Neal-Cooper, buyer, was engaged in the business of selling grain and fertilizer. They used large quantities of phosphates and potash, most of which were supplied by Texas Gulf Sulphur Co., seller. On November 20, 1969 the buyer received from the seller some printed form contracts which they were to use in making future orders. Two of the forms already bore the signature of the *seller's* general sales manager. The buyer was asked to fill in the quantities needed, sign the forms, and return them to the seller.

The buyer's agent agreed to buy 10,000 tons of coarse potash and 2,000 tons of granular potash for the period November 1, 1969 through June 30, 1970. All deliveries were to be "F.O.B. cars seller's plant, Potash, Utah." The form contained an **exculpatory clause** excusing the parties from performance caused by, among other things, the operation of statutes or law.

exculpatory clause
a clause which relieves one from liability

On December 2, 1969 the buyer placed a large order for potash to be delivered in January. The seller refused to fill the order because the Canadian government passed regulations which controlled the seller's production and price of potash so they were unable to promise any fixed tonnage for shipment in the future. (The Canadian regulations were intended to limit the production of potash and to set a minimum price of 33.75¢ (Canadian) per unit.) The seller argued that the agreement, if there was one, was thus rendered commercially impracticable, thereby excusing performance under section 2–615 of the UCC.

At the trial there was testimony that the Canadian source was the primary source of the seller's potash but not the only source. The seller did have potash mines in the U.S.
   a. Was the seller excused from performance?
   b. If the buyer had ordered all 10,000 tons of coarse and 2,000 tons of granular potash for January delivery, would the seller have an excuse for not shipping all of it at that time?
[*Neal-Cooper Grain Co. v. Texas Gulf Sulphur Co.*, 508 F.2d 283 (1974).]

10. In the case of *National Heater Company, Inc. v. Corrigan Co. Mechanical Contractors, Inc.*, 482 F.2d 87 (1973),[47] if you were the seller, what would you have done to avoid the risk of loss which the seller had in that case?

---

[47] See p. 286.

Breach of the Sales Contract, Courses of Action, and Remedies 20

After you have read this chapter, you should be able to:

1. Describe the buyer's courses of action if the seller defaults before its date of performance; then describe the seller's courses of action if the buyer defaults before its performance is due.
2. List and then define the various monetary remedies available to buyers and sellers upon the breach by the other party.
3. Describe the differences between incidental and consequential damages, give an example of each, and state the circumstances in which the court will award consequential damages.
4. List and then describe the circumstances in which the buyer may recover the goods contracted for from the seller and the circumstances in which the seller may recover the goods it has delivered to the buyer.
5. Discuss the circumstances in which the parties may limit the damage recovery of the opposing party.
6. Define what is meant by a statute of limitations and describe when the time period of this statute usually begins and ends in sales transactions.

Introduction

breach of contract
wrongful nonperformance of a contractual promise

When wrongful nonperformance and therefore **breach of contract** by a contracting party occurs, what can the innocent party do; that is, what legal remedies are available, and to what extent can their contract make provision for this?

There is probably no more important area in the study of law than the area of legal remedies. The discussions of rights and duties of the parties can seem important and complex, and the explanations of legal concepts and doctrine may seem impressive and well established, but no right or duty is important and no legal concept impressive unless there is a corresponding remedy for those affected. Issues of which remedies are available to an injured party and what the appropriate and fair measure of **damages** is, are issues of primary importance in the study of commercial law.

damages
the money judicially awarded to an injured party for another's wrongful conduct

damage
loss or harm

General Ideas Regarding Breach, Remedies, and Damages

Courts and "the law" must attempt to put the non-breaching party in the same position it would have been in had there been full performance.[1] Any remedy or measure of damage which strives to achieve something less than this creates an incentive *not* to perform exactly as promised. The entire body of our commercial law is premised on the notion that the parties to a commercial transaction desire performance.

This chapter presents an analysis of both the buyer's and seller's courses of action once they have learned of a breach by the other party and their various remedies. *The material is best read based upon the central image of two corporate merchants who have entered into an enforceable sales agreement.*

Breach of the Sales Contract by the Seller

Buyer's Courses of Action without Bringing a Lawsuit

One of the most difficult problems which arise from commercial conduct is the judgment about the other party's anticipated performance. When a doubt about the seller's performance is created in the mind of the buyer, for example, what should the buyer do? Below we consider first the possible courses of action of the buyer; then we analyze the remedies and measures of damage available to the buyer when the seller breaches. We start with the buyer's courses of conduct and remedies because, generally, the buyer faces a tougher problem in assessing the nature of the seller's performance than does the seller in assessing whether the buyer has paid or will pay.

Demand adequate assurance of performance by the seller.

The Buyer's Right to Adequate Assurance of Performance. If reasonable grounds appear which cause the buyer (or seller) to feel insecure about the seller's (or buyer's) performance, then the buyer (seller) should (1) suspend performance, (2) demand in writing an adequate assurance of performance, and (3) await a reply for a reasonable time, which is not over thirty days. If there is no adequate reply, then the buyer (seller) may treat the contract as repudiated by the seller (buyer).[2] This section was discussed more fully in chapter 19, Performance of the Sales Contract.

Rejection of the goods.

commercial unit
"such a unit of goods as by commercial usage is a single whole for purposes of sale, and division of which materially impairs its character or value on the market or in use" UCC 2–105(6)

The Buyer's Right to Reject or Accept the Goods. Generally, at the time of the seller's tender of the goods, it is the obligation of the buyer to inspect the goods and either accept or reject them. It *must* accept and pay for them if they conform to the contract. If, however, the goods fail *in any respect,* then the buyer may reject the whole, or accept the whole (with, we assume, an allowance in the price for the defect), or accept any **commercial unit** or units and reject the rest.[3] The definition of a commercial unit may vary depending upon the type of goods in question and the practices of merchants in the market for the goods. The importance of the definition of a commercial unit is illustrated by the following case.

---

[1] UCC 1–106(1).   [2] UCC 2–609.   [3] UCC 2–601.

Facts

The seller, Salinas Lettuce Farmers Cooperative located in Salinas, California, sold a truckload of various kinds of vegetables to the purchaser, Larry Ober Co., Inc., a produce broker located in Pompano Beach, Florida. The load contained 115 cartons of green cabbage, 4 cartons of broccoli and 10 cartons of romaine. When it arrived the cabbage and broccoli were badly discolored and the romaine was decaying. The purchaser accepted all of the good vegetables and rejected the cabbage, broccoli and romaine. Apparently the seller suffered more damage from this response than it would have if the purchaser would have accepted the entire truckload. So, it sued the purchaser for this damage. The court hearing the case said that the question in this case is the treatment of a mixed load of vegetables in the perishable agricultural commodities industry and whether the industry considers *each lot* of distinct vegetables to be a commercial unit or whether it considers the *entire truckload* to constitute a commercial unit?

Decision

The court held that the entire truckload was a commercial unit.

Reasoning

The court reasoned that in the market for perishable agricultural commodities, the seller lacks the ability to control what happens to its goods if they are rejected, and particularly so when a portion is accepted while another portion is not. Thus there has arisen in the industry the practice of accepting or rejecting whole truckloads. So, the court concluded that whenever there is a shipment of several perishable agricultural commodities the entire truckload (or carload) is the commercial unit. A buyer may not accept some commodities and reject others. Rather, its appropriate course of action if it accepts the goods is to accept the *entire* shipment and seek damages for breach of warranty on the inferior or spoiled goods. In this case, the purchaser became liable for the entire contract price less damages resulting from any breach of warranty by the seller. The burden is on the purchaser to establish the breach and the resulting damages.

Salinas Lettuce Farmers Cooperative v. Larry Ober Co., Inc., 28 U.C.C.Rep. 684, U.S. Dep't. of Agriculture, (1980).

Rejection of the Goods. Let us assume that the buyer has ordered one shipment of goods and it has arrived and the buyer desires to *reject* the entire shipment. How is an effective rejection made? The rejection:

1. must be made within a reasonable time after the delivery or tender of the goods (but before acceptance), and
2. is effective when the buyer seasonably notifies the seller of the rejection.[4]

These requirements of an effective rejection demand that the buyer act *promptly*. The words "reasonable" and "seasonably" are not defined in this section, so a court is left free to define them in relation to the circumstances of the case. The buyer's actions must be *precise* when rejecting goods. Any exercise of ownership of the goods by the buyer is wrongful against the seller and may cause a court to conclude that the buyer has waived its rejection.

After notice of rejection is sent, the buyer's course of action will depend on whether it has paid anything for the goods received. If the buyer *has not* paid anything for the goods, it is under a duty to hold them with reasonable care for disposition by the seller.[5] If the seller has no agent or place of business at the place where the rejection takes place, then a *merchant* buyer must follow any reasonable instructions from the seller. In the absence of such instructions, and if the goods are perishable or will quickly decline in value if not sold, the buyer *must* make reasonable efforts to sell the goods for the account of the seller, deducting from the sales price its reasonable expenses for caring for and selling the goods.[6]

---

[4] UCC 2–602(1).   [5] UCC 2–602(2)(b).   [6] UCC 2–603(1)(2).

If the buyer *has paid* something for them, whether it is the full price or just a partial payment, the buyer has a property interest in the goods in its possession or control, called a **security interest,** for the amount paid *and* expenses reasonably incurred in their inspection, receipt, transportation, care, and custody.[7] This property interest in the goods enables the buyer to sell the goods in good faith and in a commercially reasonable manner. The buyer must account to the seller for any excess money received over the amount of the security interest.[8]

Acceptance of the Goods. The alternative to rejecting the goods is to accept them. Acceptance occurs (1) after a reasonable opportunity to inspect and when the buyer signifies to the seller that the goods are conforming or that he will take them in spite of their non-conformity; or (2) if the buyer fails to make an effective rejection (after a reasonable opportunity to inspect); or (3) if the buyer does any act inconsistent with the seller's ownership.[9] Acceptance of a part of any commercial unit is acceptance of that entire unit.[10]

Acceptance of the goods has three important consequences. (1) Acceptance obligates the buyer to pay for the goods at the contract rate.[11] (2) Acceptance gives the *seller* an additional remedy for a breach by the buyer. (3) Of more importance to our inquiry into breach and damages, acceptance shifts the burden of proof for establishing non-conformity from the seller to the buyer. Whereas rejection of the goods by the buyer results in the *seller* bearing the burden of proving that the goods were conforming, if acceptance has taken place and then an alleged non-conformity is detected, it is the burden of the *buyer* to establish the nature of the seller's breach.[12]

1. The Buyer's Right to Revoke Its Acceptance. We must assume that many, if not most, of the breaches by a seller for tendering non-conforming goods are discovered after acceptance. The complexity of goods manufactured today makes it difficult to discover whether goods tendered are non-conforming by mere visual inspection or even sampling their performance. The Code recognizes this and provides a course of action for the buyer when it discovers a non-conformity after acceptance. Section 2–608 allows a buyer to revoke acceptance. It provides:

> (1) The buyer may *revoke his acceptance* of a lot or commercial unit whose non-conformity *substantially impairs its value to him* if he has accepted it
>   (a) on the reasonable assumption that its non-conformity would be cured and it has not been seasonably cured; or
>   (b) without discovery of such non-conformity if his acceptance was *reasonably induced* either by *the difficulty of discovery before acceptance* or by the seller's assurances.
> (2) Revocation of acceptance must occur *within a reasonable time* after the buyer discovers or should have discovered the ground for it and before any substantial change in condition of the goods. . . . It is not effective until the buyer notifies the seller of it.
> (3) A buyer who so revokes has the same rights and duties with regard to the goods involved as if he had rejected them. [Emphasis added.]

Rejection and revocation of acceptance have some similarities and some substantial differences. If the revocation is effective, then, as in rejection, the goods will be treated as if they were the seller's, and the buyer has the same courses of action open to it, including the right to sell the goods it possesses. Unlike a rejection, which is available in *single delivery contracts* for *any* non-conformity, a revocation of acceptance is permitted only where the non-conformity *substantially impairs* the value of the goods to the buyer.

In the following case the non-conformity of the goods did not substantially impair the value of the goods to the buyer, who was not permitted to revoke its acceptance.

---

[7] UCC 2–711(3).   [8] UCC 2–706(6).   [9] UCC 2–606(1).

[10] UCC 2–606(2).   [11] UCC 2–607(1).   [12] UCC 2–607(4).

---

security interest
"an interest in personal property or fixtures which secures payment or performance of an obligation"
UCC 1–201(37)

Revocation of acceptance.

Facts
The plaintiff, Kearney & Trecker Corp., was the seller of sophisticated industrial equipment used to make metal parts. On July 1, 1970 they agreed to sell to Fargo Machine & Tool Co., defendant, for $153,725 a metal-shaping machine with additional parts that made the machine adaptable for a number of tasks. Delivery and installation were completed in September, 1971. The machine did not operate to the full satisfaction of the buyer, and numerous service calls followed. As of January, 1972 Fargo Machine had paid $75,000 on the machine and was not content with the machine's performance but agreed to pay an additional $28,868, reducing the balance to $50,000 in return for Kearney's promise to correct specified deficiencies. In June of 1972 Kearney advised Fargo that the deficiencies had been remedied and requested prompt payment of the balance. Fargo refused to pay, stating that new deficiencies were noticed all the time. In April of 1973 the seller, Kearney & Trecker, filed suit for the balance. The buyer, Fargo Machine & Tool Company, **counterclaimed** by asserting that they wished to revoke their acceptance of the machine. Can the buyer revoke its acceptance?

Decision
The court held that the buyer could not revoke its acceptance but did allow the buyer to offset specified items of damage against the seller's claim for the balance.

Reasoning
The court relied on UCC section 2–608 and the requirement that a non-conformity must substantially impair the value of the goods to the buyer before revocation of acceptance will be ordered. The court stated that although the impairment in value is a subjective issue requiring the court to focus on the impairment of value to the particular buyer before the court, it is to be resolved based upon the objective facts of the case and not based upon personal beliefs of the buyer. The "facts" the court found persuasive were: (1) the buyer made a $28,000-plus payment after acceptance and had a reasonable opportunity to use the machine; (2) in the first two years of operation there was only one period when the machine went down, and there were no incidents where a work piece was defectively machined or finished late; and (3) in the nearly 5½ years that Fargo operated it, the machine was used to at least the same productive extent as is normally expected of such a machine. The court concluded that Fargo's extensive use of the machine is a clear indication that the effect of the malfunctions on the user was not substantially adverse. The court awarded the plaintiff $46,260, allowing the defendant to offset over $4,000 of damages for lost profits and repairs.

Fargo Machine & Tool Co. v. Kearney & Trecker Corp., 428 F.Supp. 364 (1977).

counterclaim
a claim asserted by the defendant against the plaintiff's claim in a civil action

In most situations where the goods do not conform to the contract, the buyer and seller, guided by their own notions of good faith action, and perhaps by the thought of doing business in the future, will attempt to work out an adjustment of the price for the non-conformity. If such an adjustment is not possible and the buyer has followed one of the courses of action just described and, further, desires a legal remedy for breach, then the buyer *must notify* the seller that it is claiming a breach of the agreement.[13] Upon breach of the sales agreement by the seller, the buyer may select one or more of the court-awarded remedies discussed next.

Buyer must notify seller of a breach.

Buyer's Resort to the Courts
Valuing the Expectation, Reliance, and Restitution Interests of the Injured Party

Money Damages. The law must attempt to compensate the non-breaching party so that it is put as close as possible to the position it would have been in had there been performance. Courts, as a general guide to awarding remedies, recognize three basic principles which are usually phrased in terms of the non-breaching party's *interests* in the transaction. They are, in order of importance, the *expectation, reliance,* and *restitution* interests.

No single legal principle will provide a guide for action in every situation involving a breaching party. However, given the general objective of compensation, the best principle to begin with is that courts should give the non-breaching party what it *expected* from the other party's performance. In some cases an award of money damages will do

---
[13] UCC 2–607(3)(a).

this, and in other cases an order to the seller to convey the goods will do this. The fundamental notion, though, is to give the buyer the *gain* that it had expected. When such a *gain* is given to the non-breaching party, a court is protecting the *expectation interest* of that party.

In some circumstances, however, a buyer may have incurred expenses in reliance upon the expected performance which exceed the gain from the particular breached performance. For example, a manufacturer of small steel products may have spent $1,000 for cement footings and supporting structures for a large steel stamping machine it ordered from the seller. Assume that the seller repudiates the contract and the buyer finds that it can purchase a similar machine for the same price it was to pay the first seller. However, the new machine required *new* cement footings, which cost another $1,000, and the old ones had to be removed at a cost of $500. This buyer incurred expenses of $1,500 in *reliance* on the first seller's promise and should be able to recover that amount even though the measurable *gain* to the buyer had there been no breach may have been less.

In a few cases the anticipated gain may be too speculative to measure and there may be no amounts expended by the non-breaching party in reliance on the breached promise, but the *breaching* party may have experienced a gain as a result of the transaction. In this case the courts will measure the amount of loss to the non-breaching party by allowing it to recover the breaching party's gain. Courts are protecting the **restitution** interest of the buyer in this instance. The best example of this measure of damage is a case in which the buyer pays $3,000 down on a $5,000 contract and there is a breach by the seller. For a number of reasons the buyer is unable to prove its gain had there been performance and cannot show damage caused by reliance on the breached promise (assume, for example, that a mountain ski resort had ordered a large snow-making machine the fall before a winter in which there were record snowfalls). Courts would order the return of the $3,000.

restitution
a legal remedy restoring one to his original position prior to the particular transaction

Buyer's Remedies in the Courts. Protecting the expectation, reliance, and restitution interests of the non-breaching party is accomplished by the law's recognizing one or more of the following remedies of the buyer: (1) the right to cover (buying substitute goods); (2) the right to sue for damages for non-delivery or repudiation; (3) the right to accept the goods and either deduct damages from the price or sue for damages resulting from the accepted goods; and (4) the right to require the seller to deliver the goods. In this section we analyze the different types of the buyer's monetary recovery (the first three listed remedies). In the next major section we analyze the fourth category of remedies, the right to the goods.

Before the buyer claims one of the first two remedies discussed below, it *must* give the breaching seller *notice that it is claiming a breach,* and it may also demand the return of any money paid the seller under the breached contract. If this money paid is not returned, it may be made part of the damage claim.

cover
to seek a substitute performance of a contract

1. The Buyer's Right to Cover (Procure Substitute Goods). One of the innovations in Article 2 is the buyer's remedy of "covering." After a breach (non-delivery of the goods) by the seller and notice to the seller that the buyer is claiming such a breach, the buyer may, in good faith and without unreasonable delay, make a reasonable purchase of goods in substitution for those due from the seller.[14] If the goods cost more than the buyer had agreed to pay, it may sue the seller for this added cost plus any incidental or consequential damages, but less any expenses saved in consequence of the seller's breach.[15] The section on "covering" was intended by the draftsmen of the Code to be the primary remedy of the buyer, but the buyer is not "forced" to cover (it may select any appropriate remedy). In the following case the buyer chose to cover.

---

[14] UCC 2–712(1).   [15] UCC 2–712(2).

Part 4: Sales and Consumer Law

Facts
The plaintiff, Owens, agreed to buy 143,500 feet of 6-inch pipe and 103,000 feet of 3-inch pipe from the defendant, Clow Corporation. The defendant did not make several deliveries on time, and the plaintiff suffered some damage as a result. When it appeared that the defendant would not be able to make future deliveries on time, the plaintiff "cancelled" the contract with Clow, bought the required pipe elsewhere for more than it was required to pay Clow, and sued Clow for the difference. Clow admitted that it could not fully perform the contract but argued that Owens was required to buy all the pipe Clow had before buying the pipe from another source. Was the defendant correct?

Decision
No. The appellate court affirmed a trial court finding in favor of the plaintiff, Owens.

Reasoning
In reviewing Owens' action in claiming a breach and covering, the court noted that whether it was reasonable for Owens to purchase elsewhere, after his agreement with Clow caused him damaging delays, was a classic jury issue. The court affirmed the charge to the jury on the law and quoted it as follows:

> . . . if you are reasonably satisfied from the evidence that defendant, Clow, . . . failed to furnish the materials as agreed or within a reasonable time, then Owens would be entitled to cancel the contract with Clow and purchase other materials from another supplier and set off the difference in cost against. . . Clow, provided such purchase was reasonably necessary and was made in good faith without any unreasonable delay.

Owens v. Clow Corporation, 491 F.2d 101, 104 (1974).

The Code provision for covering reads simply, but applying its provisions to a factual pattern may be complicated by the nature of the goods contracted for and the buyer's plans for the goods when received. Let us start with a simple example. Assume that B contracted to buy a quantity of apples for $5,000, payment due on delivery. S, seller, breaches and the buyer buys elsewhere the same quantity and quality apples for $4,500. This is one of those rare situations where there has been a breach but no **damage**. In such cases the court would award **nominal damages** of $1 to B should B desire to sue. The more realistic situation is one in which B must pay $6,000 for the same apples (or reasonable substitutes). In this case B could buy the apples and sue S for $1,000.

Now let us change from apples to a complex piece of machinery and assume that there are very few sellers of such machinery. If there is only one seller of such machinery, then B would attempt to get the machine itself (if it had been constructed) and would not have opted to cover. If there are a few sellers, good commercial practice would dictate that B get price quotes from them for the machinery. The identical machine need not be ordered, but the Code requires that the substitute be "commercially usable as a reasonable substitute under the circumstances of the particular case."[16]

Another factor (besides the nature of the goods) which complicates the calculation of monetary damages for the buyer is what the buyer intended to do with the goods. At this point we are going to emphasize a basic distinction in the types of monetary damages. This distinction is between incidental and consequential damages. The discussion below relates to *both* buyers' and sellers' money damages.

a. Incidental Damages. Obviously, the buyer should be able to recover all of its *expenses resulting from the seller's breach*. So, if there are added expenses in covering for inspection, receipt, transportation, care or custody of the goods rejected or later purchased, these may be recovered. These "reasonable expenses" associated with breach, Article 2 calls "incidental damages."[17] **Incidental damages** are essentially reliance losses and they must be *caused* by the seller's breach.

b. Consequential Damages. B, however, may have incurred an additional item of damage. If B had one contract to purchase apples for $5,000 before S breached and then made another contract to sell them for $5,800, B was *expecting* an $800 *gain* from the two transactions. This gain is an item of **consequential damages** and *may* be recovered from S so long as *S knew or had reason to know that the apples were being purchased for*

damage
loss or harm

nominal damages
the money judicially awarded to an injured party when no damage has occurred from another's wrongful conduct

incidental damages
the money judicially awarded to a non-breaching party for expenses reasonably incurred by the non-breaching party on the other party's breach

consequential damages
the money judicially awarded to an injured party for loss which the breaching party reasonably could foresee would be a result of his breach

---
[16] UCC 2–712, comment 2. [17] UCC 2–715(1).

resale at the time B and S contracted. Consequential damages are those resulting from the breach and the buyer's inability to fulfill general or particular requirements for which the goods were needed. Usually in a sales contract case, consequential damages refer to the lost gain or lost expectation of the parties.

When persons assert that they are entitled to consequential damages, they face a relatively tough matter of proof. First they must prove that it is more probable than not that the *breaching party* knew, or had reason to know, at the time the contract was formed the general or particular requirements for the goods which were not fulfilled. This is relatively easy to do where the buyer is a known "middleman" whose sole purpose for being in business is to purchase and resell goods. It is also relatively easy to do where the contract states that the goods are for resale. But what test should be applied by a court where these circumstances are not present? How much and what kind of "knowledge" must the seller possess to make it liable for consequential damages?

The majority of courts seem to be utilizing the same test announced in the classic case of *Hadley v. Baxendale*,[18] summarized by Professor Corbin in his classic treatise on contract law. He stated that a plaintiff may recover consequential damages if it can prove that "it is one that ordinarily follows the breach of such a contract in the usual course of events, or [is one] that reasonable men in the position of the parties would have foreseen as a probable result of breach."[19] The following case illustrates the proof necessary for a court award of consequential damages.

Facts
The plaintiff, Great American Music Machine, Inc., contracted with the defendant, Mid-South Record Pressing Company, to press some record albums from a tape made by Ralph Harrison, an unknown songwriter and singer. The plaintiff planned to have Harrison's records distributed and promoted and at the same time planned to raise additional capital through a public offering of its stock. On April 3, 1972 the plaintiff received the first shipment of records and, upon inspection, discovered that they were warped, pitted, and blistered and produced excessive surface noise. The plaintiff immediately contacted the defendant but was told that 8,000 of the records had already been distributed. In the meantime the plaintiff had contacted a brokerage firm to underwrite some of its stock. The brokerage firm agreed to underwrite $500,000 worth of the plaintiff's securities if it could get the Harrison record album "up and going." The plaintiff alleged that the defective pressing of the records virtually destroyed the market for Harrison's records and caused the failure of the brokerage firm to underwrite its stock. Can the plaintiff recover the capital lost from the projected underwriting as a measure of damages for the defendant's breach?

Decision
No. On the issue of the consequential damages, the court found for the defendant.

Reasoning
The court says that although there was "some mention" between the plaintiff and defendant of the stock offering, it does not appear from the proof that this matter was discussed in sufficient detail so that the defendant had *any idea* it might be held liable for the failure of the underwriting. Also, the court rejected the $500,000 claim because the proof was not sufficient to establish that the underwriting failed as a result of the defective record pressing.

Great American Music Machine, Inc. v. Mid-South Record Pressing Company, 393 F.Supp. 877 (1975).

c. Mitigation of Damages. The common law required the parties to mitigate (reduce, limit) their damages. This means that a non-breaching party had to choose a course of action upon breach which would limit rather than compound the damages. This policy of the law is continued in Article 2 in the requirement that a buyer can recover consequential damages under the general remedy of "covering" only where that consequential loss could not have been reasonably prevented by covering.[20]

---

[18] 156 Eng. Rep. 145 (Ex. 1854).

[19] A. Corbin, *Corbin on Contracts* 79 (1964), quoted in J. White and R. Summers, p. 316.

[20] UCC 2–715(2)(a).

2. The Buyer's Right to Sue for Damages for Non-delivery or Repudiation. The buyer is free to choose between the cover remedy just discussed and suit for damages for non-delivery under section 2–713.[21] It may not, however, "cover" *and* sue for damages under section 2–713.[22] Section 2–713 permits a buyer who has not accepted or received the goods to sue a repudiating seller for an amount of money determined by the difference between the market price of the goods at the time the buyer learned of the breach and the contract price, together with any incidental or consequential damages and less expenses saved. The place where market price is to be determined is the place where the goods were to be tendered; or, in cases of rejection or revocation of acceptance, at the place of arrival.[23]

Assume that on April 10, B agreed to pay $5,000 to S for a quantity of apples, "F.O.B. S's orchard" in Holland, Michigan, for delivery September 10. On August 10, S repudiates the contract. Further, assume that on August 10 the price for the same quantity and quality apples in Holland, Michigan (a noted apple-growing region) is $6,000. B may sue S for $1,000 plus any incidental or consequential damages, less expenses saved in consequence of the breach.

3. The Buyer's Right to Accept the Goods and Either Deduct Damages from the Price or Sue for Damages. As a last remedy for monetary recovery, the buyer may accept the goods and either (a) notify the seller of the breach within a reasonable time after the buyer discovers or should have discovered the breach, and recover damages for loss as well as incidental and consequential damages; or (b) notify the seller of his intention to deduct from the purchase price due to the seller the damages resulting from the seller's breach.

4. The Buyer's Right to Recovery of the Goods. The Buyer's Right to Specific Performance. Section 2–716(1) directs a court to award **specific performance** "where the goods are unique or in other proper circumstances." Specific performance is an order from a court decreeing that a party to a contract should perform as promised or face contempt of court charges. The old common law of contracts provided that specific performance should be decreed only where the remedy at law (usually the award of money damages) was inadequate. Recall that contracts for the sale of land were assumed to be contracts of such a special type that the remedy at law was deemed inadequate and specific performance was awarded in almost every case.

Contracts for the sale of priceless works of art or heirlooms were, at common law, and remain under Article 2, appropriate cases for the award of specific performance.[24] However, the drafters wanted section 2–716 to be read more broadly and they admonished that "this Article seeks to further a more liberal attitude than some courts have shown in connection with the specific performance of contracts of sale."[25] The only requirement is that the goods be "unique." Certainly this means that the goods could not be purchased in a reasonable fashion or for a reasonable price elsewhere. In the following case the court found that the circumstances merited a decree of specific performance.

Facts
The plaintiff, Mitchell-Huntley Cotton Co., agreed to buy from a group of merchant-farmers all of the cotton planted, produced, and ginned by the defendants through December 15, 1973. The plaintiff was engaged in the business of buying cotton from large commercial growers and selling and delivering it to textile mills and others. The contract was made on February 15, 1973 and the basic price to be paid for the cotton was $.30 per pound. Shortly after the contract was made, a drastic shortage of cotton developed, and the price for cotton increased to over $.80 per pound by the late summer of 1973. The defendants claimed that the contract was unenforceable since, by the terms of the contract, they could wait

---
[21] See UCC 2–712, comment 3.   [22] See UCC 2–713, comment 5.   [23] UCC 2–713(2).
[24] See UCC 2–716, comment 2.   [25] See UCC 2–716, comment 1.

Sue for damages.

Accept the goods and either deduct or sue for damages.

specific performance
the exact performance of a contract by a party as ordered by a court

until after December 15, 1973 to have their cotton ginned and were thus not required to perform. The plaintiff sued the defendants for breach of the contract and requested the court to order the defendants to specifically perform. Should the plaintiff be awarded the remedy of specific performance?

Decision
Yes. The court entered judgment for the plaintiff.

Reasoning
The court found that since the tradition and trade custom was to gin cotton promptly upon its maturity, the defendants were under an obligation of good faith performance to so gin all their cotton which matured prior to December 15, 1973. The court further found that, as of the fall of 1973, the "majority" of all cotton to be produced in the U.S. for 1973 had been sold, and that there were no merchantable grades of cotton in storage in the U.S. So, as of February 25, 1974 the court ordered the defendants to harvest their cotton, have it ginned and deliver it to the plaintiffs.

Mitchell-Huntley Cotton Co., Inc. v. Waldrep, 377 F.Supp. 1215 (1974).

Breach of the Sales Contract by the Buyer

Seller's Courses of Action without Bringing a Lawsuit

In most instances when a buyer's performance becomes doubtful, the seller's courses of action are going to depend upon an assessment of the buyer's solvency. The seller has contracted for *payment*, and potential insolvency threatens this promised performance. In many commercial transactions it is the tradition to pay sometime after receipt of the goods. Often the seller will have lost control of the goods when the seller learns of the buyer's insolvency or other breach. Therefore, we can imagine at least three courses of conduct based upon *who has the goods:* the seller, the buyer, or perhaps a third party to whom the buyer has transferred the goods. *The courses of action discussed below assume that the seller still has control of the goods*. Generally, where a seller has relinquished control of the goods, it must seek the assistance of a court order (a remedy) to regain them.

The Seller's Right to Adequate Assurance of Performance. If the seller still has the goods and if reasonable grounds for insecurity exist, then the seller may (1) suspend performance, (2) demand in writing an adequate assurance of performance, and (3) await a reply for a reasonable time, which is not over thirty days.[26] If the assurance—the reasonableness of which is to be determined according to prevailing commercial standards—is not adequate under the circumstances, then the buyer has repudiated the contract, and the seller may choose one of the remedies discussed below.[27]

The Seller's Right to Receive Cash Payment upon Discovery of the Buyer's Insolvency. If the seller should discover that the buyer is insolvent, then, even if the buyer is not required by the sales contract to pay cash, the seller may refuse delivery unless payment is made in cash. The seller may also ask for cash for goods already delivered and, if the goods are in transit, stop the delivery of them unless payment is made in cash.[28] If the buyer refuses to pay cash, it is in default. Section 2–702 also outlines one of the seller's *remedies* upon the discovery of the buyer's insolvency. It will be analyzed in the next section.

The Seller's Right to Withhold Goods and Stop Delivery of Goods in Transit or Otherwise. Where the buyer repudiates the contract before delivery, or fails to make a payment due on or before delivery, or wrongfully rejects or revokes acceptance of the goods, or becomes insolvent before its performance is due, the seller may withhold the goods.[29] If the goods are in the possession of *any* carrier or bailee, the seller may order the goods withheld when the seller discovers the buyer to be *insolvent;* in other instances

---

[26] UCC 2–609.   [27] UCC 2–609(4).   [28] UCC 2–702(1).   [29] UCC 2–703(a).

Margin notes: Demand adequate assurance of performance by the buyer. Get cash on the buyer's insolvency. Withhold the goods; regain them if they are in transit.

of breach such as a repudiation or failure *to make a payment due,* the seller may withhold or stop delivery *only* if the goods are shipped by the carload, truckload, planeload, or are in larger shipments of express or freight.[30]

On stoppage, the seller then pays the cost of transporting the goods in another direction other than to the buyer. However, if a *negotiable* bill of lading is outstanding (see chapter 16), *the carrier is not obligated to stop the goods in transit without surrender of the negotiable bill.*

Seller's Remedies in the Courts

Seller's Monetary Recovery. Some of the courses of action discussed above may be thought of as "remedies" in that they are attempts to minimize the seller's damages and thus, to a limited degree, compensate the seller. However, usually more is needed to compensate the seller. In this section we present the causes of action which a court would recognize in attempting to put the damaged seller in the same position it would have been in had there been performance. These remedies are presented in two broad classifications: the seller's right to monetary recovery; and the seller's right to reclaim the goods under certain conditions, discussed in the next section. The Code recognizes that there may be instances in which more than one remedy would be appropriate and specifically sanctions this by rejecting any doctrine requiring the seller to "elect" one remedy to the exclusion of another.[31]

In applying the remedies discussed below, courts will attempt to protect the *expectation* interest of the seller, and, where this is not adequate, the *reliance* interest and the *restitution* interest. Before focusing on these general guides to a remedy, a court must find that the buyer has defaulted. A default may be established by proving that the buyer: (1) wrongfully rejected the goods; or (2) wrongfully revoked acceptance; or (3) failed to make payment which was due on or before delivery; or (4) repudiated with respect to a part or the whole of the contract.[32] A "wrongful" rejection or a "wrongful revocation of acceptance" establishes a breach by the buyer and is proved by showing that the buyer has refused to accept or retain conforming goods properly tendered.[33] This is illustrated by the following case of a wrongful rejection by the buyer.

Facts
The plaintiff, E. H. Thrift Air Conditioning, Inc., contracted on October 13, 1967 with the defendant subcontractor, R. R. Waites Co., to construct large air ducts for installation in a Ramada Inn. The plaintiff was given the detailed plans for the air ducts and fabricated them exactly as the plans indicated. In December of 1968 the goods were received by the defendant, and a few days later the defendant informed the plaintiff that the goods could not be used because there was an error in the defendant's construction plans. The defendant said that it was shipping the goods back. The plaintiff informed the defendant that it should keep the goods, pay the price, and the plaintiff would help the defendant resell the goods. In May, 1969 the defendant shipped the goods back to the plaintiff and refused to pay for them. The plaintiff claimed that the goods conformed to the contract and brought an action for the full price. Should it recover?

Decision
Yes. The appellate court affirmed a decision for the plaintiff for the full price.

Reasoning
An agent of the defendant corporation testified that the delivered air ducts conformed in all respects to the plans given to the plaintiff. A tender by the seller of goods which conform to the contract in all respects gives rise to a positive duty on the buyer to accept and pay in accordance with the contract. If the goods conform to the contract, the buyer has no other option than to pay. A failure to do so gives rise to a *wrongful rejection,* which gives the seller immediate remedies for breach. The court allowed the plaintiff to recover the full contract price and said nothing about the plaintiff returning the goods to the defendant, purchaser. [We must assume, therefore, that their market value was zero.]

R. R. Waites Co., Inc. v. E. H. Thrift Air Conditioning, Inc., 510 S.W.2d 759 (Mo. 1974).

---

[30] UCC 2–705(1).

[31] See UCC 2–703, comment 1.

[32] UCC 2–703.

[33] See UCC 2–602, comment 3.

Resell.

1. The Seller's Right to Resell and Recover the Difference Between Resale Price and Contract Price. When the buyer wrongfully rejects or revokes acceptance or fails to make a payment due, the seller may resell the goods and, if the sale is made in good faith *and* in a commercially reasonable manner, recover the difference between the resale price and the contract price together with incidental damages, but less expenses saved.[34] In our simple example involving the sale of apples for $5,000, if we assume a breach by the buyer before delivery, and a resale price of $4,200 and an added expense of $50, the seller should be able to recover $850 from the buyer. If the apples were resold for $5,500, then the seller suffered no damage and may keep the profit.[35]

Today's commercial transactions are rarely this simple, however. Assume that the seller of the apples could prove that it had reasonable expenses of $4,200 in growing the apples and would have made a profit of $800 in the transaction. Assume further there were some apples of the seller that were not yet identified to any contract for sale at the time of breach. Therefore, the "resale" remedy would not be adequate because the purchaser of the "resale" apples would have purchased some of the unsold apples, and the seller would have made $1,600 on the two transactions ($800 on the sale to the breaching buyer and $800 from the resale buyer). So the "resale" remedy will not give the seller its expectation value where the seller has a relatively limitless inventory of goods to sell. The lost profit may be recovered under section 2–708(2). The point is that the appropriateness of section 2–706's applicability may be determined by an evaluation of the seller's potential to sell other goods on hand (its inventory) and the market conditions (could two sales really have been made?) together with the nature of the product (is it unique or standard?).

Sue for damages.

2. The Seller's Right to Sue for Damages for Nonacceptance or Repudiation. The seller may desire not to resell the goods identified to the contract and is not compelled to do so. For example, if the seller has agreed to sell apples in March but finds that, after a buyer breaches in September, it can make more money by converting the apples to applesauce or apple cider, then it may do so. In this instance, and in any instance where the buyer does not accept the goods or repudiates, the seller may sue the buyer for the difference between the market price at the time and place for tender and the unpaid contract price, together with any incidental damages but less expenses saved in consequence of the buyer's breach.[36]

If the buyer repudiates and the seller wishes to sue before the date of tender, it may do so. In this instance the market price for the goods will be determined at the time when the seller learned of the repudiation.[37]

If the measure of damages as calculated by the contract-price-minus-market-price formula is inadequate to compensate the seller for its expected gain, it may sue for the lost profits it would have made from full performance plus incidental damages.[38] The calculation of "lost profits" is usually measured by taking the seller's cost from the seller's list price or contract price. Utilization of this measure is appropriate only to put the seller in the same position it would have been in had there been performance. It cannot put the seller in a better position. For example, if a seller had constructed a machine at a cost of $7,000 and contracted to sell it for $8,000 and, following a breach by the buyer, realized $7,800 on resale of it, the seller's recovery is limited to $200 (plus incidental damages). It may not recover $1,000 unless it proves that it is more probable than not that it could have sold two machines (one to the breaching buyer and one to the resale buyer).

Sue for the contract price.

3. The Seller's Right to Sue for the Full Contract Price. The seller's right to sue for the full contract price can be viewed as a parallel remedy to the buyer's cause of action for specific performance. Like the buyer's cause of action for specific performance, this right

---

[34] UCC 2–706(1).   [35] UCC 2–706(6).   [36] UCC 2–708(1).

[37] UCC 2–723(1).   [38] UCC 2–708(2).

of the seller is limited rather substantially. It is available in only three circumstances. If the buyer has failed to pay the price as it becomes due, the seller may recover the price, together with any incidental damages, where:

a. the goods have been delivered and accepted by the buyer;[39] or
b. conforming goods were lost or damaged within a commercially reasonable time after risk of their loss has passed to the buyer;[40] or
c. the seller is unable, after a reasonable effort, to resell goods identified to the contract at a reasonable price, or the circumstances reasonably indicate that such effort will be unavailing.[41]

The Seller's Recovery of the Goods from an Insolvent Buyer. In most commercial transactions between merchants, at least three Articles of the UCC may apply. This is especially true in the common situation where a seller sells goods on credit. Depending upon the nature of the breach and the damages sought, Article 2, Sales, may control or Article 3, Commercial Paper, may control or Article 9, Secured Transactions, may control.

When a seller delivers goods and demands payment and payment is made by a check which is later dishonored, the seller may use one of the remedies provided in Article 3 and bring suit "on the check." These remedies are discussed in Part 5, Commercial Paper.

When a seller contracts to sell goods, it may agree to deliver the goods with payment in thirty, sixty, or ninety days after delivery. To protect itself, the seller may create an enforceable security interest in itself by complying with the requirements of Article 9. Such a seller is a "secured" party and may recover (upon breach of the **security agreement**) the goods delivered to the buyer by following the procedures outlined in Article 9. Article 9 is the subject of chapters 28 and 29 and will not be discussed here.

This section focuses upon "unsecured" sellers and the right to *reclaim* goods under Article 2. An unsecured seller is one who has no agreement with the buyer creating a **security interest** in the goods sold. Such a seller has merely a promise to pay for the goods delivered, either upon acceptance or sometime thereafter. *Except for instances in which the buyer is insolvent, Article 2 contains no section which gives the unsecured seller a right to reclaim the goods.*

Section 2–702(2) provides:

Where the seller discovers that the buyer has received goods on credit while insolvent he may reclaim the goods upon demand made within ten days after the receipt, but if misrepresentation of solvency has been made to the particular seller in writing within three months before delivery the ten day limitation does not apply.

The applicability of the first part of this section is limited substantially. Recall that if the seller knows of the buyer's insolvency before delivery, it may refuse to deliver unless it is paid in cash.[42] So the section above would probably apply only if the seller did not know of the buyer's insolvency upon delivery but found out within ten days of the receipt of the goods. In such a case the seller may reclaim the goods. This ten-day limitation does not apply, however, if the seller has received during the three months before delivery, in writing, a representation by the buyer that it is solvent.

It should be obvious that unsecured-credit sellers take substantial risks. Usually such sales are made only to buyers who are well known and trusted by the sellers.

Limitation of Remedies and Damages

Courts have long respected attempts by the parties to agree in advance what the damages will be upon breach. Where such a limitation is attempted in "the contract," the amount of damages stated is called **liquidated damages.** These liquidated damages will be awarded to a non-breaching party only if they are reasonable. An attempt to fix unreasonably large

Sue to get the goods.

security agreement
an agreement which creates or provides for a security interest

security interest
"an interest in personal property or fixtures which secures payment or performance of an obligation" UCC 1–201(37)

liquidated damages
the money judicially awarded in the amount as agreed to by the parties in their contract at the time it was made as reasonable compensation for damage which may be caused by the wrongful conduct of one of the parties in the future

---

[39] UCC 2–709(1)(a).   [40] UCC 2–709(1)(a).   [41] UCC 2–709(1)(b).   [42] UCC 2–702(1).

liquidated damages may be declared void as a penalty.[43] (For example, seller sold the buyer a fire detection system for $498. The contract provided that 1/3 of the contract price was to be paid in the event the buyer cancelled the contract. The day after the contract was signed, the buyer cancelled the contract before the seller did anything in respect to the work seller was to perform. The seller could not recover the 1/3 of the purchase price because, since no actual damage was suffered by the seller, the stipulated sum was unreasonably and grossly disproportionate to any real damage, and enforcing it would be a penalty against the buyer.) *The reasonableness of the amount is to be determined as of the time the contract is made.* Courts also will consider (1) the anticipated or actual harm caused by the breach; (2) the difficulties of proof of loss; and (3) the inconvenience or nonfeasibility of otherwise obtaining an adequate remedy.

Statute of Limitations

statute of limitations
a statute limiting the time in which a claim may be asserted in court; expiration bars enforcement of the claim

A **statute of limitations** exists for all areas of the law e.g., criminal law, tort law, contract law, and sales law. These statutes express a policy judgment by state legislatures that for the "efficient" administration of justice, plaintiffs should bring their claims to court as soon as it is reasonably possible to do so. They achieve this by simply stating in a "statute of limitations" that if the particular action is not commenced within a specified number of years, the action is barred; the legal cause of action is thus extinguished.

The heart of Article 2's statute of limitations in contracts for sale, section 2–725, provides:

An action for breach of any contract for sale must be commenced within four years after the cause of action has accrued. By the original agreement the parties may reduce the period of limitation to not less than one year but may not extend it.[44]

In most cases the four-year period begins to run from the date when a breach is *announced* by a party or the date the breaching party fails to perform.[45] For a breaching seller, this is the date of tender; for a breaching buyer, the date payment is due. But what happens when there is a breach of warranty after both parties have performed? The Code attempts to deal with this difficult problem by providing:

. . . A breach of warranty occurs when tender of delivery is made, . . .[46]

In the following case the court held that the statute of limitations had run on the plaintiff's claim from the time the defective machine was installed. However, the court sent the case back for trial because of the plaintiff's allegation that the defendant had fraudulently concealed the defect.

Facts
The plaintiff, Gates Rubber Company, ordered a large lead extrusion press from the defendant, USM Corporation. The press was installed in early 1964, a failure in the press occurred on July 23, 1968, and the plaintiff initiated suit on March 16, 1971. Illinois, the state in which this action was commenced (but in a federal court), had a five-year statute of limitations (states are free to change portions of the UCC from that originally proposed by the drafters). The trial court dismissed the plaintiff's claim for $67,000 for direct damage to property and $650,000 for damage caused by interruption of production schedules because the suit was not brought within five years from the date of installation. Was this decision correct?

Decision
The appellate court essentially agreed with the trial court, but remanded the case because the plaintiff did properly allege factual issues which should have been submitted to the jury.

---

[43] UCC 2–718(1).   [44] UCC 2–725(1).   [45] UCC 2–725(5).   [46] UCC 2–725(2).

Reasoning

The court noted that statutes of limitations are intended to accomplish two quite different policies. First, they are intended to protect defendants from false claims that might be difficult to disprove if brought after all relevant evidence has been lost or destroyed and witnesses have become unavailable. Second, our society has an interest in the efficient administration of commercial transactions, and therefore it is desirable to simply cut off possible liabilities at specific points in time. If goods are negligently made, the cause of action for such negligence accrues as of the date of the negligent act—this is the date of acceptance of the goods, not the date the injury occurred. In most cases, such as this one, the cause of action accrued at the time the defective press was installed. However, Illinois recognizes an exception to this rule. If a person liable in such a case fraudulently conceals the defect, then the cause of action may be commenced within five years from the date of discovery of the defect. In this case the defendants stated that the part which ultimately failed was designed for "low loading stress" when its engineers knew and had calculated that the part was actually "fairly highly stressed." The court held that this was a sufficient allegation of an intentional misrepresentation to warrant the submission of evidence to the jury, and dismissal of the plaintiff's claim without hearing evidence was error.

Gates Rubber Company v. USM Corporation, 508 F.2d 603 (1975).

Summary Statement

1. Generally, the damage remedies of buyers and sellers must attempt to put the non-breaching party in the same position it would have been in had there been full performance.
2. The courses of action of a buyer when it learns of a breach or potential breach are to:
   a. demand an adequate assurance of performance if the goods have not been delivered; or
   b. reject non-conforming goods; or
   c. accept the goods; or
   d. revoke acceptance of a lot or commercial unit whose non-conformity substantially impairs its value to the buyer; and
   e. *in all cases,* if the buyer wishes to pursue its legal remedies for damages, it must notify the seller that it is claiming a breach of the agreement.
3. In awarding damages to a non-breaching party, a court will attempt to protect the party's expectation, reliance, or restitution interests.
4. The buyer's possible remedies for breach of the sales agreement by the seller are:
   a. the right to cover; or
   b. the right to sue for damages for non-delivery or repudiation; or
   c. the right to accept the goods and either deduct damages from the price or sue for damages resulting from the accepted goods; or
   d. the right to require the seller to convey the goods contracted for (specific performance); or
   e. the right to the goods when the seller becomes insolvent and replevin.
5. Incidental damages are money amounts awarded by a court for *expenses* reasonably *incurred* by the non-breaching party; consequential damages are money amounts awarded by a court for loss which a breaching party reasonably could *foresee* would result from its breach.
6. The courses of action of a seller when it learns of a potential breach or a breach are to:
   a. demand an adequate assurance of performance;
   b. demand and receive cash payment upon the discovery of the buyer's insolvency;
   c. withhold the goods or stop delivery of goods in transit.

7. The seller's possible remedies for breach of the sales agreement by the buyer are:
    a. the right to resell the goods and recover the difference between the resale price and the contract price; but, if this is inadequate, to put the seller in as good a position as performance would have; then the measure of damages is the profit which the seller would have made from full performance by the buyer together with any incidental damages; or
    b. the right to sue the buyer for damages for nonacceptance or repudiation; or
    c. the right to sue for the full contract price; or
    d. the right to recover the goods from an insolvent buyer.
8. The buyer and seller may, in their agreement, limit the remedies available to the other party and the damages they may be liable for. Such limitations are enforceable so long as they are reasonable.
9. An action for breach of any contract for sale must be commenced within four years after the cause of action has accrued.
10. The time when a breach of warranty occurs is when tender of delivery is made, except that where a warranty explicitly extends to future performance, and discovery of the breach must await the time of such performance, the cause of action accrues when the breach is or should have been discovered.

In the following case involving two large corporations, the court first examined the nature of a "requirements contract" and then passed judgment on the claim for specific performance and the defense of commercial impracticability. This case will serve as a reminder that commercial contracts are intended to shift risks and one party cannot escape a contractual obligation merely because it becomes unprofitable.

Eastern Air Lines, Inc. v. Gulf Oil Corporation
415 F.Supp. 429 (1975)

King, J. The plaintiff, Eastern Air Lines, Inc. (Eastern), had been purchasing some of its aviation fuel in the south from the defendant, Gulf Oil Corporation (Gulf), for over thirty years. On June 27, 1972 Eastern and Gulf agreed that Gulf would furnish jet fuel to Eastern at certain specific cities in the Eastern system until January 31, 1977. The contract was one of Gulf's "standard form aviation fuel contracts," which was similar to contracts in general use in the aviation fuel trade. It was signed after "substantial arm's length negotiation" between the parties and considered to be favorable to both. The agreement was a "requirements contract," which provided Eastern the opportunity to demand and receive aviation fuel as their requirements dictated at the various sites. Eastern gave up the right to buy fuel from other suppliers at these locations. The "requirements" agreement provided Gulf with a long-term outlet for their jet fuel, which was needed because of the construction of a new refinery. Gulf had to be prepared to supply Eastern's reasonable good faith demands at these locations. The price of the fuel was to be set according to an indicator which was directly dependent upon the price of *domestic* crude oil. Both parties knew at the time of contract negotiations that increases in crude oil prices would be expected and were "a way of life."

The major Arabian countries producing oil (OPEC) increased their crude oil prices 400 percent between September 1973 and January 1974. The price of a portion of the U.S. domestic production also increased by this amount, but much of the domestic production was covered by a U.S. government pricing system which kept the price relatively low. The contract price of the Eastern-Gulf agreement was set by the government pricing system. As the price of aviation fuel began to climb dramatically, Eastern began buying more and more fuel from Gulf. In a requirements contract there almost always is a large measure of discretion exercised by the purchaser. In this case Eastern could fill its planes from several different suppliers, each at a different location. As the terms of the Gulf agreement became more favorable to Eastern, it ordered that more of its planes fill up at the cities served by Gulf. This practice was called "fuel freighting."

On March 8, 1974 Gulf informed Eastern that it was increasing its price for aviation fuel beyond that provided for by the price indicator in their agreement, and that if Eastern would not agree to this, Gulf would shut off Eastern's supply of jet fuel within fifteen days. Eastern responded by filing a complaint in court alleging that Gulf had breached its contract and requesting the court to enter an order of specific performance. Gulf replied by arguing three major points. (1) Eastern's practice of fuel freighting was not performance in good faith and was a breach of the agreement. (2) If the court found against it on the first point, then Gulf argued that the agreement was unenforceable because it had become commercially impracticable within the meaning of the UCC. (3) An order for specific performance was not appropriate.

The court stated that the UCC specifically approves requirements contracts. Section 2–306 (1) states:

> A term which measures the quantity by the output of the seller [called an "output" contract] or the requirements of the buyer [called a "requirements" contract] means such actual output or requirements as may occur in good faith, except that no quantity unreasonably disproportionate to any stated estimate or in the absence of a stated estimate to any normal or otherwise comparable prior output or requirements may be tendered or demanded.

Was Eastern's practice of "fuel freighting" performance in good faith? The court found that it was because it was consistent with established commercial practice. The fuel taken on by a plane depends upon the price, the weather, schedule changes, aircraft load, ground time, and many other factors. The court found these factors have been known to oil companies and have been taken into account by them in drafting their fuel contracts. "Fuel freighting" is an established industry practice inherent in the nature of the business and is not performance in bad faith.

The court responded to Gulf's second argument by pointing out that the UCC states that increases in price alone do not excuse performance unless the rise in cost is due to some unforeseen contingency which alters the essential nature of the performance. Both parties knew that the price of fuel was going to rise, and they agreed on a formula to account for this. The court used these words to find for Eastern on this issue:

> *We will not allow a party to a contract to escape a bad bargain merely because it is burdensome.* The buyer has a right to rely on the party to the contract to supply him with goods regardless of what happens to the market price. That is the purpose for which such contracts are made. [Emphasis added.]

In addition, the court stated that it could not approve the defense of commercial impracticability where Gulf had tendered no evidence on how much it cost Gulf to produce jet fuel. For all the court knew from the evidence, Gulf might still be selling jet fuel to Eastern at a profit. Indeed, the court noted that in 1973, the year in which the "energy crisis" began, Gulf had its best year ever, recording $800 million in net profits after taxes.

Finally, the court awarded specific performance to Eastern because the UCC directed courts to take a more liberal attitude toward this remedy. A party was no longer required to prove that the money damage remedy would be inadequate. In this case the issues were squarely framed and clearly resolved in Eastern's favor, and it would be a "vain, useless and potentially harmful exercise" to declare that Eastern had a valid contract but then leave it to bring another suit to determine its past and future damages.

The court found in favor of Eastern and entered an order for specific performance of the agreement.

Questions and Case Problems

1. B, buyer, has just received a large metal-working machine from S, seller. B has visually inspected the machine but it will not be ready for operation until it is installed. If B detects a defect in the machine upon visual inspection at the time of installation (assume that there is a crack in the metal casing), what should B do? If B installs the machine and it does not appear to work properly, what may B attempt to do? In what circumstances will B be successful in choosing a course of action?

2. In question 1 above, assume that B lost twenty days' production because the machine did not function properly. In what circumstances may B recover consequential damages?

3. If B, buyer, buys from S, seller, ten dozen electronic staplers for B's business-supply company to resell, and S phones B before delivery that it will not perform, carefully describe at least two of the remedies available to B.
    a. In what circumstances can B "force" S to deliver the staplers?
    b. Assume that B properly accepted the staplers once they were delivered but discovered later that they were defective. What is the measure of B's damages?

4. S, seller, has contracted with B, buyer, to sell 100 finished picture frames of various sizes and made from various kinds of rare hardwood. Describe the courses of conduct and/or remedies of S in each of the circumstances below:
    a. S has received word that B is insolvent.
    b. S has completed some and has shipped some (which are in the possession of a carrier) when it is informed by B that B is repudiating the contract.
    c. S can prove that it would have spent $2,500 to make the frames, and the contract price was $3,700. In what circumstances may it recover the lost profit?

5. M, manufacturer, manufactures small tent-campers. These are nothing but aluminum boxes placed on wheels and towed by car owners. When the owners wish to stop and camp, they unfold a tent which springs up from the aluminum box. M contracted to sell fifteen of these units for $800 each to R, retailer. M produced the units for $675 each and usually kept such a large supply of these tent-campers on hand that it could fill any order. Five days before M was to deliver the tent-campers, R telephoned M and explained that it was having trouble moving its inventory and was "reconsidering" its order.
    a. What should M do?
    b. On the date for M's performance, it tenders the goods and R refuses, saying that it is "cancelling" the order. What are M's remedies and measures of damage?
    c. Assume that M resells the very tent-camper units it had identified for the contract with R for $800 each. Has M suffered any damage? If so, what amount?

6. Burk, seller, contracted to sell about 950 head of yearling steers to Emmick, buyer. The steers were delivered and payment was made by a negotiable instrument that was dishonored when it was presented to the buyer's bank. Burk reclaimed the cattle and then resold them for less than the contract price. Burk sues Emmick for the difference between the contract price and the resale price. The buyer argues that once the cattle were reclaimed, the seller was in as good a position as it had been before the contract so the seller was not entitled to a money judgment in addition to reclaiming the cattle. What is your response to this argument? Explain your answer in detail. [*Burk v. Emmick,* 637 F.2d 1172, (8th Cir., 1980).]

7. S agreed to manufacture and deliver twelve snowmobiles to P on November 1, 1974. They were delivered on that date, inspected, and paid for by P. On the packaging, in the sales contract, and in the instructions for the snowmobiles, S stated that it would warrant that the snowmobiles would perform properly for one year from the date of delivery to P. In December 1974 P sold three of the snowmobiles to A, B, and C, individually, who received the same warranty from S. The snowmobiles of A, B, and C all malfunctioned, and S denied any liability. A filed a lawsuit against S on October 30, 1978, B filed suit exactly one year later, and C filed one year after that (October 30, 1980). Can these legal actions be maintained? Why or why not?

8. For purposes of review, this question and the one that follows contain some fundamental legal issues discussed in chapters 17–19.
    W, an oil well drilling company, contracted with S, a southwest oil company, to explore a small region of Texas for oil formations and to drill if the formations appeared to be of the type that might yield oil. The "contract" which was made was oral and provided that W would be paid expenses for exploring, would be paid $10 per foot for drilling, and would be paid what it cost W for the piping needed. W and S were to share the profits if any oil was found. W explored for oil for three weeks and found a promising location and began drilling. After it had been drilling for a week and reached a depth of 500 feet, S informed W that as far as it was concerned no contract was ever formed and it did not intend to pay W for exploration and drilling expenses. W had received several letters from S during the one month of its operation referring to their agreement. What legal problems does W have?

9. The L Corporation was engaged in the business of building lobster boats. The Maine Lobstermens' Cooperative Association, Inc. (M) ordered three lobster boats from L. M's order form stated a price of $50,000 per boat, a delivery date of April 1, 1980, and other technical information relating to the specifications and performance capabilities of the boats. L's acknowledgment form agreed in all important particulars with M's except that printed on it in large letters were the words "The parties hereby expressly agree that L will not be liable for consequential damages." Agents of M had signed L's form and returned a copy of it to M. The boats were delivered on time and, during one of the first voyages of one of the boats, the engine malfunctioned because it was not properly installed in the boat. It was out of line, and the shaft and bearing overheated and broke. The boat was swept upon the rocks and destroyed. Miraculously, the crew of the boat was saved, but there were injuries. M sued L for the value of the destroyed boat, and the injured crew sued for their injuries. What arguments would you expect from L, and do you think they will be successful?

10. In the case of *Eastern Air Lines, Inc. v. Gulf Oil Corporation,* 415 F.Supp. 429 (1975),[47] why was the court reluctant to consider the commercial impractability defense of Gulf? Why was an order for specific performance more appropriate than a remedy for money damages?

---

[47] See pp. 304–5.

21 Consumer Law
A. A Seller's Warranties, Their Waiver, Modification, and Breach

After you have read this chapter, you should be able to:

1. Define the various possible types of warranty which can be made by a seller in a sales transaction and list the elements of each or the conditions in which each is made.
2. Describe the circumstances in which each of the warranties made by a seller or merchant may be excluded or modified.
3. Outline the main purpose and the major provisions of the Magnuson-Moss Warranty Act.
4. Write a paragraph explaining the reasons for the doctrine of unconscionability and then describe the circumstances in which this legal principle is usually applied.
5. Make a list of all the major defenses which can be asserted by a manufacturer in a case by an injured consumer-plaintiff based on a breach of warranty, and briefly describe each.
6. Explain horizontal and vertical privity.

Introduction

In this chapter, we shift our focus from the situation in which a merchant contracts with a merchant to *a merchant contracting with a consumer*. The word "merchant" has already been defined, but we give the Code definition, in part, here because it is important to the subject of this chapter. A merchant is any seller

who deals in goods of the kind [sold] or otherwise by his occupation holds himself out as having knowledge or skill peculiar to the practices or goods involved in the transaction. . . .[1]

A **consumer** is a person who buys goods for use primarily for personal, family, or household purposes.[2] In short, a merchant is a person who is in business to sell goods or leads others to believe it has special knowledge about the goods sold, and a consumer is the one who buys goods for use (but not for resale).

A key to understanding the legal principles used today to resolve a merchant-consumer dispute is to realize that this transaction is probably evidenced by a form contract drafted by the merchant-seller. We emphasized in this Part that *consumers no longer bargain in the traditional sense*. They may choose from a limited variety of alternatives offered by a few merchant-sellers, but when it comes time to transact the sale, the terms are spelled out by the seller on its form, drafted, we must assume, to benefit it. This reality aids us in understanding why some of the consumer remedies discussed in the next chapter grew from *outside* contract law.

Today the words "consumer law" denote a wide variety of consumer remedies based upon state and federal statutory law and common law. These remedies may be divided into two broad categories depending upon the circumstances of the case and the nature of the damage suffered by the consumer. The first and probably the most important category of consumer remedies are those available to a consumer who suffers economic loss or personal **injury** caused by a *defective product*. The second category of remedies are those available to a consumer who suffers economic loss caused by an *illegal credit transaction*.

The remedies available to a consumer for economic loss or personal injury caused by a defective product may be divided into three very broad classifications. *First,* there are those remedies based upon a suit for a *breach of warranty* (a promise, either expressed or implied) made in the sales transaction. Since the topic of the creation of warranties, their waiver, modification and breach is important to any discussion of sales law, *we have devoted this entire chapter to this topic.* Please do not forget, though, that *this discussion of warranties applies to both merchant-consumer transactions and merchant-merchant transactions.*

A *second* category of remedies, a category becoming very important, if not already the most important area of law when one discusses consumer law, is that of the **tort remedies** for negligent manufacture and negligent design of products plus the tort remedy based on the theory of strict liability. *These tort remedies,* together with a third category of remedies, namely those created by *state and federal law,* are the subject of the *following chapter 22.*

In a particular circumstance, an injured consumer-plaintiff may argue theories of relief from *all* of the categories just mentioned. There is no inconsistency in arguing that, for example, liability may be based upon one or more of the warranties provided for in Article 2 of the UCC, upon negligent design, and also upon strict liability. The circumstances will usually favor one theory over another, however. We will explain these circumstances in the sections that follow.

---

[1] UCC 2-104(1).   [2] UCC 9-109(1).

---

consumer
a person who buys goods for use primarily for personal, family, or household purposes

injury
the wrongful invasion of another person's interest

tort
a civil (private) noncontractual wrong for which a court will give a remedy

The Warranties of Article 2 of the UCC

There are three classifications of **warranties** made by sellers or merchants; they are express warranties, implied warranties, and warranties of title and against infringement of **patent** or **copyright**.[3] Express and implied warranties are much more significant than warranties of title and against infringement, so they will be analyzed first.

Express Warranties

A seller makes **express warranties** by:

a) Any affirmation of fact or promise made . . . to the buyer which relates to the goods and becomes part of the basis of the bargain. . . .
b) Any description of the goods which is made part of the basis of the bargain. . . .
c) Any sample or model which is made part of the basis of the bargain. . . .[4]

This warranty must, simply put, be *expressed*—that is, *outwardly stated*—by the seller as an affirmation of fact or promise, or by the seller's providing a description, model, or sample. It is not necessary that the words "warrant" or "guarantee" be used or that the seller have an intention to make a warranty.[5]

The expression which the seller must make may be found in the sales agreement, in advertising, in plans or instructions furnished with the goods, in packaging, or may be made orally. This expression, however, must be more than a statement of opinion. The statement that "this car is tuned like an orchestra and will provide good service and will get 32 miles per gallon when driven at 50 miles per hour" contains just one expressed warranty—the mileage-per-gallon phrase. However, sometimes the distinction is hard to make. Consider these assertions made by a merchant in an actual case: (1) the parts are of high quality; (2) experiences and testing have shown that the frequency of repairs was very low and would remain so; (3) the purchase of machines by the buyer and leasing of them to customers would return a substantial profit to the buyer; (4) replacement parts are readily available; and (5) the goods sold will not cause fires, and the machines have been tested and they are ready. The court held only the fourth and fifth assertions were statements of fact.[6]

The opinion portion of an assertion made by a seller is labeled "puffing" by the courts and creates no liability for the seller. One of the vestiges of the doctrine of caveat emptor is that a buyer should be able to tell the difference between fact and opinion and is allowed to rely only on the former.

Section 2–313 also requires that the statement of the seller creating the express warranty become part of the *basis of the bargain*. The comments to section 2–313 state that "no particular reliance on such statements (affirmations of fact) need be shown in order to weave them into the fabric of the agreement."[7] In all probability, in a case involving a consumer plaintiff and a merchant defendant, all the plaintiff need do is allege that it relied on an express warranty in making a purchase, and this should be sufficient to submit the issue of the existence of the express warranty to the jury.[8]

---

warranty
an express or implied assurance that certain facts exist; (in sales of goods) generally, an affirmation of fact or an express promise made by a seller or manufacturer of goods, or a promise implied in a sales transaction by law, that the goods sold are of a certain quality or will perform in a certain manner

patent
a governmental grant of protection of an invention

copyright
a governmental grant of protection of original works in a tangible medium of expression

express warranty
a warranty expressed by a party

---

[3] For a discussion of patents and copyrights see pp. 851, 856.

[4] UCC 2–313(1). [5] UCC 2–313(2).

[6] *Royal Business Machines, Inc. v. Lorraine Corp.*, 633 F.2d 34 at 41–42 (1980).

[7] UCC 2–313, comment 3.   [8] R. J. Nordstrom, *Law of Sales* p. 204 (1970).

Implied Warranties

Implied warranties are those imposed on a sales transaction by statute or court decision. If certain circumstances exist, there is a tradition in our legal system which compels courts to assert that a seller has made implied warranties *whether the seller intended them or not*. Given this broad definition of implied warranties, one may conclude that Article 2 creates three classes of implied warranties: those of merchantability, fitness for a particular purpose, and title. The last warranty is not traditionally thought of as an implied warranty, nor is it labeled as such in Article 2, so it is explained in a separate section.

Implied Warranty of Merchantability. This warranty, imposed on all *merchants,* implies a promise by the selling merchant that the goods are *fit for the ordinary purposes for which such goods are used*.[9] This warranty may be excluded or modified by the agreement as discussed in a section below.

If a consumer buys a TV set, a camera, a washing machine, an auto, or whatever from a merchant, there is imposed on the sales transaction, unless waived or modified, a warranty that the goods are of a quality comparable to that generally acceptable in that line of trade. Certainly the goods must perform for the purposes for which they were intended. A TV set must show a picture, a camera must take a picture, etc. Under Article 2, section 2–314(1), "the serving for value of food or drink to be consumed either on the premises or elsewhere is a sale."

Implied Warranty of Fitness for a Particular Purpose. Section 2–315 states:

> Where the seller at the time of contracting has reason to know any particular purpose for which the goods are required and that the buyer is relying on the seller's skill or judgment to select or furnish suitable goods, there is unless excluded or modified . . . an implied warranty that the goods shall be fit for such purpose.

This implied warranty is imposed on *any seller* (not just merchants) but requires two elements of proof: (1) that the seller *knew the particular purpose* for which the goods were bought, and (2) the buyer *relied* on the seller to select the goods. *Actual* knowledge of the particular purpose is not required so long as the circumstances of the purchase are such that the seller *should* have reason to know the purpose.[10] For example, a consumer may hire a heating and cooling firm to air-condition his or her home to 75 degrees during the summer months. If the equipment fails to cool the home as provided in the contract, then this warranty is breached. Note that the air-conditioning system installed may work properly and therefore be "merchantable" but does not fulfill the particular purpose for which it was purchased.

Also, this implied warranty is significant in a large commercial transaction between merchants when the buyer submits some rough plans or basic specifications and relies on the seller to design and then manufacture an item. In the following case the two elements necessary for an implied warranty of fitness for a particular purpose were present.

Facts

The plaintiff, Michael Catania, entered the defendant's retail paint business and asked the defendant to recommend a paint to cover the exterior stucco walls of the plaintiff's house. The defendant was told that the stucco was in a "chalky" and "powdery" condition. The defendant advised the plaintiff to "wire brush" any loose particles which were "flaky" or "scaly" before applying any paint. The defendant recommended and sold to the plaintiff a paint known as Pierce's shingle and shake paint and told him to mix two or three gallons of the paint in a container and to add a thinner. The plaintiff followed the instructions, and five months after the date of the purchase, the paint on the exterior walls of the plaintiff's house began to peel, flake, and blister. Did an implied warranty of fitness for a particular purpose exist?

---

[9] UCC 2–314(2)(c).   [10] See UCC 2–315, comment 1.

Decision

Yes. The appellate court affirmed a decision by the trial court that such a warranty existed.

Reasoning

In creating an implied warranty of fitness for a particular purpose, the court acknowledged that two requirements must be met: (a) the buyer must rely on the seller's skill or judgment to select or furnish suitable goods; and (b) the seller at the time of contracting must have reason to know the buyer's purpose. In every case it is a matter of fact whether these requirements are met. In this case the jury found that these facts existed, so a decision in the plaintiff's favor was proper.

Catania v. Brown, 231 A.2d 668 (Conn. 1967).

One factual pattern or circumstance may create all three of the warranties discussed thus far. If a buyer informs a seller of a purpose for the purchased goods and relies on the seller to select it and the seller goes on to say, "These goods will fit your needs," or similar language, the statement may be an express warranty.[11] If the intended use of the goods was an *ordinary* use of the goods and the product failed to operate for this use, both the express warranty and the warranty of merchantability may have been breached. If the intended use was not an "ordinary" one and the product failed to perform, then a breach of the warranty of fitness may be argued.

Warranty of Title

When a seller contracts to sell goods, Article 2 provides that there is a warranty that the title to the goods shall be good and its transfer rightful and that the goods shall be delivered free from any security interest or other **encumbrance** of which the buyer at the time of contracting has no knowledge.[12] This provision requires the seller to defend any lawsuit against the purchaser that involves claims of ownership of the goods sold. The seller must also defend against any claims that it, the seller, infringed any patent or trademark in producing or selling the goods if it is a dealer in those goods.[13]

Exclusion or Modification of Warranties and Limitation of Damages for Breach of Warranty

Perhaps the most fundamental notion in American contract law is that there should be "freedom of contract." Generally, this means that the parties to a contract should be free to work out the terms of their agreement and courts should not interfere with the bargaining process or the terms of the contract. The function of courts should be to enforce the parties' contractual intent! As we have seen, ascertaining that intent is not always an easy task. However, if the parties intend, as evidenced by their written agreement or otherwise, to waive warranties implied by Article 2, then courts should enforce this intent unless the waiver violates the Magnuson-Moss Warranty Act described below. One place we find this freedom-of-contract notion in Article 2 is in section 2–316, which permits the parties to exclude altogether or modify the warranties just explained above.

Express warranties are supposed to arise from the negotiated or dickered terms of the parties. Words or conduct which create express warranties and words or conduct tending to limit such warranties are to be construed as consistent with one another. When the words or conduct of limitation are *unreasonable,* they are *inoperative* as a waiver of modification.[14] In short, any attempt by a seller to first make an express warranty and then later deny making it should be labeled as unreasonable conduct and will be inoperative. The way around this for the merchant is, of course, to make no express warranties but to rely on the seller's right to "puff" to make a sale.

---

[11] R. J. Nordstrom, p. 243.

[12] UCC 2–312.

[13] See UCC 2–312, comment 3.

[14] UCC 2–316(1).

Title.

encumbrance
a person's right in another person's property

Exclusion, modification, limitation of damages for breach.

The *implied warranty of merchantability* may be excluded or modified by a writing that uses conspicuous language and mentions the word "merchantability."[15] Language is conspicuous if it is so written that a reasonable person against whom it is to operate ought to have noticed it. If the language is in the text of a form contract, it is conspicuous if it is in larger or contrasting type or color.[16]

The implied *warranty of fitness for a particular purpose* may be waived or modified (1) by a writing and (2) by conspicuous language of waiver or modification in the writing. This warranty may be waived by, for example, conspicuous language which states that "there are no warranties which extend beyond the description on the face hereof."[17]

In addition, both implied warranties may be excluded if the goods are said to be sold "as is" or "with all faults" or if other language calls the buyer's attention to the exclusion of warranties and makes plain that there is no implied warranty.[18] Also, when the buyer has examined the goods *before* entering into the contract or has refused the seller's demand to examine the goods if given an opportunity, there is no implied warranty with regard to defects which such an examination ought (in the circumstances) to have revealed.[19] In some cases where the intent of the parties is not clear,[20] course of dealing or course of performance or usage of trade may result in a waiver or modification of an implied warranty.[21]

The *warranty of title* may be excluded or modified by specific language of waiver or modification or by circumstances which give the buyer reason to know that the person selling does not claim title.[22]

There can be no doubt that the sections of Article 2 providing for waiver or modification of warranties are powerful and significant when a merchant sells to a consumer. When merchants deal with one another, the warranty provisions in the sales contract, or the attempted waiver or modification of implied warranties, will be the subject of close scrutiny and negotiation. But when *you* as a consumer make a purchase from a merchant, how often do you read the seller's agreement for warranty provisions? If you did read the agreement, what would you find? And if you found conspicuous language which waived or modified the implied warranties, what could you do about it?

Consider, for example, the warranty and limitation of damages provided for on the package of Sears "Early One" Smoke and Fire Detector. This is a typical smoke and fire alarm which sells for under $20 and is intended for home installation. On the box there is the language:

FULL ONE YEAR WARRANTY ON SMOKE DETECTOR
For one year from the date of purchase, Sears will repair or replace this smoke detector free of charge, if defective in material or workmanship. This warranty shall not apply to the batteries, which are expendable. To obtain warranty service, simply return the smoke detector to your nearest Sears store throughout the United States.

In heavy black letters there follows this language:

LIMITATION ON LIABILITY
Sears will not be liable for loss or damage to property or any incidental or consequential loss or expense from property damage due directly or indirectly to occurrences which the smoke detector is designed to detect.

---

[15] UCC 2–316(2).   [16] UCC 1–201(10).   [17] UCC 2–316(2).
[18] UCC 2–316(3)(a).   [19] UCC 2–316(3)(b).   [20] R. J. Nordstrom, p. 271.
[21] UCC 2–316(3)(c).   [22] UCC 2–312(2).

Sears makes a rather generous warranty on the detector! But what would happen if the alarm failed to operate and, as a result, a home was destroyed by fire and, in addition, persons suffered injury? Damage to the property and persons in this case would be consequential damage, and a court would have to judge whether the limitation on the damages found on the box and other sales material was effective. In some states there are statutes prohibiting this, or courts have held that such a limitation is "unconscionable" and have not enforced the limitation provision. Sears does note this on the box by adding:

> Some states do not allow the exclusion or limitation of incidental or consequential damages, so the . . . limitation or exclusion may not apply to you.

The law has responded in at least two ways to aid consumers when there has been a breach of an alleged warranty and an attempted waiver of it. Congress passed legislation to help consumers cope with warranty abuse, and the courts expanded the definition of unconscionability to apply to warranty waivers and exclusions. We will first explain the federal legislation.

Federal legislation.

The Consumer Product Warranty and Federal Trade Commission Improvement Act (Also Called the Magnuson-Moss Warranty–Federal Trade Commission Improvement Act)

This Act,[23] which became law on July 4, 1975, was prompted in part because *consumers were dissatisfied with their "protection" afforded by the UCC warranties.* "Warranty abuse" was a phenomenon substantiated in 1974 when a congressional subcommittee reviewed 200 warranties from 51 major companies and found only one which offered a warranty free of ambiguous phrases, exemptions, and disclaimers.[24] This Act seeks to make warranty enforcement a reality by *providing to the consumer the information needed to pursue a claim for a breach.* The Act does not alter the warranties of merchantability or fitness for a particular purpose nor does *the Act compel a merchant to make a warranty.*

The general provisions of the Act do apply when a *written* warranty is made *and* the cost of the item purchased exceeds $15. The one who makes a warranty (called a "warrantor") is required by the Act to fully and conspicuously disclose the terms and limitations of the warranty to the consumer *before* the sale. Some of the items which warrantors should disclose are:

1. The names and addresses of the warrantors,
2. The product or parts covered, and
3. A statement of what the warrantor will do upon breach of the warranty, at whose expense the work will be done, and the period of time the warranty will last.

Perhaps the most significant provision of the Act limits the use of written warranties to disclaim the implied warranties created in a sales transaction by the UCC. As we stated in the previous section, Article 2 provides for the creation of implied warranties and it also provides for their exclusion or modification under certain circumstances. Merchants did take advantage of the waiver and modification provisions. Very generally, this conduct prompted passage of the Act under discussion which does supercede the UCC in this area of waiver and modification of implied warranties. Under this Act, a supplier *may not disclaim or modify implied warranties if* the supplier makes *any written warranty or* if the supplier either at the time of sale or within 90 days thereafter enters into *a service contract* with the consumer.

---

[23] 15 U.S.C.A. sec. 2301 et seq.

[24] W. Haemmel, B. George, and J. Bliss, *Consumer Law* (St. Paul: West Pub. Co., 1975), p. 285.

The Unconscionable Contract or Clause

Certainly the most potent weapon a consumer plaintiff has to support an assertion that a clause of a contract or an entire contract with a merchant is basically unfair is section 2–302. It provides:

If the court as a matter of law finds the contract or any clause of the contract to have been unconscionable at the time it was made the court may refuse to enforce the contract, or it may enforce the remainder of the contract without the unconscionable clause, or it may so limit the application of any unconscionable clause as to avoid any unconscionable result.[25]

This section gives the judge, not the jury, the right to "police" sales contracts for fundamental fairness. According to one legal scholar, what Karl Llewellyn had in mind when he first drafted section 2–302 was the development of an open and direct attack upon one-sided, unbargained-for, small-print clauses in standardized form contracts.[26]

The official Comments to this section state that the basic test or definition is whether "in the light of the general commercial background and the commercial needs of the particular trade or case, the clauses involved are so one-sided as to be unconscionable under the circumstances existing at the time of the making of the contract."[27] Section 2–719(3) provides that limitation in a contract "of consequential damages for injury to the person in the case of consumer goods is prima facie unconscionable."

We can best understand the notion of unconscionability by reexamining how courts respond to what could be labeled "unfair" sales agreements between a merchant seller and a merchant buyer on the one hand, and a merchant seller and a consumer on the other hand.

A sales agreement between merchants is intended to shift certain business risks. If a court is convinced that the merchants "bargained" for the provisions of the sales agreement, the provisions will be enforced even if the result is to cause severe economic loss.

Almost all instances in which there has been a successful assertion at the appellate level that a contract or clause of a contract is unconscionable involve *consumers and merchants* as the two parties.[28] The following case is such a successful assertion. This case is a classic example of how the courts use the principle of unconscionability to protect consumers against those merchants who are overzealous in their use of standard form contracts.

> Unconscionability.
>
> **unconscionable contract**
> a contract in which one of the parties is in too unequal or one-sided a bargaining position at the time the contract is made

Facts

Mr. Henningsen purchased a new Plymouth automobile from Bloomfield Motors, Inc., as a Mother's Day gift for his wife. Ten days after getting the car, Mrs. Henningsen was driving when she heard a "crack" under the hood of the car, the steering wheel spun in her hands and the car veered 90 degrees from its path into a brick wall. The car, with 468 miles on it, was totally destroyed and Mrs. Henningsen was injured. Mr. and Mrs. Henningsen sued Bloomfield Motors, Inc., and Chrysler Corporation, manufacturer of Plymouths, for personal and property damage based, among other things, on a breach of warranty theory.

The purchase order signed by Mr. Henningsen contained this language (in part):

The manufacturer warrants each new motor vehicle . . . chassis or parts . . . to be free from defects in material or workmanship under normal use and service. Its obligation under this warranty being limited to making good at its factory any part or parts thereof which shall within ninety (90) days after delivery . . . or before such vehicle has been driven 4,000 miles, whichever event shall first occur, be returned to it with transportation charges prepaid and which its examination shall disclose to its satisfaction to have been thus defective; this warranty being expressly in lieu of all other warranties expressed or implied and all other obligations or liabilities on its part. . . .

The defendants argued that the last clause of the above "warranty" barred the plaintiff, Mrs. Henningsen, from asserting a claim for personal injuries. The jury returned a verdict

---

[25] UCC 2–302(1).

[26] W. Zelermyer, *The Unconscionable Contract,* a paper read at the American Business Law Association Annual Meeting, College Park, Maryland, August 18, 1978.

[27] UCC 2–302, comment 1.   [28] J. White and R. Summers, *Uniform Commercial Code,* p. 114 (1972).

for the plaintiffs and the defendants appealed. Should the "warranty" language apparently modifying or limiting the plaintiffs' right to sue for personal injuries be a bar to the plaintiffs' claim?

Decision
No. The appellate court agreed with the trial court and affirmed the verdict for the plaintiffs.

Reasoning
The court said that the terms of the warranty are a "sad commentary" upon the automobile manufacturers' marketing practices. The manufacturer agrees to replace defective parts for 90 days or 4,000 miles, whichever occurs first, if the part is sent to the factory, transportation charges prepaid, and if examination discloses to its satisfaction that the part is defective. It is difficult to imagine a greater burden on the consumer or a less satisfactory remedy, said the court. It added that, aside from imposing on the buyer the trouble of removing and shipping the part, the manufacturer has sought to retain the uncontrolled discretion to decide the issue of defectiveness. The court called the security provided to the buyer by the warranty illusory in character and then concluded that the warranty, even though apparently agreed to by the parties, should not be enforced. It said:

The status of the automobile industry is unique. Manufacturers are few in number and strong in bargaining position. In the matter of warranties on the sales of their products, the Automotive Manufacturers Association has enrolled them to present a united front. From the standpoint of the purchaser, there can be no arms length negotiating on the subject. Because his capacity for bargaining is so grossly unequal, the inexorable conclusion which follows is that he is not permitted to bargain at all. He must take or leave the automobile on the warranty terms dictated by the maker. He cannot turn to a competitor for better security.

The attempted exclusion of all obligations except those specifically assumed by the express warranty are a studied effort to frustrate the protection given to consumers by the warranties created by law. The attempted disclaimer is so inimical to the public good as to compel an adjudication of its invalidity.

Henningsen v. Bloomfield Motors, Inc. and Chrysler Corporation, 161 A.2d 69, 94 (N.J. 1960).

The above case was decided in 1960 before the UCC was adopted in New Jersey and before the passage of the Magnuson-Moss Warranty Act. However, the court's reasoning is a classic statement of the need for the doctrine of unconscionability.

Although the above case makes clear the "policy" reasons for the doctrine of unconscionability, it does not clearly define the doctrine itself. Such a definition is difficult and varies from state to state and case to case. Generally, in finding that a contract or clause is unconscionable, courts consider these circumstances important: (1) the background of the party asserting unconscionability—such facts as age, education, economic status, etc.; (2) the "hidden" or complex nature of the language used; (3) the degree of inequality in bargaining position; and (4) the number of "meaningful choices" available to the party asserting unconscionability.

Defenses to products liability.

Privity under Article 2; Defenses to a Products Liability Claim *Based on a Breach of Warranty*

Privity under Article 2

The liability of a seller of goods for economic loss or personal injury caused by a defective product is still limited by privity in many jurisdictions today. This limitation can best be described by dividing privity issues into two major classifications: horizontal privity and vertical privity.

Horizontal Privity. Cases which involve the question of who is a *proper plaintiff* are labeled *horizontal privity cases*. These cases involve the question "to whom is the warranty made?" Typically, a consumer buys goods and either takes them home or gives them as a gift and someone else is then injured as a result of a defect. Should this injured person recover? Article 2 provides *some* guidance in answering this question with three alternative sections which may be adopted by states. The alternative adopted by most of the states provides:

A seller's warranty whether express or implied extends to any natural person who is in the family or household of his buyer or who is a guest in his home if it is reasonable to expect that such person may use, consume or be affected by the goods and who is injured in person by breach of the warranty. A seller may not exclude or limit the operation of this section.[29]

Horizontal privity, then, is a legal defense which is of varying vitality depending upon what the supreme court of the state in which the suit is brought has held on this issue.

Vertical Privity. There seems to be more agreement in state appellate decisions about *vertical privity.* This class of issues refers to which party in the chain of distribution—the manufacturer, the wholesaler, the distributor, or the retailer—is the *proper defendant* when facing a plaintiff injured by defective goods and who is relying on a breach of warranty theory. In most cases where a consumer is suing a *manufacturer,* there is no technical privity. Usually, the plaintiff is in privity only with a retailer. In most of the recent cases, the need for this privity has been discarded when a defendant higher up in the chain of distribution is sued by a consumer. There are several reasons for this. (1) It is usually the manufacturer who, through mass advertising campaigns, has created the demand for the goods, thus, it is "fair" that it be liable for injury caused by a defect. (2) If such privity were required, it might result in hardship to the plaintiff if the retailer were insolvent. (3) Requiring this technical privity would result in a multiplicity of lawsuits where the consumer sues a retailer, the retailer sues the wholesaler, etc.

Statute of Limitations and Notice of Breach of Warranties

Finally, recall that law requires that any claim for a breach of warranty be brought within, usually, four years from the date of tender of delivery (section 2–725(1)(2)) unless there is a *warranty explicitly* extending this period. Many injured plaintiffs must use a tort theory of liability because their sales-theory claim has been barred by this statute of limitations.

A closely related notion is that Article 2 imposes on a buyer the obligation to notify the seller of *any breach* within a reasonable time after it discovers or should have discovered the breach.[30] If a buyer fails to give this notice, it is barred from any remedy. This provision is applied liberally to the merchant-consumer transaction, but there are cases denying a consumer-plaintiff recovery because of failure to give notice of breach so that a merchant-defendant may act to preserve evidence essential for its defense.

Conclusion

This chapter has presented just a part of the material that is usually thought of as "Consumer Law." As you can see from the examples and some of the cases, some of this law was illusory in that it really did not help the consumer in a claim against a manufacturer for a defective product. Often, manufacturers were able to waive or modify the various warranties provided for by Article 2. Also, to some extent, the defenses of privity, based on our older notions of contract law, were used to defeat consumer claims. In response to a demand for increased consumer protection, Congress passed the Magnuson-Moss Warranty Act, and the court system relied more heavily on the notion of unconscionability to strike down unfair and burdensome contract clauses that waived or modified seller warranties. But, these were only part of the approach to this significant problem. In the next chapter we explore other approaches.

---

[29] UCC 2–318, Alternative A.   [30] UCC 2–607(3)(a).

Summary Statement

1. Briefly, a merchant is one who deals in goods or by his or her occupation holds himself or herself out as having knowledge or skill peculiar to the sale of goods. A consumer is one who buys goods for use primarily for personal, family, or household purposes.
2. In Article 2 there are provisions for the creation of four kinds of warranty. Each serves a different purpose and is made in different circumstances. These warranties are express warranties, implied warranties of merchantability, implied warranties of fitness for a particular purpose, and warranties of title including warranties against infringement of patent or copyright.
3. Some of the warranties may be modified or waived by the agreement of the parties. Like the creation of these warranties, their modification and waiver each requires different circumstances.
4. The Magnuson-Moss Warranty Act was passed by Congress to protect consumers against merchants who took unfair advantage of the waiver and modification of warranty sections of Article 2. It provides for full and limited warranties and prohibits merchants from waiving implied warranties under some conditions.
5. In many instances, when a large merchant seller attempts to modify or waive warranties or consumer remedies in a sales contract with a consumer, a court may declare such an attempt "unconscionable" and refuse to enforce it. An unconscionable clause or contract is one that, in light of the general commercial background and the commercial needs of the particular trade or case, appears so one-sided at the time the contract was made that a court in good conscience cannot enforce them.
6. Major legal defenses used by merchant sellers in a defective products liability claim *based on a breach of warranty* may include the lack of horizontal privity, failure to give notice of breach, and the running of the statute of limitations.

The following case was passed upon in some respects, on four different occasions, by two different trial courts, by the Florida Supreme Court, and by the United States Fifth Circuit Court of Appeals. Ultimately, the Fifth Circuit decided the case (409 F.2d 1166 (1969)) based upon Judge Simpson's dissenting opinion in an earlier appeal of the case, which is summarized below. Liability was not imposed upon the defendant for the decedent's lung cancer.

Green v. American Tobacco Company
391 F.2d 97 (1968)

Coleman, Circuit J. In December 1957 Edwin Green, Sr. as plaintiff brought suit against the American Tobacco Company, claiming that he had incurred lung cancer as a result of smoking the defendant's product, Lucky Strike cigarettes, for almost 31 years. On February 25, 1958 Mr. Green died, and the administrator of his estate and his widow pursued his original claim. The jury in the first trial found as fact that Mr. Green had primary cancer of the lung, that this was the cause or one of the causes of his death, and that smoking Lucky Strike cigarettes was a proximate cause or one of the proximate causes of the cancer. This finding was based upon the plaintiff's expert witnesses, who testified that one out of nine or ten heavy cigarette smokers die of lung cancer; that 30,000 or 35,000 deaths yearly in the United States are caused by lung cancer caused by cigarette smoking; and that there is a much greater incidence of lung cancer in the half of the adult population that smokes.

The plaintiffs argued that liability for Mr. Green's death should be imposed on the defendant based upon a breach of implied warranty of merchantability theory and negligence.

In the first trial the jury concluded that there was no developed human skill or foresight which could have afforded the manufacturer a knowledge of the harmful effects of smoking. So the jury initially found for the defendant.

As a result of this jury finding, the negligence theory was deemphasized in an appeal of the case, and the subsequent appeals and rehearings focused on whether cigarettes which cause lung cancer which result in death are "merchantable." The attorneys for the plaintiffs argued that the concept of "merchantability" imposes a form of strict liability on the defendant, and all the plaintiff need prove is that the product caused the injury complained of.

In response to this, the defendant argued that the cigarettes were merchantable since they were fit for the ordinary purposes for which such goods were sold—namely, smoking. They admitted that cigarettes would not be merchantable if they contained some foreign matter such as a mouse's ear or glass; but as long as they were essentially identical to other cigarettes that pass in the trade under the label "cigarettes," they are merchantable. Should a jury verdict for the defendant be affirmed? If so, on what ground?

The court noted that there never had been any evidence presented which would tend to show Lucky Strikes were more dangerous or had a greater propensity to cause lung cancer than cigarettes bearing other brand names. Nor was there any evidence that the cigarettes which Mr. Green smoked contained any foreign substance or any spoiled, contaminated, or other substandard ingredient which caused injury. The concept of merchantability does not impose *absolute* liability on the defendant when the product is shown to cause injury. It may impose a form of strict liability on the defendant in that liability will be established without regard to the defendant's intent or carefulness, *but* a defect in the goods must be proved. In this case there was no defect! The court found that the Lucky Strike cigarettes were exactly like all others of the particular brand and virtually the same as all other brands on the market.

Moreover, the court reasoned, if it adopted the plaintiff's reasoning, a seller of butter could be liable to a plaintiff damaged when his or her cholesterol count rose dangerously; or the seller of whiskey might incur liability to everyone who could prove the overconsumption of whiskey contributed to ["nonaccidental" is meant here] injury or death.

[The United States Fifth Circuit Court of Appeals overruled an earlier decision of its own, and in a final hearing en banc (all of the judges of the circuit sitting on the case), essentially affirmed a jury decision for the defendant.]

Questions and Case Problems

1. Plaintiff, manufacturer of plastic bottle caps sold to major distillers of liquor, ordered plastic liners for the bottle caps from the defendant. Before a contract was made the defendant had supplied the plaintiff with brochures, bulletins and other materials that made certain factual representations about the defendant's product. The contract itself did not contain these representations. The defendant shipped an order of bottle cap liners to the plaintiff and the plaintiff alleges they were not in conformance with the specifications and representations made in the brochures and bulletins. Do you believe the seller has made an express warranty in these bulletins and brochures? [*AFA Corporation v. Phoenix Closures, Inc.*, 501 F.Supp 224 (D. Ct., Ill., 1980).]

2. Buyer purchased a round hay baler from John Deere Company, seller, defendant, in May of 1976. About one month later, the buyer's arm was severed when it became caught in the baler. The buyer, plaintiff, sues defendant based on a breach of an express warranty that the baler was especially designed to be safe. The operator's manual stated:

   "The safety of the operator was one of the prime considerations in the minds of John Deere engineers when this baler was designed. Shielding, simple adjustments and other safety features were built into the baler wherever possible."

   Defendant, by means of conspicuous language in both the purchase order and in the attached warranty materials, disclaimed all express warranties. Do you believe that John Deere made an express warranty and, if so, was it properly disclaimed? [See, *Schlenz v. John Deere Company*, 511 F.Supp. 224 (D. Ct., Mont., 1981).]

3. John wanted to buy a new electric drill. He saw an advertisement in the local newspaper which said that Sears was having a special sale on "½ inch electric drills, reduced 20% to $15." John went to Sears to buy the drill but was very interested in whether or not the drill was double-insulated. This meant that the drill had special wiring in it so that if a short developed the drill would not shock the user. John was interested in this feature because he often worked in his basement, where the floor was damp as the result of leaky plumbing, and there was a substantial risk of electrocution. John asked the saleswoman at Sears, "Do you have double-insulated drills?" The saleswoman replied, "We have just what you want," and got for John one of the drills on sale. She said, "This drill is double-insulated." John then said, "Fine, I'll take it," and handed her his Sears credit card. The saleswoman made out the appropriate sales slip and John left with the drill.

   Answer the following questions in a series of short sentences, explaining briefly.
   a. Did Sears make an express warranty?
   b. Did Sears make an implied warranty of merchantability?
   c. Did Sears make an implied warranty of fitness for a particular purpose?
   d. Did Sears make any other warranties?

4. In question 3 above, assume that John took the drill home and one day his daughter was using it in the basement and was injured because the drill was not double-insulated. If Sears were sued for the injuries based upon a warranty theory, what might Sears argue? Would Sears be successful? Assume that John, before using the drill, had sold it to a friend visiting from another state and the friend was injured in his (the friend's) home because the drill was not double-insulated. What would Sears argue in response to a claim for injury based upon warranty theories? Would Sears be successful this time?

5. In questions 3 and 4 above, the packaging for the drill which John purchased and the instructions said in plain and conspicuous language:

   For one year from the date of purchase, Sears will repair or replace this drill free of charge if defective in material or workmanship.

   And, in larger type, it added:

   Sears will not be liable for loss or damage to property or any incidental or consequential loss or expense from property damage due directly to defects in the drill.

   Assume that all of the information in question 3 above is true, and that after John purchased the drill, he was severely injured when using the drill in his basement, which at the time was dry. You may also assume that the drill was not properly double-insulated. As a result of this defect, the drill exploded and caused John's basement to catch fire, resulting in $5,000 damage to the basement and personal injury to John. Does the above language on the packaging and directions limit John's measure of recovery to the value of the drill? What additional circumstances might help John's case?

6. Walker-Thomas Furniture Company operated a retail furniture store in the inner city of the District of Columbia. From 1957 to 1962 it contracted with Williams for the "purchase" of household items. The "agreement" of the parties read in such a way that Walker-Thomas was supposedly leasing each item to Williams for a stipulated monthly rent. It also provided that title to the goods would remain in Walker-Thomas until the total of all the monthly payments had been made on all items purchased. Also, an obscure provision added that all payments now and hereafter made shall be credited pro rata on all outstanding "leases," bills, and accounts. The effect of this last provision was to keep a balance due on every item purchased until the balance due on all items, whenever purchased, had been fully paid. This resulted in the debt created by any new credit purchase being secured by the right to repossess all items previously purchased by that purchaser. On April 17, 1962 Williams bought a stereo set for a stated value of $514.95, but she soon defaulted in her payments. Walker-Thomas seeks to repossess all items purchased by her since December 1957. What legal argument would you expect Williams to make in her defense? What circumstances might be important in establishing this defense? [*Williams v. Walker-Thomas Furniture Company*, 350 F.2d 445 (1965).]

7. Robert Jones owned a small business providing amusement rides at shopping centers. In the course of Jones' operation he had on occasion made trades of his equipment with manufacturers of the rides and with other ride operators. He believed new or different rides attracted more people. He sold one of these rides, a "pony cart" ride, to Nicole, Inc. The ride was defective and injured one of Nicole's patrons, and now Nicole sues Jones because of the defect alleging that the sale from Jones to Nicole breached the implied warranty of merchantability. Can Nicole recover from Jones on this theory? [See *Allen v. Nicole, Inc.,* 412 A.2d 824 (N. J. 1980).]

8. Plaintiff, a dairy farmer, bought 4 milking machines from the defendant for his dairy herd. The machines were delivered on Feb. 19, 1973 and installed by March 1, 1973. In 1976, the buyer's herd suffered a severe epidemic of mastitis, an udder infection, and he maintains that the cause of the epidemic was a defect in the milking machines. The plaintiff filed suit for breach of warranty on March 11, 1977. There is a 4-year statute of limitations. The defendant claims the suit is barred by the statute of limitations, and the plaintiff argues that the claim arose upon discovery of the defect in 1976. Is the plaintiff's claim barred by the 4-year statute of limitations? [*Clark v. De Laval Separator Corporation,* 639 F.2d 1320 (5th Cir., 1981).]

9. C purchased a 1955 Chevrolet Corvette from S for $2,800. Some time later C learned that a prior owner had placed a $3,600 lien on the Corvette. Describe the remedy that C has against S.

10. In the case of *Green v. American Tobacco Company,* 391 F.2d 97 (1968),[31] explain how you would try to prove *today* the defendant's cigarettes to be unmerchantable in view of the movement toward decreased nicotine content and the required labeling of cigarette smoking as dangerous to health.

---

[31] See pp. 318–19.

22 Consumer Law
B. A Manufacturer's Liability for Defective and Unreasonably Dangerous Products, and Recent Consumer Protection Legislation

After you have read this chapter, you should be able to:

1. Define the two general categories of tort law which provide remedies for injured consumers, and explain how the legal device of "res ipsa loquitur" is used in a products liability case.
2. Write a paragraph on the need for the tort theory of strict liability by emphasizing the limitations on the use of warranty-based and negligence-based theories of seller liability.
3. Define in some detail what a "defect" is and what "unreasonably dangerous" means for purposes of applying section 402A of the Restatement of Torts.
4. Briefly discuss three defenses to products liability claims.
5. Explain how market share liability provides a remedy to an injured consumer.
6. Discuss in a series of short paragraphs why federal and state legislation is needed to help deal with the products liability crisis.
7. Explain briefly the purpose and function of the Consumer Product Safety Commission and the Federal Trade Commission, and describe how they operate.
8. Explain the purpose of The Consumer Credit Protection Act, The Fair Credit Reporting Act and The Equal Credit Opportunity Act, and give an example of a violation of the last two Acts.

Introduction

In this chapter we continue our discussion of the various legal theories and remedies that an injured consumer can use to state a good claim for damages against a manufacturer or seller and the latter's defenses to products liability. The first set of theories and remedies discussed below has developed within the context of our *tort law*. Products liability and the "consumer movement" though have also moved into the *legislative arena*. So, we end this chapter with a thorough discussion of the federal and some state legislation intended to protect the consumer.

The History of Products Liability Law

Liability for defective products in the mid-to-late 1800s was almost unknown. There are two reasons for this. The first is that such liability was conceived of as a "commercial circumstance"; thus the principles creating liability should arise from contract law, not from other areas of civil liability such as negligence. Many of the appellate cases from this period held that an injured person could not even bring an action against a producer or seller unless it was in **privity** with that producer or seller. Thus, an injured consumer could not sue a manufacturer unless he or she was the one who had contracted to buy the defective good. Family members, friends and bystanders were all unable to sue for a consumer-product related injury. The notion that privity was needed to maintain an action served the industrial interests of the period and most probably eliminated numerous suits. However, under an exception to the general rule requiring privity, one could recover (if there were no privity) if the goods causing the injury were "inherently dangerous." The class of goods which were "inherently dangerous" in the mid-to-late 1800s and early 1900s included mislabeled poison, a defective scaffold ninety feet high, and a defective bottle of aerated water.

privity
a mutuality of relationship between persons or between persons and a particular transaction (usually created by contract)

The severe result of invoking the requirement of privity was lessened shortly after the turn of the century when an appellate court[1] held that a Buick automobile was negligently manufactured and, therefore, allowed an injured plaintiff consumer to maintain an action for personal injury against a defendant corporate manufacturer with whom the plaintiff had *not* contracted. We learn in this chapter how the classification of "inherently dangerous" goods grew into a significant element of one of the major theories of products liability today.

A second reason for the relatively slow development of products liability law in the late 1800s and early 1900s was the doctrine in our law of **caveat emptor.** This phrase expresses a general policy recognized by courts that the one who buys a defective product should, as against the producer or seller, suffer the loss. This is a less precise notion than privity and arose from the social and economic climate of the times. Caveat emptor denotes a general behavior of courts rather than a precise legal principle.

caveat emptor
a Latin phrase meaning "let the buyer beware"

At a time when manufactured goods were relatively simple, it was judged best to let the consumer choose the appropriate product—even try it out—and if a purchase of a product were made, then the consumer should be stuck with it even if it were defective. This was good policy because, in an economic system which encouraged the presence of numerous sellers in the market for goods, over time the producer of faulty products would go out of business as word spread about the quality of its product. However, with the increasing complexity of goods and with the trend toward concentration (fewer producers) in almost all major industrial markets, the doctrines of privity and caveat emptor were perceived as increasingly unjust.

The response of the law has been literally explosive. Today, in most jurisdictions, privity is no longer referred to, and many legal scholars would characterize products liability law as based on the premise of "*seller* beware." The predominance of these doctrines for decades, though, shaped the legal environment of today's products liability law.

---

[1] *MacPherson v. Buick Motor Co.,* 111 N.E. 1050 (N.Y. 1916).

The remedies available to an injured consumer today may come from one of three general areas: from the *warranties* provided for in Article 2 of the UCC previously discussed in chapter 21; from the *common law of torts* (here there are two chief theories of remedies based upon "negligence theory" and "strict liability theory"); and, from miscellaneous *federal and state statutory provisions* creating liability for sellers who sell defective products or deceive consumers. The last two areas are discussed in this chapter.

Tort Theories of Products Liability

Our American "civil" law is traditionally divided into the two broad categories of contract law and tort law. **Tort** law is further divided into three categories: intentional torts, negligence, and strict liability. Establishing liability based upon an intentional tort theory requires proof of the defendant's *intent* to commit a wrongful act. This theory is almost never used in products liability cases because manufacturers and sellers *intend* no harm by the sale of their product. Negligence and strict liability are today, however, widely accepted theories of products liability.

This has not always been true. As we pointed out above, until the second or third decade of this century, most courts would bar a plaintiff from asserting a claim against the manufacturer or seller unless the plaintiff could prove privity with the defendant. An exception to this general rule allowed an injured plaintiff to recover on a negligence theory if the defective goods were "inherently or unreasonably dangerous." During the 1960s, courts so expanded the classification of goods which were "inherently or unreasonably dangerous" that today these words do not mean exceptionally or especially dangerous but mean *"capable of causing harm" if the good is defective.* However, some courts may not have freed themselves entirely from this requirement and thus demand that the plaintiff at least allege that the defective goods were "unreasonably dangerous."

Today *negligence* and *strict liability* are two independent legal theories upon which an injured plaintiff may base its product liability claim. They may be alleged and proved in the *same case* in which a breach of warranty theory is argued or they may serve as the sole basis for liability. Obviously these theories cannot be defeated by an assertion that there was no privity. Nor are any arguments based upon a waiver or modification of a warranty relevant.

A chief reason for using tort theories of liability is that although the statute of limitations for personal injury is usually shorter—most jurisdictions have a three-year statute of limitations on personal *injury* claims—*the time period begins to run from the date of injury,* not the date of delivery of the good. A disadvantage of using these theories is that most courts will not permit recovery for economic loss *alone,* such as lost profits or damage to the goods. To recover for economic loss, the plaintiff must *also* show *personal injury.*[2] *Providing a remedy in the form of money damages to one who has suffered personal injury is the real purpose of our tort law.*

Negligence

To establish **"negligence"** in a products liability case, the plaintiff must prove that the *defendant's conduct in either manufacturing or designing goods produced a risk of harm greater than society is willing to accept in light of the benefits to be derived from that activity.* Simply put, the risk of harm must be unreasonable in the circumstances.[3] In almost all negligence cases the issue of the "reasonableness" of the defendant's conduct is an issue for the jury to decide. That is, most of these cases present problems of proof rather than issues of substantive law.

---

[2] See D. Noel and J. Phillips, *Products Liability in a Nutshell* (St. Paul: West Pub. Co., 1974), p. 10.

[3] J. Henderson and R. Pearson, *The Tort Process* (Boston: Little, Brown, 1975), p. 268.

tort
a civil (private) noncontractual wrong for which a court will give a remedy

negligence
(conduct) failure to use the degree of care demanded by the circumstances; (the tort) negligent conduct proximately causing injury to another person's interest

Proving that goods were negligently manufactured or designed is no easy task. Without the help of an additional legal device, it would be impossible to prove if the goods were destroyed as a result of a defect. This legal device is designated by the Latin phrase **res ipsa loquitur,** which, literally translated, means "the thing speaks for itself." This device is properly used where there is a *gap* in the plaintiff's proof of negligence caused simply by the circumstances of the case. If the plaintiff can show that (1) the injury complained of *does not normally happen* in the absence of negligence, and (2) at the *time of the alleged negligent act*—the time of the manufacture of the goods, not the time of injury—the defendant had *exclusive control* of the thing which later caused the injury, then an application of res ipsa loquitur will cause the judge to state that the plaintiff has filled the gap in its evidence, and an inference of negligence will be created. It is then up to the defendant to rebut that inference. The following classic case illustrates the use of res ipsa loquitur.

res ipsa loquitur
the thing speaks for itself

Facts
The plaintiff, a waitress in a restaurant, was severely injured when a bottle of Coca Cola exploded in her hand. She sued the bottler and alleged that it either negligently bottled the Coke (put it under too much pressure) or negligently manufactured the bottle. She was unable to show any specific acts of negligence. The bottler defended by introducing evidence that it bottled Coke in a manner all bottlers used and was therefore not acting unreasonably—that is, was not negligent. The defendant also argued that it was the plaintiff who must have mishandled the bottle. The jury returned a verdict for the plaintiff. On appeal, the defendant argued there was not sufficient evidence of negligence to submit the issue to the jury. Should the plaintiff's verdict be reversed?

Decision
No. The appellate court found in favor of the plaintiff.

Reasoning
The appellate court held that the doctrine of res ipsa loquitur applies in a negligence case if the plaintiff alleges, and the evidence could reasonably show, that (1) the defendant had exclusive control of the thing causing the injury and (2) the injury is of such a nature that it ordinarily would not occur in the absence of negligence by the defendant. The plaintiff also alleged that the bottle had not changed since it left the defendant's possession and that she was using due care at the time the bottle exploded. The court concluded that the evidence was sufficient to support a reasonable inference that the bottle was in some manner defective at the time it left the defendant's possession. The jury could properly rely on this inference in finding for the plaintiff.

Escola v. Coca Cola Bottling Co., 150 P.2d 436 (Cal. 1944).

Today, many of the products liability cases rely on a negligence theory to provide a remedy when the design of a product may have caused injury. In many of these cases there is *no defect* in the goods in that they operate as they are intended to operate. The conduct that is "unreasonable" is the *failure to design a safe product* when injury of the type complained of occurs and is *foreseeable* by the manufacturer. Below is a case that is typical of the law's approach in this area.

Facts
The plaintiff was driving a 1963 Chevrolet Corvair when the car was struck head-on by another car. The plaintiff was severely injured when the steering column was thrust into his head. The car was so designed that the steering column was one piece of steel all the way from a position directly in front of the driver to a point 2.7 inches in front of the leading surface of the front tire. The plaintiff did not contend that the design caused the accident but that, because of the design, he received injuries he would not otherwise have received. The defendant, General Motors Corporation, the designer and manufacturer of the car, argued that it has no legal duty to produce a vehicle in which it is safe to collide or which is accident-proof. The trial court dismissed the plaintiff's claim, and the plaintiff appealed. Did the plaintiff state a proper case based upon negligent design?

Decision
Yes. The appellate court reversed the trial court and held that the plaintiff did state a good cause of action based upon negligent design.

Reasoning
The court reasoned that under the present state of the art, an automobile manufacturer is under no duty to design an accident-proof vehicle, but such manufacturer is under a duty to use reasonable care in the design of its vehicle to avoid subjecting the user to an unreasonable risk of injury in the event of collision. Collisions with or without fault of the user are clearly foreseeable by the manufacturer and are statistically inevitable.

The injury of the type complained of in this case was foreseeable as an incident to the normal and expected use of an automobile, given the fact that the steering column was designed as it was. The normal risk of driving must be accepted by the user, but there is no need to further penalize the user by subjecting him to an unreasonable risk of injury.

Larsen v. General Motors Corporation, 391 F.2d 495 (1968).

In a products liability case based upon negligence, the retailer or immediate seller (if there is one) is not held liable unless it has reason to know of the defect or dangerous design and fails to warn the purchaser. To find liability, each of the defendants must have acted negligently.

The defenses of contributory negligence, assumption of risk, and lack of proximate causation, discussed below, are defenses available to the defendant. Also, the defendant may meet the plaintiff's case with proof that its conduct is not unreasonable because it conforms to the generally accepted standards of performance in the particular area of conduct. For example, Coca Cola attempted to counter the plaintiff's case in Escola by introducing evidence that the industry standard of taking a sample bottle every three hours from the manufacturing mold (this is approximately one out of every 600 bottles) and subjecting it to an internal pressure of 450 pounds per square inch, sustained for one minute, is "pretty near" infallible in guarding against defectively manufactured bottles. The Escola case presented some difficult factual issues for the jury. It was a very close case. The original fact finder in that case simply believed the plaintiff's evidence, but many negligence cases on similar evidence result in verdicts for the defendant.

Strict Liability

strict liability
absolute liability irrespective of the absence of negligence or fault

Strict liability as a tort theory used in products liability cases is of recent and increasing significance. If it has not become so already, it soon will be the dominant theory in products liability cases. A manufacturer may be strictly liable when it:[4]

. . . sells any product in a defective condition unreasonably dangerous to the user or consumer or to his property and is subject to liability for physical harm thereby caused to the ultimate user or consumer, or to his property, . . .

The basic reason for the increasing use of this theory is that there are fewer well-established legal defenses to such claims. For the reasons already stated, warranty theory and negligence theory still permit the successful assertion of defenses when a plaintiff may be injured by a product through no fault of the plaintiff. Strict liability is based on the notion that, as between an innocent injured plaintiff and a merchant, the latter should pay for an injury caused by a defect.

The Escola case discussed above was so close on the negligence issue that Judge Traynor, a famous California jurist, could have applied the theory of strict liability in that case. In a concurring opinion, he clearly stated the policy reasons for strict liability as follows:

Even if there is no negligence, . . . public policy demands that responsibility be fixed wherever it will most effectively reduce the hazards to life and health inherent in defective products that reach the market. It is evident that the manufacturer can anticipate some hazards and guard against the recurrence of others as the public cannot. Those who suffer injury from defective products are unprepared to meet its consequences. The cost of an injury and the loss of time or health may be an overwhelming misfortune to the person injured, and a needless one, for the risk

---

[4] RESTATEMENT (SECOND) OF TORTS sec. 402A (1965).

of injury can be insured by the manufacturer and distributed among the public as a cost of doing business. It is to the public interest to discourage the marketing of products having defects that are a menace to the public. If such products nevertheless find their way into the market it is to the public interest to place the responsibility for whatever injury they may cause upon the manufacturer, who, even if he is not negligent in the manufacture of the product, is responsible for its reaching the market. However intermittently such injuries may occur and however haphazardly they may strike, the risk of their occurrence is a constant risk and a general one. Against such a risk there should be general and constant protection and the manufacturer is best situated to afford such protection. [*Escola v. Coca Cola Bottling Co.,* 150 P.2d 436, 440–41 (Cal. 1944).]

There are two key concepts in the application of strict liability. The first is the definition and application of the term "defect" and the second is the term "unreasonably dangerous." We will first explain the current thinking of courts about the term defect.

Defect. The term defect is also used in both negligent manufacture and negligent design cases in that if a product is negligently manufactured it has a defect in it; and if a good is negligently designed it may also be said to be "defective." But, the term defect when used in a strict liability case has a slightly different meaning.

In a strict liability case there are two fairly well-established definitions of the term defect. That is, state supreme courts that have defined the word defect for use in a strict liability case have adopted, generally speaking, one of two definitions. These definitions are as follows:

1. A product may be found defective if it fails to perform as safely as an ordinary consumer would expect; or
2. A product may be defective if the risk of danger inherent in the challenged design outweighs the benefits of the design.[5]

As you can see, the first definition of defect takes a rather individualistic point of view. That is, it focuses on the individual and then asks, "what would an ordinary consumer expect?" The second or alternative definition of the term focuses more on the value of the product to society. This second definition appears to represent an emerging consensus.[6] In very general terms, the second definition requires a judge or jury to engage in a form of cost-benefit analysis. If the dangerousness of the product outweighs its benefit to society, then the decision-maker may conclude it was defectively designed. For example, is an ordinary butcher's knife defectively designed? Most people would say "no" even though they are inherently very dangerous. The reason is that the benefit to our society of having them outweighs the costs associated with the inherent design. The following case is an application of the above first definition of defect.

Facts

Benjamin E. Dunham, the plaintiff, was using a hammer manufactured by Vaughan & Bushnell Manufacturing Co., defendant, to drive a pin into the connector between his tractor and a manure spreader. A chip from the beveled edge of the hammer broke off and struck him in the right eye, resulting in the permanent loss of sight in that eye. The hammer was about eleven months old and had been used for ordinary tasks around the plaintiff's farm. The defendant argued that the plaintiff's reliance on strict liability was not appropriate because the evidence did not show that there was a defect in the hammer when it left the manufacturer's control. The defendant also argued that everyone knows metal "tires" with age and use and is subject to failure. No manufacturer should be expected to produce a hammer which would last forever. The trial court found in favor of the plaintiff, and the defendant argued, on appeal, that strict liability was not proved in the trial court.

---

[5] *Strict Products Liability: Giving Content to the Term "Defect" in Design Cases,* 40 Ohio St. L. J. 209 (1979).

[6] J. Henderson, *Reviewed Judicial Controversy over Defective Product Design: Toward the Preservation of an Emerging Consensus,* 63 Minn. L. Rev. 773, 775 (1979).

Decision

The appellate court affirmed a verdict for the plaintiff.

Reasoning

The court acknowledged that there must have been a defect in the goods and it must have existed when the goods left the custody of the manufacturer; this does not mean, however, that the defect must manifest itself at once. On this issue the court relied on another case in which a defective brake linkage bracket on a tractor broke over three years after it was installed in the tractor. The court also concluded that the jury could find that a defect existed because the definition of a defect rests on the premise that those products are defective which are dangerous because they fail to perform in the manner reasonably to be expected in light of their nature and intended function. A defect may be a "condition" not contemplated by the ultimate consumer, which would be unreasonably dangerous to him.

Dunham v. Vaughan & Bushnell Mfg. Co., 247 N.E.2d 401 (Ill. 1969).

Unreasonably Dangerous.   A second circumstance which must be alleged and proved in a products liability case based on strict liability is that the product was "unreasonably dangerous." Like the term, "defect," the definition of the term "unreasonably dangerous" may differ from state to state. The supreme courts of some states define an unreasonably dangerous product as one that is dangerous to an extent beyond that contemplated by the ordinary consumer who purchases it.[7]

Defenses to Products Liability Cases

contributory negligence
plaintiff's conduct which falls below the standard to which he should conform for his own protection and which is a legally contributing cause with the defendant's negligence causing the plaintiff's harm

assumption of risk
voluntarily assuming a known risk of harm

proximate cause
the cause of an injury without which the injury would not have occurred

A significant category of defenses is directed at what may be called the *plaintiff's misbehavior in using the product*. These defenses are **contributory negligence** *of the plaintiff,* **assumption of a known risk,** *misuse, hypersensitivity,* and *lack of* **proximate causation.** These defenses may be used by a manufacturer or seller in either a breach of warranty case, or negligence or strict liability cases. Moreover, the use and application of these defenses varies so widely from state to state that generalization about them is almost impossible. Some states, for example, have adopted the position that contributory negligence is *not* a defense to a claim for damage based upon a breach of warranty theory, while some other state supreme courts have held that it is an absolute defense.[8] Moreover, courts in some states could hold that, where a woman uses a hair dye when she knows she experiences severe skin reactions to hair dyes, a doctrine of "hypersensitivity" would preclude her recovery for damage. Some courts could hold that similar "misconduct" tended to prove a lack of proximate causation in that it was the plaintiff's own acts which were the primary cause, not the product. Whatever the label used, where an injured plaintiff voluntarily and unreasonably proceeds to encounter a known danger or a danger that would be known to a reasonable person, or where the plaintiff uses a product in a manner for which it was not intended, the plaintiff will most probably encounter some form of defense. The "reasonableness" of the plaintiff's conduct ultimately will be decided by the jury.

Recently, we have learned that some products we once believed were safe, were really very dangerous. Asbestos, a substance made of tiny fibers used widely as insulation and fire retardant material, was found to be cancer causing to some people exposed to it. When the manufacturers were sued by plaintiffs damaged by this substance, they pleaded that they used the most advanced technology of the time to discover the product's dangerous qualities and thus did all that could be required of them. This is called the "state of the art defense."

A majority of jurisdictions do allow a state of the art defense. This means that in a strict liability case, the courts will allow the jury to consider evidence on whether a defendant used technology that was available at the time a "defective" product was manufactured. However, in one recent development, the New Jersey Supreme Court held that

---

[7] Comment i to sec. 402A, RESTATEMENT (SECOND) OF TORTS (1958).

[8] J. White and R. Summers, p. 336.

state of the art evidence was not admissible in a strict liability suit.[9] This case, like the one discussed below involving DES, may point to areas that will represent the law of a majority of jurisdictions in the near future.

Very Recent Developments in Products Liability Law

Liability without Causation

An essential element of any plaintiff's cause of action for negligence or strict liability is that there be some reasonable connection between the negligent design or manufacture, or causing the defect and the unreasonably dangerous quality of the product produced by the defendant, and the damage that the plaintiff suffered. In short, the defendant must have caused the damage.

The DES Cases. Several recent cases, however, have indicated the establishment of a significant trend away from a strict application of the causation requirement. These cases involved the chemical diethylstilbestrol (DES).

DES was first introduced to the drug market in the late 1940s to prevent miscarriages in pregnant women. It was banned by the Food and Drug Administration in 1971, but as of that date about 200 companies had manufactured it. The drug was banned because of a high incidence of cancer contracted by the daughters of DES users. These daughters were plaintiffs in about one thousand products liability cases pending against the former DES manufacturers.

Let us consider a typical case in order to understand this recent trend of liability without causation. Assume that a daughter of a DES user is informed that she has cancer. She is obviously severely damaged and she elects to sue a manufacturer. But, which one? Because of the passage of time it is impossible to identify which manufacturer made the DES consumed by her mother. Prescriptions and the bottles they came in were discarded long ago. So, under conventional tort theories the plaintiff could not state a good case because she could not identify with reasonable certainty, the defendant that caused the injury. In the leading case, *Sindell v. Abbott Laboratories*[10] the California Supreme Court held that an injured plaintiff could state a good case so long as: (1) identification of the manufacturer is impossible through no fault of the plaintiff; and (2) the product is **fungible;** and (3) a plaintiff joined enough defendants so that a "substantial percentage" of the market for that product is represented, then the plaintiff is relieved of the burden of proving causation of a specific defendant. In addition the court held that, once the elements of the case are established, a defendant could be held liable for the proportion of the judgment represented by its share of sales in that market, unless it demonstrates that it could not have made the product which caused the plaintiff's injury. So, if a particular defendant had 10 percent of the sales in the market for DES, it would pay 10 percent of the judgment.

fungible goods every unit of goods is the equivalent of any other like unit (e.g., rice, or quantities of oil, that are of the same quality)

This new theory of "market share" liability has not yet gained wide use for other products but it could in the very near future. Some legal scholars believe that it will be used in some of the asbestos and Agent Orange cases. Moreover, some of the writers have suggested that some of the cigarette companies will be joined by plaintiffs in these cases because smoking cigarettes greatly enhances the lung damage resulting from the inhalation of asbestos, and many of these plaintiffs cannot remember which brand of cigarettes they were smoking twenty years ago or so.[11]

---

[9] *Beshada,* et al. *v. Johns-Manville Products Corporation,* 447 A.2d 539 (N.J. 1982).

[10] 607 P.2d 924 (1980).

[11] The DES Cases and Liability Without Causation, 19 AM. BUS. L. J. 519 (1983).

Recent Federal and State Consumer Product Legislation—Products

Congress and most state legislatures have passed consumer product legislation, the significant features of which are discussed in the following sections. Since 1966 Congress has passed six Acts which govern some aspect of product safety or product design. Also, the Federal Trade Commission and the Consumer Affairs Section within the Antitrust Division of the Justice Department have become much more active in pressing the interests of consumers. In the next section we will briefly explain some of the recent federal legislation and regulation.

The Consumer Product Safety Act of 1972

The Consumer Product Safety Act of 1972[12] created the Consumer Product Safety Commission (CPSC). This commission has jurisdiction over every consumer product *except* automobiles, food, and a few other items regulated by older agencies of government. The basic idea behind the creation of the CPSC was to bring order to an increasingly confusing mish-mash of federal and state consumer regulatory bodies. The commission is to collect and disseminate information relating to injuries and to conduct investigations and tests on consumer products and their use. When a consumer product creates a hazard of injury or illness, the CPSC may develop consumer product safety standards. These standards must be set forth in performance requirements. If the CPSC finds that an unreasonable risk exists and that no standard will provide protection, it may ban a product. It has banned such products as garments containing asbestos, some baby cribs, some drain cleaners, assorted types of fireworks, furniture painted with lead paint, some kinds of lawn darts, and self-pressurized products containing vinyl chloride.[13] The basic idea of the CPSC was to disseminate information about product safety and attempt to get products redesigned in light of the consumer's foreseeable ignorance and consumer misbehavior or misuse. The long case at the end of this chapter should give you some idea of how the CPSC operates. From a reading of this case, judge for yourself the value of the CPSC.

Motor Vehicle Safety Legislation.

Motor vehicle safety legislation has been on the books since 1966, but only recently have the various enforcement activities established the legislation as noteworthy. Although the National Traffic and Motor Vehicle Safety Act of 1966[14] and the Highway Safety Act[15] have been amended or altered by legislation or executive order almost every year since their adoption, they are some of the more successful attempts to regulate product safety. It has been estimated that 150,000 lives have been saved during the period 1967 to 1977 due to automobile safety legislation and the reduced speed limit necessitated by the oil shortage of 1973.[16]

The National Traffic and Motor Vehicle Safety Act of 1966 created the National Highway Traffic Safety Administration. It has the authority to promulgate rules for traffic safety, conduct research, disseminate information about vehicle safety, and, if a manufacturer will not voluntarily comply, initiate procedures resulting in the recall of automobiles which pose a threat to the public.

The Federal Trade Commission Act.

The Federal Trade Commission (FTC) was created in 1914 to deal with anticompetitive practices in business. Gradually its powers have expanded and today one of its major

---

[12] 15 U.S.C.A. sec. 2051 et seq.

[13] U.S. Consumer Product Safety Commission, *1979 Annual Report,* Appendix L.

[14] 15 U.S.C.A. sec. 1381 et seq.   [15] 23 U.S.C.A. sec. 401 et seq.

[16] *Motor Vehicle Safety* 1977, Annual Report. U.S. Department of Transportation.

functions is to regulate in the area of deceptive trade practices. This regulation primarily focuses on advertising methods and claims of businesses where the common law remedies of misrepresentation and deceit are not thought to be effective.

The FTC can issue "trade regulation rules" and then enforce these rules by demanding that an alleged offender appear before it for a hearing. The result of this hearing is usually the issuance of a cease and desist order which can be enforced by a court or a federal marshall. The following is an example of one of the more famous recent trade regulation rules.

Trade Regulation Rule Concerning Retail Food Store Advertising and Marketing Practices
16 C.F.R. Part 424 (1972)

§ 424.1 The Rule

(a) The Commission, . . . hereby promulgates as a trade regulation rule its determination that:

(b) In connection with sale or offering for sale by retail food stores of food and grocery products or other merchandise, . . . it is an unfair method of competition and an unfair or deceptive act or practice to:

(1)(i) Offer any such products for sale at a stated price, by means of any advertisement disseminated in an area served by any of its stores which are covered by the advertisement which do not have such products in stock, and readily available to customers during the effective period of the advertisement. (If not readily available, clear and adequate notice shall be provided that the items are in stock and may be obtained upon request.)

(ii) *Provided, however,* That it shall constitute a defense to a charge under subdivision i. of this subparagraph if the retailer maintains records sufficient to show that the advertised products were ordered in adequate time for delivery and delivered to the stores in quantities sufficient to meet reasonably anticipated demands.

(2) Fail to make the advertised items conspicuously and readily available for sale at or below the advertised prices.

Unless, in each of the above cases, there is clear and conspicuous disclosure in all such advertisements as to all exceptions and/or limitations or restrictions with respect to stores, products or prices otherwise included within the advertisements.

The FTC may also use a *second* method of enforcing the powers given to it by giving a firm notice that they are engaged in a deceptive trade practice and then asking them to stop. Many times the firms dispute these assertions and the issue is taken before a court.[17] Although the category of deceptive trade practices is very broad, the case below is fairly typical of the kind of cases and the kind of powers that the FTC has.

Facts
The FTC entered a final order against Fedders Corp. as a result of an investigation by the FTC that Fedders had made serious misrepresentations in the advertising claims it had used to promote sales of its air conditioning equipment. The FTC found that Fedders had claimed that its air conditioners were unique because they had "reserve cooling power," a term which was intended to imply an unusual ability to produce cold air under extreme conditions of heat and humidity. In fact, the Fedders conditioners had no technical advantage over the equipment of its competitors. The FTC determined that Fedders was engaged in a violation of the FTC Act because it misrepresented what its product could do.

Fedders petitioned the court for a review of the FTC order. Is the cease and desist order proper?

Decision
The court dismissed the petition of Fedders thus leaving the original cease and desist order in force.

Reasoning
The order challenged by Fedders had two parts. The first part prohibited Fedders from misrepresenting directly or by implication that any air conditioner on the basis of a comparison thereof with the product of other manufacturers is unique in any material respect unless such is the fact. Fedders does not appeal from this part of the order. The second part of the order prohibits Fedders

---

[17] For FTC adjudicative proceedings and judicial review, see pp. 717–18.

from making, directly or indirectly, any statement or representation in any advertisement as to the air cooling, dehumidification, or circulation characteristics, capacity or capabilities of any air conditioner, unless at the time of such representation Fedders has a reasonable basis for such statement or evidence which shall consist of competent scientific, engineering or other similar objective material or industry-wide standards based on such material. Fedders argued that this part is not valid because it is too broad and that it prohibits practices which were not sufficiently related to the unlawful practice actually found by the FTC. That is, Fedders argues that the part of the order requiring a reasonable scientific or engineering basis for their advertising claim is overly broad.

The court held that there is broad language in the FTC order and that this is proper because the FTC must have wide discretion in its choice of a remedy to cope with deceptive trade practices. So long as the remedial order is reasonably related to the unlawful practices found to exist, the FTC order should be upheld. In this case, the vague design claim relating to a reserve cooling power implicated the basic performance characteristics of the entire product. By limiting the order to unsubstantiated representations as to "cooling, dehumidification, or circulation characteristics" as opposed to any performance characteristic which might include energy usage or durability for example, the FTC has done the necessary limitation.

Fedders Corp. v. Federal Trade Commission, 529 F.2d 1398 (1976).

State legislation.

Related Federal and State Legislation

Attempts by the federal government to legislate standards for merchants and products performance have been, at best, mildly successful. It now appears that because of two related developments at the state level, a remedy of value is beginning to emerge for consumers who are damaged by merchant misconduct. Now over 39 states[18] have legislation which provides a remedy to consumers who are not dealt with in an ethical or fair way. This legislation, plus the fact that many states allow consumer-related complaints to be filed without an attorney's help in small claims courts, provide remedies within the reach of many consumers. For example, Michigan law provides that "unfair, unconscionable or deceptive methods, acts or practices in the conduct of trade or commerce are unlawful."[19] The legislation defines 29 unlawful acts. A partial listing of these specific acts is as follows:

(i) Making false or misleading statements of fact concerning the reasons for, existence of, or amounts of, price reductions.
(j) Representing that a part, replacement, or repair service is needed when it is not.
(n) Causing a probability of confusion or of misunderstanding as to the legal rights, obligations, or remedies of a party to a transaction.
(o) Causing a probability of confusion or of misunderstanding as to the terms or conditions of credit if credit is extended in a transaction.

This Michigan legislation also provides that a person who suffers loss as a result of a violation of one of the 29 listed acts may bring an action to recover actual damages or $250, whichever is greater. The legislation does not provide a remedy for the recovery of substantial amounts for personal injury as a result of a defective product but does allow recovery for minor amounts. For example, a student at Michigan State University was recently awarded $250 when he showed in the local small claims court that he was told by a merchant that his defective stereo speaker was covered by warranty and would be repaired without charge. When he went to pick up the speaker from the merchant, he was told that it would cost him $60. He paid the amount under protest and then filed his claim.

    Recently many states (about thirty) have passed legislation dealing with a very specific area of consumer complaints. This legislation applies to *new* cars that cannot be repaired properly and are thus the proverbial "lemon." These "Lemon Laws" vary from state to state but usually provide that, 1) if a new car is under warranty and it has a defect

---

[18] W. Haemmel, p. 36.   [19] 14 MICH. STAT. ANN. secs.19.418(3) et seq.

which significantly affects its value or use, and 2) if the dealer is unable to fix the defect in a stated number of tries (usually four), the owner is entitled to a new car or the return of the purchase price. Most of these laws require that an informal jury established by Better Business Bureaus in cooperation with auto dealers find facts supporting the consumer's claim.

Also, at least one state, New York, enacted in 1984 the first law in the United States to provide consumer protection for buyers of *used* cars. This law requires a dealer in used cars (defined as a person who sells 3 or more used vehicles a year) to provide a written warranty for certain parts for a period of from 30 days or 1,000 miles if the car has over 36,000 miles, to 60 days or 3,000 miles if the car has 36,000 miles or less. Such law applies to used car sales for $1,000 or more. (N.Y. General Business Law, Sec. 198-b, 1984).

The Product Liability Risk Retention Act

Finally, we explain briefly here another approach to the products liability crisis. Many manufacturers are doubtless aware and regret that their products cause the damage that they do. Also, what they are very concerned about is the uncertainty of the amount of liability. A large recovery by just one plaintiff can jeopardize the existence of a firm. Products liability insurance has gained wide acceptance, but the premiums for this insurance also reflect both the uncertainty involved and the necessary profit of an insurance company. Since manufacturers are closer to the products liability cases than the insurers, Congress thought it prudent to let the manufacturers *jointly* form "captive" or wholly owned insurance companies to cover the risks involved. On September 25, 1981, the Product Liability Risk Retention Act was passed.[20] This Act allows manufacturers, distributors, and retailers of products to form insurance companies that they own together.

Recent Federal and State Consumer Protection Legislation—Credit

A substantial amount of consumer protection legislation involves the regulation of credit transactions. Closely related to the actual sale of goods (or real property) is the manner in which the buyer pays. Quite often the buyer pays a small portion of the purchase price in cash and then promises to pay the balance plus interest on this outstanding balance until the full amount is paid. When a seller tenders a good or property to a buyer and then relies on a buyer's promise to pay in the future, it is extending credit to the buyer.

Often it is difficult for a consumer to assess the exact amount that will be paid for goods when credit is involved, and just as difficult is the computation of the cost of credit itself. Recently both Congress and state legislatures passed statutes to provide the consumer with knowledge about his or her credit transactions.

The Consumer Credit Protection Act (CCPA)

Federal legislation.

The Consumer Credit Protection Act[21] (also called the Truth-In-Lending Act) is administered by the Federal Reserve System and has been in force since 1969, when the Federal Reserve Board adopted regulations for conduct. These regulations reach all extensions of credit for personal, family, household, or agricultural purposes. The applicability of the Act is suspended if there is state legislation covering similar transactions and the requirements for disclosure are substantially similar to those imposed by the Act.

Under the 1969 regulations, the lender must furnish to the borrower, before the credit is extended, a written disclosure statement which sets forth (1) the cash price, (2) the down payment, (3) the total amount financed, (4) the dollar amount the loan will cost, (5) the approximate amount of the true annual interest rate, and (6) an explanation of the delinquency and default charges. The Act does not set any ceiling on finance charges or interest rates, nor does it affect state **usury** laws. A violator of the Act may incur both civil and criminal liability.

usury
charging a rate of interest on a loan higher than that permitted by statute

---

[20] 15 U.S.C. sec. 3901.   [21] 15 U.S.C.A. sec. 1601 et seq.

The Fair Credit Reporting Act

The Fair Credit Reporting Act became law in 1970.[22] Its purpose is to make available to consumers requesting credit the information relied upon by the merchant or the one extending the credit. This is done so that the consumer may check the accuracy of this information. The Act covers credit information supplied to potential creditors, insurers, or employers of that person. A less important goal is to help protect consumers against the discharge of such confidential information to persons who may have no legitimate use for it.

The Act focuses on the disclosure by the merchant to the consumer of the name and address of the credit reporting agency or credit bureau that made the report. If the consumer asks, the user of the information must disclose free of charge the information in the report. The consumer may require the credit reporting agency to delete any inaccurate or obsolete information from the file. If a dispute develops, the consumer may give his or her version of the dispute to the credit agency and they must put it in the file.

The consumer can require that a credit report be withheld from anyone who under the law does not have a legitimate business need for the information. Generally, the users of this information are businesses extending credit or employing the consumer. If there is a violation of the Act, the consumer may sue for damages plus punitive damages and attorney's fees.

The Equal Credit Opportunity Act

The Equal Credit Opportunity Act (ECOA)[23] was passed in 1977 to help prevent discrimination against any applicant for credit on the basis of race, color, religion, national origin, sex, or marital status. One of the strongest provisions of this Act requires the party extending credit to provide each applicant who is denied credit or whose account is terminated, the reasons for such action if the applicant requests. The Act applies to banks, finance companies, retail stores, credit card issuers, and other firms that usually extend credit. The Act does not guarantee credit to any applicant. The creditors may still set the standards, but the standards may not discriminate against one of the classes mentioned above.

Fair Debt Collection Practices Act

This Act[24] was passed in 1977 by Congress as an amendment to the CCPA discussed above in order to provide a remedy to consumers who are harassed by debt collectors. The Act can be enforced by the FTC or by damaged consumers and it applies only where there are no similar state laws applicable to the abuses of debt collectors. There are about 40 *states* with such laws, so this *federal* law applies in only a minority of the states. Generally, this law and the state laws like it, make it illegal to contact a consumer at unusual or inconvenient times and to use misleading tactics such as posing as an attorney or police officer. A debt collector who violates this Act may be liable for actual damages caused to the plaintiff; in addition, the plaintiff may be awarded punitive damages not to exceed $1,000, court costs and reasonable attorneys' fees.

Summary Statement

1. A consumer injured by a defective product may use the tort theories of negligence (negligent manufacture and negligent design of a product) and strict liability to state a good claim against a manufacturer.
2. The doctrine of *res ipsa loquitur* may help the plaintiff establish a prima facie case of negligence.

---

[22] 15 U.S.C.A. sec. 1681, et seq.   [23] 15 U.S.C.A. sec. 1691 et seq.   [24] 15 U.S.C.A. sec. 1692 et seq.

3. The theory of strict liability depends on a court's definition of "defect" and "unreasonably dangerous" as those terms are applied to products.
4. The defenses to a products liability claim based upon negligence, strict liability, and in some cases breach of warranty, include those related to the misuse of the product by the plaintiff. These defenses are contributory negligence of the plaintiff, assumption of a known risk, misuse, hypersensitivity, and lack of proximate causation.
5. Very recently courts have developed the legal principle of market share liability. This principle is used to shift the burden of causation from the plaintiff to the defendant in circumstances in which the plaintiff cannot prove with reasonable certainty which of several defendants caused the injury.
6. The Consumer Product Safety Commission was created to help collect data on defective products and related consumer injuries, and to help prevent consumer injury by the adoption of product safety standards.
7. The Federal Trade Commission can issue trade regulations and cease and desist orders to help prevent deceptive trade practices.
8. Consumer law also includes the federal and state regulation of credit. Three important federal statutes that regulate credit are The Consumer Credit Protection Act, The Fair Credit Reporting Act and The Equal Credit Opportunity Act.

The following case shows how the federal government is reacting to the products liability crisis. Generally, it does this by creating product safety standards.

Southland Mower Co. v. Consumer Product Safety Commission
619 F.2d 499 (1980).

Gee, Circuit J. Approximately 77,000 people are injured each year in the United States by contacting the blades of walk-behind power mowers. Of these injuries, an estimated 9,900 involve the amputation of at least one finger or toe, 11,400 involve fractures, 2,400 involve the tearing of flesh, there are 2,300 severe cuts and 51,400 other lesser cuts and lacerations requiring emergency room treatment. The annual economic cost inflicted by the 77,000 yearly blade-contact injuries has been estimated to be about $253 million and this figure does not include an amount for pain and suffering or for lost use of amputated fingers and toes.

To reduce these blade-contact injuries, the Consumer Product Safety Commission (CPSC) promulgated a safety standard for walk-behind power mowers. The standard consisted of three provisions: (1) a requirement that rotary walk-behind mowers pass a foot-probe test; (2) a requirement that rotary machines have a blade-control system that will stop the mower blade within three seconds after the operator's hands leave their normal operating position; and (3) a requirement, applicable to both rotary and reel-type mowers, that the product have a label of specified design to warn of the danger of blade contact. There were a few other standards not here important.

These standards were challenged by the Outdoor Power Equipment Institute (OPEI) as being too strict, severe, or inappropriate (for reasons discussed below), and by an interested consumer as being too lax. The arguments of OPEI, representing the manufacturers of power mowers, are, in part, that: the standard does include some non-consumer products within its scope; there was not substantial evidence on the record to support the foot-probe and shielding requirements; the blade-stopping requirement is a design restriction rather than a performance requirement; the technology required is currently unsafe and unreliable; and the three-second stopping time is not justified by the evidence.

Are the standards proposed by the CPSC within the jurisdiction of the Commission, are they appropriate and enforceable?

The Court held that some of the standards are appropriate and enforceable while others are not, so it affirmed the CPSC standards in some respects and vacated a few of the standards.

The legislation creating the CPSC requires that safety standards be supported by substantial evidence on the record as a whole. The foot-probe provision can be sustained only if the record contains such relevant evidence as a reasonable mind might accept as adequate to support a conclusion that an unreasonable risk of foot injury exists from blade contact at the discharge chute, that the foot-probe will lessen it, and that the benefits of this proposed reform make it reasonable in light of the burdens it imposes on product manufacturers and consumers. The determination of whether an unreasonable risk of discharge-chute injury exists involves a balancing test like that familiar in tort law: The regulation is enforceable if the severity of the injury that may result from the product, factored by the likelihood of the injury, offsets the harm the regulation imposes upon manufacturers and consumers. Under this test, even a very remote possibility that a product would inflict an extremely severe injury could pose an unreasonable risk of injury if the proposed safety standard promised to reduce the risk effectively without unduly increasing the product's price or decreasing its availability or usefulness. Conversely, if the potential injury is less severe, its occurrence must be proven more likely in order to render the risk unreasonable and the safety standard warranted. The court said that its examination of the record has failed to reveal substantial evidence that injury at the discharge-chute was sufficiently provable or likely that it made the risk addressed by the foot-probe of this area unreasonable. In a study of 36 blade-contact foot injuries conducted for CPSC, only one occurred when the operator inserted his foot into the blade path at the discharge-chute. So, this standard is unenforceable.

The blade-control system is intended to protect the operator against blade-contact injuries to both hands and feet by stopping the blade before the operator can contact it after he or she leaves the normal operating position and thus releases the deadman's control. The CPSC estimates that the blade-control provisions will eliminate approximately 46,500 operator blade-contact injuries a year. This figure represents approximately 60 percent of all blade-contact injuries and nearly 80 percent of all injuries claimed to be reduced by the standard. OPEI asserts that the standard is expressed as a design requirement rather than a performance requirement, and the Act creating the CPSC directs that a safety standard's provisions shall, whenever feasible, be expressed in terms of performance requirements. The court found that the blade-stop provisions are performance requirements. While the standard does mandate that the mower blades stop within a specified time period, it does not dictate a specific means of fulfilling this condition. Manufacturers are neither formally nor practically restricted to employing a particular design, since two existing and different mechanisms are capable of passing the blade-stop test.

Is there substantial evidence to support the selection of three seconds as the time limit within which blades must stop? The CPSC commissioned at least three studies to determine the length of time it took for a person to reach the blades after letting go of the handle. These times ranged from about .6 seconds to 4.9 seconds. In setting the blade-stop time, the CPSC considered not only the time in which an operator could reach the blade after releasing the deadman's control but also the incremental cost of successively faster blade-stop times. The record contains substantial evidence that the cost of the blade-stop mechanism varies inversely with the length of time in which the device stops the blade. The three-second requirement is not arbitrary and is supported by substantial evidence and is therefore valid.

[**Note:** The above case is a good illustration of how the federal government through one of its agencies, the CPSC, is attempting to reduce consumer-product related injuries. These types of injury are particularly difficult for the legal system to deal with because, in most cases, the injury is severe, but not severe enough to make it feasible to hire an attorney and sue the manufacturer under a rather vague and difficult cause of action of negligent design.]

Questions and Case Problems

1. Remington Arms, defendant, has sold approximately 3 million model 870 shotguns, primarily to hunters. It has sold 75 thousand model 870P shotguns to police departments, about 80% of all law enforcement agencies in the U.S. use this gun including the FBI and the U.S. secret service.

Officer Paton was unloading his model 870P at the scene of a disturbance when the gun discharged killing officer DeRosa. Officer Paton does not recall firing the weapon, but admits that he was holding it when it discharged. In subsequent laboratory tests, the gun was found to have been in good working order. The trigger pull and safety devices on the gun were set exactly as they had been designed to be.

The family of officer DeRosa sues Remington. State what argument you believe they made in their attempt to state a claim and whether you believe they would be successful. [*DeRosa v. Remington Arms Co., Inc.*, 509 F.Supp. 762 (D.Ct., N.Y., 1981).]

2. The following is the same problem as number 3 used in chapter 21. John wanted to buy a new electric drill. He saw an advertisement in the local newspaper which said that Sears was having a special sale on "½ inch electric drills, reduced 20% to $15." John went to Sears to buy the drill but was very interested in whether the drill was double-insulated. This meant that the drill had special wiring in it so that if a short developed the drill would not shock the user. John was interested in this feature because he often worked in his basement, where the floor was damp as the result of leaky plumbing, and there was a substantial risk of electrocution. John asked the saleswoman at Sears, "Do you have double-insulated drills?" The saleswoman replied, "We have just what you want," and got for John one of the drills on sale. She said, "This drill is double-insulated." John then said, "Fine, I'll take it," and handed her his Sears credit card. The saleswoman made out the appropriate sales slip and John left with the drill.

Assume that, after John purchased the drill, he was severely injured when using the drill in his basement, which was dry. You may also assume that the drill was not properly double-insulated. As a result of this defect, the drill exploded and caused John's basement to catch fire, resulting in $5,000 damage to the basement and personal injury to John. Also, assume that the drill was destroyed.

In a series of short paragraphs, first *define* and then *apply* the tort theories that John may use to help him state a good case against Sears for the injuries received.

3. The plaintiff, Philip Schemel, was a passenger in a car which was being driven within the 55 mph speed limit when it was struck from behind by a 1960 Chevrolet Impala traveling at a speed of about 115 mph. The plaintiff was injured and sues General Motors Corporation, the manufacturer of the Impala, defendant, alleging the following items:
   a. The defendant knew, or should have known, that there was no useful purpose in designing an automobile that could be driven at excessive speed.
   b. The defendant should have foreseen that the automobile would, in fact, be driven by someone at an excessive and unlawful speed, to the risk of the public in general.
   c. The defendant advertised the speed at which its automobile could be driven, thereby encouraging irresponsible persons to exceed lawful and reasonable speed limits.
   d. The defendant has a duty basically the same as that of any member of our society—the duty to act with reasonable care.
   e. Therefore, General Motors should be liable because they designed an automobile which they knew was capable of violating, and in fact would probably violate, the expressed social policy of traveling no faster than 55 mph; and the injury of the kind complained of was therefore reasonably foreseeable, given the design features of the Impala.

   The driver of the speeding car is not a party to the lawsuit, and nowhere does the plaintiff argue that the Impala was defective. Based on the material you read in this chapter, should a court dismiss the plaintiff's claim for failure to state a legally recognizable claim? [*Schemel v. General Motors Corporation*, 384 F.2d 802(1967).]

4. The plaintiff was burned severely when his General Motors pickup truck rolled over. He sued General Motors and Corbin Limited. Corbin manufactured the pants worn by the plaintiff at the time of the accident. The complaint against Corbin alleged that the "burn characteristics" of the pants enhanced the severity of the plaintiff's injuries. He alleged that the pants melted and stuck to flesh when they burned instead of disintegrating and falling away. The defendant, Corbin, has asked the court to join Burlington Industries, Inc.,

since Burlington manufactured all the fabric used by Corbin. Further, Corbin pleads that if they are found liable on a strict liability theory, then Burlington should pay the judgment. From what you know about strict liability law, do you think the plaintiff's complaint against Corbin based on a strict liability theory would be dismissed or do you think the case would be heard? Do you think a court would require the plaintiff to prove its case against Burlington, or against the seller of the pants, Corbin? [See, *Kelly v. General Motors Corp.,* 487 F.Supp. 1041 (D. Ct., Mont. 1980).]

5. The plaintiff filed a wrongful death action against Velcro USA, Inc., the defendant. The defendant makes velcro, a type of closing device used on coats, pants and other garments. It consists of one pad of plastic loops that attaches to another pad of hooks. The plaintiff's husband was killed when, it was alleged, the velcro closure installed on the deflation panel of his Raven S-55 hot air balloon failed and the balloon fell to the ground. Velcro never participated in the design, manufacture, sale or servicing of hot air balloons. Velcro alleges that, when it found out about velcro's use on hot air balloons, they attempted to bring to the attention of the aviation community the inherent dangers of such usage. Velcro tried to have the Federal Aviation Administration issue a directive about the dangers in the use of velcro in aviation devices, but the agency refused. In addition, Velcro sent a direct warning to all registered owners of balloons known to use velcro. There is evidence the deceased received the warning but failed to pay attention to it.

    The plaintiff attempts to state a claim based on breach of express and implied warranties, negligence and strict liability. Do you think evidence of Velcro's attempt to warn users of its product should be admitted as evidence of a valid defense? [*Temple v. Velcro USA., Inc.,* 196 Cal.Rptr. 531 (Cal. 1983).]

6. P had taken a common medicine used to relieve the symptoms of the flu. Following repeated use of the medicine, P developed cataracts in her eyes. The doctors said, and subsequent tests proved, that there was a link between the cataracts and the medicine. P cannot recall the manufacturer or brand name of the medicine, and the place where she bought it sells many such medicines. Can P state a claim in court against a manufacturer of the medicine? What is the legal issue in this case and how would P respond to the arguments of the defendant?

7. In your own words and from a consumer's perspective, list some of the shortcomings of using the two major tort theories of products liability. Aside from the loss of money, what objections would a manufacturer who distributes nationwide have to these theories? How does the Model Uniform Product Liability Act propose to deal with these shortcomings and objections?

8. What is the function of the Federal Trade Commission, and how does it carry out its tasks with regard to protecting consumers?

9. Juan Maldonado, a Puerto Rican born American male, applied to Standard Oil Company for a credit card. He did own a home and a car but was planning on buying a new VW convertible. He had no debts out of the ordinary for a person who bought some of his consumer items on credit. Standard denied him a credit card and gave no reason for this. What are his remedies, if any, and how might Standard respond to avoid liability?

10. In the case of *Southland Mower Co. v. Consumer Product Safety Commission,* 619 F.2d 499 (1980),[25] what arguments did the petitioners (OPEI) use to attack the safety standards of the CPSC? In your opinion is such federal regulation worthwhile?

---

[25] See pp. 335–36.

Ethics and Business Law in Part 4
Sales and Consumer Law

Introduction

This end-of-Part discussion, like the others in this book, is designed to encourage students to begin forming personal beliefs about what is right or wrong conduct in business. The discussion here builds on the material in the first end-of-Part discussions on pages 58 to 69; you may find it helpful to review that.

This material has several goals. The "sampling of ethical issues" section immediately following is designed to help you see the range of ethical issues associated with this area of the law. The in-depth discussion is intended to provide you with a background for forming your own beliefs about a single very important ethical issue in business. The problems at the end of this Part are designed to build your skill in ethical analysis while exploring further the in-depth issue.

A Sampling of Ethical Issues in Sales and Consumer Law

In many ways, the ethical issues in the law of sales are similar to those discussed for the law of contracts. Thus, promise keeping is again a critical issue which arises when a promise does not constitute a contract. The statute of frauds, or the statute of limitations, may make the promise unenforceable in court. But does this eliminate your ethical duty to fulfill your promise?

Products liability law raises another classic ethical issue. If both the manufacturer and the buyer of a product are without fault, who ought to pay for an injury? If the buyer pays for the injury, this reduces the manufacturer's costs, perhaps allowing lower prices. Since more people benefit from lower prices, utilitarians prefer this outcome. On the other hand, Kant's philosophy is likely to condemn this approach because it uses the injured buyer exclusively as a means to lower prices.

Another ethics issue is associated with the extent of the manufacturer's obligation to make products safe. For example, how much money should auto makers be required to spend to make their cars safe? If they can save one life by spending an additional $10,000 should they be required to do so? Most of us would say yes. But what if the cost to save the one life rose to $50,000, or $250,000, or $10,000,000? Can we attach a financial value to a human life?

Warranty law and freedom of contract also raise ethical issues. Since merchants can waive warranties such as the warranty of merchantability, many do. Consumers often purchase certain products without an awareness of the presence or absence of a warranty. Does the fact that consumers are not paying attention to this part of the transaction justify merchants in modifying the implied warranties? Does the idea of "freedom of contract" protect this practice by merchants?

Section 2-302 of the UCC makes clauses or contracts unenforceable if they are unconscionable. This is an attempt to give judges flexibility and the opportunity to assess particular transactions against an uncertain, but clearly ethical, standard as opposed to the usually clear legal standard. Notice that the uncertain standard here in the law creates social costs because many more people cannot determine whether their agreements are enforceable. Is it better to have a legal system with clear, precise rules which may produce some unfair results, or is it better to have a system which is uncertain and allows greater judicial flexibility but produces fewer unfair results?

In-Depth Discussion of a Basic Issue: Is Legal Always Ethical?

Does the legality of an act always make it ethical? To illustrate, your study of both sales and contract law has equipped you to determine whether the courts will enforce one of your promises. This discussion is designed to help you decide whether you believe, for example, that you are bound to your promises even when they do not constitute a contract and thus are not enforceable in court. In a sense, we are asking whether or not conduct which may be unethical by some standards, can be justified because it is legal. The following section describes some of these ethical standards.

The Egoist Views

Many who believe that there is not an ethical obligation in business, beyond obeying the law, justify this conclusion with egoistic reasoning. Thus, this group simply asks what course of conduct generates for them the greatest benefit. They often see that there are great benefits associated with ignoring the effect of their conduct on others and seeking only their own self-interest. For example, persons in this group would be willing to deceive others as long as it does not constitute fraud. The reality is that in many business situations, deception—which does not necessarily constitute fraud—is often profitable. Similarly, this group in dealing with a naive person might *orally* contract to sell wheat at the market price when delivery is to take place 60 days later. If during the 60 days the price goes down, these egoists would assert the statute of frauds making the contract unprovable and, therefore, unenforceable. If the price goes up, they would not assert the statute and would enforce the wheat contract. For convenience we will refer to this group as "open egoists."

Another group of egoists follow typical ethical standards in business because they conclude that this conduct makes good business sense. This group has decided that—in a practical sense—you always, "reap as you shall sow" or that, "what goes around, comes around." That is, you maximize your self-interest by always appearing to be ethical. This group would not assert the defense of the statute of frauds on the wheat transaction because they believe this would injure their business reputation. We can call this group "timid egoists."

Other egoists reject the views described above. They believe that they must *generally* appear to be ethical but that they can profitably act very self-interestedly *in some situations*. The focus here is on the careful evaluation of each situation to determine whether it is profitable to *appear* clearly self-interested. If a transaction is *public,* then one acts with *apparent* ethics. On the other hand, if a transaction is *not visible* and the other party is one not likely to be a source of future business, then it makes sense for the egoist to do things such as asserting the statue of frauds in the wheat transaction. We will refer to this group as "disguised egoists."

Utilitarian Views

Some utilitarians reach the same conclusions about conduct as many kinds of egoists, but for different reasons. They believe that ethics ought not to play a role in business decision making; that it is the role of the legal system to ensure that profitable and legal conduct benefits society. These persons sometimes assert that they are unable to decide what is best for society and, therefore, they should only try to decide what is best for themselves. They justify self-centered action on the basis that the legal system functions with sufficient perfection so that society's interests and their self-interests are the same. When legal imperfections are obvious, this group often concludes that self-centered action which exploits the imperfection leads to its cure. That is, by engaging in acts which appear to be unethical, these utilitarians draw attention to the flaws in the legal system and thereby promote reforms which make such future conduct illegal. This group of utilitarians clearly acknowledges that there are imperfections in our legal system. But they see no need to evaluate obligations beyond obeying the law because they see self-interest and the utilitarian interests as the same. We can call this group "quasi-utilitarians."

"Pure utilitarians" reject the line of reasoning which is used to purportedly justify exploitation of legal imperfections. This reasoning is condemned as a form of rationalizing—a way to espouse utilitarian views while acting as an egoist. Pure utilitarians believe that each individual must try to forecast the consequences of each act and only do those things which will generate the greatest good for the greatest number. For these utilitarians, it is clear that the law is only one of many ethical constraints on business behavior.

Kantian and Religious Views

In general the Kantian and Religious views, like that of the pure utilitarian, clearly conclude that there are duties in business beyond simply obeying the law. These groups derive their ethical obligations from sources independent of the law. For Kantians, the source is duty, identified by making acts or rules universal. For religious persons, the source is usually a sacred writing or the teachings of a prophet or church. For these groups, compliance with the law is only one part of a much broader range of ethical duties.

To Which Group Do You Belong?

One way to begin thinking about your beliefs about whether there is a duty beyond simply obeying the law is to assess how you would react to working for supervisors who were open egoists, timid egoists, disguised egoists, quasi-utilitarians, pure utilitarians, Kantian, or Religious. Do you find some of these ethical orientations more appealing in a supervisor than others? Similarly, you might ask yourself whom you would want to be doing business with on a regular basis?

Solving Ethics Problems

Like the other end-of-Part discussions in this book, this one presents problems for you to consider. These problems have three goals. The first is to give you the opportunity to further explore the in-depth issue. The second goal is to give you experience in ethical reasoning about the law and about related management problems. The third goal is to let you see how thinking critically about the law can increase your ability to make ethical decisions. To facilitate this, the problems begin by asking you to analyze the law for its ethical content and then shift to looking at related problems in managerial ethics.

For a discussion of the ethical roles of markets and the law, and examples of the four styles of ethical reasoning—egoism, utilitarianism, Kant's philosophy, and religious ethics—read the business ethics material at the end of Part 1.

Problems

1. Review the case of *Philipp Brothers v. El Salto, S.A.*, on page 248. Assume that El Salto's statements are true, that there was an oral agreement whereby Philipp would advance the $750,000. Do you think it is ethical, making these assumptions, for Philipp to assert the parol evidence rule?
2. Suppose someone decided to buy a used car and began following the want ads for a particular model in the *The New York Times*. After following the ads for two months and inspecting many of the cars he became very aware of the values of these models. One day an ad appeared offering a car for sale for $2,100. After looking at it the buyer decided that it was worth $4,400. The seller was a bright

college student who was just unaware of the market for this car. The buyer bargained with the student and agreed on a purchase price of $1,750. Later the student discovered the true value of the car and sued, claiming lack of consideration. Who prevails in the lawsuit? Assess the buyer's conduct in the context of our imperfect legal and economic systems using the four styles of ethical reasoning. Do *you* believe the conduct of the buyer was ethical?

3. Assume that you have entered into a contract for the purchase of a year's supply of exterior base paint for your painting business which you operate part-time during the school year and full time during summers. The contract price is $6.75 per gallon, about fair market value for a large wholesale purchase. You know that the seller's profit on the transaction is about seventy-five cents per gallon. Further you know that the paint has been ordered, delivered and is in storage at the wholesaler's warehouse. Later, you learn that another paint supplier is on the verge of bankruptcy and is willing to sell the same paint for $3.75 per gallon. What is the amount of your legal liability if you breach your contract? What is the amount of your savings if you breach and purchase from the near bankrupt supplier? Evaluate this conduct using the four basic styles of ethical reasoning. Which style of ethical reasoning do you find most appealing?

4. Suppose you were the owner of a mail-order house specializing in small farm implements such as shovels, hoes, spades, and brooms. A buyer outside your target market, a manufacturer, ordered 144 specialized shovels which he intended to use in his firm's production process. After he received the shovels it took him almost 6 months to try them out and discover that they would not do what he had hoped they would. As a result he is now asking to return the shovels and get his money back. You have discussed the matter with your lawyer and he informs you that you have no legal liability to do anything. Your profit on the transaction is about $1,000. If you refund the whole amount, you would lose all of your profit on the transaction, but you could resell the shovels in a year. Since the manufacturer has no use for specialized shovels you can probably buy them back for about half what you sold them for. If you do that, you can resell them and earn a total profit of $1,500. How would a disguised egoist analyze this transaction? How would a religious person analyze it? What do you think is the right thing to do? Why?

PART 5 Commercial Paper

23. Introduction to Commercial Paper and Banking Operations
The concept of the negotiable instrument and how its creation is dependent upon matters of form. Relationships and duties assumed by parties associated with negotiable instruments are explored. You will see how these instruments are processed by the banking industry.

24. Transfer and Negotiation
How rights existing in negotiable instruments can be transferred to third persons and how additional rights by warranty become associated with the instrument.

25. Holder, Holder in Due Course, and Defenses
The concept of the holder in due course, the most favored status with regard to rights associated with negotiable instruments, and the limitations placed upon the holder in due course status by personal and real defenses.

26. Banks, Checks, and Customer Relations
The relationship of a bank to its customer, especially the bank's liability to its customer. Transactions involving checks are viewed from all dimensions and special cases are examined.

27. Deadlines and Discharge
The establishment of duties that the parties owe on negotiable instruments, and discussion of how these duties are discharged.

Summary

Over the centuries it was recognized that it was much more convenient, and in many ways safer, to use paper which could transfer *rights to payment* than to use money. If the paper qualified as "negotiable" as opposed to "non-negotiable," it could pass to an innocent purchaser *greater rights* than are normally transferred to another by assignment. "Commercial paper" under Article 3 of the Uniform Commercial Code may be either negotiable or non-negotiable. Our main concern in Part 5, Commercial Paper, is with that kind of commercial paper called the "negotiable instrument." A negotiable instrument is a signed writing, containing an unconditional promise or order to pay, a sum certain in money, on demand or at a definite time, to the order of someone or to the bearer of the instrument. If any of these elements is missing, the paper is non-negotiable. Keep in mind that the paper is still legal and enforceable as a contract, but it is simply not negotiable.

Negotiable instruments are in the form of checks, drafts, promissory notes, and certificates of deposit. Some instruments—payable to bearer in form—can be "negotiated" by their delivery to a "holder." Other instruments—payable to order in form—require for their negotiation an indorsement coupled with delivery. If the indorsement is not proper, the recipient will be only a **transferee,** not a holder. A mere transferee cannot be a holder in due course with rights superior to those of an assignee.

The holder in due course is a holder who takes the instrument "in due course"—i.e., for value, in good faith, and without notice of various improper circumstances which would destroy the justification for conferring greater rights in the holder.

We will see that parties to negotiable instruments and those holding such instruments have rights and duties toward each other.

Banks have an important role in the collection of checks. They have rights and duties toward each other and toward their customers.

An understanding of Article 3 of the Uniform Commercial Code is essential to learning the law of commercial paper.

Business ethics as it relates to the text material in this Part is considered at the end of the Part.

transferee
one to whom another has transferred something

23 Introduction to Commercial Paper and Banking Operations

After you have read this chapter, you should be able to:

1. Understand the concept of negotiability.
2. Recognize practical applications of negotiable instruments.
3. Relate the flow of commercial paper to banking operations.
4. Identify the various types of negotiable instruments.
5. Discuss the formal requirements of negotiable instruments.

Introduction

Most people take negotiable instruments for granted, and there are very good reasons for this. Each time someone writes a check for the purchase of goods and services, or signs a promissory note for a loan or for a purchase on credit, in all likelihood that person has created a negotiable instrument.

The **negotiable instrument** is a **formal** written **contract** used extensively in everyday business transactions. It is a means by which a person called a "holder in due course" can get "greater rights" against the party who made or drew the instrument than would be the case if liability depended simply on the law of contracts. Accordingly, it becomes extremely important to learn about negotiable instruments as a kind of commercial paper.

Negotiation and Assignment Compared

A familiar illustration can quickly identify and compare the qualities of negotiation with an *assignment,* a legal concept that was introduced in Part 2, Contracts. Suppose that Mary buys *for business use* a $600 electric typewriter from Pete on credit. The sales contract may allow her a period of time—six months, for example—before she is required to pay the purchase price. Prior to the due date, however, Pete is entitled to sell or assign his rights in the contract to a third party.

Assume that Pete sells his rights in the $600 contract to Community Bank for $500 cash—a $100 discount. In this event, Community, the assignee, simply steps into the shoes of Pete, assignor. Community receives all of Pete's rights, but it is also subject to all of the defenses against Pete which Mary might raise under the original contract. If, for example, Pete had warranted the typewriter and the warranty is breached, Mary's defense in refusing to pay under the original contract will be valid against Community just as it would have been against Pete if he had never made the assignment. Community may then recover from Pete under the terms of the assignment contract or on the basis of an implied warranty.

Now, consider the difference in outcome if the credit terms of the sale to Mary are embodied in the form of a negotiable promissory note[1] payable to the order of Pete. Mary would be the "maker"[2] of the note and Pete the "payee" to whom it was payable. He could then indorse and transfer the note in a manner that would create in the Community Bank the rights of a **holder in due course**[3] **(HIDC).**

If the note was not voluntarily paid at maturity, Community could enforce it against Mary despite the breach of warranty defense mentioned above and most other defenses that she could raise.[4] Mary would then be compelled to bring a warranty action against Pete to rescind the contract or to recover money damages for getting the typewriter fixed.

In either event, notice that the responsibility for the breach ultimately falls on Pete, as it should. However, when a negotiable promissory note is used as a credit instrument, HIDCs like the bank can be confident of getting a judgment against the primary party-maker, Mary, or, as will be discussed later, against the secondary party-indorser,[5] Pete.

The HIDC Concept

From the point of view of HIDCs then, negotiable instruments are a great advantage over mere assignment. *Greater rights can be obtained by an HIDC of a negotiable instrument than by an assignee of a contract right.* Indirectly they benefit debtors too, because many sales would not be made unless the seller-payee could depend on negotiating the instrument for cash to some third party, typically a bank or finance company.

This transaction is known as *discounting.* The seller-payee will normally receive less than face value for the note—e.g., a $1,000 note may sell for $980 (a low discount) or for $800 or less (a high discount).

negotiable instrument
a writing signed by the maker or drawer containing an unconditional promise or order to pay a sum certain in money payable on demand or at a definite time to order or to bearer

formal contract
a contract which must be in a certain form

A negotiable instrument as a credit device.

holder in due course (HIDC)
the holder of a negotiable instrument who takes it for value, in good faith, and without notice that the instrument is overdue or has been dishonored or of any defense against, or claim to, the instrument by any person

Discounting.

---

[1] UCC 3–104(1).   [2] UCC 3–413(1).   [3] UCC 3–302.

[4] UCC 3–305.   [5] UCC 3–414(1).

The difference between face value and the discount price is the margin or yield. The purpose of this margin is to compensate the third party for its risk. This margin will vary, depending on the credit rating of the debtor, the length of time until maturity, and the security or collateral which stands behind the instrument in the event of default.

Negotiable Instruments As a Substitute for Money

Negotiable instruments can be used as substitutes for money just as, in the previous example, a promissory note was used as a credit device. The *check*, which is a form of a **draft** drawn on a bank and payable on demand, is the most familiar illustration.[6] (See figures 23.1–23.3.)

Assume that David, who has money on deposit in a checking account with Hometown Bank, draws a $25 **check** payable to the order of Pineville Bookstore, payee, for the purchase of textbooks. An authorized agent of the bookstore, usually the cashier who handles the transaction, will indorse on the back of the check with a rubber stamp: "Pay to Community Bank, For Deposit, Pineville Bookstore."[7]

As a routine matter, this check, along with other items,[8] will be placed in Pineville's depositary bank,[9] Community. Pineville Bookstore will be given a $25 provisional credit[10] in its checking account, and the check will be forwarded through bank channels to David's Hometown Bank, known as the **drawee,** payor bank.[11]

If there are sufficient funds on deposit in **drawer** David's checking account, the item will be debited, or charged, against his balance. Periodically, David will receive through the mail a statement of his account and often his cancelled checks.

The provisional credit that **payee** Pineville Bookstore received at Community becomes final since the check was paid from David's account by Hometown. Pineville Bookstore can now draw on that account as it wishes—e.g., to pay its bills, replenish its inventory, or expand its operations.

If David did not have sufficient funds on deposit with Hometown, the drawee-payor bank, or if for some reason David stopped payment on his check,[12] the check would be returned through channels to Community. Community would then reverse the provisional credit with an offsetting debit entry and return the check to Pineville Bookstore.

At this stage Pineville would have to collect on the check from David, perhaps resulting in a lawsuit. Keep in mind that the payment of debts with checks or notes is conditional payment only—conditioned on the instrument being paid.[13]

You can see that an assignment of contract rights would be very awkward in this situation. Checks, however, are tailor-made for such transactions. With very little change, if Community Bank permitted Pineville to withdraw the funds represented by David's check prior to its being "bounced," or returned, Community Bank may become an HIDC of the check since it paid value for it by advancing money to Pineville. In that capacity, Community could proceed against David, the drawer, on the check, and most defenses that David could raise would be ineffective against Community as an HIDC. The HIDC Community Bank could, and probably would, first make every effort to collect from its customer Pineville, the payee-indorser; but the status of HIDC is very valuable because it practically assures Community of a judgment against David.

---

draft
a negotiable instrument containing an unconditional order, (e.g., "pay")

check
a negotiable "draft drawn on a bank and payable on demand" UCC 3–104 (2)(b)

drawee
the person on whom a draft is drawn and ordered to pay

drawer
the person who initially draws or creates and signs a draft

payee
the person to whose order the instrument is originally written

---

[6] UCC 3–104(2)(b).

[7] This indorsement is "special," UCC 3–204(1), because it names the person to whom it is indorsed; it is also "restrictive," 3–205(c), because it limits the things that the indorsee Community Bank can do with it. The bank can place this for deposit only in the Pineville Bookstore's account and forward the check for collection.

[8] UCC 4–104(1)(g).   [9] UCC 4–105(a).   [10] UCC 4–201(1).

[11] UCC 4–105(b).   [12] UCC 4–403.   [13] UCC 3–802(1)(b).

Figure 23.1 Check Flow Chart

Figure 23.2 Sample Check

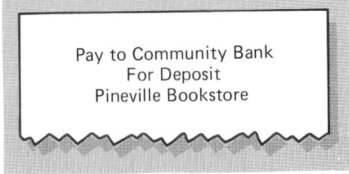

Figure 23.3 Deposit Stamp on Back of Check

```
Pay to Community Bank
     For Deposit
   Pineville Bookstore
```

Types of Negotiable Instrument—Notes and Drafts

Many new terms were introduced during the previous discussion of the concept of negotiability. In this part of the chapter we will elaborate on these terms and observe further the importance of negotiability as we discuss:

1. the types of instrument;
2. the parties and banks that deal with them;
3. the form which all instruments must have in order to be negotiable.

All instruments are either notes or drafts.[14] Notes *promise* payment and are promissory instruments, while drafts *order* payment and are order instruments. Notes are *two-party* instruments in which a maker, such as a credit purchaser or borrower, promises to pay money to a payee. A certificate of deposit, shown in figure 23.4, is a particular kind of note in which a bank acknowledges receipt of money and engages to repay it.

Notes are promises, drafts are orders.

Notes are two-party instruments.

[14] UCC 3–104(2).

Figure 23.4   Certificate of Deposit

```
┌─────────────────────────────────────────────────────────────────────────┐
│                      ╭─── CERTIFICATE OF DEPOSIT ───╮                   │
│  NO INTEREST PAID AFTER DUE DATE    INVESTMENT—SAVINGS                  │
│                                                            No. 2382     │
│            HILLSBORO, MASSACHUSETTS _____                    │
│                                                                         │
│   THIS CERTIFIES THAT _____  │
│                            HAS DEPOSITED WITH                           │
│                              Hometown    HILLSBORO,                     │
│                             State Bank   MASSACHUSETTS   $ _____     │
│                                                                         │
│   _____ DOLLARS   │
│   PAYABLE _____ DAYS-MONTHS AFTER DATE IN CURRENT FUNDS ON RETURN │
│   OF THIS CERTIFICATE PROPERLY ENDORSED WITH INTEREST                   │
│   AT THE RATE OF _____ PER CENT PER ANNUM.                            │
│   THIS CERTIFICATE SHALL BE CONSIDERED RENEWED AUTOMATICALLY FOR THE    │
│   SAME LENGTH OF TIME AND INTEREST RATE FROM ITS ORIGINAL MATURITY AND  │
│   THEREAFTER FOR SUCCESSIVE PERIODS OF TIME OF THE SAME LENGTH, UNLESS  │
│   PRESENTED FOR REDEMPTION WITHIN TEN (10) DAYS AFTER THE END OF THE    │
│   ORIGINAL TERM OR ANY SUBSEQUENT TERM. THE BANK MAY REDEEM THIS        │
│   CERTIFICATE AT ANY ORIGINAL OR SUBSEQUENT MATURITY DATE BY TEN (10)   │
│   DAYS WRITTEN NOTICE TO THE PAYEE AT HIS ADDRESS SHOWN BY THE BANK'S   │
│   RECORDS. IF SUCH NOTICE IS GIVEN, THIS DEPOSIT WILL NOT BEAR INTEREST │
│   AFTER THE REDEMPTION DATE. SUBJECT TO THE FOREGOING, THIS CERTIFICATE │
│   IS CONTINUOUS; NO RENEWAL NECESSARY.                                  │
│   TAX I.D. NO.         ADDRESS                                          │
│   ☐ DEPOSIT INTEREST TO ACCOUNT                                         │
│   ☐ ADD INTEREST TO PRINCIPAL UPON RENEWAL    _____   │
│                                               EXEC. ASSISTANT CASHIER—  │
│                                                     VICE PRESIDENT      │
│                      ╰─── NOT SUBJECT TO CHECK ───╯                     │
└─────────────────────────────────────────────────────────────────────────┘
```

Drafts are three-party instruments.

Drafts are *three*-party instruments in which a drawer orders the drawee to pay to a payee. A check is a special form of a draft which is *drawn on a bank,* drawee. The drawee bank is ordered to pay the money *on demand.*

Notes and drafts may or may not be negotiable. If not negotiable, they are still legal and enforceable as contracts, and they may be transferred by *assignment;* but they cannot be negotiated.

Negotiability Is a Matter of Form

The form which notes and drafts must assume in order to qualify as negotiable will be discussed in detail later; but, to aid in understanding the various types of commercial paper, notice that *all negotiable instruments must comply with all of the following requirements:*

1. the instrument must be in writing and signed by the maker or drawer;
2. each instrument must contain an unconditional promise or order to pay a sum certain in money;
3. the time of payment must be on demand or at a definite time; and
4. each instrument must be payable to order or to bearer.[15]

Negotiable Promissory Notes

Recall the previous hypothetical situation in which Mary purchased a typewriter on credit and financed the unpaid balance by creating a $600 negotiable promissory note to the order of Pete, payee. The note had two parties, **maker** and *payee,* and a promise to pay. The instrument gave a definite time before the maker, Mary, was required to pay.

maker
the person who initially makes and signs a promissory note

This illustrated the use of a negotiable note as a credit device.[16] If the terms had called for payment on demand,[17] Pete could have required payment at any time after the

---
[15] UCC 3–104(1).   [16] UCC 3–109.   [17] UCC 3–108.

Part 5: Commercial Paper

Figure 23.5 Promissory Note

PROMISSORY NOTE

NAME John Robinson   NO. 471-00-3322 $ 1000.00

DUE Demand   SECURITY Signature   HILLSBORO, MASSACHUSETTS Current Date , 19 _____

On demand, or if no demand is made, then   Six Months   after date, without grace,

I, we or either of us, as principals, promise to pay to the order of Hillsboro State Bank, Hillsboro, Massachusetts,

the sum of One Thousand Dollars & 00/100 ——————————————————————— Dollars

with interest at the rate of 10% percent per annum from date until paid, at its offices in Hillsboro, Massachusetts.
  And in the event default is made in the payment of this note at maturity and it is placed in the hands of an attorney for collection, or suit is brought on same, then a reasonable additional amount shall be added as attorney's and collection fees.
  The makers and endorsers hereof hereby severally waive all notices, demands for payment, presentation hereof for payment, protest in case this note is not paid at maturity, and agree to all extensions and partial payments before or after maturity without prejudice to holder, and further agree that any one of them, acting individually, may renew this note and thereby extend the time for payment of any portion of the principal and accumulated interest due and agree to pay an interest rate to be determined at the time of such renewal. Makers agree that each of them shall be and remain obligated as principals during any such extended period for payment. The death or loss of capacity of any of the makers hereof shall not revoke or terminate, as to the other makers, the authority of each to renew and extend this note for and on behalf of all other surviving or non-incapacitated makers.

(signed) *John Robinson*   Address Hillsboro, Mass.
(signed) *Larry Cox*   Address Hillsboro, Mass.
(signed) *Richard Nelson*   Address Hillsboro, Mass.
Form 77B Revised

Promissory Note
1. Which party or parties occupy a position analogous to that of Mary in the textbook example?
2. Which party most closely resembles Pete, the person who sold Mary the car?
3. If John Robinson receives the entire $1000, what function do the signatures of Cox and Nelson serve?
4. What is an acceleration clause? Does this instrument have an acceleration clause?
5. Since three parties have signed this note payable to the order of the bank, does that fit the definition of a note as a TWO PARTY instrument and a PROMISE to pay?

note was issued to him.[18] This would not have suited the needs of the parties quite as well, but on some occasions the only way a maker can induce the payee to lend money or to sell on credit is by promising to pay on demand.

Mary, the maker of the note, is undertaking a direct and personal obligation to pay Pete the $600 at maturity. No one else is being ordered to pay on her behalf. Since the maker is absolutely liable, she is described as a "primary party."[19] (Figure 23.5 shows an example of a promissory note.)

Negotiable Drafts

If the terms of an instrument include three parties—a *drawer* who orders a *drawee* to pay money to a *payee*—the instrument is a draft. (Figure 23.6 shows an envelope draft.) Suppose that a draft is used to finance the credit sale of $1,000 worth of goods. The seller may draw a six-month time-draft on the *buyer-drawee* ordering the buyer to pay $1,000 to a payee. The payee may be the seller, the seller's bank, or any person designated by the seller.

This type of draft is known as a *trade acceptance*. When the instrument is drawn by the seller ordering the buyer to pay and it is signed as accepted by the *buyer,* the buyer becomes an **acceptor,** and now is a *primary party* with liability on the instrument similar to that of the maker of a note.[20] Primary parties are directly liable on the instrument they sign; unlike secondary parties, they do not expect someone else to pay on their behalf.

acceptor
the drawee on a draft who has assented in writing on the draft to pay it

---

[18] UCC 3–122(1)(b). [19] UCC 3–413(1). [20] UCC 3–413(1).

Figure 23.6 Envelope Draft

Customer's Draft

Hillsboro State Bank

On Demand/at Sight   HILLSBORO, MASSACHUSETTS   Current Date _____ 19___

PAY TO THE ORDER OF __Payee-Seller_____ $ __1,000.00__

One Thousand Dollars and No/100 ———————————————————— DOLLARS
VALUE RECEIVED AND CHARGE TO ACCOUNT OF   WITH EXCHANGE

ENCLOSURES Invoice in triplicate airway bill of lading; marine and war risk insurance; non-negotiable airway bill of lading.

TO __Drawee-Buyer_____

THROUGH __Seller's Bank_____   ____Drawer-Seller____

FORM 163

Envelope Draft

1. This draft is in the form of an envelope that will enclose the invoice, insurance policies, and bill of lading. The drawee-buyer is entitled to examine these documents before paying the $1000.
2. This draft is payable *on demand* or *at sight*. While the buyer can examine the enclosed documents to see that they are in proper order, the buyer must not use them to pick up the goods at the carrier's depot until the buyer has paid the draft.
3. A trade acceptance is a draft that would have given the buyer a *credit period* after his signature or acceptance of the draft. The time period would be, for example, six months after date. There is no place for the drawee-buyer's signature on this draft, but on the typical trade acceptance there will be a designated line.
4. A bank acceptance is a draft resembling a trade acceptance, except, by prior arrangement, the buyer's bank agrees to become the drawee-acceptor and to sign or accept on behalf of its customer.

If the *bank* accepts the draft—usually by prior arrangement between the buyer and his bank—the instrument is known as a *banker's acceptance*.

The importance of this distinction becomes apparent if you visualize a situation in which the payee needs cash before the instrument matures in six months. If the payee should decide to **negotiate** the instrument—i.e., indorse and discount the draft for as much cash as it will bring on the market—do you suppose the payee will receive a higher price (low discount from face value) if the instrument has been accepted by a bank rather than accepted by the buyer alone? Chances are that a purchaser of the paper will pay more for a banker's acceptance. Other things being equal, the bank's financial status and reputation will make this instrument more desirable than a trade acceptance.

negotiate
to deliver a negotiable instrument to a holder

Of course, most buyer-drawees will discharge their liability at maturity by full payment, but the financial reputation of the party who accepts can make an important difference. If a seller-payee wants to be assured of a ready and willing market for the draft, and also of a high price (low discount), a banker's acceptance normally is preferable to him.

Not all drafts are time drafts with a definite maturity date. Some are sight drafts payable "at sight" or "on demand" when presented to the drawee.

A check is the most common example of a draft payable on demand. Remember that a check is a special form of draft that is always drawn on a bank.[21] In the normal course of things it is expected that the drawee bank will pay on demand the amount designated in the check. Then the bank will charge or reduce the drawer-depositor's account by that amount.

---

[21] UCC 3-104(2)(b).

Other forms are the **cashier's check** and the *traveller's check*. A cashier's check is drawn by a bank officer (cashier) on the bank itself as drawee and payable to the order of a payee. It resembles a note since the one drawing the draft (the drawer) and the one expected to pay (the drawee) are the same party. The bank drawer of a cashier's check cannot stop payment on it, as is illustrated by the following case.

cashier's check
a check drawn by a bank on itself and payable to the order of a payee

Facts
Reinhard purchased goods from the plaintiff, Moon Over the Mountain Ltd. He paid for them by delivering to the plaintiff's agent a cashier's check which he had purchased from the defendant, Marine Midland Bank, where he was a customer. The check was drawn by the defendant payable to the plaintiff's agent, who indorsed and delivered it to the plaintiff. It was then deposited for collection in the bank where plaintiff had its account. Meanwhile, Reinhard decided to stop payment on the check and directed the defendant to do so. The check was returned to plaintiff's bank marked "Payment Stopped." Plaintiff sued the defendant on the check and obtained a judgment. Defendant appealed.

Decision
Affirmed for plaintiff.

Reasoning
Since under UCC 3–802(1)(a) the payee loses its right against its debtor when a cashier's check is taken in payment of an underlying debt, the bank drawer cannot refuse payment on the instrument. The bank here has drawn and issued the cashier's check; it is primarily liable thereon and cannot stop payment.

Moon Over the Mountain Ltd. v. Marine Midland Bank, 87 Misc.2d 918 (N.Y. 1976).

A traveller's check may name as drawee a financial institution that is not a bank. Strictly speaking, then, it is not a check at all but a draft.

In its original form, the traveller's check does not name a payee. The payee will be specified later when the owner or "traveller" decides to use or cash the check; the owner will then insert the name of the payee. The "traveller" will also be required to sign the instrument when it is used. This gives the recipient payee, perhaps a hotel or airline, an opportunity to verify the owner's written signature at that time by comparing it with the owner's written signature on the instrument as it was originally issued.

A *letter of credit* (shown in figure 23.7) is neither a draft nor a note. It is a promise by a bank or other person to honor or to pay drafts drawn in accordance with its terms. For example, a Texas merchant who is not well known beyond the borders of his home state may bargain with his bank to guarantee payment of drafts drawn upon it by Mexican or Japanese exporters. This will allow the Texas businessperson to make purchases of goods that would not have been sold to him on the strength of his credit alone.

Parties

By this time most of the parties and banks that deal with negotiable instruments have been introduced. To review and reenforce one's knowledge of this material, it will be discussed in more detail under the subheadings "Primary Parties," "Secondary Parties," and "Other Parties," including banks.

Primary Parties

Primary parties are *makers* of *notes* and *acceptors* of *drafts*.[22] The party or parties who purchase on credit or borrow money and sign promissory notes as makers are primary parties. Acceptors of drafts—such as drawee banks that certify checks[23] or buyer-drawees that agree to be bound on trade acceptances by signing and accepting them[24]—are primary parties also.

primary parties
parties (maker and acceptor) on a negotiable instrument who are absolutely liable for its payment according to the terms at the time they sign

---

[22] UCC 3–413.   [23] UCC 3–411.   [24] UCC 3–410.

Figure 23.7 Letter of Credit

```
CABLE ADDRESS                HILLSBORO STATE BANK                    IRREVOCABLE
HILLSBANK                     HILLSBORO, MASSACHUSETTS              COMMERCIAL CREDIT


                                    HILLSBORO,              NO.    A-524
                                    MASSACHUSETTS           UP TO  $10,186.50
SELLER'S NAME  Po Lung-Yu
Tachibana Bldg., 1083 Ikebukuro,
2-chome, Toshima-ku, Tokyo, Japan   DATE OF ISSUE


GENTLEMEN:

    WE HEREBY AUTHORIZE YOU TO DRAW ON   HILLSBORO STATE BANK

FOR ACCOUNT OF  NAME OF BUYER-CUSTOMER OF HILLSBORO STATE BANK, HILLSBORO, MASS. 86543

UP TO AN AGGREGATE AMOUNT OF   **TEN THOUSAND ONE HUNDRED EIGHTY SIX AND 50/100***


AVAILABLE BY YOUR DRAFTS AT   Sight
ACCOMPANIED BY   Airbill, marked Freight Prepaid; Commercial Invoice, signed in
triplicate; Packing List in Triplicate; Insurance policy or certificate endorsed
in blank, for 110% of the invoice cost including: The Institute War Clauses, and
the Institute Cargo Clauses (All Risks) and the Institute Strikes, Riots and
Civil Commotions Clauses. Claims to be payable in the United States of America in
the currency of drafts. Airbill should be made out to order and blank endorsed
and marked "Notify the above mentioned applicant."

No partial shipments allowed.

Shipping Expiration: 60 days.

Document Negotiation: 90 days.

Bank: Dai-Ichi Kangyo Bank, Tokyo, Shinbashi Branch

Reference: Attached copy of Refiners & Producers Marketing, Inc. purchase order
which becomes a part of this Letter of Credit.




     DRAFTS MUST BE DRAWN AND NEGOTIATED NOT LATER THAN Expiration Date of Letter. EACH DRAFT
MUST BE MARKED "DRAWN UNDER LETTER OF CREDIT NO.       A-524        OF HILLSBORO STATE
BANK, HILLSBORO, DATED     Date of Issue      " AND THE AMOUNT OF EACH DRAFT SO DRAWN ENDORSED
BY THE NEGOTIATING BANK ON THE REVERSE SIDE HEREOF. WHEN PRESENTED BY THE MAKER DIRECT TO THE DRAWEE
BANK, THE DRAFTS MUST BE ACCOMPANIED BY THIS LETTER OF CREDIT FOR THE PURPOSE OF SUCH ENDORSEMENTS
BEING MADE THEREON.
     WE HEREBY AGREE WITH THE DRAWERS, ENDORSERS AND BONA FIDE HOLDERS OF DRAFTS DRAWN UNDER AND IN
COMPLIANCE WITH THIS CREDIT THAT SAME SHALL BE DULY HONORED UPON PRESENTATION TO THE DRAWEE BANK AS
SPECIFIED ABOVE.
                                    YOURS VERY TRULY



                                    SIGNATURE OF BANK OFFICIAL
                                    ─────────────────────────────
                                              AUTHORIZED SIGNATURE
```

These parties promise to pay the instrument according to its tenor or terms at the time the instrument is created or the time of acceptance. If the instrument is incomplete at the time of acceptance, a person takes a risk in accepting it. If the instrument is later filled in properly, there is no problem.[25] For example, if a buyer-drawee on a trade acceptance accepts it with his or her signature and authorizes the seller to fill in the blank space with the amount of the purchase price, the acceptor has no ground for complaint when the correct amount is inserted as authorized. If an excessive, unauthorized amount is filled in, however, the acceptor will be liable for that sum to a subsequent HIDC.[26] The acceptor is responsible for the incompleteness since the acceptor gives the wrongdoer a golden opportunity to materially alter the instrument. After paying the HIDC, the acceptor has a right of recovery against the wrongdoer.

Keep in mind that neither primary parties nor secondary parties, which you will study in the next section, are liable on the instrument forever. They may be discharged from liability based on the state statute of limitations that controls the original transaction between the parties. Our chapter-ending case, *Tepper v. Citizens Federal Savings and Loan Association* will explain this in greater detail.

Secondary Parties

If a person's signature on a negotiable instrument is *other than as maker or acceptor*, that person is a **secondary party.** The drawer and indorser are secondary parties.

Drawer. It is easy to be trapped by the comparison of a secondary party-drawer who initiates a draft with a primary party-maker who initiates a note. Be careful—the analogy is misleading.

In the normal course of events, the *drawer* of a draft or check expects the drawee to pay. When a person writes a check, it is an *order* from the drawer to the drawee bank to pay out of the money on deposit in the drawer's checking account. When the maker of a note borrows money, however, or purchases on credit, the maker does not order someone else to pay,[27] he himself *promises* or undertakes to pay.

A drawer does obligate himself to pay the instrument *if* the holder takes the proper three steps:

1. **Presentment**. The instrument is properly presented to the drawee for payment.
2. **Dishonor**. The instrument is dishonored by the maker's or drawee's refusal to pay it.
3. *Notice*. The drawer is given proper notice of nonpayment or dishonor.[28]

The drawer may avoid or disclaim this liability by drawing the draft "without recourse."[29] However, it is difficult to find people who are willing to do business with a drawer on this basis because they do not have recourse—i.e., do not have the right of recovery—against the drawer on his or her signature if the draft is dishonored by the drawee.

Indorser. **Indorsers** are secondary parties who sign notes and drafts in the process of negotiation. They do not sign as makers or acceptors. Generally speaking, *every indorser makes a conditional or secondary promise to pay the holder of the instrument if the*

secondary parties
parties on a negotiable instrument who are liable on the instrument only if certain conditions occur

presentment
"a demand for acceptance or payment made upon the maker, acceptor, drawee or other payor by or on behalf of the holder" UCC 3-504(1)

dishonor
the refusal of the drawee to accept the draft, or of the drawee, acceptor, or maker to pay the draft or note

indorser
the person who signs on an instrument (or on a paper attached to it) other than as a maker, drawer, or acceptor

---

[25] UCC 3-115(1).

[26] UCC 3-407(3). For material alteration of incomplete instruments, see pp. 401-2.

[27] Some states have adopted UCC 3-121, Alternative A, which makes a note payable at a bank "the equivalent of a draft drawn on the bank payable when it falls due out of any funds of the maker or acceptor for such payment."

[28] UCC 3-501.   [29] UCC 3-413(2).

usual three steps of presentment, dishonor, and notice are followed. Qualified indorsers ("without recourse" indorsers)[30] disclaim their signature as indorsements with secondary liability if the instrument is dishonored, but they are exceptions to the rule.

Discharge of Secondary Parties for Failure to Observe the Conditions of Presentment, Dishonor, and Notice of Dishonor.

These preliminary three steps are conditions for holding an indorser secondarily liable. They are the same as those for holding a drawer secondarily liable, but there is a very important difference. If these conditions do not occur, the indorser is completely discharged, but the drawer is discharged only if the drawee becomes insolvent *during the delay* in *presentment for payment* or *notice of dishonor*.[31]

If the drawee does become **insolvent,** the drawer is discharged to the extent that his claim against the drawee is reduced. For example, assume that a $100 check would have been paid by the drawee if the instrument had been properly presented. However, if the holder of the check is late in presenting it to the drawee for payment, and the drawee becomes insolvent during the delay, then the drawer is discharged from any further liability by assigning all of the drawer's rights to the holder. The holder may be able to recover a fraction of the $100 check from the insolvent drawee. Thus, if the drawee's creditors eventually receive twenty cents on the dollar, the holder of the check will be entitled to collect $20.

Study carefully *Tepper v. Citizens Federal Savings and Loan Association* at the conclusion of this chapter for the effect of the state statute of limitations on the liability of secondary parties, and of primary parties as well.

Other Parties

Payee. The *payee* is the person to whose order the instrument is originally written. This person must be identified with reasonable certainty.[32] The payee normally becomes an indorser-secondary party when the payee signs on the instrument so that it can be negotiated to some other person.

Indorsee. The **indorsee** is the person named in the **indorsement**—e.g., "Pay to A [indorsee], [signed] B [indorser]"; or "Pay to Community Bank [indorsee], [signed] Pineville Bookstore [indorser]."[33]

For the time being, please note that these indorsements which *name* the indorsee are called *special indorsements*—the indorsement is to a "special" person. If the last or only indorsement of an instrument is a special indorsement, the instrument is *order paper*. This means that the indorsee *must* indorse before the paper can be further negotiated.[34]

An additional point to observe here is that the word "order" does not necessarily have to appear in the special indorsement. If not present, it is simply assumed to be there—i.e., the indorsement is read as if the word *order* appeared in it as follows: "Pay to [the order of] A, [signed] B."

Remember that we are speaking here of an *indorsement*. If words of negotiability—that is, "order" or "bearer" or their equivalents—do not appear on the *face* or front of the instrument, it is not negotiable to begin with.

Holder. A **holder** is a person who is in *possession* of an instrument which has been originally drawn or issued to him or his order, or later specially indorsed to him.[35] Merely *naming* someone as payee or indorsee is not sufficient to make the person a holder. That person must be *in possession* of the instrument as well.

---

[30] UCC 3–414(1). [31] UCC 3–502(1). [32] UCC 3–110(1).
[33] UCC 3–204(1). [34] UCC 3–204(1). [35] UCC 1–201(20).

---

insolvent
"a person is insolvent who either has ceased to pay his debts in the ordinary course of business or cannot pay his debts as they become due or is insolvent within the meaning of the federal bankruptcy law" UCC 1–201(23)

indorsee
the person named by an indorser on an instrument to whom it is to be paid

indorsement
the indorser's signature on an instrument (or on a paper attached to it)

holder
the person in possession of an instrument which flows to him either initially, by indorsement, or as the bearer of the instrument

Further, a holder may be a person who is in possession of an instrument which is **bearer** paper *originally*, e.g., on the face of the paper it reads "Pay to the order of *Bearer*," or "Pay to the order of *Cash*." Another possibility is that the holder may be in possession of an instrument that was *originally* order paper, but which has become bearer paper because the last or only indorsement is a *blank* indorsement—e.g., the indorser simply signs his or her name, "Jarrett Hudnall," but does not name an indorsee. A blank indorsement is an indorsement without any accompanying words. Because of the risk of a bearer instrument being lost or stolen and getting into the hands of a holder who can then collect on the instrument, one should be very careful when indorsing an instrument in blank.

bearer
the person in possession of an instrument payable to bearer or indorsed in blank (a signature without additional words)

Bearer.[36] A bearer is a holder who is in possession of an instrument which is bearer paper on its face—i.e., it is made out to "Bearer," or to "Cash," or to the equivalent of these, discussed later. A bearer may also be a person who is in possession of an instrument on which the last or only indorsement is a blank indorsement.

Holder in Due Course (HIDC). An HIDC must first qualify as a holder. In addition, this holder must acquire the instrument "in due course," which means purchase for value, in good faith, and without notice that the instrument is overdue, has been dishonored, or that there is an outstanding claim of ownership on or defense against the instrument.[37] A bank can become an HIDC (a) if it is a holder, and (b) to the extent that credit has been withdrawn.

Special Relationships
Accommodation Party. An **accommodation party** may be primarily or secondarily liable. This depends on whether the party signs as an accommodation maker, accommodation drawer, accommodation acceptor, or accommodation indorser.[38] The purpose of such a signature is to lend the name and financial resources of the accommodation party to the instrument. The accommodation maker and acceptor are primarily liable. The accommodation drawer and indorser are secondarily liable.

accommodation party
a person who signs commercial paper as an accommodation to another person whose signature is on the instrument for the purpose of assisting the latter to obtain credit

The accommodation party is never liable to the party accommodated.[39] In the event an accommodation maker is required to pay the instrument, the accommodation maker can recover from the *accommodated* party.

The same is true of an accommodation indorser. The accommodation indorser who is required to pay the instrument, has a right to recover such payment from the accommodated indorser or from any prior person who has become liable as a secondary party.

Guarantor. A person who uses the words "payment guaranteed" or an equivalent phrase with that person's signature is bound according to the terms of the instrument if it is not voluntarily paid at maturity. There is no need for the holder to pursue or to give notice to any other party.[40]

A person may undertake a less demanding guaranty obligation by merely guaranteeing collection. "Collection guaranteed" obligates the signer only if the primary party is insolvent or if the holder has gone into court and received a judgment on the instrument and is now unable to collect on the judgment.[41]

Words of guaranty will be interpreted to mean that *payment* is guaranteed unless collection is specified. Any words of guaranty make unnecessary presentment, dishonor, and notice, which are normally required before secondary parties become liable on their indorsement contracts.[42]

---

[36] UCC 1–201(5). [37] UCC 3–302. [38] UCC 3–415(2). [39] UCC 3–415(5).
[40] UCC 3–416(1). [41] UCC 3–416(2). [42] UCC 3–416(5).

Figure 23.8 Diagram of Check Collection Process

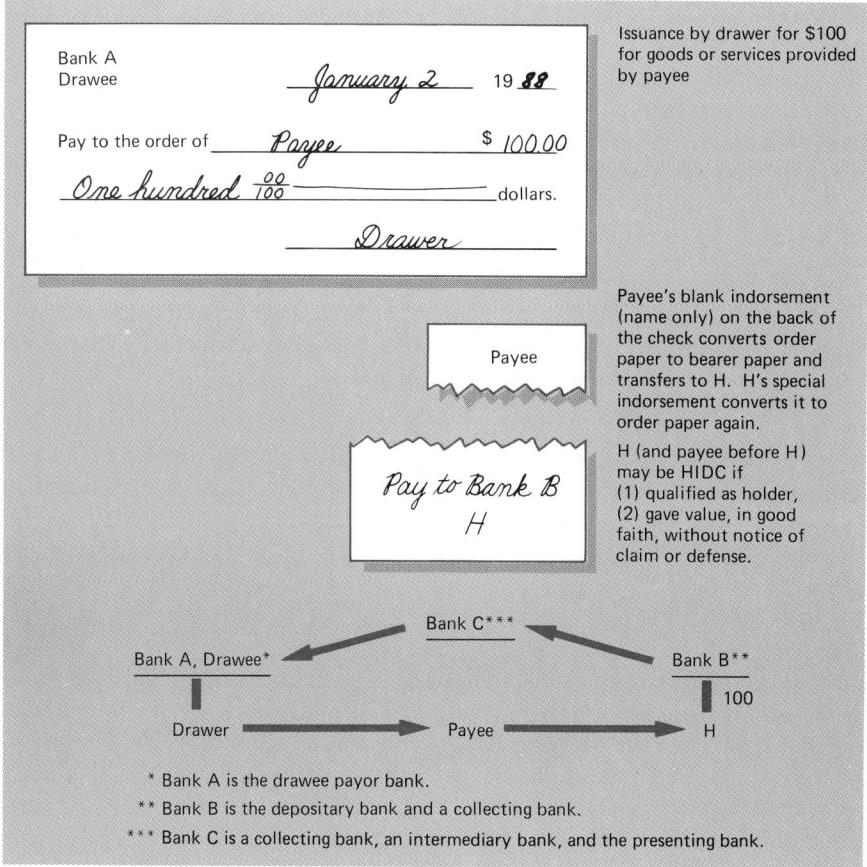

The Banking Process

depositary bank
"the first bank to which an item is transferred for collection even though it is also the payor bank"
UCC 4-105(a)

Depositary Bank

The *first* bank in which one deposits a check to *begin* the collection process is the **depositary bank.**[43] (Figure 23.8 diagrams the entire collection process.) The first bank may also be the drawee-payor bank. The depositor will receive a provisional or temporary credit in his or her checking account, and the item will be forwarded to the next bank for collection. If the check does not bounce within a prescribed deadline—i.e., if it is not returned to the depositary bank or if notice is not sent to the depositary bank that there are "not sufficient funds" to pay the check or that payment has been "stopped"—the provisional credit will be made final. If the check is properly returned or if notice is sent within the deadline, the depositary bank will reverse the provisional credit.

Remember, from the depositor's point of view, the depositary bank in which the depositor has an account is the drawee bank. Whenever this depositor writes a check, he or she will be drawing on this account and ordering the depositor's drawee bank to pay money to a payee.

The depositary bank could give value and perhaps become an HIDC if it allowed its customer-depositor to cash another person's check or to withdraw funds represented by another's check before the collection process was completed. Of course, the depositary

---

[43] UCC 4-105(a).

bank would have to meet all the requirements for becoming an HIDC in addition to giving value. This could become very important if the other person's check bounced and, instead of proceeding against its own depositor-customer, the bank chose to pursue the drawer.

Payor Bank

In the check collection process, items are transferred from the depositary bank through intermediary banks to the **payor bank.** The payor bank holds the checking account of the drawer. From the point of view of the drawer, the payor bank is synonymous with the drawee.[44] (See figure 23.8.)

Assuming that there are sufficient funds on deposit in the drawer's account, the item will be paid and the depositor's account will be debited or charged. If funds are not sufficient or if payment has been stopped, the item will be returned to the depositary bank.

When a check reaches the payor bank through collection channels, it has until the midnight deadline[45]—midnight on the next banking day following receipt of an item—to decide whether to pay or to return the check. If the payor bank fails to examine its customer's account within the allotted time, and it discovers after the midnight deadline has passed that there are not sufficient funds to pay the check, the payor bank will be accountable for the amount of the item to the collecting banks.[46] It is penalized for failing to act within the prescribed time limits established by law. The payor bank then has recourse against its customer, the person who overdrew his or her account.[47]

Keep in mind that some drafts are not drawn on bank-drawees—e.g., a trade acceptance. In that case the payor may be an individual or a business firm.

payor bank
"a bank by which an item is payable as drawn or accepted"
UCC 4–105(b)

Collecting Banks

This term includes all banks, even the depositary bank, forwarding a check for collection to a payor bank.[48] It does not include the payor bank.

collecting bank
"any bank handling the item for collection except the payor bank"
UCC 4–105(d)

Presenting Bank

This is the last bank in the collection process. It turns the check over to a payor bank for final disposition.[49]

presenting bank
"any bank presenting an item except a payor bank"
UCC 4–105(e)

Intermediary Bank

Intermediary banks are "in between" the depositary and the payor banks. Neither the depositary nor the payor bank is included, but the presenting bank does fall within the definition.[50]

intermediary bank
"any bank to which an item is transferred in course of collection except the depositary or payor bank"
UCC 4–105(c)

Formal Requisites of Negotiable Instruments

"Commercial paper" may be negotiable or non-negotiable. We are primarily interested in the negotiable instrument. If the instrument is not negotiable, it is still valid and enforceable as a contract, but no one can become an HIDC.

The basic elements that are common to all negotiable instruments were introduced briefly in the discussion of the various types of instrument. The final portion of this chapter will deal with each of these components in detail:

1. *Written and signed*. The instrument must be in writing and signed by the maker or drawer.
2. *Unconditional promise or order—sum certain in money*. Each instrument must contain an unconditional promise or order to pay a sum certain in money.

Formal requisites.

---

[44] UCC 4–105(b).   [45] UCC 4–104(h).   [46] UCC 4–302(a).   [47] UCC 4–401(1).

[48] UCC 4–105(d).   [49] UCC 4–105(e).   [50] UCC 4–105(c).

3. *Demand or definite time.* The time of payment must be on demand or at a definite time.
4. *Order or bearer.* Each instrument must be payable to order or to bearer.[51]

The writing.

Written

Oral contracts to pay money may or may not be enforceable, depending on the statute of frauds and its exceptions. Negotiable instruments, however, must be in writing.

Writing includes printing, typewriting, handwriting, or any other method of committing words to paper. The UCC permits the writing to be on anything, but as a practical matter, the writing will be on a convenient-to-handle printed form. Writing in pencil is permissible, but most prudent people will guard against that because of the opportunities for fraudulent material alteration of the instrument.

Signed.

Signed

The signature of the maker or drawer may be written at any place on the instrument. Usually it appears at the bottom-right of the paper, but it may be incorporated in the language of the instrument itself. For example, a *handwritten* negotiable note may recite that "I, Jane Rhymes, promise to pay $100 to bearer on demand." Here Rhymes is clearly identified as the maker who engages or undertakes to pay. Unless clearly identified as a maker, drawer, or acceptor, the person who signs will be treated as a secondary party indorser.[52]

The signature may consist of any mark, stamp, or symbol adopted by a party with a present intention to authenticate the writing.[53] It could be an X mark, for example, if it is the genuine intention of the signer to use such a symbol for this purpose.

Marks and symbols present practical problems. All X marks are basically alike, whereas a signature is a highly individualized symbol associated and identified with only one person. A payee of a note or draft may be quite satisfied upon witnessing Wayne Mondy, as maker or drawer, authenticate an instrument with an X. However, if the payee attempts to negotiate such an instrument to a third party, particularly one who was not present at the original transaction, that party may decline to pay out hard-earned cash for an instrument signed with an X.[54] If you were the third party, would you have any reluctance?

Signature by Authorized Agent or Representative. A person's signature may be placed on the instrument by an authorized agent in a manner that obligates only the principal. If it is the intention of an agent operating within the scope of the agent's authority to obligate the principal alone, the agent should do one of the following:

1. Sign the name of the principal, but not the agent's own name.
2. Disclose the principal and clearly show that the agent is signing in a representative capacity.[55]

For example, if Lane Feazel is the authorized agent of World Services, Inc., he can obligate *only* his employer by signing in these examples:

1. "World Services, Inc."
2. "World Services, Inc., by Lane Feazel, Secretary-Treasurer," or "Lane Feazel, Secretary-Treasurer for World Services, Inc."[56]

---

[51] UCC 3–104(1).   [52] UCC 3–402.   [53] UCC 1–201(39).

[54] Some states require that a person who is capable of signing place his or her signature on the instrument as a witness.

[55] UCC 3–403(2)(b).   [56] UCC 3–403(3).

One can feel confident that personal liability is avoided by following alternative 1 above because a *person cannot be held liable on the instrument unless his signature appears on it.*[57]

If a signature appears, even though it may be forged or unauthorized, the actual signer is personally liable. Forgers and unauthorized signers are, thus, personally liable even though their *real* signatures do not appear at all;[58] the improper signature becomes that of the person who wrongfully signed. For example, if the payee is Jones, and Smith forged Jones' signature as indorser, Smith is now liable as an indorser.

If the authorized agent follows alternative 2 above, the agent can obligate the principal only by disclosing the name of the principal before or after the name and office of the agent. When an agent puts his own name on an instrument, he simply invites problems upon himself unless he both (a) discloses the principal and (b) clearly shows his representative capacity. In the event he does only one of these things, the agent may prove his representative capacity by parol evidence if he is being sued by an "immediate party"—e.g., a payee.[59]

No such opportunity for defense will be available against one who is not an immediate party. The reason for this rule is that these parties, who were not present at the original transaction, are entitled to assume that there are two parties liable on the instrument—the principal, and the agent who did not take appropriate steps to show that he or she is operating in a representative capacity.

As a practical matter, it makes a great deal of sense to take precautionary measures that can avoid a lawsuit in the first place. Even those suits that are eventually won involve the expenditure of a great deal of time, money, and anxiety in the process.

The Promise or Order

The Promise.   The promise contained on the face of a note to pay money simply discloses an intention to be bound or an engagement to pay. Synonyms such as "undertake" or "obligate" or "engage" would do just as well,[60] but when important sums of money are in the balance, why invite litigation by using such unusual terms?

The promise.

Since most of the instruments that you will be called upon to sign are printed forms anyway, this does not present much of a problem. The word "promise" is typically used, and there is no necessity to discuss the matter.

Remember, however, that a mere acknowledgment of a sum due or payable in the future—"IOU $100, [signed] John Bonhomme"—while legal, enforceable, and assignable under the law of contracts, is not a sufficient promise under the Code and cannot be a negotiable instrument.

The Order.   An order is an instruction or direction to pay, issued by the drawer to the drawee.[61] For example, in every check the drawer orders the drawee bank to pay money. The drawer is entitled to do this because the relationship between the depositor and the drawee bank is creditor/debtor. The drawee is the drawer's debtor to the extent of the drawer's checking account balance. The contractual arrangement was agreed to when the drawer-depositor first opened that checking account.

The order.

The instruction, direction, or order must be more than a mere request or authorization. In other words, it must leave nothing to the discretion of the drawee. For example, on a check the first word addressed to the drawee bank is "Pay." The drawee must be identified with reasonable certainty, and may be addressed with words of courtesy, e.g., "Please pay."

---

[57] UCC 3–401(1).   [58] UCC 3–404(1).   [59] UCC 3–403(2)(b).

[60] UCC 3–104, comment 5. [61] UCC 3–102(1)(b).

The promise or order must be unconditional.

Unconditional. The promise or order must be absolute, unconditional, iron-clad. It must be a general and unreserved commitment on the maker's or drawer's resources—no condition, escape clauses, or cop-outs.

Anything less than a full and total dedication of the maker's or drawer's financial strength would destroy the instrument's unique capacity to function as a substitute for money or as a credit device. It is obvious that potential purchasers of commercial paper would be less willing to spend their money on instruments that are hedged with excuses and alibis than on instruments that are not so limited.

Only *express* conditions destroy negotiability. Implied conditions do not.[62] Nor is negotiability affected by the mere mention of, or reference to, the underlying consideration which supports the original contract.[63]

For example, "I promise to pay $1,000 to the order of J. T. Bain on demand, subject to his faithful performance of Contract #61382. [signed] Merrill Goodwyn." The express condition, "subject to his faithful performance of Contract #61382," makes the promise conditional and destroys negotiability.

One must be able to determine *from the face of the instrument* whether the commitment to pay is absolute and unconditional.[64] The above promise does not measure up to the standard of negotiability because the maker is entitled to avoid payment if the contract is not performed, and whether or not performance has occurred *cannot be determined from the face of the instrument*. The fact that Bain may have actually performed the contract does not make the instrument negotiable because that fact *cannot be determined by examining the instrument*.

Consider, however, a modification of the above note which simply mentioned that it was given in return for, or in consideration of, or in reference to, Contract #61382. One might say there was an implied condition that the maker not be liable contractually if Bain failed to perform, but this does not destroy negotiability.

If Bain does not perform the underlying transaction referred to, that is a matter to be taken up *outside* the scope of the negotiable instrument. The maker or drawer is absolutely committed *on the instrument* despite the implied condition that the payee may not perform and the maker or drawer may later have to sue the payee for breach of contract. An instrument may be negotiable even though it refers to the transaction which gives rise to the instrument.

A statement in an instrument that it is secured—by a mortgage or in some other way—does not destroy negotiability.[65] This operates to the creditor-holder's benefit and simply adds to the salability or marketability of the instrument.

If, for purposes of bookkeeping convenience, the instrument mentions a particular fund to be debited or charged, negotiability is not affected.[66] This rule favoring negotiability holds true for commercial paper that is limited to a particular fund backed by a governmental unit or limited to payment from the entire assets of a partnership, unincorporated association, trust, or estate.[67] It is assumed that instruments issued by these entities will carry sufficient assurance of payment to encourage their acceptability.

Keep in mind that instruments *expressly* made *subject* to, or *governed* by, some other agreement—e.g., subject to Contract #61382—are not negotiable. Neither are instruments that are strictly limited to payment out of a particular fund.[68]

---

[62] UCC 3–105(1)(a).   [63] UCC 3–105(1)(b)(c).

[64] If an instrument states that it is void if drawn for more than a particular amount or void if presented for payment after a particular date, negotiability is *not* destroyed because that condition can be determined from the face of the instrument.

[65] UCC 3–105(e).   [66] UCC 3–105(f).   [67] UCC 3–105(h).   [68] UCC 3–105(2).

To illustrate: if Jack Sorenson limits or restricts payment of his note to "the proceeds from next year's corn crop," the instrument would be non-negotiable. His general credit is not committed to payment, and no one can tell from examining the *face* of the note whether "next year's corn crop" will even be planted, much less whether it will be sufficient to pay the note.

A governmental unit can limit its obligation to payment out of a particular fund without affecting negotiability because it is assumed that tax revenues will always be sufficient. A similar exception is made in favor of instruments by partnerships, unincorporated associations, trusts, and estates when all their assets are committed.

Sum Certain in Money

Sum Certain. The reason for this requirement is obvious. Every potential purchaser will insist on knowing how much money will be received at maturity. No serious buyer or investor wants to play guessing games on the amount of money involved.

<small>The sum certain.</small>

As a general rule, the sum is sufficiently certain if, *at the time of payment,* it can be computed from the information that appears on the face of the instrument.[69] This means that the sum certain is *unaffected* by:

1. payment with interest or in installments;
2. payment with interest at different rates before and after default;
3. payment with a discount before a fixed date or with an addition afterward;
4. payment with (or less) foreign exchange rates to protect the constant value of an instrument;
5. payment with collection or attorney's fees in the event of default in payment.[70]

Keep in mind that the crucial time is the *time of payment,* and the computations must be made from what appears on the *face* of the instrument. It cannot be known at the time of issuance whether there will be a default, whether payment will be accelerated, or whether an attorney or collection agency will be needed; but these facts will be available at the time of payment.

An instrument with interest payable at the *legal rate or judgment rate, as fixed by state law,* is negotiable even though the actual rate of interest is not specified. An interest term which calls for application of the *bank rate or current rate,* however, does not satisfy the requirement of sum *certain.*

Money. Money means a medium of exchange authorized or adopted by any government as part of its currency.[71] The medium of exchange must qualify as money *at the time the instrument is issued.* The reason for this, of course, is to give assurance to a potential purchaser right from the start that the instrument will be paid in the currency of a recognized government.

<small>Money.</small>

Keep in mind that for *certainty of sum,* the important time is the *maturity date.* For the purpose of *qualifying as money,* however, the important time is *when the instrument is issued.*

Note here as well that negotiable instruments are not the equivalent of money, and that a person cannot compel another to take commercial paper in payment of debts. Generally speaking, negotiable instruments are *conditional payment* contingent upon being honored at maturity. The *obligation* on the basis of which the instrument was given is suspended pending payment of the instrument on the due date. If not paid when due, then suit may be based on the *instrument* or on the *obligation* for which the instrument was given.[72]

---

[69] See UCC 3–106, comment 1. [70] UCC 3–106(1).

[71] UCC 3–107(1). [72] UCC 3–802(1)(b).

Unless the instrument requires otherwise, a promise or order to pay in foreign currency may be satisfied by payment at maturity of the *dollar* amount that the foreign currency will buy at the exchange rate. For example, an instrument payable in Belgian *francs,* Japanese *yen,* or Chilean *pesos* may be satisfied with the number of U.S. dollars that the foreign currency could buy at current exchange rates. If the instrument *requires* payment in the foreign currency, an attempt to discharge one's obligation in U.S. dollars will not be sufficient.[73]

No other promise or order *except payment of money* is sufficient to establish negotiability. Promises or orders of payment in seal skins, wampum, or gold dust destroy negotiability because they are not money; the money value is not readily apparent on the *face* of the paper. Certain other promises are permitted, without affecting negotiability, because of one thing in common—they promote acceptability and marketability of the paper.

As an example, some instruments include a term that allows the holder or creditor to **confess judgment** against the debtor when an instrument is not paid at maturity.[74] This strengthens the creditor's position by expediting enforcement of the paper upon default. The creditor can get a judgment on the unpaid instrument without giving notice of the proceedings to the debtor. Whether or not a confession of judgment is illegal has no effect on the *negotiability* of the instrument.

Promises that give collateral security to an instrument, promises to protect or increase collateral should it decline in value, and promises that relinquish the benefit of debtor protection laws—all add to the advantage of the holder.[75] Since they encourage and promote the flow of negotiable paper rather than impede it, the law permits these extra promises to be made.

Time of Payment

If a prospective user of a negotiable instrument cannot tell from the face of the paper when it is due, this naturally will diminish its acceptability. To encourage a ready and open market for commercial paper then, a negotiable instrument must be made payable *on demand* or *at a definite time.*

> **confession of judgment**
> a party's consent to jurisdiction and judgment of a court without a trial in a civil case

> On demand.

On Demand. An instrument is payable on demand if it expressly states that it is payable on demand, if it calls for payment at sight or presentation, or if no time for payment is stated.[76]

A check falls into the last category—no time for payment is stated. It normally contains the date of issue but no maturity date. It is the absence of a maturity date that makes it payable on demand.

From the point of view of the *maker or drawer* of an instrument, the time of payment is not certain, but that is not the controlling factor. The *prospective buyer* or holder is the one that the law wants to encourage, and it seeks to do that by allowing that person to collect on demand. It was held in the following case that blank spaces for installment payments on a note did not cause the note to be non-negotiable for failure to state a definite time when it was payable; it was payable on demand.

Facts

Defendants executed four negotiable promissory notes to plaintiffs totalling $21,000. The notes specified neither time nor place of payment. The notes contained the date of issue, but each had an unfilled blank after the printed word "Due." Defendants argued that the notes were due only when they were financially able to repay the loans. Plaintiffs contended that the notes were payable on demand.

---

[73] UCC 3–107(2).

[74] UCC 3–112(d). A note with such a term is called a "cognovit note."

[75] UCC 3–112(b)(c)(e).   [76] UCC 3–108.

Decision
Judgment for plaintiffs.

Reasoning
Instruments payable upon demand include those in which no time for payment is stated. A cause of action against the maker of a demand instrument accrues upon the instrument's date, or if no date is stated, on the date of issue. A written condition that a note is payable "if and when able to pay" creates an obligation to pay it within a reasonable time.

A promissory note executed without a maturity date is deemed to be a completed demand instrument, so testimony about a contemporaneous oral condition cannot vary that term of the instrument.

Ranieri, et al. *v. Terzano*, et al., 457 N.E.2d 906 (Ohio 1983).

Definite Time. The common link among each of the following requirements for definite time is *the face of the paper.* Time of payment is definite if it can be determined from the terms appearing on the instrument itself.

The requirement of definite time is met if the instrument is payable on a fixed date, before a fixed date (frequently these are combined as "on or before 31 December 1999," for example), or a fixed period after a fixed date (one year from the date of the instrument).[77] A term which recites that the paper is payable "on or before the expiration of one year from the date of issue" sets a maximum length of time but allows the *maker or drawer* to make payment before the end of a full year and thereby save money on interest.

The requirement for certainty of time is also satisfied if the instrument is payable "a fixed period after sight" or "a fixed period after acceptance."[78] This can be very useful in a sales transaction that allows an extended credit period to the buyer—i.e., the drawee on a trade acceptance drawn by the seller. The draft will be presented to the buyer-drawee by the seller or the seller's agent; if the buyer properly "accepts" the instrument by signing it and returning it to the seller, the goods will be delivered to the buyer. The seller keeps possession of the negotiable instrument; then, when the fixed period after sight or acceptance expires, the seller presents the instrument to the buyer for payment.

If maturity of an instrument is made to depend on an act or event uncertain as to time of occurrence, the time requirement is not satisfied even though the event later occurs.[79] Examples are: promises to pay when a person attains a stated age, when a certain building is built, or on the death or marriage of a certain person. The standard, once more, is the *face* of the paper. If time is not certain on the face of the instrument, then time is not certain for purposes of negotiability.

Acceleration Clauses. The Code approves of a definite time subject to *any acceleration.*[80] Normally the holder of an instrument is given the option of accelerating time of payment if the debtor defaults on an installment. The reason behind this rule is that the debtor "brings it upon himself" by not living up to his agreement and this is a reasonable way of assuring the creditor that he can take appropriate action now to protect himself.

Other acceleration clauses allow the *holder* to declare the full amount to be due and payable at any time he in good faith deems himself to be insecure.[81] This term is not particularly advantageous to the debtor, but he may not be given any choice in the matter—take it or leave it, the creditor tells him. For purposes of negotiability, such acceleration clauses do not destroy certainty of time.

Extension Clauses. Clauses which give the debtor an additional period of time for payment are extension clauses and are just the opposite of acceleration clauses. They are permitted on the following terms:

1. At the option of the *holder* (this simply means that the creditor-holder can give the debtor more time to pay if the holder so chooses).

Definite time.

Acceleration clauses.

Extension clauses.

---

[77] UCC 3–109(1)(a).
[78] UCC 3–109(1)(b).
[79] UCC 3–109(2).
[80] UCC 3–109(c).
[81] UCC 1–208.

2. At the option of the *maker or acceptor* to a further definite time (except for this limitation, enforceability of the paper could be frustrated indefinitely).
3. Automatically upon the happening of a specified event (e.g., "maturity shall be extended by one year, if crop yields fall below eighty bushels per acre").[82]

The Words of Negotiability: To Order or To Bearer

Unless an instrument contains one of the "magic words" of negotiability— "to *order* of," "to *bearer*," or the equivalent—it is not negotiable and can be transferred only by assignment. "Pay to the order of A" is different from "Pay to A," the latter phrase causing the instrument to be non-negotiable.

To Bearer. An instrument is payable to *bearer* when the terms specify "bearer," or "the order of bearer."[83] The latter phrase, "the order of bearer," normally occurs on a form that is printed to read "Pay to the order of _____," and the word "bearer" is inserted in the blank space. Until the space is filled in, the paper is incomplete in a necessary respect and, therefore, is non-negotiable and unenforceable.[84]

The instrument is payable to bearer if the paper reads "Pay to Cash," or "Pay to the order of Cash," or any other word besides "cash" that does not designate a payee capable of making a signature.[85] An instrument which reads "Pay to the order of One Keg of Beer" or "Pay to Two Crates of Pop" shows that the maker or drawer is not interested in having a "payee" indorse! If the "payee" or the object designated instead of a payee is not capable of indorsing, then the instrument becomes payable to bearer.

Another illustration of bearer paper is one which names "a specified person or bearer" as payee.[86] The bearer provision takes precedence, and it is a bearer instrument; e.g., "Pay to the order of John Jones or bearer."

When an instrument is *order* paper either on its face, or because of a special indorsement, e.g., "Pay to A, [signed] Payee," a subsequent blank indorsement, which consists only of the signature of the indorser, e.g., "A," changes the instrument to bearer paper.[87]

To order.

To Order. An instrument meets this requirement when it is payable to the order, or to the assigns, of *any person reasonably identified,* or to that person or that person's order.[88] For example, "Pay to the order of A," or "Pay to A or his order." This indicates that the maker of the note or drawer of the draft intends that the payee be able to negotiate the instrument to some other party. An instrument on its face reading "Pay to Lee Young" is non-negotiable; the words "order of" or "bearer" are missing.

On all *drafts,* the drawer first *orders* the drawee to pay money. To take the process a second step, the drawee may be ordered to pay "to the order of Rich Soland"—i.e., to the named payee Rich Soland or to whomever the payee may indicate in his indorsement.

If Rich Soland to whom the instrument flows indorses in blank with only his name, then the drawee will be directed to pay the bearer, i.e., the holder, of the instrument. If he indorses specially, "Pay to Fran Zappa, [signed] Rich Soland," the drawee will be directed to pay the named indorsee.

Instruments may be made payable to the order of the following payees:

1. The maker or drawer; e.g., the seller who is the drawer of a trade acceptance may name himself as payee, or the drawer of a check may name himself as payee.
2. The drawee; e.g., the drawer of a check in paying a debt that the drawer owes to the drawee bank will name the drawee bank as payee.
3. A payee who is not a maker, drawer, or drawee (this covers the great majority of transactions).

---

[82] UCC 3–109(1)(d).   [83] UCC 3–111(a).   [84] UCC 3–805.   [85] UCC 3–111(c).
[86] UCC 3–111(b).   [87] UCC 3–204(2).   [88] UCC 3–110(1).

4. Two or more payees *jointly*—e.g., A *and* B—or two or more payees in the *alternative*—e.g., A *or* B.
5. An estate, trust, or fund (in this event, the instrument is payable to the order of the representative—e.g., a check payable to the order of United Fund would be treated as payable to the order of its authorized agent, perhaps the treasurer, who would indorse on behalf of the fund).
6. An office or officer by his title, in which event it is payable to the incumbent officer or his successor; e.g., Travis County Tax Collector.
7. A partnership or unincorporated association.[89]

An instrument made payable both to order *and* to bearer is payable to order unless the "bearer" word is handwritten or typewritten. The reason for this is that on a printed form, "Pay to the order of _____ or bearer," the word "bearer" is likely to be overlooked when the name of a payee is inserted. To avoid an unintended result, the paper will be bearer paper only if the drawer or maker has shown that that is the desired objective by writing in the word "bearer."[90]

Summary Statement

1. Negotiable instruments are either notes or drafts. Notes are two-party instruments in which a maker-primary party promises to pay money to a payee. Drafts are three-party instruments in which the one who creates it, the drawer, orders the drawee to pay money to a payee.
2. A certificate of deposit is a special kind of note in which a bank borrows money from a customer, acknowledges receipt of it, and promises to repay. This is a reversal of the norm because usually the customer is borrowing from the bank.
3. A check is a special kind of draft which is drawn on a bank and payable on demand.
4. Frequently you come across a trade acceptance and a banker's acceptance in the financing of sales transactions. These are simply drafts drawn by the seller on the drawee, who is either the buyer or the buyer's bank, payable to the order of a payee. These drafts usually give the buyer some time or credit period in which to pay. Typically, the buyer or the buyer's bank will accept by signing the draft and returning it to the seller; the goods which are being sold on credit will be turned over to the buyer at that point, and at the end of the credit period the instrument will be presented to the acceptor for payment.
5. Notice that the drawee becomes a primary party when the drawee accepts the instrument by signing it. A check will have the drawee bank as a primary party only if the bank certifies the check.
6. Primary parties are makers of negotiable notes and acceptors of drafts. As a general rule, everyone else who signs an instrument is a secondary party.
7. Watch out for accommodation parties, however! An accommodation party may be an accommodation *maker* or an accommodation *acceptor,* in which event the accommodation party would be a *primary* party; or the accommodation party may be an accommodation *drawer* or *indorser,* and thus be a *secondary* party.
8. Primary parties are absolutely liable on the instrument according to its terms. Secondary parties expect to be called upon to pay only if, at maturity, the instrument is properly presented, dishonored, and notice of dishonor is given to the secondary party.

---

[89] UCC 3–110(1).   [90] UCC 3–110(3).

9. Other important parties are the *bearer* (a person in possession of bearer paper) and the *holder* (a person who must be in possession of an instrument that has been drawn, issued, or indorsed to him or her, or who is in possession of bearer paper). HIDCs are holders who have, in addition, given value, in good faith, and without notice of a claim or defense, or that the instrument is overdue or has been dishonored.
10. In the collection process, the banks with which one most frequently comes in contact are depositary banks—the first bank to receive a check and initiate the bank collection process—and the payor-drawee bank. The payor-drawee is the bank at the end of the line. It pays the check if its customer-depositor has sufficient funds on account and has not issued a stop-payment order; otherwise it returns the check by its midnight deadline to avoid being held accountable for it.
11. It is important to remember that any kind of writing will do—pen, pencil, typewriter, or some other form. The signatures can be written by an authorized representative as well as by the person who actually becomes a party on the instrument. It is crucial, however, that the signature, whether it be in the form of an X mark or a written name, actually be intended to validate the paper.
12. The instrument must not have any express conditions to the liability of the person creating it. Otherwise no one is likely to be willing to accept it as a credit device or as a substitute for money. Keep in mind that the holder must be able to determine from the *face* of the instrument that the person who issued it has absolutely committed his or her general credit to payment at maturity.
13. The money that is designated on the draft or note must be backed up by a recognized government, and the amount must be certain. The reason for this is to assure the prospective purchaser that he or she is receiving something of value.
14. From the *holder's* point of view, the time of payment must be certain. This requirement can be satisfied by maturity on a fixed date, before that date, a fixed time after a fixed date, a fixed date subject to *any* acceleration, and a fixed date with *some* extensions of time. It may be a bit confusing that demand instruments satisfy the time requirement; but remember, it is the holder who must be induced to accept these instruments. From that perspective, time is certain, and the person who issued the instrument must simply contend with this feature.
15. Every negotiable instrument must contain the "magic" words of negotiability—"to order," "to bearer," or their equivalents. This permits the payee or the holder to whom the instrument is first issued to negotiate it to some other party. That party may subsequently hold the instrument to maturity or further negotiate it to someone else.

In the following case a check was wrongfully dishonored by the drawee bank and the court had to decide when the statute of limitations began to run against the drawer.

Tepper v. Citizens Federal Savings and Loan Association
448 So.2d 1138 (Fla. 1984)

Ferguson J. The sole question presented is when does the statute of limitations begin to run against a drawer in an action for wrongful dishonor of a check—on the date of issuance of the check or the date of presentment and dishonor?

Rose Tepper (appellant) was adjudicated an incompetent in December, 1982. On examination of her personal effects, a court-appointed guardian discovered a check for the sum of $6,068, dated January 4, 1974. The check was drawn to Rose Tepper by Citizens Federal Savings and Loan Association against its account with Jefferson National Bank.

On December 20, 1982, appellant's representative presented the check to the drawee bank, Jefferson National (not a party to this action), which refused payment. The representative then advised the drawer, Citizens Federal (appellee), of the dishonor. Citizens Federal orally notified appellant's representative that it would neither honor nor refund the instrument. The guardian instituted this action against the drawer on July 12, 1983.

The trial court dismissed the guardian's complaint on appellee's motion, holding that "the statute of limitations began to run on the date of issuance of the check herein sued upon, [so the] action is barred by the applicable five year statute of limitations." We reverse upon a holding that the statute of limitations begins to run against a drawer of a check on the date of presentment and dishonor.

A draft is a three-party instrument whereby the drawer orders the drawee to pay money to the payee. A draft is also called a check when the drawee is a bank and the instrument is payable on demand. A drawee is not liable on the instrument until there has been an acceptance. The drawee may, by accepting in writing on the instrument, agree to honor it as presented. By contrast, a drawee may reject the instrument, as by stamping insufficient funds on a check where the drawer's deposited funds are less than the amount of the instrument. The act of accepting the instrument renders the drawee primarily liable as an acceptor. Because there are no conditions precedent to its liability, a cause of action accrues against an acceptor in the case of a demand instrument on the date of the instrument or date of issue.

The drawer, on the other hand, is only secondarily liable on the instrument, in that there are conditions precedent to liability. The normal conditions precedent include presentment to the drawee, dishonor, and notice of dishonor. Therefore, a cause of action against the drawer of a draft accrues only upon demand following dishonor of the instrument. Notice of dishonor constitutes a demand. This latter section is clearly dispositive of the issue presented, as a cause of action against the drawer herein, Citizens Federal, thus did not accrue until appellant's representative received notice of dishonor from the drawee, Jefferson National Bank.

A cashier's check is a check on which the issuing bank acts as both the drawer and the drawee. Its own act of issuance renders the bank a drawee who has accepted the draft; thus the issuing bank becomes primarily liable as an acceptor. Presentment of a negotiable instrument is not necessary in order to establish liability against parties who are primarily liable. In such a case the statute of limitations begins to run on a demand instrument at the moment of issuance. As to parties secondarily liable, however, such as the drawer herein, there is no instant liability and thus no cause of action until demand following presentment and dishonor.

The distinction between a cashier's check where the issuing bank is primarily liable and other drafts, where the drawer is secondarily liable, is stated:

[U]nder the Code, a cause of action against a certifying bank or a bank issuing a cashier's check accrues on the date of the check (or date of issue if the check is undated). This means that the statute of limitations begins to run at that time and suit against the bank will be barred after the statute of limitations has run. But a cause of action against a drawer of a check does not accrue until demand following dishonor. This theoretically means that the time for bringing action against the drawer may be deferred indefinitely if there is no presentment for payment.

Under Florida law an action may not be deferred indefinitely in all instances; instead, a drawer will be discharged from its liability if presentment is unreasonably delayed and the drawee bank becomes insolvent during the delay.

In that appellee herein was the drawer of the instrument which is the subject of this action, and therefore only secondarily liable, a cause of action did not accrue against it until after demand following presentment and dishonor on December 20, 1982. The action for wrongful dishonor of the instrument was commenced timely.

[Reversed, for appellant's representative.]

Figure 23.9 "Handmade" Instrument

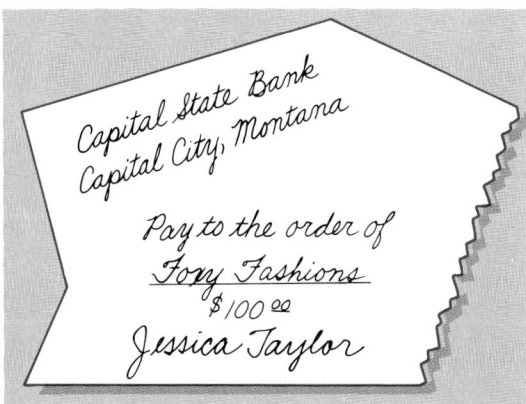

Questions and Case Problems

1. Defendant, McManus, signed a note of the corporation that employed him. His signature and that of another officer followed the stamped name of the corporation, but there was no designation of a representative capacity. McManus is being sued personally by the payee. Discuss the outcome. Would your answer be the same if McManus were being sued by an HIDC who took the instrument by negotiation from the payee? What if the payee negotiated the note to someone who did not qualify as an HIDC? Could that person get a judgment against McManus? [*Leahy v. McManus,* 206 A.2d 688 (Md. 1965).]

2. Assume that Jessica Taylor sees a $100 coat that she wants to purchase at Foxy Fashions. When she opens her personalized check book supplied by her bank, Capital State, she discovers that there are no more blank checks left in the book. Before the sales clerk can object, Jessica simply writes on a piece of scratch paper as in figure 23.9. The sales clerk consults the manager, who refuses to accept Jessica's "check."
    a. Is this really a check?
    b. Is it negotiable?
    c. Is it enforceable—on the assumption that someone will take it—even if it is not negotiable?
    d. What is the effect on negotiability of the omission of a date on it?
    e. When is the instrument payable?
    f. What is the effect on negotiability of Jessica's failure to spell out $100 in words in addition to putting it into figures?
    g. If the instrument is negotiable, can Jessica legally compel Foxy to take the instrument in payment for the coat?
    h. If the instrument is negotiable, is it really a check or a draft?
    i. On the assumption that this instrument is negotiable, will Foxy Fashions' indorsement be necessary to negotiate it?
    j. Is Capital State properly classified as a depositary, presenting, drawee, or payor bank?

3. A note was drafted in duplicate. The original was signed by the maker and, with the use of carbon paper, the maker's signature was impressed on the duplicate copy. Since the original cannot be found, can the payee enforce the duplicate with a carbon copy of the maker's signature as a negotiable instrument? [*Chrismer v. Chrismer,* 144 N.E.2d 494 (Ohio 1956).]

4. The City of Concord acquired certain real property in the city by tax sale and wanted to auction it off to the highest bidder. The municipal ordinance and the announced terms of the auction sale require the bid to be accompanied by "cash or certified check." The newspaper advertisements required that all bids be accompanied by "cash or certified check in an amount to at least 10% of the bid price." Perry's high bid was accompanied by a bank draft of the New Hampshire Savings drawn on the Mechanics National Bank and payable to George West, Tax Collector. The second high bid, submitted by Henry J. Love, was accompanied by a cashier's check of Concord National Bank payable to the City of Concord. The third highest bid was submitted by Pasquale Alosa and accompanied by U.S. currency. Lockwood Realty Co. submitted the fourth highest bid accompanied by its check certified by the Mechanics National Bank. Who is the highest bidder that conformed to the terms of the auction and is, therefore, entitled to the property upon full payment of his bid price? [*Perry v. West,* 266 A.2d 849 (N.H. 1970).]

5. Defendant, Samuel Feinberg, signed a promissory note personally and as the representative of Sain Builders, Inc., which is now involved in bankruptcy proceedings. Feinberg argues that the phrase "as per contract" contained in the note destroys the requirement of an unconditional promise and that the plaintiff-indorsee, D'Andrea, is not an HIDC because he must have been aware of the underlying contract between Sain Builders and payee. Judgment for whom and why? [*D'Andrea v. Feinberg,* 45 Misc.2d 270 (N.Y. 1965).]

6. An instrument in all other respects negotiable related in part as follows: "It is agreed that this note is to be paid in Elks Club #8 Second Mortgage real estate bonds." Does this sentence render the entire note non-negotiable? Why or why not? [*Moore v. Clines,* 57 S.W.2d 509 (Ky. 1932).]

7. A note provides that it is payable in sixty days, or sooner if certain property is sold. Is the note negotiable or does this acceleration provision destroy certainty of time? [*Fox v. Morris,* 496 P.2d 158 (Nev. 1972).]

8. A note with a definite maturity date provided that the holder could accelerate payment at any time the holder felt insecure. When the holder accelerated on the basis of this term, the maker of the note defended on grounds that there was no reason for the holder to feel insecure. Result?

9. Defendant, South Sea Apartments, Inc., issued a note to the order of payee in return for services that were to be performed by payee in the future. At the time payee negotiated the note to plaintiff it was not disputed that plaintiff knew of this agreement. Since the agreement was later breached by payee, defendant refuses to pay at maturity and claims that the plaintiff's knowledge of the agreement imports a condition which destroys negotiability of the note. In the alternative, defendant asserts that plaintiff's knowledge of the agreement either destroys its good faith or puts it on notice of a defense, and as a result plaintiff is a mere holder, not an HIDC. Evaluate these defenses. [*Gordon Supply Co. v. South Sea Apts., Inc.,* 257 N.Y.S.2d 237 (1965).]

10. Among other things, *Tepper v. Citizens Federal Savings and Loan Association,*[91] 448 So.2d 1138 (Fla. 1984), discussed the importance of the state statute of limitations to negotiable instrument law. When does the statute of limitations begin to run against primary parties? Against secondary parties?

---

[91] See pp. 368–69.

24 Transfer and Negotiation

After you have read this chapter, you should be able to:
1. Speak confidently of the meaning and importance of "negotiation."
2. Be familiar with the methods of negotiating a negotiable instrument.
3. Recognize the types of indorsements, their common features, and the legal consequences of each.
4. Illustrate the "shelter provision" and its exceptions.
5. Explain the legal effect of reacquisition of an instrument by a prior owner.
6. Understand the importance of warranty liability and its relationship to indorsement liability.
7. Determine the legal effect of forged instruments, forged indorsements, and the signatures of impostors.
8. Discover when payment of an instrument is "final."

Introduction

We noted in chapter 23, Introduction to Commercial Paper and Banking Operations, that a negotiable instrument, which is a type of formal contract, has the potential of conferring upon another "greater rights" than could be obtained under a simple contract by assignment. This chapter is important because it tells you *how* these greater rights become vested in another. It is not enough to know that these greater rights exist. If *you* are to derive the benefits or avoid the burdens associated with commercial paper, you must know how to use the law of commercial paper effectively.

Negotiation

At the outset of this inquiry it is important to fix firmly in mind that "order" paper requires an indorsement and delivery for a **negotiation**.[1] However, no indorsement is necessary for the negotiation of "bearer" paper; it can be negotiated by delivery alone.[2]

negotiation
the delivery of negotiable paper to a person who thereby becomes a holder

Order and Bearer Paper

Identification of Order Paper
An instrument can be identified as order paper:

1. if it names a payee that is capable of indorsing—e.g., "Pay to the order of Greenery USA"[3]—or
2. if the last or only indorsement is a special indorsement (one that names an indorsee)—e.g., "Pay to Ruston State Bank, [signed] Charles Ogden."[4]

In each of these illustrations the named party, *Greenery USA* or *Ruston State Bank*, must indorse and deliver the instrument before it can be further negotiated by the holder.

Identification of Bearer Paper
Bearer paper expressly states that it is payable to bearer, to the order of bearer, or it names no payee that is capable of making an indorsement, e.g., "Pay to *Bearer*," "Pay to the order of *Bearer*," or "Pay to the order of *Cash*."[5] Order paper may even be converted into bearer paper if the last or only indorsement is in blank (blank indorsements consist of the signature of the indorser only; no indorsee is named).[6]

While the holder of bearer paper can legally negotiate it without further indorsement, people who are willing to receive negotiable paper normally require an indorsement. This will facilitate recovery against the indorser on the instrument in the event of later dishonor of the instrument. Also, a person who negotiates without an indorsement makes certain transfer warranties, but only to the *immediate recipient*. If the recipient indorses and transfers the instrument, he or she then incurs indorsement liability as well as warranty liability.[7]

Order and Bearer Paper in Action
To put this in a realistic focus, assume that Dorothy Adams, owner of a landscape firm, purchases a selection of plants from *Greenery USA*. By way of payment, she draws and issues a $4,800 check on her drawee bank, Pinnacle State, payable to the order of Greenery, the payee-supplier (figure 24.1).

Greenery may either deposit the check for credit in its account, use the check to pay off its trade creditors, or discharge an obligation on a loan. The possibilities are far too numerous to pursue, but, for purposes of illustration, suppose that an authorized representative of Greenery indorses it "Without Recourse, Greenery USA, by Jack Ingram,

---

[1] UCC 3–204(1). [2] UCC 3–204(2). [3] UCC 3–110. [4] UCC 3–204(1).
[5] UCC 3–111(2)(6). [6] UCC 3–111(c), 204(2). [7] UCC 3–417(2).

Figure 24.1   Check

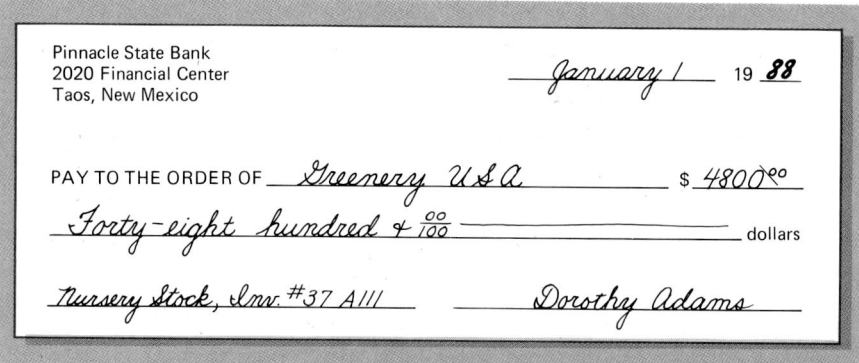

Figure 24.2   Indorsements on Check

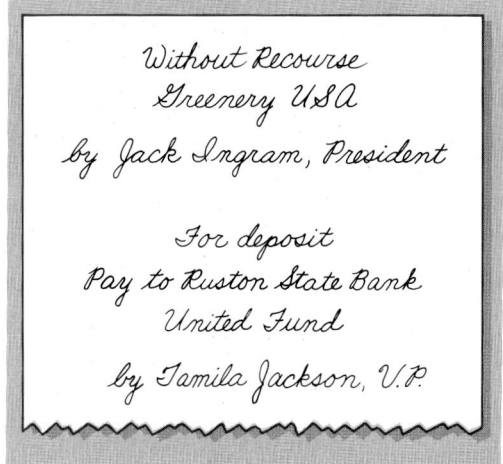

President" and donates it to United Fund. "Without recourse" is discussed later; briefly, it means that the indorser will not be liable as an indorser if the instrument is not paid when due.

In all likelihood United Fund will indorse the check for deposit in its bank—e.g., "For deposit, Pay to Ruston State Bank, [signed] United Fund, by Tamila Jackson, V.P." (figure 24.2)—and the bank will then forward the check through collection channels to Pinnacle State. If funds are sufficient and no stop-payment order has been issued by Dorothy Adams, the check will be paid by the drawee-payor bank, Pinnacle State Bank.

Indorsements

All Indorsements Are Multifaceted (Many-Sided)

Dorothy Adams' first delivery ("issue")[8] of her check to Greenery makes Greenery a holder.[9] A close look at the indorsements placed on the instrument by Greenery and United Fund will be helpful in illustrating certain elements that are common to all indorsements.

---

[8] UCC 3–102(1)(2).   [9] UCC 1–201(20).

Figure 24.3 Blank (and Qualified) Indorsement

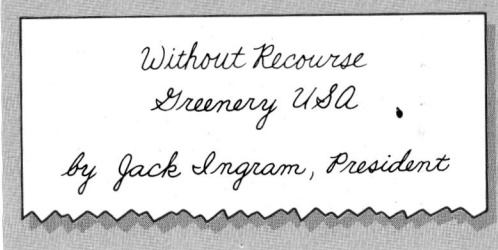

Figure 24.4 Special (and Restrictive) Indorsement

All indorsements, from the simplest to the most complex, are hybrid (mixed) in nature and may be analyzed on the following basis:

1. blank or special—determines the method to be used in subsequent negotiations;
2. restrictive or nonrestrictive—determines the type of interest being transferred;
3. qualified or unqualified—determines the liability of the indorser.

Blank Indorsement

A **blank indorsement** consists simply of the indorser's signature.[10] For example, in figure 24.3 the payee's signature, Greenery USA, appears on the instrument without naming an indorsee.

blank indorsement an indorsement which does not specify any particular indorsee

Since a business firm can act only through its agents, the fact that Greenery's signature was placed there by Jack Ingram does not change things in the least. Nor, for that matter, does the qualifying phrase "Without Recourse" (see the discussion below on qualified indorsements).

The instrument is now bearer paper because the last or only indorsement is in blank. United Fund is the bearer and can negotiate it by delivery alone. Since a bearer instrument which is lost or stolen may get into the hands of an HIDC, a cautious party will be well advised to write above the signature of Greenery any contract or instructions consistent with the character of the indorsement.[11]

No title or ownership can be transferred by a *forgery* of a required indorsement. While C, an innocent party, may purchase an instrument in good faith and without notice of a forgery of a required indorsement, C cannot be an HIDC because C is not, first, a holder. To qualify as a holder, C would have to be in possession of an instrument *indorsed* to C or in blank—that means a genuine indorsement, not a forgery. (P is the payee of a check. T stole it, forged P's blank indorsement, and delivered it to you. Although you possess the check, ownership cannot flow to you without P's indorsement.)

Usually an indorsement (or other signature) by a mark—e.g., "X"—must be witnessed by two or more people and signed by them as witnesses.

Special Indorsement

A **special indorsement** names the indorsee.[12] For example, when United Fund indorsed "Pay to Ruston State Bank," it named the bank an indorsee and, therefore, the indorsement is special (figure 24.4). A special indorsement need not use the word "order"; it will be implied.[13]

special indorsement an indorsement which specifies a particular indorsee

The fact that the "For Deposit" language limits or restricts the use of the instrument has no bearing on the issue of special versus blank indorsements. Nor is it relevant to special or blank indorsements that the signature was made by an agent, Tamila Jackson, Vice President.

---

[10] UCC 3–204(2).   [11] UCC 3–204(3).   [12] UCC 3–204(1).   [13] UCC 3–204(1).

Before the instrument can be further negotiated, the special indorsee must indorse. If joint payees or indorsees are named ("A and B"), both must indorse; if payees or indorsees are named in the alternative ("A or B"), either may indorse.[14]

Blank and Special Indorsements: A Summary

All indorsements are either blank or special. If an indorsement consists of the indorser's name without designating an indorsee, it is a blank indorsement.

Do not be in the least bit surprised to find that the blank or special characteristics of an indorsement exist alongside the restrictive/nonrestrictive and qualified/unqualified elements of the same indorsement. An analysis of any indorsement will reveal each of these components, which will now be discussed.

Restrictive Indorsement

restrictive indorsement
an indorsement which determines the type of interest in the instrument being transferred

Keep in mind that a **restrictive indorsement** determines the type of interest being transferred. It will either *condition* the indorser's liability on the instrument (transfer a conditional interest) or *regulate* the things that the recipient, who may be an agent or trustee, can do with the instrument (transfer a limited interest).[15]

Restrictive Indorsements That Impose Conditions. It is important to point out that *no* indorsement destroys the negotiable character of a negotiable instrument. While the original promise or order on the *face* of a negotiable instrument must be absolute and unconditional, an indorser may make his or her indorsement contract depend on the performance of an express condition.[16] The right to impose a condition makes the instrument more adaptable to the indorser's needs. For example, the payee may indorse "Pay to Del Wells upon performance of contract #61387, [signed] David Reitzel."

Notice that the indorsement is special as well as restrictive, so Del Wells must indorse before the instrument can be further negotiated. The fact that the indorsement is both special and restrictive simply reenforces the earlier observation that all indorsements are hybrid (mixed) in nature. All parties including depositary banks (but not intermediary or drawee-payor banks)[17] must recognize the existence of the condition.

In order to become an HIDC, the person who receives such an instrument must pay in accordance with its terms.[18] In other words, you could not become a holder *for value*—one of the requirements of an HIDC—if you do not pay consistent with this indorsement.

An exception was noted above for nondepositary intermediary and drawee-payor banks.[19] These banks simply handle too many thousands of checks daily in the clearinghouse or collection process to be responsible for this type of indorsement. They must, however, obey the terms of the indorsement of the bank that forwarded the item for collection.

To make certain that payment at maturity discharges the person who pays from further liability on the instrument, the condition must be obeyed. If the instrument that the payee, Reitzel, indorsed restrictively to Wells was a $1,000 *note* that you had issued, you could discharge your liability on the instrument only by paying the holder, Wells, in a manner "consistent with the terms of such restrictive indorsement."[20]

This restrictive indorsement should be a warning signal to you, the maker-primary party. If you expect to be fully discharged by your payment to Wells, you should inquire of the payee, Reitzel, to determine whether contract #61387 has been performed. If it has not been performed, payment should be withheld. Otherwise you may be compelled by the payee, Reitzel, to pay a second time.[21]

---

[14] UCC 3–116.

[15] UCC 3–205.

[16] UCC 3–205.

[17] UCC 3–206(2), 4–205(2). See pp. 358–59 for definitions of these banks.

[18] UCC 3–206(3).

[19] UCC 3–206(2), 4–205(2), 4–105(a)(c).

[20] UCC 3–603(1)(6).

[21] UCC 3–603(1).

Restrictive Indorsements That Purport to Prohibit Further Negotiation. The indorsement "Pay A only, [signed] Indorser" *purports* to prohibit further transfer or negotiation of the instrument, but the UCC does not give it that legal effect.[22] It is treated as if it were a special *and* nonrestrictive indorsement instead.

Restrictive Indorsements for Deposit and Collection. The most frequent type of restrictive indorsement is one which reads "For Deposit" or "For Collection" along with the indorser's signature.[23] That is what the agent of United Fund did with the check received from Greenery USA (figure 24.4).

If you will consult the back of the cancelled checks your drawee-payor bank may send to you each month with a statement of your account, you will find another common form of restrictive indorsement: "Pay any bank" or "Pay any bank, banker, or trust co."[24] These are placed on the check by depositary and collecting banks, and they are the only indorsements to which banks in the collection process have to pay any attention.[25]

Once these indorsements have locked an instrument into bank collection channels, "outsiders" are put on notice. No one can become a holder for value unless payment for the instrument is applied consistent with this indorsement, i.e., the money is deposited into the account of the indorser.[26] A drawee-payor bank may be held liable for not complying with the restrictive indorsement.

Restrictive Indorsements in Trust. A restrictive indorsement may establish a trust for the use or benefit of the indorser or some other person.[27] For example, the indorsements "Pay to T for the use of P, [signed] P" and "Pay to T in trust for M, [signed] P" establish T as the trustee for a beneficiary, who is either the indorser, P, in the first instance, or some other person, M, perhaps a minor child, in the second instance.

The party who receives the instrument from T—i.e., the "first taker" following such an indorsement—must pay or apply the money consistent with the indorsement. If this is done, and if all of the other requirements are met, the first taker may qualify as an HIDC. Subsequent parties are not in any way affected or given notice by such an indorsement, unless they have actual knowledge that the trustee, T, has violated his or her duty in negotiating the instrument.[28]

Qualified Indorsements or Indorsement without Recourse

Whenever a person transfers an instrument for consideration, the transferor makes certain implied transfer warranties,[29] discussed later. If the transfer is made with an indorsement, the holder receives, in addition to the implied warranties, a right of recourse against the indorser if the following steps are taken:

1. Presentment: the instrument is properly presented for payment or acceptance.
2. Dishonor: payment or acceptance is refused.
3. Notice of dishonor: the indorser is given timely notice of dishonor.[30]

It is possible for the indorser to avoid this conditional liability under the indorsement contract *if the indorser so indicates expressly on the instrument*. The use of the phrase "without recourse" along with the indorser's signature has this effect.[31] The phrase means that, in the event of dishonor, no recourse can be made against that indorser because of such dishonor. The implied transfer warranties of such an indorser are now comparable to those of an assignor under the common law.

qualified indorsement
an indorsement which disclaims or qualifies the liability of the indorser on the instrument

---

[22] UCC 3–205(b), 3–206(1) and comment 2.

[23] UCC 3–205(c). [24] UCC 3–205(c). [25] UCC 3–206(2), 4–205(2).

[26] UCC 3–206(c), 4–201(2). [27] UCC 3–205(d). [28] UCC 3–206(4), 3–304(2).

[29] UCC 3–417(2). [30] UCC 3–414(i). [31] UCC 3–414(1).

Figure 24.5 Qualified Indorsement

Figure 24.6 Irregular Indorsement

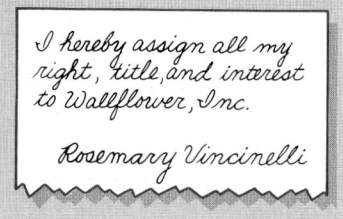

From the indorser's point of view, "without recourse" is an excellent way of escaping the normal liability that accompanies one's signature as an indorser on a negotiable instrument. The difficulty is in finding someone who will take such an indorsement.

You should be cautious in receiving instruments indorsed in this manner. If the holder is not able to collect from the debtor at maturity, the holder must rely on breach of implied warranty by the transferor.

Assume that P receives a check from D in return for the sale of merchandise. P indorses "without recourse" to H and delivers the check to H. Then D notifies the drawee bank to stop payment on the check (a stop-payment order). H will be able to recover from P only if H can prove some breach of the implied transfer warranties by P.

If H sued P on the basis of P's transfer warranties to H, H would attempt to prove that:

1. P did not have good title to the instrument. (*But he did!*)
2. Signatures were not genuine or authorized. (*But they were!*)
3. The instrument has been materially altered. (*But it was not!*)
4. P had knowledge of some defense. (*Assume that P did not.*)
5. P had knowledge of D's insolvency. (*Assume that D was not insolvent or that P had no knowledge of it.*)[32]

In many situations H will simply be unable to recover a single penny from P. However, H may proceed against D. The stop-payment order does not mean that D is certain to be successful in a suit by H. A qualified "without recourse" indorsement will not prevent the qualified indorser from being liable for breach of warranty of no knowledge of any defense good against him.

Qualified indorsements are most likely to be used when the indorser has no personal interest in the instrument—e.g., the instrument has been made payable to an agent rather than to the principal (the agent's employer) and the agent simply indorses it over to the principal—or when the recipient has no bargaining power—e.g., the instrument is conveyed as a gift, such as the one by Greenery USA to United Fund (figure 24.5).

Irregular Indorsements

A negotiable instrument may be "assigned" by an irregular indorsement of assignment (figure 24.6). Rosemary's words of assignment do not affect the character of her signature as an indorsement.[33]

---

[32] UCC 3–417(2)(3).

[33] UCC 3–202(4).

Transfers

Transfers without a Required Indorsement

By way of review, recall the manner in which negotiable paper is negotiated: bearer paper by delivery; order paper by indorsement and delivery. On some occasions, and normally because of forgetfulness, order paper will be transferred without an indorsement. For example, you may rush into a familiar store on the way to school or work to cash a payroll check or pay a bill and forget to indorse the instrument. In situations like these, the transferee or recipient is entitled to your unqualified indorsement.[34] The negotiation takes place when you finally indorse. *At that time* the store becomes a holder and, if all the other requirements are met, an HIDC.

Transfers for Less Than the Full Amount

An indorsement can be effective as a negotiation only if it conveys the full amount of the instrument or the unpaid balance. A $1,000 instrument indorsed $400 to A and $600 to B is quite legal and enforceable, but neither of the parties would qualify as a holder. They would be treated instead as assignees of the indorser's interest.[35]

Shelter Provision

shelter concept
obtaining rights by claiming "through" or "under"

The transfer of a negotiable instrument conveys to the recipient-transferee all the rights of the transferor.[36] If, for example, the transferor was an HIDC, the transferee would receive all the rights of an HIDC; the transferee can claim through the HIDC using the HIDC as a shelter. This result will follow even though the transferee could not meet all the requirements for being an HIDC.

When Greenery USA donated a check to United Fund, United Fund could not qualify as an HIDC because it did not give value. Nevertheless, United Fund received the rights of Greenery, and, if Greenery qualified as an HIDC, United Fund would be entitled to exercise those rights as well.

The same result follows despite the fact that the transferee takes the instrument either:

1. after it is overdue;
2. with notice of its previous dishonor;
3. with notice of a claim to it; or
4. with notice of a defense against it.

For example, if a draft or note payable to the order of P, payee, is negotiated to an HIDC, the rights of the HIDC pass to the transferee, X, even though:

1. X gave no value; or
2. X received the instrument after it was overdue; or
3. X had notice of a defense against the instrument, such as fraud by the payee on the maker or drawer of the instrument; or
4. X had notice that the instrument had been previously dishonored, such as by the drawee-payor or maker refusing to honor the instrument.

There are two easily recognized exceptions to this shelter provision. The transferee does not receive the transferor's rights:

1. where the transferee was a *party* to fraud or illegality affecting the instrument, or
2. where the transferee as a *prior holder* had notice of a claim or defense.

---

[34] UCC 3–201(3).   [35] UCC 3–202(3).   [36] UCC 3–201(1).

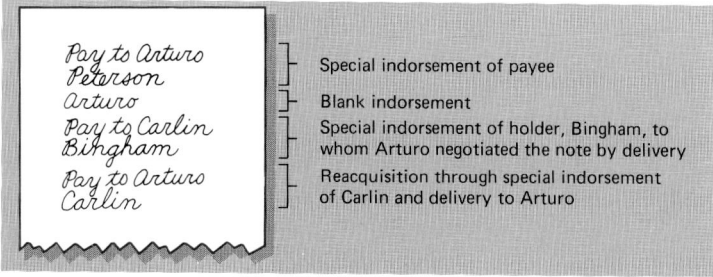

Figure 24.7 Reacquired Instrument by Arturo

Figure 24.8 Instrument Renegotiated to Arturo

The justification for these exceptions is readily apparent.

a. A wrongdoer should not benefit from his wrongdoing. Therefore, if X collaborated with P in the fraud illustration above, X should not subsequently profit from the shelter provision by claiming through the HIDC.
b. If X was a prior holder before the HIDC—e.g., if the instrument went from M to P to X (assume that X knew of P's fraud or illegality with regard to M although X played no part in it), and then *from X to an HIDC before coming back to X*—X cannot improve his status as a mere holder and he cannot claim through the HIDC. In other words, a *reacquirer* cannot "whitewash" or "launder" the instrument by running it through the hands of an HIDC.

Reacquirers

Reacquisition of an instrument by a prior party.

Generally speaking, when a party reacquires an instrument that he formerly held, he may reissue or further negotiate it.[37] For example, a negotiable note issued by Mackey, the maker, to Peterson, the payee, could be negotiated initially to Arturo and then back to Arturo with the following indorsements as shown in figure 24.7.

Arturo is a reacquirer. Even if the note is now overdue, he can still negotiate it. On the assumption in the above example that he further indorses and negotiates it to X, the liability of Bingham and of Carlin is discharged (1) against Arturo, the reacquiring party, and (2) against subsequent holders *not* in due course.[38] It would be foolish not to discharge Bingham and Carlin because, if Arturo or a subsequent holder *not* in due course collected from one of them, the one who paid would in turn proceed back against Arturo, as diagrammed in figure 24.8.

The reacquiring party can cancel any indorsement which is not necessary to that party's title or ownership.[39] If so inclined, Arturo could mark out the special indorsements of Bingham and Carlin. This would leave only Peterson's special indorsement and Arturo's blank one. If Arturo then negotiated the instrument to anyone who qualified as an HIDC, Bingham and Carlin would not be liable as indorsers. In effect, Arturo has made a gift to Bingham and Carlin by discharging them from further liability.[40]

---

[37] UCC 3–208.   [38] UCC 3–601(3)(a).   [39] UCC 3–208.   [40] UCC 3–605(1)(a).

Part 5: Commercial Paper

Forgeries and Unauthorized Signatures

Nobody is liable on a negotiable instrument unless his or her signature is on the instrument. The **forgery** of a signature or the unauthorized use of a signature (by an agent, for example) does not obligate the party whose name is wrongly used unless:

1. the party ratifies the transaction (after learning all the facts, he OK's the transaction by word or other conduct); or
2. the party is precluded or estopped from denying it (engaged in conduct that makes it unfair to permit the party to avoid or disown the transaction).[41]

forgery
the unauthorized act of imitating or altering a writing with the intent to defraud and impose liability

To illustrate each of the above, (1) a mother might ratify the forgeries of her signature on checks by a daughter, and (2) an employer might be precluded or estopped by its negligent supervision of a check-writing machine from disclaiming the conduct of an agent who abused his or her position and wrongfully placed the employer's signature on a company blank check.

In the following case the court held that the negligence of the payee of checks substantially contributed to the payee's agent unauthorizedly making the payee's indorsements on the checks.

Facts
Payee's general credit manager, Curie, took six checks payable to payee (Dunham-Bush), indorsed the name of the payee, and then indorsed them for deposit into his personal account at the Connecticut Bank and Trust Company (CBT), defendant. As general credit manager, Curie was responsible for handling accounts receivable, posting those accounts, and for issuance of reminder billing statements. Annual audits by Haskins and Sells for the year of these events, and for three previous years, recommended separation of the function of handling receivables, posting, and issuing reminders. These recommendations were not implemented.

Hartford Accident and Indemnity Company, surety of payee Dunham-Bush, reimbursed payee for its losses and proceeded, as plaintiff, against depositary bank, CBT. Since CBT took the check on the forged or unauthorized indorsement of payee, it will be liable to payee (or, in this case, payee's surety, Hartford) unless it can prove that payee's negligence substantially contributed to the forgery and that it acted in good faith and in accordance with reasonable commercial standards of the banking industry. Judgment was rendered for defendant, and plaintiff appealed.

Decision
Judgment affirmed for defendant, Connecticut Bank and Trust Company.

Reasoning
On the facts found, CBT has carried its burden of proof. Dunham-Bush's daily office procedure for handling receipts of its receivables at the time the defalcations occurred, the concentration in one person of authority for dealing at three levels with receivables, and the failure to act on the auditor's recommendations, which specifically addressed the procedures under which the defalcations took place, constituted that degree of negligence which substantially contributed to the making of the unauthorized indorsements. The procedure followed by CBT in the handling of its deposits is reasonable in the context of modern banking where checks have taken on a new importance as an accepted exchange medium. A multiplicity of teller stations have evolved to handle this volume and the evolution has led us into an electronic mode operation. As a result, banking procedure at the teller level focuses on the last indorser. This is the one who has received the proceeds of the check and to whom the electronic trail will lead. Modern banking practice considers the available safeguards and has structured its procedures accordingly.

Hartford Accident and Indemnity Company v. Connecticut Bank and Trust Company, 476 A.2d 1083 (Conn. Super. 1982).

You will want to make a distinction between two types of forgeries: (a) instruments that are completely forged from the very outset—e.g., X forges D's signature as drawer on a check; and (b) forged indorsements—e.g., X steals a check drawn originally by D to the order of P and X forges P's blank indorsement. The first of these forged instruments

---
[41] UCC 3-404, 3-406.

Figure 24.9 Forged Instrument

(a) can be negotiated to innocent HIDCs. Forgery of a *drawer's* signature does not prevent the otherwise negotiable instrument from being negotiable. The instrument *is* signed, although the drawer whose signature is forged is not liable thereon. However, following a forged required *indorsement* (b), no title passes, and no one can become a holder or an HIDC.

At maturity, M will refuse to pay A, an HIDC, because M's signature does not appear on the instrument and, indeed, M did not know of its existence prior to the HIDC's demand for payment. No *contract* has ever existed between *M,* on the one hand, and either X, P, or A, on the other hand; therefore, M is not liable on the instrument and has a "real" defense which is valid against anyone, including an HIDC. (See figure 24.9.)

M would be liable if M ratified X's forgery or if M negligently supervised X's use of a check-writing machine. However, as matters stand, A, the HIDC, must seek recovery against P or X; but since M did not sign the instrument, M is not liable on the instrument. As a rule, the loss will fall upon the person who dealt with the forger unless the forger can be found and made to pay.

An unauthorized signature operates as the signature of the unauthorized signer; *the latter* did sign it. So X's forgery of M's signature causes X to be liable as the maker; if X had forged P's indorsement, X would also be liable as an indorser.[42]

The fact that A is an HIDC does not assist him in these collection efforts. He will be pursuing X on his liability as a *maker,* and P as an *indorser* and as a *warrantor.* Accordingly, while X's real name does not appear on the instrument, the forgery obligates him nevertheless. The drawee bank cannot charge its depositor drawer's account when the latter's signature was forged on the check.

As shown in figure 24.10, M signs a negotiable promissory note with P as the payee. X steals the note, forges P's blank indorsement, and transfers the note to A, who, *except* for the forgery, meets the requirements for being an HIDC. At maturity, M refuses to honor the note, asserting P's claim to the note. (UCC 3–603(1)(a))

In this situation, A is neither a holder nor an HIDC. A is in possession of an instrument, but it has not been properly indorsed so as to flow to him so he cannot become a holder nor an HIDC even if he met all of the other requirements. A can proceed against X on the forged indorsement and on the breach of transfer warranty, but P still owns the instrument.

If P is sued as an indorser by A or a subsequent party that has received the instrument through A, the forgery operates as a *real defense* for P, if we assume no ratification or estoppel by P. On the other hand, if P decides to take the initiative, P could assert a *claim of ownership* against A or anyone else to recover possession of the instrument.

---

[42] UCC 3–404(1).

Figure 24.10 Forged Indorsement

Figure 24.11 Impersonator Receives an Instrument

Figure 24.12 Indorsement by Impersonator

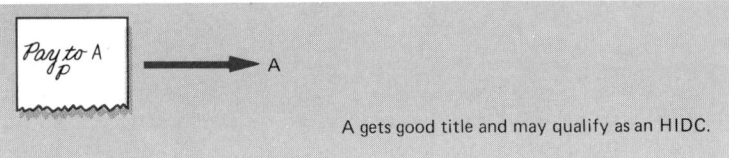

Impostors

Impersonation.

When an **impostor** payee induces issuance of an instrument, *anyone can indorse in the payee's name*. Thus, if X impersonates P and induces M to issue a negotiable instrument to the order of P (the person who is being impersonated), *anyone* can indorse in P's name. X's indorsement of P's name is not treated as a forgery. In other words, X can indorse P's name and negotiate such an instrument to A, who may qualify as an HIDC. (See figures 24.11 and 24.12.) The HIDC as a plaintiff will prevail against M if M refuses to pay the instrument at maturity.[43] While M is guilty of no wrongdoing, M nevertheless intended to create a negotiable instrument despite the trickery of X. This led to the purchase of the instrument by a completely innocent person, A, who had no opportunity to prevent or detect the original fraud. By way of justification of this rule, it can be said that, when one of two innocent persons must suffer (M or A), the loss falls on the one who had an opportunity to detect the wrongdoing or the opportunity to insure against it. Furthermore, A has the right to proceed against the wrongdoer, X. A cannot collect from P, the party who has been impersonated, because P's signature never really appeared on the instrument.

impostor (impersonator) a person who misrepresents himself (herself) as another person

This same result will follow: (1) if an employee supplies the maker or drawer with the name of a real or fictitious payee that the employee *does not intend should have any interest in the instrument;* or (2) if an agent with authority to sign does sign on behalf of the agent's employer but with the intention that the real or fictitious payee *have no interest.*[44]

---

[43] UCC 3–405(1)(a). [44] UCC 3–405(1)(b)(c).

Figure 24.13 Negotiable Promissory Note Indorsed in Blank by P, Payee, and Delivered to A, to B, to H

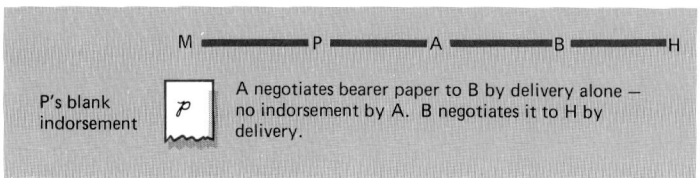

What the employee or agent really intends is to take the instrument which has now been made out to a phony supplier-creditor or to a fictitious name added to the payroll list, indorse the payee's name, and pocket the cash. The innocent purchaser of such an instrument is protected, and once again the loss falls on the person who had an opportunity to prevent the deception, or to insure against it. Here, that person would be the employer.

However, if the person who deals with the impersonator acts negligently in cashing the checks, that person may be liable instead of the employer.

Warranties

warranty
an express or implied assurance that certain facts exist

Various **warranties** implied by law under the Code are made by persons transferring a negotiable instrument and by persons who obtain payment or acceptance of the instrument.

Transfer warranties.

Transfer Warranties

If M issues a negotiable instrument payable to the order of P, P may indorse and deliver it to a holder, A, in payment for goods or services. In this situation, P becomes conditionally or secondarily liable on his or her indorsement contract to the holder, A. P impliedly agrees that the instrument will be honored. If M refuses to pay the note at maturity and A gives timely notice of dishonor or nonpayment, P is liable to A for the face amount. This is the liability of an indorser *as a secondary party.*

P may be liable to A for breach of implied *transfer warranties* as well. When a person transfers an instrument and receives a consideration, certain implied transfer warranties are created automatically or by operation of law. If the transferor has indorsed the instrument, these warranties extend to all subsequent transferees. However, if bearer paper is negotiated by delivery alone, transfer warranties are made to the immediate recipient only.[45] In other words, for the situation diagrammed in figure 24.13:

1. P's transfer warranties extend to A, B, and H.
2. A's transfer warranties extend *only* to B, not to H.

Transferors warrant as follows:

a. The transferor has good title or is authorized by the owner to collect.
b. All signatures are genuine or authorized.
c. No material alterations of the instrument.
d. No defense of any party is valid against the transferor.
e. No *knowledge* of insolvency proceedings against the drawer of an unaccepted instrument (secondary party) or against the maker or acceptor (primary party).[46]

---

[45] UCC 3–417(2).   [46] UCC 3–417(2) (a)–(e).

Figure 24.14 Overlap of Indorsement Liability and Warranty Liability

In the following case the depositary collecting bank fulfilled its warranty of good title and authority.

Facts
Pan American World Airways (Pan Am) is a member of the Air Transport Association of America. One of the functions of the Association is to appoint travel agents for its member carriers and to provide these travel agents with printed forms for flight tickets and other documents connected with air travel and related services. Travel agents then issue drafts drawn on member airlines (in this case Pan American), payable to themselves, in return for services that travel agents render to the member carriers. These services are for other than air transportation, e.g., promotional efforts, bookkeeping and so forth.

The Air Transport Association authorized a unique way of drawing these drafts—by the use of special embossing or validating plates. Eight drafts bearing the proper validating plates were issued by defunct travel agents and delivered to Roadway International. That company deposited them in its account at Continental National Bank of Miami (Continental Bank), defendant. The bank initiated the collection process against Pan Am. Proceeds in excess of $82,000 were paid by Pan Am to the account of Roadway.

Pan Am sued Continental Bank for the return of that sum. Judgment was rendered for Continental Bank and Pan Am appealed.

Decision
Affirmed for defendant Continental Bank.

Reasoning
Continental Bank's warranty of good title is limited to a finding that the draft was presented for payment with no forged indorsements. Even if issue of these drafts was unauthorized, Pan Am or Air Transport Association allowed that to happen. Continental played no role in the selection or supervision of these agents and is not responsible for their lack of authority.

Pan American World Airways, Inc. v. Continental National Bank of Miami, 444 So.2d 1073 (Fla. 1984).

Typically, a party's indorsement liability and warranty liability will overlap, as shown in figure 24.14. Suppose that X forged M's signature as maker of a negotiable promissory note with X as the payee; X then indorsed and negotiated the note to A, and A subsequently indorsed and delivered the note to H. M is justifiably entitled to refuse payment to H (assuming no ratification or estoppel by M). Given timely notice of dishonor by H, A is liable to H on his indorsement contract. A would be liable also as warrantor because M's signature is not genuine.

If A negotiated bearer paper by delivery alone, or if A indorsed but H failed to properly present for payment or give notice of dishonor following A's indorsement, H would have to rely solely on breach of implied transfer warranty. Warranty liability, therefore, has a value over and above indorsement liability.

Keep in mind also that, if A indorses "Without Recourse," he is not liable as an indorser but he is liable on transfer warranties. In that case the transfer warranties are modified somewhat. The qualified indorser warrants that he has *no knowledge* of a defense that is valid against him.[47] All other indorsers warrant against valid defenses rather than no knowledge of defenses.

---

[47] UCC 3–417(3).

Presentment warranties.

Presentment Warranties

When an instrument is presented to the proper party at maturity for payment or acceptance (certification), the person presenting warrants:

1. he or she has good title or is authorized to collect for the owner;
2. he or she has *no knowledge* that the signature of the maker or drawer is forged or unauthorized; and
3. the instrument has not been materially altered.[48]

The general rules are basically straightforward and easily justified. For example, M makes a promissory note. X steals it from the payee, P, forges the payee's blank indorsement, and sells and delivers it to A. A does not have good title to the note. If M innocently pays A, then M should be able to recover from A.[49] After all, A is not the holder nor the owner of the instrument. The payee is still the owner and is entitled to payment from M.

The instrument has been "converted"[50] (explained later) if M pays following a forged indorsement. M is liable to P, so M should be entitled to recover from A any mistaken payment that M has made to A. The following case illustrates, in the case of a check, the liability of a depositary collecting bank on its warranty of title to the payor bank.

Facts
Defendant, Zions First National Bank, presented two cashier's checks for $12,500 to plaintiff Valley Bank & Trust Company and received payment. These cashier's checks, on which Valley Bank was drawer and drawee, were payable to "Peck & Shaw Fine Cars" and to an individual joint payee, Steven J. Gibbs on one check and Jeffrey Olson on the other. When paid by Valley Bank, each check was indorsed with the name of both joint payees and also bore Zions Bank's notation, "PEG" (prior endorsements guaranteed). After Valley Bank learned that the Peck & Shaw indorsements were forgeries, it brought this action against Zions Bank to recover on Zions' guaranty of valid indorsements or for breach of Zions' warranty of good title as provided in UCC 3–417(1)(a) and 4–207(1)(a). Trial court held for Valley Bank. Zions Bank appealed.

Decision
Affirmed for Valley Bank.

Reasoning
It is settled beyond argument that a collecting bank obtaining payment on a cashier's check bearing a forged indorsement is liable upon its warranty of good title and its guaranty of indorsements to the payor bank. This statutory liability under UCC sections 3–417(1) and 4–207(1) duplicates the liability incurred by the PEG guaranty of prior indorsements which Zions Bank entered upon these cashier's checks.

Valley Bank & Trust Company v. Zions First National Bank, 656 P.2d 425 (Utah 1982).

Implicit in the second presentment warranty—no knowledge of a forged maker's or drawer's signature—is the thought that the one who is paying (the maker, acceptor, or drawee) is in a better position to recognize a forgery than the presenter.[51] If the maker's signature has been forged on a note but that person does not recognize the forgery when the instrument is presented at maturity for payment, the money cannot be recovered from the innocent HIDC who received payment. Similarly, the drawee or acceptor who pays a check or draft on the drawer's behalf, despite the forgery of the drawer's signature, is penalized because of this negligence or carelessness. Such persons do have the right to pursue the wrongdoer, however.

Material alteration,[52] which will be discussed in a later chapter, is a "real" or "universal" defense that is valid *even against a holder in due course.* The thought behind this rule is that a contracting party on an instrument should not be liable for more money than he or she has originally agreed to pay.

---

[48] UCC 3–417(1).   [49] UCC 3–417(1)(a).   [50] UCC 3–419(1)(c).

[51] UCC 3–417(1)(b)(i)—(iii).   [52] UCC 3–417(1)(c).

Carefully note the exceptions to presentment warranty rules—(1) no knowledge, and (2) material alterations—in favor of an HIDC acting in good faith. To summarize these exceptions, an HIDC who is acting in good faith—i.e., one who continues to be innocent of any knowledge of a forged maker's or drawer's signature or a material alteration when the HIDC presents for payment or acceptance—does not always make these warranties. Therefore, the HIDC is entitled to keep the money—the one who pays has recourse against the wrongdoer.

Finality of Payment or Acceptance

Payment or acceptance of an instrument is "final" in favor of an HIDC *or* one who in good faith changes his or her position in reliance on payment.[53] This rule is easily enough understood in its protection of an HIDC. However, if a person has not given value or does not otherwise qualify as an HIDC but has made some irrevocable commitment on the strength of this payment, then it is made final in that person's favor as well.

There are two exceptions to this rule. Payment may be recovered if a presentment warranty has been breached,[54] and if certain provisions of the Article on Bank Deposits and Collections are violated.[55]

Conversion

An instrument is **converted**—controlled by someone other than the rightful owner—when it is cashed on a forged indorsement.[56] If X steals from P a $1,000 check drawn payable to the order of P, forges P's indorsement, and passes it to an innocent party, A, who collects on it from the drawee, the drawee has converted P's instrument. If P acts within the time limits, P can assert his claim of ownership against the drawee for $1,000.[57] P can proceed against X and A as well in order to obtain a full recovery.

Since the drawee did not know what the payee's signature looked like (it has a copy of the drawer-customer's signature, which it is supposed to recognize, but not the payee's), it is entitled to charge back against collecting banks for breach of the presentment warranty of good title.[58]

If a forged signature of a drawer-customer is not detected, the bank is not likely to recover on grounds of a presentment warranty. It is penalized for its negligence or oversight, and as a rule, the drawee can recover from the wrongdoer only.[59]

Agents or representatives, including depositary and collecting banks, may advance checks through bank channels following a forged indorsement of the true owner's signature. If they have acted in good faith and in accordance with reasonable business standards, they are not liable to the true owner beyond the amount that remains in their hands.[60] For example, if X steals P's $1,000 check, forges P's indorsement, and transfers the check to A, A may indorse it for collection to the depositary bank (not the payor-drawee bank) and withdraw $500 before P discovers the theft and forgery. In such an event, the depositary bank is liable to P for the remaining $500. It may also have to account to the drawee bank for breach of the presentment warranty of good title.[61] (See *Pan American World Airways, Inc. v. Continental National Bank of Miami*,[62] in which the drawee could not recover against the collecting bank; no indorsements were forged.)

conversion
the tort of intentional interference with another's right to possession, control, and dominion of a chattel

chattel
a tangible, movable thing

---

[53] UCC 3-418.
[54] UCC 3-417(1).
[55] UCC 4-213, 4-301.
[56] UCC 3-419(1)(c).
[57] UCC 4-406(4).
[58] UCC 3-417(1)(a), 4-207(1)(2).
[59] UCC 3-417(1)(b), 4-207(1)(b).
[60] UCC 3-419(3).
[61] See UCC 3-419, comment 6.
[62] See p. 385.

Summary Statement

1. Bearer paper is negotiated by delivery alone. Order paper is negotiated by indorsement and delivery.
2. To identify bearer paper, examine its face. If the face of the paper expressly states that it is payable "to Bearer" or "to Order of Bearer," or it names no payee capable of making a signature—e.g., "Cash"—then it is bearer paper. Don't stop there, however. If the instrument has been indorsed, examine the last (or only) indorsement. A blank indorsement means that the instrument is still bearer paper. A special indorsement converts it to order paper.
3. Order paper will name as payee on the face of the instrument a natural person—e.g., Willie Nelson—or some legal entity that is capable of making a signature through an agent—e.g., Ruston State Bank. Examine the reverse side of the instrument as well as the face, however. If the last or only indorsement is special, the instrument continues to be order paper. If the last or only indorsement is in blank, the instrument becomes bearer paper. If it was bearer to begin with, the special indorsement converts it into order paper.
4. All indorsements are hybrid in nature. Each one will contain elements of the following:
    a. Blank or special. These indorsements determine the method to be used in subsequent negotiations.
    Delivery alone if the last or only indorsement is blank; indorsement plus delivery if the last or only indorsement is special.
    b. Restrictive or nonrestrictive. These indorsements determine whether the interest conveyed is conditional or limited.
    One form of restrictive indorsement contains an express condition—e.g., "Pay to A when he finishes painting my house, [signed] P." The other important form makes the indorsee an agent or trustee—e.g., "Pay to ABC Bank for deposit, [signed] P," or "Pay to T in trust for M, [signed] P."
    c. Qualified or unqualified. These indorsements determine the liability of the indorser.
    When one indorses qualifiedly or without recourse and transfers for a consideration, he makes certain warranties but is not liable as an indorser.
5. The "shelter provision" transfers to the recipient of the instrument all the rights that the transferor had to convey. If the transferor was an HIDC, the transferee gets the rights of an HIDC. This rule opens up the market for commercial paper and makes it easier to sell. However, where the transferee was a party to fraud or illegality affecting the instrument, or where the transferee as a holder *prior* to the HIDC had notice of a claim or defense, the shelter provision rule is ineffective.
6. Forgeries and unauthorized *signatures* do not obligate the party whose name was wrongly used, unless that party ratifies the signature or is precluded or estopped from denying it. *Forged instruments* can get into the hands of HIDCs, but the forger and all indorsers incur signature liability as well as warranty liability. If a *required indorsement* is *forged,* no subsequent party can become a holder or an HIDC. The forger and all indorsers that follow do incur signature and warranty liability, however, and the true owner of the instrument will have a valid claim against the person in possession of the instrument.
7. An impersonator's signature of the name of the individual being impersonated is not a forgery. It operates as a valid signature and subsequent holders can qualify as HIDCs. The wrongdoer is responsible for his or her conduct but, if recovery against the wrongdoer is not practicable, the party who issued the instrument to the impersonator is liable for it.

8. Each time an instrument is *transferred* for a consideration, and each time one is *presented* and payment or acceptance is obtained, certain warranties are made. If the instrument is indorsed by the transferor, the warranties run in favor of all subsequent parties; if the instrument is negotiated by delivery alone, the transfer warranties extend only to the immediate recipient.
9. Warranty liability is different from indorsement liability but is compatible with it. Indorsement liability is discharged if the instrument is not presented for payment at the proper time or if timely notice of dishonor is not given. Warrantors continue to be liable, however. Their obligation is not conditioned on presentment, dishonor, and notice of dishonor.
10. A bank is supposed to know the status of its customers' accounts. When it honors a check—even one creating an overdraft—payment is, generally speaking, *final* in favor of an HIDC or one who in good faith changes his or her position in reliance on payment.
11. If an *indorsement* has been forged, the drawee bank that pays the check is liable to the true owner. Then it may proceed against a collecting bank for violation of a presentment warranty. If a *customer-drawer's signature* is forged, the bank should detect it. Payment of such a forged instrument makes the payor bank liable to its customer. The bank may then proceed against the wrongdoer, but not against collecting banks.

This chapter has emphasized the various rights and duties that can arise when commercial paper is negotiated. The following case presents us with an example of how the principles of law (one is that a bank is required to know its depositor's signature) can be modified by equitable considerations (contributory negligence by one innocent party causing another innocent party to suffer loss).

Neely Enterprises, Inc. v. American National Bank of Huntsville
403 So.2d 887 (Ala. 1981)

Adams, J. Mr. and Mrs. Neely, the owners and operators of J. Gordon Neely Enterprises, Inc., [(Neely), plaintiff,] are doing business as Midas Muffler. Mrs. Neely became acquainted with Bradshaw [a defendant,] in 1976 when, as a Kelly Girl, [Bradshaw] was hired by the company's stockholder accountant to assist him with their account. Mrs. Neely became friendly with Bradshaw and hired her parttime to teach [Bradshaw] how to keep the corporate books. Since 1960, Mrs. Neely had performed all of the in-house bookkeeping duties by herself.

* * *

On Bradshaw's recommendation, Neely opened an account for payroll in American National Bank of Huntsville, a defendant, where Bradshaw kept her personal checking. Neely maintained its corporate account at First Alabama Bank of Huntsville where it had banked for a number of years. Mr. and Mrs. Neely signed the bank signature card and the [firm's] corporate resolution, which stated, among other things, that American National was authorized to pay out funds, on either bearer or order paper, to any of the signatories. Bradshaw was entrusted with these documents to return them to the bank, and without the knowledge or authorization of the Neelys, signed the signature card and added her name in a noticeably different type.

Bradshaw filled out checks drawn on the First Alabama account, except for two drawn on the American National account, made payable to American National and with a large space to the left of the amount written on the designated lines. Mrs. Neely signed these checks being fully aware of these large gaps. She admitted that she never left spaces like that on her personal or corporate checks because it could facilitate alterations, but Mrs. Neely never questioned Bradshaw's practice of doing so because she yielded to Bradshaw's superior knowledge.

Bradshaw altered the checks either by adding a digit or two to the left of the original amount, or by raising the first digit after using liquid erasure. She then made a split deposit by depositing the original amount into Neely's American National payroll account, and depositing to her [own] account the difference between the original and altered amounts. On some occasions she took the difference in cash without depositing it to her account. On those checks that were not raised, she either cashed them and kept the money, or deposited them to her account, or deposited part of the check into the Neely account and kept the rest.

* * *

After Bradshaw picked up the [firm's] monthly statements and items, she realtered them to reflect the original amounts by using liquid erasure. Together, the two women reconciled the statements with Mrs. Neely calling out the information from her journal entry and with Bradshaw responding from the bank statements and items. Consequently, Mrs. Neely never saw the altered checks or the statements. Even when the statements were mailed, Mrs. Neely never opened them and she never reconciled the statements without Bradshaw. A new accountant hired in the latter part of 1977 discovered the defalcations, totalling $17,005.18.

Neely filed a complaint against Bradshaw and American National for [the tort of] conversion. The trial court entered a judgment in favor of American National from which Neely appeals.

* * *

First, Neely contends that the bank converted its funds because it paid out proceeds to Bradshaw when she was not named as payee. We disagree. The checks at issue were made payable to the order of American National as opposed to being drawn to J. Gordon Neely Enterprises, and none of them was indorsed restrictively "For Deposit Only" into Neely's specially designated and numbered account.

* * *

Neely also relies heavily upon the proposition that

It is generally held that a check or draft drawn to the order of a bank precludes the diversion of the proceeds of it to a use other than that of the drawer, and that such diversion can be justified only by proof of authority from drawer.

10 Am.Jur.2d *Banks* § 560 (1963).

However, overlooked by Neely, cited within the same paragraph from which it quotes, is the following:

[B]ut . . . if the drawer has clothed his agent with apparent authority to receive the proceeds of such check, the bank is not negligent in, and is not liable to the drawer for, paying, in reliance upon such apparent authority, the proceeds of such check to such agent contrary to his actual authority, if the agent should misappropriate such proceeds.

10 Am.Jur.2d *Banks* § 560 (1963).

* * *

Next, Neely alleges that American National is liable for paying out on altered instruments. Both parties rely upon Code § 3-406.

* * *

Neely argues that American National did not pay the instruments according to commercially reasonable standards because the checks allegedly bore visible marks of alteration. American National contends that Neely is precluded from asserting the material alterations as a basis for liability because Neely's negligence substantially contributed to the alterations by leaving large spaces to the left of the amount designation, and by entrusting the same employee with writing the checks and reconciling the bank statements without the protection of internal corporate controls.

We must first resolve whether American National acted in a commercially reasonable manner, because unless the bank acted reasonably it cannot assert the defense that Neely's negligence substantially contributed to the alterations. American National produced expert witnesses testifying that although some of the words and numbers on the amount designation lines were slightly misaligned, and although a few checks visibly contained liquid erasure, the bank did not violate reasonable commercial standards when it paid out on these particular checks to Bradshaw. It was stated that the decision of whether to pay a particular check that may have appeared to be somewhat irregular on its face was based entirely upon a judgment call under the particular circumstances of that check. Based upon the judgment call surrounding the decision to pay each check, and after examining the checks exhibited, the trial court concluded that American National had acted in a commercially reasonable fashion under the circumstances. Inasmuch as this fact issue was found in favor of American National, the nonjury finding will stand on appeal because it was not plainly and palpably erroneous.

After resolving the threshold question of the commercial reasonableness of the bank's actions, we must next determine whether Neely, by its negligence, substantially contributed to the facilitation of the alterations. The Uniform Commercial Code does not define the negligence which will support the defense of § 3-406, and instructs that it is an issue strictly left to the fact-finder on a case by case approach. The official comment does advise, however, that "[n]egligence usually has been found where spaces are left in the body of the instrument in which words or figures may be inserted." It is undisputed that Mrs. Neely signed the checks fully aware of the large gaps in front of the amount.

Similarly, two other examples of negligence are supported by the record: no inquiry was made into Bradshaw's veracity, although it was rumored that previously she had been in trouble with embezzlement in Tennessee, and Neely failed to maintain internal controls so that the employee writing the checks was not also the principal person reconciling the bank statements.

Affirmed for American National Bank of Huntsville.

Questions and Case Problems

1. A negotiable instrument was indorsed in blank by P, the payee, and negotiated to A. The indorsement of A was placed on the instrument by an unauthorized party and then the instrument was transferred to P. Does P qualify as a holder? [*Westerly Hospital v. Higgins*, 256 A.2d 506 (R.I. 1969).]

2. Jensen Movers drew a check on Union Bank payable to the order of Lewittes Furniture Enterprises, Inc., plaintiff, and delivered it to plaintiff. A thief, Joel Simpson, stole the check, forged Lewittes' indorsement, and transferred it to Margaret Marino. She deposited the check, containing plaintiff's forged indorsement, into her joint account with Peter Marino at Bankers Trust, defendant. Bankers presented the check to Union and it was paid. Plaintiff sued the defendant for recovery of the proceeds of the check. The plaintiff's case was based on its rights as assignee of the drawee bank to go against defendant collecting bank for breach of its implied (statutory) and express warranties of the genuineness of prior indorsements. Decision? [*Lewittes Furniture Enterprises, Inc. v. Bankers Trust of Suffolk*, 372 N.Y. S.2d 830 (N.Y. 1975).]

3. Cole drew a check on Buffalo Bank payable to the order of Wyoming Homes. An agent for Wyoming Homes deposited it in a Gillette bank without an indorsement. The bank stamped the check "First National Bank, Gillette, Wyoming, For Deposit Only" and collected it for the payee, Wyoming Homes. Buffalo Bank charged Cole's account. Cole then proceeded against the First National Bank of Gillette, contending that it was only a transferee of the check (not a holder or an HIDC) and that it took the check subject to Cole's defenses of fraud and failure of consideration against Wyoming Homes. Decision? [*Cole v. First National Bank of Gillette*, 433 P.2d 837 (Wyo. 1967).]

4. A negotiable note was created by the defendant-maker payable to the order of "Greenlaw & Sons Roofing & Siding Co." and indorsed in blank "Greenlaw & Sons by George M. Greenlaw." The plaintiff, a later indorsee of the note for value, is confronted with the defense that, since the note was not properly indorsed, the plaintiff cannot be a holder or a holder in due course. If the defendant is correct—he points to UCC 3-203 and 3-307 to substantiate his argument—any defense will be sufficient to defeat plaintiff's claim. Discuss. [*Watertown Federal Savings & Loan Association v. Spanks*, 193 N.E.2d 333 (Mass. 1963).]

5. Plaintiffs, partners in a Tacoma barbershop, have maintained a partnership checking account with the defendant, Puget Sound National Bank, since October 1964. The signatures of both partners were required for withdrawal from the account. Mr. Nash, a longtime employee of the plaintiffs, was occasionally left alone and in charge of the barbershop. He had no formal managerial responsibilities and no authority to write partnership checks. Between September 16, 1968 and January 3, 1969, Mr. Nash forged plaintiffs' signatures on numerous checks. Defendant bank honored these checks. In early January of 1969, plaintiffs discovered the forgeries. This action was then commenced to recover the monies paid. Are plaintiffs entitled to recover? [*Terry v. Puget Sound National Bank,* 492 P.2d 534 (Wash. 1972).]

6. A check was made payable to the order of payees A and B. After the check was certified by the drawee bank, it was indorsed by B only and cashed. When the check was eventually presented to the drawee bank, it refused payment because A did not indorse. Was the bank justified in its refusal to pay? [*Clinger v. Continental National Bank* et al., 503 P.2d 363 (Colo. 1972).]

7. Feldman Construction Company drew a check on Union Bank (defendant-drawee) payable to the order of "A Corp. and B Supply." A Corp. indorsed and cashed the check at Union Bank without B Supply's indorsement. Since B Supply was not paid, it filed a lien against Feldman's property. Feldman satisfied B Supply's lien and then proceeded against Union on the ground that the check had not been properly indorsed. Decision? [*Feldman Construction Co. v. Union Bank,* 104 Cal.Rptr. 912 (Cal. 1972).]

8. D issues a $100 check to P. P raises the check to $1,000 (a material alteration) and has it certified by the drawee bank. P then indorses the check "Pay to H, [signed] P" and negotiates it to H. H, an HIDC, cashes the check for $1,000. When D discovers these facts (immediately upon examining his monthly bank statement and cancelled checks), he compels the drawee to reinstate his account for $900. UCC 4–401(2)(a). Can the drawee bank recover the $900 from H? If not, can it recover from P? Discuss the application of UCC 3–417 to this fact situation.

9. D draws a $1,000 check on D-Bank payable to the order of P. X steals the check and forges P's blank indorsement. A receives the check from X for value, before maturity, and without knowledge of the forgery. A deposits the check in A-Bank, which forwards it to D-Bank for collection. D-Bank pays the check and returns it to D at the end of the month. P then discovers the wrongdoing and notifies D. Discuss P's rights against D, D-Bank, A-Bank, A, and X.

10. In *Neely Enterprises, Inc. v. American National Bank of Huntsville,* 403 So.2d 887 (Ala. 1981),[63] the court related that unless American National acted in a commercially reasonable manner, it could not assert as a defense that Neely's negligence substantially contributed to the alterations. How was the issue of the bank's conduct resolved?

---

[63] See pp. 389–91.

Holder, Holder in Due Course, and Defenses 25

After you have read this chapter, you should be able to answer the following questions:

1. What is a holder? What are the rights of a holder?
2. What is a holder in due course? What are the rights of a holder in due course?
3. What is "value"? Is value the same thing as consideration?
4. Is "notice" of a claim or a defense the same thing as "knowledge" of a claim or defense?
5. What does the phrase "good faith" mean? Can a person be in good faith if he or she has notice of a claim or a defense?
6. What is the difference between a claim and a defense?
7. What claims or defenses are valid against a holder? Are these valid against a holder in due course as well?

Introduction

Chapters 23 and 24 illustrate the possibility of obtaining "greater rights" in a negotiable instrument by its negotiation. This chapter centers on the person who occupies the most favored position, namely, the *holder in due course* (HIDC). Therefore, since the negotiable instrument is used so commonly in business as *the* means of payment, and since many defenses cannot be asserted against a person who is an HIDC, it becomes necessary to understand fully how you can become an HIDC. HIDC status gives you as much protection as possible in being able to enforce payment on the instrument.

Holder and Holder in Due Course

An HIDC must first be a holder.

A *holder* is a person in possession of a negotiable instrument "drawn, issued, or indorsed to him or to his order, or to bearer, or in blank."[1] The holder may qualify as an HIDC if the instrument is taken (1) for value, (2) in good faith, and (3) without notice of any claim or defense or that it is overdue or has been dishonored.[2]

A payee may qualify as an HIDC,[3] but, if there is any defense on the instrument, normally the payee will know about it. For example, a retailer-payee who has sold defective merchandise to a consumer probably will not qualify as an HIDC because of bad faith and notice of a defense—e.g., breach of contract, failure of consideration.

Even on the assumption that the payee did meet all the requirements of an HIDC, HIDCs are subject to the *assertion* of defenses—real or personal—of those parties with whom they have dealt.[4] While a seller-payee may be in good faith and quite innocent of any notice of a defense at the time of the sale, the purchaser-drawer could still assert that defense against the seller-payee at a later time.

As a practical matter, the payee can benefit from the HIDC status only if the payee is somehow insulated from the transaction which gives rise to the defense of the maker or drawer of the instrument. Assume that D draws a $1,000 check without inserting the name of a payee. If D entrusts the check to his agent, A, to deliver it to XYZ Corporation, but instead A inserts the name of one of his personal creditors (P), P may become an HIDC if P meets all of the requirements.[5]

The Status of a Holder Is Fixed at the Time He Becomes a Holder
If he becomes a holder in due course and *later learns* of facts which, if known before he became a holder, would have prevented him from becoming an HIDC, he *continues* as an HIDC.

For value.

Value
Consideration is a "bargained for" exchange—a legal detriment that a promisee gives or promises to give in return for the promisor's promise. If A has promised to sell B a $400 Honda on credit, and B accepts, then B's consideration is his promise to pay. Until B has actually paid, his promise is executory, i.e., it has not been executed or fulfilled.

When the word "value" is used in connection with the law of Negotiable Instruments, it means *consideration* that has been performed,[6] and also a *past debt*. In the illustration above, if a negotiable promissory note is substituted for the Honda and is sold by A to B, B becomes a holder for value when B pays A the $400. If B makes only partial payment, B becomes a holder for value to the extent actually paid.

---

[1] UCC 1-201(20).   [2] UCC 3-302(1).   [3] UCC 3-302(2).
[4] UCC 3-305(2).   [5] See UCC 3-302, comment 2(g).   [6] UCC 3-303(a).

If the $400 note was being sold by A to B at a discount—say, for the price of $387—B would be a holder for full face value upon payment to A of the agreed sum, $387. On the assumption that all the other requirements were met, B would qualify as an HIDC as well.

However, if B has paid A only $200 of the $387 discount price, and then receives notice of a defense of the maker to payment on the note, B could not qualify as an HIDC for the remainder. B would be limited in his HIDC status to $200. B is not required to pay the additional $187 because he is not getting what he originally bargained for.

One who acquires a **security interest** in an instrument may become a holder for value.[7] For example, P, the payee of a $1,000 note due in one year, may need cash immediately. Instead of selling the note at a steep discount, the payee may pledge it as collateral security for a $600 loan. In that event, the one who advances the $600 on the security of P's $1,000 note is a holder for value to the extent of the loan.

security interest
"an interest in personal property or fixtures which secures payment or performance of an obligation"
UCC 1-201 (37)

A holder may give value if an instrument is taken for an antecedent or preexisting claim whether the claim is due and matured or not. An easy illustration of this is the payment of a debt with a check. The **cancellation** of the debt in return for the check constitutes value.[8]

cancellation
the nullification of a contractual obligation

Keep in mind that "payment" with negotiable instruments is really only "conditional" payment. That is, the debt is considered paid only if the instrument is honored or paid. If the check "bounces" (is dishonored and returned) or the note is not paid at maturity, the debt is now enforceable in the courts.[9] A full discharge from an obligation occurs only in those situations where a *bank* is a maker, drawer, or acceptor of an instrument and the party who uses it to satisfy the obligation does not indorse.[10] For example, if Bert Jones purchased athletic equipment from Spaulding Company and paid for it with a cashier's check issued by Ruston Trust Company payable to the order of Spaulding, Jones would not be liable on the instrument if he did not indorse it. The debt is solely that of Ruston Trust, the primary party.

Value is given if negotiable instruments are exchanged—e.g., if a check is given in purchase of a note, or if an irrevocable commitment is made to a third party in return for an instrument.[11] The latter is illustrated by the issuance of a letter of credit by a bank in return for a note or check of its customer.

Banks give value, and may become HIDCs upon meeting the other requirements, to the extent they acquire a security interest.[12] Security interests arise to the extent that the credit given for an item has been withdrawn.[13] For example, if a bank that is in the process of collecting a $1,000 item for its customer-depositor allows the immediate withdrawal of $500, it will be a holder for value for $500 if the check later bounces.

A bank may give its customer an unreserved right of withdrawal prior to the time an item is collected. In this event, the bank is an HIDC for the full amount even if none of the credit has been drawn upon[14] because of the customer's right of immediate withdrawal and contingent liability of the bank.

Good Faith

There is a simply stated test for the good faith of a holder—"honesty in fact in the conduct or transaction concerned."[15] The test is entirely *subjective* in nature, i.e., the holder is not judged by an objective standard of reasonableness or anything else. Even though a reasonable person would or should have suspected some defense or claim, if the holder honestly did not, the holder can satisfy the good faith test.

Good faith.

---

[7] UCC 3-303(a), 4-209.   [8] UCC 3-303(b).   [9] UCC 3-802(1)(b).

[10] UCC 3-802(1)(a).   [11] UCC 3-303(c).   [12] UCC 4-209.

[13] UCC 4-208(1)(a).   [14] UCC 4-208(1)(b).   [15] UCC 1-201(19).

The good faith test, sometimes characterized as "empty head–honest heart," means that a holder can meet this criterion even though the holder negligently or carelessly turns a deaf ear to facts and circumstances that would put a reasonable person on notice of a defense. Such disregard for suspicious circumstances, however, may cause one to flunk the "notice"[16] test. In the following case the court held that the carelessness of the holder did not constitute bad faith.

Facts
The defendant, Leo's Used Car Exchange, Inc. (Leo), is being sued for stopping payment on two checks totaling $15,150 which were issued to payee, Villa's Auto Sales, Inc., in payment for two cars. An authorized agent of Villa's indorsed the checks and cashed them at the plaintiff bank, Industrial National. Normal procedure at Industrial National calls for the manager to approve corporate checks drawn on another bank. The manager would approve if he knew the person cashing the check and knew his business. But these two checks were cashed by a teller at National Industrial Bank without the manager's approval being sought. The plaintiff bank will qualify as an HIDC and be successful in its suit against Leo if it purchased the two checks in good faith.

Decision
For the plaintiff, Industrial National.

Reasoning
The defendant argued that the plaintiff failed to exercise ordinary care by violating its own rule of management, and that this is evidence of lack of good faith. However, good faith only requires "honesty in fact in the conduct or transaction concerned." Nothing in the definition suggests that, in addition to being honest, the holder must exercise due care as well. In those situations where the UCC has required more than "honesty in fact," it has explicitly so stated.

This is not to say that negligence has no role in the determination of one's HIDC status. Evidence of negligence goes to the notice requirement, however; it is not relevant to the issue of good faith.

Industrial National Bank of R.I. v. Leo's Used Car Exchange, Inc., 291 N.E.2d 603 (Mass. 1973).

Notice.

The Notice Requirement
If a holder takes an instrument with notice that there is a claim or defense against it, or that it is overdue or has been dishonored, then the holder cannot qualify as an HIDC.[17] A holder has notice of one of these facts if:

1. he has actual knowledge of it; or
2. he has received[18] a notice or notification of it; or
3. from all the facts and circumstances *known to him at the time in question,* he has *reason to know* that it exists.[19]

Effective notice must allow a reasonable time to act.[20] To illustrate, assume that H is in good faith—i.e., that he honestly does not know that M, the maker of a note, has a defense of fraud against P, the payee. If H has received notification of this defense through the mails, and, while it has not actually come to his attention, the letter has been delivered to his business address in ample time for receipt of such communications,[21] then H has legal notice of the defense and cannot qualify as an HIDC.

Next—and still on the assumption that H is in good faith—suppose that two days before maturity he pays $100 for a $1,000 note which has been in circulation, with interest compounded, for ten years. The reason P, the payee, is willing to sell the instrument so cheaply is that P has defrauded the maker. Since H honestly does not know of the fraud, will he qualify as an HIDC? Not likely. The sale of this instrument at *such a large discount* is a fact "known to him at the time in question" and will probably be sufficient to give H "reason to know" that some defense exists.[22]

---

[16] UCC 1–201(25).   [17] UCC 3–302(1)(c).   [18] UCC 1–201(25).   [19] Ibid.

[20] UCC 3–304(6).   [21] UCC 1–201(26).   [22] UCC 1–201(25)(c).

Claims exist when the owner has been wrongfully deprived of the instrument. In the previous illustration, H would not qualify as an HIDC if, at the time he became a holder, he had notice of a *claim* rather than notice of a *defense*. The owner of an instrument would have a claim if it were stolen by someone and transferred to H. On the assumption that the instrument was *bearer* in form at the time it was stolen, H could be an HIDC if he had no notice of the owner's claim, and if all the other requirements were met.

If the instrument was *order* in form, however, the thief would have to forge the owner's indorsement, and in that event, H could not become an HIDC because he would not be a holder—the instrument did not flow to him by indorsement. Even in those situations where H is in good faith and has no notice of the forgery, title does not pass to him through the unauthorized indorsement of the forger.[23]

Notice of a Claim or Defense. The following are illustrative of those events that will give notice of a claim or defense and prevent a holder from becoming an HIDC:[24]

1. Visible evidence of forgery, alteration, or other irregularity (such as wholesale incompleteness) that calls into question the validity, terms, or ownership of the instrument.
2. Information that the obligation of some party is voidable—e.g., the party was induced by fraud or mistake to sign the instrument—or, information that all parties have been discharged—e.g., all signatures have been cancelled or the instrument has been paid.
3. Knowledge that the **fiduciary** has negotiated in breach of duty—e.g., an instrument indorsed "Pay to T in trust for P, [signed] P" was negotiated by T to H in payment of T's personal debt.

fiduciary
a person with a duty to act primarily for the benefit of another

In the following case the drawee bank was held to be on notice of the payee's agent acting contrary to his fiduciary duty, thereby precluding the drawee from being an HIDC.

Facts
The Mott Grain Company had signed an agreement with the First National Bank & Trust Co. of Bismark to allow any one of three of Mott's men to indorse the checks received by the company and have them deposited in the company's account at the bank. One of these men, Vernon Baszler, indorsed some $40,520.93 of such checks and, instead of having them placed in the company's account, he had them placed in his own account at the same bank. Vernon Baszler was later convicted of criminal charges, and the Mott Grain Company sued to get its money back from First National.

Decision
For the plaintiff, Mott Grain Company.

Reasoning
The court held that Baszler was depositing third-party checks payable to the grain company in his personal account and thus "for his own benefit." Thus, the bank did have notice and does not qualify as a holder in due course. The purchaser has notice of a claim against an instrument when he has knowledge that a fiduciary has negotiated the instrument in payment of or as security for his own debt or in any transaction for his own benefit or otherwise in breach of duty.

Mott Grain Company v. First National Bank & Trust Co. of Bismark, 259 N.W.2d 667 (N.D. 1977).

Notice That the Instrument Is Overdue or Dishonored. A purchaser is given notice that an instrument is overdue or dishonored if the purchaser has *reason to know:*

1. that the **principal,** or any part of it, is overdue, or that there is an uncured **default** in payment of another instrument of the same series; or
2. that acceleration of the instrument has been made; or
3. that a demand instrument is being taken after a previous unsuccessful demand for payment, or after an unreasonable length of time following issuance (a reasonable period of time for an uncertified check drawn and payable in the U.S. is presumed to be thirty days).[25]

principal
(in money) the capital sum of a money debt

default
a failure to perform a legal duty

---

[23] UCC 3–404. [24] UCC 3–304(1)(2). [25] UCC 3–304(3).

Chapter 25: Holder, Holder in Due Course, and Defenses

There are some events which do not convey notice. The public filing or recording of a document which relates to a negotiable instrument does *not* give notice sufficient to prevent a purchaser from becoming an HIDC.[26] Nor does knowledge of the following facts give notice of a claim or defense:[27]

1. the instrument was antedated or postdated;
2. the instrument was issued in exchange for an executory (unperformed) promise;
3. the instrument has an accommodation signature;
4. completion of an incomplete instrument, without notice of impropriety;
5. negotiation by a fiduciary but without knowledge that the fiduciary is breaching a duty;
6. default in payment of interest on the instrument or in payment of another instrument (except a default on an instrument of the same series).

Rights of a Holder in Due Course

A holder who qualifies as an HIDC takes the instrument

1. free of *all claims*—e.g., the true owner of lost or stolen bearer paper cannot reclaim it from an HIDC;
2. free of all defenses, except real or universal defenses and defenses of those parties who dealt with the HIDC.[28]

Real or Universal Defenses

real or **universal defense**
a defense to *contractual* liability on an instrument

While a negotiable instrument is, for all appearances, a formal written contract, it may not be *contractually* binding on various parties because either they don't have the capacity to contract, or they assert other defenses which preclude or relieve them of contractual liability on the instrument.[29] Defenses to *contractual* liability on an instrument are called **real** or **universal defenses.** The following are examples of real defenses.

Minority

This defense is allowed against an HIDC to the same extent that state law will allow it against anyone else.[30] For example, in most states a minor has the option to disaffirm any contract made with an adult. If the minor disaffirms the purchase of a *necessary* item, he or she is liable for the reasonable value. For *nonnecessaries,* the minor simply returns or offers to return what is left of the item (if anything) and is entitled to receive back all of the money he or she paid for the item. The adult is generally not permitted to retain any part of the money for wear and tear, damage, or depreciation.

Those states which follow the majority view outlined above would allow the minor a full defense against an HIDC if the minor purchased nonnecessaries. The HIDC would have to recover from other parties to the instrument on their indorsement contracts or their transfer warranties.

If the minor purchased a necessary item, he or she would be liable to the HIDC for an amount equaling the reasonable value of the item. For the amount between the reasonable value and the larger amount on the face of the instrument, the HIDC would have to pursue other parties to the instrument.

Insanity or Duress Precluding Contractual Liability

adjudicate
to determine by judicial authority

A person who has been judicially committed to a mental institution has been **adjudicated** not to have capacity to contract, and, therefore, cannot be contractually liable as a party

---

[26] UCC 3–304(5).   [27] UCC 3–304(4).   [28] UCC 3–305.

[29] UCC 3–305(2)(a)–(e).   [30] UCC 3–305(2)(a).

to a negotiable instrument. Such a person who made or drew a negotiable instrument, which was later negotiated to an HIDC, could assert the real defense of lack of capacity.

The effect of **duress** (coercion) in influencing someone to sign a negotiable instrument depends upon the law in each particular state. In some instances the duress causes the contract to be voidable, in which case duress is a "personal defense" (discussed later) not assertable successfully against an HIDC. In other instances the duress prevents the transaction from being a contract, in which case it is a real defense assertable successfully against all parties. For example, T threatens D that, if D doesn't sign the check as drawer, T will urge the district attorney to prosecute D's wife for the commission of an alleged crime. D signs the check. D is liable on the check as a voidable contract, which he can avoid; he has a "personal defense." However, if T pointed a loaded gun at D's head, compelling D to sign the check, while the instrument is negotiable on its face, it is *not a contract* binding *D* as a party to it because D did not intentionally or voluntarily create it. This is a form of duress precluding contractual liability; it is a real defense, and D is protected from any liability on the check. But the instrument can be negotiated by P to an HIDC, and *P* would be liable thereon as a contracting party. The HIDC will have to recover from the wrongdoer or some indorser or transferor subsequent to the wrongdoer.

duress
wrongful inducement to do that which a reasonable person would have been unable to resist

Illegality

Illegality also may be a real defense. For example, some states prohibit the enforcement of any contract or instrument given in connection with a gambling transaction. These obligations are treated as **null** and void because gambling is thought to be inimical to the public interest and, therefore, contrary to public policy. In such a state, an HIDC would be confronted with a real defense if the maker or drawer of an instrument can prove that it was issued in payment of a gambling debt.

null
of no legal effect

Another common illustration of illegality as a real defense is **usury.** Some states penalize the charging of an excessive rate of interest on a loan by absolutely denying the enforcement of usurious instruments. The remedy of an HIDC in such cases is against the indorser or warrantor.

usury
charging a rate of interest on a loan higher than that permitted by statute

In each of these examples the nature of the defense—whether or not it is a real defense—depends on state law. In some states—Nevada for instance—gambling may be no defense at all. In some states illegality merely makes the contract voidable. Accordingly, where illegality makes the transaction *void,* it is a *real defense.* When illegality makes the transaction *voidable,* it is a *personal defense.*

In the following case the maker of a negotiable promissory note issued it pursuant to a transaction declared illegal by statute and therefore the maker had a real defense on the ground of illegality.

Facts
Gateway Financial Service, a defendant, a corporation licensed to deal in secondary mortgages, made a loan to plaintiffs that was secured by a mortgage on their home. The transaction was governed by the New Jersey Secondary Mortgage Loan Act. Gateway sold the note and mortgage to Security Pacific Finance Corp., a defendant, also a corporation licensed to deal in secondary mortgages. At the closing of the loan by Gateway to the plaintiffs, a $3,000 deduction was made for credit life insurance; however, Gateway never acquired a policy of insurance because Gateway never caused the premium to be submitted to the insurance company. In addition, plaintiffs assert that they were forced to buy the insurance. They also say that the $800 attorney's fee charged at the closing was unlawfully high. In these ways, argue plaintiffs, the loan transaction violated various provisions of the Act.

Plaintiffs' suit against Gateway and Security Pacific seeks a judgment declaring that their note and mortgage are void and unenforceable by defendants. They also seek return from Security Pacific of all periodic payments plaintiffs made to it since the filing of the complaint, and a judgment against Gateway for the amount of the deducted insurance premium.

The N.J. Secondary Mortgage Loan Act of 1979 was adopted in response to numerous abuses in the secondary mortgage market. It provides, in part, as follows: Any obligation on the part of the borrower arising out of a secondary mortgage loan shall be void and unenforceable unless such secondary mortgage was executed in full compliance with the provisions of this Act.

Decision
For plaintiffs.

Reasoning
Assuming that Security Pacific is a holder in due course of plaintiffs' note and mortgage, what are its rights if, because of noncompliance with the Act's requirements, the note and mortgage are "void and unenforceable"? The answer lies in the policy of the Act and in the words of the Uniform Commercial Code as adopted in New Jersey. It is plain that the policy of the Act is to give generous protection to borrowers in regulated transactions. The Act recognizes that second mortgagors are frequently persons seeking loans of last resort, that they are usually in no position to bargain over the terms of the loan or to have any real idea what they might bargain about. The Act recognizes that lenders of last resort are frequently persons whose methods ought to attract careful scrutiny and that their customers are peculiarly unfit to perform that function. Thus, the Act not only creates monetary penalties for persons violating its terms, but it also authorizes the Commissioner of Banking to suspend or revoke the license of violators. The Act goes further and makes noncomplying loans void and unenforceable.

What does "void and unenforceable" mean to a holder in due course? UCC Section 3–305(2) says that a holder in due course takes the instrument free of all defenses of any party with whom he has not dealt except. . . .

(b) such other incapacity, or duress, or illegality of the transaction, as renders the obligation of the party a nullity.

* * * *

Surely, the legislature was conscious in 1970 of the need to harmonize the terms of the new Act with the already existing Code. Therefore, when the legislature decided that a noncomplying loan should be void and unenforceable, it must have had its eye on the Code provision that subjects even holders in due course to the defenses of "such . . . illegality of the transaction, as renders the obligation . . . a nullity." It is inconceivable that the legislature thought there was some difference between "void and unenforceable" in the Act and "a nullity" in the Code. The words are interchangeable. Surely, the legislature meant to say that a noncomplying secondary mortgage would be a nullity as the word is used in UCC 3–305(2).

Westervelt v. Gateway Financial Service, et al., 464 A.2d 1203 (N.J. 1983).

Fraud in the Procurement (Fraud in the "Factum," "Execution," or "Essence")
A person who has signed an instrument has a real defense if he has been deceived to the extent that

1. he *does not know* that he signed *an instrument, or* he *knows* that he signed an instrument, but is completely *tricked and deceived* regarding its essential *terms; and*
2. this person has not acted negligently or carelessly.[31]

If a country-western music fan rushes up to Willie Nelson to get his autograph, Willie will have a real or universal defense against a subsequent HIDC if that signature was placed on a negotiable note cleverly hidden in an autograph pad. It is clear that Willie did not intend to create the note, and, on the assumption that under these circumstances he was not negligent, he will be protected if the "fan" negotiates the instrument to an HIDC.

This defense would arise as well if the person who knowingly and intentionally signed an instrument did not have knowledge or reasonable opportunity to obtain knowledge of its essential terms. For example, assume that M is given one note to read and become familiar with while the salesperson is filling in the blanks of a supposedly identical note. Actually there are new and unfavorable terms in the salesperson's note, but M has been told that they are identical. Finally, the salesperson switches notes with M, and M innocently signs the one with the unfavorable terms. This will give M a real defense even if the salesperson negotiates the note to an HIDC.

---

[31] UCC 3–305(2)(c).

The common features in these two examples of the real defense of fraud—sometimes called fraud in the *procurement, factum, execution,* or *essence*—are

1. no intent to create a negotiable instrument, *or* no knowledge of the terms, *and*
2. no negligence.

In effect, *no contract has been created,* so there is no legal ground for liability.

If, on the other hand, a person really intends to create a negotiable instrument but has been *induced* to do so by P's fraud and deceit—e.g., P has lied to M regarding some essential component of a stereo unit—M would have only a personal or limited defense, which would not be valid against an HIDC. Such a defense of fraud in the inducement would be successful against a mere holder or assignee but not against an HIDC, who could get a judgment against M. M would then have to seek recovery against P, the person who defrauded M. This "personal" or "limited" defense of fraud—where M really intends to create the instrument and is not so defrauded that he does not know what he is signing—is known as *fraud in the inducement.*

Unauthorized Signatures

A forgery or unauthorized signature does not obligate the person whose name has been wrongfully used, unless that person ratifies the signature or is precluded by his negligence from denying the signature.[32] The rationale for this rule is obvious. Since the person whose name has been forged had no intention of creating the instrument or parting with ownership, he or she is not obligated by the forgery. The person has not agreed to any contract, and is not liable on the instrument because *his or her signature does not appear thereon.* If the real owner's *indorsement* has been forged, the owner still has a claim to the instrument. The recipient of such an instrument, which is later reclaimed by the true owner, can attempt to recover from the wrongdoer on the forged indorsement[33] or on the transfer warranties.[34]

Remember to distinguish *forgery* from the signature of an *impostor,* because the signature of an impostor does pass good title to the holder. The holder may even qualify as an HIDC, but there can never be a holder or an HIDC following a required indorsement which has been forged.[35]

Material Alteration

The real or universal defense of **material alteration** can best be understood by considering, first, its definition, then its general effect, and finally its effect on an HIDC.[36] Keep in mind, however, that a defendant's *negligence* can deprive the defendant of this defense just as it can deprive one of the defense of forgery,[37] and further that any party may assent to or *ratify* a material alteration.

Any change in the contract of any party to the instrument in *any* respect is a material alteration. It may be only a slight change such as the addition of one cent to the amount payable or an advance of one day in the date of payment.[38] This definition includes, but is not limited to, unauthorized filling in the blanks on an incomplete instrument as well as adding to or deleting from the instrument.

For example, an incomplete instrument may be issued to a payee-creditor with instructions to fill in the amount with the balance due. If this *holder* fills in an excessive amount, that would be a material alteration. It would be a material alteration as well if

material alteration
"any alteration of an instrument is material which changes the contract of any party thereto in any respect" UCC 3–407(1)

---

[32] UCC 3–404, 406.   [33] UCC 3–404(1).   [34] UCC 3–417(2).

[35] For examples and discussion of these distinctions, see pp. 381–84.

[36] UCC 3–407.   [37] UCC 3–406.   [38] See UCC 3–407, comment 1.

this person added, changed, deleted, or in any way modified terms of a complete instrument to which the issuer previously had become bound. In the following case the unauthorized completion of an incomplete instrument in the amount payable was a material alteration not assertable against the HIDC.

Facts
Elias Saka, defendant, gave Weaver Levy a signed check that was blank regarding the amount. Levy was instructed to complete it for $800 and make payment to the payee, Sahara Hotel, plaintiff, on a $3,046.03 bill charged to Affinity Pictures, Inc. Instead, Levy completed the check for the full amount of $3,046.03 and delivered it to the Sahara. Saka stopped payment on the check, and this suit was instituted by Sahara for the full amount. Saka alleges by way of defense (1) that the payee Sahara is not an HIDC because it had notice that the charges were disputed and (2) that the completion of the check by Levy in a different handwriting from that of the drawer, Saka, was sufficient to put Sahara on notice of irregularity.

Decision
Judgment for Sahara.

Reasoning
A payee may be an HIDC, UCC 3–302(2), but, as a practical matter, this is the exception rather than the rule. Since the payee is an immediate party to the underlying transaction, under normal circumstances he cannot claim this status because he necessarily knows of any defenses to the contract. However, Saka's evidence was not sufficient to raise the issue that the hotel had notice of a dispute.

The fact that the body of the check was completed in a different handwriting from that of the drawer's signature did not impose on Sahara the duty to make further inquiries, nor did it destroy Sahara's good faith because UCC 3–304(4)(d) provides that knowledge that an incomplete instrument has been completed by another does not of itself give the purchaser notice of a claim or defense unless the purchaser has notice of any improper completion.

Elias Saka v. Sahara-Nevada Corporation, 558 P.2d 535 (Nev. 1976).

The next inquiry concerns the *effect* of a material alteration. If a *holder* makes a material alteration *and* if it is made with a *fraudulent* purpose, any party whose contract is thereby changed receives a discharge from any further liability on the instrument. This means that, if the payee of an instrument raised the amount from $100 to $1,000, the maker or drawer is fully discharged.

If this instrument was issued by a buyer for merchandise, the buyer could retain the goods without making further payment to the seller payee-creditor. The payee-creditor is penalized for his fraud. To carry this example one step further, the payee and the issuer would be discharged if the material alteration was made by a *subsequent* holder. Those persons on the instrument *prior* to the material alteration are the ones whose contract and liability on the instrument are so affected.

Alterations that are not made by *holders,* or alterations that are made by holders *without any fraudulent intent,* do not discharge anyone. To illustrate: if a holder extended the time of payment with the purpose and effect of benefiting the debtor, there would be no fraudulent material alteration, and the debtor would not be discharged. Nor would anyone be discharged if the change was made by a person who did not qualify as a holder.

Material alterations do not deprive a subsequent HIDC of the right to enforce the instrument for the *original amount,* or *for the amount that was fraudulently inserted on an incomplete instrument.* If a payee raised a $100 instrument to $1,000 or improperly filled in the amount of $1,000 on an incomplete instrument, the issuer would be liable to an HIDC for $100 on the *raised* instrument, and for $1,000 on the *improperly completed one.*

Discharge
If at the time the instrument is received the HIDC has notice that a party has been discharged, the discharge will operate as a real defense against the HIDC. Discharge in insolvency proceedings is a real defense even if the HIDC has no notice of it.

Personal or Limited Defenses

Defenses which seek to *avoid* liability on the instrument (*voidable* contract) are called **personal** or **limited defenses**. Such defenses cannot be asserted successfully against an HIDC. Examples are:

1. fraud inducing the making of an instrument;
2. failure of consideration;
3. want of consideration;
4. defenses to liability on a contract, a valid claim to the instrument by anyone;
5. nonperformance of any condition precedent;
6. nondelivery of the instrument;
7. delivery for a special purpose which has not occurred and the instrument was unauthorizedly delivered; and
8. generally other defenses which are not real defenses, just discussed.

> **personal** or **limited defense**
> a defense which is not to *contractual* liability on an instrument but, rather, is to *avoid* liability on an instrument; any defense which is not a real defense

To illustrate: suppose D issues his check to P to pay for goods which P promised to deliver to D. P never delivered the goods and never intended to do so. D has the personal defenses of fraud and failure of consideration, which D can assert successfully against P and later holders but not against a subsequent HIDC. If D issues a check to P as a gift, there is a *want* of consideration.

HIDC and the Federal Trade Commission

The FTC issued a rule in 1976 that has the effect of *denying the rights of an HIDC* to a holder who receives an instrument given in a *consumer credit transaction*. The rule declares that it is an unfair and deceptive practice within section 5 of the Federal Trade Commission Act for the credit-seller of personal, family, or household goods or services to natural persons to use *any* method of financing *that separates the seller's duty to perform from the buyer's duty to pay.*

> The Federal Trade Commission and consumer credit transactions.

In at least ten-point boldface type, the seller must include the following *notice #1* in any consumer credit contract executed by the buyer, and *notice #2* in any direct loan financing agreement which the seller arranges for the buyer.

Notice #1
ANY HOLDER OF THIS CONSUMER CREDIT CONTRACT IS SUBJECT TO ALL CLAIMS AND DEFENSES WHICH THE DEBTOR COULD ASSERT AGAINST THE SELLER OF GOODS OR SERVICES OBTAINED PURSUANT HERETO OR WITH THE PROCEEDS HEREOF. RECOVERY HEREUNDER BY THE DEBTOR SHALL NOT EXCEED AMOUNTS PAID BY THE DEBTOR HEREUNDER.

Notice #2
ANY HOLDER OF THIS CONSUMER CREDIT CONTRACT IS SUBJECT TO ALL CLAIMS AND DEFENSES WHICH THE DEBTOR COULD ASSERT AGAINST THE SELLER OF GOODS OR SERVICES OBTAINED WITH THE PROCEEDS HEREOF. RECOVERY HEREUNDER BY THE DEBTOR SHALL NOT EXCEED AMOUNTS PAID BY THE DEBTOR HEREUNDER.

The rule covers sellers who in the ordinary course of business sell or lease goods or services *to consumers*. It does *not* include the following:

1. sales for industrial or commercial uses;
2. transactions by legal entities other than natural persons;
3. purchases of realty, commodities, securities, farm equipment, or services of public utilities; and
4. consumer goods or services where the purchase price is more than $25,000.

To illustrate: assume that a consumer enters into a credit purchase of a stereo with a local retailer. Prior to the FTC rule, the consumer may have been required to sign a negotiable promissory note for the unpaid balance, and the note may have been negotiated to an HIDC. If so, the HIDC could get a judgment against the consumer who defaulted upon payments even though the stereo never functioned properly.

Today *the consumer preserves all his or her defenses,* and these defenses may be asserted *against the retailer or against a third party* who, except for the FTC rule, would have had the rights of an HIDC. The third party is treated as an *assignee* of the retailer-assignor's rights. The third party assignee or transferee simply stands in the shoes of the retailer and *is subject to all the consumer's defenses that are available against the retailer.*

Summary Statement

1. An HIDC is a holder who has given value for a negotiable instrument in good faith and without notice of a claim or defense to the instrument or that the instrument is overdue or has been previously dishonored. A payee may qualify as an HIDC. Personal defenses cannot be asserted successfully against an HIDC, but real defenses can be asserted against the HIDC. However, even an HIDC is subject to the defenses (real or personal) of a party *with whom the HIDC has dealt.*
2. *Value* means that the consideration promised in exchange for an instrument has been executed or performed. It may also consist of an antecedent (preexisting) claim (past debt), whether the claim is due or not, or of a security interest acquired by any party (including a bank). Value is given when negotiable instruments are exchanged and when one party makes an irrevocable commitment to another in reliance on a negotiable instrument.
3. The *good faith* required of an HIDC simply means that the HIDC must have acted *honestly in fact* in the transaction in which he or she purchased the instrument. This standard is completely *subjective* and is applied on a case-by-case basis.
4. *Notice* of a claim or defense to the instrument, or that the instrument is overdue or previously dishonored, is a more rigid or *objective* standard than good faith. A holder has notice of one of these and is prevented from becoming an HIDC: (a) if he has actual knowledge; or (b) if he has received notice even though he has not actually read it within a reasonable time after receipt; or (c) if from all the facts and circumstances *known to him at the time in question* the holder has *reason to know* that one of these defects exists.
5. One may be confronted with notice of a claim or a defense, or that an instrument is overdue or dishonored, by information which appears on the face of the instrument or from outside sources. However, *no notice* is conveyed: (a) by the filing of a document which affects the instrument; (b) by antedating or postdating; (c) by issuance of the instrument for an executory promise; (d) by knowledge of accommodation signatures; (e) by completion of an incomplete instrument; (f) by the negotiation of a fiduciary (T negotiates to you an instrument previously indorsed restrictively, "Pay to T in trust for X, [signed] Billy Carter," and you are without knowledge of any breach of trust by T); or (g) by default in payment of interest or in payment of another instrument.
6. Basically, a mere holder takes an instrument subject to all claims and defenses that may exist, but an HIDC is free from all claims and free from all defenses *except* real defenses and defenses of parties with whom the HIDC has dealt. Real defenses arise when the basic obligation for which the instrument was originally issued is *null* and *void*. This may be because the initial transaction—e.g., gambling "contracts" in some states—was completely illegal and prohibited by

statute, or because a "contract" never really existed in the first place—e.g., extreme duress or other lack of capacity, fraud in the procurement or factum, forgery, or fraudulent material alteration. A discharge in insolvency proceedings is a real defense, and the same is true of any other discharge that the HIDC has notice of when taking the instrument.
7. The Federal Trade Commission has adopted a rule which has the effect of eliminating HIDCs from consumer credit transactions. Those parties who would normally qualify as HIDCs under the UCC are subjected to the same defenses as a retailer who has made a credit sale of personal, family, or household goods or services to a consumer.

This chapter has emphasized the benefits of the status of a holder in due course. The following case illustrates how this status can be ignored by the court in the absence of legislation when the court senses that this status is being abused and justice and equity demand such action.

Matthews v. Aluminum Acceptance Corp.
137 N.W.2d 280 (Mich. 1965)

Fitzgerald, Judge. If ever the elements of a classic case involving an aluminum siding company and its subsequent assignee were before an appellate court, that case unravels here. It could be drawn from the files of almost any practising lawyer, or it might be the complaint of the next client in the waiting room.

In this action to enjoin defendant from enforcing any claims against plaintiffs and from foreclosing the mortgage upon plaintiffs' home, the questions on appeal are whether constructive forgery or fraud was established and whether the entire transaction was shot through with usury.

In April of 1962, plaintiffs Robert and Katherine Matthews were approached by representatives of All-Style Builders, aluminum siding applicators. They allege that All-Style indicated that their modest home had been chosen as a demonstration site for aluminum siding for that area. New siding was to be applied over the tar paper on their home, and in addition they were to be given a loan of $650 in cash to fix their tractor, and the total price of this was to be $3,250. Further, they were to receive $100 to apply against their contract for each potential customer which All-Style brought to view their newly sided home.

To the Matthews, the alleged inducements were sufficiently alluring that they signed up for the package. The siding was applied, they were given $650, but to time of trial no one had even shown up to view the siding as a potential customer.

When the smoke cleared, so to speak, the Matthews learned that the instrument they had signed included a promissory note and mortgage calling for 84 equal monthly installments at the rate of $61.04 per month for a grand total of $5,127.36, not the $3,250 they had anticipated, and the instruments had been assigned to defendant Aluminum Acceptance Corporation, a firm specializing in financing siding application.

All-Style Builders is not a party to this suit, and defendant Aluminum Acceptance claims it is a bona fide holder of the paper, denies fraud, and further claims that the instruments are not usurious because the agreement provided for a cash price, whereas the note and mortgage represent a "time price" and a discount transaction.

As to the transaction itself, Mr. Matthews says that he was unable to read any but the largest print, and that only with difficulty, and Mrs. Matthews was able only to read the printed portion with her glasses and that the papers were stacked one on top of another at the time of signing and with the upper portions covered, leaving visible only the area to be signed. The papers, they further allege, were blank at the time of signing.

Plaintiffs made only one payment and now seek to enjoin foreclosure of the mortgage, and defendant counterclaims seeking foreclosure, deficiency, and such other relief "as shall be agreeable to equity and good conscience."

The latter phrase is a little difficult to digest when the record is studied closely.

Judgment was entered canceling the mortgage and giving defendant judgment on its counterclaim in the sum of $3,250. Aluminum Acceptance Corporation appeals this judgment. The rule in Michigan is that a signature deceptively procured is in law a forgery, and those who subsequently acquire interest under the forged instrument are in no better position than if they had purchased with notice.

Appellant corporation also urges that if, as the defendant, it is a holder in due course, it is immaterial whether or not there was fraud in the inducement with respect to the promissory note.

The agreement gave defendant notice of the agreed contract price of $3,250 while the note and mortgage stated the sum of $5,127.36. Such a disparity furnishes ample notice of the infirmity of the instrument and that it was usurious, rendering it impossible for defendant to be a holder in due course and to avail itself of such defenses as a holder in due course might have.

The judgment of the court is affirmed.

Questions and Case Problems

1. Defendant, Arena Auto Auction, Inc., created a problem by twice mailing checks to the wrong payee. After the wrong payee received the first check, he indorsed it in the name of the named payee and cashed it with the plaintiff, Park State Bank. Park State knew the wrong payee, had cashed his checks and loaned him money in the past, and allowed him to withdraw the money before the check cleared.

    Payment on the check was stopped, but, instead of correcting its error, the drawer-defendant (Arena Auto Auction) innocently issued another check to the same wrong payee. He attempted to cash it as well, but when Park State refused to cooperate, he hastily left town.

    Is Park State liable for the amount of the first check because it dealt with a forger, or not? Discuss.

2. Temple drew a draft payable to the order of Yin-Li. Yin-Li indorsed in blank and lost it. The draft was found by Vasquez, who indorsed specially to Robel and negotiated it to Robel who gave value, in good faith, before maturity, and without knowledge of the preceding facts.
    a. Does Robel qualify as an HIDC?
    b. If Robel is an HIDC, is he subject to any valid claims or real defenses?
    c. If Vasquez retained the instrument, would he be a holder, HIDC, and subject to any claims or defenses?
    d. If Vasquez stole the instrument instead of finding it, discuss Robel's rights against Temple. All other facts remain as stated.

3. The Berenyis, defendants, bought carpeting from Kroyden Industries. The sales representative offered to *give* the Berenyis the carpeting, valued in the contract at $44 per square yard, without making any payments on their $1,520 note as long as they referred prospective customers to Kroyden. At the time of this offer, Kroyden was under an injunction to refrain from making such offers. The Berenyis signed a negotiable promissory note for $1,520, which was later negotiated to the plaintiff, New Jersey Mortgage and Investment Corp., who sued the defendants on the note. Result? [*New Jersey Mortgage and Investment Corp. v. Andrew and Anna Berenyi*, 356 A.2d 421 (N.J. 1976).]

4. Holler sold stolen goods to the unsuspecting defendant company, which gave Holler a check. The check was eventually negotiated to plaintiff company, an HIDC. When plaintiff sued defendant for nonpayment of the check, defendant raised the defense that the goods had been previously stolen. Result? [*Star Provision Company v. Sears, Roebuck & Company*, 92 S.E.2d 835 (Ga. 1956).]

5. Defendant drew a check and payee indorsed it to plaintiff. Defendant stopped payment on the check and plaintiff sued defendant. Defendant raised the defense of failure of consideration and plaintiff replied that it was an HIDC. Defendant claimed that plaintiff was not a HIDC because it learned of a defense before it deposited the check in the bank. Discuss. [*Kemp Motor Sales Inc. v. Statham*, 171 S.E.2d 389 (Ga. 1969).]

6. A drawee bank was sued by one of its depositors on a check originally drawn in payment for services in the amount of $1.25. Actually, the depositor allowed the payee to fill out the amount of the check for her signature. Given this opportunity, the payee wrote the figures of $1.25 far to the right side so that the number 684 could be added to the left of $1.25, and the words "One 25/100" were written close to the printed word "dollars" on the check blank so that "Six Thousand-Eight hundred-Forty" could be inserted ahead of the words, causing the check to read $6,841.25. The drawee honored the check for $6,841.25. Must the drawee reimburse the customer's account for the full (or any) amount? Discuss. [*Williams v. Montana National Bank of Bozeman*, 534 P.2d 1247 (Mont. 1975).]

7. Corporation drew a check for $1,400 payable to the order of a customer of plaintiff bank. The customer deposited the check in his account and plaintiff gave him provisional credit. The bank also allowed the customer to withdraw $140 before it discovered that the corporation had stopped payment on the check and then the check was dishonored. Meanwhile, the customer had "skipped," leaving no credits in his account on which to charge the $140. The bank sued the corporation, after it refused to pay. Result? [*Falls Church Bank v. Wesley Heights Realty, Inc.*, 256 A.2d 915 (D.C.App. 1969).]

8. Carolyn Brazil entered into a contract with the payee of her check to make certain home improvements. The payee made false representations to her regarding the purchase of construction materials for the job and cashed the check that same day. When she discovered the deception, she stopped payment by the drawee. The plaintiff-depositary bank, Citizen National, which is acknowledged to be an HIDC, instituted this action against Brazil. Result? [*Citizens National Bank of Quitman v. Carolyn Brazil*, 233 S.E.2d 482 (Ga. 1977).]

9. Defendant Blackburn issued a check to Vanella for the purchase of a used car. Vanella deposited the check in plaintiff bank and received cash and credit. Blackburn stopped payment when he learned that Vanella misrepresented that the automobile was free of liens. Plaintiff received partial repayment of the value it advanced to Vanella and brings this action against Blackburn to recover the balance. It is conceded that the plaintiff bank is an HIDC. Discuss. [*Marine Midland Trust Co. of Rochester v. Blackburn*, 50 Misc.2d 954 (N.Y. 1966).]

10. In *Matthews v. Aluminum Acceptance Corp.*, 137 N.W.2d 280 (Mich. 1965),[39] why did the defendant feel it was a holder in due course and on what basis in law, not equity, did the court refute this contention?

---

[39] See pp. 405–6.

26 Banks, Checks, and Customer Relations

After you have read this chapter, you should be able to:

1. Recognize the contractual relationship between the bank and its customers.
2. Assess a bank's liability for the wrongful dishonor of an item.
3. Determine when a bank may charge a customer's account.
4. Understand the importance and effectiveness of stop-payment orders.
5. Appreciate the customer's duty to examine cancelled checks and the risk involved in failing to do so.
6. Explain the bank's alternatives when confronted with stale checks and checks issued by customers who later become deceased.
7. Compare certified with uncertified checks.
8. Examine bank collection indorsements and checks with missing indorsements.

Introduction—The Nature of a Check

As individuals conducting personal business and transacting business for proprietorships, partnerships, and corporations, we will write checks and deal with banks. It is important to recognize that there is a body of law that governs banks and that has its impact on negotiable instruments. Our study of commercial paper would be incomplete, therefore, without an examination of the law of banking to the extent that it relates to checks and drafts.

The relationship between a drawee bank and its customer is debtor/creditor. The customer's check is a draft on the bank for the amount the bank owes the customer. A check is simply a "draft drawn on a bank and payable on demand."[1] It is assumed that there are sufficient funds on deposit with the drawee bank to cover any check which is issued; no such assumption is made with other drafts.

The demand nature of a check may be altered by postdating, but this does not affect its negotiability.[2] Since the drawee bank is under contract to follow orders of the depositor-drawer, it must not pay the check until the date arrives. The effect, then, of postdating is to change a check into a time draft.

A check does not operate as an assignment of funds in the hands of the drawee for payment of the holder. In fact, the holder has no rights against the drawee at all unless the drawee has accepted or certified the instrument.[3] If the drawee wrongfully dishonors an uncertified instrument, the holder can only pursue prior parties on their indorsements and warranties.

The Contract between the Bank and Its Customer

When a check is deposited for collection, the bank becomes the agent or subagent of the owner; any settlement given for the item is provisional and may be charged back until the check is finally honored by the payor bank.[4] The bank must use ordinary care in forwarding any item for collection.[5] If it does, the bank will not be liable for the insolvency, neglect, misconduct, mistake, or default of another bank or person or for loss or destruction of an item in transit or in the possession of others.[6]

These and all other provisions of Article 4, Bank Deposits and Collections, can be changed by agreement of the bank and its customer. However, no agreement can disclaim the bank's liability for its lack of good faith or failure to exercise ordinary care; nor can an agreement limit the measure of damages for such lack of good faith or failure to exercise ordinary care. The bank and its customer may agree on reasonable **standards** of responsibility by which the conduct of the bank is to be judged.[7]

standard
an established measure

Banks that participate in the collection process are supposed to take proper action on an item before the midnight deadline.[8] A bank acts seasonably or within the midnight deadline if it does so by midnight on the banking day following the one on which it receives the item.[9] *Failure to act within this time limit can make the bank accountable for the face amount of an item.*[10]

When an item has been finally paid or honored by the payor bank,[11] the relationship between the depositary bank and its customer becomes that of a debtor to its creditor. The bank is the debtor of its depositor to the extent of the money held on account. This is the basis of the customer's right to "order" its bank to pay one person or another.

---

[1] UCC 3–104(2)(b).   [2] UCC 3–114(1).

[3] UCC 3–409(1). No one is liable on a negotiable instrument unless his signature is on it. UCC 3–401.

[4] UCC 4–201(1), 4–212.   [5] UCC 4–202(1).   [6] UCC 4–202(3).   [7] UCC 4–103(1).

[8] UCC 4–202(2).   [9] UCC 4–104(h).   [10] UCC 4–302.

Wrongful Dishonor

A bank is not liable on a check or other draft unless it certifies or accepts the item.[12] At that time it becomes a *primary* party and agrees to pay a holder according to the terms of the instrument.[13] Holders cannot compel the drawee bank to honor an uncertified or unaccepted instrument; their recourse is against prior parties on the instrument.

If the drawee bank does refuse to honor a properly payable item—i.e., refuses to pay a check that has not been stopped, that is regular in form, and one for which there are sufficient funds on deposit—then the customer is entitled to recover from the drawee bank for damage proximately caused to the customer by the wrongful dishonor.[14]

The customer must prove the extent of the customer's damage, just as he or she must prove the other facts of his or her case. This may include an amount for the customer's arrest or prosecution or other consequential (indirect) damages. To illustrate: the direct damages proximately caused by wrongful dishonor might be the loss of profit on a transaction; consequential damages could be the permanent loss of that customer or damage to one's reputation.

When a Bank May Charge a Customer's Account

A bank may charge against its customer's account any item that is *properly payable*. This is true even though the charge creates an overdraft, because the issuance of the check itself carries authority to pay and the implied promise to reimburse the bank.[15]

Since the bank is under a contract with its depositor, it is supposed to know and record the status of each account and to follow its depositor's orders. When an overdraft is paid, the recipient is protected and the drawee is repaid by its customer. Except for recovery of bank payments[16] and for violation of presentment warranties,[17] the rule to remember is that payment is *final* in favor of an HIDC and those who have in good faith substantially changed their position in reliance on the payment.[18] This is illustrated by the following case where, because of such reliance, the real defense of forgery cannot be asserted.

Facts
A customer of the defendant-depositary bank forged the signature of one of the drawers of a check on the plaintiff-drawee bank. The depositary bank had no notice of suspicious circumstances when it received the check from the customer and it initiated collection. After the depositary bank received final payment from the drawee bank, it allowed its depositor (the forger) to withdraw the amount of the check. Drawee bank seeks to recover from the depositary bank the amount paid under the forged drawer's signature.

Decision
For defendant-depositary bank.

Reasoning
Under UCC 3–418, payment or acceptance of an instrument is final in favor of a holder in due course or a person who has in good faith changed his position in reliance on the payment.

Fireman's Fund Insurance Company v. Security Pacific National Bank, 85 Cal.App.3d 797 (Cal. 1978).

In keeping with the protection of an HIDC (see Real or Universal Defenses in chapter 30), a bank which in *good faith* makes payment to a *holder* may charge its customer's account for

tenor
what is stated as meant

1. the original **tenor** or amount of a materially altered item, or
2. the final or completed tenor of an item that was originally issued incomplete, unless the bank has notice that completion of the item was improper.[19]

---

[11] UCC 4–213. [12] UCC 3–410, 4–411. [13] UCC 3–413(1).

[14] UCC 4–402. [15] UCC 4–401(1). [16] UCC 4–213, 4–301.

[17] UCC 3–417(1), 4–207(1). [18] UCC 3–418. [19] UCC 4–401(2).

To give an example, if the drawee-payor bank innocently charges a customer's account with an uncertified check that has been materially altered from $100 to $1,000, the customer can compel the bank to reimburse the account for $900. Material alteration is a real defense against an HIDC to the extent of the $900 alteration.[20] Since banks in the collection channel make transfer and presentment warranties, the drawee-payor bank would then be entitled to charge back against the presenting bank $900 for breach of material alteration warranty.[21]

If the bank in good faith pays an item that was originally issued incomplete, it can charge the customer for the full amount. In the absence of notice to the bank of improper completion, the customer takes responsibility for these instruments.

Stop-Payment Orders

A customer may order its bank to stop payment on a check, but the bank must be given a reasonable time to put the order into effect.[22] A matter of hours may be a reasonable period of time. However, the drawer will be liable to a HIDC on a stopped check.

An *oral* stop order is effective for *fourteen calendar* days. *Written* orders, or *written* confirmations of oral orders, are valid for *six months* and may be renewed.[23] A slight error in the information given to the bank may not defeat the customer's right of recovery, as is illustrated in the following case.

Facts
FJS Electronics, Inc., plaintiff, brought this action to recover the amount of a check drawn on defendant-appellant Fidelity Bank. The president of FJS phoned Fidelity and requested that payment be stopped on the check. The amount given in the phone conversation was $1,844.48; the actual amount was $1,844.98.

A written confirmation from defendant of plaintiff's oral stop payment containing the incorrect information was received in the mail by FJS. The confirmation included the following language: "PLEASE ENSURE AMOUNT IS CORRECT." FJS did not correct the information. The trial court concluded that defendant Fidelity Bank had a reasonable opportunity to stop payment and rendered judgment for plaintiff. Defendant appealed.

Decision
Affirmed for FJS Electronics, plaintiff.

Reasoning
It is clear that the order here was timely received. The court below determined that even though it contained an error, the order was given in such manner as to give the bank a reasonable opportunity to act. Fidelity, in essence, asserts that the UCC 4–403(1) should be read to require compliance with the procedures of a particular bank, regardless of what they are and regardless of whether the customer has been made aware of them. Fidelity argues that since its technique for ascertaining whether payment had been stopped required absolute accuracy as to the amount of a stopped check, this section would require absolute precision in order for the notice to be reasonable. Such a narrow view is not consistent with the intent of Section 4–403, expressed in Comment 2 following the section:

The position taken by this section is that stopping payment is a service which depositors expect and are entitled to receive from banks notwithstanding its difficulty, inconvenience and expense. The inevitable occasional losses through failure to stop should be borne by the banks as a cost of the business of banking.

FJS Electronics, Inc. v. The Fidelity Bank, 431 A.2d 326 (Pa. 1981).

If the bank pays despite a valid stop order, the customer can compel the bank to reimburse the account by proof of the fact and amount of the loss.[24] The bank is then **subrogated** to the customer's rights against the payee or any other holder of the check.[25] If this approach does not prevent unjust enrichment of the drawer-customer at the expense of the bank, the bank is subrogated to the rights of an HIDC, holder, or payee against the *drawer*.

subrogation
the substitution of one person for another with reference to a claim or a right

---

[20] UCC 3–407.

[21] UCC 3–417, 4–207.

[22] UCC 4–403(1).

[23] UCC 4–403(2).

[24] UCC 4–403(3).

[25] UCC 4–407(c).

Assume that D purchases merchandise from P and issues a $45 check on ABC Bank (drawee) in payment. If, without any legitimate reason, D simply decides not to pay and issues a valid stop order to ABC Bank, P would be successful in a lawsuit against D. D has made a contract with P and has no legal grounds to avoid payment.

If ABC Bank paid the check despite the stop order, its customer, the drawer, could not compel ABC Bank to reimburse his account because he has suffered no loss. Even if the bank initially reimbursed the account to appease its customer, it could subsequently charge back. Remember that the bank is subrogated to the rights of an HIDC, holder, or payee against the drawer to avoid a loss and prevent the drawer from being unjustly enriched. After all, there is no good reason to allow D to keep the merchandise and, simply at his whim, stop payment on the check issued to pay for it.

On the assumption that D has legal grounds for stopping payment—e.g., P never delivered the merchandise to D—the bank's negligence in paying despite the order will cause D a loss. In this event, D can compel ABC Bank to reimburse his account, and ABC will be subrogated to D's rights against P.

However, if P negotiated to an HIDC, the bank's conduct (negligent or not) in paying the check would not be the cause of D's loss. D had a personal defense only—failure of consideration—and an HIDC would have succeeded in an action against D in spite of this defense. Thus the bank would be subrogated to the HIDC's rights and could charge D's account. On the other hand, if D could prove a real defense, the bank's conduct in paying the check would cause D to suffer a loss, so it would have to reimburse D's account.

Stale Checks

When an uncertified check has been in circulation more than six months, the drawee is *not obligated* to pay it. Normally it will consult its depositor on such checks, but it has the option to pay them without consultation if it acts in good faith.[26] For example, the check may be issued in payment of dividends by one of the bank's corporate customers and held by one of the stockholders for more than six months. This check could be paid in good faith without consultation with the corporate issuer.

Death or Incompetence of a Customer

Neither death nor adjudication of incompetence of a customer of either a collecting or payor bank affects that bank's authority to accept, pay, or collect an item or to account for its proceeds until the bank *knows* of the death or adjudication and has a *reasonable opportunity to act* on it.[27] Even with knowledge of the death of a customer, a bank may certify or pay checks (but not other items) for a period of *ten days after death*.[28] A person claiming an interest in the account—e.g., a relative or the executor of the decedent's will—may order the bank to stop further payment. The reason for this exception is that "there is almost never any reason why they should not be paid, and that filing in probate is a useless formality, burdensome to the holder, the executor, the court and the bank."[29]

Customer's Duty to Examine Cancelled Checks

Periodically the bank will send to each customer a statement of account supported by the cancelled or paid items that have been charged (debited) to the account. The customer must then exercise reasonable care and promptness in examining the materials for unauthorized signatures and for alterations. The bank is entitled to prompt notice if any irregularities are discovered.[30]

---

[26] UCC 4–404.　　[27] UCC 4–405(1).　　[28] UCC 4–405(2).

[29] UCC 4–405, comment 3.　　[30] UCC 4–406(1).

The bank is protected, and the customer must pursue other means of recovery, when an item bearing the customer's unauthorized signature or an alteration is paid if all of the three following conditions are satisfactorily proved:

1. the bank establishes that the customer failed in his duty to examine the checks and report his unauthorized signatures or alterations;[31] *and*
2. the bank establishes that it suffered a loss because of the customer's breach of duty;[32] *and*
3. the customer is not able to show that the bank failed to exercise ordinary care in the payment of these items.[33]

If the bank fails to establish either 1 or 2 above, or if the customer is able to establish the bank's failure in 3, then the bank is liable for the unauthorized signature or the altered item. This is exactly what one would expect. After all, the bank is under contract with its customer, it has a copy of the customer's signature, and it is supposed to follow the customer's orders—no forgeries or alterations, please. Since a certain number of these are bound to occur, the bank must train its employees to detect as many of these items as possible, and it must absorb the loss or losses that do materialize or insure against them.

If the same wrongdoer undertakes *subsequent* forgeries, unauthorized signatures, or alterations which the bank pays in good faith after the first check (or "first batch," if two or more items are involved) has been forwarded to its customer, the bank is once more protected. The customer must pursue other means of recovery if the customer failed within a reasonable period of time (not exceeding fourteen calendar days) to detect the "first batch" of irregularities and notify the bank. In this way the customer is penalized for his or her breach of duty in not promptly examining his or her checks and reporting irregularities.[34] The bank is not protected, however, and the customer may recover if the bank did not exercise ordinary care in paying the "second batch."[35]

Without regard to the exercise of reasonable care by either the customer or the bank, there is a statute of limitations on the customer's right to assert these irregularities against the bank. For unauthorized customer-drawer signatures and for alterations, the period is one year from the time the statement of account and supporting items are made available to the customer. Since the customer is not likely to recognize the forged or unauthorized signature of an indorser, the statute of limitations is three years, rather than one, from the time the materials are made available to the customer.[36]

Certified Checks

There are no primary parties on a check as it is normally issued. The drawer is a party secondarily liable, and the drawee and payee are not liable until their signatures are on the item. The check is not an assignment of funds for the benefit of the payee or any subsequent holder,[37] and for this reason the bank cannot be compelled to pay by a holder. It is, however, liable to customers for wrongful dishonor of checks and other items.[38]

When a bank certifies a check, it becomes a primary party analogous to a maker of a note.[39] The certification or acceptance will be written or stamped on the instrument and signed by an authorized officer of the bank.[40] The bank is not obligated to provide this service,[41] so it will normally charge a fee when certification is requested.

---

[31] UCC 4–406(1).   [32] UCC 4–406(2)(a).   [33] UCC 4–406(3).

[34] UCC 4–406(2)(b).   [35] UCC 4–406(2)(b), (3).   [36] UCC 4–406(4).

[37] 3–409.   [38] UCC 4–402.   [39] UCC 3–413(1).

[40] UCC 3–410(1).   [41] UCC 3–411(2).

Certification obtained by a *holder* has the effect of discharging the drawer and all indorsers *prior to the holder* who is having the check certified.[42] For example, if D issued a check to P, who indorsed to A and so on to H, a certification by the drawee bank at the request of H would discharge D, P, and A from further liability on the check. The reason for this is that the instrument is now the primary debt and responsibility of the certifying bank. Certification is analogous to cashing the check; and it is easy to see that if the drawee had paid H cash, all parties prior to H would be discharged. Anyone who indorses it following the certification, however, will incur the usual secondary liability.

When a *drawer* has an instrument certified, no one is discharged. Obviously there is no one prior to the drawer to be discharged.

Missing Indorsements and Bank Collection Indorsements

In an effort to speed up the collection process and make it more efficient, depositary banks may supply any necessary indorsement of a customer, unless the item expressly requires the *payee's* indorsement. Generally, the bank's written statement on the instrument that it was deposited to the customer's account is sufficient.[43] Also, the drawee/payor bank may charge its customer's account for any item which is properly payable from that account even if the charge creates an overdraft.[44] This is illustrated in the following case.

Facts
The plaintiffs, Barretts, are husband and wife. Mr. Barrett made a check payable to Aquatic Industries on July 19, 1975 for $1,500 drawn on their joint checking account at the drawee defendant bank. Aquatic Industries did not indorse the check when it deposited the check in its account at the Rosewell Bank. The Rosewell Bank, failing to add Aquatic's indorsement as it was authorized to do by UCC 4–205(1), sent the check through banking channels to the defendant bank. Upon receiving the check, the bank debited plaintiffs' account and returned it to them. Plaintiffs contended that the check should not have been paid because it was never indorsed.

Decision
For the drawee bank.

Reasoning
The check was properly payable. Since it was properly payable, a bank may charge against its customer's account any item which is otherwise properly payable from that account even though the charge creates an overdraft. UCC 4–401(1). The absence of the payee's indorsement and the failure of the collecting Rosewell Bank to supply the missing indorsement as it was authorized to do did not affect the payor bank's right to pay this check and to debit the plaintiffs' account. In absence of the indorsement of the payee, the instrument was not transferred by negotiation, and any subsequent transferee of the instrument could not acquire the status of a holder in due course. UCC 3–201(1).

First National Bank of Gwinnett v. Gerald Barrett, 233 S.E.2d. 24 (Ga. 1977).

Intermediary banks and nondepositary payor banks are not in any way given notice or affected by any restrictive indorsement except that of its immediate transferor. For example, if P indorses restrictively in trust for M, "Pay to T for the benefit of M, [signed] P," the depositary bank must exercise due care in receiving this instrument from T, but subsequent banks in the collection channel need not pay any attention to it. They need only obey the instructions contained in the restrictive indorsement *of the bank* which transfers the check to them.[45]

Lost, Destroyed, or Stolen Instruments

If an instrument has been lost, stolen, or destroyed, the owner may still sue on it and recover from any party who is liable. This person, now a plaintiff in a lawsuit, will have

---

[42] UCC 3–411(1). Their contract that the instrument would be honored is performed by the certification.

[43] UCC 4–205(1).   [44] UCC 4–401(1).   [45] UCC 3–206(2)(3)(4), 4–205(2).

to prove his ownership, the facts which prevent his production of the instrument (e.g., if it was destroyed by fire, this would have to be proven), and the terms of the instrument.[46]

Keep in mind that a contract is really more than the paper on which it is written. Even if the paper is destroyed, the contract, with its rights and duties agreed upon by the parties, continues to exist. It is now much harder to prove, but witnesses can be called and the owner's own testimony is admissible.

In order to protect the one who pays from having to pay a second time (assuming that the instrument eventually surfaces in the hands of a legitimate party), the court may require security. This protection against fraud or mistake could be in the form of a bond or insurance policy which the owner would have to post before the court will allow the owner to collect.

NOW Accounts: Negotiable Orders of Withdrawal and the Consumer Checking Account Equity Act

Effective since 31 December 1980, U.S. financial institutions have been able to offer the practical equivalent of interest-paying checking accounts at rates as high as 5¼%. Congress authorized depositary institutions to permit their savers to make withdrawals (**NOW**'s) by means of negotiable check-like instruments.[47] Savings and loan associations, mutual savings associations, credit unions as well as commercial banks can treat NOW drafts in the same manner as checks under the Uniform Commercial Code.[48]

NOW account
a negotiable order of withdrawal

NOW accounts are available only to *individuals* and to *non-profit* religious, philanthropic, charitable, and educational *organizations*. This means that individuals who operate sole proprietorships are entitled to hold NOW accounts, but not partnerships, corporations, or any other type of for-profit organizations. In an effort to clarify this important area of the law, the Federal Reserve Board supplied a listing of those eligible to maintain NOW accounts at member banks:

1. individuals;
2. sole proprietors;
3. husband and wife operating unincorporated businesses;
4. local housing authority;
5. residential tenants' security deposits;
6. independent school districts;
7. redevelopment authority;
8. escrow funds (provided entire beneficial interest is held by individuals or qualifying organizations);
9. labor unions;
10. trust and other fiduciary accounts (provided entire beneficial interest is held by individuals or qualifying organizations);
11. pension funds;
12. trade associations.

In sum, the changes made by Congress in the Consumer Checking Account Equity Act do not introduce any significant new problems for those engaged in the study of the *Uniform Commercial Code*.

---

[46] UCC 3-804.

[47] Consumer Checking Account Equity Act of 1980, Pub. L. No. 96-221, Title III, sec. 303, 94 Stat. 143 (1980) (codified at 12 U.S.C. sec. 1832 (a) et seq.).

[48] 45 Fed. Reg. 64,164 (1980).

Summary Statement

1. Checks are demand drafts drawn on banks. The drawer is entitled to order the drawee bank to pay money from the checking account because of the contractual relationship that exists between them. The bank is the debtor of its customer, the drawer, to the extent of the checking account balance.
2. A bank becomes an agent of its customer in the check clearing process. It will forward checks through bank channels to the drawee-payor for collection. Each bank that participates in the process must take proper action on the check before its midnight deadline—midnight of the next banking day following receipt of an item—or be held accountable for the amount of the check.
3. A holder cannot compel a drawee bank to honor a check, but if the drawee wrongfully dishonors, it is liable to the customer for actual damage, direct and consequential, proximately caused by such dishonor. The drawee may honor an item even though it creates an overdraft, and, generally speaking, payment of a check (whether it creates an overdraft or not) is final in favor of an HIDC and those who have in good faith substantially changed their position in reliance on payment. A drawee bank may charge its customer for the original tenor of a materially altered item or for the completed tenor of an item that was issued incomplete.
4. Once a check has been issued, the drawer may (for any reason) direct the bank to stop payment. Oral stop orders are valid for fourteen calendar days; written orders for six months. When the check "bounces" back into the hands of the holder or HIDC, the drawer must be ready to prove a personal or real defense; otherwise a judgment may be entered against the drawer.
5. If the drawee overlooks the stop order and through negligence pays the check anyway, the drawer-customer may recover from the drawee upon proof of the amount of loss caused by the drawee's negligence.
6. A drawee bank is not obligated to honor uncertified checks that have been in circulation more than six months, but it may do so in good faith. Death of a customer does not automatically terminate the drawee's right to pay checks that were drawn previously. Even with knowledge of death and an opportunity to act on it, the drawee may for ten days after date of death pay or certify such checks unless ordered to stop by a person claiming an interest in the account.
7. When the drawee periodically mails its customer a statement of account along with the customer's cancelled checks, the customer has a duty to examine the checks promptly and put the bank on notice of irregularities. If the customer does not act reasonably and promptly in the performance of this duty, and if such negligence or breach of duty causes the bank to suffer a loss, the customer will be responsible for the loss. However, if the drawee bank itself has been negligent, then the customer will *not* be responsible for the loss.
8. There are no primary parties on a check as originally issued, and the check does not operate as an assignment of funds for the payee or anyone else. When a check is certified, the drawee becomes a primary party-acceptor analogous to the maker of a note. All parties *prior* to the one having the check certified are discharged from further liability on the instrument.
9. An intermediary or a nondepositary payor bank is not in any way affected by a restrictive indorsement *except* that of its immediate transferor. Depositary banks are entitled to indorse for deposit on behalf of their customers unless the item expressly requires the payee's signature.
10. The owner of a lost, stolen, or destroyed instrument may still recover on it with proof of ownership, of the facts which prevent its production, and the terms of the instrument. To protect the payor against the possibility of a second payment, the court may require the owner to provide security for the payor's benefit.

In the following case the court held that the drawers' negligence in not detecting forgeries of their signatures on their checks relieved the drawee bank from liability for paying some of the forged checks.

K & K Manufacturing, Inc., and Knight v. Union Bank
628 P.2d 44 (Ariz. 1981)

Hathaway, C. J. In this case we must apply Articles three and four of the Uniform Commercial Code to determine who should bear the risk of loss when a dishonest employee forges her employer's name as drawer on a number of checks on his business and personal checking accounts, then appropriates the proceeds for her personal use.

Appellant Bill J. Knight is the president and majority stockholder of both K & K Manufacturing, Inc. and Knight Foundry & Manufacturing, Inc. Knight Foundry employed about 80 people at the time of trial, while K & K Manufacturing, appellant, which was formed to accomplish the contracting, buying and selling for the foundry business, employed only two persons when the events which form the basis of this action occurred. These two employees were Knight and a bookkeeper, Eleanor Garza. The bookkeeper's duties at K & K Manufacturing were very broad, including picking up the company mail and Knight's personal mail from a common post office box, preparing checks for Knight's signature to pay both company and personal bills, and making entries in a cash disbursement journal reflecting the expenses for which the checks were written. Most importantly, it was her responsibility to reconcile the monthly statements prepared and sent by appellee Union Bank, where Knight kept both his business and personal checking and savings accounts. No one shared these duties with Miss Garza.

Between March 1977 and January 1978, Miss Garza forged Knight's signature on some 66 separate checks drawn on his personal or business accounts at Union Bank. The majority of these checks were made payable to her. The total amount of the forgeries on the K & K Manufacturing account was $49,859.31. The total on Knight's personal account was $11,350. The bank paid each such check and Miss Garza received or was credited with the proceeds.

We need not concentrate on the details of the fraud, except to comment that it proved to be effective for nearly one year.

* * *

Eventually, an in-house audit showed the discrepancies in the 1977 disbursements. Appellants brought this action against appellee for breach of contract, seeking repayment of the funds the bank paid out on checks with unauthorized signatures. After a court trial, judgment was entered in favor of appellant Knight for $5,500, representing the amount paid out of his personal account on forged checks from March 28 to May 20, 1977. This figure included eight forged checks paid by the bank prior to the mailing of its monthly statement containing a record of the payments and the checks themselves to Knight on May 6, plus a 14-day period. Since no forged checks on the K & K Manufacturing account were paid prior to May 20, judgment was entered [for Union Bank].

* * *

The concept of which party bears the loss in a forgery situation such as the one presented here is addressed in Articles three and four of the Uniform Commercial Code, covering commercial paper and bank deposits and collections. [UCC 3–406, 4–406].

* * *

These provisions impose a duty on the depositor to check his monthly statement for unauthorized signatures or alterations on checks. If the depositor fails to do so, after the first forged check and statement relating thereto is sent to him, plus a reasonable period not exceeding 14 days, he is precluded from asserting the unauthorized signature or alteration against the bank. UCC Sec. 4–406, comment 3. The burden of proof of depositor's negligence is on the bank. Even if the bank succeeds in establishing the depositor's negligence, if the customer establishes that the bank failed to exercise ordinary care in paying the bad checks, the preclusion rule . . . does not apply. UCC Sec. 4–406, comment 4.

We first address the issue of whether appellee met its burden of proof of showing that appellants "substantially contributed" to the forgeries or failed to exercise "reasonable care and promptness" in examining the monthly statements. The record shows that appellants trusted Miss Garza completely with both writing checks and reconciling the monthly statements. No spot checks were made by Knight or the controller at Knight Foundry, both of whom had access to the banking records. Knight was informed by a bank officer that his personal account was overdrawn on 12 occasions in 1977, yet did nothing to discover the reasons therefor. Knight testified he was aware Miss Garza's work was often inaccurate as well as tardy in 1977 and 1978.

* * *

We adopt the majority view that the depositor is chargeable with the knowledge of all facts a reasonable and prudent examination of his bank statement would have disclosed if made by an honest employee. . . .

Secondly, we turn to the question of whether appellants met their burden of proof of demonstrating appellee did not exercise ordinary care in paying the bad checks, and did not act in good faith and in accordance with reasonable commercial standards. There appears to be no dispute regarding the good faith of appellee in paying the forgeries. The issue is whether its method of ascertaining unauthorized signatures on its depositor's checks met the standard of care under the circumstances.

Implied in the debtor/creditor relationship between a bank and its checking account depositor is the contractual undertaking on the part of the bank that it will only discharge its obligations to the depositor upon his authorized signature. The mere fact that the bank has paid a forged check does not mean the bank has breached its duty of ordinary care, however.

At trial, an operations officer for appellee testified as to the methods employed during the period the forgeries occurred to discover unauthorized signatures on depositor's checks. She testified that checks were organized so that a bundle from the same account could be compared with the authorized signature on the bank's signature card. A staff of five filing clerks handled an average of approximately 1,000 checks each per hour in this manner. She testified it was common for a file clerk to become familiar with the drawer's signature in large accounts such as appellants'. An official of a large Arizona bank testified that tellers and file clerks are not trained to be handwriting experts. He testified that in his opinion, because most large banks have completely abandoned physical comparison of checks with the signature card, the system employed by appellee was better than the norm of the banking community in Southern Arizona.

In view of this and other evidence, we conclude that there was sufficient evidence to support findings 13 and 14 and the judgment entered below. Similar methods of comparing drawer's signatures have been upheld as constituting ordinary care and being within reasonable commercial standards across the country. . . . Appellant Knight and his controller admitted the forgeries were quite good. Appellants also argue that because the bank tellers recognized Miss Garza was cashing large checks made to herself and her boyfriend and that she was driving an expensive sports car, they had a further duty to check the validity of the drawer's signature. This evidence was balanced by testimony that Miss Garza thoroughly explained the reasons for the large checks as increased salary, bonuses, and payment of Knight's expenses while he was out of town. Knight and Miss Garza were in the bank together on a regular basis and the tellers knew Miss Garza was authorized to handle large amounts of Knight's money.

Finally, there was evidence that some K & K Manufacturing checks were forged with a rubber stamp facsimile of Knight's signature, which was only authorized for use with the Knight Foundry account. Appellants argue appellee fell below the standard of ordinary care in honoring these checks. The trial court personally examined appellee's expert witness on this subject. There was testimony that if facsimile signatures appear "all of a sudden" on the checks, the depositor may be contacted, but there was sufficient evidence that the piecemeal use of the stamp here, which was at times authorized by appellants, was not such that appellee should be held to bring it to their attention. The finding of fact that appellee's acts, including those regarding the facsimile signature, did not fall below ordinary care or reasonable commercial standards was not clearly erroneous.

Affirmed.

Questions and Case Problems

1. D purchased inventory from P with a $5,000 check. Drawee Bank wrongfully dishonored D's check, and P repossessed the inventory. This caused D much embarrassment and at least $1,000 in good will. In addition, D lost a $2,000 breach-of-contract suit to X for failure to deliver merchandise. If D's inventory had not been repossessed, D could have fulfilled the contract with X. D then sued Drawee Bank. Result?

2. D issued a $100 check on Drawee Bank payable to the order of P. P materially altered the amount (words and figures) to $1,000 and negotiated it to an HIDC. The HIDC forwarded it to Drawee Bank for collection and received $1,000. When these facts were revealed by D's examination of her monthly statement and cancelled checks, she proceeded against Drawee Bank to reinstate her account. Result?

3. Faye Zappacosta, bookkeeper for Arrow Builders, drew checks on defendant-drawee (Royal National Bank) purportedly representing social security and income taxes withheld from the wages of Arrow's employees. For twenty-three months she drew fifty-four such checks. Twenty-three were properly applied and the others were presented individually by Zappacosta and honored by the defendant-drawee (Royal National). This scheme could have been detected by Arrow's chief accountant after the first month's embezzlement if Zappacosta's work had been properly supervised. Arrow proceeded against defendant Royal National after these facts came to light. Result? [*Arrow Builders Supply Corp. v. Royal National Bank,* 288 N.Y. S.2d 609 (N.Y. 1968).]

4. The plaintiff, Tusso, delivered a check to the payee for the sum of $600 on July 24, 1972. The following morning at 9:00 A.M. the plaintiff appeared and placed a stop-payment order on the check. The same morning at 10:30 A.M. the payee appeared at the defendant Security National Bank, drawee, the same bank where the plaintiff had placed the stop order, and had the check certified. The bank charged the plaintiff's account immediately. Plaintiff sued to have the defendant Security National Bank reimburse his account. Result? [*Tusso v. Security National Bank,* 76 Misc.2d 12 (N.Y. 1973).]

5. Granite filed a written stop order with the drawee Hempstead Bank on a check issued to Overseas Equipment Co. Granite then delivered a new check to Overseas. More than a year later the first check was presented to Hempstead and paid. Granite claimed that the drawee bank is liable to it for paying the first check. Result? [*Granite Equipment Leasing Corp. v. Hempstead Bank,* 326 N.Y. S.2d 881 (N.Y. 1971).]

6. Depositor, Palmer, brought action against his bank to recover for the alleged wrongful dishonor of several checks. Jury found for the plaintiff and awarded actual and punitive damages, and the defendant appealed.

    The trial court jury answered several issues, which were: (1) that someone forged Palmer's signature as an indorser on a $275 check; (2) that thereafter the bank intentionally refused payment of checks written by Palmer; (3) that the bank attempted to collect an overdraft resulting from the chargeback against the account of the $275 check, and for insufficient check fund charges resulting from its dishonor of Palmer's checks after it knew or should have known that the indorsement was a forgery; (4) that Palmer had suffered actual damages of $2,000; (5) that Palmer was entitled to punitive damages of $3,500; and (6) that the dishonor of the checks was not the result of a mistake. Result? [*Northshore Bank v. Palmer,* 525 S.W.2d 718 (Tex. 1975).]

7. Atlantic Telec, Inc., drawer, recovered on a $13,000 check that its drawee bank, Southeast First National Bank, failed to stop on an oral order. The check had been given by Atlantic to the payee pursuant to a contract between Atlantic and the payee. The bank presented testimony to show that the payee had breached its contract with Atlantic. The bank did not object to the oral order. It appealed, arguing instead that Atlantic failed to show it had a right to stop payment. Result? [*Southeast First National Bank of Satellite Beach v. Atlantic Telec, Inc.,* 389 So.2d 1032 (Fla. 1980).]

8. Empire Packing Co., Inc. drew a check on its bank (Illinois National Bank and Trust Company, the drawee-payor) to the order of the plaintiff, Rock Island Auction Sales, Inc. in payment for cattle. The drawee-payor bank, Illinois National, received the check through clearinghouse channels for collection but held it for five days on assurance from Empire that funds would soon be deposited to cover it. Shortly afterward, the check was returned by the drawee-payor marked "Insufficient Funds." A petition in bankruptcy was filed against Empire. The plaintiff, Rock Island, was successful against Illinois National in the District Court, and Illinois National appeals.

    Plaintiff argues "that [as] the payor bank [Illinois National] became liable for the amount of the check because it held the check without payment, return or notice of dishonor, beyond the time limit fixed in UCC 4-302. . . ." Result? [*Rock Island Auction Sales, Inc. v. Empire Packing Co., Inc.,* 204 N.E.2d 721 (Ill. 1965).]

9. Plaintiff drew and delivered to Santo his check for $3,000 drawn on the defendant bank payable to the order of Santo on November 10, 1964. On December 10, 1964, plaintiff gave written notice to defendant to stop payment on the check. On December 24, 1964, defendant ignored the stop payment order and made payment of the check. Plaintiff sued defendant for the amount of the check and the bank raised the defense that plaintiff had not shown that he was damaged by the payment of the check. Discuss. [*Cicci v. Lincoln National Bank and Trust Company of Central New York,* 46 Misc.2d 465 (N.Y. 1965).]

10. In *K & K Manufacturing, Inc. v. Union Bank,* 628 P.2d 44 (Ariz. 1981),[49] why was Bill Knight, President of K & K, entitled to recover on the first eight forged checks ($5,500) his bookkeeper drew, but neither he nor the corporation was entitled to recover on subsequent forgeries?

---

[49] See pp. 417–18.

Deadlines and Discharge 27

After you have read this chapter, you should be able to:

1. Distinguish between presentment for payment and presentment for acceptance.
2. Learn when presentment is necessary.
3. Become familiar with the mechanics of presentment—how it is made, to whom, and the length of time allowed.
4. Recognize the importance of giving notice of dishonor, and find how such notice is to be given.
5. Review the methods of discharging one's liability on an instrument.

Introduction

The duties one assumes and the rights brought into existence by the creation of a negotiable instrument do not last forever. The same law that provided for the creation of commercial paper also provides for its ending. It was important for you to know how to create a formal contract, and it is equally important to know how to discharge (end) the formal contract.

Once an instrument has been created negotiable in form and issued to a payee under some contractual arrangement, it may be further negotiated to a holder or an HIDC. At maturity, the holder will expect to be paid, so the holder will take the very practical step of "presenting" it to the maker, acceptor, or, if it is a nonacceptable draft, to the drawee.

When a holder of an instrument is finally paid according to its terms by one of these parties, the holder is satisfied and the liability of all parties to the instrument is discharged. If it is not paid—if the instrument is dishonored—then the holder may institute a lawsuit and be faced with an array of real or personal defenses.

Instead of bringing suit immediately and undergoing the expense and anxiety that it entails, the holder may seek other avenues of recovery. After all, the holder had no part of the potential defendant's dispute with the payee.

At this stage, the holder will think of the secondary or conditional liability of the drawer or indorsers. These secondary parties, or any of them, will be liable on the instrument if the holder takes the preliminary steps of timely presentment for payment and, if the instrument is not paid, notice of dishonor.

This chapter deals with the procedures that must be followed to bind primary and secondary parties, and with the ways in which a party can discharge his or her liability on an instrument.

Presentment, Dishonor, and Notice—In General

presentment
"a demand for acceptance or payment made upon the maker, acceptor, drawee or other payor by or on behalf of the holder" UCC 3-504(1)

dishonor
the refusal of the drawee to accept the draft, or of the drawee, acceptor, or maker to pay the draft or note

Presentment of an instrument *for payment*[1] at the proper time[2] and, under some circumstances, presentment *for acceptance* prior to payment,[3] is the first step a holder must take to preserve the liability of secondary parties—drawers and indorsers. Once *any* presentment has been made (whether presentment for acceptance or for payment, and whether presentment is necessary or optional), the instrument is **dishonored**[4] if the responsible party does not accept or pay within certain time deadlines.[5] Secondary parties engage to be liable only if the instrument is *duly presented* for acceptance or payment to the drawee, acceptor, or maker. Therefore, it is essential that presentment be made if, on dishonor of the instrument, they are to be held liable by the holder.

Finally, the *holder* must *give notice of dishonor* to secondary parties,[6] and this notice must be *sent* prior to midnight of the *third* business day following dishonor or receipt of notice of dishonor.[7] For *banks,* the deadline is midnight of the *next banking day* following dishonor or receipt of notice of dishonor.[8]

Presentment

How Made

Presentment—that is, the demand for payment or acceptance—is made upon the maker, acceptor, or drawee by or on behalf of the holder. It may be made by mail, through a clearinghouse, or personally at the place designated in the instrument. If no place is specified, then the business address or residence is acceptable. Presentment is excused if no one can be located at any of these places to accept or pay the instrument.[9]

---

[1] UCC 3-501(1)(b). [2] UCC 3-503. [3] UCC 3-501(1)(a), 3-503(1)(a).

[4] UCC 3-507(1)(a). [5] UCC 3-506. [6] UCC 3-501(2).

[7] UCC 3-508(2)(4). [8] UCC 4-104(h). [9] UCC 3-504.

Rights of the Party to Whom Presentment Is Made

The maker, acceptor, or drawee (or their authorized agent) may require the following things *without dishonoring* the instrument:

(a) exhibition or physical display of the note or draft;
(b) reasonable proof of identification and, if the presenter is an agent, reasonable proof of the agent's authority;
(c) presentment at the specified place, or, if none is specified, at a place reasonable in the circumstances; and
(d) a signed receipt on the instrument for full or partial payment, and surrender of the instrument if paid in full.[10]

Failure to comply with any of these requirements invalidates the presentment. However, the presenter must be given a reasonable time to comply—e.g., the presenter who is an agent may need some time to produce proof of this authority to act on behalf of the owner.[11]

Time Allowed for Acceptance or Payment

The instrument is not dishonored if *acceptance* is deferred until the close of the next business day following presentment. Even beyond that, the *holder* may allow postponement for an additional business day in a good faith effort to obtain acceptance.[12] As a general rule, *payment* may be deferred while reasonable steps are taken to determine whether the instrument is properly payable; but payment must be made before the close of business *on the day of presentment* to avoid dishonor.[13]

Time of Presentment

When an instrument contains a *due date*, presentment *for payment* should be made on that date.[14] If payments have been accelerated, presentment for payment is due within a reasonable time after acceleration.[15] Any presentment *for acceptance* must be made on or before the date when payment is due.[16]

Presentment for payment or acceptance of *all other instruments*—i.e., those without due dates—is due within a reasonable time after date or issue or after the secondary party becomes liable.[17] Otherwise the secondary party is discharged.

A reasonable period of time is determined from the nature of the instrument, banking or **trade usage,** and the facts of the particular case. For uncertified checks drawn and payable in the U.S., a reasonable period of time for presentment or for the initiation of the bank collection process is *presumed* to be

(a) 30 days after date or issue (whichever is later) with respect to the *drawer's* liability, and
(b) 7 days after indorsement with respect to an indorser's liability.[18]

Effect of Late Presentment

The holder's failure to make a proper and timely presentment,[19] as well as the holder's failure to give proper and timely notice of dishonor,[20] has the effect of discharging *secondary* parties. Indorsers will be fully discharged under these circumstances; drawers *may* be fully or partially discharged.

usage of trade
"any practice or method of dealing having such regularity of observance in a place, vocation, or trade as to justify an expectation that it will be observed with respect to the transaction in question" UCC 1–205(2)

---

[10] UCC 3–505(1).
[11] UCC 3–505(2).
[12] UCC 3–506(1).
[13] UCC 3–506(2).
[14] UCC 3–503(1)(c).
[15] UCC 3–503(1)(d).
[16] UCC 3–503(1)(a)(b).
[17] UCC 3–503(1)(e).
[18] UCC 3–503(2).
[19] UCC 3–503(1)(e), 3–502(1), 3–501(b)(c).
[20] UCC 3–501(2), 3–502(1).

The *drawer* of a domiciled instrument—one payable at a particular bank—will not automatically receive a full discharge. The discharge is limited to the extent that funds placed on deposit in that bank and intended for payment of a domiciled instrument have "shrunk" because of the bank's insolvency during the delay, i.e., the period of time beyond thirty days. To qualify for this discharge, the drawer must make a written assignment to the holder of all the rights the drawer has against the now insolvent bank.[21]

To illustrate, suppose that the drawee originally held sufficient funds to pay a customer-drawer's $1,000 check, but that the payee or subsequent party held the check for more than thirty days before presenting it or initiating the bank collection process. If the drawee bank becomes insolvent during the delay (the period in excess of thirty days) and only $500 are ultimately available to pay the check, the drawer may discharge his liability by written assignment to the holder of his rights against the bank for $500.

Indorsers of uncertified checks are fully discharged if the instrument is presented or the collection process begun more than seven days after their indorsement. In essence, the payee or holder is being penalized because of the failure to make a timely presentment.

Notice of Dishonor

> Banks have shorter deadlines than their customers.

Notice of dishonor may be given by the holder or by his bank or agent to anyone who may be liable on the instrument.[22] Notice to one partner is notice to all partners. To be effective, any notice of dishonor must be given *by a bank* before its one-day midnight deadline (midnight on its next banking day following the banking day on which it receives the item or notice of its dishonor), and *by all other persons* before the three-day midnight deadline (midnight of the third business day after dishonor or notice of dishonor).[23]

Failure to give timely notice of dishonor will result in the discharge of *secondary* parties in the same manner as a failure to make a timely presentment.[24] While memorizing dates and deadlines can be quite a chore, it could be very beneficial to a person in the long-run to remain familiar with this one.

Notice may be given in any reasonable manner, written or oral. It must be sufficient to identify the dishonored instrument. A misdescription which is not misleading will still be effective as a notice.[25]

Notice operates for the benefit of all who have rights against the party notified.[26] For example, if H presents an instrument at maturity and it is dishonored, one notice by H to indorsers A and B is all that is needed. If H recovers from B, B can pursue A without giving further notice to A. If H gives notice to B only, then B has a full three-day period to notify A.

Written notice is given when *sent* although it is never received.[27] It may consist of the instrument itself with the stamped or written statement that acceptance or payment has been refused.[28]

Protest

> **protest**
> a formal certificate, issued by a properly authorized person, certifying that a foreign or international draft was duly presented for acceptance or payment and that it was dishonored

Protest is a formal method of preserving proof that presentment was made and that the instrument was dishonored.

Protest is required for drafts which, on their face, appear to be drawn or payable outside the states and territories of the United States and the District of Columbia.[29] Such drafts at times are called "international" or "foreign" drafts. On all other drafts, protest

---

[21] UCC 3–503(1)(b). [22] UCC 3–508(1). [23] UCC 3–508(2), 4–104(h).

[24] UCC 3–501(2), 3–502(1). [25] UCC 3–508(3). [26] UCC 3–508(8).

[27] UCC 3–508(4). [28] UCC 3–508(3). [29] UCC 3–501(3).

is optional. It is a certificate of dishonor made by a U.S. consul, vice consul, notary public, or other authorized person according to the law of the place of dishonor. The protest must identify the instrument, and it may certify that some or all of the parties have been notified.[30]

Delayed, Waived, or Excused Presentment, Protest, or Notice

Delay
Delay in presentment, protest, or notice of dishonor is excused if the party does not know that it is due—e.g., the holder received it after acceleration by a prior party but without notice of the acceleration.[31] Delay is also excused if it is caused by circumstances beyond the party's control and the party exercises reasonable diligence after the cause of the delay ceases.[32]

Waiver or Excuse
Presentment, protest, or notice of dishonor is completely excused if:

(a) it has been expressly or impliedly waived;
(b) the party has dishonored or countermanded (stopped) payment or otherwise has no reason to expect or right to require that the instrument be accepted or paid; or
(c) presentment, protest, or notice cannot be given by the exercise of reasonable diligence.[33]

Presentment alone is excused if the maker, acceptor, or drawee is dead or insolvent. If payment or acceptance is refused for reasons other than the want of a proper presentment—e.g., the holder is told by the maker that he will not pay at maturity because the payee defrauded him—then presentment is excused because it would simply be useless.[34]

Waiver of protest is a waiver of presentment and notice of dishonor as well, even though protest is not required. *Waiver of presentment, notice, or protest embodied in the instrument itself is binding on all parties.* If it is written above the signature of one or more indorsers, it binds those only.[35]

Discharge

A party is **discharged** from liability on an instrument by any act or agreement with the other party that would discharge a simple contract for the payment of money.[36] It is sometimes said that payment discharges the instrument, as is illustrated in the following case.

discharge
(in contracts) the termination of a contractual duty to perform a promise

Facts
Bruce Small, minor son of the defendant, Genevieve, purchased an automobile from the plaintiff, George Allen, for $225. He paid $100 down, and a note for the balance was signed by Bruce and Genevieve. Bruce paid the note, and it was marked "Paid in full, George S. Allen" and delivered to Bruce Small, who had the lien on the automobile discharged of record. Later Bruce Small, still a minor, by written notice rescinded his contract with the plaintiff. He assigned his ownership to the plaintiff by transferring the ownership using the form provided on the registration certificate. He then returned the car to the plaintiff's garage and demanded that the plaintiff return the $225, which plaintiff refused to do. Bruce Small successfully sued the plaintiff, who then returned the $225 to him. Plaintiff later sued Genevieve on the note, contending that Genevieve is liable to him on the note to the extent of its face amount. He argued that since Bruce rescinded his contract with the plaintiff, the lien note was restored to its former status as far as the defendant was concerned, she being an accommodation maker.

---

[30] UCC 3–509.   [31] UCC 3–511(1).   [32] UCC 3–511(1).   [33] UCC 3–511(2).
[34] UCC 3–511(3).   [35] UCC 3–511(5)(6).   [36] UCC 3–601(2).

Decision
For defendant, Genevieve Small.

Reasoning
There is no question that the note was fully paid according to its terms and tenor, and the court so found. Payment is the final act which extinguishes a negotiable instrument and transmits it into a cancelled voucher. There is no longer a holder of the instrument and no suit may thereafter be maintained.

The findings establish that the defendant signed the note to insure its payment. The full payment was made. The surrender of a note by the holder to the maker, with intent thereby to discharge it, does discharge it. Whatever acts Bruce Small took on his own behalf, as a minor, were between him and the plaintiff and could not affect the rights of the defendant.

George S. Allen d/b/a Allen's Garage v. Genevieve Small, 271 A.2d 840 (Vt. 1970).

The following methods of discharge are exclusive insofar as the provisions of UCC Article 3 are concerned, but the Article does not prevent or affect discharge arising from other rules of law, e.g., bankruptcy:

satisfaction
the discharge of an obligation by paying what is due

renunciation
the abandonment of a right by a person

1. payment or **satisfaction** (Section 3–603); or
2. tender of payment (Section 3–604); or
3. cancellation or **renunciation** (Section 3–605); or
4. impairment of right of recourse or of collateral (Section 3–606); or
5. reacquisition of the instrument by a prior party (Section 3–208); or
6. fraudulent and material alteration (Section 3–407); or
7. certification of a check (Section 3–411); or
8. acceptance varying a draft (Section 3–412); or
9. unexcused delay in presentment or notice of dishonor or protest (Section 3–502).[37]

The liability of *all parties* is discharged when one who has no right of action—i.e., no recourse against anyone on the instrument—reacquires it or is himself discharged.[38] For example, a note issued from M to P and negotiated from P to A to H may be reacquired by M prior to maturity or paid by M at maturity. Both reacquisition and payment discharge all parties to the instrument at that time.

If M chooses to reissue the note he purchased before maturity, he will of course be liable to subsequent parties. Intervening parties, P, A, and H, are discharged with respect to M and subsequent holders *not* in due course. If their indorsements are cancelled, they will not be liable even to an HIDC.[39]

Effect of a Discharge
No discharge *provided by Article 3* is effective against a subsequent HIDC unless the HIDC has notice of the discharge when he takes the instrument.[40] Discharges provided by *other* rules of law, e.g., bankruptcy, are effective despite lack of notice.

Payment or Satisfaction
In order to receive the benefit of a discharge, payment or satisfaction must be made to a *holder* or the holder's authorized agent. Payment offered in full settlement may be accepted in partial settlement only. Always consult your state law. In the following case the payee's cashing of a check marked "in full satisfaction" but payable only for a lesser amount did not constitute consent by the payee *who wrote on the check to that effect.*

Facts
During 1971 the plaintiff, Wesley Scholl, did work for the defendants, Clinton and Virginia Tallman. As of February 18, 1971 plaintiff's books indicated that the Tallmans owed him $2,927.37. The Tallmans made payments during the course of 1971-72, but as of November 4, 1974 they allegedly still owed $2,077.37. Defendants believe plaintiff's figure to be too high; they felt that several hundred dollars in cash payments had not been credited to their account. They then sent a $500 check to Scholl with the words "Wesley Scholl Settlement in Full for all Labor and Materials to Date" typed on the back of the check. No further payments were made.

---

[37] UCC 3–601(1).   [38] UCC 3–601(3).   [39] UCC 3–208.   [40] UCC 3–602.

A short time later Scholl cashed the check but not until he had scratched out the typing on the back and wrote "Restriction of payment in full refused. $1,826.65 remains due and payable." He then brought this suit to collect payment.

The trial court found in favor of the defendants on **accord and satisfaction.** It was proved that the plaintiff had failed to record two checks, but the cash payments were not proved. The plaintiff appealed.

Decision
Reversed. For the plaintiff, Scholl.

Reasoning
The question before the court is whether there has been an accord and satisfaction of the disputed claim. The offer and consideration are not disputed here; the controversy involves acceptance. South Dakota's version of the UCC addresses the issue: "Part performance of an obligation . . . when expressly accepted by the creditor in writing in satisfaction . . . extinguishes the obligation."

The question is whether indorsement of the check with knowledge of the condition on the face of the check constitutes acceptance in writing under the statute. UCC 1–207 provides: "A party who with explicit reservation of rights performs or promises performance or assents to performance in a manner demanded or offered by the other party does not thereby prejudice the rights reserved. [Such words as 'without prejudice,' 'under protest' or the like are sufficient.]" The case was remanded for determination of how much was due to the plaintiff.

Scholl v. Tallman, 247 N.W.2d 490 (S.D. 1976).

accord and satisfaction
a new contract (accord) which discharges a party from a previous contractual obligation; the old contract is discharged (satisfied)

Jus Tertii: The Law of the Third Party

The maker, acceptor, or drawee is discharged even though payment is made with knowledge that some other party has a claim of ownership on the instrument unless, prior to payment, the party with the claim either (1) secures or indemnifies the one seeking a discharge, or (2) gets a court order (injunction) against payment.[41]

To illustrate: suppose that the payee, P, is fraudulently induced to negotiate a note to A; or, if P is a minor, simply assume that P indorses the paper to A in a transaction for goods. In either case, P will have a claim on the instrument. Knowledge of this claim, however, will not affect the maker-M's right to pay A or a subsequent holder at maturity and receive a full discharge. After all, the maker has *no defense of his or her own* against the payee or the holder. The maker expects at maturity to be able to pay a *holder* and receive a discharge, and the maker does not want to be drawn into a dispute between P and A. Payment and discharge can be prevented only if P, the party with the claim, (1) posts security or **indemnity** for M, or (2) gets an injunction against payment.[42]

Payment at maturity does *not* result in a discharge if it is made in bad faith or with knowledge that the holder acquired by theft or acquired through a thief. However, bearer paper could be stolen and still be negotiated to an HIDC. If this happens, payment to an *HIDC* who innocently acquired through a thief is a discharge even though this fact is known to the payor at the time of payment.[43]

Finally, no discharge results if payment is inconsistent with the terms of a restrictive indorsement.[44] Assume that P indorses a note issued by M as follows: "Pay to A upon completion of contract #61384, [signed] P." If A presents this instrument to M for payment at maturity, M must take reasonable steps to determine that the contract has been completed. If it has not been completed, payment to A will not discharge M from liability to P.

You will recall, however, that intermediary banks and payor banks that are not also depositaries are only affected by the restrictive indorsement *of their transferor*. In the situation described above, these banks would not have to be concerned with P's restrictive indorsement.[45]

indemnity
an absolute obligation to pay for another's loss

---

[41] UCC 3–603(1).   [42] UCC 3–306(d).   [43] UCC 3–603(1)(a).   [44] UCC 3–603(1)(b).

[45] UCC 3–206(2), 4–205(2). See pp. 376–77.

tender (verb)
to proffer, make available

Tender of Payment

Tender or offer of full payment *at maturity or at a later time* discharges the tendering party *only to the extent* of all subsequent liability for interest, costs, and attorney's fees.[46] A tender *before maturity* has no effect, unless the terms permit a party who is liable on the instrument to accelerate payment and avoid the running of interest. For example, a note may provide that the maker promises to pay "on or before" the due date.

If the holder refuses tender of payment by a party (M, maker, for example), any party on the instrument who has a right of recourse against the tendering party (M) is fully discharged.[47] On an instrument issued by M and indorsed from P to A to H, H's refusal of M's tender completely discharges P and A because H had a chance to get his money and refused to take it.

The primary party on a time instrument makes tender if he is ready and able to pay at every place designated at maturity. Tender of payment of a domiciled note or draft—one payable at a bank—can be made at maturity if funds are available at that bank and instructions have been given to pay.[48]

Cancellation and Renunciation

A holder may discharge the liability of any party on the instrument in any manner apparent on the face of the paper or the indorsements.[49] Since this discharge is in the nature of a gift, no consideration is necessary.

The holder who is discharging a party from further liability may do so by intentionally cancelling the instrument or the party's signature.[50] The holder may renounce his or her rights either in a signed writing which is delivered to the party being discharged or by surrender of the instrument to that party.[51] Neither cancellation nor renunciation affects the title to the instrument unless it is surrendered.[52]

recourse
a right to resort to some one or thing

collateral
property subject to a security interest UCC 9–105(1)(c)

Impairment of Recourse or of Collateral

Assume that M issued P a $1,000 note that was subsequently indorsed to A and, finally, to H. If M dishonored at maturity and A was held secondarily liable to H on the indorsement contract, A could normally expect to seek reimbursement from P. After all, P was the one who got him into this fix to begin with.

However, what if H released or discharged P? Is A left to seek recovery against M alone? M, remember, already refused to pay once, and he is likely to refuse again. Does it seem fair then for H, acting unilaterally and without A's consent, to defeat A's initial expectation of falling back on P?

No! One's gut reaction is that this is not fair, and the Code reenforces this conclusion.[53] A is fully discharged if H releases P. However, if H released P and *reserved his rights against A* at the time P was discharged, A would remain liable to H but A would be entitled to recourse against P.[54] The basic thought to keep in mind is that A's right to seek reimbursement from prior parties cannot be jeopardized or destroyed by the unilateral conduct of H. In the following case the holder's undue extension of time of payment on a note discharged the nonconsenting accommodation co-maker on the note.

Facts

Adamson, defendant, was an accommodation co-maker of a $13,000 negotiable promissory note that was in default. The loan was for the mushroom business of Wick, Adamson's son-in-law. Originally the Holcomb State Bank, plaintiff, would not make the loan to Wick. Then the Bank president suggested that Adamson sign as co-maker, which he did. On the note was handwritten, "For use in Wick's Mushroom Business," and "This is Wick's Note & Adamson is co-signer." The Bank credited the money to the mushroom company account. Adamson did not receive any of the proceeds from the loan.

---

[46] UCC 3–604(1).   [47] UCC 3–604(2).   [48] UCC 3–604(3).

[49] UCC 3–605(1)(a).   [50] UCC 3–605(1)(a).   [51] UCC 3–605(1)(b).

[52] UCC 3–605(2).   [53] UCC 3–606(1)(a).   [54] UCC 3–606(2)(c).

When the note came due, Wick paid the interest but not the principal. Later, Wick entered into an agreement with the bank on a four month extension of the note, but Adamson refused to sign the extension form. On the note's default, plaintiff bank sued the defendant on the note. The trial court gave judgment for plaintiff bank, and defendant appealed.

Decision
Reversed, for the defendant Adamson.

Reasoning
Under UCC 3–601(a)(1), an agreement by the holder bank to suspend the right to enforce a promissory note against the maker, without the consent of the accommodation co-maker, defendant, and without an express reservation of rights against him, discharges the accommodation co-maker from liability.

Holcomb State Bank v. Adamson, 438 N.E.2d 635 (Ill. 1982).

This principle holds true in situations where H releases collateral security that A was depending on as well. Modify the M to P to A to H hypothetical to the extent that M pledges valuable goods, jewels, stocks, or commodities (or mortgages property) as security for the note. If H releases this security without the consent of A, or of P, they are discharged to the extent of their injury or loss. If $500 worth of security was **pledged** or mortgaged to strengthen the note, A or P would be discharged to that extent if H released or surrendered the security. Once again, the reason for this rule is that H cannot unilaterally inflict harm or alter the contract of those parties who precede him.

pledge
the possessory security interest in bailed goods acquired by the bailee when there is a bailment for the purpose of security

Reacquisition of the Instrument by a Prior Party

Suppose that D drew a check payable to the order of P. The check was then negotiated by the indorsement of A, B, and C to P. A, B, and C are discharged because, on dishonor, they are liable to P, the holder, who as payee is, in turn, liable to them. In this way, persons who are liable to another, who then becomes liable to them, are spared the problem of circuity of action.

Summary Statement

1. When an instrument is *presented* by a holder to a maker, acceptor, or drawee for *payment* at maturity, or for *acceptance* at or prior to maturity, the instrument is *dishonored* if it is not paid or accepted within the deadline. Presentment for *payment* should be made on the due date or, if the instrument has been accelerated, within a reasonable time after acceleration. Presentment for *acceptance* must be made on or before maturity. *Any other presentment*—i.e., presentment of an instrument without a due date—must be made within a *reasonable time* after date or issue or after a secondary party becomes liable.

2. A reasonable period of time depends on the type of instrument, usage of trade, and the facts of the particular case. For an *uncertified check* drawn and payable in the U.S., a reasonable period of time is presumed to be *thirty days from issue* with respect to the *drawer's* liability and *seven days from indorsement* for a *secondary party's* liability. Failure to make a proper presentment, unless excused, will *fully* discharge *indorsers.* The drawer, acceptor, or maker of an instrument *payable at a bank* may be *fully or partially discharged* if the drawee-payor bank becomes insolvent during the delay depending on the extent of such insolvency.

3. Once an instrument has been dishonored, the *holder* must send notice of dishonor to secondary parties by midnight of the *third* business day following dishonor; *for banks,* the period is trimmed to midnight of the *next banking day.* Notice may be given in any reasonable manner, written or oral, which sufficiently identifies the instrument. It is effective if *sent* within the deadline even though it is never received. Failure to give proper notice, unless excused, will *fully* discharge *indorsers;* the drawer, maker, or acceptor of an instrument payable at a bank may be fully or partially discharged if the drawee-payor bank becomes insolvent during the delay, depending on the extent of such insolvency.

4. Protest, made in the presence of an authorized official, is a formal way of preserving proof of presentment, dishonor, and notice of dishonor. It is required on "international" or "foreign" drafts.
5. A party is discharged from all liability on an instrument by any act or agreement that would discharge a simple contract, e.g., payment to a holder at maturity. If a person reacquires an instrument, *all intervening parties* are discharged from liability to the reacquirer; intervening parties will *not* be liable to subsequent holders, but they will be liable to subsequent HIDCs *unless* their indorsements are cancelled.
6. No discharge under Article 3 is effective against a subsequent HIDC unless the HIDC has notice of it at the time he takes the instrument. To be effective, payment or satisfaction must be made to a *holder* or the holder's authorized agent. The discharge is available even though payment is made with knowledge that some party has a claim of ownership on the instrument unless, prior to payment, the party with the claim either (a) secures or indemnifies the one seeking a discharge, or (b) gets an injunction against payment. Payment at maturity will not result in a discharge if it is made with knowledge that the holder acquired by theft or through a thief (unless the holder has the right of an HIDC). Neither will payment at maturity amount to a discharge if it is inconsistent with the terms of a restrictive indorsement.
7. Tender of full payment at or after maturity discharges the tendering party from liability for interest, costs, and attorney's fees. If the holder refuses a proper tender, all parties who had a right of recourse against the one making tender are discharged.
8. A *holder* may discharge the liability of any party by intentionally cancelling the instrument or the party's signature. If the holder releases a previous signatory against whom some intervening party has a right of recourse, the release will have the effect of discharging the intervening party as well, *unless* the holder reserves rights against the intervening party. In the event that the holder does reserve such right of recourse against the intervening party, the intervening party retains his or her original right to seek recovery against the one that the holder discharged. Similarly, if the holder releases collateral that a party on the instrument had access to as security for the party's original obligation on the instrument, that party will be discharged to the extent of injury or loss caused by such release.

In the following case note how the court held that, when the holder of a note impaired the collateral security for the note without the consent of the co-makers of the note, since the note did not indicate that either of them was an accommodation co-maker surety for the other, the impairment did not discharge them from their liability as co-makers—primary parties absolutely liable on the note.

United States v. Unum, Inc.
658 F.2d 300 (5th Cir. 1981).

Politz, Circuit Judge. The Small Business Administration (SBA) filed suit to collect the balance due on a promissory note executed by Unum, Inc., and Lance W. Dreyer. Defendants-appellants admitted the obligation, but claimed a discharge from liability because the SBA had unjustifiably impaired the collateral securing the debt by releasing its lien to a third-party purchaser for $1,000. The district court rejected the defense of unjustifiable impairment, and this judgment was affirmed on appeal.

Unum and Dreyer purchased three Lockheed Constellations from the SBA that it had acquired in a foreclosure sale. The sale was financed by a $61,000 note that Unum and Dreyer issued to SBA, and secured by chattel mortgages on the planes. One of these planes was eventually seized and auctioned off by the Anchorage International Airport to pay for delinquent space rental and tie-down fees.

Aviation Specialties was high bidder at the airport auction sale. It purchased the plane for $3,670.00, the amount of the fees, subject to SBA's chattel mortgage. Later, for payment of $1,000.00, the SBA released its mortgage on the plane and credited the money to the original note. Aviation Specialties, meanwhile, made $20,000.00 improvements to the plane.

The United States filed suit on the note. Unum and Dreyer admitted the debt but advanced an affirmative defense claiming discharge from the obligation to the extent of the fair market value of the sold airplane. They predicated their defense on UCC Section 3-606, arguing that the SBA's release of its lien for $1,000 unjustifiably impaired the collateral:

(1) The holder discharges any party to the instrument to the extent that without such party's consent the holder

* * *

(b) unjustifiably impairs any collateral for the instrument given by or on behalf of the party or any person against whom he has a right of recourse.

At first blush, this section appears to provide a defense. However, a maker of a note, as opposed to a surety, is not entitled to invoke this defense.

This interpretation of 3-606 is soundly based. The maker of a note is always primarily responsible for the debt with no recourse except against co-makers. Sureties, whether accommodation makers or indorsers, are only secondarily liable; they retain a right of recourse against the primary obligor. Fairness dictates that if the risk a surety has agreed to undertake is increased through impairment of the securing collateral by the person to whom payment is due, the surety should be discharged to the extent of the impairment.

In the present case, the face of the note reflects that Dreyer and Unum are both makers. There is no evidence that Dreyer was an accommodation maker. Consequently, they may not seek relief under Section 3-606.

Affirmed for the Small Business Administration.

Questions and Case Problems

1. Bermes was required by state law to file his accident claim with the Industrial Commission within one year after *final payment* for his injuries under an insurance policy. The insurance company drew a draft to the order of Bermes which he received on May 3 and which was honored or paid in cash on May 6. He filed his claim with The Industrial Commission on May 4 of the next year. Did he file in time? [*Consolidated Freightways v. The Industrial Commission,* 269 N.E.2d 291 (Ill. 1971)].

2. The defendant, New House Products, Inc., offered to make part payment at maturity of a promissory note that it had issued to the payee, Commercial Plastics. The offer was rejected. Commercial then instituted this suit for the entire amount of the principal, interest, and attorney's fees. What was the effect of New House's tender? [*New House Products, Inc. v. Commercial Plastics and Supply Corp.,* 233 S.E.2d 45 (Ga. 1977).]

3. Two promissory notes payable to Beermann "Quality" Fertilizers, defendant, were executed on October 2, 1967 by the maker, David Vavra. Each of the notes provided on the face that "the makers, sureties, and guarantors of this note hereby severally waive presentment for payment, notice of nonpayment, protest, and notice of protest, and diligence in bringing suit against any party thereto and consent that time of payment may be extended without notice thereof." The notes were indorsed in blank by the defendant and transferred before maturity by the payee to the plaintiff bank for their full value. The payee, Beermann Brothers, is a defendant.

    Payment was not made at maturity, and Vavra executed two extension notes to the plaintiff which set maturity *21 days longer than the original period.*

    Does this extension have any effect on the liability of defendant-payee, Beermann Brothers? [*Citizens State Bank v. Beermann Brothers,* 198 N.W.2d 458 (Neb. 1972).]

4. Glover and Ferguson, partners, signed a ninety-day $20,000 note to the plaintiff-payee bank, National Bank of Commerce of the Pine Bluff. Before the note was due, Ferguson bought Glover's partnership interest. Glover informed the bank that Ferguson was assuming all partnership obligations. Glover further related that he did not want the note extended nor would he sign a renewal.

Five months later Ferguson was discharged in bankruptcy, and the bank proceeded against Glover for the balance. Glover *alleged* that the bank agreed not to sue Ferguson and that this had the effect of discharging him (Glover) from any further liability under UCC 3–606(1)(a). Glover further *alleged* that the bank was estopped from pursuing him because Ferguson's checking account on several occasions exceeded the overdue and unpaid balance and the bank failed to off-set against it. Result? [*Glover v. National Bank of Commerce of the Pine Bluff,* 529 S.W.2d 333 (Ark. 1975).]

5. Security Pacific National Bank (Security), plaintiff-depositary bank, brought this action against Associated Motor Sales (A.M.S.), payee, to recover on overdrafts of $188,000 caused by the dishonor of $312,000 in checks by various payor banks which A.M.S. had deposited with Security. A.M.S. defends on the basis that the checks were not timely dishonored.

   Security's evidence of dishonor consisted of copies of returned checks with payor bank stamps of dishonor, of the deposit ticket accompanying each deposit, and of Security's written notice of dishonor to payee-A.M.S. Security's assistant cashier Olga Skoro also declared that she was present when Mr. Levine, president of A.M.S., was advised of the returned checks within one day after they were ''bounced'' back to Security. Has Security given proper notice within the prescribed time? [*Security Pacific National Bank v. Associated Motor Sales,* 106 Cal.Rptr.App.3rd 171 (Cal. 1980).]

6. The plaintiff secured a judgment on a promissory note executed by the defendants, Paul W. McAtee and McAtee Builders, Inc. and the defendant, Paul McAtee, appealed. The note was secured by a mortgage executed by the defendant, McAtee Builders, Inc., on real property owned by McAtee Builders, Inc. Paul McAtee's defense was that he was discharged from his obligation because the plaintiff, without Paul McAtee's consent, released the mortgage given by McAtee Builders. The relevant statutory authority, UCC 3-606 provides as follows:

   (1) The holder discharges any party to the instrument to the extent that without such party's consent the holder

   (b) unjustifiably impairs any collateral for the instrument given by or on behalf of the party or any person against whom he has a right of recourse.

   Result? [*Christensen v. McAtee,* 473 P.2d 659 (Or. 1970).]

7. Mrs. Fischer indorsed a $2,000 check payable to the drawer and drawn on Clayton Bank. Nevada State Bank cashed the check for the payee/drawer and initiated collection through Valley Bank the same day. Ninety days later Valley Bank notified Nevada Bank that the check had been dishonored because the original was lost in transit. Nevada Bank immediately debited Mrs. Fischer's account by $2,000 and notified her of the payor bank's dishonor. It was apparent that one of the several banks in the collection process had violated its midnight deadline in giving notice of the dishonor. Had that bank acted timely, Mrs. Fischer would have learned in a reasonable time that the check had been dishonored. Is Mrs. Fischer liable as an indorser? [*Nevada State Bank v. Fischer,* 565 P.2d 332 (Nev. 1977).]

8. M issued a negotiable instrument to P for $100. P raised the amount to $200 and presented it to M for payment at maturity. M detected the alteration and refused to pay any amount. Is M liable to P for the original $100?

9. M issued a negotiable promissory note payable to the order of P for $800. P negotiated to A, and the instrument was subsequently negotiated to B, to C, then back to A, and finally to H. H did not qualify as an HIDC, however, because he received the instrument as a gift. At maturity, M refused to pay, and H gave timely notice to all indorsers. B and C claim that they have been discharged by A's reacquisition. Result? Would your response be the same if H qualified as an HIDC?

10. In *United States v. Unum, Inc.,* 658 F.2d 300 (5th Cir. 1981),[55] why did the court conclude that release or impairment of the collateral did not relieve defendants of liability on the note?

---

[55] See pp. 430–31.

Ethics and Business Law in Part 5
Commercial Paper

Introduction

This end-of-Part discussion, like the others in this book, is designed to encourage students to begin forming personal beliefs about what is right or wrong conduct in business. The discussion here builds on the material in the first end-of-Part discussion on pages 58 to 69; you may find it helpful to review that.

This material has several goals. The "sampling of ethical issues" section immediately following is designed to help you see the range of ethical issues associated with this area of the law. The in-depth discussion is intended to provide you with a background for forming your own beliefs about a single very important ethical issue in business. The problems at the end of this Part are designed to build your skill in ethical analysis while exploring further the in-depth issue.

A Sampling of Ethical Issues in Commercial Paper

Holder in Due Course Doctrine
The holder in due course (HIDC) doctrine is a core concept of commercial paper law. At first blush, the ethical character of this doctrine appears mysterious, difficult to perceive. In effect, this doctrine deprives a maker or drawer of commercial paper of the ability to assert personal defenses against a holder in due course. Thus, if you issued a check to a local retailer as payment for living-room furniture, and the retailer negotiated the check to its wholesaler who is an HIDC, you would have to pay the check even if you did not receive the furniture from the retailer. This is because non-delivery of the furniture is "failure of consideration," only a personal defense. This may appear very unfair.

But notice that both you and the wholesaler have done nothing wrong. It is the retailer who has broken a promise. Therefore, as between you and the wholesaler, the moral weight of the claims is about equal. The effect of the holder in due course doctrine is to shift the burden to one of these innocent parties, the maker or drawer of the instrument on the one hand, or the HIDC. In doing this, the law advances the interests of the majority by making commercial paper similar to currency, by making it easy to collect on the note or draft, so people will more readily accept commercial paper. This benefits almost everyone by making it easier for transactions to occur. In effect, the maker or drawer is required to first pay the note or draft, and then sue persons like the retailer for breach of contract.

But sometimes the innocent maker or drawer gets stuck. If the retailer has gone into bankruptcy, or disappeared, or died, the innocent drawer or maker may never see the furniture and never get the money back. Thus, this party pays a price to benefit everyone else who enters into commercial paper transactions. Do you think it is ethical for our legal system to cause injury to innocent makers or drawers so that the whole system works better? Is there any other realistic alternative?

Commercial Paper Time Limits
Another ethical issue in commercial paper law is associated with the *time* requirements for certain actions. If commercial paper is to play a role similar to currency, then the delays associated with the paper must be minimized. Therefore, an unexcused delay in

presenting an instrument will discharge any indorser thereon. Similarly, payment or acceptance of a check by a bank must occur within one business day or the instrument is deemed to be dishonored. Notice of dishonor must be given by the holder of the instrument within three business days or indorsers are discharged. Similarly, banks are not required to honor checks more than 6 months old.

These rules in effect punish those who are tardy in the performance of their commercial paper obligations. Sometimes the punishment is significant. Clearly, the goal is to speed the flow of commercial paper and make it more like currency. But in order to do this the law sometimes imposes time limit penalties on parties who are innocent of any wrongdoing except tardy action. In an ethical sense, these persons are sometimes sacrificed so that the whole system can operate more effectively. Do you think it is ethical to impose disproportionate penalties on a few individuals to benefit the many others who participate in the commercial paper system? Do you think it is ethical to punish for time delays those who are unaware of these time requirements?

In-Depth Discussion of a Basic Issue: Order and Ethics

While *negotiable* paper is often made "to the order of," here we use the word "order" in a different sense. In the following discussion, "order" refers to that characteristic of the law which produces stability, predictability, and consistency.

Order is the idea that societies need peace, stability, and predictability in important legal, business, and political matters.

Order and Arbitrariness

In many instances laws designed to create order also create some amount of arbitrariness. Thus, to achieve order, we have created the arbitrary rule that we must drive on the right side of the road. Laws aimed at creating order sometimes seem designed only to develop a predictable procedure, and usually one which is easily enforceable. For example, the law that oral stop orders are good for only 14 calendar days seems quite arbitrary. Anyone would have a difficult time arguing that 14 days is good while 13 or 15 days are bad or wrong. What is needed is an arbitrary standard, one which is easily enforced. For many persons, the arbitrary attribute of this and similar laws deprives them of their legitimacy and thus they don't comply. The 55 mile per hour speed limit is another example of a law with an arbitrary component.

Positive Law: Legitimacy Based on Order or Power

In the first end-of-Part discussion, we stated that positive law has as its philosophic goal the creation of order. However, not all thinkers seek to justify positive law by the fact that it usually generates order.

Some positive law thinkers believe that natural law and historical law do not provide bases for judging the legitimacy of laws. In this view, the only standard for judging legitimacy is whether or not a law has gone through the law making process of the government in power. Sometimes this jurisprudence is expressed as "might makes right." Because the government has the power to put you in jail, you must obey its laws. And *under this jurisprudence,* the laws which promote slavery, apartheid, and Hitler's holocaust are entirely just. To a very large extent, this is a view of the law as divorced from morals. Because this positive law, justified only by power, is arbitrary, it is easy to confuse it with positive law justified by order. Arbitrariness is an attribute common to both.

Natural Law: Order as an Ethical Principle

Order itself is definitely a moral good, something essential to organized society and civilization itself. Unless we are able to understand when the law seeks order, the law can seem to us unfair, harsh, arbitrary, and not deserving of our loyalty and compliance. To think about the law in philosophical ways, we need to be able to weigh the importance of order in various legal situations. Sometimes we need to compare order with other principles of justice and with the desires of those governed. Unless we develop this skill we can misunderstand the law and not see what it is really trying to accomplish.

If we see that order is essential to society, then it is very easy to assert that order is a part of the natural law, resting on the moral ideas that we ought to treat others equally, and in predictable ways.

Order can also flow from other ethical principles. For example, the requirement that we not harm others can lead us to require that everyone drive safely. And this may result in a law like the 55 mile per hour speed limit. As we think about such a law, it is important to see its constituent parts. Thus, the basic thrust of this law is aimed at avoiding harm while another part identifies an exact speed (55 mph). This latter part is clearly arbitrary but it allows the law to be easily enforced. Thus, while a small part of this law is arbitrary, the major thrust of it is aimed at creating order and promoting safety.

In a similar way, the UCC requires that commercial paper, to be negotiable, must identify a "sum certain." Without this requirement, parties would be uncertain of their obligations and courts would be entangled in prolonged disputes over the intent of the parties. Therefore, the requirement promotes order.

The requirement that we drive on the right side of the road is often cited as a law which is completely arbitrary and is only justified because it produces only order. Hans Kelsen, an important legal philosopher, has articulated the idea that arbitrariness, used to achieve order, can be justified by non-positivist thinking. Kelsen used the Kantian procedure of making a rule universal to evaluate whether we are obligated to obey laws which appear arbitrary. He concluded that not obeying cannot be made universal; if everyone disobeyed every arbitrary law, there would be chaos.

Order and Other Legal Goals

Legal Imperfections and Order

Because laws which promote order often must be arbitrary they sometimes create opportunities for injustice. People can sometimes take advantage of an arbitrary law to gain unfair advantage. Recall that the statute of frauds makes some contracts unenforceable because they cannot be proved by a writing. If one party to a transaction knows this and the other doesn't, then for practical purposes one party thinks the contract can be enforced against each party, while the other party knows that the contract is unenforceable against either party. Thus, the arbitrary character of this law allows it to be used to obstruct justice in some instances.

Solving Ethics Problems

Like the other end-of-Part discussions in this book, this one presents problems for you to consider. These problems have three goals. The first is to give you the opportunity to further explore the in-depth issue. The second goal is to give you experience in ethical reasoning about the law and about related management problems. The third goal is to let you see how thinking critically about the law can increase your ability to make ethical decisions. To facilitate this, the problems begin by asking you to analyze the law for its ethical content and then shift to looking at related problems in managerial ethics.

For a discussion of the ethical roles of markets and the law, and examples of the four styles of ethical reasoning—egoism, utilitarianism, Kant's philosophy, and religious ethics—read the business ethics material at the end of Part 1.

Problems

1. Review the case of *K & K Manufacturing, Inc. and Knight v. Union Bank* on pages 417–18. Is this case really about the negligence of Knight in failing to discover that his trusted bookkeeper, Garza, was forging his signature? Or is it more about creating an arbitrary rule for determining who shall bear a loss, the bank or the customer, when there has been a forgery and both parties are innocent? What style of ethical reasoning can be used to justify this law?

2. Suppose you are a banker with two customers, one large and one small. The small customer is more of a nuisance to the bank than the valued customer. A conflict arises between the two customers, and the small customer places an oral stop payment order on a check for $15,000 he issued to the large customer just before leaving for a three week vacation in Europe. You know that the large important customer will be appreciative if you do not tell the small customer that the oral stop order is only good for 14 calendar days. Ought you to tell the small customer about the effect of the oral stop order? Do you think it is ethical to use laws which promote order by using arbitrariness, to your own advantage?

3. Suppose someone is negotiating to you a check which you intend to negotiate to another party. Because you are familiar with commercial paper law, you know you can avoid liability for some indorsement warranties by asking that the check be indorsed in blank so that your indorsement is not required for further negotiation of the check. Do you think this conduct is ethical? What ethical reasoning supports this conduct?

4. If you were the manager of a large work crew of 65 laborers who were required to punch a time clock each morning, would you be justified in creating a rule which stated that those more than 6 minutes late would be docked an hour's pay? Would such a managerial policy be justified by a desire to create order? What ethical reasoning can you articulate which justifies such a managerial policy?

PART **6** Secured Transactions, Bankruptcy, and Insurance

28. **Creation of Security Interests in Personal Property**
    The concept of security interests in tangible (e.g., goods) and intangible (e.g., accounts receivable) personal property, including fixtures; creation and perfection of security interests and the legal effect of perfection.

29. **Enforcement of Personal Property Security Interests; and Suretyship**
    The priorities of security interests in personal property among secured parties and subsequent purchasers of the collateral. Remedies of a secured party on the debtor's default. The law of suretyship, and its creation, frequency of occurrence, and importance in business transactions.

30. **Bankruptcy under the Bankruptcy Reform Act of 1978**
    A current analysis of the 1978 federal bankruptcy law, as amended in 1984, with its extensive changes in format, substance, procedure, and judicial administration.

31. **General Principles of Insurance Law**
    The reason for the creation of the concept of insurance, the kinds of property and life insurance, and the great importance and place of insurance in our everyday business and private lives. Insurance company organization, governmental monitoring and regulation of the insurance industry, and the rights and duties of the insured and the insurer.

32. **Life, Fire, and Automobile Insurance Law**
    The kinds and extent of life and property insurance policy coverage and exclusions.

Summary

In this Part we will examine four legal topics that are important to most individuals and businesses—secured transactions involving personal property, suretyship, bankruptcy, and insurance. A secured transaction is one in which an interest in personal property, such as a car, is given as collateral for a loan. While we hope that bankruptcy law will not affect you individually, the law is extremely important to businesses forced to write off many thousands of dollars worth of debts discharged in bankruptcy.

Insurance involves the shifting of risks from one party, the insured, to another party, the insurer. Insurance has become so important that it has an impact on virtually every personal or business transaction, from birth (which is covered by health insurance) to death (which is covered by "life" insurance).

Business ethics as it relates to the text material in this Part is considered at the end of the Part.

28 Creation of Security Interests in Personal Property

After you have read this chapter, you should be able to:

1. Describe a secured transaction.
2. List the three major types of collateral.
3. Define after-acquired property and future advances.
4. Describe the floating lien.
5. List two methods used to *create* a security interest.
6. Describe the four methods used to *perfect* a security interest.
7. Discuss the rules regarding perfection that apply to multi-county and multi-state transactions.

Introduction

As consumers increase their use of credit in making purchases, the law of Secured Transactions becomes especially important. In most consumer transactions the creditor will want something more than the mere promise of the consumer to repay the debt. Many creditors will require the consumer to give the creditor a security interest in property which the consumer owns. Some creditors will require, additionally, the promise of another person, a surety, to pay the debt on the consumer's default. In this chapter and the next we will discuss these two credit transactions: the personal property secured transaction, and suretyship.

Although secured transactions are important for the consumer, they are especially important for the person in business. This is because a person in business will often enter into a secured transaction as a debtor in acquiring goods and will enter into a second secured transaction as a creditor in selling goods to a consumer.

The law of secured transactions is at times technical and complicated. However, it is important to keep in mind as you read these chapters that this material is especially important to the person who is not an attorney. This is because, in most cases, the person entering into a secured transaction does not retain an attorney but, instead, acts as his or her own attorney. While this practice is not recommended, it is often necessary because secured transactions are so common that it would usually be impractical and expensive to retain an attorney.

Definitions

After graduating from college, Rufus decided to buy a new car. The average price of new cars was $11,000; however, Rufus had only $4,000 in his savings account. Consequently, Rufus went to First Bank and borrowed $7,000, giving the bank a note in that amount. At this point Rufus becomes a *debtor* and First Bank is a *creditor*.

If the bank required nothing more than the note from Rufus, the law of secured transactions would be unnecessary. However, creditors like the bank usually do want something else: they want the right to repossess Rufus' property if Rufus fails to make his agreed payments or if he goes into bankruptcy. In this case the bank would want such an interest, called a **security interest,** in Rufus' car. A creditor with a security interest is called a **secured party,** and the whole transaction would now be described as a **secured transaction.**

In many cases the creditor extends credit in order that the debtor may purchase the property which is then used as **collateral** for the loan. This is called a **purchase money security interest.** In Rufus' case, he has given the bank a purchase money security interest in the car because he used the loan to purchase the car. If he had borrowed money to buy the car but had given the bank a security interest in only his speedboat, the security would *not* be a *purchase* money security interest.

Source of Law

The law of secured transactions is found in Article 9 of the Uniform Commercial Code. Because the UCC has been adopted in all states but Louisiana, the law of secured transactions is generally uniform throughout the United States.

The UCC provides that Article 9 applies "to any transaction (regardless of its form) which is intended to create a security interest in personal property or fixtures. . . ." (Section 9–102(1)(a).) This statement has two major consequences. First, if the creditor asks for real estate as security instead of personal property, the transaction is not a secured transaction but, instead, is a *mortgage*. Mortgage law is derived from real estate cases and statutes and has been discussed in Part 10, Real Property.

---

security
a creditor's interest in specific property, or in the obligation of a third person, as assurance for the performance of the debtor's obligation

security interest
"an interest in personal property or fixtures which secures payment or performance of an obligation" UCC 1–201(37)

secured party
a creditor with a security interest

secured transaction
a transaction used to create a security interest

collateral
the personal property subject to a security interest

purchase money security interest
"a security interest is a 'purchase money security interest' to the extent that it is (a) taken or retained by the seller of the collateral to secure all or part of its price; or (b) taken by a person who by making advances or incurring an obligation gives value to enable the debtor to acquire rights in or the use of collateral if such value is in fact so used." UCC 9–107

The second consequence is that, regardless of what a transaction is called by the debtor and the creditor, it is a secured transaction if the parties intend to create a security interest in personal property or fixtures. For example, a lease of goods with an option to buy for a nominal consideration may be, in substance, a secured transaction.

Types of Collateral

The personal property which is subject to a security interest is called *collateral*. The types of personal property which may be used as security are either *tangible* (e.g., goods) or *intangible* (e.g., accounts receivable) and may be broken down into three major categories: tangible goods, intangibles, and paper. These categories will become important later when we discuss methods of "perfecting" a security interest and priorities among several secured parties.

Tangible Goods
Goods are generally defined as tangible things which are movable when the security interest is created or which are fixtures. Specifically, there are four types of goods.

Consumer goods.

Consumer Goods. *Consumer goods* are goods which are used or bought for use primarily for personal, family, or household purposes. (UCC 9–109(1).) If Rufus purchased his car primarily for a personal or family purpose, the car would be considered a consumer good.

Equipment.

Equipment. Goods which are used or bought for use primarily in business (including farming or a profession) are classified as *equipment* (UCC 9–109(2)). If Rufus was a travelling salesman and used the car primarily for travelling to customers, the car would be equipment.

Inventory.

Inventory. Goods which are held for sale or lease are considered to be *inventory*. If Waldo were a car dealer and bought his car for purposes of resale, the car would be inventory.

Farm products.

Farm Products. Crops, livestock, and supplies used or produced in farming operations which are in the possession of a debtor engaged in farming fall under the heading of *farm products*.

Intangibles
Account. Two types of intangibles, one specific and one general, can be used as security. The specific type of intangible is the **account**. Accounts include the *account receivable,* a right to payment for goods which have been sold or leased or for services which have been rendered. Accounts also include a right to payment under a contract even where the right has not yet been earned by performance. (UCC 9–106.)

account
a right to payment under a contract

1. Assignment of Accounts. Because of the increasing use of accounts as security for loans, the UCC allows accounts to be assigned freely. The UCC policy is reflected in UCC 9–318(4), which permits **assignment** even when the contract between the debtor and creditor prohibits it.

assignment
the transfer of a contract right

The **assignee** must bear in mind two factors which will affect the ability to collect an account. *First,* unless the debtor has made an enforceable agreement not to assert claims or defenses, the rights of the assignee are subject to such claims and defenses. *Second,* the debtor is authorized to make payments to the creditor until receiving notification of the assignment *and* notice that payment is to be made to the assignee. Unlike the common law discussed in chapter 13,[1] the UCC provides that notice of assignment alone is not enough to change the debtor's obligation to pay the creditor; such notice must include a demand that future payments be made to the assignee.

assignee
the person to whom a contract right is transferred

---

[1] See above, pp. 183–84.

General Intangibles. The other type of intangible is **general intangibles** which includes all personal property other than the property which we specifically list in this section. For example, goodwill, copyrights, patents, and trademarks would be considered general intangibles because they do not fall within the other categories.

general intangibles
a catchall category covering a variety of personal property

Paper

In many cases a right is evidenced by a piece of paper, and the paper may be used as a security. The UCC specifically provides that a security interest may be created in the following three types of paper.

Chattel Paper. Chattel paper is defined as a writing or writings which evidence both a monetary obligation and a security interest in or lease of specific goods. (UCC 9–105(1)(b).) Suppose, for example, that Rufus, instead of financing his car at the bank, had financed the purchase at the dealership under the type of security arrangement called a **conditional sale,** whereby the seller reserves title to the car until the buyer completes making payments. Under this arrangement Rufus would sign both a note and a contract, and these writings together are chattel paper.

conditional sale
a sale in which the seller reserves title until the buyer completes payments; now called a secured transaction under UCC 9

In many cases the dealership cannot wait three or four years for Rufus to pay because the dealership needs cash to purchase more automobiles. Consequently, the dealer might go to a bank, borrow money, and give the bank a security interest in the chattel paper. The bank would then have a security interest in the dealership's security interest, and, if the dealer defaulted in his payments to the bank, the bank would then begin receiving payments from Rufus.

Instruments. An **instrument** is any writing, apart from a security agreement or lease, which evidences a right to payment of money. One common type of instrument is the *negotiable instrument* (covered in Part 5, Commercial Paper), which includes drafts, checks, and notes. Another instrument is the *certificated security,* which is a share or other interest in property or in an enterprise of the issuer which is represented by an instrument in bearer or registered form and which is commonly dealt in on securities exchanges or commonly recognized as a medium for investment. (UCC 8–102(1)(a).)

instrument
a writing which evidences a right to payment of money, including negotiable instruments, and also certificated securities

Documents of Title. A document of title is a document which entitles the person in possession of it to hold and dispose of the document or the goods it covers as the person sees fit. Common examples are the *bill of lading,* a document issued by a carrier which evidences receipt of goods, and a *warehouse receipt,* a receipt issued by a person in the business of storing goods.

Proceeds and After-Acquired Property

In addition to the categories of goods, the security interest might also cover proceeds and after-acquired property. **Proceeds** cover whatever the debtor receives upon selling, exchanging, or otherwise disposing of the collateral. Although there are a number of specific rules governing proceeds, the general rule is that a security interest in collateral also covers identifiable proceeds when the debtor disposes of the collateral. For utmost protection, however, a secured party should file a financing statement, described below, which specifically covers proceeds.

proceeds
what the debtor receives when he disposes of collateral

After-acquired property refers to property acquired after the debtor and creditor have entered into a security agreement. UCC 9–204 specifically provides that the security agreement may cover after-acquired collateral. The section also provides that the security agreement may include future loans made by the secured party. The combination of these two provisions allows a secured party to create a **floating lien** to cover present and future advances and acquisitions with the agreement.

after-acquired property
(in security) property acquired after the security agreement is made

The floating lien is especially useful when the collateral is inventory. Suppose, for example, that Alpha Appliance Store borrows cash from First Bank and gives to the bank a security interest in present and future inventory. The security agreement also covers

floating lien
a security device which covers after-acquired property and future advances

Chapter 28: Creation of Security Interests in Personal Property future advances by the bank and proceeds. One day Alpha sells a new stove to a customer in exchange for cash and an old stove is taken as a trade-in. Alpha then borrows money from the bank and purchases another new stove from a manufacturer. There is no need for the bank to create a new security interest because, under the floating lien concept, the original agreement covers the old stove (proceeds), the new stove (after-acquired property), and the new loan (future advances).

Creation of Security Interests

In order to acquire rights in the debtor's property, the creditor must create a valid security interest. However, in order to create rights that are superior to those of other creditors and to ensure that he or she is paid first when the property is sold, the creditor must *perfect* the security interest. First we will discuss *creation* of the security interest, and then we will discuss *perfection* of the security interest.

Form

Two methods are used to *create* a security interest. By the *first method,* the creditor and debtor might enter into a **security agreement**, an agreement which must, under the Code,[2] (1) be in writing, (2) be signed by the debtor, and (3) contain a description of the collateral.

> **security agreement**
> "an agreement which creates or provides for a security interest" UCC 9–105(1)(l)

The following excerpt from a security agreement has been taken from the following Massachusetts case:

[The debtor does] hereby grant, sell, assign, transfer and deliver to Grantee the following goods, chattels, and automobiles, namely: The business located at and numbered 574 Washington Street, Canton, Mass. together with all its goodwill, fixtures, equipment and merchandise. The fixtures specifically consist of the following: *All contents of luncheonette including equipment such as: booths and tables; stand and counter; tables; chairs; booths; steam tables; salad unit; potato peeler, a U.S. Slicer; range; case; fryer; compressor; bobtail; milk dispenser; silex; 100 Class air conditioner; signs; pastry case; mixer; dishes; silverware; tables; hot fudge; Haven Ex.; 2-door stationwagon 1957 Ford A57R107215* together with all property and articles now and which may hereafter be, used or mixed with, added or attached to, and/or substituted for, any of the foregoing described property.

The most common legal question regarding such agreements involves the question of whether the description of the collateral is sufficient, as is illustrated in the following early case.

Facts
On November 18, 1960, Firestone & Co., defendant, made a loan to Kozy Kitchen, and Kozy Kitchen signed the security agreement quoted above, giving Firestone a security interest, of which Firestone filed notice the same day. On November 19, 1960, National Cash Register (NCR), plaintiff, delivered a cash register to Kozy Kitchen under a conditional sales contract, and a month later NCR filed notice of its security interest. Kozy defaulted on its loan and on its sales contract. Firestone then took possession of the cash register and sold it. NCR sued Firestone for the tort of **conversion,** claiming that it should receive the proceeds from the sale because Firestone's security agreement does not mention the cash register.

> **conversion**
> the tort of intentional interference with another's right to possession, control, and dominion of a chattel

Judgment was rendered for the plaintiff in the trial and appellate courts, and the defendant appealed.

Decision
Reversed, for defendant, Firestone.

Reasoning
This case is one of first impression for this court under the UCC. Firestone's security agreement was broad enough to cover the cash register. "All contents of luncheonette" includes the cash register. Also, at the end of the agreement there is reference to after-acquired property, which would include the cash register.

National Cash Register Company v. Firestone & Co., Inc., 191 N.E.2d 471 (Mass. 1963).

---

[2] UCC 9–203(1)(a).

The *second method* used to *create* a security interest is the **pledge**, whereby the secured party actually takes *possession* of the collateral.[3] In most cases the pledge is not used, because the debtor wants to keep possession of the property for the debtor's own use and enjoyment. However, the pledge is the preferred method of creating a security interest when paper is used as collateral.

pledge
the possessory security interest in bailed goods acquired by the bailee when there is a bailment for the purpose of security

Requirements

Regardless of whether the security agreement or pledge is used, the UCC imposes three requirements which must be met if the security interest is to *attach* to the collateral—that is, if it is to be enforceable by the creditor. *First,* the debtor and creditor must agree that it will attach. This requirement would automatically be met if a security agreement was used. *Second,* the creditor must give value. **Value,** generally, means *any consideration* sufficient under contract law. Under the UCC, value is also specifically defined[4] to include a creditor's *binding commitment to extend credit* and a creditor's taking security for *a pre-existing claim*. *Third,* the debtor must have rights in the collateral although, as we discussed above, the security interest may attach to after-acquired property.[5]

value
(UCC, in part) any consideration sufficient to support a contract, or a commitment to extend credit, or a past debt

Perfection of Security Interests

When the three requirements for attachment have been met, the secured party may enforce his interest against the debtor. But often another party besides the debtor may claim an interest in the collateral. Suppose, for example, that Heidi purchased a refrigerator under a conditional sales contract from Bill's Appliance Store and that Bill's security interest attached to the refrigerator. Heidi used the refrigerator in her grocery store, thus making the refrigerator *equipment.* In each of the following three cases a third party might claim an interest in the collateral. (1) Heidi might sell the refrigerator to a friend who had no knowledge of Bill's security interest. (2) Another creditor might obtain a lien on the refrigerator, that is, a legal right in the refrigerator as security for the debt. (3) Heidi might go into bankruptcy and the trustee in bankruptcy would claim that the value of the refrigerator should be divided evenly among all her creditors.

In each of the three cases Bill's interest would be subordinate to that of the third party, even though the interest would be enforceable against Heidi alone. In order for Bill to gain rights superior to such third parties, he must give **constructive notice** (notice by law) to them that he has a security interest. This is called **perfection of a security interest.** *Four* common methods are used to *perfect* security interests.

constructive notice
knowledge of a fact presumed or imputed by law

perfection of a security interest
when the creditor complies with Article 9 of the Uniform Commercial Code's requirements for perfection

Financing Statement

The *first* and the *most common method* used commercially to *perfect* security interests *is to file* a short document called a **financing statement** either locally in a county office, such as the registrar's office, or centrally with the Secretary of State. The place of filing depends on the type of collateral and on the law in each particular state. For instance, in some states if an automobile is used as collateral, the financing statement should be filed locally unless the automobile is considered to be inventory, in which case there must be a central filing. Regardless of the place of filing, the financing statement is effective for *five years* from the date of filing; and after that time it lapses, unless a *continuation statement* is filed before the lapse.

The formal requirements for the financing statement are simple. The statement must: (1) list the names and addresses of the debtor and of the secured party, (2) be signed by the debtor, and (3) contain a statement describing or indicating the types of the collateral. Today, the following fairly well accepted Uniform Commercial Code form of financing statement (see figure 28.1) is recognized countrywide with the name of the particular state indicated at the top of the form.

financing statement
a document which is filed by the secured party to give public notice of the security interest in personal property

---

[3] UCC 9–203(1)(a). See p. 447.   [4] UCC 1–201(44).   [5] UCC 9–204(1)(2).

Figure 28.1   State of Colorado, Uniform Commercial Code, Financing Statement

Secured parties often, through ignorance of the law or laziness, attempt to use a security agreement as a financing statement or the financing statement as a security agreement. Two different documents should be used because the requirements differ. For instance, a security agreement cannot be used as a financing statement because the financing statement contains the additional requirement that the addresses of the parties be indicated. And the financing statement does not meet the requirements for a security agreement, as illustrated by the following early case.

Facts

On February 21, 1962 American Card Company executed a note for $12,373 payable to H.M.H. Co. American Card and H.M.H. both signed a financing statement which was properly filed. However, a written security agreement was never signed. Receivers for American Card contend that the claim of H.M.H. as creditors is not a valid security interest because the financing statement did not contain a grant of a security interest by American Card. H.M.H. claims that the financing statement may serve as the security agreement. The lower court held in favor of the Receivers, and H.M.H. appealed.

Decision
Affirmed, for the Receivers.

Reasoning
While it is possible for one document to serve as both the financing statement and the security agreement, the separate requirements for each must be met by the document. The financing statement in question did not contain the required agreement by the debtor that H.M.H. be granted a security interest.

American Card Co. v. H.M.H. Co., 196 A.2d 150 (R.I. 1963).

Going back to our original example of Bill's sale of a refrigerator to Heidi, if Bill had filed a financing statement covering Heidi's refrigerator, Bill would be giving constructive notice to the world of his security interest in the refrigerator. It is important to note the practical implication of this rule: when you purchase property from someone outside the normal course of business, you should first check to determine whether the property is subject to a security interest. If there is a perfected security interest, the secured party of the seller may repossess the property from you, an innocent buyer. However, the secured party will be protected only when the financing statement is filed and indexed properly. In the following case the financing statement was filed under the wrong name.

Facts
Kenston Corporation sold dry cleaning equipment under a conditional sales agreement to Matthew R. Leichter, who did business under the name Landman Dry Cleaners. Leichter signed a financing statement "Landman Dry Cleaners, By: Matthew R. Leichter." Kenston filed the financing statement under the name of Landman Dry Cleaners, not under Leichter's name. When Leichter went into bankruptcy, the trustee in bankruptcy claimed that the security interest was not properly perfected.

Decision
For the trustee.

Reasoning
Filing under a trade name alone is a major error. Later creditors looking under "Leichter" would not find the financing statement filed under "Landman."

In re *Leichter,* 471 F.2d 785 (1972).

Pledge
A *second method of perfection* is the *pledge,* whereby the secured party takes *possession* of the goods. The pledge gives clear notice to the world of the security interest by virtue of the secured party's possession.

The pledge obviously cannot be used when one of the three types of collateral, namely intangibles, is used as security because by its very nature there is nothing to physically possess. On the other hand, the pledge in most cases must be used when the collateral is *paper* because of long-standing commercial practices. For instance, the UCC provides that, with few exceptions, a security interest in instruments can be perfected only by the secured party taking possession. A security interest in the other two types of paper—namely, chattel paper and negotiable documents—may be perfected by filing; but to be absolutely safe, the creditor should still take possession because certain purchasers are given priority over the secured party who has perfected by filing.

Automatic Perfection
In cases where a person purchases *consumer* goods and gives a creditor a *purchase money security interest* in those goods, the secured party's security interest will be perfected *automatically.* However, it is still a safe practice for the secured party to perfect the security interest by filing a financing statement because, if the statement is not filed, a *buyer* from the consumer takes the goods free of the security interest if: (1) the buyer buys without knowledge of the interest; (2) the buyer pays value; and (3) the buyer buys for his personal use. For example, in the situation where Bill sold the refrigerator to Heidi, Bill's security interest would be automatically perfected if, instead of equipment, the refrigerator was a consumer good bought for Heidi's personal use. Since there is perfection, Bill's security interest would prevail over other *creditors* and the *trustee in bankruptcy.*

But if Heidi sells the refrigerator to a friend who has no notice of Bill's security interest and who buys for the buyer's own personal, family, or household purposes, the friend will take the refrigerator free and clear of the security interest. In the following case the purchase money security interest in consumer goods was not defeated by the debtor's gift of the collateral since the donee did not give value.

Facts
Rike-Kumber sold a diamond ring to Nicolosi on July 7, 1964. Nicolosi signed a purchase money security agreement, but a financing statement was not filed. Nicolosi gave the ring to his fiancee and later declared bankruptcy. Now Rike-Kumber claims the ring.

Decision
For Rike-Kumber.

Reasoning
Rike-Kumber's security interest was automatically perfected. The fiancee did not give value and, therefore, is not a buyer for value.

In re *Nicolosi,* 4 UCC Rptr. 111 (Ohio, 1966).

Certificate of Title Laws

In most states there are certificate of title laws which cover automobiles and may also cover other vehicles such as trailers, mobile homes, boats, and farm tractors. If goods are subject to such laws, filing a financing statement is not effective to perfect a security interest; instead, the security interest is perfected by notation on the certificate of title.

Multi-County and Multi-State Transactions

In our mobile society it is common for debtors to move from one county to another or from one state to another, taking with them the property that is subject to a perfected security interest. When such a move takes place, does the security interest continue to be perfected? When the move is *from one county to another in the same state,* the states follow two different approaches. In some states if the financing statement was originally filed properly, it continues to be effective in the new county to which the debtor moves. In other states the secured party must file a copy of the financing statement within four months in the new county; otherwise the security interest becomes unperfected.

When the move is *from one state to another state,* there are two general UCC rules which apply, although these rules are subject to a number of exceptions. *First,* under section 1–105, the parties may agree that the laws of a particular state or nation are to govern their rights and duties if the transaction bears a reasonable relation to such state or nation. *Second,* there is a provision governing perfection to the effect that perfection is governed by the law of the state where the collateral is located when the *last* event occurs which is necessary to perfect the interest. This event will usually be filing the financing statement. If the security interest in the collateral is perfected under the law of that state and then the collateral is moved to another state, it will remain perfected if, *within four months,* the secured party perfects the interest in the *new* state. The UCC also has detailed rules governing: accounts (e.g., accounts receivable); general intangibles (e.g., patents, copyrights); mobile goods of a type which are equipment, or inventory for lease by the debtor to others, which are *normally* used in *more than one jurisdiction* (e.g., trucks, rolling stock, airplanes, commercial harvesting machinery); goods covered by a certificate of title (e.g., automobiles); chattel paper; and minerals. With respect to accounts, general intangibles, and such mobile goods, the law applicable is the law of the state *where the debtor is "located,"* which is the debtor's place of business if the debtor has one, or at the debtor's chief executive office if the debtor has more than one place of business, otherwise at the debtor's residence. Ascertaining the applicable law is important when you, as a secured creditor, must file a financing statement or when you must determine whether a previous secured creditor has filed one.

Summary Statement

1. A secured transaction is one in which a debtor gives to a creditor an interest in property owned by the debtor.
2. There are three major classifications of collateral: (a) tangible goods, (b) intangibles, and (c) paper.
3. The Uniform Commercial Code specifically provides that the security agreement may cover after-acquired property and future advances. This allows a secured party to create a floating lien with one security agreement.
4. A security interest may be created by (a) security agreement or (b) pledge.
5. The most common methods used to perfect a security interest are the pledge and filing a financing statement.

In the following case the court discusses the general policy of the UCC regarding description of collateral in a security agreement.

In re Amex-Protein Development Corporation
504 F.2d 1056 (1974)

Per Curiam. Plant Reclamation claimed a security interest in personal property held by Amex-Protein, which was in bankruptcy. Plant Reclamation claimed that the security interest was created by a promissory note which included the following language: "This note is secured by a Security Interest in subject personal property as per invoices." The invoices referred to in the note were submitted by Plant Reclamation when it sold equipment to Amex-Protein. Plant Reclamation also filed a financing statement listing the equipment.

per curiam
by the court, all the judges

The appellate court adopted the opinion of the District Judge:

I. Did the Promissory Note "Create or Provide for" a Security Interest?

"Security interest" means an interest in personal property or fixtures which secures payment or performance of an obligation. . . .

No magic words or precise form are necessary to create or provide for a security interest so long as the minimum formal requirements of the Code are met. . . . This liberal approach is mandated by an expressed purpose of the secured transaction provisions of the Code:

"The aim of this Article is to provide a simple and unified structure within which the immense variety of present-day secured financing transactions can go forward with less cost and with greater certainty. . . .

"The Article's flexibility and simplified formalities should make it possible for new forms of secured financing, as they develop, to fit comfortably under its provisions. . . ." Comment to UCC and Cal.Com.C. section 9101.

Accordingly, the promissory note herein qualifies as a security agreement which by its terms "creates or provides for" a security interest.

II. Adequacy of Description of the Collateral

There is nothing in the Uniform Commercial Code to prevent reference in the security agreement to another writing for particular terms and conditions of the transaction. There is also nothing in the Uniform Commercial Code to prevent reference in the Security Agreement to another writing for a description of the collateral, so long as the reference in the security agreement is sufficient to identify reasonably what it described. In other words, it will at times be expedient to give a general description of the collateral in the security agreement and refer to a list or other writing for more exact description. In addition, the security agreement could itself consist of separate parts, one a general description of the obligation secured and the rights and duties of the parties, and the other a description of the collateral, both such writings being signed by the debtor and stated to comprise a single security agreement or referring to each other. [Footnotes omitted.] Id. section 109 at 387–388. . . .

The judgment is affirmed [for Plant Reclamation].

Questions and Case Problems

1. The comptroller of Fibre Glass Boat Corporation sent the following letter to a creditor, Teleflex: "Pursuant to our telephone conversation, please find a duly executed copy of a financing statement received from your company, wherein the Fibre Glass Boat Corporation agrees to guarantee all inventory used in the production of boats, limited in the amount of fifteen thousand dollars, in order to cover all merchandise that may be purchased from your company." Teleflex later claimed that this letter created a security interest. Is Teleflex correct? [In re *Fibre Glass Boat Corporation,* 324 F.Supp. 1054 (1971).]

2. Alpha purchased a pair of skis from her roommate Beta. Alpha agreed to make monthly payments on the skis over a period of six months and entered into an oral agreement with Beta that, in the event of a default on any payment, Beta could repossess the skis. Alpha later defaulted. May Beta legally repossess under their security agreement? Why?

3. Willard signed a security agreement giving Popular Finance Company (PFC) a security interest in "1 2-pc. living room suite, wine; 1 5-pc. chrome dinette set, yellow; 1 3-pc. panel bedroom suite, lime oak, matt. & spgs." The agreement provided that this property was to be kept at Willard's residence and the address was stated in the agreement. When Willard later declared bankruptcy, it was claimed that the security interest was invalid because the description of the property was insufficient. Is the description sufficient? [In re *Drane,* 202 F.Supp. 221 (1962).]

4. Elmer borrowed money from Friendly Finance (FF) and gave FF a security interest in all of his lawn equipment. FF filed a financing statement covering the equipment. Later Elmer sold his lawn mower to his next door neighbor, Rufus, who bought the mower in good faith, paid value, and was unaware of FF's security interest. If Elmer defaults in his loan payments, may FF repossess the mower from Rufus? Why?

5. Mitchell and Donelson were partners operating a clothing store under the name of Marby's Fashions. Marby's borrowed $25,000 from a bank and signed a security agreement covering the store's equipment. Marby's also signed a financing statement that covered equipment, inventory, and accounts receivable, and the bank filed the statement. Does the bank have a perfected security interest in Marby's equipment, inventory, and accounts receivable? [*Mitchell v. Shepherd Mall State Bank,* 458 F.2d 700 (1972).]

6. A creditor took a security interest in the crops of a farmer. The security agreement included the kind of crops, the names of the farms where the crops were grown, and legal descriptions of the farms. A financing statement was filed that covered the farmer's crops "which are now growing or are hereafter planted, grown, and produced on land owned or leased by debtor in Cherokee County, Kansas." Later the farmer sold the crops to a third party, who claimed that the financing statement was insufficient to perfect a security interest in the crops and, therefore, the creditor had no lien on the crops. Is the third party correct? [*Chanute Production Credit Ass'n. v. Wier Grain & Supply, Inc.,* 499 P.2d 517 (Kan. 1972).]

7. Excel Stores, Inc., a Connecticut corporation engaged in the business of selling toys and other merchandise, purchased six cash registers on credit from National Cash Register Company (NCR). NCR took a security interest in the cash registers. However, in signing the security agreement, the treasurer of Excel Stores inadvertently used the name "Excel Department Stores," and this name was also used on the financing statement. Does NCR have a perfected security interest? [In re *Excel Stores, Inc.,* 341 F.2d 961 (1965).]

8. A bank agreed to lend money to a company, and the company signed a security agreement covering all existing and future accounts receivable. The bank filed a financing statement which described the collateral as "Accounts Receivable." The company later went into receivership, and the Receiver claimed that the security interest was unperfected as to accounts receivable which arose after the date of the financing statement because the financing statement did not mention *future* accounts receivable. Is the Receiver correct? [*South County Sand & Gravel Co. v. Bituminous Pavers Co.,* 256 A.2d 514 (R.I. 1969).]

9. The United Bank of Denver loaned $2,400,000 to Smith Enterprises and took a security interest in Smith's "inventory, accounts, contract rights, equipment and machinery." Later, when a bankruptcy petition was filed against Smith, the bank claimed that the security interest covered Smith's eggs and chickens. Is the bank correct? [In re *K. L. Smith Enterprises, Ltd., Debtor,* 2 B.R. 280, 28 UCC Rptr. 534 (Colo. 1980).]

10. In the case of In re *Amex-Protein Development Corporation,* 504 F.2d 1056 (1974),[6] the court concluded that a promissory note could be used to create a security interest. What Code policy is served by this liberal approach?

---

[6] See p. 449.

29 Enforcement of Personal Property Security Interests; and Suretyship

After you have read this chapter, you should be able to:

1. Determine which of two secured parties has priority when both have perfected by filing a financing statement.
2. Discuss the rights of a secured party against a mortgagee who claims a fixture.
3. List the procedure which a secured party will follow after the debtor's default.
4. Define the three parties involved in a suretyship arrangement.
5. Explain the distinction between strict surety and guarantor, and the importance of this distinction under the statute of frauds.
6. Describe how the suretyship contract is created.
7. Explain the types of defense which are available to a surety.
8. Discuss the three options available to a surety after paying the creditor.

Introduction to
Enforcement of Personal Property Security Interests

In chapter 28 we examined three basic questions relating to the law of secured transactions: (1) What type of collateral may be used as security? (2) How is a security interest created? (3) How is a security interest perfected? However, even when a creditor meets all the requirements for creating and perfecting a security interest, it is possible that other creditors will have better rights to repossess the collateral when the debtor defaults. We will begin this chapter with a discussion of the rules which determine which creditor has priority upon the debtor's default. These rules are litigated frequently and are very important because a creditor can lose thousands of dollars in collateral if a court determines that the creditor does not have priority. Once a determination is made as to which creditor has priority, there is one key security question left to consider: What right does the creditor with priority have to repossess and to sell the collateral?

After concluding our examination of the law of secured transactions, we will look at another type of security arrangement, suretyship. This arrangement—under which the creditor obtains the promise of another person, a surety, to repay the obligor's debt (or to perform some other obligation of the obligor)—requires an understanding of the law of Suretyship.

Priorities

The problem of priorities.

George owned a $1,000 stereo. In need of cash, he borrowed $2,000 from Andy and gave Andy a security interest in the stereo. Later, having spent the $2,000, George borrowed another $2,000 from Kay and gave Kay a security interest in the same stereo. If George defaults on both of his loan payments, who has the right to repossess the stereo, Andy or Kay? As noted in chapter 28, a secured party with a perfected security interest has priority over unperfected security interests. Thus, if Kay had perfected her security interest and Andy did not perfect, Kay would in most cases be entitled to the stereo. Many cases, however, cannot be resolved this easily, and the decision will depend on additional factors. Eight common fact situations which raise priority questions will be discussed below.

Creditors Perfect by Filing

If both creditors have perfected their security interests by filing a financing statement, *the first secured party to file has priority*.[1] This rule illustrates the importance of filing the financing statement as soon as possible, even before the loan is made. For example, on June 1 Andy promised to lend George $2,000, took a security interest in the stereo, and filed a financing statement. On July 1 Kay loaned George $2,000, took a security interest in the stereo, and filed a financing statement. On August 1 Andy made his promised loan. Who has priority? The answer under the above rule is that Andy has priority because he filed his financing statement first, even though he did not lend the money until after Kay's loan. Before extending credit on July 1, Kay should have checked the public records and, if she had done so, would have discovered that the stereo was already subject to a security interest.

Creditors Perfect Using Different Methods

If each creditor uses a different method of perfection, the creditor who has either filed a financing statement or perfected first has priority.[2] Let us suppose that on June 1 Andy loaned $2,000 to George and took a security interest in George's stereo. On July 1 Kay

---

[1] UCC 9–312(5)(a). [2] UCC 9–312(5)(a).

loaned $2,000, took a security interest in the stereo, and perfected by taking possession—that is, by pledge. On August 1 Andy filed a financing statement covering the stereo. Kay would have priority because her interest was *perfected* first, even though her security interest was not the first to attach. Andy's security interest had *attached* on June 1, but his *perfection* did not occur until August 1.

Neither Creditor Perfected

If neither Andy nor Kay had perfected his/her security interest, the secured party who first created a security interest will prevail.[3] This rule will be rarely used because as soon as a secured party realizes that other security interests exist, he or she will immediately attempt to perfect his or her security interest, thus making the case subject to the above rules.

Fixtures

fixture
a chattel which, under real estate law, has become permanently attached to realty and thus ceases to be a chattel and becomes part of the realty; it still can be used as collateral for a security interest

A **fixture** is property which, although at one time personal property, has been attached to real estate in such a way that it is legally considered to be part of the real estate, although it still may be used as collateral in a secured transaction. Because it is legally part of the real estate, a new type of creditor now enters the picture: a creditor with a mortgage covering the real estate. To illustrate, we might assume that our debtor, George, lives in a house that he has mortgaged to First Bank. If he builds his stereo system into a wall in such a way that it is considered to be a fixture, the stereo, as part of the real estate, becomes subject to the mortgage of First Bank. If the mortgage is foreclosed, First Bank can claim not only the house and land but also the stereo.

The situation becomes complicated when George gives a creditor, *Second Bank,* a security interest in the stereo to secure another loan. If George defaults on both loans, who has priority: the creditor with a mortgage or the secured party? Although the rules governing this situation are very complex and subject to exception, it may be generally stated that to gain priority over a creditor with a recorded mortgage, the secured party must have a *purchase money security interest, and* the security interest must be perfected by a fixture filing *before* the goods become fixtures or *within ten days after* they become fixtures. A **fixture filing** is a filing of the financing statement in the office where mortgages are recorded.[4]

fixture filing
filing a financing statement in the office where mortgages are recorded

Noninventory Financing

Noninventory financing is especially important to a person in business and to creditors who lend to businesses. To illustrate a typical situation, we might assume that George runs a business—a restaurant—and that he borrows $2,000 from First Bank, giving First Bank a perfected security interest in all of the *equipment* which he now owns or may acquire later. As discussed in chapter 28, after-acquired property may be included in a security agreement. George then buys a stereo on credit from a local store, Loud Sounds, and gives Loud Sounds a security interest in the stereo. George uses the stereo to play music to customers. If George defaults on his payments to First Bank and to Loud Sounds, who has priority with regard to the stereo? In most cases, First Bank, with its prior, perfected security interest, prevails. However, there is a major exception which protects secured parties with a *purchase money security interest* such as that of Loud Sounds. If there is a purchase money security interest, the purchase money creditor has priority if it *perfects within ten days after the debtor receives possession of the collateral.*[5]

---

[3] UCC 9–312(5)(b).   [4] UCC 9–313.   [5] UCC 9–312(4).

Inventory Financing

One might think initially that inventory financing should be treated in the same manner as equipment financing; that is, the secured party with an interest in *after-acquired property* should have priority over all other creditors except for the purchase money security interest. However, in practice, inventory financing differs from equipment financing in that inventory is bought and sold more frequently than equipment and, to finance the continuing purchase of new inventory, lenders often will automatically make periodic loans to a business. Loans made under this arrangement are secured by a security agreement covering both future advances and after-acquired inventory, as noted in our discussion of the floating lien in chapter 28. A secured party with such a perfected security interest will have priority over later security interests in after-acquired inventory, *except* a *subsequent* secured party who: (1) acquired a *purchase money security interest* in the same after-acquired inventory; (2) *perfected* the security interest *before* the debtor receives possession; and (3) gave *written notice,* within certain specified times, to the holder of the prior conflicting security interest *if that holder had previously filed a financing statement,* that he has, or expects to acquire, a purchase money security interest in the after-acquired inventory of the debtor.[6] Since the earlier secured party now has notice, the latter will not make the usual periodic advance, knowing that the loan is not required since the purchase has been financed under the later purchase money arrangement.

To illustrate, George now operates a stereo store and has given First Bank a perfected security interest covering all present *and future inventory.* George later purchased a truckload of RCA stereos on credit, giving RCA a purchase money security interest in the stereos. In order to gain priority over the earlier perfected security interest of First Bank, RCA must do two things *before delivering* the stereos: (1) give notice to First Bank of its intention to acquire a security interest in the stereos, and (2) perfect its security interest in the stereos.

Buyers in Ordinary Course of Business

If a customer, Mary, visited George's stereo store, she might be unaware that the RCA stereos in the store are subject to the security interests of both First Bank and RCA. Does this mean that, if Mary buys a stereo, it might be repossessed by one of the creditors if George defaults on his payments? Such a result would have a detrimental effect on commerce, so the UCC specifically provides that a **buyer in the ordinary course of business,** such as Mary, buys free and clear of security interests created *by the seller.* This protection extends even to a case where the security interest is perfected or the buyer knows of the security interest.[7] The buyer did not prevail in the following case.

buyer in ordinary course of business
"a person who, in good faith, . . . buys in ordinary course from a person in the business of selling goods of that kind. . . ." UCC 1–201(9)

bailment
a delivery of goods by a bailor to a bailee which are to be returned to the bailor or as the bailor directs in accordance with the bailment agreement

Facts
Chemical Bank, plaintiff, financed the purchase of a motorboat by Muller, defendant, who was not a boat dealer. The bank filed a financing statement. Muller later transferred the boat to Miller Yacht Sales, which sold it to a customer. Muller defaulted on his payments to the bank, and the bank sued Miller Yacht Sales for damages.

Decision
Judgment for the bank.

Reasoning
Miller Yacht Sales was not a buyer in the ordinary course of business because it purchased the boat from Muller, who was not in the business of selling boats.

Chemical Bank v. Miller Yacht Sales, 413 A.2d 619 (N.J. 1980)

---

[6] UCC 9–312(3).   [7] UCC 9–307(1).

Bailee's Liens

In many cases the interest of a secured party will conflict with that of a **bailee** who has repaired or improved the collateral and who claims a **bailee's lien** in order to secure payment for services rendered and for materials supplied to the collateral. In such cases, a bailee *in possession* of the collateral and with a valid bailee's lien under the relevant state law, takes priority over a previously perfected security interest,[8] as is illustrated in the following case.

bailee
the person to whom goods are bailed

bailee's lien
the bailee's legal right to retain possession of the bailed goods as security for the obligation owing to the bailee, usually payment for the bailee's services and for materials supplied to the bailed goods

artisan's lien
a person's possessory lien on goods owned by another and improved at the owner's request

Secured party's rights on default.

Facts
Nelms, a defendant, borrowed money from the Gulf Coast State Bank, petitioner, in order to purchase a car, and the bank took a perfected security interest in the car. Later the car was damaged in an automobile accident and taken to an auto repair shop, also a defendant. After the car was repaired, Nelms did not pay the repair bill, and the repair shop claimed a bailee's lien on the car. Since Nelms' car payments were in arrears, the bank claimed possession of the car from the repair shop, which refused, asserting that its **artisan's lien** had priority over the bank's perfected security interest under the UCC.

The bank claimed that its perfected security interest had priority. The trial court held for the bank, the appellate court reversed in favor of the repair shop, and the bank appealed.

Decision
Affirmed, for the repair shop.

Reasoning
A bailee with a lien upon goods in its possession has priority unless the state lien law expressly provides otherwise. The Texas lien law did not change the UCC rule.

Gulf Coast State Bank v. Nelms, 525 S.W.2d 866 (Tex. 1975).

Rights of Secured Party on Default

When a debtor defaults in making payments, the secured party with priority will normally take two courses of action: (1) repossess the collateral and (2) either retain or sell the collateral.

Repossession

Dolly obtained financing from First Bank to purchase a new car and gave the bank a security interest in the car. Dolly parked the car every night in her driveway, which was her private property. One morning she discovered that the car was gone and, after calling the police, learned that the bank had repossessed the car during the night because she had missed two payments. Are such repossessions legal?

The answer is to be found in UCC 9–503 which provides: "Unless otherwise agreed a secured party has on default the right to take possession of the collateral . . . without judicial process if this can be done without breach of the peace." As interpreted by the courts, this allows a secured party to trespass secretly onto the debtor's property in the middle of the night in order to remove the collateral so long as there is no breach of the peace.

A **breach of the peace,** as defined by most courts, results from an act of violence or an act which is likely to produce violence. Using this definition, secured parties have been allowed to remove a car from a private driveway and an airplane from an open hangar. No breach of the peace occurred in the following case.

breach of the peace
a disturbance of public order by an act of violence, or by an act likely to produce violence, or which, by causing consternation and alarm, disturbs the peace and quiet of the community

Facts
The Bank of Babylon, defendant, entered into a security agreement covering property owned by Elwood Auto Parts, the debtor. The agreement gave the bank the right, on the debtor's default, to enter the debtor's premises and take away the property with or without legal process. After Elwood's default, the bank entered the premises, using a key obtained from a locksmith, and removed the property. Cherno, plaintiff, representing creditors of the debtor, sued the bank contending that the bank committed a breach of the peace by the way it removed the property.

---
[8] UCC 9–310.

Decision
This was not a breach of the peace.

Reasoning
Even though the bank might have committed a "breaking" into the premises, the bank did not commit an act of violence and did nothing to disturb the peace and quiet of the community. Also, in this situation the use of the key was not likely to result in violence.

Cherno v. Bank of Babylon, 282 N.Y. S.2d 114 (N.Y. 1967).

In addition to self-help repossession, a secured party might also commence an action to obtain a court order that the debtor turn over collateral. Because court proceedings involve state action, the due process clause of the federal Constitution requires that the debtor be given notice of the court hearing and an opportunity to present a defense before the property is seized. In a few states, courts have decided that even self-help repossession involves state action, and these courts require a court hearing before the collateral is seized.

After Repossession

A secured party who has possession of the collateral through self-help or a court order has two options. First, the secured party may sell the collateral at a public or private sale. The sale must be commercially reasonable with regard to the method, manner, terms, place, and time of sale. Furthermore, although subject to specific exceptions, such as a sale of perishable goods, the secured party must give reasonable notification of the sale to the debtor and to other secured parties who have sent written notice (to the repossessing secured party) claiming an interest in the collateral. If the sale of the collateral results in a surplus after secured parties have been paid, the debtor is entitled to the surplus. But if the proceeds are not sufficient to cover the secured debt, the debtor is liable for any deficiency.

The other option is for the secured party to keep the collateral in full satisfaction of the debt. This option will be used most frequently by a secured party when the collateral is worth more than the unpaid debt. In order to protect the debtor and prevent unfair enrichment of the secured party, the UCC provides that in most cases the secured party must send written notice to the debtor, and to other secured parties claiming an interest in the collateral, proposing to keep the collateral in satisfaction of the debt. If the debtor or another secured party objects within 21 days after the notice was sent, the repossessing secured party must sell the collateral. If no objection is raised, the secured party may keep the collateral in satisfaction of the debt.

Compulsory resale.

The UCC provides special protection for the debtor where the collateral is *consumer goods* and the debtor has paid *sixty percent* of the loan or of the price. In such cases, the creditor must obtain from the debtor a written, signed statement under which the debtor allows the creditor to retain the collateral. A creditor without this statement must sell or dispose of the collateral within ninety days after taking possession.

Introduction to Suretyship

On the day when he reached the age of eighteen and legally became an adult, Junior decided to purchase a used car from Dealer. Junior selected a car and signed a conditional sales contract whereby he was to make monthly payments to Dealer for two years. But Dealer decided that he wanted more than Junior's promise to repay the debt; he wanted some type of security to protect him in the event of Junior's default.

There are two common types of security arrangements used in business. One type is the secured transaction discussed above where the debtor gives the creditor a security interest in certain collateral. The other security arrangement, which may be used separately or in conjunction with the secured transaction, is **suretyship**. Under this arrangement another person—for example, Junior's Father—would also sign Junior's note and promise to pay the debt.

suretyship
a legal relationship in which one person (surety) and another person (principal, the debtor) are obligated to perform the same obligation to a third person (creditor) who is entitled to only one performance, and as between the surety and the principal the latter is to perform the obligation and is ultimately liable therefor

Definitions

principal
(in suretyship) the debtor in a suretyship arrangement

surety
a person who promises the creditor to pay the principal's debt or to perform his obligation on the principal's nonperformance

surety bond
a promise by a professional surety to pay if the principal defaults or commits a wrongful act

guarantor
a type of surety

guaranty
a type of suretyship

In security arrangements using a surety, there are typically three parties. The **principal** or *principal debtor* is the debtor, in our case Junior. The principal is indebted to the *creditor,* Dealer. The **surety** (Father in the above example) is a third party who agrees to become liable on the debt of the principal (Junior).

A very common business arrangement is the **surety bond** under which a professional surety promises to make payment if a principal defaults or commits a wrongful act. In many cases surety bonds are required by contract. For example, a person building a new office building might require the contractor to furnish a construction bond to cover a possible failure of the contractor to complete the contract or to pay the subcontractors. Other bonds are required by statute. These include bonds required of public officials, bonds required of fiduciaries such as the executor of an estate, and bail bonds.

In some states a distinction is made between two categories of surety: one is the *strict surety* and the other the **guarantor.** The strict surety is a *co-debtor* with the principal. For example, a son wants to buy an automobile on credit, but the seller will not sell to the son without the father as surety. Accordingly, the father and son sign the contract and promissory note for *their* purchase, on credit, of an automobile for the son, with the agreement between *them* that the son is to pay for the automobile. *As to the creditor seller,* the father and son are the *co-debtor purchasers; as between the father and son, the son is the principal* and *the father is the strict surety.* However, if the automobile had been sold to the son as the purchaser and the father agreed with the *seller* to be responsible for the son's payment and liable on his default, the father would be a guarantor, liable only on the son's default.

A guarantor is liable only in accordance with the terms of the suretyship contract. There are various types of **guaranty** differing only in their contract terms, two of which will be considered here.

The *absolute guaranty* is a contract that the guarantor will perform only on the principal's *default.* A common example is the "guaranty of payment," such as X's written statement to Z, "Extend credit to A, and if A does not pay, I will." At the maturity date, if A does not pay, Z can recover from X.

The *conditional guaranty* states a condition which must occur before the surety is liable to the creditor. A commonly used example is the "guaranty of collection," when the guarantor must pay only if the debt is *uncollectible*—that is, the creditor cannot collect it from the principal. It is uncollectible when the creditor has sued the principal, the resulting judgment cannot be paid, and the surety is notified of this within a reasonable time.

Statute of Frauds

The distinction between a strict surety and a guarantor is important under the statute of frauds. The contract of a strict surety is *not within that portion of the statute of frauds* which provides that a promise to answer for the duty (debt, default, or miscarriage—e.g., an employee's embezzlement of a firm's cash) *of another* is unenforceable without a proper writing. Since the strict surety is a *co-debtor* with the principal, *as to the creditor* they are both co-debtors and co-principals. The co-debtor strict surety does not condition its liability on the default by the other co-debtor principal. They are both liable to the creditor as co-debtor principals.

In contrast, the guarantor promises to pay or perform the principal's obligation *only on the principal's nonperformance* and, therefore, a contract of guaranty is within the statute and unenforceable without a proper writing. (S requests C to extend credit to D, stating that if D doesn't pay C then S will pay C. C then extends credit to D, who later defaults. S's contract with C is within the statute of frauds and is unenforceable unless there is a proper writing.[9]) The writing may be the signed contract itself, or a note or memorandum of an oral contract signed by the party to be charged with performance (the guarantor) or by that party's lawfully authorized agent.

The Suretyship Contract

A suretyship contract is created in the same manner as other contracts and must meet basic contractual requirements in addition to the statute of frauds, such as offer and acceptance, consideration, and legality. Contract law is covered in Part 2.

Surety's Defenses

Complete Defenses

Both the principal and the surety may have defenses against the creditor when the creditor seeks to enforce their contracts with him. There are the usual contract defenses (discussed in Part 2, Contracts) such as fraud, duress, coercion, and undue influence, which the principal and surety may assert against the creditor in their respective contracts. If Father is a *strict surety* with the principal Junior on a note signed by them for the purchase of a car from Dealer but Dealer never delivered the car, neither would be liable on the note because of failure of consideration—Dealer's failure to render the agreed consideration, namely, delivery of the car. If Father were a *guarantor,* he could also assert Junior principal's defenses in a suit against him by Dealer.

Complete defenses of the surety against the creditor.

It must be emphasized that all of the principal's defenses which are not personal to the principal are also available to the surety (guarantor). For example, assume that Dealer fraudulently induced Junior to buy the car. On Junior's default by his nonpayment, Father surety (guarantor) can assert the fraud if he is sued by Dealer.

There are a few contract defenses, however, which are personal to the principal and cannot be raised by the surety. These include the principal's discharge in bankruptcy, the principal's power of avoidance resulting from the principal's infancy or insanity, and the running of the statute of limitations on the principal's obligation.

There are special defenses which are unique to the suretyship arrangements. When the creditor and the principal agree to a *modification of their contract* without the consent of the surety, if the modification agreement is binding on them (e.g., there is consideration), *and* it would increase the possibility of the surety's risk, the surety is discharged from the suretyship obligation. However, all modifications will not result in discharge, as is the case in situations involving a *paid* surety, such as an insurance company surety.

The surety will also be discharged in cases where the creditor does not perform the suretyship contract—for example, by failing to mail copies of the principal's bills to the surety. Furthermore, the surety will be discharged when the principal's debt is paid or when a proper tender of payment is rejected by the creditor.

Partial Defenses

We have considered the surety's defenses which *completely discharge* the surety. However, there are some defenses which only partially discharge the surety. A few are:

Partial defenses of the surety against the creditor.

1. When the creditor has property as security as well as a surety and the creditor surrenders the property to the principal or wrongfully impairs its value, the surety is discharged only to the extent of the value of the surrendered property or of its impairment.
2. When the creditor releases one of various co-sureties without the consent of the others, thereby causing them to lose their contributive shares from the released co-surety in the event the principal defaults, the other co-sureties are discharged to the extent of the loss of such contributive shares.

---

[9] For a proper writing, see pp. 158–59.

3. When there is a guaranty of collection, if the creditor *delays* in collecting from the principal or *delays* in giving notice of uncollectibility to the surety so as to cause loss to the surety in the surety's effort to be reimbursed by the principal, the surety is discharged to the extent of such loss.

Surety's Rights

In cases where the surety has no defense or only a partial defense and must pay the creditor on the principal's default, there are four options available to the surety. *First,* the surety has the right of **exoneration.** The debtor may induce a person to become a surety for him by his express or implied *promise to the surety* that the debtor will perform his obligation to the creditor and, if the debtor should fail to do so, the debtor will make the surety whole for the surety's performance of his suretyship obligation. Should the debtor so promise and, on the debtor's nonperformance, the creditor legally seek to enforce the surety's obligation to him, the surety can obtain a court order compelling the debtor to perform his promise to the surety to the extent of the debtor's available assets. The surety is still liable to the creditor on his suretyship contract but, to the extent of the debtor's available assets, the surety can be exonerated, that is spared loss and inconvenience in the performance of his suretyship obligation. For example, John requests Frank to be surety on the purchase that John is to make from Henry, Frank becomes a surety, and then John defaults on his debt. When Henry sues Frank as a surety, Frank can obtain a court order making John's assets available to pay his debt to Henry.

Second, the surety is entitled to **reimbursement** from the principal for expenditures made by the surety in performance of the debtor's obligation. For instance, if Father as surety paid Dealer on Junior's failure to pay Dealer, Junior would be liable to Father for those payments.

Third, the surety is entitled to be subrogated to the rights of the creditor. With a **subrogation,** the surety steps into the shoes of the creditor and takes over all the creditor's rights to collect the debt. We might assume, for example, that Junior had given Dealer a security interest in his car. If Junior defaulted and Father paid off Dealer, Father would succeed to Dealer's rights, in this case the right to collect the debt and to repossess the collateral.

Finally, in cases where there are several sureties (co-sureties) for the same debt, the liability of the co-sureties is joint and several; that is, a creditor may collect from all co-sureties jointly, or may decide to sue and collect from only one of the co-sureties. If the creditor collects from less than all of the co-sureties, those who pay are entitled to **contribution** from the other co-sureties. If the co-sureties *have contracted together* to be co-sureties, their contract will provide how their respective contributive shares will be determined. If they have *not contracted together,* the contributive share of each co-surety is determined by the maximum liability of each co-surety. In the latter event, if each of the co-sureties is *liable for the same maximum amount,* then their contributive shares are equal. If each of the co-sureties is *not liable for the same maximum amount,* then the contributive share of each co-surety is determined by the *proportion* which that co-surety's maximum liability bears to the total maximum liability of *all* the co-sureties. (A is a co-surety with a maximum liability of $5,000, B for $10,000, C for $15,000. On the principal's default of her $10,000 debt, B paid the creditor $10,000. A's share of the liability is 5,000/30,000, B's is 10,000/30,000, and C's is 15,000/30,000 of the $10,000 paid by B. Thus, A's contributive share is 1/6 of $10,000, B's is 1/3 of $10,000, and C's is 1/2 of $10,000.)

Surety's rights against the principal.

exoneration
(in suretyship) the surety's right to have a court compel the debtor to perform his promise to the surety to perform the debtor's obligation to his creditor to the extent of the debtor's available assets.

reimbursement
(in suretyship) the surety's right to recover from the principal

subrogation
(in suretyship) the surety succeeds to the creditor's rights against the principal

Surety's rights against his co-sureties.

contribution
(in suretyship) the right of sureties who have paid the creditor to collect part of the payment from other sureties

Summary Statement

Enforcement of Personal Property Security Interests
1. When two or more creditors claim an interest in the same collateral and all creditors have perfected by filing a financing statement, the first creditor to file has priority.
2. A secured party will prevail over a mortgagee who claims a fixture if the secured party has a purchase money security interest and has perfected by a fixture filing either before the goods become fixtures or within ten days after the goods become fixtures.
3. A perfected security interest in *equipment* is subject to the priority of a purchase money security interest which has been perfected within ten days after the debtor receives the collateral.
4. A perfected security interest in *after-acquired inventory* has priority over later security interests, except as against a secured party with a purchase money security interest in the same after-acquired inventory, who has perfected the security interest before the debtor obtains possession, and who has given proper notice to the holder of the conflicting security interest.
5. Buyers in the ordinary course of business take property free from a previously perfected security interest in the property created by the seller.
6. Generally a bailee's lien has priority over a previously perfected security interest in the bailed goods.
7. After a debtor defaults, a secured party will (a) repossess the collateral through self-help or court order and (b) sell the collateral or, subject to certain limitations, keep the collateral in full payment of the debt.

Suretyship
8. Three parties are involved in a suretyship relationship: (a) a principal, who is the debtor; (b) a creditor; and (c) a surety who promises the creditor to pay the debt either as a co-debtor with the principal or as a guarantor on the principal's default.
9. A strict surety is a co-debtor with the principal on their contract with the creditor and the surety's contract is not within the statute of frauds. A guarantor's contract is within the statute.
10. A guaranty of collection is enforceable only when the debt is uncollectible.
11. All of the principal's defenses which are not personal to the principal may be asserted by the surety against the creditor on the principal's default.
12. Defenses personal to the principal are (a) the principal's discharge in bankruptcy, (b) the principal's power of avoidance resulting from the principal's infancy or insanity, and (c) the running of the statute of limitations on the principal's obligation.
13. Binding modification of the principal's contract by the principal and the creditor without the surety's consent, which increases the possibility of the surety's risk, discharges the surety.
14. The surety has partial defenses and is partially discharged by the creditor's (a) surrendering or impairing property security held by the creditor, (b) releasing a solvent and available co-surety without a reservation of rights, and (c) delaying either collection or in giving notice of uncollectibility to the surety on a guaranty of collection causing loss to the surety.
15. A surety who has paid the creditor is entitled to (a) reimbursement from the principal, (b) subrogation to the creditor's rights, and (c) contribution from other co-sureties.

In the following case the court considers the constitutionality of self-help repossession under the Uniform Commercial Code.

Frost v. Mohawk National Bank
74 Misc.2d 912 (N.Y. 1973)

Edward S. Conway, Justice. This is a motion by the plaintiff for a preliminary injunction and temporary restraining order enjoining the defendants during the pendency of the action from continuing to deprive plaintiff of the use and benefit of a certain 1971 Fiat automobile and for an order directing defendants to return it to the plaintiff.

Plaintiff purchased a certain 1971 Fiat automobile from Hickey Ford Sales on July 7, 1971. The purchase was financed by defendant Mohawk National Bank under a retail installment contract which called for 36 monthly installments of $55.45 each, commencing August 20, 1971 and ending on July 20, 1974.

After the plaintiff had failed to make the payments due for April and May under the installment contract, the defendant Mohawk National Bank repossessed the automobile through its agent, defendant Edward F. Dunleavy, by removing it from its parking place on First Street in Troy.

There is no longer any question but that where repossession is obtained through judicial process under the **replevin** statutes, a person must be afforded notice and an opportunity to be heard prior to any taking, except in extraordinary circumstances. . . .

In the opinion of this Court, the rationale of the Sniadach and Fuentes cases is that in the exercise of "due process" by the state, notice and an opportunity to be heard must be given where the object of the action is the taking of property in which the possessor has a significant property interest, except in extraordinary circumstances.

The Court has examined the retail installment contract in the instant case and finds that there is a clause which allows the seller, in the event of a default, the right without notice or demand, to enter upon any premises where the vehicle may be found and take possession of and remove the vehicle without process of law.

Section 9–503 of the Uniform Commercial Code provides in part:

> Unless otherwise agreed a secured party has on default the right to take possession of the collateral. In taking possession a secured party may proceed without judicial process if this can be done without breach of the peace or may proceed by action. . . .

Many text writers on the Uniform Commercial Code have expressed opinions that "self-help" under section 9–503 of the Code may very well be struck down under the rationale of *Sniadach v. Family Finance Corp.,* . . . and *Fuentes v. Shevin.* . . . However, they all make a distinction between "self-help" and replevin prior to a hearing even though both involve a "taking" of the debtor's property before any judicial determination of the validity of the taking. Most of them make a distinction when self-help repossession is authorized by a private contract and the consumer has contracted for the security interest.

It is the opinion of this Court that an agreement entered into in compliance with section 9–503 of the Uniform Commercial Code must be held to be legal, especially where the debtor has expressly authorized the "self-help" provisions of the contract. Such an agreement cannot be held to be unconscionable when such terms are expressly authorized by statute. To stretch the rationale of the Sniadach case and later cases following it to include a prohibition of "self-help" under a security agreement would require this Court to go beyond the point permitted by good reason under the circumstances of this case.

The motion of the plaintiff is therefore denied, and the order of this Court to show cause, dated June 6, 1973, is vacated.

replevin
a common law form of action to regain possession of specific chattels

---

Questions and Case Problems

Enforcement of Personal Property Security Interests

1. Burrows purchased livestock from Bailey on an installment sale arrangement. Burrows later borrowed $80,000 from Walker Bank, which took a perfected security interest in the livestock Burrows was purchasing. Bailey then filed a financing statement covering the livestock being sold to Burrows. Does the bank have a security interest that is prior to Bailey's interest? [*Walker Bank and Trust Co. v. Burrows,* 507 P.2d 384 (Utah 1973).]

2. Central Bank had a perfected security interest in "equipment now owned or hereafter acquired" by Galleon. Lewyn sold a machine to Galleon on credit, keeping title to the machine until Galleon made payment. The machine was delivered to Galleon, and Lewyn did not file a financing statement. Who has priority to the machine—Lewyn or Central Bank? Why? [*Galleon Industries, Inc. v. Lewyn Machinery Co., Inc.,* 279 So.2d 137 (Ala. 1973).]

3. Carol works for First Bank as a lending officer. Carol is considering making a loan to Disco Duds Clothing Store (DD) to enable the store to purchase a new stock of inventory, in which First Bank will take a security interest. However, Carol learns that Second Bank already has a perfected security interest in Disco's present and future inventory. Can First Bank gain priority over Second Bank's interest? If so, how?

4. National Shawmut Bank had a perfected security interest in a car owned by Wever. Wever sold the car to Hanson-Rock, an automobile dealer, who resold the car to Jones. Now National Shawmut wants to repossess Jones' car. May it? [*National Shawmut Bank of Boston v. Jones,* 236 A.2d 484 (N.H. 1967).]

5. Corbin Deposit Bank had a perfected security interest in Foreman's car. Foreman took his car to King, who was in the business of repairing cars, for repair work. Foreman did not pay King for the repair work, and King claimed a lien on the car, which was still in his possession. Foreman also failed to pay his debt to the bank. The car was sold. Who is entitled to the proceeds? [*Corbin Deposit Bank v. King,* 384 S.W.2d 302 (Ky. 1964).]

6. Walter signed two combination notes and security agreements giving Citizens State Bank a security interest in his automobile and boat. After Walter defaulted on his payments on both notes, the bank repossessed the collateral and sent Walter a notice that the automobile would be sold. The bank then sold the automobile and boat, and sued Walter for a deficiency judgment. Is the bank entitled to the deficiency? [*Citizens State Bank v. Hewitt,* 279 S.E.2d 531 (Ga. 1981).]

7. Moody gave Sherman County Bank a perfected security interest in property used in his farming operation, including after-acquired property. Moody later bought equipment from an implement company on an installment basis. The company took a security interest in the equipment and later filed financing statements. When Moody defaulted on his payments, the bank claimed that it was entitled to the equipment Moody purchased from the implement company because, in fact, the implement company did not file the financing statements within ten days after the installment contract was signed. Is the bank correct? [*Sherman County Bank v. Kallhoff,* 288 N.W.2d 24 (Neb. 1980).]

Suretyship

8. Kennedy agreed with Exxon to guarantee the account of Plastifax, Inc. When Plastifax filed for bankruptcy, Exxon sued Kennedy on the guaranty. Does the Plastifax bankruptcy discharge the guarantor Kennedy? [*Exxon Chemical Americas v. Kennedy,* 295 S.E.2d 770 (N.C. 1982).]

9. Cardwell guaranteed purchases by McPeters from Failing. The guaranty provided that Failing would promptly mail copies of all invoices to Cardwell. Failing waited seven months after one purchase before mailing the invoice. If McPeters fails to pay the invoice, is Cardwell liable? [*George E. Failing Co. v. Cardwell Investment Co.,* 376 P.2d 892 (Kan. 1962).]

10. In 1933, Keyes signed a note promising to pay a debt to Laney. Dyer was a surety on the note. When Keyes failed to pay the note, Dyer paid Laney in 1946 and sued Keyes for reimbursement in 1948. Keyes defended by claiming that Dyer could not bring suit on the 1933 note in 1948 because the statute of limitations requires lawsuits to be brought within three years after the cause of action arises. Is Keyes correct? [*Keyes v. Dyer,* 243 P.2d 710 (Okla. 1952).]

30 Bankruptcy under the Bankruptcy Reform Act of 1978

After you have read this chapter, you should be able to:

1. Discuss the source of bankruptcy law.
2. Describe the bankruptcy administrative framework.
3. Distinguish between voluntary and involuntary bankruptcy.
4. Describe the property in the debtor's estate.
5. Discuss the distribution of the estate after liquidation.
6. Suggest two alternatives to bankruptcy.

Introduction

In recent years the use of credit to finance the purchase of property and services has become extremely popular with both consumers and businesses. The popularity of credit purchases, however, has resulted in an unfortunate and unexpected consequence for many borrowers—a trip to bankruptcy court. In a typical year well over 200,000 Americans file for bankruptcy. *Bankruptcy is not a crime; it is a legal remedy affecting debtors who are experiencing financial difficulty.*

In this chapter we will examine what happens when an individual files for "liquidation" bankruptcy and the effect of the bankruptcy on the debtor and the creditors. We will also examine two alternative courses of action available under the bankruptcy law: wage earner plans for individuals with regular income, and reorganization plans for businesses.

Source of Bankruptcy Law

Federal jurisdiction over bankruptcy law.

The United States Constitution, Article I, Section 8, provides that "the Congress shall have power . . . to establish . . . uniform laws on the subject of Bankruptcies throughout the United States." This means that bankruptcy is a *federal* matter and that the states do not have the power to enact bankruptcy laws.

Congress has used its power to enact bankruptcy Acts five times—in 1800, 1841, 1867, 1898, and 1978. The current one, the *Bankruptcy Reform Act of 1978* repealed the 1898 Act and made a number of changes in bankruptcy law. The Bankruptcy Reform Act of 1978, as amended in 1984 and 1986, will be the primary source for the following discussion of bankruptcy law. Many attorneys refer to the Act as the "Bankruptcy Code" in order to distinguish it from the old 1898 Act.

Bankruptcy Reform Act of 1978—the law governing bankruptcy effective October 1, 1979.

Administrative Framework

Under the 1978 Act, a new bankruptcy system was created. Bankruptcy courts were established as adjuncts for each federal district court. As a result of *Northern Pipeline Construction Company v. Marathon Pipe Line Company,* 102 S.Ct. 2858 (1982), in 1984, Congress amended the law to provide that (1) U.S. Courts of Appeals are to appoint bankruptcy judges for fourteen year terms and (2) bankruptcy judges are not, absent agreement of the parties, to decide matters going beyond bankruptcy issues.

Bankruptcy judges are not allowed to administer the debtor's estate. For example, the Act provides in section 341 that the bankruptcy judge may not preside at—and cannot even attend—the first meeting of creditors to plan for the administration of the debtor's estate because the judge might learn something at the meeting that would bias the judge's later judicial decisions. Consequently, the administration of the estate is handled by a separate officer, the **trustee** in bankruptcy.

trustee
(in bankruptcy) the officer responsible for administering the debtor's estate

Trustees are initially appointed by the bankruptcy judge from a panel of private trustees. However, at the first meeting of creditors, a new trustee may be elected if the election is requested by creditors holding at least twenty percent of the unsecured claims. The trustee generally serves as the representative of the debtor's estate and handles a wide range of administrative duties, such as collecting and selling the debtor's property, investigating the financial affairs of the debtor, and making a final report and accounting to the court.

Title 11 of the U.S. Code containing the new bankruptcy Act has eight chapters. We will discuss three chapters of primary concern to individuals and businesses. Chapter 7 has the title "Liquidation," Chapter 11 "Reorganization," and Chapter 13 "Adjustment Of Debts Of An Individual With Regular Income." Chapter 7, often called "straight bankruptcy," involves the collection, liquidation, and distribution of the debtor's **estate**.

estate
(in bankruptcy) the debtor's legal or equitable interest in property on the date the case commences

Chapters 11 and 13 are concerned with plans for full or part payment of creditors. The person who is the subject of a "bankruptcy case" is called a "debtor," not a "bankrupt." A debtor may be an individual or a business, and each of Chapters 7, 11, and 13 is concerned with various kinds of debtor.

Before 1986, it was difficult for family farmers to use Chapter 13 because of the low debt requirements (see page 470). Chapter 11 was also unattractive because it is often time-consuming and expensive. As a result, a 1986 law created Chapter 12, entitled "Adjustment of Debts of a Family Farmer with Regular Annual Income." To qualify for Chapter 12 a family farmer's debts must not exceed $1,500,000.

Chapter 7 "Liquidation"

To illustrate the procedure followed in a typical bankruptcy case, let us assume that Micawber, a young college graduate, has made a number of purchases on credit and suddenly discovers that he has $10,000 in debts and only $2,000 worth of assets. Micawber is unable to make the installment payments on his debts as they become due and he is afraid that his wages will be subject to **garnishment.** He is now considering filing for bankruptcy.

Commencement of the Case

A bankruptcy case is commenced with the filing of a petition by a *debtor,* which is called a **voluntary case,** or by the debtor's creditors, which is called an **involuntary case.** The term "debtor" includes "persons" who are individuals, corporations, or partnerships that reside, or have a domicile, a place of business, or property in the United States.

In a *voluntary case,* the debtor may be any person except, primarily, a railroad, bank, insurance company, savings and loan association, or building and loan association. Insolvency of the debtor is not required. The petition may be filed by husband and wife jointly. The voluntary filing of a petition automatically acts as an *order for relief* under the bankruptcy law—that is, an order adjudicating bankruptcy of the debtor. Under the 1984 amendments, however, the court is permitted to dismiss the petition where the debts are mainly consumer debts and granting relief would constitute a "substantial abuse" of bankruptcy law.

In an *involuntary case,* the debtor may be any person except the above five types of organization excluded in a voluntary case and except a farmer or a charitable corporation. If the debtor has twelve or more creditors, the petition may be filed by three or more creditors whose *unsecured* claims total at least $5,000. If there are fewer than twelve creditors, the petition may be filed by one or more of such creditors whose total claims amount to at least $5,000. The debtor, Micawber in our case, may choose not to contest the petition, in which case the court will order the relief requested in the petition. If the debtor does contest the petition, the court will order relief only if, after a trial, it is determined that the debtor is not paying his or her debts as they become due, or that a custodian was appointed or took possession of the debtor's property within 120 days before the filing of the petition. If the court dismisses the petition, it may award the debtor costs, attorney's fees, and damages, including, in some cases, **punitive damages.**

The filing of the petition acts as an automatic **stay** of (1) judicial, administrative, or other proceedings against the debtor; (2) the enforcement of a judgment against the debtor; and (3) the creation or enforcement of any lien against the debtor's estate. Thus, Micawber's creditors could not start a suit or enforce their judgments by garnishment or otherwise after a petition is filed. There are, however, certain actions that are excluded from the operation of the stay, including criminal proceedings, the collection of alimony or support, and an action of the Department of Housing and Urban Development to foreclose a mortgage insured under the National Housing Act. Also, under section 361 of the Code, certain measures, such as requiring cash payments to creditors, may be taken to provide adequate protection for creditors harmed by the stay.

---

garnishment
a statutory proceeding begun by a judgment creditor to reach the intangible assets of the judgment debtor—e.g., the debtor's right to his salary—by writ of garnishment

voluntary case
a bankruptcy case in which the petition is filed by the debtor

involuntary case
a bankruptcy case in which the petition is filed by the creditors

punitive (or exemplary) damages
the money judicially awarded to an injured party in excess of compensatory damages to punish for malicious, wanton, or intentional wrongful conduct

stay
(noun) a halt

Creditors' Claims

Within a reasonable time after the order for relief, there will be a meeting of the creditors. The debtor, here Micawber, is required to appear at this meeting and to testify under oath if any creditor wants to question him. As previously noted, the judge is not allowed to attend this meeting and the creditors in certain cases may elect a trustee to replace the one appointed by the court. The creditors may also elect a **creditors' committee** that may consult with, and make recommendations to, the trustee and submit questions to the court regarding administration of the case.

Each creditor may file a **proof of claim,** which is automatically allowed unless an objection is raised by a party affected by the bankruptcy. If there is an objection, the court will allow the claim unless it determines that the claim falls within a specified list of claims that are not allowed, such as claims that are unenforceable against the debtor, claims for unmatured interest, and unmatured alimony and support that is not discharged by the bankruptcy.

If a **claim** is **contingent** or unliquidated, the court may estimate the value of the claim to determine the amount of the allowance. And when a creditor has a claim secured by a security interest or other lien on the debtor's property, the allowance is treated as a secured claim to the extent of the value of the property and an unsecured claim to the extent that the claim exceeds the property value. For example, C has a $10,000 claim against D and has D's office furniture worth $6,000 as security. C's unsecured claim is for $4,000.

creditors' committee
(in bankruptcy) a committee elected by the creditors to advise the trustee in bankruptcy

proof of claim
the claim filed by a creditor in a bankruptcy case

contingent claim
a claim not certain of occurring, depending on a possible future event

The Estate

The trustee is responsible for collecting the property of the debtor's estate, reducing the property to money, and closing the estate in a manner that serves the best interests of the parties. The estate generally includes all legal or equitable interests which the debtor has in property *as of the date the case was commenced*. There are, however, three ways in which additional property might be added to the estate even though the debtor had no interest in the property on commencement of the case.

First, the estate includes property acquired by the debtor within 180 days after the petition was filed (1) by inheritance, bequest, or devise; (2) as a beneficiary on a life insurance policy; or (3) as the result of a property settlement agreement with a spouse for a divorce.

Second, if the debtor, while insolvent, made a preferential transfer of the debtor's property before the bankruptcy petition was filed, called a "voidable preference," the trustee has the right to avoid the transfer and reacquire the property for the estate. A **preference** is a transfer of property to a creditor for a debt owed before the transfer was made. The transfer must have been made while the debtor was **insolvent** (defined as a financial condition where the debts are greater than the assets, exclusive of fraudulent transfers and property exempted under the Code) and within ninety days before the petition was filed; however, there are special rules governing transfer to insiders such as a relative of an individual debtor or a director of a corporation. It also must be shown that the transfer enabled the creditor to receive preferential treatment. Additionally, the trustee may avoid fraudulent transfers made by the debtor within a year before the petition was filed and also transfers voidable under state law. The following case illustrates the preferential treatment requirement.

preference
(in bankruptcy) a debtor's transfer of his property, made when insolvent and within ninety days before a petition in bankruptcy was filed, which gives a creditor preferential treatment

insolvency
(in bankruptcy) when the debtor's assets are less than his liabilities

Facts
Freelin filed a voluntary Chapter 7 bankruptcy petition on September 30, 1980. From June 30, 1980, to September 30, 1980, Freelin made three car payments to BancOhio, which held a security interest in his car. The trustee alleged that these payments constituted voidable preferences, but presented no evidence that the value of the debt was greater than the value of the car.

Decision
The car payments are not voidable preferences.

Reasoning

Trustees may avoid only pre-bankruptcy transfers that enable one creditor to recover a greater amount of the debt than other similar creditors. In this case the trustee was unable to prove that the car payments allowed BancOhio to obtain a larger percentage of the debt than it would have received upon distribution of the debtor's property after the filing.

In re *Conn, Debtor,* 9 B.R. 431 (Ohio 1981).

There are several important exceptions to the rules allowing the trustee to avoid preferences. For example, the trustee may not avoid a transfer: (1) that was a contemporaneous exchange for new value given to the debtor; (2) that was in payment of a debt incurred in the ordinary course of business and made according to ordinary business terms (e.g., payment of monthly utility bills); (3) that created a purchase money security interest in property acquired by the debtor that secured new value which is perfected within ten days after the debtor received the property; (4) to a creditor to the extent that, after the transfer, the creditor gave new value not secured by an unavoidable security interest; (5) that created a perfected security interest in inventory or receivables or the proceeds of either; or (6) in a case involving an individual with primarily consumer debts if the total value of the property transferred is less than $600.

The *third* possibility for adding property to the estate is for the trustee to use his or her rights as a **lien creditor** to avoid certain transfers by the debtor. The trustee's rights include the power of: (1) a creditor who has a judicial lien; (2) a creditor who has obtained a writ of execution that was returned unsatisfied; and (3) a bona fide purchaser of real property from the debtor. To illustrate the trustee's rights, we might assume that our debtor, Micawber, gave an unperfected security interest in his boat to a creditor, Heep. Because Heep's security interest in the boat is not perfected, a lien creditor would have priority with regard to the boat. Thus, the trustee, with the powers of a lien creditor, can avoid Heep's interest in the boat. Heep's only recourse is to file a claim as an unsecured creditor and share Micawber's assets with other unsecured creditors.

Although the trustee may make additions to the estate by avoiding preferences and by exercising his or her rights as a lien creditor, certain property is exempt and will not be included in the estate. A debtor may choose to use the **exemptions** listed in the federal bankruptcy statute or, *alternatively,* may elect the exemptions available under state law, although *the states have the right to require the debtor to use the state exemptions.* At this date, over half the states have decided to require the use of their own exemptions. Property *exempt under the federal law* is very extensive and includes the following: (1) the debtor's residence up to a maximum interest of $7,500; (2) *one* motor vehicle up to $1,200 in value; (3) household furnishings, wearing apparel, appliances, books, animals, crops, or musical instruments held for personal, family, or household use up to a maximum $200 value for *each* item and a total value of $4,000; (4) up to $500 in jewelry; (5) implements, professional books, tools of the debtor's trade up to $750 in value; (6) an unmatured life insurance contract owned by the debtor other than credit life insurance; (7) prescribed health aids; (8) various state and federal benefits including social security, unemployment compensation, local public assistance, veterans' and disability benefits; (9) private benefits including the debtor's right to alimony and support payments, pension, profit-sharing and other plans, to the extent reasonably necessary for the support of the debtor; and (10) the debtor's right to receive certain payments such as an award under a law compensating victims of a crime, a payment under a life insurance policy on a person of whom the debtor was a dependent, and a payment of up to $7,500 on account of personal injury. The debtor is also entitled to exempt any other property up to a value of $400, plus any unused amount under (1) above up to $3,750. Thus, under this last provision, a debtor who is not a homeowner may exempt $4,150 in any property.

The state exemption laws are not uniform and, if the debtor elects the state exemptions, the debtor's rights will vary considerably, depending on the state of the debtor's

---

lien creditor
a creditor with a judicial lien or a writ of execution

exemption
(in bankruptcy) a debtor's property that is not liquidated and not distributed to creditors in bankruptcy

residence. Additionally, many of the state laws were drafted many years ago and the exemptions are not as useful today as they once were. For instance, the Michigan law exempts, among other property, 10 sheep, 2 cows, 5 swine, 100 hens, 5 roosters, and enough hay and grain to feed the animals and poultry for six months!

Distribution of the Estate

After the trustee has collected and liquidated the debtor's property, the property will be distributed according to the following **priorities:** (1) administrative expenses and specified fees and charges; (2) unsecured claims, in an involuntary case, arising in the ordinary course of business after the case was commenced but before the order for relief or the appointment of trustees; (3) unsecured claims up to $2,000 for wages, salaries, or commissions earned by an individual within ninety days before the filing of the petition or the cessation of the debtor's business; (4) unsecured claims for contributions to employee benefit plans arising from services rendered within 180 days before the petition was filed or the debtor ceased doing business, but only to the extent of $2,000 per employee less amounts paid for wage claims and to other employee benefit plans; (5) unsecured claims (up to $2,000 per individual) of grain producers and fishermen against grain and fish storage businesses; (6) unsecured claims up to $900 owed to individuals who have deposited money for the purchase of consumer goods or services which were not delivered or provided; and (7) unsecured tax claims of governmental units. Any property remaining after priority claims and expenses have been paid will be distributed on a pro rata basis to unsecured creditors who have filed a proof of claim.

priorities (in bankruptcy) claims that are paid first after the estate has been liquidated

Discharge

After the estate has been liquidated and distributed, the court will order a **discharge.** However, a discharge will not be allowed if the case falls within one of seven main categories. *First,* discharges are allowed only to *individuals,* not to corporations or partnerships. However, corporations and partnerships may utilize Chapter 11 of the Code on business reorganization or they may liquidate under state law. *Second,* a discharge is not allowed if the debtor has transferred, destroyed, or concealed property within one year before, or any time after, the petition was filed with the intent to hinder, delay, or defraud creditors. *Third,* a debtor who has concealed, destroyed, falsified, or failed to preserve recorded information relating to the debtor's financial condition or business transactions will not be granted a discharge unless the act was justified. *Fourth,* a debtor who fraudulently makes a false oath, presents a false claim, gives or receives property for acting or failing to act, or withholds recorded information from officials is not entitled to a discharge. *Fifth,* a discharge is not allowed when the debtor has failed to explain satisfactorily a loss or deficiency of assets. *Sixth,* a debtor who refuses to obey a lawful order of the court will not be discharged. *Finally,* a discharge is not allowed if the debtor has been granted a discharge in an earlier bankruptcy case commenced within six years before the petition in the current case was filed. The following case illustrates one of the discharge provisions.

discharge (in bankruptcy) a court order releasing the individual debtor from his debts after the estate has been liquidated and distributed

Facts
Dennis and Anne, husband and wife, filed a Chapter 7 bankruptcy petition. Documents filed by the couple contained numerous false statements. When creditors sought to prevent their discharge, the couple conceded that the statements were false. Dennis, who was involved in real estate development and sales, claimed that they misinterpreted a question in the documents.

Decision
The debtors are not entitled to discharges in bankruptcy.

Reasoning
The filing of correct documents is important to ensure that the trustee and creditors receive dependable information. False statements that result from mere mistakes will not prevent a discharge; fraud is required. In this case, given the intelligence and experience of the witness Dennis, the court concluded that his explanation was not credible and that he did not honestly misinterpret the question.

In re *Mazzola, Debtors,* 4 B.R. 179 (Mass. 1980).

If these exceptions do not apply and the *discharge* is granted, it serves to release the debtor from debts that arose before the date of the order for relief. The discharge also voids judgments relating to such debts and operates as an injunction against the collection of the debts.

However, even after a discharge, certain types of debts must still be paid by the debtor. These include: (1) certain taxes—e.g., taxes for which the debtor failed to file a return or filed a fraudulent return; (2) debts incurred in obtaining property or services by false pretenses or false financial statements reasonably relied on by creditors; (3) debts owed to creditors whose names were not given to the court by the debtor; (4) debts resulting from breach of fiduciary duty, larceny, or embezzlement; (5) debts owed for alimony or support; (6) debts resulting from a willful and malicious injury caused by the debtor; and (7) certain debts owed to a governmental unit, including educational loans owed to a governmental unit or nonprofit institution which became due within five years of the bankruptcy petition filing, unless the debt is causing undue hardship on the debtor; and (8) debts owed for injuries resulting from the debtor's drunk driving. In addition, certain debts are presumed to be nondischargeable, in order to prevent a debtor from buying luxury goods immediately before the bankruptcy. These are: (1) debts totalling more than $500 for luxury goods and services purchased within forty days before the filing and certain cash advances totalling more than $1,000 obtained within twenty days before the filing.

Prior to the Code, debtors who were previously discharged were subjected to much pressure from former creditors to reaffirm (promise to pay) discharged debts. In order to correct this abuse, Congress made it more difficult for former creditors to obtain such promises to resume liability. Thus the Code provides that *reaffirmation* can occur *no later than* when a discharge is granted in bankruptcy proceedings. In cases where an individual wants to reaffirm a debt, the bankruptcy court must inform the debtor at a hearing that the reaffirmation is not required under law and of the legal effect of the reaffirmation. Unless an individual is represented by an attorney, the court must also determine that the reaffirmation does not impose undue hardship on the debtor and is in the debtor's best interest. If the debtor is represented by an attorney, the attorney must file an affidavit which states that the agreement does not impose undue hardship. Even when these requirements are met the debtor is entitled to rescind the agreement within sixty days after it is filed with the court.

The Code prohibits governmental units from discriminating against a person who has gone through bankruptcy. The 1984 amendments provide that debtors are also protected from discrimination by private employers; for example, a private employer may not fire a person because of the bankruptcy.

Chapter 13 "Adjustment of Debts of an Individual with Regular Income"

Chapter 13 plan
a plan for the payment of debts proposed by an individual as an alternative to a straight bankruptcy

As an alternative to the straight bankruptcy procedure described above, which leads to liquidation and distribution of the debtor's estate, it is possible for a debtor to propose a plan for the payment of debts under Chapter 13 of the Code. A **Chapter 13** case, commonly called a "wage earner's plan," is commenced by the filing of a *voluntary petition,* which operates as an automatic stay of proceedings in the same manner as a straight bankruptcy petition. Only *individuals* (except a stock broker or a commodity broker) with *regular income,* and with less than $100,000 in unsecured debt and less than $350,000 in secured debt, are eligible for Chapter 13 proceedings.

The debtor then proposes a plan which provides for the submission of future income to the control of the trustee and provides for payments to creditors, including full payment of the claims entitled to priority discussed above. Chapter 13 contains a number of provisions that may be included in the plan, including the modification of the claims of secured creditors. The plan may not provide for payments over a period exceeding three years unless the court feels that there is cause to extend the plan an additional two years. The debtor retains title to, and possession of, the property unless the plan provides otherwise.

After the debtor has filed the plan, the court will schedule a **confirmation hearing,** at which time creditors may object to the plan. The plan must be accepted by each secured creditor unless an exception applies, such as when the property subject to the security interest is surrendered to the creditors or the claims are paid in full. The plan must be accepted by unsecured creditors unless the plan provides for payment of the claim in full or unless all of the debtor's disposable income is to be applied to payments. The court will decide whether or not to confirm the plan after considering various requirements set forth in section 1325 of the Code. If the plan is confirmed and the debtor makes all payments promised under the plan, the debtor will be discharged of the debts provided for by the plan, although there are certain exceptions, such as alimony and support payments.

confirmation hearing
the hearing at which a Chapter 13 plan is considered by the court

As the following case shows, some debts that are not dischargeable under Chapter 7 are dischargeable under Chapter 13.

Facts
Kevin is employed as a city planner and Frederika as a college instructor. Both are well educated and they have a total debt of $27,802 of which $22,351.62 is for student loans. When they filed a Chapter 13 petition, their plan called for payment of $7,152.51 of the student loans. Confirmation of the plan is now at issue. Is payment of the student loan amount substantial and meaningful and therefore made in good faith not taking advantage of existing generous laws; and is the unpaid amount dischargeable?

Decision
The plan is confirmed, the payment is made in good faith, and the unpaid amount is dischargeable.

Reasoning
Bad faith is not present. Under Chapter 7 the student loans would not be dischargeable. However under Chapter 13 such loans are not included among the kinds of debts that cannot be discharged. "The Court is, or ought to be, bound by the law. Any remedy lies with Congress."

In re *Rowe, Debtor,* 17 B.R. 870 (Va. 1982).

Chapter 11 Business Reorganization

As an *alternative to bankruptcy,* a business may choose to reorganize under **Chapter 11** of the Code. A Chapter 11 proceeding may be commenced by the filing of either an involuntary petition, or a voluntary petition by a debtor as defined in a Chapter 7 proceeding (but not a stockbroker or a commodity broker) or by a debtor railroad. Once a petition is filed, only the debtor may file a plan for 120 days after the order for relief unless a trustee has been appointed, in which case any party in interest may file a plan. The court may order the appointment of a trustee for cause (including fraud, dishonesty, incompetence, or gross mismanagement) or if the appointment is in the interest of creditors, security holders, or other interests of the estate.

Chapter 11 plan
a plan for the reorganization of a business

In addition to the possible appointment of a trustee, the court is also required to appoint a creditors' committee as soon as possible after the order for relief. The creditors' committee consults with the debtor or trustee concerning administration of the estate, investigates all matters relevant to the formulation of a plan, participates in the formulation of a plan, and performs other services as representative of other creditors.

After the plan is formulated, it will be transmitted, along with a written disclosure statement approved by the court, to holders of claims, who may accept or reject the plan. The court will then schedule a hearing and will confirm the plan if it complies with Chapter 11. If the plan is fair and equitable, it may be confirmed even though all classes of claims have not accepted the plan; once confirmed, it binds all interested parties.

Summary Statement

1. Under the U.S. Constitution, bankruptcy is a federal matter; states do not have the power to enact bankruptcy laws.
2. Under Chapter 7, if it is a voluntary bankruptcy the petition is filed by the debtor, while in an involuntary bankruptcy the petition is filed by creditors. In an involuntary bankruptcy if the debtor contests the petition, the court will order relief if it determines that the debtor is not paying his or her debts as they become due.
3. The debtor's estate includes all legal or equitable interests which the debtor has in property as of the date the case was commenced.
4. After liquidation under Chapter 7, the estate will be distributed first to creditors with priority and then to unsecured creditors.
5. As an alternative to Chapter 7, an individual might file a plan under Chapter 13, and a business might file a reorganization plan under Chapter 11.

In the following case the court discusses the question of whether student loans are dischargeable in bankruptcy.

In re Conard, Debtor
6 B.R. 151 (Ky. 1980).

Merritt S. Deitz, Jr., Bankruptcy Judge. For the first time under the new Bankruptcy Code we are asked to consider "undue hardship" as an affirmative defense in a suit seeking to have a federally-guaranteed student loan excepted from discharge.

Section 523(a) of the Code provides that a bankruptcy discharge will not extend:

(8) to a governmental unit, or a nonprofit institution of higher education, for an educational loan, unless . . .

(B) excepting such debt from discharge under this paragraph will impose an undue hardship on the debtor.

* * * * *

Paul Conard, 31, a substitute teacher for the Jefferson County Board of Education, was terminated as a full-time history teacher in April, 1979. His gross income for 1979 was $6,000; for 1978 $9,941. When called as a substitute, he is paid $33 per day.

Conard filed for relief under the Bankruptcy Code in October, 1979, listing $37,354 in liabilities and $25 in assets.

His obligations consisted of a loan executed in connection with a business venture, Double Dip Ice Cream; signature loans; revolving credit card accounts, and a student loan of $4,125.79.

The United States initiated this action to have Conard's student loan obligation excepted from his discharge in bankruptcy. Conard raised the affirmative defense under § 523(a)(8)(B) of the Code that to enforce repayment of the debt would impose an undue hardship.

* * * * *

The following facts were developed at the trial, at which Conard was the only witness:

Upon being discharged from military service, Conard used the G.I. Bill of Rights to obtain a college education. His thirst for knowledge led him through five different colleges.

At some point in his academic travels the wellspring of benefits from the G.I. Bill was depleted, and Conard applied for and obtained a series of three federally-guaranteed, long-term, low-interest loans with which he could complete his collegiate journey. He obtained a bachelor's degree in education at Western Kentucky University, and there studied toward, but did not obtain, a postgraduate degree.

Conard, unmarried with no dependents, lives at the home of his 75-year-old mother. Having no car of his own, he drives her van.

Accurately describing himself as "overweight", Conard testified that his physical appearance "turns off a lot of people", including potential employers. The weight problem—and it is a severe one—has not been diagnosed as having any medical origin. Conard attributes it to "a different metabolic rate"

Conard has unsuccessfully sought sales jobs. He has *not* applied for employment at any private schools in Jefferson County, nor has he applied at any schools, public or private, in surrounding counties. He apparently is content to await recall by the county board of education, and he ranks low on the recall roster.

With his elderly mother as a guarantor, Conard obtained a $5,000 loan from Union Trust Bank this summer, some months after filing bankruptcy. Curiously, he is using the loan proceeds only to retire as they become due the $150 monthly payments on that same loan.

* * * * *

This claim of undue hardship rests upon two asserted facts: (1) Conard must support and provide for his elderly mother, and (2) he is unable to obtain employment because of his physical appearance.

Upon the first point, we have some question as to who is supporting whom. The mother, who gave birth to this healthy young man while in her 44th year, and who fancies a mode of transportation generally associated with drivers two generations her junior, may be a vital woman indeed. Although the record does not indicate the extent of her income or financial substance, it is at least clear that the Union Trust Bank would not extend credit to the son without the mother's hand being put to the note.

Upon the second point we must observe with neither cynicism nor cruelty, that corpulence is a condition which may swiftly diminish with continued impecuniosity.

This unemployed former president of the Double Dip Ice Cream Company, having double-dipped the available federal subsidies to obtain a superior education, should consider some alternatives. Enlightened self-interest would seem to suggest the virtue of a vigorous and energetic search for a proper workshop in which to use those intellectual tools which have been well honed at federal expense. Productivity is preferable to living off the substance of the land. In order to stimulate some reflection upon such heretical theories of individual enterprise, it is hereby

ORDERED, that the indebtedness of Paul George Conard to the Department of Health, Education and Welfare, United States of America, is not dischargeable in bankruptcy. This is a final order. Judgment shall be entered accordingly.

Questions and Case Problems

1. A debtor had net take-home pay of approximately $432 per month and also received help in paying his expenses from his fiancee, with whom he shared an apartment. He was trained as a diesel mechanic and had worked as a hypnotist, but his future employment prospects were clouded because he was a convicted felon. Should his student loan which he owes to the Wisconsin Higher Educational Aids Board be discharged in the debtor's bankruptcy? [In the Matter of *Tobin, Jr., Bankrupt,* 18 B.R. 560 (Wisc. 1982).]

2. Pauline paid a sum of money to the Wyatts in return for their promise to support her. They used the money to purchase a house, where Pauline resided temporarily. The Wyatts later stopped supporting Pauline and filed a Chapter 13 petition. Under state law, the Wyatts hold legal title to the property while Pauline holds equitable title. Should the house be included in the debtors' estate? [*Collomb v. Wyatt,* 6 B.R. 947 (N.Y. 1980).]

3. Robert, who was granted bankruptcy discharges in 1960 and 1967, petitioned for a third bankruptcy in 1973. He kept few records of his financial transactions because he dealt almost exclusively in cash and because he did not like banks. Should the court grant Robert's discharge? [In the Matter of *Horton, Bankrupt,* 621 F.2d 968 (9th Cir. 1980).]

4. Sam, who operated a fencing company as a sole proprietor, filed a Chapter 7 bankruptcy petition on April 11, 1980. During January and February, 1980, Sam drew checks totalling $4,300 from the business made payable to his wife. Sam was unable to explain what happened to these funds beyond stating that they were used for "personal expenses." He claimed monthly recreational expenses of $720. He also failed to provide a satisfactory explanation for the loss of cash drawn from his business in January and February of 1980. Should Sam's discharge in bankruptcy be allowed? [In the Matter of *Sam Ramos, Debtor*, 8 B.R. 490 (Wisc. 1981.)

5. Clara had two elderly aunts, Millie and Tillie. Under Millie's will, Clara was to receive all of Millie's property. Tillie named Clara as the beneficiary in her life insurance policy. Clara was deeply in debt and decided to file for bankruptcy under Chapter 7 in order to discharge her debts and avoid using the inheritance and insurance money to pay her creditors. A petition under Chapter 7 was filed on January 15. Aunt Tillie died the following May 15 and Aunt Millie died the following November 15. Are the inheritance and the insurance proceeds included in Clara's estate and thus available to creditors? Why?

6. Kermit filed a voluntary bankruptcy petition under Chapter 7. Sixty days before filing the petition, Kermit had given a security interest in his boat to First Bank, at which time First Bank made a $1,000 loan to Kermit. At the time of this transaction, Kermit was not insolvent. The trustee now wants to avoid the security interest. First Bank claims that the trustee cannot avoid the interest because (1) Kermit was not insolvent and (2) the bank gave new value to Kermit. Who wins? Why?

7. A debtor had been recently divorced and his wife received all his property. He had no savings account, no car and only $40 in his checking account. Although he made several attempts to find a job, he was temporarily unemployed and lived with his parents. Should the debtor's educational loans of over $4,000 be discharged in bankruptcy? [*United States v. Hemmen*, 7 B.R. 63 (Ala. 1980).]

8. A jury entered a verdict against Joseph in the amount of $86,704. After the verdict Joseph transferred notes worth $93,337 to his father-in-law in exchange for $54,400. He then transferred $40,000 to a corporation owned by his children in exchange for a $40,000 note which was to be repaid over a 36-year period. During the same year an involuntary Chapter 7 petition was filed against Joseph. Can the trustee recover the property transferred by Joseph? [In re *Newman, Debtor*, 6 B.R. 798 (N.Y. 1980).]

9. Jenkins earned most of his income from farming. Although he engaged in commodities trading on a regular basis, mainly in pork bellies, he did not realize an income from it. For example, during the first three months of 1978, Jenkins suffered a loss of $560,000 from trading. A brokerage firm to whom Jenkins owed $224,280 commenced an involuntary bankruptcy proceeding against him. If Jenkins challenges the petition, should he be adjudged a bankrupt? [*Jenkins v. Ray E. Friedman & Company*, 664 F.2d 184 (8th Cir. 1981).]

10. A limited partnership developed a plan of reorganization under Chapter 11. Only one creditor, a bank which held a first mortgage on the only substantial asset held by the partnership, objected to the plan. The court decided that the rate of interest to be paid the bank under the plan was not fair and equitable, but also that it was not feasible for the debtor to pay a higher rate of interest. Should the plan be confirmed? [Matter of *Landmark at Plaza Park Limited*, 7 B.R. 653 (N.J. 1980).]

General Principles of Insurance Law 31

After you have read this chapter, you should be able to:

1. List the major types of insurance.
2. Define insurance.
3. Describe the regulation of insurance transactions.
4. Explain what is meant by an insurable interest and indicate when the insurable interest must exist.
5. Explain why warranties, representation, and concealment are important and how they are used as defenses by insurance companies.
6. Indicate what is meant by subrogation and when it is applicable.

Types of insurance.

Introduction

A knowledge of insurance is extremely important to every individual on both a personal and a business level. Like death and taxes, insurance is certain to affect you at some time during your life. If you own an automobile, a house, or a business, or wish to provide financial security for your family, insurance represents a key element in personal, business, and estate planning.

In this chapter we will examine the general principles of the law relating to insurance contracts. In chapter 32 we will examine closely the three most common types of insurance: (1) life insurance, (2) homeowner's insurance, and (3) automobile insurance.

To illustrate both the importance and the various types of insurance, we might assume that a recent college graduate, Fred, is married, has a child, and has recently purchased a small clothing store. There are many different kinds of insurance that Fred should consider in his personal and business transactions.

Types of Insurance

Homeowner's Insurance

Fred and his wife should purchase a homeowner's policy that will provide coverage for losses due to damage or destruction of their home. As discussed in chapter 32, the policy should also protect them in the event they are sued by someone whom they accidentally injure or who is injured while on their property.

Life Insurance

Fred and his wife should create an estate plan that includes a will and life insurance, and possibly also a trust and lifetime gifts. The types and form of life insurance policies will be discussed in chapter 32.

Health Insurance

Health care costs are rising faster than the costs of most products and services. In some communities the charge for spending one night in the hospital runs into hundreds of dollars, not including medical treatment and other services. Consequently, it is extremely important that Fred obtain insurance covering hospital expenses, medical and surgical fees, and other services such as X rays, radiological treatment, and laboratory tests. It is common for individuals to supplement their health insurance with a major medical insurance policy that provides coverage for extended illness, which might cost more than the coverage provided by the primary insurance policy.

Disability Insurance

If Fred should become ill, his health insurance will pay for hospital and medical treatment, but a source of income will be needed to support the family until his recovery. A disability insurance policy can be purchased that will provide a monthly income for Fred until he recovers.

Annuity

annuity
an insurance policy that pays the insured a designated amount periodically, beginning at a date set in the policy

In planning for his eventual retirement, Fred might decide to purchase an **annuity** policy. An annuity is a type of insurance policy that will pay Fred a designated amount periodically, the payments to begin at a date set in the policy. Fred might choose to purchase a fixed dollar annuity that pays a set amount—e.g., $10,000 per year. Alternatively, he might choose a variable annuity where the annuity premiums are invested in stocks or bonds and the benefit rises or falls, depending on the current value of the portfolio.

Automobile Insurance

Fred and his wife will need either regular or no-fault automobile insurance for their car. Both types of insurance will be discussed in chapter 32.

Title Insurance

When Fred and his wife purchased their home, it is likely that they purchased **title insurance,** which protects them in the event that the person who sold them the house did not have clear title to the property. For instance, there might be a deed on record with a hidden defect, such as a voidable deed signed by a minor. Title insurance will protect Fred and his wife for as long as they own the property. With title insurance, only one premium is paid—at the closing—although if the owner or owners mortgage the house, the bank usually will require the purchase of a second policy to protect the bank's interest.

title insurance
insurance that covers the title to real estate

Social Insurance

Today approximately ninety percent of workers are covered by social security, even when they are self-employed; and almost all of our country's population over 65 years of age is covered by Medicare, which is provided by the federal government. Workmen's (sometimes called "workers'") compensation laws protect workers who are injured on the job.[1]

Business Insurance

In addition to workers' compensation insurance, there are several types of insurance that Fred will need for his business. Fred should purchase fire and liability insurance for his business as well as automobile insurance if automobiles are used in the business. Fred might purchase **business interruption insurance,** which will reimburse him for lost revenues in the event he has to close his business temporarily because of property damage. If Fred ships his clothing in the ordinary course of business, he will want to purchase **inland marine insurance** to cover against loss while the goods are in transit. *Crime insurance* can be purchased to protect Fred from dishonesty of his employees or theft by outsiders. A number of the personal insurance coverages discussed above can be purchased by the employer as a fringe benefit for the employees, including group life, medical disability, and retirement insurance. Finally, if Fred is considered the key person in his business, the business should purchase key employee life insurance coverage to cover financial losses suffered by the company when Fred dies.

business interruption insurance
insurance that covers lost revenues when a business is closed as the result of property damage

inland marine insurance
insurance that covers goods that are being shipped

Malpractice Insurance. If Fred was engaged in a profession, such as medicine, law, or accounting, he would also need malpractice (also called professional liability) insurance which would provide liability coverage in the event he is sued by a patient or client for failing to meet the duty of care demanded by the profession. In the professions that have been deeply involved in malpractice litigation, notably medicine and accounting, insurance is difficult to obtain and very expensive. For example, the Wall Street Journal (May 30, 1985) reported that, in accordance with recent premium boosts, some Big Eight accounting firms may pay as much as $10 million a year in annual premiums.

Excess Liability Insurance

Damage awards to injured persons have increased greatly in recent years, and liability coverage under standard homeowner's automobile and business policies is often inadequate. For instance, homeowner's insurance usually provides liability coverage for $50,000; if Fred injures someone—for example, by accidentally hitting someone in the eye with a golf ball—the damages could easily run over $100,000. Consequently, it is wise to purchase an excess liability policy, sometimes called an "umbrella" policy, which will provide liability coverage for at least $1 million.

---

[1] For further discussion of Social Security and Workmen's Compensation, see Chapter 37.

Self-Insurance

When insurance coverage becomes too expensive, many businesses and organizations use some type of self-insurance mechanism. Some companies simply "go bare"; they purchase no insurance and use company assets to pay losses. Some companies self-insure for most losses but purchase supplementary catastrophic loss insurance. Other companies or organizations group together to form insurance "pools" and thus spread their losses among the group. Finally, many companies in recent years have formed subsidiaries, called "captive" insurance companies, and then purchase coverage from the captives, thus avoiding brokerage commissions and other costs.

Definition of Insurance

insurance
a contract in which the insurer agrees to pay the insured for losses affecting the insured's interests

insurer
the person who assumes another's risk (in the insurance contract)

insured
the person whose risk has been assumed by another (in the insurance contract)

Insurer organization.

Before we proceed further, it will be useful to define insurance. There are two different types of insurance definitions. *First,* most courts have adopted a very general definition: **insurance** is a contract, usually called an insurance policy, where one party (called the **insurer** or underwriter) agrees to pay another party (the **insured**) for losses affecting the insured's interests (the insurable interest). The consideration which the insurer receives for contracting to pay for such losses is called the *premium.*

Second, state insurance commissioners are guided by specific statutory definitions of insurance which they use in deciding whether a particular activity is subject to insurance regulation. For example, section 22 of the California Insurance Code defines insurance as a "contract whereby one undertakes to indemnify another against loss, damage, or liability arising from a contingent or unknown event." Plans for prepaid legal services are not insurance, generally.

Organization of Insurers

Many insurance companies, especially those that write fire and casualty insurance, are organized as typical business corporations. That is, they authorize, issue, and sell stock to shareholders, who own the business and receive dividends. However, two other methods of organization are also commonly used by insurance companies.

First, a substantial amount of insurance at the international level is underwritten by Lloyd's of London. Lloyd's is not a company but, instead, is a society with thousands of members who join together to form syndicates, each of which specializes in a certain type of insurance. A person who purchases insurance from Lloyd's is really purchasing insurance from one or more of these individual syndicates. In an effort to make American insurers more competitive with Lloyd's, the state of New York enacted legislation in 1978 that provides for the creation of the New York Insurance Exchange, which is modeled after Lloyd's.

mutual company
a company owned by the insureds

Second, many American insurers—especially those that underwrite life insurance—are mutual companies. A **mutual company** is one that is owned by the insureds, with the result that the insureds are purchasing insurance at cost since there are no shareholders to be paid. A few mutual companies sell assessable policies, which means that the policyholders must pay an amount in addition to the premium if the company suffers losses. For example, after a Colorado insurance company failed in 1975, the policyholders, many of whom were unaware that their policies were assessable, were charged an average of $500 to cover the company's losses.

In addition to the type of organization, insurance companies can be classified by the type of insurance they sell. At one time an insurance company could sell only one type of insurance—fire, life, or casualty. Today, however, all states allow multiple-line underwriting under which a nonlife insurer can sell all types of insurance except for life insurance. Most states today have gone one step further and allow all-line companies to sell all types of insurance.

Insurance Regulation

Government regulation.

Unlike most contracts, the contract of insurance is closely regulated by the government. Insurance regulations govern the financial condition of insurers, policy premiums, policy forms, and the licensing of insurers and their agents. The overriding legal question with regard to insurance regulation has been whether the individual states or the federal government should be primarily responsible for regulating insurance. The question arises because the commerce clause of the United States Constitution, Article I, Section 8, provides that Congress has the power to regulate *interstate* commerce. The federal McCarran-Ferguson Act recognized state regulation of insurance unless a federal law is specifically directed toward the insurance industry. The Act also provided that federal antitrust Acts[2] would not apply to the insurance industry if states established their own regulations. Most states have developed their own regulations and, consequently, today insurance is regulated chiefly by the states.

Insurable Interest

One of the key distinctions between an insurance contract and other types of contract is the requirement that the insured have some type of interest, called an **insurable interest,** in the risk covered by the insurance contract. There are three reasons why the law requires the insured to have an insurable interest. *First,* insurance is usually considered to be a contract of indemnity; that is, the purpose of insurance is to provide compensation for losses suffered by the insured. Without the requirement of insurable interest, a person could insure property he or she does not own and thus be overindemnified for a loss.

insurable interest an interest the insured has in the risk covered by the insurance contract

Second, the insurable interest requirement is designed to prevent gambling contracts, which are void in most states. For example, if Jack insures something in which he has an interest (as when he purchases collision insurance on his own car), he is not gambling but, instead, is merely shifting an existing risk to the insurer in exchange for his payment of premiums. However, if Jack purchased collision insurance on Sam's car, a car in which he had no interest, the insurance "contract" would be a wager; Jack would be betting the company that Sam's car will be damaged in a collision.

Third, an insurable interest is required because of the moral risks that would be created by allowing a person to insure a risk in which the person has no interest. For instance, if we allow Jack to insure Sam's life or car when Jack has no interest in either, Jack will be tempted to destroy the car or even to murder Sam in order to collect on the policies.

Although these reasons underlie insurable interest theory, in practice the theory is applied differently for life and property insurance. *With life insurance,* insurable interest means that the insured has a reasonable expectation of *economic benefit* or a *legal interest* in the life being insured. To illustrate, if Clyde took in a young orphan with the intention of caring for and supporting him, the orphan would have an insurable interest in Clyde's life based on the reasonable expectation of economic benefit provided by Clyde, even though the orphan was not legally adopted. If Clyde legally adopted the orphan, the orphan would have an even better case because of his legal relationship to Clyde under which Clyde is required to provide support. Thus, the orphan could take out a policy of life insurance on Clyde's life.

Insurable interest in *life*.

With life insurance, the insurable interest must *exist when the policy is purchased,* but it is not required that there be an interest at the time of the loss. Once an insurable interest is established, the insured may purchase any amount of life insurance on the insured which the insurer is willing to sell. In the following case the insurable interest in life existed when the policy was purchased but not at the time of death.

---

[2] For a discussion of antitrust, see chapter 47.

Facts
Jack, the decedent, was employed by Pioneer Foundry Co., Inc., defendant, for nine years. During Jack's employment, the company had an insurable interest in Jack's life, and it purchased a $50,000 policy on his life, the company being named as beneficiary on the policy. When Jack later left the company, the company continued to pay the premiums on the policy until Jack's death, when the insurance proceeds were paid to Pioneer. Jack's widow, plaintiff, sued Pioneer for the proceeds, contending that Pioneer's insurable interest in Jack's life ceased at the time he left Pioneer and, therefore, the proceeds belong to Jack's estate administered by the plaintiff. The lower court dismissed the case, and the plaintiff appealed. Is the company, which had no insurable interest at the time of Jack's death, entitled to recover $50,000 on the policy?

Decision
Yes. Affirmed, for the defendant, Pioneer.

Reasoning
The company is entitled to keep the proceeds. If the insurable interest requirement is met when the policy is issued, the policy proceeds must be paid even if there is no insurable interest at death. The company is not limited in its recovery to the amount of its financial loss, which in this case was nothing.

Secor v. Pioneer Foundry Co., Inc., 173 N.W.2d 780 (Mich. 1970).

Insurable interest in property.

There are two views as to what constitutes an insurable interest in *property*. In some states the insured must actually have some type of *legal or equitable interest* in the insured property. For instance, Jack obviously has an insurable interest in his own car if he is the legal owner of the car. In other states an insurable interest exists if a person expects to *suffer an economic loss* if the property is destroyed. Under this theory, if Jack owned a pizza shop and often borrowed his friend Sue's car to make deliveries, Jack would have an insurable interest in Sue's car because Jack would suffer an economic loss if Sue's car were destroyed (a loss of sales because he would be unable to make deliveries).

In the following very early case the court applied the legal interest test.

Facts
New Holland Turnpike Road Co., plaintiff, voluntarily contributed one-third of the cost of a public bridge used by persons traveling on the turnpike. The company then purchased fire insurance on the bridge. When the bridge was later destroyed by fire, the company suffered a loss of tolls and sued to collect on its insurance policy from the insurer, Farmers Mutual Insurance Co., defendant. Judgment was rendered for the plaintiff in the lower court, and defendant appealed contending that the plaintiff did not have an insurable interest in the bridge at the time of its destruction.

Decision
Reversed, for the defendant insurance company.

Reasoning
The turnpike company may not collect on the policy. The company does not have an insurable interest. In this state (Pennsylvania), the interest of the insured must arise from a legal title. The company's voluntary contribution when the bridge was built does not give it such an interest in the bridge.

Farmers Mutual Ins. Co. v. New Holland Turnpike Road Co., 15 A. 563 (Pa. 1888).

Unlike life insurance, with property insurance the insurable interest must *exist at the time of loss,* and the insured may recover *only up to the value of his or her interest* at the time of loss. For instance, if Jack purchased automobile insurance on his car but later sold the car, his insurable interest would cease at the time of sale. He could recover nothing if the car were destroyed after the sale.

Insurers' defense against payment.

Insurance Company Defenses

It is a common belief that insurance companies often refuse to make payment on their policies because of fine print provisions in the policies—or, stated another way, "the large print giveth and the fine print taketh away!" While this is, of course, an exaggeration, there are many cases where a company has a legitimate defense in its refusal to pay. Most of these defenses fall within one of three categories.

Warranties

A **warranty** is a statement of fact or a promise made by the insured *which is part of the insurance contract* and which must be true if the insurer is to be liable on the contract. Under the common law, the insurance company would be justified in rescinding the policy if the warranty was untrue. For example, if Jack purchased insurance on his frame house and warranted in the policy that the house was brown when it actually was pink, under the common law rule he could not recover for fire losses because his statement was untrue. This harsh rule has been changed in most states by statutes which provide that, unless the contract provides otherwise, statements of fact or promises made by the insured are interpreted to be representations.

warranty
(in insurance) a statement of fact or a promise made by the insured which is part of the insurance contract and which must be true if the insurer is to be liable on the contract

Representations

A **representation** is a statement of fact made by the insured *during negotiations* with the insurer before the policy is issued. It is *not a part of the insurance contract* and normally is made in the application for insurance. For instance, when Jack applied for fire insurance, he might have stated that his house was brown, but the statement might not be incorporated into the policy. If Jack's representation is not true—i.e., if the house is pink—may the company avoid liability on the policy? In the absence of fraud, the general rule is that the company may not *avoid* liability unless the representation was *material* to its decision whether to issue the policy. In other words, the question is whether the company would have issued the policy even if the representation had not been made. The color of Jack's house would not be material and, therefore, Jack's misrepresentation would be no defense. However, if Jack had represented that the house was made of stone when in fact it was a frame house, the company could *avoid* liability because of the misrepresentation of a material fact. The following case illustrates this.

representation
(in insurance) a statement of fact made by the insured which is not a part of the insurance contract but, during negotiation, is made to induce formation of the contract

Facts
In applying to Countryside Casualty Co., plaintiff, for automobile insurance, Orr, defendant, stated in his application that he had no arrests for offenses other than traffic violations, that he had not been fined or convicted for a moving violation, and that he did not use alcoholic beverages. In fact Orr had a number of convictions for traffic violations, forgery, and drunkenness. The company issued the policy, and Orr's car was later involved in an accident. Orr was not driving the car at the time of the accident. The company instituted an action to have the policy declared void because of Orr's misrepresentations, and to be relieved of any liability for the car accident. The lower court held for the plaintiff, and the defendant appealed. May the company cancel the policy and avoid liability because of Orr's false statement?

Decision
Yes. Affirmed for the plaintiff, company.

Reasoning
Orr's misrepresentations were material to the risk. Consequently, the policy was void and the company is not liable.

Countryside Casualty Co. v. Orr, 523 F.2d 870 (1975).

Concealment

Concealment occurs when the insured intentionally fails to disclose a *material fact* to the insurer. Generally the insured must disclose material facts and may not recover on the policy if such facts were concealed with the intention of defrauding the company. In the following case the information not disclosed by the insured was material to the insurer's decision to insure.

concealment
(in insurance) the insured's intentional failure to disclose a material fact to the insurer

counterclaim
a claim asserted by the defendant against the plaintiff's claim in a civil action

Facts
Tate, defendant, husband of the decedent wife, was listed as the beneficiary in a $25,000 life insurance policy on his wife, issued by the plaintiff, Massachusetts Life Insurance Co. When the policy was originally issued, the wife failed to disclose "that she had received advice from or attendance or treatment by physicians, other practitioners or psychologists" as requested by the application form. She had consulted a psychiatrist, who had treated her for depression, psychiatric disorder, and alcohol addiction. Shortly after applying for the insurance, she was hospitalized for severe depression and died of pneumonia two years after the policy was issued. The company then instituted an action to rescind the policy because of the wife's misrepresentations.

The defendant **counterclaimed** for the value of the policy. The trial court rendered judgment for the plaintiff, the appellate court reversed, and the plaintiff appealed.

Decision
Reversed, for the plaintiff, company.

Reasoning
The insured (wife's) intentional material misrepresentation by nondisclosure of her consultation with a psychiatrist concerning her condition and of his treatment of her depression and alcoholism justified rescission of the policy. The fact that the wife died from another cause does not disprove the increase of risk.

Massachusetts Mutual Life Insurance Company v. Tate, 369 N.E.2d 767 (N.Y. 1977).

Subrogation

subrogation
the substitution of one person for another with reference to a claim or a right

Subrogation is generally defined as the substitution of one person for another with reference to a claim or a right. In insurance law, subrogation is the substitution of the insurance company for the insured (after the company has paid the loss) with reference to the insured's rights or claims against the party who caused the loss.

Insurance companies generally have the right of subrogation in property insurance policies but not in life insurance policies. For example, let us assume that Jane purchased an automobile policy from No-Dent Insurance Company and that she was named as the beneficiary on her husband's life insurance policy, which was issued by Deep Pockets Insurance Company. If her husband was killed and her car damaged in an accident caused by Leroy, Jane would collect under both policies. No-Dent would then be subrogated to Jane's rights against Leroy, but Deep Pockets would have no right of subrogation.

Summary Statement

1. There are several types of insurance that directly affect the average person. Among the most important types are life insurance, homeowner's insurance, and automobile insurance.
2. Insurance is generally defined as a contract where one party agrees to pay another party for specified losses.
3. Under the federal McCarran-Ferguson Act, the regulation of the insurance business is primarily a matter for individual states.
4. An insured person must have an insurable interest in the risk covered by the contract to acquire insurance.
5. For life insurance, the insured must have an insurable interest in the insured life at the time the contract is formed; while for property insurance, the insured must have an insurable interest in the property at the time of property loss.
6. In most cases an insurance company cannot raise a warranty or representation as a defense unless the statement was material to its decision whether to issue the policy.
7. Insurance companies generally have the right to subrogation in property insurance policies, but not in life insurance policies.

The following case illustrates the application of the legal rules regarding misrepresentation by an applicant for insurance.

Vaughn v. American National Insurance Company
543 P.2d 1404 (Okla. 1975)

Lavender, Justice. Action brought by beneficiary on life insurance policy providing coverage of $5,000 as to ordinary life and an additional coverage of $5,000 for accidental death. The insured, Marvin Edward Vaughn, was the son of the beneficiary, Wanda Mae Vaughn. She was the plaintiff. April 4, 1972, the insured died from an automobile accident. It was an accidental death. American National Insurance Company (insurer) refused coverage on its life policy based on misrepresentations found in the application. By cross-petition, insurer sought cancellation of its policy. Trial court rendered judgment for insurer on its cross-petition to rescind. Court of Appeals reversed the judgment of rescission. The case was appealed.

In *Massachusetts Mutual Life Ins. Co. v. Allen* . . . (1965) this court said:

> A "misrepresentation" in negotiations for a life insurance policy under 36 O.S. 1961, section 3609, is a statement as a fact of something which is untrue, and which the insured knows or should know is untrue . . . and which has a tendency to mislead, where such misrepresentation is material to the risk.

False information given by the applicant in the application of his not being hospitalized and of no consultation or treatment by a physician, except for flu, concealed from the insurer true facts. These true facts, if revealed, would have given the insurer knowledge requiring a prudent insurer to investigate and would have led to the discovery of applicant's prior emotional problems.

We hold that false information was a misrepresentation. That misrepresentation was material to the acceptance of the risk on the life of the applicant. The insurer is entitled to a judgment of rescission.

Decision of the Court of Appeals vacated and judgment of the trial court affirmed.

Questions and Case Problems

1. A home appliance service company sold plans to homeowners who were planning to sell their homes. Under the plans the company performed a check on the appliances in the home and agreed to repair the appliances during a one-year period if the home buyer experienced problems with them. Is this plan a contract of insurance? [Opinion No. 78–20 of the New Mexico Attorney General, October 4, 1978.]

2. Baum discussed forming a corporation with Cook and extended over $16,000 worth of credit to Cook. Baum purchased key man life insurance on Cook from New York Life Insurance Company. Shortly after issuance of the policy, Cook formed a corporation with someone else. Does Baum, who was not included in the corporation, have an insurable interest in Cook's life? [*New York Life Insurance Co. v. Baum,* 700 F.2d 928 (5th Cir. (1983).]

3. Because of poor health, Stefan and Justina transferred title to their residence to their son Stephen. They continued to reside in the house and insured the property with Excelsior Insurance Company of New York. Stephen was not named in the insurance policy. When the house was damaged by fire, Excelsior claimed it was not liable because the parents had no insurable interest in the property. Is Excelsior correct? [*Etterle v. Excelsior Insurance Company of New York,* 428 N.Y.S.2d 95 (1980).]

4. Mary purchased an insurance policy on the life of her husband, Steve, in the amount of $600,000. Mary and Steve were later divorced, but Mary continued to pay premiums on the insurance policy. Later, when Steve died, the company refused to pay Mary on the grounds that (1) she had no insurable interest in Steve's life because of the divorce or (2) if she did have an insurable interest, its value was only $300,000 as determined by the size of Steve's alimony payments and his life expectancy. Is the company correct on either of these grounds? Why?

5. A husband and wife purchased a lot in a beach subdivision for $12,500. A street bordering the property gave the couple access to the lot. When they bought the property, the couple also obtained title insurance. After the purchase, they learned that their lot and the adjoining street are covered by high tide water every spring and fall. Does title insurance cover their loss? Why? [*Title & Trust Company of Florida v. Barrows*, 381 So.2d 1088 (Fla. 1979).]

6. An automobile that had been stolen in Ohio was sold to an innocent purchaser in Alabama. The purchaser bought an automobile insurance policy on the car, including fire and theft coverage. The car was later stolen from the purchaser and was destroyed by fire. The insurance company claimed that the purchaser was not entitled to collect on the policy because he had no insurable interest in the car. Is the company correct? Why? [*Ex parte Granite State Insurance Company v. Lowe*, 362 So.2d 240 (Ala. 1978).]

7. A mortgage company obtained a mortgage on real estate and purchased fire insurance on the property. The company immediately assigned the mortgage to the Federal National Mortgage Association (FNMA) and promised FNMA to maintain insurance on the property. When the property was later destroyed by fire, the insurance company refused to pay for the loss, claiming that the mortgage company had no insurable interest. Is the insurer correct? [*Capital Mortgage Corporation v. Michigan Basic Property Insurance Assoc.*, 261 N.W.2d 5 (Mich. 1977).]

8. A woman who was covered by a health insurance policy fell from a horse and suffered serious skull and brain injuries. As a result, the woman had to undergo surgery and therapy, which were paid for by the insurer. The insurer later sent the woman a life insurance application, which was completed and returned to the insurer. On the application it was stated that the woman had received head injuries but had recovered. The insurer issued the policy and shortly thereafter the woman died after undergoing another skull operation. The company claimed that it was not liable on the policy because of the misrepresentation. The beneficiary claimed that the company was liable because it knew of the woman's condition, having made payments under the health insurance policy. Who is correct? [*Murray v. Montgomery Ward Life Insurance Company*, 563 P.2d 20 (Colo. 1977).]

9. Arthur, in completing an insurance application, answered "no" to the following question: "Have you ever had or been told by a physician or other practitioner that you had . . . heart trouble?" In fact, Arthur had been told—and had been treated for a heart condition. When Arthur died, the company refused to pay the insurance proceeds to Arthur's widow. May the widow recover the proceeds? Why? [*Weeser v. Provident Mutual Life Ins. Co.*, 322 So.2d 230 (La. 1975).]

10. In the case of *Vaughn v. American National Insurance Company*, 543 P.2d 1404 (Okla. 1975),[3] would the decision have been different if the court had concluded that the applicant's answers in the application were warranties rather than representations? Why?

---

[3] See p. 483.

Life, Fire, and Automobile Insurance Law 32

After you have read this chapter, you should be able to:

1. Describe the three most common types of life insurance and explain their coverages.
2. Discuss the legal effect of a conditional receipt.
3. Define the term "incontestability" as it is used in an insurance contract.
4. List the types of homeowner's insurance policy forms and explain their coverages.
5. Compare traditional and no-fault automobile insurance.

Introduction

In chapter 31 we examined the general principles of insurance law, including the different types of insurance, the definition of insurance, the methods of organization used by insurers, insurance regulation, the concept of insurable interest, and various defenses used by insurers. In this chapter we will focus on the three most important types of insurance for the average person: (1) life insurance, (2) fire insurance, and (3) automobile insurance. Fire insurance is usually purchased as part of a multi-coverage package known as homeowner's insurance, which will be discussed below.

Life Insurance

Types of Life Insurance

There are three general types of life insurance policies. **Term insurance** is insurance sold for a specified time period. If the person dies within the time period, the company will pay the face value of the policy. If the insured does not die within the term, the insurance terminates and the company usually has the right to keep all premiums—i.e., there is no cash value.

term insurance
insurance sold for a specified time period, with no cash value

Whole life insurance (sometimes called straight life, ordinary life, or permanent life insurance) provides coverage throughout the life of the insured. Whole life insurance includes cash values which build up through the years. The policyholder is entitled to borrow money from the company up to the cash value or to turn in the policy to the insurance company for cash.

whole life insurance
insurance for the entire life of the insured, with cash values that increase through the years

Endowment insurance is insurance that pays the policyholder a lump sum of money at a date specified in the policy. If the insured person dies before that date, the money is paid to the beneficiary at death. This type of policy is popular with persons who will need a large sum of money at a future date—e.g., for college expenses or retirement. However, because of inflation, the money eventually received by the insured or the beneficiary may be inadequate to buy what it was originally expected to be able to buy.

endowment insurance
insurance that pays the policyholder a lump sum at a specified date

Conditional Receipts

Although **conditional receipts** vary in form, the most common type of receipt provides that coverage is effective on the date of application unless the company determines that the applicant was not an acceptable or insurable risk according to company rules and standards on that date. If, under company rules and standards, the applicant is considered insurable, there is coverage even when the applicant dies before company approval of the policy, as is illustrated by the following case.

conditional receipt
a receipt that provides an applicant for life insurance with temporary coverage until the application is approved by the company

Facts
On March 14, 1974, a man applied for a $125,000 life insurance policy with Provident Life & Accident Insurance Co., defendant. He paid the first month's premium and was given a conditional receipt stating that he was covered immediately if the company was satisfied that he was insurable on that date. The next day he was examined by a physician who recommended the man as a first class risk. On March 19, before the application reached the company's home office, the man was killed in an automobile accident. The company refused coverage, and the beneficiaries of the policy, plaintiffs, sued for the proceeds. The lower court rendered judgment for the plaintiffs, and the defendant appealed.

Decision
Affirmed, for the plaintiffs, beneficiaries.

Reasoning
The man was an insurable risk on March 14. Consequently there was coverage under the conditional receipt, and the company was wrong in refusing coverage.

Vernon v. Provident Life & Accident Insurance Co., 222 S.E.2d 501 (S.C. 1976).

Incontestability

Let us assume that Clyde purchased a life insurance policy naming his wife as beneficiary. Clyde died after the policy had been in effect for nine years. After his death the company refused coverage, claiming that Clyde had lied about his health on the application. The company's refusal obviously puts the beneficiary in a difficult position; it will be hard to prove what Clyde's health was nine years ago, and the person best able to testify, Clyde, is dead. To avoid undue burden on beneficiaries, state law usually requires insurance companies to include an **incontestability clause** in life insurance policies. This clause provides that the company may not contest the coverage, except for non-payment of premiums, after the policy has been in effect for a stated time period, usually one or two years.

incontestability clause
a clause in a life insurance policy providing that the company may not contest coverage after the policy has been in effect for a stated time period

Suicide

Life insurance policies usually contain a clause stating that if the insured commits suicide within a certain period (e.g., two years) from the date the policy was issued, the company is not liable. Such clauses are upheld by the courts, which have decided that the public policy of enforcing the contract and providing for the beneficiary outweighs the public policy of discouraging suicide. Furthermore, when death occurs within the two-year period, there is a presumption that the death was not a suicide. In the following case it was held that suicide did not occur because the death was not intentional.

Facts
A twenty-year-old Marine served in a fighter squadron as a radar technician. He was familiar with .45 calibre automatic pistols and had given instructions on their use. The Marine was a happy-go-lucky, cheerful person who sometimes tried to "shake up" his friends by placing a .45 to his head and pulling the trigger. One day when the Marine was apparently in good spirits, he suddenly put a pistol to his head, said "Here's to it" to a friend, and pulled the trigger. The gun fired, killing the Marine. Government Personnel Life Insurance Company, defendant, that insured him claimed this was a suicide and refused to pay on the policy. The Marine's mother, plaintiff, the beneficiary under the policy, sued for the policy proceeds. The lower court rendered judgment for the plaintiff, and the defendant appealed.

Decision
Affirmed, for the plaintiff, mother.

Reasoning
The death is not a suicide. The company must prove that the death was intentional. The burden of proof was not met here.

Angelus v. Government Personnel Life Insurance Co., 321 P.2d 545 (Wash. 1958).

Beneficiaries

The **beneficiary** in an insurance policy is the person designated to receive the death benefit after the insured dies. Most policies provide for the designation of second beneficiaries, who will take the death benefit if the first beneficiary is not alive when the insured dies.

Although, as a general rule, contract rights of a third party beneficiary cannot be altered,[1] the insurance contract is an exception to this rule. In most policies the contract stipulates that the policy owner reserves the right to change the beneficiary and can do so by following a procedure set forth in the policy. The change of beneficiary is usually not effective unless the company records the change at its home office.

As a general rule under common law, a person will not be allowed to benefit from his or her own wrongful act. As applied to the insurance contract, this rule means that a beneficiary who murders the insured cannot recover on the insurance policy.

beneficiary
(in insurance) the person designated in a life insurance policy to receive the death benefit

---

[1] See pp. 187, 190–91.

Homeowner's Insurance

The purchase of a house represents the largest investment ever made by most individuals. Consequently, it is extremely important that this investment is protected with the proper insurance coverage. Most homeowner's policies today represent a package of property and liability coverages.

Policy Forms

Four types of policy forms are commonly used today. The *Basic Form* provides protection for eleven types of perils, including fire,[2] windstorm, hail, explosion, and vandalism. The *Broad Form* policy, probably the most popular policy, adds coverage for five additional perils: (1) the weight of ice and snow, (2) the collapse of a building, (3) accidents from steam or water systems, (4) accidents from electrical equipment, and (5) falling objects such as trees. The *Comprehensive Form* is "all-risk" coverage; that is, all perils are covered with very few exceptions, such as earthquake, tidal waves, war, and nuclear radiation. Finally, a *Special Form* provides Comprehensive Form coverage on the real estate and Broad Form coverage on personal property.

Property Coverage

Three types of property are covered by a homeowner's policy. First, of course, the *dwelling* itself is protected from loss by the above perils. Second, *appurtenant structures* such as a garage or storage sheds are normally covered for an amount equal to ten percent of the coverage on the dwelling. Third, *personal property* such as furniture, clothing, and jewelry is normally covered up to an amount equal to fifty percent of the coverage on the dwelling.

In addition to these property coverages, the standard policy will provide an **additional living expense** in an amount up to twenty percent of the coverage on the dwelling. This is used to cover living expenses incurred by a homeowner who is forced to leave the home while repairs are being made.

additional living expense
a homeowner's insurance policy provision that covers living expenses incurred by a homeowner forced to leave the home while repairs are being made

Liability Coverage

The standard homeowner's policy includes comprehensive **personal liability coverage.** Most individuals are protected under their automobile insurance policies if they injure someone while driving a car. However, many accidents are not caused by the use of an automobile. For example, if Sam is playing golf and hits another player with a ball, or if a visitor slips on the carpet in Sam's house, Sam might be liable for substantial damages. The personal liability coverage protects the homeowner in the event such claims are made.

As additional protection, the standard homeowner's policy will pay reasonable medical expenses to persons injured in the house or as a result of the insured's activities away from the house. For example, if Gloria slipped on the sidewalk when visiting Sam's house, the policy would pay Gloria's medical expenses up to a certain amount, even though Sam was not legally responsible for the accident.

personal liability coverage
a homeowner's insurance policy provision covering liability for accidents on or away from the insured property

Exclusions

The standard homeowner's policy contains certain express exclusions from both property and liability coverage. Examples of exclusions from *property coverage* are losses resulting from volcanic eruptions, earthquakes, landslides, floods, and water that backs up through sewers. Exclusions from *liability coverage* include losses covered by workers' compensation laws; liability resulting from the use of aircraft, motor vehicles, and watercraft; and liability resulting from business pursuits.

---

[2] By "fire" is meant a "hostile" fire, which is a fire burning in a place where it was *not* intended to burn. A fire in a place where it was intended to burn is a "friendly" fire (e.g., a fire set in a fireplace), which is not covered by the insurance policy.

In addition to the express exclusions from coverage, certain exceptions from coverage will be implied by the courts. A "friendly fire" exception occurred in the following case.

Facts
Youse, plaintiff, wrapped her star sapphire ring in a handkerchief and placed it on her dresser with some Kleenex tissue. Her maid later inadvertently threw the Kleenex and the handkerchief into a wastebasket. Another servant then emptied the wastebasket into a trash burner and burned the trash. The ring, which was later discovered in the trash burner, was damaged to the extent of $900. Youse claimed that her homeowner's policy, issued by Employers Fire Insurance Co., defendant, covered the loss because personal property was insured "against all direct loss or damage by fire." Judgment was rendered for the plaintiff in the lower court, and the defendant appealed.

Decision
Reversed, for the defendant, company.

Reasoning
This loss is not covered. The policy's clause of loss by fire means by a hostile fire. There is an implied exception in homeowner's policies for "friendly fires." Friendly fires are those lighted and contained in a usual place for fire such as a fireplace, an incinerator, or a trash burner. Here, the loss was caused by a friendly fire.

Youse v. Employers Fire Insurance Co., Boston, Mass., 238 P.2d 472 (Kan. 1951).

Replacement Cost or Coinsurance

Many homeowner's policies contain a provision that may trap an unsuspecting homeowner and result in a loss of thousands of dollars in coverage. This is a provision that requires a homeowner to carry insurance equal to a certain percentage (usually eighty percent) of the full replacement cost of the house. If the owner meets the eighty percent requirement, he is covered for the full cost of the replacement *up to the amount of coverage*. If the coverage is less than eighty percent, then the homeowner receives the larger of: (1) the actual cash value of the part of the building damaged, or (2) the proportion of the replacement cost which the amount of insurance coverage bears to the required eighty percent of the full replacement cost.

Automobile Insurance

There are two basic automobile insurance mechanisms in our country to cover injuries and property damage resulting from such accidents: traditional automobile insurance, and no-fault automobile insurance.

Types of automobile insurance.

Traditional Automobile Insurance

Traditional automobile insurance is a package of four basic types of coverages. *First,* and probably most important, the policy provides **liability insurance** which covers you for damages you might have to pay if you injure someone or damage someone's property in an automobile accident. In several states, financial responsibility laws require owners of automobiles to purchase liability insurance. The purpose of such laws is to protect the public from losses caused by motorists who are not financially responsible. Liability coverage insures not only the named insured and residents of the insured's household, but also other persons using the automobile with the permission of the named insured.

The *second* basic coverage is for *medical payments,* including all reasonable expenses for medical, surgical, and hospital services incurred within one year from the date of the accident. Covered persons include the named insured, relatives, and guests riding in the automobile.

The *third* basic coverage provides insurance for *physical damage to the automobile*. Most automobile owners purchase two types of property insurance. **Collision insurance** pays for damage to the insured automobile when it is involved in a collision. **Comprehensive insurance** covers damage to the insured automobile resulting from causes other than collision, such as falling objects, fire, theft, explosion, earthquake, windstorm,

automobile liability insurance
insurance that covers a driver who injures someone, or damages someone's property, in an automobile accident

collision insurance
insurance covering damage to the insured automobile resulting from a collision

comprehensive insurance
insurance covering damage to the insured automobile resulting from causes other than collision

hail, flood, or riot. Both collision and comprehensive insurance are often sold with a deductible—e.g., $100. This means that if there is physical damage to the automobile, the owner pays the first $100 and the company pays losses above that amount.

The *fourth and last type* of basic coverage is *uninsured motorist* coverage. It is possible that the insured owner of an automobile, member of the insured's family, or guests in the automobile might be injured in an accident caused by a person who does not have liability insurance as required by law or who is a "hit and run" driver. In such cases **uninsured motorist coverage** pays all sums which the insured is entitled to recover for bodily injury caused by the accident. A "hit and run" accident is defined as one in which there is physical contact between the automobiles at the time of the accident and the identity of the other driver cannot be determined. In the following case no such physical contact occurred.

> **uninsured motorist coverage**
> insurance that pays all sums that the insured is entitled to recover when he is injured by an uninsured or a "hit and run" driver

Facts
An unidentified car stopped suddenly at an intersection. This caused the following car to stop abruptly and a motorcycle to run into the following car. The motorcycle was driven by Hensley, plaintiff, who claimed that he was entitled to recover under the uninsured motorist coverage in his insurance policy issued by Government Employees Insurance Company, defendant. The lower court rendered judgment for the defendant, and plaintiff appealed.

Decision
Affirmed, for the defendant, company.

Reasoning
This was not a hit and run accident, and consequently the motorcyclist is not covered and cannot recover. There was no physical contact between the motorcycle and the unidentified first vehicle.

Hensley v. Government Employees Insurance Company, 340 So.2d 603 (La. 1976).

No-Fault Automobile Insurance

No-fault automobile insurance has been enacted in one form or another in approximately half of the states and now covers over half the population of the United States. Appellate courts in a number of states have approved the no-fault concept and have declared it to be constitutional.

The basic no-fault concept is simple, although the details may vary, depending on the state. No-fault, in essence, gives victims of automobile accidents the right to be paid by their own insurance policies for *personal injury,* no matter who caused the loss (personal injury protection). But no-fault laws also take away the right to sue the person who caused the accident. The net result is that to recover under no-fault you no longer must prove that another person is "at fault."

To illustrate no-fault, we might assume that twins, Jack and Jill, are involved in similar automobile accidents. In both cases the cars driven by Jack and Jill are rear-ended by careless drivers and their cars, each worth $2,000, are totally destroyed. Both Jack and Jill suffer broken right legs and their out-of-pocket losses total $4,000 for medical care and $3,000 in lost wages. The only difference is that Jack is injured in Detroit and, as a Michigan resident, is covered by the most liberal no-fault law in the United States. Jill, an Ohio resident, is injured a few miles south of Detroit in Toledo and is not covered by no-fault.

> Advantages of no-fault insurance.

Under the Michigan no-fault system, victims of automobile accidents are entitled to recover from their own insurance companies all charges for medical and hospital care and lost wages for up to three years. In addition to this *required* coverage, drivers have the option, also available in states without no-fault, of purchasing collision coverage for their cars. In our case, Jack would immediately collect from his company $4,000 for medical care, $3,000 for lost wages and, if he had purchased enough optional collision coverage, $2,000 for the car.

> Disadvantages of no-fault insurance.

But in no-fault states like Michigan, a victim cannot sue the person who caused the accident unless the damages are greater than the benefits provided under the law (or unless the victim dies, has bodily functions seriously impaired, or is seriously disfigured).

Thus, in our case, Jack cannot sue the other driver and will receive no compensation for his pain and suffering. Also, if he has no collision coverage, he will recover nothing from the other driver for the damage to his car.

Jill, living in a state without no-fault, could recover the value of her car and at least part of the cost of medical care from her own insurance company if she had elected to include these coverages. But even if she had no insurance coverage, she could sue the other driver and might recover not only her out-of-pocket losses, but also a substantial amount for pain and suffering. According to one study, the amount paid in the average settlement is 2.4 times the amount of actual loss, or in this case $21,600.

Consequently, if neither Jack nor Jill had purchased collision coverage, Jack would be limited to a total of $7,000 under no-fault, which he can collect only from his own company, while Jill might recover $21,600 from the person who caused the accident.

However, is Jill really in a better position than Jack? Under the *fault* system, in order to recover from the other driver, Jill must prove that the other driver is at fault. If we assume that this can be proven, in many states Jill will still recover nothing if the other driver proves that Jill's own carelessness contributed in even a small way to the accident. Regardless of the final outcome, Jill will have to wait more than five years in some metropolitan areas for her case to come to trial, and in the meantime must pay her own bills. And, if Jill wins the case, it is possible that as much as fifty percent of her recovery will be used for attorney's fees and related costs. Considerations such as these have caused Congress and the states without no-fault to continue the debate as to whether no-fault systems should be adopted.

Advantages of the "fault" system of insurance.

Disadvantages of the "fault" system of insurance.

Some Trends in Insurance

In the business world there exists the potential for large, powerful organizations to take advantage of relatively powerless individuals. In these situations the law often serves as an equalizer and thus prevents, to a large extent, unethical behavior. For example, three trends have developed in recent years to protect insureds from companies which might attempt to insert "fine print" clauses in insurance contracts or which are tempted to act unfairly in paying claims.

First, state insurance commissioners in several states have adopted regulations requiring certain types of policies to be readable. For example, the purpose of the Pennsylvania regulation, section 64.1, "is an auto insurance policy that is understandable to a person of average intelligence and education." To carry out this purpose, the regulations require the use of a certain size type, short sentences, and simple words.

Second, courts in several states have developed the doctrine of "reasonable expectations" to protect the insurance consumer. Under this rule, persons who have reasonable expectations that they are covered by an insurance policy will, in fact, be covered—even though they did not read the policy and the fine print of the policy denies coverage.

Third, courts in many states, led by California, have decided that insurance companies have a duty to act in good faith when dealing with insureds. Insurance companies that breach this duty are often required to pay millions of dollars in punitive damages.

Summary Statement

1. The three most common types of life insurance are term insurance, whole life insurance, and endowment insurance.
2. A conditional receipt is used to provide insurance coverage between the date of application and the date the company approves the policy, provided that the applicant was insurable on the application date.

3. The incontestability clause in life insurance policies prevents the company from contesting coverage after the policy has been in effect for a specified time, normally one or two years.
4. There are four common types of homeowner's insurance. The most popular type is the Broad Form, which provides coverage for sixteen specific perils.
5. Traditional automobile insurance is a package of four coverages: liability, medical payments, property, and uninsured motorist.
6. With automobile no-fault insurance, persons injured in automobile accidents are compensated by their own insurance companies and, in most cases, cannot sue the person who caused the accident.

The following case illustrates the problems faced by a person who is injured by an uninsured motorist—even when there is uninsured motorist coverage.

Taft v. Sweeney
373 A.2d 712 (N.J. 1977)

per curiam
by the court, all the judges

Per Curiam. At issue in this appeal is the availability of Uninsured Motorists coverage (UM) issued to plaintiff as a source of compensation for injuries he received in an automobile accident where the total proceeds of the liability policy insuring the culpable defendant to the statutory minimum has been tendered to and accepted by plaintiff. Plaintiff contends that, since the value of the injuries received in the accident exceeds the amount of liability coverage available, defendant must be regarded as uninsured to the extent of such excess and he is therefore entitled to tap his UM coverage for the excess. The trial judge granted the motion for summary judgment interposed by Safeco Insurance Company, the carrier which provided the UM coverage. This appeal ensued. We affirm.

The facts of the underlying accident and the available insurance policies are not complex. On September 29, 1974 an automobile driven by plaintiff collided with defendant Sweeney's automobile. There seems little doubt but that the collision was caused by the negligence of Sweeney, who was charged with operating his vehicle while under the influence of alcohol and subsequently pleaded guilty to the charge. At the time of the accident Sweeney was insured by defendant Transamerica Insurance Company through a liability policy which limited coverage to $15,000 per person and $30,000 maximum for each accident, the minimum amounts required by N.J.S.A. 39:6B-1. . . .

Fundamental to the issue raised in this appeal is the meaning to be attributed to the word "uninsured" in N.J.S.A. 17:28-1.1 which sets forth the requirement for uninsured motorists coverage.

Uninsured motorists coverage . . . becomes available only when the insured is injured by an *uninsured* motor vehicle or a hit and run automobile. Neither is involved in this case. [Emphasis added]

Defendant Sweeney was insured to the statutory minimum. Nothing in N.J.S.A. 17:28-1.1 suggests that UM coverage is to be made available as excess insurance whenever a liability policy, meeting the statutory minimum limits of coverage, proves an inadequate source of compensation to the injured insured. The essential requirement for such coverage is lack of insurance, not inadequate insurance.

Affirmed.

Questions and Case Problems

1. Tom and Mary, a young married couple, have just purchased their first home after obtaining a twenty-year mortgage from First Bank. Tom and Mary both work and need their incomes to make the mortgage payments. However, they are afraid that if one of them should die, the other would be unable to make the payments. What type of insurance protection would you recommend for Tom and Mary? Why?

2. An attorney represented an engineering company for a fee of $300 a month and was provided coverage under the company's group life insurance plan. Although the engineering company did not withhold taxes for the attorney and she was not listed on the

payroll, the company did send a letter to the insurer listing her as an employee. However, the attorney did not meet the definition of employee within the policy because she was not employed on a full-time basis. The attorney died after the policy had been in effect for two years, and the insurer refused to pay the beneficiary. Must the insurer pay? Why? [*Bonitz v. Travelers Insurance Company,* 372 N.E.2d 254 (Mass. 1978).]

3. A life insurance company issued a policy on Edward's life. One day Edward's wife, Angela, discovered Edward dead in their bedroom. Edward had been shot in the temple, but there was no evidence that he had held the murder weapon. Angela was charged with murder but acquitted. The insurance company claimed that Angela was not entitled to the proceeds because this was a suicide within two years of the date of the policy. Is the company correct? [*Lincoln Income Life Ins. Co. v. Parker,* 224 S.E.2d 781 (Ga. 1976).]

4. An insured owned a life insurance policy which named certain beneficiaries. The insured executed a will in which he provided that persons other than the named beneficiaries were to receive the insurance proceeds. He died the day after signing the will. Who should receive the proceeds—the beneficiaries named in the will or the beneficiaries named in the policy? [*Pena v. Salinas,* 536 S.W.2d 671 (Tex. 1976).]

5. A homeowner (with homeowner's liability insurance coverage) worked at a research center. One of his duties at the center was to take care of a wolf named Sophie and, in order to fulfill this duty, he kept Sophie at his home. One day while at the home Sophie bit a child. The insurance company claimed that the homeowner had no liability coverage for the bite. Is the company correct? Why? [*North River Insurance Company v. Poos,* 553 S.W.2d 500 (Mo. 1977).]

6. Charlie's car would not start. He borrowed his friend Evelyn's car in order to charge the battery. While Charlie's battery was being charged through jumper cables attached to Evelyn's vehicle, the battery exploded and injured Charlie. Evelyn's insurance provides coverage for liability resulting from "ownership, maintenance and use" of her vehicle. Is Charlie entitled to recover damages from Evelyn's insurer? [*McNeill v. Maryland Insurance Guaranty Association,* 427 A.2d 1056 (Md. 1981).]

7. A truck driver, in making a delivery of goods, learned that the goods could not be unloaded for a couple of days. He unhitched the trailer and on the following day picked up several strangers and began to visit a number of local bars. After he had around nine beers, the driver drove the truck into a utility pole, which caught fire and damaged a school. The company that insured the owner of the truck claimed that there was no coverage. Is the company correct? [*Louisville Gas and Electric Company v. Employer's Mutual Liability Insurance Co.,* 548 S.W.2d 843 (Ky. 1977).]

8. William owned a 1977 Plymouth. He allowed his son Robert to use the car but instructed Robert not to let anyone else drive the car. One night Robert used the car to drive two friends to a particular destination. When they were ready to leave, Robert's friends went to the car, found the keys, and decided to drive the car to where Robert was standing. Robert did not give them permission to drive the car. On the way to Robert, the car was involved in a collision. Does William's insurance provide coverage? [*Western States Mutual Insurance Company v. Verucchi,* 363 N.E.2d 826 (Ill. 1977).]

9. Suzanne was driving her car west on a highway when an approaching car crossed the center line and forced her off the highway. She crashed into several trees and another automobile. The approaching car, which did not strike her car, did not stop and was not identified. Suzanne now claims that her own insurer must pay the damages, which she claimed were $27,500, under her uninsured motorist coverage. Is she correct? Why? [*Jett v. Doe,* 551 S.W.2d 221 (Ky. 1977).]

10. In the case of *Taft v. Sweeney,* 373 A.2d 712 (N.J. 1977),[3] assume that four passengers riding with Taft were seriously injured in the accident along with Taft. Would Taft and the passengers be entitled to collect under Taft's uninsured motorist coverage? Why?

---

[3] See p. 492.

Ethics and Business Law in Part 6
Secured Transactions, Bankruptcy, and Insurance

Introduction

This end-of-Part discussion, like the others in this book, is designed to encourage students to begin forming personal beliefs about what is right or wrong conduct in business. The discussion here builds on the material in the first end-of-Part discussion on pages 58 to 69; you may find it helpful to review that.

This material has several goals. The "sampling of ethical issues" section immediately following is designed to help you see the range of ethical issues associated with this area of the law. The in-depth discussion is intended to provide you with a background for forming your own beliefs about a single very important ethical issue in business. The problems at the end of this Part are designed to build your skill in ethical analysis while exploring further the in-depth issue.

A Sampling of Ethical Issues in Secured Transactions, Insurance, and Bankruptcy

One ethical issue is the extent to which unethical conduct by one party may justify another party in also engaging in unethical conduct. Often in business, one firm feels justified in engaging in unethical conduct because a competitor does it and failure to respond in kind will result in a loss of business. The right to repossess raises this same issue. UCC 9-503 allows creditors to repossess property without going to court if they do so without a "breach of peace." If repossession places persons in danger of physical harm, this would impose a burden on them which far exceeds the benefit to the repossessor and therefore would be illegal. But many repossessions involve some form of trickery. Often cars are repossessed late at night, by breaking into them and using a master key to start them and drive them away. In one case a "repo man" tricked the debtor into driving his car into a dealership to determine whether he was behind in his monthly payments. While the debtor was inside a dealership office, the car was taken and locked up in a storage area.

When the debtor sued the creditor for the tort of conversion, the judge concluded that the repossession had been in violation of UCC 9-503, stating that "to allow repossession in these circumstances would be to encourage practices abhorrent to society: fraud, trickery, chicanery, and subterfuge. . . ." Do you think unethical conduct on the part of someone else (such as a debtor failing to pay a just debt) is valid justification for you to engage in questionable conduct (such as repossessing with the use of trickery)?

Insurance raises a basic ethical issue: ought persons to be able to escape responsibility for their own behavior? Some forms of insurance have this effect. For example, workers compensation insurance shifts the responsibility for a safe workplace away from the employer. When an injury occurs the insurance pays rather than a negligent employer. Do you think it is right to allow people and organizations to escape personal responsibility through insurance?

Another insurance issue involves the ethics of adjusting rates for differing classes of risk. Thus, most non-drinkers and non-smokers can purchase life insurance at a discount because they have a lower risk of early death. Smoking and drinking are factors over which most potential insureds *have control.* And the lower insurance rates provide an incentive for healthy conduct. You probably think this type of rating is ethical.

In many other instances, individuals are rated on the basis of factors over which they have *no control.* Thus, if you applied for life insurance and disclosed that both of your parents and one brother died before age 50, you would likely be declined or charged a very high rate. Do you think this type of rating is ethical?

A recent case in bankruptcy illustrates an ethical dilemma for the legal system. In the case, In re *Graham, Debtor* 21 B.R. 235 (Iowa, 1982), a radiologist, age 59, who earned over $200,000 per year filed for voluntary bankruptcy under Chapter 7, showing debts of over $1,000,000. His nonexempt property was worth about $97,000. One of the unsecured creditors petitioned to convert the case from Chapter 7 to Chapter 11 to allow for repayment of the debts. The court denied the petition stating that Dr. Graham was entitled to make a fresh start and that society was better off by encouraging him to work rather than discouraging him by using his wages to fund a Chapter 11 plan. Do you think Chapter 7 was intended to help persons in Dr. Graham's position? Or do you think Dr. Graham was exploiting the legal system? If you were in Dr. Graham's position would you seek Chapter 7 or Chapter 11 protection?

In-Depth Discussion of a Basic Issue: Are People Only Economic Entities?

The issue addressed here is the moral status of other human beings and what this implies for the way the law and managers treat them. Stated another way, is it ethically right to treat others as exclusively economic entities?

What the Law Implies

Clearly, the law recognizes that individuals are, at least in part, economic entities. Thus, the law allows them to contract, to be financially liable for breach of contract, and to be obligated to financially compensate those whom they tortiously injure. In allowing individuals to give security interests in their property, and allowing that property to be repossessed and sold to satisfy the debt, the law again acknowledges that people are at least in part economic entities.

On the other hand, the law imposes limits on the economic injury which persons can be compelled to endure. For example, there are substantial procedural obstacles to collecting an unsecured debt. Thus, the debtor must be sued and the debt proved in court before the available property can be seized and sold. Even when the unsecured debt has been proven in court, there are some items of the debtor's property, called *exempt property,* which are not available to satisfy the unpaid debt. The existence of the exempt property category suggests that the legal system places limits on the extent to which individuals can be treated as economic entities.

The whole idea of allowing an individual's debts to be forgiven without repayment (bankruptcy) again illustrates the law's conclusion that there are limits to the economic entity idea. The presence of an exempt property category for bankruptcy further reinforces this idea. In effect, the general thrust of this body of law is to allow persons to escape their economic obligation in order to preserve their human dignity.

In the following paragraphs we examine these concepts of exempt property and bankruptcy using the four styles of ethical reasoning. Our objective is to see the way these styles of ethical reasoning lead to differing conclusions about the ethical character of individuals.

Egoism

For egoists, the moral worth of exempt property and forgiveness of legitimate debts varies, depending on the status of the individual egoist. Debtors evaluate these legal concepts as ethically good while creditors evaluate them as ethically bad.

Most fundamentally however, an egoist almost by definition views all others as entities which have value only in proportion to the pleasure they generate for him or her. This is almost the same as viewing persons exclusively as economic entities.

Utilitarianism

At some times in history, debtors could be jailed for failure to repay their obligations. If such a severe penalty were to exist today, default on a debt would likely be a rare event. Because of its rarity, the risks and expenses of lending money are reduced. This is likely to lead to lower interest rates which affect the majority of persons positively. Consequently, a utilitarian could justify treating individuals as exclusively economic entities.

Kant's Philosophy

This style of ethical reasoning accords distinctive status to individuals. Kant sees people as unique because of their capacity to engage in ethical reasoning. Therefore, he concludes that we may never use persons "exclusively as a means to an end." Therefore, the exclusively utilitarian approach to people, as for example treating them only as economic entities, is, in Kant's view, ethically wrong.

Religious Ethics

Religious persons reach a conclusion similar to Kant's, but for different reasons. This ethic generally sees humans as made in the image of God, possessing an eternal soul, and with God-given dominion over the other forms of life on the earth. Further, in many religious traditions, the poor occupy a status which entitles them to special treatment. Certainly this orientation would reject the conclusion that individuals can be exclusively economic entities.

Solving Ethics Problems

Like the other end-of-Part discussions in this book, this one presents problems for you to consider. These problems have three goals. The first is to give you the opportunity to further explore the in-depth issue. The second goal is to give you experience in ethical reasoning about the law and about related management problems. The third goal is to let you see how thinking critically about the law can increase your ability to make ethical decisions. To facilitate this, the problems begin by asking you to analyze the law for its ethical content and then shift to looking at related problems in managerial ethics.

For a discussion of the ethical roles of markets and the law, and examples of the four styles of ethical reasoning—egoism, utilitarianism, Kant's philosophy, and religious ethics—read the business ethics material at the end of Part 1.

Problems

1. Review the case of In re *Conard, Debtor* on page 472. There Conard filed for bankruptcy and sought relief from a student loan on the grounds of undue hardship. Try to assess the style of ethical reasoning implicit in portions of the Bankruptcy Code which exempt student loans from discharge and the section which allows discharge for undue hardship. Also try to compare the judge's style of reasoning along with that of Paul Conard.

2. You are a student just completing an undergraduate degree in business. You have a job offer from your father's firm for $24,000 per year, to begin in 6 months. During your years as a student you incurred personal debts which require monthly payments of $750 per month. If you file bankruptcy, all of these debts will be forgiven. Ought you to do this? Why or why not?

3. Suppose you are a loan officer of a small bank in charge of small business loans. One of your borrowers is encountering severe financial difficulty. This person bought a franchised computer store in the early 1980's and competition has, through no fault of the franchisee, made this business much less profitable than in the past. You have a security interest in all the store's inventory. The franchisee is in default and asking you for extra time to make up the past due amount. You judge that if you repossess the inventory and drive him out of business you will recover about 80 cents for every dollar loaned. On the other hand, if you wait you judge that there is a 25% chance he will turn the business around and you will collect both principal and interest; however there is a corresponding risk of 75% that he will still go under. If he does, you will collect only 60 cents on the dollar. In making your decision, should you consider the impact of this decision on the franchisee's personal life? If you think you should, how much weight should this be given? What would you do?

4. Suppose you have a subordinate who has worked for you for 2 years, who has usually done a very good job, but who is currently going through a protracted, emotionally draining, divorce. As a consequence, his productivity has fallen dramatically. In thinking carefully you conclude that your department would be substantially ahead financially if you fired this employee and hired someone whose life is more stable. Ought you to fire and rehire? Why or why not?

PART 7 Agency and Employment

33. **Nature and Creation of Agency**
    The legal relationship that occurs when a party transacts business affairs with a person acting on behalf of another.

34. **Duties of Principal and Agent to Each Other**
    The limits of authority and power that the agent has in changing legal relationships between the principal and third parties. This chapter also investigates the idea that the creation of the agency relationship brings into existence rights and duties between principal and agent.

35. **Agency and the Law of Contracts and Torts**
    How the legal environment in the substantive law areas of contracts and torts is impacted for both the principal and agent by the operation of the agency. How the agent can limit his or her exposure to the legal environment.

36. **Termination of Agency**
    Terminating the agency relationship by acts of the parties, by operation of law, and when equity and fairness require. How the law prevents premature termination of the agency relationship.

37. **Employment**
    Various state and federal laws affecting employers and employees, employer use of detection tests, and unfair discrimination against women in the workforce because of their sex. Labor law is covered in chapter 49.

Summary
An agency relationship is created by agreement for the purpose of transacting business affairs by one party with a person acting on behalf of another. The primary objective of the agency is to give authority and power to an agent to create a contract between the principal and a third person. In the process, various rights, duties, and liabilities are created on the part of the principal, agent, and third person.

As with other legal relationships, the law provides for termination of the agency relationship through freedom of individual action and by operation of law.

Any discussion of employment involves not only the agency relationship between employer and employee, covered in chapters 33–36, but also an examination of the regard which society has for employees as reflected in federal and state legislation affecting their employment, protection from injury, compensation for injury, and financial security. Chapter 37 is concerned with such legislation.

Business ethics as it relates to the text material in this Part is considered at the end of the Part.

33 Nature and Creation of Agency

After you have read this chapter, you should be able to:

1. Define the agency relationship and identify the source of agency law.
2. Describe the relationship of agency law to business transactions.
3. Understand how an agent's conduct may affect the liabilities of the agent, the principal, and the third person.
4. Explain why it is important to determine whether an agent is a servant.
5. Distinguish an agent from
   a. an independent contractor,
   b. a real estate broker,
   c. a bailee,
   d. a trustee.
6. Distinguish a general power of attorney from a limited power of attorney.
7. Describe the relationship of agency law to business associations.
8. Explain who may be a principal and who may be an agent.
9. Distinguish a general from a special agent.
10. Explain how an agency is created.
11. Define ratification and describe its five elements.
12. Explain who must prove the agency relationship.

Introduction and Nature of the Agency Relationship

The laws of **agency** enter into all forms of business activities, such as the corporation, partnership, and sole proprietorship. The rights and duties of the parties involved in agency create a series of potential lawsuits. In order for you to recognize an agency problem, it is necessary to distinguish other types of somewhat similar business relationships.

agency
a legal relationship between two persons who agree that one is to act on behalf of the other, subject to the other's control

Agency Concept

Business associations rely on their employees and other representatives to contract and to act on the association's behalf in the delivering of goods and services. The relationships formed by this process have legal consequences governed by agency law.

Source of Agency Law

The source of agency law is the common law created through each state's judicial system where the agency agreement was made.[1] Rights and duties conflict in this three-party relationship (the business or individual is referred to as the **principal** in agency law; the representative acting under the authority and on behalf of the principal is called the **agent**; and the person with whom the agent contracts is called the *third party*).

principal
a person who has authorized an agent to act on his behalf and subject to his control

agent
a person authorized to act on behalf of another and subject to the other's control

Throughout Part 7, Agency and Employment, reference will be made to the *Restatement of Agency,* which is an authoritative general compilation of the common law of agency throughout the country and constantly referred to in judicial decisions and opinions.

Business Organizations and Agency Law

Agreements that are commonly made in dealings with business associations frequently involve agency issues. For example, a salesperson (agent) who contracts with the customer (third party), on behalf of a company (principal), is acting pursuant to an agency relationship, and a consequent series of rights and duties arises for all parties to the transaction.

The laws governing the *operation* of the corporation, partnership, and the sole proprietorship illustrate the application of agency laws.

Corporations

The **corporation** is an artificial person or legal entity created by law.[2] Ordinarily, the officers of a corporation and certain other designated employees are those agents through whom the corporation acts.[3] The board of directors is not an agent of the corporation because it is not under the direct control of the stockholders, and the board makes its own managerial decisions.[4]

corporation
a legal entity created by statute authorizing an association of persons to carry on an enterprise

---

[1] Restatement (Second) of Conflict of Laws sec. 291 (1969).

[2] *Black's Law Dictionary,* Rev. 5th ed., 307 (1979); see Part 8B, Business Organizations: Corporations. In *The Trustees of Dartmouth College v. Woodward,* 4 Wheat (U.S.) 518,636, 4 L.Ed. 629,659 (1819), Chief Justice Marshall stated, "A corporation is an artificial being, intangible, and existing only in contemplation of law."

[3] Revised *Model Business Corporation Act,* sec. 3.02, General Powers: "Each corporation shall have power to conduct its business, carry on its operations, . . . to elect directors and appoint officers, employees, and agents of the corporation [and] define their duties . . . ;" and *Phoenix Savings and Loan, Inc. v. Aetna Casualty & Surety Co.,* 266 F.Supp. 465 (1966).

[4] Restatement (Second) of Agency sec. 14C. (1958): "Neither the board of directors nor an individual director . . . is an agent of the corporation."

Partnerships

partnership
an association of two or more persons to carry on as co-owners of a business for profit

Partnerships are governed by the Uniform Partnership Act[5] and the owners' partnership agreement. The U.P.A. sec. 9(1) provides: "Every partner is an agent of the partnership for the purpose of its business . . ." and thus establishes the statutory foundation for the application of agency law to partnership transactions.[6]

Sole Proprietorships

A sole proprietor has the legal right to and exclusive ownership of his or her business. The agency relationship occurs when the proprietor owner hires employees or other representatives to contract with customers on the proprietor's behalf. For example, a real estate broker who owns houses (principal) hires a salesperson (agent) to sell the houses. The contract that the agent (salesperson) makes with the buyer (third person) to sell the buyer a house will bind the proprietor principal (broker).

Most business transactions involve one person acting for another person and, therefore, agency law applies. All parties concerned in the agency relationship should understand the legal consequences of their actions. This chapter will help you to identify the agency issues.

Definition of Agency

fiduciary
a person with a duty to act for the benefit of another

Agency is a **fiduciary** relationship based upon an express or implied *agreement* whereby one party, the agent, is authorized to act *on behalf* and *under the control* of another, the principal, when the agent consents so to act.[7] Basically, agency is a legal relationship between two persons who agree that one (agent) is to act on behalf of the other (principal), subject to the other's control. Throughout Part 7, Agency and Employment, we will often use the following abbreviations: P (principal), A (agent), T (third party). This relationship may be diagrammed as in figure 33.1.

Employer and Employee or Master and Servant Relationship

To the extent that a person has the right of control, or exercises control, over another person, he or she is liable for the other person's conduct. The principal's control may or may not be over the agent's *physical* conduct. If control is not over *physical* conduct, then the principal is not liable for the agent's *physical* conduct. (P retains A, a real estate broker, to produce a willing and able buyer of P's house and land. A drives his own car negligently and hits X, a pedestrian. P is not liable to X; only A is liable to X. P did not have the right to control the *physical* conduct of A, a special agent, in driving A's automobile.)

However, if a principal has the right to control, or exercises control, over the *physical* conduct of the principal's agent, the principal is liable to third persons for *physical* harm caused to them by the agent's wrongful *physical* conduct. Such an agent is called a "servant," or often "employee," and the principal is called a "master," or often "employer." (P's truck driver negligently drives into T while delivering P's goods. Since P has the right to control A's *physical* conduct, A is a servant and P is liable to T for T's *physical* injury caused by A's negligence.) Most agents are servants.

---

[5] The Act has been adopted in all states except Louisiana.

[6] See Part 8A, Business Organizations: General Partnerships and Special Ventures.

[7] RESTATEMENT (SECOND) OF AGENCY sec. 1 (1958); and *Tonka Corp. v. Commissioner of Taxation,* 169 N.W.2d 589, 593 (Minn. 1969).

Figure 33.1   Relationships among Principal-Agent-Third Party

The terms of *master* and *servant* are used in the *employment* relationship only to determine the liability of an employer principal for the *physical harm* caused to third persons by the servant employee's *torts*. This legal relationship exists when the master (principal) controls the *physical conduct* of the servant (agent). The master is held responsible for the negligence of the servant causing physical injury to the third party[8] while the servant was acting within the scope of his or her employment.[9]

Agency Distinguished from Other Business Relationships

Independent Contractor

For agency to exist, the principal must have the *right* to exercise *control,* or *actually* exercise *control,* over the agent. An **independent contractor** hired to accomplish a physical *result* is not an agent primarily because the independent contractor is not under the *supervision and control* of the hiring party. The independent contractor acts independently on his own and makes his own contracts. Notice the court's reasoning in the following case in making the legal distinction between employees and independent contractors.

independent contractor
a person who contracts independently for himself to render a result, and who is not acting on behalf of another nor subject to another's control

Facts
Gerald Resnik, plaintiff, worked for Day as a licensed real estate salesperson from February 24, 1976, to November 4, 1977, pursuant to a written contract. Day failed to pay Resnik $478.41 that was part of a commission as a result of a real estate listing he obtained for Day. Day made motions for dismissal of Resnik's action due to lack of jurisdiction claiming that Resnik was not an employee of Day. The motions were denied although the trial court made findings that Resnik's contract with Day stated a relationship of independent contractor between the parties. Was Resnik an independent contractor or an agent/employee?

Decision
An agent/employee. Judgment for Resnik affirmed.

Reasoning
The critical legal distinction between employees and independent contractors is the right to control the manner and means by which the agent conducts his business. A bona fide contractor is customarily engaged in an independently established business and retains the right to control the manner in which he performs his contract. An employee, on the other hand, is subject to the absolute control and direction of his employer. A real estate salesman cannot contract in his own name; he can only be employed by a licensed real estate broker, he cannot be employed by any person other than the broker under whom he is at the time licensed, and his license must remain in the posession of his broker employer. We conclude, therefore, that a salesman, insofar as his relationship with his broker is concerned, cannot be classified as an independent contractor.

Gerald Resnik v. Anderson and Miles 167 Cal.Rptr. 340 (Cal. 1980).

An independent contractor may become an agent if he or she is subject to the *control* of the principal in the performance of service. The degree of control the principal exercises over the hired party is decisive, and the courts will disregard the professional status of the hired party and examine the facts of the situation on the issue of control.

---

[8] *Smalich v. Westfall,* 269 A.2d 476 (Pa. 1970).

[9] See pp. 532–33 for a full discussion of the master-servant relationship.

broker
a person authorized to represent another and to negotiate for him with others

auctioneer
a person licensed by law to sell property of another at a public sale

factor
a person in business for himself with authority to buy goods, or to sell goods in his possession, in his own name for another

bailment
delivery of goods by a bailor to a bailee which are to be returned to the bailor or as the bailor directs in accordance with the bailment agreement

trustee
a person who holds title to property in trust for the benefit of someone

trust
a legal device whereby legal title to property is held by one person (a trustee) for the benefit of a beneficiary

settlor
the person who has created an express trust

Some independent contractors retain their status when retained to act. Examples are doctors, certified public accountants, and engineers. If control should be exercised over their conduct, then they become agents. Examples are hiring a doctor to be an employee in the employer's plant, hiring the C.P.A. as the treasurer or comptroller of a firm, and hiring the engineer as a member of the employer's staff.

Some independent contractors lose this status as such while they are retained to do a job; they become agents. Examples are lawyers, real estate **brokers, auctioneers,** and **factors.** They become "special agents" or "professional agents."

Real Estate Broker. A real estate broker is licensed by the state to represent sellers in the sale of their real property (land). The broker is compensated for this service on a commission basis. A real estate broker has very limited authority—generally to state the asking price and identify the owner's property—and in such capacity the broker is an agent. The broker may be given authority to represent the seller and to contract on the seller's behalf rather than just to negotiate for the seller.[10]

Bailee

Bailed property is goods delivered by a bailor to another, the bailee, to be returned to the bailor or as the bailor directs.[11] As business associations continue to rent equipment, the incidents of bailed property become very common. A bailee is not an agent, but he can become an agent if the bailee has possession with authority to buy, sell, or otherwise deal with the bailed goods on behalf of the bailor.

Trustee

A **trustee**[12] is a party to whom the legal title of property has been transferred for the purpose of managing the property for a beneficiary.

Although the trustee acts on behalf of the beneficiary, generally the trustee is not an agent because:

1. the trustee has title to the property held in **trust,** while an agent normally does not have title to any property;
2. the trustee does not have authority to make the beneficiary a party to a contract with anyone, while an agent has the authority to make the disclosed principal a party to the contract;
3. the trustee acts in its own name as trustee, while the agent usually acts in the name of the principal; and
4. the trust is not revocable by the trustee, while an agency usually is revocable by the agent or the principal.[13]

The following case illustrates that the **settlor** unlike a principal has no control over the trustee nor the property in the trust unless the trust instrument so provides.

---

[10] *Knudson v. Weeks,* 394 F.Supp. 963 (Okla. 1975).

[11] See Part 3, Personal Property and Bailments; and *English v. Dhane,* 286 S.W.2d 666 (Tex. 1956).

[12] See Part 11, Wills and Decedents' Estates, and Trusts, chapter 55.

[13] See Joseph L. Frascona, *C.P.A. Law Review,* 7th ed. (Homewood, Ill.: Richard D. Irwin, 1985), p. 556; *Cassedy v. Connecticut Gen. Life Ins. Co.,* 56 Misc.2d 970 (N.Y. 1968); and RESTATEMENT (SECOND) OF TRUSTS sec. 8 (1957).

Facts
On September 29, 1965, the settlor gave the lessee-optionee, defendant, a 50-year lease and an option to purchase, during the sixth year of the lease, on 31 acres of land. Extentions on the options to purchase were made and on March 1, 1976, the settlor signed an instrument purporting to grant the lessee-optionee another five-year extension of its option to September 29, 1981. The trustee, plaintiff, was unaware of this action and did not participate in it. On July 3, 1979, the trustee brought this action against the lessee-optionee to determine the validity of the attempted extension of the last option. Can a settlor who has created a trust by conveying property that is subject to an option to sell thereafter extend the period of the option without the participation or consent of the trustee?

Decision
No. Judgment for the plaintiff, trustee.

Reasoning
A trust is a form of ownership in which the legal title to property is vested in a trustee, who has equitable duties to hold and manage it for the benefit of the beneficiaries. The trustee under a valid trust deed has exclusive control of the trust property, subject only to the limitations imposed by law or the trust instrument. Once the settlor has created the trust, he is no longer the owner of the trust property and has only such ability to deal with it as is expressly reserved to him in the trust instrument.

Continental Bank & Trust Company v. Country Club Mobile Estates, 632 P.2d 869 (Utah 1981).

Power of Attorney

A written authorization to act as an agent is called a **power of attorney.** There are two types based upon the extent of the authority given to the agent: the limited power of attorney, and the full or general power of attorney.

power of attorney
written authority by a principal to an agent

Limited Power of Attorney
When the power to act or contract is *restricted* to a certain period of time and to specific transactions, it is a *limited power of attorney* (see figure 33.2). For example, P authorizes A to withdraw a specified amount of money from P's personal checking account while P is in the hospital. The restrictions here are to a certain amount and during hospitalization.

General Power of Attorney
An authorization to do any and all things necessary to carry on with the principal's legal affairs is a *general power of attorney* (see figure 33.3). In the following case notice how the court strictly interprets the terms of the power of attorney.

Facts
Plaintiff, Gunder Mehus, was the son of Artha Mehus, deceased. In February, 1969, Artha appointed Gunder as her attorney-in-fact, granting to him the power to indorse and deposit checks and to draw checks on her account for the payment of taxes, farm-related expenses, and living and medical expenses. Gunder testified his mother gave him a check and told him to purchase a joint savings certificate in their names. The personal representative of the decedent, defendant, claims that Gunder did not have the authority and that the joint savings certificate belongs solely to the decedent's estate. Did Gunder Mehus have the authority to purchase the savings certificate in joint tenancy with himself and Artha Mehus?

Decision
No. Judgment for defendant.

Reasoning
A power of attorney is an instrument in writing authorizing another to act as one's agent. The power of attorney given to Gunder in this case was restricted in the authority it bestowed. It did not include a power to draw checks on Artha's account for all purposes or more specifically for the purpose of making gifts either to the attorney-in-fact or to others. Nor did the power of attorney authorize the attorney-in-fact to manage the private financial affairs of Artha.

In re *Estate of Artha Mehus,* 278 N.W.2d 625 (N.D. 1979).

Figure 33.2   Limited Power of Attorney

| Form **2848** (Rev. October 1982) Department of the Treasury Internal Revenue Service | **Power of Attorney and Declaration of Representative** ▶ See separate instructions | OMB No. 1545-0150 Expires 9-30-85 |

Part I   Power of Attorney

Taxpayer(s) name, identifying number, and address including ZIP code (Please type or print)

hereby appoints (name(s), CAF number(s), address(es), including ZIP code(s), and telephone number(s) of individual(s))*

For IRS Use Only
File So.
Level
Receipt
Powers
Blind T.
Action
Ret. Ind.

as attorney(s)-in-fact to represent the taxpayer(s) before any office of the Internal Revenue Service for the following tax matter(s) (specify the type(s) of tax and year(s) or period(s) (date of death if estate tax)):

Type of tax (Individual, corporate, etc.)	Federal tax form number (1040, 1120, etc.)	Year(s) or period(s) (Date of death if estate tax)

The attorney(s)-in-fact (or either of them) are authorized, subject to revocation, to receive confidential information and to perform any and all acts that the principal(s) can perform with respect to the above specified tax matters (excluding the power to receive refund checks, and the power to sign the return (see regulations section 1.6012-1(a)(5), Returns made by agents), unless specifically granted below).

Send copies of notices and other written communications addressed to the taxpayer(s) in proceedings involving the above tax matters to:
  1 ☐ the appointee first named above, or
  2 ☐ (names of not more than two of the above named appointees) _____

Initial here ▶ .... if you are granting the power to receive, but not to endorse or cash, refund checks for the above tax matters to:
  3 ☐ the appointee first named above, or
  4 ☐ (name of one of the above designated appointees) ▶

This power of attorney revokes all earlier powers of attorney and tax information authorizations on file with the Internal Revenue Service for the same tax matters and years or periods covered by this power of attorney, except the following:

(Specify to whom granted, date, and address including ZIP code, or refer to attached copies of earlier powers and authorizations.)

Signature of or for taxpayer(s)
(If signed by a corporate officer, partner, or fiduciary on behalf of the taxpayer, I certify that I have the authority to execute this power of attorney on behalf of the taxpayer.)

_____ (Signature)   _____ (Title, if applicable)   _____ (Date)

_____ (Signature)   _____ (Title, if applicable)   _____ (Date)

*An organization, firm, or partnership may not be designated as a taxpayer's representative.

For Privacy Act and Paperwork Reduction Act Notice, see page 1 of separate instructions.   Form **2848** (Rev. 10-82)

Figure 33.3 Full Power of Attorney

FULL POWER OF ATTORNEY

1. *Appointment of Attorney-In-Fact.* KNOW ALL MEN BY THESE PRESENTS, that I, ..., residing at .... make, constitute, and appoint ...., residing at .... to be my lawful attorney-in-fact for me and to do any and all acts which I could do if personally present.

2. *No Limitation on Attorney-In-Fact's Powers.* I intend to give my attorney-in-fact the fullest powers possible and do not intend, by the enumeration of his powers to limit or reduce them in any fashion.

3. *Enumeration of Attorney-In-Fact's Powers.* Among the powers granted to my attorney-in-fact are:

(a) *Receive Goods and Money.* To demand and sue for and recover and receive all debts, rents, interest, money, goods, and chattels due to me or that may become due to me or which belong to me or to which I may be entitled to possession. In connection with these powers my attorney-in-fact is authorized to execute and deliver receipts, releases, and discharges. My attorney-in-fact is also empowered to make, endorse, accept, or deliver in my name or his name commercial paper, agreements, and other instruments that he deems necessary to carry out the powers granted to him by these presents.

(b) *Conduct Business.* To carry on the business of .... presently conducted by me under the trade name "..................." at .... In connection with the conduct of my business, my attorney-in-fact may recover all debts due or that become due to the business, pay all debts that the business may owe or which may become due to others, enter into agreements and other written instruments, employ people to further the conduct of the business, pay all taxes due from the business, and do all other acts that my attorney-in-fact deems necessary to carry on the business.

(c) *Appear in Actions and Suits.* To appear, answer, and defend all actions and suits that may be brought against me in my name, and in my stead, to compromise, settle or adjust them or any other claims against me in any manner that my attorney-in-fact deems proper.

(d) *Sell, Transfer, or Purchase Securities.* To purchase, sell, or transfer stocks and bonds of any kind in my name or that of my attorney-in-fact and to execute and deliver any instruments required in connection with the purchase, sale, or transfer.

(e) *Manage Real Estate.* To take possession of any real estate that belongs to me or to which I may be entitled to possession and to receive any rents or profits that may be due from the real estate. In connection with these powers, my attorney-in-fact is empowered to enter into new leases for any term, renew or extend existing leases for any term, and to sell, convey, or mortgage any real estate affected by these presents. My attorney-in-fact is also empowered to commence and prosecute for me and in my name any suits or actions for the recovery of the possession of any real estate belonging to me or to which I may be entitled and for the rents and profits due from such real estate or from any other real estate which is the subject of these presents.

(f) *Appoint Other Attorneys-In-Fact.* To constitute, appoint, and authorize in my attorney-in-fact's place and stead with full power of revocation other attorneys-in-fact for me to exercise any or all of the powers granted to my attorney-in-fact by these presents.

4. *Closing Paragraph.* IN WITNESS WHEREOF, I have hereunto set my hand and seal the .... day of ...., 19....

....
Principal

Durable Power of Attorney

The common law provides for the termination of a power of attorney upon the principal's incapacity.[14] This rule presents two potential problems: (1) the agent may be held personally liable on a contract made with a third party on behalf of an incompetent principal under the agent's implied warranty to the third party that the agent's principal has contractual capacity; and (2) the principal's intent to provide for the management of his or her assets in the event of an emergency physical or mental disability will not be accomplished.

To resolve this dilemma, the majority of states authorize by statute a **durable power of attorney** defined in the Uniform Probate Code as a writing that ". . . contains the words 'this Power of Attorney shall not be affected by the subsequent disability or incapacity of the principal' . . . or similar words showing the intent of the principal that the authority conferred shall . . . continue beyond the principal's incapacity." Both principal and agent must be of legal age and competent at the time the power of attorney was signed.

The durable power of attorney remains in duration until either the principal revokes it, it expires by its terms, or the principal or agent dies. Consider the business use of a durable power of attorney by an elderly person, or its importance to an individual going to a hospital for serious surgery or to a healthy person, to include a durable power of attorney as part of a complete estate plan in the event of an unforeseen emergency. In each instance both the principal and the agent know the powers granted will not terminate upon incapacity.

durable power of attorney
a statutory written power of attorney that will not terminate upon the principal's incapacity

Capacity to Be Principal, Agent

Principal

Generally, if a person has the legal capacity to act, the person can act through an agent.[15] If the principal has limited capacity, the appointment of an agent is void or voidable in accordance with contract law. For example, P, a minor, authorizes A, an adult, to purchase in P's name a television set from a merchant. Both the appointment of the agent and the purchase contract made under it are voidable by the minor. The contract may be ratified by the minor after the minor reaches majority.

Agent

Any person may act as an agent, even if he or she lacks contractual capacity. The contract is between the principal and the third party; the agent is not a party to the contract. Thus, although a minor/agent can avoid the contract with the principal who appointed the minor as an agent, the minor has the power to bind the principal with a third party. The minor's power of avoidance is personal to the minor and is not available to the principal. By statutory law an agent may be a partnership or a corporation.

Classification of Agents

Agents are classified in accordance with the extent of their authority. There are two classes of agents, "general" and "special," both of whom receive a delegation of authority from the principal to perform on its behalf. If an agent exceeds the scope of the agent's authority, the agent is personally liable and the principal is not bound.

---

[14] See p. 544.

[15] See chapter 9, Capacity/Ability to Create a Contract.

General Agent

A **general agent** has been defined as "an agent authorized to conduct a series of transactions involving a continuity of service."[16] An example of a *general agent* is the manager of a retail hardware store employed to perform all the acts connected with managing the store. Limiting the agent's authority to the hardware store does not make the agency special. The *continuity of service* would involve such acts as personnel responsibility, buying merchandise, and dealing with customer relations on a daily basis. Other examples of general agents are sales personnel, truck drivers, secretaries, and clerks on salary.

general agent (universal agent)
an agent authorized to conduct a series of transactions involving a continuity of service

Special Agent

"A **special agent** is an agent authorized to conduct a single transaction or a series of transactions not involving continuity of service."[17] A power of attorney given by a stockholder to a broker to sell a stock certificate is an example of a special agency. The single transaction of selling stock will terminate the broker's authority. There is no continuity of service involved in the sale transaction.

A universal agent is a sort of unlimited general agent, and is an agent authorized by the principal to transact all business of every kind. This is usually given in an emergency situation and can be created only by clear and unambiguous language. It is rarely used but, if used, it should be limited to a stated period of time. For example, "to do anything that must be done during my stay in the hospital."

special agent
an agent authorized to conduct a single transaction or series of transactions not involving continuity of service

Creating the Agency

Appointment—Consent of the Principal and Agent

The agency relationship is based on an implied or express agreement between the principal and the agent, as found in the facts of each case. For example, P expressly appoints A to act for and on behalf of P, and A consents. An agency relationship may be created in an informal manner without compensation being paid to the agent. Although the agency relationship usually is contractual, it may be a *gratuitous* undertaking by the agent.[18] If the agency is created by a *contract* between the principal and the agent, the law of contracts applies to its enforcement.[19]

Form

Unless state statutory law requires a writing, the appointment of an agent may be oral or by conduct. For example, if P authorizes A *to sell P's land,* by statute the appointment must be in writing.

Ratification

Ratification by one person of an unauthorized act by another person does *not* create agency because there is no *initial* agreement between the two persons that one is *to* act for the other. In agency one is *to* act for another in the future, however short or long a period of time.

"Ratification is the affirmation by a person of a prior act which did not bind him but which was done on his account and is given effect as if originally authorized by him."[20]

ratification
(in agency) a person's manifested consent to be bound by another's previously unauthorized act made in his name and not binding on him

---

[16] Restatement (Second) of Agency sec. 3 (1958); and *Kelly v. U.S. Steel Corporation and The Thew Shovel Company,* 170 F.Supp. 649 (1959).

[17] Restatement (Second) of Agency sec. 3 (1958).

[18] *Groh v. Shelton,* 428 S.W.2d 911 (Mo. 1968).

[19] *Automotive Finance Co. v. Kesk, Inc.,* 200 So.2d 136 (La. 1967).

[20] Restatement (Second) of Agency sec. 82 (1958).

The doctrine of ratification may be useful when a principal, with knowledge of the unauthorized transaction, accepts the benefit or affirms the "agent's" conduct and thereby becomes bound with the same effect as though the agent had authority so to act. (An unauthorized real estate agent, in P's name, signs a purchase and sale agreement with T to sell P's house above its appraised market value; if P wants the benefit of this contract, P's subsequent written ratification will bind P and T.)

The court in the following case refused to apply the doctrine of ratification because the principal did not have full knowledge of the unauthorized transaction.

Facts
On June 21, 1971, Mrs. Thropp, plaintiff, opened a margin trading account with Bache Halsey Stuart Shields, Inc., a securities brokerage firm, defendant, placing in its care securities worth approximately $40,000.00. Mrs. Thropp opened the Bache account in her name alone.

Between September 21, 1971, and April 21, 1972, Jack Thropp ordered Gregory, a broker in Bache's Columbus, Ohio office, to sell his wife's stock for cash, in a series of transactions which eventually depleted the margin account. During this seven-month period, Jack Thropp ordered Bache to issue seven checks in his wife's name, which he picked up at Bache's operations section. He then forged his wife's indorsement, cashed the checks, and spent the money.

In 1975 plaintiff first learned of Gregory's involvement, and in December, 1975 she filed this suit against Bache for negligence in handling her security account. Bache claimed as a defense Mrs. Thropp ratified the actions of Jack Thropp and Bache.

The District Court described Bache's duty in terms of Mrs. Thropp's "right to rely on Bache's not taking instructions from a third party in her account without a duly executed power of attorney on file," and rendered judgment for plaintiff. Defendant appealed.

Decision
Affirmed, judgment for plaintiff, Mrs. Thropp.

Reasoning
We see no reason to disturb the finding that Mrs. Thropp did not learn of Gregory's involvement until 1975. Thus, it cannot be said that she ratified Bache's actions. Nor can it be said that she ratified her husband's forgeries. The fact that she remained his wife is not the sort of "action" ratification requires.

Phyllis Ann Thropp v. Bache Halsey Stuart Shields, Incorporated, 650 F.2d 817 (1981).

Elements of Ratification. For ratification, the principal must *intend* to affirm the transaction and the following conditions must be satisfied:

1. The principal must have had *legal capacity* both when the unauthorized transaction was made by the agent, and when ratification occurred.
2. The principal must ratify the *entire* contract; P cannot accept the benefits and reject the obligations. For example, A, without authorization, sold P's merchandise on credit, payable in installments. P cannot ratify the sale and exclude the installment sale provision. P has to ratify the contract in its entirety or not at all.
3. The transaction to be ratified must be *legal*. For example, a loan unauthorizedly obtained by A on P's behalf that violates a usury statute cannot be ratified.
4. The agent must disclose to the third person the identity of the principal on whose behalf the agent *purports* to act. It is not necessary that the person who is acting as an agent have any authority at this time. Ratification will not apply in the case of an undisclosed principal. For example, if A never informed T that he was selling a boat on P's behalf, P cannot ratify the contract made by A with T. The reason is that T never intended to contract with P, and it would be unfair to permit P to impose himself upon T by ratification. T intended to contract with A.
5. The ratification must occur before the third person withdraws. For example, if T sues A for breach of contract because A never had the authority, P cannot then decide to ratify the contract.

Agency by Operation of Law
The courts will infer an agency if it appears from the facts that there was an implied intention to create one.

Marital Relationship. The marital relationship does not, in itself, create authority for one spouse to act for the other. However, if a wife customarily orders household supplies, authority or apparent authority to purchase things needed in the household can be inferred.[21] A husband is under a legal duty to financially provide the necessities of life for his family. A wife or child to whom a husband or parent has failed to provide the necessities has the power to contract for the purpose of necessities.[22]

Proving the Agency Relationship

When an agency question is relevant to a case, the burden of proving that the agency relationship existed is on *the party who claims it existed*.[23] As illustrated in the combinations of agency liability, this may be the principal, agent, or third party. The agency relationship is not presumed and must be proved by the evidence. For example, if T sues P, claiming that A acted as P's agent, T has the burden of proving the agency between P and A.

Burden of proof.

Summary Statement

1. The source of agency law is the common law.
2. Corporations, partnerships, and sole proprietorships all act through agents.
3. Agency is a fiduciary relationship based on an express or implied agreement whereby one party, the agent, is authorized to act on behalf and under the control of the principal.
4. If a principal has the right to control, or exercises control, over the *physical* conduct of the agent, the principal is liable to third persons for *physical* harm caused to them by the agent's wrongful *physical* conduct. Such an agent is called a "servant" or "employee," and the principal is called a "master."
5. The terms "master" and "servant" are used in the employment relationship only to determine the liability of an employer principal for the physical harm caused to third persons by the servant employee's torts.
6. An independent contractor is hired to accomplish a physical result and is not under the direct supervision and control of the hiring party.
7. A real estate broker is an independent contractor but, when retained by a client, the broker becomes a special agent and generally has authority only to state the asking price and identify the owner's property.
8. A power of attorney is a written authorization to act as an agent. A limited power is restrictive, a general power is not.
9. Any person with legal capacity to act can act through an agent.
10. Any person can act as an agent even if the person lacks contractual capacity.
11. A "general agent" is authorized to conduct a series of transactions involving a continuity of service.
12. A "special agent" is authorized to conduct a single transaction or a series of transactions not involving continuity of service.
13. The agency relationship is based on an implied or express agreement between the principal and the agent.
14. The relationship of master and servant is a type of agency. One can be a servant even though the service is gratuitously performed.

---

[21] Restatement (Second) of Agency sec. 22, comment b (1958); and *Melton v. Mire*, 268 So.2d 123 (La. 1972).

[22] Restatement of Restitution sec. 113 (1937).

[23] *Reed v. Bunger*, 122 N.W.2d 290 (Iowa 1963).

15. Ratification is a person's affirmation of an unauthorized act having the effect of binding the ratifying party as though the act had been authorized previously.
16. The agency relationship is not presumed, and the burden of proving it is on the party who claims it exists.

In the following case notice how the court requires that the party seeking to benefit from the agency relationship prove its existence.

McLaughlin v. Chicken Delight, Inc.
321 A.2d 456 (Conn. 1973)

Bogdanski, Associate Justice. This is an action where McLaughlin, administrator of decedent's estate, plaintiff, alleged that the motor vehicle which struck and killed the decedent was owned by the defendant, franchisor, Chicken Delight, Inc., and that the operator of the vehicle was its agent. The superior court held that the vehicle was not owned by the defendant but by the franchisee Food Caterers, Inc., and that the operator of the vehicle was not the agent of the franchisor, defendant, and rendered its judgment for the defendant. Plaintiff appealed.

The following is a summary of the facts found by the court. The defendant was the franchisor, and Food Caterers, Inc. was the franchisee, under the terms of an agreement whereby the defendant granted solely to Food Caterers, Inc. the right to use at its store in East Hartford the name, symbols, methods, and systems of operations of "Chicken Delight." The **franchise** agreement was designed to control the quality and taste of all "Chicken Delight" products sold to the public. It provided that the defendant should have the privilege of complete inspection of the business and books of the franchisee. Under the agreement, the franchisee was required to deliver promptly and at the time designated by the customer hot and freshly prepared foods from the "Chicken Delight" store. The franchisee agreed to purchase or lease an adequate number of delivery vehicles and to "maintain a free and adequate delivery system." There are seven such franchises in Connecticut and 400 throughout the United States.

The franchisee owned and operated the East Hartford store already mentioned. Above its entrance was a sign with "Chicken Delight" in large letters and "free delivery" in smaller letters. The motor vehicle in question was owned by the franchisee. There were no markings, printing, or signs on it. Inside the vehicle at the time of the accident and next to the operator was a cardboard box imprinted with the words "Chicken Delight." Next to the carton was a heater to keep the food products warm during delivery to customers. At the time of the accident, the heater was in operation and Carfiro was in the process of making a delivery to a customer. Carfiro was hired by Mrs. Joyce Morrison, widow of Robert Morrison, who, prior to his death, managed the business. While Morrison was alive, he instructed operator employees how to make deliveries. After his death Mrs. Morrison took over the task. There was no evidence that Carfiro was hired, paid, or instructed by or known to the defendant.

The packaged foods to be sold were limited and the only name that could be used was "Chicken Delight," the place of business had to be known as "Chicken Delight," and the precise method and manner of cooking was specifically defined. The franchisee had to purchase numerous articles and equipment stated by the franchisor to be essential. This equipment had to be purchased from the franchisor or meet the standards prescribed by it. The franchisee was required to sell its food in a container bearing the trademark "Chicken Delight" and buy its entire requirements for the various packaging kits defined by the franchisor. The business could be conducted only at an approved location, and its construction and remodeling had to meet the franchisor's standards. The preparation and cooking of all foods had to meet specific standards.

It is the plaintiff's contention that the facts found by the trial court show beyond dispute that, at the time of the accident resulting in the death of the decedent, Carfiro in operating the delivery vehicle was acting in furtherance of and for the "benefit" of the business affairs of the defendant, Chicken Delight, Inc.

---

franchise
a business relationship between a "franchisor" who markets goods or services through a "franchisee" who has the right to use the franchisor's trade name, trademark, and methods of operation

An essential factor in an agency relationship is the right of the principal to direct and control performance of the work by the agent.

The question presented to this court is whether it must be held as a matter of law that the trial court, on consideration of all the evidence in the case, could not reasonably and logically have reached any conclusion other than that Carfiro was the agent of Chicken Delight. The question of the existence or nonexistence of any agency relationship is ordinarily one of fact to be determined by the trier of fact. The above findings . . . by the court amply support its conclusion that the plaintiff failed to establish the requisite agency relationship claim.

Questions and Case Problems

1. This action was initiated by the plaintiff, the Jay County Rural Electric Membership Corporation, (hereinafter REMC), against the Aetna Casualty & Surety Company, defendant, seeking recovery on a comprehensive dishonesty, disappearance and destruction bond for the period of time from 1948 to 1965, alleging fraudulent and dishonest acts committed by the REMC's general manager, Harold Floyd, also a defendant. Plaintiff alleged that Floyd was indebted to REMC for funds expended by Floyd for his personal use, excess salary, payment of Floyd's personal expenses, and for work performed by REMC employees on Floyd's personal residence. Floyd points out that the corporate minutes show three resolutions authorizing certain types of expenditure and a general clause for each meeting indicating that the board of directors had read and approved a list of checks written during the previous month. Did the board of directors ratify the general manager, Harold Floyd's, conduct? [*Harold Floyd, The Aetna Casualty & Surety Company v. Jay County Rural Electric Membership Corporation,* 405 N.E.2d 630 (Ind. 1980).]

2. Daniels, without Mathews' consent, signed a contract on Mathews' behalf to sell Mathews' boat to Marcos for $15,000 payable in three equal monthly installments. Mathews later agreed to its terms except the installment payments. Mathews claims he ratified the contract and wants to hold Marcos liable. Decide.

3. Plaintiff's mother, Janice McComey, resided in an apartment building owned by defendant, Robert Christopher Company, a partnership comprised of Robert Carangi and Josephine Carangi. Mr. Carangi hired Victor Vinney to paint and repair the building. As plaintiff and her mother returned from shopping they entered the building and noticed the common entrance way was very dark. As plaintiff placed her foot on the second step, she stepped on a tool, her body rolled and she fell. After plaintiff fell, she and her mother noticed that the light fixtures in that portion of the common area had been disconnected. They also noticed two tools on the floor between the front door and steps. Thereafter, plaintiff filed a complaint for damages to recover for the injuries she sustained in the fall. Defendant answered the complaint denying any liability as the negligence, if any, was that of an independent contractor. Was the employer/defendant liable for the negligence of Vinney, the independent contractor? [*Nikki Cordet v. Robert Christopher Company,* 210 Cal.Rptr. 517 (Cal. 1985).]

4. Plaintiff, Bicknell, Inc., sued John J. Havlin, defendant, an insurance agent, alleging negligence in failing to place proper insurance coverage on two buildings leased to Bicknell. Havlin described himself as experienced in the insurance business. Havlin made recommendations for particular types of coverage and, when asked what would be sufficient coverage for the buildings, he stated "let's slap fifty-thousand on each building."

    A fire broke out on June 3, 1974, in one of Bicknell's two new rented warehouses. The fire loss amounted to $103,275.91. The insurance carrier paid Bicknell $50,000.00, the amount of the endorsement of April 4, 1974. Did Havlin, as Bicknell's insurance agent, violate a duty of care in not providing Bicknell with sufficient insurance coverage? [*Bicknell, Inc. v. John J. Havlin,* 402 N.E.2d 116 (Mass. 1980).]

5. The plaintiffs are husband and wife. The defendant firm is engaged in the business of acting as a real estate broker representing buyers and sellers of real property. Plaintiffs contend that, as a result of seeing one of defendant's signs on a lot, they contacted the defendant, and one of defendant's agents, John Pate, came to their residence and after observing that they were black refused to show them the dwelling. The defendant's president approved of Pate's action. They allege that this refusal to show the home was a violation of the Fair Housing Act. Plaintiffs seek damages against the defendant and also an injunction permanently restraining and denying defendant from refusing to show, negotiate and sell real estate to plaintiffs and others in similar situations. Defendant contends that it has not violated any provisions of the Fair Housing Act and also asserts that Pate was an independent contractor and not an agent of John M. Brabham Agency, Inc. Decide. [*Roland and Ernesteen Bradley v. John M. Brabham Agency, Inc.,* 463 F.Supp. 27 (S.C. 1978).]

6. Walker, a 16 year old minor, authorized his 21 year old friend Harry to purchase a TV set in his name. After the TV set was delivered to Walker in good working order he used it for three months and then decided to return the set and get his money back. May he do so? Explain.

7. The appellant, Fielding Home for Funerals, brought suit to collect the proceeds of a life insurance policy from the respondent insurance company. Although it is undisputed that the policy had lapsed prior to the death of the named insured due to non-payment of premiums, the appellant contends in its complaint that the respondent is estopped to assert the lapse of the policy since it had represented to appellant that the policy was in force and, as a consequence of reliance on such representation, the appellant acted to its detriment. The appellant accepted assignment of the proceeds of the policy from the policy beneficiary as payment for the funeral and burial expenses of the insured. A former employee of appellant testified she had called the respondent insurance company on the telephone to ascertain whether the policy in question was in force and was informed by the person answering that it was. The issue is whether a presumption to speak for the respondent can arise even though the person who was called is not identified by name. Can it be presumed that a person is authorized to speak for a business as its agent when the caller cannot identify the person by name? [*Fielding Home for Funerals, as Assignee for the Life Insurance Policy of Debra Green v. Public Savings Life Insurance Company,* 245 S.E. 2d 238 (S.C. 1978).]

8. Defendant, Bay State Harness Horse Racing and Breeding Association, Inc. (Bay State), entertained its patrons when they were not absorbed in watching the races by broadcasting music supplied by Music Box, Inc., an independent contractor, pursuant to its contract with defendant. Bay State's president and treasurer was unwilling to obtain a license from the American Society of Composers, Authors and Publishers (ASCAP), of which the plaintiffs are members, and had instructed his subordinates in Bay State not to play any ASCAP copyrighted music. Despite this admonition, such music was played at a time when ASCAP had monitors in the field to spot and record such transgressions. Was Bay State responsible for the infringing performances by an independent contractor? [*Famous Music Corp.,* et al. *v. Bay State Harness Horse Racing and Breeding Association, Inc.,* 554 F.2d 1213 (1977).]

9. Sierra Pacific Industries, plaintiff, purchased a ten acre parcel in Willow Creek on which five duplexes and two single family units are located. After the acquisition, Sierra Pacific requested the assistance of Joseph H. Carter, defendant, a real estate broker, in selling the Willow Creek parcel. Acting in reliance on Carter's representation as to the value of the Willow Creek parcel, Sierra Pacific commissioned him to sell it for an asking price of $85,000 of which Sierra Pacific would receive $80,000 and Carter $5,000. Carter sold the property for that amount to his daughter and son-in-law and retained a $5,000 commission without informing Sierra Pacific of his relationship with the buyers. Sierra Pacific instituted a fraud action against Carter for the $5,000 commission paid to Carter based on the foregoing facts. Decide. [*Sierra Pacific Industries v. Joseph H. Carter,* 163 Cal.Rptr. 764 (Cal. 1980).]

10. The case of *McLaughlin v. Chicken Delight, Inc.*, 321 A.2d 456 (Conn. 1973)[24] held that the person (plaintiff) claiming that an agency existed (between the driver and the defendant) had the burden of proving an agency. It also held that, while a third person, defendant, may benefit from an agency (between Food Caterers, Inc. and its driver), nevertheless the third person is not a principal of the person providing the benefit (the driver). Discuss the court's holding in light of the fact that, in proving agency, actually two parties (the defendant and Food Caterers, Inc.) are benefiting from services rendered by an agent (the driver) but only one of the parties benefited is the principal.

---

[24] See pp. 512–13.

34 Duties of Principal and Agent to Each Other

After you have read this chapter, you should be able to:

1. Define the following kinds of authority:
   a. express authority,
   b. implied authority,
      i. incidental authority,
      ii. customary authority,
   c. apparent authority.
2. Know whose duty it is to determine the extent of the agent's authority.
3. Explain the effect of limitations on the agent's authority.
4. Explain the instances when an agent may delegate authority to another.
5. List and explain the five duties an agent owes to a principal.
6. List and explain the four duties a principal owes to an agent.
7. Explain the effect of proper exercise of the agent's authority.
8. Explain the meaning of a fiduciary.

Introduction

In the preceding chapter of this Part we discussed the nature of agency, its creation, and how it is distinguished from other business relationships, particularly the independent contractor. In this chapter, we will discuss the various kinds of authority, apparent authority, and the duties of principal and agent to each other.

Agent's Authority

Scope of Agent's Authority

An agent may properly contract with a third party *only if authorized by the principal* in words or other conduct. Agents have no power to create their own authority nor extend its scope. The essence of **authority** is a person's (principal) consent to another (agent) to act on the principal's behalf.

The following types of authority will help you to identify authority and decide whether the agent is acting with the principal's consent.[1]

Express Authority. If the principal orally or in writing specifies what the agent is to do, the agent has **express authority** to act. For example, if P tells his stockbroker A to sell P's stock at a certain price, A has been given *express authority* to sell the stock at a specified price.

Implied Authority. The agent's duty is to carry out his express authority *as reasonably understood by the agent*. The agent must interpret the principal's words of consent in order to understand what they mean. The principal's words *imply* to the agent, and the agent *infers* from those words what the agent reasonably understands he or she is to do. Thus we have **implied** (or inferred) **authority.** Implied authority can be described as incidental or customary.

1. *Incidental Authority.* An agent is authorized from the circumstances to perform those acts that are reasonably necessary to carry out the express authority. Suppose an agent is authorized to use a company car on a business trip to effect a sale with a third party. The salesperson/agent has implied **incidental authority** to charge the gasoline used to the principal.
2. *Customary Authority.* The traditional trade or professional practice in which the agent acts creates an implied authorization to conform with the general custom. This is referred to as **customary authority.**

By agreement between the principal and the agent, the agent *may not* have incidental and customary authority.

Some common examples of implied authority may be helpful.

1. In *authority "to sell" personal property,* if the agent has *received possession* of the property, then the agent's implied authority is to *contract* in the principal's name and sell and transfer the *title* to the property. If the agent has *not received possession,* the agent's implied authority is solely to *produce a willing and able buyer.* In *authority "to sell" real property,* if the agent's *authority is in writing* (e.g., power of attorney) and there is *nothing* to the contrary, the implied authority is to *contract* in the principal's name and sell and transfer the *title* to the property. If the authority is *oral,* the implied authority is solely to *produce a willing and able buyer.*

---

[1] See RESTATEMENT (SECOND) OF AGENCY sec. 7, comment c (1958) where express and implied authority are discussed.

authority
an agent's power to act for the principal in accordance with the principal's manifestation of consent to the agent

express authority
an agent's authority specifically expressed in the principal's manifestation to the agent

implied authority
an agent's authority which the agent reasonably can understand he has from his principal's manifestation to him, but not expressed therein

incidental authority
implied authority to do what is incidental in carrying out the express authority

customary authority
implied authority to do those acts that conform to the general custom or usage

2. *Authority to receive payment* implies authority to receive only *cash* for the entire amount or to take a *check as conditional payment*—on condition that it is paid. Authority to receive payment does not authorize the agent to accept credit.
3. *Authority to sign checks and other negotiable instruments in the name of a principal* is not implied easily, in the absence of special circumstances (e.g., emergency).

Apparent Authority.[2]   Agency and authority are created by the principal's expression of consent *to the agent.* If P represents *to T,* a third person, that A is P's agent, there is no agency nor authority because P never expressed consent *to A* that A was to be P's agent. But as far as T is concerned, A *apparently* is P's agent because of P's representation *to T.* Therefore, A is an *apparent agent* with **apparent authority** to act for P in accordance with P's representation *to T.* The extent of A's apparent authority will depend upon *T's* reasonable understanding of P's representation to T. If A acts within the scope of A's apparent authority, P will be bound to T by A's conduct with the same effect as though A had authority so to act. Under apparent authority, sometimes called "ostensible authority," *the principal's expression of consent is to the third person* rather than to the agent. Apparent authority has replaced estoppel when P's manifestation to T is that *A is P's agent.*

apparent authority
the power of a person (A) to act as though he were an agent, created by another's (P's) manifestation to a third person (T) that A is P's agent

A person may be an agent with authority and, at the same time, have apparent authority. For example, P employs A as a salesperson in P's store, and P informs T that A is P's salesperson. A's authority and apparent authority are to act as a salesperson is reasonably expected to act.

An intent to authorize an act may be found from the *principal's conduct.* For example, a store clerk who reasonably appears to a vendor/third party to have authority to purchase supplies from the vendor has apparent authority to do so, and the owner of the store will be liable to the vendor on a sale.

The following case illustrates how the agent's apparent authority can take the form of conduct which reasonably causes the third party to believe that the principal consents to the agent acting on its behalf.

Facts
In June of 1973, Oak Hill Raquet Club contracted with Emmark Collaborative, Inc., for the design, construction and construction management of the Oak Hill project. Emmark then entered into a subcontract with Emmenegger Construction Company, Inc. Emmenegger was to do the concrete work on the project. Emmark was the construction manager for the Oak Hill project. Fred Alsbach was the job superintendent for the project and directed activities on the job site. There is some dispute as to who is Alsbach's employer. Ames, plaintiff, a concrete worker, was not certain for whom he was working. He dealt exclusively with Alsbach and did not meet or talk to Emmenegger. Ames has not been paid for his concrete work and claims that his contract was with Emmenegger, which is denied by Emmenegger.

The trial court found that Alsbach was an employee of Emmenegger and that Alsbach hired Ames to do some of the concrete work. The existence of this authority is the main issue before us on appeal. Did Alsbach have authority to bind Emmenegger to the contract with Ames? Judgment was rendered for Ames and Emmenegger appealed.

Decision
Yes. Affirmed, judgment for Ames.

Reasoning
Ames' bill for the January work was made out to "Emmenegger Constr. Co.," and was submitted by Ames to Alsbach in the trailer. This bill was approved for payment by Leo Kuntz, Emmenegger's corporate vice president, and was later submitted for payment by Alsbach on an Emmenegger purchase order. If doubt existed as to Alsbach's authority to bind defendant, it was removed by Kuntz' action in approving the January bill for payment. This indicated consent by the principal (Emmenegger) to actions of its agent (Alsbach).

Emmenegger Construction Co. Inc. v. Frank King, et al., 431 N.E.2d 738 (Ill. 1982).

---

[2] See RESTATEMENT (SECOND) OF AGENCY sec. 8 (1958), where apparent authority is discussed; also see Warren A. Seavey, *Agency* (St. Paul: West Publishing Co., 1964), p. 43.

Legal Effect of a Contract Properly Executed by an Agent

If an agent acts within the express or implied authority in the name of the principal, there is a contract between the third party and the principal. Accordingly, a salesperson is not personally liable for a breach of warranty for goods made to a customer/third party because the sales contract is made *with the principal* through the agent; the agent is not a party to the contract.

Third Party's Duty to Determine the Extent of the Agent's Authority

The third party is under a legal obligation not only to identify the *existence* of the agent's authority but also to determine the *extent* of the agent's authority. If the agent exceeds this authority, the principal will not be bound. Suppose a life insurance agent changes the terms of a life insurance contract without the consent of the company. It is the customer/third party's responsibility to determine whether the agent had the power to change the insurance contract. A third party who fails to do so acts at its peril.

The third party cannot rely upon statements made by the agent unless the principal has invited the third party to do so. For example, a customer is invited by the store owner to rely upon the salesperson's statement of the price of goods.

Limitation on the Agent's Authority

As between the principal and the agent, any expressed limitations on the scope of the agent's authority are valid. However, a third party without knowledge of the private and *secret* limitations is not bound by them. The third party has the duty of determining the extent of an agent's authority, but since the third party cannot determine the secret limitations on such authority made by the principal, the limitations are not effective as to the third party. If the agent has *express, implied,* or *apparent authority* to act, the agent can make a contract with the third party that will bind the principal.

For instance, if it is customary in the used car trade to warrant a used car for thirty days and the principal instructs the salesperson/agent to warrant the car for only fourteen days, unless disclosed to the customer/third party the latter can assume that the agent has authority to give a thirty-day warranty. The agent has such *apparent authority*.

In the following case the court found no apparent authority on the part of an attorney/agent to settle his client's case.

Facts

Plaintiff was allegedly injured when the vehicle in which she was a passenger was struck by a vehicle driven by defendant. Plaintiff retained John D. Logsdon, an attorney, to represent her in a personal injury action. Unknown to all parties or the court, Logsdon had apparently forged plaintiff's indorsement to the settlement draft made payable to plaintiff and to Logsdon as her attorney, and he received the proceeds. Plaintiff brought this action to set aside the judgment. The trial court denied the plaintiff's motion to set aside the judgment and dismissed her action. Plaintiff appealed. Did the attorney, Logsdon, have apparent authority to settle the action?

Decision

No. Reversed, motion to set aside the judgment allowed.

Reasoning

Apparent authority, or ostensible authority as it is also called, is that which, though not actually granted, the principal knowingly permits the agent to exercise or which he holds him out as possessing. An apparent agent is one who, with or without authority, reasonably appears to third persons to be authorized to act as the agent of another.

In the present case there is no evidence of apparent authority on the part of Logsdon to settle plaintiff's case other than his retention as her attorney. There being no evidence, other than Logsdon's employment as plaintiff's attorney, of Logsdon's apparent authority to settle plaintiff's action, we hold that the trial court abused its discretion in denying plaintiff's motion to set aside the judgment of dismissal.

Miotk v. Rudy, 605 P.2d 587 (Kan. 1980).

Delegation of Authority by Agent

When a principal selects an agent to contract with others on its behalf, the principal does so on the *personal qualifications* of the agent.³ The agent generally will exercise *discretion, special skill,* or *judgment* in the performance of the agent's contract with the principal and the agent's *fiduciary duties* on behalf of the principal. Hence, it usually is held that an agent does not have implied (or apparent) authority to delegate the agent's authority to another (subagent) without the consent of the principal.

If the agent's discretion, special skill, or judgment are not required for the agent's performance, unless the principal has indicated to the contrary, the agent has implied (and apparent) authority to **delegate** his performance to a **subagent.** On delegation, the subagent is an agent both of the agent appointing him or her and also of the agent's principal. The subagent has two principals who are both liable for the subagent's conduct, the appointing agent being ultimately liable. For example, P insurance company appoints A as its general manager in a particular geographical area, A agreeing to be *responsible* for personnel hired by A. A employs insurance salespersons working out of A's office. The salespersons sell insurance in P's name to third persons, binding P to them. The salespersons are subagents with A and P as their principals. Both A and P are liable for the salespersons' conduct but, as between A and P, A is ultimately liable.

An agent's *delegation* of his authority to a *subagent* is different from an agent's *appointment* of *another agent*. The appointed agent and the appointing agent have only one principal—namely, the person who created the original agency. For example, P owns a retail store and employs A as general manager. A appoints S as a salesperson in the store. P is the principal, and both A and S are the principal's agents. S is not an agent of A, who is *not liable* for S's conduct. Only P is liable for the conduct of A and S.

An agent may delegate his authority in the following four instances.

1. *Ministerial or Mechanical Duties.* In certain cases the act to be performed by the agent does not require anything more than a ministerial (nondiscretionary) or mechanical duty. For example, a general agent parking attendant may delegate the duty to collect parking tickets because it requires no special skill, discretion, or judgment. The principal may prohibit the delegation of even a ministerial act, providing it is clearly indicated to the agent. It is usually good practice to do so because the principal is responsible to compensate the subagent.

2. *Business Custom.* It is implied that the agent has authority to delegate if the trade or profession in which the agency is to be performed has an established custom to employ subagents. In the following case, a limited partner brought suit against his attorneys for negligent representation. The attorneys claim they delegated their duty to subagents. There is no professional custom for attorneys to employ subagents.

delegation
the transfer of one's duty to another, the transferor still being responsible for the duty

subagent
the person appointed by an agent and as to whom the appointing agent is a principal

Facts
In 1980, plaintiff, Quintel Corp. (Quintel), commenced an action against Citibank and others, defendants, for their alleged violations of federal securities laws in connection with Quintel's investment in Flag Associates, L. P. (Flag), a real estate limited partnership. The complaint alleges that the general partners of Flag and Citibank made certain misrepresentations to Quintel upon which it relied in investing in Flag.

In 1982, Quintel commenced a separate action against Arnold S. Alperstein, and Goldstick, Weinberger, Feldman, Alperstein & Taishoff, P. C., attorneys who represented Quintel in connection with Quintel's investment in Flag. Quintel alleges that the Alperstein defendants were negligent in their representation.

An agreement was reached between Citibank, Alperstein and Conboy, which resulted in the allocation of the legal work that had to be completed on behalf of the Limited Partnership and Quintel. Pursuant to that agreement Alperstein and Goldstick relied upon Conboy and Citibank to protect the limited partner's (Quintel) interest in the Flag transaction.

---

³ See RESTATEMENT (SECOND) OF AGENCY secs. 17, 18, and 19 (1958) where delegable acts and powers are discussed.

Did Alperstein and Goldstick have authority to delegate their fiduciary duty to the subagents Conboy and Citibank without the principal's (Quintel) consent?

Decision
No. Judgment for plaintiff, Quintel.

Reasoning
It is a rule of the first importance governing the conduct of a lawyer that his relationship to his client should be personal; that his responsibility should be direct. Without specific authority from his principal, an agent has no power to delegate his trust. The relationship of principal and agent does not exist between the principal and a subagent. The complaint does not allege that Quintel, as Alperstein's client, was a party to the agreement or consented to it.

Quintel Corporation v. Citibank N.A., 589 F.Supp. 1235 (1984).

For example, if it is customary in the real estate agency business to have subagents show the house and accept counteroffers, the agent would be authorized to do so.

3. Unforeseen Emergency. If the circumstances surrounding the agent's acts create a sudden emergency, and it is impracticable for the agent to communicate with the principal, the agent may appoint a subagent to protect the principal's interest and do what the agent reasonably can believe the principal would want done if the principal were aware of the circumstances. To illustrate, if the principal delivers perishable food to a carrier/agent with instructions to transport and sell it to a third party, if the carrier/agent cannot communicate with the principal that the third party refuses to purchase it and if the food will be worthless unless refrigerated in a warehouse, the carrier/agent has authority to store it and charge the principal's account, the warehouseman being a subagent of the principal to care for the food.

4. Contemplated Conduct of Principal's Business So Requires. Although not expressed in the agency contract, if it is reasonably inferred from the principal's business that the parties contemplated the appointment of subagents, then the agent may delegate his or her authority. For example, a general insurance agent ordinarily has the power to appoint subagents to sell insurance for the company. Also, an agent corporation has implied authority to act through its officers and other employees, and an agent partnership through its partners.

Duties and Liabilities of Principal and Agent

Agent to Principal

The basis of liability resulting from an agency relationship is contractual. The agreement, express or implied, between the agent and the principal creates a series of rights and duties.[4] An understanding of this contract is necessary for both parties to perform properly. The following duties are imposed upon the agent in compliance with the contract and the **fiduciary** relationship. They may be expressed in the contract, but frequently are implied. The principal may sue the agent in contract or tort, depending on the nature of the duty violated. In general, the agent has five duties to the principal.

1. Loyalty. The agreement between the principal and agent creates a *fiduciary relationship*. An agent acts solely for the benefit of the principal, and the agent thereby incurs a duty of loyalty which is imposed on all fiduciaries.

For example, if A has been authorized to negotiate the sales price and sell a house for P, and A sold the house to a friend, T, below the fair market value, A has committed a breach of duty to P.

An agent cannot enter into a contract with a third party that would create a *conflict of interest* with the principal. The purpose of the agent's contracts with others is to benefit the principal. Even though this may not be expressed in the agency contract, it is implied by the fiduciary relationship.

A's duties to P.

fiduciary
a person with a duty to act primarily for the benefit of another

A's duty to be loyal to P.

---
[4] See RESTATEMENT (SECOND) OF AGENCY secs. 376 to 409 (1958) for a discussion of the duties an agent owes to a principal; also see Warren A. Seavey, *Agency* (St. Paul: West Publishing Co., 1964), pp. 234–52.

For instance, if A is P's agent and A convinces P to sell his product to T, a corporation in which A owns a substantial amount of stock, of which P is unaware, A has violated A's duty of loyalty to P. A is liable even if A acts in good faith and believes the transaction is appropriate. However, if P knew of A's interest in the corporation, there is no breach. Notice how the court in the following case requires an *ethical and moral responsibility* on behalf of a real estate broker dealing with his client.

Facts
Dahl sued Black, a real estate salesman, and his broker, Mallot, as a consequence of Dahl's attempt to utilize Black's services to sell his leasehold interest in Illiamna Lake Lodge.

Black conferred with Dahl almost daily during the following weeks and revealed that he had two potential buyers, Prichard and Sears, who were interested in purchasing the leasehold as partners. Dahl did not look for other buyers once the agreement with Black had been reached. Black repeatedly assured Dahl that the partnership intended to go through with the purchase of his interest. In fact, the partners were not prepared to close the deal at that time. Moreover, according to Sears, one of the partners, Black had informed him that if the partners delayed ten to fifteen days they would be able to acquire the leasehold for $10,000 less than the $50,000 Dahl required.

The complaint alleged that Black had willfully or negligently failed to inform Dahl of any conflict of interest, failed to ensure that the proceeds of the sale would accrue to Dahl, and delayed the closing of the original deal, all of which constituted a breach of the fiduciary duty owed by Black to Dahl. Judgment was rendered for Dahl, and the defendants appealed. Was there a breach of fiduciary duty owed to Dahl?

Decision
Yes. Judgment affirmed for plaintiff, Dahl.

Reasoning
There flows from this agency relationship and its accompanying obligation of utmost fidelity and good faith, the legal, ethical, and moral responsibility on the part of the listing broker, as well as his subagents, to exercise reasonable care, skill, and judgment in securing for the principal the best bargain possible; to scrupulously avoid representing any interest antagonistic to that of the principal in transactions involving the principal's listed property, or otherwise self-dealing with that property, without the explicit and fully informed consent of the principal. The court's findings here amply demonstrate a breach of these obligations. We hold that in light of the high standard of care owed by real estate agents to clients, the trial court's conclusion of law was correct.

Richard Black aka Del Black and Mallot v. Frank Dahl, 625 P.2d 876 (Alaska 1981).

A's duty to obey P and to perform A's contract with P.

2. *Obedience and Performance.* The contractual relationship between the principal and the agent may be an ongoing process creating a variety of *instructions* the agent is obligated to follow. An agent generally is obligated to comply with the principal's reasonable instructions. If A violates the instructions, causing harm to P, even if acting in good faith, A is liable to P. Accordingly, if A, acting in good faith, sells to an unauthorized company in violation of P's instructions, A is liable to P for any resulting injury to P.

The agent is never obligated to perform illegal or unethical acts. Codes of trade practice and professional responsibility will determine whether the principal's instructions are reasonable. For example, a stockbroker may engage in proper customary trade practice in the sale of stock without objection by the principal/customer.

A's duty to exercise reasonable care.

3. *Reasonable Care.* An agent is not only subject to the express and implied contract terms with the principal, as well as the fiduciary obligations imposed by the common law, but also the tort law of negligence as it applies to the transaction. The agent has a duty to exercise proper care in acting as an agent. For example, if A, a real estate agent, does not advertise an exclusive listing, A may be liable to P for not complying with the local trade practice.

A's duty to account to P.

4. *Accounting.* One of the implied fiduciary duties requires the agent to keep an account of all the property and money belonging to the principal. Whatever an agent receives during and as a result of the agency, the agent holds in trust for the principal. He cannot secretly keep profits from the agency; they belong to the principal. For example, if T owes P money and T pays P's agent, A, who has authority to receive such payments, A holds the money in trust for P and cannot secretly keep it for himself.

If the agent is sued by the principal for failure to properly account, the agent has the burden of proving that he or she paid the principal. For example, if A should deposit corporate funds in A's personal checking account, the corporation could claim the funds in A's account.

The agent has a duty to keep a separate account of the principal's funds. The agent will be held personally liable for the loss of any commingled funds.

5. Information. An agent has a duty to communicate information to the principal even though not instructed to do so under the express terms of the contract. For example, a counteroffer made to a real estate agent by T, the prospect, must be communicated to P, the home owner.

> A's duty to inform P.

Principal to Agent

The contract between the principal and agent creates the duties the principal owes to the agent.[5] The implied terms of the contract common to this relationship may create duties of the principal to pay the agent for the performance of services, to reimburse the agent for authorized advances and expenses, and to indemnify the agent against liability to third parties. In general, the principal has four duties to the agent.

> P's duties to A.

1. Duty of Compensation. An agent is entitled to the agreed compensation or the fair value of the agent's services. If the agent is hired by the principal, the resulting employment contract will determine the *compensation* and duration of the agency. For example, if a stockbroker is hired without an agreed commission rate, the stockbroker is entitled to the customary trade commission.

> P's duty to compensate A.

2. Duty to Comply with the Agency Contract. The principal has a duty to comply with the terms of the agency contract and to allow the agent to perform under the contract. If a real estate agent is given an "exclusive agency" to list the principal's house for sale for ninety days, the principal cannot terminate the agency before that time nor employ another agent for the same purpose. Under an "exclusive sale contract," only the agent may make the sale.

> P's duty to perform P's contract with A.

3. Duty of Reimbursement. The intent of the principal and the agent as *expressed in their contract* determines the right of the agent to recover expenses incurred while *authorizedly* performing the agency contract.

> P's duty to reimburse A.

If the principal *requests* the agent to expend the agent's own money in the performance of the agency, the agent has the authority to do so and the principal has a duty to **reimburse** the agent for such expense. The principal's request may be express, or implied from performance pursuant to the agent's authority which required the agent to incur expense. A typical example is a principal's request that the agent is to do something which will require the agent to travel and incur travel expense.

> **reimbursement**
> one person's right against another to be repaid money paid on the other's behalf for which the latter was responsible

4. Duty of Indemnity. **Indemnity** is an obligation to pay for another's loss. A principal has the duty, unless their contract provides otherwise, to indemnify the agent for the agent's *payment of damages to third persons* because of the proper performance of the agency contract or a resulting tort. A principal has an implied duty to indemnify the agent for the payment of damages the agent was required to make for loss the agent sustained without the agent's fault while acting pursuant to the agent's authority.

> P's duty to indemnify A.
>
> **indemnity**
> an absolute obligation to pay for another's loss

---

[5] See RESTATEMENT (SECOND) OF AGENCY secs. 432–441 (1958) for a discussion of the duties a principal owes to the agent; also see Warren A. Seavey, *Agency* (St. Paul: West Publishing Co., 1964), pp. 263–72.

Summary Statement

1. *Express authority* occurs when the principal specifies, either orally or in writing, what the agent is authorized to do.
2. *Implied authority* is customary or incidental, and consent for the agent to perform occurs when the agent reasonably believes that it is necessary to carry out the express authority.
3. *Incidental authority* occurs from the circumstances allowing the agent to perform those acts that are incidental to perform the agent's express authority.
4. *Customary authority* is found when the trade or professional practice in which the agent acts creates an implied authorization to conform with the general custom.
5. *Emergency authority* occurs when the agent is confronted with circumstances that the agent reasonably can believe the principal did not foresee would occur and that require action which the agent reasonably believes is what the principal would do if aware of the circumstances.
6. *Apparent authority* occurs when the principal's words or other conduct addressed to a third party reasonably cause the third party to believe that someone is the principal's agent with authority. Under this theory, it is sometimes said that the principal is "estopped" from denying such agency and authority.
7. The third party is under a duty to determine the extent of the agent's authority.
8. A third party is not bound by secret limitations on the agent's authority. However, as between the principal and the agent, any express limitations on the scope of the agent's authority are valid.
9. Generally, an agent cannot delegate to another the agent's authority to act for the principal. However, if the agent's special skill, discretion, or judgment are not involved, the agent may delegate:
    a. ministerial or mechanical duties,
    b. when there is an established custom to employ subagents,
    c. if an unforeseen emergency arises making it impracticable to communicate with the principal, and
    d. if it is reasonably inferred from the principal's business that the parties contemplated the appointment of subagents.
10. As a result of the fiduciary relationship, an agent owes to the principal the following duties:
    a. loyalty,
    b. obedience and performance,
    c. reasonable care,
    d. to account for agency funds, and
    e. to keep the principal informed.
11. The principal owes to the agent the following duties:
    a. to compensate the agent,
    b. to comply with the agency contract,
    c. to reimburse the agent for expenses authorizedly incurred, and
    d. to indemnify the agent for losses caused to the agent by the agency relationship through no fault of the agent.
12. The agency relationship creates a fiduciary obligation on the agent toward the principal. A fiduciary is a person with a duty to act primarily for the benefit of another. The law imposes special duties to perform with a high degree of care.

The following case interrelates the master-servant relationship (see chapters 33, Nature and Creation of Agency, and 35, Agency and the Law of Contracts and Torts) with the doctrine of apparent authority. Note how liability can be found under either legal theory.

Chevron Oil Company v. Sutton
515 P.2d 1283 (N.M. 1973)

McManus, Chief Justice. Sutton sought damages for death by wrongful act against Chevron Oil Company (Chevron), Lee Sharp (station lessee for Chevron), and Herbert R. Buss (Sharp's employee). Sutton's wife had died from injuries sustained in a car accident when a wheel of a car repaired by Buss came off the vehicle.

The main issue before this court is whether Chevron asserted enough control over its lessee to constitute a master-servant relationship. If such relationship is present, then Chevron could be found liable under the doctrine of **respondeat superior**. . . .

The fact in dispute is whether or not Chevron exercised such control over Sharp as to bring the doctrine of respondeat superior into play. Independent stations of the appellant (Chevron) were required to: (1) diligently promote the sale of Chevron's brand products; (2) remain open for certain hours and days and "meet the operating hours of competitors"; (3) keep the premises, restrooms and equipment in a "clean and orderly condition"; (4) present a "good appearance"; and (5) promote Chevron's image to the motoring public. In addition, Sharp also (6) sold Chevron products and dispensed gasoline and oil provided by the Chevron organization; (7) received the benefit of Chevron advertising; (8) wore uniforms containing the Chevron emblem; (9) used calling cards which billed the station as "Lee Sharp Chevron and Four Wheel Drive Equipment" (apparently with Chevron's consent); and (10) the customers of the Sharp station were permitted to charge purchases of both products and repairs on Chevron credit cards.

Even if there were not a material issue as to whether or not Chevron asserted enough control as to create an actual master-servant relationship, there still exists a material issue as to whether or not Chevron had clothed the lessee with apparent authority.*

Here, Chevron knew of and allowed Sharp to conduct his Four Wheel Drive Fixit Shop; and it would be reasonable to assume that, if Chevron did not want Sharp to continue such a business, it should have forbidden such activities or at least have put the public on notice that Sharp did not have the authority to make repairs and that it would not be responsible for such repair activities. Instead of putting the public on notice that Sharp did not have the authority to make such repairs, Chevron advertised in the telephone directory that its stations performed auto repairs, and that its repairmen were skillful.

Sutton relied on such statements, in addition to relying on signs, uniforms and credit card privileges which indicated to the public that Sharp was under the control and was an agent of Chevron. . . . Thus, because Sutton relied on such statements and indicia of authority, there is a material question of fact present as to whether or not Sharp had been clothed with apparent authority by Chevron to act as Chevron's agent. . . .

The cause [case] is reversed and remanded to the District Court of Bernalillo County for action consistent with this opinion.

*[Emphasis added.]

respondeat superior let the master (superior) be responsible for the torts of his servant committed while acting within the scope of his employment

Questions and Case Problems

1. Bromber, the general manager of a hotel, offered a $1,000 reward in a newspaper for information leading to the arrest and conviction of the person who killed the hotel clerk during a hotel robbery. Plaintiff, Jackson, claimed the reward, and the defendant, hotel owner Goodman, denied that Bromber had the authority to make the reward offer. Was there sufficient evidence to present a jury question that Bromber, as the hotel manager, had apparent authority to make the reward offer? [*Jackson v. Goodman,* 244 N.W.2d 423 (Mich. 1976).]

2. Wood checked into the Holiday Inn and tendered payment for his room by using his Gulf Oil Company credit card. Sometime during the early morning Jessie Goynes, the "night auditor" of the Holiday Inn, called National Data in order to confirm the plaintiff's credit card number and receive an authorization to extend credit on the basis of the card. He received a communication from National Data advising him: "Do not honor this sale. Pick up the credit card and send it in for reward." After getting the directive from National Data, he telephoned the plaintiff's room at 7:00 A.M. and advised him that he was unable to obtain credit authorization and requested plaintiff to surrender the card. Goynes said that Wood voluntarily complied. Goynes was offensive, abusive, and insulting to Wood. Wood then paid in cash and left the motel. Upon returning home, Wood called Gulf and explained that he used the card for business purposes. He complained that his account was current, and his credit was immediately reinstated. Wood sued the Gulf Oil Corporation, Holiday Inns, Inc., and Jessie Goynes. Goynes denied any negligence or wrongful conduct and asserted by way of cross-claim that he was acting under the direction of Gulf and was therefore entitled to indemnification by Gulf.

    (a) Was the Holiday Inn clerk the agent of the Gulf Oil Company? (b) Is Gulf liable for the clerk's tortious conduct? (c) Is Gulf required to indemnify the Holiday Inn for its clerk's negligence? [*Wood v. Holiday Inns, Inc.*, 508 F.2d 167 (Ala. 1975).]

3. Must a third party who paid a traveling salesperson, authorized to solicit orders for the salesperson's principal, who never turned the money over to the principal, pay the money again to the principal?

4. The owner of land appointed a real estate agent to sell his land. The real estate agent owned 80% of the stock in a company to whom he sold the land at its appraised fair market value. When the seller discovered the real estate agent's interest in the company that bought the land he sued the company demanding it return the land to the seller. Did the real estate agent violate any duty owed to the seller?

5. Davis was a salaried outside salesperson of defendant, International Playtex Corporation. His duties included selling Playtex products to retail stores. He worked out of his home and was required to own and operate a motor vehicle for business use. He had no set hours of employment and was urged by Playtex's district manager to work evenings and weekends. While traveling to his girlfriend's home to do paperwork for Playtex, Davis was involved in a collision with Barnum, who died from his injuries. Rappaport, the plaintiff, the executor of Barnum's estate, brought this suit against Playtex. Was Davis acting within the scope of his employment at the time of the accident? [*Rappaport v. International Playtex Corporation,* 352 N.Y.S.2d 241 (N.Y. 1974).]

6. Rushing, King and Kenney, defendants, are the owners of an undivided three-fourths interest in the real property in question. Garrett, plaintiff, the owner of the remaining one-fourth undivided interest, filed suit in the Circuit Court for **partition** and for specific performance of an alleged contract of sale to him of their interests in the real property. The court below found that a series of letters written by counsel for the plaintiff and the defendants during the course of the partition suit constituted a written binding contract for the sale of defendants' interest in the property to plaintiff. There was no proof that defendants had given to their attorney any express authority to contract for the sale of their interests in the property. Does an attorney employed by a party in litigation such as in the instant case, have implied authority to execute a written agreement for the conveyance of property? [*Rushing, King and Kenney v. Garrett, Jr.,* 375 So.2d 903 (Fla. 1979).]

partition
a division of property between joint owners

7. Anglo-American Clothing Corporation, plaintiff, brought an action against Marjorie's of Tiburon, Inc., dba under the trade name of Rebel Jeans, defendant, alleging that Rebel Jeans was indebted to Anglo-American Clothing, by virtue of a contract of sale in which Rebel Jeans purchased from plaintiff 132 jackets at a total purchase price of $2,739.00. Rebel Jeans defended on the basis that approximately 40 jackets were defective and that they had attempted a proper rejection of said items upon the grounds that the transaction was a sale or return transaction. Although Anglo-American's agents do not have actual authority to enter into such type of transactions, both witnesses testifying for Rebel Jeans indicated that statements made to them by Anglo-American's agent led them to believe that he had such authority by virtue of owning an interest in the business. The testimony disclosed that Anglo-American's agent did not however own any interest in the business. Did Anglo-American's agent have implied or apparent authority to enter into a sale or return contract? [*Anglo-American Clothing Corporation v. Marjorie's of Tiburon, Inc., dba Rebel Jeans,* 571 P.2d 427 (Okla. 1977).]

8. Plaintiff, Mr. Ford, a black, visited the "Bud" Orth Real Estate Agency owned and operated by Ellsworth C. "Bud" Orth, a licensed real estate broker. Ford asked Ken Orth, a licensed salesperson on duty at the agency, to show him a particular piece of property as advertised for sale. The property, owned by Donald and Joanne McMahon, was in an area of the city in which few, if any, blacks owned property or resided. Ken Orth, in the presence of Ford and his family, made a phone call to the McMahons informing them that Ford wanted to look at the property as a prospective purchaser and that he was a black. After the telephone call Orth informed Ford that the owner did not want to show the property to black persons and therefore he could not see it. Ford told Ken Orth that he was discriminating and left the agency. Ford filed a complaint with the Wisconsin Real Estate Examining Board, alleging in substance that E. C. "Bud" Orth, a licensed broker, was guilty of racial discrimination. Was Ken Orth, acting as an agent under the explicit instructions of his principal, the seller, guilty of discrimination? [*Ford v. Wisconsin Real Estate Examining Board,* 179 N.W.2d 786 (Wis. 1970).]

9. The Hagues, husband and wife, defendants, owned a 160 acre quarter-section of land. Hilgendorf, plaintiff, was a real estate broker. The Hagues listed the land with Hilgendorf for sale at a stated price. This listing gave Hilgendorf the exclusive right to sell the land for a period of twelve months at a 6% commission. The Hagues later sent Hilgendorf a letter purporting to terminate the listing on the 160 acre parcel. Hilgendorf did not acquiesce in Hagues' termination of the listing. Hilgendorf produced several buyers who were willing and able to buy the 160 acres on the terms indicated by the Hagues, but the Hagues ignored their offers. The Hagues secured another real estate broker who, sold the 160 acres. Hilgendorf sued the Hagues for damages for breach of the listing contract, the damages being measured by the commission. Did the Hagues have the right to terminate the listing contract? [*Hilgendorf v. Mervin and Joan Hague,* 293 N.W.2d 272 (Iowa 1980).]

10. In the case of *Chevron Oil Company v. Sutton,* 515 P.2d 1283 (N.M. 1973),[6] the court referred the case back to the trial court on the ground that the facts pleaded could result in a finding of a master-servant relationship and of apparent authority. In light of this opinion, what do you think can be done to avoid the risk of liability on the basis of master-servant relationship, and apparent authority with respect to auto repairs on the station premises?

---

[6] See p. 525.

35 Agency and the Law of Contracts and Torts

After you have read this chapter, you should be able to:

1. Explain the three things an agent must do to be protected from personal liability on a breach of contract suit.
2. Know the application of the parol evidence rule to:
   a. simple (informal) agency contracts with a third party and an agent.
   b. formal contracts with a third party and an agent.
3. Understand when an agent may agree to be held personally liable to a contract with a third party.
4. Explain an implied warranty of authorization.
5. Explain an implied warranty of the principal's capacity.
6. Define a disclosed principal and a partially disclosed principal, and explain when these principals are personally liable under the agent's contract.
7. Define an undisclosed principal, and explain when the undisclosed principal is and is not personally liable under the agent's contract.
8. Explain when a third party's payment to the agent will bind the principal, and when it will not bind the principal.
9. Distinguish a servant from a nonservant agent, and explain the reason for and the importance of this difference.
10. Explain when the principal is liable for the torts of its agent, and when the principal is not liable.
11. Determine a public accountant's status, duties, and the extent of liability to the client for breach of contract and, to certain third persons, for negligent or fraudulent misrepresentation in connection with the accountant's examination of the client's business.
12. Determine the status and liability of independent auditors.

Introduction

In the preceding chapters of this Part we discussed the concept of agency, the authority and apparent authority of an agent, and the duties of the principal and the agent *to each other*. In this chapter we will discuss the impact *on third persons* of an agent's conduct resulting in contractual and tort liability of the agent and of a disclosed and an undisclosed principal.

This chapter is important because it gives you insight into how increased exposure to risk in the legal environment brought about by agency can be limited.

Basically, two substantive areas of law are impacted significantly by the agency relationship: contracts and torts.

Contract Liability of Agents

Liability of Agent As a Party to a Contract

The agent must do the following three things to be protected from contractual liability:

1. Disclose the principal. The disclosure of the agent's capacity and the fact that the agent is acting on behalf of a particular principal may be expressed in any manner. The third party must be aware that the agent is acting on behalf of another.
2. Have authority to act. The agent must be authorized by the principal to act on the principal's behalf. The authority may be express or implied, or there may be apparent authority.[1]
3. Have any written contracts properly executed. If an agent signs a written contract with the third party, the agent must disclose his or her *representative capacity* on the contract. For example, if Jane Arnold is acting for Peter Powers, a proper signature would be, "Peter Powers by Jane Arnold." If the agent simply signed "Jane Arnold," even though the third party knew she was acting for her principal, the *parol evidence rule* may apply and prevent verbal testimony to explain the agent's capacity.

The *parol evidence rule*[2] has the following applications:

1. **Simple contracts.** If the written contract is *simple* (i.e., not under seal, or not a negotiable instrument such as a promissory note or a check), the agent may testify concerning the fact that the third party *knew* he was acting on behalf of the principal, although the written contract does not disclose this.
2. **Formal contracts.** If the contract was under seal or negotiable commercial paper (e.g., a check), the parol evidence rule will prevent the agent from giving testimony concerning the third party's knowledge that the agent was acting on behalf of the principal.

simple contract
a contract which need not be in any particular form

formal contract
a contract which must be in a certain form

Agent May Agree to Personal Liability

The agent may agree to be held personally liable at the request of the third party. For example, if T requests A to stand behind a sales contract, the agent (A), in order to effect a sale and receive a commission, may agree to be held personally liable in the event of a breach.

---

[1] See pp. 517–18, for discussion of authority and apparent authority.

[2] See pp. 156–57, for discussion of the parol evidence rule.

Agent's Implied Warranties

An agent makes two implied **warranties** on the contract made by the agent for the principal with third persons: (1) implied warranty of authorization, and (2) implied warranty of the principal's capacity to contract.

The agent will be held personally liable if the agent breaches either warranty even though acting in good faith.

warranty
an express or implied assurance that certain facts exist

Implied Warranty of Authorization. When an agent contracts with a third party, the agent impliedly warrants having the authority to contract for the principal. If the agent does not have this authority, or *exceeds the scope of such authority,* the agent is liable to the third party for **damages** for breach of implied warranty of authority.

In the following case a corporate president made an offer to sell corporation property without the approval of the board of directors or stockholders. The court held he was in breach of an agent's implied warranty of authorization.

damages
the money judicially awarded to an injured party for another's wrongful conduct

Facts
Plaintiff sued D. C. Craig, defendant, as president of Craig Industries, Inc., for breach of warranty of authority.
   Plaintiff had long expressed interest in purchasing the plants of Craig Industries to augment its business of producing and selling charcoal briquets. On September 19, 1977, Mr. Craig telephoned Mr. Gideon, plaintiff's vice president, to inquire if the plaintiff corporation was interested in buying one of Craig Industries' plants. In anticipation of a deal being made, plaintiff's lawyer had prepared a partially completed typewritten "Letter Offer to Purchase."
   On September 27, 1977, the attorneys for Craig Industries, Inc., wrote the plaintiff's lawyer that the corporation's board of directors had met that date and "voted to reject the offer." Mr. Gideon's uncashed $25,000 check was returned with the letter. Plaintiff thereafter commenced suit. Judgment was rendered against both defendants, and Mr. Craig appealed. Did Mr. Craig breach his implied warranty of authority?

Decision
Yes. Judgment affirmed for the plaintiff, Husky Industries, Inc., against Mr. Craig only.

Reasoning
Having represented himself as an agent of a disclosed principal, an individual who purports to contract in the name of his principal without or in excess of his authority to do so, becomes personally subject to liability to the other contracting party. Unless the agreement also expressly binds him personally, the liability of the agent is not predicated upon the contract itself, but rather upon the agent's breach of the express or implied covenant or warranty of authority.
   Nothing was mentioned or discussed regarding the apparent authority Mr. Craig was using to contract on behalf of the corporation. Mr. Craig, representing himself as an agent, undertook to contract in the name of his disclosed principal without or in excess of his authority to do so; plaintiff's agents were unaware of such lack of authority; and plaintiff was damaged by defendant Mr. Craig's breach of his express or implied covenant or warranty of authority.

Husky Industries, Inc. v. Craig Industries, Inc. and D. C. Craig, 618 S.W.2d 458 (Mo. 1981).

Implied Warranty of Principal's Capacity. The agent impliedly warrants to the third party that the principal has capacity to be contractually bound. For example, if the agent acts for a dissolved corporation, the former corporation will not be liable *under any contract,* but the agent can be held liable for *breach of the agent's implied warranty of the principal's capacity.* However, if the agent acts on behalf of a minor/principal and does not represent that the principal has full capacity, the agent is not liable if the minor avoids the contract.

Contract Liability of Principals

Whether a principal is disclosed, undisclosed, or partially disclosed to the third person depends upon the third person's knowledge of a person as a principal and the principal's identity. When the third person knows that the agent is acting for a principal but the third person does not know the principal's identity, the latter is a **partially disclosed principal.** In this book, unless otherwise indicated, reference to a disclosed principal includes a partially disclosed principal, because the third person intends to contract with the *principal* whoever it may be *and the agent.*

Liability of Disclosed Principal or Partially Disclosed Principal As Party to a Contract
Once the agent has **disclosed** to the third party the identity of the **principal** for whom the agent is *authorized to contract,* or the third person reasonably should be aware of the principal's identity, the principal becomes liable on the subsequently made contract.[3] However, if the agent is not authorized, or if the agent exceeds the scope of his or her authority, the principal may ratify[4] the contract and thus become liable on the contract with the effect as though it were initially authorized. Accordingly, if there is a principal with contractual capacity, and the agent with authority properly executed the contract with the third party, a contract exists only between P and T. If the principal is partially disclosed, both the principal and the agent are parties to the contract with the third person.

Liability of Undisclosed Principal As Party to a Contract
If the third party is not aware and reasonably should not be aware that the agent is acting for anyone, the principal is called an **undisclosed principal.** The parties to the contract are the agent and the third party. However, if the third party breaches the contract, the assets of the third party are available to satisfy a judgment obtained by the agent against the third party. Because the agent then holds such assets in trust for the benefit of the principal, the law causes the *undisclosed principal also, along with the agent, to be a party to the contract* authorizedly made by the agent so that the principal's assets are available to the third party if the agent breaches the contract. So there are *three* parties to the contract—namely the agent, principal, and third party—unless the undisclosed principal is excluded from being a party to the contract either (1) expressly by the contract, (2) by the contract being under seal, or (3) if the contract is a negotiable instrument in which the principal's name does not appear. Each of the three parties is liable as a contracting party. For example, when P authorizes A to purchase property on P's behalf without disclosing that A is representing anyone and A, intending to act for P, authorizedly contracts with T to purchase the property in A's own name, P (as well as A) is liable on the contract.

Effect of Agent's Improper Purpose
If an agent makes a contract for the disclosed or undisclosed principal as the agent is *authorized* to do, but with an *improper purpose* of which the third party does not have notice, the principal is bound on the contract as though the agent had a proper purpose. For example, payment by the third party to the agent of funds due to the principal, the agent having authority to receive such funds, will bind the principal even if the agent never remits the payment. This rule applies only if the third party acted in good faith and did not know the agent would act improperly. For example, P appoints A to collect rents on P's behalf. T, a tenant, paid the rent to A, who kept the money. P would have to give credit to T for the monthly rent.

The reasons for this rule are that T cannot ascertain A's improper purpose, and public policy requires P to select the agent carefully for loyalty to P.

---

[3] See RESTATEMENT (SECOND) OF AGENCY sec. 4 (1958) for a general discussion of a disclosed, partially disclosed, and undisclosed principal.

[4] See pp. 509–10, on the rules of ratification in agency.

---

partially disclosed principal
a person whose identity is not disclosed to a third person who knows, or reasonably should know, that an agent is, or may be acting as, an agent for that principal whoever it may be

disclosed principal
a person known, or who reasonably should be known, by a third party to be a principal for an agent

undisclosed principal
a person not known, or who is not reasonably known, to be a principal for an agent by a third party

Effect of Agent's Unauthorized Misrepresentation
of What the Agent Was Authorized to Represent Truthfully

If an agent makes a contract for the disclosed or partially disclosed principal as the agent is *authorized* to do, but misrepresents *matters in connection with the contract* of which the third party does not have notice, the principal is liable on the contract and also for such misrepresentations. For example, a salesperson misrepresents the fabric content of a sweater sold to an innocent store customer third party. The store owner principal is liable to the customer for the agent's untruthful statement.

Tort Liability

The three-party relationship created by an agency contract frequently involves an injury arising from tort liability. If the principal directs its agent to commit a wrongful act, the *principal* is liable in tort to the injured third party. The principal is also liable for all other tortious acts committed by the agent while acting within the scope of the agent's authority.

Even though the agent may injure the third party while acting for the principal, the *agent* may also be held liable. An agent is liable to third parties for the agent's torts irrespective of whether or not his principal is also liable and whether or not the agent was acting within the scope of the agent's authority. The injured third party may select the principal or the agent as liable for the agent's torts committed within the course and scope of the agent's authority. Also, it is possible that the third person may be liable *to the agent* for torts caused by the third person's improper conduct.

misfeasance
misdoing

nonfeasance
not doing

While an agent is liable to a third party for the agent's misdoing, called **misfeasance,** the agent is not liable for not doing anything, called **nonfeasance,** in the absence of any legal obligation to act. He has no duty to the third party, and so has no liability for nonfeasance. But once an agent begins to act, the law imposes a duty upon the agent to act carefully, as it does for everyone, and also imposes liability for misfeasance.

Principal's Liability for Torts of the Agent while Acting within the Scope
of the Agent's Authority

Let us briefly examine the *principal's* tort liability within the three-party relationship.

servant
an agent whose physical conduct his master (principal) has the right to control or controls

master
a principal who has the right to control, or controls, the physical conduct of his servant agent

An agent may be a **servant** or a *nonservant* agent. We have defined an agent as a person authorized to act on behalf of another and subject to the other's control. The principal's degree of control over the conduct of the agent may vary. If the principal has the right to control, or exercises control over, the *physical conduct* of its agent, the agent is called a *servant* and the principal is called a **master.** Often courts refer to them as principal and agent. Most agents are servants.

The reason for distinguishing between servants and nonservant agents is that the principal's liability varies as the degree of the principal's control over the conduct of the agent. Thus, a *master* is liable for the *tortious physical harm* (or loss) to third persons caused by the servant while acting within the *scope of the servant's employment* (servants are usually called *employees*). A principal is liable for the *nonphysical* torts of its *nonservant agent* while acting within the *scope of the agent's authority*.

For example, independent contractors who become special agents (e.g., brokers, lawyers) are nonservant agents, and because the principal does *not* control their *physical conduct,* the principal is not liable for their tortious physical harm to third persons. (P retains A, a real estate broker, to produce a prospective buyer of P's land. While A is driving A's auto showing the land to a customer, A drives negligently and injures the customer. P is not liable for A's tortious physical harm to the customer because A is a nonservant agent.) (A, P's truck driver, while delivering P's goods, negligently injures a pedestrian. P is a master and liable for the tortious physical harm to the pedestrian caused by A, P's servant.) Accordingly, let us first consider torts by servants and then torts by nonservant agents.

A principal or master is not liable to third persons for **punitive damages** for the acts of the agent unless either (1) the act was previously authorized by the principal, (2) the act was later ratified or approved by the principal, (3) the principal was reckless in employing an unfit agent, or (4) the act occurred while the agent was acting in the scope of the agent's employment in a managerial capacity.[5]

Torts by Servants. The doctrine of a master's liability for the **torts** of the servant committed while acting within the scope of the servant's employment is called **respondeat superior**. "Scope of employment" is a broad phrase, but in general it means *in furtherance of the master's business*. In certain instances a master is liable even when the servant has *not* acted within the scope of the servant's employment.

1. *Torts committed within the scope of employment.*
   Once tortious physical harm has occurred, the *first step* is to determine if the wrongdoer is an *agent*. If the wrongdoer is, the *next step* is to decide if the wrongdoer is a *servant*. If the agent is, then the *last step* is to see if the servant was acting within the *scope of the servant's employment* when the tort was committed. The court in the following case held an employer was not responsible for its employee's act causing injury to another because the employee was not discharging his duty owed to the employer at the time of its occurrence.

punitive (exemplary) damages
the money judicially awarded to an injured party in excess of compensatory damages to punish for malicious, wanton, or intentional wrongful conduct

tort
a civil (private) noncontractual wrong for which a court will give a remedy

respondeat superior
let the master (superior) be responsible for the torts of his servant committed while acting within the scope of his employment

Facts
Plaintiff, alleges that a welder, an employee of defendant, one of the Natkin companies, contractors, stuffed paper into the ends of a pipe the plaintiff was welding, filled the pipe with acetylene gas from his welding rig and caused the gas to explode. Plaintiff claims that the explosion caused him to contract a rash, ringing and deafness in both ears, nausea and dizziness. The defendants filed motions for summary judgment on the grounds that no Natkin employee was authorized to use acetylene gas for any purpose other than the cutting of steel. The lower court allowed the motion and plaintiff appealed.

Decision
Motion for summary judgment affirmed.

Reasoning
The employee setting off the explosion with acetylene gas, had temporarily abandoned the interests of his employer and was acting in a purely personal manner and contrary to the policy and instructions of his employer.

Larry R. Williams v. Natkin & Company et al., 508 F.Supp. 1017 (1981).

In what is known as the "independent frolic" or "detour" cases, the chief question is whether the servant's deviation from the servant's authority is sufficient to cause the servant's conduct not to be within the scope of the servant's employment.

2. *Torts committed beyond the scope of the servant's authority.*
   The master is not liable to the third party for torts committed by the servant when the servant acts beyond the scope of the servant's employment. If the servant is no longer acting for the benefit of the master and has dealings with the third party outside the servant's employment relationship with the master, the injured third party generally has no recourse against the master. When a servant engages in an independent frolic or detour which is not within the servant's scope of employment, there is much difficulty and difference among the cases in determining at what point in time and space the servant returns into the employ of the master.

Torts by Nonservant Agents. The principal is not liable for tortious physical harm committed by a nonservant agent because the principal has no control over the agent's physical conduct. However, the principal is liable for the agent's nonphysical torts committed while acting within the agent's authority or apparent authority. For example, if the agent intentionally misrepresents to a customer third party regarding the subject matter authorized or apparently authorized to be sold by the agent, the principal may be liable for the tort of **deceit**.

deceit
briefly, a tort consisting of contractual fraud (for a full definition see the Glossary)

---

[5] See RESTATEMENT (SECOND) OF AGENCY sec. 217C.

It should be noted that an agent is not liable for the torts or breach of contract committed by the principal in connection with a transaction authorizedly made by the agent. The following case is an example.

Facts

The plaintiffs, Mr. and Mrs. Dorkin, contracted with the defendant, American Express Company, for a European tour. While being transported from Antwerp to Amsterdam in Holland, Mrs. Dorkin sustained personal injuries when the tour bus in which she and her husband were riding braked abruptly, causing her to be thrown to the floor. The plaintiffs claimed that the negligence of the defendant was a failure to exercise reasonable and prudent care in providing safe equipment and careful personnel in the discharge of its contractual obligation to supply a safe, entertaining European vacation. The plaintiffs contend that the defendant was the agent of the various hotels and transportation companies as principals who supplied the services abroad and that the defendant as agent is liable for their tortious conduct. Defendant denies that it is so liable. Was American Express liable for the injury of Mrs. Dorkin?

Decision

No. Judgment for defendant, American Express.

Reasoning

In the absence of agreement or acts indicating an intention of the contracting parties to superadd the responsibility of the agent, there is no such responsibility of the agent to third parties for tortious acts of the principal. Similarly, there is no liability on the part of the agent for breach of contract by the principal. Defendant performed its contract with plaintiffs and, as an agent, is not liable for the tortious conduct of its principals. Further the defendant is really an independent contractor and not an agent.

Dorkin v. American Express Company, 74 Misc.2d 673 (N.Y. 1974).

The Status and Liability of Public Accountants

Status

A public accountant is an **independent contractor.** A public accountant certified by the state is called a "certified public accountant" (CPA). However, a public accountant may become an agent for a principal if the principal controls or has the right to control the accountant, or the accountant has authority to contract for a principal. If the accountant becomes an agent, then the law of agency is applicable and determines the liability of the accountant to the principal and to third persons in contract and in tort.

Liability

To the Client. The public accountant is a professional person, either an individual or a firm of accountants, with the overall responsibility and duty, pursuant to contract, to exercise reasonable care in the examination of the recorded business affairs of the client and, as a result, to disclose all material relevant financial information in a manner that is not misleading. This responsibility does not include the discovery of irregularities, e.g., defalcations (defection, misappropriation of money), unless otherwise agreed. However, if the accountant discovers suspicious circumstances, the accountant then has the responsibility to investigate further. Also, the accountant may be liable if the accountant's negligence prevents such discovery.

The accountant's disclosure to the client must be made in terms and manner which the particular client reasonably can understand. Failure to provide the agreed-upon careful quality of work is a **breach of contract** by the accountant with the client. An illustration of such a breach is the accountant's failure to render the services contracted for within the express, or if not express then within a reasonable, time. The accountant's material breach of contract precludes any right to compensation for services which have been rendered.

The accountant does not have a common law **possessory lien** on the client's materials possessed by the accountant as security for payment for services rendered. However, some states provide for a statutory lien on such materials. The accountant's working papers and his own copies of data belong to the accountant.

---

independent contractor
a person who contracts independently for himself to render a result, and who is not acting on behalf of another nor subject to another's control

breach of contract
wrongful nonperformance of a contractual promise

lien
a legal right in another's property as security for the performance of an obligation

possessory lien
a lien which includes the right to possession of the property which is subject to the lien

To Third Persons. We have stressed the accountant's responsibility and liability to *the client* for negligent misrepresentation and resulting breach of contract; but is the accountant responsible and liable to *third persons* for the accountant's services to the client? Because there is no contract between the accountant and third persons, there is no **privity** between them. However, if the accountant has *reason to believe that, through the client, the accountant's product* (e.g., financial statement, other materials) *will be made available to third persons,* a duty of care by the accountant toward such third persons springs into being, and the accountant is liable to the third person for *negligent misrepresentation* in the accountant's product which proximately causes harm to that third person.

The extent of such duty of care by the accountant to the third person depends upon whether or not the accountant knows the identity of the particular third person *and* that the third person may rely on the accountant's product. If the third person's identity is *known* by the accountant, then the accountant's duty of care toward such known third person is for simple **negligence** producing misrepresentation in the accountant's product—that is, failure to exercise ordinary reasonable prudent care. This is the same duty of care that the accountant owes to the client. However, if the third person's identity *is not known* to the accountant, then the accountant is liable for damage proximately caused by the accountant's **fraud,** or gross negligence amounting to "actual" or "constructive" fraud. If the accountant *intends* to mislead (called "scienter"), then there is actual fraud. Constructive fraud exists if there is reckless disregard for the truth.

It should be carefully noted that it is the accountant's *negligent or fraudulent misrepresentation in the accountant's product* which subjects the accountant to liability to the client for breach of contract, and to liability to certain third persons who have relied on such misrepresentation.

privity
a mutuality of relationship between persons or between persons and a particular transaction

negligence
(conduct) failure to use the degree of care demanded by the circumstances

fraud
(in contracts) a misrepresentation of fact, known to be false, intentionally made to induce another person to make or refrain from making a contract, and reasonably relied on by the other person

The Status and Liability of Auditors

A "certified public accountant" (CPA) in providing the audit function reviews financial statements and reports to determine whether they are in accordance with generally accepted accounting principles. This obligation is one of ten generally accepted auditing standards. As auditors are often professional agents, the preceding material on the status and liability of public accountants applies to the CPA as an agent engaged in auditing.

The auditor's special function is to assist management by providing it with verifiable reports to be used by third parties.[6] Hence, to a great extent auditor's liability involves claims by the third party as the primary beneficiary of the auditor's report. For example, a person about to sell her business retains an auditor to prepare financial statements for a known potential buyer. The buyer is a foreseen third party that can hold an auditor liable for ordinary negligence in preparing the report. Courts have held auditors liable for negligent misrepresentations reasonably relied on by the foreseen third parties.[7] Hence, an auditor's liability extends to all third parties whom the auditor should reasonably foresee as recipients. An auditor's risk of liability includes those third parties who commonly use auditors' reports such as buyers of a business, bankers and investors.

The following case considers the common law standards governing the liability of independent auditors for failing to detect fraud by the management of the audited company.

---

[6] AICPA Professional Standards, vol. B, sec. 5102

[7] *Rusch Factors, Inc. v. Levin,* 284 F.Supp. 85 (1968); *Citizens State Bank v. Timm, Schmidt & Co. and General Casualty Company of Wisconsin,* 335 N.W.2d 361 (Wis. 1983).

Facts

Between 1970 and 1975, managerial employees of Cenco Incorporated engaged in a massive fraud. The fraud was eventually discovered by a newly hired financial officer at Cenco who reported his suspicions to the Securities and Exchange Commission. Cenco's independent auditor throughout the period of the fraud, the accounting partnership of Seidman & Seidman (Seidman), either never discovered the fraud or if it did it failed to report it. The fraud primarily involved the inflating of inventories in the Medical/Health Division far above their actual value. This increased the apparent worth of Cenco and greatly increased the market price of its stock (when the fraud was unmasked, the market price of its stock plummeted by more than 75 percent).

The unmasking of the fraud led to the filing of a class action in federal district court against Cenco, its corrupt managers, and Seidman. The class was composed of purchasers of Cenco stock during the period of the fraud, when the stock price was inflated. The suit charged the defendants with having violated various federal securities laws and SEC rules, and common law strictures against fraud and related misconduct. Cenco filed a cross-claim against its co-defendant Seidman, alleging that Seidman was liable to Cenco under both federal and state common law for having failed to prevent the fraud by Cenco's managers.

Plaintiffs settled their claim by Seidman's payment of $3.5 million. The dispute is now between Cenco and Seidman. Was Seidman entitled to use the wrongdoing of Cenco's managers as a defense against the charges of breach of contract, negligence and fraud?

Decision:

Yes. Cenco's cross-claim against the auditors, Seidman, dismissed.

Reasoning

Breach of contract, negligence, and fraud, when committed by auditors, are a single form of wrongdoing under different names. The contract in question here consists of the letters between Seidman and Cenco outlining the terms of Seidman's annual retention to audit Cenco's books.

The tort of negligence in the context of auditing is likewise a failure to use professional care and skill in carrying out an audit. And if such care and skill are not used, then the audit reports to the client will contain misrepresentations, either negligent or, if the auditor knows that the representations in the reports are untruthful or is indifferent to whether or not they are truthful, fraudulent.

Here the uncontested facts show fraud permeating the top management of Cenco. In such a case the corporation should not be allowed to shift the entire responsibility for the fraud to its auditors.

Cenco Incorporated v. Seidman & Seidman, 686 F.2d 449 (1982).

Summary Statement

1. To be protected from personal liability, an agent must:
    a. disclose the principal,
    b. be authorized by the principal to act on its behalf,
    c. have any written contract with a third party properly executed by the agent.
2. The parol evidence rule will allow an agent who signed a *simple* contract to testify that the third party with whom the agent contracted knew the agent was acting on behalf of a principal. A simple contract, as contrasted with a formal contract, is not in any required form (e.g., a check).
3. If the agent signed a *formal* contract, the parol evidence rule will prevent the agent from giving testimony concerning the third party's knowledge that the agent was acting on behalf of the principal.
4. If requested by the third party, the agent may agree to become personally liable on the contract.
5. The circumstances surrounding an agent's contract for a principal with a third person create an implied warranty of authorization. This means that the agent warrants he or she has authority and has not exceeded its scope.
6. Also, the agent impliedly warrants that the principal has capacity to be contractually bound.

7. An *undisclosed principal* is a principal not known to the third party who is unaware of any agency. The undisclosed principal has authorized the agent to act for the principal's benefit and on the principal's behalf. The undisclosed principal is liable to the third party on a simple contract, as is the agent also.
8. A *disclosed principal* is a principal that is known to the third party. The principal is liable to the third party if the principal has capacity to contract and if the agent was authorized or apparently authorized to act on its behalf or if the contract was ratified by the principal.
9. If the agent makes an authorized contract for the disclosed or partially disclosed principal but with an *improper purpose,* of which the third party does not have notice, the principal is bound on the contract.
10. If the agent makes an authorized contract for the disclosed or partially disclosed principal and *misrepresents* matters in connection with the contract, of which the third party did not have notice, the principal is liable on the contract and for such misrepresentations.
11. A principal is liable for the nonphysical torts of its nonservant agent when they are committed within the course and scope of the agent's authority or apparent authority. The principal (master) is also liable for the tortious physical harm to third persons committed by the principal's servant while acting within the scope of the servant's employment. This rule is based on the theory that the servant, although acting wrongfully, is acting for the benefit of the principal (master). It is known as the doctrine of "respondeat superior."
12. A public accountant may be liable to the client for breach of contract and, to certain third persons, for negligent or fraudulent misrepresentation in connection with the accountant's examination of the client's business.
13. An independent auditor is liable to all third persons who the auditor can reasonably forsee will be recipients of the auditor's false information if the auditor fails to exercise reasonable care or competency in obtaining or communicating the information.

In the following case the *master* was held to be vicariously (substitutively) liable under the doctrine of *respondeat superior* for the negligence of its *servant*. This personal injury action for negligence was brought against the owner of a tavern and its employee by a customer, plaintiff, who lost an eye when the employee, in demonstrating self-defense with a pocketknife in the tavern, caused the blade to come in contact with the customer's eye. Note the court's reasoning in finding the tavern employee was not acting "outside the scope of his employment" at the time he injured the customer's eye.

Riviello v. Waldron and Raybele Tavern, Inc.
391 N.E.2d 1278 (N.Y. 1979).

Fuchsberg, J. Plaintiff, Donald Riviello, a patron of the Pot Belly Pub, a Bronx bar and grill operated by the defendant, Raybele Tavern, Inc., lost the use of an eye because of what was found to be negligence on the part of Joseph Waldron, also a defendant, a Raybele employee as chef.

Living nearby, Riviello had frequented the establishment regularly for some years. One night Riviello gravitated to the end of the bar near the kitchen, where, during an interval when Waldron had no food orders to fill, Waldron and another patron and mutual friend were chatting. Riviello joined in the discussion which turned to street crime in the neighborhood. In the course of the conversation, Waldron exhibited a knife containing a small blade and screwdriver attachment, which he said he carried for protection. At this point Waldron went to the kitchen to fill a food order. Several minutes later, while Waldron was returning from his chore to rejoin Riviello, Riviello suddenly turned and, as he did so, his eye unexpectedly came in contact with the blade of the knife which Waldron still had in his hand while demonstrating self-defense. Riviello sued Waldron and the Tavern.

The issue is whether, as a matter of law, Waldron's negligence, which Riviello sought to impute to Raybele on the theory of "respondeat superior", was outside the scope of his employment. The trial court found for the Tavern, defendant, and against Waldron. Riviello appealed the judgment in favor of the Tavern.

The Pot Belly was the arena in which Waldron worked, and the evening was the time when he did so. The route from the kitchen where he would hold forth as chef to the patrons in the public room in which he performed his other functions could hardly be claimed to be a physical deviation. We turn to the extent of Waldron's departure, if it may be so characterized, from the normal methods of his performance, and to whether the specific act of carrying the pocketknife in his hand was one that the employer could reasonably have anticipated. Initially, it bears noting that, for an employee to be regarded as acting within the scope of his employment, the employer need not have foreseen the precise act or the exact manner of the injury as long as the general type of conduct may have been reasonably expected. It suffices that the tortious conduct be a natural incident of the employment. Hence, general rather than specific foreseeability has carried the day even in some cases where employees deviated from their assigned tasks. It was permissible to find as a fact that Raybele could have anticipated that, in the course of Waldron's varied activities in the pursuit of his job, he might, through carelessness, do some injury. The specifics of the act, though it was not essential that they be envisaged, could be, as here, the product of an inattentive handling of the pocketknife that injured Riviello.

Judgment reversed.

Questions and Case Problems

1. Claude I. Bennett, a partner in Bennett Dairy, a partnership, pursuant to his authority, executed a contract in Claude's name with Putney, who was to erect a silo on the Bennett farm and build a foundation on which the silo could be placed. Putney built the foundation but never erected the silo. Bennett Dairy alleges that it is the undisclosed principal of Claude, and it sued Putney for damages for breach of contract. May the partnership as the undisclosed principal sue on the agent Claude's contract? [*Bennett Dairy v. Putney*, 362 N.Y.S.2d 93 (1974).]

2. The plaintiffs claim damages to their motor vehicle of $1,113.68 and $61.00 in medical expenses incurred by Edna Mittlesteadt, one of the plaintiffs, as the result of a traffic collision involving a vehicle owned by the Arkansas Highway and Transportation Department that was backed onto the highway into the path of plaintiff's vehicle. Upon a trial to a jury, judgment in the amount of $1,174.68 was entered in behalf of the plaintiffs. After the entry of the judgment, defendants filed a motion for a new trial which was overruled by the trial court. The defendants argue that the trial court was without jurisdiction. They contend that this suit was against the State of Arkansas and constituted a matter which should be filed with the State Claims Commission. Plaintiffs claim that the case was filed against the defendants, the State employees who caused the accident, as individuals and does not attempt to subject the State to any liability whatsoever. May a State employee, while acting within the scope of his employment, be held personally responsible for his negligence occurring upon a highway? [*James Arvel Ralls*, et al. v. *Martin Mittlesteadt*, et al., 596 S.W.2d 349 (Ark. 1980).]

3. Jerry and JoAnn Cameron, plaintiffs, sought to purchase a home. They contacted a real estate salesperson who showed them several homes. In the process of showing homes to the Camerons, this agent allowed them to look at a multiple listing book which contained a description of the property they ultimately bought. That description stated that the home was 2,400 square feet. After the purchase the Camerons learned in fact that there were

only 2,245 square feet. The Camerons filed suit against Terrell & Garrett, defendants, the real estate agents of the seller, who had submitted the information for the multiple lising book. Terrell & Garrett had obtained the square footage information from the seller and were unaware of the misrepresentation. Judgment for whom? [*Cameron v. Terrell & Garrett, Inc.*, 599 S.W.2d 680 (Tex. 1980).]

4. A 10 year old boy got into a fight with an 11 year old neighbor. Must the 11 year old's father pay for the medical bills incurred as a result of this fight?

5. Tube Art, defendant, the owner of a sign agreed to transport and reinstall it on a building's parking lot. Tube Art's service manager and another employee went to the proposed site and took photographs and measurements. A Tube Art employee laid out the exact size and location for the excavation by marking a 4 by 4 foot square on the asphalt surface with yellow paint. The dimensions of the hole, including its depth of 6 feet, were indicated with spray paint inside the square. After the layout was painted on the asphalt, Tube Art engaged a backhoe operator, defendant Richard F. Redford, to dig the hole. The bucket of Redford's backhoe struck a small natural gas pipeline. After examining the pipe and finding no indication of a break or leak, he concluded that the line was not in use and left the site. The following morning, an explosion and fire occurred in the building serviced by that gas pipeline. As a result of the gas pipeline break, two people in the building were killed and most of its contents were destroyed. Massey and his associates, plaintiffs, as tenants of the building, brought an action for negligence against Tube Art and Richard Redford. Was Tube Art vicariously liable for the negligence of Redford? [*John Massey and Thomas J. Downey, et al. v. Tube Art Display, Inc.*, 551 P.2d 1387 (Wash. 1976).]

6. David Hall engaged Wagner Company Realtors to sell Hall's house. Mrs. Silva was the sales agent for Wagner. Hall alleged that Silva received a $1,000 down payment for the house from Flores, buyer, and illegally kept $900, and for this reason Flores rescinded the contract. Hall further alleged that, because of this, Hall's property was not sold to Flores and had to be sold to another person at a reduced price causing loss to Hall. Hall sued Wagner Company Realtors for such loss and punitive damages caused by the alleged Silva **conversion** of $900. Is the Wagner Company Realtors liable in punitive damages for its sales agent, Mrs. Silva's, conversion? [*Wagner v. Hall*, 519 S.W.2d 488 (Tex. 1975).]

conversion
the tort of intentional interference with another's right to possession, control, and dominion of a chattel

7. In 1970, an agreement was entered between Crane-Maier and the Sherrill Trust whereby the Trust's real property located in Galveston County would be subdivided, developed and sold by Crane-Maier. Bruce Advertising, Inc., plaintiff, dealt with Crane-Maier by supplying services to them on a contractual basis for development of the realty. Bruce Advertising was not aware that the Sherrill Trust owned the property which Crane-Maier was developing. Suit was brought by Bruce Advertising against Crane-Maier, defendant, for the services rendered by Bruce Advertising when payment was not forthcoming. After suit was instituted, Crane-Maier by way of its pleadings informed Bruce Advertising that the Sherrill Trust was owner of the property which Crane-Maier was developing. The trial court sitting without a jury entered judgment against both Crane-Maier and the Sherrill Trust, now also a defendant, holding them jointly and severally liable for the services rendered by Bruce Advertising. The Sherrill Trust appealed. Can Bruce Advertising recover a judgment against both the principal, Sherrill Trust, and the agent, Crane-Maier? [*M. A. Sherrill, Trustee of the William W. Sherrill Trust v. Bruce Advertising, Inc.*, et al., 538 S.W.2d 865 (Tex. 1976).]

8. A principal hired an agent to drive his truck and deliver goods for his business. On the agent's return from a delivery he stopped at his house to attend his daughter's birthday party. The children at the party jumped into the truck for a ride, and one child—while riding on the truck fender—fell under the truck wheel and was injured. May the child's parent sue the principal for the agent's negligence?

Chapter 35: Agency and the Law of Contracts and Torts

9. Leo Joiner, defendant, employed J. F. Carter to make a custom application of pesticide by means of an aircraft in flight to his crops in the immediate vicinity of the fish pond of the plaintiffs. The plaintiffs' lake was built at a cost of approximately $15,000 and was stocked with game fish and used as a recreation area for fishing and water pleasure and added to the value of the adjoining real estate. Large numbers of fish started dying in the plaintiffs' pond as well as in another pond in the vicinity of plaintiffs' pond, and the fish continued to die until all of the fish in the pond were dead. Plaintiffs' complaint charged that spraying operations were conducted on nearby farm land owned by defendant Joiner, the pesticide was permitted to escape or drift onto the property of plaintiffs and into plaintiffs' fish pond and, as a proximate consequence, the lake was contaminated and the fish died and the value of the plaintiffs' land was depreciated. The complaint also alleged that Carter was an independent contractor employed by Joiner to do this spraying. Was Joiner responsible for the negligent acts of his independent contractor? [*Boroughs* et al. *v. Leo Joiner*, 337 So.2d 340 (Ala. 1976).]

10. The case of *Riviello v. Waldron and Raybele Tavern, Inc.*, 391 N.E.2d 1278 (N.Y. 1979)[8] established that a master is liable for the torts of his servant when the tortious conduct is a natural incident of the employment. What is the objective of this rule of law?

---

[8] See pp. 537–38.

Termination of Agency 36

After you have read this chapter, you should be able to:

1. List and explain the five methods by which agency is terminated by acts of the parties.
2. List and explain the six methods by which agency is terminated by operation of law.
3. Distinguish agency coupled with an interest in the subject matter of the agency from agency given as security.
4. Explain the effect of the principal terminating the agency without giving notice to third parties.
5. Explain the effect of terminating the agency between the principal and agent when notice is not given to third parties.

Introduction

Now that agency with its express, implied, and apparent authority has been created, how is the agency and such kinds of authority terminated? Basically, how is an agent's *power* to act for a principal terminated so that the principal cannot be made liable any longer by an agent's conduct?

If the agent knows, or reasonably should know, that if the principal knew of changed circumstances the principal would not want the agent to act, then the agent's power is terminated. In the case of apparent authority, the same is true, if the third party so knew or reasonably should know this.

Our concern here is under what circumstances does agency, the agent's authority, and apparent authority terminate. As it is important for you to know how an agency relationship is created, it is also important for you to know how it ends.

Termination by Acts of the Parties

Acts of the parties.

There are five ways by which agency power may be terminated by acts of the principal and agent: expiration, mutual agreement, option, revocation, and renunciation.

Expiration pursuant to the terms of the agency contract.

Expiration of the Agency Contract

The contract between the principal and the agent may specify that it will terminate upon the happening of a certain event or at the end of a time period. For instance, a contract with a real estate broker that creates an exclusive agency to list the principal's house for sale for ninety days. At the expiration of the ninety-day period the contract is terminated, even though the purpose of the contract has not been accomplished.

Mutual agreement.

Termination by Mutual Agreement

The common law principles of the law of contracts relative to termination of a contract are applicable to terminating an agency contract.[1] Hence, the parties by mutual consent may terminate an agency contract.

Exercise of option to terminate.

Option of a Party

An agency contract, by its terms, may allow either the principal or the agent to terminate by giving advance notice to the other. Exercising this option will have the effect of a termination. For example, a life insurance agent may, under the employment contract with the insurance company, have the option to terminate by giving the company thirty days notice.

P's revocation.

"Revocation" by the Principal

Once the principal has authorized the agent to perform on the principal's behalf, the principal always *retains the power* to "revoke" (terminate) the authority. Even though the principal may be liable to the agent for damages sustained due to *wrongful revocation,* the principal nevertheless has the *power to revoke.* For example, the agency contract may provide that it cannot be terminated by either party. The contract can still be revoked, although revocation will subject the principal to damages for its breach.

Unless the parties have otherwise agreed, the principal's revocation is ineffective to terminate the agency unless the agent has actually received notice of the principal's intent so to terminate, or other facts reasonably cause the agent to believe that revocation has occurred. (P mails a letter to A, P's agent, stating that the agency is at an end. Before A received the letter he made a contract in P's name with T pursuant to A's authority. P is bound on the contract.)

---

[1] See pp. 173–74.

In the following case a loan broker sues its principals for a broker commission, claiming that the principals wrongfully revoked their contract after the broker had performed in accordance with the contract. Notice how the court distinguished between the principals' *power to revoke* and their *right to revoke*.

Facts
Plaintiff, Sunshine Exploration Company, sued defendants, Manos and Muncey, doing business as Manos and Muncey Architects, a partnership, for breach of a loan brokerage contract. Plaintiff claims that, as defendants' agent, it obtained a loan commitment in accordance with the contract, but defendants refused to accept it and wrongfully terminated the contract prior to the expiration of the thirty-day period provided in the contract. Did the defendants as a principal *wrongfully revoke* the agency with Sunshine?

Decision
Yes. Judgment for plaintiff, Sunshine.

Reasoning
The principal may, of course, revoke a unilateral offer, but there is a distinction between his power to revoke and his right to revoke. He may at any time before full performance revoke the authority of an agent so the agent will lose his authority to bring the principal into legal relations with a third party. However, if he has no right to revoke it, he will be liable for damages suffered by the agent by reason of the wrongful revocation.

Having failed to establish a right of revocation, the defendants are liable for their breach of contract.

Sunshine v. Manos, 496 S.W.2d 195 (Tex. 1973).

"Renunciation" by the Agent

A's renunciation.

The agent maintains the same power as the principal to terminate the agency contract, regardless of its terms, called a power to "renunciate" or "renounce."

If under the terms of the agency contract the agency is terminable at the will of the agent, the agent can renounce at any time without incurring damages for breach of the agency contract. If the principal's instructions are illegal, the agent has the right to renunciate.

The agent will be liable for damages for breach of the agency contract. An example is when the agency contract is for a stated period of time and the agent wrongfully renounces the contract. Thus, an exclusive ninety-day real estate listing will terminate when A notifies P two weeks after accepting the listing that the agent is listing the house with other brokers.

Unless the parties have otherwise agreed, the agent's renunciation is ineffective to terminate the agency unless the principal has notice, or other facts reasonably cause the principal to believe, that renunciation has occurred.

The following case illustrates how an "indefinite duration agency" may be terminated at the will of either the principal or the agent; however, the agent may be entitled to damages.

Facts
Plaintiff sues for an accounting for five percent commission on all business obtained for defendant within plaintiff's geographic sales area arising out of an alleged oral contract which called on the plaintiff to obtain his old business associates as customers for the defendant. The parties agreed that plaintiff was to work for defendant to obtain for defendant prior customers of plaintiff.

Plaintiff performed his obligations for seven months, brought to defendant a monthly average of $10,000 in business, and spent $3,600 in expenses. After seven months, defendant discharged plaintiff without good cause. Was this a rightful termination of the agency?

Decision
No. Judgment for plaintiff.

Reasoning
Agreements between principal and agent for an indefinite time generally may be terminated at will of either party. There is a limitation on the power to terminate an agency, namely, that the principal is liable to the agent for the value of services and reasonable expenses incurred up to the time of revocation.

Want v. Century Supply Company, 508 S.W.2d 515 (Mo. 1974).

Operation of law.

Termination by Operation of Law

When an agency contract is terminated by *operation of law,* it ends, regardless of the parties' consent. The law brings about the result even though the principal or the agent may have another intent.

There are six ways by which agency power may be terminated by operation of law: death, insanity, bankruptcy, war, destruction of the agency subject matter, and change of law or other circumstances.

Death of P or A.

Death

Since agency is a personal service contract,[2] because the agent is a fiduciary acting primarily on behalf of the principal, the authority given to the agent terminates without any notice to the agent upon the principal's death. The agent cannot act for a nonexistent person. An ordinary contract, however, will not terminate upon the obligor's death, but rather becomes an estate obligation.[3] In the following case a valid power of attorney without an agent's security interest (discussed later) terminated at the death of the principal.

Facts
Plaintiff is the executrix of the estate of the decedent, her sister, Ethel Mae Schull, who entered the hospital in early March, 1975, for an ailment soon diagnosed as terminal cancer. On March 31, 1975, after she was informed of her condition and while still in the hospital, the decedent executed a power of attorney in favor of her stepson, the defendant, Andrea C. Schull. After she executed the power of attorney, she told the defendant where she had hidden her will and several savings account passbooks and instructed him to retrieve them. The defendant obtained possession of these items and, with the power of attorney, withdrew the funds from the savings accounts, depositing the money in accounts in his name, his wife's name, or both. The total sum of money involved amounted to $25,001.64 which the plaintiff now seeks to recover from the defendant and his wife.

Did the agency relationship created by the power of attorney survive the death of the stepmother, Ethel Mae Schull?

Decision
No. Judgment for the plaintiff.

Reasoning
Unless the agency is coupled with an interest, which is not the case here, the well-settled rule is that the agency relation created by this power of attorney terminated at the death of the principal.

There is no doubt in the court's mind that a legal power of attorney was executed by the decedent and that within the authority of that instrument the power of attorney terminated with the author's death and the balance of the monies disbursed by the defendant and his wife belong to the estate.

Mary Long, Executrix v. Andrea C. Schull, et al., 439 A.2d 975 (Conn. 1981).

However, some state statutes and a few courts take the position that the agent has power to bind the deceased principal's estate until the agent receives notice of death. Examples are statutes that relate to principals who are in the armed forces and banks that have authority to pay checks drawn by the principal or the agent before the principal's death.[4]

Insanity of P or A.

Insanity

The principal who appointed the agent to act on the principal's behalf must be capable of maintaining supervision over the agent. Therefore, the insanity of the principal will terminate the agency, as is illustrated by the following case.

---

[2] See pp. 185–86.

[3] *Commercial Nursery Co. v. Ivey,* 51 S.W.2d 238 (Tenn. 1932).

[4] See p. 412.

Facts
The decedent, Margaret Berry, was admitted to the hospital in February 1970. On March 26, 1970, she executed a power of attorney designating her niece, Irene Montanye, as her agent. Thereafter, the decedent was discharged from the hospital. On April 29, 1970, the decedent suffered a stroke and was readmitted to the hospital. She remained in a comatose or semicomatose condition until her death on June 30, 1971. On April 30, 1971, Mrs. Montanye, acting under the power of attorney, transferred some $109,000 of the decedent's funds into a trust account in the name of the decedent in trust for Ann R. Scully, administratrix of this estate.

Distributees of the decedent and their assignees objected that the alleged agency created by the power of attorney was void because at the time of the transfer and thereafter the decedent was mentally incompetent by reason of being in a comatose or semicomatose state and, therefore, the agency was suspended or revoked. Can an agency be terminated by the mental incompetency of the principal?

Decision
Yes. Permission is given to distributees to file verified objections to prove decedent's mental incompetency.

Reasoning
If the objectors prove that, at the time of the agent's transfer of the funds, and thereafter, the decedent was mentally incompetent or incapacitated by reason of her alleged comatose or semicomatose state, then the agency would have been suspended or revoked. The court finds that the proposed amended objections raised valid issues of law and fact and granted permission to file amended objections.

In re *Berry's Estate,* 329 N.Y.S.2d 915 (1972).

The agent's insanity that occurs after the agent's appointment will terminate the agency as a matter of law. Some courts have held that, once the incapacity has been removed, the agency relationship can be restored.

Bankruptcy

The bankruptcy of the principal will terminate the authority of the agent to act with respect to property related to the bankruptcy if the agent reasonably can believe that, because of the bankruptcy, the principal would no longer want the agent to have such authority.

The agent's bankruptcy will also, generally, terminate the relationship. The credit of the agent is frequently related to the principal's reputation in the business community. Thus, the agent's authority to act will terminate if the agent reasonably can believe that, if the principal knew the facts, the principal would not want the agent's authority to continue.

Bankruptcy of P or A.

War

The outbreak of a war in the country where the agent has been authorized to transact the principal's business will terminate the agent's authority if the agent reasonably can believe that, if the principal knew the facts, the principal would not want the agent's authority to continue. The large number of multinational corporations and international trade could be affected by this rule. For example, if a U.S. corporation is selling its equipment in country X, and a war unexpectedly breaks out in X, the corporate agent's authority to sell in X may terminate.

War.

Impossibility by Supervening Destruction of the Agency Subject Matter

If performance by the agency becomes impossible, the agent's authority is terminated. For example, a marine broker who is authorized to sell P's boat would lose his authority if the boat were destroyed by a storm.

Impossibility of performance of the agency by supervening destruction of the agency subject matter.

Impossibility by Supervening Change of Law or Other Circumstances

The agent's authority is terminated by a change in law or other circumstances that would make performance impossible. For instance, if A, a construction contractor, must substantially change his contract because an amended building code requires fireproof material, his authority to act on behalf of P is terminated without P's specific consent.

Impossibility of performance of the agency by supervening change of law or other circumstances.

"Irrevocable Agency"

Termination of Authority Coupled with an Agent's Security Interest

Authority coupled with an agent's security interest.

We have learned that *agency* and *authority* can be terminated by either the principal or the agent, and that if the termination of the agency contract is wrongful the terminating party is liable for breach of the contract. However, there are two situations when the principal cannot terminate the *power* of the agent to act and affect the principal. These are often called "irrevocable agency" situations, meaning that the *power* of the agent cannot be terminated by the principal, as distinguished from termination of *agency* and *authority* which the principal can do at any time.

These two situations occur when the *power* given to the agent is *security* to assure the agent that the principal will perform his or her promise to the agent. In one situation "authority" or power is *given as security,* and in the other the "authority" or power is *coupled with an interest in the subject matter of the agency.*

Authority given as security.

"Authority Given As Security." When the principal *gives* authority *as security* to the agent *in exchange for consideration then given by the agent,* there is a *contract* between them and the principal cannot revoke that authority. (On January 6, *P requests a $200 loan from A,* P promising to repay the loan on January 24 and that, on his default, A has authority to sell P's electric typewriter. The loan is made and there is now a *contract* between P and A. P defaulted and informs A that his authority to sell is terminated. A's *power* to sell is not terminated and A can sell the typewriter. P's authority to A was given in exchange for the *new* consideration of a loan of $200 made to P by A, creating a *contract* between them.) However, if *P already owes money to A* and P *later* gave A authority to sell P's typewriter on P's default, P's authority was not given to A in exchange for any new consideration from A; since there is *no contract* between them, P can terminate A's authority because it is *not given as security.* For there to be a contract, the authority must be given as security in exchange for consideration *then given* by A. In many states, death of the principal will not terminate this power.

Authority coupled with an interest in the subject matter.

"Authority Coupled with an Interest in the Subject Matter of the Agency." An agent has an irrevocable, vested *security interest* in and power over *property transferred to the agent* by the principal *with authority* to dispose of the property if the principal should default on an obligation owing by the principal to the agent. (*P owes A $200*. On February 6, P promises to repay the loan on February 24 and that, on default, A has authority to sell P's calculator. P *delivers* the calculator to A. A's power to sell on P's default is irrevocable by P.) A contract is not required here to make the agency irrevocable. Death of the principal will not terminate this power.

Effect of Termination of Agency and Authority

The principal's termination of agency or of the agent's authority is immediately effective *between them when the agent actually receives notice* of the principal's intent so to terminate. But what is the effect of such termination on third parties? We have learned that third parties have the duty to determine whether agency exists and the extent of the agent's authority.

The necessity of notice to T of termination of agency and authority.

If the principal (P) has represented to third persons (T) that someone (A) is P's agent, A has *apparent authority* to act for P within the scope of A's apparent authority with the same effect as though A had authority so to act. If P wishes to terminate such apparent authority, he must give proper notice of termination of authority to those *third persons to whom P had so represented* creating the apparent authority.

The *extent* of such notice varies. If A is a *special agent,* P need not give any notice *to such third persons,* with certain exceptions when notice is required: (1) A is a specially accredited agent, specially accredited to deal with T on a continuing basis; or (2) P has notice that A has begun to deal with T; or (3) A has a written authorization to be exhibited to T; or (4) P knows of the termination of an event on the continuance of which A's authority depends. If A is a *general agent, P must give notice of termination to such third persons.* For example, P appointed A as P's agent for the purpose of selling and handling fire insurance for P. A sold a fire insurance policy of P to T. A few months later, P informed A that the agency was terminated. Subsequently T has a fire and reported it to A. Since A still has apparent authority to act as P's agent, which includes authority to receive fire reports from insured third persons, T's report to A was made to P.

The *kind* of such notice varies. If T has dealt with P *on credit,* T must receive *actual notice* of termination of authority; otherwise *reasonable notice* is sufficient by either: "(a) advertising the fact in a newspaper of general circulation in the place where the agency is regularly carried on; or (b) giving publicity by some other method reasonably adapted to give the information to such third person."[5]

Summary Statement

1. An agency may be terminated by *acts of the parties*. The methods for so doing are by:
    a. contractual agreement,
    b. mutual agreement,
    c. option of a party in giving advance notice to the other,
    d. revocation by the principal, and
    e. renunciation by the agent.
2. An agency may be terminated by *operation of law,* which will end the relationship regardless of the parties' consent. The methods are:
    a. death of either the principal or the agent,
    b. insanity of either the principal or the agent,
    c. bankruptcy,
    d. war,
    e. impossibility by supervening destruction of the agency subject matter, and
    f. impossibility by supervening change of law or other circumstances.
3. When the principal *gives* authority *as security* to the agent *in exchange for consideration then given by the agent,* there is a *contract* between them and the principal cannot revoke that authority.
4. An agent with *authority coupled with an interest in the subject matter of the agency* has an irrevocable vested *security interest* in and power over the property transferred to the agent, with authority to dispose of the property if the principal should default on an obligation owing to the agent.
5. As between the principal and agent, the question of notice to third parties of termination of the agent's authority is of no consequence. The agent may have the *power* but not the right to act on behalf of the principal.
6. The principal's termination of agency or of the agent's authority is immediately effective between them when the agent actually receives notice of the principal's intent so to terminate.
7. If the principal wishes to terminate apparent authority, he must give proper notice to those third persons to whom P has represented and thereby created apparent authority.
8. If the agent is a *general agent,* the principal must give notice of termination to third persons to whom the principal has represented that a person is an agent in order to terminate the agent's apparent authority.

---

[5] See RESTATEMENT (SECOND) OF AGENCY sec.136(3)(a)(b) (1958).

9. If the agent is a *special agent,* the principal need not give any notice to such third persons unless:
    a. A is specially accredited to deal with T on a continuing basis; or
    b. P has notice that A has begun to deal with T; or
    c. A has a written authorization to be exhibited to T; or
    d. T knows of the termination of an event on the continuance of which A's authority depends.
10. If T has dealt with P *on credit,* T must receive *actual* notice of termination; otherwise *reasonable* notice is sufficient.

In the following case a hospital terminated a ten-year agency contract with its medical director which recited that it "may not be revoked or altered by The Hospital for a term of ten years." The medical director claims that the contract created an agency coupled with an interest, and the hospital has neither the right nor the power to terminate during its term.

Sarokhan v. Fair Lawn Memorial Hospital, Inc.
199 A.2d 52 (N.J. 1964).

["J.A.D." means Judge, Appellate Division]

interlocutory order
an intermediate court order pending a final decision

Kilkenny, J.A.D. Defendants, Fair Lawn Memorial Hospital, Inc., and its directors and officers, appeal from an **interlocutory order** of the Chancery Division, restraining them from terminating plaintiff's services as medical director and director of surgery of defendant hospital, and from interfering with his rendition of such services. . . .

Defendant corporation operates for profit a private 63-bed hospital in Fair Lawn, New Jersey. Plaintiff is a doctor and a surgeon. . . .

On April 19, 1962 plaintiff entered into a written agreement with defendant hospital, under the terms of which he was appointed medical director and director of surgery of the hospital for a term of ten years. No salary is specified for these services. The agreement recites that it "may not be revoked or altered by The Hospital during that period" and that plaintiff is bound to the performance of the duties undertaken by him for the ten-year term of the contract.

Until September 1963 plaintiff performed his duties without interference by the board of directors. On October 8, 1963 defendant, Nicholas DeVito, president of the hospital, wrote a letter to plaintiff inquiring why two men were not appointed assistant medical directors. A reply was received from plaintiff's counsel, stating that plaintiff alone could appoint members to the professional staff and that under no circumstances was he to be considered the agent of the board of directors, or of the president of the hospital. The first count, alleging several acts of allegedly wrongful interference by defendants in the performance of his duties and the exercise of his contractual rights, seeks injunctive relief of the kind specified in the temporary injunction now under review.

After plaintiff instituted this suit, defendant hospital notified him that all association by him with the hospital was at an end. The hospital is dissatisfied with his services, believes that he is responsible for its poor financial condition, and it does not want him any more as its medical director and director of surgery. . . .

Defendants feel that they have just cause to terminate plaintiff's services; and, even if just cause were lacking, they have the power to terminate the agency or employment relationship, subject only to an action for damages if, in so doing, there is a wrongful breach of contract. Plaintiff's position is that defendants created an agency coupled with an interest and have neither the right nor the power to terminate during its ten-year term.

The mere fact that the appointment recites that it will be irrevocable during the term of the appointment does not preclude the principal from exercising the power to revoke it. This does not mean that the principal may breach such a contract with impunity. For a wrongful breach, the agent may sue at law and recover money damages.

The law has recognized, as an exception to the general rule, that "an agency coupled with an interest" cannot be revoked by the principal during the term fixed for its existence.

Defendants concede that, if the contract herein created an agency coupled with an interest, they would not have the power to revoke it. They maintain that such an agency was not created. We agree.

If the agency is given *as security* for a debt or obligation, it is regarded as an agency coupled with an interest.

The agency herein was not given as security for some obligation due plaintiff. He had no interest in the subject matter of the power independent of the power conferred. The power conferred by defendant hospital was not one "coupled with an interest." Accordingly, it is not irrevocable, despite the terminology used by the parties.

We conclude that the contract in issue did not create an agency coupled with an interest and that defendants had and have the power to terminate it. . . . We make no determination as to whether defendants breached any contractual right of plaintiff in terminating his relationship with the hospital.

The order under review is reversed.

Questions and Case Problems

1. Clinkenbeard responded to Central Southwest Oil Corporation's (Central) advertisement in Argosy Magazine, which described the possibilities for individuals to win valuable oil leases in the monthly non-competitive leasings of federal land by the Department of the Interior. Central offered to select valuable tracts coming up for leasing, handle the paper work involved in entering the individual's name in the running for the leasing of such tracts, and notify the entrant if he had won a lease. Clinkenbeard accepted the offer and dutifully sent in approximately $40 per month from September 1971 to October 1972. His lucky day arrived on June 5, 1972, when he received a call from Tom Allen, President of Central, informing him that he had won a lease. Central paid Clinkenbeard $7,020 for the lease. In fact the lease was one of the most heavily filed upon in the lottery and there was evidence that, at least as of the time of trial, it was worth several times what Central had paid. Did the fiduciary duty owed by Central to Clinkenbeard exist at the time of the assignment? [*Clinkenbeard v. Central Southwest Oil Corporation,* 526 F.2d 649 (1976).]

2. The plaintiff, Nathan Francis, is a co-lessee with defendant, Ted Bartlett, who managed a gravel mining operation. Bartlett gave a power of attorney to Francis as the manager authorizing Francis to pay Bartlett his portion of the royalties from the operation. Bartlett claims that the royalty due him for the past two years was five cents per cubic yard of gravel instead of two-and-a-half cents, at which rate he was paid. Bartlett accepted such reduced payments during the past two years without complaint. Bartlett then sued Francis for the additional amount of royalty allegedly due him. Was Bartlett correct? [*Francis v. Bartlett,* 121 So.2d 18 (La. 1960).]

3. A principal gave her agent a power of attorney to sell her building that stated "the agency shall continue for ninety days and will not be revoked during that period." A month later the principal gave her agent notice that the agency was revoked. The agent later made a contract with a buyer, who knew the agency was revoked, to sell the land. May the buyer eject the principal from the building and purchase the land?

4. P owned a building and authorized A, a real estate broker, to keep it rented and deduct a 6 percent commission on the amount collected and send the balance to P. A, in P's name, leased to T, who paid rent to A for several years. P died but T had no notice or knowledge of P's death. For the next year T continued to pay A the rent, with which A absconded. The executor of P's estate sued T for the year's rent due from the time of P's death. T claimed that T's payment to A even after P's death is a defense. Is T correct?

5. A was the general manager of a hardware store owned by P, who was declared insane by a court. G, appointed by the court to be P's guardian, immediately terminated A as the manager and agent of P. Did G have the right to do so?

6. The sole proprietor of a restaurant hired an agent to manage the business. The sole proprietor later filed voluntary bankruptcy. The bankruptcy court appointed a trustee in bankruptcy to manage the sole proprietor's assets. Does the agent continue to have authority to manage the restaurant?

7. William Mubi, husband of Sharon Mubi, plaintiff, commenced a civil suit against Walter W. Tribble and Jane Doe Tribble, defendants, for personal injuries and property damage resulting from a motor vehicle collision. On August 5, 1970, after this action was filed, defendants through their attorney filed an answer and an Offer of Judgment in the amount of $3,150.00. Under the Rules of Civil Procedure, this offer had to be accepted within ten days or it was deemed withdrawn. William Mubi died at approximately 9:00 a.m. on August 11, 1970, six days after the offer was made. Prior to his death he had requested his wife, Sharon Mubi, plaintiff, to accept the Offer of Judgment of $3,150.00, and she, in turn, advised the secretary of William Mubi's attorney, Robert Spillman, that the offer was accepted. Because Spillman was out of town on vacation he did not receive the notice of the Offer of Judgment until 2:00 p.m. on August 11, whereupon Spillman authorized an office associate to immediately accept the Offer of Judgment. Although the decision to accept the Offer was communicated to decedent's attorney before he died, the attorney's written acceptance was not made until after William Mubi's death. Did the power of attorney, given by William Mubi (through his wife) to his attorney, Spillman, to answer on his behalf, terminate at his death? [*Mubi v. Broomfield,* 492 P.2d 700 (Ariz. 1972).]

8. P, a casualty insurance company, made A its general agent to write casualty insurance in P's name. A wrote T's casualty insurance on T's business. Thereafter, and without notifying T, the general agency of A was revoked by P. T later incurred a loss and promptly notified A. T had neither notice nor knowledge of the revocation of A's authority by P. A notified P one year later and P refused to honor the claim because P was not notified by the insured, T, within a reasonable time after the loss. T sued P on the policy issued by A. Can T recover?

9. Decedent was the widow of Arnold Friedman, an artist of some repute. She transferred almost the entire collection of her late husband's art works to the respondent, an art dealer, for exhibition and sale. The respondent was to act as the sole sales agent for the works of Arnold Friedman, retaining one-half of any purchase price realized as his "commission." Pursuant to the terms of their written agreement, decedent "sells, transfers and assigns all of the works of the late Arnold Friedman, now in her possession . . . absolutely and forever" to the respondent. In consideration for same respondent agreed to accept these art works; prepare them for sale and exhibition; "put forth his best efforts to sell", and pay over to the decedent one-half of the sale price as these art works were sold. The petitioner, administratrix of the estate of the decedent, brought this action to recover the art works claiming that title never passed to the respondent. Did the written agreement constitute a sales contract or a consignment creating an agency relationship? [*Estate of Wilhelmina Friedman, Deceased,* 397 N.Y.S.2d 561 (1977).]

10. In the case of *Sarokhan v. Fair Lawn Memorial Hospital, Inc.,* 199 A.2d 52 (N.J. 1964),[6] the court indicates that an example of an "irrevocable agency" is an agency coupled with an interest. Irrevocable agencies are created because of the needs of justice and fairness. Why does an agency coupled with an interest meet these needs?

---

[6] See pp. 548–49.

Employment 37

After you have read this chapter, you should be able to:

1. Indicate what kind of discrimination in employment is prohibited by the federal Equal Employment Opportunity Act.
2. State those circumstances when discrimination in employment is not prohibited or unlawful under the above Act.
3. Recognize the age groups of employees which are, or are not, protected from age discrimination in employment under the federal Age Discrimination In Employment Act.
4. Explain how the federal Wage-Hour Law applies to:
   a. child labor.
   b. maximum daily and weekly hours of employment.
   c. wages.
5. Discuss the common law basis for liability by an employer for injury experienced by his employees and compare it with the current basis for employer liability for such injury under state workmen's compensation statutes.
6. Explain the purpose of the federal Occupational Safety and Health Act and how business is affected by the Act.
7. Describe how the following federal programs operate under the Social Security Act:
   a. Old Age, Survivors, and Disability Insurance.
   b. Medicare.
   c. Unemployment Insurance.
8. Become more aware of the widespread emergence of employer tests to detect employee lying, and employee use of drugs and alcohol and their adverse economic effect in the marketplace.
9. Discuss the current status and rights of women in the work force and unfair discrimination against them because of their sex.

Introduction

Society is concerned that people have proper and equal opportunity to obtain employment and that the terms of employment are reasonable and do not constitute an invasion of any employee's legal rights, particularly, here, that employment be lawfully non-discriminatory and that fair labor standards apply. This area will be discussed under the heading The Employment Contract.

Another concern of society is that proper reasonable standards are established to ensure the safety and health of employees while engaged in their work, and that reasonable compensation is provided for any injury they may sustain in their work. This area will be discussed under the heading Protection and Compensation for Injury.

Society is also concerned about the financial status of employees on their retirement, disability, hospitalization, and unemployment. This area will be discussed under the heading Social Security.

Lastly, society is concerned with employer use of detection tests to determine employee lying and use of drugs and alcohol, and with unfair discrimination against women in the work force because of their sex.[1]

employee
as generally used, a servant agent, although some statutes are interpreted to give it a wider meaning

employer
a principal, or more specifically a master

The term "**employee**" as generally used in statutes (e.g., Employers Liability Acts, Workmen's Compensation Acts) and in court decisions means a servant agent, although some statutes (e.g., social security, unemployment insurance, minimum age, and fair labor statutes) are interpreted to give the term employee a wider meaning. The term "**employer**" is a principal, or more specifically a master.[2]

The Employment Contract

An employer's common law right of freedom of contract—basically to employ at his will and, in the absence of employment contract provision to the contrary, to fire at will—has given way to public policy in the form of federal and state legislation limiting that freedom. Judicial interpretation and enforcement of such legislation thus becomes very important to you as a present or probable employee or employer.

Non-discrimination.

Non-discriminatory Employment

The two major pieces of federal legislation amending the federal Civil Rights Act of 1964 to ensure equal non-discriminatory opportunity for employment are the Equal Employment Opportunity Act of 1972 and the Age Discrimination in Employment Act of 1967, with their later amendments.

EEOA.

Equal Employment Opportunity Act (EEOA). This federal Act applies to persons as employers engaged in an industry in or affecting interstate commerce with fifteen or more employees for each working day in each of twenty or more calendar weeks in the current or preceding calendar year, and any agent of such person. It also applies to: state and local governments; government agencies; political subdivisions; the District of Columbia department and agencies; employment agencies; labor organizations; apprenticeship programs; and in advertising.

Prohibition of discrimination on the basis of race, color, religion, sex, or national origin.

The Act prohibits employers from *unlawfully* discriminating in employment and makes it

an unlawful employment practice for an employer (1) to fail or refuse to hire or to discharge any individual, or otherwise to discriminate against any individual with respect to his compensation, terms, conditions, or privileges of employment, *because of* such individual's race, color, religion, sex, or national origin; or (2) to limit, segregate, or classify his employees or applicants for

---

[1] See Title 29 Code of Federal Regulations, Part 1604, for Guidelines on Discrimination Because of Sex and on Sexual Harrassment.

[2] See pp. 502–3 for the terms servant and master.

employment in any way which would deprive or tend to deprive any individual of employment opportunities or otherwise adversely affect his status as an employee, *because of* such *individual's* race, color, religion, sex, or national origin. [Emphasis added.]

In the following first case of its kind to be decided by the Supreme Court of the United States, the court had to decide whether the difference in longevity between men and women employees could justify a valid difference in the contributions to a pension fund required to be made by those employees.

Facts
The Los Angeles Department of Water and Power, defendant, determined that its female employees would, as a class, outlive its male employees. Accordingly, the Department required its female employees to make significantly larger pension fund contributions than the males, with the result that each female employee took home less pay than a male earning the same salary.

A class action suit was brought by Marie Manhart, a woman employee in the Department, on behalf of all women employed and formerly employed by the Department, plaintiffs, seeking an injunction against this action by the Department and retroactive relief. The federal district court and, on appeal, the federal court of appeals, decided in favor of the plaintiffs, except that retroactive relief was denied. The Department, defendant, brought this matter before the Supreme Court of the United States.

Decision
Affirmed, for plaintiffs, without retroactive relief, and sent back for further proceedings.

Reasoning
The Equal Employment Opportunity Act makes it unlawful "to discriminate against any *individual* with respect to his compensation, terms, conditions, or privileges of employment, because of such *individual's* race, color, religion, sex, or national origin." The statute's focus on the individual is unambiguous.

An employment practice that requires 2,000 individuals to contribute more money into a fund than 10,000 other employees simply because each of them is a woman rather than a man is in direct conflict with both the language and the policy of the Act. It constitutes discrimination against every individual woman employed by the Department, and is unlawful unless exempted by the Equal Pay Act of 1963 or some other affirmative justification.

City of Los Angeles Department of Water and Power, et al. *v. Manhart,* et al., 435 U.S. 702 (1978).

In a recent decision the Supreme Court of the United States further implemented the concept in the above case. The court held that it is unlawful discrimination on the basis of sex in violation of Title VII of the Civil Rights Act of 1964 for an employer to offer its employees the option of receiving retirement benefits from one of several companies selected by the employer, all of which pay a woman lower monthly benefits than a man who has made the same contributions. The court also held that all retirement benefits derived from contributions made after its decision must be calculated without regard to the sex of the beneficiary, that its decision is not retroactive, and that, under the Arizona deferred compensation plan involved, benefits derived from contributions made *prior* to its decision may be calculated as provided by the existing terms of the Arizona plan. (*Arizona Governing Committee for Tax Deferred Annuity and Deferred Compensation Plans v. Natalie Norris,* 463 U.S. 1073 (1983). Whether considerations of sex should be barred from *all* insurance plans, *including individual purchases of insurance,* is an issue which is presently being considered by Congress.

In still another recent decision of importance to employers and employees, the Supreme Court of the United States held that it is unlawful sex discrimination based on pregnancy in violation of Title VII of the Civil Rights Act of 1964 as amended by the Pregnancy Discrimination Act of 1978: (1) for an employer to exclude pregnancy coverage from an otherwise inclusive employee health insurance benefits plan; and (2) for an employer's employee health insurance benefit plan to provide hospitalization benefits for pregnancy-related conditions to its female employees but less extensive pregnancy benefits for spouses of male employees, such being discrimination against female spouses of male employees and therefore also discrimination against male employees. (*Newport News Shipbuilding and Drydock Company v. EEOC,* 462 U.S. 669 (1983).

The U.S. Supreme Court has made it clear in *Dothard v. Rawlinson,* 433 U.S. 321 (1977)[3] that, in cases of alleged *unlawful* discrimination in employment on the basis of an individual's race, color, religion, sex, or national origin, there are three steps to be considered. (1) The employment standards or requirements must produce a *result* or *effect* that is discriminatory or disparate (unequal). If they do, then there *is discrimination.* Otherwise there is *no* discrimination. (2) If there is discrimination, then *the employer has the burden* of showing that the standards or requirements are *job-related* in that they have a definite relationship to the particular job for which they are established. If they are *not* job-related, then the discrimination *is unlawful.* (3) If they *are* job-related, then the complaining person, *plaintiff, must show* that *other selection devices* (other means) *without a similar discriminatory effect* would also serve the employer's legitimate interest in efficient and trustworthy workmanship. If the plaintiff *can* show this, then the discrimination *is unlawful.* Otherwise, the discrimination is *not* unlawful. A *discriminatory effect* together with a *discriminatory intent* results in *unlawful* discrimination.

However, it is not unlawful:

bona fide
in good faith

1. for an employer to employ an employee on the basis of religion, sex, or national origin in those certain instances where religion, sex, or national origin is a **bona fide** *occupational qualification* reasonably necessary to the normal operation of that particular business or enterprise;
2. for any *educational institution of learning* to employ employees of a particular religion if such institution is, in whole or in substantial part, owned, supported, controlled, or managed by a particular religion or by a particular religious corporation, association, or society, or if the curriculum of the institution is directed toward the propagation of a particular religion;
3. for an employer to apply different standards of compensation, or different terms, conditions, or privileges of employment pursuant to a *bona fide seniority or merit system,* or to a system which measures earnings *by quantity or quality of production,* or to employees who work in *different locations*—so long as such differences are not the result of an *intention* to discriminate because of race, color, religion, sex, or national origin. The employer may give and act upon the results of any *professionally developed ability test* so long as the test, its administration, or action upon the results is not designed, intended, or used to discriminate because of race, color, religion, sex, or national origin. However, the test must be job-related in order not to be *unlawfully* discriminatory. Also, the employer may legally differentiate on the basis of sex in determining the amount of wages or compensation if it is authorized by the federal Fair Labor Standards Act of 1938, as amended in 1974.[4] [Emphasis added.]

The EEOA further provides that *nothing* in the Act shall be interpreted to *require* any employer to grant *preferential treatment* to any individual or group because of the race, color, religion, sex, or national origin of such individual or group on account of an *imbalance* which may exist with respect to the total number or percentage of persons of any race, color, religion, sex, or national origin employed by any employer in comparison with the total number or percentage of persons of such race, color, religion, sex, or national origin in any community, state, section, or other area or available work force there. The fact that an employer has no minority people among the employees does not of itself mean that *illegal* discrimination has occurred. However, it raises a strong inference of such illegality. In order to dispel such an inference, many employers employ only a few minority employees so as to create an impression of nondiscrimination when, in fact, their intention is to discriminate illegally.

---

[3] This case is on pp. 566–68.

[4] See section 703(e) and (h) of Title VII, 78 Stat. 256–57.

However, of great importance to employers and employees is a dramatic change in the law *permitting racial prejudicial discrimination under the limited circumstances of a bona fide affirmative action plan.* This change occurred by the recent decision of the United States Supreme Court in the 1979 landmark case of *United Steelworkers of America,* et al. *v. Weber,* et al., 443 U.S. 193 (1979). The italicized word "require" in the first sentence of the last paragraph above was the pivot of the court's majority decision that the federal Act did not "forbid private employers and unions from voluntarily agreeing upon bona fide affirmative action plans that accord racial prejudices in the manner and for the purpose provided in the Kaiser-USWA plan" (p. 200). "The purposes of the plan mirror those of the statute. Both were designed to break down old patterns of racial segregation and hierarchy. Both were structured to 'open employment opportunities for Negroes in occupations which have been traditionally closed to them' " (p. 208).

Presidential Executive Orders prohibit discrimination on the basis of race, creed, color, national origin, and sex by the federal government and by persons doing business with the federal government. Pursuant to Executive Order 11246, employers having contracts with the federal government are required to file affirmative action plans initially and yearly updates with the Office of Federal Contract Compliance Programs in the federal Department of Labor.

The Civil Rights Act establishes an Equal Employment Opportunity Commission (EEOC), appointed by the President, to administer the Act. This federal commission has power to bring civil actions in federal courts against employers where there is reasonable cause to believe that an unlawful employment practice has occurred and attempts to conciliate the matter have failed. Usually states and cities have fair employment practices agencies, and if you as an employee have a complaint for illegal discrimination, you should apply to the latter agencies before the federal commission will consider the matter. In the case of illegal discrimination against *federal* employees, enforcement of the law is done by the EEOC.

Age Discrimination in Employment Act (ADIEA). This federal Act of 1967 as amended in 1978 and 1986 has for its purpose "to promote employment of older persons based on their ability rather than age; to prohibit arbitrary age discrimination in employment; to help employers and workers find ways of meeting problems arising from the impact of age on employment."

ADIEA.

Prohibition of discrimination on the basis of age.

The Act applies to employers with at least 20 employees. It provides in section 623(a)(1)(2) that it is unlawful for an employer engaged in an industry in or affecting interstate commerce

> (1) to fail or refuse to hire or to discharge any individual or otherwise discriminate against any individual with respect to his compensation, terms, conditions, or privileges of employment, because of such individual's age;
> (2) to limit, segregate, or classify his employees in any way which would deprive or tend to deprive any individual of employment opportunities or otherwise adversely affect his status as an employee, because of such individual's age.

Note that this section refers to age discrimination against the *individual.* Employers' *blanket* mandatory retirement rules are not *illegal* age discrimination if the employer can prove that the stated retirement age is a bona fide occupational qualification.

The prohibition of age discrimination applies to nonfederal employees who are at least 40 years of age. Under certain conditions, the prohibition does not apply to bona fide executives or high policymakers who have been employed for a 2-year period immediately before retirement. The Act also provides that employees of the federal government who are at least 40 years of age are free of any discrimination based on age.

With certain exceptions, there is no maximum 70 years of age limit for federal employees. The federal Equal Employment Opportunity Commission is responsible for administering the federal part of the Act.

In the following case the court established the test "of function and not of pay" in determining whether the employee was in the bona fide executive or high policymaking position exemption under ADIEA, 29 U.S.C. section 631(c)(1).

Facts
Plaintiff, Whittlesey, 65 years of age and the Chief Labor Counsel of defendant, Union Carbide Corporation, was compulsorily retired by the defendant after having been employed by the defendant as an attorney since 1953. Plaintiff brought an age discrimination action against the defendant in the United States District Court of New York for violation of the federal Age Discrimination in Employment Act. Defendant claimed that the plaintiff was in a bona fide executive or a high policymaking position and therefore exempt under the Act. The Court found in favor of the plaintiff and the defendant appealed to the United States Court of Appeals.

Decision
Affirmed for the plaintiff, Whittlesey.

Reasoning
This case is among the first to test the scope of the exemption. The central liability issue was whether Whittlesey was exempt from ADIEA protection as a "bona fide executive or high policymaking employee" under 29 U.S.C. § 631(c)(1). Judge Leval correctly rejected the argument that Whittlesey's high salary and title of chief labor counsel automatically removed him from coverage. . . . He determined that congress intended the test for the exemption to be "one of function, not of pay." From the evidence concerning Whittlesey's duties at Union Carbide, Judge Leval found that Whittlesey was not a "bona fide executive", but "was primarily an attorney doing legal work, giving legal advice, giving attention to the effect of statutes, regulations and administrative action upon company practices and attending to litigation." While Whittlesey had "some administrative or executive responsibility over the functioning of this small [labor law] section", his supervisory duties nevertheless "were quite minimal and occupied a very small portion of his time."

Nor did Whittlesey lose his ADIEA protection under the "high policymaking employee" prong of the exemption, for Judge Leval found that "Union Carbide did not encourage or invite its house lawyers to play a dynamic policy-creating role" and that "they were employed to do legal work". He further found that when Whittlesey did contribute to corporate policy, his "role in connection with policy formulation was minor" and did not rise to the exemption level contemplated by the statute and regulations. Since these findings by Judge Leval are amply supported by the record, we affirm his determination that Whittlesey was not exempt from ADIEA protection by § 631(c)(1).

John W. Whittlesey v. Union Carbide Corporation, 742 F.2d 724 (1984).

The Act contains one general exception to this prohibition: when age is shown to be "a bona fide occupational qualification [BFOQ] reasonably necessary to the normal operation of the particular business," sec. 623(f)(1), an employee may be terminated on the basis of his age before reaching age 70. It should be noted that in October 1986, the ADIEA was amended exempting *state* and *local* firefighters and law enforcement officers from the ADIEA.

FLSA.

Fair Labor Standards Act
This federal Act of 1938 as amended, also known as the Wage-Hour Law, has for its purpose "the establishment of fair labor standards in employment in and affecting interstate and foreign commerce, and for other purposes." For example, if you are an employee of a manufacturer of goods which are shipped outside the state of manufacture for the purpose of doing interstate business, you are covered under the Act. It is administered by the Secretary of Labor. We are generally concerned here with the Act's provisions for child labor, minimum wages, and maximum hours of employment. Many states have laws in these areas.

Child Labor. The Act prohibits "oppressive child labor" as the employment of an employee under the age of sixteen years, other than by a parent under certain circumstances; or the employment of an employee between the ages of sixteen and eighteen in an occupation particularly hazardous to, or detrimental to the health and well-being of, such persons in that age group. Many states require persons below eighteen years of age to obtain a work permit.

Maximum Hours. An employer can compel an employee to work more than the usual forty hours per week, but the employer must pay the employee no less than one and one-half times the regular rate at which the individual is employed. However, exceptions are made in special situations, such as for employees under the terms of a collective bargaining agreement, and for wages at piece goods rates.

Many states limit the hours of work permitted for persons under sixteen years of age, with a maximum of eight hours per day and forty hours per week, although other states vary concerning the maximum weekly hours of labor.

Minimum Wages. The Act establishes a minimum hourly wage which must be paid to an employee; this amount is periodically revised by Congress. Under the Equal Pay Act amendment, wage discrimination on the basis of sex is prohibited except when such pay is made pursuant to a seniority system, a merit system, a system which measures earnings by quantity or quality of production, or a differential based on any other factor other than sex.

The term "wages" includes the reasonable cost to the employer of furnishing such employee with board, lodging, or other facilities, if they are customarily furnished by such employer to the employees. However, such cost is not included in wages to the extent that a collective bargaining agreement applicable to that particular employee excludes it as a part of wages.

Exemptions from the Above Provisions. The above hourly and minimum wage provisions of the Act do not apply in many instances with certain exceptions, some of which are: an employee in a bona fide executive, administrative, or professional capacity, or generally as an outside salesperson; generally an employee in a retail or service establishment if more than 50% of such establishment's annual dollar volume of sales of goods or services is made within the State in which the establishment is located; generally an employee in an amusement or recreational establishment not operating for more than seven months in a calendar year; an employee generally employed in agriculture. (See U.S.C., Title 29, sec. 213, as amended.)

Unions and Collective Bargaining

This subject is discussed in detail in chapter 49, Labor Law, to which reference should be made at this time. Beginning with the Norris-La Guardia Act of 1932, the movement to recognize and strengthen unions of employees started as an important part of the labor-management process. Subsequent federal labor legislation, discussed in chapter 49, attempted to attain a just and legal balance regarding the rights, duties, and conduct of labor and management, respectively. The various unfair labor practices by employees and unions as well as by employers are listed and discussed in that chapter.

Protection and Compensation for Injury

State Workmen's Compensation Statutes

Common law established various duties of employers toward their employees regarding their work. Generally, they were: to provide reasonably safe working conditions, which included reasonably safe tools and equipment; to exercise reasonable care in the selection of competent and adequate number of fellow servant employees; and to exercise reasonable care in operating the business and in the establishment of reasonable operating rules.

common law principles of nonstatutory law reflecting the customs and usages of society found in judicial decisions

An employer was liable to his employees for injury caused to them *by his negligence,* with three exceptions. The first exception was the *fellow-servant rule,* when the injury to an employee was caused not by the employer's negligence but, rather, by the negligence of a fellow-servant employee. The second exception was the *servant's contributory negligence rule,* when the injury to an employee was caused by the injured employee's contributory negligence. The third exception was the *servant's assumption-of-risk rule,* when the injured employee knew of the risks of injury from the job and assumed them by entering upon the employment with such risks.

The law is different today as a result of public policy that the risks of injury to employees *arising out of, and in the course of, employment* should be that of the employer. The cost of paying for such injury should be a part of the operating expense of the business. An employee's contributory negligence and his noncompliance with his employer's rules will not preclude the employee from recovering for any injury which arose out of and in the course of the employment. (The company policy required workers using a lathe to wear protective eye goggles supplied by the company. A, an employee working over a lathe, did not wear any goggles, and A's eyes were injured by sparks from the lathe. A can recover for the injury.)

There has been much concern among businesses and some conflict among state courts on the meaning and application of the phrases "arising out of" and "in the course of" employment. In the following well reasoned and often cited case, the phrases "arising out of" and "in the course of" employment were interpreted and determined to be not synonymous but, rather, two separate elements both of which are necessary for recovery of workmen's compensation. Once it is determined that "*arising* in the course of employment" means "*originating* in the course of employment," then we look to see whether the employee's injury had its *genesis* or origin at the workplace in order to determine if "course of employment" is present. The case is concerned primarily with "course of employment."

Facts

The Florida statute defines injury, for purposes of the workers' compensation act, as "personal injury or death by accident arising out of and in the course of employment, and such diseases or infection as naturally or unavoidably result from such injury." Strother, plaintiff, a cashier at Morrison's Cafeteria, defendant, was charged with the responsibility of handling the payment of food bills from customers from mid-afternoon to closing at nine each night. Although not a part of her regular employment, on two occasions she drove the cafeteria's manager to the bank to deposit the day's receipts. On the two days preceding the incident which resulted in the injury for which she now seeks workers' compensation, Strother observed two men in the cafeteria who were not customers or employees. On the evening of the incident, she noticed the same two men enter the cafeteria in the same manner as they had entered on the two previous days. This evening, she left work and drove directly home (some fifteen or twenty minutes' drive from the cafeteria) where she was assaulted by, and her purse was taken by, the men whom she had observed in the cafeteria. They thought she was carrying the cafeteria's money since they demanded "the money or deposits."

Plaintiff filed a claim with the Florida Commission for workmen's compensation under the Florida statute. The Commission's judge of industrial claims ordered workmen's compensation to the plaintiff on the basis that the circumstances of the plaintiff's employment exposed her to a greater risk than that of a regular cashier and that the assault *arose out of and in the course of her employment.* However, the Industrial Relations Commission reversed the order of the judge of industrial claims and denied workmen's compensation on the basis that, while the plaintiff's injuries *did arise out of her employment,* they were *not sustained in the course of her employment.* The plaintiff petitioned the Supreme Court of Florida claiming that she sustained the injuries *in the course of her employment.*

Decision

The Commission's decision is quashed [void], and the order of the judge of industrial claims reinstated, for plaintiff.

Reasoning
The plaintiff's injuries from the assault had their origin and cause entirely within the course of her employment and arose out of her employment. The *"arising out of" requirement refers to causation,* only incidentally related to considerations of time and space, and must be satisfied by a showing of causal connection between work and "injury". The "course of" requirement, on the other hand, *refers to continuity of time, space and circumstances,* only incidentally related to causation. *This requirement must be satisfied by a showing of an unbroken course beginning with work and ending with work and ending with injury under such circumstances that the beginning and the end are connected parts of a single work-related incident.*

We hold that, to be compensable, an injury must *arise* out of employment in the sense of causation and be *in the course of employment in the sense of continuity of time, space, and circumstances*. This latter factor may be proved by showing that the causative factors occurred during the time and space limits of employment. Plaintiff's injuries resulting from the assault had their genesis at the place of employment since the assailants were actually on the business premises, casing it so to speak, and, then when the plaintiff left, they followed her to her home and there assaulted her and robbed her of her purse which they thought contained the cafeteria's cash receipts. The time bomb began ticking while she was on the business premises and during working hours and went off at a time and place remote from the place of employment.

Strother v. Morrison Cafeteria, et al., 383 So.2d 623 (Fla. 1980).

There must be a *substantial* causal relationship between the employment and the injury experienced by the employee. Also, if the injury arises out of or in the course of employment, any *new* injury which flows from and is a consequence of the initial injury is covered by workmen's compensation.

In order to ensure that there is proper and adequate financial security to cover this risk—i.e., to indemnify the injured employee—employers must comply with state workmen's compensation laws. Usually employers are required either to take out insurance through a state insurance fund or a private insurance company, or to deposit adequate securities with the state workmen's compensation committee. Employees who are domestic servants or farm laborers usually are not covered by workmen's compensation statutes. Also, an employer is not liable for injury self-inflicted by the employee or resulting from the employee's intoxication. Since workmen's compensation coverage must be provided by the employer, an employee cannot waive such coverage. Also, since the employee is covered by workmen's compensation, in many states the employee cannot sue the employer, although in states which permit such suit the common law defenses become available to the employer if sued by an employee. The employee can sue a third person who wrongfully injured the employee. For example, the employee can sue the driver of a vehicle for the driver's negligence causing injury to the employee while the driver was transporting the employer's goods. The state laws have detailed schedules specifying the limited money amounts payable for various injuries.

Health and Safety Laws
Society is concerned about the health and safety of employees while on the job. Various state and federal laws and administrative rules and regulations have as their purpose to set *standards* to reduce preventable hazards to employees in the place of work and to provide for safe and healthful working conditions.

On the state level, there are departments of labor or of health which have the responsibility for determining whether an employer is complying with the state health and safety statute and administrative rules and regulations.

On the federal level is the Occupational Safety and Health Act (OSHA) of 1970 as amended, administered by the Secretary of Labor. The Act provides for and directs the Secretary of Labor to establish and publish specific mandatory and occupational safety and health *standards* with which employers in a business in or affecting interstate commerce must comply. The specification of standards does not relieve an employer, in the

OSHA.

promulgate
proclaim

Chapter 37: Employment

absence of a specific standard, from the duty to furnish a place of employment which will not expose employees to a recognized risk of death or serious bodily harm. The Act provides for employer record keeping of illness, injury, and death experienced by employees and for employer reports to the Secretary of Labor under certain conditions.

The OSHA division of the Department of Labor is responsible for making inspections of an employer's business premises and working conditions and for issuing citations for alleged violation of OSHA. Employers may appeal from such citations to the OSHA Review Commission and, after exhausting their administrative remedies, they may seek judicial relief in the U.S. Court of Appeals. At the present time, there is much public concern about allegedly lessened governmental enforcement of OSHA. Illustrative of this cause for concern are the numerous lawsuits for large amounts of money brought by present and former employees as asbestosis sufferers.

Pursuant to the purpose of the Act to reduce safety hazards and improve working conditions, 29 U.S.C. section 654 provides:

(a) Each employer—
  (1) shall furnish to each of his employees employment and a place of employment which are free from *recognized* hazards that are causing or are likely to cause death or serious physical harm to his employees;
  (2) shall comply with occupational safety and health standards **promulgated** under this chapter.
(b) Each employee shall comply with occupational safety and health standards and all rules, regulations, and orders issued pursuant to this chapter which are applicable to his own actions and conduct. [Emphasis added]

This section is called the "general duty" provision of the Act, and is intended as a catchall provision to cover dangerous conditions of employment *not specifically covered* by existing health and safety standards promulgated by the Secretary.

Section 660 (29 U.S.C.) provides for civil and criminal penalties for serious and nonserious violations of section 654 and of occupational safety and health standards promulgated by the Secretary. Subsection (j) defines a *serious* violation:

(j) For purposes of this section, a serious violation shall be deemed to exist in a place of employment if there is a substantial probability that death or serious physical harm could result from a condition which exists, or from one or more practices, means, methods, operations, or processes which have been adopted or are in use, in such place of employment unless the employer did not, and could not with the exercise of reasonable diligence, know of the presence of the violation.

In the following case the court had to decide whether there was a *violation of the standard* published in the rule of the Secretary of Labor *and therefore a violation of the general duty provision (section 654)*, and, if there was a violation, whether it was a serious one.

Facts

Petitioner, Everglades Sugar Refinery, Inc. (company), engages in the refining, packaging, and shipping of cane sugar. Decedent Carter, and Sauls, company employees, were assigned one weekend to do routine maintenance and cleanup operations, which included cleaning up "mud" from the syrup process. They could do this by using a small pickup truck and shovels. They knew that a particular payloader vehicle needed repair and was inoperable because of a disconnected throttle linkage and that they were not authorized to use or attempt to repair it. They felt they could do the cleaning up faster if they could repair the payloader and use it. They had mechanical ability. While trying to make the payloader work, Sauls accidentally bumped the boom release and the heavy bucket with a 300-pound load fell upon Carter who was underneath trying to make repairs and killed him. A regulation promulgated by the Secretary of Labor, a **respondent** here, stated as a standard "Any power-operated industrial truck not in safe operating condition shall be removed from service. All repairs shall be made by authorized personnel." The Secretary issued a citation to the company

respondent (appellee)
a party against whom an appeal is taken

for violation of the regulation and of section 654 (29 U.S.C.). The matter was heard by an Administrative Law Judge, and, on appeal, by the Occupational Safety and Health *Review* Commission, also a respondent here, both affirming the Secretary's citation. The company appeals.

The issues are as follows: 1. Was there a violation of the regulation and, therefore, of section 654? The Secretary interprets the regulation to mean that a repair made by unauthorized personnel on an inoperable industrial truck constitutes a violation without the truck being *initially* in an unsafe operating condition, *provided the attempted repair may result in creating an unsafe condition.* Also, that the second sentence of the regulation applies to the repair of *all* power-operated trucks, whether or not the truck is in a safe or unsafe condition under the circumstances. 2. If there is a violation of the regulation and, of section 654, is the violation a serious one? The Secretary contends the company reasonably *could foresee* that what happened could occur *irrespective of whether or not negligence might occur.*

Decision
Affirmed, for the respondents, Secretary and Commission.

Reasoning
The Secretary's interpretation of its own regulation should be upheld. The Secretary's interpretation of an OSHA regulation is entitled to great deference. [The court quoted from another case], "We have held that the promulgator's interpretation is controlling as long as it is one of several reasonable interpretations, although it may not appear as reasonable as some other." In this case the Secretary's interpretation of the regulation was a reasonable interpretation governing unauthorized repairs. The company violated the regulation and, therefore, section 654. The violation was a serious one. The company cannot avoid its responsibility to adhere to the regulations because Carter himself was negligent in what he did. Further, under the circumstances the company could conceive that an employee could injure himself in repairing the loader. Foreseeability is an expectation which a person, experienced in the circumstances, could conceive would happen.

Everglades Sugar Refinery, Inc. v. Raymond J. Donovan, Secretary of Labor, and Occupational Safety and Health Review Commission, 658 F.2d 1076 (United States Court of Appeals, Fifth Circuit) (1981).

Social Security

Society is further concerned about the financial impact upon employees by reason of their retirement, disability, death, hospitalization, and unemployment. These are areas of grave financial risk to an employee, and the federal and state governments participate in a program of insurance to cover this risk. The key federal law on this subject is the Social Security Act of 1935, as amended.

Employees who are included under the Act are: employees of private business; new federal employees hired in 1984 and thereafter; employees of nonprofit organizations; and employees of only those States which are currently under Social Security. Non-federal employers currently under Social Security cannot withdraw from its coverage.

Old-age, Survivors, and Disability Insurance (OASDI)

OASDI.

Both the employer and the employee contribute, as taxes, under the Federal Insurance Contributions Act (FICA) to help pay for: the loss of income benefits on retirement at age 65, or earlier at age 62 at a reduced benefit if early retirement is chosen by the employee; survivor benefits on death of the employee; and financial benefits to employees under 65 years of age who are physically disabled. Persons who are self-employed must financially contribute to this insurance program and thereby participate in the insurance coverage.

FICA.

Congress enacted legislation in 1983 which increases the current retirement age of 65 to 67 in two steps. Beginning in the year 2000, the retirement age will advance by two months each year until it reaches 66 in the year 2005. Then beginning in 2017, the retirement age will resume its advance by 2 months each year until it reaches 67 in 2022.

The Tax of Employee and Employer. An employer is required to withhold the necessary contributions *from the employee's wages* as he or she is paid, and the *employer also makes a similar contribution* and makes deposit and payment of both such funds as required by law. This involves the employee's annual wage base and the percentage of tax on that base.

1. *The Employee's Annual Wage Base.* The basis for the employee's contribution is called the employee's *annual wage base,* which is the maximum amount of an employee's *wages* that are subject to the tax. For example, A's annual wage is $48,000. For the calendar year 1987, the first $46,800 is taxable as the annual wage base. The Secretary of the Treasury has the authority to adjust the maximum contribution by the percentage of increase in "average wages," as measured by the Department of Labor in its review of hourly wages paid nationally.
2. *The Percentage of Tax on That Base. The percentage of tax on the employee's annual wage base* is fixed by the statute. The OASDI and Hospital Insurance Taxes on the annual wage base are: 1986 and 1987, 5.70% (OASDI) + 1.45% (Medicare) = 7.15% (total); 1988 and 1989, 6.06% + 1.45% = 7.51%; 1990 and thereafter, 6.20% + 1.45% = 7.65%. When any employee has more than one job and is paid wages by two different employers, the tax on both wages is withheld from each employer and the *employee* is entitled to a refund for the excess tax paid by him or her; neither employer is entitled to any refund. Also, the employee's tax is not a deductible item on the employee's annual federal income tax return. The *employer's contribution* will be in the same amount as that of its employee.

The Self-Employment Tax. The self-employment tax *percentage* (before tax credits) will be the same as the above *combined* employee and employer tax percentages. For example, the rate of tax for 1987 is 14.30% (before tax credit). But the *amount* of the tax will increase as the amount of the above employee's annual wage base increases. However, only for the self-employed, there is a special *tax credit* of 2.0% of the self-employed's income for 1986 through 1989, and a *deduction*—not a tax credit—for the taxable year of an amount equal to 1/2 of the taxes imposed for 1990 and each year thereafter.

Benefits. Old-age, survivors, and disability benefits are fixed by the statute, and the extent of such benefits depends on various factors. Benefits increase automatically, subject to limitations, with an increase in the cost-of-living of a statutorily prescribed percent as indicated by the consumer price index. Delayed retirement adds an increase in benefits by statutorily specified percentages.

Recipients of benefits are subject to tax on their Social Security benefits. *Up to 1/2 of the benefits* will be taxed if a recipient's adjusted gross income exclusive of Social Security benefits, plus 1/2 of his or her Social Security benefits, exceeds a certain base amount—$25,000 for single retirees, and $32,000 total for a married couple filing a joint return.

On retirement, the employee's earnings beyond a certain maximum reduce retirement benefits until age 70. Until 1990, benefits are reduced $1 for every $2 of "*earned* income" above the base of $6,600 which is indexed annually. Beginning in 1990, the penalty is $1 for every $3 earned above the base. Earned income means *work income* earned in the form of wages or by self-employment. It does not include other income such as (but not limited to) retirement pay, investment income (other than by a dealer in securities), interest from savings accounts, capital gains, rental income from owned real estate (other than a real estate dealer), payments from certain trust funds and annuity plans, royalties from patent or copyright. Statewide federal social security offices are available to provide all social security information to the public.

Employee Pension Plans Controls
Pension plans for employees have been established by many employers. It has become very apparent that there was a need for close governmental supervision over such plans in order to ensure greater protection of the interests of employees covered by such plans. The federal Employees Retirement Income Security Act (ERISA) of 1974 serves this purpose. The Secretary of Labor has the responsibility for operation and supervision of such pension plans.

ERISA.

Hospital Insurance (Medicare)

Medicare.

The federal *Medicare Handbook* describes *Medicare* as a federal "health insurance program for people 65 or older, and some under 65 who have been disabled. It is a federal government program administered by the Social Security Administration. Medicare has two parts. One part, Part A, is called *hospital insurance.* The other part, Part B, is called *medical insurance,*" which assists the patient in his or her payment of *doctor's* expenses. Most people who have Medicare hospital insurance do not have to make monthly payments for this protection. They have hospital insurance because of credits for work under social security. Persons who have Medicare *hospital insurance* are eligible to obtain federal *medical insurance* on payment of small monthly premiums, payable quarterly, while working but then withheld monthly from benefit checks when not working, but which rise as the cost of medical care rises.

Unemployment Insurance
The purpose of the Federal Unemployment Tax Act (FUTA) is to provide temporary financial assistance to a former employee with a sufficient number of credits from former employment during a period of unemployment, provided he or she is ready, able, and willing to take a suitable full-time job that becomes available. Refusal to take such a job which the state employment office indicates is available may well disqualify the unemployed person from receiving unemployment insurance benefits. The cost of the operation of the unemployment insurance program is administered by the federal government out of part of the tax collected, but each state and the District of Columbia administers the program in its own area.

FUTA.

Under FUTA, employers who are within the provisions of the Act and not exempt are taxed annually by the federal government. Each state also taxes the employer, the state tax being at least 5.4 percent in most states. The employer can receive an offset credit against the federal tax up to 5.4 percent of the state unemployment tax. While the federal government does not require that an employee pay a tax while he is employed, a few states do impose a tax on the employee when the state has a supplemental program. Taxes are collected by the employer and submitted to the state, which deposits them with the federal government, where an Unemployment Insurance Fund is maintained with an account for each state and subject to withdrawal by the particular state solely for the payment of benefits. The federal tax is based on a percentage of a wage-base amount. A tax of 6.2% (before tax credits) is imposed on the first $7,000 of wages paid in 1985 and 1986 to a covered employee by such an employer. An employer with a low rate of unemployment may benefit by having a good experience rating and thereby further reduce the employer's *state* tax and still retain the federal offset against the federal tax of 5.4 percent.

Employer Use of Lie, Drug and Alcohol Detection Devices

Use of Lie Detection Devices
Employer use of lie detection (polygraph) devices on their employees is a subject of much current public discussion and controversy. A number of states, by statute, prohibit employers from using lie detection tests as a condition of employment or of continuing employment. But law enforcement, government agencies, and drug dispensing firms often

are exempted from such prohibition. However, the institution of a requirement that employees submit to a lie detection test has been held by some courts to be a proper subject for collective bargaining.

Use of Drug and Alcohol Detection Devices

Employee use of drugs and alcohol and its probable cause of impairment on the job has led to widespread reaction from employers and federal and state governments in the form of tests to detect such use. Often opposition to the use of such tests is based on alleged invasion of the federal constitutional right of privacy and the right against unreasonable searches and seizures. Testing may be pre-employment, random, or screening of employee use.

Private employers are tired of paying the enormously high bill for substance (drug) abuse in the workplace, reflected for example in high absenteeism, accident rates and medical expenditures, increased theft, and lower productivity. Many major corporations in the United States currently screen prospective employees for drug abuse. Many employers are encouraging employees to use Employee Assistance Programs—company sponsored efforts that offer a host of medical and counseling services to troubled employees.

In the public domain, the federal government is engaged in a determined effort to combat drug abuse. The President's Commission on Organized Crime, after more than two years of study, prescribed widespread drug testing of public and private employees as an important weapon in the war against drugs. Because the railroad industry has been wracked in the past few years by a series of drug and alcohol influenced accidents, the industry, working in conjunction with the Federal Railroad Administration, is in the process of promulgating rules that include: post-accident toxicological testing of railroad employees; authorization to "test for cause" if on-the-job impairment is suspected; and pre-employment screening.

Women's Rights

It seems appropriate that, in discussing Employment, a comment be made on the subject of the current status and rights of women in the work force as they overcome unfair discrimination against them because of their sex.

During the last several years, a long overdue recognition of women's rights, particularly in freedom from unfair discrimination solely because of their sex, has emerged in federal and state legislation and in judicial decisions as well as in general business and societal acceptance. Difficulty lies in wide business acceptance and in greater governmental and legal enforcement, and particularly in greater opportunity for advancement to higher paying jobs and positions of greater responsibility.

Two excellent relatively up-to-date references on the current status of women's rights are published by the Women's Bureau of the U.S. Department of Labor. They are: (1) "Time for Change: 1983 Handbook on Women Workers," Bulletin 298; and (2) "A Working Woman's Guide To Her Job Rights," Leaflet 55, January 1984. These two publications enumerate and discuss federal and state legislation in the area of women's rights.

Some statistics concerning the number and status of women in the work force would probably surprise many people and businesses. For example:

1. Women accounted for more than 3/5 of the increase in the civilian labor force in the last decade.
2. Sixty-three percent of all women 18 to 64 years of age, or nearly 46 million women, were in the civilian labor force in 1983.
3. Women accounted for nearly 44% of all persons in the civilian labor force in 1983.

4. Between 1972 and 1982, women accounted for 68 percent of the 14 million increase in employment in white collar occupations. However, they continue to constitute large proportions of workers in traditionally female occupations. In 1983, they were 80 percent of all administrative support (including clerical) workers but only 8 percent of precision production, craft, and repair workers; and 70 percent of retail and personal sales workers but only 32 percent of managers, administrators, and executives.
5. The proportion of married-couple families with the wife in the paid labor force rose from about 40 percent to 52 percent between 1972 and 1983.
6. The more education a woman has the greater the likelihood she will seek paid employment. Among women 25 to 64 years of age with 4 or more years of college in March 1984, 78 percent were in the labor force.
7. The average woman worker is nearly as well educated as the average male worker. In March 1984, the median number of years of school women had completed was 12.7 compared with 12.8 for men.
8. About 61 percent of all mothers with children under 18 years of age (19.5 million mothers) were in the labor force in March 1984; 52 percent of mothers with preschool children (8 million mothers) were labor force participants.

Probably the major issue for women in the 1980s will be that of equal pay for different work of *comparable worth,* that is, equal remuneration for different work of equal value performed by men and women. This concept is presently the subject of much controversy. The Equal Employment Opportunity Commission (EEOC), in its first decision on this subject (Decision No. 85–8, June 17, 1985), decided that the theory of comparable worth is not within the scope of Title VII of the Civil Rights Act of 1964. "We find that sole reliance on a comparison of the intrinsic value of dissimilar jobs—which command different wages in the market place—does not provide a violation of Title VII. . . . We are convinced that Congress never authorized the government to take on wholesale restructuring of wages that were set by non-sex based decisions of employers—by collective bargaining—or by the market place." In that case the muncipal employer's administrative staff (predominantly female) had claimed that they were being paid less than the employer's maintenance staff (predominantly male) even though the duties performed by the female employees in the administrative staff required equal or more skill, effort, and responsibility than the duties performed by employees in the maintenance classification.

Summary Statement

1. The federal Equal Employment Opportunity Act (EEOA) specifies what is and what is not an unlawful employment discriminatory practice by an employer on the basis of an individual's race, color, religion, sex, or national origin. There are three steps necessary to determine when there is unlawful discrimination in employment because of an individual's race, color, religion, sex, or national origin under EEOA.
2. The federal Age Discrimination In Employment Act (ADIEA) prohibits arbitrary age discrimination in employment mainly with respect to nonfederal employees between the ages of 40 and 70 years, with certain exceptions.
3. The federal Fair Labor Standards Act (FLSA), also known as the Wage-Hour Law, establishes fair standards for the employment of child labor, maximum hours of employment, and minimum wages. Oppressive child labor is prohibited.
4. State Workmen's Compensation Statutes changed the common law basis for employer liability for injury to employees arising out of and in the course of employment.

5. The federal Occupational Safety and Health Act (OSHA) provides for promulgation by the Secretary of Labor of specific mandatory occupational safety and health standards for employers in the workplace. Sections 654 (general duty provision) and 660 (29 U.S.C.) are particularly applicable.
6. Irrespective of OSHA's specific standards, an employer has a duty to so maintain the workplace as not to expose employees to a recognized risk of death or serious bodily harm.
7. The broad federal Social Security Act includes in its coverage the following:
   a. Old-Age, Survivors, and Disability Insurance (OASDI). Provision is made for financial assistance to employees on their retirement, benefits to the survivors of employees, and benefits in the event of disability.
   b. Employee's Retirement Income Security Act (ERISA). This Act serves to provide needed federal governmental supervision over pension plans for the benefit of employees.
   c. Hospital insurance (Medicare) as a health program for eligible persons 65 years of age or older, and some under 65 who are disabled.
   d. Federal Unemployment Tax Act (FUTA). This Act provides temporary financial assistance to former employees who are eligible, with sufficient credits from former employment, and who are unemployed and are ready, able, and willing to take a suitable full-time job.
8. Widespread employee abuse of drugs and alcohol has triggered a variety of employer tests aimed at detecting their use and relieving their disruptive economic effect in the marketplace.
9. Women's rights, particularly in freedom from unfair discrimination solely on the basis of their sex, is now the subject of increasing favorable legislation and judicial decisions, as well as of general business and societal acceptance.

In the following long authoritative case, the Supreme Court of the United States clearly explained the process by which illegal discrimination in violation of the federal Civil Rights Act was determined. Observe carefully the court's approach to the question and how the burden of proof shifts from the employee, initially, and then to the employer.

Dothard, Director, Department of Public Safety of Alabama, et al. v. Rawlinson, et al.
433 U.S. 321 (1977)

Mr. Justice Stewart. Appellee Dianne Rawlinson sought employment with the Alabama Board of Corrections as a prison guard, called in Alabama a "correctional counselor." . . .

I

At the time she applied for a position as correctional counselor trainee, Rawlinson was a 22-year-old college graduate whose major course of study had been correctional psychology. She was refused employment because she failed to meet the minimum 120-pound weight requirement established by an Alabama statute. The statute also establishes a height minimum of 5 feet, 2 inches.

After her application was rejected because of her weight, Rawlinson filed a charge with the Equal Employment Opportunity Commission and ultimately received a right-to-sue letter. She then filed a complaint in the district court on behalf of herself and other similarly situated women, challenging the statutory height and weight minima as violative of Title VII and the Equal Protection Clause of the Fourteenth Amendment. . . . [The District Court decided in her favor. Defendants, the Director of Public Safety of Alabama and others, as appellants, brought this action before the Supreme Court.] While the suit was pending, the Alabama Board of Corrections adopted Administrative Regulation 204, establishing gender [male] criteria for assigning correctional counselors to maximum-security institutions for "contact positions"—that is, positions requiring continual close physical proximity to inmates of the institution. Rawlinson amended her class-action complaint by adding a challenge to Regulation 204 as also violative of Title VII and the Fourteenth Amendment.

Like most correctional facilities in the United States, Alabama's prisons are segregated on the basis of sex. Currently the Alabama Board of Corrections operates four major all-male penitentiaries . . . [and] the Julia Tutwiler Prison for Women [. . . all of which] are maximum-security institutions. Their inmate living quarters are for the most part large dormitories, with communal showers and toilets that are open to the dormitories and hallways.

A correctional counselor's primary duty within these institutions is to maintain security and control of the inmates by continually supervising and observing their activities. To be eligible for consideration as a correctional counselor, an applicant must . . . fall between the minimum height and weight requirements of 5 feet 2 inches, and 120 pounds, and the maximum of 6 feet 10 inches, and 300 pounds. Appointment is by merit, with a grade assigned each applicant based on experience and education. No written examination is given.

The Board of Corrections employed a total of 435 people in various correctional counselor positions. . . . Because most of Alabama's prisoners are held at the four maximum-security male penitentiaries, 336 of the 435 correctional counselor jobs were in those institutions, a majority of them concededly in the "contact" classification. Thus, even though meeting the statutory height and weight requirements, women applicants could under Regulation 204 compete equally with men for only about 25 percent of the correctional counselor jobs available in the Alabama prison system.

II

In enacting Title VII, Congress required "the removal of artificial, arbitrary, and unnecessary barriers to employment when the barriers operate invidiously to discriminate on the basis of racial or other impermissible classification." . . . The district court found that the minimum statutory height and weight requirements that applicants for employment as correctional counselors must meet constitute the sort of arbitrary barrier to equal employment opportunity that Title VII forbids. The appellants assert that the district court erred both in finding that the height and weight standards discriminate against women, and in its refusal to find that, even if they do, these standards are justified as "job related."

The gist of the claim that the statutory height and weight requirements discriminate against women does not involve an assertion of purposeful discriminatory motive. . . . *to establish a prima facie case of discrimination, a plaintiff need only show that the facially neutral standards in question select applicants for hire in a significantly discriminatory pattern. Once it is thus shown that the employment standards are discriminatory in effect, the employer must meet "the burden of showing that any given requirement [has] . . . a manifest relationship to the employment in question" [job related]. If the employer proves that the challenged requirements are job related, the plaintiff may then show that other selection devices without a similar discriminatory effect would also "serve the employer's legitimate interest in 'efficient and trustworthy workmanship.'"*

When the height and weight restrictions are combined, Alabama's statutory standards would exclude 41.13 percent of the female population while excluding less than 1 percent of the male population. Accordingly, the district court found that Rawlinson had made out a prima facie case of unlawful sex discrimination. . . . *We cannot say that the district court was wrong in holding that the statutory height and weight standards had a discriminatory impact on women applicants.*

We turn, therefore, to the appellants' argument that they have rebutted the prima facie case of discrimination by showing that the height and weight requirements are job related. These requirements, they say, have a relationship to strength, a sufficient but unspecified amount of which is essential to effective job performance as a correctional counselor. . . . The appellants produced no evidence correlating the height and weight requirements with the requisite amount of strength thought essential to good job performance.

If the job related quality that the appellants identify is bona fide, their purpose could be achieved by adopting and validating a test for applicants that measures strength directly. Such a test, fairly administered, would fully satisfy the standards of Title VII because it would be one that "measure[s] the person for the job and not the person in the abstract." . . . But nothing in the present record even approaches such a measurement.

. . . *The district court was not in error in holding that Title VII of the Civil Rights Act of 1964, as amended, prohibits application of the statutory height and weight requirements to Rawlinson and the class she represents. [Emphasis added]*

III

Regulation 204 explicitly discriminates against women on the basis of their sex. In defense of this overt discrimination, the appellants rely on sec. 703(e) of Title VII, . . . which permits sex-based discrimination "in those certain instances where . . . sex . . . is a *bona fide occupational qualification* reasonably necessary to the normal operation of that particular business or enterprise." The district court rejected the bona fide occupational qualification (bfoq) defense. . . . In the particular factual circumstances of this case *we conclude that the district court erred in rejecting the state's contention that Regulation 204 falls within the bfoq exception.*

The environment in Alabama's penitentiaries is a peculiarly inhospitable one for human beings of whatever sex. Indeed, a federal district court has held that the conditions of confinement in the prisons of the state, characterized by "rampant violence" and a "jungle atmosphere," are constitutionally intolerable. . . . The record in the present case shows that . . . no attempt is made in the four maximum-security male penitentiaries to classify or segregate inmates according to their offense or level of dangerousness. . . . Consequently, the estimated 20 percent of the male prisoners who are sex offenders are scattered throughout the penitentiaries' dormitory facilities.

. . . In the usual case, the argument that a particular job is too dangerous for women may appropriately be met by the rejoinder that it is the purpose of Title VII to allow the individual woman to make that choice for herself. More is at stake in this case, however, than an individual woman's decision to weigh and accept the risks of employment in a "contact" position in a maximum-security male prison. [Emphasis added]

The essence of a correctional counselor's job is to maintain prison security. A woman's relative ability to maintain order in a male, maximum-security, unclassified penitentiary of the type Alabama now runs could be directly reduced by her womanhood. There is a basis in fact for expecting that sex offenders who have criminally assaulted women in the past would be moved to do so again if access to women were established within the prison. There would also be a real risk that other inmates, deprived of a normal heterosexual environment, would assault women guards because they were women. In a prison system where violence is the order of the day, where inmate access to guards is facilitated by dormitory living arrangements, where every institution is under-staffed, and where a substantial portion of the inmate population is composed of sex offenders mixed at random with other prisoners, there are few visible deterrents to inmate assaults on women custodians.

. . . The likelihood that inmates would assault a woman because she was a woman would pose a real threat not only to the victim of the assault but also to the basic control of the penitentiary and protection of its inmates and the other security personnel. The employee's very womanhood would thus directly undermine her capacity to provide the security that is the essence of a correctional counselor's responsibility.

There was substantial testimony from experts on both sides of this litigation that the use of women as guards in "contact" positions under the existing conditions in Alabama maximum-security male penitentiaries would pose a substantial security problem, directly linked to the sex of the prison guard. On the basis of that evidence, we conclude that the district court was in error in ruling that being male is not a bona fide occupational qualification for the job of correctional counselor in a "contact" position in an Alabama male maximum-security penitentiary.

The judgment is accordingly affirmed in part and reversed in part, and the case is remanded to the district court for further proceedings consistent with this opinion.

It is so ordered.

Questions and Case Problems

1. Explain the three steps necessary to determine when there is unlawful discrimination in employment because of an individual's race, color, religion, sex, or national origin under the federal Equal Employment Opportunity Act.

2. Thirteen of the fourteen black employees at the defendant power plant brought this action, claiming that the defendant's requirement of a high school diploma or passing of intelligence tests as a condition of employment in, or transfer to, jobs at the plant was an illegal discrimination in violation of the federal Civil Rights Act of 1964. There were 95 employees at the particular plant involved. There was no proof of discriminatory purpose by the diploma and test requirements. The tests were not directed or intended to measure the ability to learn to perform a particular job or category of jobs. The requisite scores used for both hiring and transfer approximated the national median for high school graduates. Whites registered far better than blacks. The diploma and test requirements were not shown to be related to job performance. Judgment for whom? [*Griggs, et al. v. Duke Power Co.*, 401 U.S. 424 (1971)].

3. Professor Scott, a black faculty member of the University of Delaware, who does not have a Ph.D. degree, brought a class action against the University, alleging illegal employment discrimination in violation of the federal Civil Rights Act of 1964, resulting in the University's failure to renew his contract. Among the various reasons for his assertion of illegal discrimination was that the University's requirement that an individual have a Ph.D. degree or equivalent to attain an assistant professorship had a disparate (unequal) impact upon blacks in the areas of hiring, contract renewal, promotion, and tenure. There was insufficient evidence to prove any intent by the University to discriminate against blacks by this requirement. He asserted that this requirement is not justified by the legitimate needs of the University. The University emphasized scholarship and the advancement of knowledge and sought people for its faculty who had "the capabilities of making significant contribution to scholarship that would bring recognition to the University." Was the Ph.D. degree or equivalent requirement related to job performance and justified by the legitimate interest of the University? [*Scott v. The University of Delaware*, 455 F.Supp. 1102 (1978).]

4. Cactus Craft of Arizona is a firm which manufactures and distributes novelty and souvenir gift items, including cactus lamps, jewelry, and numerous other items. An employee between the ages of sixteen and eighteen years of age operated a power tool for drilling part of the time under supervision, which included shaping and forming of pieces of wood so that they could be used for lamps. The Secretary of Labor issued a regulation prohibiting employment of minors between sixteen and eighteen years of age in the operation of power-driven wood-working machines, which are defined as "all fixed or portable machines or tools driven by power and used or designed for cutting, shaping, forming (or) surfacing wood." A power tool for drilling is not specifically mentioned in the regulation. The Secretary of Labor contends that the defendant violated the Fair Labor Standards Act concerning child labor. Was this oppressive child labor under that Act? [*Hodgson v. Cactus Craft of Arizona*, 481 F.2d 464 (1973).]

5. Explain when wage discrimination on the basis of sex is not prohibited under the federal Equal Pay Act.

6. Sam Dell's Dodge Corp. is an automobile dealership. Salespersons received a base pay and commissions on sales of cars, trucks, accessories, etc. The company furnished many of the salespersons with demonstrator cars. These cars were used primarily in connection with the salespersons' duties at the company. The cars were parked on the lot during the day. Salespersons used them for demonstration rides for their customers. Occasionally the cars would be lent to other salespersons for the same use. Salespersons were permitted to drive the cars for personal use when not working; however, they were specifically told that the cars were not for their families. For each week that a car was provided to a salesperson, the company deducted money from that salesperson's earnings for insurance. The value of the use of the cars was not included on the salesperson's W-2 tax statements or the company's pay records. The mileage accumulated by the salespersons when driving for personal use apparently was significant when compared with business use. The Secretary of Labor claims that the company employer violated the minimum wage requirements of the Fair Labor Standards Act. Were the demonstration cars furnished for salespersons' use "wages" under the Act? [*Marshall v. Sam Dell's Dodge Corp.*, 451 F.Supp. 294 (1978).]

7. How did state workmen's compensation statutes change the common law liability of the employer for injuries suffered by its employees while on the job?

8. Reese was employed by Gas Engineering and Construction Company as a pipeline welder. While working under a large pipe, the scaffolding collapsed and the pipe fell, crushing Reese's left knee. This type of injury is included in the Kansas Workmen's Compensation Statute schedule of injuries for which compensation will be paid. As a result of this injury, Reese favored his left leg and now has a sore back strain and pain and shin splints on his right leg. Reese filed a claim under the Kansas Workmen's Compensation Statute, and the examiner awarded fifty weeks of temporary total disability and 40 percent permanent partial general disability. The company appealed. Should workmen's compensation for general bodily disability be awarded, such disability being a separate and distinct injury resulting from the scheduled injury under the state's workmen's compensation Act? [*Reese v. Gas Engineering and Construction Company*, 532 P.2d 1044 (Kan. 1975).]

9. Davis, the decedent, was a new employee working his fourth day with Republic Creosoting Company. He was hired to sort and stack railroad wood ties after completion of the unloading process of getting the ties off the delivery trucks. The unloader (fork lift) operator suggested to Davis that he come to the unloading so that he could help sort the ties after they had been unloaded. Davis had never witnessed the unloading operation before nor had it been described to him. However, the field superintendent, when hiring Davis, told Davis not to get around the trucks and that the unloader did all the unloading. During the entire operation of unloading, all the company's employees, other than the unloader operator, remained a safe distance from the truck, as did Davis on this occasion. The usual unloading process began with the removal of the chains holding the packages of ties onto the truck. The unloader operator then would move the unloader into position so that it supported a package of steel banded ties holding 25 to 45 ties. Only after the unloader was supporting a package did the truckdriver cut the band of the package to be unloaded. Under no circumstances would the band be cut before the unloader was in position. The unloader then removed the loosened ties from the truck.

   On the day of the accident, the chains had been removed from the truck but the unloader had not yet been moved into position. Without being ordered to do so and without informing anyone of what he intended to do, Davis went up to the truck and, while standing on the ground next to the truck, cut the steel band on a package of ties with an ax. As a result, five of the ties fell on Davis, killing him.

   The Secretary of Labor claimed that the company had violated the Occupational Safety and Health Act general duty clause by failing to instruct and supervise properly an untrained employee regarding the hazards of unloading railroad ties. The Occupational Safety and Health Review Commission decided that there was no violation. The Secretary, Brennan, appealed. Did the company commit such a violation with respect to Davis? [*Brennan v. Occupational Safety and Health Review Commission*, 501 F.2d 1196 (1974).]

10. In the case of *Dothard, Director, Department of Public Safety of Alabama*, et al. *v. Rawlinson*, et al., 433 U.S. 321 (1977)[5] the court had a very definite approach in the case determining whether an illegal discrimination in violation of the federal Civil Rights Act had occurred. Explain that approach.

---

[5] See pp. 566–68.

Ethics and Business Law in Part 7
Agency and Employment

Introduction

This end-of-Part discussion, like the others in this book, is designed to encourage students to begin forming personal beliefs about what is right or wrong conduct in business. The discussion here builds on the material in the first end-of-Part discussion on pages 58 to 69; you may find it helpful to review that.

This material has several goals. The overview section is designed to help you see the range of ethical issues associated with this area of the law. The in-depth discussion is intended to provide you with a background for forming your own beliefs about a single very important ethical issue in business. The problems at the end of this Part are designed to build your skill in ethical analysis while exploring further the in-depth issue.

Overview of Ethical Issues in Agency and Employment

Agency

Agency law raises a variety of ethical issues for persons in business. Many arise from the existence of the *fiduciary relationship*. Because the agent's fiduciary duties are owed to the principal, the principal can reasonably expect that the agent will look out for the principal's best interests. Occasions arise, however, when the agent may be tempted to place his or her best interests above those of the principal. There is no ethical standard, except egoism, which could justify this.

Because the fiduciary duty of loyalty compels the agent to place the interests of the principal above that of the third party, other ethical issues arise. Sometimes, the agent must assess the principal's ethical conduct. For example, if the third party is being legally injured by the principal, what ought the agent to do? One alternative is to withdraw from the agency relationship. Of course this raises the risk of liability for breach of an agency contract.

When a professional agent is appointed, such as an attorney or an accountant, the agent is legally obligated to perform in accordance with external ethical standards of a profession. These may prevent the agent from withdrawing. In these situations then, the professions decide what actions are generally ethical rather than leaving it to the individual agent.

Confidential information can create an issue for agents when they are tempted to use the information for their own benefit.

Employment

The doctrine of *respondeat superior* makes the employer liable for the physical harm caused by the torts of employees who are acting within the scope of their employment. Is this always an ethical outcome? Suppose the employer is completely faultless? Also, do you think it is ethical for an employee to disclose trade secrets of a former employer to a new employer if this might well result in a promotion for the employee?

571

As you have read in this Part, society feels that it is morally unfair and unjust to subject workers to discrimination in employment based mainly on an individual's race, color, religion, sex, national origin, and age, as is reflected in the EEOA and the ADIEA. Landmark federal and state case opinions are now occurring frequently clarifying what is unethical conduct in this area. One ethically intense issue is affirmative action. In effect this legal doctrine gives preferential treatment to one group, over another, in order to remedy prior discrimination. Employers are experiencing extensive economic loss because of employee use of drugs and alcohol, as well as from employee theft. Explosive ethical issues arise currently concerning employer use of lie, drug, and alcohol detection devices. Employer need for necessary information concerning such employee abuse is countered by employee arguments concerning invasion of privacy.

In-Depth Discussion of a Basic Issue: Ethical Treatment of Co-Workers

The purpose of this in-depth discussion is to give you an opportunity to begin deciding for yourself what you believe ought to be your style of relating to those with whom you work—superiors, subordinates, and other co-workers.

Notice that agency law, particularly the agent's fiduciary duties described in chapter 34, creates a legal system which allows one party to wisely trust another in a business transaction. The basis for this trust is the force of law; if parties who are required by law to be trustworthy are not, they can be legally liable. In a sense, agency law describes a distinctive moral style for relating to certain co-workers.

In contrast with agency or fiduciary relationships, most commercial relationships are said to be *at arm's length*. This means that the law assumes that the parties to a transaction will look out for their own self-interests. The law described in Part 2, contract law, describes the way arm's-length relationships work. In general, this body of law does not recognize the importance of trust in anywhere near the same way as agency law. Thus, a used-car dealer might sell a five-year-old Volkswagen for 25 percent more than its fair market value, and, as long as there has been no misrepresentation or deception, the courts will enforce the agreement because the parties must look out for their own self-interests.

Perspective
Recall that, in the first end-of-Part discussion, we made a distinction between ethical views which seek a good for one's self, such as egoism, and views which seek the good of others, such as utilitarianism, Kant's philosophy, and religious ethics. We labeled this attribute "perspective." This idea of perspective also distinguishes arm's-length from fiduciary relations. The fiduciary relationship is "other" oriented while the arm's-length relationship is basically self-oriented.

Styles of Ethical Reasoning
Egoistic. Clearly, egoists would have a preference for the arm's-length way of relating to co-workers because this allows them to exploit others and thereby increase their material well-being. Of course some sophisticated egoists might modify their appearance and project themselves as other-oriented if that would suit their purpose. For example, a common egoist strategy is to adopt an apparent fiduciary relationship with superiors while openly treating peers and subordinates in an arm's-length fashion.

Utilitarianism. This style of reasoning illustrates an important difference between the results of legal analysis and personal ethical analysis. Notice that the law classifies most business relationships as arm's-length. That is, the majority of business relationships are assumed by the law *not* to be based on trust. Why does the law do this? Probably for utilitarian reasons such as the following. If persons were legally required to look out for the interests of others in the majority of business transactions, then there would likely be a great deal more litigation over business transactions thereby burdening the courts. Reasoning in a similar way, if persons left it to the legal system to look out for their self-interests, they might become lax, perhaps more vulnerable, and become easy prey for the ruthless in society. For these reasons, the *legal system* can justify encouragement of arm's-length relationships.

But the reasoning which is valid for the legal system may not be valid for an individual embracing utilitarianism. On the individual level, it is likely that the greatest good for the greatest number arises when you treat others in ways more similar to the fiduciary style, at least with complete openness and honesty.

Kant's Philosophy and Religious Ethics. These views both stress great respect for individual human dignity. This aspect of both styles of moral reasoning makes it very unlikely that they could justify the extreme version of arm's-length relations. Both would require that we be open and honest, make full disclosure, and respect the informed choices of our co-workers.

The Law As a Constraint on Relating to Co-workers

As you think about fiduciary and employment relationships perhaps you can see that while they articulate an other-oriented perspective they also compel, as the other side of the coin, a self-oriented perspective. Thus, in the fiduciary relationship, the agent's way of relating to the third party is definitely not aimed at aiding the third party. In fact, the reverse is closer to the truth. Thus, if the agent advances the interests of the third party adverse to the interest of the principal, that would be a breach of the agent's fiduciary duty of loyalty. Accordingly, agents and employees may be more constrained in their conduct than those who act independent of these legal relationships.

Solving Ethics Problems

Like the other end-of-Part discussions in this book, this one presents problems for you to consider. These problems have three goals. The first is to give you the opportunity to further explore the in-depth issue. The second goal is to give you experience in ethical reasoning about the law and about related management problems. The third goal is to let you see how thinking critically about the law can increase your ability to make ethical decisions. To facilitate this, the problems begin by asking you to analyze the law for its ethical content and then shift to looking at related problems in managerial ethics.

For a discussion of the ethical roles of markets and the law and examples of the four styles of ethical reasoning—egoism, utilitarianism, Kant's philosophy, and religious ethics—read the business ethics material at the end of Part 1.

Problems
1. In chapter 37, you read the case of *Strother v. Cafeteria,* et al. In that case a cashier working in a cafeteria was followed home from work by criminals who intended to steal from her the receipts of the cafeteria. At her home she was assaulted and her purse stolen. She filed for workmen's compensation. On appeal the claim was denied after a careful interpretation of the statutory language which defines when an injury *arises* in, and *originates* in, the course of employment. Assume that you owned the cafeteria. Would you feel that your duty to this employee had been extinguished because her legal claim had been denied? Is this a case where legal analysis and ethical analysis reach opposite conclusions? If you viewed your ethical relationship with employees as more fiduciary than arm's-length, what would this imply for your treatment of the cashier?

2. A highly talented subordinate of yours is doing an outstanding job and making you look like an excellent manager, but your boss does not know about this superstar. Suppose your boss indicated that one of your peers—a manager on the same level as you—is leaving and that your boss is looking for a replacement. Would you recommend the superstar for the other management position? Notice that if this subordinate leaves your department, its performance will decline. Also note that by elevating the star you will make *your* relative performance look worse. Assume there would be a promotion available to you or one of your peers in the next 18 months and that, if you recommended the star for the immediate promotion, in all likelihood the star would get the next promotion too. Would you recommend the star to your boss? In other words, would you relate to this subordinate as a fiduciary or at arm's-length? What do you think the law requires you to do in this situation? Do you think the legal requirement is one which is likely to be litigated if it is not met?

3. Assume that you have learned that one of your employees has contracted AIDS. There is no risk that anyone else can contract this deadly disease from this person. However, staff morale and customer relations are likely to suffer if you allow this person to continue working for your organization. What ought you to do and why?

4. You are the supervisor of an engineering group for a large aerospace organization. One of your key subordinates, a Ph.D. chemist, approached you with the news that he has a job offer from a competing firm. To help him in making a decision, he is asking you about his future with the company. You ask for time to discuss the matter with your boss. Your boss informs you that the project that the subordinate is working on will be concluded in three months. At that time, all the people on that project, including the subordinate, will be laid off. Your boss also tells you that this subordinate is critical to the successful conclusion of the project. The boss therefore tells you to inform the subordinate that he is highly regarded by the management, but to say nothing to him about the project, its termination, and lay-off of persons working on the project. The fact that the subordinate is highly regarded by top management is technically true and, without the information about the project's upcoming termination and consequent personnel layoffs, will lead him to the wrong conclusion about his future with the company. What will you do, and why?

PART

8 Business Organizations
A. General Partnerships and Special Ventures

38. Creation and Termination of General Partnerships
The nature of a partnership; kinds of partnership; how a partnership is created, dissolved and terminated; and how partnership assets are distributed on dissolution.

39. Partnership Management and the Authority of Partners
The express, implied, and apparent authority of partners in the management of a partnership, in the absence of partnership agreement to the contrary.

40. Rights, Duties, and Remedies of Partners among Themselves
The inter-partner relationship with respect to the rights, duties, and remedies of the partners among themselves, with particular reference to the Uniform Partnership Act.

41. Special Ventures
Other noncorporate forms of business entity distinguished from the general partnership.

Summary

The oldest known form of business organization is the partnership. Although partnerships are easy to create, their structure is complex with consequent exposure to liability. If you ever become a partner, these chapters will help you understand the managerial problems you can expect to encounter. As a partner you will have many legal rights and duties to your co-partners as well as to third persons dealing with your firm. These chapters explain the resulting rights and duties.

Chapter 41, Special Ventures, will acquaint you with various types of noncorporate business ventures, such as the limited partnership, joint venture, mining partnership, business trust, unincorporated association, joint-stock company, and the franchise.

Business ethics as it relates to the text material in this Part is considered at the end of Part 8B.

38 Creation and Termination of General Partnerships

After you have read this chapter, you should be able to:

1. Identify the source of partnership law.
2. Define a general partnership.
3. Explain the legal distinction between the aggregate and entity theories of partnership.
4. List and explain the classifications of partnerships.
5. List and explain the classifications of partners.
6. Explain what is necessary to create a partnership.
7. Explain what is generally found in the Articles of Partnership.
8. Explain who may be partners.
9. Explain and define partnership by estoppel.
10. Discuss what is meant by partnership property.
11. List and explain the five characteristics of tenancy in partnership.
12. Discuss partnership dissolution.
13. List and explain the three methods of dissolution by acts of the partners.
14. List and explain the two methods of dissolution by operation of law.
15. List and explain the five instances when a partnership can be dissolved by decree of the court.
16. Explain when and why notice of dissolution must be given to partners and to third parties.
17. Discuss the winding up of partnership affairs.
18. Explain the order of distributing partnership assets after dissolution.

Introduction

Partnership is one of the oldest forms of business organization. Hammurabi, a king of Babylon, made reference to the regulation of partnerships in the 20th century B.C. The development of ancient partnership law has its origin with the Italian merchants of the late Middle Ages.

However, modern partnership law, as it exists in the United States, evolved from the English law. The civil law, the law merchant, the common law, and equity all contributed to a confused state that demanded a statutory body of partnership law. The result in England was the adoption of the *Partnership Act of 1890*. In the United States the *Uniform Partnership Act* (U.P.A.) was approved by the Conference of Commissioners on Uniform States Laws in 1914 and has been adopted by most states.[1]

The purpose of the U.P.A. is to codify the principles of partnership law for **general partnerships,** as distinguished from limited partnerships, which are discussed in chapter 41, Special Ventures. *Unless stated otherwise, reference to "partnership" is to the general partnership.* Unless the Act provides otherwise, the common law rules of contract and agency will govern partnership transactions.[2] The law governing partnerships is essentially the *state* statutory law of the Uniform Partnership Act. The Uniform Partnership Act is reproduced as Appendix B of this book.

general partnership
a partnership as defined by the U.P.A.

Nature of Partnership

A **partnership** has been defined in U.P.A., section 6, as "an association of two or more persons to carry on as co-owners a business for profit." It is a contractual agreement between competent parties to pool their capital and/or services in a business and to share the profits and losses. Our concern will be limited to the legal relationships between the partners and between the partnership and third parties. The Uniform Partnership Act will be cited as the applicable law throughout the text. You may refer to it in Appendix B.

partnership
(general partnership) "an association of two or more persons to carry on as co-owners a business for profit" U.P.A., sec. 6

Aggregate and Entity Theories of Partnership

You, as an individual, are endowed by the law with a legal personality. In that capacity your personal rights and property are protected. You can make contracts on your own behalf, sue and be sued; you are a legal entity. State legislatures and the Congress can create a legal entity such as a business corporation. The **common law** regarded the partnership as a group of individuals and not as a legal group entity. The **law merchant** took the view that a partnership was a legal entity having a legal personality of its own, apart from the individual partners. The Uniform Partnership Act appears not to have solved the problem as to whether a partnership is an aggregate of persons or a legal entity.[3] There are, however, functional operations of a partnership that support the *legal entity theory.* For example, the partnership can own and convey **property,** both real and personal, in the firm name;[4] the partnership is the principal of the partners who are its agents;[5] each partner is accountable to the firm as a fiduciary;[6] books and records are kept for the firm;[7] contributions and advances are made to the firm and are returnable by it;[8] and a partnership is defined as an association—a person.[9]

common law
principles of nonstatutory law reflecting the customs and usages of society and found in judicial decisions

law merchant
a body of law which developed by the customs and usages of merchants and which later became part of the common law

property
a thing; also an interest or right in a thing

---

[1] The U.P.A. has been adopted by all states except Louisiana and Georgia.

[2] U.P.A., sec. 4.

[3] See Jensen, *Is a Partnership under the Uniform Partnership Act an Aggregate or an Entity?* 16 VAND. L. REV. 377 (1963).

[4] U.P.A., secs. 8, 25.   [5] U.P.A., sec. 9(1).   [6] U.P.A., sec. 21.

[7] U.P.A., sec. 19.   [8] U.P.A., secs. 18(a), 38(1).   [9] U.P.A., sec. 2.

Torts committed by a partner within the scope of the partner's authority are based upon the *aggregate theory* (of persons) and hence the unlimited liability of partnerships for the acts of those persons. For instance, each partner and the partnership could be held liable to satisfy the claims of an injured party.

The Internal Revenue Code requires the partnership to file an information return, and each partner must report and pay his or her share of partnership income in their individual tax returns, hence, treating the partnership as an aggregate of persons.

Kinds of Partnership

Partnerships have been divided into several classes regarding their extent of business activity and the nature of their employment. This classification is helpful in determining whether a partner has customary authority as an agent to bind the partnership with third parties, as discussed in chapter 39.

A partnership is a **trading partnership** when it *buys and sells property*. Some trading partnerships—e.g., plumbing contractors or T.V. repair shops—combine the sale of goods with the furnishing of services.

trading partnership
a partnership in the business of buying and selling property

A **nontrading partnership** engages in providing only services, generally on a fee-for-services basis, such as one of lawyers, physicians, and accountants.

nontrading partnership
a partnership in the business of selling only services

This classification shows that the customary authority of a partner in a trading partnership will be substantially broader than in a nontrading partnership. The implied authority of partners in trading and nontrading partnerships is discussed in chapter 39.

Kinds of Partners[10]

A *dormant partner* is one who is not active in the business and is not known to the public as a partner. An example would be a retired accountant still sharing in the firm profits after having sold his or her practice.

A *nominal partner* is not a partner but holds himself out as a partner or allows others to hold him out as a partner—as, for example, by permitting his name to appear on firm stationery as a member of the partnership. To illustrate, if a partnership is purchased, it may be helpful to retain the name of the selling partner. He is not a partner. Because he is held out to be a partner, he may be held liable as such by "estoppel."

A *secret partner* takes an active part in firm management but is not known to the public as a partner.

An *ostensible* or *public partner* holds himself out, or permits himself to be held out, as a partner and actively engages in the partnership business. If he does not actively so engage, he is a *silent* partner.

A *general partner* is an *ordinary* partner in a general partnership or in a limited partnership.

A *limited partner* is a partner in a limited partnership who is not a general partner. He is sometimes called a "special partner."[11]

Creation of the Partnership

Requisites for a partnership.

A partnership is generally created by the express or implied contractual agreement of the parties. If the parties intended to create a partnership, and they comply with the U.P.A. requisites, as between each other there is a partnership. However, when the question concerns the firm's liability to third parties, a partnership may be implied in law by the courts, regardless of the parties' intent to form a partnership.

---

[10] See Alan R. Bromberg, *Crane and Bromberg on Partnership,* (St. Paul: West Publishing Co., 1968), pp. 141–42 for a general discussion on the many kinds of partners.

[11] See pp. 614–15 for a discussion of limited partnership.

Form

Unless the state statutory law requires a writing, no particular form is required to create a partnership agreement. If it falls within the statute of frauds,[12] there must be written evidence of the partners' contract. For example, an accounting partnership agreement should be in writing under the statute of frauds, as it will normally exist for a specified time of more than one year. It is always desirable to have a written partnership agreement to avoid a misunderstanding regarding its terms. (See figure 38.1.)

Articles of Partnership

The partnership contract is called the *articles of partnership*. The agreement generally includes the date of formation, the names and addresses of the partners and the partnership, its purpose and duration, the capital contribution of each partner, the proportions by which the partners share in the profits and losses, salaries and drawing accounts, the duties and restrictions on managing the firm, the method of accounting and the fiscal year, rights and duties on voluntary termination, disability, retirement, death of a partner, and dissolution procedures.

The agreement.

Firm Name

The partnership may select any name it desires provided it complies with state statutory law. It may use a fictitious trade name or the names of the partners. The name cannot be *deceptively similar* to an existing business. State statutes usually require the partnership to file a *business certificate* in a local government office (e.g., city hall, county clerk's office), where the firm is located, indicating the name and location of the partnership and the names and addresses of the partners. The purpose of this is to allow a party who wants to sue the firm to discover who the partners are who own the business.

Illegality

A partnership agreement must comply with contract law concerning the legality of its operation. If the agreement is illegal under statutory law or court decision for public policy reasons, it is a void agreement. The courts will attempt to separate the legal portion of the partnership agreement from its illegal part and allow the partnership to exist only for its legal purpose.

U.P.A. As Part of the Partnership Agreement

Unless the parties agree to change the effect of the U.P.A., where allowed the U.P.A. becomes part of the partnership agreement. For instance, *unless the partnership agreement provides otherwise,* all partners have equal rights in the management and conduct of the partnership business regardless of their capital contribution.[13]

The U.P.A. becomes part of the agreement unless changed by the partners.

An Association

You recall that section 6 of the U.P.A. defined a partnership "as an association of two or more persons. . . ." An association as partners is not a master/servant or employer/employee relationship. It is a relationship that makes each member a coprincipal and a general agent for the firm in transacting partnership business. Although it does not pay tax itself, a partnership is a unique entity for tax purposes and is required to calculate its income or loss and file an information return. This taxable income or loss is then passed through to the partners,[14] who show it on their individual tax returns.

---

[12] See pp. 152–56 for a discussion of the statute of frauds.

[13] U.P.A., sec. 18(e).

[14] See Int. Rev. Code of 1954 ch. 1, subch. K (26 U.S.C.A.) for the tax effect of partnership transactions.

Figure 38.1 General Partnership Agreement (Short Form)
Source: Reprinted with permission from Edmund O. Belsheim's "Modern Legal Forms." Copyright © 1971 by West Publishing Co.

GENERAL PARTNERSHIP AGREEMENT (Short Form)

Agreement, made this _____ day of _____, 19 ____, by and between John Doe, of _____, and Richard Roe, of _____.

Whereas, Richard Roe has acquired an undivided one-half interest in the real estate and insurance business heretofore owned and conducted by John Doe, with office and place of business located at _____;

It is agreed as follows:

1. **Name and Duration.** The parties hereby agree to continue the operation of said business as partners under the name of _____, the partnership to continue for an indefinite time and until terminated as herein provided or as may be mutually agreed upon.

2. **Capital.** The amount of capital contributed to the partnership by the parties is hereby agreed to be the sum of $ _____ each, and is represented by the following personal property: [here describe].

3. **Reserve Fund.** An additional sum of _____ dollars ($ _____) shall be set up and reserved from the profits of the partnership business, and shall become and be a part of the invested capital, it being agreed that not less than _____% of the net earnings shall be so reserved until said amount is accumulated.

4. **Banking.** The funds of the partnership shall be deposited in its name in the _____ Bank of _____, and all trust funds shall be deposited in such bank in a separate account. All such funds, partnership or trust, shall be subject to withdrawal only by check made in the name of the partnership and signed by either partner.

5. **Duties.** Each partner shall devote all his time and attention to the business of the partnership, and shall not, directly or indirectly, engage in any other business without the consent of the other partner.

6. **Books.** Full and accurate accounts of the transactions of the partnership shall be kept in proper books, and each partner shall cause to be entered therein full and accurate accounts of all his transactions in behalf of the partnership. Such books shall be kept at the place of business of the partnership, and each party shall at all times have access to and may inspect and copy any of them.

7. **Drawings.** Each party shall be entitled to withdraw such amounts and at such times, from the partnership earnings, as shall from time to time be fixed and agreed upon.

8. **Profits and Losses.** At the end of each calendar year, a full and accurate inventory shall be prepared, and the assets, liabilities, and income, both gross and net, shall be ascertained, and the net profits or net losses of the partnership shall be fixed and determined. The net profits or net losses shall be divided equally between the parties, and the account of each shall be credited or debited with his proportionate share thereof.

9. **Limitations.** Neither party shall, without the written consent of the other, make, execute, deliver, indorse or guaranty any commercial paper, nor agree to answer for, or indemnify against, any act, debt, default or miscarriage of any person, partnership, association or corporation, other than that of the parties hereto.

10. **Termination.** The partnership may be terminated by either party upon giving 60 days notice to the other party of his desire to withdraw, in which event an accounting shall be had and a division of the partnership assets made, provided, however, that the party to whom notice is given shall have the right to acquire the whole interest of the partnership at a price not to exceed the book value thereof, on such terms as may be agreed upon, and to continue the partnership business under the same name.

In Witness Whereof, the parties have signed this agreement.

_____   _____
[Signatures]

Two or More Persons. The "two or more persons" requirement immediately will distinguish the partnership from the sole proprietorship, where one person earns the profits and bears all losses. The "person" under U.P.A., section 2, "includes individuals, partnerships, corporations, and other associations." However, the *person* must have the *capacity to contract.*

Infants or Minors. Under most state laws, a minor may be a partner with partnership rights. The minor's agreement is voidable by the minor during minority or a reasonable time thereafter. The minor can disaffirm and withdraw during that time without incurring liability for breach of contract. The minor may also disaffirm his or her individual liability on partnership contracts with third parties, although some states will not allow a minor of an insolvent partnership to withdraw the minor's capital contribution.

Insane Persons. The state law governing competency of the mentally ill to contract will determine their ability to be partners. Generally, their contracts will be voidable, unless they have been adjudicated to be insane, in which case they have no capacity to contract and cannot be partners.[15]

Corporations. Modern corporation laws and the U.P.A., sections 2 and 6(1), permit corporations to become partners.[16]

Carrying on a Business for Profit

Partners must "carry on as co-owners a business for profit." To illustrate, if X and Z invested in an apartment building and agreed to share the rental income, this in itself will not create a partnership;[17] it is not a business. A business must carry on a number of *continuous commercial transactions* as an enterprise. A fraternity or sorority or other nonprofit organization cannot be a partnership.

Co-owners of a Business

U.P.A., section 7(2) lists a number of forms of co-owned property which do not, in themselves, establish a partnership. Joint tenancy, tenancy in common, tenancy by the entirety, joint property or part ownership—even if the co-owners share profits made by use of the property—are not partnerships.

Sharing Profits. The *sharing of profits* is *prima facie evidence* that a person is a partner in a business. However, under U.P.A., section 7(4), no such inference may be drawn when profits are received in payment: (a) as a debt, by installments or otherwise; (b) as wages of an employee or rent to a landlord; (c) as an annuity to a widow or representative of a deceased partner; (d) as interest on a loan; or (e) as the consideration for the sale of the goodwill of a business. However, in any of these instances, if the recipient of the profits also has the *right to participate in the management of the business,* there is *a co-ownership* and a resulting partnership.

---

[15] See pp. 129, 132 on capacity to contract.

[16] See Revised MODEL BUSINESS CORPORATION ACT sec. 3.02(10).

[17] U.P.A., sec. 7(3).

Partner by Estoppel

Partnership liability of a nonpartner by estoppel.

estoppel
a principle of law that when one person "holds out" (represents) a material fact to another person, who changes his position materially to his prejudice in reasonable reliance on the holding out, the first person is "estopped" (prohibited) to deny what he had asserted previously

A person who is not a member of a partnership may incur partnership *liability* to a third party *as though* the person were a partner under the doctrine of *partnership by estoppel.* This occurs when a person who is not a partner by words or conduct *represents* himself, or permits himself to be represented, to anyone as a partner and a third party *relies* on that representation[18] and *extends credit* to the partnership in reasonable reliance on the holding out. The person is really not a partner and does not become a firm member but is a *nominal partner* and cannot deny liability. By estoppel, he is liable to third persons as a partner. For example, Jones permits Moran to inform Peters that Jones and Moran are partners when, in fact, they are not partners. Moran tells Peters that Jones is his partner, and Peters, in reliance on Moran's statement, extends credit through Moran to the apparent Jones/Moran partnership. Jones is estopped to assert that she and Moran are not partners, and Jones is liable as a partner to Peters.

The following case illustrates how an associate in an accounting firm may be held out to the public as being a partner, but *between members* the associate is not a partner. Partnership by estoppel applies only to a *third party's claim* that a person is a partner.

Facts
In 1964 Kelley and Galloway were partners in an accounting business. Smith came to work for them for three-and-one half years. In 1968 when he left the firm he made a claim that he was entitled to a fixed percentage of the profits.

There was no writing evidencing a partnership agreement. However, during the years Smith worked for the firm he was held out to the public as a partner. In a contract entered into between Kelley, Galloway, Smith, and a third party, Smith was designated a partner. Partnership tax returns listed him as such; so did a statement filed with the Kentucky Board of Accountancy. In a suit filed in the circuit court against a third party, he was designated a partner.

On the other hand, there was no agreement that Smith would be a partner or have a right to share in the profits; he made no contribution to the assets of the partnership; he took no part in the management; he had no authority to hire or fire employees or to make purchases for the firm; he did not sign any notes when the firm was borrowing money; and he was not obligated to stand any losses of the firm.

Smith sued the partnership and claimed that he was a partner and was entitled to a twenty percent interest in the profits. Was Smith a partner?

Decision
No. Judgment for the defendant firm.

Reasoning
The conduct of the parties over a three-and-one-half-year period confirms the conclusion that, though Smith was held out to the public as a partner, between themselves a partnership relationship was not intended to be and was not created.

Smith v. Kelley, 465 S.W.2d 39 (Ky. 1971).

Partnership Property

Partnership assets and property.

The *assets* of a partnership consist of the *partnership property* and the *contributions of the partners necessary for the payment of the partnership liabilities.* U.P.A., section 8(1) defines partnership property as "all property originally brought into the partnership stock or subsequently acquired by purchase or otherwise, on account of the partnership."

Creditors

Charging order.

Firm Creditors. The issue of partnership property is important when the firm is insolvent and its creditors are seeking satisfaction of their claims.

Individual Creditors. The partners of a firm in their individual capacity may incur personal debts. A partner's personal creditors, in that instance, may reach that partner's interest in the firm by means of a *charging order.*[19]

---

[18] U.P.A., sec. 16(1).   [19] U.P.A., sec. 28.

For example, a personal creditor of a partner must first reduce the claim to a judgment, and then request the court: to charge the interest of the debtor partner in a share of the partnership profits and any other money due the debtor from the partnership; and to appoint a **receiver** and direct the receiver to collect such moneys from the partnership and pay them to the judgment creditor until the judgment is satisfied. It then becomes necessary to determine what is firm property.

receiver
a person appointed by a court to receive, preserve, and manage property which is involved in litigation

Title to Partnership Property
A partnership may hold title to **personal property,** and under U.P.A., section 8(3) to **real property,** in the firm name. A majority of states allow the partnership to hold title to real property under a fictitious name.

personal property (personalty)
a movable thing, along with interests and rights in the thing

Transfer of the Partnership Property
Personal Property. Any partner with express, implied, or apparent authority may transfer personal property owned by the firm to another party. For example, X, a partner in a construction firm, may sell a truck owned by the partnership to Z without the actual authority of the co-partners if there is **customary authority** in that business to sell equipment.

real property (realty)
land and immovable things attached to land, along with interests and rights in the land; also a freehold interest in land

Real Property. If title to the real property is in the name of the partnership on the deed, the title can be transferred by any partner executing the deed in the partnership name. The partner must have authority or **apparent authority** to make the conveyance. If the partner does not, the partnership can recover the property.

customary authority
implied authority to do those acts that conform to the general custom or usage

Title to Partnership Property Held in the Name of an Individual Partner. An individual partner may have the title to partnership property in that partner's own name. For example, the partner may have owned property before the partnership was formed and contributed that property to the firm but failed to transfer record title to the partnership. The partner holds the title as a trustee, in constructive trust, for the benefit of the co-partners.

apparent authority
the power of a person (A) to act as though he were an agent, created by another's (P's) manifestation to a third person (T) that A is P's agent

Tenancy in Partnership
Each partner has a property interest in firm property and is a co-owner in such property. Title to firm property is held by the partners as a *tenancy in partnership.*[20]

This concurrent ownership has characteristics that distinguish it from a **tenancy in common** and a **joint tenancy.** For example, a joint tenant has full survivorship rights upon the death of a co-tenant; a surviving partner does not.

tenancy in common
a form of ownership of property by more than one person without survivorship

The characteristics of a tenancy in partnership are as follows:

1. A partner, subject to any agreement between them, has an equal right with the other partners to *use specific* partnership property for partnership purposes.
2. A partner's right in *specific* partnership property cannot be transferred by the partner (sold, assigned, or mortgaged) without the consent of all the other partners.
3. A partner's right in *specific* partnership property is not subject to attachment by the partner's *personal* creditors.
4. On the death of a partner, the decedent partner's right in *specific* partnership property vests in the surviving partners; except that when the deceased is the last surviving partner, then the decedent's right in such property vests in the legal representative of the decedent,[21] who holds it in trust for partnership purposes.
5. A partner's right in *specific* partnership property is not subject to any interest of the partner's surviving spouse.

joint tenancy
a form of ownership of property by more than one person with the right of survivorship

---

[20] U.P.A., sec. 28.   [21] U.P.A., sec. 25(d).

The following case illustrates that a personal creditor of a partner may reach only a partner's interest in the firm and not the assets of the partnership.

Facts
Amerco, the plaintiff, after it secured a judgment against Bohonus, the defendant, sought a charging order from the court. The court granted the request for a charging order and as a part of that order mandated the sale of Bohonus' interest in the assets and property of the partnership business. Defendant appealed. May the trial court order the sale of partnership property to satisfy the individual debt of a partner?

Decision
No, only the partner's interest. Reversed, for defendant.

Reasoning
On due application to a competent court by any judgment creditor of a partner, the court which entered the judgment may charge the interest of the debtor partner with payment of the unsatisfied amount of such judgment debt with interest thereon. Only the "interest in the partnership" may be charged and we find no provision therein for sale of assets or property of the partnership.

Bohonus v. Amerco, et al., 602 P.2d 469 (Ariz. 1979).

We have seen what a partnership is and how it comes into existence. The operation of a partnership may be interrupted by any number of events resulting in its *dissolution* or in *termination* of its legal entity as a partnership. These are now to be discussed.

Dissolution, Winding up, and Termination

Termination of partnership entity after dissolution and winding up.

The termination of the partnership is a process involving the sale of its assets, the payment of its liabilities, ultimate distribution of cash to the partners, and ending with the termination of the partnership entity. Termination is preceded by *dissolution* and *winding up,* which occur in that order.

Dissolution

Dissolution.

Dissolution is defined by U.P.A., section 29 as follows:

> The dissolution of a partnership is the change in the relation of the partners caused by any partner ceasing to be associated in the carrying on as distinguished from the winding up of the business.

The "change in the relation of the partners" may be the result of a partner leaving the firm, or of a partner's disability, retirement, or death. The well-designed partnership agreement will provide for the continuance of the partnership business, giving the remaining partners the right to purchase the leaving partner's interest and a pay-off of his or her distributive share of the profits.

The legal effect of dissolution is to terminate all authority of any partner to act for the partnership[22] except to wind up the partnership business. After dissolution, the partnership remains obligated to pay its liabilities. For instance, a deceased partner's estate is liable for the deceased partner's share of the partnership debts.

It is important to recognize that the partnership entity is *not* terminated by dissolution. The partnership will continue in accordance with the partnership agreement during the winding up of its affairs.

In the following case the court held that a partnership may be sued in its own name following dissolution but prior to termination.

Facts
Commonwealth Capital Investment Corporation, plaintiff, brought an action against Leland R. McElmurry and several others, defendants. McElmurry was a general partner of MHS Enterprises, a dissolved partnership and also a defendant, which had guaranteed performance on a promissory note and loan agreement. The court granted the plaintiff summary judgment against

---
[22] U.P.A., sec. 33.

McElmurry in his capacity as a general partner of MHS. McElmurry appeals, alleging that because MHS had been dissolved prior to plaintiff's suit no judgment could be rendered against it and he could not, therefore, be held liable on the void judgment.

Decision

Judgment for plaintiff affirmed.

Reasoning

A partnership is not terminated upon dissolution. It continues on until the winding up of partnership affairs is completed. The winding up includes the satisfaction of debts against the partnership. Therefore, a partnership may be sued in its own name following dissolution but prior to termination. The judgment against MHS was not void and McElmurry, as a former general partner, could properly be held liable.

Plaintiff properly sued the partnership as an entity. Consequently, the judgment entered against the partnership was not void, and defendant could be held liable as a general partner of the partnership.

Commonwealth Capital Investment Corporation v. McElmurry, 302 N.W.2d 222 (Mich. 1980).

Causes for Dissolution. Dissolution is effected by the acts of the partners, by operation of law, and by decree of court.

1. By Acts of the Partners.

a. Agreement. The partnership agreement may provide for its dissolution upon a specified period of time or the occurrence of an event.[23] For example, a partnership may have been created for the purpose of buying, developing, and selling a condominium. When the dissolution occurs in accordance with the partnership agreement, there is no further liability for any partner.

b. Withdrawal. For any number of reasons, a partner may decide to withdraw from the firm in *violation* of the partnership agreement. Although the partner has the power to withdraw, by doing so the partner may thereby incur damages for breach of the partnership agreement. Usually the partnership agreement will provide for a partner's withdrawal by giving proper advance notice to the associates. U.P.A., section 31(b), states: "Dissolution is caused by the express will of any partner when no definite term or particular undertaking is specified."

c. Expulsion. A partner may be expelled by the co-partners for cause. The partnership agreement may specify certain reasons for dismissal. A partnership is dissolved by the expulsion of any partner for cause.[24]

2. By Operation of Law.

a. Death. U.P.A., section 31(4) provides for the automatic dissolution of the partnership upon the death of a partner.

b. Bankruptcy. Bankruptcy of any partner or of the partnership will cause the firm to dissolve.[25] The partner or firm in bankruptcy cannot *carry on* the partnership business.

3. By Decree of Court. An individual partner may petition the court to obtain its dissolution under certain circumstances. The issue before the court is whether or not the firm can continue to *carry on* partnership business. U.P.A., section 32 provides upon petition that the court *shall* decree a dissolution whenever any of the following occur:

a. Insanity. A partner has been declared a lunatic in any judicial proceeding or is shown to be of unsound mind.

b. Incapacity. A partner becomes in any way incapable of performing part of the partnership contract. For example, if a partner suffered a physical disability that prevented the partner from providing services, that fact would allow the court to dissolve the partnership even over the disabled partner's objections.

---

[23] U.P.A., sec. 31(1)(a).   [24] U.P.A., sec. 31(1)(d).

[25] U.P.A., sec. 31(5). As noted in chapter 30, Bankruptcy under the Bankruptcy Reform Act of 1978, a partnership is not entitled to a discharge in bankruptcy.

c. *Misconduct.* The conduct of a partner which tends to affect prejudicially the carrying on of the business is ground for another partner to petition for a dissolution. For instance, the conduct of a partner who continues to cause a disruption in the working relationship affecting the carrying on of the business is ground for dissolution.

d. *Operation Only at a Loss.* The statutory definition of a partnership (U.P.A., section 6) is to carry on the business for a profit. When the business of the partnership can be carried on only at a loss, a partner may petition the court for dissolution.

e. *Equitable Necessity.* U.P.A. provides a "catch all" provision in section 32(f), which allows dissolution "whenever other circumstances render a dissolution equitable." An example is, when a person is fraudulently induced to enter a partnership based on a misrepresentation in its financial statements.

Notice of Dissolution. The legal effect of dissolution is to terminate all authority of any partner to act for the partnership, except so far as may be necessary to wind up the partnership affairs.[26]

Notice to Partners. When dissolution is caused by an act of a partner (for instance, a partner who became disabled and could not continue working), the partner must give notice to the other partners of intent to withdraw from the firm. If the partner fails to give notice of withdrawal, the partner is liable to the other partners for his or her share of any liability created by any partner acting for the partnership as if the partnership had not been dissolved.

Notice to Third Parties. While dissolution terminates the authority of partners to continue to act for the partnership and continue the partnership business, nevertheless third persons who know of the partnership may not know that the partnership has been dissolved. As to them, the partners have *apparent authority* to continue the partnership business.

Also, with respect to the winding up process there is an apparent authority problem. The winding up process may be done only by partners who have not wrongfully caused a dissolution. They have *implied authority* to sell the partnership assets and pay off the various firm creditors with the proceeds. A partner who has wrongfully caused a dissolution (for example, by a withdrawal in violation of the partnership agreement) may have *apparent authority* to engage in the winding up process with third parties who knew of the partnership's dissolution but did not know which of the partners were ineligible to engage in the winding up process.

In order to eliminate the above instances of such apparent authority, notice must be given to those third parties of dissolution and partner ineligibility, except that no notice of dissolution is required when the dissolution is caused by operation of law (e.g., a partner's death or bankruptcy). There may be "actual notice" or "constructive notice."

1. Actual Notice. Third parties who have *extended credit* to the partnership (for example, past creditors) must be given actual notice; that is, they must actually receive notice that the firm has been dissolved and of partner ineligibility. This will destroy the apparent authority.

2. Constructive Notice. To third parties who knew of the partnership but never had extended credit to the firm, general notice, such as by local newspaper publication, is sufficient to eliminate the apparent authority. A third party is held to have notice without ever having read the notice.

---

[26] U.P.A., sec. 33.

Winding up Partnership Affairs

The winding up of partnership affairs is the orderly liquidation of partnership assets and the distribution of proceeds to partnership creditors and then to the partners themselves. Throughout the winding up process the partners continue to owe a fiduciary duty to each other. They are prevented from taking on new partnership business.

Right to Wind up Partnership Affairs.   U.P.A., section 37 provides that "unless otherwise agreed the partners who have not wrongfully dissolved the partnership or the legal representative of the last surviving partner, not bankrupt, have the right to wind up the partnership affairs." A court-appointed receiver will wind up the partnership if the dissolution is by court decree. A surviving partner is entitled to reasonable compensation for services rendered in winding up the partnership affairs.

Upon dissolution, each partner has the right to be paid his or her interest in the partnership. To prevent a liquidation, partners commonly enter into a "buy and sell" agreement that provides for a method to evaluate and pay the partners' interests.

In the following case the court was bound by the buy-sell provision of the partnership agreement that did not mention discounts in determining the value of a deceased partner's interest.

Winding up.

Facts
On July 1, 1950, Burt Marshall, defendant, Roy Marshall and Blanche Olsen executed a partnership agreement forming the M & M Investment Company. Blanche Olsen died October 29, 1971. Seattle-First National Bank (Seattle-First), plaintiff, was named executor of her will.

In valuing Olsen's partnership interest as part of her estate, Seattle-First valued the partnership's land only, without taking into account other assets or any liabilities. The partnership agreement contains a buy-sell provision: in the event of the death of one of the partners, the surviving partners would purchase the interest of the deceased partner. Marshall contends that the value of the partnership interest should have been discounted by sales costs, minority interest, and capital gains taxes to be paid upon sale of the partnership interest. Although these discount factors are not mentioned in the partnership agreement, Marshall's position is that these discounts are inherent in the concept of "current market value."

The trial court stated it was bound by the partnership agreement which does not mention such discounts in determining the value of a deceased partner's interest. Judgment for plaintiff. Defendant appealed.

Decision
Judgment of the trial court affirmed, for plaintiff Seattle-First.

Reasoning
In light of the considerations underlying a buy-sell provision, it is not unreasonable to conclude that the parties to the M & M Investment Company partnership agreement intended an outgoing partner's interest to be valued as indicated, without discounts. Because the partnership agreement setting forth the method of valuing a deceased partner's interest makes no allowance for discount factors, the trial court properly refused to discount the value of Olsen's partnership interest.

Seattle-First National Bank as Executor v. Burt W. Marshall, et al., 641 P.2d 1194 (Wash. 1982).

Distribution of Assets.   U.P.A., section 40 establishes the rules for settling accounts between the partners after dissolution as a part of the winding up process. The partners may by their own agreement change the statutory order of payments *among themselves*. Under 40(b), distribution of partnership assets is made: first, to creditors who are not partners; second, to partners for their advances to the partnership; third, to partners of their capital contributions; and fourth, to partners of their respective shares of the profits.

Insolvent Partnership with Solvent Partners.   Assume you are X, an equal partner in XYZ partnership. Your partnership agreement states "all partners are to share equally in the profits." The partnership has assets of $35,000 consisting of partners' capital contributions, and liabilities of $95,000, hence a partnership loss of $60,000. You and your partners are solvent, how will firm creditors be paid? To what extent may firm creditors reach your personal assets? Assume you, as Partner X, made a capital contribution of $20,000; Y, $10,000; and Z, $5,000. Firm creditors will be paid from partnership assets. Section 40(a) of the U.P.A. defines partnership assets as partnership property and the contributions of the partners necessary for the payment of partnership liabilities. Keep in mind that each partner must contribute toward the partnership losses according to his or her share in the profits.[27] From your personal assets you as partner X would pay firm creditors nothing; Y must pay $10,000; and Z $15,000, as illustrated by the following:

XYZ Partnership

Partnership Loss = $60,000

	Partner X	Partner Y	Partner Z
Capital contribution	$20,000	$10,000	$ 5,000
Personal payment to creditors	-0-	$10,000	$15,000
	$20,000	$20,000	$20,000

Insolvent Partnership with a Personally Insolvent Partner. If Partner Z and your XYZ firm are insolvent, as between the firm creditors and personal creditors of Partner Z, who will be given preference on firm assets? A court with equity powers will segregate the assets and liabilities of the partnership and of the individual partners. The court will apply the *doctrine of marshaling of assets*. Under U.P.A., section 40(i), the *partnership creditors* of the insolvent firm are entitled to be paid first from *partnership property*. The Bankruptcy Code, in section 723(a), provides that if there is a deficiency of partnership assets to pay in full the partnership creditors, then each general partner *is personally liable* for the full amount of such deficiency. The *individual personal creditors* of an insolvent partner are entitled to be paid first from the property of their *debtor/partner*. An insolvent partner must distribute his or her personal property in the following order: (1) personal creditors are to be paid first; (2) partnership creditors second; and (3) then partners who paid partnership creditors an amount in excess of their share of partnership liabilities. Personal creditors have no claim against the personal property of the other partners.

Marshaling of assets.

Summary Statement

1. A partnership is an association of two or more persons to carry on as co-owners a business for profit. Each element in this definition must be satisfied for there to be a partnership.
2. With the exception of Louisiana and Georgia, the Uniform Partnership Act is the statutory source of partnership law.
3. Under the aggregate theory of partnerships, each partner is personally liable for partnership claims; the partnership is legally viewed as a group of individual persons. Under the legal entity theory, the partnership has a legal status of its own apart from the individual partners.
4. Partnerships are classified as trading and nontrading.
5. General partners are classified as dormant, nominal, secret, and general.
6. The Articles of Partnership or Partnership Agreement generally include many items so that there is no uncertainty about the terms of the partners' relationship.
7. Any person competent to contract may be a partner; another partnership or a corporation may also become a partner.

---

[27] U.P.A., sec. 18(a); on dissolution, see sec. 40(d).

8. A partnership is a contractual relationship, and hence the parties must agree to its creation.
9. A partnership by estoppel occurs when a person by words or conduct represents himself, or permits himself to be represented, as a partner, and the third party in reasonable reliance on that holding out extends credit to the partnership.
10. Partnership property is held as a *tenancy in partnership* with the following characteristics:
    a. Any partner may use it for partnership purposes.
    b. A partner may not, without the consent of the other partners, transfer his or her interest in it.
    c. Personal creditors of a partner may not attach that partner's right in it.
    d. Upon a partner's death, the decedent partner's right in partnership property vests in the surviving partners.
    e. The surviving spouse of a partner has no interest in the deceased partner's property.
11. Dissolution is the change in the relation of the partners caused by any partner ceasing to be associated in the carrying on of the business. Upon dissolution, no partner is authorized to act for the partnership except to wind up partnership business.
12. Dissolution does not terminate the partnership entity.
13. Dissolution may be caused by the acts of the partners or by operation of law.
14. Actual notice of dissolution, and ineligibility to participate in the winding up process, must be given to third parties who had extended credit to the partnership, and constructive notice (e.g., newspaper publication) to third parties who knew of the partnership but had never extended credit to the firm.
15. Winding up of a partnership is the liquidation of partnership assets and distribution of proceeds to partnership creditors and then to the partners themselves.
16. After dissolution, partnership assets are distributed as follows:
    a. firm creditors who are not partners,
    b. partners' advances,
    c. partners' capital contributions,
    d. remaining assets are distributed as profits.

In the following case the court must determine if a partnership existed. Notice that the parties must agree to share profits and losses, and that at the trial the burden of proof is on the party seeking to prove that a partnership existed.

In re Wells' Will
321 N.Y.S.2d 200 (1971)

Gabrielli, Justice. Frank Wells died on March 10, 1969 and was survived by three sons and five daughters. By his will executed on September 13, 1968 he devised and bequeathed his estate to the petitioner, in trust, for the benefit equally of his eight children with the remainder to their issue. The principal assets are three farms valued at $267,300 and livestock and farm equipment valued at $14,950, the last-mentioned not being the subject of any controversy on these appeals. All three farms, recorded in decedent's name, had been worked as a dairy farm, and the livestock and equipment referred to were used on the farm.

The executor-trustee (petitioner) has filed a petition for the judicial settlement of its intermediate account and seeks a determination of the title to the farm and the ownership of the livestock and farm equipment, as well as a declaration that it has general authority to sell the farm. Objections to the account were filed by the three sons (objectants), in which they assert they were partners with decedent in the operation of the farm, and they also claim title thereto, including the livestock and farm equipment thereon. Decedent's daughters (respondents) filed replies controverting these objections.

... Decedent purchased the three farms separately, the first acquisition having occurred in 1937. The other two farms were acquired in 1939 and 1944, title being taken in the name of decedent and his wife, who later predeceased him. Thereafter title to all three farms continued in his name. When each son attained the age of fourteen, he quit school and went to work full time on the farm. They have continued to work there since. As each married, he received $50 a month, his maintenance, and the free use of a residence on the farm. Thereafter and for some six years prior to decedent's death, he paid each son a salary of $300 per month plus the free use of a residence. Throughout all this time decedent made all decisions relating to the financial operation and management of the farm, and objectants performed the required labor to operate it. All income realized from the sale of produce and milk sold from the farm was received by and paid to decedent, and all the proceeds from the operation of the farm went into his personal account. Decedent consistently filed individual personal and farm income tax returns which showed deductions for wages paid to the sons. No partnership tax return was ever filed. Additionally, all real estate taxes were paid by decedent and taken by him as an income tax deduction. It also appears that the objectants filed individual returns and never, of course, deducted any losses from the farm operation or reported any profits therefrom, reporting as income only the salary paid by decedent. Of further interest, each continued to receive his salary, despite business losses sustained by decedent during certain years. Significantly, decedent recited in paragraph VI of his will that "I presently own certain farm properties which are being operated by [my] sons for me," following which he made certain provisions for the continuance of the operation of the farm.

... Naturally, a partnership may result not only from an express agreement, but from circumstantial evidence as well. An indispensable requirement of a partnership is "a mutual promise or undertaking of the parties to share in the profits of the business and submit to the burden of making good the losses." Even if we were to conclude that the decedent and objectants are considered to have placed their money, efforts, and skills in a common business, they have not divided the profits nor borne the losses in any proportion, and objectants have not sustained their burden of showing the existence of a partnership. The evidence clearly establishes (and objectants concede) that missing are the indispensable essentials of a mutual promise to share the profits and an undertaking to assume the burden of making good the losses, without which no contract of partnership can be created under either the Common Law or statutory law of New York.

The decree should be modified by deleting so much therefrom as (1) declares that a partnership existed among decedent and objectants and (2) directs that there be an accounting of the assets and profits thereof, and as so modified, it should be affirmed.

Questions and Case Problems

1. In late February or early March of 1977 Gregory Walsh, plaintiff, contacted Chet Ellingson at the Ellingson Agency, defendant, an insurance and real estate corporation, concerning an advertised parcel of real estate. After finding the price prohibitive on this piece of property, he detailed his needs to Ellingson. Ellingson showed Walsh a lot that he thought might meet Walsh's needs. Ellingson told Walsh that he owned the property with "some partners" and that it was for sale for $30,000. On March 17, 1977, Walsh returned to the Ellingson Agency and told Ellingson that he wished to buy the property for $29,000 cash. A buy-sell agreement was drafted and signed by both parties, and Walsh gave Ellingson $1,000 in earnest money. A closing date of April 5, 1977 was set. Prior to March 17 the other owners of the property had not been disclosed. Shortly after March 17, 1977 Walsh received a title insurance policy which revealed that the property was owned by the Ellingson Agency and Four Seasons Motor Inn, also a defendant, as tenants in common. This is the first time that Walsh learned who the other "partners" were. On April 5, 1977, Walsh went to the Ellingson Agency and told Ellingson that he was ready to write a check pursuant to the buy-sell agreement. Ellingson told Walsh that he could not get his partners to sell, and he offered to return the $1,000. Walsh would not accept the return of his earnest money. Ellingson testified that he had no authority to act for the Four Seasons but that he thought the sale would be acceptable to the Four Seasons. Testimony was also adduced concerning a prior land holding between Ellingson Agency and Four Seasons.

According to the testimony, the two corporations had purchased another parcel of land which was sold in 1975. Ellingson was approached by an individual concerning the sale of the first parcel. He testified that he talked it over with the directors of Four Seasons and they decided on a price to offer the prospective buyer. The offer was accepted and the proceeds were equally divided between the Ellingson Agency and the Four Seasons. Plaintiff Walsh filed a complaint against the two defendants seeking the execution and delivery of a warranty deed to the subject property or in the alternative a quitclaim deed of Ellingson's interest in the property and actual damages as reimbursement for expenses occasioned as a result of the defendants' refusal to perform. Plaintiff alleged that Ellingson represented that he was a partner and agent of the other partners, and was authorized to contract to sell the property. Was there a partnership between the Ellingson Agency and the Four Seasons Motor Inn, and if so, are defendants bound by the buy-sell agreement? [*Gregory J. Walsh v. Ellingson Agency and Four Seasons Motor Inn,* 613 P.2d 1381 (Mont. 1980).]

2. In 1959 plaintiff met Philip Miller. Later, Mr. Miller asked plaintiff to marry him, to move to Jackson, and to help him run the nursery business. Plaintiff gave up her well-paying job to move to Jackson. The business was close to failing at the time of their marriage. By 1974, the time of Mr. Miller's death, the business was prosperous. Plaintiff did not make any capital contribution to the partnership, although she held a management position in the nursery business and did physical labor. She kept all the books and hired and fired employees. In 1960 a business registration certificate was filed for the nursery listing it as a partnership. Annual tax forms listed the business as a sole proprietorship and plaintiff's occupation as a housewife. There never was any formal written partnership agreement. Mrs. Miller, the plaintiff, sued defendant bank, her husband's executor, claiming that she was a partner in the nursery business with her deceased husband. Was there a partnership? [*Miller v. City Bank and Trust Company,* 266 N.W.2d 687 (Mich. 1978).]

3. X owns a building with a restaurant rented to Z. Z is the manager of the restaurant and is authorized by X to make all food purchases in X's name. In addition to rental payments, Z pays X 15 percent of the monthly net profits. Y, a creditor of the restaurant, sued X and Z as partners. Are they partners?

4. A claim was filed and recited that the claimant, a dissolved law partnership, had rendered legal services on behalf of decedent during his lifetime; that decedent had acknowledged the debt and had paid part of it before his death. Claimant alleged that the balance was $24,750. The court dismissed the claim and stated that since claimant was not in existence, it could not file a claim. Claimant maintains that in dismissing the claim the court failed to perceive the distinction between dissolution and termination of a partnership. Did the court err in dismissing the claim? [*Horton, Davis & McCaleb v. Richard Howe, Ex'r of the Estate of Earl E. Howe,* 85 Ill.App.3d 970 (1980).]

5. Juanita Bailes and Fred Bailes were married in 1953. They began operation of a business, Bailes Best Made Dog Food, as a partnership in 1958, and continued such operation until Fred Bailes died intestate (without a will) in 1969. Surviving him were Juanita, his wife, and an only son Fred, Jr., by a previous marriage. Plaintiff, Fred, Jr., claims that all the assets of the business should become part of the estate of his father and should be distributed according to the law of descent and distribution. Juanita Bailes, defendant, objects. Is plaintiff entitled to his father's interest in the partnership? [*Bailes v. Bailes,* 549 S.W.2d 69 (Ark. 1977).]

6. X, Y, and Z were doctors who owned their medical building as partners. The building was owned free and clear of any mortgage debt. Z died and his widow sued X and Y for her husband's interest in the medical building. Decide.

7. Plaintiff, a judgment creditor of defendant partner, seeks to impose and foreclose (enforce) a **lien** on defendant's undivided interest in *partnership* real estate. The court held that foreclosing on real estate of a partnership to satisfy the judgment debt of an individual partner was legal. Plaintiff appealed. You decide. [*Buckman v. Goldblatt,* 314 N.E.2d 188 (Ohio 1974).]

lien
a legal right in another's property as security for the performance of an obligation

8. Plaintiff, Gus N. Jebeles, and defendant, Gus V. Costellos, entered into an oral partnership agreement under the business name of "Dino's Hot Dogs." A rift was created between plaintiff and defendant and the defendant ceased to remit any sums to plaintiff as his share of the profits of the partnership, changed the locks on the doors to the establishment and has failed or refused to furnish plaintiff with an accounting of the partnership business. Because of the unhappy and hostile attitude that exists between plaintiff and defendant, it is evident that these two men cannot engage in a business undertaking in a manner which would continue the contacts that normally exist between partners in an active business. Jebeles filed his complaint seeking a dissolution of the partnership and a full and complete accounting by Costellos for all profits received. Costellos counterclaimed that there was no partnership agreement, but that, if there was one, Jebeles breached it. The court ordered an accounting, but refused to dissolve the partnership. Should the court have dissolved the partnership? [*Gus N. Jebeles v. Gus V. Costellos* and *Gus V. Costellos v. Gus N. Jebeles,* 391 So.2d 1024 (Ala. 1980).]

9. An agent for Marvil Properties (Marvil), plaintiff, a general partnership, entered into a contract in the name of the partnership with Fripp Island Development Corporation (Fripp), defendant, for the sale by Fripp to Marvil of certain real estate. This action for specific performance of the sales agreement was brought by Marvil in the partnership's name without naming the partners. Does a general partnership have the capacity to sue in its name? [*Marvil Properties v. Fripp Island Development Corp.,* 258 S.E.2d 106 (S.C. 1979).]

10. In In re *Wells' Will,* 321 N.Y.S.2d 200 (1971),[28] if you were one of the sons of the decedent, what would you have done while your father was alive so as to be able, after his death, to establish that there was a partnership?

---

[28] See pp. 591–92.

Partnership Management and the Authority of Partners 39

After you have read this chapter, you should be able to:

1. Identify the source of law regarding the management of a partnership.
2. Identify trading and nontrading partnerships.
3. Explain the source of a partner's implied authority.
4. Explain what is meant by the implied authority of a partner, and list and give examples.
5. Discuss the express authority of a partner.
6. List and explain the five prohibited transactions under the U.P.A. on a partner's implied authority to bind the firm.
7. Explain what is meant by a partner's apparent authority.
8. Explain when a majority is required to effect a partnership decision; explain when a unanimous vote is required.

Introduction

Partnerships engage in a broad spectrum of business activities ranging from the small hardware store to the New York Wall Street law offices. The management problems and contractual relationships encountered by each partnership will vary, depending upon the size and nature of the partnership.

This chapter examines the legal procedures established by the Uniform Partnership Act to manage the partnership and engage in contracts with third parties. The law of **agency** as discussed in Part 7, Agency and Employment, will apply.[1]

Actual Authority of the Partners

*Each partner is an **agent** of the partnership for the purpose of carrying on, in the usual way, the partnership business.*[2] Hence, all partners have **actual authority** to bind the firm with third parties unless prohibited by the partnership agreement. The partners also have equal voice in the internal management of the business, unless denied by the agreement.[3] In addition to the actual authority, a partner may have *apparent authority* to bind the firm with third parties as that partner carries on the partnership business in the usual and customary manner.

Express Authority

Partners have, by virtue of their agreement, **express authority** to act on behalf of the partnership. Thus, a managing partner of a retail department store has *express authority* to purchase inventory on credit and thereby obligate the firm. The partnership agreement will determine the extent of the individual partners' express authority but not their apparent authority.

Implied Authority

A partner may have **implied authority** to bind the firm with third parties. This may occur even if the partnership agreement or the partners do not give him or her any authority. The extent of the partner's implied authority will depend upon the scope of the firm's business and its character as a "trading" or "nontrading" partnership.[4] A *trading* partnership is engaged in buying and selling *property*. A *nontrading* partnership is engaged in selling *services*. The following are common examples of a partner's implied authority to contract with third persons on behalf of the partnership.[5]

Contracts to Buy and Sell.   The authority of a partner to buy or sell the firm's assets depends upon whether the firm is a trading or nontrading partnership. A partnership engaged in manufacturing, wholesaling, or retailing is a trading partnership. Partnerships of lawyers, accountants, and doctors are nontrading partnerships. In the following case the court characterized the partnership operations as nontrading and found that a partner was not acting within the scope of the business when he sold lumber to the plaintiff.

---

[1] U.P.A., sec. 4(3), and *Rice v. Jackson,* 171 Pa. 89 (1895).

[2] U.P.A., sec. 9(1).   [3] U.P.A., sec. 18(e).

[4] See p. 580 for classification of partnerships.

[5] See Alan R. Bromberg, *Crane and Bromberg on Partnership,* (St. Paul: West Publishing Co., 1968), p. 280 for a discussion of trading and nontrading partnerships.

---

agency
a legal relationship between two persons who agree that one is to act on behalf of the other, subject to the other's control

agent
a person authorized to act on behalf of another and subject to the other's control

actual authority
express and implied authority

express authority
an agent's authority specifically expressed in the principal's manifestation to the agent

implied authority
an agent's authority which the agent reasonably can understand he has from the principal's manifestation to him, but not expressed therein

Facts

Bole, the plaintiff, instituted this suit against Lyle, Peters, and Barton, partners of the Cherokee Box and Handle Company, to recover funds advanced to defendants for the purchase of lumber which was never delivered. Barton, the managing partner, signed the sales contract on behalf of the partnership. Bole paid Barton for the lumber. The partnership received no part of the proceeds of the check, and the other partners knew nothing of the transaction until plaintiff's claim was made after the dissolution of the partnership. Is each of the partners liable for the claim?

Decision

No. Judgment for defendants.

Reasoning

Sales made by a partner in a trading firm are not viewed with the same strictness as in nontrading firms, such as here involved, because in trading firms sales are usually within the scope of the business while in nontrading firms they are exceptional and only incidental to the main business. In this case there was nothing in the firm name to suggest that it was in the business of selling lumber. Plaintiff, Bole, chose to deal with Barton without knowing anything of the nature of the partnership, and the non-participating partners were in no way responsible for his loss; recovery should be against Barton alone.

Bole v. Lyle, et al., 287 S.W.2d 931 (Tenn. 1956).

To Borrow Money and Execute Commercial Paper. A trading partnership that is buying and selling inventory will have frequent needs to borrow money and execute promissory notes in the firm name. A partner in such a firm has implied authority to do both and to pledge partnership property, provided that it is reasonably necessary to carry on the partnership business. A partner in a nontrading partnership does not have this implied authority unless an emergency requires it or it is customary for that business to borrow money and sign notes.

Employment. Partners have implied authority to employ personnel whose services are necessary to carry on the partnership business.

Firm Debts. A partner has implied authority to pay the *partnership's creditors* with partnership funds. However, a partner may not pay his or her *personal creditors* with firm funds.

Settle and Compromise Claims. A partner has implied authority to settle and compromise a claim of a partnership creditor.

Representations and Admissions. A partner has implied authority to make representations and admissions that may bind the firm, provided that they are made in the ordinary and usual course of firm business. For example, X, a partner, admitted to Z, a firm creditor, that Z's claim was owed. X's admission will bind the firm.[6]

Notice to a Partner. A partner has implied authority to receive notice on any matter relating to partnership affairs, and such notice will bind the partnership, except in the case of fraud.[7] To illustrate, if a landlord gave notice of an increase in the partnership rent to a partner, the notice will bind the firm.

Limitation on Authority

Partners have no implied authority to perform acts that are not customary and usual in the carrying on of the partnership business. The partnership agreement, however, may give a partner express authority to do acts not for the carrying on of usual partnership business. However, certain transactions are prohibited under U.P.A., section 9(3).

A partner may not assign the partnership property for the benefit of creditors. If a partner made such an assignment, it would prevent the firm from conducting its usual business. The U.P.A. allows an assignment if authorized by the other partners.[8]

---

[6] U.P.A., sec. 11.   [7] U.P.A., sec. 12.   [8] U.P.A., sec. 9(3)(a).

confession of judgment
a party's consent to jurisdiction and judgment of a court without a trial in a civil case

A partner may not dispose of the goodwill of the business. A partner has no implied authority to sell the partnership goodwill, because this would cause a discontinuance of firm business. Partnership authorization would be required from *all* the other partners.[9]

A partner may not do any act which would make it impossible to carry on the ordinary business of the partnership. For example, an individual partner has no implied authority to sell an office computer that is required to process its monthly billings.[10]

A partner may not **confess a judgment.** An individual partner has no implied authority to admit that a claim is due, because the partners have the right to defend the claim in court.[11] For example, in a malpractice claim against a medical partnership, an admission of liability by a doctor partner who treated the patient will not bind the firm.

A partner may not submit a partnership claim to arbitration. A partner cannot submit a firm dispute to arbitration without the consent of the other partners unless the firm has ceased doing business.[12] Since arbitration is becoming a common method of resolving disputes[13] and is found in many contracts, third persons dealing with a partnership should insist on unanimous consent in a contract that provides for arbitration.

Apparent Authority

Partners have apparent authority[14] to carry on in the usual way the partnership business, and third persons who reasonably rely on such authority can bind the firm.[15] A partner without actual or apparent authority cannot bind the firm with third parties. If the third person knows of the lack of authority, he cannot bind the firm for the partner's unauthorized acts.

Firm Management

The internal management of the partnership is accomplished by the partners' vote in the decision-making process.

Ordinary Business

At a partnership meeting the *decision of the majority* will govern, provided that it is an *ordinary business* matter and the vote does not contradict an agreement between the parties. Hence, the majority may decide those business affairs that are *normal and customary* in carrying on the firm's business.[16] For example, in a construction firm, the majority may decide to rent construction equipment over the objection of the minority. All of the partners will be bound under the equipment lease. Half of the partners is not a majority.

Extraordinary Business

A *unanimous vote* by the partners is necessary for a business decision that would change the partnership agreement.[17] Thus, changing the location of the firm is a matter all the partners must agree to, unless the partnership agreement provides otherwise.

In the following case the partners incorporated part of the business without the consent of one partner, who brought suit to reach his partnership interest in the corporation.

---

[9] U.P.A., sec. 9(3)(b).

[10] U.P.A., sec. 9(3)(c). [11] U.P.A., sec. 9(3)(d). [12] U.P.A., sec. 9(3)(e).

[13] See p. 16 for a discussion of arbitration.

[14] For the concept of apparent authority, see p. 518.

[15] U.P.A., sec. 9(1). [16] U.P.A., sec. 18(h). [17] U.P.A., sec. 18(h).

Facts
Fortugno, plaintiff, a member of a family partnership that was organized to collect and sell manure, brought an action for its dissolution. The partnership, Hudson Manure Company, sold its manure to mushroom growers in southeastern Pennsylvania. In the course of its operation, the partnership found it convenient to put certain of its activities in corporate form in order to limit the liability of the individual partners. Fortugno refused to authorize the corporate division of the partnership and claimed that the enterprises constitute a single integrated partnership, whether or not any phase of the business was conducted in corporate form. He sought to be paid in cash for his partnership interest in both the partnership and the corporation and requested the court to order the sale of the corporate assets. May the partnership property be traced into the corporation?

Decision
Yes. Judgment for Fortugno.

Reasoning
Less than all the partners may not bind the partnership by an act not performed for the purpose of carrying on the usual partnership business, unless authorized by the other partners. Because Fortugno never ratified the act of incorporating part of the partnership, no assets of the partnership may remain in the corporation.

Fortugno v. Hudson Manure Company, 144 A.2d 207 (N.J. 1958).

Summary Statement

1. Partnership management is governed by the Uniform Partnership Act and agency law. The partners by agreement may change the effect of the U.P.A., which states that "all partners have equal rights in the management and operation of the partnership business" (sec. 18(e)).
2. The extent of a partner's contribution to the firm does not affect that partner's equal voice in management.
3. The partnership agreement grants to each partner *express authority* to act as an agent on behalf of the partnership.
4. Implied authority of a partner to act on behalf of the firm depends upon whether it is a trading or nontrading firm.
5. The implied authority of a partner depends on the nature of the firm; some common examples of a partner's implied authority are authority to:
    a. buy and sell inventory in a trading partnership;
    b. borrow money and execute commercial paper in a trading partnership;
    c. employ personnel;
    d. pay firm debts with partnership funds;
    e. settle and compromise claims;
    f. make admissions that will bind the firm if made in the ordinary and usual course of firm business; and
    g. receive notice on any matter relating to partnership affairs.
6. Unless authorized by *all* the other partners, or unless they have abandoned the business, a partner may not:
    a. assign the partnership property in trust for creditors;
    b. dispose of the partnership's goodwill;
    c. do any other act which would make it impossible to carry on the ordinary partnership business;
    d. confess a judgment; or
    e. submit a partnership claim to arbitration.
7. A majority vote is required to effect *ordinary* business decisions connected with the partnership business.
8. A unanimous vote of the partners is required to change the partnership agreement or any material agreement between the partners.

In the following case the court held that a partner had actual authority to execute notes for partnership obligations that bind the partnership and its individual partners.

Leo Womack, Adminstrator v. First National Bank of San Augustine, Texas
613 S.W.2d 548 (Tex. 1981)

J. W. Summers, Chief Justice. The First National Bank of San Augustine, Texas, (bank), plaintiff, sued Charles C. McClanahan (Charles) and his brother, Dr. H. Lane McClanahan (Lane), to recover upon five promissory notes. The bank alleged that the notes represented individual obligations of each of the brothers or, alternatively, were partnership obligations executed by Charles on behalf of a partnership composed of the two brothers named McClanahan Brothers. Charles answered, admitting liability and claiming that the notes were partnership notes. Dr. H. Lane McClanahan filed a general denial. Prior to trial, Lane died, and Leo Womack was appointed as Temporary Administrator of the decedent's estate and substituted as a party defendant. The case was tried before a jury which found that the notes were partnership obligations and judgment was rendered for the First National Bank of San Augustine, from which Womack appeals.

On August 4, 1972, the McClanahan brothers executed a partnership agreement for the express purpose of engaging in the operation of a hog farm. By this agreement, which consisted of only four provisions and covered only a half page, the brothers agreed that Charles was to devote his time to the business and in return, receive 75% of the profits and share 50% of the losses while Lane would receive 25% of the profits and share 50% of the losses. Additionally, the agreement provided that the partnership funds would be kept in a joint account and Charles agreed ". . . to keep a complete record of the business, and shall be subject to inspection by Lane at any time." The agreement does not contain any provision relative to the partners' authority, nothing limiting their authority nor defining it. No partnership name is indicated in the agreement and there is testimony that the partnership operated under the names "McClanahan Farms," "C. C. McClanahan Farms," "McClanahan Brothers," and "Sugar Bush Farms" interchangeably.

Following formation of the partnership, Lane and Charles began executing a series of notes with appellee-bank as payee. All notes reflect on their face that they were executed in contemplation of investment in the partnership business, each containing notations that they are secured by either livestock, feeding equipment or hogs. The notes are signed "Charles McClanahan" or "C. C. McClanahan" and "H. Lane McClanahan, M.D."

In full recognition of that rule (that one is not liable on an instrument unless he signs it), our supreme court has stated that there are several instances in which a non-signing partner may be liable upon a note signed by another partner. A partner's authority to bind the partnership and his partners is governed by the Texas version of the Uniform Partnership Act unless expanded or limited by the partnership agreement.

Section 9 of the U.P.A. provides that: "(1) Every partner is an agent of the partnership for the purpose of its business, and the act of every partner, including the execution in the partnership name of any instrument, for apparently carrying on in the usual way the business of the partnership of which he is a member binds the partnership, unless the partner so acting has in fact no authority to act for the partnership in the particular matter, and the person with whom he is dealing has knowledge of the fact that he has no such authority." As we construe this section, Dr. McClanahan may be held liable on the notes as a partner if they were executed for "apparently carrying on in the usual way the business of the partnership." Thus, since the partnership agreement was silent as to Charles McClanahan's authority to issue negotiable paper in the partnership name, he had the actual or express authority to do so under Sec. 9 if such act were for the purpose of "apparently carrying on" the business of the partnership in the way other firms engaged in the same business in the locality usually transacts business, or in the way in which the particular partnership usually transacts its business. Whether Dr. McClanahan was aware that Charles was executing the notes has no effect upon his authority to do so, "for it is familiar law that each partner of a partnership has, as agent, power to bind all members of his firm for an indebtedness incurred in the prosecution of his firm's business; and this is true even though members other than the acting one is (sic) without knowledge of the obligatory act." Stated another way, it has been said that an agent's authority is presumed to be co-extensive with the business entrusted to his care.

He is limited in his authority to such acts as are incident to the management of the particular business with which he is entrusted. Thus, the inquiry becomes whether Charles McClanahan executed the notes in order to conduct the business which Dr. McClanahan testified had been entrusted to his care, in its ordinary and normal manner, there being no evidence in the record as to the normal business transactions of other hog farms in San Augustine County.

We believe that there was ample evidence to support the jury's finding that Charles McClanahan had the authority to execute the notes and bind the partnership thereto. The notes themselves reflect that the monies loaned upon the notes were invested in the partnership business; the farm was initially financed over an eight month period by the execution and payment of a series of notes; the partnership agreement did not attempt, in any manner, to limit Charles McClanahan's authority. This conclusion is further buttressed by the fact that partners normally have the right to execute negotiable paper for commercial purposes consistent with the object of the partnership and for the benefit of the partnership. Where the partnership business contemplates periodical or continuous or frequent purchasing, not as incidental to an occupation, but for the purpose of selling again the thing purchased, it is usual and customary to purchase on credit and to execute paper evidencing the existence of the partnership debt. Both Charles McClanahan and Ray Neal McEachern testified that Charles would execute a note, buy hogs and feed them on the proceeds thereof, sell them and pay on the notes. Such was the customary business of the partnership. We must therefore conclude that Charles McClanahan had the actual authority to execute the notes in question as partnership obligations.

Judgment affirmed.

Questions and Case Problems

1. Voeller, the managing partner of the Pay-Out Drive-In Theatre, signed a contract with Hodge, plaintiff, for the sale of a small parcel of land belonging to the partnership. That parcel, although adjacent to the theater, was not used in theater operations. The agreement for the sale of land stated that it was between Hodge and the Pay-Out Drive-In Theatre, a partnership. Plaintiff sued the defendants, partners of the Theatre, for specific performance of the contract. The trial court found that Voeller had apparent authority to execute the contract on behalf of the partnership, and that the contract should be specifically enforced against the defendant partners. Defendants appeal arguing that Voeller did not have apparent authority to sell the property. The other partners have maintained from the inception of this controversy that Voeller did not have apparent authority to sell this property. Did Voeller have apparent authority to sell the property? [*Hodge v. Garrett, Voeller,* et al., 614 P.2d 420 (Ida. 1980).]

2. Oswald, plaintiff, and Leckey, defendant, signed a partnership agreement to conduct an accounting practice. The partnership was not harmonious and was terminated. Plaintiff seeks an accounting and claims defendant had no authority to write off uncollectible accounts without plaintiff's consent while winding up the partnership affairs. Defendant claimed he acted in good faith and has the power to compromise claims. You decide. [*Oswald v. Leckey,* 572 P.2d 1316 (Or. 1977).]

3. X, Y, and Z ran a college bookstore as partners. At a partnership meeting they agreed that X and Y would work in the store but Z would be the only partner authorized to order textbooks. A salesperson who knew that X was a partner, but did not know that she was without authority to order textbooks, took an order from her for 1,000 books. The partnership refused to accept or pay for the books. Can the textbook company collect?

4. X and Z were partners in a medical practice. Y, a patient of Z, was billed $600 for an operation. Y claimed that the bill was unfair, and Z agreed to compromise by accepting $300 as payment in full. X told Z that Z had no authority to accept less than the original bill and told Y that the partnership was going to sue for the additional $300. Y claimed that partner X was bound by the compromise. Decide.

5. A client owed an accounting partnership $200 for services rendered to her. She paid the money to a partner who used it to pay off a personal home improvement loan. Must she repay the fee to the partnership?

6. A Boston partnership engaged in the antique business desired to move the firm to Vermont. At a partnership meeting one of the three partners objected to the move. Is a majority vote sufficient to move the firm to Vermont?

7. X and Y operated a construction business as partners. Z, a customer, complained to X that the construction of his apartment building was defective. X found Z to be unreasonable but agreed to submit the dispute to arbitration. Y protested the arbitration procedure and claimed that the partnership is not bound to arbitrate. Is Y correct?

8. X, Y, and Z are partners in an accounting firm. X and Y want to rent additional space on the floor where they always operated the firm. Z feels it is too expensive to do so and votes against it. X and Y sign the lease and rent the new space. Is Z liable as a partner on the lease?

9. Feingold, plaintiff, sued William and Charlotte Davis, husband and wife and owners of Davis Nursing Home as a partnership. Mr. Davis signed a purchase and sale agreement to sell the nursing home to Feingold, including its assets and goodwill. Mrs. Davis, his co-partner, never signed nor consented to the agreement and refused to convey the property. Feingold sought specific performance of the purchase and sale agreement. Decide. [*Feingold v. Davis*, 282 A.2d 291 (Pa. 1971).]

10. After reading the case of *Leo Womack, Administrator v. First National Bank of San Augustine*, 613 S.W.2d 548 (Tex. 1981),[18] what specific provision should have been in the partnership agreement to have protected Dr. McClanahan and his estate from this lawsuit by the payee/bank?

---

[18] See pp. 600–601.

Rights, Duties, and Remedies of Partners among Themselves 40

After you have read this chapter, you should be able to:

1. List and explain the eight rights of a partner as an owner of the firm.
2. Explain the remedies of a partner.
3. List and explain the five duties of partners to each other.
4. Analyze and discuss the nature of a partner's liability on firm contracts and torts committed by a partner or an employee of the firm.
5. Explain the liability of an incoming partner entering an existing firm.
6. Explain the nature and extent of a partner's liability.
7. Explain the effect of dissolution of the firm on a partner's existing liability.
8. List and explain the three property rights a partner has in the partnership.

Introduction

This chapter explains the rights and duties of the partners among themselves as well as the partnership's liability to third persons who have dealt with the firm. The U.P.A., section 18 establishes the rules that determine the rights and duties of the partners, *unless their partnership agreement provides otherwise.* Also, since partners are general agents of the partnership, the law of agency applies[1] and spells out the common law agent duties of each partner, unless the partnership agreement provides otherwise.

Rights of Partners

Each partner, as a co-owner of the partnership, has, *unless otherwise agreed,* the following statutory rights under U.P.A., section 18.

Profits and losses.

Share Equally in Profits and Losses

Unless otherwise agreed, each partner has the right to share in the profits and surplus equally.[2] This rule is not affected by a disproportionate amount of capital and contributions or the amount of services rendered by a partner. Thus, if A contributes $10,000 and B $5,000 and C services only, they each will share the profits equally unless otherwise agreed. Unless otherwise agreed, losses are shared as profits are shared.

Participation in management.

Equal Rights in Management

Each partner has an equal right in the management of the firm.[3] Thus, a partner who provides only services has the same voice in management as the partner who made a substantial capital contribution.

Receipt of interest.

Payment of Interest

Loans. A partner who makes a loan to the firm shall be paid interest from the date of the loan. An advance by a partner, beyond the amount of capital which the partnership agreement obligated the partner to contribute, is a loan to the partnership. The lending partner is entitled to interest from the date of advance and to repayment when the loan is due. If partnership funds are insufficient to pay the note on its due date, the co-partners must contribute their share of the amount due.

Capital Contributions. A partner who makes a capital contribution shall receive interest *from the date when repayment should be made.* The contribution used in the business should be returned upon dissolution after partnership debts have been paid. If the contribution is then not returned to the partner, unless otherwise agreed the partner is entitled to interest on the amount due. In the following case a partner's skill and labor on behalf of the partnership were determined to be a part of the partner's capital contribution to the firm to which the partner was entitled on dissolution, as well as interest thereon, when the other partner refused to make payment.

Facts
Plaintiff, Thompson, was a partner with defendant, Beth, in a business organized to erect and operate a resort area. Thompson was a skilled cabinet maker and electrician who invested $400 and contributed 2,000 hours of labor in building the lake resort. Upon dissolution of the partnership, plaintiff made demand for an accounting and payment of his share of the proceeds from the sale of the property. Defendant refused. Thompson claimed he was entitled to compensation for his 2,000 hours of labor as a capital investment and to interest on his share from the date of the sale of the partnership assets.

Decision
Judgment for plaintiff, Thompson.

---

[1] U.P.A., sec. 4(3). [2] U.P.A., secs. 26 and 18(a). [3] U.P.A., sec. 18(e).

Reasoning
A partner who has been active in contributing his skill and labor on a day-to-day basis is compensated by a share in the partnership profits. This rule does not apply where the skill and labor of the partner are his contribution to the capital assets of the partnership. Here, Thompson's return of his contribution on liquidation is not remuneration, but a return on capital investment, and he is entitled to interest from the date of sale of the partnership assets.

Thompson v. Beth, 111 N.W.2d 171 (Wis. 1961).

Partnership Books

The partnership books and records shall be kept at the principal place of business of the partnership. Each partner has the right to inspect and copy the books at any time. However, the partnership agreement may prevent a partner from inspecting the books and using the information for other than partnership purposes.

Availability of partnership books.

New Partners

A new partner may be admitted only with the consent of *all* the partners unless the partnership agreement provides otherwise. Recall that a partnership is a contractual relationship, and the admission of a new member is a material change in the agreement. The new incoming partner is liable for partnership obligations before and after becoming a partner. However, the incoming partner's personal assets cannot be reached to satisfy partnership creditors whose claims existed *before* he or she became a partner.

If a new partner promises the co-partners that he or she will pay old partnership creditors, the latter will generally be entitled to enforce the new partner's promise as third party creditor beneficiaries.[4]

If the incoming partner buys a partnership interest from a retiring partner, the transaction is not within the bulk sales law because the new partner is bound to pay the old partner's debts from partnership property. However, the incoming partner must give public notice of the purchase.[5]

Admission of new partners.

Partnership Assets

Partnership *property* is what the partnership has accumulated. It is a part of the *assets* of the partnership, which consist of (1) the *partnership property* and (2) the *contributions of each of the partners* necessary for payment of all partnership liabilities.

Partnership assets.

Reimbursement and Indemnity

Provided that a partner is acting reasonably and in good faith, a partner is entitled to be **reimbursed** for payments made and reasonable personal debts incurred by the partner in properly carrying on the partnership business. For example, an accountant who paid for office supplies with a personal check, is entitled to be reimbursed by the firm. The accountant is also entitled to be **indemnified** for damage to the accountant's property while used in the partnership business.

reimbursement
one person's right against another to be repaid money paid on the other's behalf for which the latter was responsible

indemnity
an absolute obligation to pay for another's loss

Compensation

No partner is entitled to extra compensation for services rendered in carrying on partnership business. It is important for the partnership agreement to provide for salaries to be paid to the partners because sharing the profits is considered adequate compensation, unless the parties otherwise agree. It is not unusual in a professional partnership for one partner to be authorized as a general manager. For example, a law firm may designate a

Compensation for services rendered to the partnership.

---

[4] See pp. 187–88 for a discussion of third party beneficiaries.

[5] UCC 6–103(6); see pp. 281–82 for a discussion of the bulk sales law.

partner who will expend additional time in managing the law practice. Unless the partnership agreement entitles a partner to additional compensation for additional services, there is no extra compensation. The U.P.A. does provide for reasonable compensation for a *surviving* partner's services in winding up the partnership affairs.[6]

In the following case the court held that, to be awarded compensation, a partner must show that his services extended beyond normal partnership functions, in the absence of an agreement to the contrary.

Facts
From 1952 to 1973, Sydney Altman, plaintiff, and Ashley Altman, defendant, operated a number of partnerships engaged in real estate construction and management. Sydney and Ashley received identical salaries, and each brother was permitted to charge certain personal expenses to the partnerships. In January 1973, Sydney moved to Florida to establish residency in that state for the purpose of obtaining a divorce. The brothers discussed Sydney's move at this time, and they agreed that Sydney would return to Pennsylvania after his divorce and resume full-time duties with the partnerships.

When an agreement could not be reached regarding Sydney's retirement, Sydney brought this action in the district court seeking judicial dissolution of the partnerships. Judgment was rendered for Sydney and Ashley appealed. Ashley challenges the district court's holding that he is not entitled to compensation beyond his share of partnership profits for managing the partnerships between August 1973 and June 1977.

Decision
Affirmed, judgment for plaintiff, Sydney Altman.

Reasoning
A right to compensation arises only where the services rendered extend beyond normal partnership functions. Ashley, however, does not expressly contend that the services he performed went beyond normal partnership functions. In contending that it would be highly inequitable in this case to deny compensation, Ashley emphasizes that after August 1973 the entire management and supervision of the partnerships were left to him. He asserts that he not only preserved the partnerships' properties but also maximized profits during this period. However, Ashley must also show that his services extended beyond normal partnership functions.

The district court's factual finding that Ashley's services did not warrant compensation beyond his share of the partnership profits was not clearly erroneous. Affirmed, for plaintiff.

Altman v. Altman, 653 F.2d 755 (1981).

Accounting

> Formal and informal accounting.

A partner may, under limited circumstances as provided by U.P.A., section 22, require a *formal* accounting during the ordinary operation of the partnership. This right should be distinguished from the informal process of inspecting and copying the books and records. The right to a formal accounting occurs:

1. when the partner is wrongfully excluded from the partnership business, or
2. when the right to a formal accounting exists under the partnership agreement, or
3. when a partner has acquired secret profits without the consent of the other partners from any transaction connected with the firm, or
4. whenever other circumstances render it just and reasonable.

Remedies of Partners

Contracts

The partnership is liable for the contracts of its partners as agents of the firm.

Every partner is an agent of the partnership for the purpose of its business. . . . (U.P.A., section 9.)

Hence, contract liability *of the partners* in carrying out partnership business is the responsibility of the firm. As to third persons, the partners are liable *jointly* (collectively) for partnership *contracts* (U.P.A., sec. 15(b)).

---

[6] U.P.A., sec. 18(f).

A breach of the partnership agreement subjects the wrongdoer to contract liability. Generally, the usual common law remedies for breach of contract are available to partners among themselves.[7] A partner has the remedy of an *accounting* if the partner sues the partnership.

Torts

All partners are *jointly and severally* (individually) liable to third persons *for torts* committed in the ordinary course of the partnership business.

tort
a civil (private) noncontractual wrong for which a court will give a remedy

Where, by any wrongful act or omission of any partner acting in the ordinary course of the business of the partnership . . . loss or injury is caused to any person, not being a partner in the partnership . . . the partnership is liable therefor to the same extent as the partner so acting or omitting to act. (U.P.A., section 13.) All partners are liable (a) Jointly and severally for everything chargeable to the partnership under sections 13 and 14 (U.P.A., sec. 15).

To illustrate, if Doctor X is a partner in a medical partnership and negligently treats a patient, the malpractice negligence claim may be brought against Doctor X and the partnership.

The following case illustrates that a negligent partner may not obtain contribution from his or her co-partners even though the negligent act occurred in the course of the partnership business, unless the co-partners participated in the negligent act.

Facts
Plaintiffs, husband and wife, brought a medical malpractice suit for damages only against the defendant, Dr. Charles R. Moore, alleging him to have been negligent in his diagnosis and treatment of the eyes of plaintiff wife. Thereafter, defendant initiated a third-party action against his former co-partners, Dr. James T. Flynn, Jr., Dr. Robert E. Fokes, Jr., and Dr. James R. Paulk. Defendant, Dr. Moore, alleges: that he had been an equal partner with the three third-party defendants in a medical practice partnership operated under the name of "The Eye, Ear, Nose and Throat Clinic" at the time when he had diagnosed and treated plaintiff wife; that his diagnosis and treatment of plaintiff wife was performed within the course of the partnership business; that he and his co-partners shared equally in the profits and losses of the partnership; and that the three co-partners were liable to him for three-fourths of any sum which plaintiffs might recover against him in the principal suit.

Decision
Judgment for defendants, the co-partners of Dr. Moore.

Reasoning
The law of partnership is the law of agency: "Each partner being the agent of the firm, the firm is liable for his torts committed within the scope of his agency, on the priniciple of **'respondeat superior',** in the same way that a master is responsible for his servant's torts, and for the same reason [that] the firm is liable for the torts of its agents or servants. . . . Thus, where several physicians are in partnership they may be held liable in damages for the professional negligence of one of the firm."

The co-partners and defendant would be jointly and severally liable to plaintiffs if it were established that defendant in fact negligently diagnosed and treated plaintiff wife in the course of the partnership business. Therefore, plaintiffs had the choice of suing the defendant individually, or all of the partners including defendant jointly. But defendant cannot seek contribution from his co-partners simply because they are jointly liable to plaintiffs. Here, the co-partners and defendant are not joint **tortfeasors** as among themselves. For the co-partners are subjected to liability only by the doctrine of respondeat superior. Thus, defendant whose negligence, if any, was actual, cannot seek contribution from his co-partners, who are merely constructively negligent. Of course, had defendant alleged that his co-partners were actual tortfeasors, a third-party action for contribution would lie. But such is not the case. Where a partner is sued individually by a plaintiff injured by the partner's sole negligence, the partner cannot seek contribution from his co-partners even though the negligent act occurred in the course of the partnership business.

Flynn v. Reaves, 218 S.E.2d 661 (Ga. 1975).

tortfeasor
a person who has committed a tort

respondeat superior
let the master (superior) be responsible for the torts of his servant committed while acting within the scope of his employment

Of course, partners are liable to each other and to the partnership for their torts committed on each other and on the partnership.

---

[7] See pp. 191–95 for remedies on breach of contract.

Duties of Partners

Partnership Agreement

A partnership is created by a contract between the parties. Thus, each partner has a duty to comply with the terms of the partnership agreement. A partner is liable for any loss caused to the firm for violation of his or her duties.

Duty to inform.

Information

Each partner has the statutory duty to render full information of partnership matters to any partner. A similar duty is owed by agents to their principals. The duty is based on the *fiduciary status* of partners who act on behalf of the partnership. This duty to render information "on demand" extends to the legal representative of a partner.

Duty to act carefully.

Reasonable Care

Each partner is under a common law duty to exercise reasonable care and skill in transacting partnership business. A partner is personally liable to the partnership for any loss proximately caused by the partner's negligence. However, a partner is *not* liable for honest mistakes or errors of judgment.

Good Faith

fiduciary
a person with a duty to act primarily for the benefit of another

A partner's **fiduciary** status obligates a partner to act with complete *loyalty* to the firm. This fiduciary duty prohibits a partner from making a *secret profit*. A partner holds all profits in *trust* for the partnership.

Each partner is under the fiduciary duty not to compete with the firm. This obligates the partner to devote full time and effort to the partnership. The co-partners may, however, agree to a partner engaging in a competing business.

In the following case the court held that members of a leasing partnership who elected to compete with the firm, breached their duty owed to the partnership.

Facts

Plaintiffs and all named defendants are members of Whittier Leasing Company, a general partnership formed to assist Whittier Hospital in its remodeling program and general financial well-being. Some time before February 1977, defendants, Frischling, Taylor, Kraushaar B. and Kraushaar I. Akin, Hanten, Kurz, Springer and Jackson formed a competing partnership known as Friendly Hills Leasing Company (Friendly Hills). Together, these nine constituted the total Board of Directors of the hospital. Thereafter, Whittier Hospital, acting through its board, concluded all of its lease-back transactions with Friendly Hills, to the total exclusion of Whittier Leasing Company. Plaintiffs sought dissolution of the Whittier partnership, as well as an accounting, and recovery of damages, i.e., profits lost to Friendly Hills Leasing Company. Defendants **demurred,** their pleas were sustained without leave to amend and dismissal was thereupon ordered. Plaintiffs appealed.

demurrer
a pleading asserting that a preceding pleading, in whole or in part, is on its face insufficient in law

Decision

Reversed, judgment for plaintiffs.

Reasoning

It is well settled that a partner who agrees to give his personal attention to the partnership business may not engage in any other business which gives him an interest adverse to that of the firm, or which prevents him from giving to the firm business all the attention which would be advantageous to it. Clearly, the facts here alleged reflect that certain of the partners of Whittier Leasing have elected to compete with the firm itself and to thus breach one of the partnership's basic underlying tenets. We think it therefore indisputable that plaintiffs, should they be able to prove their allegations, would be entitled to a court-ordered dissolution of Whittier Leasing.

Gerald T. Olivet, et al. *v. Frederick Frischling,* et al., 164 Cal.Rptr. 87 (Cal. 1980).

Keep Accounts

Each partner has a fiduciary duty to keep accounts of the partnership business. Usually a managing partner assumes this duty on behalf of the firm.

Summary Statement

1. Unless the partners otherwise agree, each partner as an owner has the following rights:
   a. to manage the firm (U.P.A., sec. 18(e));
   b. to inspect the firm's books (U.P.A., sec 19);
   c. to share the profits and surplus (U.P.A., sec. 18 (a));
   d. to receive interest on his capital contribution from the date when repayment should be made (U.P.A., sec. 18(d));
   e. to receive interest on a loan to the partnership from the date of the loan (U.P.A., sec. 18(c));
   f. to be indemnified by the partnership for payment made and personal liabilities incurred in carrying on firm business (U.P.A., sec. 18(b));
   g. to be repaid his capital contributions by his co-partners after all liabilities are paid (U.P.A., sec. 18(a));
   h. to receive, upon dissolution, after the payment of all creditors and loans by partners, return of his capital contribution (U.P.A., sec. 40(b) III);
   i. to vote on the admission of new partners (U.P.A., sec. 18(g)).
2. Each partner, as an agent and a fiduciary, owes to his co-partners the following duties:
   a. good faith and loyalty;
   b. to act with reasonable care in transacting firm business;
   c. to keep an account and record of his partnership business (U.P.A., sec. 21);
   d. to render information to his co-partners on all important matters affecting the firm;
   e. to obey the partnership agreement;
   f. unless otherwise agreed, to share in the losses in the same ratio as they share in the profits.
3. Each partner is liable jointly with the other partners on partnership *contracts* made in its name and within the scope of the acting partner's actual or apparent authority.
4. Each partner is liable jointly and severally for the *torts* of other partners and firm employees acting in the ordinary course of the business or with the authority of the co-partners (U.P.A., sec. 13).
5. A partner admitted into an existing partnership is liable for all previously incurred firm obligations, and this liability is satisfied only out of partnership property (U.P.A., sec. 17).
6. Dissolution of the firm does not discharge the liability of the partners, unless the firm creditors agree.
7. The partnership assets are the partnership property *and* the contributions of the partners necessary for the payment of all partnership liabilities.

In the following case a suit was brought by a husband against a medical partnership for the alienation of his wife's affections by one of the physician partners. The U.P.A., section 13, provides for partnership liability where any partner acting in the ordinary course of the business caused loss or injury to any person not being a partner.

Kelsey-Seybold Clinic v. Maclay
466 S.W.2d 716 (Tex. 1971)

Walker, J. This is a suit for alienation of affections in which the trial court rendered summary judgment for the defendant, Kelsey-Seybold Clinic, a medical partnership. [Plaintiff appealed, and the appellate court reversed and sent the case back for trial. Defendant medical partnership now appeals to this Supreme Court claiming there is no issue of fact and, therefore, summary judgment is proper.] The question to be decided is whether the Clinic established conclusively that it is not liable for the damages alleged to have been caused by the acts of one of the partners.

Plaintiff alleged that Dr. Brewer and the Clinic had treated him, his wife, and their children for several years; that Dr. Brewer, who is a pediatrician and one of the partners in the Clinic, was the doctor to whom his wife had taken their children; that beginning in late 1966, Dr. Brewer conceived and entered into a scheme to alienate the affections of plaintiff's wife, Mrs. Maria Maclay; that he showered his attentions and gifts upon her until April or May, 1967, when her affections were alienated as a direct result of his actions, causing her to separate from plaintiff on or about July 25, 1967.

Plaintiff further alleged that Dr. Brewer's actions designed to alienate Mrs. Maclay's affections occurred while he was acting as a medical doctor for plaintiff's family and in the course and scope of his employment as a partner in the Clinic; that various acts of undue familiarity occurred both on and off the premises of the Clinic; that prior to April, 1967, the Clinic, through Dr. Mavis Kelsey, one of the senior partners, had knowledge of Dr. Brewer's actions; that at the time this knowledge was acquired, the Clinic was providing medical treatment for plaintiff and his entire family; and that the "partnership approved of, consented to, and ratified and condoned such conduct of its partner, Brewer, and refused to come to the aid of your plaintiff or in any way attempt to halt or disapprove the actions of Brewer." Plaintiff prayed for the recovery of damages both actual and exemplary, from Dr. Brewer and the Clinic, jointly and severally.

We are also of the opinion that the Clinic owed a duty to the families of its patients to exercise ordinary care to prevent a tortious interference with family relations. It was not required to maintain constant surveillance over personnel on duty or to inquire into and regulate the personal conduct of partners and employees while engaged in their private affairs. But if and when the partnership received information from which it knew or should have known that there might be a need to take action, it was under a duty to use reasonable means at its disposal to prevent any partner or employee from improperly using his position with the Clinic to work a tortious invasion of legally protected family interests.

The rather meager information in the present record does not necessarily indicate that the Clinic was under a duty to act or that it could have done anything to prevent the damage when Dr. Kelsey first learned of the situation. On the other hand, it does not affirmatively and clearly appear that the Clinic could or should have done nothing. Mrs. Maclay's affections may have been alienated from her husband before anyone talked with Dr. Kelsey, but the facts in that respect are not fully developed. There is no proof as to when, where, or under what circumstances the misconduct, if any, on Dr. Brewer's part occurred. Dr. Kelsey testified that he did not believe anything improper occurred at the Clinic, but the proofs do not establish as a matter of law that he was justified in not making further inquiry after his conversations with plaintiff and Mrs. Maclay's uncle. The record does not show whether there is a partnership agreement that might have a bearing on the case, and we have no way of knowing the extent to which the Clinic might have determined which patients were to be seen by Dr. Brewer or controlled his actions while on duty. Dr. Kelsey's testimony suggests that the partners might have been in a position to prevent improper conduct by one of their number on the premises of the Clinic. In our opinion the Clinic has failed to discharge the heavy, and in the case of this character virtually impossible, burden of establishing as a matter of law at the summary judgment stage that it is not liable under any theory fairly presented by the allegations of the petition. [The court held that there was *an issue of fact* as to whether the medical partnership breached its duty to use reasonable means at its disposal to prevent Dr. Brewer from improperly using his position with the Clinic to work a tortious invasion of legally protected family interests, thus precluding summary judgment. The decision of the appellate court was affirmed.]

Questions and Case Problems

1. Appellant sought compensatory relief for petitioner's violation of his fiduciary obligation as a partner in a law firm contending that petitioner, while a partner, willfully solicited clients for his own individual purpose and willfully interfered with the relationship between the firm and its clients. May a partner solicit partnerhship clients for his own purposes while a partner? [In the Matter of *Sheldon Silverberg and Ruben Schwartz,* 438 N.Y.S.2d 143 (N.Y. 1981).]

2. X and Z operated a collection agency as partners. While attempting to collect a debt for the firm, Y, a firm employee, committed an assault and battery on W. When W sued the firm, C, a new partner, was joined as a party defendant. Is C personally liable along with the other partners?

3. The partners entered into an agreement which specified how fees should be divided upon dissolution. The law partnership was dissolved, and Bovy, a partner, brought this suit to compel compliance with the agreement regarding the division of fees. The defendants claim that, during the negotiations for the agreement, Bovy had not fully disclosed the number of cases in which he claimed a contingent fee. Was Bovy subject to a fiduciary duty of disclosure to divulge the number of cases and value of their contingent fees during the negotiation of the agreement? [*Bovy v. Graham, Cohen & Wampold,* 564 P.2d 1175 (Wash. 1977).]

4. The defendants loaned money to Dalton Waldrop who later, with Thomas Waldrop, his brother, formed a partnership for the drilling of wells. Subsequently this partnership was incorporated as Waldrop Drilling & Pipe Co., Inc., plaintiff. Defendants employed Waldrop Drilling & Pipe Co., Inc., to repair one of their pumps. This repair work was completed at a reasonable cost of $2,873.75. At the request of defendants, plaintiff performed additional repair services in the reasonable amount of $710.54. Neither of these bills was paid. Plaintiff brought this action to collect the amount due. Defendants sought to offset these amounts against the balance owed to them by Dalton Waldrop. It is defendants' position that because Dalton Waldrop, the original debtor, used the loan proceeds to purchase well-drilling equipment which later became an asset of the partnership between Dalton and Thomas Waldrop, and later a corporate asset, the partnership and the corporation are liable for the original loan. Consequently, defendants contend that the repair cost should have been offset against the balance owed to them by Dalton Waldrop. Did the partnership assume the original loan obligation of Dalton Waldrop? [*Thomas E. Waldrop and Sharlyn Waldrop v. George W. Holland, Sr.,* 558 P.2d 1237 (Wash. 1979).]

5. Plaintiff, Koenig, and defendant, Huber, were partners engaged in a plumbing and heating business. They signed a partnership agreement which provided that the parties were to employ themselves diligently in the business; and that all profits would be distributed equally. Koenig filed suit for the dissolution of the partnership and an accounting. The lower court failed to consider "extra time" spent by Koenig in the partnership business while the defendant, Huber, was operating an oil station. Is a partner entitled to be paid for "extra time" spent in a partnership business? [*Koenig v. Huber,* 210 N.W.2d 825 (S.D. 1973).]

6. Weiss was one of the partners in Pike Associates that was formed to build and operate a shopping center. Weiss put up all his right, title, and interest in the shopping center as security for a personal loan made by the defendant to Weiss. Plaintiff bank also loaned Weiss money some years earlier. Defendant attempted to foreclose on its interest in the shopping center partnership after Weiss was in default on his note to the defendant. Plaintiff seeks to enjoin the foreclosure and to establish that its interest has priority because a partner cannot pledge specific partnership property for a personal loan. May a partner pledge as security an interest in the partnership assets? [*Madison National Bank v. Newrath,* 275 A.2d 495 (Md. 1971).]

7. X, Y, and Z own a partnership engaged in the collection of corporate debts. X, while attempting to collect a debt, violated a federal law on unfair debt collection practices. The debtor sued the firm. Y and Z claim that only X is liable for his unauthorized conduct. Decide.

8. A dentist was a member of a dental partnership who signed a partnership agreement that provided for a fixed annual salary. She was an ambitious person who worked evenings, weekends and gave up her summer vacation to care for the partnership patients. Is she entitled to be paid for her extra time spent in performing partnership business?

9. Harris, the president of defendant company, International Realty Ltd., formed a partnership with a group of physicians to purchase an apartment house under construction as a good "tax shelter." Harris stated the purchase price as $1,010,000 but failed to disclose that it could have been purchased for $907,500. Harris also did not disclose to his partners that the defendant, of which he was the president and major stockholder, would receive a $100,000 commission. The doctors, plaintiffs, brought this suit to require Harris to account to the partnership for the commission received by him without their consent. Harris claims that the doctors knew someone was going to make a commission and, therefore, no disclosure was required. You decide. [*Starr v. International Realty Ltd.,* 533 P.2d 165 (Or. 1975).]

10. In light of the case of *Kelsey-Seybold Clinic v. Maclay,* 466 S.W.2d 716 (Tex. 1971),[8] if you were a partner in a partnership, what basic guidelines would you help to establish and observe so that matters of partner impropriety could be so handled as to minimize the risk of partnership liability for such impropriety?

---

[8] See p. 610.

Special Ventures 41

After you have read this chapter, you should be able to:

1. Define a limited partnership.
2. Explain the liability of:
   a. a general partner.
   b. a limited partner.
3. Explain how a limited partnership is formed.
4. Define a joint venture.
5. Explain a business trust.
6. Explain an unincorporated association.
7. Define and explain a franchise.
8. Explain the relationship of a trademark to a franchise; define a trademark.

Introduction

When you enter business you will find that there are many different kinds of business all operating within some kind of formal or loose business structure. We have just discussed the general partnership, and in chapters 42–46 we will study the corporation. There are still other forms of business organization which are likely to have importance for you, either as a participant in one or more of them, or because you have dealings with them. It is therefore important for you to have an opportunity to learn about them, their character, their legal status, and their liability.

Special Venture Organizations

Limited Partnership

limited partnership
a partnership of one or more general partners and one or more limited partners formed in compliance with the Uniform Limited Partnership Act

The **limited partnership** is a noncorporate business organization that protects the capital investor from liability for firm losses beyond the investment. It is a form of partnership created only in states that have adopted the Uniform Limited Partnership Act of 1916 (U.L.P.A.), the (Revised) Act of 1976, or the new 1985 Act (the 1976 Act with amendments). This entitles a limited partner, often called a "special partner," to share profits without sharing losses beyond his or her investment. The general partners manage the business.

> A limited partnership is a partnership formed by two or more persons . . . having as members one or more general partners and one or more limited partners. (U.L.P.A., section 1.)

Notice that each limited partnership must have at least one general partner with unlimited liability.

While 5 states have adopted the 1985 Act, the remaining states except Louisiana have adopted either the 1916 or the 1976 Acts. *This text will deal only with the 1916 Act*. However, a few comments about the 1976 Act are made at the end of this section, and Appendices C and D contain the entire 1916 and 1976 Acts.

Formation. The partners must sign and swear to a limited partnership *certificate* that states the firm name, character, location, names and addresses of general and limited partners and their investment and share of the profits, and other information. The certificate must be filed with the "designated official" as required by each state (usually in the office of the Secretary of State). A limited partnership can be formed only by *complete* or *substantial* compliance in good faith with the statutory requisites.

A limited partner's *capital* contribution can be only cash or other property, but not services. The limited partner may be *employed* by the firm to render services and be paid for such work like anyone else.

Liability of a Limited Partner. The limited partners are not personally liable for firm debts *provided that they do not participate in the control or management* of the firm. They are non-participating investors. The *general* partners have the duty to control and manage the firm and, therefore, are personally liable for the firm's obligations. If a limited partner does engage in firm management and hence "takes part in the *control* of the business," he or she will be held *personally* liable for firm debts. What constitutes "taking part in the control of the business" is not clearly defined. U.L.P.A., section 5 generally prohibits the use of a limited partner's surname (last name) as part of the firm name, unless it is the same as that of a general partner or it appeared in the partnership name before he or she became a limited partner. The limited partner is liable to the partnership for capital contributions to the firm that the limited partner agreed in the certificate of partnership would be made but had not yet been made. When creditors have a claim against the firm, a limited partner cannot withdraw his or her capital contribution.

A managing general partner may desire to invest in the limited partnership and thereby become a limited partner. U.L.P.A., section 12(2) provides for this and grants to that partner all the rights and duties of a general partner.

Rights of a Limited Partner. U.L.P.A., section 10, provides that a limited partner shall have the following rights: to inspect and copy partnership books; to have on demand true and full information of all things affecting the partnership, and a formal account of partnership affairs whenever circumstances render it just and reasonable; to have a dissolution and winding up by decree of court; and to receive a share of the profits or other compensation by way of income, and to the return of his or her contribution as provided in the partnership certificate, except as otherwise provided in the U.L.P.A., sections 15 and 16.

Liquidation. Upon liquidation, each limited partner has priority over general partners in net assets. After payment to outside partnership creditors and to limited partners who have made loans to the firm, the limited partners receive their share of profits and then their capital contribution. General partners are then paid back their loans, share of profits, and, lastly, their capital contributions.[1]

(Revised) Uniform Limited Partnership Act of 1976. Presently, 24 states and the District of Columbia have adopted the 1976 Act. A few items in the Act are mentioned here. Appendix D has the entire Act.

The name of the limited partnership must contain the words "limited partnership" in full. The partnership must maintain a registered agent in the state for service of process on the partnership, at whose office certain partnership records shall be kept. The certificate of limited partnership must be filed in the office of the Secretary of State. The capital contribution of a limited partner may be the performance of services, cash, or property.

A limited partner who actively participates in the control of the business is liable only to persons who transact business with the partnership and who know of such participation and control. The Act also specifies exactly what does *not* constitute participation in the control of the business, e.g.: being a contractor for, or an agent or employee of, the partnership; consulting with and advising a partner with respect to the business; acting as surety for the partnership; approving or disapproving of an amendment to the partnership agreement; and voting on various matters, such as: dissolution; winding up; the transfer of all or substantially all of the assets, or the incurring of debt, other than in the ordinary course of the business; change in the nature of the business; removal of a general partner.

1985 Revised Uniform Limited Partnership Act. The 1985 Act follows the format of the 1976 Act and many of its provisions. Although only five states have adopted the Act it will probably soon be adopted by many more and hence a few of its provisions are worth noting: the 1985 Act does not require the certificate of limited partnership to state the limited partners' contributions (s. 201); if the partnership agreement does not provide for the admission of general partners they may do so by written consent of all the partners (s. 401); and the partnership agreement may provide for specific events causing judicial dissolutions (s. 801). The 1985 Act continues the concept that the partnership agreement should be the document that controls the operational governance of the firm while the certificate of limited partnership provides information for creditors.

Joint Venture

A **joint venture** is an association of two or more persons as co-owners to engage in a limited business transaction for a profit. Generally, it is a single undertaking for a limited duration. For example, X and Z purchase recreational property for investment purposes. They agree to share the rental income and expenses. When the property is sold, they will share the "profits" or "gains." Both X and Z have other full-time jobs.

---

[1] U.L.P.A., sec. 23.

The negligence of one joint associate is imputed to the others in a joint venture. Any associate may be held liable to injured third persons caused by the negligence of another associate.[2]

Because of the close similarity of a joint venture to a partnership, it is commonly held that their rights and duties are governed by the Uniform Partnership Act.

Business Trust

The business trust, sometimes called a Massachusetts trust, is similar to a common law trust with the trustees acting as business managers and the beneficiaries as capital investors and holders of transferable shares. The trust is formed by a trust instrument that describes the nature of the business, a description of the trust property, the trustees and their powers, the beneficiaries' interests, and the rights of creditors dealing with the trustees.

Generally, the beneficiaries will be held personally liable for trust obligations if they have power to control the trust management, and although the trust instrument will probably state that the trustees and beneficiaries cannot be held personally liable for trust debts, it has no effect against creditors who do not assent to it. For instance, if a tenant is injured due to defective stairs in a building owned and managed by a business trust, the trustees are personally liable for the damages resulting from the tort of negligence.

Notice that the court in the following case found there was no business trust because the intended trust failed to issue transferable trust certificates and, hence, the common law trust could not be sued as a legal entity.

Facts
Plaintiff, Arthur Limouze, filed suit against the defendant, the M.M. & P. Maritime Advancement, Training, Education and Safety Program (MATES Program). Defendant was established as a business trust pursuant to an Agreement and Declaration of Trust, dated January 6, 1967. The defendant, the "Trust", has not issued certificates representing shares in the Trust. Plaintiff claims that the Trust, acting through defendants Hickey and O'Callaghan, trustees, wrongfully and improperly terminated plaintiff's employment contract on May 11, 1974. The Trust filed a motion to dismiss on the basis that the Trust was not a business trust and therefore not a legal entity and lacked capacity to be sued.

Decision
The Trust's motion to dismiss was granted.

Reasoning
In the absence of issuance of certificates or shares by the defendant Trust, the defendant Trust cannot properly be characterized as a business trust. The Trust is not a person in the eyes of the law and does not have the capacity to be sued as an entity.

Limouze v. M.M. & P. Maritime Advancement, Training, Education and Safety Program, 397 F.Supp. 784 (1975).

Franchising

Franchising is a business relationship between a *franchisor,* who markets goods or services through a *franchisee,* who has the right to use the franchisor's trade name, trademark, and methods of operation. In return, the franchisee agrees to sell the services or products under the control of the franchisor.

The court in the following case upheld the right of a franchisor to compel their franchisees to buy only from designated suppliers and sell only approved products.

---
[2] *Keiswetter v. Rubenstein,* 209 N.W. 154 (Mich. 1926).

Facts
Thomas Carvel, president of Carvel Corporation, defendant, went into the ice cream business in 1934. This is an action by **franchise** operators under franchise agreements with Carvel Corporation claiming that the supplier, H.P. Hood & Sons, and Carvel Corporation violated the antitrust laws by their refusal to deal directly with them. The franchisees allege that they have the right to purchase Carvel Mix ice cream, made pursuant to Carvel's secret formula, other than on the terms Carvel Corporation prescribed in the franchise agreement. Did Carvel Corporation violate the antitrust laws by requiring its franchise operators to deal only with its supplier of ice cream, H.P. Hood & Sons?

Decision
No. Judgment for defendant, Carvel Corporation.

Reasoning
No outsider, without Carvel Corporation's approval, had the right to require the dairy companies to sell them this special formula mix. The plaintiff did not contend that Carvel Corporation engaged in any common conspiracy with the supplier, H.P. Hood & Sons.

Susser v. Carvel Corporation, 206 F.Supp. 636 (1962).

franchise
a business relationship between a franchisor, who markets goods or services through a franchisee, who has the right to use the franchisor's trade name, trademark, and methods of operation

A company that desires to franchise should acquire federal registration in the United States Patent Office of its **trademark** and trade name. Once the trademark is registered, the owner may grant to another (the franchisee) the right to use it in accordance with the franchise contract. Well-known trademarks are McDonald, Shell, Holiday Inn, etc. The franchise contract includes a provision that designates a geographical area where the franchisee can operate.

trademark
an identifying designation differentiating one's goods from those of another

"Tying Arrangement"
Many franchisors recognize the importance of a location. Hence they purchase the buildings and lease the premises to a franchisee. To ensure a standardized image and decor, the layout, design, and equipment are considered part of the trademark image. The items in the "franchise package" must all interrelate as part of the franchise outlet in order to justify its anticompetitive effect; otherwise the franchise arrangement will be held to be illegal.

Service or Product Control
The franchisor has an interest in maintaining the goodwill of the business that the purchasing public has come to associate with its trade name. Hence a common provision found in a franchising contract obligates the franchisee to purchase *all* its products from the franchisor or its authorized suppliers. Since this is "full-line" forcing—that is, a *full* line of products must be taken by the franchisee in order to obtain *any* of the franchisor's products—such an arrangement is *not* an unlawful tying under the Clayton Antitrust Act.

Federal and State Regulation of Franchising
In an attempt to remedy misrepresentations by franchisors to promote the sale of franchises, the Federal Trade Commission promulgated (published) a Trade Regulation Rule on franchising.[3] In addition, various states require the franchisor to register its franchise prospectus before offering its franchise for sale to the public.[4]

In the following case the court had to determine if a franchise agreement created a fiduciary relationship.

---

[3] FTC (16 **CFR** Part 436).

[4] As of May 1985, fourteen states have statutes requiring franchisors to register their franchise offerings by filing a prospectus: California, Hawaii, Illinois, Indiana, Maryland, Michigan, Minnesota, New York, North Dakota, Rhode Island, South Dakota, Virginia, Washington, and Wisconsin.

Facts
In September of 1971, Picture Lake Campground, Inc., plaintiff, applied to Holiday Inns, Inc., defendant, for a franchise in the Holiday Inn Trav-L-Park system, a franchised recreational vehicle campground system offering camper rental spaces, recreation, food, and other accommodations, and using Holiday Inns' trade names, trademarks, and service marks. The complaint alleges that, during several meetings between representatives of Holiday Inns and the owners of the Picture Lake property, various representations were made by Holiday Inns concerning, among other things: the favorable market conditions for recreational vehicle campgrounds; Holiday Inns' concept of a high quality, expanding system of franchise campgrounds, with developmental, promotional and maintenance support provided by the experienced Holiday Inns corporation; the suitability of Picture Lake as a site for such a campground; and the substantial income potential of the Picture Lake property as a part of the system developed under the guidance and control of Holiday Inns.

It is plaintiff's contention that a fiduciary duty may exist in a franchise relationship and, when violated, is actionable under Virginia law. Holiday Inns' motion to dismiss the complaint was granted, and the plaintiff appealed. Does a franchise agreement create a fiduciary relationship?

Decision
No. Affirmed for the defendant, Holiday Inns.

Reasoning
A franchise relationship is inherently a business relationship, not a fiduciary relationship. While Holiday Inns had a duty to deal fairly with Picture Lake, it did not have the duty of a fiduciary with all of the obligations and responsibilities pertaining thereto. Each party served the interest of the other, but each also quite properly sought its own interest.

Picture Lake Campground, Inc. v. Holiday Inns, Inc., 497 F. Supp. 858 (1980).

Termination
In the following case Mobil Oil Corporation attemped to terminate a one-year trial franchise without providing any reason for doing so.

Facts
Plaintiff, the operator of a Mobil Gasoline Service Station, seeks injunctive relief to prevent defendant, Mobil Oil Corporation, from terminating or nonrenewing his one-year trial franchise. After successfully completing a three-week course of instruction in defendant's dealer training school, plaintiff was granted a one-year trial franchise beginning May 14, 1979 and ending May 13, 1980. On February 7, 1980, defendant mailed to plaintiff by certified mail, a notice that defendant "hereby elects not to renew its franchise relationship with [plaintiff] and that relationship will terminate on May 13, 1980." Section 2804 (c)(3) mandates that the notification of nonrenewal "shall contain . . . a statement of intention to terminate the franchise or not to renew the franchise relationship, together with the reasons therefor." The notice which defendant gave to plaintiff in this case stated, "The reason or reasons for our non-renewal decision are that Mobil has determined that it does not wish to continue its franchise relationship with you." Did this notice effectively terminate the franchise?

Decision
No. Judgment for the plaintiff.

Reasoning
The notice in question wholly fails to provide any reason and so does not conform to the notification requirements of Section 2804(c). And since the statute explicitly permits a franchisor to fail to renew a trial franchise only if the notification requirements of Section 2804 have been met, it follows that plaintiff is entitled to relief.

James Clark, d/b/a Jim's Service Center v. Mobil Oil Corporation, 496 F.Supp. 132 (1980).

Figure 41.1 Comparison of Business Organizations

	General Partnership	Limited Partnership	Business Trust	Franchise	Corporation
Creation	By agreement per U.P.A.	In writing per R.L.P.A.	Filing Business Trust certificate per statute	By contract with the franchisee	Filing articles of organization per statute
Liability	Unlimited liability with respect to torts and contracts for all partners	Unlimited liability for general partners, limited partners are generally not liable for business torts and contracts	Trust beneficiaries may be personally liable if they have power to control the trust management; trustees may be held liable for business obligations	Franchisor may be liable for torts of franchisee if it maintains control over the business; generally not liable for its contracts	Shareholders are generally not liable for corporate obligations
Management	Unless changed by the Partnership Agreement, each partner has an equal vote per U.P.A.	General partners manage with equal vote, unless changed by agreement — limited partners do not manage the business	Trustees manage the trust business in accordance with the trust agreement	Franchisee manages the franchise in accordance with the franchise contract	Officers carry out the management policy determined and authorized by the board of directors
Agency	Each partner is an agent of the partnership for partnership business per U.P.A.	General partners are agents, limited partners are not	Trustees are agents for business trust purposes, beneficiaries are not	Franchisee is an agent of the franchise, franchisors are generally not	Officers are agents, directors and shareholders are not
Taxation	Not a taxable entity but files an information return	Taxed similar to a general partnership, limited partners have limited liability and are taxed as partners	Taxable entity, may be taxed as a corporation due to corporate attributes	Taxable entity, generally a corporation	Taxable entity — may qualify as an S corporation and avoid double taxation

Summary Statement

1. A limited partnership is a partnership formed by two or more persons having as members one or more general partners and one or more limited partners. A limited partner shall not become liable as a general partner unless he or she takes part in the control of the business.
2. (a) The general partners in a limited partnership are personally liable for partnership debts. (b) The limited partners are liable to the partnership for capital contributions to the firm which they agreed in the certificate of partnership that they would make but had not yet made.
3. A limited partnership must be formed by a signed and sworn certificate, which is filed as required by each state, usually in the county clerk's office or the registry of deeds where the firm business is carried on.
4. A joint venture is an association of two or more persons organized as co-owners to engage in a *limited* business transaction for a profit.

5. A business trust is formed by a trust instrument with the trustees acting as business managers and the beneficiaries as capital investors and holders of transferable shares. The beneficiaries will be held personally liable for trust obligations only if they have power to control the trust management.
6. Franchising is a contractual arrangement whereby one party, the franchisor, consents to another party, the franchisee, using its trade name, trademark, supplied products, equipment, and managerial expertise. The franchisee agrees to sell the services or products under the control and supervision of the franchisor.

The court in the following case reviewed the plaintiffs' allegation of an illegal tying arrangement to determine if the tied products were integral components of the business method being franchised.

Frank A. Principe, et al. v. McDonald's Corporation
631 F.2d 303 (1980)

Harry Phillips, Senior Circuit Judge. Plaintiffs, Frank A Principe, Ann Principe, and Frankie, Inc., a family owned corporation, plaintiffs, are franchisees of McDonald's System, Inc.

The Principes argue McDonald's is selling not one but three distinct products, the franchise, the lease and the security deposit note. The alleged antitrust violation stems from the fact that a prospective franchisee must buy all three in order to obtain the franchise. As evidence that this is an illegal tying arrangement, the Principes point to the unfavorable terms on which franchisees are required to lease their stores. Not only are franchisees denied the opportunity to build equity and depreciate their property, but they must maintain the building, pay for improvements and taxes, and remit 8.5 percent of their gross sales as rents. McDonald's responds that it is not in the business of licensing use of its name, improving real estate for lease or selling long term notes. Its only business is developing a system of hamburger restaurants and collecting royalties from their sales. The allegedly tied products are but parts of the overall bundle of franchise benefits and obligations. According to McDonald's, the Principes are asking the court to invalidate the way McDonald's does business and to require it to adopt the licensing procedures of its less successful competitors. Federal antitrust laws do not compel such a result, McDonald's contends. Judgment in the lower court was for the defendant franchisor, and the plaintiffs franchisees appeal.

There is at the outset of every tie-in case the problem of determining whether two separate products are in fact involved. Because we agree with McDonald's that the lease, note and license are not separate products but component parts of the overall franchise package, we hold on the facts of this case there was no illegal tie-in. Given the realities of modern franchising, we think the proper inquiry is not whether the allegedly tied products are associated in the public mind with the franchisor's trademark, but whether they are integral components of the business method being franchised. Where the challenged aggregation is an essential ingredient of the franchised system's formula for success, there is but a single product and no tie-in exists as a matter of law. Applying this standard to the present case, we hold the lease is not separable from the McDonald's franchise to which it pertains. McDonald's practice of developing a system of company owned restaurants operated by franchisees has substantial advantages, both for the company and for franchisees. It is part of what makes a McDonald franchise uniquely attractive to franchisees. To characterize the franchise as an unnecessary aggregation of separate products tied to the McDonald's name is to miss the point entirely. Among would be franchisees, the McDonald's name has come to stand for the formula, including all that it entails. We decline to find that it is an illegal tie-in.

Affirmed, for defendant franchisor.

Questions and Case Problems

1. Tappan Motors, Inc. (Tappan), plaintiff, has been a regularly franchised Volvo dealer. This franchise relationship with Volvo of America Corporation (Volvo), distributor, defendant, was recently reaffirmed in a contract that provided for its termination by the distributor upon 30 days' written notice to the dealer in the event that the dealer fails to correct any default in performance of its responsibilities under the foregoing provisions within 60 days after written notice of such default. A New York statute prohibits termination by a distributor of contracts for sales of new motor vehicles to a dealer except for cause. Volvo terminated Tappan's franchise and Tappan commenced the instant action; the lower court agreed with plaintiff that Volvo was not justified in terminating their agreement.

    The evidence presented at trial shows: that Tappan had repeatedly experienced problems in servicing Volvo automobiles; Tappan's facilities were neither as large nor as clean as Volvo required; some of the specialized tools required for servicing Volvos were missing from Tappan's premises; certain of Volvo's factory service manuals were also missing; Volvo customers at Tappan were subjected to inconvenience and excessive waiting times for repairs; Tappan failed or refused to keep an adequate inventory of Volvo parts; Tappan delayed installation of a computer system for the control of its parts inventory until after its termination was scheduled to take effect; and Tappan repeatedly complained about its allocation of automobiles and threatened to dissuade customers from purchasing a Volvo elsewhere if Tappan could not supply them with the Volvo model of their choice. Was this evidence sufficient to justify Volvo's decision to terminate Tappan's franchise? [*Tappan Motors, Inc. v. Volvo of America Corporation,* et al., 444 N.Y.S.2d 938 (N.Y. 1981).]

2. The plaintiff, H. C. Blackwell Company, Inc. (Blackwell), instituted this action against Kenworth Truck Company (Kenworth), under the Automobile Dealers' Franchise Act, seeking damages for claimed wrongful termination and/or non-renewal of its franchise agreement with Kenworth. On February 4, 1976, Kenworth advised Blackwell by letter that the then existing "informal arrangement" would terminate in ninety days, unless certain demands were met within ninety days, including substantial capital improvements, increased sales, and a better bookkeeping system. Kenworth's regional sales manager testified that it would have taken Blackwell at least one year to meet the demands delineated in that letter. Blackwell attempted to meet these requirements, spending approximately $90,000 in the process. Although Blackwell was unable to accomplish everything required by Kenworth within the designated ninety day time limit, it made substantial progress toward compliance with the conditions.

    On June 24, 1976, Blackwell received a letter from Kenworth stating that the franchise would not be renewed because the May inspection report was "not favorable." Unable to persuade Kenworth to re-open negotiations, Blackwell brought this suit under The Automobile Dealers' Franchise Act, which requires an automobile manufacturer to act in good faith in terminating, cancelling, or not renewing a dealership franchise. Good faith statutorily means acting in a fair and equitable manner guaranteeing freedom from coercion or threats of coercion. Did Kenworth legally, in good faith, terminate the franchise? [*H. C. Blackwell Company, Inc. v. Kenworth Truck Company,* 620 F.2d 104 (1980).]

3. Plaintiff, Polikoff, and Levy, the defendant, with others, formed a joint venture known as the State House Inn. The members, over the objection of the plaintiff, caused all of the assets to be transferred to a new corporation, the State House Inn, Inc. Polikoff brought this suit claiming that co-venturers cannot arbitrarily dispose of the assets of the venture over the objection of one co-venturer. He asked the court to have the assets disposed of by a judicial sale. You decide. [*Polikoff v. Levy,* 270 N.E.2d 540 (Ill. 1971).]

4. In May, 1979, Bailey Employment Systems, Inc. (Bailey), commenced this action seeking payment of a $10,000 note. The defendant, Clifford Hahn, admitting the existence and execution of the note, counterclaimed against Bailey and its president, Sheldon Leighton, alleging misrepresentation and fraud as well as violations of the Connecticut Unfair Trade Practices Act by Bailey in connection with the sale of a franchise to Hahn. In a written communication to Hahn prior to the sale of the franchise, Bailey claimed that during the recession years of 1974–1976 "many well managed Bailey Employment Service franchise owners enjoyed job security and financial independence with personal incomes that averaged $500+, $600+, $700+ each and every week of the recession." The financial statements of Bailey franchises made available for trial indicate that in 1975 and 1976 only four of the 19 reporting franchisees arguably realized income of as much as $500 per week and only one realized up to $700 per week. A Bailey brochure, which Hahn obtained from a business broker and which was clearly intended to entice potential franchise purchasers, set forth "Projected Earnings" of different levels of Bailey franchises. The table was clearly meant to indicate to a potential purchaser what earnings he or she could expect from a Bailey franchise. The figures in the "Projected Earnings" table are unrepresentative, and in some instances, without any reasonable basis in fact for any of the three years prior to Hahn's purchase. Did Bailey violate the Connecticut Unfair Trade Practices Act? [*Bailey Employment System, Inc. v. Clifford Hahn,* et al., 545 F.Supp. 62 (1982).]

5. Fidelity Lease Limited, defendant, is a limited partnership organized to lease restaurant locations. It is composed of 22 limited partners and a corporate general partner, Interlease Corporation. Interlease's officers, directors, and shareholders were Crombie, Kahn, and Sanders, who were also limited partners of Fidelity. Delaney, the plaintiff, is a building contractor who entered into an agreement with the limited partnership, Fidelity, acting by and through its corporate general partner, Interlease, to lease a fast-food restaurant to the partnership. Delaney built the restaurant, but Fidelity failed to take possession or pay rent. Delaney brought suit for damages for breach of the lease agreement, naming as defendants the limited partnership of Fidelity Lease Limited, its corporate general partner, Interlease Corporation, and all of its limited partners individually. Are Crombie, Kahn, and Sanders—the officers, directors, and shareholders of Interlease—personally liable? [*Delaney v. Fidelity Lease Limited,* 526 S.W.2d 543 (Tex. 1975).]

6. Plaintiff (Thorson) and defendant (Bellamy) are real estate agents. Thorson entered into a listing agreement with Grafe to sell the real estate parcel in question. The agreement gave Thorson a right to a commission if he arranged a sale. Thorson then invited Bellamy to help him sell the land and agreed to give Bellamy one-half the commission if Bellamy arranged a sale. At the time they reached the agreement, Bellamy had told Grafe that he intended to act in a cooperative arrangement with Thorson. Concerning the commission for a sale, Bellamy testified that he intended Thorson to receive a share of the commission even if Thorson did not make the sale. Thorson, relying at least partially on a memo he prepared following a telephone call, testified at trial that the two men agreed on a 50–50 split of the commission.

Bellamy eventually purchased the land himself from Grafe and immediately resold it to Harland Crawford. When Bellamy refused to acknowledge the commission and to give Thorson his share, Thorson brought this proceeding claiming a joint venture existed and, because they never reached an agreement about how to split the commission, the two men should split the commission and expenses 50–50. Bellamy argues that, because he included Thorson in the listing gratuitously, the agreement was not supported by consideration and, therefore, it is not a contract. Decide. [*Freeland C. Thorson v. Carl Bellamy,* 635 P.2d 1048 (Or. 1981).]

7. Loomis Land & Cattle Co., plaintiff, brought suit to enjoin the sale of a shopping center under the terms of a note and deed executed by Loomis Land & Cattle Co. and Richard Loomis as guarantor to the defendant, Diversified Mortgage Investors. The right to have the sale enjoined was based upon the ground that Diversified Mortgage was a Massachusetts business trust and not a recognizable entity under the laws of Texas and was, therefore, without standing in court to pursue any of the remedies arising under the sales contract. Defendant argues that it has standing to sue in the Texas courts because a Massachusetts business trust is to be treated as a partnership. May a state regard a Massachusetts business trust as a partnership? [*Loomis Land & Cattle Company v. Diversified Mortgage Investors,* 533 S.W.2d 420 (Tex. 1976).]

8. Richardson, the plaintiff and co-trustee of a business trust, brought this action to nullify an agreement executed by two of the three trustees. The instrument creating the business trust was amended to permit the powers of the business trustees to be exercised by a majority. Richardson, the plaintiff, now contends that the amendment is invalid because it deprives the trustees of their power and duty to control the operation of the business trust. May a business trust be amended to provide for majority control of trust business? [*Richardson v. Clarke,* 364 N.E.2d 804 (Mass. 1977).]

9. Both petitioner M.I.F. Securities Company (MIF), a limited partnership, and R. C. Stamm & Co. (Stamm), a general partnership, were engaged in the securities business. They entered into an agreement whereby Stamm was to operate as a division of MIF under certain limited profit and expense sharing provisions. The agreement called for Stamm to "introduce" its securities and commodities business to MIF and clear its transactions through MIF's clearing agent, for which Stamm, as compensation therefor, was to be paid 60% of the net income received by MIF from the business generated by these accounts. Stamm would not share in either the profits or expenses arising from any other portion of MIF's business. MIF would provide Stamm with office space, market information dissemination devices, telephone lines to exchange floors, and medical and life insurance for its employees. Stamm was to be responsible for its own accounts, any losses generated by those accounts, and various expenses associated with its business, including salary for its employees, Stamm stationery, separate telephone lines, separate legal and accounting fees.

   A dispute arose over Stamm's clearing charges. Was Stamm a partner? [*M.I.F. Securities Company v. R. C. Stamm & Co.,* 463 N.Y.S.2d 771 (N.Y. 1983).]

10. In the case of *Frank A. Principe,* et al. *v. McDonald's Corporation,* 631 F.2d 303 (1980),[5] the plaintiffs/franchisees alleged an antitrust violation and an illegal tying arrangement as the theory that McDonald's is selling three distinct products, the franchise, lease and note, rather than component parts of the overall franchise package. What standard did the court apply to determine there was a single product being franchised and no illegal tie-in?

---

[5] See p. 620.

PART 8 # Business Organizations
B. Corporations

42. Nature and Classes
The background, concept, and need for the corporate form of legal entity, created with permission of the state or federal governments. The various kinds of corporation are examined.

43. Creation and Termination
The statutory requirements for creation and termination of a corporation, as well as the function and liability of promoters.

44. Corporate Powers
The source, nature, and extent of corporate express and implied power or authority without which a corporation could not function. The effect of corporate conduct which exceeds its powers is also considered.

45. Corporate Stock and Shareholders
The meaning of corporate stock owned by shareholders, the various kinds of shares, rights of shareholders, and transferability of shares; Securities Regulations; and Foreign Corrupt Practices.

46. Corporate Management
How a corporation actually operates; the functions of the board of directors and corporate officers who participate in that operation as managers, and their duties, powers, and liability. The managerial function of shareholders is examined also.

Note: These chapters on Corporations are keyed to the 1984 REVISED MODEL BUSINESS CORPORATION ACT (RMBCA). All references to the Act, and all quotations of selected sections from the Act are reproduced with the permission of the American Bar Foundation which has the copyright for the Act.

Summary
The need for corporations in a government-regulated free-enterprise system is discussed, followed by a brief history of the corporation and descriptions of the various kinds. You will see how a corporation is formed and dissolved. The powers granted to a corporation by the state are reviewed. As you will probably own stock in a corporation, the rights of stockholders are explained as well as the few instances when a shareholder may be held personally liable. Finally, the managerial functions of a corporation's officers and directors are discussed from a legal viewpoint.

Business ethics as it relates to the text material in this Part is considered at the end of the Part.

42 Nature and Classes

After you have read this chapter, you should be able to:

1. Define a corporation.
2. Explain "limited liability."
3. Identify the source of corporation law.
4. Explain the contribution to corporate law from the following:
   a. Roman law.
   b. Canon law.
   c. Civil law.
   d. Common law.
   e. Overseas trading companies.
   f. Revised Model Business Corporation Act (1984).
5. List and explain the classification of corporations.
6. Explain what is meant by "doing business" in a foreign state.
7. List activities that generally do not constitute transacting business in a foreign state.
8. Explain what is a "registered agent" and what is his purpose.
9. Explain how private corporations are regulated by the government.
10. Explain the constitutional restrictions on government regulation of a corporation.
11. Explain what is meant by disregarding the corporate entity and when the court may do so.
12. List and explain the corporate attributes.
13. Explain what is a (Subchapter) S corporation.
14. Explain what is meant by "piercing the corporate veil."

Figure 42.1 Structure of the Corporation

Introduction

You are one of five people who wish to engage in business together but who have two main problems: they need capital, the money to get the business started and operating; and they don't want to have the risk of their individual properties being available to pay creditors of the business. They also want to be able to transfer their shares or interests in the business easily to other persons without affecting the continuation of the business. The corporation came into being as a result of these and other needs.

Nature

A **corporation** is a legal entity created by statute authorizing an association of persons to carry on an enterprise. The corporation exists as a *legal person* with many powers. For example, it can own property, real and personal, in its own name; make contracts; incur debts; issue stocks and bonds; and sue and be sued. As a legal person, its owners, the **shareholders** or stockholders, are distinct from the legal entity and cannot be sued for corporate liabilities. This is known as *limited liability*—that is, the corporate investor's risk is limited to the loss of his or her investment. A shareholder cannot be held personally liable for corporate debts. For example, if you purchased **shares of stock** for $5,000, corporate creditors could not sue you personally, although your investment may be lost.

A corporation is granted its existence by the state or the federal government. The formation of a corporation, under modern statutory law, is accomplished by submitting to the Secretary of State a document called the *articles of incorporation*. The articles, discussed in a later chapter, identify the name and location of the corporation, the nature of its business, the incorporators, sometimes the directors, and officers, and authorized capitalization (see figure 42.1).

corporation a legal entity created by statute authorizing an association of persons to carry on an enterprise

shareholder (stockholder) the owner of a unit of interest in a corporation

share of stock a unit of interest in a corporation

Historical Background

Roman Law
The concept of the government creating an "artificial person" with certain characteristics having legal status has an ancient origin. During the early Roman Republic various religious, educational, and governmental groups began to develop. The Roman Empire's rulers, desiring control over these groups, granted them legal authorization only by express approval. This created the origin of a business association requiring governmental authorization.

Canon Law
The law of the Roman Catholic Church affected corporate law by regulating ecclesiastical property ownership. Pope Innocent IV (1243–1254) developed the concept of an "artificial person" that would own church property and permit its use without personal ownership by the clergy, thus creating the principle of a legal entity separate and distinct from its owners.

Civil Law
A codified legal system based on the Roman law also recognizes the corporation as a separate entity. The codification of the civil law in some European countries adopted many characteristics of the Roman law.

Common Law
In England, as early as the 14th century, many ecclesiastical, charitable, and municipal corporations developed. Their most common trait was *perpetual existence,* which became a corporate characteristic.

Overseas Trading Companies
The British government granted powers to explore, trade with, and colonize foreign territory. The British East India Company (1600), the Virginia Company (1609)—which founded the Virginia Colony and brought the Pilgrims to America—and the South Sea Company (1711) are examples of business associations that were the prototypes of the modern business corporation.

In the United States
Corporate laws were enacted in the United States as early as 1795 in North Carolina. A 20th century demand to incorporate created a need to modernize corporate law, which led to the development of the Model Business Corporation Act (MBCA) first published as a complete Act in 1950. The Act was last revised in 1984. Many states have amended their corporate law statutes substantially in accordance with the MBCA prior to its last revision. Today, in most states, filing the articles of incorporation, paying the necessary fee, and getting state approval cause the creation of an "artificial legal person"—the corporation.

Classification of Corporations

The needs of our society are commonly provided for by corporate institutions. For example, educational and health care needs are served by colleges and hospitals that may be *nonprofit corporations*. When the general public is served by the corporation—for example, a municipality—it is a *public corporation.* If substantial business is carried on in interstate commerce, it is a *foreign corporation* in other than its state of incorporation.

Public, Private, and Quasi-Public Corporations
A *public corporation* is one organized by the state or federal government to administer government affairs. An example is the Federal Deposit Insurance Corporation (FDIC). The government may then employ recognized business procedures in such matters as the purchase of property and management of its functions. For example, a city is a *municipal public corporation* granted authority to operate by the state.

Private corporations are created by private parties and may serve a profit or nonprofit purpose but not a governmental function. For instance, the national corporations that constitute our free-enterprise system are private corporations although their stock is sold to the public. They engage in business for a *profit* and to provide a return on the stockholders' investment by way of a *dividend*. Private corporations are now highly regulated by governmental agencies such as the Department of Labor and the Federal Trade Commission.[1] Most of our discussion in these chapters on corporations will be concerned with the private corporation organized for a profit and selling its stock to the public. They are "business corporations" and sometimes referred to as "public" because of their stock ownership.

Quasi-public corporations are known as "public service corporations." They provide services that the general public has an interest in, such as supplying gas and electricity and operating railroads. Because of their public involvement, they are subjected to greater governmental regulation than private corporations.

Domestic and Foreign Corporations

A *domestic corporation* is a corporation formed and created under the laws of the state that granted its corporate charter. In all other states or countries it is a *foreign corporation*. For example, if you were to incorporate in Massachusetts but did extensive business in New York and Florida and all the stockholders reside in Connecticut, you would be a domestic corporation in Massachusetts and a foreign corporation in New York and Florida.

It is not unusual for many large corporations to do business in several states. When a foreign corporation transacts business in a *substantial and continuous manner as opposed to a casual transaction,* it must obtain permission for this intrastate business in the foreign state. For example, if a corporate representative procured purchase orders in Texas that would be accepted by a Massachusetts corporation in Massachusetts, where its permanent corporate office was located, it would not be "doing business" in Texas.

In the following case the court found a professional law association was not doing business in a foreign state based on an isolated transaction.

Facts
Defendant, Dr. Reisman, is a medical doctor and general surgeon. The plaintiff is an Arizona professional association comprised of approximately 18 lawyers. In November of 1977 Dr. Reisman contacted Edwin Hendricks, a member of plaintiff, seeking legal advice and representation in a dispute between himself and Floyd County Medical Center (hospital) in Georgia. The hospital had restricted Dr. Reisman's privilege to use its facilities by requiring him to consult with another surgeon before scheduling a patient for surgery and to have another surgeon present during surgery. . . . The total bill for Hendricks' services, including travel costs and professional services of several of Hendricks' associates who also worked on the case, was $21,438.14. Dr. Reisman had made advances of $15,000 but failed and refused to pay the balance. Plaintiff sued Dr. Reisman and judgment was rendered for the plaintiff. Dr. Reisman appealed, urging that the trial court erred in denying his motion for a directed verdict based upon appellee law association's failure to register as a foreign corporation in Georgia.

Decision
The trial court properly denied Dr. Reisman's motion for a directed verdict.

Reasoning
Under these circumstances, there is ample basis for the court's conclusion that the appellee had neither extended its business into Georgia on a continuous basis nor engaged "in a number of repeated transactions of like nature" within the state. Affirmed, for plaintiff.

Reisman v. Martori, Meyer, Hendricks & Victor, an Arizona Professional Association, 271 S.E.2d 685 (Ga. 1980).

State corporate statutes require a foreign corporation that intends to do intrastate business to procure a *certificate of authority*. The application generally requires filing the foreign corporation's articles of incorporation with the Secretary of State and paying the filing fee. Of most importance is the name and office address of the corporation's registered agent to receive service of process in the event the foreign corporation is sued. Foreign corporations are subject to the foreign state regulating agencies and corporate state taxation.

---

[1] See chapters 47–49 on government regulation of business.

Close Corporations

It is a common misconception that the corporate organization with its many advantages is reserved for "big business." Many small companies desire to incorporate and thereby obtain limited liability. In a *close corporation* the stock is generally owned by one individual or his or her family. Hence, the managerial control of the corporation is in the owners. The closely held stock is not traded publicly, and the business is referred to as a close corporation. It has a separate corporate entity with all the corporate attributes of any corporation. Many state statutes authorize one person to incorporate, own all the stock, and serve as sole director and president.[2]

(Subchapter) S Corporations

Profits earned by a corporation normally are taxed two times! First the *corporation* is taxed on the profits and then, on distribution of the profits as corporate dividends to shareholders, the *shareholders* must include such dividends as taxable income in their income tax returns.

Under the federal Internal Revenue Code, shareholders of certain closely held *small* business corporations may elect to be *individually* taxed as partners. If the corporation qualifies, the individual shareholders are taxed on their shares of the corporation's income, or can deduct their proportionate share of its losses. The corporation, as an entity, pays no *federal* income tax. (It may have to pay a state corporate income tax.) Hence, the shareholders are relieved of the double-tax burden on corporate income—namely, a corporate tax on the profit when made and also a tax on the dividend when the profits are distributed.

Subchapter S Revision Act of 1982

The Subchapter S Revision Act of 1982 allows income deductions, losses and credits of the corporation to pass through to each of the shareholders the same way such items pass through to partners. To be eligible for Subchapter S treatment under the new Act, the following must be satisfied:

1. the number of permitted stockholders must not exceed 35;
2. only one class of stock, voting as well as non-voting common stock, is allowed;
3. all shareholders must consent to the election, however a person who becomes a shareholder after the initial election of Subchapter S status will be bound by the intitial election until the election is terminated;
4. passive investment income (e.g., royalties or rental income) is now allowed for corporations which do *not* have accumulated earnings and profits at the close of the taxable year; for those that *do* have such accumulated earnings and profits, a corporate level tax of 46 percent will be imposed on the excess of passive investment income over 25 percent of gross receipts, and the election will be terminated when the corporation has excessive passive investment income for three consecutive years;
5. the election for Subchapter S may be revoked by those shareholders holding a majority of the corporation's voting stock;
6. income and losses are passed through the corporation and allocated to shareholders on a per-share basis.

Professional Corporations

As the result of professional groups attempting to obtain various corporate advantages by way of tax-sheltered qualified pension and profit-sharing plans and other employee fringe benefits, every state has enacted corporate legislation allowing professionals to incorporate their practice. Members of the professions have found themselves annually confronted with a substantial tax liability because of their status as employers or

---

[2] See, for example, Mass. Gen. Laws, ch. 156, A sec. 8 (1963).

proprietorships or partnerships. By incorporating their practice, they become owner-employees and are thereby eligible to participate in employee fringe benefits such as pension and profit-sharing plans. Contributions to these plans are tax deductible by the professional corporation, and the trust income invested is tax free until distributed to the employees at retirement.

Creation of the corporation does not exempt the professional shareholder employees from liabilities which they otherwise would have had. That is, generally a shareholder individual who renders professional services as an employee of a professional corporation is liable for any negligence in which the individual personally participated to the same extent as if the individual were a sole practitioner. However, such individuals would not be liable for the conduct of other employees unless such individuals were at fault in appointing, supervising or co-operating with them. For example, doctors X,Y, and Z form a professional medical corporation. X engages in a malpractice procedure with patient, P. P may sue the corporation and also X as an individual. Generally, P would not be allowed to recover personally from doctors Y and Z. The Revised Model Professional Corporation Act provides for alternative theories of stockholders' liability.[3] Generally, this diminution in liability is an advantage over the unlimited liability of a partnership. The following case illustrates this principle.

Facts
Zagoria and Stoner were co-shareholders in a professional corporation, Zagoria and Stoner, P.C., all of whom are defendants. The corporation was organized for the practice of law under the Georgia Professional Corporation Act. At a real estate closing, Zagoria issued a check on the escrow account of Zagoria and Stoner, P.C., for $3,130 to the plaintiff, DuBose Enterprises, Inc., for commission as real estate broker. DuBose deposited the check that was subsequently returned unpaid.

DuBose sued the professional corporation and Zagoria and Stoner individually to recover on the check. DuBose contends that Stoner as a shareholder of the professional corporation should be individually liable for the dishonored check and should not be allowed the protection of the corporate shield from liability for the professional corporation's debts. Are Stoner and/or Zagoria personally liable for the corporation's debt? Is the corporation liable?

Decision
No. Judgment for defendants.

Reasoning
Stoner rendered no services in connection with the transaction in which the check was issued, and further, there was no evidence that DuBose was the client of the professional corporation in the real estate transaction. An attorney-shareholder of a professional corporation who does not participate in the rendering of the services out of which a claim arises will be free from personal liability for that claim. DuBose alleges that Zagoria is individually liable under the Georgia Professional Corporation Act. There was no evidence that DuBose was the client represented by Zagoria in the real estate closing. The law applicable to business corporations and professional corporations alike is that shareholders enjoy limited liability, but they will be liable individually for their own tortious or wrongful acts. Plaintiff DuBose presented no evidence to show that Zagoria issued the check with *knowledge* that it would be dishonored. DuBose alleged that the corporate escrow account on which the check was drawn was closed but presented no evidence on this point. However, DuBose also claimed that the professional corporation was liable. Any acts on the part of Zagoria which may have caused DuBose losses were ***ultra vires,*** unauthorized or beyond the scope of any authority to act for the professional corporation.

Zagoria v. DuBose Enterprises, Inc., 296 S.E.2d 353 (Ga. 1982).

ultra vires,
beyond the powers

---

[3] Cf. Revised Model Professional Corporation Act, sec. 34 and official comment thereto that provide for three alternatives regarding shareholder's liability: (1) limited liability as in a business corporation; or (2) complete vicarious personal liability as in a partnership; or (3) personal liability limited in amount conditioned upon financial responsibility in the form of insurance or a surety bond established by the licensing authority for each profession as security required as a condition for limiting liability of shareholders.

Nonprofit Corporations

A *nonprofit* (eleemosynary) corporation is organized for charitable purposes, examples being colleges and hospitals. Because they are given preferential tax treatment, special statutes govern their formation and operation.[4]

Corporate Regulations

Our economy may be described today as a highly regulated free-enterprise system. If you were to incorporate, state statutory law would grant you various corporate powers. However, as a domestic corporation in the state of formation, your company would be subject to the state tax laws and state regulating agencies. For example, if you were manufacturing raw materials, the state environmental protection agency would regulate the extent of the allowed pollution caused by the company. If you were "doing business" in a foreign state, the company would be subject to the regulating agencies and tax law of that state also. Interstate business would require you to comply with the regulations of the federal agencies, such as the Federal Trade Commission.

Constitutional Restrictions

State and federal administrative agencies are subject to certain constitutional restrictions in regulating a corporation's activities.

Corporation As a Legal Person

When a corporation comes into existence by filing the necessary documents with the appropriate state office, a legal entity is formed that exists independently of its owners. Today the corporation is highly regulated by various state and federal administrative agencies that have the right to review not only its books and records (e.g., the Internal Revenue Service), but also its operational procedures (e.g., the Department of Labor). As a legal person it has constitutional rights to protect itself from arbitrary governmental intervention. For example, an administrative summons issued by the I.R.S. to review corporate books and records is subject to a court "show cause" hearing.

The United States Constitution allows the corporation the right of the "people" under the Fourth Amendment (to be secure against unreasonable searches and seizures), the Fifth Amendment (right not to be deprived of liberty or property without due process of law), and the Fourteenth Amendment (the right not to be denied the equal protection of the laws). State constitutions commonly have similar restrictions.

Disregard of Corporate Entity

The corporation as a legal entity distinct from its shareholders is the basis for limited liability. Notice the court's reasoning in the following case why it would not pierce the corporate veil and disregard the corporate entity.

Facts

Jones, defendant, operated a sheet metal business as a sole proprietorship until it was incorporated. At that time, Jones transferred the assets of that business to the corporation in exchange for an equal amount of stock for himself and his wife. Pierson, plaintiff, was an employee of the corporation and loaned the corporation $80,571.42.

Jones assigned corporate accounts receivable of $34,000 to Pierson. The corporation filed bankruptcy at which time it owed Pierson $33,187.64. This action was instituted by Pierson against Jones personally to recover that sum. Judgment was rendered for Jones, and Pierson appeals.

Pierson contends that Jones did not have authority to borrow money for the corporation and that the trial court erred in not piercing the corporate veil. Does the evidence justify piercing the corporate veil?

---

[4] See the Revenue Act of 1978 (Pub. L. 95–600), sec. 341, and amendments thereunder.

Decision
No. Judgment for defendant, Jones, affirmed.

Reasoning
To justify piercing the corporate veil, it must also be shown that there is such a unity of interest and ownership that the individuality of such corporation and such person has ceased; and it must further appear from the facts that the observance of the fiction of separate existence would, under the circumstances, sanction a fraud or promote injustice.

Pierson also asserts that the corporation was undercapitalized at the time he lent it money and that this is a justification for piercing the corporate veil. We disagree.

Undercapitalization is one factor to be considered in determining whether or not to pierce the corporate veil. However, financial inadequacy is measured by the nature and magnitude of the corporate undertaking or the reasonableness of the cushion for creditors at the time of the inception of the corporation. Here the corporate accountant testified that at the time of its inception the corporation was not undercapitalized. Clearly, a corporation adequately capitalized at its inception can become undercapitalized at a later time for any of a variety of legitimate reasons.

John A. Pierson v. Gail Jones, 625 P.2d 1085 (Id. 1981).

The corporation serves as a form of legal entity to answer the needs of business society. It serves small as well as large businesses. However, because it is formed with the permission of society, it is subject to societal constraints and cannot do what society condemns. When it attempts to do so, the courts will "pierce the corporate veil" that is, look behind the corporate legal entity to determine such impropriety. For example, if shareholders X, Y, and Z formed a closely-held corporation without adequate capital to support its transactions, commingled corporate and their personal funds, and never held director or stockholders' meetings, the corporation is vulnerable to the *doctrine of piercing the corporate veil.* When the doctrine is applied by a court, the shareholders' personal assets may be reached by a corporate business creditor, or by a tort claimant suing the shareholders for a personal injury that occurred on the corporate premises. Another example would be an undercapitalized **subsidiary corporation** owned by a parent corporation that is sued by a business creditor of the subsidiary. A court may hold the parent liable for the obligations of the subsidiary.

subsidiary corporation
a corporation owned by another corporation

In some instances in order to obtain credit, the shareholders may have to make themselves personally liable for the corporate debts. For example, a bank may ask them to individually sign a corporate note.

The courts will always "pierce the corporate veil" when the stockholders form the corporation to perpetuate a fraud or to accomplish an illegal purpose. The following case illustrates a wrongful death claim based upon the negligent operation of a leased swimming pool operated by a corporation. Notice the reason why the court disregarded the corporate entity and held the owner personally liable.

Facts
Plaintiff, Minton, is the father of a girl who drowned in a public swimming pool leased and operated by Seminole Hot Springs Corporation. Defendant, Cavaney, was the director and secretary of the corporation. Seminole never issued any stock, had any assets, or functioned as a corporation. Was Cavaney personally liable for the claim?

Decision
Yes. Judgment for plaintiff, Minton.

Reasoning
The terms "alter ego" and "disregard of the corporate entity" are generally used to refer to the various situations that are an abuse of the corporate privilege. The equitable owners of a corporation, for example, are personally liable when they treat the assets of the corporation as their own and add or withdraw capital from the corporation at will, when they hold themselves out as being personally liable for the debts of the corporation, or when they provide inadequate capitalization and actively participate in the conduct of corporation affairs.

In the instant case the evidence is undisputed that there was no attempt to provide adequate capitalization. Seminole never had any substantial assets. It leased the pool that it operated, and the lease was forfeited for failure to pay the rent. Its capital was trifling compared with the business to be done and the risks of loss.

Minton v. Cavaney, 364 P.2d 473 (Cal. 1961).

Subsidiaries

A subsidiary corporation has a majority of its outstanding and issued stock owned by a parent corporation. When the parent corporation owns all the stock it is a wholly owned subsidiary. For example, a new line of merchandise may involve such a substantial risk to a corporation that it desires to fragment its liability by forming a subsidiary to sell the new products. Generally, the officers and directors of the parent corporation will also serve in the subsidiary corporation. If the parent corporation exercises control over the wholly owned subsidiary, it will usually be liable for the contracts and torts of the subsidiary.

Summary Statement

1. A corporation is a legal entity created by statute authorizing an association of persons to carry on an enterprise.
2. The corporation as a legal person is a distinct legal entity and hence the corporate stockholders cannot be sued for corporate liabilities. This is known as "limited liability." A stockholder's risk is limited to the loss of his or her investment.
3. Corporation law is found in state or federal statutory law. Each state has its own corporation laws, and many have modernized them to comply substantially with the former Model Business Corporation Act.
4. Roman law required government approval for a corporation.
5. Canon law developed the concept of an "artificial person" that could own property in its own name.
6. Civil law recognized the corporation as a separate entity.
7. Common law established the perpetual existence of a corporation.
8. Corporations may be classified as:
    a. public,
    b. private,
    c. quasi-public,
    d. domestic, or
    e. foreign.
9. A foreign corporation is one that is "doing business" in a substantial and continuous manner where it was not originally incorporated.
10. A foreign corporation must maintain a resident agent in the foreign state to receive service of process in the event the corporation is sued.
11. Private corporations are highly regulated by the state and federal governments. As a "legal person," a corporation is entitled to many constitutional rights.
12. The courts may disregard the corporate entity and "pierce the corporate veil" whenever necessary to prevent fraud.
13. A corporation that qualifies under the Internal Revenue Code may elect to be taxed similarly to a partnership. It is referred to as a "Subchapter S corporation."
14. Corporations have numerous attributes that make them a very popular form of business, namely:
    a. perpetual succession;
    b. centralization of management;
    c. no shareholder liability for corporate obligations;
    d. power to sell their stock to raise capital;
    e. ease of transferring corporate stock; and
    f. under the legal entity theory they are liable for their own obligations.

In the following case the court analyzed the factors involved in piercing the corporate veil.

United States of America v. Healthwin-Midtown Convalescent Hospital and Rehabilitation Center, Inc. and Israel Zide
511 F.Supp. 416 (1981)

Maletz, Judge. On September 14, 1971, the Healthwin Corporation was organized in California for the purpose of operating a health care facility. From that date, until November 30, 1974, it participated as a provider of services under the Medicare Act, and received periodic payments from the United States Department of Health, Education and Welfare (HEW) for the services provided Medicare beneficiaries by Healthwin. Audits by HEW showed that a series of overpayments had been made to Healthwin in 1972, 1973 and 1974 in the total amount of $30,481.55. It is this sum, plus interest, that the United States, plaintiff, seeks to recover here.

The issue here is whether defendant Zide, president and administrator of Healthwin Corporation, is personally liable for the Medicare overpayments to Healthwin. As a basis for such liability, plaintiff first argues that the corporate entity should be disregarded under the alter ego theory of liability. Plaintiff's alter ego claim must be analyzed in accordance with state law. Under California law, "issues of alter ego do not lend themselves to strict rules and prima facie cases. Whether the corporate veil should be pierced depends upon the innumerable individual equities of each case." Generally, however, the corporate veil may be pierced when it is shown: that there . . . [is] such unity of interest and ownership that the separate personalities of the corporation and the individual no longer exist and that if the acts are treated as those of the corporation alone, an inequitable result will follow.

With regard to the "unity of interest and ownership" test, the evidence at trial showed that at all times relevant here, Zide was a fifty percent shareholder of the Healthwin corporation. In addition, Zide had a fifty percent interest in a partnership which owned both the realty in which Healthwin's health care facility was located and the furnishings used at that facility.

Other factors the courts consider in determining whether the corporate veil should be pierced include: the inadequacy of the corporation's capitalization or its insolvency; the failure to observe corporate formalities; the absence of regular board meetings; the nonfunctioning of corporate directors; the commingling of corporate and noncorporate assets; the diversion of assets from the corporation to the detriment of creditors; and the failure of an individual to maintain an arm's length relationship with the corporation.

All these factors are present here. . . . The necessary conclusion from all this is that Zide handled Healthwin's finances so as to accommodate his own business interests. Treatment of corporate assets in this fashion has long been considered a significant factor supporting the piercing of the corporate veil.

Another factor present here is that the operations of Healthwin were marked by an essential disregard of corporate formalities. Thus board meetings were not regularly held and, with the exception of the first board meeting, Zide and his wife were the only directors or shareholders present.

There is the final consideration that the court should not pierce the corporation's veil unless necessary to prevent an inequitable result. As to this, it is not necessary that plaintiff prove actual fraud; it is enough if the failure to pierce the corporation's veil would result in an injustice. Given the situation present here, the court must conclude that it would be unjust not to pierce the corporate veil. For one thing, Healthwin's undercapitalization subjected all its creditors, including plaintiff, to inequitable risks regarding Healthwin's obligations to them.

In view of the foregoing considerations, the court holds that Healthwin's corporate entity should be disregarded under the alter ego theory of liability. Judgment for plaintiff.

Questions and Case Problems

1. Planet was the beneficial owner of 66 acres of unimproved land, held in trust, and CT&T as trustee was the legal owner. Planet borrowed $7,622,956.71 from Bankers securing the loan by a first mortgage on that land. The loan was also personally guaranteed by Romano, the president and sole shareholder of Planet, and by his wife, Barbara, who owned no interest in Planet. Planet defaulted on the loan, and Bankers instituted foreclosure proceedings against CT&T. Romano was neither a named defendant nor made a party to this action. Hartenfeld filed his petition to intervene asserting a $150,000 equitable lien on the land for the following reasons: Hartenfeld and Romano had entered into a written agreement whereby Hartenfeld was to receive $200,000 for performing legal services for Romano; the contract provided that "whenever during 1973, you (Romano) successfully accomplish a new land loan on any of your parcels of real estate, I will be paid immediately all fees then owed me under this letter agreement." After notice to all interested parties, the subject land was sold at a sheriff's sale to Bankers, the sole bidder, for $7,622,956.71, the principal amount of the loan. Hartenfeld claims that the loan by Bankers to Planet must be construed as a loan to Romano under a "reverse" piercing of the corporate veil. The court allowed an imposition of an equitable lien in Hartenfeld's favor and Bankers appealed. May the court pierce the corporate veil of Planet and hold Romano personally liable to Hartenfeld? [*Bankers Trust Company,* et al. *v. Chicago Title & Trust Company,* et al., 412 N.E.2d 660 (Ill. 1980).]

2. The plaintiff, The Village Press, Inc., negotiated with Stephen Blum, as agent for the Stephen Edward Co., Inc., to prepare mail order catalogues for Pridecraft, Inc. Stephen Blum controlled both the Stephen Edward Company and Pridecraft. The parties entered into an agreement whereby the plaintiff would print the Pridecraft catalogues and bill Stephen Edward Company, Inc. Plaintiff delivered the catalogues, but due to a dispute over their quality, neither corporation tendered payment. No evidence was presented at trial that indicated that Blum suppressed the fact that his businesses were incorporated. In fact, the exhibits show that Blum mailed all of his correspondence on letterheads of the Stephen Edward Co., Inc. and signed them "Stephen Blum, President." Moreover, no evidence was offered that Blum ever made any agreement to hold himself personally responsible for his corporations' debts. Plaintiff argues that Blum personally controlled the corporations, making them, in effect, his alter egos. Plaintiff concludes therefrom that Blum is personally liable for their debts. Is Blum personally liable for the debts of the two corporations he controlled? [*The Village Press, Inc. v. Stephen Edward Company, Inc.,* et al., 416 A.2d 1373 (N.H. 1980).]

3. Colin sought to evict a tenant under a rent control regulation. The building was owned by 130 West 112th Street Corp. and all the stock was owned by Colin. Colin claimed that he desired the apartment for his own personal use. The rent commissioner denied the application on the ground that Colin had no standing (no legal status in the case) because he was not the owner of the building, and the rental regulations do not recognize a corporation as having a necessity to occupy housing. Colin claimed, because he owned all the stock, the court should disregard the corporate entity. May the corporate veil be pierced for the benefit of the corporation or its stockholders? [*Colin v. Altman,* 333 N.Y.S.2d 432 (1972).]

4. This is an action filed by The Associated Press to collect for the breach of two contracts executed by the defendant, Briarcliff Communications Group, Inc., one a news service and membership contract and the other a wirephoto contract. The Associated Press is a non-profit, New York corporation which is engaged in the business of gathering and disseminating news and literary property to its members. It has not registered with the Georgia Secretary of State to do business in Georgia. Does the interstate nature of the plaintiff's business render it exempt from the Georgia statutory registration requirement by virtue of the supremacy of the commerce clause of the United States Constitution? [*Briarcliff Communications Group, Inc. v. Associated Press,* 268 S.E.2d 356 (Ga. 1980).]

5. Linton & Company, Inc., (Linton) plaintiff, is a consulting firm engaged primarily in urban planning and environmental studies, maintaining its principal office in Washington, D.C. Defendant, R. L. Reid, is an officer and shareholder of Robert Reid Engineers, Inc., (Engineers), defendant, that performs engineering services and maintians its principal offices in Houston, Texas. The present dispute between the parties related to work done incident to the planned construction of the Red Mountain Expressway in Birmingham, Alabama. Linton executed a subcontract with Engineers in Washington, D.C. to prepare an environmental impact statement.

    During the time of negotiating the subcontract as well as performing upon it, Linton had three or four employees who came to Alabama to collect data for the environmental impact statements for the proposed Red Mountain Expressway project. During the entire two and a half year period that Linton was involved in this project, Linton's employees made approximately twelve trips to Alabama. The average duration of a trip was two or three days with the employees staying in hotels while in Alabama and returning to Linton's Washington offices. At least seventy-five percent of Linton's work pursuant to the subcontract was performed in Linton's offices in Washington, D.C.

    Although Engineers was paid by the state on March 6, 1979, Engineers has refused to pay anything to Linton. Consequently Linton initiated this suit in the U.S. District Court in Alabama to recover money for breach of contract and work and labor done. Plaintiff has never qualified to do business in Alabama. Defendant claims that this failure precludes plaintiff from bringing this action. Decide. [*Linton & Company, Inc. v. Robert Reid Engineers, Inc.,* 504 F.Supp. 1169 (1981).]

6. S. & L. Painting Contractors, Inc., plaintiff, does virtually all its business in Mississippi and less than 1% of its business in Arkansas. It is not registered to do business in the State of Arkansas as is required by law; the company's officers did not know of the requirement. Its agents came to Arkansas and entered into a contract in Arkansas to do some work on a residence near Lake Village. Plaintiff was not paid for its work and filed an action to impose a lien against the Arkansas residence. The owners, J. D. Vickers and Susan Smith Vickers, were joined as parties defendants. May plaintiff, a foreign corporation, enforce its contract in Arkansas? [*S. & L. Painting Contractors, Inc. v. J. D. Vickers,* et al., 589 S.W.2d 196 (Ark. 1979).]

7. X, Y, and Z are stockholders of a real estate business they operate as a corporation. They have purchased a building for office use and formed a separate corporation to own the building. The real estate office and other tenants will pay rent to the corporation that owns the building. P, a client, brought suit against the real estate corporation for return of her down payment and has attached the building owned by the separate corporation. May the court disregard the corporate entity that owns the building and allow P's attachment?

8. X owned a small department store as a sole proprietor. X had many personal and business creditors. In an attempt to save his business, he incorporated the store and purchased all the stock. X's personal creditors sought to reach the corporate assets to collect their claims. X claimed that the store as a corporation owned assets distinct from his personal assets. Decide.

9. Diversacon, Industries, Inc. (Diversacon), plaintiff, a Florida corporation with its principal place of business in that state is a wholly owned subsidiary of United States Industries, Inc. (USI) a Delaware corporation. USI maintains an administrative office in Jackson, Mississippi at the headquarters of Con-Plex, one of its subdivisions. A bid was submitted in the name of Diversacon to the State of Louisiana to construct an interstate highway, listing Con-Plex post office address and telephone in Jackson. Diversacon was awarded the contract. Subsequently, all administrative support necessary to the Louisiana construction project was handled out of the Con-Plex office in Jackson by USI personnel. Diversacon obtained a surety agreement with the defendant, National Bank of Commerce of Mississippi, by which the Bank was to reimburse it for funds expended on the subcontractor's behalf.

When the sub-contractor defaulted and abandoned the Louisiana project in 1975, the Bank refused to honor its obligation for over $600,000 which Diversacon spent to complete the construction. Diversacon's suit against National Bank of Commerce of Mississippi followed. The Mississippi Federal District Court found Diversacon's activities to constitute "doing business" in that state, which required it to qualify as a foreign corporation under Mississippi law in order to have access to its courts. Was Diversacon doing business in Mississippi? [*Diversacon Industries, Inc. v. National Bank of Commerce of Mississippi,* 629 F.2d 1030 (1980).]

10. In the case of *United States of America v. Healthwin-Midtown Convalescent Hospital and Rehabilitation Center, Inc. and Israel Zide,* 511 F.Supp. 416 (1981),[5] the court held the defendant Zide, a director/shareholder, personally liable for Medicare overpayments made to his corporation and pierced the corporate veil on the theory that he was the alter ego of the corporation. What should Zide have done to have prevented this result?

---

[5] See p. 635.

Creation and Termination 43

After you have read this chapter, you should be able to:

1. Define and explain the function of a promoter.
2. Explain why a promoter is a fiduciary.
3. Explain the information required in the articles of incorporation.
4. Define and explain a *de jure* corporation.
5. Define and explain a *de facto* corporation.
6. Define and explain a so-called "corporation by estoppel."
7. Explain involuntary dissolution by the state.
8. Explain when the incorporators may dissolve a corporation.
9. Explain when the shareholders may dissolve a corporation.
10. Distinguish a merger from a consolidation.
11. Explain the legal effect of a merger or a consolidation.
12. Explain the legal effect of a "stock exchange."

Introduction

After you have decided to join with other persons to form a corporation, where would you look to determine how to form the corporation, and what societal limitations exist to your doing so? You probably will want to retain an attorney to give you this advice. It may come as a surprise to learn that a corporation can be formed only by permission of the state and, therefore, only by compliance with the laws of the state. Also, only the state can terminate corporate existence. You and your associates are called *promoters,* and all of you assume certain duties and liabilities in connection with organizing the corporation and contracts made before the corporation came into existence. We will begin with a discussion of promoters.

Creation

Promoters

If you were to plan the incorporation of a business venture, it would be necessary to consider whether contracts have to be signed *before* the corporation is formed. For example, will it own or lease its place of operation? Who will invest in the business? Or will it have to borrow funds from a bank? Planning the corporation and attending to its organization is the function of a **promoter.**

promoter
a person who organizes and brings a corporation into existence

Promoter's Liability. Because the promoter performs various functions *before* formation of the corporation, the promoter is not its agent. Accordingly, the promoter is personally liable on contracts made on behalf of the proposed corporation. For example, as a promoter, you would be personally liable if you signed an office lease on behalf of a nonexisting corporation. If the corporation later occupied the premises, it may also be liable; however, this would not relieve you, the promoter, from your liability to the landlord.

After incorporation, the corporation may become bound *to the terms* of the preincorporation contract, but the courts differ on how this may be accomplished. One theory is *adoption,* whereby the corporation adopts or assumes the obligation of performing the preincorporation contract either by corporate resolution of its board of directors or impliedly by knowingly accepting the benefits of the contract. The promoter is still liable as a party to the contract. A second, and the most used, theory is **novation,**[1] whereby the nonpromoter party to the preincorporation contract agrees to discharge the contract and, by a new contract, take the corporation in place of the promoter. A third theory is *continuing offer,* whereby the preincorporation contract is construed to be a continuing offer to the corporation by the nonpromoter party, and the corporation on its creation can accept it and be bound. A fourth theory, not legally sound, is *ratification,* whereby the corporation seeks to authenticate the making of the contract on its behalf retroactively as of the time the preincorporation contract was made. The ratification theory is not sound because the corporation was not in existence at the time the preincorporation contract was made and, therefore, could not at that time appoint an agent nor authorize the contract to be made.

novation
a new contract in which one of the parties was not a party to the old contract and which immediately discharges the old contract

Although the promoter is not an agent for the proposed corporation, the promoter is under a duty to act for its benefit and hence is a **fiduciary,**[2] and in that capacity the promoter owes the corporation being promoted and its stock subscribers a high degree of care.

fiduciary
a person with a duty to act primarily for the benefit of another

---

[1] See pp. 188–89 for a discussion of novation.

[2] See pp. 521–23 for an explanation of the implied duties of a of fiduciary.

Incorporators

State corporate laws require the **incorporator** to sign and file the articles of incorporation with the Secretary of State. While some states insist on three incorporators, the modern trend requires only one. Generally, the statutes require the incorporators to be natural persons, and often citizens of the state or of the United States. Because incorporation is a contractual undertaking, the incorporators must not be minors, with their limited capacity to contract. The modern statutory trend is to allow a corporation to act as an incorporator.

incorporators
the persons who sign the articles of incorporation

Articles of Incorporation

State corporate statutes establish the procedures involved in incorporating a business. The **articles of incorporation** is the written application to the state for permission to incorporate. It must be filed with the Secretary of State and generally must have the following information.

articles of incorporation
the written application to the state for permission to incorporate

The Name of the Corporation. The incorporators must select a name that is distinguishable from other corporations upon the records of the Secretary of State.[3] State statutes generally allow for the reservation of the corporate name (for three or four months) in advance of the filing date.[4] This may be a convenient way of assuring the organizing members that the selected name will qualify. The name must contain one of the following words or its abbreviation: "corporation," "company," "incorporated," or "limited."

The Purpose. There must be a statement of the purpose for which the corporation is organized. As we previously discussed under the classification of corporations, the members may incorporate for a profit, nonprofit, professional, or charitable purpose. State statutes establish the rules to qualify as a special class of corporation. For example, separate laws exist for the incorporation of a professional medical practice because of its stock ownership by the licensed physicians and medical purpose to deliver health services.

Capital Stock Authorization. The amount and class of shares the corporation shall have authority to issue is stated in the articles of incorporation. This is not the amount of stock the corporation must issue. For example, the corporation may initially issue 5,000 shares of stock although it is authorized 25,000 shares, the remaining 20,000 shares may be issued at a later date. The 5,000 are referred to as *issued and outstanding*.

Any restrictions placed on the transfer of shares of stock are also specified. For instance, closely held corporations commonly provide that a shareholder who desires to sell his or her stock must first notify the directors of the selling price and grant the corporation the option to redeem the shares at the same price. This method assures control of the voting stock by the owner-directors of the small corporation. The transfer of stock is discussed in a later chapter.

Place of Business. The post office address of the *initial* principal office of the corporation must be listed. This establishes that it is doing business as a *domestic* corporation in that state.

Directors and Officers. Most states require a listing of the names and addresses of the initial directors and officers of the corporation.

The directors need not be residents of the state of incorporation nor shareholders of the corporation. The directors may be one or more in number, and they may be increased or decreased by amending the articles of incorporation. The initial directors hold office until the organizational stockholders' meeting, when they are ratified or new directors are elected by the stockholders. Each director will hold office generally until the next annual stockholders' meeting or until a successor is elected. A director may resign prior to that time or be terminated by the stockholders for cause. After approval of the articles of

---

[3] RMBCA, sec. 4.01(b).   [4] RMBCA, sec. 4.02.

charter
articles of incorporation approved by the state

incorporation by the state, which is now called the corporate **charter,** the directors named therein hold an organizational meeting for the purpose of adopting the bylaws, electing the corporate officers,[5] and transacting whatever other business comes before the meeting—e.g., approve of any previous contracts entered into by the promoters.

The officers appointed by the board of directors generally consist of a president, one or more vice presidents, a secretary, and a treasurer. Many states allow the same person to be both secretary and treasurer. The directors and officers are discussed in a later chapter.

Incorporators. The incorporator must sign and file the articles of incorporation under the penalties of **perjury,** stating that the information they contain is correct.

perjury
knowingly falsely swearing under oath, or affirming, in a judicial or quasi-judicial proceeding

Registered Agent. The name and address of the registered agent is placed in the articles to provide a claimant access to whom and where legal service can be made. The articles of incorporation are a matter of public information in the office of the Secretary of State and may be viewed there by anyone. A person desirous of suing the corporation may send legal process to the resident agent or a corporate officer. Many states require a resident agent only when the applicant is a foreign corporation.

Bylaws. The rules and regulations of a corporation for its internal management and operation are its **bylaws.** They implement the charter and must be reasonable and not contrary to law. The shareholders have the right to enact bylaws, in the absence of statute and charter to the contrary. The Revised Model Business Corporation Act gives to the incorporators or initial directors the power to enact the initial bylaws[6] and also, in most states, the power to amend and repeal them in the absence of statute or charter to the contrary.

bylaws
(in corporations) rules and regulations of a corporation for its internal management and operation

Certificate of Incorporation

Upon the filing of the articles of incorporation and payment of the filing fee, a certificate of incorporation is issued by the Secretary of State. In most states, and under the Revised Model Business Corporation Act, corporate existence then begins.[7] The approved articles of incorporation are now called the charter. At this stage, creditors deal with the corporation as an entity separate from its stockholders, and the officers may do business in their respective capacities to avoid personal liability. The first order of business will be an organizational meeting for the stockholders to elect the directors, who will appoint the officers. The directors then adopt the bylaws, open a corporate checking account, and commence the management of the business.

Defective Incorporations

de jure corporation
a corporation which has completely or substantially complied with the mandatory requirements of a valid state incorporation statute

De Jure Corporation. Upon issuance of the corporate certificate, the corporate entity is formed. Although minor errors occur in attempting to comply with the statutory requirements for incorporation, a *de jure* (by law) **corporation** exists. For example, an incorporator may have failed to list a director's address in the articles of incorporation, or the seals required by statute to be next to the signatures of the incorporators may have been omitted.

de facto corporation
a corporation which has not complied substantially with the mandatory requirements of a valid state incorporation statute but has made a colorable attempt to do so, in good faith, and has begun to operate as a corporation

De Facto Corporation. When a *de jure* corporation cannot be found, the courts will determine if a defective incorporation is in "sufficient compliance" with the *mandatory* provisions of the corporation law. If it finds (1) a colorable attempt (i.e., real effort) in good faith (2) to comply with the mandatory provisions (3) of a valid corporate law for its incorporation and (4) business use of the corporation beyond just the organizational meeting, a *de facto* (by fact) **corporation** has been formed. It exists in fact although not by law, and a *de facto* corporate debtor cannot avoid liability on the basis of its being defective. Although a *de facto* corporate defendant may not attack its legal existence for

---

[5] RMBCA, sec. 2.05.   [6] RMBCA, sec. 2.06.   [7] RMBCA, sec. 2.03.

the reason stated, the state may do so. The certificate of incorporation is conclusive evidence of corporate existence. Often the phrase "colorable compliance" is used to describe "colorable attempt," and it means that some real effort has been made to comply, but the compliance is less than substantial, although getting close to it.

Corporate status, whether *de jure* or *de facto,* is very important with respect to the liability of the corporate members (shareholders) because, with the corporate status as a shield, the members are not liable for corporate obligations. Without corporate status, they are personally liable for their contractual obligations. This is illustrated in the following case where the court held that there was no colorable attempt to comply with the state corporate statute and, therefore, since there was no *de facto* corporation, the members were personally liable.

Facts
Conway, the plaintiff, entered into a contract with Trend Set Construction Corporation for remodeling work on Conway's home. Samet, the defendant, signed the contract as president of Trend Set Construction Corporation. Conway subsequently learned that Trend Set had never filed a certificate of incorporation. Suit was then brought against Samet personally. Samet defended on the ground that her attorney was supposed to have incorporated the business. The attorney told Samet she was incorporated and gave her a corporate seal. Her attorney had all the necessary information to incorporate and was paid the incorporation fees. Samet claimed she had a *de facto* corporation. Was this a *de facto* corporation?

Decision
No. Judgment for the plaintiff, Conway.

Reasoning
More is required to establish the *de facto* corporation defense than giving instructions to an attorney to incorporate. There must be a colorable attempt to comply with the statute governing incorporations made before the contract. Without any certificate of incorporation having been even prepared or acknowledged, there can be no *de facto* corporation.

Conway v. Samet, 300 N.Y.S.2d 243 (1969).

Corporation by Estoppel

The so-called "corporation by **estoppel**" occurs when business associates hold themselves out as being a corporation to third persons who materially changed their position in reasonable reliance on the misrepresentation. The estoppel prevents such associates from later denying corporate existence, but it does not create a corporation. There is an estoppel to deny corporate status.

Notice how the court in the following case decided that the doctrine of corporation by estoppel is distinct from a *de facto* corporation.

estoppel
a principle of law that when one person "holds out" (represents) a material fact to another person, who changes his position materially to his prejudice in reasonable reliance on the holding out, the first person is "estopped" (prohibited) to deny what he asserted previously

Facts
Bukacek, the plaintiff, and three others were the incorporators of Pell City Farms, Inc., the defendant. Pursuant to an agreement between the incorporators and Pell City Farms, Inc., Bukacek conveyed his 300-acre tract to Pell City Farms, Inc. Bukacek then claimed that Pell City was incapable of taking legal title to the property as a corporation because it had not filed its articles of incorporation. Bukacek executed the deed, transferring his interest in the land to the corporation; he was an incorporator, officer, director, and stockholder of the corporation and participated in the business activities of the corporation relating to the land after the articles of incorporation were filed. May Bukacek have the corporation's title to the land set aside?

Decision
No. Judgment for defendant, Pell City Farms.

Reasoning
The incidence of corporate existence may exist *as between the parties* by virtue of an estoppel. Corporations by estoppel are not based upon the same principles as corporations *de facto.* A *de facto* corporation cannot be created by estoppel. The only effect of an estoppel is to prevent the raising of the question of the existence of a corporation.

Bukacek was one of the incorporators who dealt with the corporation as a corporation both before and after the articles of incorporation were filed. Bukacek is estopped to deny the existence of the corporation at the time he voluntarily executed a deed transferring property to the corporation even though the articles of incorporation had not been filed at that time.

Bukacek v. Pell City Farms, Inc., 237 So.2d 851 (Ala. 1970).

Termination

The state creates corporate existence, and only the state can authorize its dissolution. Unlike a sole proprietorship or a partnership, a corporation will not terminate upon the death of an owner. When a stockholder dies, his or her shares, as personal property, become an asset of the decedent stockholder's estate. As previously discussed, this continuity of the corporation is called "perpetual succession." Our discussion will focus on methods of terminating a corporation either voluntarily by the incorporators or shareholders, or involuntarily by the state, shareholders, or creditors. By the term "dissolution" is meant the termination of the existence of a corporation as an entity.

Voluntary Dissolution

A corporation has statutory power to voluntarily terminate, provided that it complies with the state corporate laws. In some instances the incorporators may dissolve the corporation; however, it is usually the shareholders. The directors have no power to dissolve without the stockholders' approval.

By Incorporators or Initial Directors. After having filed the articles of incorporation and being granted the corporate charter by the state, the corporation may be unable to issue its stock and, therefore, may decide not to commence business. The incorporators or initial directors may file *articles of dissolution*.[8]

Upon approval, the Secretary of State will issue a *certificate of dissolution,* and corporate existence will terminate.

By Shareholders. The shareholders may, by following state corporate law, dissolve the corporation for any reason. The board of directors adopts a resolution recommending dissolution that is submitted to a vote at a shareholders' meeting. In most states, at least a majority vote is required. Articles of dissolution are then filed, and the certificate of dissolution will be issued by the Secretary of State.

In most states and under the Revised Model Business Corporation Act section 14.05, the dissolved corporation may not carry on any business except that necessary to wind up and liquidate its business affairs. The corporation must notify and pay the creditors, pay any taxes due, collect the receivables, liquidate the assets, and distribute the remainder of the assets to the shareholders.

Involuntary Dissolution

The court, on a petition brought by the shareholders or the state, may dissolve the corporation.

By Shareholders. The shareholders may bring a petition to dissolve the corporation for gross mismanagement *by the board of directors* (e.g., voting for plant expansion with insufficient funds to finance the venture); on the ground of unfair advantage by the majority over the minority stockholders; or on the grounds of dissension and deadlock.

In the following case the court refused to dissolve a solvent corporation whose shareholders were deadlocked in electing a board of directors for two successive years.

Facts

Cooper-George, Inc., the defendant, was created in 1950 by J. L. Cooper, Henry George and John George, for the primary purpose of building an apartment house. The shares were divided evenly between the Cooper family and the George family.

. . . The George family, plaintiff, initiated this suit for dissolution. Judgment was rendered for the plaintiff, and defendants Cooper-George, Inc. and various shareholders appealed.

The Cooper-George apartment house, a 13 story apartment building in downtown Spokane, is the sole asset of the corporation. The defendants contend that RCW (statute) 23A.28.170(1)(c) does not require a dissolution when a company has been in

---

[8] RMBCA, sec. 14.01.

business for 28 years, operates a major apartment building, is solvent, is not being mismanaged, is not deadlocked at the board of director level regarding transaction of business, is not denying to any shareholder requested information, and is not causing any shareholder to benefit to the financial detriment of another. The plaintiff maintains that the mere fact that the shareholders were deadlocked in electing a board of directors for two successive years is all that is required under RCW to dissolve a corporation.

Decision
Reversed. Judgment for defendant, Cooper-George, Inc., and its appealing shareholders.

Reasoning
In determining whether to grant dissolution under either the common law or statute, the principal inquiry appears to be whether dissolution would be beneficial to the shareholders and not injurious to the public. We conclude that our present statute contemplates that the trial court, in its discretion, shall determine whether there exist equitable grounds for ordering dissolution of the corporation. In so ruling, the trial court should consider business profitability despite the deadlock. In this case, the trial court erroneously ruled that Cooper-George should be dissolved merely on the basis that the jurisdictional requirements were met. We remand the matter to the trial court to determine, after considering the best interests of all the shareholders, whether dissolution is warranted.

Henry George & Sons, Inc. v. Cooper-George, Inc., et al., 632 P.2d 512 (Wash. 1981).

By State. The state, acting through the attorney general's office, may cause an involuntary dissolution for a corporation's failure to pay state taxes, for not filing annual reports, for fraudulently filing articles of incorporation, for the failure of a foreign corporation to appoint a resident agent, or for abuse of its corporate authority.

Bankruptcy
A corporation may voluntarily elect to file for bankruptcy, or its creditors may commence involuntary bankruptcy proceedings by petitioning the bankruptcy court. The corporate assets will then be liquidated and applied to creditors' claims, or a repayment plan will be considered by the bankruptcy court, depending on the nature of the bankruptcy case. Once bankruptcy proceedings have commenced, a board of directors' resolution to dissolve adopted by a majority of the shareholders will effect a dissolution.[9]

Mergers, Consolidations, and Exchange of Stock

Merger
In a **merger,** one corporation is absorbed by another corporation, which continues to exist as the surviving corporation while the other terminates. State corporate statutes have specific procedures that must be followed. Generally, each board of directors involved adopts a plan of merger that is approved by its stockholders[10] (see figure 43.1).

In the following case, a shareholder contested a sale of the corporation on the grounds that it was, in fact, a merger and that the merger statute, which required a two-thirds shareholders' vote, was not followed.

merger
(in corporations) the absorption of one corporation by another corporation

Facts
Applestein, the plaintiff, a shareholder of United Board and Carton Corporation, the defendant, sought to enjoin a proposed sale of 40 percent of the corporation's stock to Epstein, the sole shareholder of Interstate Corporation, in exchange for all of Interstate's stock. Interstate would then cease to exist, and United would then take over all its assets and liabilities. Applestein argued that this was a merger rather than a sale and hence, required a vote of approval of two-thirds of the stockholders. United claimed that it had the right to purchase stock without shareholders' approval.

Decision
Judgment for plaintiff, Applestein.

---

[9] See chapter 30, Bankruptcy under the Bankruptcy Reform Act of 1978. A corporation is not entitled to a discharge in bankruptcy in a Chapter 7 case.

[10] RMBCA, sec. 11.01.

Figure 43.1   Statutory Merger

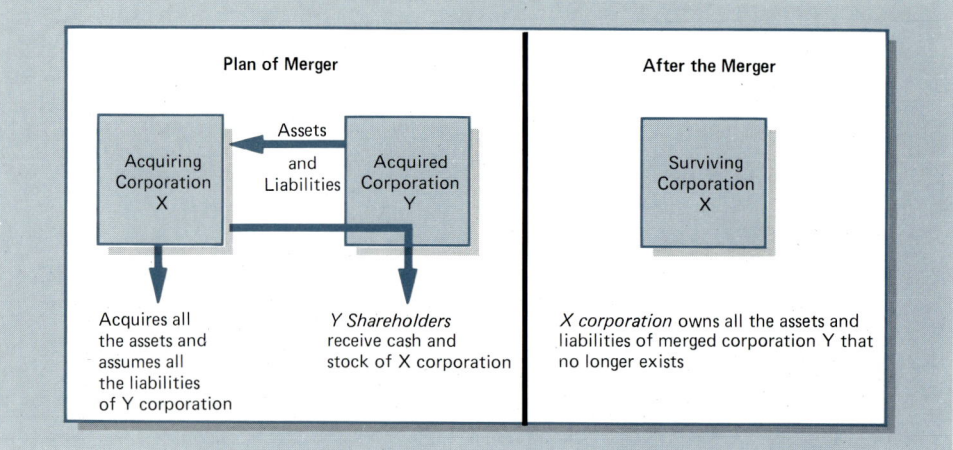

Reasoning

A merger of two corporations contemplates that one will be absorbed by the other and go out of existence but the absorbing company will remain. As a consequence of the legislative power to legalize mergers, the state can prescribe the terms and conditions for a valid merger. This is more than a simple purchase by United of the assets of Interstate. In substance, the transaction is a merger. Accordingly, the shareholders of United were entitled to be notified of their statutory rights of dissent. The failure of the corporate officers of United to take these steps to obtain stockholder approval of the agreement by the statutory two-thirds vote at a proper stockholders' meeting would render the proposed corporate action invalid.

Applestein v. United Board and Carton Corp., 159 A.2d 146 (N.J. 1960).

Consolidation

consolidation
(in corporations) the combination of two or more corporations forming a new corporation

In a **consolidation,** two or more corporations combine together, forming a *new* corporation (see figure 43.2). In a merger, the corporations combine together, resulting in a *surviving corporation* rather than a *new* corporation that is formed under a *plan of consolidation.* Thus, X and Y corporations combine with and *merge* into Z corporation, the surviving corporation; but when X, Y, and Z *consolidate* they form a new corporation, C corporation.

However, the legal effects of a merger, consolidation and exchange of stock are similar.

When a share exchange takes effect, the shares of each acquired corporation are exchanged as provided in the plan, and the holders of the shares are entitled only to the exchange rights provided in the articles of share exchange.

Exchange of Stock

All of the issued and outstanding shares of a corporation may be acquired through the exchange of these shares by another corporation pursuant to a plan adopted by the board of directors and approved by the stockholders of the acquired corporation.[11] For example, Corporation X acquires the stock of Corporation Z, both corporations maintaining their legal entity. Corporation Z becomes a subsidiary of Corporation X, whose board of directors governs the operations of the acquired Corporation Z. The tax consequences of a merger, consolidation or stock exchange are referred to as a "reorganization" under the Internal Revenue Code and would be carefully examined by tax counsel in any of these situations.

---

[11] Cf. RMBCA, sec. 11.02.

Figure 43.2   Statutory Consolidation

Some Reasons for Merger, Consolidation, or Exchange of Stock. A corporation may wish to merge with another to acquire a related or unrelated line of merchandise in order to diversify and reduce some of its economic risks; or it may wish to invest accumulated income rather than pay a dividend or tax as it is. If the effect is to lessen interstate competition, it may violate a federal antitrust law. For example, a large computer corporation may acquire a smaller one for all of the above reasons. There are always significant tax consequences to any merger, consolidation, or exchange of stock.

Summary Statement

1. Promoters plan the corporation and attend to its organization. In doing so, they frequently sign preincorporation contracts, on which the promoter is personally liable to third parties thereon.
2. A promoter is a fiduciary because a promoter is under a duty to act for the benefit of the corporation. He or she is liable to the corporation for any secret profits made while acting as a promoter.
3. The articles of incorporation must be filed and approved by the Secretary of State's office. The corporate name, purpose, capital stock authorization, place of business, names and addresses of directors and officers, fiscal year, and resident agent are listed in the articles of incorporation that are signed by the incorporators.
4. A defectively formed corporation may be given legal status in certain circumstances.
5. A *de jure* (by right) corporation exists by complete or substantial compliance with the statutory requirements for incorporation.
6. A *de facto* (in fact) corporation exists when there was a good faith colorable attempt to organize under a state corporation law and there is business use of the defectively formed corporation.
7. A corporation by estoppel does not create a corporation, but prevents the denial of corporate existence by associates who held themselves out as being a corporation to third parties who materially changed their position in reasonable reliance on the misrepresentation.
8. The state, acting through the attorney general's office, may dissolve a corporation that fails to act legally.

9. Shareholders may voluntarily dissolve the corporation by voting to adopt the board of directors' resolution to dissolve, or the corporation may be involuntarily dissolved with court approval.
10. A merger is the absorption of one corporation by another corporation, which continues to exist while the other terminates.
11. A consolidation is the combination of two or more corporations forming a new corporation.
12. The legal effect of a merger or consolidation is the termination of all corporations except the surviving corporation (merger) or new corporation (consolidation); the surviving or new corporation has all the rights and duties of a corporation, and the rights of creditors are not impaired.
13. An exchange of stock is a legal process whereby, pursuant to the directors' plan being approved by the shareholders, all the issued and outstanding shares of a corporation are acquired through the exchange of shares in another corporation; the acquired corporation becoming a subsidiary of the acquiring corporation.

In the following case the court held a defective corporation was liable on a note that was executed by its officer when, after legal incorporation, the company accepted the benefits of the contract with the knowledge of its terms.

Framingham Savings Bank v. Joseph Szabo, Trustee
617 F.2d 897 (1980)

Coffin, Chief Judge. In February 1977, George Sulak purchased all of the assets of the Framingham Lumber Company for a new enterprise he was forming, to be entitled Framingham Lumber Company, Inc. The new company carried on a business essentially identical to that of the old company on the same site. The same month Sulak signed Articles of Incorporation for the new company in his role as president and treasurer. However, when the Articles were mailed to the Secretary of State of Massachusetts, they were rejected by the Secretary and returned to Sulak's attorney. More than one year later, in October, 1973, an employee of Sulak's attorney hand delivered the Articles to the office of the Secretary; they were again rejected because the name of the new company was too similar to that of the old, and the procedure was explained whereby the defect in incorporation could be cured. These procedures were never followed. However, the Articles were finally accepted and filed in October 1975, and Sulak's corporation commenced its legal existence at that time.

In August, 1974, Sulak's company purchased a 1974 White truck with purchase money furnished by plaintiff Framingham Savings Bank (bank). The bank took a promissory note and a security interest in the truck; Sulak signed the documents as an officer of the corporation. In July, 1975, the bank again advanced the corporation purchase money, on this occasion for a 1974 Audi automobile, taking a similar note and security interest in the vehicle. The corporation defaulted on its payments to the bank in June 1976, went bankrupt, and the bank repossessed the two vehicles and sold them for $25,675 and $3,450 respectively. The bank brought this action against the corporation's trustee in bankruptcy to establish its entitlement to these proceeds, based on its security interests in the vehicles. The trustee defended on a number of grounds, including the contention that the security interest was invalid because the corporation did not exist at the time the agreement was formed.

Most states hold that a corporation can be bound to a pre-incorporation agreement by knowing ratification or adoption of the contract. The rationale for the contrary Massachusetts rule stems from the premise that the individual executing the contract could not act as an agent for the not yet existing corporation. Therefore, the corporation could not become bound to the contract by ratification or adoption of the putative agent's bargain. Rather, to bind itself the corporation must introduce "into the transaction such an element as would be sufficient foundation for a new contract." The corporation can become liable on the terms of the original contract, but only if its post-incorporation acts are sufficient independently to bind it to a new contract. The bank made its offer to the corporation not Sulak. Indeed, the entire transaction was carried out by both parties on the assumption that the contract was between the bank and Framingham Lumber Co., Inc. The bank looked to the corporation, not to the individual,

Sulak, to perform the obligations of the contract. The corporation's name appeared on the security agreement and the certificates of title for the vehicles; the checks used to pay loan installments were drawn on the corporation's bank account. Moreover, the corporation, after its legal status was secured, used the vehicles and paid installments with knowledge of the terms of the contract.

Thus, we hold that the agreement between the bank and Sulak, acting on behalf of the defectively incorporated firm, created a continuing offer to the putative corporation, and when the corporation entered into legal life and, with knowledge of the terms of the agreement, availed itself of the benefits of the bank's performance, it obligated itself to perform those terms just as if it had explicitly promised to do so. We hold the corporation in this case is bound and therefore reverse the judgment of the district court.

Questions and Case Problems

1. Emmick approached J. B. Morris with a plan whereby Morris' ranch would be incorporated and through Emmick's managerial skills made to show a profit. At approximately the same time, Emmick approached Golden and proposed that Golden contribute some farm machinery and livestock to Oahe Enterprises, Inc., the corporation to be formed for the operation and management of the Morris ranch. At this meeting, it was concluded that Oahe shares would be given a $50 par value. As Emmick's payment for the Oahe's shares he transferred 6,514 shares of Colonial Manors, Inc., stock (CM stock) to Oahe Enterprises, Inc. Emmick is a director and shareholder of Colonial Manors, Inc., an Iowa corporation that is involved in the promotion and management of nursing homes throughout the Midwest.

    In October 1966, Golden agreed to transfer various items of equipment to Oahe in exchange for shares in the corporation. Golden's complaint is that Emmick was allowed to use as the value of his CM stock a value arbitrarily affixed by the CM board of directors for a strictly internal purpose—that of raising badly needed funds for CM by offering stock options at a desperate juncture in its corporate life. This value admittedly bore no relationship to the book value of CM stock, which was forty-seven cents per share. Did Emmick, as a promoter of Oahe Enterprises, Inc. violate a fiduciary duty owed to Golden? [*Warren Golden v. Oahe Enterprises, Inc.*, 295 N.W.2d 160 (S.D. 1980).]

2. Neal was an incorporator for Main Street Electric Company, Inc. He filed the articles of incorporation with the Secretary of State in Texas. The articles were refused because there already existed a Main Street Electronic Company, Inc. in Texas. May the Secretary of State refuse an application on these grounds?

3. *On July 24, 1975,* plaintiff Bankers Trust Company of Western New York (formerly Banker's Trust Company of Rochester) entered into an equipment security agreement with Roseberry Inn, Inc., for the purpose of securing loans totaling $30,000 which were deposited by Bankers Trust into Roseberry Inn's corporate checking account on July 24 and September 30, 1975, February 13 and May 17, 1976. On October 1, 1977, Roseberry Inn, Inc., defaulted on the loans and the sum of $11,136.31 plus interest became due and owing plaintiff. The security agreement covered certain restaurant equipment which was placed in a building operated as the Roseberry Inn. These premises were owned by Harry Chudnofsky, President of Roseberry Inn, Inc. On or about January 13, 1978, defendants bought the premises in question, including the equipment at a mortgage foreclosure sale. On October 6, 1978, and again on December 8, 1978, plaintiff Bankers Trust demanded of defendants that it be permitted to repossess the restaurant equipment, but the defendants refused. Plaintiff thereafter instituted this suit alleging conversion and unjust enrichment. Defendants raise the defense that the plaintiff acquired no interest in the equipment because Roseberry Inn, Inc. was not a legally existing entity at the time the security agreement was entered into on *July 24, 1975* as it had not yet filed a *certificate of incorporation* with the Secretary of State.

On July 21, 1975, prior to the date the articles of incorporation were executed and the security agreement entered into, a *certificate or reservation of the name* Roseberry Inn, Inc. was filed with the Secretary of State by or on behalf of Harry Chudnofsky. On July 24, 1975, the Board of Directors of Roseberry Inn, Inc. executed a certificate of incorporation, passed a corporate borrowing resolution and issued a "certificate of resolutions" authorizing the security agreement. *On July 30, 1975,* Roseberry Inn, Inc. filed a certificate of incorporation with the Secretary of State. On August 4, 1975, Roseberry Inn, Inc. applied for a liquor license using its corporate name. On March 2, 1976 the corporation entered into a lease agreement with Cable-Wiedemer, Inc. which lease was signed by Chudnofsky both in his individual capacity and as president of Roseberry Inn, Inc. Was Roseberry Inn, Inc., a *de facto* corporation? [*Bankers Trust Company of Western New York v. Robert F. Zecher,* et al., 103 Misc.2d 777 (N.Y. 1980).]

4. Defendant, Morgan, executed a note in Georgia on 19 November 1970 as president of Beefmastor, Inc. Beefmastor, Inc. was subsequently incorporated on 31 December 1970. The note was in partial payment for a business located in Georgia and all payments on the note were to be made in Georgia. After making some payments, Beefmastor, Inc. defaulted on the note. Can defendant be held personally liable on a note that he executed as president of a corporation which had not yet been formed, but which was subsequently incorporated and which made payments on the note until default? [*Smith v. Morgan,* 50 N.C.App. 208 (N.C. 1980).]

5. Levin, an incorporator, filed the articles of incorporation and named the corporation "Levin's, Limited." The Secretary of State's office refused to accept the articles because "limited" would not indicate to the public that the business is a corporation, and hence the name is improper. Decide.

6. Martin Stern, Jr., plaintiff, brought this action for architectural services rendered to Nathan Jacobson, defendant, in Jacobson's development of a hotel and casino, known as the Kings Castle, on the north shore of Lake Tahoe, Nevada. In January, 1969, Jacobson contacted Stern and asked him to draw plans for Jacobson's new hotel/casino at Lake Tahoe.

   On May 1, 1969, Jacobson acquired all of the stock of A.L.W., Inc., a corporation which had previously operated a casino on this site, and which was to operate the Kings Castle. After May 9, 1969, A.L.W., Inc. operated the hotel and casino. All monies were subsequently paid and received through A.L.W., Inc. Stern billed Jacobson beginning in June of 1969. All of the checks were drawn on the account of A.L.W., Inc.; only one of the checks was signed by Jacobson. The Kings Castle opened in July 1970. On February 3, 1972, A.L.W., Inc., as owner of Kings Castle and Casino, filed its petition for arrangements under Chapter 11 of the Bankruptcy Act. Jacobson contends that his obligations were adopted by A.L.W., Inc., and such adoption constitutes a novation and Jacobson was released from his obligation. Decide. [*Nathan Jacobson v. Martin Stern, Jr.,* 605 P.2d 198 (Nev. 1980).]

7. Colorado Indoor Trap Shoot, Inc., the plaintiff, sued Tucker, defendant, doing business as Consolidated Sales Company. Plaintiff was to purchase from defendant the necessary equipment to open and operate one of the indoor trap shoot establishments in Colorado. Plaintiff was to pay the defendant $2,100,000 for the exclusive rights to sell, lease, and distribute all such indoor trap shoot equipment in the State of Colorado for a maximum period of five years. Defendant claims that the contract was entered into on behalf of its company which was to be formed by him as a promoter, and this was known to the plaintiff. Is Tucker, as a promoter, personally liable on the preincorporation contract? [*Tucker d/b/a Consolidated Sales Co. v. Colorado Indoor Trap Shoot, Inc.,* 471 P.2d 912 (Okla. 1970).]

8. The plaintiff, Stephens Wholesale Bldg. Supply Co., sold merchandise to the defendant, Norman R. Harris, individually, and doing business as Bessemer Building and Improvement Company. Prior to the filing of incorporation papers by defendant, Harris, on April 2, 1969, a corporate checking account was opened, a lease for corporate office space and a bid on a construction job were made in the name of the corporation. Harris opened his business relationship with Stephens in an individual capacity, although he subsequently operated as a corporation. Was Harris personally liable under contract with Stephens before he incorporated? [*Harris v. Stephens Wholesale Bldg. Supply Co., Inc.*, 309 So.2d 115 (Ala. 1975).]

9. Plaintiffs prepared the lease in the name of Sunshine Greenery, Inc., as the tenant, and it was signed by Brunetti as president of that named entity. Mr. Cantor, acting for plaintiffs, knew that Brunetti was starting a new venture as a newly formed corporation known as Sunshine Greenery, Inc. Although Cantor had considerable experience in ownership and leasing of commercial property to individuals and corporations, he did not request a personal guaranty from Brunetti, nor did he make inquiry as to his financial status or background. Without question, he knew and expected that the lease agreement was undertaken by the corporation and not by Brunetti individually, and that the corporation would be responsible thereunder. The lease was repudiated by a letter from counsel for Sunshine Greenery, Inc. dated December 17, 1974. On November 21, 1974, the corporate name of Sunshine Greenery, Inc. had been reserved for Brunetti by the Secretary of State and on December 3, 1974 a certificate of incorporation for that company was signed by Brunetti and Sharyn N. Sansoni as incorporators. The certificate was forwarded by mail to the Secretary of State on that same date with a check for the filing fee, but for some unexplained reason it was not officially filed until December 18, 1974, two days after the execution of the lease. Was Brunetti individually liable for the lease? [*Edward A. Cantor v. Sunshine Greenery, Inc.*, 165 N.J.Super. 411 (N.J. 1979).]

10. In the case of *Framingham Savings Bank v. Joseph Szabo, Trustee*, 617 F.2d 897 (1980),[12] the court held the defectively organized corporation liable on a note rather than the officer who signed on its behalf. What should the bank have done if it intended the officer and the corporation to be liable on the note?

---

[12] See pp. 648–49.

44 Corporate Powers

After you have read this chapter, you should be able to:

1. Explain the function of the "purpose clause" in the articles of incorporation.
2. Explain the source of the corporation's *express powers*.
3. Discuss the *implied powers* of a corporation.
4. List and explain the corporate statutory powers.
5. Explain the function of corporate bylaws.
6. Explain the doctrine of *ultra vires*.
7. Explain the remedies for *ultra vires* acts.

Introduction

While the corporation may exist as a legal entity by permission of the state, it cannot function without authority or power. The state is the source of all corporate power and determines what a corporation may and may not do. Accordingly, it is necessary to consider the nature and extent of corporate powers.

Nature of Corporate Powers

In the planning stages of the corporation it is necessary to determine the purpose of its formation. This is described in the *purpose clause* of the articles of incorporation. Once authorized by the state to function as a corporation, it has the consequent **express powers** as stated in the *articles of incorporation* and the *corporate statutes* to carry out its business purpose. For instance, as an "artificial person" the corporation may, in its own name, own property, sell stock, borrow money, and hire employees. If the incorporators anticipate a new line of business, the purpose clause should be broadly descriptive of its express powers so as to avoid a later necessary amendment of the articles of incorporation, requiring stockholders' approval.

corporate express powers
those powers specifically stated in the corporation's articles of incorporation and in the corporation statutes

Many states and the Revised Model Business Corporation Act in section 3.01(a), allow a purpose clause authorizing the corporation to engage in any lawful business transaction. For example, a typical purpose clause for a restaurant business may state that the purpose is "to engage in the restaurant business and any legal business transactions related thereto." The powers that are reasonably necessary to carry out the express powers are called **implied powers.** *Corporate officers have no authority to bind a corporation without express, implied, or statutory power.* This is illustrated in the following early case.

corporate implied powers
those powers reasonably necessary to carry out the express powers

Facts
Plaintiff, Brinson, was a shareholder of defendant corporation, Mill Supply Co. He sued to prevent it from paying a guaranty contract. A. F. Peterson was the president and secretary of defendant corporation, who signed, in the corporate name, a contract of guaranty of a promissory note signed by Alfred Peterson in his individual capacity. Brinson claimed that the president had no authority to have the corporation guarantee payment of Peterson's personal note.

Decision
Judgment for plaintiff, Brinson.

Reasoning
For a contract executed by a corporate officer to be binding on the corporation, it must appear that (1) it was incidental to the business of the corporation; or (2) it was expressly authorized; and (3) it was properly executed. The powers granted to the corporation under the articles of incorporation do not expressly or impliedly authorize it to issue accommodation paper or to guarantee the obligations of a third party. To permit the payment of the claim would clearly result in an invasion of the assets of the defendant corporation.

Brinson v. Mill Supply Co., 14 S.E.2d 505 (N.C. 1941).

Corporate Statutory Powers

The state where the corporation is organized gives it various statutory powers. These powers are the reasons why the corporation is the most desirable way of operating a business. Under section 3.02 of the Revised Model Business Corporation Act, "unless the articles of incorporation provide otherwise, every corporation has the same powers as an individual to do all things necessary or convenient to carry out its business and affairs, including without limitation power:"

Perpetual Succession. "(1) to have perpetual duration and succession in its corporate name."

The death of a shareholder or a change in management will not affect its perpetual existence. The stability provided by this attribute makes it the only proper business form for the larger corporations with many shareholders.

To Sue and Be Sued in Its Corporate Name. "(2) to sue and be sued, complain and defend, in its corporate name."

Sole proprietors and partners are sued and sue in their own names. The corporation as a distinct and independent legal person sues in *its* own name. This is a significant advantage because the owners and managers are not personally liable for corporate debts.

To Have a Corporate Seal. "(3) to have a corporate seal. . . ."

The seal is commonly used on important documents to evidence corporate authorization of the transaction. Banks generally require a corporate seal when a corporate checking account is opened, and the certificate of stock normally has the corporate seal on it.

To Make and Alter Bylaws. "(4) to make and amend bylaws, not inconsistent with its articles of incorporation or with the laws of this state for managing the business and regulating the affairs of the corporation."

Bylaws determine the policy of the corporation and establish the authority of the officers, directors and stockholders. The initial bylaws are usually adopted by the board of directors who have the power to alter or amend unless the articles of incorporation reserve that to the stockholders.[1]

To Acquire and Deal with Property. "(5) to purchase, receive, lease, or otherwise acquire, and own, hold, improve, use, and otherwise deal with, real or personal property, or any legal or equitable interest in property, wherever located."

The property then becomes a corporate asset, subject to the rights of creditors. For example, a corporate restaurant, that does not pay its debts and owns its own kitchen equipment, may have the equipment attached and liquidated by its creditors and the proceeds used to satisfy their claims.

To Dispose of Its Property. "(6) to sell, convey, mortgage, pledge, lease, exchange, and otherwise dispose of all or part of its property."

Once authorized, it is the corporation, as a legal person, who sells the property, and not the board of directors or corporate officers who act for the corporation.

To Acquire, Dispose of, and Deal in Interests in Other Corporations. "(7) to purchase, . . . or otherwise acquire; own, hold, vote, use, sell, mortgage, lend, pledge, or otherwise dispose of; and deal in and with shares or other interests in, or obligations of, other domestic or foreign corporations, associations, partnerships . . . , and individuals, the United States, a state, or a foreign government."

This power clearly identifies the investment potential of the corporation beyond its own business purpose. A corporation may own, in its own name, stock or bonds in another business or government.

To Make Contracts, Incur and Secure Its Obligations. "(8) to make contracts and guarantees, incur . . . obligations, and secure any of its obligations by mortgage or pledge of any of its property, franchises, or income."

This corporate power to engage in debt financing is commonly used to meet cash flow demands. The ability to raise money by the issuance of bonds and notes is an essential statutory power.

---

[1] RMBCA, sec. 2.06.

To Lend and Invest. "(9) to lend money, invest and reinvest its funds, and receive and hold real and personal property as security for repayment."

Prudent investment of corporate profit is an obligation of the board of directors.

To Be a Member of Another Enterprise. "(10) to be a promoter, partner, member, associate, or manager of any partnership, joint venture, trust, or other entity."

This power permits a corporation to be a general partner in a general or limited partnership with unlimited liability for the partnership's obligations.[2]

To Engage in Intrastate and Interstate Business Activities. "(11) to conduct its business, locate offices, and exercise the powers granted by this Act within or without this state."

Many corporations carry on business activities, not only in its state of formation, but in many others. Our economy could not function without this power.

To Have Directors and Agents, and Financially Assist Its Employees. "(12) to elect directors and appoint officers, employees, and agents of the corporation, define their duties, fix their compensation, and lend them money and credit."

The corporation may use corporate funds for the benefit of its directors and employees who may wish to borrow. The corporation could assist in the establishment of corporate credit unions for its employees who can borrow from the credit union.

To Establish Incentive, Pension, and Other Benefit Plans. "(13) to pay pensions and establish pension . . . plans, and benefit and incentive plans for any or all of its former or current directors, officers, employees, and agents."

Planning for retirement is essential to the well-being of our labor force. The Employee Retirement Income Security Act[3] governs the procedure and tax advantages of the pension area. Many small business associations have elected to incorporate to obtain these benefits.

To Make Donations for the Public Good. "(14) to make donations for the public welfare or for charitable, scientific, or educational purposes."

This power allows the corporation to make tax deductible charitable contributions. Our society, with its numerous nonprofit organizations (e.g., colleges and hospitals) relies upon substantial corporate contributions for their funding.

To Aid Public Policy. "(15) to transact any lawful business that will aid governmental policy."

The board of directors, as the principal governing body of the corporation, will be discussed in a later chapter. The directors are generally elected by the stockholders and their number is fixed by the bylaws.

To Have All Implied Powers to Effect Its Purposes. "(16) to make payments or donations, or do any other act, not inconsistent with law, that furthers the business and affairs of the corporation."

This is a broad statement of the corporation's implied power and authority.

The following early case illustrates how a court will extend the power to contract beyond the corporation's immediate *expressed* purpose, provided that the contract is within the corporation's implied powers and authority, is executed, and is not contrary to public policy.

---

[2] See chapter 38 and pp. 614–15 for a discussion of both general and limited partnerships.

[3] 29 U.S.C., ch. 18, and amendments thereto.

Facts
Plaintiff, Miller, sued the defendant, Temple Lumber Company, for breach of a contract to construct a dwelling house for plaintiff. Temple Lumber was to furnish all labor and materials in the construction of a house for Miller and was to do the construction according to a set of plans and specifications. Temple Lumber's corporate charter set out the purpose of the corporation as that of "manufacturing lumber and the purchase and sale of material used in such business and doing all things necessary and incident to such lumber business." Temple Lumber claimed it was not liable on the contract since construction of a building was not an act within its "purpose" clause and, therefore, was beyond the powers of the corporation.

Decision
Judgment for plaintiff, Miller.

Reasoning
An act of a corporation is *ultra vires* when it is beyond the scope either of the express or implied power of the charter. If the act is not one prohibited by law or public policy, and it enures to the direct benefit of the corporation, and is executed, it is not, strictly speaking, *ultra vires*. Acts which are not enumerated in the purpose clause of the charter of a corporation but are not prohibited and are appropriate, convenient, and suitable in carrying out the purposes for which the charter was expressly granted are the "implied powers and authority" of a corporation.

Temple Lumber Co. v. Miller, 169 S.W.2d 256 (Tex. 1943).

The above corporate powers are the *general* powers of a corporation. RMBCA section 3.03 states the *emergency* powers of a corporation; "an emergency exists for the purposes of this section if a quorum of the corporation's directors cannot readily be assembled" (section 3.03(d)).

Unauthorized Corporate Acts

Ultra Vires Acts

ultra vires
beyond the powers

A corporation may perform only those acts that are authorized by its express, implied, or statutory powers. These powers are derived from the state of incorporation as established in corporate statutory law, the articles of incorporation, and its reasonably implied powers. If it should engage in an unauthorized act, it is **ultra vires**—that is, beyond the powers of the corporation. For example, if the board of directors of a computer corporation were to authorize the expenditure of funds to purchase conservation land in order to protect the wild life, although this may be socially desirable, it would be beyond the authority of a computer corporation and *ultra vires*.

***Illegal Acts Distinguished from* Ultra Vires.** Corporate action in excess of *corporate* authority is *ultra vires,* but it is not *illegal* unless it is contrary to statute or public policy as declared by the courts. For example, in the above illustration, while the board action was in excess of *corporate authority,* such action was not illegal as contrary to *public law.* However, if the board had *bribed* a Congressman to vote in Congress to make the land available to the corporation, this would be contrary to federal statute and public policy, be illegal, and be a crime.

Legal Effect of* Ultra Vires *Acts. At common law, *ultra vires* business transactions were void because they were performed without legal authorization. Under modern statutory law, the defense of *ultra vires* is abolished in a suit for breach of contract by or against a corporation. The official comment to section 3.04 of the Revised Model Business Corporation Act states it is unnecessary for persons dealing with a corporation to inquire into limitations on its purposes or powers that may appear in its articles of incorporation. A person who is unaware of these limitations when dealing with the corporation is not bound by them.

The following case illustrates this when the defendant's corporate president acted beyond his authority.

Facts
Southeastern Beverage & Ice Equipment Company, Inc., the plaintiff, brought suit against the Free For All Missionary Baptist Church, Inc., the defendant, for rent due under a lease for liquor dispensing equipment. The lease was signed by the president and secretary of the defendant corporation. The church contends that the lease was *ultra vires* and unauthorized.

Decision
Judgment for plaintiff.

Reasoning
Incapacity or lack of power on the part of the church corporation does not make the lease invalid, and the defense of *ultra vires* is not available. The State Business Corporation Code abolished the doctrine of *ultra vires* as a means of avoiding a transaction which the corporation later claims is beyond its capacity or power. The corporation is not relieved of liability to any third persons for acts of its officers by reason of any limitation upon the power of the officers not known to such third persons. There is no evidence that Southeastern Beverage as lessor knew of any limitation upon the power of the Baptist Church president.

Free For All Missionary Baptist Church, Inc. v. Southeastern Beverage & Ice Equipment Company, Inc., 218 S.E.2d 169 (Ga. 1975).

Many courts will allow *ultra vires* as a defense where the contract is executory—that is, not yet performed. If the corporation or the other party has received full performance of the contract, they cannot avoid liability by the defense of *ultra vires*. This occurred in the following case.

Facts
Plaintiff, Total Automation, Inc., was a corporation with a checking account in the defendant bank, Illinois National Bank & Trust Co. The bank operated a travel department that was owed money by Total Automation. The bank deducted the amount owed to the travel department from Total's checking account. Plaintiff claims that the bank had no right to setoff because the operation of a travel agency by a national bank is an *ultra vires* act.

Decision
Judgment for defendant, Illinois National Bank & Trust Co.

Reasoning
The defense of *ultra vires* is not favored by the courts where it is raised by a private party seeking to avoid payment for a benefit received. Total Automation is not aggrieved as a private person by having to pay for services it used, nor can it be heard to say it is aggrieved as a member of the public by a departure from sound policy relating to banking, since it voluntarily entered into the *ultra vires* transaction and reaped its benefits.

Total Automation, Inc. v. Illinois National Bank & Trust Co. of Rockford, 351 N.E.2d 879 (Ill. 1976).

Remedies for* Ultra Vires *Acts. The corporation may be protected from *ultra vires* activity engaged in by the officers or directors. A corporation's lack of power to act may be challenged: in a proceeding by a shareholder against the corporation to enjoin the act; in a proceeding by the corporation, directly, derivatively, or through a receiver, trustee, or other legal representative, against an incumbent or former director, officer, employee, or agent of the corporation; or in a proceeding by the Attorney General if it establishes that the corporation obtained its articles of incorporation through fraud or the corporation has continued to exceed or abuse the authority conferred upon it by law.[4]

Summary Statement

1. The "purpose clause" of the articles of incorporation give it express and implied powers to engage in the stated purpose.
2. The *express powers* of a corporation are found in the articles of incorporation and the corporate statutory law.
3. The *implied powers* grant to the corporation authority to perform those reasonably incidental acts in carrying on corporate business.

---

[4] RMBCA, sec. 3.04 and sec. 14.30.

4. The corporate statutory powers give to a corporation the implied authority:
   a. of perpetual succession,
   b. to have a corporate name,
   c. to sue and be sued in its corporate name,
   d. to have a corporate seal,
   e. to acquire and dispose of its property,
   f. to financially assist its employees,
   g. to buy and sell stocks and bonds in other corporations, etc.,
   h. to make contracts and incur debts,
   i. to lend and invest,
   j. to engage in intrastate and interstate business activity,
   k. to have officers and agents,
   l. to make and alter bylaws,
   m. to make charitable contributions,
   n. to transact lawful business,
   o. to establish incentive plans,
   p. to be a member of another enterprise,
   q. to elect a board of directors,
   r. to have all implied powers to effect its purposes.
5. The bylaws regulate the internal affairs of the corporation. They establish the authority of the directors, officers, and shareholders as well as procedures for calling meetings.
6. Acts of the corporation outside the scope of the corporate authority are *ultra vires*. Executed corporate contracts are valid, and the creditor cannot use the defense of *ultra vires;* if executory, either party may use the *ultra vires* defense.
7. If officers or directors propose an *ultra vires* act, the shareholders may enjoin the act, the shareholders in a representative suit may sue the officers or directors personally, or the attorney general may bring a proceeding to dissolve the corporation.

Notice how the court in the following case examines the nature of the contract signed by the corporate president and found it to be "unusual and extraordinary," thus requiring express authority to execute.

Goldenberg v. Bartell Broadcasting Corporation
262 N.Y.S.2d 274 (1965)

Wilfred A. Waltemade, Justice. In the case on trial, the plaintiff sets forth two causes of action, both of which seek recovery of damages for an alleged breach of a written contract of employment. The first cause of action is against the defendant Bartell Broadcasting Corporation, an entity incorporated under the laws of the State of Delaware. It is alleged in substance that on or about March 16, 1961, the plaintiff and the defendant Bartell Broadcasting Corporation entered into a written contract wherein the plaintiff was engaged as an assistant to Gerald A. Bartell, the president of the defendant Bartell Broadcasting Corporation. The plaintiff's primary duties were to engage in corporate development in the field of pay television. The contract, which was for a period of three years, provided for (1) payment to the plaintiff of $1,933 per month; and (2) for the delivery to plaintiff of 12,000 shares of "Free Registered" stock of defendant Bartell Broadcasting Corporation, which stock was payable in three installments of 4,000 shares each in the months of January 1962, 1963, and 1964; and (3) the payment of plaintiff's traveling and living expenses in connection with the services to the employer; and (4) that the defendant Bartell Broadcasting Corporation would provide the plaintiff with a private office and proper office facilities; and (5) that the agreement would be binding on any successor corporation or any corporation with which defendant Bartell Broadcasting would merge.

This written contract was signed by the plaintiff and by Gerald A. Bartell in his capacity as the president of Bartell Broadcasting Corporation. It is further claimed that on or about May 1961, this contract was amended to increase plaintiff's monthly compensation from $1,933 to $2,400. It is further contended that the plaintiff was not paid his monthly compensation commencing with the month of November 1961; that the defendant Bartell Broadcasting Corporation failed to deliver 4,000 shares of stock allegedly due in January 1962; and that in July 1962, the defendant Bartell Broadcasting Corporation denied the validity of plaintiff's employment contract. . . .

The authority of an officer to act on behalf of a corporation may be express, implied, or apparent. There has been no proof offered in this case indicating that Gerald A. Bartell, as president of the defendant Bartell Broadcasting Corporation, had express authority to enter into the agreement, dated March 16, 1961, which is the subject of the first cause of action.

Did Gerald A. Bartell then have either implied or apparent authority to execute the contract?

Implied authority is a species of actual authority, which gives an officer the power to do the necessary acts within the scope of his usual duties. Generally the president of a corporation has the implied authority to hire and fire corporate employees and to fix their compensation. However, the president of a corporation does not have the implied power to execute "unusual or extraordinary" contracts of employment. . . .

The agreement of March 16, 1961 not only provides for the payment of a substantial monthly compensation, but also requires the delivery of 12,000 shares of "free registered" stock of the defendant Bartell Broadcasting Corporation. While the payment of the monthly compensation would not make the contract of March 16, 1961 "unusual or extraordinary," the Court is of the opinion that the inclusion in the contract of the provision requiring the delivery to plaintiff of 12,000 shares of "free registered" stock does bring the agreement within the category of being an "unusual and extraordinary" contract.

With the varied and broad business experience acquired by the plaintiff in his wide business association as evidenced by his career resumé furnished to the defendants . . . and by plaintiff's own testimony, it can be truly said that he not only was presumed to have knowledge of the statutory provisions of the law pertaining to corporations, but that he apparently also had actual knowledge of such laws. It is reasonable to infer that the plaintiff was aware, or at the least had reason to be aware, that the authority for the issuance of corporate stock rests solely within the powers of the Board of Directors of the corporation, and that in the absence of express authority, the president of a corporation does not have the implied or apparent authority to enter into an employment contract which provides for the issuance of corporate stock as compensation.

The Court concludes, after a careful analysis of the evidence and the application of the law reviewed herein, that the plaintiff has not made out a prima facie case of express, implied, or apparent authority of the president of the defendant Bartell Broadcasting Corporation to execute the contract of employment.

Accordingly, the motion by the defendants to dismiss the complaint is granted.

Questions and Case Problems

1. The "purpose clause" of Z Corporation stated that it was organized to operate a sporting goods store. The directors authorized the corporate purchase of an apartment. S, a shareholder of Z Corporation, brought an action against the corporation, claiming that it was about to perform an *ultra vires* act. The directors claim they have the statutory power "to purchase real property wherever situated." Is the shareholder correct?

2. X Co., Inc. was a life insurance agency. X Co. purchased a car wash and began its operation. X Co. had ten shareholders who knew of the car wash purchase and did not object although X Co. never amended its articles of incorporation. X Co. purchased various shop products from S on open account and owed it $5,000. When sued by S, X Co. defended on the ground that, as a life insurance agency, the entire car wash business was *ultra vires,* and hence it is not liable under any contract with S. Decide.

3. The plaintiff is a member in good standing of the defendant non-stock Connecticut corporation. The certificate of incorporation sets forth that the sole purpose of the corporation is to provide facilities for the serving of luncheon or other meals to members. Neither the certificate of incorporation nor the bylaws of the corporation contain any qualifications for membership, nor does either contain any restrictions on the guests members may bring to the club. The club is one of the principal luncheon clubs for business and professional people in the city, and is a gathering place where a great many of the civic, business and professional affairs of the community are discussed in an atmosphere of social intercourse.

    The plaintiff sought to bring a female to lunch with him, and both he and his guest were refused seating at the luncheon facility. The plaintiff claims that the corporation and its directors have acted *ultra vires* in that they have exceeded the powers conferred upon them by the certificate of incorporation, the bylaws, and the state statutes regulating corporate powers and in so doing they have breached the plaintiff's rights as a member of the corporation in refusing to allow plaintiff to bring female guests to the corporation's facility. Decide. [*Cross v. The Midtown Club, Inc.*, et al., 365 A.2d 1227 (Conn. 1976).]

4. Legal Aid Services, Inc., plaintiff, brought an action against American Legal Aid, Inc., defendant, to enjoin it from using the term "Legal Aid" in defendant's business transactions on the grounds that it was deceptively similar to plaintiff's name. There was considerable evidence that many people were confused about the two corporations. Defendant claims that it has the express statutory power to have its own corporate name. Decide. [*American Legal Aid, Inc. v. Legal Aid Services, Inc.*, 503 P.2d 1201 (Wyo. 1972).]

5. The president of a corporation was very friendly with the deceased vice-president's family. Without approval of the corporate board of directors he paid $5,000 per month to the family as a corporate benefit. When the shareholders discovered this they sued the president for the corporate loss. Did the president have authority to make this charitable contribution?

6. Marsili and other shareholders, plaintiffs, brought a derivative action against Pacific Gas & Electric Company, defendant, and allege that a contribution to Citizens for San Francisco was *ultra vires* because neither defendant's articles of incorporation nor the state law permits a corporation to make political donations. The Citizens group was an association organized to defeat a local ballot proposition that would prohibit the construction of buildings exceeding seventy-two feet unless approved in advance by the voters. Did the board of directors have authority to make the contribution? [*Marsili v. Pacific Gas & Electric Company*, 124 Cal.Rptr. 313 (1975).]

7. A contract was made between plaintiff American Heritage Investment Corporation (American) and defendant Nathan Hale Investment Corporation (Hale Investment). The latter agreed to transfer to American its shares in Nathan Hale Life Insurance Co. (Hale Life) in exchange for which American agreed to pay Hale Investment $750,000 or transfer to Hale Investment 500,000 of Hale Investment's own shares or make payment by both shares and cash with the shares valued at $1.50 each. On May 24, 1977, plaintiff filed suit seeking specific performance of the contract. Defendant Hale Investment answered the complaint setting forth as an affirmative defense the provisions of the Illinois Business Corporation Act which prohibits a corporation from purchasing its own shares. May Hale Investment raise the defense of *ultra vires*? [*American Heritage Investment Corporation v. The Illinois National Bank of Springfield*, et al., 68 Ill.App.3d 762 (1979).]

8. National Organization for Women, Essex County Chapter, plaintiff, brought this action against Little League Baseball, Inc. to admit girls aged eight to twelve to participate in local Little League baseball teams. Plaintiff claims that Congressional Charter of Little League Baseball, Inc. with a purpose clause "to promote, develop, supervise and voluntarily assist in all lawful ways to interest boys who will participate in Little League baseball" violates the New Jersey statutory policy of sex discrimination in places of public accommodation. Decide. [*National Organization for Women, Essex County Chapter v. Little League Baseball, Inc.*, 318 A.2d 33 (N.J. 1974).]

9. Alfalfa Electric Co-op, Inc., plaintiff, brought this action against First National Bank & Trust Co. of Oklahoma City, defendant, to determine if a loan granted by the bank to plaintiff was unlawful. Alfalfa claims that its board of directors had no authority to encumber a portion of its assets by pledging them as collateral for loans to a nonprofit development corporation created by the plaintiff. Alfalfa seeks a declaratory judgment to determine whether the loan was *ultra vires* and, if so, it requests return of the encumbered assets from defendant, First National Bank. Is pledging corporate assets as collateral for a corporate loan within the powers of the corporation? [*Alfalfa Electric Co-op, Inc. v. First National Bank & Trust Co. of Oklahoma City,* 525 P.2d 644 (Okla. 1974).]

10. In the case of *Goldenberg v. Bartell Broadcasting Corporation,* 262 N.Y.S.2d 274 (1965),[5] the court held that the corporation had acted *ultra vires*. Discuss the court's holding and explain how the court reached this conclusion.

---

[5] See pp. 658–59.

45 Corporate Stock and Shareholders

After you have read this chapter, you should be able to:

1. Define a share of stock.
2. List and explain the rights of a shareholder.
3. Distinguish the two basic kinds of stock.
4. Explain cumulative voting by shareholders.
5. Explain voting by proxy.
6. Define and explain a voting trust.
7. Define a dividend and explain a "surplus" for its payment.
8. Distinguish a "certificated security" from an "uncertificated security" and explain the transferring of each.
9. Explain the procedures for restricting the transfer of stock.
10. Explain a shareholders' derivative suit.
11. Give examples when a shareholder may be held personally liable to corporate creditors.
12. Explain the function of the state and federal regulation of stock issuance.
13. Define a wasting asset corporation.
14. Explain the purpose and function of the Foreign Corrupt Practices Act.
15. Explain the purpose of the Securities Act of 1933.
16. List and explain the statutory exemptions to the registration process required under the Securities Act of 1933.
17. Explain the purpose of the Securities Exchange Act of 1934.
18. Explain what is meant by an "insider transaction."

Introduction

We have learned that the corporation is a legal entity separate and distinct from its shareholders. As a result, shareholders are not liable for obligations of the corporation; the obligations are not obligations of the shareholders. The corporate stock is owned by the shareholders and, therefore, it becomes important to discuss what is meant by corporate stock and to understand the rights of the shareholders.

Corporate Stock

Nature

When you purchase shares of stock in a corporation, a stock certificate (see figure 45.1) is generally issued as evidence of your fractional ownership in the business.[1] "**Share** means the units into which the proprietary interests in a corporation are divided" (Revised Model Business Corporation Act, sec. 1.40(22)). As an owner you would have numerous rights, depending on the kind of stock purchased. Generally, a **shareholder** (stockholder) has: (1) the right to share in the profits of the corporation by way of a dividend distribution; (2) the right to share in the surplus upon dissolution; (3) the right to vote at stockholders' meetings; and (4) the right to transfer his or her stock. However, because the corporation owns the assets in its own name, as a shareholder you do not have any interest in *specific* corporate property. A corporation's ability to raise substantial capital by dividing its ownership into shares of stock that may be sold to the general public is part of the foundation of our free-enterprise system.

share of stock (stock)
a unit of interest in a corporation

shareholder (stockholder)
the owner of a unit of interest in a corporation

Purchase of Stock

While persons may purchase stock from shareholders, they may also subscribe to purchase stock from a corporation either to be formed or already in existence. The purchaser who signs a "preincorporation" subscription agreement, usually prepared by the promoter, is making an offer to purchase shares from the corporation when it comes into existence. Under RMBCA section 6.20(a), the offer is irrevocable for six months unless otherwise provided in the subscription agreement. On incorporation, the purchaser immediately becomes a shareholder for the subscribed number of shares. The purchaser who signs a "postincorporation" subscription agreement, usually prepared by the existing corporation, thereby accepts the corporation's offer to sell to the purchaser the specified number of shares.

Classes of Stock

The articles of incorporation require the incorporators to state the initial capitalization of the corporation—that is, the number of shares and kind of stock the corporation will have the authority to issue. A selection of the kinds of stock will depend upon the nature of the business. The capitalization may subsequently be changed by amending the articles of incorporation with the stockholders' approval.

Common Stock. The two basic kinds of stock are *common* and *preferred*. **Common stock** has the ordinary rights of participation in a corporation, such as the right to vote at shareholders' meetings, share in the dividends, and share in the distribution of corporate assets on dissolution.

common stock
corporate stock with the ordinary rights of participation in a corporation

---

[1] Revised Article 8 of the Uniform Commercial Code (1978) has been extended to cover a registered security interest not represented by a written instrument called an "uncertificated security." See pp. 665, 670 for further discussion.

Figure 45.1 Example of Certificate of Stock (Front)

Par value stock is stock with a certain minimum dollar price when issued—e.g., $1 par value means that each share is to be sold by the corporation at not less than $1 as determined by the board of directors, payable by the purchaser to the corporation. *No-par value* stock is stock issued for any price as determined by the board of directors, in the absence of charter provision to the contrary.

preferred stock
corporate stock with a preference over the common stock

dividend
a portion of corporate net profits or surplus set aside for distribution to the shareholders

Preferred Stock. A holder of **preferred stock** is given preferential rights over a holder of common stock. These rights make the stock more attractive to an investor. Generally, they give preference in the payment of **dividends** and in the distribution of assets upon dissolution. Although these rights do not have a *promise* of receiving a dividend, dividends will be paid to preferred shareholders before the holders of common stock. The articles of incorporation generally deny holders of preferred stock the right to vote.

Cumulative preferred stock entitles the holder to a certain dividend distribution each year, which, if not paid, accumulates over the years until funds become available. When a dividend is declared, it cannot be paid until all back accumulations are paid first. *Non-cumulative preferred stock* does not have such an accumulation, but it does have priority over dividends declared on common stock. *Participating preferred stock* entitles the holder to participate with the holders of common stock in any dividend distribution remaining after dividends are first paid on the preferred stock. *Non-participating preferred stock* is not entitled to participate in the surplus that is distributed to the holders of common stock. Even preferred shareholders have no right to demand a dividend when the directors honestly decide not to declare one.

Rights of Shareholders

A shareholder has a contractual relationship with the corporation whereby it agrees to give the shareholder certain rights for the consideration (selling price) of the stock. "Consideration for shares may consist of cash, promissory notes, services performed, contracts for services to be performed or any other tangible or intangible property. If shares are issued for other than cash, the board of directors shall determine the value of the consideration received as of the time the shares are issued." [RMBCA, sec. 6.21(c).]

However, the Revised Model Business Corporation Act in section 6.21(c) permits promises of future services to serve as consideration for the issuance of shares.

As evidence of the contractual relationship, the shareholder may receive a stock certificate (certificated security) duly executed by the corporate officers, generally the president and secretary.

The shares of a corporation shall be represented by certificates or shall be uncertificated shares.

As an owner of the stock, the shareholder may generally sell it at any price, transfer the shareholder's title to another as a gift, or pledge it as security for a loan.

Stockholders usually have the following rights: (1) the right to vote at shareholders' meetings; (2) the right to receive a dividend; (3) the right to inspect the corporate books; (4) pre-emptive rights; (5) the right to transfer the stock; (6) the right to sue the corporation or third parties for improper action; and (7) the right to share in the profits upon dissolution.

Right to Vote

Shareholders have the right to vote for the directors and on other appropriate matters at their annual meeting or at any duly called special stockholders' meeting. The right to vote may be denied to any class of stock in the articles of incorporation, in which event a stockholder has *nonvoting shares*. Changes in the articles of incorporation require directors' and stockholders' approval and the amended articles to be filed at the office of the Secretary of State.[2] For example, a corporate name change or recapitalization generally requires approval by a majority of the stockholders. Treasury shares—i.e., its own shares reacquired by the corporation—do not have any voting rights. The corporation may reacquire its shares in various ways, such as by buying them.

Who May Vote. The corporation maintains a stock transfer book that records the shareholders who are entitled to receive notice of all meetings. Generally only those recorded shareholders may vote.[3]

A shareholder may desire to **pledge** the stock to obtain a loan. In that event the shareholder retains the right to vote unless the shares are *transferred* to the pledgee.[4] For example, if a bank required you to pledge your IBM stock as security for a $5,000 loan, you would maintain voting rights during the term of the loan. If you defaulted and transferred the shares to the bank, it would have voting rights.

Nonvoting shareholders[5] may have the statutory right to vote as a class upon certain amendments to the articles of incorporation. Examples of such amendments are: (1) an increase or decrease of the aggregate number of authorized shares of the nonvoting stock;

pledge
the possessory security interest in bailed goods acquired by the bailee when there is a **bailment** for the purpose of security

bailment
a delivery of goods by a bailor to a bailee which are to be returned to the bailor or as the bailor directs, in accordance with the bailment agreement

---

[2] See RMBCA, sec. 10.01, 10.02, and 10.03 for procedures to amend articles of incorporation.

[3] UCC 8–207(1).

[4] UCC 8–207.

[5] The official comments to sec. 7.21 of the RMBCA state the articles of incorporation may provide that some classes of shares are nonvoting.

(2) an increase in the number of authorized shares having superior rights to the nonvoting stock; or (3) a cancellation of accrued dividends of the nonvoting stock that have not been declared.

Number of Votes. Under the common law a shareholder was entitled to only one vote regardless of the number of shares the shareholder owned. Today by statute a stockholder may vote as many shares of voting stock as he or she owns.

State statutes generally provide for **cumulative voting** by shareholders in the election of directors. The articles of incorporation will grant this right that entitles a shareholder to as many votes as he or she has shares of voting stock multiplied by the number of directors to be elected. Your vote = number of shares you own x number of directors to be elected. For example, if the corporate board consisted of 10 directors and you had 100 shares of voting stock, you may have 1,000 votes that may be cast for any one director or in any other manner. The minority shareholders are thereby given an indirect voice in the management of the corporation that could otherwise be denied to them by 51 percent of the voting shareholders.

cumulative voting
a method of voting whereby a shareholder has as many votes as he has shares of voting stock multiplied by the number of directors to be elected

Voting by Proxy. Many shareholders of large corporations do not desire to personally attend the annual shareholders' meeting and other special meetings but wish to exercise their voting right. The shareholder may, by written **proxy**, authorize another to vote for him or her.[6]

proxy
a shareholder's written authorization to another person to vote his shares at a corporate meeting; also the person with such authority

Minority shareholders of large corporations occasionally engage in a proxy fight in an attempt to vote as a block for a particular issue or to elect directors. Proxy solicitation is now regulated by the Securities and Exchange Commission, which requires that sufficient information be provided shareholders regarding the nature of the proxy fight.[7]

Voting Trust. The shareholders may agree to pool their voting stock in an attempt to control the management of the corporation. Shareholders' voting agreements were valid under the common law. A **voting trust** is a trust created by an agreement among the shareholders to transfer legal title to their voting stock to a party serving as a trustee who is authorized by the trust to vote the stock as a unit.[8] The trustee is a **fiduciary** with implied duties owed to the stockholders to protect their interest and with limited powers to act in accordance with the voting trust agreement.

voting trust
a trust created by an agreement between the shareholders to transfer legal title to their voting stock to a party (trustee) who is authorized to vote the stock as a unit

In the following case a voting trust agreement was held to be unenforceable because it was contrary to the state's voting trust statute.

fiduciary
a person with a duty to act primarily for the benefit of another

Facts
Plaintiffs, individually and as trustees, are the owners of 76% of the outstanding stock of the defendant Oceanic Exploration Company (Oceanic). Plaintiffs entered into a written agreement whereby 50% of the company's stock was placed into a "voting trust agreement" which gave their voting rights in the stock to others and an option in favor of the corporation which gave it the right for a period of 5 years to purchase "all or any part" of plaintiffs' stock. Plaintiffs attempted to have the "voting trust agreement and purchase option agreement" declared void so as to regain control of the corporation because it imposed an illegal restraint on their right to alienate their stock interests. The court found for the defendant and plaintiffs appealed.

Decision
Reversed, judgment for plaintiffs.

---

[6] RMBCA, sec. 7.22(c) states no proxy shall be valid after eleven months from the date of its execution unless otherwise provided in the proxy.

[7] Securities Exchange Act of 1934, sec. 14(a).

[8] RMBCA, sec. 7.30(b). Under the Act, a voting trust agreement may not be for a period exceeding ten years.

Reasoning
A voting trust is a stockholder pooling arrangement with the criteria that voting rights are separated out and irrevocably assigned for a definite period of time to voting trustees for control purposes while other attributes of ownership are retained by the depositing stockholders.

While we do not suggest that the mere fact that the corporation is a party removes a trust from the statute, we do find that the final contract in issue here including a stock purchase option agreement running from an already unified majority shareholder group to the corporation may be so foreign to the stockholder voting trust agreement that it is beyond the contemplated scope of the statute on voting trusts. Given the scope of this agreement it may be that the voting rights are not separated from the other retained attributes of ownership. We conclude the court erred in holding the contract in this case to be, as a matter of law, a voting trust.

Oceanic Exploration Company v. Jack J. Grynberg, et al., 428 A.2d 1 (Del. 1980).

Dividends

If you were to invest in a corporation as a stockholder, you would expect a return on your investment by way of a **dividend** and an increase in the market value of the stock. A dividend is a portion of the corporate net profits or *surplus* set aside for distribution to the shareholders. It is within the discretion of the directors to declare a dividend, but it is not to be declared when the corporation is insolvent. *Until a dividend is declared by the board of directors, the stockholders have no right to receive one.* If the directors refuse to declare a dividend and have clearly abused their discretion by continuously voting against a "declaration," a court may require the payment of a dividend. This is illustrated by the following well-known case.

dividend
a portion of corporate net profits or surplus set aside for distribution to the shareholders

Facts
Plaintiffs, shareholders in the Ford Motor Company, defendant, brought an action to compel the company's board of directors to declare a special dividend. The company had made substantial profits over the years, and a regular quarterly dividend of five percent per month on its capital stock had been paid since 1911, with additional special dividends of from $1 million to $10 million per year from 1911 to 1915. In 1916 the board of directors decided to continue the regular five percent per month dividend but no longer to make any additional special dividends. At that time the company's surplus was $112 million, its yearly profits $60 million, its liabilities including capital stock less than $20 million, and its cash on hand $54 million. The company had planned improvements costing $24 million. Judgment was for the plaintiffs, and the company appealed.

Decision
Affirmed in part for plaintiffs and reversed in part for defendant.

Reasoning
A business corporation is organized and carried on primarily for the benefit of its stockholders. The powers of the directors are to be exercised in the choice of means to attain that end and do not extend to a change in the end itself, to the reduction of profits or to the nondistribution of profits among stockholders in order to devote them to other purposes. It is not within the lawful powers of a board of directors to shape and conduct the affairs of a corporation for the merely incidental benefit of shareholders and for the primary purpose of benefiting others. There was a large daily, weekly, monthly receipt of cash. The output was practically continuous and was continuously, and within a few days, turned into cash. Moreover, the contemplated expenditures were not to be immediately made. It would appear that, accepting and approving the plan of the directors, it was their duty to distribute on or near the 1st of August 1916 a very large sum of money to stockholders.

Dodge v. Ford Motor Co., 170 N.W. 668 (Mich. 1919).

However, the courts are hesitant to substitute their judgment for the dividend policy of the directors who were elected by the shareholders to use their discretion in managing the corporation.

Fund for Declaration of Dividends. A dividend is declared when the board of directors votes to approve a resolution on a dividend and announces its distribution. There must be a "surplus" for the payment—that is, an amount of assets that exceeds the liabilities and the issued and outstanding shares.

The shareholders entitled to the dividend then become *general creditors* of the corporation and may enforce the debt if the corporation should become insolvent prior to distributing the dividends. Once the dividend has been declared, announced, and set aside, the fund is held in trust for the benefit of the shareholders. Corporate creditors cannot reach the assets in this fund. If the stock is transferred to a new owner *after* the dividend is *declared* but *before* the announced *record date for payment,* the transferee is generally entitled to receive the dividend.

As an exception to the rules discussed regarding the need for a surplus before the directors can declare a dividend, a *wasting assets corporation* may pay dividends out of current net profits. For instance, an off-coast oil drilling venture is a wasting asset corporation because it is organized to exhaust or use up the assets (oil) of the corporation, in contrast to an industrial corporation organized to manufacture computers on a continuing basis.

Effective Date of Dividend Distribution. As the owner of stock, you generally have the right to sell it at any time. If the directors declare a dividend, the question arises as to whom it should be paid if the holder transferred the stock *after* the declaration date. For example, the board may declare a dividend today *(declaration date)* to be effective in one month *(effective date)* and payable to the stockholders of record in two months *(payment date).* The vote to declare a dividend is irrevocable and the *registered holder on the effective date* will be sent the dividend on the payment date. If the corporation is not aware that a transfer took place and paid the *registered holder* who sold the stock to a transferee, the corporation is protected and the transferee must sue the transferor for the money received, *not the corporation.*[9]

Right to Inspect Corporate Books

The common law granted to a shareholder the right to inspect the corporate books and records at reasonable times for a proper purpose. It is the "proper purpose" aspect of this right that frequently causes a problem. For example, may a public interest group, such as the environmentalists, purchase a block of stock (100 shares) in a corporation and demand the right to review the minute book of the board of directors and shareholders? Generally no, because a shareholder does not demonstrate a "proper purpose" by disapproving of a corporate activity such as a manufacturing company causing a high rate of pollution. The federal Environmental Protection Agency has authority to regulate air standards; it would be the proper party to investigate the alleged illegal act.[10]

If the corporation improperly refuses an inspection of the records, the shareholder may seek court action. In the following case plaintiff was allowed to see a breakdown list of stockholders for the purpose of soliciting their proxies.

Facts
Hatleigh Corporation, plaintiff, is the record holder of 1,000 shares of common stock of Lane Bryant, Inc., defendant. Hatleigh requested Lane Bryant, Inc. to provide Hatleigh with a stockholder list of Lane Bryant. Lane Bryant contends that the demand was not bona fide because Hatleigh had not formed an intention to actually solicit proxies but was seeking the list of stockholders for a different purpose. A number of shares of Lane Bryant are listed on the books of the corporation as being held by "CEDE & CO." This denotes a recognized system whereby various brokerage firms hold stock that is actually owned by their customers in the name of CEDE & CO. or in the name of other similar firms organized to hold shares of stock for others. Hatleigh filed a demand with the court to inspect and copy a list of the stockholders of Lane Bryant.

Decision
Judgment for plaintiff, Hatleigh Corporation.

---

[9] UCC 8–207.

[10] See pp. 714–15 for a discussion of administrative regulations.

Reasoning
When the breakdown of shares is disclosed, the identity of the brokerage firms holding stock under the name of "CEDE & CO." can be learned and contact can then be made with them in order to ascertain the number of beneficial owners on whose behalf they hold stock in the street name so that a proper amount of informational materials may then be forwarded to the brokerage firms for distribution to the beneficial owners. Plaintiff seeks this "breakdown" list as to CEDE in order that plaintiff too may get its proxy solicitation materials into the hands of the beneficial owners in ample time for the annual meeting. Such information should be made available to the plaintiff forthwith so that its list of stockholders for its proper purpose of soliciting their proxies is at least equivalent, in this aspect, with the list available to the corporation for the same purpose.

Hatleigh Corporation v. Lane Bryant, Inc., 428 A.2d 350 (Del. 1981).

Most states have statutory laws regulating the inspection right. Some give the shareholder the absolute right while others go beyond the "proper purpose" limitation of the common law. The Revised Model Business Corporation Act sec. 16.02 grants the right only to shareholders of record to examine and copy at the shareholders' expense (1) excerpts from minutes of meetings of the board of directors and stockholders, (2) the accounting records of the corporation, and (3) if demand is made in good faith and with a proper purpose a list of the corporate shareholders.

A shareholder may authorize an attorney or other agent to inspect the books on the shareholder's behalf.

In the following case the court held that stockholders could inspect corporate books only at reasonable times.

Facts
Plaintiffs are minority shareholders in Schwartzman Packing Company, a New Mexico closely held family corporation. They alleged that the defendant, the majority shareholders of the company, engaged in various willful acts of oppressive conduct toward the plaintiffs resulting in damages to the corporate entity and to themselves. The defendant corporation informed plaintiffs more than two months before trial that it would cooperate with plaintiffs and permit a reasonable inspection of corporate books and records. Plaintiffs delayed almost two months from the time this notice was given until the date they scheduled their examination to begin. After examination had begun the corporation felt that the scope of examination being pursued by the plaintiffs was placing a severe burden upon the operations of the corporation because plaintiffs were sending teams of three to six accountants or bookkeepers to examine books and records of the corporation during normal business hours. Plaintiffs, appellants, contend that the trial court limited plaintiffs' request for inspection and review of the defendant's corporate records to such an extent that it constituted a violation of the law.

Decision
Affirmed judgment for defendants.

Reasoning
The right of a shareholder to examine books and records is not unlimited. Inspection must be made at "reasonable times." What is reasonable and proper necessarily depends upon the circumstances of each case and must be determined by the exercise of the discretion of the court enforcing the right. A trial court must of necessity have some discretion in determining when and in what manner the right of examination should be exercised. Under the facts in this case, it was not an abuse of discretion for the trial court to limit examination to regular business hours in addition to the 222 hours of examination which had previously been allowed.

J. C. Schwartzman, et al. v. Schwartzman Packing Company, 659 P.2d 888 (N.M. 1983).

Financial Statements
An inspection of the corporate books may include the minutes of the directors' and stockholders' meetings, the stock transfer books, and the books of account. Due to their personal nature, we have seen most states require a "proper purpose" to inspect. There is generally no such limitation to the shareholders' right to receive financial statements showing the corporation's assets, liabilities, and operations.[11]

---

[11] RMBCA, sec. 16.02.

Pre-emptive Rights

You will recall that the incorporators established the original *authorized* capitalization in the articles of incorporation filed with the Secretary of State. The corporation then had the right to issue shares up to the authorized amount. If the corporation desires to exceed that initial authorization, it must amend the articles by the directors voting a resolution and having it approved by a majority of the voting shareholders. When the amended articles of incorporation are filed and approved by the state, new stock may be issued. A **pre-emptive right** is the right of the voting stockholders of record to purchase the new stock in proportion to their old stock interest before the new stock may be offered to the public. Hence, a shareholder may maintain his or her relative voting power and dividend interest.

Most states prohibit the pre-emptive right for an issuance of **treasury stock** or for an issuance to employees as a part of a stock purchase plan.

The Revised Model Business Corporation Act is generally in accord with the modern trend of corporate law which limits or abolishes the pre-emptive right.[12]

pre-emptive right
a shareholder's right to subscribe to a newly authorized issue of stock proportionate to his holdings in the corporation

treasury stock
corporate stock reacquired by the issuing corporation

Transfer of Shares

The rights and duties of corporations and stockholders to transfer stock is governed by Article 8 of the Uniform Commercial Code. Article 8 was revised in 1977 to include a security investment not represented by a written certificate defined as an "uncertificated security."[13] The issuance of an "uncertificated security" is *registered* upon the security transfer book maintained by the corporation. An *initial transaction statement* is then sent to the shareholder. The Official Comment to the Uniform Commercial Code, section 8–101 states: "This Article does not purport to determine whether a particular issue of securities should be represented by certificates, in whole or in part. That determination is left to the parties involved, subject to federal and state law."

Transfer of Uncertificated Securities. An uncertificated security is transferred by the transferor (seller) instructing the corporation to issue a *transaction statement* to the new owner (or pledgee) and register the transaction on its transfer ledger. *Within two business days after the registration of a transferred uncertificated security,* the corporation must send the new registered owner (or registered pledgee) and the transferor a *transaction statement*. The transaction statement serves as registration notice to the new owner and a reduction of interest notice to the transferor-seller.

A *periodic statement* must be sent at least annually to the registered owners describing the issuance of which the uncertificated security is a part.[14]

Transfer of Certificated Securities. To effect a proper transfer of a certificated security (stock certificate), the transferor-seller must deliver the certificate and if necessary indorse it over to the purchaser. If the transfer is of a temporary nature (e.g., a pledge of the stock as security for a bank loan), the owner may make the assignment on a separate instrument which requires delivery of both the separate document pledging the stock and the stock certificate.[15]

bona fide purchaser
(in corporations) a purchaser for value in good faith and without notice of any adverse claim, and who is either a holder of a certificated security or registered on the corporate books as the owner

"Bona Fide Purchaser." Article 8 of the Uniform Commercial Code deals with "investment securities" that include stock and bonds. These securities may be transferred to a **bona fide purchaser** who may acquire greater rights than the transferor-holder.[16]

A bona fide purchaser is a purchaser for value in good faith and without notice of any adverse claims . . . (UCC 8–302).

---

[12] RMBCA, sec. 6.30. [13] UCC 8–102(1)(b).

[14] UCC 8–408. [15] UCC 8–309.

[16] Although a security is a negotiable instrument, its transfer is not governed by Article 3 on Commercial Paper but rather by Article 8 of the Uniform Commercial Code.

This is a change from the common law of assignments that limited the transferee's rights in the stock to those of the transferor. Article 8 allows the "bona fide purchaser" to defeat a claim by the owner of the stock that could be asserted against the transferor; for example, if the stock was acquired by fraud, deceit, or without consideration by the transferor from the owner.

Example 1: A fraudulently induced O, the owner of a stock certificate for 100 shares of X corporation, to indorse and deliver the certificate to A. O can avoid the transaction and reacquire the certificate. However, if A had sold and delivered the certificate to B, a bona fide purchaser, B acquired the title to the certificate and the shares represented thereby.

Example 2: T steals O's certificate of stock and sells and delivers it to Z, an innocent purchaser for value. Since O never indorsed the certificate, nobody can later become a **holder.** Therefore, no later person can become a bona fide purchaser. However, if O had indorsed it (signed O's name) making it a bearer certificate, and then T had stolen it and sold and delivered it to Z, Z would be a holder and become a bona fide purchaser with title to the certificate and the shares represented thereby.

holder
(in corporations) the person in possession of a certificated security which flows to him either initially or by indorsement

Statute of Frauds. If you orally contracted to *sell* your stock, it would be unenforceable regardless of the selling price under UCC 8–319, a special statute of frauds provision. Under the Code, if the contract *for sale* of securities is in writing, it is enforceable. If it is oral, it is unenforceable unless proved in one of four ways. Reference should be made to section 8–319 of the Code.

Restrictions on Transfer. The incorporators of a closely held corporation may decide to issue its stock to select shareholders. For instance, a family business may desire to keep control of its ownership and management. The articles of incorporation and the bylaws may state a restriction allowing the corporation or its shareholders the right to purchase the stock before it is offered to outsiders. The selling price may be established in accordance with a specified formula stated in the text of the restriction or it may be the current market price. Restrictions on the transfer of stock are generally valid if they are conspicuous and reasonable. Because a purchaser is generally not aware of restrictions in the articles of incorporation or bylaws, the stock certificate must conspicuously note the restriction, unless the buyer has actual knowledge of it, in order for it to be effective.

In order to be conspicuously noted, the Code requires it to be written so that a reasonable person ought to have noticed it, as a printing or heading in capitals or in larger or contrasting type or color.[17] The stock certificate need not state the terms of the restriction, but the purchaser must have the right to read the full text that generally appears in the articles of incorporation or the bylaws.

If the security is uncertificated, the *initial transaction statement* sent to the registered owner must note the restriction.[18]

Shareholders' Remedies

As a stockholder, you own a fractional portion of the corporation with contractual rights. If the directors act wrongfully and deprive the stockholders of their rights, they may sue for breach of contract. For example, the stockholder may sue the directors for not being permitted to exercise any of his rights previously discussed, such as his right to a dividend when one should have been declared, to vote at meetings, to inspect the corporate books for a proper purpose, or to exercise his pre-emptive right. In any of these instances, more than one stockholder will be *individually* injured and any one, on behalf of the others, may bring a *derivative* suit against the corporation.

---

[17] UCC 1–201(10). [18] UCC 8–204(b).

Stockholders' derivative suit.

Stockholders' Derivative Suit. As a shareholder you may individually, or with other minority shareholders, bring an action on behalf of the corporation against the directors and officers on the basis of breach of their managerial fiduciary duties resulting in a depletion of corporate assets. You must procedurally first prove that, on proper demand, the corporation refused to bring suit against the officers and/or directors for mismanagement. This means you must first exhaust your internal corporate remedies. You do this by first requesting the board of directors to take proper action, unless it would be futile to do so (e.g., a majority of the board are involved in the wrong, or are prejudiced). If such a request is unsuccessful or futile, then you must request the shareholders at a corporate meeting to take proper action, unless it would be futile to do so (e.g., a majority are involved in the wrong, or a majority are biased). You may also bring an action on behalf of the corporation against an outside person if the corporation wrongfully refuses to do so. Such actions are called "derivative" actions. In both instances the right to sue and damages awarded belong to the corporation.

In the following well reasoned case the plaintiffs, stockholders of the defendant corporation, brought this individual class action rather than a stockholders' derivative suit. On appeal, the court reversed the certification of the suit as a class action.

Facts
Plaintiffs Donald J. Richardson, Grove L. Cook and Wayne Weaver are stockholders of Major Oil Corporation (Major Oil) who brought this action individually and on behalf of all other stockholders of Major Oil. The original complaint named as defendants Arizona Fuels, Inc.; Eugene Dalton; and Deanna J. Dalton, the legal or beneficial owners of 47% of the issued and outstanding shares of stock of Major Oil. Eugene Dalton is alleged to be the controlling stockholder, officer and director of Arizona Fuels and the controlling officer and director of Major Oil. Deanna Dalton is alleged to be an officer and director of both Major Oil and Arizona Fuels. The issue is whether the district court erred in certifying this matter as a class action.

Decision
Yes. Judgment for plaintiffs reversed.

Reasoning
A class action and a derivative action rest upon fundamentally different principles of substantive law. A derivative action must necessarily be based on a claim for relief which is owned by the stockholders' corporation. Indeed, a prerequisite for filing a derivative action is the failure of the corporation to initiate the action in its own name. A recovery in a class action is a recovery which belongs directly to the shareholders. However, in a derivative action, the plaintiff shareholder recovers nothing and the judgment runs in favor of the corporation. Suits which are said to be derivative, and therefore come within the rule, are those which seek to enforce any right which belongs to the corporation and is not being enforced, such as the liability of corporate officers or majority shareholders for mismanagement, to recover corporate assets and related claims, to enforce rights of the corporation by virtue of its contract with a third person and to enjoin those in charge of the corporation from causing it to commit an *ultra vires* act. On the other hand, [if] the injury is one to the plaintiff as a stockholder and to him individually, and not to the corporation, as where the action is based on a contract to which he is a party, or on a right belonging severally to him, or on a fraud affecting him directly, it is an individual action.

The first causes of action allege injury to the corporation only. The injury alleged can be asserted by plaintiffs only derivatively as stockholders on behalf of the corporation. The cause of action alleges initially that the defendants "breached their fiduciary duties to Major Oil and to its stockholders."

The claim for relief belongs to the corporation. The cause of action then goes on to allege that the defendants "mismanaged the corporate and prudential affairs of Major Oil." Mismanagement of the corporation gives rise to a cause of action in the corporation. Therefore, any compensatory damages belong to the corporation and not to the stockholders individually.

Donald J. Richardson, et al. v. *Arizona Fuels Corporation*, et al., 614 P.2d 636 (Utah 1980).

Stockholders' Direct Suit. If as a shareholder you were deprived of a rightful incident of share ownership (e.g., the right to vote,[19] a claim to compel dividends wrongfully withheld,[20] a claim that a corporate action is *ultra vires*,[21] an action to inspect corporate books and records[22]) you would have a direct action claim against the corporation. Damages are awarded to you as an individual in a direct action suit. If such a wrong were perpetrated upon other shareholders as well as yourself, you could bring an action on behalf of yourself and the other shareholders against the corporation. This is called a "class" or "representative" action.

Shareholders' Liability

Shareholders are not liable for *corporate* contracts or tort claims because the corporation, as a legal entity, is separate and distinct from its owners, the shareholders. However, shareholders contract with the corporation in the purchase of stock and are obligated to pay *to the corporation* the full consideration of the shares.

Corporate creditors who cannot satisfy their claims from corporate assets may bring a "bill in equity" against a stockholder who failed to pay his or her subscription price. In this way the price, or corporate right to the price, as an asset of the corporation becomes available through the corporation to the corporate creditors.

Watered Stock
You recall that the consideration for stock issuance of shares may be paid in property or services actually performed or, under the RMBCA sec. 6.21(c), to be performed for the corporation. If such property or services are overvalued and worth less than the par value of the share, the share is diluted; hence the name "**watered stock**." Par value stock may also be issued for less than par value for (1) insufficient cash; (2) payment of a stock dividend without transferring the surplus to the capital account;[23] (3) a stock bonus; or (4) a gratuitous issue. In such events, both the corporation and the stockholders are liable in tort for deceiving the corporate creditors who relied upon the misrepresented outstanding par value capital stock as having been paid for in an amount of at least its par value. However, the innocent purchaser for value of watered stock, unaware of the previous watering, takes the shares free and clear of any liability for such watering.

watered stock
corporate stock reduced in value by the issuance of par value shares for less than their par value

Securities Regulations

State Blue-Sky Laws
Suppose a corporation in which you are a stockholder is in need of capital. The accountant for the corporation has prepared statements indicating its present financial status. If you, the other stockholders, and the corporate board desire to sell additional stock to *state residents,* the corporate attorney would have to assure compliance with the state "blue-sky" laws. The phrase "blue-sky" comes from persons praising the stock to the blue sky.

Intrastate sale of securities.

---

[19] *Reifsnyder v. Pittsburgh Outdoor Advertising Co.,* 173 A.2d 319 (Pa. 1961).

[20] *Tankersley v. Albright,* 80 F.R.D. 441 (1978).

[21] *Eisenburg v. Flying Tiger Line, Inc.,* 451 F.2d 267 (1971).

[22] *Kahn v. American Cone & Pretzel Co.,* 74 A.2d 160 (Pa. 1950).

[23] See pp. 667–68 on Fund for Declaration of Dividends.

Each state has enacted statutes established to assure public protection from a fraudulent issuance of stock. A stock sale that intentionally violates the law can subject the corporate board, officers, and the corporation to criminal prosecution and an injunction against the corporation preventing future stock sales. A stockholder may rescind a stock sale made in violation of a blue-sky law. Generally, the corporation that desires to sell its stock (issuer) must file corporate information with the appropriate state official for registration. Keep in mind that the *interstate* sale of stock to the public requires compliance with the federal statutes, and state blue-sky laws relate only to an *intrastate* sale.

Federal Securities Laws

The Securities Act of 1933. The federal Securities Act of 1933 section 5, requires registration with the Securities and Exchange Commission (SEC) of securities offered to the public through the use of the *mails* or any means of *interstate* commerce, unless there is a specific statutory exemption. The *registration statement* must disclose necessary financial and other information, which is also in a *prospectus* furnished to each prospective investor allowing the latter to make an intelligent investment decision based upon the merits of the security. The SEC does not approve or disapprove of the offering; it simply requires disclosure of relevant information about the corporation. The stock offered for sale may be worthless, but the prospectus information must be true.

The Registration Process. The statute provides for a pre-filing, waiting, and post-effective period. During the pre-filing period, the corporation or an underwriter (a person who sells the stock on behalf of the issuer) may make an offer to sell its stock that complies with prospectus requirements, providing that acceptance is postponed. The waiting period is 20 days after the registration statement is filed before the registration statement becomes effective. During the post-effective period (after the 20 days waiting period has expired) the stock may be sold by providing the investor with a prospectus that contains information in the registration statement. It is unlawful to sell the securities before the post-effective period.

Statutory Exemptions.
  1. Regulation D (Private Sales Offerings). In 1982 the SEC promulgated Regulation D composed of rules 501 through 506 to simplify the exemptions for private sales of stock and eliminate the necessity of filing a formal registration statement with the SEC.

  Rule 501 defines the terms of Regulation D.

  Rule 502 establishes conditions that apply to all offerings under Regulation D. Of great importance are those that prohibit advertising to the general public, require the issuing corporation to "legend" the stock by stating on it they are *restricted securities* and can be resold only by a full registration or in an exempt registration transaction and making information about the offering available to certain investors.

  Rule 503 requires *notice* of a Regulation D offering be filed with the SEC in Washington, D.C., regardless of the amount of the issuance.

  Rule 504 allows the corporation to issue an *aggregate sale of securities within 12 months that does not exceed $500,000 to any number of purchasers,* without providing them with any information. Local state law may require a disclosure document concerning the corporation be furnished to the buyers. In that event the offering may be advertised and the stock need not be restricted as required under Rule 503.

  Rule 505 allows a corporation to sell securities not in excess of $5,000,000 per issue, in any twelve month period to any number of accredited investors, and up to thirty-five other purchasers. The accredited investors do not receive a formal registration statement describing the nature of the offering, however, any of the thirty-five other purchasers must.

  The term *accredited investor* is defined in Rule 501 to include (1) any bank, insurance company, investment company, or employee benefit plan, (2) any business development company, (3) any charitable or educational institution with assets of more than $5 million, (4) any director, executive officer or general partner of the issuer, (5) any person who purchases at least $150,000 of the securities being offered, provided the purchase does not exceed 20% of his net worth, (6) any person with a net worth of more than $1 million, and (7) any person with an annual income of more than $200,000.

Rule 506 allows a corporation to offer any *unlimited amount of securities to any number of accredited investors* and up to thirty-five others provided they (the thirty-five non-accredited investors) *are capable of evaluating the risks involved.* This rule will allow a large corporation to issue substantial numbers of stock to *accredited investors* without formally registering as a public offering. However, the corporation must be sure its purchases are from the group defined in Rule 501. Any purchaser outside the group places a burden on the corporation to persuade the SEC that the non-accredited investors understand the risk involved.

2. Regulation A (Small Public Offerings). If a corporation wished to offer up to 1.5 million dollars of securities to the general public in any twelve-month period, it could do so as a *small public offering* without a full registration statement being filed with the SEC. The corporation, as the issuer, would have to file a "notification" and an "offering circular" to the investor and the SEC regional office disclosing relevant information. Regulation A filings are less detailed, are processed faster, and are less costly than full registration.

Regulation A.

3. Short-term Commercial Paper. If your corporation issued a promissory note, a draft, bill of exchange, or any other type of commercial paper, they would be exempt from registration with the SEC, provided the issuance arises out of a current business transaction and has a maturity date of not more than nine months. The paper may not be advertised for sale to the public.

SEC Section 3(a) 3.

4. Intrastate Issues. If you were sure each purchaser of your securities was a resident of the state where your business was incorporated, there is another exemption from registration with the SEC. To qualify, at least 80 percent of your corporation's gross revenues must come from operations within the state of incorporation.

SEC Section 3(a) 11 and Rule 147.

5. Non-profit Organizations. If your corporation was organized for educational, health, recreational, or charitable purposes, there is an exemption from registration in the sale of its securities. For example, a college that issues tax-exempt bonds need not file with the SEC.

Liability. Civil. If you (1) signed the registration statement, or (2) were a director of the corporation that issued the security, or (3) with your consent were named in the registration statement as a person about to become a director, or (4) served as an accountant who assisted in the certification or preparation of the statement, you could be held personally liable if the Registration Statement contained an untrue statement of a material fact or omitted necessary material information. However, a director may reasonably rely on statements made by the corporate CPA or legal counsel.

Criminal. Any *willful* violation of the Act will subject the wrongdoer to criminal liability of up to five years in prison and/or a fine of up to $10,000. Keep in mind that if the issuance must comply with the SEC registration, the corporation will also have to register in each state where it sells its securities.

SEC Section 24.

The Securities Exchange Act of 1934. The 1934 Act in addition to creating the Securities and Exchange Commission (SEC) regulates the trading by the stock exchanges of securities after a company has "gone public." Holders of securities listed on national stock exchanges are protected, as "public companies" must file periodic reports that update information in the original registration statement. Examples are the annual Form 10-K and the quarterly Form 10-Q. (See figure 45.2.)

Figure 45.2   Form 10-Q

SECURITIES AND EXCHANGE COMMISSION
Washington, D.C. 20549
FORM 10-Q

QUARTERLY REPORT UNDER SECTION 13 OR 15(d) OF THE SECURITIES EXCHANGE ACT of 1934

For Quarter Ended March 31, 1981   Commission File Number 1-2345

FORGE INDUSTRIES CORPORATION
(Exact name of registrant as specified in its charter)

DELAWARE	12-3456789
(State or other jurisdiction of incorporation or organization)	(I.R.S. Employer Identification No.)

FORGE BUILDING, HEAVY DRIVE, ANYTOWN, DELAWARE 99999
(address of principal executive offices and zip code)

Registrant's telephone number, including area code (777) 555-0000

Indicate by check mark whether the registrant (1) has filed all reports required to be filed by Section 13 or 15(d) of the Securities Exchange Act of 1934 during the preceding 12 months (or for such shorter period that the registrant was required to file such reports), and (2) has been subject to such filing requirements for the past 90 days.   Yes   X   No _____

Indicate the number of shares outstanding of each of the issuer's classes of common stock, as of the latest practicable date.

Class	Outstanding at April 30, 1981
Common Stock, par value 66-2/3¢ per share	7,020,531

FORGE INDUSTRIES CORPORATION
INDEX

	Page No.
Part I. Financial Information:	
Consolidated Condensed Balance Sheets—March 31, 1981 and December 31, 1980	3
Consolidated Condensed Statements of Income—Three Months Ended March 31, 1981 and 1980	4
Consolidated Condensed Statements of Changes in Financial Position—Three Months Ended March 31, 1981 and 1980	5
Notes to Consolidated Condensed Financial Statements	6–7
Management's Discussion and Analysis of the Financial Condition and Results of Operations	8
Exhibit 11—Calculation of Earnings Per Share	9
Part II. Other Information	10–11
Index to Exhibits	12

Insider Transactions.   If you were a director, officer, or the owner of 10 percent or more of the corporate stock listed on a national stock exchange, you are an "insider" and subject to special regulations under section 16(b) of the 1934 Act. Suppose you purchased stock in the corporation as an officer or director and sold it within six months from the date of purchase, or sold the stock and then repurchased the stock within six months from the date of its sale, any profits you may have realized could be recovered by the corporation. The purpose of this rule is to prevent "short-swing" trading based upon inside information not made available to the public.

Short-swing trading Section 16(b).

The 1934 Act imposes both criminal and civil liability for its violations similar to the 1933 Act.

SEC Rule 10b-5 (Full Disclosure Rule).   The SEC issued Rule 10b-5 implementing section 10(b) of the Act. There are no exceptions to compliance with SEC Rule 10b-5. The Rule makes unlawful an intentional material misstatement or an omission by a person buying or selling any security. The rule applies to *any* person and is not limited to officers, directors, or owners of 10 percent or more of the corporation's stock. For example, if you had "inside information" concerning a stock, you have a duty to disclose this information to buyers or sellers of the security.

Section 10(b) and Rule 10b-5.

Proxy Solicitation Rules.   The SEC requires a registered company in advance of a stockholders' meeting to furnish each stockholder with a "proxy statement" and a form of a proxy where the stockholder can vote on each proposal that will be presented at the meeting. Rule 14 a-3 requires the proxy statement be accompanied by the annual report when they are solicited for the election of directors at the annual stockholders' meeting.

Tender Offers.   A corporation that makes an offer to purchase the stock of another corporation is often opposed by the "target corporation's" management. Anyone that acquires more than 5% of a registered security must file an information statement with the SEC under section 13(d). A tender offer is a public invitation to a corporation's shareholders to purchase their stock and does not include stock purchases on the open market.

The Insider Trading Sanctions Act of 1984

On August 10, 1984, President Reagan signed the Insider Trading Sanctions Act. Investors owning publicly traded securities are now protected by federal statutory law from traders who take advantage of material inside non-public information. It is an unethical practice for insiders to frustrate an investor's reasonable expectation that a fair securities market will make information available to all traders at the same time.

Under the Act, the Securities and Exchange Commission may seek an injunction against an inside trader and require the defendant to pay any profit made or loss avoided to the corporation. A federal district court has authority to require a defendant who traded a security with material non-public information to pay as damages up to three times the profit gained or loss avoided. There is a five year statute of limitations on SEC claims seeking treble damages. Criminal liability may be imposed with fines up to $100,000.

The Act extends liability to non-trading "tippers" who engage in "aiding and abetting" the violation of the "tippee." Hence, brokers and dealers who advise their customers to trade based on non-public material inside information may be liable under the Act. However, the Act eliminates the liability of a securities salesperson who executed a stock transaction for a customer knowing the customer had inside information.

The brokerage firm that employed the securities salesperson is not liable if its agent traded on inside information or disclosed it to a customer. This is a change from agency law that generally holds a principal (employer) liable for the negligence of its agents (employees). Section 21 (d)(2)(B) of the Securities Exchange Act of 1934 states that no person is liable under the Act ". . . by reason of employing another person who is liable" for the new sanctions.

In the following highly publicized and important case notice the reason why the court found a "tippee" investment analyst was *not* under a duty to abstain from using inside information.

Facts

In 1973, Dirks was an officer of a New York broker-dealer firm who specialized in providing investment analysis of insurance company securities to institutional investors. On March 6, Dirks received information from Ronald Secrist, a former officer of Equity Funding of America. Secrist alleged that the assets of Equity Funding, a diversified corporation primarily engaged in selling life insurance and mutual funds, were vastly overstated as the result of fraudulent corporate practices. Secrist also stated that various regulatory agencies had failed to act on similar charges made by Equity Funding employees. He urged Dirks to verify the fraud and disclose it publicly.

Dirks decided to investigate the allegations. The senior management denied any wrongdoing, but certain corporation employees corroborated the charges of fraud. Neither Dirks nor his firm owned or traded any Equity Funding stock, but throughout his investigation he openly discussed the information he had obtained with a number of clients and investors. Some of these persons sold their holdings of Equity Funding securities, including five investment advisers who liquidated holdings of more than $16 million. During the two-week period in which Dirks pursued his investigation and spread word of Secrist's charges, the price of Equity Funding stock fell from $26 per share to less than $15 per share. This led the New York Stock Exchange to halt trading on March 27.

Recognizing that Dirks "played an important role in bringing [Equity Funding's] massive fraud to light," the SEC only censured him. Dirks appealed the SEC's ruling but the U.S. Court of Appeals entered judgment against Dirks. The case is now before the U.S. Supreme Court on certiorari.

Decision

Reversed, judgment for Dirks.

Reasoning

The test is whether the insider personally will benefit, directly or indirectly, from his disclosure. Absent some personal gain, there has been no breach of duty to stockholders. And absent a breach by the insider, there is no derivative breach.

We find that there was no actionable violation by Dirks. It is undisputed that Dirks himself was a stranger to Equity Funding, with no preexisting fiduciary duty to its shareholders. He took no action, directly or indirectly, that induced the shareholders or officers of Equity Funding to repose trust or confidence in him. There was no expectation by Dirks' sources that he would keep their information in confidence. Nor did Dirks misappropriate or illegally obtain the information about Equity Funding.

As the facts of this case clearly indicate, the tippers were motivated by a desire to expose the fraud. In the absence of a breach of duty to shareholders by the insiders, there was no derivative breach by Dirks.

We conclude that Dirks, in the circumstances of this case, had no duty to abstain from use of the inside information that he obtained.

Dirks v. Securities and Exchange Commission, 463 U.S. 646 (1980).

Foreign Corrupt Practices Act of 1977

Investigations by the Securities and Exchange Commission disclosed corrupt foreign payments by over 300 U.S. corporations involving hundreds of millions of dollars. Congress responded to these corporate abuses by enacting the Foreign Corrupt Practices Act of 1977. The Act amends section 13 (b) of the Securities Exchange Act of 1934 to require reporting corporations to comply with certain *accounting standards*. The Act also makes it unlawful for such reporting corporations *or any domestic concern (i.e., any business association) not subject to the Securities Exchange Act* to engage in *corrupt practices* with foreign officials. Finally, the Act further contains provisions on *disclosure.*

Accounting Standards

The accounting standards provision applies only to reporting corporations subject to SEC jurisdiction. It requires them to *keep books, records, and accounts which, in reasonable detail, accurately and fairly reflect the transactions and dispositions of corporate assets.* Foreign bribery is often paid from off-the-books slush funds that are made illegal by the

Act. Corporations subject to the SEC are also required *to devise and maintain a system of internal accounting controls* sufficient to provide reasonable assurance that transactions are executed in accordance with management's specific authorization and are recorded as necessary to permit preparation of financial statements in conformity with generally accepted accounting principles or other applicable criteria and to maintain accountability for its assets. Access to assets is permitted only in accordance with management authorization, and the recorded accountability for assets is compared with existing assets at reasonable intervals. The Act requires appropriate action to be taken with respect to any differences.[24]

Foreign Corrupt Practices
This portion of the Act applies to reporting corporations subject to the SEC, their officers, directors, employees, agents (of the corporation), or stockholders, and to any individuals of a domestic concern (any business association), who make use of the mails or any means of interstate commerce to corruptly pay any official of a foreign government or a foreign political party for the purpose of influencing any decision in order to obtain or retain business.

Disclosure
This portion of the Act may be cited as the Domestic and Foreign Investment Improved Disclosure Act of 1977. It supplements the Securities Exchange Act of 1934 relative to the requirement of disclosure in connection with filing periodic and other reports with the SEC. More detail is required to be disclosed by the same beneficial owners. The disclosure requirements are very detailed.

The Foreign Corrupt Practices Act places full responsibility on a firm's board of directors to assure that there is compliance with the Act's requirements for proper recordkeeping and a system of internal accounting controls, and to make provision for their continual review so as to detect illegal payments in violation of the Act.

Penalties for Violation
A corporation may be fined up to $1,000,000 for violation, and an individual may be fined up to $10,000 and imprisoned for a term of up to five years or both. The fine of an individual may not be paid by the corporation.

Summary Statement

1. Stockholders have a contractual relationship with the corporation with consequent rights.
2. Generally, a stockholder has the following rights:
    a. to vote for the election of the directors and on other appropriate matters at a meeting of the stockholders;
    b. to receive a declared dividend;
    c. to inspect corporate books for a proper purpose;
    d. to transfer the stock subject to any restrictions;
    e. to sue the corporation for improper action when authorized by corporate state law;
    f. to purchase new stock in proportion to the shareholder's old stock held before the new stock issue is offered to the public (pre-emptive right) in the absence of statute, charter, or bylaw to the contrary; and
    g. to share in the profits upon dissolution of the corporation.

---

[24] 15 U.S.C., sec. 78q–1(b).

3. Common stock is the ordinary voting stock of the corporation.
4. Preferred stock has preference over other kinds of stock with respect to dividends and, generally, a priority on distribution of the profits upon dissolution. Preferred stock may be:
    a. cumulative,
    b. non-cumulative,
    c. participating,
    d. non-participating.
5. Cumulative voting entitles a stockholder to as many votes as the stockholder has shares of voting stock multiplied by the number of directors to be elected.
6. Proxy vote is written authorization given to another to vote on behalf of a shareholder. The SEC regulates proxy solicitation.
7. A voting trust is a stockholders' agreement whereby title to their stock is transferred to a trustee who votes the stock as a unit.
8. A dividend is a portion of the corporate net profits or surplus set aside for distribution to the shareholders. It is declared by the directors.
9. An "uncertificated security" is not represented by a stock certificate. The shareholder receives a transaction statement from the corporation as evidence of his registered interest.
10. Stock transfer may be restricted if the terms are conspicuous and reasonable.
11. A stockholder may sue the directors if wrongfully deprived of his or her rights.
12. Stockholders may be held personally liable to corporate creditors if they fail to pay the full consideration of the purchased shares or for the purchase of "watered stock."
13. The Securities Act of 1933 requires registration with the SEC of securities offered to the public, unless there is a specific statutory exemption.
14. Some statutory exemptions for filing a registration statement with the SEC for the sale of stock are (a) a Regulation D private sale offering, (b) a Regulation A small public offering, (c) short-term commercial paper, (d) intrastate issues, and (e) non-profit organizations.
15. Short-swing trading by "insiders" is prohibited by the Securities Exchange Act of 1934.
16. The Foreign Corrupt Practices Act of 1977 is an antibribery law concerned with corrupt payments to foreign government officials.

The following case illustrates how the court construes the term "security" to include an investment of money in an enterprise with the expectation of profits. Notice how the court finds an investment contract even though the investor contributed some effort to obtain a return on his investment.

Securities and Exchange Commission v. Glenn W. Turner Enterprises, Inc.
474 F.2d 476 (1973), cert. denied, 414 U.S. 821 (1973)

Duniway, J. This is an appeal from an order granting the Securities and Exchange Commission a preliminary injunction. The injunction prohibits offering and selling by appellants [defendants in the lower court] of certain of their "Adventures" and "Plans," and also any withdrawal by appellants of funds from the assets of the corporate defendants other than in the regular course of business. Dare to Be Great, Inc. (Dare), a Florida corporation, is a wholly owned subsidiary of Glenn W. Turner Enterprises, Inc. The individual defendants are, or were, officers, directors, or employees of the defendant corporation.

The trial court's findings, which are fully supported by the record, demonstrate that defendants' scheme is a gigantic and successful fraud. *The question presented is whether the "Adventures" or "Plans" enjoined are "securities" within the meaning of the federal securities laws.*

In *SEC v. W.J. Howey Co.*, the Supreme Court set out its by now familiar definition of an investment contract: "The test is whether the scheme involves an investment of money in a common enterprise with profits to come solely from the efforts of others." . . .

For purposes of the present case, the sticking point in the Howey definition is the word "solely," a qualification which of course exactly fitted the circumstances in Howey. All the other elements of the Howey test have been met here. There is an investment of money, a common enterprise, and the expectation of profits to come from the efforts of others. Here, however, the investor, or purchaser, must himself exert some efforts if he is to realize a return on his initial cash outlay. He must find prospects and persuade them to attend Dare Adventure Meetings, and at least some of them must then purchase a plan if he is to realize that return. Thus it can be said that the returns or profits are not coming "solely" from the efforts of others.

Strict interpretation of the requirement that profits to be earned must come "solely" from the efforts of others has been subject to criticism. . . . Adherence to such an interpretation could result in a mechanical, unduly restrictive view of what is and what is not an investment contract. It would be easy to evade by adding a requirement that the buyer contribute a modicum of effort. Thus the fact that the investors here were required to exert some efforts if a return were to be achieved should not automatically preclude a finding that the Plan or Adventure is an investment contract. To do so would not serve the purpose of the legislation. Rather we adopt a more realistic test, whether the efforts made by those other than the investor are the undeniably significant ones, those essential managerial efforts which affect the failure or success of the enterprise.

In this case, Dare's source of income is from selling the Adventures and the Plan. The purchaser is sold the idea that he will get a fixed part of the proceeds of the sales. In essence, to get that share, he invests three things: his money, his efforts to find prospects and bring them to the meetings, and whatever it costs him to create an illusion of his own affluence. He invests them in Dare's get-rich-quick scheme. What he buys is a share in the proceeds of the selling efforts of Dare. Those efforts are the sine qua non of the scheme; those efforts are what keeps it going; those efforts are what produces the money which is to make him rich. In essence, it is the right to share in the proceeds of those efforts that he buys. In our view, the scheme is no less an investment contract merely because he contributes some effort as well as money to get into it.

Our holding in this case represents no major attempt to redefine the essential nature of a security. Nor does our holding represent any real departure from the Supreme Court's definition of an investment contract as set out in Howey. We hold only that the requirement that profits come "solely" from the efforts of others would, in circumstances such as these, lead to unrealistic results if applied dogmatically, and that a more flexible approach is appropriate.

Affirmed.

Questions and Case Problems

1. Blackhawk Holding Corp., the defendant, when organized issued Class A common stock and Class B common stock. Owners of Class B stock were not entitled to dividends or to participate in the distribution of assets but did have the right to vote. Class B stock represented 28 percent of the total stock issuance. Stroh, a Class B stockholder and plaintiff, claimed that Class B stock was not valid because there was no economic interest in the corporation associated with its ownership. Is stock that only confers a right to vote valid? [*Stroh v. Blackhawk Holding Corp.*, 272 N.E.2d 1 (Ill. 1971).]

2. X Corporation had 50,000 shares of issued and outstanding Class A voting common stock and 10,000 shares of issued and outstanding Class B nonvoting stock. The board of directors voted to submit to the shareholders a plan to increase the aggregate number of authorized shares of the nonvoting stock. The Class A shareholders voted in favor of the increase. Class B shareholders were not permitted to vote, and they claim that the increase was not validly approved. Decide.

3. XYZ Corp.'s board of directors never declared a dividend in its fifteen years of business. The company always earned a profit, but the directors believed a large cash account was much safer than declaring dividends. The shareholders sued the company to force a dividend. Decide.

4. Plaintiff, the Vista Fund (Vista), is a Minnesota partnership formed to invest in promising new enterprises. In December 1967, Vista purchased shares in defendant RayGo, a Minnesota corporation. At that time RayGo included a division known as the Deltak Division, which engaged in the design and sale of waste heat recovery units and fire heaters. In September of 1972 the defendants, officers and directors of RayGo, formed a new corporation which they controlled and named the Deltak Corporation. On September 29, 1972, these defendants caused Deltak Corporation and RayGo to enter into a purchase agreement whereby RayGo conveyed to Deltak Corporation the entire Deltak Division of RayGo for $1,601 of Deltak stock, an amount allegedly far below the fair market value of the assets conveyed. The record indicates that plaintiff was apprised of, and expressed concern about the Deltak transactions. On March 26, 1974 RayGo entered into a plan of merger with Foster Wheeler Acquisition Corporation, a wholly-owned subsidiary of Foster Wheeler. When Foster Wheeler's board of directors refused to bring suit against RayGo, Inc., plaintiff purchased 100 shares of Foster Wheeler stock and commenced this stockholder's derivative suit on its own behalf. Must a plaintiff be a shareholder at the time he commences a stockholder's derivative action and, if so, must such ownership be continuous and uninterrupted from the time of the alleged wrongs to the time suit is brought? [*The Vista Fund v. Gordon O. Garis,* et al., 277 N.W.2d 19 (Minn. 1979).]

5. Plaintiff's principal, George Delmarmo, a 13% stockholder of defendant, sought and was denied access to the stockholders list prior to the commencement of this litigation. According to defendant, Delmarmo's purpose was to solicit purchase of stock from other stockholders in order to gain control and assume management himself, to accomplish his employment by defendant as a consultant, to merge or sell defendant or initiate a public offering of its stock. Was plaintiff entitled to the stockholders list? [*Delmarmo Associates v. New Jersey Engineering & Supply Co.,* 424 A.2d 847 (N.J. 1980).]

6. Minority stockholders of a close corporation, filed a stockholders' derivative action against the majority stockholders and the corporation alleging that the majority stockholders, acting as corporate directors and officers, purchased from themselves and for the corporation shares of capital stock of the corporation at a price in excess of its market value. The complaint alleged that, while the purchase was made from retained corporate earnings, it so financially depleted the corporation that the corporation was required to borrow $10,000 back from the majority stockholders. The trial court dismissed the complaint as failing to state a cause of action and the minority shareholders appealed. Decide. [*John E. Tills, Sr.,* et al. *v. United Parts, Inc.,* et al., 395 So.2d 618 (Fla. 1981).]

7. Wilkes, the plaintiff, and three individual defendants organized a corporation to run a nursing home. Each party was an equal shareholder and director. They all received $100 per week for services rendered to the nursing home. The business was successful for fifteen years, when the plaintiff and another shareholder had a misunderstanding. The relationship degenerated to the point where in January of 1967 plaintiff gave notice to sell his shares for their appraised value. At the board of directors' meeting in February 1967, plaintiff's salary was cancelled and at the annual stockholders' meeting in March he was not re-elected as a director or officer. Plaintiff sued the corporation and the individual defendants for damages for lost salary and for breach of the fiduciary duties owed to minority shareholders. Decide. [*Wilkes v. Springside Nursing Home, Inc.,* 353 N.E.2d 657 (Mass. 1976).]

8. Skoglund and Ackerly, plaintiffs, brought an action against Ormand Industries, Inc. to inspect their books. Ormand Industries is engaged in the outdoor advertising business in California. Skoglund had bought and sold several communication corporations engaged in the outdoor advertising business. Ackerly is the president of Ackerly Communications Inc., a closely held Seattle outdoor advertising company in which Skoglund is a major shareholder. Skoglund and Ackerly are substantial shareholders of Ormand. They believed that Ormand was being mismanaged and requested an inspection of the corporate books and a list of the shareholders. Ormand refused because the plaintiffs failed to show a proper purpose, and because they are in a competitive position with Ormand because of their outdoor advertising interests in the Seattle area. Decide. [*Skoglund v. Ormand Industries, Inc.*, 372 A.2d 204 (Del. 1976).]

9. F.H.T. was formed in 1968 by Jerald Feuerhelm, Burton Hutton and Hayden Thompson, the sole stockholders, directors, and officers of the corporation, with Thompson and Feuerhelm each receiving a 40% interest. At a stockholder meeting held on or about December 1, 1972, a stock transfer restriction resolution was entered between Thompson and Feuerhelm with the purpose to restrict "the sale or transfer of shares of the company both during the lifetime and at the death of any of the stockholders in order to assure the continuity of the ownership of the company," and requiring the shareholders to first offer their shares for sale to the company. The resolution also contains a buy-out provision to be effective upon the death of a stockholder. The resolution was endorsed by Thompson and Feuerhelm as both officers and shareholders of the corporation. Jerald Feuerhelm died on June 5, 1980.

   This action arises from a dispute among the parties concerning the validity of the 1972 stock transfer resolution. This action was brought on behalf of F.H.T., seeking an injunction to enforce the buy-out resolution. The Feuerhelm estate has refused to sell its shares back to F.H.T. and has counterclaimed on behalf of F.H.T., alleging the 1972 resolution as void, unenforceable as being an unreasonable restraint on alienation, or as being waived or rescinded by subsequent acts of Jerald Feuerhelm and Hayden Thompson. The court found the stock transfer resolution to be valid and properly executed by Feuerhelm and Thompson and not waived or abandoned by them. The court ordered specific performance of the 1972 resolution and ordered the administrator of the estate of the decedent, to comply with the resolution by delivering the stock to the corporation. The administrator appealed. What decision? [*F.H.T., Inc. v. James S. Bailey*, et al., 320 N.W.2d 772 (Neb. 1982).]

10. In the case of *Securities and Exchange Commission v. Glenn W. Turner Enterprises, Inc.*, 474 F.2d 476 (1973), cert. denied, 414 U.S. 821 (1973),[25] the court briefly quotes a sentence from the case *SEC v. W.J. Howey Co.* Discuss the court's holding in the Turner Enterprises case and explain how that case can be distinguished from the quoted sentence in the Howey case.

---

[25] See pp. 680–81.

46 Corporate Management

After you have read this chapter, you should be able to:

1. Explain the managerial function of a shareholder.
2. Explain when stockholders' approval is necessary for corporate management.
3. Define a quorum.
4. Explain the managerial role of the directors.
5. Explain how board action may be taken without a formal meeting.
6. Explain the significance of a director being a fiduciary.
7. Give an illustration of a director's breach of a fiduciary duty.
8. Explain how directors are elected and removed.
9. Explain what is meant by the indemnification of a corporate officer or director.
10. Explain the managerial role of the corporate officers.
11. Explain when a corporate officer may be held personally liable.
12. Explain the business judgment rule and the public policy for the rule.

Introduction

Society today, more than ever before, depends upon efficient management of its corporate institutions. You may serve as an employee for a corporation and depend upon it for your livelihood, well-being, and a dignified retirement. To administer to these needs, corporate policy must be clearly defined and implemented. State corporate laws, the articles of incorporation, and the corporate bylaws grant authority to the stockholders, the board of directors, and the corporate officers to effectively manage the corporation. Our discussion will focus on the managerial functions of each group and their respective roles therein.

Shareholders

Shareholders are given their authority from state corporate law, the articles of incorporation, and the bylaws. In the last chapter we discussed the rights of a shareholder as a fractional owner of the corporation and his or her concern with making a profit from the investment. This was generally accomplished by a dividend and an increase in the market value of the stock. The principal managerial function of the shareholder is to elect the board of directors at a legal shareholders' meeting. Hence, they are not directly involved with policy decisions, which are reserved to the board of directors. A voting majority of shareholders dissatisfied with corporate policy may elect a new board of directors.

Authority.

Limited managerial functions.

Managerial decisions that would substantially change the nature of the corporation require approval by the voting stockholders; for example, changes in the articles of incorporation such as the corporate name, changes in its authorized stock, changes in corporate purpose, or a merger or a consolidation.

Shareholders' Meetings

The shareholders may vote and act legally only at a duly called and properly held regular or special stockholders' meeting.[1]

Voting at shareholders' meeting.

Time. The time of the annual stockholders' meeting is fixed in the articles of incorporation and the bylaws. Most state statutes require a regular annual meeting.[2] Notice to the stockholders of the annual meeting is often not required but is usually given. However, *advance written notice* of a *special* meeting is required. The notice must indicate the time, place, date, and purpose of the meeting.

The bylaws generally allow a majority of the stockholders the right to call a special meeting of the stockholders.

A closely held corporation may find it burdensome to give written notice of the meeting to its few shareholders. Most statutes allow a written *waiver of notice* signed by the shareholders either before or after the meeting.

In the following case the court held that attendance at a stockholders' meeting will not waive proper notice.

Facts

Darvin, the plaintiff, brought this action to set aside actions taken at the stockholders' meeting of defendant, Belmont Industries, Inc. Darvin and four other stockholders owned all of the shares in Belmont Industries, Inc. They were also directors and officers of the corporation. A dispute over corporate management arose between Darvin and the other directors, who no longer wanted Darvin in the corporation. Accordingly, a special meeting of the stockholders and directors was scheduled for September 12, 1969.

Darvin received notice of the meeting on September 11. At the meeting Darvin was eliminated as a director and officer. The bylaws of the corporation provided that shareholders shall receive notice "at least ten days prior to any meeting." Darvin claims that the actions taken at the meeting are ineffective because he was given notice only one day in advance. Was Darvin's attendance at the meeting together with the nonvoting of his shares sufficient participation to waive the notice requirement?

---

[1] RMBCA, secs. 7.01 and 7.02.   [2] See, for example, MASS. GEN. LAWS ANN. ch. 156, sec. 28.

Decision
No. Judgment for plaintiff, Darvin.

Reasoning
The purpose of the time-notice requirement is to provide a shareholder with sufficient opportunity to study contemplated action at the shareholders' meeting and the legality thereof. Darvin's mere attendance at the meeting coupled with the nonvoting of his shares was not sufficient participation to waive the notice requirement.

Darvin v. Belmont Industries, Inc., 199 N.W. 2d 542 (Mich. 1972).

quorum
the number of persons necessary to be present, or shares necessary to be represented, at a meeting in order to transact business

Quorum. A legal stockholders' meeting requires a quorum to transact business. A **quorum** is a specified number of shareholders required to be present or a specified number of shares required to be represented before the shareholders' meeting can begin. State statutes, the articles of incorporation, and the bylaws determine the specific number, generally a majority of the voting stockholders or shares represented.[3] A shareholders' meeting that opens with a quorum may generally continue to transact corporate business even after a sufficient number of shareholders leave the meeting and break the quorum. This provides for a continuation of the meeting over the objection of dissident stockholders who have left. [RMBCA, sec. 7.25.]

Shareholders' Action without a Meeting. Small closely held corporations may wish to transact business that requires shareholders' approval, but decide not to call a special meeting. Most corporate statutes allow this if the shareholders sign their consent to the action taken without a meeting.

Directors

Corporate management.

The directors elected by the shareholders manage the business and establish corporate policy. In that capacity they do not carry on the day-to-day business. The authority of the board to manage the corporation is derived from state statutes, the articles of incorporation, and the bylaws.[4]

Powers of Directors
The *board* of directors acts on behalf of the corporation. While acting within the scope of their authority the directors *as a board* has the power to bind the corporation *with respect to corporate matters voted on by the board, but not with respect to contracts with outside parties* because the board is not an agent of the corporation for such an operational or administrative purpose. The board delegates the administration of corporate policy to the officers authorizing them to carry out the day-to-day business. The board votes on policy and functions *only as a body;* individual members have no authority to act without board consent.

Number of Directors
Most state corporate statutes require at least three board members. The articles of incorporation or the bylaws will fix the exact number. To accommodate the closely held corporation and the professional corporations, many states allow as few as one director.[5]

---

[3] RMBCA, secs. 7.25 and 7.27.

[4] RMBCA, sec. 8.01(c) provides that a corporation having 50 or fewer shareholders may dispense with or limit the authority of a board of directors by describing in its articles of incorporation who will perform some or all of the duties of a board.

[5] RMBCA, sec. 8.03.

Qualifications
Generally, any person may be a director, including a nonresident, minor, or nonshareholder. Corporate statutes, the articles of incorporation, or the bylaws may place restrictions on eligibility. It is not unusual for the bylaws to impose stock ownership requirements on the directors. Larger corporations encourage "outside directors" to serve as board members.

Directors' Meetings

Board acts only through board meetings.

The directors may vote on corporate matters only at a legally held board meeting. A quorum is necessary for a meeting, and must continue for action to be taken. The bylaws may provide for regular board meetings to be held with or without notice. Special meetings require notice to the directors unless it is impracticable to do so. If proper notice was not sent and a director should attend a meeting, he or she may be deemed to have waived the notice requirement. Board action may be taken without a meeting when all the directors sign a *consent statement* that recites the action taken.[6] This is especially convenient in a closely held corporation where the directors and stockholders are the same parties. Bylaws may require the meetings to be held at a particular place, but most states allow meetings within or without the state of incorporation.

In the following case the court held directors having a personal interest in the matter before the board could not be counted toward the quorum.

Facts
Plaintiff, an Illinois corporation, is a medical clinic located in Harvey, Illinois. Defendants are two physicians, Kim and Ladpli, licensed to practice medicine in Illinois. On October 10, 1972, and April 11, 1973, Kim and Ladpli, respectively entered into employment agreements with plaintiff containing restrictive covenants. There were 12 shareholders, of whom 7 were elected directors. All seven directors were present at the meeting of the board of directors on February 3, 1977. Four of these directors, including Ladpli, had written employment contracts containing the restrictive covenant. The corporate minutes of the meeting read in relevant part: "After some discussion, to make it easier for physicians being 'eased out' of the clinic under the incentive system to leave and to make it easier for future physician recruitment, it was unanimously decided that the 'restrictive covenant' on all existing contracts be removed."

Plaintiff urges that the four personally interested directors having restrictive covenants in their employment contracts cannot be counted toward the quorum and majority vote of plaintiff's board of directors.

Plaintiff sued to enforce the restrictive covenant provision in the employment contracts of the two defendants.

Decision
Judgment for plaintiff.

Reasoning
At the time of the resolution in issue, plaintiff's bylaws provided for 13 directors; thus seven directors constituted a quorum. Where there is no quorum because of the disqualification of directors, a contract executed pursuant to a resolution of the board of directors is voidable and may be rendered valid by shareholder ratification. We conclude that the directors with restrictive covenants in their contracts were clearly disqualified to vote this benefit of removal to themselves.

Weiss Medical Complex, Ltd. v. Sun C. Kim, M.D., et al., 408 N.E.2d 959 (Ill. 1980).

Liability of Directors

Directors as fiduciaries.

Directors may be held personally liable to the corporation or to the shareholders in the management of the corporation if they violate a duty owed to either of them causing a financial loss. This duty is based upon the director being a *fiduciary* that manages the company on behalf of the corporation and the shareholders. A director's dissent to board action, made at the board meeting or by registered mail to the secretary immediately thereafter, protects the director from liability for such action.

---

[6] RMBCA, sec. 8.21.

Directors have a common law duty to exercise the standard of care of an ordinary prudent director in a similar business, and are held liable for their negligent acts.[7] Directors are not liable for honest errors of judgment if they acted in good faith and with due diligence. For example, if the board of directors in exercising its discretion votes to adopt a new line of merchandise that results in a financial loss, the directors cannot be held personally liable.

Duty of care standard.

Business Judgment Rule. Corporate directors and officers have a duty of care that must be exercised in the performance of their corporate functions. They must perform in *the best interest of the corporation and with the care that an ordinary prudent person would reasonably be expected to exercise under similar circumstances.*[8] What are the functions of an officer or director and where are they found? The corporation itself may impose duties found in the certificate of incorporation, bylaws, or directors' and stockholders' resolutions. If a director or officer accepts a position on a corporate committee (e.g., audit committee), there is a consequent responsibility to perform those committee functions with a duty of care consistent with the reasonable prudent person standard. An employment contract between a corporation and corporate officer will also define corporate duties.

In all of these instances independent business judgments must be made by the officer or director involving risks. Public policy demands that, in exercising the duty of care in the performance of their functions as officers and/or directors, an independent business judgment must be made safe from hindsight review simply because the decision was unsuccessful. Case law has established what is known as the *business judgment rule that allows a director or officer to make an honest and rational informed business decision that turns out to be wrong without being personally liable for its consequences.*

Business judgment rule.

The "safe harbor" provided by the business judgment rule is illustrated in the following case.

Facts
Plaintiff, Cramer, brought a shareholder's derivative action stemming from the making of illegal overseas payments to foreign government officials and private persons. A committee that acted in good faith and with the full authority of the board of directors of General Telephone & Electronics Corporation (GTE) found no illegal activity on behalf of the corporation. The four directors, defendants, claim that the committee's determination was a business judgment of GTE's management and that the derivative suit should not proceed—a business judgment which is insulated from judicial review and which bars the maintenance of the derivative suit. In the lower court the plaintiff's claim was dismissed because of plaintiff's failure to comply with the requirement of an initial demand on the corporate directors to sue.

Plaintiff claims that defendant corporate directors so dominated the board as to make a demand futile.

Decision
Judgment for defendant directors.

Reasoning
Absent bad faith or some other corrupt motive, directors are normally not liable to the corporation for mistakes of judgment. We do not think that the defendants herein so dominated the board of directors as to make a demand on the board futile. At the time Cramer commenced this suit, there were 14 individuals on GTE's board of directors. Only four of these were named as defendants in this action. The remaining ten directors had not been involved in the allegedly fraudulent activities. Indeed, several of the directors had not even been members of the board at the time the questionable transactions occurred. We believe that unless the plaintiff's complaint alleges some facts tending to show why a demand would be futile, such a demand should be required. The complaint should be dismissed. We affirm the district court's dismissal of Cramer's claim.

Cramer v. General Telephone & Electronics Corporation, 582 F.2d 259 (1978).

---

[7] *Atherton v. Anderson,* 99 F.2d 883 (1938) and *Murphy v. Hanlon,* 79 N.E.2d 292 (Mass. 1948).

[8] See RMBCA, sec. 8.30 and Tentative Draft No. 1, *Principles of Corporate Governance and Structure: Restatement and Recommendations,* A.L.I. (1982), sec. 4.01.

State corporate statutes commonly provide duties that establish a director's liability with respect to an illegal declaration of dividends, purchase of treasury stock, or the illegal distribution of assets during corporate liquidation.

Director's Breach of Fiduciary Duties

A director, as a fiduciary, must account to the corporation for *secret profits* received in violation of the director's *duty of loyalty* as well as *secret profits* made by using inside information acquired at a board of directors' meeting. A director will be protected from suit for breach of a fiduciary duty if the director makes a *full disclosure* of any financial interest the director may have in the contract to the board of directors or to the voting shareholders, who approve. The corporation or the shareholders may sue the director for breach of a fiduciary duty and compel the director to pay any secret profits to the corporation. In the following case the corporation sued its former director for breach of his fiduciary duty to disclose material facts to the corporation.

Facts
Plaintiff, Aero Drapery of Ky., Inc., brought suit against Engdahl, the defendant, an officer and treasurer of Aero. While employed by Aero, the defendant entered into a contract with several of Aero's key employees to leave and form a new corporation in direct competition with it. Engdahl and the other employees then quit and began competing with Aero, who alleged breach of fiduciary duties against Engdahl.

Decision
Judgment for plaintiff, Aero Drapery of Ky., Inc.

Reasoning
Engdahl as a director and officer was a fiduciary of Aero. Whenever a fiduciary possesses information and the withholding of that information will damage the corporation, it is his duty to fully disclose these facts to the corporation. Engdahl should have terminated his duties as director and treasurer when he first began preparation to directly compete with Aero.

Aero Drapery of Ky., Inc. v. Engdahl, 507 S.W.2d 166 (Ky. 1974).

Removal of Directors

The stockholders may call a meeting to remove a director or the board of directors. State statutory law generally provides specific grounds for a director to be removed "for cause." Generally, a majority of the shareholders may remove a director "without cause."

Corporate Officers

State corporate statutes require corporations to have officers, elected and removed by a board of directors. These officers carry out, on a day-to-day basis, the policy established by the board (see figure 46.1). The kinds of officers, as well as the term of office and the duties of the officers, are stated in the bylaws. They usually consist of a president, secretary, and treasurer and as many vice-presidents as are required in the bylaws.

Function of corporate officers.

Powers of Officers

The powers of corporate officers are determined by the law of agency because they are agents of the corporation. The board of directors, the articles of incorporation, and the bylaws delegate authority to the officers. An officer must not misuse his or her powers so as to breach the officer's duty of loyalty to the corporation.

Agency law applicable.

Liability of Officers

The officers are acting on behalf of the corporation and, therefore, are *fiduciaries*. Similar to directors, the officers have a duty to exercise that degree of care that an ordinary prudent officer would exercise under the circumstances.

Fiduciaries with duty of care.

Figure 46.1 Corporate Management

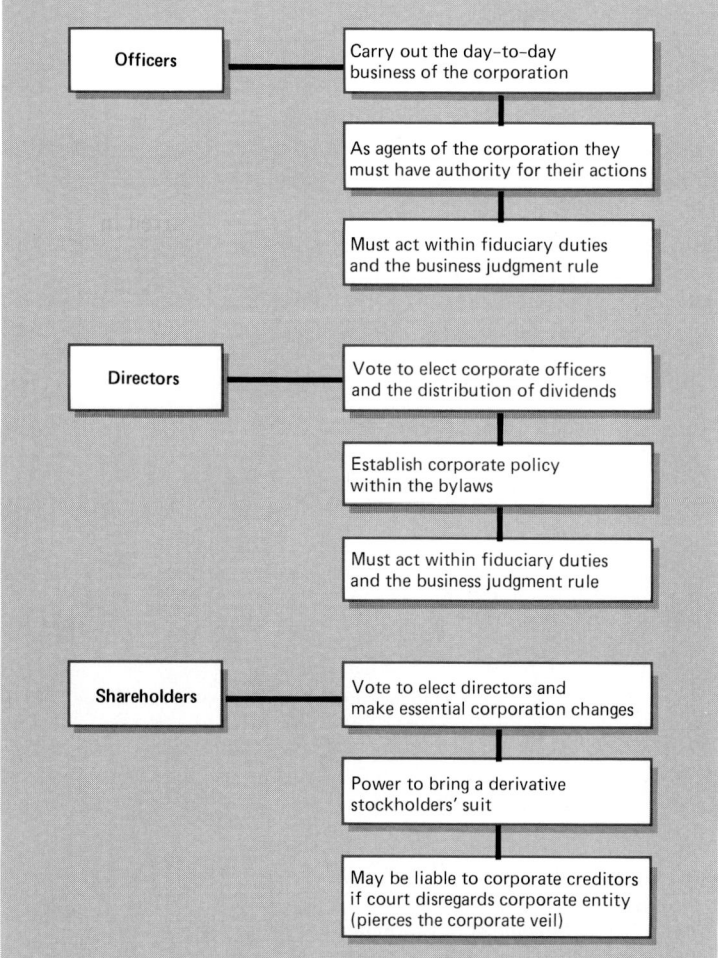

Indemnification of Officers, Directors, Employees, and Agents

Corporate officers or directors may believe that they are acting in good faith but still may be sued by shareholders or other aggrieved parties. The cost of defending the lawsuit and the risk of being found liable may discourage competent individuals from accepting such an office. Under the common law, the expenses involved in defending a director or officer in a suit were borne by them. Today many state statutes, following the Model Business Corporation Act, authorize the corporation to indemnify a corporate officer, director, or agent. Insurance companies will write indemnification policies to cover this loss. The articles of incorporation and bylaws should state the terms of indemnification.

Summary Statement

1. Shareholders indirectly manage the corporation by voting to elect the board of directors at the shareholders' meeting.
2. Managerial decisions that substantially change the nature of the corporation require approval by the shareholders.
3. A quorum is a specified number of shareholders or shares represented required to be present before the shareholders' meeting can begin.
4. Directors manage the business affairs and establish corporate policy.

5. Board action may be taken without a meeting when all directors sign a *consent statement* that recites the action taken.
6. A director is a fiduciary because a director manages the company on behalf of the stockholders. Directors are not liable for honest errors of judgment if they act in good faith.
7. A director, as a fiduciary, is liable for secret profits received in violation of a director's duty of loyalty.
8. The stockholders elect and may remove the directors.
9. A corporation may *indemnify* directors or officers for any loss incurred in connection with a suit, provided that they acted in good faith.
10. Corporate officers are elected by the directors to carry out the day-to-day business of the corporation.
11. Officers act on behalf of the corporation and are fiduciaries. They can be held liable for breach of a fiduciary duty of loyalty.
12. The business judgment rule allows an officer and/or a director to make an honest business decision that turns out to be wrong without being personally liable for its consequences. Public policy demands that officers and/or directors in performing their functions in good faith must be safe from lawsuits because their decisions were unsuccessful.

As you read the following long case, carefully notice the various duties a director owes to a company.

Francis, *et al.* v. United Jersey Bank, *et al.*
432 A.2d 814 (N.J. 1981)

Pollock, Judge. Plaintiffs are trustees in bankruptcy of Pritchard & Baird Intermediaries Corp. (Pritchard & Baird), a reinsurance broker (one who arranges for a contract of one **insurer** to indemnify another insurer against loss which the first insurer may suffer). Defendant Lillian P. Overcash is the daughter of Mrs. Lillian G. Pritchard and the executrix of her estate. At the time of her death, Mrs. Pritchard was a director and the largest single shareholder of Pritchard & Baird. Because Mrs. Pritchard died after the institution of this lawsuit but before trial, her executrix was substituted as a defendant. United Jersey Bank is joined as the administrator of the estate of Charles Pritchard, Sr., who had been president, director and majority shareholder of Pritchard & Baird.

insurer
the person who assumes another's risk (in the insurance contract)

This litigation by the plaintiffs to recover misappropriated funds paid out by Pritchard & Baird focuses on payments made by Pritchard & Baird to Charles Pritchard, Jr., and William Pritchard, who were sons of Mr. and Mrs. Charles Pritchard, Sr., as well as officers, directors and shareholders of the corporation.

The trial court, sitting without a jury, characterized the payments as fraudulent conveyances and entered judgment of $10,355,736.91 plus interest against the estate of Mrs. Pritchard. The judgment is appealed by the executrix concerning the liability of Mrs. Pritchard as a director.

The initial question is, was Mrs. Pritchard negligent in not noticing and trying to prevent the misappropriation of loss and premium funds held by the corporation in an implied trust for the corporation's clients, the insurers. Generally, directors are accorded broad immunity and are not insurers of corporate activities. The problem is particularly nettlesome when a third party asserts that a director, because of nonfeasance (not doing), is liable for losses caused by acts of insiders, who in this case were officers, directors and shareholders. Determination of the liability of Mrs. Pritchard requires findings that she had a duty to the clients of Pritchard & Baird, that she breached that duty and that her breach was a proximate cause of their losses.

It is incumbent upon directors to discharge their duties in good faith and with that degree of diligence, care and skill which ordinarily prudent men would exercise under similar circumstances in like positions. As a general rule, a director should acquire at least a rudimentary understanding of the business of the corporation. Accordingly, a director should become familiar with the fundamentals of the business in which the corporation is engaged.

Because directors are bound to exercise ordinary care, they cannot set up as a defense lack of the knowledge needed to exercise the requisite degree of care. Directors are under a continuing obligation to keep informed about the activities of the corporation. Otherwise, they may not be able to participate in the overall management of corporate affairs. Directors may not shut their eyes to corporate misconduct, and then claim that because they did not see the misconduct they did not have a duty to look. The sentinel asleep at his post contributes nothing to the enterprise he is charged to protect.

A director may require legal advice concerning the propriety of his or her own conduct, the conduct of other officers and directors or the conduct of the corporation.

A director may have a duty to take reasonable means to prevent illegal conduct by co-directors; in an appropriate case, this may include threat of suit.

A director is not an ornament, but an essential component of corporate governance. Consequently, a director cannot protect himself behind a paper shield bearing the motto, "dummy director." All directors are responsible for managing the business and affairs of the corporation.

In general, the relationship of a corporate director to the corporation and its stockholders is that of a fiduciary. Shareholders have a right to expect that directors will exercise reasonable supervision and control over the policies and practices of a corporation.

The most striking circumstances affecting Mrs. Pritchard's duty as a director are the character of the reinsurance industry, the nature of the misappropriated funds and the financial condition of Pritchard & Baird. The hallmark of the reinsurance industry has been the unqualified trust and confidence reposed by ceding [the insurers acquiring reinsurance] companies and reinsurers in reinsurance brokers. Those companies entrust money to reinsurance intermediaries with the justifiable expectation that the funds will be transmitted to the appropriate parties. Consequently, the companies could have assumed rightfully that Mrs. Pritchard, as a director of a reinsurance brokerage corporation, would not sanction the commingling and the conversion of loss and premium funds for the personal use of the principals of Pritchard & Baird. Affirmed, for the plaintiffs, trustees.

Questions and Case Problems

1. Two creditors of an insolvent corporation sued its sole stockholder and chief officer to recover on their money judgments against the corporation. Defendant, Robert J. Fleming, was the president and sole stockholder of Fleming Sheet Metal Company (Fleming Metals), a heating and ventilating business incorporated in 1965. Rather than sell additional stock to finance the corporation, Fleming would advance money through loans, retained salary or payment of corporate debts; and these advances were reflected on an "officer's due" account from which Fleming was paid with corporate assets. Plaintiffs contend that Fleming breached a fiduciary duty by favoring himself over other creditors. Decide. [*Snyder Electric Co. v. Robert J. Fleming*, 305 N.W.2d 863 (Minn. 1981).]

2. Barr, the plaintiff and shareholder of Talcott, a corporation, brought a derivative shareholders' suit against Wackman and other directors of Talcott. Because of the self-dealing and breach of fiduciary duties of Talcott's directors, First Capital, a subsidiary of Gulf and Western had been able to obtain board approval of an unfair stock offer. Wackman claims that the derivative action cannot be maintained since no demand was made on the board to rescind the offer. Must demand be first made on the directors before the stockholders bring a derivative suit? [*Barr v. Wackman*, 329 N.E.2d 180 (N.Y. 1975).]

3. Smith, a director of XYZ Corporation, attended a corporate board meeting when a dividend was declared. Due to an inadequate surplus, this was an illegal dividend. Smith did not vote against the dividend. The next day Smith decided she should vote against the declaration of the dividend and sent a registered letter to the secretary. Creditors of XYZ Corporation sued the directors, including Smith, for declaring an illegal dividend. Is Smith liable?

4. Jones, the president of XYZ Co., with the directors' approval, franchised a successful business throughout the east coast. As a result of this new franchising venture, the corporation overextended and became insolvent. A shareholders' suit was brought against Jones, alleging a breach of his fiduciary duty as the chief executive officer to transact business in a reasonable manner. Decide.

5. Segal and Martinez were two physicians who formed plaintiff corporation, Patient Care Services, to provide comprehensive health services to a hospital. Both physicians were directors, officers, and stockholders of Patient Care Services. The hospital that engaged its services did not renew the contract. A new medical corporation formed, owned, and managed by Segal was awarded the new contract. Segal informed Martinez of his intent to negotiate with the hospital on behalf of his corporation. Was Segal liable for breach of his fiduciary duty of loyalty? [*Patient Care Services, S.C. v. Segal,* 337 N.E.2d 471 (Ill. 1975).]

6. Jones, the president of XYZ Corporation, developed a competing corporation during his office as president. The directors knew of this but never attempted to stop Jones. XYZ Corp. became insolvent because of this competition. The shareholders brought suit against Jones and the directors for breach of their fiduciary duty of loyalty. The directors claim that they are not liable because they did not participate in the competing company. Decide.

7. Gimbel, plaintiff and shareholder of Signal Companies, Inc., defendant, sued to enjoin the sale of its stock in a subsidiary corporation. Gimbel represents a minority group of shareholders who object to a proposed sale of all the capital stock of Signal Oil, a wholly owned subsidiary of defendant corporation. A special meeting of the defendant's board of directors was called without notice of its purpose. Three of the four outside directors were unaware of the proposed sale prior to the meeting. A handwritten outline of the transaction was handed to the directors and an oral presentation was made supporting it. The tax consequences of the sale were discussed. The general financial status of Signal Oil Co., including its sales, income, cash flow, balance sheet, projected expenditures, and risks were also reviewed. Gimbel attacked the proposed sale on the grounds that the directors recklessly authorized the sale without informed reasonable deliberations. Judgment for whom? [*Gimbel v. Signal Companies, Inc.,* 316 A.2d 599 (Del. 1974).]

8. The Pintura Corporation was an Illinois corporation engaged in the business of finishing and installing dry wall in construction projects. Nieto was its president and sole shareholder. Wille Building Materials Corporation (Wille), was an Illinois corporation which supplied Pintura with dry wall and other supplies. Plaintiff National Acceptance Company of America (NACA) was and is in the busines sof making commercial loans. On May 23, 1974, Pintura assigned to Wille the balance of all monies to become due to Pintura from one Highland Construction Co., for work performed on a project in Elgin, Illinois. The assignment recites that it was given in consideration for Wille's continued extension of credit to Pintura. On September 27, 1974, in order to secure Wille's indebtedness to NACA, Wille assigned to NACA its right in the Pintura-Wille assignment. Subsequently, Highland issued five checks, totaling $35,322.73 payable jointly to Pintura and Wille. All checks were deposited in Pintura's corporate account. Defendant Nieto indorsed three checks in Pintura and Wille's names, and he directed an authorized indorsement and deposit of the other two checks in Pintura's behalf. May defendant Nieto, a corporate officer, be held individually liable for conversion committed by him in behalf of and for the sole benefit of the corporation? [*National Acceptance Company of America v. Pintura Corporation,* et al., 418 N.E.2d 1114 (Ill. 1981).]

9. McCrary Engineering Corp. (McCrary) specializes in the planning, design and supervision of construction of water and sewerage projects for municipalities, counties and industry. Defendant Hood became its president in 1972. In 1976, Hood caused defendant Southeast Consultants, Inc., (Southeast) to be chartered, with Hood as principal stockholder and president. Unknown to McCrary's directors, Southeast used McCrary's office as its office and used McCrary's equipment, supplies and personnel in its engineering operations. In 1979 Hood left McCrary.

McCrary sued Hood and Southeast Consultants, Inc., for damages and injunctive relief, alleging that defendant Hood had breached his fiduciary duties to McCrary by forming a competing engineering firm without notice and by improperly using McCrary's resources to set up and operate the new firm, and by usurping current and future business opportunities belonging to McCrary, particularly for contracts to design sewer and water systems and contracts to supervise completion of projects for which McCrary had prepared the initial designs. Did Hood take unfair advantage of a corporate opportunity? Decide. [*Southeast Consultants, Inc. v. McCrary Engineering Corp.*, 273 S.E.2d 112 (Ga. 1980).]

10. In the case of *Francis*, et al. *v. United Jersey Bank*, et al., 432 A.2d 814 (N.J. 1981),[9] the court carefully reviews the duty a director owes to a company. Chances are that you may, during your business career, be asked to serve as a director. Based on the findings of this case, establish a list of duties a director owes to a corporation.

---

[9] See pp. 691–92.

Ethics and Business Law in Part 8
Business Organizations

Introduction

This end-of-Part discussion, like the others in this book, is designed to encourage students to begin forming personal beliefs about what is right or wrong conduct in business. The discussion here builds on the material in the first end-of-Part discussion on pages 58 to 69; you may find it helpful to review that.

This material has several goals. The "sampling of ethical issues" section immediately following is designed to help you see the range of ethical issues associated with this area of the law. The in-depth discussion is intended to provide you with a background for forming your own beliefs about a single very important ethical issue in business. The problems at the end are designed to build your skill in ethical analysis while exploring further the in-depth issue.

A Sampling of Ethical Issues in Business Organizations

Partnerships

Partners owe fiduciary duties to the partnership. But this duty often conflicts with self-interest. For example, assume that you were one of 10 partners and you came across a business opportunity which should, by law, be turned over to the partnership, but which you could secretly take for yourself. Would this tempt you? Suppose the opportunity would generate a secret profit for you of $30,000, but only $3,000 for you if you turned it over to the partnership. Can you see how great the temptations can be in partnerships and, therefore, how important trust and ethical character are among partners?

Another ethical issue stems from the nature of partnership law. It makes partners *jointly and severally* liable for the torts of the partnership. Sometimes this may appear unjust. Suppose there are 3 partners each worth, respectively, $5,000, $10,000, and $1,000,000. If the partner worth $5,000 commits a partnership tort which results in a judgment of $500,000, practically all the money could be collected from the wealthiest partner. Do you think this result is just? Can you articulate a style of ethical reasoning which supports this aspect of partnership law?

In partnership law, partners share profits and losses equally unless the partnership agreement is to the contrary. This is true despite unequal capital contributions and unequal work for the partnership. Can you see that in a new two person partnership, especially one without a written partnership agreement, it is possible for one partner to contribute 80% of the capital and the work yet be legally entitled only to 50% of the profits? Can you articulate a style of ethical reasoning which supports this aspect of partnership law?

Special Ventures

Limited partners share in the profits of the partnership but are not personally liable, beyond their capital contributions, for the claims against the partnership. This is true as long as they don't participate in the management of the partnership. Do you think that non-participation in management is a strong enough ethical basis for limiting liability? If a *general* partner became inactive in the management of an accounting partnership, should this eliminate liability on his part?

Corporations

The basic goal of corporate conduct is an important and controversial ethical concern. Some argue that maximizing shareholder wealth is the only ethical goal. Others claim corporations must be "socially responsible" to be ethical.

Social responsibility is the idea that we must evaluate the impact of corporate action, not just on shareholders, but on all parts of society—employees, suppliers, consumers, neighbors, even future generations.

The conflict between shareholder wealth maximization and social responsibility becomes very visible when large corporations engage in acts of charity such as making gifts to hospitals or educational institutions. Some shareholders criticize this because they claim it reduces their dividends. Others criticize it because corporate managers are giving away money which is not theirs; charity decisions should be made by *owners* of property, such as shareholders, not by mere managers. In contrast, the social responsibility camp argues that corporations are chartered by society to serve the public good. Often society, and even the corporations, are benefitted more by using profits for charitable activities rather than just for dividends. What is your view on this issue?

Another ethics issue in corporation law centers on the duty of loyalty owed by officers to the corporation and thereby to shareholders. When mergers, buy-outs, or hostile takeovers are on the horizon, officers rightly often fear losing their jobs. This fear sometimes causes them to place their own self-interest above that of the corporation.

"Golden parachutes" provide large severance payments to officers if their corporation is taken over and they are fired. Some argue that golden parachutes are necessary to keep talented officers with a firm which is vulnerable to a takeover. Others claim that golden parachutes are merely a way for officers to enrich themselves at the expense of shareholders. What do you think?

"Poison pills" are devices which make hostile takeovers more risky. They work by authorizing existing shareholders to purchase additional shares at a low price in the event a hostile purchaser acquires more than, e.g., 25% of the firm's stock. Since the hostile party cannot buy these new shares, they in effect dilute, and reduce the value of, the hostile party's investment. A poison pill reduces the risk of takeovers and thereby preserves the jobs of officers. But shareholders are injured when a poison pill is used because, in the typical takeover, shares increase in value 25% to 40% and this the shareholders have lost. Do you think poison pills are ethical?

In-Depth Discussion of a Basic Issue: What Moral Obligations Do We Owe Employing Organizations?

What *moral,* as opposed to *legal* obligations, do we owe to partnerships, corporations and other business organizations? To a large extent the answer turns on what we define organizations to be in a *moral* sense. If you conclude that business organizations are the same as persons, then you would conclude that you owe many obligations to the organization beyond mere contractual duties. For example, in an organizational emergency you might feel morally bound to work extra hours without pay. In contrast, if you conclude as many do, that business organizations do not exist in a moral sense, you owe the business organization no duties beyond your legal obligations. Thus, in an organizational emergency you might try to extort a very high rate of pay for your extra work.

Juristic Entities
Persons are considered "legal entities" in the sense that they are recognized by the law as able to assume legal rights and incur legal duties. They may be individuals, or in the eyes of the law nonhuman legal entities called "juristic entities." Many business organizations, such as corporations, are juristic entities. In many ways, the law treats corporations the same as it treats individuals. Thus, it places individuals and corporations on the same legal level. The implication is that we owe similar moral duties to organizations as well as to individuals.

The Historical View
Historically in western civilization, individuals have been the main moral entities. This flows out of our Judeo-Christian tradition, from the belief that individuals are made in the image of God and that the things of the earth have been given to mankind. As a consequence, we feel free to kill cows for food, cut down trees for housing, pick flowers to decorate a table and in other ways destroy life. Whales can be harvested for their economic value and horses can be rendered into dog food. In contrast, it is wrong to do even minor injury to other human beings. Certainly we cannot eat them. And even if they ask us, we cannot help them take their own lives. In the Judeo-Christian tradition, and in most but not all major religions, persons and churches are the only moral entities besides God. Churches were among the first recognized juristic entities and corporation law has grown from this source. The following sections discuss the way the moral status of business organizations would be analyzed using the four styles of ethical reasoning.

An Egoistic View
The egoist will not recognize business organizations as moral entities. For the egoist even other human beings do not exist in an ethical sense. Employers, co-workers, even spouses, are solely means to the end of the egoist's self-satisfaction. Therefore, an egoist who is a director of a corporation can justify taking a director's fee without exercising the due care required by law if there is no risk of liability on his part.

A Utilitarian View
Utilitarians generally recognize other persons as moral entities. They must weigh the impact of *their* ethical decisions on other persons. The act which benefits the *majority of persons most* is the act which the utilitarian feels he ought to do.

Utilitarian views of organizations are sometimes articulated in terms of *mission.* That is, because we operate in an imperfect social system some organizations generate more social good than others and some utilitarians therefore accord them more moral stature. A hospital may be highly regarded while a firm manufacturing cigarettes might be viewed very negatively. A utilitarian nurse might work extra hours for free for the hospital while refusing to work for the cigarette company even for double the pay.

A Kantian View
In Kant's thinking, man is entitled to distinctive moral treatment because of the capacity to engage in moral reasoning. This is the attribute which distinguishes humans from other life forms. In Kant's view, we can eat hamburgers because the cows can't engage in moral reasoning. Since each individual has the potential to engage in moral reasoning, each is entitled to moral dignity.

A debate is now raging among serious philosophers about whether, in a Kantian sense, some organizations are able to engage in moral reasoning. If one concludes that they can, then by Kantian reasoning, these organizations would be entitled to treatment similar to that accorded to human beings. Some argue that organizations perceive, transmit information, evaluate the information, *and as an organization* make ethical decisions. They argue that an organization's decisions can have attributes different from the decisions made by individual persons in the organization. The sense that there is an ethical culture to an organization points to its Kantian existence. Perhaps you have seen an organization keep employed a disabled worker long after the person has become unable to carry on his or her share of the organization's responsibilities; this might suggest that the organization is engaging in moral reasoning and thus "exists" in a Kantian sense.

A Kantian who believes organizations are moral entities might be compelled to quit, or advocate that he be laid off, if he concluded that was the best thing for the organization.

Religious Views

The religious view is that persons are the only moral entities, other than churches and God. As a consequence, organizations are viewed as non-existing and as simply a grouping of existing individuals. Thus, an analysis of a problem confronting a college is resolved by analyzing its impact on students, faculty, alumni, staff, and administrators.

Kantians might reach a different conclusion than religious thinkers. For example, if all of the people associated with a college were given pay raises or reduced tuition, that might benefit these people yet do injury to the university by limiting its ability to transmit ethical values academically in the future. Thus, Kantians sometimes see organizations as entities to which they owe moral obligations while religious individuals sometimes see only other people.

Conclusion

The way we think about organizations as moral entities greatly influences the types of ethical decisions we make about them. Some view organizations as non-existing, others see their existence in their mission, some see existence in the ability to engage in moral reasoning, and some see organizations as simply groups of people. Which of these views of organizations—egoist, utilitarian, Kantian, or religious—do you find most appealing?

Solving Ethics Problems

Like the other end-of-Part discussions in this book, this one presents problems for you to consider. These problems have three goals. The first is to give you the opportunity to further explore the in-depth issue. The second goal is to give you experience in ethical reasoning about the law and about related management problems. The third goal is to let you see how thinking critically about the law can increase your ability to make ethical decisions. To facilitate this, the problems begin by asking you to analyze the law for its ethical content and then shift to looking at related problems in managerial ethics.

For a discussion of the ethical roles of markets and the law, and examples of the four styles of ethical reasoning—egoism, utilitarianism, Kant's philosophy, and religious ethics—read the business ethics material at the end of Part 1.

Problems

1. Review the case of *Francis,* et al. *v. United Jersey Bank,* et al., on pages 691–92. There, the court held that Mrs. Prichard's estate was liable for fraudulent payments made by the company while she was a director, even though she was also the largest shareholder. Try to characterize Mrs. Prichard's philosophic orientation toward organizations. How do you classify the director's liability law articulated in this case; is it egoistic, utilitarian, Kantian, or religious in nature? Or is it some combination?

2. Seon Cab Corporation had one shareholder, Carlton. The only assets of this corporation were 2 taxicabs which were operated in New York City. Carlton was also the principal shareholder in 9 other corporations. Each of these also owned 2 taxicabs operated in New York City. A cab owned by Seon Cab Corporation was operated negligently and as a result ran over Walkovszky. Walkovszky sued only Carlton. Do you think Seon Cab Corporation is a moral entity? Do you think Walkovszky should be allowed to recover from Carlton's other corporations if he had sued them? Why or why not?

3. Assume you are the business manager of a research hospital which does important work on finding cures for certain types of cancers. Because you've worked for them for a long time, you are quite effective and the work of the organization would be slowed down significantly for about a year if you were to leave. You make $60,000 per year. An auto parts chain has asked you to join their organization and is offering you $85,000 per year. You know the hospital is unable to pay you any more. Is this hospital a moral entity? Ought you to take the new job? Why or why not?

4. Suppose you are the manager of marketing for a firm which makes high quality stereo sound systems for installation by automobile manufacturers. Your product is superior to that of any competitor. One of your subordinates has a serious drinking problem. As a result, your organization has lost an important customer and its profits will therefore be 3% lower this year. Your organization contributes to the March of Dimes, sponsors excellence in a local grade school with poor students, and employs an unusually high percentage of handicapped persons. Is this organization a moral entity? How do you weigh the rights of your organization in comparison to the needs of this alcoholic employee? Should you fire him? How would this situation be analyzed by an egoist, a utilitarian, a Kantian, and a religious individual?

PART

9 Government Regulation of Business

47. **Antitrust Law**
    Various major federal antitrust laws and their development as society's response to undue concentration of business power.
48. **Administrative Law**
    How the federal administrative agencies operate in administering the federal antitrust laws.
49. **Labor Law**
    The various federal laws designed to control labor-management relations.
50. **Environmental Law**
    Federal legislation to control further unwarranted and socially undesirable intrusion by business in upsetting the human and physical environment in which we live.

Summary
The purpose of federal governmental regulation of business is fundamentally to protect our freedom to do business by curbing and preventing abuses. The government regulation discussed in chapter 47 is intended to protect free enterprise and fair competition. Administrative agencies, as discussed in chapter 48, have the responsibility to monitor business and establish rules and regulations to carry out the federal laws.

In chapter 49 the laws that identify and protect the rights of labor to organize and of management to manage are discussed. Laws to protect the human and physical environment from private and public abuse and unnecessary waste are discussed in chapter 50.

Business ethics as it relates to the text material in this Part is considered at the end of the Part.

47 Antitrust Law

After you have read this chapter, you should be able to:

1. Define pure monopoly and pure competition.
2. Explain the reason for the Sherman Act of 1890.
3. Explain why group boycotts are illegal.
4. Explain why Congress passed the Clayton Act.
5. Explain exclusive dealing contracts, tying arrangements, stock acquisitions designed to lessen competition, and horizontal versus vertical constraints.
6. Identify the Federal Trade Commission and its primary functions.
7. Understand the Robinson-Patman Act of 1936.
8. Understand the major defenses against the Robinson-Patman Act of 1936.

Introduction

Imagine that you are an entrepreneur in a small midwestern town. Your company sells oil to consumers within a forty-mile radius and has been expanding rapidly since you began it ten years ago. You are finally making a decent living from the business. Suddenly you discover that your competitors are involved in a scheme which will allow them not only to control the industry but to wipe out your firm.

The stockholders of your larger competitors are turning their power to vote in corporate matters over to a select group of people called trustees. These trustees thereby gain enormous power in many firms at once and can control the supply (and so the price) of oil for the entire nation, including the area in which you have traditionally done business. By raising the price of oil in one state and making a great deal of profit, they can lower the price in another area, even to the point of taking a loss for a while, to drive out competition—including your firm. How would you feel?

This scheme is far more than a story. During the late 1800s and early 1900s, such business trusts were common. People like John D. Rockefeller and Cornelius Vanderbilt made their fortunes using schemes just like this one. The public became greatly concerned as business power became more and more concentrated in the hands of a few individuals. They therefore turned to law for help.

Freedom to compete is a healthy concept and goes hand in hand with the principles of freedom and liberty on which the United States was founded. The early governmental policy of laissez faire (governmental noninterference with business) made it possible for such freedoms to be abused as business sought to increase its power. The policy had to be modified by federal statute to check the increasing tide of unreasonable restraint of trade which interfered with free enterprise and fair competition.

Accordingly, the issue became—how to balance free enterprise and fair competition on the one hand with governmental regulation of business on the other hand. The same issue exists today. This chapter analyzes the strains of public and private interests and the government's current reaction to them in controlling monopolies, combinations, and unfair restraints in business.

We shall see in this chapter the purposes of the various major antitrust statutes, how these statutes have worked, the type of business activities restrained, and the impact of the federal courts in interpreting and enforcing these statutes.

The Response of Law to Undue Concentration of Business Power

The United States was created with the intention of providing maximum opportunity for free competition in business. The doctrine of **laissez-faire**—that is, to let business alone—was dominant and worked well, at least until the industrial expansion after the Civil War. Then, with business growing by leaps and bounds, it became necessary to monitor the activities of some firms.

laissez-faire
government's policy of not interfering with business

The amount and type of government regulation of business has always been hotly debated in the world of work, but such regulation does exist. In this chapter we will examine the major federal antitrust laws: the Sherman Act of 1890; the Clayton Act of 1914; the Federal Trade Commission Act of 1914; and the Robinson-Patman Act of 1936 amending the Clayton Act. Students should be aware that a number of other laws also regulate business, but they are somewhat less important.

What is it we want to regulate? Anyone who has followed a winning baseball team knows that things tend to get exciting when the competition is a little too close for comfort. When your team is leading by four or five runs the game can become boring, but when the lead is cut to one and the opposition has a tying run on third base with no outs, the situation is entirely different. For many people, the world of business provides the same kind of excitement. Competition forces firms to do their best to stay ahead, and by and large this is a good thing for all of us. Firms come up with new products, increase their sales, and improve current products—all to be the leader of the industry. Once in a while, however, a firm becomes as strong or stronger than its competitors and can drive its rivals completely out of business. If this happens, the leader becomes the *only* one with a particular product and can establish any price it wants, no matter how exorbitant.

The difficulty for the government is to determine *when* the law should exert control over competition. When there are many firms of equal strength, control may not be needed. When there is but one firm, and that firm is in a position to hurt the public, control is clearly needed. But what about the case in the middle, where a few firms control an industry? And, what about the case of an industry where one firm rather than many would be desirable? For example, it would be useless to have thirty or forty different telephone companies competing in the same city. Think of all the wires the telephone company now puts up. Could you imagine thirty times as many wires? As you can see, finding an answer is not easy. The government has set down some guidelines on when they will exert control and when they will not. Before we can examine those laws, you need to understand two terms: pure monopoly and pure competition.

Pure Monopoly versus Pure Competition

On rare occasions a firm discovers that it has no competitors. For example, most utility companies are unlikely to have competition in a given town. One gas company or one electric company satisfies the needs of the entire community; duplication is simply unnecessary. In a small community, one barber shop may be enough to cut everyone's hair. In these cases, it is either impossible for a competitor to enter the market or merely improbable or unlikely. The more improbable or unlikely competition is, the closer the market is to a **pure monopoly**—a market situation where only one firm is producing a product or providing a service.

pure monopoly
a market in which there is a single firm with no competitors

More often, however, a number of firms compete with each other for business. On occasion, the products are so similar that consumers cannot distinguish between the goods of different firms. There may also be so many sellers that the size of the market for each firm is small, and an individual company cannot have any meaningful influence over the price of the goods. If both things happen at the same time, we approach **pure competition.**

pure competition
a market in which many firms compete and no one firm has very much power

The market for wheat is an example of nearly pure competition. Many farmers produce wheat, and there is little if any difference between their end products. Furthermore, no individual farmer can influence the price very much because the market is so large. If one farmer tried to get $.10 more per bushel, buyers would merely move on to the next farmer. Thus, we can say that there is pure competition for wheat.

Federal statutory modification of laissez-faire.

Controlling Monopolies, Combinations, and Unfair Restraints

As you can imagine, monopolies in key industries can become enormous and wield tremendous power. Unfortunately, this power is not always used to benefit consumers. The first example in this chapter pointed out how some firms try to drive out competition in the hope of ultimately forming a monopoly. The practice of giving controlling blocks of stock to trustees was the first target of federal regulation and the genesis of today's **antitrust laws.**

antitrust laws
laws that limit monopolies, combinations, and unfair restraints to help prevent the undue concentration of economic power

Sherman Act of 1890

It is highly unlikely that any firm will be an absolute monopoly, so the United States government had to develop a law to control situations that were *approaching* monopolistic competition. The first law to do this was the Sherman Act of 1890. The two major sections of this law are:

Section 1: Every contract, combination in the form of trust or otherwise, or conspiracy, in restraint of trade or commerce among the several States, or with foreign nations, is hereby declared to be illegal. . . .

Section 2: Every person who shall monopolize, or attempt to monopolize, or combine or conspire with any other person or persons, to monopolize any part of the trade or commerce among the several States, or with foreign nations, shall be deemed guilty of a felony. . . .[1]

Section 1, as later interpreted by the U.S. Supreme Court, makes unreasonable restraint of trade illegal. Section 2 goes on to explain that individuals who engage in such restraint can be prosecuted for their actions.

The United States Supreme Court recently held that agreement among competing physicians setting, by majority vote, maximum fees for payment from participants in specified insurance plans was per se unlawful under section 1 of the Sherman Act. (*Arizona v. Maricopa County Medical Society,* et al., 457 U.S. 332 (1982).

Boycotts. Part of the Sherman Act has been interpreted by the courts to limit the opportunity for firms to join in not doing business with another company. Although any company can decide with whom it will or will not deal, if many firms get together in a concerted effort to boycott one firm, they are participating in a **group boycott,** which is a violation per se (of itself) of the Sherman Act. This is illustrated by the following case.

group boycott
a concerted effort by a number of firms to avoid doing business with a particular individual or firm

Facts
Klor's Inc., plaintiff, was a San Francisco retail store, and Broadway-Hale Stores, Inc., defendant, was its principal competitor. The owners of Klor's accused Broadway-Hale of trying to get the manufacturers of household appliances to agree not to sell to Klor's or to discriminate against Klor's by the method of offering Klor's goods at unreasonably high prices. Judgment for plaintiff. Defendant appealed.

Decision
Affirmed, for plaintiff, Klor's.

Reasoning
The plaintiff's contention that this concerted effort on the part of Broadway-Hale, Inc. and others violated the Sherman Act was sustained. Mr. Justice Black wrote: "Group boycotts . . . have long been held to be in the forbidden category. . . . Plainly the allegations of this complaint disclose such a boycott. This is not a case of a single trader refusing to deal with another, nor even of a manufacturer and a dealer agreeing to an exclusive distributorship. Alleged in this complaint is a wide combination consisting of manufacturers, distributors and a retailer. It deprives the manufacturers and distributors of their freedom to sell to Klor's at the same prices . . . made available to Broadway-Hale. . . . It clearly has, by its nature and character, a monopolistic *tendency.*" [Emphasis added.]

Klor's Inc. v. Broadway-Hale Stores, Inc., 359 U.S. 207 (1959).

Violations of the Sherman Act may be punished by a jail sentence or a fine or both. Over the years, Congress has increased the fine by amending the Act.[2] Today, a corporate violator can be required to pay $1 million, and individuals to pay as much as $100,000. The government also has the power to enjoin violators from further action. Finally, individuals whose businesses have been injured by a violation of the Act can sue for treble (triple) the amount of injury sustained, plus related court costs.

The Clayton Act of 1914
The Sherman Act did not succeed in halting all of the abuses that Congress had hoped it would cover. As a result, Congress passed the Clayton Act of 1914. Among the more important parts of the Act are provisions dealing with exclusive-dealing contracts, tying sales, and stock acquisition designed to substantially lessen competition or tending to create a monopoly, discussed below.

Exclusive-Dealing Contracts. If you were a manufacturer, you might want to get retailers to agree not to sell the products of your competitors. Some retailers might even find the arrangement beneficial. The retailer would get to know your product very well

---
[1] See Sherman Act, 15 U.S.C.A., secs. 1–7.   [2] Amendments to Sherman Act, sec. 2.

and could depend on you for a constant supply. If enough retailers agreed to such an arrangement, you could effectively wipe out your competition. If your firm were powerful enough to exert some influence on the retailer, you might consider forcing the retailer into such an arrangement. Whatever its effect on the retailer, such an arrangement *might* substantially decrease competition. The Clayton Act prohibits this kind of activity and labels it an **exclusive-dealing contract.**

exclusive-dealing contract
an agreement between a seller or lessor and a purchaser or lessee that the latter shall not use or deal in the products of a competing seller or lessor

tying arrangement
an agreement between a seller or lessor and a purchaser or lessee that a sale or lease of a product to the latter is contingent upon the latter's purchase or lease of another product of the seller or lessor

Tying Arrangements. A **tying arrangement** is another technique "to substantially lessen competition" or "tending to create a monopoly." Here is how a tying contract works. Suppose you were the owner of a medium-size manufacturing plant. You decide to purchase 1,000 fountain pens from Ajax Pen Company. Ajax gives you a good deal on the fountain pens, but as part of that deal makes you sign a contract agreeing to purchase only Ajax *ink* for those pens. Clearly, if Ajax has a monopoly on pens and can get its customers to sign such agreements, it soon will have a monopoly on ink as well. Tying contracts are regulated by section 3 of the Clayton Act. They have been declared illegal where the contract will "*substantially* lessen competition or *tend* to create a monopoly in any line of commerce." [Emphasis added.] See the excellent detailed court opinion in *United States of America v. Mercedes-Benz of North America, Inc.,* 517 F.Supp. 1369 (1981).[3]

The law does not require that there be a monopoly in an industry before it will step in to regulate the firms involved. It merely requires that the action substantially lessen competition by foreclosing competitors from substantial volume of the tied market. In the case above, Ajax would be lessening competition by limiting the ability of other ink companies to sell their products. But how large a volume of tied sales is necessary to effectively limit competition? In the landmark case,[4] the court decided that tied sales should amount to at least $500,000 to require regulatory action.

Stock Acquisitions Designed to Lessen Competition. It was suggested earlier in this chapter that the courts often face difficult questions as to *when* a firm becomes large enough to wield a great deal of power. One problem that has been particularly perplexing is whether the *sheer size* of the firm should dictate governmental control, or whether the firm must actually *use* that power to restrain trade in some way. The government's answer came in section 7 of the Clayton Act as amended by the Cellar-Kefauver Act of 1950:

No corporation shall acquire, directly or indirectly, the whole or any part of the stock or other share capital and no corporation subject to the jurisdiction of the Federal Trade Commission shall acquire the whole or any part of the assets of one or more corporations engaged in commerce, where in any line of commerce in any section of the country, the effect of such acquisition, of such stocks or assets, or of the use of such stock by the voting or granting of proxies or otherwise, *may* be substantially to lessen competition, or *tend* to create a monopoly. [Emphasis added.]

Notice that such acquisition need not *result* in substantially lessening competition or creating a monopoly in order to be unlawful. All that is required is that it "may" or "tend to" produce the unlawful result.

merger
(in corporations) the absorption of one corporation by another corporation

Corporate acquisition of stock may result in a horizontal or vertical **merger,** and if it *may* substantially lessen competition or *tend to* create a monopoly, it is unlawful. The following example illustrates the concept of horizontal and vertical mergers. Stop Time, Inc. is a firm that manufactures and sells pocket watches. To manufacture these watches, Stop Time must purchase the raw materials, put them together as pocket watches, and sell the watches to retailers, who sell to the public. Stop Time probably competes with companies such as Timex, Westclox, and Benrus, to name a few. A diagram of Stop Time's competitive situation would probably look like figure 47.1.

---

[3] Pp. 864–67.   [4] *International Salt Co., Inc. v. United States,* 332 U.S. 392 (1947).

Figure 47.1 Diagrammatic Representation of Stop Time, Inc.'s Competitive Situation

If Stop Time purchased stock in Timex, Benrus, or Westclox, that would be a **horizontal merger**; Stop Time would be combining forces with its competitors. On the other hand, if Stop Time bought a controlling interest in all retailers of pocket watches or in all sources of raw materials, that would be a **vertical merger**.

According to section 7 of the Clayton Act, horizontal mergers were illegal; vertical ones were not. Today, because of complex case law and vast and overlapping administrative rules and regulations, students are advised to see a legal specialist if their problem seems to extend beyond this brief description. Although both types of combinations could cause problems, the Act limited only horizontal mergers. This was an important weakness in the law.

A third kind of merger occasionally ends up in litigation. It is called a *conglomerate merger*. A conglomerate merger is one in which there is little or no distinguishing connection between the output or industry of the firms which are brought together. An example of a conglomerate merger would be the union of a book publisher with a manufacturer of canned pineapple. As with other types of mergers, the court looks at the merger and asks what the impact is likely to be. If an unfair advantage is likely to result, the merger will probably be declared illegal.

horizontal merger
a merger of competing firms

vertical merger
a merger between a firm and one of its major suppliers or customers

The Federal Trade Commission Act

The **Federal Trade Commission** was created in 1914 when Congress passed the Federal Trade Commission Act. Congress intended the FTC to monitor two areas: (1) unfair methods of competition, and (2) unfair or deceptive acts or practices in or affecting commerce. The FTC also has the power to enforce antitrust laws.

Federal Trade Commission May Act on Its Own Initiative. If the Federal Trade Commission believed that a firm is using some unfair method of competition, it would probably try to prosecute the firm under an appropriate section of one of the major antitrust laws.[5] However, on many occasions the FTC has moved on its own to stop deceptive acts in commerce, as in the following case.

Federal Trade Commission
a government body that monitors unfair competition and commercial practices

Facts
The case arose out of Colgate's attempt to prove on television that its shaving cream, Rapid Shave, outshaves them all. Colgate had three one-minute commercials designed to show that Rapid Shave could soften even the toughness of sandpaper. The announcer informed the audience that "to prove Rapid Shave's super-moisturizing power, we put it right from the can onto tough, dry sandpaper.

Apply . . . soak . . . off in a stroke." It appeared that sandpaper was being used, but it was really a "simulated sandpaper" made of plexiglass to which sand had been applied. The Federal Trade Commission found that the commercial was a material deceptive device. Colgate appealed.

Decision
Affirmed, for the Federal Trade Commission.

---

[5] For FTC administrative procedures and techniques for dispute resolution, see pp. 716–18.

Reasoning
The court had to decide whether it was a deceptive practice under section 5 of the FTC Act to represent falsely that a televised test, experiment, or demonstration provides a viewer with visual proof of a product claim. The court held: "We agree with the Commission that the undisclosed use of plexiglass in the present commercials was a material deceptive practice, independent and separate from the other misrepresentations found. We find unpersuasive Colgate's other objections to this conclusion. They claim that it will be impractical to inform the viewing public that it is not seeing an actual test . . . but we think . . . that the ingenious advertising would well be able . . ., if it so desires, to conform to the Commission's insistence that the public not be misinformed."

Federal Trade Commission v. Colgate-Palmolive Co., 380 U.S. 374 (1965).

If a firm is found to be violating the law, a number of punishments are available, ranging from civil penalties to criminal prosecution. The FTC has generally used a combination of consent decrees and orders. These are similar to settlements with the offending firm and are not nearly as severe as criminal prosecution.

Robinson-Patman Act of 1936

Section 2(a) of the Clayton Act was difficult for both courts and businesses to understand. In an attempt to clear the air, Congress passed the Robinson-Patman Act of 1936, amending section 2(a). This Act was specifically designed to deal with **price discrimination**. Experts today contend that the Robinson-Patman Act has not actually clarified the issue to the satisfaction of all interested parties. It does, however, state that it shall be "unlawful to discriminate in price between different purchasers of commodities of like grade and quality, where . . . the effect of such discrimination may be (a) to substantially lessen competition, or (b) to tend to create a monopoly in any line of commerce or (c) to injure, destroy, or prevent competition with any person who either grants or knowingly receives the benefit of such discrimination, or with customers of either of them."[6]

price discrimination the practice of offering the same product to different competing customers at different prices

The Uses of the Robinson-Patman Act. The Act is used to eliminate a number of unfair practices. One of these is to lower the price of goods in a geographical area to drive out the competition. A second practice is to give discounts on goods to one seller but not to another, where the only reasonable explanation of the discount is an intent to destroy competition or create a monopoly. A third practice is to discriminate against purchasers by charging inordinately high freight costs with the intent to destroy competition. In the following case the FTC held that the firm's charging lower prices for its product in certain geographical areas drove out competition and was violative of the Clayton Act.

Facts
"Dean Milk Co. maintain [ed] its executive offices in Franklin Park, Illinois, and [was] engaged in the processing and sale of fluid milk . . . in a number of states. . . . Its prices in Evansville, Indiana . . . and Lexington, Kentucky, all of which are served by the Louisville processing plant, were lower than prices in Louisville." The FTC had to decide whether the price difference reflected a violation of section 2(a) of the Clayton Act.

Decision
Dean's price difference was such a violation.

Reasoning
The dairy argued that evidence of a "reasonable possibility" of adverse competition effects on competition is not enough to issue an order to cease. The FTC disagreed, "Congress clearly intended to prevent in their incipiency practices which might harm the competitive process and thus explicitly provided that a showing of actual injury was not necessary. [Here] we think the conditions . . . in the market—the low profit margins and the high mortality rate in the smaller dairies—support a conclusion that there is a reasonable possibility that continued sales . . . where they cannot realize a reasonable profit . . . will cause the demise of other small dairies.

Respondent [Dean Milk Co.] will be ordered to cease charging lower prices . . ."

In re *Dean Milk Company*, 68 FTC 710 (1965).

---

[6] Robinson-Patman Act, (1936) 15 U.S.C., sec. 13.

Resale Price Fixing. Resale price fixing occurs when the price is fixed at which the purchased product is to be resold by the buyer. When two or more competing suppliers agree to so fix the price, there is *horizontal* price fixing. When the supplier so agrees with his or her buyer, there is *vertical* price fixing. Both are illegal today. Some manufacturers try to avoid the consequences of vertical price fixing by merely *suggesting* retail prices to buyers rather than entering into an agreement (conspiracy to restrain trade) with the buyers concerning prices.

Defenses against a Charge under the Robinson-Patman Act. Not all price differences or discounts are violations per se of the Robinson-Patman Act. If a buyer purchases such a large quantity of goods that the manufacturer can save money on production or on purchase of raw materials, a discount may be offered. If a change in conditions makes the goods sell for more (or less), this would not be a violation. If you can demonstrate that you did not attempt to lessen competition, but merely acted in good faith to challenge your competitors, you will be safe. This was the point of the following case, which held that there was no violation of the Robinson-Patman Act.

Facts
Defendant, Standard Oil Co., sold gasoline to four comparatively large "jobbers" (customers) in Detroit at a lower price per gallon than it sold to many comparatively smaller service-station customers in the same area. Defendant appealed from a judgment in favor of the FTC.

Decision
Reversed, for the defendant, Standard Oil Co.

Reasoning
Standard Oil Co. argued that it lowered prices in good faith to retain jobbers as customers—that is, it met the lower prices of competitors to retain customers. The Supreme Court ruled: "It is enough to say that Congress did not seek, by the Robinson-Patman Act, either to abolish competition or so radically to curtail it that a seller would have no substantial right of self-defense against a price raid by a competitor. The heart of our national economic policy long has been faith in the value of competition . . ., which it sought to protect, and monopoly, which it sought to prevent.

Judgment of lower court reversed. . . . We agree [that] the lower price was justified."

Standard Oil Co. v. FTC, 340 U.S. 231 (1951).

Cost-price comparisons are not conclusive as to predatory pricing. The U.S. Court of Appeals[7] has well stated that "the ultimate question is 'Did the justification for the defendant's price depend upon its anticipated destructive effect on competition, or was the price justified as a reasonably calculated means of maximizing profits, minimizing losses, or achieving some other legitimate end?' This is the standard analysis of alleged predatory pricing, not rigid adherence to a particular cost-based rule."

Summary Statement

1. With a stated belief in free competition, the United States has grown from an agrarian economy to the world's foremost industrialized nation. Sometimes competition becomes extremely stiff, and weak, ineffective firms are driven out of the market. This may lead to a monopoly. Not all monopolies are evil and not all require governmental regulation. In some circumstances, however, the government may wish to intervene.
2. The major federal antitrust laws are: the Sherman Act of 1890; the Clayton Act of 1914 with the Cellar-Kefauver Amendment; the Federal Trade Commission Act of 1914; and the Robinson-Patman Act of 1936 amending section 2(a) of the Clayton Act. Some defenses against the Robinson-Patman Act were noted in order to

---
[7] *William Inglis & Sons Baking Co.,* CA-9, CCH-Trade Regulation #504, paragraph 64, 229, August 25, 1981. Also see *Matsushita Electric Industrial Co. Ltd., et al. v. Zenith Radio Corporation,* et al., 106 S.Ct. 1348 (1986).

emphasize that firms sometimes discriminate among their customers for good commercial reasons, with the apparent result of hurting competitors. The government is not trying to eliminate competition, it is trying to regulate abuses.
3. The Federal Trade Commission has an important role in today's antitrust regulations. The Commission monitors performance of companies around the criteria of the Sherman and Clayton Acts.
4. The Robinson-Patman Act is used to eliminate unfair practices such as unfair discounts or discrimination in pricing.
5. Under the Robinson-Patman Act there are certain violations that can be defended against by showing that the actions taken were just good business and not designed to lessen competition.

In the following well-known case the court found a tying arrangement in violation of the Sherman Act.

Siegel v. Chicken Delight, Inc.
448 F.2d 43 (1971), cert. denied 405 U.S. 955 (1972)

Before Madden, Judge of the United States Court of Claims, and Merrill and Hufstedler, Circuit Judges.

Merrill, J. This antitrust suit is a class action in which certain franchisees of Chicken Delight seek treble damages for injuries allegedly resulting from illegal restraints imposed by Chicken Delight's standard form franchise agreements. The restraints in question are Chicken Delight's contractual requirements that franchisees purchase certain essential cooking equipment, dry-mix food items, and trademark bearing packaging exclusively from Chicken Delight as a condition of obtaining a Chicken Delight trademark license. These requirements are asserted to constitute a tying arrangement, unlawful per se under section 1 of the Sherman Act. . . .

*****

II. The Existence of an Unlawful Tying Arrangement

In order to establish that there exists an unlawful tying arrangement plaintiffs must demonstrate: First that the scheme in question involves two distinct items and provides that one (the tying product) may not be obtained unless the other (the tied product) is also purchased. . . . Second, that the tying product possesses sufficient economic power appreciably to restrain competition in the tied product market. . . . Third, that a "not insubstantial" amount of commerce is affected by the arrangement. . . . Chicken Delight concedes that the third requirement has been satisfied. It disputes the existence of the first two. Further it asserts that . . . there is a fourth issue: whether there exists a special justification for the particular tying arrangement in question. . . .

A. Two Products

The District Court ruled that the license to use the Chicken Delight name, trademark, and method of operations was "a tying item in the traditional sense," the tied items being the cookers and fryers, packaging products, and mixes.

The hallmark of a tie-in is that it denies competitors free access to the tied product market, not because the party imposing the arrangement has a superior product in that market, but because of the power or leverage exerted by the tying product.

Sale of a franchise license, with the attendant rights to operate a business in the prescribed manner and to benefit from the goodwill of the tradename, in no way requires the forced sale by the franchisor of some or all of the component articles. . . .

. . . The relevant question is not whether the items are essential to the franchise, but whether it is essential to the franchise that the items be purchased from Chicken Delight. This raises not the issue of whether there is a tie-in but rather the issue of whether the tie-in is justifiable, a subject to be discussed below.

We conclude that the District Court was not in error.

B. Economic Power

Under the per se theory of illegality, plaintiffs are required to establish not only the existence of a tying arrangement but also that the tying product possesses sufficient economic power to appreciably restrain free competition in the tied product markets.

. . . It is not the nature of the public interest that has caused the legal barrier to be erected that is the basis for the presumption, but the fact that such a barrier does exist. Accordingly we see no reason why the presumption that exists in the case of the patent and copyright does not equally apply to the trademark.

C. Justification

Chicken Delight maintains that, even if its contractual arrangements are held to constitute a tying arrangement, it was not an unreasonable restraint under the Sherman Act. Three different bases for justification are urged.

First, Chicken Delight contends that the arrangement was a reasonable device for measuring and collecting revenue.

Second, Chicken Delight advances as justification the fact that when it first entered the fast food field in 1952 it was a new business and was then entitled to the protection afforded by *United States v. Jerrold Electronics Corp.* . . .

The third justification Chicken Delight offers is the "marketing identity" purpose, the franchisor's preservation of the distinctiveness, uniformity and quality of its product.

We conclude that the District Court was not in error in holding as matter of law (and upon the limited jury verdict) that Chicken Delight's contractual requirements constituted a tying arrangement in violation of section 1 of the Sherman Act. . . . [J]udgment is affirmed.

The District Court judgment was reversed and remanded for limited trial on several damage questions.

Questions and Case Problems

1. Soft Top Ice Cream, Inc. sells franchises that allow the purchaser of the franchise to sell several different flavors of soft ice cream. However, Soft Top Ice Cream, Inc. demands that retailers purchase a special machine from them to make the product. They explain that only the combination of their special machine and special mix will produce the product which is sold as "Soft Top Ice Cream." Is this a violation of the Clayton Act? [*Engbrecht v. Dairy Queen Co. of Mexico, Missouri,* 203 F.Supp. 714 (1962).]

2. Car Carriers, Inc. is in the car transport business. The company and other related enterprises brought antitrust action against Ford Motors Co. which had terminated Car Carriers contract in favor of a second car transport company. Among all the firms in the area, Car Carriers could prove injury only to themselves. Given these facts, does Ford Motors Co. participate in wrongful monopolization? Explain. [*Car Carriers, Inc.,* et al. *v. Ford Motors Company,* 745 F.2d 1101 (1984).]

3. Assume that, in the question above, the consumers of the car transport business were injured because of diminishing competition resulting from Ford Motors Co.'s action. Would this be considered when deciding whether Ford is engaging in anti-competitive acts? [*Car Carriers, Inc. v. Ford Motors Co.,* 745 F.2d 1101 (1984).]

4. Lynch Business Machines, Inc. filed a complaint based on antitrust action. The defendant, manufacturer of office products, had acquired stock in a company manufacturing cosmetics. This acquisition enhanced competition in this particular market. Plaintiff claims that defendant's acquisition of the stock violates the Clayton Act. Do you agree or disagree with plaintiff's claim? Explain. [*Lynch Business Machines, Inc. v. A. B. Dick Company,* 594 F.Supp. 59 (1984).]

5. A manufacturer unilaterally fixed a suggested resale price for its products. However, he refuses to deal with any distributor that sells his products at a price other then that which he suggested. Does this manufacturer engage in a per se unlawful resale price maintenance scheme? [*Spray-Rite Service Corp. v. Monsanto Co.,* 684 F.2d 1226 (1982).]

6. Bristol-Myers Company is the manufacturer of the non-prescription product "Bufferin." In advertising for Bufferin, Bristol-Myers referred to the results of scientific tests or studies claiming that Bufferin is twice as fast and twice as strong as aspirin in relieving pain in addition to implying that "Doctors specify Bufferin for minor pain more than any leading brand of pain reliever you can buy." However, Bufferin's faster action claim has not been established. Is this legal? Explain. [In the Matter of *Bristol-Myers Company*, et al., 102 FTC 21 (1983).]

7. Borden Inc., a producer of processed lemon juice, chose to price this product below its variable cost in order to promote sales. Why may this be considered as wrongful pricing? [In the Matter of *Borden, Inc.*, 102 FTC 1147 (1983).]

8. On May 10, 1982, the three companies—Coca-Cola, Associated Coca-Cola, the Root Company (wholly owned subsidiary of Coca-Cola), and Chapman S. Root—Chairman and CEO of Associated Coca-Cola and the beneficial owner of all the capital stock of the Root Company—entered into a stock purchase agreement in which Associated Coca-Cola will purchase all the shares of Associated beneficially owned by the Root Company. This represented approximately 57.5% of the shares outstanding. Does this transaction violate any antitrust laws? Explain. [In the Matter of *The Coca-Cola Company*, 102 FTC 1102 (1983).]

9. Aladdin Tire Co. had certain accounts called "commercial accounts." These accounts operated through a number of stores in greater Boston; coincidentally Aladdin owned and operated these stores. Prices of tires were lower at these stores than elsewhere. Illegal? [In re *U.S. Rubber Co.*, et al., 28 FTC 1489 (1939).]

10. In the case of *Siegel v. Chicken Delight, Inc.*, 448 F.2d 43 (1971), cert. denied 405 U.S. 955 (1972),[8] the court said that "the relevant question is not whether the items are essential to the franchise, but whether it is essential to the franchise that the items be purchased from Chicken Delight. This raises not the issue of whether there is a tie-in but rather the issue of whether the tie-in is justifiable." Discuss this statement by the court and explain how a business may so operate as to avoid violation of this part of the Sherman Act.

---

[8] See pp. 710–11.

Administrative Law 48

After you have read this chapter, you should be familiar with all of the following terms:

1. Administrative Procedures Act of 1946.
2. Administrative investigations.
3. Informal settlements.
4. Adjudicative procedures.
5. Judicial review.
6. Substantial evidence test.
7. Administrative reparations.
8. License.

Introduction

Most of us assume that when we purchase a drug prescribed by our family physician, it will be pure and safe when taken as directed. But did you ever wonder who sets the standards against which the drugs are measured? Often we were told in elementary civics courses that legislators make laws and, therefore, the laws establishing drug standards must have been passed by legislators. But is it that easy? Let us stop and consider that statement for a moment.

Let us think of all the drugs currently on the market. Many of them have names that a layperson can barely pronounce—and much less can a layperson understand their chemical makeup and action. How many of our senators or representatives have degrees in pharmacology? Obviously, very few, if any! Then how do they have the expertise necessary to legislate on the safety of each and every drug? Obviously they do *not* have the expertise—and they do *not* legislate on each drug. Even if the legislature were inclined to begin the impossible task of passing laws about each drug, do you think they would have the time to complete the job and do all the other things legislators are supposed to do? Again, obviously, the answer is no!

So how are the standards established to assure our safety when we take a prescribed medicine? The bulk of the work is delegated to administrative agencies. Some of the major federal administrative agencies that you may have heard about are: the Federal Trade Commission (FTC); the Federal Communications Commission (FCC); the National Labor Relations Board (NLRB); the Federal Reserve Board; the Internal Revenue Service; and the group that regulates the safety of medicine, the Food and Drug Administration (FDA). In this chapter we look at the range and limits of activities of our federal administrative agencies. There are also state administrative agencies concerned with state matters.

Congress provided for the creation of federal administrative agencies because it needed help to implement legislation it enacted. These agencies have the following responsibilities: (1) creating administrative rules and regulations; (2) establishing administrative procedures necessary for administrative action; (3) monitoring and providing for administrative investigation of industries for violations of antitrust laws and for consumer protection; and (4) adjudicating violation of such laws and administrative rules and regulations.

In this chapter we will consider the establishment and growth of federal administrative agencies, and observe how they operate. We will note again the problem of how far government, through its administrative agencies in the fulfillment of their responsibilities, should interfere in our daily business and private life. As you read this chapter, you should keep in mind the fact that every state has administrative agencies which may affect a particular business. However, as the wide diversity of these state agencies makes summary in this text impossible, we will be concerned only with federal administrative law.

Response of the Law

Administrative agencies.

Administrative agencies are so numerous today that just listing them with a brief description of the function of each would take up the rest of this book and a major portion of another. A more manageable task for us is to present an overview of the growth of administrative agencies and provide some idea of how they operate. We will therefore examine the foundation upon which administrative law has grown from the federal Administrative Procedures Act of 1946, 60 Stat. 237 (1946).

Administrative agencies do far more than set standards. Once standards are set in the form of rules, these rules are law and must be enforced. Note that administrative agencies establish rules, not statutory laws, which are made only by Congress as a legislative body authorized by the U.S. Constitution. Agencies monitor performance. If persons do not meet their standards, the agencies often have the power to levy fines or revoke previously granted privileges. These powers are not unlimited and, on occasion, agency decisions are overturned by courts of law through a process known as "judicial review."

Both the number and the domain of concern of administrative agencies have grown rapidly in the past twenty years. In reading the materials that follow, students should recall the question asked at the beginning of Part 9, Government Regulation of Business: How great an involvement do we, as managers of major industries and as private citizens, want the government to have in our lives?

Delegation

The Problem of Time

In the opening of this chapter we suggested that elementary civics texts traditionally told students that legislators make laws. We then went on to say that this was not always the case. Administrative agencies also have the power to create law in the form of rules and regulations, which all of us must obey. Where does that power come from? Article I, section 1 of the United States Constitution states: "All legislative powers herein granted shall be vested in a Congress of the United States, which shall consist of a Senate and a House of Representatives." Reading on, you simply never come across a section stating that there shall be a Federal Trade Commission.

<small>Source of administrative agency power.</small>

The power comes from a concept familiar to management students known as "delegation." Suppose you were to start a small business, perhaps a gas station. At first you might be able to handle all of the issues that come up during the day. You can pump gas, change the tires, and fix all of the engines that need fixing. As the business grows, however, you may be faced with growing lines of customers demanding gasoline. As you spend more and more time at the pumps, you get further and further behind on your repairs. You might throw up your hands in disgust and shout, "There aren't enough hours in a day to do all of the things I would like to do." So you might hire an assistant to pump gas—i.e., you delegate the responsibility to someone else, thus freeing you to do the more enjoyable task of fixing broken Mercedes and Jaguars.

<small>Delegation.</small>

Congress did the same thing when it delegated the responsibility for rule-making to administrative agencies. It simply did not have the *time* to create all the rules necessary for the smooth operation of our nation. It may not lack the interest, but it very well may have far too many other things to do.

<small>One reason for delegation is lack of time.</small>

The Problem of Expertise

If we go back to our gas station example: suppose the assistant gas pumper works out well, and you go back to the job of fixing engines. Then a customer approaches you with a Classic 19XX Stutz Bearcat. If you have never been trained in making repairs on classic automobiles and if you thought that such repairs might become a significant part of your business, you would consider delegating the responsibility for repairs. Certainly you would want to keep your role as owner and manager of the work of your assistants, but, if others have expertise which you lack, you delegate to them the responsibility for getting the job done.

Once again, Congress sought to delegate its responsibility when it discovered that it did not have nearly as much collective specialized knowledge about particular areas as could be marshalled in an administrative agency. This combination of pressures on Congress—too little time and insufficient expertise—led to the creation of the huge number of federal administrative agencies. At first, some people considered this delegation a potential violation of the Constitution. But the power to delegate responsibility downward

<small>Another reason for delegation is lack of expertise.</small>

from Congress to administrative agencies has long been guaranteed. The case which follows is a classic because it is one of the very few instances of a delegation downward from Congress being held *invalid*. It has come to be known as the *Hot Oil* case.

Facts
In 1933, the United States was in the midst of a great depression. However, in the state of Texas, huge oil reserves were discovered. This led to a vast oversupply of oil in the marketplace. Through the National Industrial Recovery Act, section 9(c), President Roosevelt was authorized to prohibit transportation in interstate commerce of petroleum and the products thereof . . . (48 Stat. 200 (1933)). The Panama Refining Company sued (ultimately to the Supreme Court), claiming that section 9(c), and therefore the President's Executive Order implementing it, and the Regulations of the Secretary of the Interior were unconstitutional delegations of power, notwithstanding sections of the law which declared this to be a national emergency and saying that action had to be taken to conserve national resources. Were they unconstitutional and, therefore, void?

Decision
Yes. Judgment for Panama Refining Co.

Reasoning
"Thus, in every case in which the question has been raised, the court has recognized that there are limits of delegation which there is no constitutional authority to transcend. We think that section 9(c) goes beyond these limits. . . . The power sought to be delegated is legislative power, and nowhere in the statute has Congress declared or indicated any policy or standard to guide or limit the President when acting under such delegation. . . . There is such a breadth of authorized action as essentially to commit to the President the functions of a legislature rather than those of an executive or administrative officer executing a declared legislative policy."

Panama Refining Co. v. Ryan, 293 U.S. 388 (1935).

Administrative Procedures

Administrative procedures necessary for administrative action.

While agencies vary somewhat in the procedures they use, it is still possible to create a composite picture of what happens when it is necessary for an agency to take action against a business firm for violation of a rule. In the next few pages we shall examine some typical administrative techniques for dispute resolution. The agency we shall examine is the Federal Trade Commission (FTC).

You will recall that, in the previous chapter, the FTC was identified as the agency responsible for monitoring industries for violation of antitrust laws. In addition to having that responsibility, the FTC is actively involved in consumer protection. For example, the FTC has consistently prosecuted individuals involved in false advertising or those who make deceptive claims, as is illustrated in the following case.

Facts
Charles of the Ritz Distributors Corporation, a manufacturer, produced a cream designed for cosmetic use. According to its own claims, the cream "restores natural moisture necessary for a live, healthy skin"; "your face need know no drought years"; and the preparation brings to the user's "skin quickly the clear radiance . . . the petal-like quality and texture of youth." The cream is called "Rejuvenescence Cream." The Federal Trade Commission sued to stop the use of the name "Rejuvenescence Cream." Is the name deceptive in that it would lead people to believe that the cream would actually rejuvenate skin?

Decision
Judgment for the Federal Trade Commission.

Reasoning
Representations merely having the capacity to deceive are unlawful. The Federal Trade Commission had produced an expert who testified that the average woman, conditioned by talk in magazines and over the radio . . . might take rejuvenescence to mean that "this is one of the modern miracles" and is something which would actually cause her youth to be restored.

Charles of the Ritz Distrib. Corp. v. FTC, 143 F.2d 676 (1944).

Investigations

In order to do its job effectively, administrative agencies need to have the power to investigate instances in which they believe rules have been violated. The Federal Trade Commission has that power. Typically, federal agencies have large groups of staff members who spend their time continuously collecting data on the industry or industries being monitored. Therefore, it is likely that instances of deviation from the rules would rapidly come to the attention of the agency staff. If the problem becomes acute, the enforcement arm of the agency can initiate some action.

The Federal Trade Commission, like most other agencies, has the power to compel people to testify before it. To accomplish this task, it may issue what is known as a **subpoena.** Subpoenas are designed to elicit testimony from particular witnesses, but they may be insufficient and unrealistic as a technique for gathering the quantity of information constantly needed for monitoring purposes. Therefore, administrative agencies also have the power to demand the periodic filing of reports. While some businesspeople complain about the volume of paperwork, the advantage of these reporting procedures is that a wide range of activities can be carefully monitored at once.

Administrative investigation.

subpoena
an order to appear before a judicial or proper administrative body for the purpose of giving testimony

Informal Settlements

In chapter 2, Organization of the United States Legal System, we mentioned that, when a dispute arises, lawyers rarely try to bring the case to court immediately. Rather, they try to discuss the problem with the adversary in the hope of arriving at some mutually satisfactory settlement. The Federal Trade Commission and most other agencies have mechanisms which facilitate informal enforcement of standards.

Needless to say, the degree to which the agency is willing to settle informally depends upon the nature of the infraction (is it a major offense?) and the number of infractions which that firm had been involved in previously. If an agreement is struck between the parties, the FTC requires that a formal affidavit be filed detailing the nature of the complaint and providing the agency with written assurance that there will be no further violations of the rules.

Attempt for informal settlements.

Adjudicative Proceedings

Certainly not all matters can be settled informally. Therefore, agencies have established adjudicative procedures designed to formally decide cases of alleged violations of administrative rules.

Adjudicative proceedings.

Complaint. An administrative agency issues a complaint. This is a document designed to serve as notice to the business involved that the agency believes that the business has violated a particular standard. The Federal Trade Commission, for example, issues an "adjudicative complaint." (Also known as a Part III complaint since it is issued pursuant to Part III of the FTC's rules.)

Hearings. At first glance, administrative hearings appear to be much like any courtroom trial. However, closer examination reveals several significant differences. Just as in formal courts, administrative hearings are presided over by a judge. The judges are called "administrative law judges," and they are employees of the agency. They are *not* members of the state or federal judiciary.

At the hearing, the administrative law judge allows each side to present evidence. In FTC proceedings, parties may cross-examine witnesses and make motions and objections. In fact, in the case of an indigent (poor person), the FTC can make arrangements to have counsel appointed to represent the indigent. Once all of the evidence has been presented, the judge issues an opinion. As we will see shortly, this opinion may be appealed to a higher authority if deemed necessary.

Chapter 48: Administrative Law

Evidence. One major difference between formal state and federal courts, on the one hand, and administrative agencies, on the other, is in the kind of evidence which they will find acceptable. Formal court systems tend to be more restrictive about the kinds of evidence they will receive. The formal courts have grown up with a system which is based upon exclusionary rules of evidence. That is, the courts have rather rigorously tended to exclude evidence if it may in any way be undependable—the classic example being the courts' reluctance to accept **hearsay**.

hearsay
matter not personally known but heard from others

Administrative hearings are conducted less formally than state or federal court hearings. They also allow evidence of a much broader scope. The federal Administrative Procedures Act defines the scope of acceptable evidence in section 7(c):

> Any oral or documentary evidence may be received, but every agency shall as a matter of policy provide for the exclusion of irrelevant immaterial or unduly repetitious evidence and no sanction shall be imposed or rule or order be issued except upon consideration of the whole record or such portions thereof as may be cited by any party and as supported by and in accordance with the reliable, probative and substantial evidence.

This means that evidence which would otherwise be unacceptable in a court may be included as part of an administrative hearing for its probative value, as is illustrated in the following case.

Facts
Powers was an employee of Cities Service Oil Company. As shipping master, Powers interviewed applicants for jobs. Powers often questioned potential employees about their union affiliations and told people that he would not hire members of the National Maritime Union. This is a violation of potential employees' rights under the National Labor Relations Act. Was the NLRA trial examiner wrong in accepting or rejecting testimony concerning Powers' behavior if such testimony is hearsay?

Decision
No. Judgment for the NLRB.

Reasoning
Counsel admits that the evidence is hearsay and, while the Board is entirely free to accept such evidence, we cannot say that it commits reversible error in excluding it.

NLRB v. Cities Service Oil Co., 129 F.2d 933 (1942).

Decision. The administrative judge considers all of the evidence and issues an opinion. This opinion is usually subject to review by the entire administrative agency and they may either accept the opinion or reject it. However, notice that the original decision is made by the administrative judge and that there is no right to a jury trial. The opinion may contain a recommendation for a sanction. For example, the Federal Trade Commission judge may decide that a particular business advertising practice should not continue, and therefore a cease and desist order may be issued.

Judicial review of administrative adjudications.

Judicial Review

Decisions made by administrative agencies are reviewable. By this we mean that if you, as an aggrieved party, are not satisfied with a decision made by an agency, you may appeal the decision to a court of law. However, courts do not automatically have to hear your case. Indeed, there is a tendency on the part of federal courts to resist review in favor of relying on the administrative agencies' expertise.

Substantial evidence test.

The standard which the courts use in deciding whether or not to review an administrative agency's decision is the *substantial evidence* test. This test declares that courts will review issues that involve questions of law. However, questions of fact are reviewed only if the decision violates a test of reasonableness. While this is the dominant view today, there are some *state* statutes which give the courts the right to have a trial *de novo*[1] (new trial). The argument in favor of allowing *de novo* trials is that this assures that the courts

---

[1] See 82 AM. JUR.2d Workmen's Compensation, sec. 618 (1962); and Ohio Rev. Code, Title 41, *Labor and Industry*, sec. 4123.519.

will have an opportunity to provide a somewhat stronger check on arbitrary administrative action. Finally, the Administrative Procedures Act, section 706, provides useful guidance on the scope of judicial review. The following case illustrates the substantial evidence test.

Facts
Edward Taylor was employed by the Equal Employment Department of the State Employment Security Agency. He was given notice of dismissal by the Employment Security Department stating that he had violated Rule XII of the Rules for Personnel Administration: (a) disgraceful personal conduct which impairs job performance or causes discredit to the agency,
(b) incompetence or inefficiency,
(c) discourteous treatment of the public or fellow employees while on duty, and
(d) dishonesty. The Personnel Advisory Commission upheld the dismissal and Taylor petitioned for judicial review. The District Court reversed and ordered Taylor's reinstatement, and the Department appealed. In reviewing the decision of an administrative agency, the question presented asks whether the agency's decision was based on substantial evidence.

Decision
Affirmed for Taylor; the decision of the agency was not based on substantial evidence.

Reasoning
The charges all arise out of his conduct at two meetings. While his actions were inappropriate they do not give rise to the level of violating the rules noted above. The District Court said that the evidence did not support the reasons given for Taylor's termination. Moreover, in this agency, except when the seriousness of the offense warrants, dismissal is proper only after other forms of disciplinary action have proved ineffective. No disciplinary measures were taken against Taylor until he was terminated.

State of Nevada v. Taylor, 683 P.2d 1 (Nev. 1984).

Types of Powers Held by Administrative Agencies

Administrative agencies have several different ways in which to exert control over their respective companies. It is, of course, possible for an administrative agency to simply use the power of moral persuasion to obtain compliance with its rules. However, the chances of this technique working satisfactorily are quite limited. Perhaps the most common technique used is to *fine* rule-breakers. Another form of sanction is to force the regulated party to pay *reparations* to the injured party. Finally, a third technique employed by administrative agencies is the granting, revocation, and withholding of a *license*.

At the state level, one example of a licensing requirement is the license you must earn to drive your car. A driver's license is a privilege granted to you after you have demonstrated a rudimentary understanding of automobile safety and handling. If you violate too many driving laws, your license can be suspended or revoked.

Administrative exercise of power by moral persuasion, fine, reparations, grant of a license.

Summary Statement

1. Federal administrative agencies are a creation born of necessity. Although the federal Constitution specifies that legislators make laws, reality dictates that rule-making procedures be delegated to administrative agencies.
2. While it is impossible to outline all of the different structures of the many administrative agencies which exist, there is a substantial body of federal laws guiding their actions. The most important of these laws is the Administrative Procedures Act.
3. Administrative agencies investigate violations of rules and may take informal action to settle disputes. However, there are more formal alternatives available. Agencies may hold hearings, complete with elaborate procedures (formal or informal), and may issue decisions which the regulated groups must follow.

4. The decisions of administrative agencies may be appealed to courts of law, but courts are reluctant to use their power of *judicial* review.
5. Finally, agencies vary in their strength. Some agencies can fine, and impose reparations upon, rule violators; others have the power to grant, withhold, and revoke licenses.

As was discussed earlier, decisions made by administrative agencies are reviewable, but the courts understand that administrative agencies are competent to review even complex administrative matters. The case which follows illustrates the judiciary's appropriate use of an administrative law judge.

Mackowiak v. University Nuclear Systems, Inc.
735 F.2d 1159 (1984)

Wright, Circuit Judge. Mackowiak, a quality control inspector for University Nuclear Systems, Inc. (UNSI) was terminated in a reduction of force in January, 1982. He asserts that the termination occurred because he was an overly zealous inspector and because he identified safety problems to the Nuclear Regulatory Commission (NRC). He filed a complaint under the "Whistleblower" protection statute of the Energy Reorganization Act.

After a hearing, an administrative law judge concluded that the termination was not caused by protected conduct and recommended dismissal. The Secretary of Labor found a *prima facie* case of discrimination. Nevertheless, he dismissed the complaint because he found that UNSI would have terminated Mackowiak even if he had not engaged in protected conduct.

In his petition for review by this court, Mackowiak argues that the Secretary's decision was not supported by substantial evidence.

Mackowiak is a sheet metal worker certified as a welding inspector by the American Welding Society. . . .

Bechtel Incorporated told UNSI, its subcontractor, that it had to lay off approximately 8% of its work force. The union contract provided: in cases of layoff, the last employee hired shall be the first laid off providing the ability and efficiency of the employee is substantially equal.

UNSI determined that Mackowiak's "attitudinal problems" made him inferior to other inspectors with less seniority, despite his admitted technical confidence. He and three junior inspectors were terminated on January 19.

The question is whether Mackowiak was discriminated against *because* he participated in a Nuclear Regulatory Commission proceeding. The administrative law judge held that Mackowiak failed to establish a *prima facie* case of discrimination. He found that UNSI was unaware of Mackowiak's contact with the Nuclear Regulatory Commission investigators. The Secretary questioned this finding, noting that there was adequate evidence in the record "to support an inference that UNSI was motivated in part by Mr. Mackowiak's protected conduct."

"The presence or absence of retaliatory motive is a legal conclusion and is provable by circumstantial evidence even if there is testimony to the contrary by witnesses who perceived lack of such improper motive."

The record contains circumstantial evidence to support a finding that UNSI was motivated in part by Mackowiak's contact with the Nuclear Regulatory Commission investigators. UNSI's quality assurance manager knew that Mackowiak talked to the Nuclear Regulatory Commission's investigators. The sequence of events was suspicious. . . .

We sustain the Secretary's conclusion that Section 5851 protects quality control inspectors from retaliation based on internal safety and quality control complaints.

The Whistleblower provision in the Energy Reorganization Act is modeled on, and serves an identical purpose to, the provision in the Mine Health and Safety Act.

They share a broad, remedial purpose of protecting workers from retaliation based on their concerns for safety and quality.

The rationale for the rule is stronger here. Quality control inspectors play a crucial role in the Nuclear Regulatory Commission's regulatory scheme. The NRC regulations require licensees and their contractors and subcontractors to give inspectors the "authority and organizational freedom" required to fulfill their role as independent observers of the construction process. In a real sense, every action by a quality control inspector occurs "in a Nuclear Regulatory Commission proceeding," because of their duty to enforce the Nuclear Regulatory Commission's regulations.

At times, the inspector may come into conflict with his employer by identifying problems that might cause added expense and delay.

There is substantial evidence to support the Secretary's conclusion that Mackowiak was a difficult employee who created some friction in his relations with co-workers and superiors. What is less clear, however, is the extent to which his troublesomeness arose from his persistence in following Nuclear Regulatory Comission approved procedures and in identifying quality and safety problems.

On this record, we cannot determine whether UNSI could meet its burden of proof. We remand the case to allow the Secretary to resolve the issue. He may hold evidentiary proceedings or remand for a new hearing before an administrative law judge. In either event, the Secretary must determine independently whether UNSI would have terminated Mackowiak even if he had not engaged in conduct protected by Section 5851. Unless UNSI can meet its burden of proof on this issue, the Secretary must find for the petitioner.

Petition granted. Remanded for further proceedings.

Questions and Case Problems

1. A trade association representing a group of community antenna television systems petitions the U.S. Supreme Court for review of a revised fee schedule which set the annual fee at $.30 per subscriber. May Congress delegate its job of lawmaking to others? [*National Cable Television Ass'n., Inc. v. United States*, 415 U.S. 336 (1974).]

2. Must all agencies attempt to resolve disputes informally before moving to a hearing?

3. Bergen Pines County Hospital is challenging the validity of the Department of Human Services' regulations. These regulations are prescribing how the hospital should fix the rates paid to it for caring for medicaid patients in its long-term medical care facility. The hospital is arguing that the administrative agency is not qualified to make such rules. What qualifies administrative agencies to make rules? Why should not the legislature do it? [*Bergen Pines County Hospital v. N.J. Department of Human Services*, 476 A.2d 784 (N.J. 1984).]

4. Petitioner challenges a final decision of the District of Columbia Department of Employment Services (DOES) disqualifying him from unemployment compensation benefits for a ten week period on the ground that he was discharged from his most recent job because of "dishonesty" amounting to "misconduct." Having reviewed the record, the judge observed that the formal rules of evidence were not closely followed. Does this mean the decision may be reversed? Explain. [*Jadallah v. District of Columbia Department of Employment*, 476 A.2d 671 (D.C. 1984).]

5. Describe the purpose of a complaint issued by an administrative agency.

6. Employer filed a request for reconsideration of final unemployment liability determination by the Department of Economic Security *after* the statutory 15-day period for filing such a request. The unemployment Insurance Appeals Board refused to reconsider the determination and the employer appealed. Based on your understanding of administrative law, is the employer entitled to a judicial review? Explain. [*Sun Valley Express Moving and Storage, Inc. v. Arizona Department of Economic Security*, 680 P.2d 841 (Ariz. 1984).]

7. William Pector, a liquor law enforcement agent, testified that although he was not a member he entered the Yacht Club and purchased a "VO and Coke." He claims that he placed a sample of the drink in a vial, which sample was later sent to the state chemist for testing. Based on Pector's testimony and the toxicology report, the Utah Liquor Control Commission suspended the Club's liquor license and operations for thirty days because the Club had made an unlawful sale of an alcoholic beverage to a nonmember. The state chemist's toxicology report on the alcoholic content of a specimen drink allegedly sold to nonmembers of the Club was admissible under exception to the hearsay rule for reports and findings of public officials. Is hearsay evidence admissible in an administrative agency hearing? Explain. [*Yacht Club v. Utah Liquor Control Commission,* 681 P.2d 1224 (Utah 1984).]

8. The plaintiff, Gerald Fenus, seeks judicial review of a decision of the Secretary of Health and Human Services denying him disability benefits. The plaintiff applied for disability benefits initially on Nov. 6, 1978, alleging a work related back injury. He was denied disability status and reapplied in 1980 and 1982 with the same result. Since the plaintiff has substantial medical evidence from both his physician and hospital visits, may he manage to get the facts reviewed? [*Fenus v. Scheweiker, Secretary of Health and Human Services,* 584 F.Supp. 45 (1983).]

9. The Funeral Directors and Embalmers Examining Board appeals from the trial court's order vacating the Board's decision suspending Calvin Monroe's license to practice as a funeral director and embalmer. The Board concluded him to be of unprofessional conduct, obnoxious behavior and gross negligence. On judicial review, how much weight should be given to the decision rendered by the agency? [*Monroe v. Funeral Directors and Embalmers Examining Board,* 349 N.W.2d 746 (Wis. 1984).]

10. In the case of *Mackowiak v. University Nuclear Systems, Inc.,* 735 F.2d 1159 (1984),[2] it is argued that there was substantial evidence to support the finding of the administrative agency. Do you agree?

---

[2] See pp. 720–21.

Labor Law 49

After you have read this chapter, you should be able to identify all of the following terms:

1. AFL-CIO.
2. Criminal conspiracy.
3. Injunction.
4. Yellow dog contract.
5. Norris-La Guardia Act.
6. Wagner Act.
7. Taft-Hartley Act.
8. Unfair labor practices.
9. Bargaining unit.
10. Boulwarism.
11. Executive Orders 10988 & 11491.
12. Hot Cargo.

Introduction

sole proprietorship
a business owned and operated by one person

partnership
(general partnership) "an association of two or more persons to carry on as co-owners a business for profit" U.P.A. sec. 6

corporation
a legal entity created by statute authorizing an association of persons to carry on an enterprise

If you were to work for a small firm, e.g., a **sole proprietor**, there is an excellent chance that you would know the owner personally. If you had a problem concerning your wages, hours, or the conditions of employment, it would be relatively easy to bring your concern to the proper authority. Further, in a small organization, since your labor is a significant part of the whole, management has a great deal of interest in your well-being.

As the organization grows, e.g., a **partnership,** there may be a division of work among the partners such that one partner manages the firm while the other participates largely through investment of capital. As an employee, you may rarely see one of the partners. **Incorporated** firms have the potential of growing to be huge organizations. Examples of organizations in this category abound and include Ford, General Motors, IBM and General Mills. It is highly unlikely that people working on the assembly line will know anyone in top management. If problems arise concerning wages, hours, or conditions of employment, an employee might raise his or her concern with a foreman and perhaps with the personnel department, but the employee's voice is just one among the crowd. Unlike the situation in a sole proprietorship, one employee rarely makes up a significant part of the workforce.

The question of how an employee can be heard in a large organization has been answered in the United States by labor unions. Labor organizations such as the American Federation of Teachers, the United Auto Workers, and the American Federation of State, County, and Municipal Employees have flourished in the past several decades in response to employees' needs for representation in the workplace.

Not only have these unions pressed employers for better labor contracts, but they have also been instrumental in pressing legislators to pass pieces of legislation which have improved our lives immeasurably.

Response of the Law

Unions were not always welcome additions to the world of work. Indeed, at first they were strenuously resisted by employers. Today, unions are generally accepted as part of the work environment, but many employers resist union organizing efforts because they believe unions will drive up wages or take away management prerogatives. We, the authors, do not take any position on the impact of unions in the workplace. Our job is to present, educationally, the labor union as a present-day factor in business, except to note that the issue is certainly unresolved. This chapter presents an overview of the major federal laws which govern labor-management relations.

At first, employers resisted unions by dismissing employees who exhibited pro-union tendencies, and the courts were supportive of employers' actions for many years. Gradually, as we shall see, the courts and the legislators have sought to strike a balance between the unions' right to organize employees and the employers' right to manage the business free from outside interference. Laws such as the Wagner Act, Taft-Hartley, and Landrum-Griffin Acts are frequently referred to by contemporary labor relations specialists as they attempt to discern the best course of action in resolving a labor dispute.

The law has also attempted to provide benefits to employees of the federal government. For example, the following pieces of federal legislation are all part of the domain of Labor Law: (a) Executive Order 10988 and (b) Executive Order 11491, discussed later.

In this chapter we will examine some of these laws in order to understand their impact on employees and management.

Contemporary Unions

The American Federation of Labor (AFL) grew under the early leadership of Samuel Gompers. Gompers was concerned about representing the skilled craftsmen. The AFL craft locals represent craft autonomy, that is, for each particular skill there is a union group which represents their interests. Gompers, for example, was a member of the cigar-makers. Other craft-oriented unions include the carpenters, the plumbers, and the electricians.

American Federation of Labor.

Industrial unions were formed because people like John L. Lewis, of the coal miners union, believed that the AFL was ineffective in representing the interests of workers who were semi-skilled or unskilled in mass production industries. In the 1930s people were able to join with others in massive organizing campaigns which resulted in large numbers of people joining labor unions. The AFL and the CIO were not always joined in one organization, as they are today. In fact, for many years a bitter rivalry existed between the two groups. At first, the CIO was called the Committee (later Congress) of Industrial Organizations and was a branch of the AFL. Internal disputes and rivalries over organizing strategies led to a split which lasted until 1955, when new leaders of each organization were brought together by a man named Arthur Goldberg. (Mr. Goldberg subsequently was a member of the U.S. Supreme Court and then U.S. Ambassador to the United Nations.)

Congress of Industrial Organizations.

Today unions within the AFL-CIO and independent unions are rivals for control of a major group of largely unorganized employees. These are white-collar workers, professionals, and government employees. As we shall see, the law has had a significant impact upon the growth of unions in our country, and we can expect further growth of unions among government employees to be shaped by social control exerted through law.

AFL-CIO.

Early Attempts to Control Labor Unions

Criminal Conspiracy

Employers have traditionally resisted union organizing attempts. The earliest strategy adopted by employers to quash a union was to accuse the union of having unlawfully combined into a **criminal conspiracy** to control wages. The logic of this argument was that, if wages were driven up, eventually the consuming public would suffer, since prices would rise. Thus, any time a worker joined with others to ask for a wage increase the worker was risking a court action. During the first half of the nineteenth century this doctrine was quite effective.

criminal conspiracy a combination of persons for the purpose of committing an unlawful act

Then, in a landmark decision, the courts of the state of Massachusetts decided the following case.

Facts
The defendants were bootmakers who were organized into a union group. They were accused by the Commonwealth of Massachusetts of having committed the crime of unlawfully attempting to extort great sums of money from the employer by means of organizing a union. Was the formation of a union an unlawful conspiracy?

Decision
No. Judgment for the defendants.

Reasoning
The manifest intent of the association is to induce all those engaged in the same occupation to become members of it. Such a purpose is not unlawful. . . . An association may be formed, the declared object of which is innocent and laudable. If the plaintiff wanted to demonstrate that this union was formed for criminal purpose, it should have brought this forward as part of the evidence.

Commonwealth v. Hunt, 4 Metcalf 111 (Mass. 1842), 44 Mass. Reports.

The criminal conspiracy doctrine, which began with an incident involving shoemakers in Philadelphia in 1806, ended following the *Hunt* case just noted. It was a powerful weapon for its time but finally yielded to the injunction.

Injunction

injunction
a court order requiring a person to do or not to do something

Another early weapon used against employees was the **injunction**. An injunction is an order issued by a court ordering that a person do or not do something. For example, if students decided to march and perhaps take violent action against a professor's decision to give an entire class failing grades, it would be possible for the university to obtain a stop order, an injunction. In the case of a labor dispute, if a union embarked on a course of action which seemed likely to injure the employer in any way, the employer would request an injunction. Needless to say, in the late 1800s such an order was relatively easy to obtain, the potential damage to the employer would be minimal, and the injunction would still be issued.

In 1894, the U.S. Supreme Court affirmed the use of injunctions in labor disputes when it heard *In re* Debs (158 U.S. 564 (1895)). Since that time injunctions have been used in labor disputes. However, courts are much more careful about the circumstances under which they issue a stop order.

yellow dog contract
an agreement between an employer and employee that the employee will not be, nor continue to be, a member of a union

Associated with the injunction was a tactic used by employers called the **yellow dog contract.** Under these contracts, employees had to promise their employer not to join a union. If they did join, they were automatically fired for violating a condition of employment. Such contracts are illegal because they unfairly hinder union members' ability to organize for collective action. The reason a yellow dog contract is associated with the injunction is that employers would seek an injunction from the courts to stop unions from attempting to organize workers who had previously signed yellow dog agreements. Yellow dog contracts have been declared illegal.

Contemporary Federal Labor Legislation

Norris-La Guardia Act.

Norris-La Guardia Act

Until the 1930s labor unions were at the mercy of employers. Early in the '30s, when the United States was in the midst of a severe depression, President Hoover attempted to deal with the extremely high rate of unemployment and low wages by offering workers a piece of legislation designed to give employees an advantage in the labor-management relations arena which they had not previously enjoyed. It was the Norris-La Guardia Act of 1932, and it has several noteworthy provisions. First, it declared yellow dog contracts to be illegal. Second, it guaranteed employees the right to organize into unions and to bargain collectively with their employers. This principle remains an important part of our federal labor laws today.

Wagner Act.

Wagner Act

In 1933, the Roosevelt administration was attempting to do what the Hoover administration had failed to do—that is, bring our country out of the depression. One attempt to move in this direction was the National Industrial Recovery Act. The critical section with respect to labor relations was 7(a), which specifically endorsed employees' rights "to bargain collectively through representatives of their own choosing." The Supreme Court held that the NIRA was unconstitutional.

Within two years Congress acted again to protect labor's interests. In 1935, it passed the National Labor Relations Act. The NLRA is usually referred to as the Wagner Act. It remains today as one of the most important pieces of federal labor legislation. The following case illustrates its purpose to safeguard the rights of employees.

Facts
Jones & Laughlin Steel produced steel in Pennsylvania and sold their goods throughout the United States. One of the elements defined by the Wagner Act as an unfair labor practice is the discharge of employees for union activity. Jones & Laughlin had committed this act and so were charged by the NLRB with an unfair labor practice. Jones & Laughlin fought the NLRB by arguing that the Wagner Act was unconstitutional and that their manufacturing business was not in the "stream of commerce." Is the Wagner Act unconstitutional and is Jones & Laughlin in commerce?

Decision
Judgment for NLRB.

Reasoning
We think it clear that the National Labor Relations Act may be construed to operate within the sphere of constitutional authority. The statute goes no further than to safeguard the rights of employees. Further, Jones & Laughlin clearly fits as in the stream of commerce and so is subject to federal regulations.

NLRB v. Jones & Laughlin Steel Corp., 301 U.S. 1 (1937).

As referred to in the Jones & Laughlin case, the Wagner Act defined some practices which were designed to give employees more rights to organize for labor action. These were called **unfair labor practices** by *employers*. Later the Taft-Hartley Act defined unfair labor practices by a *union*.

There are five unfair labor practices by employers. Employers may *not*:

1. refuse to bargain with employee representatives;
2. discharge an employee for filing a complaint under the Wagner Act;
3. encourage or discourage union membership or discriminate when hiring or retaining employees just because of their union leanings;
4. interfere with employees in any way in their right to determine who shall represent them; and
5. dominate or interfere with any labor organization or contribute to its support in any way.

Needless to say, such a powerful Act would not be effective unless it had some administrative support. Thus, Congress created the National Labor Relations Board to handle disputes as they arose. In addition to the unfair labor practices as enumerated, the NLRB also was charged with the task of setting up union election procedures and defining the appropriate **bargaining unit.**

The bargaining unit is a group of employees appropriately joined together for the purpose of collective bargaining. In an industrial setting, for example, the bargaining unit might be all of the employees within a particular department, or all employees doing essentially the same job. The NLRB enters the scene if there is a dispute concerning whether or not particular employees should be in the unit. Disputes often arise in this regard. For example, employers may argue that particular employees, such as first line foremen, have managerial responsibility, while the union argues that they are members of the unit.

Taft-Hartley Act
Some labor law experts argue that labor laws and labor sentiment in our country move in pendulum swings. That is, strongly pro-labor laws are passed, then strongly pro-management laws are enacted. Since the Wagner Act was clearly pro-labor, protecting employees' rights to organize, the Taft-Hartley Act would be pro-management. Indeed, it was precisely that. Passed in 1947, it was designed to redress an imbalance which Congress and the American people perceived in the labor area. It is not difficult to imagine why they believed there was a need for a law controlling labor. In the period just prior to passage of Taft-Hartley our nation was embroiled in strikes. Not only was there a nationwide coal strike, but telephone company, steel, oil, textile, and maritime workers also had work stoppages, and many other unions were involved in labor disputes of one kind or another.

unfair labor practices
tactics by an employer or a union which are legally prohibited as unfair

bargaining unit
a group of employees appropriately joined together for the purpose of collective bargaining

Taft-Hartley Act.

State Right-to-Work Provisions. One of the most controversial sections of the Taft-Hartley Act is section 14(b), the "right-to-work" section. This portion of the Act allows states to pass right-to-work laws. These laws allow companies to make contracts which have very weak union security clauses. In effect, they permit people to work in a union plant without joining the union. The merits of right-to-work laws have been argued for a number of years.

Free Speech. Taft-Hartley made several important changes in the state of labor law in the United States. First, it allowed employers to comment more freely on union organizing activities than they had been able to do in the past. Prior to Taft-Hartley, employers had to be extremely careful about what they said to employees about the union. Taft-Hartley directly addresses the subject of free speech in section 8(c), where it says that employers would not commit an unfair labor practice to speak to employees, unless they threaten reprisal or promise some benefit to employees. This is the so-called "free speech" amendment.

Unfair Labor Practices. Another important part of the Taft-Hartley Act is its section on unfair labor practices. This time the unfair practices were aimed at labor rather than at management. There are a number of such unfair labor practices by unions. First, it is an unfair labor practice for the union to try to coerce employees to join unions. In other words, no harsh tactics can be used to get an employee to join. Second, certain kinds of strikes and boycotts are unfair labor practices. Strikes or boycotts designed to make an employer assign work to a particular craft group, strikes or boycotts designed to force an employer to recognize a union without NLRB precertification, and secondary boycotts are all held to be unfair labor practices.

secondary boycott
the bringing of pressure by a union on a neutral party who will then pressure the employer with whom the union has a dispute

Secondary Boycott. A **secondary boycott** is a union attempt to place *concerted pressure* on an otherwise *uninvolved party* in order to get that party to pressure the union's real adversary into capitulating. The following case held that there was insufficient *concerted* activity present and, therefore, no secondary boycott.

Facts
The teamsters were picketing several rice mills in Louisiana, one of these being International Rice Milling Co., Inc., complainant before the NLRB. The union was charged by International Rice with an unfair labor practice of secondary boycott when the pickets told two employees of Sales & Service House, a customer of the mill, that they were on strike and that the two employees could, and should, not purchase from the mill. International Rice claimed that there was a secondary boycott by the union. The NLRB dismissed the complaint; the Court of Appeals set aside the dismissal; and the case is now before the U.S. Supreme Court. Was this a secondary boycott?

Decision
No. Judgment for NLRB.

Reasoning
The most that can be concluded is that the union did encourage two employees of a neutral customer to turn back from an intended trip to the mill. A secondary boycott involves "concerted activity" to a far greater extent than exhibited here.

NLRB v. International Rice Milling Co., Inc., 341 U.S. 665 (1951).

Other unfair labor practices defined by this Act include:

1. union attempts to charge excessive dues;
2. a prohibition against **featherbedding;** [Featherbedding is forcing an employer to keep unneeded employees, such as on jobs which no longer exist. An example is forcing a newspaper to continue to employ people to set type even though modern typesetting technology eliminates the need for this work.]
3. union refusal to bargain in good faith;
4. union attempts to force employers to discriminate against employees who are not interested in the union, in an attempt to influence union membership.

featherbedding
make-work arrangements for employees when there is no work for them to perform

The duty to bargain in *good faith* is now shouldered regularly by both the union and management, as part of the collective bargaining process. An interesting case emerged in 1964 which tested the principle of good faith bargaining. General Electric instituted a policy which has come to be known as *Boulwarism*, named after Mr. Boulware, an executive at General Electric. The case is as follows:

Facts
General Electric negotiated a contract with the International Union of Electrical Workers (I.U.E.). G.E.'s strategy involved making considerable efforts prior to negotiation to determine what was right and fair for the employees. They then presented the package to the union and made it clear that it would not make any changes which it did not consider "correct" merely because of an actual or threatened strike. The NLRB decided that G.E.'s conduct was not bargaining in good faith. G.E. petitioned for review.

Decision
Petition denied.

Reasoning
G.E.'s bargaining technique, its campaign among employees, and its conduct at the bargaining table, all complementing each other, were calculated to disparage the union. This is not bargaining in good faith.

NLRB v. General Electric Company, 418 F.2d 736 (1969).

National Emergency Strikes under Taft-Hartley. Because of all the strikes which had occurred in the period immediately preceding the Taft-Hartley Act, Congress decided to build in a provision which would give the government power to act when a vital industry was adversely affected by a labor action. In the event that a dispute in an industry (or in a substantial part thereof) "imperils the nation's health or safety," the President may appoint a Board of Inquiry to report on the dispute. This can result in an order by the court to stop the strike for sixty days and then again for another twenty days, if needed. During the second period, an election is conducted among the workers to see whether they would accept the last offer of the employer. If no progress results, the President then reports to Congress about the state of affairs and makes recommendations which the President believes to be appropriate.

Landrum-Griffin Act

The technical name for the Landrum-Griffin Act is the Labor Management Reporting and Disclosure Act of 1959. The reason for this Act was largely to clean up the internal affairs of unions. In the mid 1950s Senator McClellan began an investigation into the activities of unions and uncovered massive amounts of corruption and violence. The public was sufficiently alarmed to push for strong reform legislation, and in 1959 that is precisely what the public received in the form of the Landrum-Griffin Act.

For our purposes, the most important part of the Landrum-Griffin Act is Title I, which is also known as a "bill of rights" for union members. This is because it assures that all union members will have an opportunity to participate in the internal affairs of their organization in some meaningful way. For example, Landrum-Griffin Title I guarantees members the right to vote in union elections. Titles II–VI contain other provisions to deal with internal union problems, such as the election of officers and the prohibition of certain kinds of people (for example, certain convicted offenders) from holding union office.

Title VII of Landrum-Griffin contains amendments to Taft-Hartley. Perhaps the most important amendment was to make it an unfair labor practice to become involved in a **hot cargo agreement.** Hot cargo agreements generally were union decisions not to handle items that were produced by, or were going to support, an anti-union company.

Government Employees

The federal government has always been rather slow in managing its own labor-management relations. Although there are examples of some concerted labor activity in the federal government in the 1800s, union-management relations in the public service were

Landrum-Griffin Act.

hot cargo agreement
an agreement between an employer and a union that the employer is not to handle or otherwise deal with goods of another employer

virtually dead until President Kennedy enacted Executive Order 10988 in 1962. The thrust of this Order was to have three kinds of union recognition in the federal sector. "Informal recognition" allowed employees to gather together but management did not have to consult the group before acting. "Exclusive recognition" meant that a union represented at least 10 percent of the number of the employees in question. The union was then entitled to bargain a contract for all employees in the unit, and management had to meet with the representatives. "Formal recognition" was an intermediate step which obligated the managers to speak with the union only prior to acting.

President Nixon substantially altered labor relations in the public sector by issuing Executive Order 11491 in October 1969 and did away with all but the exclusive form of recognition. This change, in addition to other amendments, has marked a period of rapid expansion of interest of federal employees in union groups. Today, there are well over 1,000,000 government employees represented by union organizations, such as the American Federation of Government Employees.

However, the range of items and the power of federal government union groups is still rather limited.

The Strike: Public versus Private Sector

Almost all of us take for granted the right of employees to strike for higher wages. In fact, we are often surprised to learn that the courts can sometimes stop groups from striking.

In the *private* sector, the right to strike is so much a part of labor relations that it is rarely interfered with by the courts. The only time the courts will stop a private sector strike is in the event of violence.

In the *public* sector, the right to strike is much more restricted. The courts have repeatedly ruled that strikes in the public sector are illegal. The reason given by the courts is that if government employees strike they threaten the well-being of the entire community. However, there is some debate about this argument, and we may one day see legal public sector strikes.

In both the public and private sectors, management has a limited arsenal of weapons to fight the strike. These weapons include the *lockout* and the *injunction*. By the injunction, the court is ordering a group to "stop" a certain kind of behavior which may cause damage. A lockout is, as its name suggests, a closing of a plant *before* the union strikes.

Summary Statement

1. The origins of craft unionism and industrial unions are quite different. Industrial unions exist as a response to technological change.
2. Various methods have been used to control labor unions. Early attempts at labeling unions as criminal conspiracies gave way to attempts to use antitrust laws, followed by a regularized pattern of laws.
3. Today's labor laws have their roots in the Norris-La Guardia Act. However, the three major contemporary laws are the Wagner Act, the Taft-Hartley Act, and the Landrum-Griffin Act.
4. Government employees represent an ever-increasing number of potential union members. Special executive orders regulate labor-management relations between government and its employees. Supervisors and managerial employees are normally excluded from the categories of employees entitled to the benefits of collective bargaining.

The following case addresses the question of whether faculty members should be excluded from the categories of employees entitled to the benefit of collective bargaining. The decision was made by a closely divided court.

NLRB v. Yeshiva University
444 U.S. 672 (1979)

I

Powell, J. Yeshiva is a private university. . . . On October 30, 1974, the Yeshiva University Faculty Association (Union) filed a representation petition with the National Labor Relations Board (Board). The Union sought certification as bargaining agent for the full-time faculty members at 10 of the 13 schools. The University opposed the petition on the ground that all of its faculty members are managerial or supervisory personnel and hence not employees within the meaning of the National Labor Relations Act (Act).

*****

Faculty power at Yeshiva's schools extends beyond strictly academic concerns. The faculty at each school make recommendations to the dean or director in every case of faculty hiring, tenure, sabbaticals, termination, and promotion. Although the final decision is reached by the central administration on the advice of the dean or director, the overwhelming majority of faculty recommendations are implemented.

*****

II

A three-member panel of the Board granted the Union's petition in December, 1975, and directed an election in a bargaining unit consisting of all full-time faculty members at the affected schools.

*****

The Union won the election and was certified by the Board. The University refused to bargain, reasserting its view that the faculty are managerial. In the subsequent unfair labor practice proceeding, the Board refused to reconsider its holding in the representation proceeding and ordered the University to bargain with the Union. . . . When the University still refused to sit down at the negotiating table, the Board sought enforcement in the Court of Appeals for the Second Circuit, which denied the petition. . . .

The Court concluded that such [faculty] power is not an exercise of individual professional expertise. Rather, the faculty are, "in effect, substantially and pervasively operating the enterprise." Accordingly, the court held that the faculty are endowed with "managerial status" sufficient to remove them from the coverage of the Act. We granted certiorari, 440 U.S. 906 (1979), and now affirm.

*****

III

There is no evidence that Congress has considered whether a university faculty may organize for collective bargaining under the Act. . . . The Board has recognized that principles developed for use in the industrial setting cannot be "imposed blindly on the academic world." *Syracuse University,* 204 NLRB 641, 643 (1973).

*****

IV

The status of such employees, in the Board's view, must be determined by reference to the "alignment with management" criterion. The Board argues that the Yeshiva faculty are not aligned with management because they are expected to exercise "independent professional judgment" while participating in academic governance, and because they are neither "expected to conform to management policies [nor] judged according to their effectiveness in carrying out those policies." Because of this independence, the Board contends there is no danger of divided loyalty and no need for the managerial exclusion. In its view, union pressure cannot divert the faculty from adhering to the interests of the university, because the university itself expects its faculty to pursue professional values rather than institutional interests. The Board concludes that application of the managerial exclusion to such employees would frustrate the national labor policy in favor of collective bargaining.

This "independent professional judgment" test was not applied in the decision we are asked to uphold. The Board's opinion relies exclusively on its previous faculty decisions for both legal and factual analysis.

*****

V

The controlling consideration in this case is that the faculty of Yeshiva University exercise authority which in any other context unquestionably would be managerial. Their authority in academic matters is absolute. They decide what courses will be offered, when they will be scheduled, and to whom they will be taught. They debate and determine teaching methods, grading policies, and matriculation standards. They effectively decide which students will be admitted, retained, and graduated. On occasion their views have determined the size of the student body, the tuition to be charged, and the location of a school. When one considers the function of a university, it is difficult to imagine decisions more managerial than these. To the extent the industrial analogy applies, the faculty determines within each school the product to be produced, the terms upon which it will be offered, and the customers who will be served.

The Board nevertheless insists that these decisions are not managerial because they require the exercise of independent professional judgment. We are not persuaded by this argument. There may be some tension between the Act's exclusion of managerial employees and its inclusion of professionals, since most professionals in managerial positions continue to draw on their special skills and training. But we have been directed to no authority suggesting that that tension be resolved by reference to the "independent professional judgment" criterion proposed in this case.

*****

VI

The question we decide today is a mixed one of fact and law. But the Board's opinion may be searched in vain for relevant findings of fact. The absence of factual analysis apparently reflects the Board's view that the managerial status of particular faculties may be decided on the basis of conclusory rationale rather than examination of the facts of each case. The Court of Appeals took a different view, and determined that the faculty of Yeshiva University "in effect, substantially and pervasively operate the enterprise." 582 F.2d at 698. We find no reason to reject this conclusion. As our decisions consistently show, we accord great respect to the expertise of the Board when its conclusions are rationally based on articulated facts and consistent with the Act. . . . In this case, we hold that the Board's decision satisfies neither criterion.

Affirmed.

Questions and Case Problems

1. Distinguish between a craft and an industrial union.

2. Can employers still request an injunction against a union group, even though we live in an age of enlightened human resource management?

3. The Mine Workers Union was trying to obtain and enforce a collective bargaining contract's clause. This clause would limit the coal operators to subcontracting coal hauling to "contractors employing union members." In their attempt to obtain this clause, the union forced the coal operators and coal haulers to sign a contract containing the clause in question. Is this clause legal? What would you call this clause? Explain. [*Feather v. Mine Workers*, 113 LRRM, 3367 (1983).]

4. The employer told employees that the company preferred that they supported and voted for the incumbent union rather than the outside union. In return, the employees were promised wage increases, bonuses and other improvements in their working conditions. Are these promises legal? Explain. [*New York Telephone Company and Communication Workers, Local 1108, AFL-CIO,* 112 LRRM 1416 (1983).]

5. In the question above, the employer laid off one employee due to the worker's support for the outside union rather than the incumbent union. This layoff occurred after the employer had received a telegram stating that the worker was one of the outside union's supporters. Since the worker's duties still were essential and there was still a need for him in the factory, did the employer violate any laws by laying off this worker? Explain. [*New York Telephone Company and Communication Workers, Local 1108, AFL-CIO*, 112 LRRM 1416 (1983).]

6. A manager works in a parts room where he shares a desk with two other departmental employees who perform the same type of work. He occasionally works overtime and uses his own judgment as to whether to do so, but he punches the time clock and is paid time-and-one-half for overtime, as are other department employees. Lastly, he has not evaluated or disciplined employees, and his vacation and fringe benefits do not differ from those of other employees. Could this person be a member of a union's bargaining unit? Explain. [*T.L.C. Lines, Inc. and Machinists District No. 9, AFL-CIO*, 112 LRRM 1414 (1982).]

7. The International Union of Operating Engineers told their general contractor that if a nonunion supplier of ready-mix concrete made a pour, a second union that had a dispute with the supplier would establish a picket line and the members of the contracting union would honor this picket line. Since this was a subcontracting clause of the labor agreement, is the union acting lawfully? Explain. [*Local 12, International Union of Operating Engineers, AFL-CIO, and Cal Tram Rebuilders, Inc.*, 114 LRRM 1030 (1983).]

8. A union group of employees of Allis-Chalmers Mfg. Co. decides to engage in a lawful strike against Allis-Chalmers Mfg. Co. Some employee members of the union decide they do not want to participate in the strike and so they cross the picket line. The union fines them. The employees claim their rights under Landrum-Griffin have been violated. Do they have a case? [*NLRB v. Allis-Chalmers Mfg. Co.*, 388 U.S. 175 (1967).]

9. The union terminated its contract with Purex Corp. by giving adequate notice, and shortly afterwards Purex union members went on a strike against Purex. Because of the no-strike clause in this contract, Purex would like to prevent the union from walking off the job. What form of relief could be requested from the court? [*Purex Corp. v. Teamsters Local 618*, 112 LRRM 3433 (1983).].

10. In connection with the case of *NLRB v. Yeshiva University*, 444 U.S. 672 (1979),[1] the University refused to bargain with its faculty members, claiming that they were managerial employees. Do you consider faculty members to be managerial employees? What are the legal criteria for such a decision?

---

[1] See pp. 731–32.

50 Environmental Law

After you have read this chapter, you should be able to:

1. Discuss the major components of the National Environmental Policy Act.
2. Understand the purpose and function of the National Environmental Protection Agency.
3. Trace the development of the Clean Air Act and the Clean Water Act as recently amended.
4. Introduce the main concepts of the Toxic Substances Control Act, the Resource Conservation and Recovery Act, and the federal Environmental Pesticide Control Act.
5. Highlight the provisions of the Endangered Species Act and its recent amendments.
6. Distinguish state from federal land use powers.

Introduction

One student accurately defined the *environment* as "the universe, and all that surrounds it." The focus of our present inquiry is the *ecosphere*—that intricate web of the earth's living things and the thin global skin of air, water, and soil which supports its existence. The *human environment* is still more complex because it consists not merely of our physical surroundings—it encompasses the vast interplay of our emotional, intellectual, and cultural life as well.

A study of environmental law, then, is the study of mankind's efforts to regulate intrusions on the ecosphere, particularly those intrusions that stress the environment beyond its natural capacity to adjust. This chapter will be limited to an examination of environmental protective measures within the U.S. and how they interrelate to form a national strategy for maintaining the integrity of the ecosphere.

Federal Regulation—The Environmental Protection Agency

The Environmental Protection Agency (EPA) was established by a 1970 executive reorganization plan designed to *consolidate federal environmental activities into a single agency*.[1] The objective was to structure a *coordinated response to a broad range of pollutants*—air, water, noise, solid wastes, toxic chemicals, pesticides, and radiation. Generally speaking, Congress has conferred upon EPA a twofold task: (a) creating national pollution standards, and (b) enforcement of these standards (normally in conjunction with the states).

The necessity for federal regulation and the EPA.

The problems are enormous, however. First, within each area, millions of dollars in research are needed to make way for enlightened regulation. Second, environmentally sound solutions often run into opposition from energy and production-minded interests—e.g., emission control limits on automobiles sometimes frustrate fuel economy and production schedules. Finally, progress in one area may provoke difficulties in another area. To illustrate, cleaner air and water require the removal of solid and chemical wastes. Disposal of these wastes creates land-use problems that are not entirely within the jurisdiction of EPA. The cooperative efforts of federal, state, regional, and local governmental agencies are frequently essential to progress toward an environmentally acceptable solution. Such problems are not respecters of political boundaries.

National Environmental Policy Act

The National Environmental Policy Act (NEPA)[2] is the kingpin of U.S. environmental laws. Contrary to popular belief, it does not set a single pollution standard for air, water, noise, radiation, hazardous substances, or solid wastes. Neither does it establish a veto over harmful environmental projects. The Council on Environmental Quality (CEQ), which was chartered by NEPA, merely serves as the President's policy advisor. It has issued *regulations* to *all* federal agencies on the *implementation of NEPA*,[3] but it does not have enforcement powers.

NEPA.

CEQ.

---

[1] Reorganization Plan #3 of 1970, 35 Fed. Reg. 15623, 84 Stat. 2086 (1970).

[2] 42 U.S.C. secs. 4321–4347, 83 Stat. 852, Pub. L. 91–190 (1970) as amended by Pub. L. 94–52 (1975), and Pub. L. 94–83 (1975).

[3] 40 Code of Federal Regulations, secs. 1500–1508.

On the other hand, NEPA does firmly command a *rigorous decision-making process for all agencies of the federal government*. Federal agencies are required to implement these procedures to the fullest extent possible in order to achieve the environmental standards or goals set forth in section 101:

1. Safe, healthful, productive, and esthetically and culturally pleasing surroundings.
2. Preserve important historic, cultural, and natural aspects of our natural heritage.
3. Achieve a balance between population and resource use.
4. Enhance the quality of renewable resources and promote recycling of depletable resources.

Congress directed that all laws, policies, and regulations of the U.S. be interpreted and administered in accordance with NEPA. Federal agencies were ordered to utilize an interdisciplinary approach to decision making and to give environmental values appropriate consideration along with economic and technical factors.

Environmental Impact Statements

The most dramatic innovation introduced by NEPA is the section 102 requirement for Environmental Impact Statements (EIS). *These statements must accompany every proposal for legislation and other major federal actions significantly affecting the quality of the human environment.* CEQ regulations require the following format:

1. A statement of the purpose and need for the project.
2. A rigorous comparison of the reasonable alternatives.
3. A succinct description of the environment of the area to be affected by the proposed project.
4. A discussion of the environmental consequences of the proposal and of alternatives (including direct and indirect effects, energy requirements and conservation potential, mitigation measures, depletable resource requirements, impacts on urban quality and historic and cultural resources, and possible conflicts with state or local land-use plans, policies, and controls).
5. A list of the names and qualifications of the people primarily responsible for preparing the EIS and of the agencies to which the EIS was sent.
6. An appendix.

Purpose. The genius of this approach is the *early alert* it gives federal agencies. Since Congress has established as a national policy that environmental values be integrated into the decision-making process to assure an overall balance, the EIS is designed to give *advance warning* of harmful environmental consequences. Full disclosure of all the environmental, technological, and economic pros and cons should avoid wasteful expenditures on projects and proposals that have not been well thought out. The CEQ regulations introduced a "scoping process" which requires prompt and full administrative analysis of important issues. The regulations also demand a written record which documents the reasonable alternatives, the steps taken to mitigate environmental harm, and the justification for the agency's decision.

Theory and Practice. That, at least, is the way things are supposed to work. However, as everyone knows, there is frequently a big gap between theory and practice—and that is precisely the case with NEPA.

In the first place, NEPA, like the U.S. Constitution, is not self-executing. It relies upon the integrity of government bureaucracies, the alertness of concerned citizens, and the supervision of federal courts to carry out its mandate.

For example, when a federal agency undertakes a project, it must first determine whether the EIS process has been triggered—i.e., whether there is a *major federal action significantly affecting the quality of the human environment*. If, contrary to your own analysis, the agency decides that an impact statement is not necessary, there is *no one except you* or other concerned citizens to step in and do something about it. The Council on Environmental Quality is not authorized to stop the project; neither is the Environmental Protection Agency. Congress and the President have the power to influence administrative decision.

NEPA and the Courts

Some courts have found NEPA's requirements to be procedural only, but the better-reasoned decisions insist that the procedural aspects of the Act are designed to achieve a substantive national policy of environmental protection. The following case views EISs as a *means* toward the achievement of certain *ends* or *objectives*. If the impact analysis indicates that more harm will result from a project than good—that the costs outweigh the benefits—further action on such a project will be regarded by the federal courts as arbitrary and capricious. In such a case the court would have the power to enjoin (stop) the project permanently.

Facts
A citizens group, The Environmental Defense Fund, Inc., plaintiffs, sought an injunction against the U.S. Corps of Engineers, defendant, to prevent completion of a dam on the free-flowing Cossatot River in Arkansas. The U.S. District Court held that an adequate Environmental Impact Statement had been prepared and that the National Environmental Policy Act contained no substantive standards beyond the procedural step of "full disclosure" embodied in the EIS. Plaintiffs appealed.

Decision
Affirmed for U.S. Corps of Engineers.

Reasoning
The District Court found that NEPA "falls short of creating the type of 'substantive rights' claimed by the plaintiffs," and therefore "plaintiffs are relegated to the procedural requirements of the Act."

We disagree. The language of NEPA, as well as its legislative history, make it clear that the Act is more than an environmental full-disclosure law. NEPA was intended to effect substantive changes in decision making. The Act states that agencies have an obligation "to use all practical means, consistent with other essential considerations of national policy, to improve and coordinate federal plans, functions, programs, and resources to preserve and enhance the environment." To this end, section 101 sets out specific environmental goals to serve as a set of policies to guide agency action affecting the environment.

Section 102(1) directs that the policies, regulations and public laws of the United States be interpreted in accordance with these policies to the fullest extent possible. Section 102(2), of course, sets forth the procedural requirements of the Act. The purpose is to "insure that the policies enunciated in section 101 are implemented." The procedures included in section 102 of NEPA are not ends in themselves. They are intended to be "action forcing." However, since defendant's decision to complete the dam cannot be set aside as arbitrary or capricious, it is unnecessary to remand this case to the trial court because of its error.

Environmental Defense Fund, Inc. v. Corps of Engineers of the U.S. Army, 470 F.2d 289 (1972).

The Clean Air Act

Introduction

The Clean Air Act Amendments of 1977 continue the impressive but difficult task which Congress undertook in 1970.[4] Implementation of the Act necessitated separate treatment of emissions from stationary sources (factories, utilities) and from mobile sources (automobiles, trucks). Control of both types was expected to lead to the achievement of ambient (surrounding) air quality standards by certain target dates.

---

[4] 42 U.S.C. secs. 1857–1858a, 84 Stat. 1676, Pub. L. 91–604 (1970), as amended by 42 U.S.C. secs. 7401–7642, 91 Stat. 685, Pub. L. 95–96 (1977).

Stationary Sources

EPA was authorized by the 1970 Act to formulate *primary standards* to protect *public health,* and *secondary standards* to protect *public welfare*—visibility, vegetation, animal life. States were expected first to inventory their air quality and then to subdivide their geographical area into manageable air quality control regions (AQCR). Next, the states were required to hold public hearings and to formulate state implementation plans (SIPs) which described the means and methods of achieving those standards within each AQCR.

Mobile Sources

Congress dealt with emissions from automobiles by requiring that carbon monoxide and hydrocarbons be reduced by 90 percent between 1970–75 and nitrogen dioxides by 90 percent between 1971–76. EPA awarded automakers a two-year delay on these deadlines.

With regard to both stationary and mobile sources, great strides were made toward ambient air quality standards. None of them was achieved on the national level, however. This gave rise to the 1977 Clean Air Act Amendments.

The 1977 Clean Air Act Amendments

Congress extended the basic strategy of the 1970 Act in its 1977 amendments. New state implementation plans (SIPs) were required to be submitted to EPA by January 1, 1979. EPA then had six months to approve, disapprove, or seek state modification of the SIP. Attainment under these new plans was targeted for December 31, 1982. EPA regulations allow states to treat a plant as if it had a bubble over the top—the "bubble" concept—and to reduce high cost controls for a pollutant in exchange for an equal increase in the control of that pollutant in the same plant where abatement is less expensive.

For states that are seriously affected by automobile emissions and have not attained the standards by 1982, revised plans which impose all requirements to meet the standards by 1987 must be submitted. In sum, this means that the 1977 amendments extended the deadline for most pollutants until 1982 and for automobile-related pollutants until 1987.

New SIPs begin with an air quality index of each AQCR. Next, the states detailed their approach to *nonattainment* (dirty air) regions and *nondeterioration* (clean air) regions. Nonattainment regions include those AQCRs within the state that were not reaching the ambient air quality standards for one or more pollutants. Nondeterioration areas contain air of higher quality than the law demands. This may sound confusing, but a single AQCR could be classified nonattainment for one pollutant (a dirty air region for SO_2, for example) and nondeterioration for another (a clean air region for CO). It all depends on that region's mix of stationary and mobile sources.

Nonattainment Areas

If a SIP submitted after January 1, 1979 met EPA's approval, then the air quality control board could evaluate major stationary source permit **applicants** in nonattainment areas and issue permits under the following conditions:

1. The net effect is reduced emissions (existing sources are retrofitted so that they will more than offset new or modified sources within the area).
2. The source meets lowest achievable emission rate.
3. All other facilities of the applicant within the state are in compliance.

If EPA rejects the SIP, then, until a new plan meets its approval, there can be no new industrial construction within the state. Additionally, EPA and Department of Transportation funds will be withheld, except funds for safety, mass transit, and air quality improvement projects.

AQCR.

SIP.

applicant
an individual or a firm seeking governmental permission to engage in some activity

Prevention of Significant Deterioration

In those parts of the country where the air is cleaner than it is required to be under national standards, Congress established three air quality categories. Within these categories emission limitations have been established for particulates and sulfur dioxide. In August, 1980, EPA limitations for hydrocarbons, carbon monoxide, photochemical oxidants, and nitrogen oxides became effective.

In Class I, very little air pollution is tolerated. It includes international parks as well as national parks and wilderness areas in excess of 5,000 or more acres (there are occasions, however, when a plant may receive a limited variance for sulfur dioxide emissions). Class II areas are susceptible to moderate amounts of air quality deterioration. In Class III areas, degradation is permissible to the limits of national primary standards. Except for certain federal lands discussed above, procedures are available to redesignate land from Class II to Class III so that industrial expansion may be accommodated.

Enforcement

Congress placed at the disposal of EPA a variety of criminal and civil enforcement measures. The most innovative contribution of the 1977 amendments is an economic penalty that eliminates any cost advantage of being out of compliance. States can enforce their own air pollution laws if they do not substantially burden interstate commerce and if they have not been preempted by Congress. The following case illustrates this point.

Facts
Illinois passed a law prohibiting the movement, from out of state, of any spent nuclear fuel for disposal or storage in Illinois. The Nuclear Regulatory Commission (NRC), however, was given comprehensive regulatory powers over such matters when Congress passed the Atomic Energy Act. With regard to the shipment and storage of spent nuclear fuel, inter- and intra-state, it appears that the federal government has totally pre-empted, or excluded, state legislation.

Nevertheless, Illinois argues, the Clean Air Act (CAA) authorizes it to nullify NRC authority: Section 116 provides that "nothing in this Act shall preclude or deny the right of any state . . . to adopt or enforce . . . any requirerment respecting control or abatement of air pollution." Air pollution includes "radioactive substance or matter which is emitted into or otherwise enters the ambient air."

Is General Electric entitled to move spent nuclear fuel into Illinois despite this state statute?

Decision
Yes. For General Electric.

Reasoning
The Clean Air Act, Section 116, qualifies federal power under that Act only. It does not limit federal power under other statutes such as the Atomic Energy Act.

People of the State of Illinois v. General Electric Company, 683 F.2d 206 (7th Cir. 1982).

The Clean Water Act

Background

The 1977 Clean Water Act (CWA) amends the 1972 Federal Water Pollution Control Act (FWPCA).[5] The announced goals of the 1972 Act were: *no effluent discharges by 1985,* and *water clean enough for swimming and other recreational values by 1983.*

CWA.

FWPCA.

These goals were to be accomplished in stages—first, by establishing quality standards based on water use, such as human consumption, recreation, and industrial purposes; next, by treating effluents that are discharged into waters of the U.S. from *point* sources (e.g., ditches, pipes, defined channels). These effluents are controlled by EPA-specified technology. *Nonpoint,* or undefined, sources are dealt with through a planning process somewhat resembling SIPs under the Clean Air Act.

---

[5] 33 U.S.C. secs. 1251–1376, 86 Stat. 816, Pub. L. 92–500 (1977), as amended by 91 Stat. 1567, 1575, Pub. L. 95–217 (1977).

Industrial discharges were required to install the *best practicable control technology* by July 1, 1977, and the *best available technology economically achievable* by July 1, 1983. Municipalities were subjected to less stringent demands. *Secondary* treatment was required by 1977, and *best practicable* by 1983. For a fee, industrial dischargers can use municipal facilities if the effectiveness of these publicly owned treatment works is not jeopardized.

NPDES.

Both industrial and municipal discharges were required to obtain National Pollutant Discharge Elimination System (NPDES) permits prior to commencing operations. The permit system was designed to bolster the monitoring and enforcement provisions of the Act.

Funding. A *Buy America* provision requires funds to be spent on domestic construction materials. This section of the Act does not apply if EPA finds it to be inconsistent with the public interest, if costs are unreasonable, or if the materials are not available in satisfactory quality and quantity.

Effluent Requirements. The 1977 CWA classifies pollutants as conventional (sanitary waste), toxic (65 designated chemicals), and nonconventional (all other). Regarding conventional pollutants, EPA must publish regulations and set effluent limitations requiring *best conventional technology* (BCT). Industrial compliance was targeted for July 1, 1984.

For toxic chemicals, the July 1, 1984 deadline was applicable as well. However, industry must comply with more stringent effluent limitation requirements—*best available technology economically achievable* (BAT). Nonconventional pollutants had to be controlled by BAT not later than July 1, 1984, with the possibility of a variance until July 1, 1987.

Enforcement

The civil and criminal enforcement sections of the Act substantially parallel those of the Clean Air Act. While there is no provision that deprives a firm of the economic advantage of noncompliance, it resembles the Clean Air Act in that states retain some flexibility in enforcing their own statutes. The case which follows illustrates this flexibility.

Facts
The city of Chicago, defendant, adopted an ordinance providing that the sale of detergents containing any phosphorus constituted a criminal offense. The plaintiff, Proctor & Gamble, sought declaratory and injunctive relief, alleging that the ordinance violated the commerce clause of the U.S. Constitution in that it constituted an unconstitutional burden on interstate commerce.

Decision
For the City of Chicago.

Reasoning
The Proctor & Gamble Company could not prove convincingly that the Chicago City Council was wrong in its conclusion that limiting phosphorus in waters under its jurisdiction could someday be the key to clean water. The ordinance will not solve the problem, but it is a significant first step. Since interstate commerce is only slightly affected, and since states (and cities through their state-granted city charters) have Tenth Amendment powers to protect the public health, this ordinance is valid.

The Proctor & Gamble Company v. City of Chicago, 509 F.2d 69 (1975), cert. denied 421 U.S. 978 (1975).

Toxic Substances Control Act

TSCA.

The 1976 Toxic Substances Control Act (TSCA)[6] is concerned with the production and sale of toxic chemical substances. The TSCA expands, systematizes, and exploits information on production, use, and toxicity to prevent hazardous environmental and human

---
[6] 15 U.S.C. secs. 2601–2629, 90 Stat. 2003, Pub. L. 94–469 (1976).

exposure. The federal government can now control and stop the production or use of chemical substances that may present an unreasonable risk of injury to health or the environment.

Manufacturers of *new chemicals* and chemicals for *new uses* must notify EPA ninety days prior to beginning production. Manufacturers may also be required to test selected chemicals or to report production quantities, use, biological properties, and other information necessary for hazard assessment. The following criteria are used to pinpoint those substances which must undergo the rigorous testing procedures mandated by the Act:

1. Does substantial exposure to the chemical imply an unreasonable risk to health or the environment?
2. If data for predicting health and environmental effects are inadequate, testing is necessary to develop data.

EPA was authorized to require reports on the name and identity of each chemical, proposed uses, production level, by-products, adverse effects, and number of workers exposed. Trade secrets and financial data required by the Act are confidential, but health and safety information is subject to public disclosure. Records of significant adverse health effects must be kept for thirty years; information regarding environmental damage must be kept for five years.

Resource Conservation and Recovery Act of 1976

The Resource Conservation and Recovery Act[7] required EPA to identify areas with common solid waste management problems and appropriate planning units. EPA is required to publish guidelines to aid state development of solid waste management plans. Ambient air standards, groundwater quality, waste collection, open dumps, resource recovery, and markets for recovered materials are the chief considerations of these management plans. Before EPA will approve the state plan:

Resource Conservation and Recovery Act.

1. state, local, and regional responsibilities must be identified;
2. strategy for coordinating regional planning must be specified;
3. establishment of new open dumps must be prohibited and old ones must be improved or phased out;
4. nonhazardous wastes must be disposed of in sanitary landfills or used for resource recovery.

The plan's success is largely contingent upon the states' voluntary acceptance of responsibility. If a state does not present a plan that meets EPA's approval, or if it does not revise the plan to accommodate EPA's objections, EPA can impose upon the state a plan of its own.

Hazardous Wastes

One of the more significant features of the Act directs EPA to identify hazardous wastes that threaten the human environment. Once these wastes have been identified, owners and operators of hazardous waste treatment and storage facilities must apply for EPA permits (or state permits under EPA approved plans). Applications must detail composition, quantity, location, and the method and rate of disposal.

Essentially hazardous wastes are to be tracked from the manufacturing stage through transportation, treatment, storage, and disposal. It is enforced with civil *and* criminal penalties.

---

[7] 42 U.S.C. secs. 6901–6987, 90 Stat. 2796, Pub. L. 89–272, as added Pub. L. 94–580 (1976).

The Superfund

In the Comprehensive Environmental Response, Compensation, and Liability Act,[8] Congress created a "superfund" to be managed by EPA. The Resource Conservation and Recovery Act was designed to prevent the *creation* of hazardous waste disposal sites, but it did not permit the federal government to *clean up* the ones already in existence. The Superfund Law directs EPA to respond directly to releases or threatened releases of hazardous substances that may endanger public health or welfare.

Costs are covered by a $1.6 billion trust fund, 86 percent of which is financed by taxes on the manufacturers of petrochemical feedstocks and toxic organic chemicals, and the importers of crude oil. The remainder is financed from general revenues. Legal action can be taken to recover cleanup costs from those subsequently identified as responsible parties. Any person or firm liable for a release may be required to pay punitive damages (in this case, three times the government's response cost) if cleanup orders are not strictly obeyed.

Pesticide Regulation

The federal Insecticide, Fungicide, and Rodenticide Act of 1947 and the federal Environmental Pesticide Control Act of 1972[9] require registration and labeling of agricultural pesticides. The objective is to prevent unreasonable risk to human life and health and to the environment, with the social, environmental, and economic costs and benefits being taken into account.

Pesticides must be classified for "general" or "restricted" use. Those within the latter category may be used only by or under the supervision of state-certified and EPA-approved applicators.

The use of any registered pesticide in a manner contrary to labeling instructions is prohibited. EPA may issue a "stop sale, use and removal" order when a pesticide is found to be in violation of federal statutes. Such pesticides may also be seized.

Manufacturing plants must be registered with EPA, and they must furnish information on the types and amounts of pesticides produced, distributed, and sold. Federal inspectors with appropriate warrants are entitled to enter and inspect such establishments and take samples.

Criminal sanctions can be imposed on farmers, private applicators, registered manufacturers, commercial applicators, wholesalers, distributors, and retailers who knowingly violate the law.

The Endangered Species Act

The Endangered Species Act authorizes the Secretary of the Interior, in consultation with representatives from the states, to designate species of fish, wildlife, and plants threatened with extinction and those that might become endangered in the foreseeable future. Federal agencies must avoid jeopardizing endangered species. Fines can be imposed on private citizens who buy, sell, transport in interstate commerce, import, or export in violation of the Act.

Congress created a three-member review panel to examine controversial federal projects. The review is not undertaken, however, until all alternatives to the project have been pursued in good faith. After the review panel has compiled a detailed report on the merits

---

[8] 42 U.S.C. sec. 9601 et seq. (1980).

[9] 7 U.S.C. secs. 136–136y, 86 Stat. 975, Pub. L. 92–516 (1972), as amended by 87 Stat. 903, Pub. L. 93–205 (1973), 89 Stat. 754, Pub. L. 94–140 (1975).

of granting an exemption, the report is considered by a seven-person cabinet-level committee. The committee may then finally exempt a project on the basis of the following criteria:

1. benefits of the project clearly outweigh benefits of alternative action consistent with conserving the species or its critical habitat;
2. the project is in the public interest; and
3. there are no reasonable and prudent alternatives.

If the committee does not grant an exemption, the project cannot be continued.

Land Use

In the final analysis, all pollution problems come down to decisions regarding land use. If property is zoned for industrial purposes or devoted to highway or automobile-related uses, air pollution is a likely result. With less land available for food production, demands for increased yields per acre require the application of chemical fertilizers, insecticides, and pesticides—and therefore invite their related problems. Land dedicated to airport and other transportation uses will likely raise complaints about excessive noise. Sanitary landfills frequently evoke criticism based on aesthetics, odor, and, perhaps, contamination of groundwater. The following examples document the relationship between pollution and land use, and include illustrations on the state and federal level.

Zoning

Zoning of real property is discussed in detail in chapter 51, Real Property and Its Ownership.

Zoning ordinances are exercises of local *police powers*—i.e., powers reserved under the Tenth Amendment to the U.S. Constitution, designed to protect the public health, morals, and safety. If zoning regulations exceed a certain degree, they amount to a *taking*, and the owner must be paid a reasonable value for the property so condemned. While no clear and unmistakable lines are drawn between regulation and taking, the prohibition of some uses merely amounts to regulation. If all uses are forbidden, or if title to the property is transferred to someone else, then a compensable taking has occurred.[10]

Translated to *environmental* terms, this means that a state or the District of Columbia may *take* private property for the purpose of devoting it to a better balanced and more attractive community.

Private property may be *regulated* without payment of compensation to the owner. For example, the U.S. Supreme Court has upheld a zoning ordinance limiting to two the number of unrelated, unmarried persons forming a household. This caused certain landlords the loss of tenants—hence, an economic loss.

It is said, however, that if two unmarried people can constitute a "family," there is no reason why three or four may not. But every line drawn by a legislature leaves some out that might well have been included. That exercise of discretion, however, is a legislative, not a judicial, function. . . . A quiet place where yards are wide, people few, and motor vehicles restricted are legitimate guidelines in a land-use project addressed to family needs. This goal is a permissible one. . . . The police power is not confined to elimination of filth, stench, and unhealthy places. It is ample to lay out zones where family values, youth values, and the blessings of quiet seclusion and clean air make the area a sanctuary for people.[11]

---

[10] *South Terminal Corp. v. EPA,* 504 F.2d 646 (1974).

[11] *Village of Belle Terre v. Boraas,* 416 U.S. 1 (1974).

Solar Zoning

A special application of zoning regulation—and one that you may fully expect to have an immense social impact in years to come—is solar zoning. In a sense, this means parceling out the sun's rays in a manner that accommodates both public and private interests.

Suppose, for example, that you and your spouse plan to build a home utilizing solar energy for heating and cooling. Typically, this will entail the installation of solar collectors on the roof and the use of a liquid or gaseous medium to transfer the heat for direct use (hot water tank, radiator, heat pump) or indirect use (storage as chemical energy in a battery).

The technology for these systems has been available for years and is relatively simple. Depending on the part of the country you are in (the sunny Southwest versus colder climates) and the size of your house (currently solar collectors occupy roofspace which is the equivalent of 30–60 percent of your floorspace), the investment necessary for solar heating is sufficiently large to make you think twice. At a minimum, you will expect certain assurances that the solar panels will not be shielded from the sunlight by obstructions on neighboring lands. The issue is simply this—*are you entitled to the uninterrupted flow of sunlight across adjacent property?* Could you expect to win a lawsuit against an offending property owner if he caused obstruction of sunlight that would otherwise fall on your solar collectors? The following landmark case, which arose in Wisconsin a number of years ago, addresses a similar issue and reflects a movement among some courts to change the common law rule denying such relief.

Facts

Plaintiff Prah's home was the first residence built in the subdivision, and although plaintiff did not build his house in the center of the lot it was built in accordance with applicable restrictions. Plaintiff advised defendant, Maretti, that if the defendant's home were built at the proposed site it would cause a shadowing effect on the solar collectors on Prah's home which would reduce the efficiency of the system and possibly damage the system. To avoid these adverse effects, plaintiff requested defendant to locate his home an additional several feet away from the plaintiff's lot line, the exact number being disputed. Plaintiff and defendant failed to reach an agreement on the location of defendant's home before defendant started construction. The Architectural Control Committee of the subdivision and the Planning Commission of the City of Muskego approved the defendant's plans for his home, including its location on the lot. Prah's appeal presents an issue of first impression: whether the owner of a solar-heated residence states a claim upon which relief can be granted when he asserts that his neighbor's proposed residence (which conforms to existing deed restrictions and local ordinances) interferes with his access to an unobstructed path for sunlight across defendant-neighbor's property.

Decision

For plaintiff-appellant Prah.

Reasoning

The common law doctrine of private nuisance limits a landowner's right to use his property in a way that injures the rights of others. Property owners' rights are relative, not absolute; the uses by one must not unreasonably impair the uses or enjoyment of the other.

Defendant asserts that his right to develop his property in accordance with statutes, ordinances, and private covenants, without regard for the effects of such development on plaintiff's access to sunlight, stems from three fundamental public policy considerations: (1) such rights are limited only by the potential for causing physical damage, (2) loss of sunlight for aesthetic or illumination value is relatively unimportant, and (3) land development should not be restricted.

The court found these policy considerations no longer to be binding, however, and in reaching its decision for the plaintiff, concluded as follows:

"Courts should not implement obsolete policies that have lost their vigor over the course of the years. The law of private nuisance is better suited to resolve landowners' disputes about property development in the 1980s than is a rigid rule which does not recognize a landowner's interest in access to sunlight."

Prah v. Maretti, 321 N.W.2d 182 (Wis. 1982).

Despite the outcome in the Prah case, local zoning ordinances offer a more likely solution to solar zoning problems. For highly developed areas, zoning regulations in the form of building restrictions offer no easy answers. Many structures already existing would be characterized as nonconforming uses, and no controls could be installed until new ones take their place.

Zoning offers greater promise for newly developing rural and suburban areas, however. Restrictive covenants can be useful as well.[12] Height limitations placed on houses and other buildings will assure neighboring property owners of uninterrupted, direct sunlight.

Federal Land Use—Surface Mining
There is no single comprehensive piece of federal legislation that controls land use. About one-third of the nation's land is federally owned, and it ranges from wilderness areas to multiple-use lands that may be leased for minerals, timber, and grazing. In addition to the federal anti-pollution laws discussed so far, tax laws, federally guaranteed loan programs, and agricultural subsidies influence the use of privately owned land that is within the jurisdiction of state and local zoning authorities.

The Surface Mining Control and Reclamation Act of 1977,[13] based on Congress' commerce power, regulates the use of privately owned land. In line with the Clean Air Act and Clean Water Act, the regulatory functions will be carried out by the states if permanent regulatory programs meeting minimum federal standards are enacted by state legislatures. Otherwise, the program will be administered by the Department of the Interior.

<small>Surface Mining Control and Reclamation Act.</small>

As a prerequisite for eligibility to administer its own regulatory program, each state must establish a mechanism for designating certain lands as unsuitable for mining. As for the land that is appropriate for development, mine operators are required to restore topsoil and revegetate after mining, and treat harmful minerals so that groundwater and surface water will not be contaminated.

Prime farmlands cannot be mined unless the operator has the technological capacity to restore the area to equivalent or higher levels of yield. Alluvial valley floors cannot be mined if the mining would damage farming in the valleys or the quantity or quality of waters that supply the valley floors.

Reclamation plans must be filed by the mine operator as part of the permit application, and a $10,000 performance bond must be posted as well. Where federal coal lies beneath privately owned land, the consent of the owner is necessary before operations can begin. There is no legal maximum that can be demanded by the surface owner for this privilege.

A citizen suit provision allows any person who is or may be adversely affected by some failure to comply with this Act to file suit against *the responsible regulatory body*. Finally, the Act created an abandoned mine reclamation fund to repair land from previous strip operations, and it established within the Department of the Interior the Office of Surface Mining Reclamation and Enforcement to administer the Act's provisions.

---

[12] In Colorado, a sun state, some lending institutions require easements as a condition of making a loan for a solar system.

[13] 30 U.S.C. secs. 1201–1328, 91 Stat. 447, Pub. L. 95–87 (1977).

Summary Statement

1. The National Environmental Policy Act (NEPA) established high goals of environmental protection to be achieved through vigorous decision-making procedures.
2. Environmental Impact Statements (EISs) guide proposals for legislation and other major federal actions that significantly affect the quality of the human environment.
3. NEPA created the Council on Environmental Quality (CEQ) as a policy advisor to the President, and by Executive Order the President organized the Environmental Protection Agency (EPA) to exercise certain important standard setting and enforcement functions.
4. The 1977 Clean Air Act amendments reaffirm EPA's high air quality standards and, if new state implementation plans (SIPs) are approved, gave until 1982 to meet these standards. If automobile-related pollutants create the problem, the deadline may be extended until 1987.
5. The 1977 Clean Water Act continues to focus chiefly on *point* sources of pollution. It requires the application of the *best conventional technology* (BCT) for most pollutants and the *best available technology economically achievable* (BAT) for toxic and nonconventional wastes. The National Pollutant Discharge Elimination System requires the installation of this technology before permits are granted to dischargers of conventional, toxic, or nonconventional effluents. Target date for the goal of "water clean enough for swimming and other recreational values" was moved to 1984 (with a likely extension for nonconventional pollutants through 1987). The goal of no effluent discharges into waters of the U.S. was still maintained for 1985.
6. EPA has been empowered by the 1976 Toxic Substances Control Act to control and stop the manufacture or use of chemicals that may present unreasonable risk of injury to health or the environment. Manufacturers may be required to test chemicals, and their reports to EPA are public information.
7. Solid waste management problems are the subject of the 1976 Resource Conservation and Recovery Act. It embodies economic, technical, and other incentives, but success depends upon full state cooperation. Hazardous wastes are given special treatment by the Act—they are literally tracked by a permit system from manufacture through disposal.
8. The 1972 Federal Environmental Pesticide Control Act—amending earlier legislation—controls registration, labeling, and application of pesticides. Its objective is to prevent unreasonable risk to human life and health and to the environment, while taking into account the social, environmental, and economic costs and benefits.
9. The Endangered Species Act as amended authorizes the Secretary of the Interior to protect certain plants, fish, and wildlife (including their habitat) from extinction. If federal projects jeopardize the life or habitat of endangered species, a seven-person cabinet-level panel must determine the outcome.
10. State and federal governments formulate land-use policies. Whether a state is proceeding on its U.S. Constitution Tenth Amendment reserved powers, or the federal government on its Article I legislative powers, a just compensation must be paid to the private landowner for property that is *taken* for a public purpose. If the private property is merely *regulated*, for example, through local zoning ordinances or federal strip-mining controls, the landowner is not entitled to compensation.

The following long, classic case is reproduced almost in its entirety because of its clear and authoritative analysis of the National Environmental Policy Act, *which makes environmental protection a part of the mandate of every federal agency and department.*

Thus, in the following case the Atomic Energy Commission (presently named the Nuclear Regulatory Commission) must concern itself with adverse environmental effects of its actions. Notice how the court determines that it has power to decide this case.

Calvert Cliffs' Coordinating Committee, Inc. v. AEC
449 F.2d 1109 (1971)

J. Skelly Wright, Circuit Judge. These cases are only the beginning of what promises to become a flood of new litigation—litigation seeking judicial assistance in protecting our natural environment. Several recently enacted statutes attest to the commitment of the Government to control, at long last, the destructive engine of material "progress." But it remains to be seen whether the promise of this legislation will become a reality. Therein lies the judicial role. . . .

Petitioners argue that rules recently adopted by the Atomic Energy Commission to govern consideration of environmental matters fail to satisfy the rigor demanded by NEPA. The Commission, on the other hand, contends that the vagueness of the NEPA mandate and delegation leaves much room for discretion and that the rules challenged by petitioners fall well within the broad scope of the Act. We find the policies embodied in NEPA to be a good deal clearer and more demanding than does the Commission. We conclude that the Commission's procedural rules do not comply with the congressional policy. Hence we remand these cases for further rule making. . . .

[Ed. note: Following this case the Atomic Energy Commission (now the Nuclear Regulatory Commission) amended its rules to require its hearing board to conduct an independent review of staff environmental recommendations along with its recommendations on economic and technical factors.]

The relevant portion of NEPA is Title I, consisting of five sections. Section 101 sets forth the Act's basic substantive policy: that the federal government "use all practicable means and measures" to protect environmental values. Congress did not establish environmental protection as an exclusive goal; rather, it desired a reordering of priorities, so that environmental costs and benefits will assume their proper place along with other considerations. In section 101(b), imposing an explicit duty on federal officials, the Act provides that "it is the continuing responsibility of the Federal Government to use all practicable means, consistent with other essential considerations of national policy," to avoid environmental degradation, preserve "historic, cultural, and natural" resources, and promote "the widest range of beneficial uses of the environment without . . . undesirable and unintended consequences."

Thus the general substantive policy of the Act is a flexible one. It leaves room for a responsible exercise of discretion and may not require particular substantive results in particular problematic instances. However, the Act also contains very important "procedural" provisions—provisions which are designed to see that all federal agencies do in fact exercise the substantive discretion given them. These provisions are not highly flexible. Indeed, they establish a strict standard of compliance.

NEPA, first of all, makes environmental protection a part of the mandate of every federal agency and department. [Emphasis added.] The Atomic Energy Commission, for example, had continually asserted, prior to NEPA, that it had no statutory authority to concern itself with the adverse environmental effects of its actions. Now, however, its hands are no longer tied. It is not only permitted, but compelled, to take environmental values into account. Perhaps the greatest importance of NEPA is to require the Atomic Energy Commission and other agencies to consider environmental issues just as they consider other matters within their mandates. This compulsion is most plainly stated in section 102. There, "Congress authorizes and directs that, to the fullest extent possible: (1) the policies, regulations, and public laws of the United States shall be interpreted and administered in accordance with the policies set forth in this Act. . . ." Congress also "authorizes and directs" that "(2) all agencies of the Federal Government shall" follow certain rigorous procedures in considering environmental values. . . . In order to include all possible environmental factors in the decisional equation, agencies must "identify and develop methods and procedures . . . which will insure that presently unquantified environmental amenities and values may be given appropriate consideration in decision making along with economic and technical considerations."

"Environmental amenities" will often be in conflict with "economic and technical considerations." To "consider" the former "along with" the latter must involve a balancing process. In some instances environmental costs may outweigh economic and technical benefits, and in other instances they may not. But NEPA mandates a rather finely tuned and "systematic" balancing analysis in each instance.

To ensure that the balancing analysis is carried out and given full effect, section 102(2)(c) requires that responsible officials of all agencies prepare a "detailed statement" covering the impact of particular actions on the environment, the environmental costs which might be avoided, and alternative measures which might alter the cost-benefit equation. The apparent purpose of the "detailed statement" is to aid in the agencies' own decision-making process and to advise other interested agencies and the public of the environmental consequences of planned federal action.

Of course, . . . all of these section 102 duties are qualified by the phrase "to the fullest extent possible." We must stress as forcefully as possible that this language does not provide an escape hatch for footdragging agencies; it does not make NEPA's procedural requirements somehow "discretionary." Congress did not intend the Act to be such a paper tiger. Indeed, the requirement of environmental consideration "to the fullest extent possible" sets a high standard for the agencies, a standard which must be rigorously enforced by the reviewing courts.

Unlike the substantive duties of section 101(b), which require agencies to "use all practical means consistent with other essential considerations," the procedural duties of section 102 must be fulfilled to the "fullest extent possible." . . .

Thus the section 102 duties are not inherently flexible. They must be complied with to the fullest extent, unless there is a clear conflict of statutory authority. Considerations of administrative difficulty, delay, or economic cost will not suffice to strip the section of its fundamental importance.

We conclude, then, that section 101 of NEPA mandates a particular sort of careful and informed decision-making process and creates judicially enforceable duties. The reviewing courts probably cannot reverse a substantive decision on its merits, under section 101, unless it is shown that the actual balance of costs and benefits that was struck was arbitrary or clearly given insufficient weight to environmental values. But if the decision was reached procedurally without individualized consideration and balancing of environmental factors—conducted fully and in good faith—it is the responsibility of the courts to reverse. As one District Court has said of section 102 requirements: "It is hard to imagine a clearer or stronger mandate to the Courts." . . .

Questions and Case Problems

1. Congress designed Environmental Impact Statements to give an "early alert" regarding the environmental consequences of certain federal actions. How is this early alert system implemented?

2. Among the purposes of the Clean Air Act of 1970, Congress established the following:

    To protect and enhance the quality of the Nation's air resources so as to promote the public health and welfare and the productive capacity of its population . . .

    Following EPA approval of State Implementation Plans that allowed industrial expansion in previously undeveloped and underdeveloped regions, the Sierra Club brought suit alleging that this section of the Clean Air Act had been violated. EPA argued that the plans it approved promoted industrial growth and protected against air pollution below the national standards. Result? [*Sierra Club v. Ruckelshaus,* 344 F.Supp. 253 (1972), aff'd 412 U.S. 541 (1973).]

3. Discuss the strategy established by Congress in the 1970 Clean Air Act. What is the relationship between the approach to stationary and mobile sources?

4. Discuss the approach Congress took to clean air areas and dirty air areas under the 1977 Clean Air Act Amendments.

5. New York City, defendant, enacted an ordinance requiring exhaust emission controls for licensed taxicabs. The plaintiffs, fifteen licensed taxicab companies, sought an injunction prohibiting enforcement of the ordinance and a declaratory judgment that it was null and void. The cab companies argued that the New York City ordinance both conflicted with the Clean Air Act and was pre-empted by it. Result? [*Allway Taxi, Inc. v. The City of New York,* 340 F.Supp. 1120 (S.D.N.Y. 1972) aff'd per curiam 468 F.2d 624 (1973).]

6. The Eden Roc Hotel, plaintiff, in Miami Beach, Florida, objected to a fourteen-story addition by a competitor, the Fontainebleau Hotel Corp., defendant, because it shaded portions of Eden Roc's pool and beach. Plaintiff petitioned the court for an injunction restraining the defendant's construction. Eden Roc based its suit on the doctrine of Ancient Lights, an English common law concept that the uninterrupted use of light through a window for twenty years or more gave the recipient an easement that the adjoining landowner cannot terminate. Result? [*Fontainebleau Hotel Corp. v. Forty-five Twenty-five, Inc.,* 114 S.2d 357 (Fla. 1959).]

7. Since the 1972 federal Water Pollution Control Act, the U.S. no longer pins its clean-up efforts exclusively on water quality standards. It requires effluent-control technology as well. What is the difference between these two approaches? Discuss.

8. The Toxic Substances Control Act may require manufacturers to test selected chemicals. What are the *criteria* that are used to determine those substances which must undergo the testing procedures mandated by the Act?

9. Compare the approach Congress took in establishing national uniform clean air standards with its approach in establishing noise standards under the Noise Control Act of 1972.

10. In the case of *Calvert Cliffs' Coordinating Committee, Inc. v. AEC,* 449 F.2d 1109 (1971),[14] the court stated that "NEPA mandates a rather finely tuned and 'systematic' balancing analysis. . . ." How does the Act ensure that this balancing analysis will be carried out?

---

[14] See pp. 747–48.

Ethics and Business Law in Part 9
Government Regulation of Business

Introduction

This end-of-Part discussion, like the others in this book, is designed to encourage students to begin forming personal beliefs about what is right or wrong conduct in business. The discussion here builds on the material in the first end-of-Part discussion on pages 58 to 69; you may find it helpful to review that.

This material has several goals. The "sampling of ethical issues" section immediately following is designed to help you see the range of ethical issues associated with this area of the law. The in-depth discussion is intended to provide you with a background for forming your own beliefs about a single very important ethical issue in business. The problems at the end of this Part are designed to build your skill in ethical analysis while exploring further the in-depth issue.

A Sampling of Ethical Issues in Government Regulation of Business

Antitrust law is designed in large part to reduce the power which businesses have over one another and over consumers. Most basically, it raises the issue of when, and to what extent, one may ethically exercise power over another. Managers have a great deal of power over their subordinates and they must often decide when, and to what extent, they are justified in exercising that power. Under what circumstances do you think you are justified in exercising power over those with whom you do business?

Administrative law raises interesting ethical issues. One is associated with the delegation of legislative powers. Legislatures seek to advance the will of those governed. When authority is delegated to an administrative agency, the agency is not subject to the same pressures as elected representatives. Also, their technical expertise tends to give them a certain degree of freedom to do what they judge is ethically right. Do you think an administrative agency is ever justified in, for example, ignoring the desires of the electorate and doing what it thinks is ethically right? Would you ever be ethically justified in ignoring the desires of your subordinates and doing what you think is ethically right? Would you ever be ethically justified in ignoring the desires of your superiors and doing what you think is ethically right?

Administrative hearings are generally conducted with different procedures from those used in court trials. One difference is that hearsay evidence is admissible in an administrative hearing and often inadmissible in trials. What procedures do you think lead to more ethical decisions, those which completely exclude hearsay evidence or those which allow it?

Labor law is one of the most ethically intense areas of business law. A fundamental ethical issue of this body of law is its adversarial nature. Labor law creates a structure which often causes employers and employees to perceive each other as in hostile, instead of in collaborative, ways. Other countries, such as Japan and Germany, have approached labor relations law in ways which are not as adversarial and which do not create as much conflict. But doing this sometimes deprives workers of the power to shape the nature of their working lives through the threat of strikes. And some employers would certainly take advantage of workers who were less powerful. Which style of relationship do you find most ethically appealing, one of respect based on fear of a strike, or one based on trust which could be easily betrayed?

Environmental law also raises interesting ethical issues of great concern to society. There is conflict between those who advocate preservation of natural conditions of land, water, and air in the environment and those who would delimit some of these conditions for their own self-interest. For example, a company's pollution of the water in a stream, river, or harbor is caused by the necessary discharge of the by-products of its manufacturing process. Society has attempted to balance these conflicting interests by limiting the freedom to choose how to produce so that the environment is not unduly harmed.

In-Depth Discussion of a Basic Issue: Market Power

Market Failures

In studying antitrust law, labor law, and environmental law you have been examining the way the legal system addresses problems in the operation of the marketplace, or what are sometimes called "market failures." In a sense, *antitrust law* is concerned with keeping either sellers or buyers from escaping the forces of the marketplace. In large part, *labor law* arises out of the economic reality that there are very many workers and, in some locations at least, few employers; therefore employers have a large amount of power over those whom they hire. *Environmental law* is concerned with the problem of avoiding costs by shifting them to others such as those who breathe the polluted air or use the contaminated rivers.

The law has been quite effective in dealing with these major problems of market failure. However, there are in business many opportunities to exploit other, unregulated, market failures to our own benefit. Because there are opportunities, we must make decisions about whether it is ethical for us to exploit them. In order to have mature views in this area, you need a refined understanding of market power. This concept is the key to sophisticated resolution of many of the ethical dilemmas in business.

Historical Views

Many important moralists have given substantial thought to the practices of businesses and the operations of markets.

Aristotle, Aquinas, and Luther. These persons all wrote about market power. In general, their major concern has been with "extortion" and "exploitation" of poor or powerless persons in the marketplace. For some time this concern was expressed in the condemnation of what was called "usury," the charging of interest on money loaned. This condemnation occurred before people realized that there was a *time value* associated with the possession of money—that one dollar today is worth more to almost everyone than one dollar twenty-five years from today. Because these moralists did not clearly perceive this time value concept, they viewed the charging of interest as a manifestation of market power in which the party with money to lend was able to "unjustly extort" interest from a desperate borrower. Careful reading of their works reveals that it was the exercise of market power that they condemned rather than simply the collection of interest.

Adam Smith's View. In his 1776 treatise on economics entitled *The Wealth of Nations,* Adam Smith originated the now well-known phrase "the invisible hand" to describe in summary fashion one moral characteristic of free markets. In his words:

> As every individual . . . endeavors as much as he can both to employ his capital in the support of domestic industry, and so to direct industry that its produce may be of greatest value; every individual necessarily labors to render the annual revenue of the society as great as he can. He generally, indeed, neither intends to promote the public interest, nor knows how much he is promoting it . . . he intends only his own gain, and he is in this, as in many other cases, led by an invisible hand to promote an end which was no part of his intention.

Smith's ideas can be stated more directly and in more modern language as follows: Market competition among individuals pursuing self-interest, yields a socially optimal allocation of society's scarce resources. The marketplace exists when independent parties, acting freely, buy and sell from one another. If you sold this book to another student, the transaction would be viewed as occurring in a marketplace—the one for used books.

Philosophic Goals and Markets

Persons with different philosophical perspectives have differing views of the role of marketplaces. However, it is reasonably clear that the marketplaces are primarily utilitarian in character. They are *means* to some end. While we may not all agree on what that end is, or ought to be, most people in this country agree that the marketplace achieves some ends that they find desirable. To a large extent, business persons define their moral character by the marketplace ends that they elect to emphasize.

The major philosophic goals or ends are the following:

1. *Personal pleasure:* markets allow us to get rich or spend our earnings to buy things which give us pleasure.
2. *Personal liberty:* markets are created by decisions made by large numbers of producers and consumers. Thus, no person or organization has very much power over anyone else.
3. *Social wealth:* markets allocate resources in ways which maximize the material well-being of society.
4. *Service:* markets are viewed by many religious persons as vehicles for satisfying the material needs of society.

Certainly egoists would embrace the view that markets ought to maximize personal pleasure. And religious persons would see services as the market's main legitimate purpose. Personal liberty and social wealth might be a desired goal for all four groups: egoists, utilitarians, Kantians and religious persons.

Market Imperfections

As we said in end-of-Part 1, when markets work perfectly, they often cause persons with differing philosophical perspectives to behave in the marketplace in about the same way. Thus, an egoist and a religious person might act the same way in a perfect market. On the other hand, when markets work imperfectly, they often force persons to elect one of the competing philosophical perspectives over the others. Accordingly, it is important that every business person know clearly what his or her personal philosophical perspective is and that he or she be able to determine when markets are operating imperfectly.

We have identified the following imperfections:

1. *Too few* sellers or too few buyers;
2. *Barriers to entry,* which keep either new buyers or new sellers from entering a particular market;
3. *Imperfect knowledge* by either a buyer or a seller;

4. *Externalities,* that is, costs such as pollution, which are not borne by the appropriate buyer or seller.

These imperfections can also be classified as those that create market power and those that create externalities. The first three imperfections cause one party in a marketplace transaction to have *market power.*

When Market Power Exists
Market power exists when someone operating in the marketplace has, because of imperfections in a particular market, more power than he or she would have in a perfectly functioning marketplace. Market power exists when one party—buyer or seller—has more influence over the terms of the transaction than the other party. An extreme example of market power can be easily seen in a situation in which there is a single firm selling a product that cures cancer. Even if the firm's cost of research, production, marketing and distribution were only $1.00 per unit, it *could* set a much higher price. If, however, there were ten firms selling this product, the competition among them would drive down the price. Thus, with only one firm its *market power* allows it to control the price, but with ten firms the *marketplace* determines price.

The Exercise of Market Power
An individual who achieves market power must decide whether or not to exercise it. If one views personal pleasure as the basic goal of the marketplace, then it is logical to use the market power to enhance your wealth and pleasure. Suppose, for example, that you owned the only electrical generator for sale in a small town affected by a power outage. This creates an imperfection because there is only one seller and many potential buyers. You might, if egoistic pleasure were your basic goal, auction off the generator to the highest cash bidder—perhaps the wealthiest person in town.

If your view of the market is that its basic function is the *reduction of power of people over each other,* and the associated increase in *individual liberty,* you might decline to auction the generator and perhaps allow the group to draw lots to determine how to use it.

If your view of the market is that its basic function is material *service to society,* you might logically decline to auction off the generator out of a sensitivity to the fact that the imperfection in this situation—one seller—prevents the market mechanism from maximizing service to society. You might, in trying to maximize service, make a *gift* of the generator, perhaps to a local hospital.

If you consider the market's greatest goal to be *maximization of social wealth,* you might again recognize the imperfections in the marketplace and *negotiate* a fair sale of the generator, instead of auctioning it, to the largest employer in the community so jobs would be preserved.

Solving Ethics Problems

Like the other end-of-Part discussions in this book, this one presents problems for you to consider. These problems have three goals. The first is to give you the opportunity to further explore the in-depth issue. The second goal is to give you experience in ethical reasoning about the law and about related management problems. The third goal is to let you see how thinking critically about the law can increase your ability to make ethical decisions. To facilitate this, the problems begin by asking you to analyze the law for its ethical content and then shift to looking at related problems in managerial ethics.

For a discussion of the ethical roles of markets and the law, and examples of the four styles of ethical reasoning—egoism, utilitarianism, Kant's philosophy, and religious ethics—read the business ethics material at the end of Part 1.

Problems

1. Recall the case of In re *Dean Milk Company* on page 708. There Dean Milk Co. was one of the larger milk sellers in the region and smaller dairies were often going out of business. Dean charged lower prices in some markets than in others. As a result, small dairies in an area where Dean's prices were low had a difficult time operating profitably. The FTC held that this conduct violated section 2(a) of the Clayton Act which prohibits price discrimination. What is the ethical goal of this statute? If there were no law against price discrimination, do you think it would be ethical to engage in the same conduct as Dean?

2. Suppose you owned the *only* gasoline station in a rural town. Since there is only one station, you have substantial market power. Assume that many residents would gladly pay an additional fifteen cents per gallon rather than drive the fifty miles to the next town. You know that such a price increase is perfectly legal. Would you raise your price as high as you possibly, and profitably, could, or would you decline to completely exploit your market power? What styles of reasoning support your decision?

3. Suppose you are the chief purchasing agent for a large aerospace firm. One of your responsibilities is arranging for the janitorial services for the firm's local offices. The firm currently doing the work is going out of business. Three other local firms do janitorial work. After receiving sealed bids from these firms, you have the opportunity to "whipsaw" the firms, playing one against the other in the bidding process. You could call one firm and disclose the amount of the lowest bid and ask if it would be willing to do the work for at least 10 percent less than that bid. If that firm says yes, you could call a second firm and ask if it will go even lower. This process can be continued in some situations until you have driven almost all of the profit (often much of the overhead) out of the supplying firms' bids. Will you accept the first bids or will you "whipsaw?" Why or why not?

4. Suppose you are the marketing manager of a profit-making firm that has discovered a way to collect whole blood, process it into plasma, and store it for long periods of time. As a result the firm always has on hand a large inventory of blood plasma. The market for plasma is usually very stable because the rate of consumption is—most of the time—relatively uniform across the country. Occasionally there is a major disaster, such as an earthquake or a hurricane, which dramatically increases the demand by hospitals for plasma. If, as marketing manager, you carefully price your product to reflect market conditions, charging one normal price and another much higher price during emergencies, you can substantially increase the profitability of the firm. Would you recommend to your firm that it use such pricing policies? Why or why not?

PART 10 Real Property

51. Real Property and Its Ownership
The many physical characteristics of real property, the forms of co-ownership, and the various ownership interests in land.

52. Transferring Ownership of Realty
The methods by which interests in land are acquired and transferred, the documents necessary to do this, how security interests in land are created, and the steps involved in the typical sales transaction.

53. Renting Realty
The various methods of renting real property, the items that should be covered in leases, and the nature of rental relationships between landlord and tenant.

Summary

The following three chapters discuss the law of real property. This law developed earlier than almost any other body of law discussed in this text. As a result, it sometimes reflects its age and the fact that it developed in a primarily agricultural society. As you read through the chapters, see if you can spot aspects of the law which reflect these ancient and rural roots.

Another feature of real property law is that it is enormously complex. Even so, there are a very large number of transactions handled each day in every area. The great complexity causes transfer costs to be fairly high. Thus, real estate brokers typically charge four to ten percent of the sale price for helping conclude transactions smoothly. As you read through the chapters, try to think of workable ways to simplify real property transactions.

Finally, when reading the chapters think about strategies and tactics you could adopt as a prospective seller, buyer, landlord, or tenant. If you master the material in these chapters, and devise common-sense strategies, you can often dramatically improve your legal position in real estate transactions.

In summary, then, you should attempt to spot the old agricultural aspects of the law, look for ways to simplify it, and devise sensible strategies for handling these transactions which you will probably encounter many times in your life.

Business ethics as it relates to the text material in this Part is considered at the end of the Part.

51 Real Property and Its Ownership

After you have read this chapter, you should be able to:
1. Identify the physical parts of real property and distinguish them from personal property.
2. Understand the legal relationship between persons who co-own real estate.
3. Identify the powers over realty possessed by owners.
4. Identify the rights which the government may take from owners of real estate.
5. Identify the rights which the owner may give to another without actually transferring ownership.

Introduction

Problems frequently arise where the law must decide what is and what is not real property. For example, if a student leases certain "real property," has he also leased the stove and refrigerator on the premises? And if someone sells or wills "real property," exactly what passes by the sale or will? If a mother wills the family home to her daughter, will the daughter become the owner of the workbench in the garage when the mother dies?

Once we know what real property is, then we can examine the ways that more than one person can own the same **realty**. Of course, that introduces problems concerning the relationships among the owners. For example, if a husband and wife own realty together, should either be allowed to sell his or her interest without the other spouse's consent?

realty
real property

Exactly what powers should the law give to owners? Should they be allowed to cause ownership to stay forever in their family? And can an owner sell some of the ownership rights and keep the others?

How much power should be given to the government to restrict an owner's use of his or her property? If the government does restrict the use, should the owner be compensated for any loss in value of the property?

As you read through this material on real property and its ownership, ask yourself whether the rules of law seem fair and just for *all* the parties. If you disagree with the law, can you propose an alternative that will work better?

Physical Characteristics of Real Property and Related Rights

Surface Rights
The basic physical element of realty is land. The buyer of real property usually purchases the *surface rights* or the right to occupy the surface of a piece of land.

Surface rights.

Right to Air Space
The air space above the surface of the land is also part of the realty. Ownership of that space is called the *right to air space*. The ownership power, except for the right to exclude aircraft overflight,[1] extends to the upper atmosphere. Therefore, if the branch of a neighbor's tree grew into your air space, you would have the right to force its removal.

Right to air space.

Mineral Rights
In General. In addition to the surface area and the air space, realty also includes the earth beneath the surface. The right to dig or mine that earth is called a *mineral right*. In theory, ownership of mineral rights extends down from the land surface to the center of the earth. In practice, however, no one has been able to extract minerals from a depth of more than five miles. Ownership powers over minerals depend in part upon whether the minerals are *solid* or *fluid*.

Mineral rights.

Solid Minerals. Ownership of solid minerals such as coal, iron ore, copper ore, or uranium usually extends downward from the perimeter of the surface right. The owner of the mineral right has the power to remove any mineral located within that area.

Fluid Minerals. Ownership of minerals such as oil, a liquid, natural gas, a vapor, also usually extends downward from the surface area. However, the *doctrine of capture* grants ownership of these fluid minerals to the party who extracts (or *captures*) them. Thus, if a person drilled an oil well on a ¼ acre lot and began pumping from a pool of oil which extended beneath a 25 acre area, all the oil could be removed under the doctrine of capture. This is so even though the oil was originally another's property and, because of the pumping, it flowed from one location to another. Note that the well shaft itself may not extend into realty owned by other persons.

---

[1] See *United States v. Causby*, 328 U.S. 256 (1946).

Right to Lateral and Subjacent Support

Right to lateral and subjacent support.

This right means that the physical support for the land surface cannot be removed by a neighbor or the owner of the mineral right.[2] Thus, one could not excavate along the property line, thereby causing a neighbor's soil to slide into the trench. Similarly, the owner of the mineral right would be liable (to the owner of the surface right) if the support timbers for a coal mine were removed, allowing the tunnel system to cave in, causing deep depressions on the surface.

Water Rights

Water rights.

In General. Water on the surface or under the ground is a part of the realty. Control of that water is called a *water right*. In the United States there are two systems for regulating the exercise of water rights. The major system is the *riparian rights system*. A minority of states, primarily western, use the *prior appropriation system*.

riparian
relating to land abutting a body of water

Riparian Rights. This system allows those who own land *abutting* a body of water to make use of it. Thus, ownership of the adjoining land (or the land beneath the water) carries with it the right to use the water.

The riparian system limits the amount of water which the landowner may use with one of two theories. The *natural flow theory* allows use of the water on the riparian land so long as the natural condition of the stream, river or lake is maintained. In contrast, the *reasonable use theory* allows the riparian owner to use any amount of water so long as it does not interfere with uses being made by other riparian owners.

Prior Appropriation Rights. This system does not connect the right to use the water with the adjoining land. Rather, it grants the first party to use the water (for a beneficial purpose) priority in subsequent years over other potential users. The extent of the initial beneficial use determines the amount of water which may be used in later years.

navigable water
a body of water which can support commerce between states

Water Subject to Private Water Rights. Both systems of water rights regulate the use of water in *non-navigable* bodies. If a body of water is **navigable,** it is owned by the state or federal government and landowners may not use the water without the state's consent. A body of water is navigable if it can support commerce between states.

Real and Personal Property Distinguished

The ability to distinguish between real and personal property is critical to an understanding of real estate transactions.

real property (realty)
land and immovable things attached to land, along with interests and rights in the land

In General. The usual test is that **real property** is land and immovable things attached to the land. In contrast, **personal property** is a movable thing.

Sometimes real and personal property are very closely connected such as a stove (perhaps personal) and a house (real). In these situations the law uses finer tests than the general test of mobility. These are the tests of *attachment, intention,* and *annexation* which were discussed in chapter 14, Personal Property.[3]

personal property (personalty)
a movable thing, along with interests and rights in the thing

Attachment or Annexation. In some cases the permanency of the attachment of a thing to realty will determine whether it is real or personal.

Thus, crops are sometimes part of the realty and sometimes personal property. When a crop is frequently harvested, as is corn, then it is treated as personal property even while in the ground, because it is not *permanently* attached to the land. On the other hand, if the crops are *infrequently harvested,* such as Christmas trees, they are a part of the realty until severed from the ground. Avocado trees, grape vines, and rose bushes would be real property. Avocados, grapes, and roses raised by a *florist* would be personal property.

---

[2] *Empire Star Mines Co., Limited v. Butler,* 145 P.2d 49 (Cal. 1944).

[3] See above, p. 206 et seq.

Structures or buildings are part of the real property if they are *permanently* attached to the land. Thus, office buildings and college classrooms are part of the realty. However, a house trailer sitting on its wheels is usually considered personal property. Mobile homes on *rented* foundations are not *permanently* attached to the land and are also **personalty.** A small garden shed resting on top of the ground would be personalty. If the wheels of the house trailer were removed and it were set on a permanent foundation, it would be realty. If the garden shed were bolted to a cement pad, it would be realty.

Personal property like stoves and dishwashers become a part of the realty if they are permanently attached. In most cases a free-standing stove is personalty, but a built-in stove is realty. Personal property which becomes realty by permanent attachment, but still can be used as collateral for a security interest, is called a **fixture.**

Intention. Sometimes parties reach agreements about how property is to be classified. For example, a landlord and a tenant might agree that the dishwasher installed by the tenant could be removed at the end of the lease period. This would be an indication of an *intention* to treat the property as personal. Without this display of intention, the dishwasher would, if permanently attached, become realty and, therefore, the property of the landlord at the end of the lease.

The fixtures attached by business tenants are called **trade fixtures.** Unlike other fixtures, trade fixtures are treated as *personalty* because they are usually *not intended* to be permanent. Thus, if a baker permanently attached ovens to a *rented* bakery shop, they would still be treated as personalty because the landlord and tenant probably *intended* that they should be removed at the end of the lease period.

Adaptation. This test, will cause certain items to be classed as realty because they are *truly essential* to the functioning of realty. Thus, a toilet in a residence is usually attached with about the same degree of permanency as a free-standing stove (personalty). But since the toilet is more essential to the functioning of the residence, it is annexed to it and treated as realty. Similarly, the key to the front door is treated as real property in some states under the doctrine of annexation!

The following case illustrates the application of these concepts.

personalty
personal property

fixture
a chattel which, under real estate law, has become permanently attached to realty and thus ceases to be a chattel and becomes part of the realty; it still can be used as collateral for a **security interest**[4]

security interest
"an interest in personal property or fixtures which secures payment or performance of an obligation" UCC 1-201(37)

trade fixture
a chattel attached to leased realty by a business tenant; it is usually treated as personal property

Facts
Michigan National Bank, Lansing, installed night depository equipment, drive-up window equipment, vault doors and remote transaction units in 6 of its branches. The City of Lansing sought to increase the bank's real estate taxation because of these improvements. The bank claims these improvements are personal property, and thus not subject to the City's tax on real estate.

Decision
The items are real property subject to the City's tax.

Reasoning
The test to be applied in order to ascertain whether or not an item is a fixture emphasizes three factors:

1. Annexation to the realty, either actual or constructive;
2. Adaptation or application to the use or purpose of that part of the realty to which it is connected or appropriated; and
3. Intention to make the article a permanent accession to the realty.

Applying these factors to the present case necessitates the conclusion that the items in question are fixtures. All four items are physically annexed to the realty. The night depository equipment, drive-up window equipment and the vault doors are all cemented into place. Once installed, they are integrated with and become part of the wall in which they are mounted. The remote transaction units are also physically integrated with the land and the buildings. Such a unit consists of a roof-type canopy supported by pillars which extends from the building wall or roof over the customer unit.

---

[4] For security interests in secured transactions, see pp. 441, 454.

Figure 51.1 Characteristics of Co-ownership

Type of Co-ownership	Legal Characteristics					
	Right to occupy all the realty	Ownership interests must be equal	Consent required from co-owners for sale of interest	*All* interest passes to co-owners on death	Interest willable, but if not willed passes to co-owners on death	Only available to married couples
Tenants in common	✓					
Joint tenants	✓	✓		✓		
Tenants by entirety	✓	✓	✓	✓		✓
Community property	✓	✓	✓		✓	✓

The customer unit is mounted with steel bolts to a specially constructed concrete island. A pneumatic tube system runs either up into the canopy or down into the ground and then into the building.

Furthermore, each item is adapted to the use of the realty. In fact, not only is the present use of these buildings dependent on the presence of these items, none of these items can be used unless they are affixed to a building or land.

Taken together, these factors establish the petitioner's intent to permanently affix these items to the realty.

Michigan National Bank, Lansing v. City of Lansing, 293 N.W.2d 626 (Mich. 1980).

Co-ownership

Severalty and Co-ownership

When real estate is owned by one person alone, he or she is said to own the realty in *severalty.* Co-ownership exists when realty is owned by more than one person. Thus, two persons together may buy a farm and become co-owners of the property.

There are several types of co-ownership.[5] The major types of co-ownership are tenancy in common, joint tenancy, tenancy by entirety, and community property. These names are labels defining four or five characteristics of the relationships among co-owners. The characteristics generally involved are the potential number of co-owners, the possible percentage of ownership, co-owners' rights to sell their portions of ownership, and the distribution of a co-owner's interest in the realty on the co-owner's death. In general, the use of such words as "tenancy in common" in a deed or a lease is sufficient to bind the co-owners to all of the characteristics of that particular form of co-ownership.

All methods of co-ownership have a common characteristic: it is that co-owners all have equal rights to occupy all the property. Thus, one co-owner may not exclude any other co-owner from any portion of their co-owned property. (See figure 51.1.)

In **tenancy in common,** the interest of the co-owner passes on his or her death to the decedent's **heirs** or devisees (the persons named in the decedent's will to receive real property). Any number may co-own as tenants in common. They may have unequal percentage ownerships. For example, one may own 99 percent while the other co-owner owns 1 percent. Each of these co-owners may sell his or her interest without the other's consent unless there is a contract provision to the contrary.

tenancy in common
a form of ownership of property by more than one person without survivorship

heirs
persons who, by statute, are entitled to property not disposed of by a decedent's will

---

[5] For a full discussion of these types, see pp. 212–14.

In **joint tenancy,** on the death of a co-owner, the decedent's interest passes to, and is equally divided among, the remaining joint tenants. This is called the **right of survivorship.** Any number may own as joint tenants, but each must have an equal interest. Thus, if there are four joint tenants, each must own 25 percent. Each joint tenancy owner may sell his or her interest without the consent of the other co-owners, unless there is a contract provision to the contrary.

Tenancy by entirety is a form of co-ownership only for married couples. This method of co-ownership has all the characteristics of joint tenancy—including survivorship—except that a party may *not* sell his or her interest without the consent of the spouse. Further, a divorce or separation usually transforms tenancy by entirety into tenancy in common.

Both joint tenancy and tenancy by entirety must be created with special language because judges fear that these names of co-ownership do not adequately communicate the nature of the relationship among the co-owners. The following case illustrates this idea.

joint tenancy
a form of ownership of property by more than one person with the right of survivorship

right of survivorship
a relationship among co-owners where death of one owner causes the decedent's interest to be transferred to the remaining owners

tenancy by entirety
a form of co-ownership between husband and wife with the right of survivorship

Facts
Fred and Patricia Gilbert were husband and wife living in Alaska. They bought a parcel of land and received a warranty deed which described them as "Fred T. Gilbert and Patricia Gilbert, husband and wife . . . grantees." Patricia then died without a will. Later Fred sold the land to Carver. After the sale Mark, the son of Fred and Patricia filed suit against Carver to recover a portion of the land as an inheritance from his mother. Mark claimed his parents owned the land as tenants in common, and Carver argued that they owned it as tenants by entirety.

Decision
Tenancy in common existed, so Mark prevails.

Reasoning
We . . . favor the view that tenancy by the entirety is but a species of joint tenancy, their incidents being identical.

This being the case, the statutory presumption favorable to tenancy in common "unless it is expressly declared" in the conveyance that the grantees shall take as joint tenants, must be taken to apply to tenants by the entirety. So, to overcome the presumption that a man and woman named as grantees in a conveyance and described therein as "husband and wife" shall take as tenants in common, the conveyance must declare that they shall take as tenants by the entirety with right of survivorship.

Carver v. Gilbert, 387 P.2d 928 (Alaska 1963).

Some states recognize **community property**[6] as a substitute for tenancy by entirety. Again, this method of co-ownership is only for married couples. In these states, property acquired during marriage is generally presumed to be community property. However, property owned by one spouse before marriage, or received during the marriage by gift or inheritance, is presumed to be that person's *separate property.* As such, it is not community property. In many states, survivorship for community property is about the same as survivorship under tenancy by entirety.

community property
a form of ownership by husband and wife of property acquired by their efforts during their marriage

Nature of Ownership

Ownership of realty is usually acquired by purchase, gift, or inheritance. But everyone does not receive the same powers of ownership. The powers of ownership are defined by the **estate** in land which the new owner receives. Each estate is composed of a certain bundle of ownership rights. The words used in the deed, will, lease, or other instrument transferring ownership determine which estate the new owner receives. The party who gives up ownership powers is called the **grantor.** The party who receives ownership powers is called the **grantee.** A grantor can transfer only those ownership powers which the grantor owns.

One parcel of land usually supports only a single estate. For example, most owner-occupied homes involve just one estate. Occasionally, however, two or more estates exist

estate
(in realty) a bundle of ownership rights in, or powers over, realty

grant
(in realty) a conveyance by deed

grantor
the person who has made a grant

grantee
the person to whom a grant has been made

---

[6] For a further discussion of community property, see pp. 213–14. The "sharing" concept in community property law is now embodied in the new Uniform Marital Property Act (UMPA) of 1983, which is a community property Act being presently considered by at least 11 state legislatures.

Chapter 51: Real Property and Its Ownership

in the same parcel. Thus, both the landlord and the tenant own estates in the rented apartment. The tenant's ownership rights include the right to occupy the property. The landlord's ownership rights include the powers to collect the rent and regain possession at the end of the lease.

When more than one estate with more than one owner exists in a single parcel, these owners do not co-own, for example, as in tenancy in common. Rather, each owns a *separate* estate with *separate* powers of ownership. Co-owners own *together* a single estate. The following paragraphs discuss the powers of ownership of the major estates in land.

Fee Simple Absolute

fee simple absolute
the greatest bundle of ownership rights in and powers over realty

Fee simple absolute is the estate with *all* the ownership rights. The owner of this estate exercises all the power allowed by law. If this estate is present, there can be no other estate in the same land. Most buyers of homes and farms and commercial property purchase the fee simple absolute estate.

Conditional Estates

conditional estate
an estate where ownership is dependent upon some act or event

Conditional estates make the ownership conditional on some act or event. For example, ownership may exist only "so long as no alcoholic beverages are served on the premises." If scotch were served, ownership would shift from the owner of the conditional estate to the one who conditionally sold the property.

Whenever there is a conditional estate there must also be another corresponding estate. This second estate is made up of the ownership power retained by the grantor of the conditional estate. The retained power permits the grantor to receive back all the ownership rights held by the owner of the conditional estate if the condition is violated. The grantor would then have a fee simple absolute because he or she would be the owner of the only estate in the property.

Life Estates

life estate
an estate that lasts only for the length of a particular person's life

A **life estate** is ownership only for the length of a life. This owner exercises all the ownership powers except the right to permanently dispose of the property. The length of the ownership period is generally measured by the life of the holder of the life estate. For example, a husband might convey "to my wife Julia, for life." Occasionally the period is measured by the life of someone else.

When the life ends, the possessory rights return to the original grantor of the life estate or to another party designated by that grantor. Fee simple absolute, conditional estates, and life estates are called *freehold estates.*

Nonfreehold Estates

tenancy
a form of nonfreehold ownership in realty

Nonfreehold estates, called **tenancies,** involve ownership for a limited period of time. *Tenants* own nonfreehold estates. The length of ownership is specified in a lease, or indicated by the payment period, or is only for so long as the landlord desires. These estates are discussed in detail in chapter 53, Renting Realty.

Future interests.

Future Interests

reversion
a future interest which will, or may, be returned to the grantor. In contrast, a remainder goes to one other than the grantor

remainder
that remaining part of an estate in land which, on the termination of a preceding estate, passes to someone other than the grantor

Future interests are estates that usually give possession of the realty when a life or a conditional estate terminates. If the right of possession returns to the one who originally granted the life or conditional estate, the future interest is usually called a **reversion.** If the right of possession goes to another person, it is sometimes called a **remainder.** Thus, if a hunting guide were to convey his mountain cabin "to my brother Albonzo for life, and then to his son Fredrico," the son would, on his father's death, receive a remainder. If the guide conveyed simply "to my brother Albonzo for life," the law would probably conclude that the guide intended to regain ownership on Albonzo's death. The guide would receive a reversion.

Others' Rights in the Owner's Land

Liens
A **lien** is a legal right in another's property as security for the performance of an obligation. In a way it is a claim against the financial value of an estate in land. A "mortgage" is a lien; so is a "trust deed."[7] These are called *voluntary liens;* the owner of the realty consents to (or volunteers) the lien, usually because he or she receives money in return for granting the lien. These voluntary liens are discussed in more detail in chapter 52, Transferring Ownership of Realty.

Involuntary liens arise without the consent of the owner. For example, if an owner does not pay the property taxes when due, they often automatically become a lien against the property. This is called a *tax lien.* If the tax lien is not paid, the taxing authority can cause the property to be sold to pay the debt. This is called *foreclosure* and is discussed in more detail in chapter 52, Transferring Ownership of Realty.

Mechanics' liens are another example of involuntary liens. A mechanic is someone who supplies labor or material which is used to improve real property. A carpenter can be a mechanic; so can a plumber, a lumber yard, or the college student who installs lawn sprinklers. If mechanics who improve the realty are not paid, they can file with the county recorder or county clerk a mechanic's lien against the property. Usually the lien must be filed within a certain time period after the work is done, such as 60 or 90 days. If the lien is filed within the required time period, but it is not paid off, the mechanic can file suit, prove his or her claim, and cause the property to be foreclosed (i.e., sold) to pay the debt. The main feature of the mechanic's lien is that it is effective as of the date when the *work was done,* not when the lien was filed, or when the lawsuit was won. Thus, in foreclosure, the mechanic will generally have his or her lien paid *before* any other lien which arose *after* the work was done.

lien
a legal right in another's property as security for the performance of an obligation

Licenses
When someone owns a *possessory* estate in land, whether in severalty or as a co-owner, he or she controls all the ownership rights associated with that particular estate. Frequently the owner will give some right in the land to another. For example, a theatre owner may grant someone the privilege (right) to sit through one showing of a film. This kind of temporary, oral right to come upon the land of another is called a **license.** A license is a temporary, revocable right (privilege) to some limited use of another's land. It is personal, nontransferable, not inheritable, and not an estate in land. Stores grant implied licenses to their customers to enter the store to shop for goods. Dinner guests are on the host's property by right of a license.

Generally oral licenses are *revocable.* Thus, the theatre patron or the dinner guest would become *trespassers* if they failed to leave immediately when asked. The theatre patron may be entitled to a refund of money, but the partron cannot legally sit through the show when asked to leave. In many places trespass is a criminal offense and the police will assist in removing the trespasser. Usually an oral license is revoked automatically when the one who granted it sells the land.

license
(real property) a temporary, revocable right (privilege) to some limited use of another's land

Easements
Easements are usually *irrevocable* rights to some limited use of another's land. In contrast with licenses, easements are generally given for substantial periods of time, e.g., five or fifty years or forever. To comply with the statute of frauds, they should be in writing. Easements may be granted which allow another to drive across the owner's land, bury a sewer pipe, hang power lines over the land, or make any other use which does not constitute exclusive possession. Easements may be *appurtenant* or *in gross.*

easement
an irrevocable right to the limited use of another's land

---
[7] See p. 777.

Figure 51.2 Easement Appurtenant for the Benefit of Property A

Property A is the dominant tenement, while property B is the servient tenement. A is benefited because the easement makes that land more accessible. Property B is burdened because someone other than the owner of B has a right to the use of the property.

Easements Appurtenant. When easements are given to neighboring landowners and the easement *benefits* the neighbor's land, then it is called an *easement appurtenant*. Appurtenant means attached to the land. Thus an easement to drive farm equipment across another's land in order to farm an otherwise inaccessible parcel would be an easement appurtenant. (See figure 51.2.)

The land of the one who grants the appurtenant easement is called the **servient tenement.** That land is in a sense the servant of the benefited land. The servient tenement is burdened with the easement. The land benefited is named the **dominant tenement.**

Easements for access roads or water ditches are easements appurtenant. These easements are transferred with the dominant tenement. However, the servient tenement is bound after its transfer only if the buyer of the servient tenement had notice of the easement prior to the purchase. Notice can come from a recorded document or from physical signs, such as a road rut.

The following case illustrates the issue of transferability of rights to the use of the land of another.

servient tenement
property in which someone has an easement appurtenant

dominant tenement
property which is benefited by an easement appurtenant in nearby land

Facts
In 1962 Offutt, defendant, sold a house to the Wynns. The house adjoined an apartment building owned by Offutt. In the apartment building was a swimming pool. In order to induce the Wynns to purchase the home Offutt agreed in the contract of sale that "use of the apartment swimming pool to be available to purchaser and his family." No mention of the pool was made in Wynn's deed. In 1969 the Wynns sold the house to the Bunns and informed them that they had the right to use the pool. When the Bunns sought to use the pool they were denied access. Accordingly they sued Offutt for the right to use the pool.

Decision
Judgment for defendant. The Bunns did not have the right to use the pool.

Reasoning
The use of the pool was personal in nature and was not essential to the beneficial enjoyment of the Bunns' property and thus it was not transferred with the land to the Bunns.

Bunn v. Offutt, 222 S.E.2d 522 (Va. 1976).

Easements in Gross. Easements which do not benefit neighboring land, like easements for access given to a nonneighbor, or for telegraph lines and poles, are called *easements in gross*. Easements in gross pass to the buyer when the burdened property is sold. However, the person benefited generally cannot transfer his or her rights.

There are two other important types of easements called *easements by prescription* and *easements by implication*. These easements are discussed in chapter 52, Transferring Ownership of Realty.

Zoning ordinances.

ordinance
municipal legislation

Zoning Ordinances
The owner's use of his realty can also be restricted by zoning ordinances. An **ordinance** is a municipal law or legislation. Zoning ordinances may be adopted by cities or counties to regulate the location of residential, business, and industrial districts. The purpose of zoning is to ensure fair use and orderly development of land within the community.

The legal power to enact zoning ordinances comes from the Constitution of the United States, which recognizes the **police power** of the separate states. Generally the states cannot use police power except to promote the health, safety, morals, and general welfare of the community. State legislatures usually pass statutes which permit the cities and counties to enact the zoning ordinances.

The zoning power is very broad. Courts generally support the right of cities and counties to enforce community zoning goals at the expense of individual landowners. For example, a commercial area could be rezoned residential. If the zoning reduced the value of the owner's land, the owner would bear the loss and could not recover for the financial injury from the local government.

On the other hand, zoning cannot be used unreasonably to eliminate an *existing use*. Thus, a zoning ordinance restricting use of an area to residential could not be used to eliminate an already existing cemetery.[8] The cemetery in a residential zone is called a *non-conforming use*. If the city wished to eliminate the cemetery, it must go through **condemnation** procedures, which permit the city to take title to the property by paying the owners the reasonable value of the property. Recently, however, some states have begun to allow reasonable zoning ordinances which eliminate existing uses. Thus, an ordinance requiring the elimination of billboard signs within five years would be enforceable in some states.

The following case describes the law that applies to condemnations. The reader is asked to think about when the government should be required to compensate private parties when it takes from them some of their property.

police power
the power of a state or federal government to legislate reasonably for the general public welfare

condemnation
forcing a property owner to transfer property to a government in exchange for just compensation

Facts
This case presents the question whether a minor but permanent physical occupation of an owner's property authorized by government constitutes a "taking" of property for which just compensation is due under the Fifth and Fourteenth Amendments of the Federal Constitution. New York law provides that a landlord must permit a cable television company to install its cable facilities upon his property. . . . In this case, the cable installation occupied portions of appellant's roof and the side of her building. The New York Court of Appeals ruled that this appropriation does not amount to a taking.

Decision
Because we conclude that such a physical occupation of property is a taking, we reverse. . . . We conclude that a permanent physical occupation authorized by government is a taking without regard to the public interests that it may serve. . . .

Reasoning
We affirm the traditional rule that a permanent physical occupation of property is a taking. In such a case, the property owner entertains an historically-rooted expectation of compensation, and the character of the invasion is qualitatively more intrusive than perhaps any other category of property regulation. We do not, however, question the equally substantial authority upholding a State's broad power to impose appropriate restrictions upon an owner's *use* of his property.

The judgment of the New York Court of Appeals is reversed and the case is remanded for further proceedings not inconsistent with this opinion.

Loretto v. Teleprompter Manhattan CATV Corp., et al., 458 U.S. 419 (1982).

Spot zoning is the treatment of a single property in a manner inconsistent with the treatment of similar properties in the area. It is usually prohibited.[9] Further, zoning will not be enforceable if it exceeds the police power of the state. This occurs when the ordinance is clearly arbitrary, unreasonable, and without substantial relation to the public health, safety, morals, and general welfare.

---

[8] See *Lockard v. City of Los Angeles*, 202 P.2d 38 (Cal. 1949).

[9] *Smith v. County of Washington*, 406 P.2d 545 (Or. 1965).

Restrictive Covenants

Restrictive covenants.

covenant
a promise as a part of a contract

Even when there are no zoning restrictions, the owner may still be prohibited from certain uses. This occurs when a former owner created a restrictive **covenant** or when the nature of the neighborhood creates an *equitable servitude*. A restrictive covenant is a promise usually made by the buyer to the seller. It is often written in the deed or contract for sale or other recordable document. Usually the promise limits the use of the land in some way. For example, the buyer may contract with the seller, promising not to graze sheep on the land. This buyer is almost always bound by the restrictive covenant.

If the buyer who gave the covenant resells, the new owner is bound only if the covenant is the kind that **runs with the land.**

covenant running with the land
the promise of an owner of land which binds future owners of the same land

Note that sellers can extract the same promise from buyers by a restrictive covenant, or by transferring a conditional estate, or by separate contract. If the *restrictive covenant* is broken, the owner may be required to pay damages or may be enjoined from future breaches. In contrast, if the *condition of conveyance* is violated, the violator loses his or her ownership.

Equitable servitudes may arise even when there is no recorded covenant. The general building plan or scheme of development in the area may give notice to a purchaser that his or her use of the property must conform with the general use. When this occurs, the purchaser is said to be bound by an equitable servitude.

Possessor's Tort Duties

Possessor's tort duties.

A person who owns a possessory interest in land, called "possessor," may owe certain tort duties to other persons who come on the land. The extent of the duties depends upon whether the persons who come on the land are trespassers, licensees, or invitees.

Trespasser. A *trespasser* is a person who is on the land without any right to be there. Thus, when a neighbor walks upon your land without your consent, the neighbor is a trespasser. Generally, a trespasser takes the property as the trespasser finds it. The possessor does not have any duty to the trespasser to keep the land in a reasonably safe condition. However, the possessor cannot intentionally cause harm to the trespasser. Further, if the possessor knows that the trespasser is on the land, or that persons constantly trespass on the land, then various tort duties are imposed upon the possessor with respect to the condition of the land. An **attractive nuisance** *attracts* children to **trespass** and broadens the possessor's responsibility.

attractive nuisance
a dangerous and attractive condition of realty which may lure children into trespassing

trespass
(verb) to wrongfully interfere with another's possession of land or chattels

Licensee. A *licensee* is a person whom the possessor of land has permitted to be on that land. A social guest is an example. A licensee takes the premises for what they appear to be, and therefore the possessor has the duty to disclose to the licensee nonobvious dangers on the land known to the possessor and which the licensee would not be likely to discover.

Invitee. An *invitee* is a person who is either a *public invitee*—that is, a member of the public invited to enter or remain on the land by its possessor for a public purpose—or a *business visitor*—one who is invited by the possessor to enter or remain on the land for the purpose of doing business with the possessor. A person becomes a public invitee when he or she is permitted to go upon the land of another for a public meeting. When a retail store invites prospective customers to enter the store and consider making purchases, the customers become business visitors. Thus, a social guest is not an invitee because neither of the two purposes (public or business) is present. The possessor of land has the duty to keep the premises in a reasonably safe condition and to warn invitees of dangers on the land of which the possessor should, on reasonable examination, be aware and which are not reasonably discoverable by the invitee.

Summary Statement

1. The physical elements of real property include surface rights, air rights, mineral rights, and water rights.
2. Personal property becomes realty when that is what is intended, or when it is permanently attached to the realty, or when it is adapted to the realty. It is then a fixture. Trade fixtures, however, are usually personal property. Crops are classified as real or personal property according to their permanence in the ground.
3. Co-ownership can take the form of tenancy in common, joint tenancy, tenancy by entirety, or community property. All but tenancy in common have some right of survivorship.
4. The rights and powers of ownership are determined by the estate in land received by the purchaser. Fee simple absolute is the most common and greatest estate. Other major estates are conditional estates, life estates, nonfreehold estates, and future interests.
5. A license is a temporary, revocable right (privilege) to some limited use of another's land. Easements are rights to some use of another's land which cannot be revoked by the possessor. Easements may be appurtenant or in gross.
6. Zoning is an exercise of police power. Spot zoning, attempts to eliminate current uses, and arbitrary and unreasonable zoning are generally unenforceable.
7. Only those restrictive covenants which run with the land bind later purchasers.
8. Possessors of land owe tort duties to trespassers, greater duties to licensees and invitees.

The following older but well explained case confronts the problems associated with covenants which run with the land. The case is intended to illustrate the way a court will scrutinize the words creating the covenant. The reader is asked to think about whether or not prior owners should be allowed to control current use of realty.

Parrish v. Richards
336 P.2d 122 (Utah 1959)

McDonough, J. This is an action to enjoin maintenance of a tennis court and fence allegedly built in violation of a real property restrictive covenant.

The parties are contiguous owners of real property. . . . Defendants' residence is located between those of plaintiffs, Parrish and Peterson. Prior to the acquisition by any of the parties of any of the tracts of land here involved, there had been placed upon and against such lands certain restrictive covenants recorded in the office of the County Recorder of Salt Lake County, Utah. The covenant here involved reads as follows:

Use of Land: Each lot is hereby designated as a residential lot, and none of said lots shall be improved, used or occupied for other than private residence purposes, and no flat or apartment house . . . shall be erected thereon, *and no structure shall be erected* . . . other than a one-, two-, or three-car garage, and one single family residence, not to exceed one story in height. . . . [Emphasis added.]

Prior to August 1, 1955 defendants leveled their land on the south side and laid down a concrete apron in the southwest corner measuring 78 feet by 36 feet for a tennis court. Around and upon such concrete defendants placed a six-foot wire fence. Defendants testified that they do not intend to put up any overhead lights or floodlights whatsoever over the tennis court.

Plaintiffs brought suit alleging that the described construction of the tennis court is a "structure" erected and placed upon the property in violation of the above-mentioned restrictive covenant. Plaintiffs also alleged that the construction interfered with their view; that there had been no waiver of the covenant on their part; that the value of their property had diminished as a result of the construction; and they prayed for an injunction permanently enjoining the defendants from proceeding with the construction.

The trial court followed the correct doctrine that in the construction of uncertain or ambiguous restrictions, the courts will resolve all doubts in favor of the free and unrestricted use of property and that it will "have recourse to every aid, rule, or canon of construction to ascertain the intention of the parties." In applying that doctrine to the situation, the court concluded that the fence surrounding said tennis court does not violate the covenant. Garages and other similar buildings which are of solid construction are of a different character entirely. Structures of that kind, which are solid, obstruct the view for the neighborhood and crowd the area with buildings, which would reduce the beauty of it. It seems quite plain that the covenant was intended to prevent the blocking of the view and the crowding of the buildings which would reduce the beauty and utility and therefore depreciate the value of the property within the subdivision. But the objections which validly may be made against solid constructions do not exist in regard to a flat concrete slab for a tennis court. Nor does the wire fence around it obstruct the view. Based upon the foregoing, it is our opinion that the trial court was correct in its conclusion that the tennis court and fence are not the type of structure prohibited by the covenant.

Affirmed, for defendants.

Questions and Case Problems

1. In 1941 W. E. and Jennie Hutton executed a warranty deed conveying their interest in a parcel of land to the local school district. The words of conveyance stated: This land to be used for school purposes only; otherwise to revert to grantors herein.

    The property was used for a school for the period from 1941 to 1973. After 1973 the property was used by the school district for storage purposes. When this occurred the heirs of the Huttons filed suit to recover the property from the school district. Who owns the land? [*Mahrenholz v. County Board of School Trustees of Lawrence County*, 417 N.E.2d 138 (Ill. 1981).]

2. Wicks, a farmer, entered into an oral contract for the sale of four acres of uncut barley to Candle, a grocer, for $450. The parties agreed that the crop was to be severed three weeks after the agreement was made. Because the market price for barley rose nearly 60 percent, Wicks barred Candle from cutting the crop. Candle sues, and Wicks defends by citing that part of the statute of frauds which requires that a contract for the sale of an interest in land must be in writing. Who prevails?

3. Dixon and Brett were neighbors who each owned 25 acre parcels of land. Dixon drilled for oil and established a producing well. When Brett discovered this, he drilled his own well entirely on his own land and struck the same pool of oil. While 95% of the pool was under Dixon's land, Brett was able to pump out about 50% of the total amount of oil. Because of this, Dixon sued Brett claiming that he was only entitled to 5% of the oil instead of 50%. Who prevails?

4. Consiglio owned a building in West Yarmouth, Mass. He rented it to Carey for summer seasons. Carey operated a restaurant in the building called Dorsie's Steak House and paid rent of $4,500 to $8,500 per month. After Consiglio and Carey discussed the possibility of Carey's purchase of the building, Consiglio raised the rent to $35,000 per month in an attempt to encourage Carey to conclude the purchase. Instead of purchasing, Carey prepared to move to another nearby building. Consiglio then brought suit to prevent Carey from removing certain items of restaurant equipment installed by Carey on the grounds that they were real property. The equipment pertinent here are a walk-in freezer, a compressor which supplies the cold air to the freezer, two air conditioners, and a bar. The two air conditioners were installed in two of the three window casings. They were large units, and their installation necessitated removal of the sash from each casing. The freezer was twelve feet high and, being too high to be brought into the building, it was installed at the back wall of the building on an insulated concrete slab. A hole was cut in the rear wall of the building to provide access to the freezer door. The freezer is portable. The compressor is also located outside the building and is attached only to the freezer. The built-in bar is attached to the realty. Will the injunction be granted? [*Consiglio v. Carey*, 421 N.E.2d 1257 (Mass. 1981).]

5. Clarence sold to Delbert a parcel of land on which there was a home, barn, unharvested crops, and a housetrailer. Delbert protested when Clarence removed the trailer and Delbert sues to recover it. Will he prevail?

6. Mr. Thomas and Mr. Sturgeon were elderly gentlemen with heart ailments living in a home owned by them in joint tenancy in Fresno, California. On September 2nd, 1947, at about 9:00 P.M., a neighbor heard Mr. Sturgeon yell asking the neighbor to call a doctor. After calling, the neighbor went over and saw Mr. Thomas lying on the ground. The neighbor thought Mr. Thomas' body was cold and felt for a pulse but none was present. At that same time he heard a thud in the house. On investigation he found Mr. Sturgeon lying with his head on the piano pedals. Artificial respiration was administered. Within thirty minutes Mr. Sturgeon stopped breathing.

   Shortly thereafter, the fire chief arrived and observed that Mr. Thomas' body was discolored and cool while Mr. Sturgeon's body was still warm and had good color.

   At the trial between the heirs of Mr. Thomas and Mr. Sturgeon, evidence was introduced that an autopsy could not establish who had died first.

   Further, a physician testified that body temperature as felt at the scene would not be a good indication of who died first.

   California has a provision in its Probate Code which states:

   > Where there is no sufficient evidence that two joint tenants have died otherwise than simultaneously the property so held shall be distributed one-half as if one had survived and one-half as if the other had survived.

   The trial court found that Thomas died first and his heirs appealed the case. What decision by the appellate court? [*Thomas v. Anderson,* 215 P.2d 478 (Cal. 1950).]

7. Purcey gave a written easement to her neighbor Pistol allowing Pistol to run a water ditch across Purcey's property to irrigate Pistol's land. Purcey sells her property to Rifle, who fills in the ditch because "it's dangerous for my kids." Pistol sues. Who prevails?

8. Holmes was engaged in the business of raising and processing chickens. In 1963 he bought property in Clackamas County, Oregon on which he planned to erect a chicken-processing plant. To prepare for construction he spent $33,000 to install a well system, plant special grass, and run soil tests to determine where drain fields for the plant's sewage should be located. In 1967 Clackamas County enacted an ordinance zoning the property Rural Agricultural-Single Family Residential. The zoning prohibited further construction of the chicken-processing plant. Holmes continued work and the county sued. The trial court enjoined defendant from further construction and he appealed. What result? [*Clackamas County v. Holmes,* 508 P.2d 190 (Or. 1973).]

9. The Davis family rented an apartment in a complex controlled by McDougall. The laundry room in the complex contained a Maytag washing machine with tub, agitator, and roller type wringer. The roller wringer was designed to release automatically when misused. However, the release mechanism was defective. Jodi Davis, age 3½, climbed up on a stool, started the washer and inserted her hand in the roller wringer, causing permanent injuries to her fingers, hand, and wrist. Her parents sued on her behalf, alleging that the landlord maintained an attractive nuisance. The trial court granted McDougall's motion for summary judgment and ruled that the washing machine was not an attractive nuisance. Jodi's parents appealed. What result? [*Davis v. McDougall,* 480 P.2d 907 (Ida. 1971).]

10. In the case of *Parrish v. Richards,* 336 P.2d 122 (Utah 1959),[10] is there anything which suggests the kind of attitude this court has toward restrictive covenants? Explain.

---

[10] See pp. 769–70.

52 Transferring Ownership of Realty

After you have read this chapter, you should be able to:

1. Describe in detail the process of transferring ownership with deeds.
2. Describe the major methods of *financing* ownership and indicate the advantages and disadvantages of each method.
3. Identify the consequences of recording a document associated with realty.
4. Identify methods for transferring ownership other than by a sale.

Introduction

In the previous chapter of this Part we discussed the meaning of real property, forms of ownership and co-ownership, and the various interests in land that may be owned. In this chapter we will discuss the ways that ownership in realty can be transferred.

Most commonly, the seller transfers ownership, through the *deeding process,* in return for the buyer's payment of the purchase price. Since most buyers do not have enough cash to pay the full price, they usually borrow most of the money from a lender such as a bank. The lender usually protects its interest by requiring the buyer to execute an *instrument of finance,* such as a mortgage or a trust deed. These instruments generally allow the lender to collect the loan by selling the realty if payments are not made as promised.

The deeding process is not always needed to effectuate a transfer. For example, a city may *condemn* realty. In this process it forces a transfer of ownership without the consent of the private party.

This chapter examines ownership transfers by scrutinizing the deeding process and by evaluating the instruments of finance. The nonsale transfers of ownership, such as condemnation, are discussed last.

The Deeding Process

Usually a **deed** is a single piece of paper. (See figure 52.1.) All the parts of the *deeding process* must be completed before ownership is transferred. These elements of the modern deeding process are *execution, delivery,* and *acceptance.*

Execution refers to the format, language, and signing of the deed document. Many states have enacted statutes which specify a form for short, simple deeds. These are called *statutory deeds.* While all deeds are essentially similar, there are slight variations from state to state. For example, while some states require that deeds be notarized to be valid, most states do not. **Notarizing** involves marking signed documents in a way which indicates that an official of the state has determined that the signatures are valid.

By itself, execution of a valid deed does not transfer ownership. Delivery and acceptance are also required to complete the deeding process. **Delivery,** like transferring the chunk of sod, merely involves transferring possession of a properly executed deed with the *intention* of shifting ownership. The following case illustrates a situation where there was not a valid delivery because there was no intention to shift ownership.

deed
a formal document used to transfer title to real estate

notarize
verification by a proper public official of the authenticity of a signature

delivery
(in realty) the voluntary transfer of a deed with the intent thereby to transfer ownership of the realty

Facts
Mrs. Marshall was eighty-four years old and owned two parcels of real estate. Her son Ralph had great influence over her. One day Ralph asked Mrs. Marshall to go with him to an attorney's office, and she did. The attorney represented Ralph. After waiting for six hours in the attorney's office while Ralph and the attorney talked in another office, Mrs. Marshall was asked by Ralph to sign several documents. Her son, Ralph, urged Mrs. Marshall to sign. She did. Later she learned that she had signed deeds transferring title to her realty to her three sons, defendants. Later she died and other relatives, plaintiffs, sued for rescission of the deeds. The probate court granted rescission, and the sons appealed.

Decision
Affirmed, the deeds were invalid.

Reasoning
The probate judge did not err in ordering rescission of the deeds by which the eighty-four-year-old woman decedent had conveyed her two parcels of real estate to her three sons, reserving a life estate in herself. He specifically found that Ralph took the plaintiff to the attorney's office; that she was highly susceptible to Ralph's influence; that Ralph "urged his mother to execute the aforesaid instruments and that such urging constituted undue influence in view of the age of the

Figure 52.1 Warranty Deed

WARRANTY DEED

① THIS DEED, Made this Eleventh day of July, 1986, between Terry D. Alger and Kaye L. Alger, husband and wife

of the County of Jefferson, State of Colorado, grantor(s) and *

② Edward J. Conry and Anne L. Conry, husband and wife, as joint tenants with full rights of survivorship whose legal address is

1475 Lawrence Street

of the City and County of Denver, State of Colorado, grantee(s):

③ WITNESSETH, That the grantor(s), for and in consideration of
Two hundred fifty five thousand dollars ($255,000.00)------------------------------ DOLLARS,

④ the receipt and sufficiency of which is hereby acknowledged, have granted, bargained, sold and conveyed, and by these presents do hereby grant, bargain, sell, convey, and confirm, unto the grantee(s), and their heirs and assigns forever, all the real property together with improvements, if any, situate, lying and being in the City of Evergreen, County of Jefferson, State of Colorado, described as follows:

⑤ Lot 261 of the Iliwan First Filing as Filing No.372227 on July 4, 1976, in the Office of the Recorder for Jefferson County.

also known by street and number as: 1425 Iverness Street

⑥ TOGETHER with all and singular the hereditaments and appurtenances thereto belonging, or in anywise appertaining, and the reversion and reversions, remainder and remainders, rents, issues and profits thereof, and all the estate, right, title, interest, claim and demand whatsoever of the grantor(s), either in law or equity, of, in and to the above bargained premises, with the hereditaments and appurtenances.
TO HAVE AND TO HOLD the said premises above bargained and described with the appurtenances, unto the grantee(s), their heirs and assigns forever. And the grantor(s), for their heirs and personal representatives, do hereby covenant, grant, bargain, and agree to and with grantee(s), their heirs and assigns, that at the time of the ensealing and delivery of these presents, they are well seized of the premises above conveyed, have good, sure, perfect, absolute and indefeasible estate of inheritance, in law, in fee simple, and have good right, full power and authority to grant, bargain, sell and convey the same in manner and form as aforesaid, and that the same are free and clear from all former and other grants, bargains, sales, liens, taxes, assessments, encumbrances, and restrictions of whatever kind or nature soever, except

----- EASEMENTS OF RECORD AND NONE OTHER -----

and the above bargained premises in the quiet and peaceable possession of the grantee(s), their heirs and assigns against all and every person or persons lawfully claiming or to claim the whole or any part thereof, grantor(s) shall and will WARRANT AND FOREVER DEFEND.
IN WITNESS WHEREOF, the grantor(s) have executed this deed on the date set forth above.

Terry D. Alger
Kaye L. Alger

⑦ STATE OF COLORADO } SS.
City and County of Denver

The foregoing instrument was acknowledged before me in the City and County of Denver, State of Colorado this Eleventh day of July, 1986 by

My commission expires. 6-1-88
Witness my hand and official seal.

P. Notary

P. Notary
Notary Public
11253 E. Public St.
Address
Denver, Colorado

Key to Deed Sections

1. Grantors' Names
2. Grantees' Names
3. Consideration Statement
4. Words of Conveyance
5. Property Description
6. Habendum
7. Signatures and Certification

plaintiff, her susceptibility to [Ralph's] influence . . . , and her presence in the defendant's attorney's office"; and "after the plaintiff's execution of the deeds as aforesaid, [she] was chagrined to discover that she had caused the properties to be transferred to the defendants"; that she later asserted repeatedly "that she never intended to convey the properties to the defendants"; and that "the plaintiff did not know she had conveyed title to the properties to the defendants." Affirmed.

Marshall v. Marshall, 409 N.E.2d 1322 (Mass. 1980).

Delivery can be made to either the buyer or the buyer's agent. Thus, if a mother executed a deed in favor of a daughter, but the deed were left in the mother's safe-deposit box until her death, the deed would not transfer ownership because it was not delivered. Further, if a deed were delivered just as security for a debt, ownership would not be transferred because there was no *intent* to shift ownership.

Acceptance merely means that the buyer indicates a willingness to assume ownership. Retaining the deed after delivery usually constitutes acceptance.

The Deed Document

All deeds contain about the same information. The major sections of deeds include:

1. the names of the grantor(s), (often a seller);
2. the words of conveyance;
3. names of the grantee(s), (often a purchaser);
4. the consideration statement;
5. the property description;
6. the **habendum;**
7. the signatures and certifications.

Each section communicates important information about the nature of the parties or the property or the transaction. Since the deed is the heart of most real estate transactions, it must be scrutinized carefully by both the buyer and the seller if they are to protect their interests.

Grantor(s) Name(s).   The person giving up ownership is the grantor. The person receiving the deed is the grantee. The name(s) of those executing the deed as grantor(s) appears first. These persons must be owners of the estate conveyed in order for that interest to pass.

Words of Conveyance.   The words of conveyance generally determine which promises or warranties the grantor makes to the grantee. When the words "warrant and convey" or "grant and convey" are used, this indicates that the grantor promises or warrants the following:

1. that the grantor owns the estate transferred and will pay the grantee for his or her injury if it turns out that the grantee doesn't receive the estate described in the deed;
2. that there are no liens, leases, easements, mortgages, or other **encumbrances** which bind the grantee other than those disclosed in the deed.

Deeds of this type are generally called **warranty deeds** or *grant deeds*. They are the kind most frequently used.

The other major type of deed is called the **quitclaim deed.** The words of conveyance for it often include the word "quitclaim." This deed merely transfers the grantor's ownership, if any. No promises or warranties are implied in the deed. Thus, if a professor gave a student a warranty deed to the school building in exchange for $10,000, the student could sue and recover the money if it turned out that the professor did not own the building. If, however, a quitclaim deed were given, the student could not recover the money.

The deed's contents.

habendum
that portion of a deed which indicates the encumbrances burdening the estate

encumbrance
a person's right in another person's property

warranty deed
a deed conveying title and giving warranties to the grantee

quitclaim deed
a document used in transferring the grantor's interest in realty, if any, without any warranties

In many states there is a *special warranty deed* in addition to the warranty and quitclaim deeds. A special warranty deed reduces the grantor's legal risks because it warrants only that the title has not been impaired *during the time when the grantor owned the property*.

In the absence of other indications, the law generally presumes that the grantor and grantee intended the conveyance of the fee simple absolute estate. Conditional and life estates can usually be identified by examining the words of conveyance. For example, the words "warrant and convey so long as no sheep are grazed on the land" would transfer a conditional estate. The words "quitclaim for life" would convey only a life estate.

Grantee(s) Name(s). Aside from identifying the grantees, this section indicates the form of co-ownership, if it exists, and each co-owner's percentage of ownership. In community property states, a statement that the grantees are husband and wife would create a presumption that community property is the form of co-ownership with each co-owning fifty percent. Tenancy by entirety would be presumed from the "husband and wife" designation in some, but not all, states which recognize that form of co-ownership.

Where no relationship is stated and the grantees are not married, the law in almost all states presumes that the parties co-own as tenants in common with equal percentage ownerships. Of course, when the ownership percentages are stated, they will govern. Thus, one could convey to "Oliver Wendell Holmes as to ninety-nine percent (99 percent) and John Marshall as to one percent (1 percent)," and Marshall would own one percent, not fifty.

Generally, joint tenancy must be specifically identified. Some states demand extremely clear and emphatic language to create joint tenancy. Many lawyers use phrases like A to B and C "as joint tenants, with full rights of survivorship, and not as tenants in common."

Consideration. Generally, most deeds recite a fictitious amount like "ten dollars" as the stated consideration. In many cases consideration is not required for effective deeding.

Description of the Property. This section of the deed describes the physical boundaries of the parcel being conveyed. Frequently deeds must contain a legal description of the property to satisfy the execution requirement for deeding. Legal descriptions include subdivision lot descriptions, and meets and bounds descriptions. Street addresses and farm names often do not qualify as legal descriptions. Thus, in some states a deed describing property as "1600 Pennsylvania Avenue" would not be recordable even though the city, county, and state were identified.

Signature and Notarizing. Generally only the grantor(s) signs the deed. Grantees usually need not sign although some grantors may require it as proof of acceptance. In some states the grantor's signature must be witnessed and the deed notarized.

Instruments of Finance

Most buyers of realty do not have enough cash to pay the full purchase price. So buyers usually borrow part of the price. Lenders want to be very certain they will be repaid. So they almost always require that the borrower give the lender the legal right to force the sale of the property if loan payments are not made as promised. The lender then can use the money from the forced sale to pay off the loan. The three major instruments of finance used to protect lenders are the "mortgage," the "trust deed," and the "land sale contract." Realty can also be transferred with the seller's existing financing.

Mortgages

Mortgages are the most common instrument for financing the acquisition of realty. Generally, the buyer, **mortgagor,** will give a **mortgage** to a lender, **mortgagee,** such as a bank or savings and loan association. The mortgage gives the lender the legal right to file suit in court to *foreclose* (cut off) the buyer's ownership rights in the property in the event loan payments are not made as promised. After the suit is initiated and the judge hears the evidence, the judge issues a decree of **foreclosure.** After the decree is issued, a *sheriff's sale,* occurs and the property is auctioned off to the highest bidder. The money received from the sheriff's sale is used to repay the debt owed the lender. If the money received exceeds the debt, the surplus goes to the mortgagor (the borrower). If the money is not sufficient to pay the debt, the lender can usually obtain a **deficiency judgment** against the borrower for the balance due.

Mortgagors are protected in most states with rights of **redemption.** Prior to the decree of foreclosure, the mortgagor can sometimes stop the foreclosure process by simply paying all past-due installments along with those expenses incurred by the lender because of the default. This ability to stop foreclosure is generally called the "equity of redemption." After the decree of foreclosure is issued, the mortgagor is still protected in a majority of states by a redemption period—usually six months to a year—during which he or she can regain the property by paying off the *whole* amount of the mortgage along with the lender's default expenses. This is generally called the right of "statutory redemption." Mortgages sometimes contain clauses which waive rights of redemption. Generally these clauses cannot be enforced.

The process of mortgage foreclosure is usually very time consuming. The delays associated with the suit, sheriff's sale, and possible redemption can often delay the sale for one or two years.

Trust Deeds

With this method of financing the buyer first obtains the deed from the seller. The buyer then gives a **trust deed** to a **trustee.** The trustee holds the trust deed on behalf of the lender. The trust deed contains language which allows the trustee to sell the property if the buyer defaults on the loan payments. Note that a court order is not required to cause the sale, and that it is a sale conducted by the trustee rather than by the sheriff. In some states there are no redemption periods associated with trust deeds, or they are very short. For these reasons, sale after default often occurs more rapidly under a trust deed than under a mortgage. Therefore, lenders frequently prefer trust deeds to mortgages.

A mortgage with "power of sale" is similar to a trust deed. No foreclosure suit is required, and a private sale occurs. This sale is conducted by the mortgagee. Some states do not permit mortgages with powers of sale, and those states which do permit them carefully regulate by statute the conduct of the lender after default.

Land Sale Contracts

With this method of financing the lender—who often is also the seller—keeps the deed until all the contracted payments have been made. Then the lender must deliver a deed.

The land sale contract gives the buyer the right to occupy the realty and treat it as his or her own. The law refers to the buyer under a land sale contract as the *equitable owner* even though the buyer has not yet received the deed.

If the buyer defaults, the lender in some states can have the buyer removed from the property in about the same way a landlord evicts a tenant who has not paid the rent. This may involve a lawsuit, which is sometimes concluded much more rapidly than either a mortgage foreclosure or a sale by trustee. In these states the lender can sometimes treat the installment payments as though they were rental charges so that the defaulting buyer loses everything.

---

mortgagor
the person who has given a mortgage

mortgage
a security interest in realty; also the instrument which gives lenders the power to sell the mortgaged realty, to repay the debt, when the borrower defaults on the payments

mortgagee
the person to whom a mortgage is given

foreclosure
the cutting off of the owner's interest in realty by sale pursuant to court decree

deficiency judgment
a judgment after foreclosure, against the borrower, for the remaining unpaid balance of the mortgage loan

redemption
the reclaiming of a foreclosed ownership interest in realty

trust deed
a deed given to a trustee, in trust, with the power to sell the land on default of the secured obligation

trustee
(in realty) the one who holds the trust deed for the benefit of the lender

Land sale contract.

Most other states force the lender in the land sale contract to return to the defaulting buyer his or her equity in the property. The word "equity" as used here is a financial term meaning the difference between the value of something and the amount owed on it. Thus, if a buyer purchased a home for $60,000 by making a $10,000 down payment and executing a land sale contract for $50,000, the buyer's equity would be $10,000. If after a few years the balance due on the land sale contract were $40,000, the buyer's equity would be $20,000. If the buyer defaulted, most states would force the lender to return the $20,000 equity, less the rental value of the property. These states generally treat the land sale contract in the way mortgages are handled, including the grant of redemption rights to the borrower.

Lenders prefer land sale contracts in those states where they allow rapid resolution of the problems associated with a debtor in default.

Recording

Recording of realty documents.

Recording is the process of filing a document related to realty with the county clerk or commissioner of deeds. Deeds, mortgages, land sale contracts, easements, and liens are among the many documents usually recorded. In general, the purpose of recording is to give *notice* to the world and to influence **priority** with respect to any other claims against the realty.

priority
the order in which claims against realty are satisfied

Priority

Priority determines the order in which claims against the realty are satisfied. Thus, if there are two mortgages recorded against a property and foreclosure occurs, the mortgage first recorded will be paid completely before any funds are applied to the second. Similarly, if an owner gives two deeds for the same realty to different persons, in most states the grantee who first records his or her deed will become the final owner even if this grantee had received the second deed, i.e., second in time. Generally, this second grantee (whose deed was first recorded) must not have known of the first conveyance, and must have paid for the deed, in order for this grantee to receive first priority. Mechanics' liens are an exception to the general rule that time of recording determines priority. The time when the work was done determines the priority of a valid mechanic's lien.

Notice

Every buyer of realty is assumed by law to have *notice* of all claims and encumbrances recorded against the property. This is so even though the buyer did not know of the claim and did not examine the public record. This is called "constructive notice." For example, suppose that an easement for a right of way is recorded against a property which is later bought for development into a housing tract. The developer is bound by the easement, even though the developer was not actually aware of the easement, and even though it makes the development impossible. (Note that if the seller gave a warranty deed which did not indicate the easement, then the seller would be liable to the developer.)

Also, if a claim against property, like a mortgage, is *not* recorded and the property is sold, the buyer takes the property free of the claim. However, the buyer must not have had actual knowledge of the claim and must have paid value for the property. If the buyer knew of the claim, or if the property were acquired as a gift, generally the person receiving the property is bound by the unrecorded claim.

Nonsale Transfers of Ownership

Other Deed-Related Transfers

While the deeding process is generally associated with transactions involving the *sale* of realty, deeding is also involved with transfers of ownership through gifts and wills.

Ownership of realty is also transferred when one dies without a will. Decedents dying without a will are said to have died "intestate." In these cases the laws of descent and distribution will determine who among the surviving relatives will become the new owner or owners. Thus, in many states if a man dies intestate without children, all of the property goes to his surviving wife. If there are no heirs of the person who dies intestate, then his or her property **escheats** to the state. This means the state becomes the owner.

escheat
the transfer of property to the state when a person dies without heirs

Dedication

If a developer wants to give land to a local government—perhaps for use as public streets—then the developer can dedicate it. However, ownership is not transferred until the government *accepts* the transfer.

Dedication.

Condemnation

When a government wants private property for a public use, it may exercise its power of **eminent domain** and take title through condemnation if it pays the owner the *reasonable value* of the property.

Condemnation.

eminent domain
government power to appropriate private land for public use on payment of just compensation without the owner's consent

Adverse Possession

The doctrine of **adverse possession** rests on the idea that owners of realty should be aware of the use being made of their lands. If an owner is careless, and someone comes upon the land and occupies it for a *substantial period of time,* and meets certain other technical legal requirements, the occupant may acquire title to the land. The occupant would receive title under the doctrine of adverse possession. The following case illustrates the application of the doctrine of adverse possession.

adverse possession
a method of acquiring title to land by actual, exclusive, and continuous possession of land under color of title adverse or hostile to the true owner in an open and notorious manner for a statutory period of time

Facts
In 1958, Mrs. Dorothea Karell, defendant, purchased 18.9 acres of land in Tarrant County, Texas. A fence encompassed this land along with another parcel of about 3.7 acres. Mrs. Karell rented her property to tenants from 1958 until 1970. In 1970 she hired one Howe to remove the top soil from portions of the land including the 3.7 acre parcel. When West, plaintiff, owner of record of the 3.7 acre parcel discovered Howe's activities, he sued to quiet title and recover damages for the lost top soil. Mrs. Karell defended claiming title by adverse possession. Judgment was rendered for plaintiff and defendant appealed.

Decision
Affirmed for West, plaintiff.

Reasoning
It is undisputed that the property in issue was enclosed by a fence. Such enclosure gives rise to a rebuttable presumption that an adverse claim is being made by the party in possession. . . . In any event, in order for the Karells to establish a title they are required to prove continuous cultivation, use, or enjoyment of the land as well as possession and adverse claims. It is uncontroverted that the Karells never lived on the disputed acreage nor did they personally use or cultivate it. Any claim of title made by them is through the tenants by whom the property was supposedly occupied. Both Mr. and Mrs. Karell testified as to a succession of tenants from 1958 through 1972. (The tenants actually occupied a house located on the 18.9 acre tract.) Neither could testify that for a continuous ten year period each tenant used the disputed tract by cultivating crops, grazing livestock or by using the land in any manner so as to put the true owners on notice that an adverse claim of ownership of the property in issue was being made. Their testimony also shows that periods of non-occupancy would sometimes last as long as two months. The plaintiffs produced witnesses who testified that not all of the tenants had livestock or crops. In fact, one witness testified that, other than a tenant named Davis who occupied the premises for 2 or 3 years, no other tenant had livestock.

The use to which the Karells put the land did not constitute an actual and visible appropriation of the land which was continuous and unbroken.
Affirmed.

Karell v. West and Shobert, 616 S.W.2d. 692 (Tex. 1981).

Prescription

prescription
(in real property) a method of obtaining the right to use of another's land as an easement by open and continuous possession and use of the land under a claim of right to such use for a statutory period of time

The method for acquiring ownership by **prescription** is analogous to adverse possession. However, prescription applies to those "uses" which are associated with easements. Accordingly, property taxes need not be paid. In some cases where a claimant would not qualify as an adverse possessor because of failure to pay taxes, the claimant may prevail in a claim for prescription. For example, a person who reasonably believed that he or she was the owner of a pasture and grazed cattle there for thirty years, but whose property tax assessment did not include the pasture, might not qualify for adverse possession, but could probably win the prescription right to continue grazing cattle because of the previous use of the pasture.

Summary Statement

1. The deeding process is the most common method used to transfer ownership of realty. It requires execution of the deed document, delivery, and acceptance.
2. Warranty deeds warrant (assure) transfer of the indicated estate free of all encumbrances except those stated in the deed. Quitclaim deeds transfer only the grantor's interest, if any. The grantor does not warrant that he or she has an interest to transfer or that all encumbrances have been disclosed in the deed.
3. The language used in deeds determines the estate transferred, the form of co-ownership, the physical boundaries of the estate, and the limitations on the ownership of the grantee, such as restrictive covenants and mortgages.
4. Financing the purchase of realty usually involves either a mortgage, trust deed, land sale contract, or a sale with existing financing.
5. Generally, the debtor in default can be removed from the property most rapidly under a land sale contract, less rapidly under a trust deed, and most slowly under a mortgage.
6. Recording influences the priority among competing claims and gives notice of the recorded document to the whole world.
7. Escrows are contracts which direct a person to perform specific acts in connection with property, such as recording a deed. They are often used in closing a real estate sale.
8. Title insurance and abstracts of title allow a buyer to collect from someone other than the grantor when the buyer is injured by a defect of title not disclosed in the insurance policy nor in the title opinion.
9. Ownership can be transferred without using the deeding process. This can occur through condemnation, adverse possession, and prescription.

The following case illustrates the importance of the elements of the deeding process.

Parker v. Lamb
567 S.W.2d 99 (Ark. 1978)

Smith, G. R., Justice. This suit to cancel two deeds is between brother and sister; the appellant Robert J. Parker, Jr., and the appellee Mary Louise Lamb. The single question is whether the Chancellor was right in holding that the deeds, executed by the parties' parents, were ineffective for want of delivery. We agree with the Chancellor.

In 1971 the elder Parkers went to a trusted friend, who was an abstracter, for advice about the disposition of their property upon their death. The abstracter had an attorney prepare the two deeds in question, one conveying the city homeplace to the daughter and the other conveying a farm (which became quite valuable) to the son. The abstracter told the Parkers to put the deeds in envelopes, to be delivered after their death. He said that they could do anything they wanted to do with the property before they died, but if they still owned it at the time of their death it would go according to the deeds. Needless to say, the advice was erroneous.

Upon the elder Parker's death in 1974, the title passed to his widow as the surviving tenant by the entirety. Mrs. Parker kept the deeds in a storm cellar behind her home in Conway. The son, to prove delivery of the deeds, relies upon . . . [an] incident that occurred during his mother's last illness in 1976. In the . . . incident, Mrs. Parker, during the last several days of her life, told her daughter that she could go down to the cellar, get the two envelopes, and tear them up if she wanted to. The daughter declined.

No effective delivery is shown. The law wisely requires the delivery of a deed, as a positive act bringing home to the grantor that he is definitely parting with the ownership of his land. An essential element of a valid delivery is the grantor's intention to pass the title *immediately*. [Emphasis added.]

No such intention to pass title immediately could have existed in this case because there is no suggestion whatever in the proof that Mrs. Parker did not still believe that the abstracter's advice—that the envelopes be delivered after her death—was sound. There is no possibility that Mrs. Parker, relying upon that advice, could have intended an *inter vivos* delivery of the deeds.

* * *

Affirmed, for appellee, the deeds were ineffective.

Questions and Case Problems

1. Kruithoff leased 7 1/2 acres of pasture land from Mrs. Sandy on November 27, 1970, at $15 per year. They entered into a separate written agreement which allowed Kruithoff to erect a fence and take it down and keep it at the end of the lease. This agreement was not recorded. Before the end of the lease, Mrs. Sandy sold the land to Bailey and told him about the lease but not the oral agreement concerning the fence. When Kruithoff removed the fence at the end of the lease, Bailey sued him for the value of the fence. The fence was of four-strand barbed wire consisting of approximately 150 fence posts and an iron sucker rod gate. Only eight of the posts were imbedded in concrete. Who wins? [*Bailey v. Kruithoff,* 280 So.2d 262 (La. 1963).]

2. Arthur Glander received a deed to a small farm from his parents. A month after receiving that deed, Arthur executed a quitclaim deed for the property to his brother and his sister, Gladys. The deed was in proper form, signed and notarized. The deed was given to Arthur's father for him to hold. The father was to give the deed to the brother and sister if Arthur died. Gladys moved to New York. Thirteen years later, while visiting the father's home and rummaging through his papers, Gladys found the deed. She promptly recorded it. Arthur now sues, asking the court to determine who is the true owner in a quiet title action. Who prevails, Arthur or Gladys? [*Glander v. Glander,* 239 P.2d 254 (Ida. 1951).]

3. In 1919 Nix and Nix Company purchased land for a substantial sum of money from Tooele County in Utah. Title was transferred with a quitclaim deed. The Nixes paid property taxes to the county for the property for twenty years. Then they discovered that an honest mutual mistake had been made because the county never owned any interest in the land. Nix and Nix Company now sue Tooele County to recover the purchase price. Who prevails? [*Nix v. Tooele County,* 118 P.2d 376 (Utah 1941).]

4. The Kendricks owned property in Snohomish County, Washington. In 1961 they sold two houses and lots for $18,500 with a down payment of $1,100 and monthly payments of $120 under a land sale contract. The land sale contract was recorded. The buyers were Millard C. Davis and his wife. They mortgaged this interest under the land sale contract to a Finance Company to secure a loan of $1,000. In 1965 the buyers defaulted on the land sale contract. The Kendricks (the sellers) recorded and sent a Notice of Declaration of Forfeiture and Cancellation of Contract to the Davises. The Kendricks filed a **lis pendens,** which gives notice that a suit is pending, and initiated an **action to quiet title.** The Finance Company became a party to the suit and offered to pay off the balance of the land sale contract in return for acquiring ownership. The Kendricks, sellers, want clear title to the property free of the mortgage. Who prevails, the Kendricks or the Finance Company? [*Kendrick v. Davis,* 452 P.2d 222 (Wash. 1969).]

lis pendens
a suit is pending

action to quiet title
a legal proceeding initiated by a claimant to title in land affording any adverse parties opportunity to prove a claim to interest in the land or thereafter be barred from doing so

5. Erasmus Wiley occupied an old house in a commercial area for about twenty years. On his sixtieth birthday he executed a warranty deed to his neighbor, Buster Blue, in return for $200,000 in cash. Erasmus retained the right to occupy the property for an additional three months. Buster did not record his deed. After two months Erasmus executed a quitclaim deed for $150,000 in favor of Jerry Green, a politician. Jerry had no knowledge of the prior deed, and he immediately recorded his quitclaim deed. Erasmus now resides in a Brazilian resort and is incommunicado. What are the rights of the parties?

6. Winnie Selsor, a full-blood Creek Indian, owned 160 acres of unimproved, unfenced, poorly wooded mountainous land. When she failed to pay the property taxes, the county sold the property to L. P. Kelley. Later Winnie deeded the property to Eddie Cox. Kelley asked Herman Johnson to take care of the land. Johnson ran 35 to 40 head of cattle on the property and came upon the land about 50 times a year to check on the cattle and the land. Cox claims that the tax deed is void. Kelley asserts title through adverse possession. Cox counters that, while other requirements may have been met, Kelley did not possess the land. Who prevails? [*Cox v. Kelley,* 295 P.2d 1061 (Okla. 1956).]

7. Able leased a room in a home owned by widow Wilma. The parties executed a written lease for two years so Able would complete graduate school. Six months later Wilma sold the house to Professor Pickey. When Pickey discovered Able, he told him to leave because Pickey intends to use the room to display his rodent collection. Able claims he has the right to rent the room for another 1½ years. The lease was not recorded, and Pickey could not tell when he inspected the property that the one room had been rented out. Who prevails?

8. Frank Willett and George Miller owned lands on opposite shores of the Camarron River. From 1913 until 1930 the Camarron River moved about a half mile into Miller's property. Over 200 acres of Miller's former property are now on Willett's side of the river. The change was caused by several floods, each lasting about five days, which shifted the river's location as much as 300 feet. Willett and Miller now claim ownership of the property between the old location of the river and the new location. Who prevails? [*Willett v. Miller,* 55 P.2d 90 (Okla. 1936).]

9. Monte Bucks, the holder of a bachelor's degree in Business Administration, bought a large apartment house by putting $2,000 down and taking the property "subject to" an existing mortgage of about $750,000. He installed a former go-go dancer as the manager in the hope that she would lure many of her friends into renting apartments in his building. The plan worked, and occupancy approached 100 percent. However, rental receipts declined dramatically because the tenants spent all their money on things other than rent. In addition, maintenance expenses rose significantly because the new tenants treated the property harshly. Monte could not make the mortgage payments. The lender foreclosed on the mortgage and recovered $600,000 on the sale of the distressed apartment building. The lender now sues Monte for the other $150,000. Who prevails?

10. In the case of *Parker v. Lamb,* 567 S.W.2d 99 (Ark. 1978),[1] were the Parkers exercising good judgment in the way they obtained legal advice? Explain.

---

[1] See pp. 780–81.

Renting Realty 53

After you have read this chapter, you should be able to:

1. Describe the kinds of rental relationships which landlords and tenants may establish.
2. Describe the promises implied in most leases.
3. Describe the covenants and conditions which should be included in a residential lease.
4. Describe the tenant's powers to transfer their rights in leased property.
5. Describe the rights and obligations of landlords and tenants on termination of a lease.

Figure 53.1 Creation and Termination of a One Year Leasehold Estate

A initially owns a fee simple absolute; during the period of the lease A owns the reversion and is then referred to as the landlord or lessor.
B is the owner for one year of the leasehold estate and is the tenant or lessee.
The property is said to have been demised or leased or rented.

Basic Nature of the Landlord-Tenant Relationship

freehold estates
fee simple absolute, conditional and life estates

demise
(in realty) to lease or rent

leasehold estate
the estate in realty owned by tenants

lease
(of realty) a form of contract giving one person, the tenant (or lessee), the exclusive right to occupy for a period the realty of another, the landlord (or lessor)

Use of the property.

The landlord-tenant relationship arises when the owner of a **freehold estate** (e.g., fee simple absolute, a conditional estate, or a life estate) transfers to another the right to temporarily possess the realty. Generally, the right of *possession* is given in exchange for the payment of *rent*. The temporary transfer of the right of possession is referred to as **demising** or **leasing** the property. Since the transfer of possession is temporary, the owner of the freehold will eventually regain possession. This power to regain possession is called the *right of reversion.* The owner of the freehold is called the *landlord* or *lessor,* and the party receiving the temporary right of possession is called the *tenant* or *lessee.* After transfer, the tenant is said to own a **leasehold estate.** (See figure 53.1.)

When a written document evidences the relationship between the parties, the document is usually called the **lease** or *rental agreement*. Most leases constitute a blending of the law of *conveyancing* (i.e., transferring ownership of realty) and the law of contracts. The conveyancing aspect of the transaction is concerned with transferring a leasehold estate to the tenant. The contract aspects relate to the agreements between the parties on such issues as payment of the rent, who shall repair the realty, the amount of security or cleaning deposits and the conditions under which they can be returned, and limitation on uses of the property.

The law treats tenants as owners of *nonfreehold* estates. These estates do not occupy the same status in the law as freehold estates. The owners of freehold estates are said to be *seised* of the property. Owners of estates are seised when they acquire possession of a freehold with a deed. Tenants are not seised, though they do possess the realty. Because of this, the landlord retains some obligations of ownership, like the duty to pay the property taxes. Further, the tenant's estate will be treated as personalty. Thus, if a tenant dies, the tenant's leasehold interest may pass via the tenant's will to those who receive the decedent's *personalty*.

Because leases are two-party contracts, the law assumes that the parties negotiate the terms of the lease at arm's length with each party protecting his own self-interest. Accordingly, there is no standard lease document. Most printed lease documents have been prepared by the attorneys for landlords. If tenants are too shy or uninformed to negotiate changes in the printed forms, they may be severely injured.

Creation of the Rental Relationship

Oral Leases

A lease may be created in a variety of ways. It can be created orally, and is then called a **parol lease**; or it can be created without words—by implication from the acts of the parties. While oral leases are often enforceable, every state requires that certain leases be placed in writing. Generally it is the statute of frauds[1] for each state which determines which leases must be written.

parol lease
a lease not reduced to writing

Leasehold Estates

If a landlord-tenant relationship comes into being, the law will classify it as an estate at sufferance, an estate at will, a periodic estate, or an estate for years. The distinctions among the types of estates are important because the estates are terminated differently.

Estate at Sufferance. This estate arises when one rightfully takes possession of property as a lessee, but then remains in possession *after* termination of the lease. A few states allow landlords to use self-help eviction if no force is used. But most states require notice of termination of an estate at sufferance and permit eviction only by a police officer after a lawsuit.

Estate at sufferance.

Estate at Will. When someone takes possession of the realty with the landlord's consent, but *without* entering into an oral or written lease, he or she owns an *estate at will*. This usually occurs when the parties agree that the prospective tenant can move in and that the lease will be negotiated later.

Estate at will.

This landlord-tenant relationship can be terminated at any time by either party. Some states protect the lessee by requiring notice before eviction.

Periodic Estate. This relationship arises when the parties agree on the terms and conditions of the lease but *do not specify its term (length)*. For example, the parties may agree that the rent is "five dollars per day payable monthly in advance." There is a clear implication in this language that the lease is intended to run for longer than one month, yet the lease specifies no ending date. The law allows this tenant a *periodic estate*. In general, this estate continues for the *length of the payment period* and is automatically renewed unless one party gives adequate notice of termination. Often the notice of termination must equal the length of the payment period. Thus, where rent is paid every two months, most states would require a two-month notice to terminate.

Periodic estate.

The main characteristic of periodic leases is their flexibility. Since either the landlord or tenant can terminate, in most instances with a thirty-day notice, the terms of the lease are open to easy revision. For example, a landlord who wants to raise the rent 30 percent can submit a new lease to the tenant. For all practical purposes, the tenant must accept it or be forced to leave within about thirty days. On the other hand, the student who rented a periodic estate in the worst apartment in town on the first day of classes can easily move out in the middle of the semester when more attractive accommodations become available.

Estate for Years. This estate arises when the parties *agree on the beginning date and ending date for the lease*. The term "estate for years" is misleading because it can be for any length of time, such as one week, or two months, or 340 days, or five years. Because the parties know the date when the lease ends, no notice is required to terminate. Further, neither the landlord nor the tenant may terminate the lease without cause before the agreed termination date. Thus, if a student executed a nine-month lease and moved out after three months, he or she might be liable for six months' rent! That liability arises

Estate for years.

---

[1] See chapter 11, Contractual Form—Requirement of a Writing for Enforceability, Statute of Frauds.

only when the landlord has used reasonable efforts to rerent but has not found a new tenant. If a new tenant rerents after a vacancy of three months, the original tenant will be liable for the amount of rent for the three months' vacancy.

The following case illustrates the risks of premature termination and the duty to rerent.

Facts
Kridel, defendant, leased an apartment from Sommer, plaintiff, for two years for himself and his bride to be. Two weeks after Kridel was scheduled to move in, Sommer received the following letter.

> I was to be married on June 3, 1972. Unhappily the engagement was broken and the wedding plans cancelled. Both parents were to assume responsibility for the rent after our marriage. I was discharged from the U.S. Army in October 1971 and am now a student. I have no funds of my own, and am supported by my stepfather.
>
> In view of the above, I cannot take possession of the apartment and am surrendering all rights to it. Never having received a key, I cannot return same to you.
>
> I beg your understanding and compassion in releasing me from the lease, and will of course, in consideration thereof, forfeit the 2 months rent already paid.
>
> Please notify me at your earliest convenience.

Sommers later had an opportunity to relet Kridel's apartment but declined to do so. He then sued Kridel for the whole 2 year's rent.

Decision
Kridel is liable only for rent for the period of time from the beginning of the lease until the time when Sommers had an opportunity to relet.

Reasoning
While there is a split of authority over this question, the trend among the recent cases appears to be in favor of a mitigation requirement. . . . The older rule is based on principles of property law which equate a lease with a transfer of a property interest in the owner's estate. Yet the distinction between a lease for ordinary residential purposes and an ordinary contract can no longer be considered viable.

Sommer v. Kridel, 378 A.2d 767 (N.J. 1977).

Holdover Tenants. Frequently tenants remain in possession after termination of the estate. When this occurs, the landlord generally has a choice of several remedies.

The holdover tenant can be **evicted**—that is, forceably removed from the property by the sheriff. Further, the tenant is liable for reasonable rent for the holdover period. In some states the landlord can collect double or triple rent for the holdover period.

If the tenant holds over, the landlord may elect to compel the tenant to remain. This is an alternative to eviction. In general, the tenant will thereby become liable for rent for a period equal to the length of the original term. Thus, if Harvey Hardsnoz rented an apartment to Suzie Pillow for one year to terminate on January 1, and Suzie held over until January 3, Hardsnoz could, in some states, treat her as his tenant for the remainder of the second year. If, however, Suzie had a month-to-month tenancy and held over, she would be liable for only one month's rent.

eviction
the dispossession of a tenant from the leased premises

Covenants and Conditions in Leases

When parties enter into a lease agreement, there are generally numerous promises flowing from both the landlord and the tenant. For example, the lessor may promise to deliver possession on a certain date, while the lessee may promise to pay $150 as a cleaning deposit before the end of the first month of occupancy. Promises in leases can be classified as covenants or conditions. Breach of a **condition** automatically gives the other party the legal right not to perform his or her obligations. In contrast, breach of a *covenant* does not eliminate the obligation of the injured party to perform. It merely gives the injured party the right to sue for damages caused by the breach of the covenant. Leases which have been well drafted by a landlord's lawyer will make all the tenant's promises conditions. Thus, if the lease contains a condition prohibiting any pet of any kind in the residence, and the tenant kept a caged hamster, the landlord could evict the tenant. If, on the other hand, the lease did not make the tenant's promise a condition, the landlord could only sue for the damages resulting from keeping the hamster, if any can be proved. Some states have enacted statutes which cause all the tenant's promises to be treated as conditions.

condition
an uncertain event on the occurrence of which a contractual obligation is made contingent or dependent

Covenants and conditions in a lease are different kinds of promise.

In general, the law assumes that the lessor and lessee will negotiate all the covenants and conditions needed to establish a workable relationship. In many cases, however, the parties agree only on the very basic terms of the transaction, such as the rental amount and the length of the lease. In these situations the law will recognize the existence of *implied* covenants and conditions.

Implied Covenants and Conditions

In general, these implied promises favor landlords rather than tenants. Thus, most wise tenants will insist on executing a detailed written lease.

The following case illustrates the landlord's tort liability for defects in the property.

Facts
Agnes Rosebury, defendant, owned a rental unit and had a new roof installed. The roofers removed the gutters from the front of the house but failed to reinstall them. Later, Agnes leased the house to Rienecker.

One January, water ran off the front of the roof and accumulated as ice on the front steps of the house. Rienecker cleared the ice off the steps in the afternoon. Gary Borders, plaintiff, a social guest of Rienecker, arrived at 4:00 P.M. and stayed for dinner. At 9:00 P.M., while leaving, Borders slipped on a new accumulation of ice on the steps. Borders then sued Agnes Rosebury, the landlord.

Decision
For Rosebury, the landlord.

Reasoning
The landlord is liable for defective conditions of the leased property existing at the time the lease is executed only if the defect is unknown to the tenant, or the lessor maintains control of the area where the defect exists.

Borders v. Rosebury, 532 P.2d 1366 (Kan. 1975).

Habitability. At common law, tenants leased property under the doctrine of *caveat tenant,* let the tenant beware. The recent trend in landlord tenant law is to recognize an implied warranty of *habitability* and *fitness for the use intended.* Thus if a tenant leased property unseen, and it turned out to be infested with vermin, the tenant's duties would be extinguished for the landlord's violation of the warranty of habitability.

Duty to Repair. Unless the lease provides to the contrary, in the majority of states the *lessee* has the duty to make ordinary repairs to the rented property. This duty stems from the common law obligation imposed on all who temporarily occupy realty not to allow the property to *waste* (deteriorate).[2] However, if the landlord's conduct *causes* the defect, the landlord may be obligated to repair. Further, if this landlord-caused defect makes the property unfit for the intended use, and the landlord refuses to repair, the tenant may, in some states, treat the situation as a **constructive eviction** by moving out and paying no further rent. For example, if the landlord failed to repair the heating system in a large apartment complex during the middle of a very cold winter, the tenants could move out and not be liable for rent even though six months of the lease period were remaining.

Tort Duties. In the majority of states, lessees assume liability for tortious injuries to themselves and to others which occur on the leased property. An exception to this rule exists when the defective condition is known to the landlord but not disclosed to the tenant, and the tenant would not be able to identify the problem after a reasonable inspection. Further, the landlord is also liable for injuries occurring on portions of the property, such as hallways, which the landlord *controls*. In general, the landlord controls the *common areas*. These are areas used by all the tenants. Thus, if a tenant's guest is injured because of a defective diving board in the pool area of an apartment complex, the landlord is likely to be liable.

---

[2] The following states *do* require the *landlord* to keep the premises in good repair: California, Connecticut, Georgia, Indiana, Iowa, Kentucky, Louisiana, Massachusetts, Montana, New Jersey, New York, North Dakota, Oklahoma, Pennsylvania, South Dakota, and Wisconsin. But even in these states the tenant's duty to prevent *waste* generally still exists.

Quiet Enjoyment. The landlord impliedly promises that the tenant will not be dispossessed by someone with title superior to the landlord's.

Fixtures. Generally under *residential* leases, the personal property permanently affixed to leased realty becomes real property and, therefore, remains at the end of the lease as the landlord's property. Similarly, alterations and improvements of the realty accrue to the landlord, and the tenant is not entitled to compensation for their value. When the lease is for *commercial* property, the law presumes that the fixture may be removed by the tenant. However, the tenant must remove the fixture during the term of the lease; the tenant may not be able to remove it after the termination.

Emblements. An emblement is what is sown and produced on the land. A corn crop can be an emblement. When *farm* property is leased and cultivated by the tenant, the law implies a right to harvest those crops. In some states the crop may be harvested by the tenant even after the lease expires.

Taxes, Insurance, and Utilities. The law implies, in the absence of a contrary agreement between the parties, that the landlord will pay the property taxes. However, neither party is obligated to insure the property. The tenant generally must pay for utilities such as garbage, electricity, gas, and water.

Use of the Property. In the absence of a contrary agreement, the lessee may make any use of the property which is legal. Thus, a tenant cannot be evicted for having pets, giving parties, installing a hot plate, or even playing loud country-rock music unless the lease so states.

Prohibition Against Discrimination Statute. The federal Fair Housing Act of 1968, and its amendments, makes it unlawful to discriminate on the basis of race, color, religion, sex, or national origin in the *rental* or advertising of realty.

Express Covenants and Conditions

Nearly all the *implied* promises discussed above can be negated by an *express* agreement between the lessor and the lessee. However, **exculpatory clauses,** which attempt to limit the lessor's *tort* liability, have been nullified by a few states. Of course, no agreement can give the lessor the right to discriminate on the basis of race, color, religion, sex, or national origin.

Duty to Repair. Most tenants will want an affirmative promise in writing from the landlord, phrased as a condition, whereby the duty to repair rests with the lessor.

Cleaning Deposits. Most tenants should require a written promise stating that the cleaning deposit will be refunded if the premises are returned in the same condition as when leased, less normal wear and tear. The promise should also state that the landlord may only retain amounts actually paid others for cleaning prior to the rerenting of the premises.

Most cleaning deposit disputes arise because tenants do not plan their legal affairs intelligently. If they generate evidence of the condition of the premises before they move in and after they move out, their chances of recovering the full cleaning deposit are very high. For example, the lessee can walk through the property before and after occupancy with a respected mature person who would be a good witness in a small claims court. Then, if the issue is litigated, the tenant is likely to prevail even when the landlord lies. Note that, without the witness, it is the tenant's word against that of the landlord, and the tenant has the burden of proof. Therefore, the landlord is likely to win.

Security Deposits. Frequently lessors will require that tenants pay substantial rent in advance as security in the event that the leases are broken. For example, the lessee may be required to pay the first and last month's rent in advance.

Liquidated Damages. Many tenants want to limit their risk under leases so they include **liquidated damages** clauses which limit the liability for rent. For example, a freshman student executing a nine-month lease on an apartment near campus might want to be able to terminate the lease if he or she flunks out, and pay only two months' additional rent, rather than risk greater liability.

Joint and Several Liability. In many instances there are several tenants of the same rental unit. Lessors often include a term in leases with these multiple tenants to protect the lessors. This term makes each tenant jointly and severally liable on the lease. This means that the lessor has a right to collect *all* the rent or damages from any one, or collectively from all, of the tenants.

liquidated damages
the money judicially awarded in the amount as agreed to by the parties in their contract at the time it was made as reasonable compensation for damage which may be caused by the wrongful conduct of one of the parties in the future

Transfer of the Lessee's Interest

In the absence of a contrary agreement between the lessor and the lessee, the lessee generally has the legal power to transfer his or her right of possession to another. If this power exists, the lessor has no control over the tenant's choice of a new occupant. Further, the new occupant is also allowed to transfer his or her possessory interest to another. Therefore, landlords who want to carefully scrutinize tenants frequently include a clause in their leases prohibiting such transfers. These clauses are valid and enforceable. In addition, a few states have enacted statutes which prohibit such transfers without the lessor's consent.

Such transfers can be either **assignments** or **sublettings.** The rights of the parties vary significantly, depending upon which method of transfer is used. They are so distinct that the courts will often permit an assignment when the lease document prohibits just subletting. The reverse is also true.

assignment
(in realty) a transfer by the lessee of *all* the remaining term of the lease

Assignment
In order for a tenant to assign his or her interest in realty, the tenant must transfer the interest for *all* the time remaining on the lease. When this occurs, the original tenant is called the **assignor** and the new tenant is called the **assignee.**

sublet
a transfer by the lessee of a *part* of the remaining term of the lease

Subletting
Subletting occurs when the tenant transfers the right of exclusive possession to another for a period *shorter* than the remaining term of the lease. The original tenant thereby retains a reversionary interest. Therefore, at the end of the subletting period, the sublessor (the original tenant) regains possession for the remainder of the lease period.

assignor
(in realty) one who transfers *all* the remaining term of the lease

assignee
(in realty) the person to whom *all* the remaining term of a lease is transferred

Transfer of the Lessor's Interest

Landlords also have the legal power to transfer their interests in rented property. In general, the new owner takes the property subject to the rights of the tenants. Thus, a tenant can assert the same rights against the new owner that the tenant could have asserted against the old owner. For example, a new owner of a student dormitory cannot raise rents if the student tenants leased with fixed rents for the remainder of the academic year with an estate for years.

The new owner is bound by the old leases because, in most cases, the new owner has knowledge of the leases from the presence of the tenants on the property. If the tenants are not on the property, and the buyer is not aware of the lease when he or she becomes the new owner, the buyer usually takes free of the lease.

Recording the lease.

Tenants who do not visibly occupy the realty can protect themselves by *recording* their leases. This gives **constructive notice** to all the world of the lessee's interest. Thus, if a college freshman visited the college community in mid-July and found an apartment

constructive notice
knowledge of a fact presumed or imputed by law

which was a great bargain close to campus, he or she could execute a lease at that time, with possession to begin when school started. To be protected from a buyer of the realty who might want to raise the rent, the student can *record* the lease. This establishes and protects the student's ownership priority.

Termination of Leases

Leases can be terminated in a variety of ways by both the landlord and the tenant. But there must be some legal basis for termination or the lease continues to be effective. Thus, if a landlord discovered that a tenant, occupying under an estate for years (which did not prohibit pets), kept a dog in the apartment and served the tenant with an impressive looking notarized legal document titled *Notice to Vacate or Be Evicted,* the tenant could continue occupying the property, with the dog! This landlord had no basis for terminating the relationship. The following paragraphs discuss the legal basis for termination of the rental relationship.

Expiration of the lease.

Expiration of the Lease

Estates for years have well-defined ending dates. Periodic estates do not. The arrival of the ending date of the estate for years terminates the rental relationship without notice. If appropriate advance notice is given before the end of a periodic estate, the rental relationship will be terminated. The tenancy at will and tenancy at sufferance are terminated by the sale of the property or death of the landlord. No advance notice of termination is usually required.

Surrender of a lease and the landlord's acceptance of the surrender.

Surrender and Acceptance

If a lessee wants to terminate the lease before expiration of the term, the lessee can accomplish this by *surrendering* the lease to the landlord. However, to terminate the tenant's obligations, the landlord must *accept* the surrender. Surrender and acceptance are acts of the parties which clearly indicate that they both intend the obligations under the lease to be terminated. Thus, if a tenant leased an apartment for five years, and, after two and one-half years was transferred to a new city, the tenant could tell the landlord that he or she wanted to terminate the lease. If the landlord assented and took possession of the apartment, the tenant's obligations might be terminated.

constructive eviction
a tenant's moving out of leased premises because the landlord caused the premises to become unfit for their intended use by the tenant

Constructive Eviction

If, after execution of the lease, the landlord causes the leased premises to become unfit for their intended use by the tenant—as, for example, by refusing to provide water to an apartment—the tenant's obligations may be terminated if the tenant moves out because of the unfit condition.

Breach of condition.

Breach of Condition

If either party breaches a *condition* (not a covenant) contained in the lease, that relieves the other party of his or her obligations under the lease. Thus, if a tenant violates a condition prohibiting green plants on the premises, the landlord can deprive the tenant of possession through eviction. Conversely, a tenant can move out and not be liable for further rent if the landlord breaches an express *condition* promising to keep the premises in good repair.

Eviction.

Eviction

Generally, self-help eviction is available in only a few states. Landlords must almost always *sue* to evict. The proceedings are frequently called actions for *unlawful detainer.* As in all court actions, the defendant (in this situation the tenant) is given advance notice of the lawsuit. Courts try to handle this action speedily so that tenants can be dispossessed as rapidly as possible. If the landlord is, in fact, entitled to evict the tenant and the tenant fails to leave voluntarily, the *sheriff* will physically remove the tenant and the tenant's property from the premises.

In order to win the eviction proceedings the landlord must prove that the tenant's lease has been terminated.

The Uniform Residential Landlord Tenant Act (URLTA) (1972)

In General

The URLTA has been adopted in the states of Alaska, Arizona, Connecticut, Florida, Hawaii, Iowa, Kansas, Kentucky, Michigan, Montana, Nebraska, New Mexico, Oklahoma, Oregon, Tennessee, Virginia, and Washington. The Act, as its title indicates, deals only with *residential* leases, so that commercial, industrial, and agricultural leases do not come under its provisions. In general, the Act attempts to codify the existing court rulings on landlord-tenant law.

Summary Statement

1. The basic nature of the rental relationship involves a temporary transfer of possession in return for the payment of rent.
2. Oral leases are generally enforceable only if they are for a short period.
3. The rental relationships recognized by law are estates at will, estates at sufferance, periodic estates, and estates for years.
4. There are express and implied covenants and conditions in leases.
5. If one party breaches a covenant, the injured party must still perform his or her duties under the lease. If, however, a condition is breached, the injured party need not perform.
6. An assignment is the transfer of all the remaining term of a lease. A subletting is the transfer of just a part of the remaining term.
7. Buyers of realty generally are bound by the leases executed by the seller.
8. A holdover tenant may be liable for all the rent for an additional lease period.
9. A lease may be terminated by expiration of the term, surrender and acceptance, constructive eviction, and breach of condition.
10. The Uniform Residential Landlord Tenant Act (URLTA), adopted in many states, attempts to codify existing court rulings on landlord-tenant law.

The following case is presented to illustrate the legal concepts of constructive eviction, implied covenants, and the nature of the landlord's duty to repair.

Cherberg v. Peoples National Bank of Washington
564 P.2d 1137 (Wash. 1977)

Utter, Associate Justice. James Cherberg and his wife brought a claim based in part upon the tort of intentional interference with business expectancies arising from the willful refusal of the Joshua Green Corporation, as their landlord, to perform duties owed them under a commercial lease. A jury verdict for $42,000 was entered in favor of the Cherbergs. . . .

In 1967 the petitioners, James and Arlene Cherberg, leased a portion of the Lewis Building on Fifth Avenue in downtown Seattle and invested some $80,000 in the establishment and operation of a restaurant business at that location. The respondent, Joshua Green Corporation, acquired the Lewis Building in February of 1972, subject to the lease of the petitioners. In April of 1972, Peoples National Bank of Washington, the owner of the property abutting the Lewis Building on the south, commenced demolition of the existing buildings on its property for the purpose of constructing a high-rise office tower. The demolition work resulted in the exposure of the south wall of the Lewis Building. It was found to be structurally unsafe and in need of substantial repairs to satisfy requirements of the City of Seattle Building Department. The demised premises here at issue were located within the Lewis Building but did not abut the south wall.

The lease between the parties required the lessee to make necessary repairs to maintain the demised premises, excepting the outside walls and other structural components of the building, and reserved to the lessor the use of the roof and outside walls of the building. The lease does not contain an express covenant concerning the responsibility to maintain the structural components of the building.

Upon learning of the problems with the south wall, the lessor contacted the Cherbergs directly and through its attorneys, indicating that the Green Corporation would probably elect not to repair the wall and that the City might order the building closed. The Cherbergs responded that the lessor was obligated under the lease to make repairs and that they would suffer substantial damage should their tenancy be disrupted.

Thereafter, the lessor terminated the lease and informed the Cherbergs of its intention to post the building as unsafe. The Cherbergs closed their business for approximately one week. An independent consultant then informed the Cherbergs that repair of the wall was, in fact, feasible. Petitioners reopened their business when the Green Corporation failed to actually post the building and at that time reiterated their demands to the lessor. The bank, not wishing to be delayed further in its construction plans, eventually repaired the wall at its own expense (estimated at $30,000 to $50,000).

The Green Corporation viewed the Lewis Building as an adequately profitable investment under the circumstances existing at the time of purchase, but that it was the Corporation's desire to regain control of the premises as soon as possible in order to demolish the existing structure on the property and erect a new building which they felt might be more profitable. Demolition of the Lewis Building during the course of the new construction would have been of substantial economic benefit to the Green Corporation. The trial court, at the conclusion of testimony, dismissed the bank. The jury was instructed that respondent was liable for damages caused by the failure to repair the outside wall. It further instructed the jury with regard to the elements of the tort of intentional interference with business expectations and that, if the jury concluded that the defendant's actions were willful, damages for mental suffering, inconvenience, and discomfort would be compensable. The jury made a special finding of willful action and returned a verdict of $42,000. The only evidence of economic loss due to the temporary closure and attendant disruption of business was in the amount of $3,100.

The Court of Appeals . . . reversed. . . .

. . . The lessor was under a duty to make the repairs here in question. The general rule is that a landlord has no duty to make repairs to the demised premises absent an express covenant requiring such action. . . . While it is true that this lease did not contain an express covenant abrogating this common law rule, the area requiring repair was not a part of the demised premises but was an area of the building over which the landlord had expressly retained control.

A landlord has a duty to maintain, control, and preserve retained portions of the premises subject to a leasehold in a manner rendering the demised premises adequate for the tenant's use and safe for occupancy by both the tenant and his invitees. . . . Failure to fulfill this duty results in liability on the part of the lessor for injury caused thereby, . . . and failure to fulfill this duty, by omission to repair, can in a proper case constitute an actionable constructive eviction. . . .

The willful refusal to adequately maintain retained portions of a building so as to allow the tenant to enjoy the beneficial use of the demised portion of the building is a breach of an implied duty owed by the landlord to the tenant under Washington law. On these facts, this breach of duty was sufficient to constitute an actionable constructive eviction and provides a basis for the conclusion that the landlord was liable for any damages stemming from that breach. . . .

The decision of the Court of Appeals is reversed and the judgment in favor of the petitioners reinstated. It is so ordered.

Questions and Case Problems

1. Mr. Lemle leased, in 1965, a villa in the Diamond Head area of Honolulu for $800 per month. On the first night on the property Lemle, his wife and four children slept together to protect themselves from rats which infested the main dwelling and particularly the thatched roof made of coconut leaves. After attempts to trap and exterminate the rats, Lemle and his family left and Mr. Lemle sued for the return of their prepaid rent. Will he prevail? [*Lemle v. Breeden*, 462 P.2d 470 (Hawaii 1969).]

2. Industrial Investment Company is the lessee of certain real property in the State of Hawaii. Industrial then, with the lessor's consent, sublet to Mr. and Mrs. Hayashi. Later Industrial assigned its interest in the lease to Broida Properties who agreed to perform the lease and pay the rent to the lessor. The Hayashis then, with the consent of Broida, assigned their leasehold estate to Mr. and Mrs. Hanuna who, in turn, assigned the leasehold estate to Mrs. Park who agreed to pay the rent to Broida. She did not continue so to pay the rent. Broida sues the Hayashis for the rent. The Hayashis, sublessees, assert that they are not liable to Broida for the rent because there is no longer any privity of contract between the lessee, Industrial, and the lessor because of the lessee's assignment of its interest to Broida. Is there still privity of contract between the lessor and Industrial, the lessee, and must the Hayashis pay Broida? [*Broida v. Hayashi*, 464 P.2d 285 (Hawaii 1970).]

3. Garcia leased an apartment in the East Harlem section of Manhattan. The lead-based paint on the walls was peeling and flaking off. Garcia's two children were eating the lead-based paint. Consumption of this paint can cause mental retardation and death. Garcia complained to the landlord without effect. Then he bought the necessary supplies and repainted, and brought suit against the landlord for his expenses. Will he recover? [*Garcia v. Freeland Realty, Inc.*, 314 N.Y.S.2d 215 (N.Y. 1970).]

4. Fidel rented property from De Baca. The lease agreement contained a convenant against assignments. Fidel sublet a portion of the property for a period shorter than the unexpired term of the lease. De Baca sues to evict Fidel. Who prevails?

5. Dr. Eldredge leased a 45-acre farm located in Gem County, Idaho to Joseph W. Jensen and Rhea Bell Jensen for five years. After the first year, the Jensens defaulted in their rental payments but remained in possession. At the beginning of the fourth year, Dr. Eldredge sold the property to third parties. The Jensens elected to treat the sale as constructive eviction and abandoned the premises. Dr. Eldredge sued for unpaid rent of $1,200. The Jensens defended, claiming damages of $5,000 for early termination of the lease. Who prevails? [*Eldredge v. Jensen*, 404 P.2d 624 (Ida. 1965).]

6. Betty Reiman, a fourteen-year-old girl, went to the apartment of Mrs. Green, who had been ill, to assist in preparations for Mrs. Green's return from the hospital. Betty helped with the washing and drying of Mrs. Green's linen. The linen was dried by hanging it on a clothes line located on the roof of the apartment building. A skylight was also on the roof near the door giving tenants access to the clothes line area. Betty's cousin, Leah, helped her collect the clothes off the line, stacking them in Betty's arms. After stripping the line, Leah went ahead to open the door for Betty. When Leah pulled the door part way open, Betty stepped back to allow it to swing completely open. In so doing, her heel struck an object, causing her to fall backward through the skylight to the floor below. She now sues for the injuries sustained. The owner of the building, Moore, denies responsibility for the injuries. Who prevails? [*Reiman v. Moore*, 108 P.2d 452 (Cal. 1940).]

7. Sharon Fitzgerald orally leased, on a month to month basis, a house owned by Roger Parkin. At the time the lease was created, Parkin promised to make certain repairs within a reasonable time after the beginning of the lease. After repeated demands by Sharon, and the passage of 3 1/2 months, Parkin had not made the repairs. Sharon obtained an inspection from city authorities which resulted in a citation of Parkin for eight violations. One month later, Parkin served Sharon with a 30 day notice to quit the premises. About a month and half later, Parkin initiated an unlawful detainer action against Sharon. Sharon defended the action on the ground that Parkin was engaged in retaliatory eviction. Parkin claims that his reason for evicting Sharon is that one of Sharon's rent checks bounced, another rent check had been late, and that she had kept a dog on the premises in violation of the lease which prohibited having dogs on the premises. Who prevails? [*Parkin v. Fitzgerald*, 240 N.W.2d 828 (Minn. 1976).]

8. Peterson leased property from Platt for a ten-year period. Peterson operated an Arctic Circle Drive Inn on the property. When Peterson fell two months behind in the rent, Platt waited until the property was vacant, took possession of the premises, changed the locks, and denied entry to Peterson and his employees. As a consequence, certain tasty goods perished. Peterson sued Platt, claiming that Platt took possession illegally and, therefore, Platt should be liable for Peterson's injuries. Who prevails? [*Peterson v. Platt,* 400 P.2d 507 (Utah 1965).]

9. Sid Scholar leased an apartment near the women's dorms for a nine-month period. The lease agreement did not indicate who was to be responsible for repairs. When the toilet broke, Sid asked the landlord to repair it. He refused. Sid moved out five months before the end of the lease. The landlord sues Sid for the cost of repairing the toilet and for five months' rent. Who prevails?

10. In the case of *Cherberg v. Peoples National Bank of Washington,* 564 P.2d 1137 (Wash. 1977),[3] describe what motivated the landlord to refuse to make the repairs.

---

[3] See pp. 791–92.

Ethics and Business Law in Part 10
Real Property

Introduction

This end-of-Part discussion, like the others in this book, is designed to encourage students to begin forming personal beliefs about what is right or wrong conduct in business. The discussion here builds on the material in the first end-of-Part discussion on pages 58 to 69; you may find it helpful to review that.

This material has several goals. The "sampling of ethical issues" section immediately following is designed to help you see the range of ethical issues associated with this area of the law. The in-depth discussion is intended to provide you with a background for forming your own beliefs about a single very important ethical issue in business. The problems at the end of this Part are designed to build your skill in ethical analysis while exploring further the in-depth issue.

A Sampling of Ethical Issues in Real Property Law

Real property law incorporates the ongoing conflict which inevitably arises between the interests of the individual and the needs of society.

Individual Rights versus the Needs of Society

Governments have the constitutional power to condemn and rezone property. Both of these activities bring the needs of society into conflict with the interests of individual landowners. A government agency can condemn private property for a public purpose. Of course this advances the public need over the individual's interest. But since the government must pay the reasonable value of condemned property, the individual's injury is reduced. Do you think this is a reasonable balance between private interests and the public good? Can you think of situations where this process would produce an unjust result?

Zoning powers allow cities and counties to regulate the ways real property is used. There are of course limitations on this power. For example, a city could not engage in spot zoning. But zoning sometimes creates very large costs for individuals. Suppose you owned undeveloped land zoned for commercial use worth $400,000. If that land were rezoned to single family residences its value could fall to $100,000. Of course you would bear the loss rather than all the persons benefited by the rezoning. Do you think this is just? Can you articulate a justification for this law using one of the four styles of ethical reasoning? Can you decide why the law treats rezoning and condemnation in different ways?

Recording statutes also raise ethical issues. Recall that if a grantor issues two deeds to the same estate, the first to record will generally own all while the second to record will own nothing. This second party will undoubtedly try to sue the grantor. But if the grantor is bankrupt or has fled the jurisdiction, it is likely that the second grantee will recover nothing. Can you analyze this law from a utilitarian perspective? How do you think Kant would assess this law? Do you think this law is ethical?

Conditional estates and restrictive convenants also reflect the recurring conflict between individual desires and the needs of society. Our law allows owners to use restrictive covenants and conditional estates to control future use of the property. Many believe that individuals should not be able to control the use of realty which they do not have the legal right to possess. On this issue our law favors the individual. At one time such restraints were used to prevent realty from being owned by Catholics, Jews, Negroes, Asians, and/or Baptists. Today, of course such restraints are invalid. Do you think it is ethical for a former owner of realty to be able to control its use?

Exploitation of the Vulnerable

Real property law raises several issues where one party is able to gain an unfair advantage over another. For example, lessors often use their superior knowledge of landlord/tenant law to obtain a legal advantage over a naive tenant. One of the common tactics is for the lessor to have his attorney prepare a lease favorable to the lessor, then it is typeset and presented to tenants as a "standard" lease. If conflicts arise, the lessor is often coached by an attorney while the tenant often lacks the financial resources to protect his or her legal rights. If you were a landlord would you engage in such tactics? Why or why not?

Another example of exploitation occurs when a tenant moves to another part of the country. Lessors can delay inspecting the apartment until the tenant is gone, then unfairly withhold the cleaning deposit. For many tenants, it is just too expensive to come back and sue the lessor so they just forget the loss. Can you see how tempted some lessors would be in this situation? Do you think you could be tempted enough to engage in this conduct?

In-Depth Discussion of a Basic Issue: Unequal Wealth

This issue asks whether it is ethical to encourage the unequal distribution of wealth. Because many business ethics decisions involve this issue, mature business persons need clear beliefs about it.

Egoistic Views

A self-centered analysis leads to differing conclusions depending on who does the analysis. If the egoist is a wealthy person, then economic systems which allow for unequal wealth are good because they help this person.

Frequently, wealthy or talented persons argue that merit justifies unequal wealth. One form of this argument says that there is an *entitlement* for those with the most talent and energy. This argument assumes that individual differences in persons justify different treatment by society.

This view is often attacked on the ground that talent and perhaps even energy are distributed to individuals by forces over which they have no control. That is, the highly talented individual is not necessarily highly talented because of his or her own efforts. Rather it is the "role of the genetic dice" which determines talent. And since the individual is not responsible for this attribute, the individual should not be rewarded for it. This critique of merit concludes that talent ought not to entitle one to different treatment.

The egoistic analysis from the perspective of the poor person can reach the opposite conclusion of that of the rich person. Thus, economic systems which encourage unequal wealth may be viewed as bad by the poor person because they may be seen as reducing the share of the poor person's wealth.

As you can see, egoism provides little guidance for assessing this issue because it leads to differing conclusions depending on the status of the party who does the analysis.

Utilitarian Analysis

This line of analysis asks what generates the greatest good for the greatest number. For example in real property law, those injured by rezoning are generally not entitled to compensation for their losses—they must bear the loss themselves. This law generates the greatest good for the greatest number because the loss is borne by only one party instead of many.

It is fairly clear that unequal distribution of wealth benefits the majority. This is because our economic system creates incentives which encourage everyone to contribute as much as possible to society in order to achieve personal rewards. Also, by placing more of society's wealth in the hands of the most talented, we increase the chance that it will be used most productively, thereby increasing total social wealth. Notice that the rewards are not justified as entitlements, but rather by contribution, which causes the total pie of wealth in society to increase. There is substantial evidence that the financial incentives which produce the unequal wealth do in fact increase total wealth.

The objection to this line of analysis is that what benefits the majority—the increase in total wealth—may come at the expense of the minority of persons with either little talent or little opportunity to exercise their talent. While this argument may be powerful to some, it carries little weight for the utilitarian, who tests right or wrong by looking for the greatest good for the greatest number.

Kantian and Judeo-Christian Analysis

This line of reasoning generally focuses on duty or obligation. Since individuals may not be used exclusively as means to the ends of others, Kant would likely reject the rezoning law, seeing it as a way to use the landowner as a means to the ends of all the other taxpayers in the community. The real property law right to reasonable compensation for condemnation is more consistent with Kantian and religious ethics. While the majority benefit, it is not because they are able to impose the cost on a solitary landowner.

In the Kantian style of reasoning, duty is identified by the use of the three tests described in the first end-of-Part discussion: 1) persons are moral entities and cannot be used exclusively as means; 2) we may not act, or create rules (or economic systems), where different rules apply to the sovereign (the rule maker) than to the subject (those ruled by the sovereign); and 3) the acts or rules must be able to be made universal without logical inconsistency.

Religions identify duty in large part by looking at scriptures. In general, nearly every religion imposes a duty on believers to accord special treatment to the poor. This is clearly true in the Judeo-Christian tradition and in most of the major religions of the world. The scriptural statement, "What you do unto the least of my brothers, you do unto me," exemplifies this view.

The religious view of the poor, and the Kantian requirement that we not use individuals exclusively as means, call into question the utilitarian analysis of economic systems. While utilitarians can justify unequal wealth by concluding that the majority are benefited, the special concern of religious and Kantian thinkers for members of society who are in minority positions prevents them from accepting the utilitarian argument. They conclude that those in economic minority positions cannot be exploited even if it benefits the majority.

John Rawls, a philosopher at Harvard, has articulated a system which justifies unequal distribution of wealth for religious and Kantian thinkers. Rawls concludes that the test of the rightness or wrongness of an economic system is its impact on the least advantaged members of society. If the consequence of the unequal wealth is that these least advantaged members are better off, then the system is good. If the consequence of the unequal wealth is that this group is worse off, then the system is not morally justified. Capitalism creates unequal wealth. But if it causes the total economy to grow rapidly, so that the least advantaged members of the capitalist society are better off than with equal division of wealth, the unequal wealth is, according to Rawls, justified.

Conclusion

Can you see that egoism tests rightness or wrongness by looking at the impact on one individual, utilitarianism judges by looking at the impact on the majority, and Kantian and religious thinking on this issue look at the impact on the minority? Which line of reasoning do you find most persuasive?

Solving Ethics Problems

Like the other end-of-Part discussions in this book, this one presents problems for you to consider. These problems have three goals. The first is to give you the opportunity to further explore the in-depth issue. The second goal is to give you experience in ethical reasoning about the law and about related management problems. The third goal is to let you see how thinking critically about the law can increase your ability to make ethical decisions. To facilitate this, the problems begin by asking you to analyze the law for its ethical content and then shift to looking at related problems in managerial ethics.

For a discussion of the ethical roles of markets and the law, and examples of the four styles of ethical reasoning—egoism, utilitarianism, Kant's philosophy, and religious ethics—read the business ethics material at the end of Part 1.

Problems

1. Review the case of *Loretto v. Teleprompter Manhattan CATV Corp.*, et al. on page 767. There, the state of New York enacted a statute which in effect made $1.00 the maximum fee a landlord could charge a cable TV company for installing cable in common areas in order to serve tenants. One landlord sued in federal court and the statute was declared unconstitutional as a violation of the "Taking Clause." Evaluate the ethical character of both the New York statute and the "Taking Clause."

2. Review the case of *Karell v. West and Shobert* on page 779. There, Mrs. Karell sought to assert ownership of a 3.7 acre parcel of land because it had been enclosed with her property by a fence for a substantial period of time. Her claim was denied because of insufficient proof that her use was continuous for the required period of time. Do you think this law seeks to allocate the land on the basis of merit (or social contribution), or the greatest good for the greatest number, or with concern for the interests of the weakest members of society, or a combination of these? Does order play a role in this case?

3. You are the president of a large conglomerate with 5 major lines of business. Four are highly profitable and one is losing money for the corporation. This weak division is located in a part of the country which is undergoing economic difficulties. If you close down this division about 1,000 people will be thrown out of work with little chance of finding other employment unless they relocate to more prosperous areas of the nation. If you don't close this division, profits will decline by about 30%. What ought you to do and why?

4. Your firm allocates bonus money to each department head for distribution to subordinates as he or she judges best. You have received a pot of $10,000 to be allocated among your 5 subordinates. One is a highly talented person who accounts for about 40% of the department's productivity. Two others carry their fair share, each contributing about 20% each to the department's productivity. The remaining two contribute about 10% each. Of these latter two, one is just not very bright and the other is bright but going through some personal problems at this time. How will you allocate this bonus money—by ability, by contribution, equally, or by using a combination of these methods? How do you justify your distribution method?

PART 11 Wills and Decedents' Estates, and Trusts

54. Wills and Decedents' Estates
General state statutory law concerning the transfer of property on death by will and by intestacy (without a will).

55. Trusts
The various kinds of trust, particularly the express trust which is so widely used as a means of transferring property either during lifetime or by a will.

Summary

The event of death has an immediate legal effect on the ownership of the decedent's property. In chapter 54, the importance of making a will, the formal requisites of a will, beneficiaries, revocation of a will, proof of a will's validity (probate), and administration of the decedent's estate with and without a will are discussed.

Chapter 55 considers the trust as a legal device for the transfer of property, made either during lifetime or on death, to be administered for the benefit of a beneficiary. Various kinds of trust are examined, especially the express trust, and their creation, administration, modification, and termination are discussed.

Business ethics as it relates to the text material in this Part is considered at the end of the Part.

54 Wills and Decedents' Estates

After you have read this chapter, you should be able to:

1. Explain why a will is desirable.
2. Briefly discuss the Uniform Probate Code and where it differs from the non-Code general law.
3. Indicate which state has jurisdiction over a decedent's will and estate.
4. Enumerate and explain the usual requisites for making a will.
5. Describe who may be beneficiaries of a will.
6. Explain how a will may be revoked by the testator/testatrix and by operation of law.
7. Discuss what is meant by a codicil and its effect.
8. Briefly discuss the legal procedure to probate a will.
9. Explain the meaning and effect of intestacy on the transfer of a decedent's estate.
10. Explain how a decedent's estate is administered.

Introduction

Background

Like most persons you desire to acquire and enjoy property during your lifetime, whether acquired by your own efforts or by inheriting from your parents or other persons. You also probably would like to leave some of your property to other persons on your death. Accordingly, it is of importance that you acquire some knowledge of the law by which your property will transfer on your death.

Persons may own **property** and dispose of it as they wish either during their lifetime (inter vivos—among living persons) or at the time of their death. Nevertheless the state is concerned and interested in seeing that, to a certain extent, various persons closely related to the **decedent** must not be overlooked (disinherited) by the decedent in the distribution of his or her property at the time of death. For example, states generally prohibit the decedent's disinheritance of his or her spouse. Accordingly, state **statutory** law governs the validity of the decedent's will and the distribution of the decedent's property.

Transfer of Property on Death. A **will** is a formal document which governs the transfer of property at death. It is a testament to the decedent's intent to transfer the decedent's property on his or her death, often called a "testamentary disposition." The person executing a will is called a **testator** if a man and a **testatrix** if a woman. A person who executes a will dies "testate," and a person who dies without a will dies "intestate." A will provides not only for the transfer of property on death but for other matters which must be attended to, such as a designation of who is to represent the decedent in the administration of the decedent's estate or who is to be the **guardian** of the decedent's minor children. Also, the will may provide for a **trust,** called a "testamentary trust" because of its inclusion in the will, which is a legal device whereby legal title to property is held by one person (a trustee) for the benefit of a beneficiary. Unless otherwise indicated, use of the word "testator" or "testatrix" includes the other.

The Uniform Probate Code

The Uniform Probate Code (UPC) was approved by the National Conference of Commissioners on Uniform State Laws and the American Bar Association in 1969. By 1982, the UPC was adopted by only fifteen states: Alaska, Arizona, Colorado, Florida, Hawaii, Idaho, Kentucky (Article VII, Part 1), Maine, Michigan, Minnesota, Montana, Nebraska, New Mexico, North Dakota, and Utah. Because of such limited adoption, limited reference to the UPC will be made as the general non-UPC state law is discussed in this chapter.

The Will

Formal Requisites

Generally, seven elements must be considered in making a will: the law applicable to wills; testamentary capacity; testamentary intent; the writing; the signature; attestation; and publication. There are also special types of will to be considered.

The Law Applicable to Wills. The statutory law of the state where the testator was **domiciled** at the time of his death governs the making of his will. However, if the testator has a legal interest in land located in another state, then the law of the state where the land is located governs the validity of the will regarding the disposition of the land located there. UPC 2–506 makes an important change providing for a choice of law as to execution.[1]

property
a thing; also an interest or right in a thing

decedent
one who is dead

statute
law created by a legislative body and approved by the executive

will
a formal document which governs the transfer of property at death

testator (testatrix)
a man (woman) who executes a will

guardian
a person legally entrusted with the custody and/or the property of another

trust
a legal device whereby legal title to property is held by one person (a trustee) for the benefit of a beneficiary

Uniform Probate Code.

domicile
the state in which a person has his or her permanent home, not merely a residence

---

[1] "A written will is valid if executed in compliance with Section 2–502 or 2–503 or if its execution complies with the law at the time of execution of the place where the will is executed, or of the law of the place where at the time of execution or at the time of death the testator is domiciled, has a place of abode or is a national." UPC 2–506.

Testamentary Capacity. The testator must be of a minimum statutory age and he must have testamentary capacity to make a will. In most states and UPC 2–501, the legal age is eighteen years and he must be of "sound mind" *at the time the will is executed.* Generally, by sound mind is meant that the testator has sufficient mental capacity to make a will if he has the *ability* to know: that he is making a will to dispose of his property on his death; the nature and extent of his property; and the "natural objects of his bounty," namely members of his immediate family (e.g., spouse, children), and persons for whom he has affection. *There is a legal presumption of testamentary capacity.* Contestants who question the testator's testamentary capacity have the burden of proving that it did not exist at the time of the will's execution. In the following case, the court decided that the decedent had lucid moments when he had testamentary capacity.

Facts

Ralph Mangan died August 22, 1972 at age 72, a widower with no children. On November 16, 1971 Ralph sustained a gunshot wound and was hospitalized until December 22, 1971 when he was removed to a nursing home. On February 26, 1972 he resided with his brother, Edward, the petitioner, until April 5, 1972 when he was hospitalized with a bleeding ulcer, arteriosclerotic cardiovascular disease and other secondary ailments. On May 9, 1972 Ralph returned to the nursing home, on June 6, 1972 he was adjudicated an incompetent, and he died while in the nursing home.

While in the nursing home from December 1971 to February 26, 1972, he executed a will on February 23, 1972. The will was filed for probate and is contested by the petitioner as invalid on the ground that Ralph lacked testamentary capacity, alleging that Ralph: was thoroughly disoriented because of his advanced age, arteriosclerosis, and the trauma of the gunshot wound; and had devised property to a person he named as his nephew when there was no such nephew.

Witnesses testified that during Ralph's first stay in the hospital and later at the nursing home he was self-reliant and attended to all his business affairs even after the will was executed. At Ralph's request, his attorney had gone over the will in detail with Ralph. The attorney testified that Ralph was of sound and disposing mind, knew what he wanted and what the objects of his bounty were, mentioned dollar amounts and street addresses, and went over various names mentioning a number of nephews, cousins, and others.

Two physicians testified that at times Ralph was confused and disoriented as a result of cerebral arteriosclerosis and medication. They also testified that patients suffering from cerebral arteriosclerosis enjoy periods of lucidity, that Ralph was given a drug to improve his cerebral circulation, but they were unable to state with reasonable certainty that Ralph lacked testamentary capacity on February 23, 1972.

The lower court found that Ralph had testamentary capacity on February 23, 1972 and that the will was valid.

Decision
Affirmed.

Reasoning
The physicians stated that patients suffering from cerebral arteriosclerosis enjoy periods of lucidity, that Ralph was given a drug to improve his cerebral circulation, and that they were unable to state with reasonable certainty that Ralph lacked testamentary capacity on February 23, 1972. Ralph's attorney gave evidence of Ralph's testamentary capacity at the time he executed the will. Ralph had many kinsmen, and he could have testamentary capacity without knowing whether all of them were alive and without remembering the names of all of his nephews.

Edward L. Mangan v. Joseph J. Mangan, Jr., et al., 554 S.W.2d 418 (Mo. 1977).

undue influence
unfair persuasion by one who, because of his relationship with another, dominates the other

Testamentary Intent. The "will" is an expression of the testator's testamentary *intent* (will) to dispose of his property on his death. Testamentary capacity (ability) must be accompanied by this intent. The will must manifest in writing the testator's intent to make the writing his will in order to transfer his property as indicated in the writing. **Undue**

influence[2] or fraud practiced on the testator, and sometimes the testator's mistake, invalidates the writing as an intent to make it his will. In the following case, the court held that there was no undue influence, because an illicit relationship did not constitute such undue activity as to unduly influence the testator in making his will.

Facts
Mack Reed was a bachelor who died at age 74. He executed a will on June 30, 1964 leaving his real estate to Mary Shipp, as trustee, in trust for, and apportioned by description among, her three minor children; his household furnishings to his unmarried sisters, Lula and Bertha, with whom he lived; and the residue equally and directly to Mary's three children. Lula and her sister, Fannie, petitioners, contest the will asserting that it is invalid because of undue influence exercised by Mary on Mack. The lower court directed a verdict that there was no undue activity amounting to undue influence by Mary on Mack and that the will was valid. Petitioners claim that the will is invalid and appeal.

There was evidence that Mary and her husband, Cary, were neighbors of Mack while he was living with Lula and Bertha and they worked for Mack during the last 25 years of his life. A neighbor witnessed Mary and Mack having sexual relations in the barn. They were together daily in the fields, in the truck going and coming from town, and at the livestock shows in towns nearby. Mack spent considerable time with Mary's children, carrying them in his arms when they were small, playing with them, buying for them, and referring to them as his children. Additional evidence was that Mary employed the attorney who drew Mack's will.

Decision
Affirmed.

Reasoning
In order to raise a question of fact for the jury of undue influence affecting the validity of the will, the contestants must prove: (1) a confidential relationship; (2) a person must have been favored under the will or must have done something which causes people close to her (Mary) to be favored under the will; *and* (3) the favored beneficiary or someone else must have done and performed some undue activity in and about the procurement of the will. All that is needed to submit the case to a jury is a mere scintilla from which the jury can infer some undue activity in the procurement or execution of the will.

There was sufficient evidence regarding (1) and (2). The only question is with regard to (3) as to whether an inference is raised by the evidence that Mary was "active" in and about the execution and preparation of the will, as undue activity is legally defined. Illicit relations are shown between the testator and the person (Mary) who is favoring a beneficiary (Mary's children), but the illicit relationship is insufficient of itself to prove undue influence. Undue influence must be such as, in some manner, to destroy the free agency of the testator, and to prevent the exercise of that discretion which the law requires a party should possess as essential to a valid testamentary disposition of his property.

No presumption of undue activity in the procurement of a will amounting to undue influence arises from the mere disposition by the testator of his property to these children whom he loved and treated as his own. If they were his children, or if he thought they were, this may have influenced him to provide for them; but *unduly influenced,* as that term is legally understood, is entirely another matter.

Lula Nannie Ella Reed and Fannie Reed Simmons v. Mary Shipp, et al., 308 So.2d 705 (Ala. 1975).

---

[2] "A presumption of undue influence arises when it is shown that (1) a confidential or fiduciary relationship existed between the testator and the beneficiaries; (2) the beneficiary or beneficiaries were given a substantial bequest or devise; (3) the beneficiary or beneficiaries were active in procuring the execution of the will. . . . Nevertheless, the law does not ban as undue the natural influence of affection or attachment or the desire to gratify the wishes of one beloved or trusted by the testator, . . . and the fact that the testator made an unequal or even unjust distribution of his property does not of itself support an inference of undue influence. A man has the right to will his property to whomever he chooses, and the beneficiary in his will is not bound to account for the choice. . . ." *Edward L. Mangan v. Joseph J. Mangan, Jr.,* et al., 554 S.W.2d 418 (Mo. 1977).

**margin terms:**

nuncupative will
an oral will as permitted by statute

personal property (personalty)
a movable thing, along with interests and rights in the thing

holographic will
a will which is entirely in the testator's handwriting

attest
to witness

The Writing. The will need not be formal, as long as it substantially complies with the statutory requirements. Statutes require that, with one exception, the will must be in writing. The exception is the **nuncupative** (oral) **will,** which is subject to certain limitations. The testator's spoken words manifesting his intent to make them his will must be made during the testator's last sickness in his home or in the place where he died, his words must be published (spoken) to the requisite number of witnesses present as such at his request who must commit the testator's words to writing within a specified number of days thereafter. In this way, by the statute, soldiers in military service and sailors at sea can make nuncupative wills. Only **personal property** can be transferred by a nuncupative will.

If a will and its signature are entirely handwritten by the testator it is called a **holographic will.** UPC 2–503 requires that the holographic will's "material provisions" and signature be made by the testator.

The will may be handwritten, typed, printed, in ink or pencil, or be a combination of these. It may consist of one or more pages as long as they are clearly designated as being part of the single instrument. Also, in most states written papers not attached to the will and without the formal requisites of a will may be included as a part of the will if: the will clearly and unambiguously identifies them and indicates an intention that they are to be a part of the will; and they are in existence at the time the will is executed. For example, the papers may list various items of property designating which items are to go to the various named persons, e.g., furniture, china, silverware, pictures. This doctrine is called "incorporation by reference." However, UPC 2–513 permits the separate writing identifying certain tangible personal property to be "prepared before or after the execution of the will; it may be altered by the testator after its preparation. . . ."

The Signature. The will must be "signed" by the testator, although in most states his signature may be made for him by another person at the testator's request and direction and in his presence. The word "sign" is different from "subscribe," the latter word meaning that the signature must appear at the end of an instrument. In most states and the UPC 2–502 the testator's signature may appear anywhere in the will, subscribing is not required. Any writing, initials, mark, print, or impression which the testator intends to be his signature is such.

Attestation and Publication. In order to authenticate the signature as that of the testator, either made by him or acknowledged by him as his signature, the making of the signature must be witnessed (**attested**) by the required number of people at the testator's request, usually two and sometimes three depending on the state. UPC 2–502 requires at least two witnesses. The witnesses must be competent to testify later to the occasion of the signing, that is, the circumstances at the time, the testamentary capacity and the testamentary intent of the testator. They are to "sign" as witnesses, although their signatures usually occur at the end of the will. Generally, all of them do not have to be present at the same time nor to sign as witnesses in each other's presence, although they usually do. While an attestation *clause* of what occurred is not required in most states nor the UPC, nevertheless it usually appears in most wills. In most states and UPC 2–503, a holographic will does not require any witnesses. The testator is not required to make a "publication" (declaration) that the instrument is his will nor is he required to disclose the contents of the will to the witnesses.

In most states the fact that a person is an "interested party" under the will, namely a *direct* beneficiary, does not disqualify that person from being an attesting witness to the will. However, if that person's testimony as a witness is necessary to prove the will, in most states that person loses his or her interest as a beneficiary *under the will,* but still has a right to any statutory intestate share due him or her as though there were no will at all. For example, if the testator's daughter is named as a beneficiary in the will and, as one of the two required witnesses her testimony is necessary to prove the will, the daughter will lose her beneficial share under the will but she may now inherit a statutory intestate share of her father's estate as though there were no will. A person with an *indirect* beneficial interest under a will is not an interested party, e.g., a member of an association which has been named as a beneficiary in a will. Under UPC 2–505, any person may serve as an attesting witness without thereby invalidating the instrument as a will and without loss of his or her beneficial interest under the will.

Beneficiaries

A person who acquires as a gift property of a decedent on death is a "beneficiary." Personal property is "given" or "bequeathed" by a will to a beneficiary called a **legatee.** Real property is "devised" by a will to a beneficiary called a **devisee,** although under UPC 1–201(7)(8) a **devise** and devisee are concerned with real *and* personal property.

A named beneficiary may renounce his or her beneficial interest under the will, often either for tax purposes or in order to receive a greater share of the estate, sometimes called a "forced share." Because of the state's concern that certain persons, e.g., those closely related to the decedent such as spouse or children, not be disinherited by the decedent, statutes provide for limitations on such disinheritance and require that such persons have a right to a specified minimal share in the estate. Generally, a beneficiary who murders the decedent cannot receive any of the decedent's property under the will or by intestacy.

The beneficiary must survive the testator in order to take under the will on the testator's death. If the beneficiary and the testator should die simultaneously because it cannot be determined who died first, under section 1 of the Uniform Simultaneous Death Act, each decedent is treated as having survived the other and the property of each is so distributed. However, under section 2, if the will provided that the beneficiary must survive the testator and there is insufficient evidence that they died other than simultaneously, then the beneficiary is not presumed to have survived the testator.

Under section 6 of the Act, the Act does not apply "where provision is made for distribution of property different from the provisions of this Act, or where provision is made for a presumption as to survivorship which results in a distribution of property different from that here provided." Also, under section 3 of the Act, if the parties hold title to property as **joint tenants** with the right of survivorship, e.g., husband and wife as joint tenants of their home, and there is insufficient evidence that they died other than simultaneously, then each party receives a pro rata share of the property, e.g., if husband and wife are joint tenants each receives one-half of the property as if the other spouse had survived.

If the will provides for a **testamentary trust,**[3] the trust beneficiary must be definitely identified or can be identified within the period of the rule against perpetuities.

Revocation

Since a will speaks and is effective as of the time of the testator's death it can be revoked (terminated) at any time prior to his death. Revocation may occur in two ways: by act of the testator, or by operation of law.

By Act of the Testator. The testator revokes his will when he properly *expresses an intent* that, from that moment, he no longer wants the instrument to be his will. State statutes prescribe the two ways by which such an intention of revocation can be expressed: (1) by the testator's subsequent writing expressly or impliedly manifesting an intent thereby to revoke his will; and (2) by the testator's physical act to the instrument with the intent thereby to revoke it as his will.

1. By a Subsequent Writing. In most states, the testator's subsequent written manifestation of revocation must have the same formality as that required for the

---

[3] See pp. 803, 823. For the rule against perpetuities, see pp. 824–25.

legatee
the beneficiary of a testamentary gift of personal property

devise
a testamentary gift of real property

devisee
the beneficiary of a testamentary gift of real property

legacy
a testamentary gift of personal property

joint tenancy
a form of ownership of property by more than one person with the right of survivorship

testamentary trust
a trust created by the will of a decedent

execution of his will. A subsequent nuncupative will does not revoke a prior written will. The subsequent writing may be a new will. If the new will expressly states that it revokes a prior will, then the prior will is revoked.

A subsequent writing may also be a **codicil,** which is a writing executed with the same formality as a will; it expressly refers to a prior will, by its terms it either partially revokes or adds to the prior will by making changes or additions to the will and thereby becomes a supplemental part of the will to the extent of such change or addition, or it entirely revokes the prior will. The codicil's wording determines its legal effect. Any proper subsequent writing of revocation may revoke a prior will and its later codicils.

codicil
a writing executed with the same formality as a will, expressly referring to a prior will, by its terms either partially revoking or adding to the prior will by making changes or additions to the will and thereby becoming a supplemental part of the will to the extent of such changes or additions, or entirely revoking the prior will

2. By Act to the Instrument. Again, the testator's physical act of mutilating the will must be in exact compliance with the statute in order to effect a total or partial revocation of his will. The testator's act must be done with the intent thereby to revoke the will. The physical act may be by burning, tearing, cancelling, obliterating, or destroying the will. In the following unusual older case, selected for its excellent simplicity and directness, the court held that an attempt to destroy a will was not the same as actual destruction as required by the state statute.

Facts
J. T. Payne, the testator, executed his will on June 29, 1934, which was offered for probate after his death. A witness testified that: she, the testator and his wife were in a room in the testator's home during July 1934; the testator told his wife "I am going to get rid of this damn will right now"; he then threw the will into the fireplace where there were some live coals and he immediately turned around and walked out; the testator's wife jerked the will out of the fireplace; only one end of the will landed in the fire and the will was smoking on one end when the wife removed it from the fireplace; the wife put the will in her apron pocket and immediately left the room. Except for slight singeing of the edges of the will, not a single word was destroyed, obliterated, or even rendered obscure in the slightest degree.

The New York State statute provides that revocation of a will may be expressly effected by destruction or obliteration of it by the testator, or by someone else at his direction, with an intention to revoke it. The will is contested as invalid on the ground that the testator revoked the will offered for probate by throwing it into the fire with the intent thereby to revoke it. The lower court held that the will had been destroyed and, therefore, revoked. The proponent of the will made a motion for a new trial, which was denied. The proponent appealed.

Decision
Judgment reversed, new trial ordered.

Reasoning
The will was never destroyed and, therefore, never revoked. The statute clearly requires two things for a testator's revocation of a will by his act to the document, namely his intent to revoke the will and actual destruction or obliteration of the will. Here, while the testator intended to revoke his will, no revocation occurred by his attempt to destroy it. An attempt to destroy would open wide the gate to fraud and defeat the wholesome purpose of the statute requiring these two things.

Vance Payne v. J. T. Payne, Jr., 100 S.E.2d 450 (Ga. 1957).

The physical act may be performed by the testator or by someone in his presence and by his direction. In the absence of proof of the testator's intent to the contrary, it is presumed that the testator's physical act revoking the will was made with the intent thereby to revoke any codicils. Some states permit partial revocation of a will by the testator's physical act to the will, as by crossing out words or provisions in the will as long as the rest of the will makes sense and complies with the statute. However, nothing can be added without compliance with the formal requisites for making a will.

By Operation of Law. After a testator has made his will, his circumstances may so change as to create a presumption that he impliedly no longer has an intention to have the entire instrument be his will or that a portion of his will no longer continue because of such change. The states and UPC 2–508 differ in many respects with respect to the legal effect of some of these circumstances. A few of the more important circumstances and their legal effect will be briefly considered.

By statute in many states, the testator's marriage subsequent to his making his will revokes the will, unless the will expressed that it was made in contemplation of the subsequent marriage or the will made provision for the surviving spouse. Under UPC 2–508, the subsequent marriage does not revoke *the will;* but if the testator, by will, does not make provision for his surviving spouse, under UPC 2–301 the surviving spouse would take her *intestate share* as though the decedent had died without a will. Under that section, no change of circumstances other than a divorce or annulment revokes a will.

Subsequent marriage.

By statute in most states, the testator's divorce or annulment of his marriage occurring subsequent to his making his will does not revoke either his will or any provision therein for his surviving spouse. However, if the divorce or annulment provided for a property settlement, such provision would impliedly revoke only that portion of the will which made a gift for the surviving spouse.

Subsequent divorce or annulment.

By statute in most states and UPC 2–302, the birth of the married testator's child subsequent to his making a will does not revoke his will. The UPC 2–302 and most states by statute provide that a later-born child will receive its intestate share as if there were no will.

Later-born child.

Probate, and Administration of the Decedent's Estate

A decedent dies either with a will (testate) or without a will (intestate). If the decedent had executed an instrument which is alleged to be the decedent's will, then its validity as a will must be proved. This involves **probate** (proof). Whether the decedent died testate or intestate, the decedent's estate must be administered under the authority of a proper state court. Accordingly, we will first consider probate if the decedent died testate, then the effect of intestacy, and finally the administration of the decedent's estate.

probate
the procedure of proving to a proper court that an instrument is the will of a decedent

Probate

Procedure. Probate is the procedure of proving to a proper court that an instrument is the will of a decedent. An instrument can be effective as a will only on the testator's death. The instrument is submitted to the proper state court where it is subject to probate. This court is usually called a **probate court** or "surrogate court." The state in which the decedent was domiciled has jurisdiction over the will of the decedent and the decedent's property, except that if any of the decedent's real property is located in another state then the latter state has jurisdiction to determine the validity of the will to the extent of such real property. The will is probated in the probate court in the county where the decedent was domiciled. Once it is probated and found valid there, the probate is effective in all other states, except for real property in another state.

probate court
a court which has jurisdiction over the estate of a deceased person

The probate proceeding is begun by the filing of a petition for probate with the proper court by any interested party, usually the person who is named in the will as the personal representative desired by the decedent. All interested parties are notified of the proceeding.

The attesting witnesses to the will testify under oath as to the execution of the will. If they are not available, or if the original of the will is lost or destroyed by other than the testator, statutes make special provision for probate under these circumstances by other evidence, e.g., the testimony of other people and proof of a copy of the alleged lost or destroyed will. When the instrument is approved by the court as being the last will and testament of the decedent, "letters of administration" or "letters testamentary" are issued by the court to the person named in the will as desired by the testator to be appointed by the court to represent the testator and administer his estate. The instrument can be contested as not being the will of the decedent, and if it is found to be invalid as a will and there is no other instrument proved as a valid will, then the decedent has died intestate.

In states where the UPC has been adopted, reference should be made to it because of its provision for flexibility in handling probate of decedents' estates.

Intestacy

Death without a will causes the decedent to die intestate. State statutes of "descent and distribution" specifically provide for the distribution of intestate property to persons according to their marital or blood relationship to the intestate. Persons who, by statute, are entitled to property not disposed of by a decedent's will are called **heirs.** This is the same meaning as under UPC 1–201(17).

With respect to a person's *marital* relationship with the intestate (husband and wife), state statutes on descent and distribution differ. Generally, they provide that a surviving spouse will receive a fractional share of the intestate property, the extent of the share depending on whether or not there are surviving children and their number.

With respect to a person's *blood* relationship with the intestate, the statutes of descent and distribution in the various states usually have a pattern of *first* applying a *descending* line of inheritance and *then* an *ascending* line of inheritance for the purpose of intestate succession. **Per capita** (by heads) means that all persons who stand in the same degree of relationship to the intestate share equally in the estate without consideration of any right of representation. **Per stirpes** (by stocks, or by roots) means that the survivors of their parent represent their parent and take the parent's share in an intestate's estate by such representation for division among themselves.

Administration of the Decedent's Estate
The Personal Representative

1. Appointment. The probate court will appoint a person to represent the decedent and to administer the decedent's estate, called the **personal representative.** This person has a variety of names in the absence of statute to the contrary depending on various circumstances. If the decedent died testate and designated such a person in his will, the court usually will appoint that person the **executor** (man) or **executrix** (woman) who therefore becomes the personal representative. If the will does not so designate any such person, or the person so designated is unavailable (e.g., dead, or refuses) or is unqualified to be the personal representative, the court will appoint someone else as the personal representative called an **administrator** (man) or **administratrix** (woman) **with the will annexed.** If the decedent died intestate, the court will appoint an **administrator** (man) or **administratrix** (woman). If the personal representative cannot complete his (her) duties, the court will appoint a new personal representative called an "administrator or administratrix de bonis non." While these terms refer to men and women, nevertheless often a legal entity other than an individual, e.g., a bank, may become a personal representative, known as an "executor." Under UPC 1–201(30) all of these persons are called a "personal representative." UPC 1–201(29) defines a person as "an individual, a corporation, an organization, or other legal entity."

2. Responsibilities. The responsibility of the personal representative is to "administer" the decedent's estate in accordance with the legally valid directions as expressed by the testator in his will, or in accordance with the statute of descent and distribution with respect to an intestate estate. Briefly, this involves the collection of the decedent's property which forms the decedent's estate, payment of claims against the estate, and expeditious distribution of the remaining property as provided in the will or pursuant to the statute on descent and distribution. The personal representative must post a bond to assure that he or she properly carries out his or her responsibility, unless the will expressly waives the requirement of a bond. In the following case, the court held that executors will be surcharged for their breach of duty for not distributing the estate promptly.

---

heirs
persons who, by statute, are entitled to property not disposed of by a decedent's will

per capita
"by heads"; all persons who stand in the same degree of relationship to the intestate share equally in the estate without consideration of any right of representation

per stirpes
"by stocks, or by roots"; the survivors of their parent represent their parent and take the parent's share in an intestate's estate by such representation for division among themselves

personal representative
a court-appointed person to represent a decedent and administer his estate

executor (executrix)
a court-appointed man (woman) designated in a decedent's will as the decedent's personal representative

administrator (administratrix) with the will annexed
a court-appointed man (woman), who was not designated in a decedent's will, as the decedent's personal representative

administrator (administratrix)
a court-appointed man (woman) as an intestate's personal representative

Facts

Mrs. Katherine McCrea died testate on March 24, 1961. Her will divided her estate among six children, Katherine, William, Sarah, Elizabeth, Margaret, and John. Her will named as executors John, William and Sarah, all of whom were law school graduates. At her death Mrs. McCrea owned several farms. Some structures on the property were rental units, and others were converted into rental units by the executors. Following Mrs. McCrea's death in 1961, John and William continued operation of the properties.

The executors made no attempt to file an account and wind up the estate for twelve years when, in late 1973, William filed his First Account. Katherine petitioned and the court removed the executors and substituted Farmers Trust Company. The Company filed its First Account requesting the imposition on the previous executors of a surcharge of 3.5 percent per year on the value of the property. The lower court approved of this Account and imposed the surcharge, except as to Sarah who relied solely on the advice of her brothers. Appeal is from the court's approval of this Account. Margaret died before these proceedings were begun.

The appellants contend that the lower court improperly imposed the surcharge, asserting that there was no loss to the estate and its beneficiaries since the real estate had appreciated in value since Mrs. McCrea's death from $39,000 to $218,000.

Decision

Affirmed.

Reasoning

As to the surcharge, an executor is required to exercise the same degree of judgment that a reasonable person would exercise in the management of his own estate. This duty includes the responsibility to distribute the estate promptly. If the executor breaches this duty, he may properly be surcharged for interest on the assets not expeditiously distributed.

The former executors, through their position of trust, took control of the farm operations and all the accompanying realty. They made no effort to distribute the estate promptly. They delayed the final settlement of the estate for twelve years, and allowed the property to remain unproductive. This delay is inexcusable, particularly in view of their legal training. This breach of duty has deprived one devisee, Margaret, who died before the proceedings began, of all benefits; it has deprived the others of their benefits until now. The increase in the value of real estate is not surprising. Nonetheless, the beneficiaries have been denied its beneficial enjoyment by this unwarranted delay.

In re *Katherine Jane Wiest McCrea, Deceased,* 380 A.2d 773 (Pa. 1977).

In order to carry out this responsibility, the personal representative has many duties, a few of which are the following. The personal representative must exercise that degree of prudent care which a person in such a position is expected to exercise. Careful and accurate records of receipts and disbursements must be kept; all estate funds collected and placed in a safe depository; all proper claims against the estate paid; and the estate dealt with pursuant to the will's directions or as ordered by the court. The personal representative is personally liable for any contracts made in his or her own name as a contracting party which concern the administration of the estate. The personal representative has a right of reimbursement out of the estate for expenditures and of indemnity for loss sustained. In most states, in paying debts of the estate, the personal representative is to use first the estate personal property and then, if necessary, the estate real property as required by the will or pursuant to statute or court order.

When the statutory time has expired in which claims against the estate may be presented and after they have been paid, the personal representative must file with the court a final account of the administration of the estate. Proper notice of such filing must be given to all interested parties. After a court hearing, if all is proper the court will approve of the final account, issue a "decree of final settlement," and order distribution of the property in the estate to the proper persons. After such distribution the personal representative is discharged and the estate "closed."

Taxes

Federal and state laws provide for the imposition of taxes on the transfer of property. Accordingly, the transfer of the property in a decedent's estate becomes subject to these tax laws. A federal "estate tax" is imposed *on the estate* depending on the net value of the estate. In contrast, in addition to the federal estate tax, most states impose an "inheritance tax" on the inheriting recipient measured by the value of the property inherited or by the recipient's blood or other relationship with the decedent. State inheritance tax statutes vary widely. The federal law provides for certain exemptions and tax credits to soften the estate tax bite.

Summary Statement

1. State statutory law governs the validity of a decedent's will and the distribution of a decedent's property.
2. The Uniform Probate Code has been adopted in a minority of states and seeks to simplify and make more effective the law concerning decedents' estates.
3. A testator (testatrix) must be of a minimum statutory age, and must have testamentary capacity to make a will, meaning he must be of sound mind having the ability to know what he is doing.
4. A will is an expression of the testator's testamentary intent to dispose of his property on his death.
5. A will must be in writing, except for nuncupative wills which can be made only under certain conditions and can dispose of only personal property.
6. A holographic will is entirely handwritten by the testator.
7. "Sign" is different from "subscribe," and in most states a will must be "signed."
8. A will must have the proper number of attesting witnesses, except for a holographic will for which attesting witnesses are not required.
9. A "direct" beneficiary is not disqualified from being an attesting witness, but the beneficiary may lose his or her beneficial interest under the will if the beneficiary's testimony is necessary to prove the will.
10. A beneficiary under a will may be a legatee of personal property and/or a devisee of real property.
11. A written will may be revoked by the act of the testator in a subsequent writing such as a new will or codicil, by his act to the instrument, by his subsequent marriage. A subsequent divorce or annulment of the marriage and a later-born child of the marriage do not revoke a prior will.
12. Probate of a will occurs in the state and county where the decedent was domiciled, except that the state where a decedent's real property is located has jurisdiction to determine the validity of a will regarding the disposition of the real property located there.
13. State statutes of descent and distribution govern the distribution of a decedent's intestate property according to a recipient's marital relationship to the decedent, or according to the recipient's blood relationship to the decedent per capita or per stirpes.
14. The personal representative appointed by the court may be an executor/executrix, administrator/administratrix, administrator/administratrix with the will annexed, or administrator/administratrix de bonis non. A legal entity other than an individual may become a personal representative.
15. The responsibility of the personal representative is to administer the decedent's estate, which involves the collection of the decedent's property, payment of claims against the estate, and proper distribution of the remaining property.
16. A decedent's estate is subject to the laws on federal estate taxes and state inheritance taxes.

In this chapter we observed how important it is that a person have testamentary capacity in order to make a will. The following case illustrates the problem of *three* courts in determining whether the evidence established that the decedent lacked mental capacity to make a will.

J. Lake Hellams v. Pauline Ross
233 S.E.2d 98 (S.C. 1977)

Lewis, C. J. The issues involve the validity of the will of the late Marvin Robert Bass and, particularly, his testamentary capacity at the time he executed the instrument.

The testator died in Laurens County on March 9, 1975, leaving a will dated May 2, 1974 under which he devised all of his property to the Rabon Creek Baptist Church to the exclusion of his wife, the respondent herein. He had no children.

The respondent-widow objected to the probate of the will upon the grounds that the testator lacked testamentary capacity to make it. . . . The Probate Court subsequently overruled the attack upon the validity of the will and admitted it to probate. However, upon appeal to the Circuit Court, a jury found that . . . he did not have sufficient mental capacity to make a will on May 2, 1974, the date upon which he signed the instrument offered for probate.

The executor (appellant) took the position at the trial that there was no evidence to sustain the conclusion that the deceased was mentally incompetent . . . at the time of the execution of the will and, accordingly, moved for a directed verdict in favor of the will upon that ground. This motion was refused. . . . This appeal by the executor is from the denial of the foregoing motion[s]. The charge that the lower court erred in denying the motion[s] for a directed verdict present[s] the sole issue of whether there was any evidence to support the finding of the jury that the testator lacked mental capacity to make a will. . . .

It is conceded that the will was properly executed. The charge of testamentary incapacity was based upon allegations that the excessive use of alcohol and drugs had affected the testator's mental faculties. The testimony showed that the testator had been a heavy consumer of alcoholic beverages for a number of years. In fact, it is inferable that his consumption of intoxicating beverages had reached a point that he was an habitual drunkard; but the testimony shows conclusively that the testator was not under the influence of intoxicants on the date of execution of the will. The issue then is whether there was any evidence from which a reasonable inference could be drawn that the testator's intemperance had so affected his mental faculties as to render him incompetent to make a will even though he was not actually intoxicated at the time he executed it.

The burden of proof was upon respondent, as the contestant, to show a lack of mental capacity. This principle was more fully stated in . . . :

"It is the settled law of this state that when the formal execution of a will is admitted or proved, a prima facie case in favor of the will is made out, and that, as a general rule, the burden is then on the contestants to prove undue influence, incapacity or other basis of invalidation, and such burden remains upon the contestants throughout. In determining whether the contestants sustained such burden, the evidence has to be viewed in the light most favorable to the contestants."

The general principles governing the determination of testamentary capacity apply in cases where it is charged that the testator was affected by the use of alcohol or drugs. Therefore, the capacity of the testator to make a will is tested by whether he (1) knew his estate, (2) knew the objects of his affections, and (3) knew to whom he wished to give his property. . . .

Since intoxication is a temporary condition, even an habitual drunkard is presumed to be competent, when sober, to make a will; and the person, who asserts that the excessive use of intoxicants rendered a testator incompetent to make a valid will, must affirmatively show either (1) that at the time the will was made the testator's use of intoxicants had so impaired or deranged his mind that he lacked testamentary capacity even when he was not under the immediate influence of intoxicants or (2) that he was in fact incompetent due to intoxication existing at the time of the making and execution of the will. . . .

A careful review of the record convinces us that the evidence failed to show mental incapacity of the testator at the time the will was made. Although the testimony is undisputed that the testator was a heavy drinker and would sometimes, when on one of his frequent drinking sprees, fire his gun into the ceiling of the house and through the windows, there was no evidence of probative value that his drinking had produced a derangement of his mental faculties when he was not under the influence of intoxicants.

One of the witnesses to the will was dead, but the other two testified. One was the attorney who prepared and supervised the execution of the will and the other was the attorney's secretary. Both certified that the testator came to the attorney's office and requested that the will be prepared, giving directions as to the disposition to be made of his estate. These witnesses were positive in their testimony that the testator was sober, normal in his actions, and possessed of testamentary capacity when he signed the will.

We find no evidence of probative value to counter the positive testimony of the attesting witnesses that the testator was possessed of testamentary capacity when he signed the instrument. The lower court was therefore in error in refusing to grant appellant's motion for a directed verdict.

The fact alone that the testator disposed of property contrary to what others usually consider fair is not sufficient to declare his will void. This principle is thus stated in . . . : "The right to make a will carries with it the right to disregard what the world considers a fair disposition of property. In the case of . . . we find: 'That a will is unjust to one's relations is no legal reason that it should be considered an irrational act. The law puts no restrictions upon a man's right to dispose of his property in any way his partialities, or pride, or caprice may prompt him.'"

There was also testimony that the testator bought two trailers for considerably more than they were worth; took the sink and some furniture from his home and put it in a rental house; and that about five (5) years before his death he expressed a belief that, if he gave his money to the church, he would go to heaven. Respondent argues that the bad business deal, using articles from his home to fix rental property, and the belief that by giving his property to the church he would go to heaven constituted some evidence that the testator was of unsound mind. The belief that the giving of his property to the church would, within itself, get him into heaven might have been inaccurate but we are not prepared to say that it was evidence of an unsound mind. Neither does the bad business deal nor using his household articles to furnish his rental property reach, under this record, probative value on the question of testamentary capacity.

The judgment is accordingly reversed and the cause remanded to the lower court for entry of judgment in favor of the validity of the will.

Questions and Case Problems

1. Darrell Gentry served in the United States Army from 1952 to 1954, and again from 1956 to 1958, when he was discharged after six months' confinement in the psychiatric ward at Walter Reed Hospital. He was admitted to the Roseburg Veterans Administration Hospital in 1959.

    In 1965 Darrell, while still a patient at this facility, was adjudicated incompetent to manage his own affairs by the circuit court of Douglas County, Oregon, and placed under guardianship, with Pioneer Trust Company named as guardian.

    Dr. Esperson, the ward physician under whose care Darrell was placed while Darrell was at the Veterans Administration Hospital from 1967 to 1973, testified that Darrell suffered from a psychosis diagnosed as schizophrenia; that his mental illness was largely controllable by psychiatric medication; that he was generally lucid so long as he took his prescribed medication, but when allowed to leave the hospital for any extended period would stop taking his medicines and would shortly become psychotic and sometimes obstreperous; that he would then have to be returned to the hospital. The record shows that this pattern of behavior was repeated again and again almost from the beginning of Darrell's hospitalization at Roseburg until his death. Not infrequently Darrell would go AWOL from the hospital. Dr. Esperson expressed the opinion, however, that Darrell was mentally competent to execute a will if not in one of his deranged intervals, and that he was capable of executing the instant will.

In a letter received by Pioneer Trust Company September 29, 1969, three days before the challenged will was executed, Darrell wrote to Mr. E. E. Smith, a trust officer who was handling his financial affairs at Pioneer Trust Company, stating in part that "I want my mother to inherit my 4 or 5 thousand." This was reiterated by Darrell on other occasions, including in a letter to his mother postmarked October 6, 1969. In a letter dated September 30, 1969, apparently in response to the letter received from Darrell, Trust Officer Smith wrote Darrell informing him that if he was serious about having his estate go to his mother he should go to some attorney in Roseburg and have him prepare a valid will, taking care to inform the attorney that he was "living currently at the Veterans Administration Hospital at Roseburg."

The attorney who drafted the will, and who was an attesting witness, testified that Darrell came to him on October 2, 1969 apparently bearing the above described letter from Smith; that he, the attorney, spent approximately 25 to 30 minutes discussing the details with Darrell, including the nature and extent of his property, the persons who were the natural objects of his bounty and the effect of his will prior to drafting the will; that he, the attorney, was fully aware that Darrell was under guardianship; that notwithstanding Darrell appeared to be mentally competent when the will was executed.

The sole beneficiary under Darrell's will was his mother who, when requested by Darrell, came to his assistance when he had psychiatric or financial difficulties while out of the hospital or on furlough or AWOL. Darrell was divorced and the petitioner is Darrell's 22-year-old daughter who, after age 15, lived with her maternal grandparents. She rarely saw her father as she was growing up. Darrell's will was executed by him October 2, 1969. He died February 2, 1978.

The will is filed for probate and the petitioner contested the will on the ground that it was invalid because Darrell was mentally incompetent to make a will. You decide, explaining the reasons for your decision. [In re *Darrell Elmer Gentry, Deceased,* 573 P.2d 322 (Or. 1978).]

2. Victor and Agnes were very happily married and lived together for many years until Agnes died. They were childless, but Agnes had six brothers and sisters and many nieces and nephews. They owned two houses and a farm. Sandra Cook was Agnes' great niece, and Sandra and her family lived next door to Victor and Agnes in a house rented from them. In late 1974 or early 1975 Victor and Agnes gave a parcel of land to Sandra and they also loaned Sandra $20,000 for her to build a new house. Sandra was to pay $200 per month to Victor and Agnes on the loan.

When Agnes died May 2, 1976 Victor was in very poor health. Two weeks after Agnes' death Sandra and her family moved into Victor's home. A month later Victor's furniture was sold, and Victor, Sandra and her family moved into Sandra's new home on the farm now owned by Victor. While Victor was living with Sandra, it was agreed that Sandra would not make payments on the $20,000 loan and she discontinued these payments two months after Agnes' death. In late 1976 Sandra bought a new car and a Jeep with Victor's funds. She said Victor gave her the money because her Volkswagen was too small and the road to the house was impassable in the winter.

On December 22, 1976 Victor consulted an attorney about making a will, and a few days later he returned to the attorney's office and signed the will. Sandra accompanied Victor both times. On the second visit, she read the will to Victor, and he went into another room with two witnesses to sign it. The new will left his entire estate to Sandra. Victor and Agnes had executed previous wills on January 23, 1975, each will having the same provisions, each leaving his and her property to each other unless either predeceased the other, in which event the estate was to go to various individuals including some of Agnes' relatives. On leaving the attorney's office, Victor took home both the 1975 and 1976 wills and tore up the 1975 will before throwing it into the trash. He told Sandra that he was upset with his other relatives for trying to put him in a nursing home. Several parties testified that both Victor and Agnes had a severe aversion to living in a nursing home. Sandra admitted that she told Victor that others were going to put him in a nursing home; however, witnesses testified that they did not know of anyone who planned to do so.

In February of 1977, a guardianship hearing for Victor was held. At this hearing, Victor expressed his belief that the hearing was to put him into a nursing home. Dr. Jefferson Streepy admitted that he had told Sandra on September 30, 1977 that Victor should be put into a nursing home, but he did not recall any earlier conversations on the subject. Victor died February 2, 1978.

The 1976 will was filed for probate and the petitioners contested the will on the ground that it was invalid because of undue influence. You decide, explaining the reasons for your decision. [*Cook v. Loftus,* et al., 414 N.E.2d 581 (Ind. 1981).]

3. Hendrick Baarslag, Sr., executed his will in 1968 and died in 1972. The fourth paragraph of the will provided that the testator gave "the bulk of my property" to seven named "devisee-trustees" in an "unlimited trust" to be used "for certain purposes which are dear to my heart, and which are known to my Executor and the devisees-trustees hereinafter named, in accordance with oral and written directions that I have given to them. . . . [They] shall execute the wishes and purposes which I have in mind and with respect to which I have given written and oral instructions as guide lines to them." An undated document written in the testator's handwriting entitled "Guidelines for some persons named in My last will and testament" was found with the testator's will. The handwritten guidelines were in existence at the time the will was executed. The will was filed for probate and was valid, except that the fourth paragraph was challenged as being invalid and not admissible to probate. Does the fourth paragraph of the will incorporate by reference the handwritten guidelines and should that paragraph be admitted to probate? You decide, explaining the reasons for your decision. [*Baarslag, Jr.,* et al. *v. Hawkins,* et al., 531 P.2d 1283 (Wash. 1975).]

4. Mrs. Bottoms died December 21, 1944. At her request an officer at the bank which was holding her securities prepared for her a living trust agreement and her will. The residuary clause in the will reads as follows: "I give, bequeath and devise to Texarkana National Bank of Texarkana, Texas, to be added to and become a part of, and subject to all the terms and conditions of living trust created by me under date of January 27th, 1944, all of my estate remaining after paying all debts legally chargeable to same, including fees to my executors." On January 27, 1944 Mrs. Bottoms appeared at the bank to sign both documents which were already prepared and on a table. She signed them in the presence of two witnesses, who were unable to say which document she signed first.

The will of Mrs. Bottoms and the trust agreement were filed for probate. There is no objection to the validity of the will, but there is objection to the trust agreement being admitted to probate as a part of the will. You decide, explaining the reasons for your decision. [*Montgomery,* et al. *v. Blankenship,* et al., 230 S.W.2d 51 (Ark. 1950).] (This older case is authoritative, highly respected by the courts, and cited in many of their case opinions.)

5. At his request, a will was prepared for Joseph McCready who was blind and a resident of a home for the blind. The occasion for his execution of the will at the home was supervised by an attorney who was an attesting witness. The attorney first read the will aloud to Joseph McCready in the presence of the two additional attesting witnesses. Joseph stated that the said will met with his approval and declared the instrument to be his will. With the assistance of one of the attesting witnesses, Joseph made a cross mark for his signature. This witness wrote on the instrument after the cross mark "(Joseph McCready) his mark by Lillian T. MacKinnon." At the request of Joseph and after the reading aloud of the attestation clause of the will (which recites the facts just stated) the three attesting witnesses signed their names in the presence of Joseph. Was the will duly executed? You decide, explaining the reasons for your decision. [In re *Joseph McCready, Deceased,* 369 N.Y.S.2d 325 (1975).]

6. Wallace E. Kelley executed a will witnessed by three people one of whom was the executor named in the will. The state statute provided that, for a will to be valid, it must be subscribed in the presence of the testator by "three credible witnesses, not beneficially interested" thereunder. A paragraph in the will reads "I direct my executor to dispose of my clothing and other personal articles and effects as he in his sole discretion may deem best." Wallace died 26 days later having no wife or children. The will expressly disinherited his heirs-at-law because he felt, in his words in the will, "that they are capable of caring for themselves."

    The will was filed for probate and was contested as not being a valid will because it was not duly attested. You decide, giving the reasons for your decision. [In re *Kelley's Estate,* 92 A.2d 724 (Me. 1952).] (This older case was selected for its excellent simplicity and directness.)

7. Explain what a codicil is and the reasons for making one.

8. H. Eugene Kraus, testator, executed two valid wills, one on August 11, 1964 and the other on November 7, 1973. On December 10, 1975 Eugene telephoned his attorney who had possession of the 1973 will and directed him to destroy the 1973 will immediately by tearing and discarding it. This was done. Eugene had told the attorney that he wanted a new will drawn by another attorney. Eugene died April 3, 1976 without making another will.

    The 1964 will and a conformed copy of the 1973 will were filed for probate. Which of these two documents is Eugene's will? You decide, explaining the reasons for your decision. [In re *Eugene Kraus, Deceased,* 385 N.Y.S.2d 933 (1976).]

9. Emma C. Lindberg, testatrix, died July 1, 1950 survived by four children who were to share equally in her estate under her will. Her elderly daughter was the executrix. The estate consisted of a small bank account and two parcels of real estate. For approximately eight years, the executrix collected the rents, paid the taxes, made repairs, and in general managed the real estate.

    On July 7, 1956 the executrix filed a final account and report on the estate which was approved by order of the county court on July 26, 1956. The respondent, one of the children, objected to the order and appealed to the circuit court, and on June 25, 1958 the appeal was discussed and the matter was remanded to the county court for further proceedings. In 1958 the executrix sold the two parcels of land, collected the proceeds, and on July 11, 1958 she filed a supplemental final account and report. Respondent objected to this report alleging mismanagement, but the account was ordered approved November 14, 1958. On December 2, 1958 respondent filed a petition to vacate this order by reason of the death of one of the beneficiaries. The order was vacated September 25, 1959. On October 2, 1959 the executrix filed her second amended supplemental final account reflecting the distribution of the share of the deceased beneficiary to his heirs. On November 17, 1959 respondent objected to this account alleging various matters with respect to the executrix's management of the estate. On November 5, 1964 respondent petitioned to compel respondent's attorney to withdraw and to require the executrix to file a new final account and report, which the executrix did. At the hearing on February 26, 1965 the respondent's attorney withdrew and no date was set for a further hearing.

    On August 2, 1974 the executrix served notice for a hearing on August 15, 1974, seeking approval of a new final account. Respondent filed objections to this account and, at this time, claimed interest for the failure of the executrix to make earlier distribution of his share of the estate. On March 12, 1975 the court conducted a hearing on this account and report and, after modification, it was approved by an order entered on September 26, 1975; this order denied respondent's claim for interest. Furthermore, the executrix was 83 years old at the time of the last hearing in 1974; her attorney who was jointly on the estate bank account passed away in 1967; the executrix in no way profited by the delay in distribution as the funds remained in a checking account at all times. The executrix tried to make partial distribution to the beneficiaries, and sent checks to one of the respondent's former five attorneys, but the checks were lost.

Respondent appeals from the last court order of September 26, 1975 and demands that the court impose a surcharge of 10 percent interest on the executrix for delays in making distribution of the estate under the above circumstances. The state statute provides for such surcharge, unless for good cause shown no surcharge should be imposed.

Should a surcharge be imposed on the executrix for such delay? Give your reasons for your answer. [In re *Emma C. Lindberg, Deceased*, 364 N.E.2d 555 (Ill. 1977).]

10. The case of *J. Lake Hellams v. Pauline Ross*, 233 S.E.2d 98 (S.C. 1977)[4] dealt with a determination of whether or not the decedent had testamentary capacity under particular circumstances to make a will. Explain what you learned about testamentary capacity from the facts in that case.

---

[4] See pp. 813–14.

Trusts 55

After you have read this chapter, you should be able to:

1. Explain the trust concept.
2. Distinguish a trust.
3. Enumerate the methods by which an express trust can be created.
4. Explain the importance and form of the settlor's manifestation in order to create an express trust.
5. Discuss the testamentary trust.
6. Explain the significance of the trust purpose.
7. Indicate what is meant by trust property and discuss the importance of its transfer to the trust.
8. Discuss who may be a trustee and who a beneficiary.
9. Explain the trustee's various duties to the beneficiary.
10. Discuss the trustee's powers.
11. Discuss the liability of the trustee and indicate how the beneficiary may limit or remove such liability.
12. Explain how a trust may be modified and terminated.
13. Describe a charitable trust.
14. Distinguish the express trust from resulting and constructive trusts.

Introduction

Background

In the law of trusts, **property** is an interest or right in a thing; not the thing itself. For example, you may have title to, or the right to possess, a truck. Your title or right is property in the truck. Property may be transferred in many ways and for different purposes, as has been discussed in previous chapters in this book. In some instances you may wish to transfer the title to your property without any limitations on its use and on its later transferability, as by a **sale** of goods. On the other hand, you may wish to transfer only the right to possession, as by a **bailment**.

However, there are occasions when you would want to transfer the title to your property to a person to hold and administer the property for the benefit of someone who either is incapable of managing the property or who does not want to take the responsibility for managing it, as in the case possibly of your spouse or child. For example, X delivers property to Y to hold in trust for the benefit of Z, to distribute the income from the property to Z during Z's lifetime and on Z's death to transfer the property to D.

This is the trust concept, namely the transfer of the legal title to property to a person to hold for the benefit of someone who thereby acquires an "equitable interest"[1] in the property for what it produces or for its use in any other way. Possibly the outstanding characteristic of a trust is its flexibility of suitability for a variety of purposes. It is necessary that *both* the legal title to the property *and* the beneficial interest in the property be transferred to create a trust.

A **trust** is a legal device whereby legal title to property is held by one person (a **trustee**) for the benefit of a **beneficiary,** usually another person. A beneficiary is a person who is to receive a benefit. A **fiduciary** relationship exists between the trustee and the beneficiary in that the trustee has the duty to administer the trust property solely for the benefit of the beneficiary. The trustee has the power to transfer the **trust property** (the property held in trust) in order to carry out the requirements of the trust. The trust is a legal entity administered by the trustee. It is for this reason that often a trust is created so as to shift property out of the owner into a trust when the tax on the income from the trust property will be less than if the property had remained in the original owner.

Trust Distinguished. A trust is easily distinguished from other legal relationships[2] by considering the various characteristics of a trust. A trust may be of real or personal property. Legal title to the trust property passes to the trustee. The trustee is not subject to anyone's control. Death of the trustee or beneficiary ordinarily does not terminate the trust. There is a fiduciary relationship between the trustee and the beneficiary. The trustee cannot subject the beneficiary to liability to third persons. The beneficiary has an equitable interest in the trust property in that the property is to be administered in accordance with the terms of the trust solely for the benefit of the beneficiary. The trustee is governed by the terms of the trust.

The subject of trusts deals with various kinds of trust, which can be classified as the express trust, the resulting trust, and the constructive trust. Although the charitable trust is very much like the express trust it will be considered separately. We will first consider the commonly used express trust, and conclude with a brief examination of the charitable trust, the resulting trust, and then the constructive trust in that order.

---

[1] Principles of equity are applicable to an interest in trust property.

[2] See RESTATEMENT (SECOND) OF TRUSTS, 1959, secs. 5–16C.

---

property
(in trusts) an interest or right in a thing; not the thing itself

sale
the transfer "of title from seller to purchaser for a price" UCC 2-106(1)

bailment
a delivery of goods by a bailor to a bailee which are to be returned to the bailor or as the bailor directs in accordance with the bailment agreement

trust
a legal device whereby legal title to property is held by one person (a trustee) for the benefit of a beneficiary

trustee
a person who holds title to property in trust for the benefit of someone

beneficiary
a person who is to receive a benefit

fiduciary
a person with a duty to act primarily for the benefit of another

trust property
the property held in trust, sometimes called the "trust res"

The Express Trust

Creation of an Express Trust

Methods of Creation. The Restatement (Second) of Trusts, sec. 17, describes various ways by which an **express trust** may be created:

> A trust may be created by
>
> (a) a declaration by the owner of property that he holds it as trustee for another person; or
> (b) a transfer *inter vivos* by the owner of property to another person as trustee for the transferor or for a third person; or
> (c) a transfer by will by the owner of property to another person as trustee for a third person; or
> (d) an appointment by one person having a power of appointment to another person as trustee for the donee of the power or for a third person;[3] or
> (e) a promise by one person to another person whose rights thereunder are to be held in trust for a third person.

The Settlor's Capacity. An express trust is created by a person called a **settlor**; he settles the trust. While a trust may be created in the above five ways, the settlor must have the legal capacity to create the trust. With respect to (a) and (b) above, the settlor must have legal capacity to transfer the property to another living person (**inter vivos**). With respect to (c) above, the settlor must have legal capacity to transfer the property by will, meaning the settlor must have testamentary capacity, discussed previously in chapter 54, under Wills and Decedents' Estates.[4] With respect to (d) above, the person with the power of appointment must have the legal capacity to make the appointment. For example, X transfers property to Y in trust for Y to receive the income therefrom for Y's life, with power in Y to appoint how the property is to go on Y's death. Y has legal capacity and can appoint Z as trustee of a trust for the benefit of beneficiaries designated by Y. With respect to (e) above, the contracting promisor must have the legal capacity to make a contract so that his or her promise to transfer property in trust is enforceable by the promisee who holds this contract right in trust for the benefit of the beneficiary. For example, X is contractually bound to Y on X's promise to pay Y $25,000 as trustee for Z. Y holds this contract right against X in trust for Z.

The settlor must not be under any disability, e.g., incompetency, intoxication. Also, the inducement to create a trust by illegal or improper conduct (e.g., duress, fraud, undue influence) on the part of the trustee, beneficiary, or anyone else may prevent creation of a trust because the transaction then was made involuntarily.

Usually, a person is presumed to be competent with mental capacity to create a trust, and persons who assert incompetency have the burden of proving it. Once incompetency is established, the burden of proving competency shifts to those persons who assert competency during a brief interval by clear and convincing evidence and that a trust was created during that brief, lucid interval. Mental capacity is best determined by a person's spoken words, acts, and conduct at a particular point in time. In the following older, well-known case, selected for its particular facts and clear judicial opinion, the court found that those persons alleging the settlor to have been incompetent could not perform their burden of proving the settlor incompetent *at the time she executed the inter vivos trust instruments.*

---

[3] E.g., W conveys land to X for X's life, the remainder to be determined by X. X creates a trust of the remainder for the benefit of Z, naming Y as trustee.

[4] See p. 804.

express trust
a fiduciary relationship between persons in connection with property whereby one person called the "settlor" by his manifestation of intention causes property to be held by a person called the "trustee" for the benefit of a person called a "beneficiary" or *"cestui que trust,"* the trustee being under a duty so to deal with the property

settlor
the person who has created an express trust

inter vivos
among living persons

Facts
Plaintiff is the named trustee under a declaration of trust made by Margaret Higgins dated October 2, 1931 and an amendment thereto dated November 23, 1931. Margaret was 77 years of age on those dates and lived in her own home until she died February 16, 1933. Plaintiff seeks a declaratory judgment that the trust is valid. Defendants are the daughter of Margaret and the daughter's adopted son. They contend that Margaret was of unsound mind at the time of her execution of these two instruments. Margaret executed the declaration of trust and amendment at the office of the trustee when she was actually caring for herself and her property and apparently enjoying life. Until her execution of the declaration of trust and the amendment, she carried on her own business affairs including dealing in real property, building a house, managing her own household, and handling normal transactions.

In September 1931, Margaret consulted an officer of the plaintiff bank indicating that she wanted to save the cost of probating a will and described what she wanted in a written inter vivos trust. She said she felt her daughter was improvident and would not act wisely if allowed to draw upon the corpus of the trust and she (Margaret) did not want the trust to permit this. At her request the bank prepared and she executed the declaration of trust and, later, the amendment to provide for her last illness and burial expenses. The declaration of trust provided that the net income was to be paid to Margaret for her life and, on her death, was to be paid 75 percent to the daughter and 25 percent to her adopted son, defendants, during their lifetimes, with the remainder to Margaret's nieces. Dr. Fraser attended Margaret during her last illness from December 29, 1932 until her death in 1933. He testified at the earlier trial that on December 29, 1932 she was "mentally active."

Defendants presented the following evidence to prove Margaret's alleged incompetency on October 2 and November 23, 1931. Margaret had arteriosclerosis, high blood pressure, mental impairment evidenced by lack of memory at times, inability to concentrate at times, doing eccentric things at times, and delusions at times. Margaret did not include an emergency clause in her declaration of trust to allow for drawing on the trust corpus. A doctor who first saw Margaret on December 29, 1931, on the basis of hypothetical questions, testified at the earlier trial "I don't think anyone with a delusion is competent." But the doctor admitted that lucid intervals could occur in cases of mental disturbance like Margaret's case. Another doctor stated that Margaret was not competent even though he had never seen her, but he admitted, on the basis of information available to him, she knew what she was doing when she executed the trust instrument. Nonexpert witnesses testified Margaret had her good and bad cycles, but none saw her on October 2 and November 23, 1931.

The lower court found Margaret incompetent to make a trust on October 2 and November 23, 1931, and the plaintiff trustee appeals.

Decision
Reversed, for the plaintiff, trustee.

Reasoning
The evidence was insufficient to show that Margaret was suffering from any delusion on October 2 and November 23, 1931 or that any delusion bore directly upon or influenced the creation and terms of the trust. The testimony of the defendants' witnesses was unsubstantial on the issue of general mental incompetency. None of them saw Margaret on the days in question and none could testify as to whether she was having a so-called bad cycle when the instruments were executed. The declaration of trust provided for an entirely natural disposition of the trust estate and the proceeds thereof in favor of the natural objects of the bounty of Margaret. Margaret's belief of the defendant daughter's improvidence and her resulting trust provision concerning this belief is not a delusion.

American Trust Co. v. Dixon, et al, 78 P.2d 449 (Cal. 1938).

The Settlor's Intent.   The settlor must manifest an intention to create a trust. The express, inter vivos trust *must come into existence at the time of the manifestation,* not in the future. The manifestation must indicate an intent to impose legally enforceable duties on the trustee. Words suggesting, hoping, or wishing that the transferee of the property to be held in trust will use the property for the benefit of someone, leaving it to the discretion of the transferee, do not impose legally enforceable duties on the transferee. Such words are called "precatory" words.

The Form of the Settlor's Manifestation.   The settlor's manifestation of an intent thereby to create a trust may be by the settlor's spoken or written words or conduct and may be in any form, in the absence of statute to the contrary. The word "trust" need not be used, although use of the word "trust" does not of itself establish a trust; other elements are necessary, e.g., the transfer of trust property and identifiable beneficiaries.

A statute may require the settlor's manifestation of intent to be proved by a proper writing because the trust property is an interest in land or the trust is being created by a will. Most states have a "statute of frauds" which is a statute requiring such written proof in these instances. Without such written proof there is no trust.

A will is a testamentary disposition and may provide for a trust, called a **testamentary trust.** The subject of wills was discussed in chapter 54 on Wills and Decedents' Estates. Inasmuch as a will is ineffective until the death of the testator, i.e., the person who made the will, the trust cannot come into existence until the death of the testator. Since the trust is provided for in the will, the will must be a valid will complying with the law of the testator's domicile, or with the law in the state where the testator's real property is located.

Testamentary disposition.

testamentary trust
a trust created by the will of a decedent

A will creating a trust must be in writing, signed by the testator, and attested to by witnesses, effective on the testator's death. An inter vivos trust can take effect only *prior* to the settlor's death. If property is transferred in trust by the transferor during his lifetime but the trust is to *take effect* only on the transferor's *death,* there is no trust inter vivos or on his death because it is an attempted testamentary disposition which has not complied with the requirements of being a will. To have a testamentary trust, the testator must have manifested in the will his intent to create a trust in the will and designated the trust property; and the beneficiaries and the trust purposes must be capable of being identified from the will. The testator may, by his will, add ("pour over") property into an inter vivos trust created by him prior to his death.

Under the law of wills, in many states written papers not attached to the will and without the formal requisites of a will may be included as a part of the will if the will identifies them and indicates an intention that they are to be a part of the will. This doctrine is called "incorporation by reference." In some states the testamentary trust may be included in such papers under this doctrine.

Purposes of the Trust. The settlor's manifestation of an intent to create a trust must indicate the definite purposes of the trust. The purposes must not be **illegal**, i.e., contrary to law. If the trust purpose is illegal, then the intended trust is void. If only a trust provision is void for illegality, the otherwise valid trust may exist as a trust if separation of the illegal provision would not defeat the valid purpose for which the trust was created. Otherwise the intended trust would be void. If the trust purpose is to commit a **crime** or a **tort,** the intended trust is void. If a trust provision in a valid trust requires the trustee to perform an act which was valid when the trust was created but the performance of which would later become a tort, the provision, but not necessarily the trust, becomes unenforceable. If the carrying out of the trust purpose or of a trust provision would be against public policy other than a crime or tort, the intended trust or provision would be void for illegality. The comments to section 62 of the Restatement (Second) of Trusts, indicate various illustrations of purposes which are against public policy, some of which are: inducing the commission of a crime or tort; encouraging immorality, divorce or separation, and neglect of parental duties; restraining religious freedom. Also, if the intended trust is for a fraudulent purpose, e.g., to defraud third persons, it is invalid as a trust.

illegal
contrary to law

crime
an act, committed or omitted, in violation of a public law governing it

tort
a civil (private) noncontractual wrong for which a court will give a remedy

No Consideration Required. Consideration is not required in order to create a trust. The settlor may declare himself or herself trustee, or deliver trust property to a person, gratuitously. However, if a promise is made to create a trust, it is not binding as a contract unless it is supported by consideration. If legal consideration is rendered for the promise and the law of contracts is complied with, the promise *to* create a trust is specifically enforceable.

Transfer of Property. A trust establishes a beneficial interest in property, and a trust cannot be created until property is transferred. In the law of trusts, property is an interest (e.g., title) or right in a thing; property is not the thing itself. The thing may be tangible (land, **chattels**) or intangible (a **chose in action** such as a contract right or an account receivable). Thus, transferable *interests* in life insurance, patents, and copyrights can be trust property. The interest in property must be definite and existing, and capable of being transferred, *at the time the trust is created.* For example, a declaration of trust of corporate shares in a corporation *to be formed* fails to create a trust because the corporate shares and the declarant's interest in them have not yet come into existence and the declarant cannot transfer the shares as yet. When the corporation is formed and the declarant becomes the owner of the shares, the declarant then can create a trust of the shares.

Notice to, and Acceptance by, the Trustee and the Beneficiary. A trust may be created without any notice to the trustee or the beneficiary that a trust has been created, and without their acceptance. If the named trustee refuses to accept transfer of trust property to him or her *directly,* there is no trust. However, if trust property *has been transferred* to the trustee in trust and the trustee later **disclaims** the title to the property, the title goes back to the transferor who holds it in a constructive trust[5] for the intended beneficiary with a duty to transfer the title to a new trustee. Similarly, if disclaimer is by a testamentary trustee, the property will be held in constructive trust by the testator's executor who must transfer the property to a new trustee. If the beneficiary disclaims any beneficial interest in the trust, the trust terminates.

The Trustee. Property must be transferred to a person in trust, called a trustee, in order to create a trust. A settlor can name himself or herself as trustee without any transfer. However, if a transfer is ineffective *only* because a trustee is not named in the instrument of conveyance of the property (e.g., deed of real property) or, if named, the intended trustee is dead or not capable of taking the title to the property, such lack of name, death, or incapability does not prevent the creation of a trust.

Any person who has legal capacity to take, hold, *and* administer property for himself can be a trustee. He has capacity to administer if he can transfer, and make contracts concerning, the trust property. A beneficiary can be an individual, including a married man or woman, an infant, a **juristic** person (e.g., corporation), a state, the federal government, the settlor. However, a person cannot be the sole beneficiary and at the same time the sole trustee.

The Beneficiary. A trust involves the transfer of property to a trustee for the benefit of someone and, therefore, the trust requires a beneficiary, sometimes called a **cestui que trust.** The beneficiary is indicated in the settlor's manifestation of an intent to create a trust for the benefit of *that* beneficiary. Anyone not indicated in the manifestation who may incidentally benefit from the performance of the trust is an incidental beneficiary and is not a beneficiary of the trust. For example, X delivers money to Y in trust to pay X's debts. X is the beneficiary of the trust, not X's creditors, because X is primarily benefiting from the payment of his debts. Any person with the legal capacity to take legal title to property can be a beneficiary, although if subsequently that person no longer has such capacity he or she can no longer be a beneficiary. A trust may have more than one beneficiary.

A trust cannot be created unless, from the settlor's manifestation, the beneficiary is definitely identified or can be identified within the period of the **rule against perpetuities.** The beneficiary may be specifically named in the settlor's manifestation, or can be ascertained from facts in existence at the time the trust is to be created or which come into

---

[5] For constructive trust, see p. 832.

---

chattel
a tangible, movable thing

chose in action
intangible, personal property, such as an account receivable

disclaimer
denial of an obligation or a claim

juristic
by law

cestui que trust
the beneficiary of a trust

rule against perpetuities
the beneficiary of a trust must be identifiable at the time the trust is created or, in most states, within a period for the life of a person or persons in existence at the time the trust is created and twenty-one years after the death of such person or persons

existence within the period of the "rule against perpetuities." In most states the rule against perpetuities means a period of time measured by the life of a person or persons in existence at the time the trust is created *and* twenty-one years after the death of such person or persons. For example, X delivers money to Y in trust to pay the income therefrom to Z during Z's life and, on Z's death, to pay the principal to Z's children who are then living at the time of Z's death. A trust has been created irrespective of whether or not Z has any children at the time of the settlor's manifestation creating the trust. The members of a definite class of persons can be the beneficiaries of a trust. The settlor may be the beneficiary or one of the beneficiaries of the trust. For example, X delivers money to Y in trust for X.

Administration of an Express Trust
The trustee has various duties to the beneficiary and powers in the administration of the trust. These are determined: by the terms of the trust contained in the settlor's manifestation of intent to create the trust, subject to the settlor's exercise of any power reserved by him in connection with the trust; and by implication from the trustee's relationship to the beneficiary of the trust in the absence of trust terms to the contrary.

However, the trustee has no duty to perform trust terms which the trustee reasonably should know are illegal or the performance of which would be either illegal or materially detrimental to the interest of the beneficiary.

Also, a change in circumstances not considered or anticipated by the settlor may cause performance of the trust terms to defeat or substantially impair the purpose of the trust. In such an event, the trustee can apply to a court and, by court order, deviate from the trust terms to the extent that the trust does not prohibit such deviation. Examples of such a change in circumstances are: a change in law making performance of a trust term illegal; an economic depression causing the sale of trust property as required by the trust to be ruinous. Another instance of action by a court ordering a trustee not to comply with the trust terms is when the financial plight of the beneficiary may justify payment to the beneficiary before the time prescribed in the trust.

Duties of the Trustee to the Beneficiary. The trustee's duty to the beneficiary is to properly administer the trust. The trustee is a fiduciary toward the beneficiary with the duty of loyalty to the beneficiary to administer the trust property for the sole benefit of the beneficiary's interest. If the trustee deals with the beneficiary for the trustee's benefit, the trustee has the duty to make full disclosure to the beneficiary of all material facts of which the trustee should be aware. Because of the trustee's personal fiduciary relationship with the beneficiary, unless the trust provides otherwise, the trustee has the duty not to delegate to third persons the performance of trust terms which the trustee personally can perform. Thus, acts which require the trustee's discretion cannot be delegated.

The trustee has many other duties. The trustee has the duty to keep accurate accounts of his or her administration, make them available to the beneficiary, and, on the beneficiary's request, provide full information concerning the trust property. The trustee is to exercise the same care that an ordinary prudent person would exercise regarding that person's own property, and if, when appointed as trustee, the trustee represented having a greater skill, there is a duty to exercise such greater skill. The trustee must take and retain control of the trust property and use reasonable care to preserve it, designate it as trust property of that particular trust unless the trust provides otherwise, carefully select a bank for the deposit of trust funds designated as such. The trustee must act reasonably to enforce any claims held as trustee and to defend in any action which, if successful, could cause loss to the trust estate. The trustee has a duty, unless the trust provides otherwise, to make the trust property productive, which means the trustee must use reasonable care in the retention, transfer, and investment of the trust property. This is illustrated in the following case.

Facts

Henry F. Nussbaum, testator, made a residual bequest and devise of his estate in his will to his niece, Jane Ann Blair, as trustee, "in Trust however, for the education of my grandchildren (children of my daughter, Dorothy Janice Witmer) living at the time of my decease, or born within a period of nine months thereafter."

Henry died in 1960. The trust estate came into the hands of the trustee in 1961, consisting of $1,905 in checking and savings accounts, $5,700 in certificates of deposit and a house valued at $6,000.00. The house was sold in 1962, netting $4,467 to the trust estate. That amount was deposited in a trust checking account. In 1963, $2,000 in certificates of deposit were acquired by the trust and $500 was so invested in 1964. As of December 31, 1970, the trust fund assets consisted of $5,847 in checking account, $506 in savings account and $8,200 in certificates of deposit. In 1971 and 1972, the checking account balance was reduced by transfers to the savings account.

Plaintiff-appellant Marguerite Janice Witmer was the only grandchild of the testator who became a beneficiary of the trust. She was born September 3, 1953. At the time of the trial, she was 23 years of age. She had not attended a college or university. However, various sums of money had been expended from the trust for her benefit, including a typewriter, clothes, glasses, modeling, school tuition and expenses, and a tonsillectomy. These expenditures totalled some $1,225.00. The trust also provided $350 for dentures for the mother, Dorothy Witmer.

The trustee kept no books for the trust, which she handled rather informally. An accountant who testified calculated that between the opening of the trust and 1971, when college for Marguerite would have been a realistic possibility, had the trust funds, in excess of $100 checking account and approximately $800–1,000 savings account, been invested in one-year certificates of deposit, the trust would have earned additional interest of $2,840.

Marguerite, a plaintiff, brought an action seeking an accounting, removal of the trustee, and actual and punitive damages for breach of fiduciary duties. After trial to the court, the court ordered an accounting and removal of the defendant as trustee and entered judgment against defendant for $309 for unaccounted for funds, but found against plaintiffs on their claim for damages for breach of fiduciary duties. Plaintiffs appeal from this portion of the decree.

Decision

Judgment reversed insofar as it denied plaintiff's claim for actual damages. Remanded with directions to enter judgment for plaintiff for $2,840 actual damages.

Reasoning

There has been a breach of trust by the trustee in this case and her good faith is not a defense to appellants' claim. When the respondent came into possession of the trust estate in 1962, appellant Marguerite was some nine years of age. Respondent was aware of her age. Obviously there was no prospect of the beneficiary's attending college for a number of years. Respondent's failure to invest a large portion of the trust corpus during such time may not be justified on the grounds that during such time she acceded to requests of the beneficiary's mother to provide small sums for the beneficiary or her mother. Such expenditures were not authorized under the trust. A breach of duty by the trustee in that regard cannot justify her further breach of duty to invest the trust corpus.

The trustee should be held liable for the $2,840 which, according to the measure of damages, invoked by appellants, might have been earned by investment of the trust between 1962 and 1971.

Marguerite J. Witmer, et al. *v. Jane A. Blair*, 588 S.W.2d 222 (Mo. 1979).

Unproductive trust property and wasting trust property, i.e., property subject to depletion (e.g., patents, copyrights) should be disposed of. Investments should be diversified in order to reduce or distribute risk of loss, proper investments should be retained and improper investments disposed of. In most states the trustee may invest in United States securities and, subject to limitations, in bonds of states, cities, and counties, as well as in corporate shares. In many states, a trustee may invest in "common trust funds" whereby trust property of different, usually small, trusts is put into a common pool for investment. Courts differ on whether or not a trustee has a duty to amortize the depreciation or obsolescence of a building.

One of the troublesome areas for a trustee is compliance with the duty to make proper allocations and charges to the principal and income accounts. Under the 1962 Revised Uniform Principal and Income Act, section 3 a, b, "income is the return in money or property derived from the use of principal," while "principal is the property which has been set aside by the owner or the person legally empowered so that it is held in trust eventually to be delivered to the remainderman while the return or use of the principal is in the meantime taken or received by or held for accumulation for the income beneficiary." *Ordinary current* administrative and operative expense is chargeable to income (e.g., insurance on the trust property, trustee insurance bond premiums, ordinary repairs to trust property). Expense that is *not ordinary and current* is chargeable to principal (e.g., expense in setting up the trust, the cost of purchasing and selling investments). Prepaid rent by tenants of trust real property is allocated to income. Proceeds from insurance for loss to trust property (e.g., fire insurance) are allocated to principal.

Often investments are purchased at a premium. If the *trustee* makes such a purchase, the trustee must amortize the premium out of the income from the investment and the amortization fund is principal. If the *settlor* had made such a purchase, the trustee has no duty to amortize the premium, unless the trust provides otherwise, and all income from the investment is income available to the income beneficiary. If the investment was made at a discount, the benefit of the discount usually is principal and available to the principal beneficiary. But when treasury bills are redeemed at a discount, the amount of the discount is income.

The Restatement (Second) of Trusts, sec. 236, states the rules for determining whether *receipts from shares of stock* are principal or income:

Except as otherwise provided by the terms of the trust, if shares of stock of a corporation are held in trust to pay the income to a beneficiary for a designated period and thereafter to pay the principal to another beneficiary, the following rules are applicable:

(a) Except as stated in Clauses (e) and (f), dividends payable in cash or in property other than in shares of the declaring corporation, including ordinary and extraordinary dividends, are income, if payable to shareholders of record on a designated date which is within the period; or, if no such date is designated, if declared at a date within the period.
(b) Dividends payable in shares of the declaring corporation are principal.
(c) If the trustee has the option of receiving a dividend either in cash or in shares of the declaring corporation, the dividend is income irrespective of the choice made by the trustee.
(d) Rights to subscribe to the shares or other securities of the declaring corporation and the proceeds of any sale of such rights are principal, but rights to subscribe to the shares of other corporations are income.
(e) Upon the total or partial liquidation of the corporation during the period, amounts paid as cash dividends declared before such liquidation occurred or as arrears of preferred or guaranteed dividends are income; all other amounts paid upon corporate shares on distribution of the corporate assets to the shareholders are principal.
(f) A distribution by a corporation which is a return of capital and not a distribution of earnings is principal.
(g) The earnings of a corporation not distributed by the corporation during the period are not income.

Powers of the Trustee. The powers of the trustee not in violation of the trustee's duties to the beneficiary are either expressly stated in the trust terms, or are implied in order to carry out the trust purposes unless the trust provides otherwise. Previous text discussion of the meaning of the phrase "trust terms" is applicable here.[6] The duties of the trustee to the beneficiary, just discussed, indicate, in part, the trustee's powers which the trustee must exercise in order to carry out the trustee's duties. The trustee also has the power to incur expenses (e.g., for managing and making repairs and improvements to the trust property), to lease the trust property on reasonable terms and conditions, and to sell the trust property. The trustee has the power to settle claims affecting the trust, and to exercise the powers of a holder of securities with respect to trust securities. Except when the trust terms or state law permits, the trustee normally cannot mortgage or pledge trust property. When there is more than one trustee, they must agree unanimously, unless the trust terms provide otherwise.

---

[6] See p. 825.

By the trust terms and in order to carry out his or her duties, the trustee may have discretionary powers, such as whether or not, when and how to exercise the trustee's powers. While the trustee's *proper* exercise of the trustee's discretionary powers is not subject to a court's substitution of its preference in its exercise, nevertheless the court serves as a control mechanism to assure that there is no abuse of this power. The court will act if it is necessary to control the trustee in the trustee's dishonest use of the power, as when acting with an improper motive, or when acting arbitrarily failing to use his or her judgment.

Liability of the Trustee. The trustee has the duty to the beneficiary to properly administer the trust and, as discussed previously,[7] has many duties to the beneficiary in this regard. The trustee's violation of any trust duty owing to the beneficiary is a **breach of trust** for which the trustee is liable to the beneficiary. Only the beneficiary or the beneficiary's representative can sue the trustee for equitable relief for the trustee's breach. If there is more than one beneficiary, any beneficiary can sue the trustee for relief to that beneficiary.

breach of trust
a trustee's violation of a trust duty

The beneficiary may be precluded from holding the trustee liable for the trustee's breach of trust. The beneficiary is precluded if, prior to or at the time of the trustee's breach, the beneficiary consented to the wrongful conduct of the trustee, with the following exceptions. Such consent is ineffective if (a) the beneficiary was fraudulently induced to give consent, or (b) the beneficiary did not know of his or her rights and of material facts of which the trustee should reasonably have known, or (c) the beneficiary lacked capacity to consent, i.e., the beneficiary had no legal capacity to contract. Similarly, a beneficiary's release of the trustee or of the beneficiary's contract to discharge the trustee is effective unless at the time of such release or discharge (a), (b), or (c) above with respect to such release or discharge occurred, or (d) the trustee did not act fairly and reasonably in a transaction. Also, if a beneficiary with the option to reject or affirm (ratify) a transaction by the trustee which is a breach of trust subsequently affirmed the transaction and is thereby precluded from holding the trustee liable, nevertheless such affirmance is ineffective if, at the time the beneficiary affirmed, (a), (b), (c), or (d) above with respect to his or her affirmance occurred.

exculpatory clause
a clause which relieves one from liability

bad faith
dishonesty in fact in the conduct or transaction concerned

An **exculpatory clause** in the trust terms will relieve the trustee of liability for the trustee's breach of trust, except that it is ineffective if the trustee committed the breach in **bad faith,** intentionally, indifferent to the beneficiary's interest, or for any profit the trustee acquired from the breach.

If there is more than one trustee, no trustee is liable for a breach by a co-trustee unless he or she participated in the breach, was negligent in not preventing it, or neglected to obtain redress from the wrongful trustee.

For properly administering the trust, the trustee is entitled to be compensated out of the trust estate for services rendered, unless the trust terms are to the contrary or the court denies compensation because of the trustee's breach of trust. Also, while properly administering the trust the trustee may become personally liable to third persons. The trustee is personally liable for contracts made by the trustee with third persons, and has a right to **indemnity** from the trust estate for the trustee's expenditures and loss sustained while acting properly in administering the trust. If the trustee has breached the trust, the court may reduce or deny compensation for acting as trustee.

indemnity
an absolute obligation to pay for another's loss

Modification and Termination of the Trust

Modification. A settlor may modify or revoke a trust only if the settlor reserved powers to do so in the trust terms. If the trust terms do not have such a reservation, but at the time the trust was created the settlor intended to include these powers which were omitted

---

[7] See pp. 825–27.

by mistake, the settlor can show sufficient circumstances evidencing such mistake and obtain a court order reforming the trust terms so as to include these powers. A circumstance creating an inference that the settlor intended to reserve the power to revoke is when the settlor declares himself trustee and deposits money in a bank account in his own name as trustee for another person. If the settlor received consideration for transferring property in trust, the law of contracts regarding mistake becomes applicable and the mistake is insufficient to set aside the transfer.

The settlor's reservation of the power to revoke ordinarily is interpreted to include the power to modify, and the settlor's reservation of the power to modify without any limitations includes the power to revoke.

If fraud, duress, undue influence, or mistake have induced the settlor to create the trust, the settlor can rescind the trust or have it reformed as in the case of other transfers of property so induced.

Termination. The trust may terminate in various ways. The trust terms may specify a period of time for its duration, or that it is to end on the occurrence of a particular event. Also, a trust may terminate if, under the circumstances, a particular trust purpose no longer need be carried out. The expiration of the period or the occurrence of the event terminates the trust. If the entire purpose of the trust cannot be carried out because of supervening (later) impossibility or illegality, the court will order termination of the entire trust. However, if only some of the purposes cannot be carried out because of such supervening impossibility or illegality, the court will, when possible, permit the trustee to deviate from such purposes.

Destruction of the trust property terminates the trust, with two exceptions. The destruction may be caused by the fault of the trustee, in which event the trustee will have to pay the amount of the loss and hold such amount in trust as trust property. The destruction may be caused by the wrongful act of a third person, in which event the trustee will hold the claim against the wrongdoer as trust property.

Circumstances not known to the settlor and not anticipated by the settlor at the time the trust was created may occur which would cause performance of the trust terms to defeat or substantially impair compliance with the trust's purpose, in which event the court will order the trust to terminate.

All the beneficiaries may consent to termination of the trust and compel its termination, unless termination would violate a material purpose of the trust. An example of a material purpose is a "spendthrift trust," when the trust terms prohibit a beneficiary from voluntarily or involuntarily being deprived of his or her beneficial interest by the beneficiary or by creditors of the beneficiary. If the settlor and all the beneficiaries consent to terminaton of the trust, the trust can be terminated irrespective of the non-accomplishment of the trust's material purpose. Merger of the beneficial interest with the legal title to the trust property in one person terminates the trust.

If the trustee named in the trust terms no longer continues as trustee, the trust does not terminate and another trustee will be appointed. But if the settlor's manifestation of intent was that the trust was to continue only so long as the named trustee continues as such, that trustee's discontinuance terminates the trust.

The Charitable Trust

A **charitable trust** is created for a *charitable purpose*. Much of the law applicable to an express trust is applicable to a charitable trust, but there are major differences. Because of such differences, and solely to distinguish the express trust from the charitable trust, the express trust is often called a "private trust."

charitable trust
a trust for a charitable purpose

The methods of creating an express trust[8] are the same for a charitable trust, except that the purpose is charitable. Purposes are charitable if they are beneficial to the *community*. The Restatement (Second) of Trusts, sec. 368 states *specific* charitable purposes.

Charitable purposes include:

(a) the relief of poverty;
(b) the advancement of education;
(c) the advancement of religion;
(d) the promotion of health;
(e) governmental or municipal purposes;
(f) other purposes the accomplishment of which is beneficial to the community.

Under section 373: "A trust for the erection or maintenance of public buildings, bridges, streets, highways, parks or other public works or for other governmental or municipal purposes is charitable."

Examples of other non-specific charitable purposes beneficial to a community are: the promotion of temperance; relief of animals; protection of national security; various patriotic purposes; community purposes (e.g., city beautification, community swimming facilities); for persons of limited opportunities; erection and maintenance of tombs or monuments to commemorate notable persons; and to change existing law by legal means.[9] If the property or its income intended for a charitable trust is to be for a private use, there cannot be a charitable trust.

The trust terms must specify a *particular* charitable purpose for the creation of a charitable trust. However, it is sufficient if the trust terms leave to the trustee the power to select any unnamed charitable purpose. Also, unlike the express trust, a charitable trust cannot have a named beneficiary in the sense of being a particular *person*. The trust states only a *purpose* which must be for the benefit of a *community*. When the settlor had manifested *both* a *general* charitable purpose and a *particular* charitable purpose and the particular charitable purpose cannot be carried out, under the doctrine of **cy pres,** meaning "as near as possible," the court will order that the trust property be applied to a charitable purpose within the *general* charitable purpose as nearly as possible in accordance with the settlor's intent. However, if there is no general charitable purpose, or if the settlor's manifestation provides that, if the *particular* charitable purpose cannot be accomplished then the trust is to end, on failure of the particular purpose cy pres will not be applied. Cy pres will not be applied to defeat the settlor's intent. If the purpose of a charitable trust is accomplished and some trust property remains, the court will apply the remaining property to a charitable purpose within the settlor's general charitable intention. In the following case the court held that cy pres could not be applied and the trust had terminated.

cy pres
an equitable trust doctrine applicable particularly in charitable trusts whereby, by court order, the general trust purpose will be carried out as *nearly as possible* in accordance with the settlor's intent when the particular trust purpose cannot be carried out

Facts
The testator created a testamentary trust in his will in 1969 under the terms of which he devised and bequeathed money to Drake University and Parsons College, in equal shares, for scholarship purposes only, only the income therefrom to be used to assist needy students to receive a college education, and if either or both of these institutions failed to carry out these trust provisions then the trust or trusts shall fail and shall be cancelled and revoked, the principal to go to the testator's heirs at law. Testator died in 1974. After the execution of the will but prior to the testator's death, Parsons College became bankrupt and no longer operated as an educational institution. Drake University urges that the court should apply cy pres and that Drake University serve as trustee for the entire fund. Dorothy Simmons, executor of the testator's estate, brought an action to have the court construe the will as it relates to these two trusts for Drake University and Parsons College. Parsons College, Drake University, and the testator's heirs at law are the defendants. The lower court held for the heirs at law and Drake University appealed.

---

[8] See p. 821. [9] See RESTATEMENT (SECOND) OF TRUSTS, 1959, comments to sec. 374.

Decision

Affirmed, for the heirs at law.

Reasoning

The bequest to Parsons College in trust for the purposes set out in the testator's will has failed because Parsons College is unable to administer the trust. It is of no import that the trust failed at the outset rather than after it had been under administration for some time. Cy pres will not apply here. Courts may not ignore the testator's intent in order to give effect to doubtful trust provisions by invoking the doctrine of cy pres. Cy pres is simply a liberal rule of construction used to carry out, not defeat, the testator's intent. The cy pres doctrine is inapplicable when the testator has anticipated the possible failure of the trust and has made alternative disposition of his property to meet that contingency. Under such circumstances the testamentary intent may be ascertained without such extrinsic help. This is the case here where the testator stated unequivocally that the assets which would have gone to the trust should then go to his heirs at law.

Dorothy Simmons v. Parsons College, et al., 256 N.W.2d 225 (Iowa 1977).

State statutes govern charitable trusts, and the states vary in their restrictions concerning charitable trusts, such as how much property can be owned by a charitable trust, how much property a decedent may transfer by will to a charitable trust, and to what extent a charitable trust is exempt from taxation. Since the community receives the beneficial interest, usually the state Attorney General or other public officer is responsible for the enforcement of charitable trusts. A co-trustee also can enforce the charitable trust.

Two Trusts Implied by Law

An express or charitable trust is created by the settlor's manifestation of an intent to create a trust, transfer of the settlor's legal title to property to a trustee, and the transfer of the beneficial interest in the property either to a named beneficiary in the case of an express trust, or for the purpose of benefiting a community in the case of a charitable trust. However, two trusts are implied by law where all three of these elements are not present. They are the "resulting trust" and the "constructive trust."

The Resulting Trust

In an express trust, the trustee to whom the property is transferred normally is not intended to have the beneficial interest in the trust property. The settlor's manifestation intended the beneficial interest to go to a third person as the beneficiary. If the beneficial interest in transferred property is not transferred, the *result* is that there is no trust, and the person to whom the property was transferred holds the property in trust for the person who transferred or caused the transfer of the property and who still retains the beneficial interest in the property. Thus, we have the "resulting trust." While no manifested intent to create a trust has been made, nevertheless it is *presumed by law* that the parties intended to create a trust for the benefit of the person retaining the beneficial interest.

A resulting trust can arise in various ways. One way is where the express or charitable trust fails. Since the beneficial interest in the property transferred has not been transferred to anyone and the person holding the property is not intended to have the beneficial interest in it, the *result* is that the person holding the property is intended to hold it in trust for the original owner.

Another way for the resulting trust to arise is where an express or charitable trust has been performed but some of the trust property remains undisposed of. Since there no longer is any beneficial interest of the intended beneficiary in the remaining trust property and the trustee is not intended to have a beneficial interest in the property, the *result* is that the trustee is presumed by law to be intended to hold the property in a resulting trust for the settlor who has the remaining beneficial interest in the property.

A third and very common way for the resulting trust to arise is in connection with the purchase of property. When property is sold, the buyer pays the purchase price to the seller, and at the direction of the buyer the legal title is transferred to a third person.

Unless circumstances are to the contrary, it is presumed that the buyer had no intent that the transferee holder of the title was to have the beneficial interest in the property. Rather, it is presumed by law that the intention of the parties was that the transferee holder of the property was to hold the property in trust for the buyer. Thus, a resulting trust has been created. This type of resulting trust is often called a "purchase money trust."

The presumption of intending a purchase money resulting trust may be rebutted by evidence showing that the person paying the money intended to lend the money to the holder of the property so that the holder might acquire the property, or to make a gift to the holder of the property. The presumption of a resulting trust is also rebutted if, in the absence of a contrary intent, the property is transferred to a close relative (e.g., spouse, child) of the payor, or if the transfer was intended to satisfy a debt of the payor to the transferee holder.

The Constructive Trust

The "constructive trust" created by law does not arise, like the resulting trust, by any legal presumption of an intention to create a trust. Rather, it is created to impose an equitable duty upon a person to hold and transfer property to another because the holder's retention of the property for himself or herself would be wrongful and the holder would be unjustly enriched. The constructive trust usually is employed to remedy a wrong committed by a person in the acquisition of another's property, e.g., by fraud, duress, undue influence. For example, Y fraudulently or unduly influenced X to transfer X's property to Y. Y holds the property in constructive trust for X.

Summary Statement

1. A trust is a legal device whereby legal title to property is held by one person (a trustee) for the benefit of a beneficiary.
2. A trust is distinguished.
3. There are five ways to create an express trust.
4. The settlor must have legal capacity to create an inter vivos or testamentary trust.
5. A person is presumed to be competent with mental capacity. Persons who assert incompetency have the burden of proving it.
6. Mental capacity is best determined by a person's spoken words, acts, and conduct at a particular point in time.
7. The settlor of an express inter vivos trust must manifest an intention to create a trust, effective at the time of the manifestation. It may be in any form, unless the statute of frauds is applicable, as when the trust property is an interest in land.
8. A testamentary trust is a trust in a will, and it cannot come into existence until the death of the testator.
9. The settlor's manifestation of intent to create a trust must indicate the definite, legal purposes of the trust.
10. A trust cannot be created without a transfer of property.
11. Notice to, and acceptance by, the trustee and the beneficiary are not required in order to create a trust.
12. Any person who has legal capacity to take, hold, and administer property for himself or herself can be a trustee.
13. A trust must have a beneficiary definitely identified or identifiable under the rule against perpetuities.
14. The trustee has many trust duties to the beneficiary and, as a fiduciary, the trustee is to act solely for the benefit of the beneficiary's interest in administering the trust.
15. The trustee is to exercise the same care that an ordinary, prudent person would exercise regarding his or her own property.

16. The trustee is to make proper allocations and charges to the principal and income accounts.
17. The trustee is liable to the beneficiary for breach of trust.
18. A settlor may modify or revoke a trust only if the settlor reserved powers to do so in the trust terms.
19. A trust may terminate in various ways, as by expiration; supervening impossibility or illegality; destruction of the trust property; merger in one person of the beneficial interest in, with the legal title to, the trust property.
20. A charitable trust is created for a particular charitable purpose for the benefit of a community.
21. Cy pres means "as near as possible," and may be applied to further the general charitable purpose indicated in the trust terms if the specified particular charitable purpose fails.
22. A resulting trust may occur when the title to property is transferred but the beneficial interest in the property has not been transferred.
23. A constructive trust usually is employed to remedy a wrong committed by a person in the acquisition of another's property.

The following long case, frequently cited in later cases, illustrates the careful consideration given by the court to all the facts and the shifting of the burden of proof in determining whether or not there was a lucid period of competency when capacity was present to execute a written trust agreement.

In re Meyers
189 A.2d 852 (Pa. 1963)

Jones, J. This proceeding seeks to rescind an inter vivos deed of trust wherein Miriam H. Girsh [appellant] and Myers L. Girsh [Mr. Girsh], *then* husband and wife, were the settlors, appellant the principal beneficiary, and Joseph Goldstein, appellant's father, was the sole trustee. The vital, although not the sole, issue is the mental competency of appellant on June 29, 1950, the date upon which she executed the trust deed.

In 1947, appellant became mentally ill, her illness being diagnosed as "paranoid schizophrenia," . . . With the *possible* exception of a comparatively short period of time beginning March 5, 1948, it seems clear that, during the latter part of 1947 and throughout 1948 and 1949, appellant was mentally incompetent and a patient in mental institutions. . . .

Appellant remained at the 44th Street division [of Pennsylvania Hospital] until April 23, 1950 when she was permitted to "go out on visit," in the company of two nurses specially trained in psychiatry, to a hotel in New York "to determine whether a change in environment would result in an improvement in her mental illness."

On five occasions—April 29, May 6, May 13, May 20 and May 27—Dr. Hughes visited appellant in New York and on five occasions—May 2, June 1, June 8, June 24, and June 27—appellant, accompanied by one of her nurses, went to Philadelphia and consulted with Dr. Hughes. . . .

On June 28, 1950 Mr. Goldstein in New York City presented [a] written [trust] agreement to appellant for execution. . . . The trust agreement, although dated June 28, 1950, was executed by appellant on June 29, 1950 and witnessed by Mr. and Mrs. Goldstein. The validity of the execution of this trust agreement is herein attacked. . . .

On June 30, 1950, appellant, accompanied by Mrs. Goldstein and a graduate nurse, went to Johnstown, appellant's hometown and the place of abode of her father and stepmother, where she remained until November 3, 1950. During this period apellant remained under the care of Dr. Hughes and, on at least one occasion, July 14, 1950, went to Philadelphia for an examination by Dr. Hughes.

On November 3, 1950 appellant was admitted, under Dr. Hughes' care, to Roseneath Sanitorium near Philadelphia, an institution which cared for mentally-ill patients. Appellant's condition deteriorated and in January, 1951 she was readmitted, as a patient of Dr. Alpers, to the Institute where she remained continuously until May 23, 1955, a period of four and one-quarter years, at which time she was discharged. It is undisputed that since May 23, 1955 appellant has been mentally competent and has made a remarkable recovery.

Under the trust agreement, Mr. Joseph Goldstein was named as the sole trustee but . . . Mr. Meyers now serves in that capacity. Mr. Meyers, as trustee, has filed three accounts, . . . the third account on June 28, 1960. At the audit of the third account, appellant filed this petition to rescind the trust and to have the balance in the hands of the trustee awarded to her on the ground that she was mentally incompetent at the time she signed the trust agreement on June 29, 1950. . . .

After hearings . . . , the Orphans' Court of Cambria County concluded: (1) that, on June 28, and on June 29, 1950, when appellant executed . . . the trust agreement, she was mentally competent; (2) that, by her conduct since 1955, appellant has ratified . . . the trust agreement; (3) . . .; (4) that the . . . trust agreement [is] valid; (5) that the petition to rescind the trust must be dismissed. Appellant filed exceptions. . . . After argument, the court . . . affirmed the prior adjudication. From such decree this appeal was taken.

On the evidence of record, did the court err in finding that appellant on June 29, 1950 was mentally competent to execute this trust agreement? . . .

First, as to the burden of proof. *Ordinarily,* the mental competency of a person who executes an instrument is presumed and the burden of proof is upon the person who alleges incompetency. . . .

Therefore, in the case at bar, the *initial* burden of proof of incompetency was upon appellant. In assumption of that burden, the appellant proved that, prior to June 28 and June 29, 1950, she had been confined in mental institutions for approximately 21½ months out of 32½ months and that as late as June 10 and June 11, 1950, although there was reason to hope for a remission in her condition, appellant's condition was "such that she could not enter into any legal contract or relationship," and that, *subsequent* to June 28 and June 29, 1950, (beginning *at the latest* in November, 1950) appellant was hospitalized in one or another mental institution for the next four and one-quarter years. The record is clear that appellant was suffering from "schizophrenia, paranoid" which has been defined as a "disintegration of the individual's mind and personality, characterized by disturbances of thinking, * * * hallucinations and similar manifestations." . . . Under such circumstances, did the burden of proof shift to the appellees to prove the mental competency of appellant? In . . . it was said: "If however general or habitual unsoundness of mind be once established, the burden of proving a lucid interval or a restoration, at any particular time, is thrust upon those who allege the fact."

On the state of the instant record, it is clear beyond question that, *very shortly* before the date upon which this trust agreement was executed, appellant suffered from the "most serious form of mental illness known to psychiatry," an illness which had existed for upwards of two years; that, prior to, at the time of, and subsequent to the time of execution of the trust agreement, appellant was under the care of psychiatric nursing; that, for a period of over four years thereafter, appellant was continuously a patient in mental institutions. In its adjudication the court below stated: "There is no doubt that [appellant] was incompetent before this period and relapsed into incompetency some time later." The record not only fully supports this statement but indicates that the time interval between the date of execution of the trust agreement and the previous and succeeding incompetency was short in duration. Under such circumstances, appellant's previous and subsequent mental incompetency was of such *recent* and *serious* nature and *apparent* permanence as to impose upon appellees the burden of proving that, on the date the trust agreement was executed, appellant possessed mental competency.

In its adjudication the court below, properly held that the burden of going forward with evidence was upon appellees.

Under the instant circumstances, it being definitely appellees' burden to prove that, on the date of execution of the trust agreement, appellant possessed mental competency, i.e., the ability to understand and appreciate the nature and effect of the trust agreement, to sustain such burden required the production not of a preponderance of evidence but of proof *clear* and *convincing* in nature. . . .

Was the court below correct in finding that appellees' evidence was *clear* and *convincing?* . . . *The matter of credibility is for the trial court.* . . . [W]here mental capacity is at issue, the real question is the condition * * * at the very time he executed the [instrument], although evidence of capacity or incapacity for a reasonable time before and after the making of the [instrument] is admissible as indicative of capacity or lack of it on the particular day. . . .

The critical or crucial time at which appellant's mental competency must be determined [is] June 29, 1950—when the trust agreement was executed. . . .

To that which transpired on June 28 and June 29 the sole witnesses were Mrs. Goldstein, who witnessed [the] agreement, and Misses Warwick and Hunt, the nurses. All three witnesses testified to the events which transpired on both dates; Mr. Goldstein's arrival at the hotel apartment with the agreement, the discussion, sometimes in loud tones, between appellant and Mr. Goldstein of the contents of the agreement, the reading at length of the agreement by appellant, . . . the deletion by appellant from the trust agreement of references therein to a certain law firm and her refusal to execute the trust agreement until such references were deleted in a redrafted agreement, the execution on June 29 of the trust agreement redrafted to suit appellant's wishes, appellant's actions on both dates subsequent to Mr. Goldstein's departure, etc.

We have said that a person's "mental capacity is best determined by his spoken words, his acts and conduct." . . . These witnesses did outline and describe the words, acts, and conduct of the appellant and, from their observation of such words, acts, and conduct, they all concluded that the appellant *on those dates* did possess sufficient mental capacity to understand and appreciate the meaning and nature of the agreements which she executed. . . .

According to Dr. Hughes, . . . during the latter part of June, 1950 and July, 1950, appellant entered a period of remission to the extent that she had regained full mental competency to execute this agreement. Dr. Hughes gave his opinion that, both on the dates when the agreement [was] executed as well as on July 14, 1950, appellant was mentally competent.

Morton Meyers, Esq., a member of the bar, on June 25, 1950 visited appellant in New York, found appellant "indeed improved," "pleasant," and she "talked intelligently" to him; he discussed with her the pending agreement. . . ."

The fact is that, in the case at bar, Judge Nelson . . . *believed* the oral testimony of the nurses and Dr. Hughes. With that belief we cannot interfere. . . .

A review of this record clearly indicates, as found by the court below, that shortly *before* and *after* June 29 appellant was mentally incompetent. Our task is to ascertain from this record whether the evidence clearly demonstrates that in the *interim* period appellant was in such a state of remission and was experiencing such a lucid interval that she was then mentally competent.

If Mrs. Goldstein, the nurses, Dr. Hughes, and Attorney Meyers are to be believed, on June 29 appellant was in a state where her mental illness had abated and she was then in possession of sufficient mental capacity to execute the trust agreement. Assuming, as we must, the credibility of their testimony, such testimony bears the qualities of proof requisite in this area of the law and appellees have sustained their burden of showing that on June 29 appellant was mentally competent. . . .

. . . Our conclusion [is] that appellant did have sufficient mental capacity to execute this trust agreement. . . .

Decree affirmed. . . .

Questions and Case Problems

1. Salkin claims that he is the trustee under a trust instrument executed by Lipin. Lipin claims that when he executed the instrument he did not know that Salkin was the attorney for conflicting interests which Salkin did not disclose to Lipin. Some time after the instrument was executed by Lipin, Lipin also executed two documents amending the instrument—an informal accounting prepared by Salkin, and a release of Salkin as trustee—without fully understanding these documents and in reliance on Salkin's false representations that they were routine business papers prepared by Salkin to protect Lipin's interest. Salkin later demanded that Lipin add $20,000 to the trust property or Lipin's participation in the trust would be reduced pro tanto, i.e., to a certain extent. Lipin instituted a judicial proceeding to obtain an order staying the trustee's threatened action. When he could not obtain such an order, he had to choose between making the payment or suffering a serious financial loss. Lipin paid the $20,000.

    Lipin then instituted an action to have the instrument cancelled as a trust instrument, and to have the other documents executed by him declared to be invalid. Salkin claims that Lipin's payment with knowledge of all these facts was a ratification of the instrument and the documents. Salkin made a motion for a **summary judgment** in favor of Salkin without the necessity of a trial on the facts. The motion was granted. Lipin appeals claiming the granting of the motion for summary judgment was improper, the instrument is not a trust, and asking for cancellation of the instrument and the amending documents. You decide, explaining the reasons for your decision. [*Lipin v. Salkin,* 175 N.Y.S.2d 119 (1958).] (This older case was selected because of its excellent simplicity and directness.)

2. Albert A. Berges, the decedent, provided in part in his will: "I do hereby give, devise and bequeath to Jim Feliz, as trustee, the sum of $600.00 for each of his children, and I do hereby give, devise and bequeath to Josephine Feliz Dawson, as trustee, the sum of $600.00 for each of her children at the time of my **demise**. Said trusts shall terminate when each of said children, attain the age of eighteen years." Do these words create a testamentary trust on Berges' death? Give reasons for your decision. [In re *Albert A. Berges,* 142 Cal.Rptr. 635 (1977).]

3. In 1952 Ann B. duPont made a gift of her home, later called "Memorial House" to The Executive Council of the Protestant Episcopal Church in the Diocese of Delaware, a Delaware corporation. She died in 1963. Her will provided in part:

    "I give and bequeath to The Executive Council of the Protestant Episcopal Church of the Diocese of Delaware the sum of five hundred thousand dollars ($500,000) for the maintenance and care of, and the operations carried on in the property known as 'Memorial House,' at 56 Oak Avenue, Rehoboth, Delaware, which I have heretofore given to said Executive Council, the expenditures for such maintenance, care, and operation to be as the Bishop and Standing Committee of said Diocese shall determine in their discretion."

    Is there a testamentary trust? Give reasons for your decision. [*The Executive Council of the Protestant Episcopal Church in the Diocese of Delaware, Inc. v. Robert A. Moss,* et al., 231 A.2d 463 (Del. 1967).]

4. Aaron E. Rentz named his sister, Myrtis R. Polk, as executrix and trustee in his will, which provides in part:

    "V. I give, devise, and bequeath all the rest and residue of the property of which I may die possessed, including, but not limited to bank accounts, real estate, mortgages, choses in action, growing crops, money, and life insurance policy benefits unto Myrtis R. Polk, IN TRUST, nevertheless, under the following terms and conditions: . . . "VI. Upon the death of my Mother-in-law, Danna H. Kinard, my Trustee shall turn over the corpus of the trust to my beloved wife, Lennis, in its entirety. Should my beloved wife predecease her Mother then, and in that event, my Trustee shall turn over the corpus of the trust to my son, Danny, ten (10) years after my death."

    Is there a testamentary trust here? Give the reasons for your decision. [*Lennis K. Rentz and Danny Rentz v. Myrtis R. Polk,* 228 S.E.2d 106 (S.C. 1976).]

---

summary judgment
a judgment rendered on a motion by a party in a civil action that, solely on the basis of the pleadings with affidavits, if any, there is no genuine issue as to any material fact and the moving party is entitled to judgment as a matter of law without the necessity of a trial on the facts

demise
death

5. The testatrix's will created a testamentary trust which provides in part:
   1. the trust shall continue for twenty years from the date of the decedent's death, at which future date, if the decedent's two named grandchildren and her great-grandchild shall not all have come to the United States of America to live, then said trust shall terminate and the trustee shall distribute the corpus of the trust estate to said two grandchildren and great-grandchild, share and share alike, if they be living at that time.
   2. if either of her two grandchildren or her great-grandchild should come to the United States of America to live before the time of the expiration of the trust, the trustee was directed to pay to said grandchild, grandchildren, or great-grandchild, so living in the United States of America, one-third of the net income from the trust, with at least one payment being made annually, and that when all of the said grandchildren and great-grandchild have come to the United States of America to live, then the trust should end and the trust estate be divided equally among said grandchildren and great-grandchild.

   At the time of the execution of the testatrix's will and at all times subsequent thereto, the plaintiffs were, and still are, residents of Rumania and Hungary. The testatrix died February 28, 1956.

   The plaintiffs petition to have the testamentary part of the will be construed. They contend that they are entitled to immediate distribution of decedent's estate because, they argue, the trust created by the language in the will was merely a method and/or device relied upon by the testatrix to ensure the transfer of the funds of said legacies to the plaintiffs, and to safeguard their receipt against confiscation or seizure by the government in Rumania, and that this possibility no longer exists.

   Is the trust still in existence or has it terminated? Give reasons for your decision. [*Elizabeth Kiljan, et al. v. Norman F. Hoover,* 221 N.E.2d 387 (Ohio 1965).]

6. The testatrix's will, executed October 18, 1941, devised a specific parcel of improved real property to her trustees in trust "to furnish my daughter, Anna * * * with one of the apartments in said premises * * * rent free during her lifetime," and to pay the balance of the net income therefrom in equal shares to Anna and Daniel, with Daniel's share of the income payable to his issue if he predeceased Anna. The will nominated them as co-executors and trustees, but Daniel renounced his appointment and Anna has acted in both capacities. The language in the will indicates clearly that the primary and dominant purpose of the testatrix was to furnish Anna with an apartment in the family home rent free for life. Testatrix died September 13, 1954. In 1964 Anna vacated the apartment provided her by the will, and in 1965, because of the continued vacancy of the building and the general deterioration of the surrounding area, the trust realty was sold with the consent of the interested parties.

   Anna petitions that the testamentary part of the will be construed, contending that the trust has been terminated and that the proceeds should be distributed to the beneficiaries named in the will. You decide, giving reasons for your decision. [In re *Frank's Will,* 57 Misc.2d 446 (N.Y. 1968).] (This older case was selected for its excellent simplicity and directness.)

7. The testator had constructed a hospital in 1916 in his name called the George M. Hoffman Memorial Hospital. His will created a testamentary trust under the terms of which trust income was to be paid to the trustees solely for maintenance of the hospital, and if the hospital failed to operate as a hospital for one year the trust fund with accumulated interest or income from the fund is to be distributed to, and become the absolute property of, the testator's friend, George Green, if living, otherwise to his friend's heirs. Testator died in 1931. By 1972 the hospital building could no longer be licensed as a hospital and the Hoffman Memorial Hospital ceased to operate. In 1975 the trustees of the Hoffman trust asked the court to construe the will as it relates to this testamentary trust and to determine ownership of the assets held in the testamentary trust. Is the cy pres doctrine applicable? Give reasons for your decision. [*Kenneth J. Nelson and Homer Sharpe v. Mary Kring,* 592 P.2d 438 (Kan. 1979).]

8. Distinguish a resulting trust from a constructive trust.

9. A & M Records, Inc. is a California corporation which commercially manufactures and sells recorded musical performances in the form of disc phonograph records and prerecorded magnetic tapes. Heilman has admitted advertising and selling record and tape "albums" which included performances of songs duplicated from recordings owned and manufactured by A & M Records without making payments to A & M Records or to any of the musicians involved. Gross receipts from the sale of pirated A & M Records' performances totaled at least $80,000.

   On what legal basis does A & M Records have a claim against Heilman? Explain. [*A & M Records, Inc. v. David L. Heilman,* 142 Cal.Rptr. 390 (1978).]

10. In the case of In re *Meyers*, 189 A.2d 852 (Pa. 1963),[10] the court discussed the shifting of various burdens of proof in establishing incompetency and competency in the execution of the written trust agreement. Explain how the court did this.

---

[10] See pp. 833–35.

Ethics and Business Law in Part 11
Wills and Decedents' Estates, and Trusts

Introduction

This end-of-Part discussion, like the others in this book, is designed to encourage students to begin forming personal beliefs about what is right or wrong conduct in business. The discussion here builds on the material in the first end-of-Part discussion on pages 58 to 69; you may find it helpful to review that.

This material has several goals. The "sampling of ethical issues" section immediately following is designed to help you see the range of ethical issues associated with this area of the law. The in-depth discussion is intended to provide you with a background for forming your own beliefs about a single very important ethical issue in business. The problems at the end are designed to build your skill in ethical analysis while exploring further the in-depth issue.

A Sampling of Ethical Issues in Wills and Trusts

All of the law you have studied so far in this book has been the product of elaborate legal decision-making processes. The case law mechanism, in particular, is uniquely rigorous in making the *process* as utterly fair, impartial, and free of emotion as possible. In contrast, the study of wills and trusts is the examination of topics where individual decision making is loaded with emotion. Because this decision-making process is often vulnerable to emotion, it is quite easy to make the wrong decisions. This accounts for the formal requirements for creating a will. The general requirement for a writing, a signature, and attestation are, at least in part, designed to ensure that the testator has the appropriate mental capacity or free will. Similarly, many business ethics issues must be decided in contexts which make high quality decision making difficult. Can you see that in some ethically intense situations you may need to use different procedures to ensure that you make a high quality decision.

Sometimes it is impossible to ensure an ethical outcome. In these instances we often are compelled to rely just on *procedures* which are ethical. In a sense this is what the law does in the area of wills and trusts. The law prescribes formal procedures to ensure that the process is as fair as possible because there is no practical way to ensure that the disposition of a decedent's property by will is ethical. Can you see that managers must sometimes rely on just an ethical procedure because they can't compel an ethical result?

Can you see that the selection of beneficiaries for one's estate is an activity which reflects an ethical orientation? Some take a purely egoistic approach and leave their property to persons who have given them the most pleasure. Sometimes pets are recipients of the benefits of estates of egoists. Utilitarians might leave everything to a college, university, or research institute in hopes of generating the greatest good for the greatest number. Kant's philosophy might suggest that we have a duty to help take care of those whom we have produced, namely our offspring. Religious ethics might require that we leave our estate to a church or a charitable organization which helps the poor.

In-Depth Discussion of a Basic Issue: Mental Capacity and Free Will

This body of law addresses the issue of mental capacity directly. To make a will or create a trust a person must have mental capacity and be free of undue influence. Mental ability is also a prerequisite to the creation of ethical decisions. An understanding of modern psychology can help us avoid pitfalls and make high quality decisions so that our ethical desires translate into ethical conduct.

Business ethics is played out in markets. And markets allow individuals to seek their own self-interest and at the same time to advance the common good. But when markets and other social systems, such as the law, function imperfectly, morally sensitive business persons often must elect between advancing their self-interest or advancing the common good. For many, alternating their perspective from self to others is an insurmountable psychological challenge. The need to alternate perspectives can trigger several of the processes identified by modern psychology which cause us to misperceive, or misthink, so that our actions do not match our beliefs about what is right or wrong.

Rationalization

This process has its roots in the idea that we have difficulty simultaneously maintaining two psychologically conflicting ideas. When our minds try to resolve the conflicts, they sometimes ignore reality. For example, car buyers typically collect information about various models and, prior to the purchase, accurately absorb information about each car's strengths and weaknesses. After a purchase, they see their purchase behavior as psychologically inconsistent with the fact that their car has weaknesses. To resolve the conflict, many respond by ignoring their car's weaknesses. Thus, the decision maker rationalizes, devises after the fact, self satisfying but incorrect reasons for the purchase—the Cadillac becomes the perfect car rather than what it is in reality, a compromise between good comfort and poor mileage. It is a form of self deception. Similarly, the father who decides to leave all of his wealth to a poor daughter thereby disinheriting a financially successful son may suffer from psychological conflict over this action. One potential way to reconcile the treatment of the son is to decide that he has been disinherited for other reasons. In the search for other reasons, the father may incorrectly conclude that he has not been a good son.

Business ethics decisions can be plagued by rationalization. Since the ideas of concern for one's self and concern for others are, for some, psychologically inconsistent, they rationalize their moral behavior. Some rationalize self-interested behavior as "other" oriented. For example, radar detector users and manufacturers often declare that the detectors reduce highway speed by causing users to slow down when the buzzer goes off. But most of us recognize that their motivation is not to slow down but, rather, to be able to speed without getting a traffic ticket.

Rationalization can push some people in the opposite direction. They engage in conduct which is other oriented but describe it to themselves as self oriented. When contributing to a relief fund for Mexico City after the earthquake in 1985, the contributors say, "What goes around comes around." But we know they will not receive any financial return on this investment. Their impulse is fundamentally other oriented, but they have a hard time seeing themselves in this way. These people need to come to grips with the idea that they are impelled by strong concerns for others and, therefore, they sometimes suppress their self-interest.

Selective Perception
This is a process similar to rationalization in that it allows us to maintain our ego, or self image, by altering the way we perceive reality. In a famous experiment, college students who heard many classmates falsely describe line A as longer than line B, came to perceive the lines in the way their classmates described them rather than the way they actually were. Similarly, a son or daughter left out of a will may wrongly recall that the testator lacked testamentary capacity at the time the will was executed.

Sometimes subordinates are judged with selective perception. Only the mistakes are noticed and contributions don't seem to capture the supervisor's attention. Often a stereotype based on race, sex, accent, appearance or education causes one to view another negatively. So the negative image must be reconciled with the good work performance. Selective perception solves this psychological problem by causing us to see only the negative. As a result a good worker can be unfairly evaluated.

In part, the doctrine of undue influence derives from this reality of human nature. If an elderly person is being cared for by a close relative, the elderly person frequently appreciates the person so much as to stop seeing reality clearly. If there are conflicts between the close relative and other family members, the dependent elderly party often favors the relative on whom she or he is most dependent. Often wills leave a high percentage of an estate to the person who took care of the decedent last.

Groupthink
This is a phenomenon where close knit groups lose their ability to objectively evaluate reality. The group pressures its members to conform to its beliefs in the face of evidence that the group is wrong. Dissent is suppressed and members protect the group from "unpleasant" information which conflicts with the group views. Maintaining membership and cohesion seem to be more important than perceiving reality. In business, competitors are sometimes seen as subhuman "sharks." Unhappy consumers are "the crazies." When the group uses these labels, its members are able to reconcile treating the ones labeled in ways they would not treat "real persons." Families sometimes feud and this can create camps where groupthink prevails.

Solving Ethics Problems

Like the other end-of-Part discussions in this book, this one presents problems for you to consider. These problems have three goals. The first is to give you the opportunity to further explore the in-depth issue. The second goal is to give you experience in ethical reasoning about the law and about related management problems. The third goal is to let you see how thinking critically about the law can increase your ability to make ethical decisions. To facilitate this, the problems begin by asking you to analyze the law for its ethical content and then shift to looking at related problems in managerial ethics.

For a discussion of the ethical roles of markets and the law, and examples of the four styles of ethical reasoning—egoism, utilitarianism, Kant's philosophy, and religious ethics—read the business ethics material at the end of Part 1.

Problems

1. Review the case of *Lula Nannie Ella Reed and Fannie Reed Simmons v. Mary Shipp* on page 805. In that case try to determine who, among the parties to this case, was most likely to have misthought or misperceived. Was it Mack, or Mary or Lula and Fannie? If there was misperception, what type was it?

2. Review the case of *J. Lake Hellams v. Pauline Ross* on pages 813–14. There the will of the late Marvin Ross was contested on the basis that he was a drunkard. The will was upheld on the ground that the party attempting to break a will has the burden of proving the lack of testamentary capacity. Ross had entered into bad business transactions, expressed the view that he could buy his way into heaven, and left nothing to his family. What is the philosophic purpose of this law?

3. Suppose you have a strong belief requiring compliance with the law. Also assume you are aware that copying applications software without permission is illegal because it violates the copyright laws. If you were a new employee in an organization that made a practice of buying one copy of applications software then illegally duplicating it for use by 20 to 30 other people, what would you do? Can you see how intense the pressure on you would be to rationalize, or selectively perceive, or engage in groupthink? Suppose you were asked to do the illegal duplication. How do you think you would respond? Can you devise any strategies to keep from getting into such situations?

4. Assume you had worked for IBM for 10 years in its new product development laboratory. One of its competitors has tried to lure you away. While you know many trade secrets which it would be illegal to disclose to the competitor, they give you assurances that they are not hiring you for that information and that they would not pressure you to disclose such information if you came to work for them in their research laboratory. If you accepted their offer, do you think you would suffer any dissonance in the new job? Do you think you might lose touch with ethical reality and begin disclosing IBM's trade secrets after inventing some false justification for doing so? How could you protect yourself from such psychological traps?

PART 12 Business Law in the International Marketplace

56. Business Law in the International Marketplace
Transnational business done by persons (firms and individuals) in the United States and abroad.

Summary

Part 12 of this text is an exposure to that part of private international law concerned with transnational business, that is the transfer of property among persons across national boundary lines. International export and import of property is a necessity for a healthy, progressive national economy, and is subject to the business law and governmental regulations of the various countries. You will, in all probability, be in a business which directly or indirectly handles property for export or property which has been imported, or both.

Part 12 opens with an introduction to the subject, followed by a discussion of: methods of operating transnational business abroad; the contract between the parties in a transnational business transaction; protection of industrial property interests located abroad; and antitrust laws applicable to transnational business.

Business ethics as it relates to the text material in this Part is considered at the end of the Part.

56 Business Law in the International Marketplace

After you have read this chapter, you should be able to:

1. Explain how a letter of credit is used to assure contract performance of payment and delivery of goods.
2. Describe the nature of a foreign agent.
3. Distinguish a foreign distributor from a foreign agent.
4. Understand the use of a turn-key operation.
5. Recognize the legal significance of a parent firm establishing a branch or a subsidiary abroad.
6. Understand what is meant by technology.
7. Discuss the impact of foreign law on domestic (United States) technology exported abroad.
8. Explain the significance and importance of the various clauses that should be considered for inclusion in a transnational business contract.
9. Understand the meaning of industrial property interests and the need and means for their protection.
10. Discuss the impact of United States and foreign antitrust laws applicable to transnational business.
11. Explain the origins of the European Economic Community, its structure and operation.

Introduction

You or your American firm is about to engage in business transactions outside the United States. There are many things of which you should be aware *before* engaging in such transactions. This chapter should orient you into some of the various factors that you should consider.

Persons have a "freedom to contract," subject to the legal limitations imposed by the State as sovereign. In this chapter, unless otherwise indicated, the word "State" is used to describe a nation in the international family of nations and not one of the fifty states in the United States of America. This entire book is a discussion on the various legal areas of limitations on that freedom to contract which, internationally, differ widely from State to State.

The law in the various nations limiting this freedom takes on differing forms. In the United States we have the **common law,** statutory, administrative, constitutional, and **case law** in each state and in the federal government. This is true also in other countries with a common law background, e.g., Canada, England, Australia. Most other nations have the same forms of law but with one very important exception, namely, code law or civil law based on Roman law instead of the common law. Code law is an all-inclusive system of law stated in each national code, quite different from the common law which consists of principles of law evolving from judicial decisions rendered in the absence of any statutory (legislative or constitutional) provision.

common law
principles of non-statutory law reflecting the customs and usages of society and found in judicial decisions

case law
the law that comes from decided cases

These differences become extremely important when American business firms contemplate doing business abroad. The conclusion is obvious that, in order to avoid unnecessary risk of financial loss and to ensure knowledge of the law of the nation in which one desires to engage in business, *competent legal advice and business expertise are absolutely necessary.* Further, these must be supplemented with foreign legal advice and foreign business expertise available in the particular country.

At this point, you should begin to understand the great impact of the law on transnational business which, basically, is business law in the international marketplace of whatever is being sold. In the United States, particular attention should be given to the impact of the antitrust laws,[1] federal (and state) securities laws,[2] the Foreign Corrupt Practices Act of 1977[3] and anti-boycott regulations.[4] Domestic and foreign taxation is always a major factor for consideration in transnational business.[5]

Only a limited exposure to the subject of this chapter is possible because of shortage of space. Our approach to the subject will be to consider the following selected areas and, as each area is discussed, deal with the legal ramifications affecting each of them:

1. methods of operating transnational business abroad;
2. the contract between the parties in a transnational business transaction;
3. protection of industrial property interests located abroad;
4. antitrust laws applicable to transnational business.

---

[1] See pp. 702–12.   [2] See pp. 673–78.   [3] See pp. 678–79.

[4] United States anti-boycott regulations prohibit and make illegal activities by United States (domestic) "persons" (which includes those persons who control others, e.g., controlled subsidiaries) in interstate and foreign commerce of the United States which has the effect of furthering or supporting certain international boycotts by one or more foreign countries of another foreign country. Any request to participate in such a boycott or for information about that domestic person's business interest which is boycott related, made to that domestic person, *must* be reported by that domestic person to the United States Department of Commerce and the Treasury Department.

[5] Reference should be made to two alternative provisions in the federal Tax Code which are concerned with the exemption and deferment of federal tax on income resulting from doing transnational business. One is concerned with a Domestic International Sales Corporation (DISC), and the other with an FSA Corporation. Both are designed to further and encourage American transnational business.

Methods of Operating Transnational Business Abroad

Transnational business is concerned with the transfer of **property** among persons across *national* boundary lines. Property consists of things which are either tangible or intangible. Tangibles are those things which can be touched, such as land and **goods**. Intangibles are things which cannot be touched, that is rights, such as a contract right, an account receivable for money owed, or a copyright or patented right in some thing. Technology is concerned with both intangible things, such as ideas and processes related to material things, and tangible material things resulting from those ideas and processes, such as machines and tools. **Technology** is owned by the originator. Our main concern here is with the international business transfer of goods and technology, not land.

There are various methods of operating abroad in the transfer of property. We will consider first the sale of goods and then the licensing of technology.

Sale of Goods

Whether to produce goods in the United States for sale abroad, or to arrange for their foreign manufacture and sale, are decisions to be made only after considering established commercial procedures, cost which includes domestic and foreign taxes, risks, and foreign laws.

Domestic Production. Direct Export Sales.   If the product is to be made in the United States for direct sale to a foreign customer, the domestic seller has the same concerns of how and when to ship the goods and of definite and prompt payment of the purchase price as are in a sale made to a customer in the United States. Unless the seller has absolute trust in the foreign buyer's *unsecured* credit, the normal and safe procedure is that the parties will require two intermediaries for their mutual protection to assure shipment of the goods and definite prompt payment. The seller will not part with possession or title to the goods, nor the buyer with payment, without such assurances.

The sales agreement between the domestic seller and the foreign buyer will provide for the following procedure. The buyer is to obtain a **letter of credit** issued by a bank in the buyer's country. A letter of credit is an agreement by that bank (the issuing bank) to pay a stated amount of money on presentation to it of a **document of title** (e.g., a **bill of lading**) which itemizes the goods that have been shipped, such itemization of goods being the same as in the letter of credit. Also, the buyer is to arrange with a bank in the United States, satisfactory to the seller, which is to confirm the letter of credit—this means that the confirming bank will honor the letter of credit and pay the seller on delivery to it of a bill of lading with the same itemization of products as in the letter of credit. In this way, the seller ships the goods, obtains a bill of lading and delivers it to the confirming bank which immediately pays the seller the agreed sales price. The confirming bank then delivers the bill of lading to the issuing bank which immediately reimburses the confirming bank and delivers the bill of lading to the buyer.

Suppose the buyer complains that the goods are not as agreed. The intermediate banks have no responsibility for any loss sustained by the buyer. Their only responsibilities were for the confirming bank to pay the seller and the issuing bank to reimburse the confirming bank on the basis of the bill of lading having the same itemization of goods as in the letter of credit. The buyer will have to negotiate with the seller and, possibly, resort to legal proceedings against the seller.

Sale by a Foreign Agent.   It is normal business practice for a foreign commercial agent to be appointed by an American manufacturing firm (principal) to assist in the sale of its products abroad. The agency law in foreign countries is different in many respects from that in the United States.[6] Foreign laws, particularly in civil or code law countries, often provide for different kinds of agent and define their authority in their commercial

---

[6] For the American law of Agency, see chapters 33–36.

codes. The agency agreement must be carefully drawn; stating that there is an agency relationship is not enough.[7] An explanation of what the agent is to do must not include functions which preclude an agency relationship. Generally, sales are made by the American firm as the principal and the agent is paid a commission on those *sales which resulted from the agent's efforts.* The agent does not buy the goods and does not have title to the goods. In some countries, an agent for a foreign principal with authority to make contracts of sale for the principal or to accept orders for its goods is considered to be doing business in that country with various legal effects, one of which is to subject the principal to local taxes. Agents generally do not have this authority.

There are other important differences in foreign agency law. In some countries the law requires that only their own nationals may be agents for foreign principals, while in other countries goods may be imported only through their governmental agencies. Many American firms might be surprised to learn that in many countries agency contracts with foreign principals must be registered with the proper governmental agency and, in some countries, the law limits the amount of commission that an agent may receive under the agency contract. Payment by the principal of a higher commission, irrespective of how disguised, may constitute a violation of the United States Foreign Corrupt Practices Act of 1977.

In some countries, the national interest to protect their people who represent foreign principals is shown in various labor laws. Some host countries have laws which require that commercial agents for foreign principals must have *exclusive* rights to represent the principal in that country. Such agents often are treated as employees with the many legal effects of such status. There are also laws regarding the termination of such agency relationships, such as requiring advance notice before termination, and providing for an indemnity payment to be made by the principal to the agent either in the form of a lump sum or in an amount reflecting the amount of business brought to the principal by the agent's efforts.

Sale by a Foreign Distributor. A foreign **distributor** is an **independent contractor**.[8] A distributor, rather than an agent, is appointed usually when the American manufacturer wishes to engage *extensively* in business in the foreign country. This often involves considerable American expense because the distributor, *in acquiring title to the goods,* will need to establish an inventory and often need training for its employees if the product is technological (e.g., machines, and technical equipment). The American firm may prefer appointing a distributor in order not to make a large foreign investment by establishing a foreign branch or subsidiary, and to avoid foreign labor laws applicable to commercial agents for foreign firm principals. Also, as an independent contractor with title to the goods, the foreign distributor, not the American firm, shoulders the risk of establishing good business relationships in the foreign country and of reselling the goods at a profit. The distributor is an independent legal entity with an independent business, and the American firm is not a party to any contracts made by the distributor.

The appointment of a foreign distributor normally grants the right to *exclusive* distribution of the goods in *one specific country.* Exclusivity of distribution may well raise antitrust problems in some countries. An agreement that the American firm can fix the resale price of the goods to be resold by a *foreign* distributor apparently is not a violation of *United States* antitrust law, but it is a violation of the antitrust laws *in some countries.* The agreement should provide for a *specified* distributorship period during which, except for *specified* cause, the relationship cannot be terminated by the American firm.

In order to avoid problems of foreign labor law regarding the possible status of an agent or a distributor *as an employee,* it should help considerably if the American manufacturer could induce its representative to incorporate.

distributor
an independent contractor who sells on his own account, independent of the seller of goods to him

independent contractor
a person who contracts independently for himself to render a result, and who is not acting on behalf of another nor subject to another's control

---

[7] See *Lamb v. Goring,* [1932] 1 K.B. 710 for an excellent discussion of "agency" in that case.

[8] For a discussion of an independent contractor, see pp. 503–4.

Other Organizational Methods for Transnational Sale of Goods Domestically Produced. There are other organizational methods for transnational sales of goods. One method is a "turn-key" operation, whereby an American firm provides what is necessary in establishing a foreign business enterprise, e.g., manufacturing, supplying equipment, management and personnel training, and licensing of technology, and the firm then "turns" over to a foreign firm the operation of the enterprise. Another method is the creation of a **joint venture** between American and foreign firms for a business purpose in a foreign (host) country.

joint venture
an association of two or more persons as co-owners to engage in a limited business transaction for a profit

The extent of the American seller's activity or of the application of foreign tax laws may justify consideration of establishing either a branch or a subsidiary of the American firm in the host country. This means the establishment of a foreign presence in the host country and, therefore, consequent possible submission of itself to foreign jurisdiction and its problems. The following well-known case is an illustration of an American court's jurisdiction over a parent foreign corporation with a sub-subsidiary corporation in the United States.

Facts
Defendant, Rolls-Royce of England, Ltd. **[Ltd.]**, is a British corporation which manufactures and sells motor cars and airplane engines, and sells parts and gives service to its customers. These products are sold world-wide and customers get service at many places. Rolls-Royce of England, Ltd., owns all the stock of Rolls-Royce of Canada, Ltd., a Canadian corporation, and this Canadian company owns all the stock of Rolls-Royce, Inc. **[Inc.]** which operates in New York State.

The business of **Inc.** is solely in the sale of products manufactured by **Ltd.** and in the servicing of the products for purchasers. All sales literature used by **Inc.** is written and published by **Ltd.** All three companies have some directors in common, and key executive personnel in **Inc.** were former executives of either the English or the Canadian company and were assigned to their positions by the parent English company. There are frequent conferences among executives of the three companies at which the policies of **Inc.** are determined. **Inc.** employees who require technical training are given it by **Ltd.** in England. **Inc.** owns no automobiles, and when a car sale is made to a customer **Inc.** buys a car from **Ltd.** in England and imports it. As to airplane engines, compensation for service is paid to **Inc.** by the Canadian company. All net income of **Inc.** goes to the Canadian company and appears on that company's balance sheet, and ultimately on the balance sheet of **Ltd.**

Plaintiff, Taca International Airlines, a corporation of San Salvador, sued the defendant, **Ltd.,** and served a summons on **Inc.** as being a part of **Ltd.** Plaintiff's suit is for damage to its airplane allegedly caused by the negligence of **Ltd.** and **Inc.** Defendant, **Ltd.,** made a motion to set aside the summons and dismiss the suit, alleging that **Inc.** is a distinctly separate corporate entity and that service of a summons on **Inc.** is not service on **Ltd.** Plaintiff contends that **Inc.** is a mere incorporated division or arm of **Ltd.** and a subsidiary of **Ltd.** Is **Inc.** an independent entity, or a sub-subsidiary and a mere department of **Ltd.**?

Decision
Judgment for plaintiff; defendant's motion denied.

Reasoning
Inc. is **Ltd.'s** wholly owned sub-subsidiary, which sold and serviced **Ltd.'s** products in New York, is a mere sales agent department of **Ltd.** rather than an independent entity, and service of a summons on **Inc.** was sufficient service on **Ltd. Ltd.** was doing extensive business in New York through its local department separately incorporated as **Inc.**

Taca International Airlines v. Rolls-Royce of England, Ltd., 204 N.E.2d 329 (N.Y. 1965)

Such foreign jurisdiction includes the American firm's required compliance with the host's laws, resolution of disputes in the host's courts, and taxation problems, to mention only a few of its features. Branches or subsidiaries may be established only with the permission, or at the request, of the host country. It is important that a firm consider the tax consequences in the United States and abroad before deciding whether to have branches or subsidiaries.

The Transnational Transfer of Technology

Technology is a particular kind of property concerned with material things. It signifies that *tangible* material thing which is the result of innovation (e.g., machine, computer, factory); and also that which is the *intangible* innovative process itself, sometimes called "intellectual property" (e.g., ideas, processes, inventions). As property, technology can be transferred. We have already discussed the *sale* of goods, which includes the sale of tangible technology. Here, we will briefly consider a few other methods by which a transfer of technology may be made together with legal restrictions on such transfer.

In both kinds of technology (tangible and intangible) governmental legal restrictions are applied to their transnational business transfer because of their international importance, national security, and need in foreign countries. Legal restrictions on, or affecting the export or import of, technology in the United States and foreign countries are either in the form of domestic or foreign statutory or administrative law, or in international accords such as treaties and agreements. For example, in the United States the Export Administration Act of 1969 and the Department of Commerce Export Regulations restrict the export of technology. Some technology can be exported under the general **license** provisions of the Department of Commerce without applying for any license, while the export of other technology is prohibited without applicaton for and issuance of a *validated license*.

Some technology is subject to protection from infringement abroad, such as patents and trademarks.[9] Many foreign national laws and international accords provide a certain amount of protection, but opportunity for violation is always present. However, in some countries certain items are not patentable (e.g., medical devices, food, energy controls), and owners' rights are limited. Many countries require that governmental agencies must approve technology transfer agreements, and some have the power to modify such agreements. A suggested method of owner protection is to provide in the agreement that such modification will, at the election of the owner, void the agreement.

A careful examination should be made of the antitrust laws of the United States and of the foreign country where the recipient of the technology transfer is located. For example, the owner's restriction on the foreign recipient's use of the technology, substantial effect of the technology on American export or import, and contracts and combinations abroad intending and accomplishing restraint of foreign commerce with the United States may well be subject to United States antitrust law. Clearance with proper foreign and United States governmental agencies should be obtained in advance. A type of activity which is fraught with possible violation of foreign antitrust laws, as it is in the United States, is the **tying** or "tie-in" **arrangement** whereby a seller's agreement with a buyer for the sale of a particular product makes such sale contingent on the buyer's agreement to purchase another of the seller's products. The development of technology products abroad causes foreign countries often to require that local nationals be employed by the licensee or that local materials be used by the licensee in the development of the technology.

The Contract between the Parties in a Transnational Business Transaction

It is surprising how different the foreign political climate and concepts of doing business are from those of the United States. These must be considered carefully and in detail *before* preparing the contract. There is a wide difference in the meaning of business terms as used in the United States and abroad.

---

[9] For patents and copyrights, see pp. 310, 856.

---

technology
a particular kind of property concerned with material things

license
permission to do something

tying arrangement
an agreement between a seller or lessor and a purchaser or lessee that a sale or lease of a product to the latter is contingent upon the latter's purchase or lease of another product of the seller or lessor

A Writing

The contract should be in writing. If the contract is oral as a result of oral or written communications, a written confirmation of the oral contract and its terms should be made and approved by the parties. Unlike the Uniform Commercial Code in the United States, which fills gaps in the agreement of the parties by provisions reflecting realistic common business understanding and practice concerning intention and interpretation, there apparently is no such similar help abroad at the present time. However, it should be realized that contracts of this nature may be judged on the basis of the civil code or religiously based law of conduct in various countries.

Language. There should be only one official draft in only one official language, and the contract should so specifically provide. If at all possible, the language should be English. However, if a foreign language is to be used, and a foreign country by law may require only its own language or that a translation copy accompany the English version, then local foreign co-counsel should be retained to assure that the intended understanding of the parties is reflected in the writing. The contract should provide for a written "official" translation to be ratified by the parties for guidance and reliance in their contractual performance. Where it is necessary to have a foreign language *in addition* to English, *both* language versions should be made "official," if at all possible.

Definition of Terms. Because of differences in the meaning of words, particularly in the use of different languages and in differing business concepts, the contract should provide its own definitions of terms. To the extent necessary, it should provide that, as a part of the contract, standard terms used in a specified outside reference shall control. Probably the most complete and widely used international reference set of standard terms is *Icoterms* by the International Chamber of Commerce.

Price and Legal Compliance. There should be carefully drafted clauses concerning how payment is to be made, the kind of currency, how price is to be determined, and the responsibility for compliance with local foreign law concerning the contemplated business transaction. Some countries will not permit their currency to leave the country without governmental permission.

A way out of this dilemma is to provide in the contract that the foreign party in such country will have the responsibility to procure governmental permission and to make arrangements with an agreed outside financial institution (e.g., a bank), and that the domestic party to receive payment has no obligation to perform under the contract until all this is done. That same foreign party should also have the specified responsibility to comply with that country's laws: for registration, and procurement of governmental approval, of the contract; for obtaining a license for the business to be done, where such is required; and for the payment of necessary government taxes and fees in that connection.

"Force Majeure." Every contract should have a "force majeure" clause which, in French, signifies "irresistible or impossible force." This suggests the phrase "act of God" but its international business meaning is much more extensive. The clause should provide for those specified occasions beyond the control of the parties when a party will not be liable for failure to perform the contract.

Jurisdiction—Clauses for Choice-of-Law and Choice-of-Forum. Disputes may occur among the parties to a transnational business contract requiring resolution by a court. The law of the place where the legal proceedings occur (the forum) has **jurisdiction** over the matter to be adjudicated. However, what substantive law is the court to apply?

If the contracting parties provide in their contract a choice-of-*law* clause specifying the law of which State shall apply, the court of the forum usually will apply that specified law, unless it is contrary to the fundamental policy of the forum State. In the absence of

jurisdiction
the power of a court to hear and decide a case involving a person or subject matter properly brought before the court

Figure 56.1 RESTATEMENT (SECOND) CONFLICT OF LAWS Section 187

> § 187. Law of the State Chosen by the Parties
>
> (1) The law of the state chosen by the parties to govern their contractual rights and duties will be applied if the particular issue is one which the parties could have resolved by an explicit provision in their agreement directed to that issue.
>
> (2) The law of the state chosen by the parties to govern their contractual rights and duties will be applied, even if the particular issue is one which the parties could not have resolved by an explicit provision in their agreement directed to that issue, unless either
>
> > (a) the chosen state has no substantial relationship to the parties or the transaction and there is no other reasonable basis for the parties' choice, or
> >
> > (b) application of the law of the chosen state would be contrary to a fundamental policy of a state which has a materially greater interest than the chosen state in the determination of the particular issue and which, under the rule of § 188, would be the state of the applicable law in the absence of an effective choice of law by the parties.
>
> (3) In the absence of a contrary indication of intention, the reference is to the local law of the state of the chosen law.

such a clause, the court may apply the law of either the State where the contract was made or where contractual performance was to occur. A similar problem arises with respect to which State courts shall be the *forum* for the adjudication of the matter in dispute. Here, again, the parties can provide a choice-of-*forum* clause in their contract specifying which State shall be the forum. Various international and regional conventions approve of the validity and enforceability of such clauses.

In the United States. United States law on choice-of-*law* clauses is reflected in the *Restatement (Second) of Conflict of Laws* section 187 and the Uniform Commercial Code section 1–105(1). For choice-of-*forum* clauses it is the same Restatement, section 80 supplemented by sections 81–90. United States courts generally recognize such clauses as valid and enforceable.

Choice-of-Law. The choice-of-law clause should be drafted carefully after an examination of section 187 of the Restatement (see figure 56.1) and the facts surrounding the transnational business contract. The clause by itself is not sufficient for validity and enforceability.

In the following case the court found a choice-of-law clause in a contract to be valid and enforceable after a careful application of section 187.

Facts
Dr. Pirkey, a Colorado physician, plaintiff, was employed by Hospital Corporation of America, defendant, an international recruiting and hospital management company, to render medical services at the King Faisal Hospital in Saudi Arabia. The written contract provided "This agreement shall be construed in accordance with the Laws and Regulations of the Kingdom of Saudi Arabia." Before Dr. Pirkey was to leave for Saudi Arabia, the defendant learned that Dr. Pirkey did not include in his employment application information regarding his 1974 conviction for shoplifting. The defendant then terminated his employment. Plaintiff sues the defendant in Colorado federal district court for damages for breach of contract, alleging that the choice-of-law clause is part of an **adhesion contract** and should not be respected. The defendant contends it is not an adhesion contract and the clause is valid and enforceable. Is the clause valid and enforceable?

Decision
Yes. Judgment for the defendant hospital corporation.

adhesion contract
a standard form contract in which the weaker party has no realistic choice or opportunity to bargain

Reasoning
The court referred to section 187 of the *Restatement (Second) of Conflict of Laws*. The forum should apply the law chosen by the parties unless there is no reasonable basis for the choice. Saudi Arabia bears enough of a relationship to this transaction to remove doubts that there was not a reasonable basis for the parties' choice. Dr. Pirkey's services were to be rendered in Saudi Arabia. Choice-of-law provisions such as the one contained in this employment agreement are ordinarily given effect; they are a clear manifestation of the parties' intentions.

This is not an adhesion contract. Although the agreement is a printed form apparently prepared by the King Faisal Hospital, this alone does not define adhesion contracts. Plaintiff does not show that there was no opportunity for negotiation. Further this is not a case involving a party with superior bargaining power attempting to take advantage of a weaker party who is incapable of fully understanding the contract provisions. Dr. Pirkey signed the contract with full knowledge of its contents; he did not protest the inclusion of this choice-of-law provision in the contract at the time he signed it or subsequently prior to this action. Since Dr. Pirkey did not lack any opportunity to negotiate the provision, nor is the provision oppressive or offensive, this is not an adhesion contract.

Finally, application of the Saudi Arabian law chosen by the parties to determine their rights and duties under the contract will not be contrary to a fundamental policy of Colorado. A fundamental policy must be a substantial one, which is not the case here.

Pirkey v. Hospital Corporation of America, 483 F.Supp 770 (1980).

Choice-of-Forum. Section 80 of the Restatement provides "The parties' agreement as to the place of the action cannot oust a State of judicial jurisdiction, but such an agreement will be given effect unless it is unfair or unreasonable." This is illustrated in the following leading United States Supreme Court case when this court first departed from the rigid common law doctrine which refused to honor choice-of-forum clauses.

Facts

respondent (or appellee) a party against whom an appeal is taken

exculpate to relieve from liability

prima facie at first sight

Petitioner, Unterweser, a German corporation, entered into an international towage contract with the **respondent,** Zapata Off-Shore Co., a Texas corporation, to tow Zapata's ocean-going drilling rig from Louisiana to a point off Italy in the Adriatic Sea. The contract, submitted by Unterweser with changes subsequently negotiated by the parties, contained the provision "Any dispute arising must be treated before the London Court of Justice." The contract also contained two clauses to **exculpate** Unterweser from liability for damage to the towed rig. The rig while being towed by Unterweser's tug, the Bremen, was seriously damaged in a storm in the Gulf of Mexico, and Zapata instructed the Bremen to tow the damaged rig to Tampa, Florida, the nearest port of refuge.

Zapata sued Unterweser in the federal District Court in Tampa for $3,500,000 damages for alleged negligent towage and for breach of the towage contract. Unterweser invoked the forum clause of the contract, and made a motion to dismiss the case for lack of jurisdiction or on grounds of inconvenience. Before the District Court acted on the motion, Unterweser sued Zapata in the High Court of Justice in London for damages for breach of the towage contract as the contract provided. Zapata challenged the High Court's jurisdiction of the case, but the Court held that the forum clause conferred jurisdiction on the Court and would be enforced, absent a showing that it would not be fair and right to do so. The federal District Court then denied Unterweser's motion to dismiss and, on appeal, the decision was affirmed, following the traditional American judicially established view that "agreements in advance of controversy whose object is to oust the jurisdiction of the courts are contrary to public policy and will not be enforced." Unterweser petitioned the United States Supreme Court for review.

Decision
Reversed, for the petitioner, Unterweser. Remanded to the District Court for further proceedings consistent with the Supreme Court's opinion.

Reasoning
Forum selection clauses are **prima facie** valid and should be enforced unless enforcement is shown by the resisting party to be "unreasonable" under the circumstances. The approach substantially followed in other common-law countries including England is "that parties to a contract may agree in advance to submit to the jurisdiction of a given court, to permit notice to be served by the opposing party, or even to waive notice altogether." It is the

view adopted by the Restatement (Second) of Conflict of Laws, section 80. It accords with ancient concepts of freedom of contract. The language of the forum clause is clearly mandatory and all-encompassing, and the courts of England plainly meet the standards of neutrality and long experience in admiralty litigation. The choice of that forum was made in an arms-length negotiation by experienced and sophisticated businessmen, and absent some countervailing reason it should be honored by the parties and enforced by the courts. A freely negotiated private international agreement, unaffected by fraud, undue influence, or overwhelming bargaining power, as is the one here, should be given full effect.

Nevertheless, to allow Zapata opportunity to carry its heavy burden of showing not only that the balance of convenience is strongly in favor of trial in Tampa (that is, that it will be far more inconvenient for Zapata to litigate in London than it will be for Unterweser to litigate in Tampa), but also that a London trial will be so manifestly and gravely inconvenient for Zapata that it would be effectively deprived of a meaningful day in court, we remand for further proceedings.

The Bremen v. Zapata Off-Shore Co., 407 U.S. 1 (1972).

Section 82 of the Restatement provides that a State will not exercise jurisdiction, which has been obtained by fraud or unlawful force, over a defendant or his property. Also, section 84 provides that a State will not exercise jurisdiction if it is a seriously inconvenient forum for the trial of the action.

In Foreign States. Regional and international conventions recognize choice-of-law and choice-of-forum clauses as valid and enforceable.

Transnational Commercial Arbitration. **Arbitration** is a process of resolving a dispute by using a third party chosen for his or her neutrality and expertise to decide the disputed issue or issues. The parties must agree to be bound by the decision of the intermediary. It is a method of resolving disputes without the necessity of court proceedings, although judicial appeal from arbitration decisions is available. This method of resolving disputes relating to transnational business contracts is used increasingly and widely because of: convenience; reduction in expense; timeliness; arbitrators with expertise in the subject of the dispute and with experience in arbitration; reduced adversary confrontation with increased preservation of amicable business relations between the parties; and continued performance of the contract during arbitration proceedings.

arbitration
a method for deciding disputes outside of the court by persons called arbitrators, appointed by the disputing parties

Commercial arbitration clauses often are included in transnational business contracts. The clause should have exact language and, among other items, probably should: provide a choice-of-forum clause and possibly a choice-of-law clause; specify the particular kind of arbitrator expertise required; and, where necessary, specify the issues which are *not* subject to arbitration.

Examination should be made of the formal rules and procedures, as well as commercial arbitration clauses and associated costs, available from some of the existing arbitration groups. Some of these groups are regional, such as the Inter-American Commercial Arbitration Commission. Others are world-wide, such as the American Arbitration Association (AAA) and the International Chamber of Commerce (ICC) with its Court of Arbitration. Each has its own formal rules and procedures.

Most countries recognize transnational commercial arbitration clauses as valid and enforceable, and they will enforce valid transnational commercial arbitration awards in their courts. The United Nations 1958 Convention on the Recognition and Enforcement of Foreign Arbitration Awards, to which the United States is a party and which is widely adopted, recognizes the validity and enforceability of arbitration clauses in transnational business contracts, and provides for the enforcement of valid arbitration awards with the same effect as local judicial judgments. Some countries refuse to enforce transnational business arbitration awards unless the arbitration clause requires that arbitration is to occur only in those particular countries.

Protection of Industrial Property Interests Located Abroad

A State has sovereign jurisdiction over all persons, property, and actions that occur within its geographical borders. Transnational business investment in a foreign State subjects the firm's industrial property interests to that State's jurisdiction. Risk of loss to such interests always exists, principally from three sources: (1) foreign governmental action, as by **expropriation** or other change in law having an adverse effect on such interest; (2) damaging conduct by the foreign contracting party, as by its breach of the transnational business contract; and (3) by other foreign persons, as by their improper, unauthorized use of the owner's inventions, patents, and trademarks.

expropriation
the taking of an owner's property by the government

Foreign Expropriation

If foreign State expropriation of physical and other property of the investing firm occurs without adequate compensation, the investing firm has only three sources of relief. One is the Overseas Private Investment Corporation (OPIC), established by the United States Government to encourage United States private investment and private skills in the economic and social development of certain specified less developed friendly countries. It issues insurance to eligible investors, and on the occurrence of loss the Corporation will pay the investing firm, and the United States Government will then seek repayment from the foreign country.

A second source of relief consists of the various insurance programs of the Export Import Bank of the United States, available through its agent the Foreign Credit Insurance Association (FCIA).

The third source of relief is to use the investing firm's State courts, sue the foreign country, and enforce the judgment against the foreign country's assets located in the local country where the judgment was obtained. This can occur only if the forum court has jurisdiction over the matter and power to enforce its judgment.

Intangible Industrial Property Interests (Rights)

The association in the consumer's mind of goods with a trademark or brand name can be of great value in the marketing of such goods. The same is true of processes, **patents, copyrights,** and other kinds of intangible industrial property interests. The pirating or use of such property without a license from the owner is world-wide.

patent
a governmental grant of protection of an invention

copyright
a governmental grant of protection of original works in a tangible medium of expression

Under the common law, the *first user* of industrial property interests becomes their owner. Often there is difficulty in establishing priority of use. However, the law is different in many foreign code countries where the law requires registration of trademarks, brand names, patents, and other industrial property interests, the *first to register* becoming the owner.[10] However, various regional and international conventions provide recognition and protection of ownership of industrial property interests by compliance with the convention requirements. Of particular interest is the International Convention for the Protection of Industrial Property, of which the United States is a member, under which a single registration in the home country assures recognition of the registering party's ownership and protection of the registered property interests by all the member States without the necessity of repeated registrations in those States.

Antitrust Laws Applicable to Transnational Business

The United States antitrust laws have been discussed previously in chapter 47, Antitrust Law.[11] Reference should be made to that material at this time to provide background and avoid unnecessary repetition. There the main thrust was the application of such laws to domestic business transactions. Here we will relate those laws to transnational business

---

[10] For patents and copyrights, see pp. 310, 851.   [11] See pp. 702–12.

[12] *Continental Ore Co. v. Union Carbide & Carbon Corp.*, 370 U.S. 704 (1962).

transactions. First we will see antitrust law in operation in the United States, and then we will briefly consider foreign antitrust law particularly as it is applied and enforced in the European Economic Community.

Antitrust in the United States

The philosophy of the United States is that free competition is the best means to stimulate progress and to achieve higher living standards. Antitrust laws are designed to eliminate the abuses which militate against this philosophy.

The Sherman Act provides in section 1 that every contract, combination, or conspiracy in unreasonable restraint of trade or commerce among the several states or with foreign nations is illegal. In section 2, it is illegal for any person to monopolize, attempt to monopolize, or combine or conspire with any other person or persons, to monopolize any part of the trade or commerce among the several states or with foreign nations. The Clayton Act states that specific business practices which produce the prohibited results are (per se) illegal. Section 4 provides, "Any person who shall be injured in his business or property by reason of anything forbidden in the antitrust laws may sue therefor in any district court of the United States in which the defendant resides or is found or has an agent, with respect to the amount in controversy, and shall recover threefold the damages by him sustained, and the cost of suit, including a reasonable attorney's fee." The word "person" has been construed to include a foreign nation, as well as a natural person and a **juristic person,** e.g., corporation. Foreign governments can be sued for violation of United States antitrust laws.

juristic person
an artificial person created by law

"A conspiracy to monopolize or restrain the domestic or foreign commerce of the United States is not outside the reach of the Sherman Act just because the conduct complained of occurs in foreign countries."[12] Similarly, if a United States person improperly uses its advantages in a particular product domestic market to attempt to restrain competition of that same product in the international market, the United States antitrust laws are applicable. This is illustrated by the following case.

Facts
Plaintiffs, three subsidiaries of the International Telephone and Telegraph Company, allege that Western Union Telegraph Company (WU), defendant, has violated and continues to violate sections 1 and 2 of the Sherman Act by: (1) refusing to interconnect with plaintiffs' domestic and international telex transmission lines; (2) using its monopoly over domestic telex service to gain a competitive advantage in the provision of international service; and (3) entering into a contract with TRT, an international telex carrier, assuring TRT at least 50,000,000 minutes of outbound international telex traffic from the WU network and gaining TRT's assistance in WU's provision of international telex service. WU made a motion to dismiss some portions of the complaint relating to WU's provision of international telex service on the ground that the allegations fail to state a claim upon which relief can be granted.

Decision
WU's motion is denied.

Reasoning
First, the complaint alleges WU's entry into the international telex service market as part of a more general scheme by WU to restrain competition in both the domestic and international telex markets. Even if WU's international telex service and contracts with TRT were in themselves legal, "they lose that character when they become constituent elements of an unlawful scheme." Second, the complaint alleges that WU used its domestic telex monopoly to gain a competitive advantage in the provision of international telex service. "The use of monopoly power attained in one market to gain a competitive advantage in another is a violation of section 2, even if there has not been an attempt to monopolize the second market." A competitor in the market in which another company is unfairly using its monopoly power to gain a competitive advantage has standing to sue. Third, the complaint alleges that WU and TRT agreed that WU would guarantee 50,000,000 minutes

of outbound international traffic and that TRT would assist WU's entry into the international telex market, thereby foreclosing plaintiffs from competing for that portion of the market. It is established that, if a contract effects an unreasonable restraint of trade, a company foreclosed by that contract may bring an antitrust action under section 1 of the Sherman Act. The central questions are whether the contract was in furtherance of a more general scheme to unreasonably restrain trade in the international telex market, and whether the restraint was reasonable in the circumstances of the particular market structure.

ITT World Communications Inc., et al. v. Western Union Telegraph Company, 524 F.Supp. 702 (1981).

per se
in and of itself

In the absence of specified **per se** illegal conduct in violation of antitrust law, conspiring by a person in a foreign country with an American person to restrain trade subjects both parties and the matter to the jurisdiction of the United States courts.[13] Alleged antitrust violation for unreasonable restraint of trade must have *substantial effect* on United States commerce before United States courts will exercise jurisdiction and apply United States antitrust law. The fact that illegal antitrust acts occur *abroad* does not preclude United States courts from taking jurisdiction so long as there is a significant or substantial effect on the foreign or interstate commerce of the United States. Also, the line of product to be monopolized illegally may include a product imported into the United States.

Among the frequent instances of per se antitrust violations are resale price fixing and tying contracts. Attempts to restrain when and how a customer disposes of a product often are antitrust violations. There are also cases where a domestic firm's restraint on a United States distributor not to export in order to prevent competition with an exclusive foreign distributor is an antitrust violation. But it would be a violation if the domestic firm joined in a foreign **cartel** with a substantial restraining effect on commerce in the United States, such as causing an increase in the price of imports or excluding products from the American market.

cartel
a combination of private enterprises or States to control production, price, or distribution of like commodities or services

An agreement between manufacturers and potential competitors to allocate and divide world markets is illegal antitrust conduct. However, a parent corporation's allocation of territorial markets and setting prices for its subdivisions, if the parent really *controls* the subsidiary, is not a violation of *United States* antitrust laws.

Persons in foreign countries are included among those persons protected by, and also subject to, United States antitrust laws. Foreign competitors and foreign consumers are protected under United States antitrust laws from violations of such laws committed by United States persons. Foreign persons, including foreign governments, have the right to sue for treble damages under United States antitrust laws. Also, a foreign person can sue another foreign person in United States courts for violations of United States antitrust laws. The presence of a United States person with a foreign person in a conspiracy to restrain trade involves such contact with United States commerce as will subject both persons to United States jurisdiction under its antitrust laws.

The Export Trading Company Act of 1982. The purpose of the federal Export Trading Company Act is "to increase United States exports of products and services by encouraging more efficient provision of export trade services to United States producers and suppliers."

The Act provided for the establishment of the Office of Export Trade in the Department of Commerce under the Secretary of Commerce to "promote and encourage to the greatest possible extent feasible the formation of export trade associations and export trade companies." (Sec. 102(b)) An export trading company (ETC) is an individual, association, or organization operated for profit or nonprofit, doing business under the laws of the United States or any of its states, and for the principal purposes of "exporting goods or services produced in the United States; or facilitating the exportation of goods or services produced in the United States by unaffiliated persons by providing one or more export trade services." (Sec. 103(4))

---

[13] *National Bank of Canada v. Interbank Card Association,* 507 F.Supp. 1113 (1980).

Under the Act, the Secretary of Commerce is to promulgate regulations implementing the Act's policy. The Federal Reserve Board is made responsible for assisting in the financing and development of export trading companies in the United States.

Export Trade Certificates of Review. Title III of the Act provides that persons who wish to establish an ETC can apply to the Secretary of Commerce for a "certificate of review," which in effect is a certificate of antitrust immunity. The certificate will be issued, after concurrence of the United States Attorney General, if the applicant establishes that its specified export trade, export trade activities, and methods of operation will not be illegal or unfair. See Sec. 303(a).

The effect of this certificate is to confer certain specified antitrust protection upon the recipient of the certificate. The recipient of a certificate of review must submit annual reports to the Secretary of Commerce.

Amendments to the Sherman Act; and the Federal Trade Commission Act. Title III amends the Sherman Act and the Federal Trade Commission Act (FTC) by providing that the Sherman Act shall not apply to conduct, and the FTC shall not apply to unfair methods of competition, involving United States export trade or commerce with foreign nations unless such conduct or methods of unfair competition "have a direct, substantial, and reasonably foreseeable effect" on domestic commerce and domestic competition which gives rise to a claim for damages thereunder. (Secs. 402, 403.)

Accordingly, ETCs have a choice of utilizing either: (1) the certificate of review process under Title III, with its advantages of a specific detailed set of four standards and no treble damages for violation, as opposed to the disadvantages of cost, and the required extensive disclosure of detailed financial and marketing information which competitors could use to their advantage; or (2) the much broader standard of no "direct, substantial, and reasonably foreseeable effect" on domestic commerce and domestic competition, but with the disadvantage of treble damages for violation.

Antitrust in the European Common Market

Background. We should be aware, initially, that individual nations and groups of nations differ among themselves and from the United States concerning their economic and political conditions, goals, and methods used to accomplish those goals. For example, while the more advanced industrial nations seek protection by monopoly of their industrial property interests (e.g., patents, licensing, processes of production), generally the less developed countries (LDCs) are opposed to this concept, will disregard foreign national or international treaties because of their need for such property to further their goal of national development. It is not surprising therefore that these latter countries pay particular attention to transnational business agreements which may militate against their goal.

After World War II, the western European nations decided that it was necessary to integrate themselves economically by creating a single integrated system for the purpose of eliminating the public (e.g., tariffs) and private (e.g., restrictive agreements by and among business firms in those nations) barriers, and create an agreed *common* market for its members. The concept reflected what has always been the case among European nations—protection of local business and industry from foreign competition. This concept is quite different from the United States policy of free trade. Business conduct permitted among themselves may well be prohibited to outsiders whose conduct may interfere with such economic unity. The result was the Treaty Establishing the European Economic Community signed in Rome in 1957. This economic group of nations is often called the Common Market or EEC.

Structure. This treaty established the Commission of the European Communities (Commission) located in Brussels. It is the body to enforce Articles 85 and 86 of the treaty, which are probably the most important and frequently used sections on prohibited business restraint of trade. Complaints of violation are made to the Commission which,

Figure 56.2   EEC Treaty Article 85

> Article 85 states:
>
> "1. The following practices shall be prohibited as incompatible with the Common Market: all agreements between undertakings, all decisions by associations of undertakings and all concerted practices which are liable to affect trade between Member States and which are designed to prevent, restrict or distort competition within the Common Market or which have this effect. This shall, in particular, include:
> (a) the direct or indirect fixing of purchase or selling prices or of any other trading conditions;
> (b) the limitation or control of production, markets, technical development or investment;
> (c) market-sharing or the sharing of sources of supply;
> (d) the application of unequal conditions to parties undertaking equivalent engagements in commercial transactions, thereby placing them at a competitive disadvantage;
> (e) making the conclusion of a contract subject to the acceptance by the other party to the contract of additional obligations, which, by their nature or according to commercial practice, have no connection with the subject of such contract.
>
> "2. Any agreements or decisions prohibited pursuant to this Article shall automatically be null and void.
>
> "3. The provisions of paragraph 1 may, however, be declared inapplicable in the case of:
> — any agreement or type of agreement between undertakings,
> — any decision or type of decision by associations of undertakings, and
> — any concerted practice or type of concerted practice which helps to improve the production or distribution of goods or to promote technical or economic progress, while allowing consumers a fair share of the resulting profit and which does not:
> (a) subject the concerns in question to any restrictions which are not indispensable to the achievement of the above objectives;
> (b) enable such concerns to eliminate competition in respect of a substantial part of the goods concerned."

either as a result of such complaints or on its own initiative, under its very broad powers investigates and determines whether a violation has occurred. The Commission has power to order cessation of continued illegal violations and to impose fines for violations. Appeal and review from the Commission's decisions is to the European Court of Justice in Luxembourg. It is possible for private persons in the member countries to bring actions for violations of Articles 85 and 86 in their national courts, but this is not a usually desirable method.

Article 85. Articles 85 and 86 differ in their thrust and coverage. Article 85 is concerned with a statement of the *policy regarding prohibited business conduct,* and Article 86 with *abuse by a dominant enterprise position.*

Article 85 is reproduced above, figure 56.2. You will observe that paragraph 1 has two parts. The first part is an overall statement of prohibited business practices followed by an (a) through (e) enumeration of particular, but not exclusive, prohibited business practices. This structure is similar to the overall prohibition stated in section 1 of the United States Sherman Act, and the particularity of the Clayton Act as amended by the Robinson-Patman Act. The specific prohibited conduct in the second part of paragraph 1 is, in effect, per se violations, as are those enumerated in the Clayton Act. The word "undertakings" is a synonym for "enterprises" (businesses) and signifies that the Article applies to subsidiaries which are *independent* of their parent, and not to dependent subsidiaries. Agreements between parent and subsidiaries reflecting duties and functions of the subsidiaries are normal for dependent subsidiaries. Paragraph 2 declares null and void agreements and decisions prohibited by section 1.

Paragraph 3 reflects a policy of making exceptions to conduct which otherwise would be prohibited under paragraph 1 if the excepted business agreement, decision, or practice would, without eliminating competition substantially, benefit the member countries and their nationals by the improvement of production or distribution of goods or promote technical or economic progress. The Commission will issue such a statement of inapplicability of paragraph 1 where appropriate when *notified* by the interested party *before* the occurrence of the particular business activity under consideration. Subsequent notification is too late.

Figure 56.3 EEC Treaty Article 86

> Article 86 states:
> "Any improper exploitation by one or more undertakings of a dominant position within the Common Market or within a substantial part of it shall be deemed to be incompatible with the Common Market and shall be prohibited, in so far as trade between Member States could be affected by it. The following practices, in particular, shall be deemed to amount to improper exploitation:
> (a) the direct or indirect imposition of any unfair purchase or selling prices or of any other unfair trading conditions;
> (b) the limitation of production, markets or technical development to the prejudice of consumers;
> (c) the application of unequal conditions to parties undertaking equivalent engagements in commercial transactions, thereby placing them at a commercial disadvantage;
> (d) making the conclusion of a contract subject to the acceptance by the other party to the contract of additional obligations which by their nature or according to commercial practice have no connection with the subject of such contract."

Notice the "effect" principle at the heart of paragraph 1 ". . . which are liable to affect . . . or have this effect." We are reminded of the "substantial effect" principle of United States antitrust law. Note paragraph 1(a)'s prohibition of direct or indirect fixing of purchase or selling prices as having such a prohibited effect. The European Court of Justice has held that selective distribution systems for the sale of products which are capable of affecting trade between member States and have, as their object or effect, the prevention, restriction, or destruction of competition, are violative of Article 85, paragraph 1.

Article 86. Article 86 (figure 56.3) is concerned basically with *enterprise market or geographical dominance and prohibited abuse by the exercise of such dominance.* The Article has two parts, the first paragraph establishing the *prohibitive policy of improper exploitation through dominance,* and the subdivisions (a) through (d) enumerating, without exclusion, *forms of abuse constituting improper exploitation which are prohibited.* It should be noted that the prohibited anti-competitive conduct enumerated in Article 85(1), e.g., improper price fixing, improper control over distributors, tying, by dominant enterprise, is such an abuse.

Several important terms and phrases in Article 86 need clarification. The phrase "dominant position" is not defined. Decisions of the Commission and of the European Court of Justice have provided some guidelines. Many factors are considered in determining dominant position, such as: percent of product (at least 30 percent) and geographical market share; extent of trademark, technological, and patent recognition and consumer acceptance; production and marketing strength; financial strength and sources; vertical and horizontal integration; independence of the enterprise; know-how; and the effect of combinations of enterprises, e.g., joint ventures. Monopoly of property industrial rights are not per se a violation of Article 86, e.g., exclusivity of trademarks, patents, and licenses; it is their *abuse* constituting "improper exploitation" which causes the *conduct* to be prohibited.

The Commission's Regulation 17 pursuant to its power to regulate trade permits parties who are uncertain of the validity of their business agreement to request the Commission, on the basis of presented facts, for a "negative clearance." If granted, such clearance confirms that the agreement and the projected activity are not a violation of Articles 85 or 86, and that the Commission will not "intervene." If not granted, there is still the opportunity to request an exemption under Article 85(3), previously discussed.

The Commission is concerned with the preservation of free trade among the EEC members, and with conduct within as well as outside the Community which affects the free movement of goods in the Community. It is an "effects" approach again between conduct and result. With respect to Article 86, it is a question of whether there is abuse by dominance causing the prohibited result or effect.

The "Effect" and "Single Enterprise" Theories in the United States and the EEC
We have seen in this chapter that the United States and the EEC are concerned about transnational business operation which has a prohibited restraining "effect" on commerce. The local firm in the United States and the local firm in the EEC causing this effect were subject to the jurisdiction of the federal courts in the United States and the Commission and the Court of Justice in the EEC. However, a jurisdictional problem arose if the local firm in the United States and the local firm in the EEC were subsidiaries of foreign parents. How could the foreign parent come within the jurisdiction of the United States and the EEC?

In the United States, where the law places great responsibility on persons for *control* of an activity, we have seen that the United States acquired jurisdiction over the foreign parent as well as the local subsidiary as *separate legal entities* for the purpose of jurisdiction, *if the parent has control over its subsidiary.* The parent and its subsidiary were then really one person. If there was *no control* and the subsidiary were an "independent" legal entity, then the parent was not subject to federal jurisdiction; jurisdiction was *only over the subsidiary.* Accordingly, the concept of a "single entity" arose whereby, *if there were control,* the subsidiary was but a part of the parent, they were treated as a single entity, a single firm. Thus the foreign parent was locally present *in the form of its controlled subsidiary* and, therefore, completely subject to federal jurisdiction. Service of process on the subsidiary was service upon the parent. Touching the corporate arm was touching the corporate body. But the element of control still was of crucial importance to establish the "single entity."

The EEC was faced with the same problem of control. If the foreign parent did not have control over the subsidiary located in the Community, then the parent was not subject to the jurisdiction of the Commission and the Court of Justice for the prohibited restraint of trade effect caused by the subsidiary. Because of the difficult burden of establishing the necessary control, the Commission asserted jurisdiction over a foreign parent merely by showing that the prohibited conduct performed by the local subsidiary was really the *act of the foreign parent without attempting to prove any control at all.* The burden was placed on the foreign parent to prove *absence* of control, and not only is it almost impossible to bear this burden but often the foreign parent *defendant* does not even challenge the Commission on the matter of control!

The concept of "effect" on trade is very much used by the Commission, but gradually the concept of a "single enterprise" is assuming a greater basis for Commission jurisdiction over the foreign parent. However, the single enterprise theory has its limitations. One limitation is that, by using this concept, there is no competition between the parent and the subsidiary since there is a single entity and Article 85 does not apply because there is no agreement between individual enterprises causing the prohibited conduct of restraint of trade in the Community. However, the single enterprise concept assists in establishing "dominance" for purposes of Article 86. But, because of dominance, the Commission would probably issue a "negative clearance" since only one enterprise is involved. The Commission still can disregard the single enterprise concept and, by considering the parent and its subsidiary as separate legal enterprises, proceed under Article 85(1).

Let us not mistakenly conclude that our earlier discussion of distributorships is applicable here, because *an independent distributor is an independent contractor and not a subsidiary nor a part of the foreign firm or "enterprise."*

International Gift-giving and Social Courtesies Protocol

International gift-giving customs and social courtesies reflecting different cultures should be carefully observed in doing business abroad. Gift exchange in international business protocol is very important. For an American to ignore ritual would make him or her appear as either ignorant of the culture or insensitive to cultural preferences, which could lead to loss of respect, business opportunities and even violation of local or American law.

There is no substitute for local advice. The advice of a native resident or the local U.S. Consulate should be sought if one has any doubt about the proper protocol. In general[14] avoid giving the impression of bribery by spending too much on a gift. Get to know the recipient's preferences if possible. Gift-giving should be thoughtful, sincere, spontaneous and not ceremonial. Do not give a more expensive return gift.

Summary Statement

1. Common law is very different from code law.
2. One of the methods of operating abroad in the sale of goods is by domestic production and direct export sales by a foreign agent.
3. The letter of credit is used for the purpose of assuring the domestic seller and the foreign buyer of goods that payment and delivery will be made.
4. The status of a person as a foreign agent must be carefully defined in the agency contract, and the foreign law examined for different effects of an agency status.
5. A foreign distributor is an independent contractor for whose conduct the domestic principal firm is not liable abroad.
6. The establishment of a foreign branch of a firm possibly submits the firm to the jurisdiction of the State in which the branch is located, depending on whether the parent firm has "control" over the branch.
7. Technology is a particular kind of property concerned with material things. It may be intangible or tangible. Its transfer abroad is subject to careful examination by foreign governments and may be a violation of foreign antitrust laws.
8. Transnational business contracts should be in writing, be in only one official language, provide for carefully defined terms, ensure compliance with the foreign law concerning pricing and currency payment, and include the following clauses: force majeure, choice-of-law and forum, and commercial arbitration.
9. Industrial property interests transferred abroad are subject to many risks and all means should be used to protect such interests. Some risks are foreign expropriation, and the infringement and pirating of intangible property interests.
10. Under the common law, the first user of industrial property interests is the owner. Under the code law in many foreign countries requiring registration of such interests—particularly trademarks, brand names, and patents—the first to register becomes the owner. However, various regional and international conventions provide recognition and protection.
11. The United States Sherman and Clayton antitrust laws, and the Federal Trade Commission Act, are designed to eliminate the abuses which militate against the American philosophy of free competition.
12. Under the Sherman Act, violations are basically for unreasonable restraint of trade and for monopolies. The Clayton Act specifies per se antitrust violations. The Federal Trade Commission Act prohibits unfair methods of competition.
13. The Export Trading Company Act of 1982 establishes a basis for eligibility of export trading companies for exemption from United States antitrust laws, and provides for federal certification of such exemptions.

---

[14] For details, see the booklet *International Business Gift-Giving Customs* published by The Parker Pen Company.

14. Foreign firms are subject to the United States antitrust laws for their antitrust conduct abroad having a substantial effect on United States commerce. Also, they and their governments can sue in the United States courts for antitrust violations by American firms adversely affecting their trade.
15. The European Economic Community was created by the Treaty of Rome in 1957. Its primary purpose was the economic integration of the member States into a single integrated system to eliminate trade barriers and restrictive trade agreements by having a common market, and to protect local business and industry from foreign competition.
16. EEC Treaty Article 85 is concerned with policy of what constitutes prohibited business conduct. Article 86 is concerned with abuse by a dominant enterprise position.
17. The Commission of European Communities (Commission) is the enforcing body of the Treaty, and appeals from its decisions are to the European Court of Justice (Court).
18. The EEC Court has held that selective distribution systems for the sale of products which are capable of affecting trade between member States and have, as their object or effect, the prevention, restriction, or destruction of competition, are violative of Article 85, paragraph 1.
19. The "Effect" and "Single Enterprise" theories have been developed by the EEC Commission and Court in order to obtain jurisdiction over foreign parent firms doing business in the EEC through their subsidiaries. Control by the parent is now presumed, the parent having a most difficult burden to overcome this presumption. In the United States, the emphasis on proof of parental control still exists as a fact to be proved by the party asserting control and instigating the legal proceeding.
20. International business gift-giving customs and social courtesies reflecting differing cultures should be carefully observed in doing business abroad.

In the following very long case the United States District Court held that there was a tying arrangement which affected a not insubstantial amount of interstate commerce. However, the arrangement would be illegal as a violation of section 1 of the Sherman Act only if the evidence at a trial to be held established that: the arrangement appreciably restrained competition in the tied product market; *and* the defendant did not demonstrate legitimate business justification for the tying arrangement. The court denied motions for summary judgment made by both parties so that these issues may be resolved in a trial.

United States of America v. Mercedes-Benz of North America, Inc.
517 F.Supp. 1369 (1981)

Patel, District Judge. This action is before the court on cross-motions for summary judgment. The government brings suit for an alleged violation of section 1 of the Sherman Act under a theory of a per se tying violation based on the Dealer Agreement between Mercedes-Benz of North America, Inc. (MBNA) and each Mercedes-Benz franchised dealer. Defendant strenuously objects to the application of a per se rule and argues that a rule of reason should apply under which MBNA has demonstrated that in fact its Dealer Agreement and actual practice do not constitute a restraint of trade. [T]he court finds it necessary to deny both motions for summary judgment. The parties must proceed to trial on the issue of defendant's economic power and, if that be established, whether defendant can demonstrate sufficient business justification for a tying arrangement.[15]

---

[15] Notice the similarity of approach here with Article 86 of the EEC Treaty, above, p. 861. First, here—defendant's economic power, 1st paragraph of 86—dominant position. Second, here and under 86(d), tying arrangement (also in Article 85(e)).

I
BACKGROUND

Defendant MBNA has been the exclusive United States distributor of Mercedes-Benz automobiles since 1965. Its company, Daimler-Benz AG [DBAG] of Stuttgart, Germany, is one of the oldest automobile manufacturers in the world. [T]he Mercedes-Benz trademark, a three-pointed star in a circle, is recognized worldwide for its representation of automotive luxury, performance and technology.

Daimler-Benz assembles Mercedes-Benz autos in its German factory and ships them through its exclusive importer Daimler-Benz of North America [DBNA] to MBNA for resale to Mercedes-Benz dealers. Parts for these autos can come from several sources:

1. DBAG manufactures certain parts for use in the assembly process and to be used for replacement of used parts;

2. Original parts may come from independent automotive parts manufacturers, called "original equipment manufacturers" (OEMs). Some of these OEMs manufacture parts for several automobile manufacturers.

There are approximately 400 Mercedes dealers in the United States. Once approved by MBNA, each dealer becomes party to a standardized written Dealer Agreement with MBNA to sell and service Mercedes passenger cars and parts.

The government rests its claim of a per se illegal tying arrangement on "Standard Provisions" subpart 9C of the Dealer Agreement. Part 9 sets out various requirements relating to customer service. Subpart 9C reads:

> Dealer shall neither sell or offer to sell for use in connection with MB passenger cars nor use in the repair or servicing of MB passenger cars any parts other than genuine MB parts or parts expressly approved by DBAG if such parts are necessary to the mechanical operation of such MB passenger cars.

"MB parts" are defined in part one of the Dealer Agreement as "parts, accessories, components, assemblies, and optional equipment for MB passenger cars supplied by MBNA, DBAG, or by DBNA."

II
THE APPLICABLE STANDARD

[P]urchasing auto replacement parts only from a limited number of sources does not have as its primary purpose increasing competition for the franchised automobile. The direct result of such a requirement is to reduce the opportunity for Mercedes-Benz dealers in exercising their independent judgment in choosing parts to consider such factors as price and availability. Restricting the source of dealer replacement parts may serve to increase the price of these parts and thereby restrain the dealers' ability to compete with independent distributors.

A per se rule long has been applied to tying arrangements because of "their pernicious effect on competition and lack of any redeeming virtue."

III
PER SE TYING STANDARD

The rule of per se restraint of trade has been applied in a number of diverse business settings under section 1 of the Sherman Act.

Essentially a tying arrangement exists where a seller with some market leverage over a (tying) product conditions the sale of that product on the purchaser also agreeing to buy a different (tied) product from the seller or foregoing such a purchase from any other source.

". . . Where tying conditions are successfully exacted competition on the merits with respect to the tied product is inevitably curbed. Indeed, 'tying agreements serve hardly any purpose beyond the suppression of competition.' They deny competitors free access to the market for the tied product, not because the party imposing the tying requirements has a better product or a lower price but because of his power or leverage in another market. At the same time buyers are forced to forego their free choice between competing products. For these reasons 'tying agreements fare harshly under the laws forbidding restraints of trade.' "

Plaintiff must demonstrate the existence of three elements to establish a per se illegal tying agreement:

1. Two separate products with the sale of one conditioned on the purchase of the other;

2. A seller with sufficient economic leverage in the tying market to appreciably restrain competition in the tied product market; and

3. A tie-in affecting a not insubstantial amount of interstate commerce. [Emphasis added]

Once the above elements have been shown, a defendant engaged in a per se tying arrangement may defend itself by an affirmative showing of business justification.

A. Separate Products Tied Together.
Two Separate Products

In the present case, it is undisputed that MBNA has separate personnel and price lists for new car and replacement part sales. Many replacement (as well as original) parts are manufactured by outside suppliers.

MBNA argues that the purchase of MBNA replacement parts is an "integral component" of its franchised business method. The essence of the Mercedes-Benz franchise is the sale of trademarked automobiles. The court rejects defendant's argument that no difference may be noticed between original parts in a new automobile and parts purchased at a later date for repair or renewal for purposes of determining whether they are separate products. ". . . [T]he relevant inquiry is not whether the two items must be used together but whether they must come from the same seller." While the use of DBAG-approved parts in the assembly of a Mercedes-Benz automobile is an important factor in producing the trademarked product, the use of trademarked Mercedes-Benz replacement parts is not necessary to carry out the essence of the franchise, that is, the sale of new Mercedes-Benz automobiles.

In the light of the foregoing discussion and in light of the actual practice of Mercedes-Benz and the industry in maintaining a separate parts division, separate prices, separate personnel and, occasionally, separate manufacturers, the court finds that the Mercedes-Benz passenger car and its replacement parts are indeed separate products.

Products Tied Together

In addition to a showing that two products are separate, it must be demonstrated that the purchase of one product is conditioned on the purchase of the other. Plaintiff relies on the express wording of the Dealer Agreement to demonstrate the tie-in. The existence of the language still acts as a powerful lever in restraint of trade. [T]he language of subpart 9C expressly refers to parts "necessary to the mechanical operation" of Mercedes-Benz cars. The wording of subpart 9C allows dealers to purchase parts "expressly approved by DBAG." An 'approved source' clause may negate a finding of an illegal tying arrangement.

This is not a case where the allegedly tied product may be obtained only from an approved source; there is no express provision in the Dealer Agreement setting forth a procedure for dealers seeking to request additional approval.

In the present case, plaintiff has presented uncontroverted evidence that no formal system for approval of non-MBNA parts exists in the DBAG/MBNA network and that crucial MBNA officers are unaware of an established procedure for testing the quality of non-MBNA supplied parts upon dealer request for DBAG approval. The evidence discloses that the approved source provision exists on paper only and does not represent a true alternative for dealers wishing to avoid the effects of tie-in.

For the foregoing reasons, the court finds that the Mercedes-Benz passenger car and its replacement parts are separate products tied together by the use of the MBNA Dealer Agreement.

B. Sufficient Economic Power.

The second factor in determining a per se illegal tying arrangement is that the seller must have "sufficient economic power to impose an appreciable restraint on free competition in the product. . . ." This standard can be met in one of three ways:

1. The seller occupies a dominant position in the tying product market. . . .

2. A product is sufficiently unique that the seller has some advantage not shared by competitors in the market for the tying product. . . .

3. A substantial number of customers have accepted the tie-in and there are no explanations other than the seller's economic power for their willingness to do so.

Looking at the third factor first, plaintiff argues that this standard is easily met because each of 400 Mercedes-Benz dealers has signed the Dealer Agreement agreeing to buy replacement parts from MBNA under subpart 9C.

In the present case, there is no identified population against which to compare the 400 Mercedes dealers. Plaintiff might argue that 400 represents an appreciable number of buyers from a total population of import car dealers or of import luxury car dealers. Plaintiff has not attempted such a showing.

The essence of any showing under this test is that defendant has leverage within the market sufficient to compel buyers to accept a tying arrangement. If plaintiff is able to show that a significant number of customers in the market have accepted the tie-in, it still must show that there are no explanations for the acceptance other than the seller's economic power. Plaintiff has failed on each of these counts.

Alternatively, plaintiff may satisfy the second factor, sufficient economic power, if it can show that the alleged tying product, the Mercedes-Benz automobile, is sufficiently unique to give defendant a competitive advantage in the tying product market. If the tying product is sufficiently desirable to consumers or is a product not easily replicated or commonly available, then the producer of the tying product is likely to have sufficient leverage to restrain the tied product market. Monopoly power is not the test for uniqueness and defendant's own authorities show themselves distinguishable. [O]wnership of a trademark is not conclusive of economic power.

In the present case, Mercedes-Benz' trademark may be a factor in determining its market leverage, but alone it is not sufficient. While Mercedes-Benz may be well-known and its products highly respected, it is not one of the industry's largest competitors. Plaintiff has failed to support its claim of uniqueness with information bearing on market characteristics. For instance, does plaintiff argue that Mercedes-Benz is an automobile unique as to other luxury cars or to other imported cars? If Mercedes is a unique automobile, would not every trademarked auto also be unique? Or all luxury/import cars?

A finding of economic power based on uniqueness of a tying product is one that must be based largely on objective market factors and partially on subjective impression. Such a result cannot be determined in the present action as a matter of law.

The court finds that there is substantial factual dispute on the question of sufficient economic power and declines to resolve the matter on summary judgment.

C. Effect on Interstate Commerce.

The third required element of a per se tying violation is that the tie-in affect a not insubstantial amount of interstate commerce. The 'not insubstantial' test is interpreted broadly. "[T]he controlling consideration is 'whether a total amount of business, substantial enough in terms of dollar-volume so as not to be merely *de minimis* is foreclosed to competitors.'"

From 1974 through 1979, the total dollar volume of MBNA replacement part sales to dealers increased from $50 million to $110 million. A determination of amount of commerce affected is based on the volume of sales *allegedly* foreclosed.

Therefore the court finds that the volume sales of mechanically necessary replacement parts to be not insubstantial and that as a matter of law, plaintiff has satisfied this third requirement.

It has thus far been established that per se tying principles are applicable to the present action. The court has found, as a matter of law, that (1) the Mercedes-Benz automobile and MBNA replacement parts are separate products tied together by language in the Dealer Agreement, and (2) the tie-in affects a not insubstantial amount of interstate commerce. However a per se illegal tying violation is not shown unless plaintiff prevails at trial on the issue of defendant's economic power.

IV
BUSINESS JUSTIFICATION

In certain circumstances, defendant may demonstrate a business justification to excuse an otherwise per se illegal tying agreement. The issue before the court is narrowed to whether defendant is justified in requiring the purchase of only mechanically necessary "MB parts" for replacement after the warranty period.

The government and the public has a legitimate interest in encouraging unrestrained trade in automotive parts, yet defendant has an important legitimate interest in protecting its trademarked automobile and public confidence in the quality and safety of the product. If parts of like quality and design are available from other sources of supply, defendant's sole justification for requiring a tie-in becomes the impermissible desire to restrict trade and maintain artificially inflated prices.

At this time, the court is unable to make a finding regarding defendant's business justification defense. If plaintiff is able to establish the final element of a per se tying violation, it remains for defendant to demonstrate the necessity for its quality control procedures and the unavailability of comparable mechanically necessary replacement parts from non-MBNA sources.

V
CONCLUSION

Based on the foregoing discussion, the court finds a genuine dispute of material fact within plaintiff's motion for summary judgment and its motion is HEREBY DENIED. In accord with this court's determination that a per se standard is applicable to MBNA's alleged tying violation, defendant's cross-motion for summary judgment is also HEREBY DENIED.

Pursuant to F.R.Civ.P. 54(d), the court finds that the following material facts exist without substantial controversy:

1. The Mercedes-Benz automobile and MBNA mechanically necessary replacement parts are separate products tied together by the terms of the MBNA Dealer Agreement; and

2. The tie-in affects a not insubstantial amount of interstate commerce.

Genuine controversy exists as to:

1. Whether MBNA has sufficient economic leverage in the tying product market to appreciably restrain competition in the tied product market; and

2. Whether MBNA has demonstrated a legitimate business justification for tying the sale of its replacement parts to that of its trademarked automobile.

IT IS SO ORDERED.

Questions and Case Problems

1. The Royal Bank of Canada is doing business in New York through its New York branch. The Canadian bank has 1,146 branches in 22 countries. The Royal Bank of Canada (France), one of those branches, is incorporated in France and is the only branch that is incorporated. All the stock in the French corporation is owned by the Royal Bank of Canada. The assets and liabilities of the French branch, like the assets and liabilities of all the other branches, are carried on the books of the Royal Bank of Canada as part of its assets and liabilities. In its general advertising, as well as on its letterheads, the bank declares that France is one of the countries in which it has branches, and the bank's annual report to its stockholders recites that the French branch was established "to conduct the business of the Bank in Paris." The deposit slips, checks, passbooks and other bank documents of the French branch are printed and standardized in Canada by the Royal Bank. The staff of the French Bank is recruited and trained by the bank in Montreal, and the principal personnel are frequently shifted about from Paris to the bank's home office and to other branches. The French branch is merely notified and not consulted on accounts which are transferred to it from other Royal Bank branches, and the moneys in those accounts are reflected only in bookkeeping entries rather than by an actual transfer of the funds to France. The Public Administrator of the County of New York, as **administrator** of a decedent's estate, has a claim against the French branch, and sued the Royal Bank of Canada and the Royal Bank of Canada (France). Service of process was made on the New York branch of the Royal Bank of Canada which was doing business in New York. Was service of process on the New York branch of the Canadian bank sufficient to give the New York court jurisdiction over the French branch? [*Public Administrator of the County of New York v. Royal Bank of Canada and Royal Bank of Canada (France)*, 224 N.E. 2d 877 (N.Y. 1967).]

   administrator
   a court-appointed man as an intestate's personal representative

2. Plaintiff, Connelly, sued Uniroyal Englebert Belgique, S. A. (hereafter called Englebert), and Uniroyal, Inc. (hereafter called Uniroyal), defendants, in an Illinois court for personal injuries he suffered when a tire manufactured by Englebert and bearing Uniroyal's trademark failed while his 1969 Opel Kadett was being operated on a highway in Colorado. The car was purchased in 1969 from a dealer in Evanston, Illinois. The tire bore the name "Uniroyal" and the legend "made in Belgium", was manufactured by Englebert, sold in Belgium to General Motors, and subsequently installed on the Opel when it was assembled at a General Motors plant in Belgium. The car was shipped to the United States for distribution by General Motors.

   Uniroyal's wholly owned subsidiary owns approximately 96% of the outstanding shares of Englebert corporation. Uniroyal gave Englebert the nonexclusive license to use its registered trade name "Uniroyal" on the tires manufactured by Englebert. Uniroyal also gave Englebert detailed information as to the methods, processes, and formulas used in the manufacture of tires and tubes and other products manufactured by Uniroyal. Uniroyal supplied technical services and instruction to Englebert, including recommendations and assistance concerning construction of its products. Englebert was required to permit Uniroyal's representatives to have knowledge at all times of the goods and manufacturing operations. Englebert maintained its own books and accounts separate and distinct from Uniroyal, had its own banking sources and line of credit, and did not share common manufacturing facilities, offices, addresses, telephone numbers or employees with Uniroyal. There were no employees of Uniroyal at Englebert's plant in Belgium, and Uniroyal had no control or direction over production at that plant. Englebert's liability insurance policy was separate and distinct from Uniroyal's insurance. There never had been any joint meetings of the separate boards of the directors of Uniroyal and Englebert. Can liability be imposed upon Uniroyal for the torts of Englebert in its manufacture of tires? [*Connelly v. Uniroyal, Inc.*, et al., 389 N.E.2d 155 (Ill. 1979).]

3. Plaintiff, Nakhleh, a Syrian lawyer and business broker, sued Chemical Construction Corporation, an American corporation doing business in New York, defendant, in a federal court in New York to recover a finder's fee for breach of an alleged oral contract to help the defendant obtain a contract to build a large fertilizer plant in Saudi Arabia. Assume that, as the plaintiff alleges, the oral contract included an agreement that the contract was to be governed by Saudi Arabian law. New York has recognized the choice-of-law principle

that the parties to a contract have a right to choose the law to be applied to their contract. New York Obligations Law prohibits enforcement of oral finders' contracts. The purpose of this law is to avoid the possibility of frequent perjury caused by employees seeking to recover from their employers for non-performed or fictitious finders' services. Defendant contends that the federal court in New York does not have jurisdiction. Does this Statute of Frauds provision against finders' contracts being oral represent such a fundamental New York policy that its courts will not honor the intentions of the parties regarding the law they intended to apply? [*Nakhleh v. Chemical Construction Corporation,* et al., 359 F.Supp. 357 (1973).]

4. Plaintiff, Copperweld Steel Company, a Pennsylvania corporation, sued DeMag-Mannesmann-Boehler, a German engineering corporation doing business in the United States, defendant, for failure to perform satisfactorily a written contract between them. The case was brought in the federal court in Pennsylvania. The contract provided that the defendant design in Germany a four strand continuous casting plant to be built for the plaintiff in Ohio. The contract contained the following clause: "Any disputes arising out of the terms of the contract shall be brought before the court of justice having jurisdiction in the area where the supplier has its main offices." All records regarding the operation of the plant, and all plaintiff's personnel who operated the plant, are in Ohio. Also, all plaintiff's personnel who engaged in the negotiation of the contract are in Ohio. Certain of the defendants' personnel involved in the sale are located in the United States. Practically everything done in connection with the transaction has been done in the English language. Almost all witnesses are English speaking. Can this federal Pennsylvania court exercise jurisdiction over this case? [*Copperweld Steel Company v. DeMag-Mannesmann-Boehler,* et al., 54 F.R.D. 539 (1972), *reh,* 347 F.Supp.53 (1972), *reh.,* 354 F.Supp. 571 (1973), *aff'd.,* 578 F.2d 953 (1978).]

5. Stumm Handel GmbH, defendant, is a German firm doing business in New York under the name of Stumm Trading Company. Gaskin, plaintiff, was employed by the defendant as manager in charge of the New York operation. The written employment contract signed by the plaintiff was fairly negotiated at arm's length and in a businesslike fashion between the parties and voluntarily entered into by the plaintiff. The contract provided that: "Any controversies arising out of this contract shall be settled by means of negotiations with the Management and, if necessary, with the remaining partners. In case of failure of such negotiations it is agreed that Essen [the Republic of West Germany] shall be the forum to which any controversy must be submitted." The contract was written in German, a language which the plaintiff neither speaks nor understands. A literal translation of the contract was conveyed to the plaintiff by a representative of the defendant. The plaintiff asserts that he was never informed that by executing the contract he was consenting to the Republic of West Germany as the forum within which he must submit all controversies, and that if he had known this he would not have agreed to this provision because it is onerous and unconscionable, and a deterrent to bringing any actions whatsoever. Plaintiff sued the defendant in the federal District Court in New York for $306,260.40 he claimed was owing to him by the defendant. The defendant moved to dismiss the action on the ground that the choice-of-forum clause required litigation under the contract in the courts of West Germany. What decision on the defendant's motion? [*Gaskin v. Stumm Handel Gmbh,* 390 F.Supp. 361 (1975).]

6. Montreal Trading Ltd., plaintiff, is a Canadian corporation which trades commodities in the international market. It has never traded potash. The defendants are United States companies which produce potash. Plaintiff sued the defendants for treble damages under the United States antitrust laws, alleging that plaintiff was unable to sell potash to its customers because the defendants were engaged in a concerted refusal to deal with plaintiff and had deliberately limited potash production to drive up prices. Plaintiff alleged that the concerted refusal was by the defendants' Canadian subsidiaries whom the plaintiff contacted and who refused to sell potash for delivery in Canada. Plaintiff had never contacted the defendants for potash. The defendants were acquitted in previous federal antitrust criminal proceedings. The plaintiff has not sustained any injury in its property or business, and cannot show that it could have resold any potash which it might have purchased. Judgment for whom? [*Montreal Trading Ltd. v. Amax, Inc.,* et al., 661 F.2d 864 (1981).]

7. Defendant, Eastman Kodak Company, of New York, is a corporation engaged in the manufacture and sale of photographic apparatus and supplies. Over the years defendant acquired property and business of competing firms and secured control of from 75 to 80 percent of the entire interstate trade in the articles in which it dealt. Defendant also, by contract with the makers, obtained entire control in the United States of the imported raw paper which was recognized as the only standard paper for the manufacture of photographic printing-out paper. Defendant's refusal to sell the imported raw paper to other manufacturers compelled several competing companies to sell or go out of business. All photographic supplies manufactured by the defendant were sold with the conditions that: dealers carry only such materials for sale to customers as were sold to them by the defendant at listed prices; no articles were to be consigned by them to others without first obtaining the permission of the defendant; and the articles sold to dealers should not be sold by them to other dealers.

    The United States brought an antitrust action in the federal District Court in New York to restrain the defendant from violating the Sherman Act, charging that the defendant and others entered into contracts and combinations in restraint of interstate trade and commerce, and with monopolizing a part of such trade. Judgment for whom? [*United States v. Eastman Kodak Co.,* et al., 226 F.62 (1915).] (This is a well-known leading case.)

8. United Brands Company (UBC) of New York, applicant, is the largest group in the world banana market and accounted for 35 percent of world exports in 1974. Its European subsidiary (UBCBV) is responsible for coordinating banana sales in all the Member States of the EEC except for the United Kingdom and Italy. UBC has 40 to 50 percent of the market in Denmark, West Germany, Ireland, The Netherlands, Belgium, and Luxembourg. UBC also controls both the growing and shipping of bananas because of its vertical integration in the control of sources of bananas in the banana producer countries. Because of UBC's extensive advertising a consumer preference for its "Chiquita" brand has been created. The bananas are shipped to Europe at two ports with little cost difference and are sold to distributors at prices varying as much as 50%. Since bananas are imported while still green and are later ripened, UBC required its distributors/ripeners not to sell bananas while still green, to whom UBC applied differing prices, the difference sometimes amounting to 138 percent. In order to maintain its scheme to control the pricing and conduct of its distributors, UBC terminated its long-standing Danish distributor, Olsen, because it had participated in the advertising campaign of a competitor (Dole). Olsen and others complained to the Commission of the European Communities, which initiated a procedure for infringement of Article 86 of the EEC Treaty against UBC and UBCBV. The Commission decided that UBC and UBCBV had infringed Article 86. UBC and UBCBV then applied to the Court of Justice of the European Communities to have the Commission's decision annulled. Should it be annulled? [*United Brands Company and United Brands Continental B.V., Applicants v. Commission of the European Communities, Defendant,* The Common Market Reporter, CCH Par. 8429 (1978).]

9. Without enumeration, explain the overall EEC policy of prohibited conduct stated in the first portion of:
    a. Article 85,
    b. Article 86.

10. In the case of *United States v. Mercedes-Benz of North America,* 517 F.Supp. 1369 (1981),[16] the court stated three elements were necessary to establish a per se illegal tying arrangement. What are those elements?

---

[16] See pp. 864–67.

Ethics and Business Law in Part 12
Business Law in the International Marketplace

Introduction

This end-of-Part discussion, like the others in this book, is designed to encourage students to begin forming personal beliefs about what is right or wrong conduct in business. The discussion here builds on the material in the first end-of-Part discussion on pages 58 to 69; you may find it helpful to review that.

This material has several goals. The "sampling of ethical issues" section immediately following is designed to help you see the range of ethical issues associated with this area of the law. The in-depth discussion is intended to provide you with a background for forming your own beliefs about a single very important ethical issue in business. The problems at the end of this Part are designed to build your skill in ethical analysis while exploring further the in-depth issue.

A Sampling of Ethical Issues in International Law

International law raises distinctive ethical issues. One stems from the fact that as we travel from one culture to another, the laws and their ethical underpinnings can change significantly. As a consequence, international business is an area where we are most likely to discover ourselves in fundamental disagreement with the laws of a country which has power over us. When this occurs, the nature of one's ethical duty to comply with the law becomes critically important. Is one ever justified in violating the law of another country? Is one ever justified in violating the law of one's own country?

Another issue is associated with business practices which, in this country, are viewed as unethical, but which are common in another country. Bribery is the best example. In many cultures everyone engages in bribing. It doesn't carry the strong negative ethical connotation which it does here. Rather, people often see it as a cost of doing business with government officials who are underpaid. Persons in these cultures see the officials as justified in trying to earn a decent living. The reality is that, if you don't engage in bribing on the same terms as your competitors, you often cannot win new business, or obtain important government help on a timely basis. In a sense, our Foreign Corrupt Practices Act imposes a handicap on American firms doing business in different cultures. Do you think your beliefs about business ethics should change depending upon the country in which you are doing business? Do you think you are justified in doing something such as bribery because others do it? Does it make a difference if the others are your competitors?

Another issue is associated with foreign laws which conflict with your ethical standards. Child labor laws are a common example. Apartheid is another. Apartheid is a form of pervasive racial discrimination practiced in the Republic of South Africa and incorporated in its laws. For some time, many serious thinkers urged businesses not to comply with these laws when operating in the Republic of South Africa. Rather, they urged that American business follow the ethical standards of our nation. More recently these thinkers have concluded that apartheid is such a moral evil that it is wrong for this country, and wrong for its businesses, to support a government which enforces apartheid laws. As a consequence they have urged economic sanctions, some of which would involve the withdrawal of American firms.

Some argue that economic sanctions against the Republic of South Africa would themselves be unethical. They claim that the persons injured by sanctions would be employed or unemployed poor black persons there rather than those who enforce racist policies. Further, they claim, it would be wrong to impose sanctions without the will of the black population.

Do you think it is wrong to do business in a country which adopts policies which you judge to be fundamentally unethical? Or do you think this is not a business issue with which business should concern itself?

Another fundamental ethical issue in international business is trade protection. Can you see that low wage rates in poor countries would attract labor intensive industries? When this occurs, wealthier countries with higher wage rates lose jobs. One response by the wealthy is to impose tariffs so that products manufactured in the low wage country cannot be imported. This keeps jobs at home.

Can you see the way that capitalism tends to benefit the most poor in international trade and is, in this aspect, consistent with Kant's philosophy and religious ethics? And can you see the way the tariffs thwart this process? Can you articulate assessments of protectionist tariffs using the four styles of ethical reasoning?

In-Depth Discussion of a Basic Issue: The Duty to Comply with the Law

Every person in business needs mature views on what they believe about the duty to comply with the law. Business affords many opportunities to sidestep the law, avoid being detected, and to profit from the violation.

In this country, an ethically mature view on one's duty to comply with the law must reflect the fact that we have the opportunity to change the law. If we were to conclude that a law is ethically wrong, then we would become obligated to try to change it. In most moral systems this responsibility to try changing the law is a required first step.

Kant's Philosophy

While the following historical incident is true, and reflects many attributes of Kant's style of ethical reasoning, it is not purely Kantian. One view on *compliance* is illustrated by the life of a man who was charged with violating the laws of his country. At his trial, the man was sentenced to death. The man and his friends believed the law he was charged with violating was wrong, and that his trial had not been fair. Because of this, while the man was awaiting execution, his friends arranged an opportunity for him to escape. When told about this opportunity, the man turned to his personal ethics to decide whether it would be right or wrong to violate the law of his country and escape the unjust sentence. In reaching his decision he weighed three arguments. First he said, we should never harm others, and by escaping he would harm the state by violating its laws. Second he reasoned, each citizen impliedly agrees to obey the laws of his or her country and by escaping he would be breaking his promise—his implied agreement to obey the law. A third reason was that one's country is like a teacher or parent and we ought, therefore, to obey our country by following its laws. The man concluded that it would be ethically wrong for him to escape; accordingly he declined the opportunity and was put to death. The man's name was Socrates. His style of reasoning about compliance with the law was based on promises, consent, and duty; its perspective is clearly "other" oriented and, in important ways, it is similar to Kant's.

The ethical belief which Socrates possessed about compliance with the law is inspiring. But it was the result of a long life devoted to reasoning about ethical issues. Most students are at the beginning of their lives and less able to reason with such assurance and commitment about ethical issues.

Egoistic Analysis

Others, such as egoists, adopt a radically different view toward compliance with the law. For an egoist, the decision to comply or not usually turns on the *risks versus the rewards*. Thus, an egoist is mainly concerned with whether or not the violation of the law would be detected, and, if so, what the penalties would be in comparison to the potential profits. For example, an egoist would weigh the decision to cheat on tax returns in this way. By claiming three extra dependent exemptions for cats (illegal conduct) there would be an after tax savings of about $1,500. On the other hand, the risk of being caught by an audit is only about 2%. If caught, there would probably be a penalty assessed at 50% of the unpaid tax for *civil* fraud and the possibility of conviction and imprisonment for *criminal* fraud. In a statistical sense, the reward for cheating ($1,500) would be compared with the potential civil risk ($1,500 + $750 = $2,250 × .02 = $45!). Since the civil reward exceeds the civil risk, the egoist would probably take exemptions for his or her cats, unless deterred by the risk of criminal prosecution.

Utilitarian Analysis

Utilitarians would be likely to conclude that *the greatest good for the greatest number* occurs when everyone obeys the law. This is especially true in this country where there are a variety of mechanisms for changing laws. Electing different legislators and initiating constitutional amendments are mechanisms for changing a law which is judged, by any philosophic standard, to be wrong.

Religious Analysis

Persons with religious orientations are generally *compelled by their religion to obey the laws* of the country where they live. Again, in our country, if there is a conflict between the beliefs of a religion and the law of our country, the law changing mechanisms are available to try to modify the law.

Sometimes utilitarians, Kantians, and persons with religious ethics conclude that a law is, by their particular ethical standard, very wrong or unjust. Political efforts to change such a law are sometimes unsuccessful. Since persons of these ethical views are generally committed to complying with law, an important law which *they believe* to be unethical presents them with a real dilemma, to comply with the unethical law or, by its violation, to betray their general commitment to compliance. In these situations, some resolve the matter by engaging in *civil disobedience*.

Civil Disobedience

Civil disobedience is another way of attempting to induce a change in the law. It is very important, however, to distinguish conduct which is egoistic from that which constitutes valid civil disobedience. Mohandus K. Ghandi of India and Martin Luther King in the United States are among the persons most widely recognized as serious philosophers and practitioners of civil disobedience. You may understand civil disobedience better by studying an incident in the life of Martin Luther King.

In early 1963, Dr. King, as leader of the Southern Christian Leadership Conference, was organizing activities to protest racial segregation in the city of Birmingham, Alabama. A judge issued an injunction prohibiting marches and other kinds of protests. In defiance of the injunction, King continued to march and was arrested. While in the Birmingham jail he wrote a now famous letter in which he explained *his* justification for *his* civil disobedience. An edited version of the letter is reproduced below.

> . . . My friends, I must say to you that we have not made a single gain in civil rights without determined legal and nonviolent pressure.**** Nonviolent direct action seeks to create such a crisis and establish such creative tension . . . to dramatize the issue [so] . . . it can no longer be ignored.**** Just as Socrates felt that it was necessary to create a tension in the mind so that

individuals could rise from the bondage of myths and half-truths to . . . objective appraisal, we must see the need of having nonviolent gadflies to create the kind of tension in society that will help men to rise from the dark depths of prejudice and racism to the majestic heights of understanding and brotherhood.

[In response to the question of how he justified violating the law, King wrote the following:]

The answer is to be found in the fact that there are two types of laws: There are *just* laws and there are *unjust* laws. I would agree with Saint Augustine that "An unjust law is no law at all."

Now what is the difference between the two: How does one determine when a law is just or unjust? A just law is a man-made code that squares with the moral law or the law of God. An unjust law is a code that is out of harmony with the moral law. To put it in the terms of Saint Thomas Aquinas, an unjust law is a human law that is not rooted in eternal and natural law.****

An unjust law is a code that a majority inflicts on a minority that is not binding on itself. This is *difference* made legal. On the other hand, a just law is a code that a majority compels a minority to follow that it is willing to follow itself. This is sameness made legal.****

I hope you can see the distinction I am trying to point out. In no sense do I advocate evading or denying the law as the rabid segregationist would do. This would lead to anarchy. One who breaks an unjust law must do it openly, lovingly, . . . I submit that an individual who breaks a law that conscience tells him is unjust, and willingly accepts the penalty by staying in jail to arouse the conscience of the community over its injustice, is in reality expressing the very highest respect for law. . . .

Can you identify the attributes of Dr. King's conduct which differentiate *his* civil disobedience from the disobedience of an *egoist*?

Solving Ethics Problems

Like the other end-of-Part discussions in this book, this one presents problems for you to consider. These problems have three goals. The first is to give you the opportunity to further explore the in-depth issue. The second goal is to give you experience in ethical reasoning about the law and about related management problems. The third goal is to let you see how thinking critically about the law can increase your ability to make ethical decisions. To facilitate this, the problems begin by asking you to analyze the law for its ethical content and then shift to looking at related problems in managerial ethics.

For a discussion of the ethical roles of markets and the law, and examples of the four styles of ethical reasoning—egoism, utilitarianism, Kant's philosophy, and religious ethics—read the business ethics material at the end of Part 1.

Problems

1. Review *Pirkey v. Hospital Corporation of America* on page 853. Can you see that the choice-of-law issue is likely to determine the outcome of this case? We might surmise that if the case were tried under Colorado law, Dr. Pirkey would prevail while under the law of Saudi Arabia he would lose. Since these two bodies of law apparently conflict, the battle over the choice of law is really the battle over who will win the case. Can you see that this is a conflict between the need for order and the need to resolve the case based on other ethical principles? Is exploiting this need for order to try to win the case a form of civil disobedience? If it is a form of civil disobedience, would Dr. King judge it to be ethical?

2. Union Carbide operated plants which manufacture the pesticide methyl isocyanate. One plant located in West Virginia was subject to stringent U.S. safety and environmental laws. This plant had a computerized safety system. Another plant was located in Bhopol, India, where safety and environmental standards were lax; this plant did not have the computerized system. In December, 1984, the Bhopol plant leaked about twenty-five tons of the gaseous pesticide. As a result, 2,000 died and 100,000 were injured. Is it ethical to build plants outside the U.S. if the sole motivation is to escape more stringent safety and environmental laws? Is complying with a lax safety law a valid moral defense to a disaster like Bhopol? Was Union Carbide under a moral obligation to use the same safety standards in both countries?
3. If you were the manager of international marketing for an American firm, would you do business in South Africa, a country which uses the law to achieve racial segregation? If you did elect to do business in that country would you comply with all of its laws?
4. If you learned that you could invest $10,000 in a company that manufactures radar detectors for use by speeding drivers and receive a 25% return on your investment each year, should you do so? Why or why not?

Appendix A
An Explanation of the Civil Trial Process

Introduction

The judicial system with its use of courts deals with the interpretation, validity, declaration, and application of law to the factual situations confronting the court. In this process law is made, indicating what is legal now and, therefore, as case precedent what applies for the future. The court acts only on matters brought before it by parties who want judicial action. It has only the jurisdiction and powers given to it by federal or state statute.

Some cases involve the federal and state constitutions, and administrative rules and regulations, while other cases involve the common law and equity in the absence of constitutional or legislative guidance. The decisions of the courts are law, providing guidance to society as to what may or may not be legally done. It is therefore important to understand the meaning of these decisions by reading and analyzing them. All too often members of the public have no concept of how their judicial system works through the courts. An explanation here of the civil trial process will be helpful.

The opinions of the courts in deciding cases are often contained in reports of those cases, which are available in libraries in court buildings, law schools, and other public places. Reference to a court opinion is called a *case citation*. For example, *Vigil v. Lamm*, 190 Colo. 180, 544 P.2d 631 (1976) refers to a Colorado case report found in volume 190 of the Colorado Reports at page 180, which may also be found in the regional Pacific Reporter in volume 544 second series at page 631. The date of the case is 1976.

One of the most important ways law is made is by the published opinions of appellate courts. Most of the abbreviated court decisions in this text are edited versions of appellate court opinions. To understand how the parties to a legal dispute get to an appellate court to have their case heard, we offer here a brief overview of the civil trial process. The process described may vary slightly from state to state, but the definitions of the terms used are widely accepted.

The Trial of a Civil Case

A civil suit is initiated by the **plaintiff,** who files several documents in a trial court of general jurisdiction (usually a county court located in the county government building).[1] The document of greatest importance is called the **complaint,** which is filed by the plaintiff. The complaint must contain the following information:

> **plaintiff**
> the party who initiates a civil suit by filing a complaint in the proper court
>
> **complaint**
> the first pleading in a civil action

1. the names of the parties to the case, the plaintiff(s) and defendant(s);
2. a statement sufficient to show that the court has jurisdiction to hear the matter; and
3. a short and plain statement of the facts, indicating:
    a. the existence of a legal duty and
    b. the breach of this duty and
    c. a claim for relief in the form of a request for a given amount of money damages and/or a claim for equitable relief, such as a request for an injunction or an order for specific performance of a contract.

> **summons**
> a writ or process served on the defendant in a civil action notifying him of the action and summoning him to appear and plead
>
> **defendant**
> the party against whom a civil suit (or criminal action) is brought

The complaint normally is filed together with a **summons,** which directs the server of the papers (usually a county sheriff if the case is filed in a county court, or a federal marshall if filed in a federal court) to the last known address of the **defendant.** Usually a copy of the complaint is included for the purpose of this *service.* When the server of the papers locates the defendant(s) or, in some states, when the server locates the permanent residence of the defending party(ies), the papers are left with someone of suitable age and discretion residing therein. The server then files a sworn statement with the court, often called a *return,* in which the server swears that the defendant(s) was (were) served.

The defendant may file a document with the court responding to the complaint, called an *answer,* within a given time period, usually twenty to thirty days. A copy of the answer is given to the plaintiff. The answer may admit all, part, or none of the facts as alleged in the complaint, and may admit or deny any or all of the legal consequences. In addition, the answer may include a claim for relief against the plaintiff, called a **counterclaim,** if the grounds exist.

> **counterclaim**
> a claim asserted by the defendant against the plaintiff's claim in a civil action

The general rule defining those persons who may be plaintiffs or defendants is that they must have a direct interest in the subject matter of the suit; that is, these persons must be directly affected by the outcome. This rule has been expanded somewhat recently by permitting *class action* suits.

Class action suits were first widely used on the federal level, but gradually states have been adopting procedures which provide for this type of litigation. The class action procedural rules provide that one or more members of a class may sue or be sued as representatives of a class of persons if: (1) the class is so numerous that joinder of all members of the class is not practicable; (2) there are questions of law or fact that are common to all members of the class; (3) the claims or defenses of the parties representing the class are typical of the claims or defenses of the class; (4) the representatives of the class will fairly protect the interests of the class; and (5) all the members of the class must be identifiable (within reason). In addition to these prerequisites, the court must find that the class action is superior to other available methods for the fair and efficient adjudication of the controversy.

If a party is properly served with the complaint and fails to file an answer within the time period provided by law, then the plaintiff may ask the court to enter a *default* judgment. If such is entered, the court is making a judgment that the plaintiff is entitled to the relief claimed in the complaint.

---

[1] Some of this material is from A. Wolfe and F. Naffzinger, *The Law of American Business Organizations* (New York, John Wiley & Sons, 1984.)

As stated earlier, a defendant may *answer,* or the defendant may challenge the plaintiff's case by **motion** before the issue is formally tried. There are several motions the parties may use to challenge the legal arguments of the other party asserted through the **pleadings** filed with the court. The first such opportunity to present such a motion is presented by the defendant, who may make a motion to the court to dismiss the complaint for failure to state a claim upon which relief may be granted. In this case the motion is made by filing a document labeled "Motion" with the court.

The filing of the "Motion to Dismiss for Failure to State a Claim" by the defendant requires the judge to rule on whether or not the plaintiff has stated the existence and breach of a legal duty. The judge must consider the complaint and the facts stated therein and resolve every inference created by the facts in favor of the plaintiff. When this is done, the court will grant or deny the motion to dismiss.

motion
a procedural device asking the court to take some action

pleadings
the formal documents filed with a court that usually include the complaint, answer, and motions regarding them

Discovery

If the defendant files an answer, then the litigation moves into a phase of the process generally called the *discovery* stage. Generally the objectives of this *pre-trial* procedure are to: (1) simplify the issues; (2) obtain admissions of fact to avoid unnecessary arguments and avoid surprise; (3) limit the number of expert witnesses; and (4) cover any other matters which would expedite the trial.

The following legal devices permit an adverse party to discover almost all information relevant to the trial of a civil suit. The best known discovery device is the **deposition.** A deposition is a sworn statement of any person, including a party to the action (the plaintiff or defendant) or any witness, which is made in response to questions from the attorneys for the opposing sides. The deposition is used to discover physical evidence, to discover what a witness will say at trial, or to discover any other matter relevant to the subject of the case. A deposition is taken under oath or affirmation, usually in front of attorneys for both parties, and is transcribed by a court reporter. The final copy is signed as a true statement by the one being deposed and is filed with the court. This signed statement may be used at the trial if the witness is unavailable, or it may be used at the trial to challenge the oral testimony of the deposing witness if such testimony varies from that in the deposition.

deposition
a written statement made by a person under oath or affirmation in a judicial proceeding where there is opportunity for cross-examination before trial

If the party or witness cannot be interviewed in person, then a series of written questions may be sent and must be answered under oath. These written questions are called **interrogatories.**

interrogatory
a written question

In addition to depositions and interrogatories, a party may ask the court to order another party, if good cause is shown, to produce documents and other items of evidence for inspection, copying, or photographing. The subject of this order may be books, papers, accounts, letters, photographs, objects or tangible things, or other items which constitute evidence relating to the subject of the suit. If the mental or physical condition of the party is in controversy, the court may order the party to submit to a physical or mental examination by a physician if good cause is shown. This latter method of discovery is used in many cases where personal injury is the subject of the case.

Courts in the various states adopted many of these discovery procedures in the 1960s so they are viewed as relatively new. This adoption has resulted in many more cases being settled out of court because the procedures allow a party to discover almost all of the relevant evidence of the opposing party. The only evidence which is not obtainable by an opposing party are those materials which are **privileged.** Generally, such materials include an attorney's work product (thoughts and research on a case) and communications between the client and his attorney or the patient and his doctor.

privileged communication
a communication between certain persons which, because of their relationship, is inadmissible in evidence without a waiver of the privilege

If the parties decide to *settle* the case out of court, the attorneys ask the permission of the judge to dismiss the case. If this dismissal is done *with prejudice,* it means that a party will be barred from filing the suit again. If the pretrial procedures do not result in settlement, then the parties usually ask the judge to rule on another series of motions

An Explanation of the Civil Trial Process   A 3

challenging the legal assertions of the adverse parties. After the pleadings are all filed, either party may make a motion to dismiss the claims of an adverse party and enter judgment for the moving party by asking for a *judgment on the pleadings* or **summary judgment.** Some procedural systems make a distinction between these two motions but, in essence, they are the same. Like the initial motion to dismiss described above, these motions require the judge to consider the arguments made in all of the pleadings, resolve every reasonable inference against the moving party, and make a finding as to whether or not the arguments made and facts asserted warrant submission of the case to the jury in a trial on the facts. Generally, if the judge finds that the legal arguments and facts presented could lead to but one reasonable conclusion, and that is in favor of the moving party, then the motion must be granted. If there are issues of fact present which would lead reasonable minds to differ, then the motion should be overruled.

A matter may be tried before a **jury** or a judge alone. If a party in a civil suit desires a jury trial, it must be demanded, usually during the initial pleading phase. In federal courts, the U.S. Constitution guarantees a trial by jury in all civil actions at common law where the value of the controversy exceeds twenty dollars. The U.S. Constitution does not guarantee the right of a trial by jury in civil cases in state courts. However, the constitutions of the states usually provide that there is such a right in cases similar to those where the common law gave such a right at the time the constitution was adopted. Practically speaking, this means that almost all matters involving judgments of fact and requests for money damages may be tried before a jury. Usually negligence cases, and other personal injury cases, are tried before a jury. On the other hand, cases involving the equity powers of the court or those involving very complex issues such as antitrust suits or breaches of industrial contracts and other cases where evaluation of the evidence requires rigorous analysis and expertise are usually tried before the judge alone. In very exceptional cases, the judge may appoint a *master* or *referee* to hear some of the evidence and make findings of fact.

The process of questioning prospective jurors to determine which of them will be permitted to sit on the jury is called **voir dire.** This phrase is French in origin and means "to speak the truth." The voir dire procedure allows the court and parties to reject a prospective juror if, after questioning, it is revealed that the person is barred by *statute* to serve in that case (e.g., wife of the plaintiff) or might be prejudiced or unable to render an impartial judgment. Usually each party is given three challenges to use for *any* reason—called *peremptory challenges;*[2] additional challenges can be made for sufficient cause (statutory cause)—called *challenge for cause.*

Trial

At the trial, the plaintiff, through the attorney representing the plaintiff's interests, presents its side of the **evidence.** After each witness is sworn and "directly" examined by the plaintiff's attorney, the defendant's attorney may "cross-examine" the witness on matters brought out on direct examination. It must be emphasized at this point that, since most of the cases which proceed to trial do involve disputes of fact, the process by which the facts are "found" is the process of *direct examination* of a witness by the attorney who initially uses the witness followed by *cross-examination* by the attorney for the other side. The jury or the judge, by watching the witnesses respond to the questions asked, must determine whether they are telling the truth or accurately recalling an event. The answers which are given by the witness are considered by the fact-finder (jury or judge) together with the witness's demeanor (facial expressions and hand movements).

Following the plaintiff's version of the facts in the case, the defendant presents the evidence relevant to its side.

---

[2] See the very recent important criminal case of *Batson v. Kentucky,* 54 U.S.L.W. 4425 (April 30, 1986), discussed on page 32.

During the trial itself, a party may challenge the entire case of an adverse party by moving for a **directed verdict.** Either party may move this, and it requires the judge to rule on whether or not there are still issues of fact present which warrant the continuation of the trial. If reasonable minds could differ about the interpretation or existence of certain crucial facts, or the inferences to be drawn from the facts, then the court will overrule the motion and the trial will proceed.

directed verdict
a jury verdict as directed by the judge

verdict
a jury's finding of fact

At the close of the defendant's case, both sides make summary arguments emphasizing the aspects of the testimony and other evidence they believe most pertinent to their arguments. Before the jury retires to make its finding of fact, the judge instructs the jury on the appropriate rules of law which the jurors are to apply to the facts as determined by them. Below is an example of the type of "instruction" the judge may give to the jury in a negligence case:

Negligence is lack of ordinary care. It is a failure to exercise that degree of care which a reasonably prudent person would have exercised under the same circumstances. It may arise from doing an act which a reasonably prudent person would not have done under the same circumstances, or, on the other hand, from failing to do an act which a reasonably prudent person would have done under the circumstances.[3]

In applying this statement of the law, each juror must decide by using his or her own life experience as a guide whether or not the defendant acted as a "reasonably prudent person" would have, given the circumstances.

The judge gives the jury instructions on each matter of law argued in the case. After the instructions, the jury retires to the jury room, where it applies all the rules stated by the judge to the facts as presented to them at the trial by the parties, witnesses, attorneys, and other evidence and reaches a verdict both as to liability (was the defendant legally at fault for a breach of a rule?) and **damages** (if the defendant was liable, what is the appropriate amount of damages that will compensate the plaintiff for the breach of the rule?).

damages
the money judicially awarded to an injured party for another's wrongful conduct

A motion for *judgment notwithstanding the verdict* may be made by an aggrieved party against whom the verdict has been announced after the trial of the issues. This motion requires the judge to rule on whether or not the jury could reasonably have reached the verdict it did, given the evidence and the court's instructions. This motion is granted only when the judge believes that the jury reached a verdict by ignoring the instructions, or where, after hearing and seeing all of the evidence, the jury could not logically have reached the verdict it did. This motion, like the one for summary judgment or the one for a directed verdict, essentially challenges the legal sufficiency of a party's case. It must not be confused with a motion for a new trial, which may be made after a verdict is reached but is granted only where substantial errors in the trial process occurred.

The Appellate Process

If either of the parties believes that there was an error during the trial and that this error caused an unfavorable verdict, the party may appeal. The error must be one in the process of introducing evidence or in the statement of the law or in the application of the rule to the facts. *Parties usually cannot appeal the finding of a fact.* For example, if the jury finds that, as a matter of fact, the defendant did *sign* an agreement in question on a given date, then this may not be appealed. However, a party may appeal the issue of whether or not signing the agreement did legally *bind* the party. This latter conclusion is one which is a mixture of fact-finding and law application and is appropriate for appeal. The reasons

---

[3] 1 New York Pattern Jury Instructions—Civil, Committee on Pattern Jury Instructions, Assoc. of Supreme Court Justices, vol. 1, 2d ed. (Rochester: The Lawyers Co-operative Pub. Co., 1974), p. 126.

for this are that a party should get only one chance to introduce the evidence the party deems appropriate. Therefore, the trial courts are set up to take evidence; all the procedures at this level are adopted to ensure the fairness of the evidence-producing process. The right to cross-examination, the right to demand and examine other evidence, and the right to object to the introduction of irrelevant or excessively prejudicial evidence all exist at the trial level.

Appellate courts are not equipped to hear testimony or inspect evidence. Appellate courts are composed of three or more judges who hear the arguments of the appealing parties as to why the statements of the rules in the trial court were erroneous or why the process of rule application was erroneous.

An appeal may be initiated by either party. The one appealing is called the **appellant** or, in some courts, the *petitioner*. The one answering the appeal is the **appellee** or the *respondent*. At the trial stage, the case is given a name or "style" (in legal language); almost always this is done by putting the name of the plaintiff first, followed by the name of the defendant. However, on appeal, some courts, but not all, put the name of the appellant first when reporting the case. So if the defendant appeals, the defendant's name goes first in the official report. You should be cautioned that the appellate case's style does not reveal who is the plaintiff or defendant in the original trial of the matter. This may be determined only by reading the appellate opinion.

The appellant must file with the appellate court at least two documents. One is the transcribed version of what occurred in the trial. During the trial a court reporter took down all of the testimony, all objections and motions, and other relevant happenings in a special form of shorthand. This shorthand version of the trial is not transcribed into prose unless it is requested and paid for by one of the parties. Together with this transcript, the appellant files a legal brief which contains the appellant's legal arguments. The appellate court considers the trial transcript, the written legal arguments (briefs) of both parties, and in many cases allows attorneys for the parties to appear before it to orally answer questions asked by the appellate court and, in general, to argue the merits of the issues advanced. For the reasons stated above, the appellate court does not consider additional evidence, cannot call new or recall the old witnesses, or, generally, view the evidence again. The *facts* as found by the trial court must be taken as given.

The appellate court then takes the matter under consideration, does considerable legal research on the matter, votes, and writes its opinion. If some of the judges do not agree with the majority of the court, they may write dissenting opinions stating their reasons. This appellate opinion is usually published and is available to all persons.

If either party is still of the belief that a *substantial* error in the statement of the rule or in the application of the rule to the facts was made by either the trial or intermediate appellate court, the party may appeal the case to the next higher level, the supreme court of the state or federal system, which is usually the highest level. Again, the party appealing this time is called the appellant or petitioner and the answering party is the appellee or respondent. The name of the appellant is usually placed first. The same general practice is followed in filing the appeals papers and hearing the arguments, except that additional arguments are made either supporting or attacking the decision of the first appellate court.

An appellate court (either intermediate or supreme court) may do one of three things with the case before it. It may *affirm* the holding of the court immediately below it and state its reasons for affirming the holding. If it affirms the decision, the same party who won the case in the court below wins again.

The appellate court may *reverse* the decision being appealed and enter its own judgment, giving the reasons. The third option is to order all or part of the case *tried again* using the interpretation of the law as stated by the appellate court. In this case, if the parties so desire, the case will be tried again. The same trial judge may preside again, but a new jury will be chosen.

---

appellant
a party who appeals a case decision against him

appellee (or respondent)
a party against whom an appeal is taken

This concludes our presentation of material on the trial and appeal of a civil case. The terms defined above and the processes outlined are crucial to our understanding of how to study law because the published opinions of appellate judges are the best source available to indicate how the law is applied. For this reason we have used in this book excerpts of mostly appellate cases to illustrate the application of important legal principles discussed in this book. We have made an attempt to edit the irrelevant portions out of these opinions and have attempted to leave in enough information so that you may discern the complete outlines of how the dispute developed and how the legal rules were applied to solve the dispute.

Briefing Appellate Cases

Some of the appellate cases excerpted in the text, especially the longer ones at the end of the chapters, are very complex and will require some effort on your part to fully understand them. We suggest that you keep notes on these cases. These notes are called "briefs" by students of the law. The briefs usually have the following components:

1. A statement of the "facts" of the case as found by the trial court and restated by the appellate court.
2. A statement of the "legal" arguments advanced by both the plaintiff and the defendant.
3. A precise statement of the legal issue or legal problem facing the court; this usually involves an application of a legal principle (rule) or principles (rules) to the facts.
4. A summary of the court's reasoning used to reach its conclusion; this is best accomplished by stating in your own words which facts the court finds are "legally operative" and then summarizing how the legal principle or rule applies to these facts.

Appendix B
Uniform Partnership Act (1914)

Part I Preliminary Provisions

Section 1. Name of Act
This act may be cited as Uniform Partnership Act.

Section 2. Definition of Terms
In this act, "Court" includes every court and judge having jurisdiction in the case.

"Business" includes every trade, occupation, or profession.

"Person" includes individuals, partnerships, corporations, and other associations.

"Bankrupt" includes bankrupt under the Federal Bankruptcy Act or insolvent under any state insolvent act.

"Conveyance" includes every assignment, lease, mortgage, or encumbrance.

"Real property" includes land and any interest or estate in land.

Section 3. Interpretation of Knowledge and Notice
(1) A person has "knowledge" of a fact within the meaning of this act not only when he has actual knowledge thereof, but also when he has knowledge of such other facts as in the circumstances shows bad faith.

(2) A person has "notice" of a fact within the meaning of this act when the person who claims the benefit of the notice:

    (a) States the fact to such person, or

    (b) Delivers through the mail, or by other means of communication, a written statement of the fact to such person or to a proper person at his place of business or residence.

Section 4. Rules of Construction
(1) The rule that statutes in derogation of the common law are to be strictly construed shall have no application to this act.

(2) The law of estoppel shall apply under this act.

(3) The law of agency shall apply under this act.

(4) This act shall be so interpreted and construed as to effect its general purpose to make uniform the law of those states which enact it.

(5) This act shall not be construed so as to impair the obligations of any contract existing when the act goes into effect, nor to affect any action or proceedings begun or right accrued before this act takes effect.

Section 5. Rules for Cases Not Provided for in This Act
In any case not provided for in this act the rules of law and equity, including the law merchant, shall govern.

Part II Nature of Partnership

Section 6. Partnership Defined
(1) A partnership is an association of two or more persons to carry on as co-owners a business for profit.

(2) But any association formed under any other statute of this state, or any statute adopted by authority, other than the authority of this state, is not a partnership under this act, unless such association would have been a partnership in this state prior to the adoption of this act; but this act shall apply to limited partnerships except in so far as the statutes relating to such partnerships are inconsistent herewith.

Section 7. Rules for Determining the Existence of a Partnership
In determining whether a partnership exists, these rules shall apply:

(1) Except as provided by section 16 persons who are not partners as to each other are not partners as to third persons.

(2) Joint tenancy, tenancy in common, tenancy by the entireties, joint property, common property, or part ownership does not of itself establish a partnership, whether such co-owners do or do not share any profits made by the use of the property.

(3) The sharing of gross returns does not of itself establish a partnership, whether or not the persons sharing them have a joint or common right or interest in any property from which the returns are derived.

(4) The receipt by a person of a share of the profits of a business is prima facie evidence that he is a partner in the business, but no such inference shall be drawn if such profits were received in payment:

    (a) As a debt by installments or otherwise,

    (b) As wages of an employee or rent to a landlord,

    (c) As an annuity to a widow or representative of a deceased partner,

    (d) As interest on a loan, though the amount of payment vary with the profits of the business,

    (e) As the consideration for the sale of a good-will of a business or other property by installments or otherwise.

Section 8. Partnership Property
(1) All property originally brought into the partnership stock or subsequently acquired by purchase or otherwise, on account of the partnership, is partnership property.

(2) Unless the contrary intention appears, property acquired with partnership funds is partnership property.

(3) Any estate in real property may be acquired in the partnership name. Title so acquired can be conveyed only in the partnership name.

(4) A conveyance to a partnership in the partnership name, though without words of inheritance, passes the entire estate of the grantor unless a contrary intent appears.

Part III Relations of Partners to Persons Dealing with the Partnership

Section 9. Partner Agent of Partnership as to Partnership Business
(1) Every partner is an agent of the partnership for the purpose of its business, and the act of every partner, including the execution in the partnership name of any instrument, for apparently carrying on in the usual way the business of the partnership of which he is

a member binds the partnership, unless the partner so acting has in fact no authority to act for the partnership in the particular matter, and the person with whom he is dealing has knowledge of the fact that he has no such authority.

(2) An act of a partner which is not apparently for the carrying on of the business of the partnership in the usual way does not bind the partnership unless authorized by the other partners.

(3) Unless authorized by the other partners or unless they have abandoned the business, one or more but less than all the partners have no authority to:

(a) Assign the partnership property in trust for creditors or on the assignee's promise to pay the debts of the partnership,

(b) Dispose of the good-will of the business,

(c) Do any other act which would make it impossible to carry on the ordinary business of a partnership,

(d) Confess a judgment,

(e) Submit a partnership claim or liability to arbitration or reference.

(4) No act of a partner in contravention of a restriction on authority shall bind the partnership to persons having knowledge of the restriction.

Section 10. Conveyance of Real Property of the Partnership

(1) Where title to real property is in the partnership name, any partner may convey title to such property by a conveyance executed in the partnership name; but the partnership may recover such property unless the partner's act binds the partnership under the provisions of paragraph (1) of section 9, or unless such property has been conveyed by the grantee or a person claiming through such grantee to a holder for value without knowledge that the partner, in making the conveyance, has exceeded his authority.

(2) Where title to real property is in the name of the partnership, a conveyance executed by a partner, in his own name, passes the equitable interest of the partnership, provided the act is one within the authority of the partner under the provisions of paragraph (1) of section 9.

(3) Where title to real property is in the name of one or more but not all the partners, and the record does not disclose the right of the partnership, the partners in whose name the title stands may convey title to such property, but the partnership may recover such property if the partners' act does not bind the partnership under the provisions of paragraph (1) of section 9, unless the purchaser or his assignee, is a holder for value, without knowledge.

(4) Where the title to real property is in the name of one or more or all the partners, or in a third person in trust for the partnership, a conveyance executed by a partner in the partnership name, or in his own name, passes the equitable interest of the partnership, provided the act is one within the authority of the partner under the provisions of paragraph (1) of section 9.

(5) Where the title to real property is in the names of all the partners a conveyance executed by all the partners passes all their rights in such property.

Section 11. Partnership Bound by Admission of Partner

An admission or representation made by any partner concerning partnership affairs within the scope of his authority as conferred by this act is evidence against the partnership.

Section 12. Partnership Charged with Knowledge of or Notice to Partner

Notice to any partner of any matter relating to partnership affairs, and the knowledge of the partner acting in the particular matter, acquired while a partner or then present to his mind, and the knowledge of any other partner who reasonably could and should have communicated it to the acting partner, operate as notice to or knowledge of the partnership, except in the case of a fraud on the partnership committed by or with the consent of that partner.

Section 13. Partnership Bound by Partner's Wrongful Act

Where, by any wrongful act or omission of any partner acting in the ordinary course of the business of the partnership or with the authority of his co-partners, loss or injury is caused to any person, not being a partner in the partnership, or any penalty is incurred, the partnership is liable therefor to the same extent as the partner so acting or omitting to act.

Section 14. Partnership Bound by Partner's Breach of Trust

The partnership is bound to make good the loss:

(a) Where one partner acting within the scope of his apparent authority receives money or property of a third person and misapplies it; and

(b) Where the partnership in the course of its business receives money or property of a third person and the money or property so received is misapplied by any partner while it is in the custody of the partnership.

Section 15. Nature of Partner's Liability

All partners are liable

(a) Jointly and severally for everything chargeable to the partnership under sections 13 and 14.

(b) Jointly for all other debts and obligations of the partnership; but any partner may enter into a separate obligation to perform a partnership contract.

Section 16. Partner by Estoppel

(1) When a person, by words spoken or written or by conduct, represents himself, or consents to another representing him to any one, as a partner in an existing partnership or with one or more persons not actual partners, he is liable to any such person to whom such representation has been made, who has, on the faith of such representation, given credit to the actual or apparent partnership, and if he has made such representation or consented to its being made in a public manner he is liable to such person, whether the representation has or has not been made or communicated to such person so giving credit by or with the knowledge of the apparent partner making the representation or consenting to its being made.

(a) When a partnership liability results, he is liable as though he were an actual member of the partnership.

(b) When no partnership liability results, he is liable jointly with the other persons, if any, so consenting to the contract or representation as to incur liability, otherwise separately.

(2) When a person has been thus represented to be a partner in an existing partnership, or with one or more persons not actual partners, he is an agent of the persons consenting to such representation to bind them to the same extent and in the same manner as though he were a partner in fact, with respect to persons who rely upon the representation. Where all the members of the existing partnership consent to the representation, a partnership act or obligation results; but in all other cases it is the joint act or obligation of the person acting and the persons consenting to the representation.

Section 17. Liability of Incoming Partner

A person admitted as a partner into an existing partnership is liable for all the obligations of the partnership arising before his admission as though he had been a partner when such obligations were incurred, except that this liability shall be satisfied only out of partnership property.

Part IV Relations of Partners to One Another

Section 18. Rules Determining Rights and Duties of Partners

The rights and duties of the partners in relation to the partnership shall be determined, subject to any agreement between them, by the following rules:

(a) Each partner shall be repaid his contributions, whether by way of capital or advances to the partnership property and share equally in the profits and surplus remaining after all liabilities, including those to partners, are satisfied; and must contribute towards the losses, whether of capital or otherwise, sustained by the partnership according to his share in the profits.

(b) The partnership must indemnify every partner in respect of payments made and personal liabilities reasonably incurred by him in the ordinary and proper conduct of its business, or for the preservation of its business or property.

(c) A partner, who in aid of the partnership makes any payment or advance beyond the amount of capital which he agreed to contribute, shall be paid interest from the date of the payment or advance.

(d) A partner shall receive interest on the capital contributed by him only from the date when repayment should be made.

(e) All partners have equal rights in the management and conduct of the partnership business.

(f) No partner is entitled to remuneration for acting in the partnership business, except that a surviving partner is entitled to reasonable compensation for his services in winding up the partnership affairs.

(g) No person can become a member of a partnership without the consent of all the partners.

(h) Any difference arising as to ordinary matters connected with the partnership business may be decided by a majority of the partners; but no act in contravention of any agreement between the partners may be done rightfully without the consent of all the partners.

Section 19. Partnership Books

The partnership books shall be kept, subject to any agreement between the partners, at the principal place of business of the partnership, and every partner shall at all times have access to and may inspect and copy any of them.

Section 20. Duty of Partners to Render Information

Partners shall render on demand true and full information of all things affecting the partnership to any partner or the legal representative of any deceased partner or partner under legal disability.

Section 21. Partner Accountable as a Fiduciary

(1) Every partner must account to the partnership for any benefit, and hold as trustee for it any profits derived by him without the consent of the other partners from any transaction connected with the formation, conduct, or liquidation of the partnership or from any use by him of its property.

(2) This section applies also to the representatives of a deceased partner engaged in the liquidation of the affairs of the partnership as the personal representatives of the last surviving partner.

Section 22. Right to an Account

Any partner shall have the right to a formal account as to partnership affairs:

(a) If he is wrongfully excluded from the partnership business or possession of its property by his co-partners,

(b) If the right exists under the terms of any agreement,

(c) As provided by section 21,

(d) Whenever other circumstances render it just and reasonable.

Section 23. Continuation of Partnership Beyond Fixed Term

(1) When a partnership for a fixed term or particular undertaking is continued after the termination of such term or particular undertaking without any express agreement, the rights and duties of the partners remain the same as they were at such termination, so far as is consistent with a partnership at will.

(2) A continuation of the business by the partners or such of them as habitually acted therein during the term, without any settlement or liquidation of the partnership affairs, is prima facie evidence of a continuation of the partnership.

Part V Property Rights of a Partner

Section 24. Extent of Property Rights of a Partner

The property rights of a partner are (1) his rights in specific partnership property, (2) his interest in the partnership, and (3) his right to participate in the management.

Section 25. Nature of a Partner's Right in Specific Partnership Property

(1) A partner is co-owner with his partners of specific partnership property holding as a tenant in partnership.

(2) The incidents of this tenancy are such that:

(a) A partner, subject to the provisions of this act and to any agreement between the partners, has an equal right with his partners to possess specific partnership property for partnership purposes; but he has no right to possess such property for any other purpose without the consent of his partners.

(b) A partner's right in specific partnership property is not assignable except in connection with the assignment of rights of all the partners in the same property.

(c) A partner's right in specific partnership property is not subject to attachment or execution, except on a claim against the partnership. When partnership property is attached for a partnership debt the partners, or any of them, or the representatives of a deceased partner, cannot claim any right under the homestead or exemption laws.

(d) On the death of a partner his right in specific partnership property vests in the surviving partner or partners, except where the deceased was the last surviving partner, when his right in such property vests in his legal representative. Such surviving partner or partners, or the legal representative of the last surviving partner, has no right to possess the partnership property for any but a partnership purpose.

(e) A partner's right in specific partnership property is not subject to dower, curtesy, or allowances to widows, heirs, or next of kin.

Section 26. Nature of Partner's Interest in the Partnership

A partner's interest in the partnership is his share of the profits and surplus, and the same is personal property.

Section 27. Assignment of Partner's Interest

(1) A conveyance by a partner of his interest in the partnership does not of itself dissolve the partnership, nor, as against the other partners in the absence of agreement, entitle the assignee, during the continuance of the partnership, to interfere in the management or administration of the partnership business or affairs, or to require any information or account of partnership transactions, or to

inspect the partnership books; but it merely entitles the assignee to receive in accordance with his contract the profits to which the assigning partner would otherwise be entitled.

(2) In case of a dissolution of the partnership, the assignee is entitled to receive his assignor's interest and may require an account from the date only of the last account agreed to by all the partners.

Section 28. Partner's Interest Subject to Charging Order

(1) On due application to a competent court by any judgment creditor of a partner, the court which entered the judgment, order, or decree, or any other court, may charge the interest of the debtor partner with payment of the unsatisfied amount of such judgment debt with interest thereon; and may then or later appoint a receiver of his share of the profits, and of any other money due or to fall due to him in respect of the partnership, and make all other orders, directions, accounts and inquiries which the debtor partner might have made, or which the circumstances of the case may require.

(2) The interest charged may be redeemed at any time before foreclosure, or in case of a sale being directed by the court may be purchased without thereby causing a dissolution:

    (a) With separate property, by any one or more of the partners, or

    (b) With partnership property, by any one or more of the partners with the consent of all the partners whose interests are not so charged or sold.

(3) Nothing in this act shall be held to deprive a partner of his right, if any, under the exemption laws, as regards his interest in the partnership.

Part VI Dissolution and Winding Up

Section 29. Dissolution Defined

The dissolution of a partnership is the change in the relation of the partners caused by any partner ceasing to be associated in the carrying on as distinguished from the winding up of the business.

Section 30. Partnership not Terminated by Dissolution

On dissolution the partnership is not terminated, but continues until the winding up of partnership affairs is completed.

Section 31. Causes of Dissolution

Dissolution is caused:

(1) Without violation of the agreement between the partners,

    (a) By the termination of the definite term or particular undertaking specified in the agreement,

    (b) By the express will of any partner when no definite term or particular undertaking is specified,

    (c) By the express will of all the partners who have not assigned their interests or suffered them to be charged for their separate debts, either before or after the termination of any specified term or particular undertaking,

    (d) By the expulsion of any partner from the business bona fide in accordance with such a power conferred by the agreement between the partners;

(2) In contravention of the agreement between the partners, where the circumstances do not permit a dissolution under any other provision of this section, by the express will of any partner at any time;

(3) By any event which makes it unlawful for the business of the partnership to be carried on or for the members to carry it on in partnership;

(4) By the death of any partner;

(5) By the bankruptcy of any partner or the partnership;

(6) By decree of court under section 32.

Section 32. Dissolution by Decree of Court

(1) On application by or for a partner the court shall decree a dissolution whenever:

    (a) A partner has been declared a lunatic in any judicial proceeding or is shown to be of unsound mind,

    (b) A partner becomes in any other way incapable of performing his part of the partnership contract,

    (c) A partner has been guilty of such conduct as tends to affect prejudicially the carrying on of the business,

    (d) A partner wilfully or persistently commits a breach of the partnership agreement, or otherwise so conducts himself in matters relating to the partnership business that it is not reasonably practicable to carry on the business in partnership with him,

    (e) The business of the partnership can only be carried on at a loss,

    (f) Other circumstances render a dissolution equitable.

(2) On the application of the purchaser of a partner's interest under sections 28 or 29:

    (a) After the termination of the specified term or particular undertaking,

    (b) At any time if the partnership was a partnership at will when the interest was assigned or when the charging order was issued.

Section 33. General Effect of Dissolution on Authority of Partner

Except so far as may be necessary to wind up partnership affairs or to complete transactions begun but not then finished, dissolution terminates all authority of any partner to act for the partnership,

(1) With respect to the partners,

    (a) When the dissolution is not by the act, bankruptcy or death of a partner; or

    (b) When the dissolution is by such act, bankruptcy or death of a partner, in cases where section 34 so requires.

(2) With respect to persons not partners, as declared in section 35.

Section 34. Right of Partner to Contribution from Co-partners after Dissolution

Where the dissolution is caused by the act, death or bankruptcy of a partner, each partner is liable to his co-partners for his share of any liability created by any partner acting for the partnership as if the partnership had not been dissolved unless

    (a) The dissolution being by act of any partner, the partner acting for the partnership had knowledge of the dissolution, or

    (b) The dissolution being by the death or bankruptcy of a partner, the partner acting for the partnership had knowledge or notice of the death or bankruptcy.

Section 35. Power of Partner to Bind Partnership to Third Persons after Dissolution

(1) After dissolution a partner can bind the partnership except as provided in Paragraph (3).

    (a) By any act appropriate for winding up partnership affairs or completing transactions unfinished at dissolution;

    (b) By any transaction which would bind the partnership if dissolution had not taken place, provided the other party to the transaction

        (I) Had extended credit to the partnership prior to dissolution and had no knowledge or notice of the dissolution; or

(II) Though he had not so extended credit, had nevertheless known of the partnership prior to dissolution, and, having no knowledge or notice of dissolution, the fact of dissolution had not been advertised in a newspaper of general circulation in the place (or in each place if more than one) at which the partnership business was regularly carried on.

(2) The liability of a partner under Paragraph (1b) shall be satisfied out of partnership assets alone when such partner had been prior to dissolution

(a) Unknown as a partner to the person with whom the contract is made; and

(b) So far unknown and inactive in partnership affairs that the business reputation of the partnership could not be said to have been in any degree due to his connection with it.

(3) The partnership is in no case bound by any act of a partner after dissolution

(a) Where the partnership is dissolved because it is unlawful to carry on the business, unless the act is appropriate for winding up partnership affairs; or

(b) Where the partner has become bankrupt; or

(c) Where the partner has no authority to wind up partnership affairs; except by a transaction with one who

(I) Had extended credit to the partnership prior to dissolution and had no knowledge or notice of his want of authority; or

(II) Had not extended credit to the partnership prior to dissolution, and, having no knowledge or notice of his want of authority, the fact of his want of authority has not been advertised in the manner provided for advertising the fact of dissolution in Paragraph (1b II).

(4) Nothing in this section shall affect the liability under Section 16 of any person who after dissolution represents himself or consents to another representing him as a partner in a partnership engaged in carrying on business.

Section 36. Effect of Dissolution on Partner's Existing Liability

(1) The dissolution of the partnership does not of itself discharge the existing liability of any partner.

(2) A partner is discharged from any existing liability upon dissolution of the partnership by an agreement to that effect between himself, the partnership creditor and the person or partnership continuing the business; and such agreement may be inferred from the course of dealing between the creditor having knowledge of the dissolution and the person or partnership continuing the business.

(3) Where a person agrees to assume the existing obligations of a dissolved partnership, the partners whose obligations have been assumed shall be discharged from any liability to any creditor of the partnership who, knowing of the agreement, consents to a material alteration in the nature or time of payment of such obligations.

(4) The individual property of a deceased partner shall be liable for all obligations of the partnership incurred while he was a partner but subject to the prior payment of his separate debts.

Section 37. Right to Wind Up

Unless otherwise agreed the partners who have not wrongfully dissolved the partnership or the legal representative of the last surviving partner, not bankrupt, has the right to wind up the partnership affairs; provided, however, that any partner, his legal representative or his assignee, upon cause shown, may obtain winding up by the court.

Section 38. Rights of Partners to Application of Partnership Property

(1) When dissolution is caused in any way, except in contravention of the partnership agreement, each partner, as against his co-partners and all persons claiming through them in respect of their interests in the partnership, unless otherwise agreed, may have the partnership property applied to discharge its liabilities, and the surplus applied to pay in cash the net amount owing to the respective partners. But if dissolution is caused by expulsion of a partner, bona fide under the partnership agreement and if the expelled partner is discharged from all partnership liabilities, either by payment or agreement under section 36(2), he shall receive in cash only the net amount due him from the partnership.

(2) When dissolution is caused in contravention of the partnership agreement the rights of the partners shall be as follows:

(a) Each partner who has not caused dissolution wrongfully shall have,

(I) All the rights specified in paragraph (1) of this section, and

(II) The right, as against each partner who has caused the dissolution wrongfully, to damages for breach of the agreement.

(b) The partners who have not caused the dissolution wrongfully, if they all desire to continue the business in the same name, either by themselves or jointly with others, may do so, during the agreed term for the partnership and for that purpose may possess the partnership property, provided they secure the payment by bond approved by the court, or pay to any partner who has caused the dissolution wrongfully, the value of his interest in the partnership at the dissolution, less any damages recoverable under clause (2a II) of this section, and in like manner indemnify him against all present or future partnership liabilities.

(c) A partner who has caused the dissolution wrongfully shall have:

(I) If the business is not continued under the provisions of paragraph (2b) all the rights of a partner under paragraph (1), subject to clause (2a II), of this section,

(II) If the business is continued under paragraph (2b) of this section the right as against his co-partners and all claiming through them in respect of their interests in the partnership, to have the value of his interest in the partnership, less any damages caused to his co-partners by the dissolution, ascertained and paid to him in cash, or the payment secured by bond approved by the court, and to be released from all existing liabilities of the partnership; but in ascertaining the value of the partner's interest the value of the good-will of the business shall not be considered.

Section 39. Rights Where Partnership is Dissolved for Fraud or Misrepresentation

Where a partnership contract is rescinded on the ground of the fraud or misrepresentation of one of the parties thereto, the party entitled to rescind is, without prejudice to any other right, entitled,

(a) To a lien on, or a right of retention of, the surplus of the partnership property after satisfying the partnership liabilities to third persons for any sum of money paid by him for the purchase of an interest in the partnership and for any capital or advances contributed by him; and

(b) To stand, after all liabilities to third persons have been satisfied, in the place of the creditors of the partnership for any payments made by him in respect of the partnership liabilities; and

(c) To be indemnified by the person guilty of the fraud or making the representation against all debts and liabilities of the partnership.

Section 40. Rules for Distribution

In settling accounts between the partners after dissolution, the following rules shall be observed, subject to any agreement to the contrary:

(a) The assets of the partnership are:
   (I) The partnership property,
   (II) The contributions of the partners necessary for the payment of all the liabilities specified in clause (b) of this paragraph.

(b) The liabilities of the partnership shall rank in order of payment, as follows:
   (I) Those owing to creditors other than partners,
   (II) Those owing to partners other than for capital and profits,
   (III) Those owing to partners in respect of capital,
   (IV) Those owing to partners in respect of profits.

(c) The assets shall be applied in the order of their declaration in clause (a) of this paragraph to the satisfaction of the liabilities.

(d) The partners shall contribute, as provided by section 18 (a) the amount necessary to satisfy the liabilities; but if any, but not all, of the partners are insolvent, or, not being subject to process, refuse to contribute, the other partners shall contribute their share of the liabilities, and, in the relative proportions in which they share the profits, the additional amount necessary to pay the liabilities.

(e) An assignee for the benefit of creditors or any person appointed by the court shall have the right to enforce the contributions specified in clause (d) of this paragraph.

(f) Any partner or his legal representative shall have the right to enforce the contributions specified in clause (d) of this paragraph, to the extent of the amount which he has paid in excess of his share of the liability.

(g) The individual property of a deceased partner shall be liable for the contributions specified in clause (d) of this paragraph.

(h) When partnership property and the individual properties of the partners are in possession of a court for distribution, partnership creditors shall have priority on partnership property and separate creditors on individual property, saving the rights of lien or secured creditors as heretofore.

(i) Where a partner has become bankrupt or his estate is insolvent the claims against his separate property shall rank in the following order:
   (I) Those owing to separate creditors,
   (II) Those owing to partnership creditors,
   (III) Those owing to partners by way of contribution.

Section 41. Liability of Persons Continuing the Business in Certain Cases

(1) When any new partner is admitted into an existing partnership, or when any partner retires and assigns (or the representative of the deceased partner assigns) his rights in partnership property to two or more of the partners, or to one or more of the partners and one or more third persons, if the business is continued without liquidation of the partnership affairs, creditors of the first or dissolved partnership are also creditors of the partnership so continuing the business.

(2) When all but one partner retire and assign (or the representative of a deceased partner assigns) their rights in partnership property to the remaining partner, who continues the business without liquidation of partnership affairs, either alone or with others, creditors of the dissolved partnership are also creditors of the person or partnership so continuing the business.

(3) When any partner retires or dies and the business of the dissolved partnership is continued as set forth in paragraphs (1) and (2) of this section, with the consent of the retired partners or the representative of the deceased partner, but without any assignment of his right in partnership property, rights of creditors of the dissolved partnership and of the creditors of the person or partnership continuing the business shall be as if such assignment had been made.

(4) When all the partners or their representatives assign their rights in partnership property to one or more third persons who promise to pay the debts and who continue the business of the dissolved partnership, creditors of the dissolved partnership are also creditors of the person or partnership continuing the business.

(5) When any partner wrongfully causes a dissolution and the remaining partners continue the business under the provisions of section 38(2b), either alone or with others, and without liquidation of the partnership affairs, creditors of the dissolved partnership are also creditors of the person or partnership continuing the business.

(6) When a partner is expelled and the remaining partners continue the business either alone or with others, without liquidation of the partnership affairs, creditors of the dissolved partnership are also creditors of the person or partnership continuing the business.

(7) The liability of a third person becoming a partner in the partnership continuing the business, under this section, to the creditors of the dissolved partnership shall be satisfied out of partnership property only.

(8) When the business of a partnership after dissolution is continued under any conditions set forth in this section the creditors of the dissolved partnership, as against the separate creditors of the retiring or deceased partner or the representative of the deceased partner, have a prior right to any claim of the retired partner or the representative of the deceased partner against the person or partnership continuing the business, on account of the retired or deceased partner's interest in the dissolved partnership or on account of any consideration promised for such interest or for his right in partnership property.

(9) Nothing in this section shall be held to modify any right of creditors to set aside any assignment on the ground of fraud.

(10) The use by the person or partnership continuing the business of the partnership name, or the name of a deceased partner as part thereof, shall not of itself make the individual property of the deceased partner liable for any debts contracted by such person or partnership.

Section 42. Rights of Retiring or Estate of Deceased Partner When the Business is Continued

When any partner retires or dies, and the business is continued under any of the conditions set forth in section 41(1, 2, 3, 5, 6), or section 38(2b) without any settlement of accounts as between him or his estate and the person or partnership continuing the business, unless otherwise agreed, he or his legal representative as against such persons or partnership may have the value of his interest at the date of dissolution ascertained, and shall receive as an ordinary creditor an amount equal to the value of his interest in the dissolved partnership with interest, or, at his option or at the option of his legal representative, in lieu of interest, the profits attributable to the use of his right in the property of the dissolved partnership; provided that the creditors of the dissolved partnership as against the separate creditors, or the representative of the retired or deceased partner, shall have priority on any claim arising under this section, as provided by section 41(8) of this act.

Section 43. Accrual of Actions
The right to an account of his interest shall accrue to any partner, or his legal representative, as against the winding up partners or the surviving partners or the person or partnership continuing the business, at the date of dissolution, in the absence of any agreement to the contrary.

Part VII Miscellaneous Provisions

Section 44. When Act Takes Effect
This act shall take effect on the .... day of .... one thousand nine hundred and ....

Section 45. Legislation Repealed
All acts or parts of acts inconsistent with this act are hereby repealed.

Appendix C
Uniform Limited Partnership Act (1916)

Section 1. Limited partnership defined
A limited partnership is a partnership formed by two or more persons under the provisions of section 2, having as members one or more general partners and one or more limited partners. The limited partners as such shall not be bound by the obligations of the partnership.

Section 2. Formation
(1) Two or more persons desiring to form a limited partnership shall
  (a) Sign and swear to a certificate, which shall state
    I. The name of the partnership,
    II. The character of the business,
    III. The location of the principal place of business,
    IV. The name and place of residence of each member; general and limited partners being respectively designated,
    V. The term for which the partnership is to exist,
    VI. The amount of cash and a description of and the agreed value of the other property contributed by each limited partner,
    VII. The additional contributions, if any, agreed to be made by each limited partner and the times at which or events on the happening of which they shall be made,
    VIII. The time, if agreed upon, when the contribution of each limited partner is to be returned,
    IX. The share of the profits or the other compensation by way of income which each limited partner shall receive by reason of his contribution,
    X. The right, if given, of a limited partner to substitute an assignee as contributor in his place, and the terms and conditions of the substitution,
    XI. The right, if given, of the partners to admit additional limited partners,
    XII. The right, if given, of one or more of the limited partners to priority over other limited partners, as to contributions or as to compensation by way of income, and the nature of such priority,
    XIII. The right, if given, of the remaining general partner or partners to continue the business on the death, retirement or insanity of a general partner, and
    XIV. The right, if given, of a limited partner to demand and receive property other than cash in return for his contribution.
  (b) File for record the certificate in the office of [here designate the proper office].
(2) A limited partnership is formed if there has been substantial compliance in good faith with the requirements of paragraph (1).

Section 3. Business which may be carried on
A limited partnership may carry on any business which a partnership without limited partners may carry on, except [here designate the business to be prohibited].

Section 4. Character of limited partner's contribution
The contributions of a limited partner may be cash or other property, but not services.

Section 5. A name not to contain surname of limited partner; exceptions
(1) The surname of a limited partner shall not appear in the partnership name, unless
  (a) It is also the surname of a general partner, or
  (b) Prior to the time when the limited partner became such the business had been carried on under a name in which his surname appeared.
(2) A limited partner whose name appears in a partnership name contrary to the provisions of paragraph (1) is liable as a general partner to partnership creditors who extend credit to the partnership without actual knowledge that he is not a general partner.

Section 6. Liability for false statements in certificate
If the certificate contains a false statement, one who suffers loss by reliance on such statement may hold liable any party to the certificate who knew the statement to be false
  (a) At the time he signed the certificate, or
  (b) Subsequently, but within a sufficient time before the statement was relied upon to enable him to cancel or amend the certificate, or to file a petition for its cancellation or amendment as provided in section 25 (3).

Section 7. Limited partner not liable to creditors
A limited partner shall not become liable as a general partner unless, in addition to the exercise of his rights and powers as a limited partner, he takes part in the control of the business.

Section 8. Admission of additional limited partners
After the formation of a limited partnership, additional limited partners may be admitted upon filing an amendment to the original certificate in accordance with the requirements of section 25.

Section 9. Rights, powers and liabilities of a general partner
(1) A general partner shall have all the rights and powers and be subject to all the restrictions and liabilities of a partner in a partnership without limited partners, except that without the written consent or ratification of the specific act by all the limited partners, a general partner or all of the general partners have no authority to
  (a) Do any act in contravention of the certificate,
  (b) Do any act which would make it impossible to carry on the ordinary business of the partnership,

(c) Confess a judgment against the partnership,

(d) Possess partnership property, or assign their rights in specific partnership property, for other than a partnership purpose,

(e) Admit a person as a general partner,

(f) Admit a person as a limited partner, unless the right so to do is given in the certificate,

(g) Continue the business with partnership property on the death, retirement or insanity of a general partner, unless the right so to do is given in the certificate.

Section 10. Rights of a limited partner

(1) A limited partner shall have the same rights as a general partner to

(a) Have the partnership books kept at the principal place of business of the partnership, and at all times to inspect and copy any of them.

(b) Have on demand true and full information of all things affecting the partnership, and a formal account of partnership affairs whenever circumstances render it just and reasonable, and

(c) Have dissolution and winding up by decree of court.

(2) A limited partner shall have the right to receive a share of the profits or other compensation by way of income, and to the return of his contribution as provided in sections 15 and 16.

Section 11. Status of person erroneously believing himself a limited partner

A person who has contributed to the capital of a business conducted by a person or partnership erroneously believing that he has become a limited partner in a limited partnership, is not, by reason of his exercise of the rights of a limited partner, a general partner with the person or in the partnership carrying on the business, or bound by the obligations of such person or partnership; provided that on ascertaining the mistake he promptly renounces his interest in the profits of the business, or other compensation by way of income.

Section 12. One person both general and limited partner

(1) A person may be a general partner and a limited partner in the same partnership at the same time.

(2) A person who is a general, and also at the same time a limited partner, shall have all the rights and powers and be subject to all the restrictions of a general partner; except that, in respect to his contribution, he shall have the rights against the other members which he would have had if he were not also a general partner.

Section 13. Loans and other business transactions with limited partner

(1) A limited partner also may loan money to and transact other business with the partnership, and, unless he is also a general partner, receive on account of resulting claims against the partnership, with general creditors, a pro rata share of the assets. No limited partner shall in respect to any such claim

(a) Receive or hold as collateral security any partnership property, or

(b) Receive from a general partner or the partnership any payment, conveyance, or release from liability, if at the time the assets of the partnership are not sufficient to discharge partnership liabilities to persons not claiming as general or limited partners.

(2) The receiving of collateral security, or a payment, conveyance, or release in violation of the provisions of paragraph (1) is a fraud on the creditors of the partnership.

Section 14. Relation of limited partners inter se

Where there are several limited partners the members may agree that one or more of the limited partners shall have a priority over other limited partners as to the return of their contributions, as to their compensation by way of income, or as to any other matter. If such an agreement is made it shall be stated in the certificate, and in the absence of such a statement all the limited partners shall stand upon equal footing.

Section 15. Compensation of limited partner

A limited partner may receive from the partnership the share of the profits or the compensation by way of income stipulated for in the certificate; provided, that after such payment is made, whether from the property of the partnership or that of a general partner, the partnership assets are in excess of all liabilities of the partnership except liabilities to limited partners on account of their contributions and to general partners.

Section 16. Withdrawal or reduction of limited partner's contribution

(1) A limited partner shall not receive from a general partner or out of partnership property any part of his contribution until

(a) All liabilities of the partnership, except liabilities to general partners and to limited partners on account of their contributions, have been paid or there remains property of the partnership sufficient to pay them,

(b) The consent of all members is had, unless the return of the contribution may be rightfully demanded under the provisions of paragraph (2), and

(c) The certificate is cancelled or so amended as to set forth the withdrawal or reduction.

(2) Subject to the provisions of paragraph (1) a limited partner may rightfully demand the return of his contribution

(a) On the dissolution of a partnership, or

(b) When the date specified in the certificate for its return has arrived, or

(c) After he has given six months' notice in writing to all other members, if no time is specified in the certificate either for the return of the contribution or for the dissolution of the partnership.

(3) In the absence of any statement in the certificate to the contrary or the consent of all members, a limited partner, irrespective of the nature of his contribution, has only the right to demand and receive cash in return for his contribution.

(4) A limited partner may have the partnership dissolved and its affairs wound up when

(a) He rightfully but unsuccessfully demands the return of his contribution, or

(b) The other liabilities of the partnership have not been paid, or the partnership property is insufficient for their payment as required by paragraph (1a) and the limited partner would otherwise be entitled to the return of his contribution.

Section 17. Liability of limited partner to partnership

A limited partner is liable to the partnership

(a) For the difference between his contribution as actually made and that stated in the certificate as having been made, and

(b) For any unpaid contribution which he agreed in the certificate to make in the future at the time and on the conditions stated in the certificate.

(2) A limited partner holds as trustee for the partnership
   (a) Specific property stated in the certificate as contributed by him, but which was not contributed or which has been wrongfully returned, and
   (b) Money or other property wrongfully paid or conveyed to him on account of his contribution.

(3) The liabilities of a limited partner as set forth in this section can be waived or compromised only by the consent of all members; but a waiver or compromise shall not affect the right of a creditor of a partnership who extended credit or whose claim arose after the filing and before a cancellation or amendment of the certificate, to enforce such liabilities.

(4) When a contributor has rightfully received the return in whole or in part of the capital of his contribution, he is nevertheless liable to the partnership for any sum, not in excess of such return with interest, necessary to discharge its liabilities to all creditors who extended credit or whose claims arose before such return.

Section 18. Nature of limited partner's interest in partnership
A limited partner's interest in the partnership is personal property.

Section 19. Assignment of limited partner's interest
(1) A limited partner's interest is assignable.

(2) A substituted limited partner is a person admitted to all the rights of a limited partner who has died or has assigned his interest in a partnership.

(3) An assignee, who does not become a substituted limited partner, has no right to require any information or account of the partnership transactions or to inspect the partnership books; he is only entitled to receive the share of the profits or other compensation by way of income, or the return of his contribution, to which his assignor would otherwise be entitled.

(4) An assignee shall have the right to become a substituted limited partner if all the members (except the assignor) consent thereto or if the assignor, being thereunto empowered by the certificate, gives the assignee that right.

(5) An assignee becomes a substituted limited partner when the certificate is appropriately amended in accordance with section 25.

(6) The substituted limited partner has all the rights and powers, and is subject to all the restrictions and liabilities of his assignor, except those liabilities of which he was ignorant at the time he became a limited partner and which could not be ascertained from the certificate.

(7) The substitution of the assignee as a limited partner does not release the assignor from liability to the partnership under sections 6 and 17.

Section 20. Effect of retirement, death or insanity of a general partner
The retirement, death or insanity of a general partner dissolves the partnership, unless the business is continued by the remaining general partners
   (a) Under a right so to do stated in the certificate, or
   (b) With the consent of all members.

Section 21. Death of limited partner
(1) On the death of a limited partner his executor or administrator shall have all the rights of a limited partner for the purpose of settling his estate and such power as the deceased had to constitute his assignee a substituted limited partner.

(2) The estate of a deceased limited partner shall be liable for all his liabilities as a limited partner.

Section 22. Rights of creditors of limited partner
(1) On due application to a court of competent jurisdiction by any judgment creditor of a limited partner, the court may charge the interest of the indebted limited partner with payment of the unsatisfied amount of the judgment debt; and may appoint a receiver, and make all other orders, directions, and inquiries which the circumstances of the case may require.

(Commissioners' Note: In those states where a creditor on beginning an action can attach debts due the defendant before he has obtained a judgment against the defendant it is recommended that paragraph (1) of this section read as follows:

"On due application to a court of competent jurisdiction by any creditor of a limited partner, the court may charge the interest of the indebted limited partner with payment of the unsatisfied amount of such claim; and may appoint a receiver, and make all other orders, directions, and inquiries which the circumstances of the case may require.")

(2) The interest may be redeemed with the separate property of any general partner, but may not be redeemed with partnership property.

(3) The remedies conferred by paragraph (1) shall not be deemed exclusive of others which may exist.

(4) Nothing in this act shall be held to deprive a limited partner of his statutory exemption.

Section 23. Distribution of assets
(1) In settling accounts after dissolution the liabilities of the partnership shall be entitled to payment in the following order:
   (a) Those to creditors, in the order of priority as provided by law, except those to limited partners on account of their contributions, and to general partners,
   (b) Those to limited partners in respect to their share of the profits and other compensation by way of income on their contributions,
   (c) Those to limited partners in respect to the capital of their contributions,
   (d) Those to general partners other than for capital and profits,
   (e) Those to general partners in respect to profits,
   (f) Those to general partners in respect to capital.

(2) Subject to any statement in the certificate or to subsequent agreement, limited partners share in the partnership assets in respect to their claims for capital, and in respect to their claims for profits or for compensation by way of income on their contributions respectively, in proportion to the respective amounts of such claims.

Section 24. When certificate shall be cancelled or amended
(1) The certificate shall be cancelled when the partnership is dissolved or all limited partners cease to be such.

(2) A certificate shall be amended when
   (a) There is a change in the name of the partnership or in the amount or character of the contribution of any limited partner,
   (b) A person is substituted as a limited partner,
   (c) An additional limited partner is admitted,
   (d) A person is admitted as a general partner,
   (e) A general partner retires, dies or becomes insane, and the business is continued under section 20,
   (f) There is a change in the character of the business of the partnership,
   (g) There is a false or erroneous statement in the certificate,

(h) There is a change in the time as stated in the certificate for the dissolution of the partnership or for the return of a contribution,

(i) A time is fixed for the dissolution of the partnership, or the return of a contribution, no time having been specified in the certificate, or

(j) The members desire to make a change in any other statement in the certificate in order that it shall accurately represent the agreement between them.

Section 25. Requirements for amendment and for cancellation of certificate

(1) The writing to amend a certificate shall

(a) Conform to the requirements of section 2 (1a) as far as necessary to set forth clearly the change in the certificate which it is desired to make, and

(b) Be signed and sworn to by all members, and an amendment substituting a limited partner or adding a limited or general partner shall be signed also by the member to be substituted or added, and when a limited partner is to be substituted, the amendment shall also be signed by the assigning limited partner.

(2) The writing to cancel a certificate shall be signed by all members.

(3) A person desiring the cancellation or amendment of a certificate, if any person designated in paragraphs (1) and (2) as a person who must execute the writing refuses to do so, may petition the [here designate the proper court] to direct a cancellation or amendment thereof.

(4) If the court finds that the petitioner has a right to have the writing executed by a person who refuses to do so, it shall order the [here designate the responsible official in the office designated in section 2] in the office where the certificate is recorded to record the cancellation or amendment of the certificate; and where the certificate is to be amended, the court shall also cause to be filed for record in said office a certified copy of its decree setting forth the amendment.

(5) A certificate is amended or cancelled when there is filed for record in the office [here designate the office designated in section 2] where the certificate is recorded

(a) A writing in accordance with the provisions of paragraph (1), or (2) or

(b) A certified copy of the order of court in accordance with the provisions of paragraph (4).

(6) After the certificate is duly amended in accordance with this section, the amended certificate shall thereafter be for all purposes the certificate provided for by this act.

Section 26. Parties to actions

A contributor, unless he is a general partner, is not a proper party to proceedings by or against a partnership, except where the object is to enforce a limited partner's right against or liability to the partnership.

Section 27. Name of act

This act may be cited as The Uniform Limited Partnership Act.

Section 28. Rules of construction

(1) The rule that statutes in derogation of the common law are to be strictly construed shall have no application to this act.

(2) This act shall be so interpreted and construed as to effect its general purpose to make uniform the law of those states which enact it.

(3) This act shall not be so construed as to impair the obligations of any contract existing when the act goes into effect, nor to affect any action or proceedings begun or right accrued before this act takes effect.

Section 29. Rules for cases not provided for in this act

In any case not provided for in this act the rules of law and equity, including the law merchant, shall govern.

Section 30. Provisions for existing limited partnerships

(1) A limited partnership formed under any statute of this state prior to the adoption of this act, may become a limited partnership under this act by complying with the provisions of section 2; provided the certificate sets forth

(a) The amount of the original contribution of each limited partner, and the time when the contribution was made, and

(b) That the property of the partnership exceeds the amount sufficient to discharge its liabilities to persons not claiming as general or limited partners by an amount greater than the sum of the contributions of its limited partners.

(2) A limited partnership formed under any statute of this state prior to the adoption of this act, until or unless it becomes a limited partnership under this act, shall continue to be governed by the provisions of [here insert proper reference to the existing limited partnership act or acts], except that such partnership shall not be renewed unless so provided in the original agreement.

(Commissioners' Note: Sections 30, 31, will be omitted in any state which has not a limited partnership act.)

Section 31. Act (acts) repealed

Except as affecting existing limited partnerships to the extent set forth in section 30, the act (acts) of [here designate the existing limited partnership act or acts] is (are) hereby repealed.

(Commissioners' Note: Sections 30, 31, will be omitted in any state which has not a limited partnership act.)

Appendix D
(Revised) Uniform Limited Partnership Act (1976)

Article 1 General Provisions

Section 101. [Definitions]
As used in this Act, unless the context otherwise requires:

(1) "Certificate of limited partnership" means the certificate referred to in Section 201, and the certificate as amended.

(2) "Contribution" means any cash, property, services rendered, or a promissory note or other binding obligation to contribute cash or property or to perform services, which a partner contributes to a limited partnership in his capacity as a partner.

(3) "Event of withdrawal of a general partner" means an event that causes a person to cease to be a general partner as provided in Section 402.

(4) "Foreign limited partnership" means a partnership formed under the laws of any State other than this State and having as partners one or more general partners and one or more limited partners.

(5) "General partner" means a person who has been admitted to a limited partnership as a general partner in accordance with the partnership agreement and named in the certificate of limited partnership as a general partner.

(6) "Limited partner" means a person who has been admitted to a limited partnership as a limited partner in accordance with the partnership agreement and named in the certificate of limited partnership as a limited partner.

(7) "Limited partnership" and "domestic limited partnership" mean a partnership formed by 2 or more persons under the laws of this State and having one or more general partners and one or more limited partners.

(8) "Partner" means a limited or general partner.

(9) "Partnership agreement" means any valid agreement, written or oral, of the partners as to the affairs of a limited partnership and the conduct of its business.

(10) "Partnership interest" means a partner's share of the profits and losses of a limited partnership and the right to receive distributions of partnership assets.

(11) "Person" means a natural person, partnership, limited partnership (domestic or foreign), trust, estate, association, or corporation.

(12) "State" means a state, territory, or possession of the United States, the District of Columbia, or the Commonwealth of Puerto Rico.

Section 102. [Name]
The name of each limited partnership as set forth in its certificate of limited partnership:

(1) shall contain without abbreviation the words "limited partnership";

(2) may not contain the name of a limited partner unless (i) it is also the name of a general partner or the corporate name of a corporate general partner, or (ii) the business of the limited partnership had been carried on under that name before the admission of that limited partner;

(3) may not contain any word or phrase indicating or implying that it is organized other than for a purpose stated in its certificate of limited partnership;

(4) may not be the same as, or deceptively similar to, the name of any corporation or limited partnership organized under the laws of this State or licensed or registered as a foreign corporation or limited partnership in this State; and

(5) may not contain the following words [here insert prohibited words].

Section 103. [Reservation of Name]
(a) The exclusive right to the use of a name may be reserved by:

(1) any person intending to organize a limited partnership under this Act and to adopt that name;

(2) any domestic limited partnership or any foreign limited partnership registered in this State which, in either case, intends to adopt that name;

(3) any foreign limited partnership intending to register in this State and adopt that name; and

(4) any person intending to organize a foreign limited partnership and intending to have it register in this State and adopt that name.

(b) The reservation shall be made by filing with the Secretary of State an application, executed by the applicant, to reserve a specified name. If the Secretary of State finds that the name is available for use by a domestic or foreign limited partnership, he shall reserve the name for the exclusive use of the applicant for a period of 120 days. Once having so reserved a name, the same applicant may not again reserve the same name until more than 60 days after the expiration of the last 120-day period for which that applicant reserved that name. The right to the exclusive use of a reserved name may be transferred to any other person by filing in the office of the Secretary of State a notice of the transfer, executed by the applicant for whom the name was reserved and specifying the name and address of the transferee.

Section 104. [Specified Office and Agent]
Each limited partnership shall continuously maintain in this State:

(1) an office, which may but need not be a place of its business in this State, at which shall be kept the records required by Section 105 to be maintained; and

(2) an agent for service of process on the limited partnership, which agent must be an individual resident of this State, a domestic corporation, or a foreign corporation authorized to do business in this State.

Section 105. [Records to be Kept]
Each limited partnership shall keep at the office referred to in Section 104(1) the following: (1) a current list of the full name and last known business address of each partner set forth in alphabetical order, (2) a copy of the certificate of limited partnership and all certificates of amendment thereto, together with executed copies of any powers of attorney pursuant to which any certificate has been executed, (3) copies of the limited partnership's federal, state and

local income tax returns and reports, if any, for the 3 most recent years, and (4) copies of any then effective written partnership agreements and of any financial statements of the limited partnership for the 3 most recent years. Those records are subject to inspection and copying at the reasonable request, and at the expense, of any partner during ordinary business hours.

Section 106. [Nature of Business]
A limited partnership may carry on any business that a partnership without limited partners may carry on except [here designate prohibited activities].

Section 107. [Business Transactions of Partner with Partnership]
Except as provided in the partnership agreement, a partner may lend money to and transact other business with the limited partnership and, subject to other applicable law, has the same rights and obligations with respect thereto as a person who is not a partner.

Article 2 Formation: Certificate of Limited Partnership

Section 201. [Certificate of Limited Partnership]
(a) In order to form a limited partnership two or more persons must execute a certificate of limited partnership. The certificate shall be filed in the office of the Secretary of State and set forth:

(1) the name of the limited partnership;

(2) the general character of its business;

(3) the address of the office and the name and address of the agent for service of process required to be maintained by Section 104;

(4) the name and the business address of each partner (specifying separately the general partners and limited partners);

(5) the amount of cash and a description and statement of the agreed value of the other property or services contributed by each partner and which each partner has agreed to contribute in the future;

(6) the times at which or events on the happening of which any additional contributions agreed to be made by each partner are to be made;

(7) any power of a limited partner to grant the right to become a limited partner to an assignee of any part of his partnership interest, and the terms and conditions of the power;

(8) if agreed upon, the time at which or the events on the happening of which a partner may terminate his membership in the limited partnership and the amount of, or the method of determining, the distribution to which he may be entitled respecting his partnership interest, and the terms and conditions of the termination and distribution;

(9) any right of a partner to receive distributions of property, including cash from the limited partnership;

(10) any right of a partner to receive, or of a general partner to make, distributions to a partner which include a return of all or any part of the partner's contribution;

(11) any time at which or events upon the happening of which the limited partnership is to be dissolved and its affairs wound up;

(12) any right of the remaining general partners to continue the business on the happening of an event of withdrawal of a general partner; and

(13) any other matters the partners determine to include therein.

(b) A limited partnership is formed at the time of the filing of the certificate of limited partnership in the office of the Secretary of State or at any later time specified in the certificate of limited partnership if, in either case, there has been substantial compliance with the requirements of this section.

Section 202. [Amendment to Certificate]
(a) A certificate of limited partnership is amended by filing a certificate of amendment thereto in the office of the Secretary of State. The certificate shall set forth:

(1) the name of the limited partnership;

(2) the date of filing the certificate; and

(3) the amendment to the certificate.

(b) Within 30 days after the happening of any of the following events, an amendment to a certificate of limited partnership reflecting the occurrence of the event or events shall be filed:

(1) a change in the amount or character of the contribution of any partner, or in any partner's obligation to make a contribution;

(2) the admission of a new partner;

(3) the withdrawal of a partner; or

(4) the continuation of the business under Section 801 after an event of withdrawal of a general partner.

(c) A general partner who becomes aware that any statement in a certificate of limited partnership was false when made or that any arrangements or other facts described have changed, making the certificate inaccurate in any respect, shall promptly amend the certificate, but an amendment to show a change of address of a limited partner need be filed only once every 12 months.

(d) A certificate of limited partnership may be amended at any time for any other proper purpose the general partners determine.

(e) No person has any liability because an amendment to a certificate of limited partnership has not been filed to reflect the occurrence of any event referred to in subsection (b) of this Section if the amendment is filed within the 30-day period specified in subsection (b).

Section 203. [Cancellation of Certificate]
A certificate of limited partnership shall be cancelled upon the dissolution and the commencement of winding up of the partnership or at any other time there are no limited partners. A certificate of cancellation shall be filed in the office of the Secretary of State and set forth:

(1) the name of the limited partnership;

(2) the date of filing of its certificate of limited partnership;

(3) the reason for filing the certificate of cancellation;

(4) the effective date (which shall be a date certain) of cancellation if it is not to be effective upon the filing of the certificate; and

(5) any other information the general partners filing the certificate determine.

Section 204. [Execution of Certificates]
(a) Each certificate required by this Article to be filed in the office of the Secretary of State shall be executed in the following manner:

(1) an original certificate of limited partnership must be signed by all partners named therein;

(2) a certificate of amendment must be signed by at least one general partner and by each other partner designated in the certificate as a new partner or whose contribution is described as having been increased; and

(3) a certificate of cancellation must be signed by all general partners.

(b) Any person may sign a certificate by an attorney-in-fact, but a power of attorney to sign a certificate relating to the admission, or increased contribution, of a partner must specifically describe the admission or increase.

(c) The execution of a certificate by a general partner constitutes an affirmation under the penalties of perjury that the facts stated therein are true.

Section 205. [Amendment or Cancellation by Judicial Act]

If a person required by Section 204 to execute a certificate of amendment or cancellation fails or refuses to do so, any other partner, and any assignee of a partnership interest, who is adversely affected by the failure or refusal, may petition the [here designate the proper court] to direct the amendment or cancellation. If the court finds that the amendment or cancellation is proper and that any person so designated has failed or refused to execute the certificate, it shall order the Secretary of State to record an appropriate certificate of amendment or cancellation.

Section 206. [Filing in Office of Secretary of State]

(a) Two signed copies of the certificate of limited partnership and of any certificates of amendment or cancellation (or of any judicial decree of amendment or cancellation) shall be delivered to the Secretary of State. A person who executes a certificate as an agent or fiduciary need not exhibit evidence of his authority as a prerequisite to filing. Unless the Secretary of State finds that any certificate does not conform to law, upon receipt of all filing fees required by law he shall:

(1) endorse on each duplicate original the word "Filed" and the day, month and year of the filing thereof;

(2) file one duplicate original in his office; and

(3) return the other duplicate original to the person who filed it or his representative.

(b) Upon the filing of a certificate of amendment (or judicial decree of amendment) in the office of the Secretary of State, the certificate of limited partnership shall be amended as set forth therein, and upon the effective date of a certificate of cancellation (or a judicial decree thereof), the certificate of limited partnership is cancelled.

Section 207. [Liability for False Statement in Certificate]

If any certificate of limited partnership or certificate of amendment or cancellation contains a false statement, one who suffers loss by reliance on the statement may recover damages for the loss from:

(1) any person who executes the certificate, or causes another to execute it on his behalf, and knew, and any general partner who knew or should have known, the statement to be false at the time the certificate was executed; and

(2) any general partner who thereafter knows or should have known that any arrangement or other fact described in the certificate has changed, making the statement inaccurate in any respect within a sufficient time before the statement was relied upon reasonably to have enabled that general partner to cancel or amend the certificate, or to file a petition for its cancellation or amendment under Section 205.

Section 208. [Notice]

The fact that a certificate of limited partnership is on file in the office of the Secretary of State is notice that the partnership is a limited partnership and the persons designated therein as limited partners are limited partners, but it is not notice of any other fact.

Section 209. [Delivery of Certificates to Limited Partners]

Upon the return by the Secretary of State pursuant to Section 206 of a certificate marked "Filed", the general partners shall promptly deliver or mail a copy of the certificate of limited partnership and each certificate to each limited partner unless the partnership agreement provides otherwise.

Article 3 Limited Partners

Section 301. [Admission of Additional Limited Partners]

(a) After the filing of a limited partnership's original certificate of limited partnership, a person may be admitted as an additional limited partner:

(1) in the case of a person acquiring a partnership interest directly from the limited partnership, upon the compliance with the partnership agreement or, if the partnership agreement does not so provide, upon the written consent of all partners; and

(2) in the case of an assignee of a partnership interest of a partner who has the power, as provided in Section 704, to grant the assignee the right to become a limited partner, upon the exercise of that power and compliance with any conditions limiting the grant or exercise of the power.

(b) In each case under subsection (a), the person acquiring the partnership interest becomes a limited partner only upon amendment of the certificate of limited partnership reflecting that fact.

Section 302. [Voting]

Subject to Section 303, the partnership agreement may grant to all or a specified group of the limited partners the right to vote (on a per capita or other basis) upon any matter.

Section 303. [Liability to Third Parties]

(a) Except as provided in subsection (d), a limited partner is not liable for the obligations of a limited partnership unless he is also a general partner or, in addition to the exercise of his rights and powers as a limited partner, he takes part in the control of the business. However, if the limited partner's participation in the control of the business is not substantially the same as the exercise of the powers of a general partner, he is liable only to persons who transact business with the limited partnership with actual knowledge of his participation in control.

(b) A limited partner does not participate in the control of the business within the meaning of subsection (a) solely by doing one or more of the following:

(1) being a contractor for or an agent or employee of the limited partnership or of a general partner;

(2) consulting with and advising a general partner with respect to the business of the limited partnership;

(3) acting as surety for the limited partnership;

(4) approving or disapproving an amendment to the partnership agreement; or

(5) voting on one or more of the following matters:

(i) the dissolution and winding up of the limited partnership;

(ii) the sale, exchange, lease, mortgage, pledge, or other transfer of all or substantially all of the assets of the limited partnership other than in the ordinary course of its business;

(iii) the incurrence of indebtedness by the limited partnership other than in the ordinary course of its business;

(iv) a change in the nature of the business; or

(v) the removal of a general partner.

(c) The enumeration in subsection (b) does not mean that the possession or exercise of any other powers by a limited partner constitutes participation by him in the business of the limited partnership.

(d) A limited partner who knowingly permits his name to be used in the name of the limited partnership, except under circumstances permitted by Section 102(2)(i), is liable to creditors who extend credit to the limited partnership without actual knowledge that the limited partner is not a general partner.

Section 304. [Person Erroneously Believing Himself Limited Partner]

(a) Except as provided in subsection (b), a person who makes a contribution to a business enterprise and erroneously but in good faith believes that he has become a limited partner in the enterprise is not a general partner in the enterprise and is not bound by its obligations by reason of making the contribution, receiving distributions from the enterprise, or exercising any rights of a limited partner, if, on ascertaining the mistake, he:

(1) causes an appropriate certificate of limited partnership or a certificate of amendment to be executed and filed; or

(2) withdraws from future equity participation in the enterprise.

(b) A person who makes a contribution of the kind described in subsection (a) is liable as a general partner to any third party who transacts business with the enterprise (i) before the person withdraws and an appropriate certificate is filed to show withdrawal, or (ii) before an appropriate certificate is filed to show his status as a limited partner and, in the case of an amendment, after expiration of the 30-day period for filing an amendment relating to the person as a limited partner under Section 202, but in either case only if the third party actually believed in good faith that the person was a general partner at the time of the transaction.

Section 305. [Information]

Each limited partner has the right to:

(1) inspect and copy any of the partnership records required to be maintained by Section 105; and

(2) obtain from the general partners from time to time upon reasonable demand (i) true and full information regarding the state of the business and financial condition of the limited partnership, (ii) promptly after becoming available, a copy of the limited partnership's federal, state and local income tax returns for each year, and (iii) other information regarding the affairs of the limited partnership as is just and reasonable.

Article 4 General Partners

Section 401. [Admission of Additional General Partners]

After the filing of a limited partnership's original certificate of limited partnership, additional general partners may be admitted only with the specific written consent of each partner.

Section 402. [Events of Withdrawal]

Except as approved by the specific written consent of all partners at the time, a person ceases to be a general partner of a limited partnership upon the happening of any of the following events:

(1) the general partner withdraws from the limited partnership as provided in Section 602;

(2) the general partner ceases to be a member of the limited partnership as provided in Section 702;

(3) the general partner is removed as a general partner in accordance with the partnership agreement;

(4) unless otherwise provided in the certificate of limited partnership, the general partner: (i) makes an assignment for the benefit of creditors; (ii) files a voluntary petition in bankruptcy; (iii) is adjudicated a bankrupt or insolvent; (iv) files a petition or answer seeking for himself any reorganization, arrangement, composition, readjustment, liquidation, dissolution or similar relief under any statute, law, or regulation; (v) files an answer or other pleading admitting or failing to contest the material allegations of a petition filed against him in any proceeding of this nature; or (vi) seeks, consents to, or acquiesces in the appointment of a trustee, receiver, or liquidator of the general partner or of all or any substantial part of his properties;

(5) unless otherwise provided in the certificate of limited partnership, [120] days after the commencement of any proceeding against the general partner seeking reorganization, arrangement, composition, readjustment, liquidation, dissolution or similar relief under any statute, law, or regulation, the proceeding has not been dismissed, or if within [90] days after the appointment without his consent or acquiescence of a trustee, receiver, or liquidator of the general partner or of all or any substantial part of his properties, the appointment is not vacated or stayed or within [90] days after the expiration of any such stay, the appointment is not vacated;

(6) in the case of a general partner who is a natural person,

(i) his death; or

(ii) the entry by a court of competent jurisdiction adjudicating him incompetent to manage his person or his estate;

(7) in the case of a general partner who is acting as a general partner by virtue of being a trustee of a trust, the termination of the trust (but not merely the substitution of a new trustee);

(8) in the case of a general partner that is a separate partnership, the dissolution and commencement of winding up of the separate partnership;

(9) in the case of a general partner that is a corporation, the filing of a certificate of dissolution, or its equivalent, for the corporation or the revocation of its charter; or

(10) in the case of an estate, the distribution by the fiduciary of the estate's entire interest in the partnership.

Section 403. [General Powers and Liabilities]

Except as provided in this Act or in the partnership agreement, a general partner of a limited partnership has the rights and powers and is subject to the restrictions and liabilities of a partner in a partnership without limited partners.

Section 404. [Contributions by General Partner]

A general partner of a limited partnership may make contributions to the partnership and share in the profits and losses of, and in distributions from, the limited partnership as a general partner. A general partner also may make contributions to and share in profits, losses, and distributions as a limited partner. A person who is both a general partner and a limited partner has the rights and powers, and is subject to the restrictions and liabilities, of a general partner and, except as provided in the partnership agreement, also has the powers, and is subject to the restrictions, of a limited partner to the extent of his participation in the partnership as a limited partner.

Section 405. [Voting]

The partnership agreement may grant to all or certain identified general partners the right to vote (on a per capita or any other basis), separately or with all or any class of the limited partners, on any matter.

Article 5 Finance

Section 501. [Form of Contribution]

The contribution of a partner may be in cash, property, or services rendered, or a promissory note or other obligation to contribute cash or property or to perform services.

Section 502. [Liability for Contribution]

(a) Except as provided in the certificate of limited partnership, a partner is obligated to the limited partnership to perform any promise to contribute cash or property or to perform services, even if he is unable to perform because of death, disability or any other reason. If a partner does not make the required contribution of property or services, he is obligated at the option of the limited partnership to contribute cash equal to that portion of the value (as stated in the certificate of limited partnership) of the stated contribution that has not been made.

(b) Unless otherwise provided in the partnership agreement, the obligation of a partner to make a contribution or return money or other property paid or distributed in violation of this Act may be compromised only by consent of all the partners. Notwithstanding the compromise, a creditor of a limited partnership who extends credit, or whose claim arises, after the filing of the certificate of limited partnership or an amendment thereto which, in either case, reflects the obligation, and before the amendment or cancellation thereof to reflect the compromise, may enforce the original obligation.

Section 503. [Sharing of Profits and Losses]

The profits and losses of a limited partnership shall be allocated among the partners, and among classes of partners, in the manner provided in the partnership agreement. If the partnership agreement does not so provide, profits and losses shall be allocated on the basis of the value (as stated in the certificate of limited partnership) of the contributions made by each partner to the extent they have been received by the partnership and have not been returned.

Section 504. [Sharing of Distributions]

Distributions of cash or other assets of a limited partnership shall be allocated among the partners, and among classes of partners, in the manner provided in the partnership agreement. If the partnership agreement does not so provide, distributions shall be made on the basis of the value (as stated in the certificate of limited partnership) of the contributions made by each partner to the extent they have been received by the partnership and have not been returned.

Article 6 Distributions and Withdrawal

Section 601. [Interim Distributions]

Except as provided in this Article, a partner is entitled to receive distributions from a limited partnership before his withdrawal from the limited partnership and before the dissolution and winding up thereof:

(1) to the extent and at the times or upon the happening of the events specified in the partnership agreement; and

(2) if any distribution constitutes a return of any part of his contribution under Section 608(c), to the extent and at the times or upon the happening of the events specified in the certificate of limited partnership.

Section 602. [Withdrawal of General Partner]

A general partner may withdraw from a limited partnership at any time by giving written notice to the other partners, but if the withdrawal violates the partnership agreement, the limited partnership may recover from the withdrawing general partner damages for breach of the partnership agreement and offset the damages against the amount otherwise distributable to him.

Section 603. [Withdrawal of Limited Partner]

A limited partner may withdraw from a limited partnership at the time or upon the happening of events specified in the certificate of limited partnership and in accordance with the partnership agreement. If the certificate does not specify the time or the events upon the happening of which a limited partner may withdraw or a definite time for the dissolution and winding up of the limited partnership, a limited partner may withdraw upon not less than 6 months' prior written notice to each general partner at his address on the books of the limited partnership at its office in this State.

Section 604. [Distribution Upon Withdrawal]

Except as provided in this Article, upon withdrawal any withdrawing partner is entitled to receive any distribution to which he is entitled under the partnership agreement and, if not otherwise provided in the agreement, he is entitled to receive, within a reasonable time after withdrawal, the fair value of his interest in the limited partnership as of the date of withdrawal based upon his right to share in distributions from the limited partnership.

Section 605. [Distribution in Kind]

Except as provided in the certificate of limited partnership, a partner, regardless of the nature of his contribution, has no right to demand and receive any distribution from a limited partnership in any form other than cash. Except as provided in the partnership agreement, a partner may not be compelled to accept a distribution of any asset in kind from a limited partnership to the extent that the percentage of the asset distributed to him exceeds a percentage of that asset which is equal to the percentage in which he shares in distributions from the limited partnership.

Section 606. [Right to Distribution]

At the time a partner becomes entitled to receive a distribution, he has the status of, and is entitled to all remedies available to, a creditor of the limited partnership with respect to the distribution.

Section 607. [Limitations on Distribution]

A partner may not receive a distribution from a limited partnership to the extent that, after giving effect to the distribution, all liabilities of the limited partnership, other than liabilities to partners on account of their partnership interests, exceed the fair value of the partnership assets.

Section 608. [Liability Upon Return of Contribution]

(a) If a partner has received the return of any part of his contribution without violation of the partnership agreement or this Act, he is liable to the limited partnership for a period of one year thereafter for the amount of the returned contribution, but only to the extent necessary to discharge the limited partnership's liabilities to creditors who extended credit to the limited partnership during the period the contribution was held by the partnership.

(b) If a partner has received the return of any part of his contribution in violation of the partnership agreement or this Act, he is liable to the limited partnership for a period of 6 years thereafter for the amount of the contribution wrongfully returned.

(c) A partner receives a return of his contribution to the extent that a distribution to him reduces his share of the fair value of the net assets of the limited partnership below the value (as set forth in the certificate of limited partnership) of his contribution which has not been distributed to him.

Article 7 Assignment of Partnership Interests

Section 701. [Nature of Partnership Interest]

A partnership interest is personal property.

Section 702. [Assignment of Partnership Interest]

Except as provided in the partnership agreement, a partnership interest is assignable in whole or in part. An assignment of a partnership interest does not dissolve a limited partnership or entitle the assignee to become or to exercise any rights of a partner. An assignment entitles the assignee to receive, to the extent assigned, only the distribution to which the assignor would be entitled. Except as provided in the partnership agreement, a partner ceases to be a partner upon assignment of all his partnership interest.

Section 703. [Rights of Creditor]
On application to a court of competent jurisdiction by any judgment creditor of a partner, the court may charge the partnership interest of the partner with payment of the unsatisfied amount of the judgment with interest. To the extent so charged, the judgment creditor has only the rights of an assignee of the partnership interest. This Act does not deprive any partner of the benefit of any exemption laws applicable to his partnership interest.

Section 704. [Right of Assignee to Become Limited Partner]
(a) An assignee of a partnership interest, including an assignee of a general partner, may become a limited partner if and to the extent that (1) the assignor gives the assignee that right in accordance with authority described in the certificate of limited partnership, or (2) all other partners consent.

(b) An assignee who has become a limited partner has, to the extent assigned, the rights and powers, and is subject to the restrictions and liabilities, of a limited partner under the partnership agreement and this Act. An assignee who becomes a limited partner also is liable for the obligations of his assignor to make and return contributions as provided in Article 6. However, the assignee is not obligated for liabilities unknown to the assignee at the time he became a limited partner and which could not be ascertained from the certificate of limited partnership.

(c) If an assignee of a partnership interest becomes a limited partner, the assignor is not released from his liability to the limited partnership under Sections 207 and 502.

Section 705. [Power of Estate of Deceased or Incompetent Partner]
If a partner who is an individual dies or a court of competent jurisdiction adjudges him to be incompetent to manage his person or his property, the partner's executor, administrator guardian, conservator, or other legal representative may exercise all the partner's rights for the purpose of settling his estate or administering his property, including any power the partner had to give an assignee the right to become a limited partner. If a partner is a corporation, trust, or other entity and is dissolved or terminated, the powers of that partner may be exercised by its legal representative or successor.

Article 8 Dissolution

Section 801. [Nonjudicial Dissolution]
A limited partnership is dissolved and its affairs shall be wound up upon the happening of the first to occur of the following:

(1) at the time or upon the happening of events specified in the certificate of limited partnership;

(2) written consent of all partners;

(3) an event of withdrawal of a general partner unless at the time there is at least one other general partner and the certificate of limited partnership permits the business of the limited partnership to be carried on by the remaining general partner and that partner does so, but the limited partnership is not dissolved and is not required to be wound up by reason of any event of withdrawal, if, within 90 days after the withdrawal, all partners agree in writing to continue the business of the limited partnership and to the appointment of one or more additional general partners if necessary or desired; or

(4) entry of a decree of judicial dissolution under Section 802.

Section 802. [Judicial Dissolution]
On application by or for a partner the [here designate the proper court] court may decree dissolution of a limited partnership whenever it is not reasonably practicable to carry on the business in conformity with the partnership agreement.

Section 803. [Winding Up]
Except as provided in the partnership agreement, the general partners who have not wrongfully dissolved a limited partnership or, if none, the limited partners, may wind up the limited partnership's affairs; but the [here designate the proper court] court may wind up the limited partnership's affairs upon application of any partner, his legal representative, or assignee.

Section 804. [Distribution of Assets]
Upon the winding up of a limited partnership, the assets shall be distributed as follows:

(1) to creditors, including partners who are creditors, to the extent permitted by law, in satisfaction of liabilities of the limited partnership other than liabilities for distributions to partners under Section 601 or 604;

(2) except as provided in the partnership agreement, to partners and former partners in satisfaction of liabilities for distributions under Section 601 or 604; and

(3) except as provided in the partnership agreement, to partners *first* for the return of their contributions and *secondly* respecting their partnership interests, in the proportions in which the partners share in distributions.

Article 9 Foreign Limited Partnerships

Section 901. [Law Governing]
Subject to the Constitution of this State, (1) the laws of the state under which a foreign limited partnership is organized govern its organization and internal affairs and the liability of its limited partners, and (2) a foreign limited partnership may not be denied registration by reason of any difference between those laws and the laws of this State.

Section 902. [Registration]
Before transacting business in this State, a foreign limited partnership shall register with the Secretary of State. In order to register, a foreign limited partnership shall submit to the Secretary of State, in duplicate, an application for registration as a foreign limited partnership, signed and sworn to by a general partner and setting forth:

(1) the name of the foreign limited partnership and, if different, the name under which it proposes to register and transact business in this State;

(2) the state and date of its formation;

(3) the general character of the business it proposes to transact in this State;

(4) the name and address of any agent for service of process on the foreign limited partnership whom the foreign limited partnership elects to appoint; the agent must be an individual resident of this State, a domestic corporation, or a foreign corporation having a place of business in, and authorized to do business in, this State;

(5) a statement that the Secretary of State is appointed the agent of the foreign limited partnership for service of process if no agent has been appointed under paragraph (4) or, if appointed, the agent's authority has been revoked or if the agent cannot be found or served with the exercise of reasonable diligence;

(6) the address of the office required to be maintained in the State of its organization by the laws of that State or, if not so required, of the principal office of the foreign limited partnership; and

(7) if the certificate of limited partnership filed in the foreign limited partnership's state of organization is not required to include the names and business addresses of the partners, a list of the names and addresses.

Section 903. [Issuance of Registration]
(a) If the Secretary of State finds that an application for registration conforms to law and all requisite fees have been paid, he shall:
   (1) endorse on the application the word "Filed", and the month, day and year of the filing thereof;
   (2) file in his office a duplicate original of the application; and
   (3) issue a certificate of registration to transact business in this State.

(b) The certificate of registration, together with a duplicate original of the application, shall be returned to the person who filed the application or his representative.

Section 904. [Name.]
A foreign limited partnership may register with the Secretary of State under any name (whether or not it is the name under which it is registered in its state of organization) that includes without abbreviation the words "limited partnership" and that could be registered by a domestic limited partnership.

Section 905. [Changes and Amendments]
If any statement in the application for registration of a foreign limited partnership was false when made or any arrangements or other facts described have changed, making the application inaccurate in any respect, the foreign limited partnership shall promptly file in the office of the Secretary of State a certificate, signed and sworn to by a general partner, correcting such statement.

Section 906. [Cancellation of Registration]
A foreign limited partnership may cancel its registration by filing with the Secretary of State a certificate of cancellation signed and sworn to by a general partner. A cancellation does not terminate the authority of the Secretary of State to accept service of process on the foreign limited partnership with respect to [claims for relief] [causes of action] arising out of the transactions of business in this State.

Section 907. [Transaction of Business Without Registration]
(a) A foreign limited partnership transacting business in this State may not maintain any action, suit, or proceeding in any court of this State until it has registered in this State.

(b) The failure of a foreign limited partnership to register in this State does not impair the validity of any contract or act of the foreign limited partnership or prevent the foreign limited partnership from defending any action, suit, or proceeding in any court of this State.

(c) A limited partner of a foreign limited partnership is not liable as a general partner of the foreign limited partnership solely by reason of having transacted business in this State without registration.

(d) A foreign limited partnership, by transacting business in this State without registration, appoints the Secretary of State as its agent for service of process with respect to [claims for relief] [causes of action] arising out of the transaction of business in this State.

Section 908. [Action by [Appropriate Official]]
The [appropriate official] may bring an action to restrain a foreign limited partnership from transacting business in this State in violation of this Article.

Article 10 Derivative Actions

Section 1001. [Right of Action]
A limited partner may bring an action in the right of a limited partnership to recover a judgment in its favor if general partners with authority to do so have refused to bring the action or if an effort to cause those general partners to bring the action is not likely to succeed.

Section 1002. [Proper Plaintiff]
In a derivative action, the plaintiff must be a partner at the time of bringing the action and (1) at the time of the transaction of which he complains or (2) his status as a partner had devolved upon him by operation of law or pursuant to the terms of the partnership agreement from a person who was a partner at the time of the transaction.

Section 1003. [Pleading]
In a derivative action, the complaint shall set forth with particularity the effort of the plaintiff to secure initiation of the action by a general partner or the reasons for not making the effort.

Section 1004. [Expenses]
If a derivative action is successful, in whole or in part, or if anything is received by the plaintiff as a result of a judgment, compromise or settlement of an action or claim, the court may award the plaintiff reasonable expenses, including reasonable attorney's fees, and shall direct him to remit to the limited partnership the remainder of those proceeds received by him.

Article 11 Miscellaneous

Section 1101. [Construction and Application]
This Act shall be so applied and construed to effectuate its general purpose to make uniform the law with respect to the subject of this Act among states enacting it.

Section 1102. [Short Title]
This Act may be cited as the Uniform Limited Partnership Act.

Section 1103. [Severability]
If any provision of this Act or its application to any person or circumstance is held invalid, the invalidity does not affect other provisions or applications of the Act which can be given effect without the invalid provision or application, and to this end the provisions of this Act are severable.

Section 1104. [Effective Date, Extended Effective Date and Repeal]
Except as set forth below, the effective date of this Act is and the following Acts [list prior limited partnership acts] are hereby repealed:
   (1) The existing provisions for execution and filing of certificates of limited partnerships and amendments thereunder and cancellations thereof continue in effect until [specify time required to create central filing system], the extended effective date, and Sections 102, 103, 104, 105, 201, 202, 203, 204 and 206 are not effective until the extended effective date.
   (2) Section 402, specifying the conditions under which a general partner ceases to be a member of a limited partnership, is not effective until the extended effective date, and the applicable provisions of existing law continue to govern until the extended effective date.
   (3) Sections 501, 502 and 608 apply only to contributions and distributions made after the effective date of this Act.
   (4) Section 704 applies only to assignments made after the effective date of this Act.
   (5) Article 9, dealing with registration of foreign limited partnerships, is not effective until the extended effective date.

Section 1105. [Rules for Cases Not Provided for in This Act]
In any case not provided for in this Act the provisions of the Uniform Partnership Act govern.

Appendix E
Uniform Commercial Code (1978 Text)

Title

An Act

To be known as the Uniform Commercial Code, Relating to Certain Commercial Transactions in or regarding Personal Property and Contracts and other Documents concerning them, including Sales, Commercial Paper, Bank Deposits and Collections, Letters of Credit, Bulk Transfers, Warehouse Receipts, Bills of Lading, other Documents of Title, Investment Securities, and Secured Transactions, including certain Sales of Accounts, Chattel Paper, and Contract Rights; Providing for Public Notice to Third Parties in Certain Circumstances; Regulating Procedure, Evidence and Damages in Certain Court Actions Involving such Transactions, Contracts or Documents; to Make Uniform the Law with Respect Thereto; and Repealing Inconsistent Legislation.

Article 1 General Provisions

Part 1 Short Title, Construction, Application and Subject Matter of the Act

Section 1-101. Short Title
This Act shall be known and may be cited as Uniform Commercial Code.

Section 1-102. Purposes; Rules of Construction; Variation by Agreement
(1) This Act shall be literally construed and applied to promote its underlying purposes and policies.

(2) Underlying purposes and policies of this Act are
  (a) to simplify, clarify and modernize the law governing commercial transactions;
  (b) to permit the continued expansion of commercial practices through custom, usage and agreement of the parties;
  (c) to make uniform the law among the various jurisdictions.

(3) The effect of provisions of this Act may be varied by agreement, except as otherwise provided in this Act and except that the obligations of good faith, diligence, reasonableness and care prescribed by this Act may not be disclaimed by agreement but the parties may by agreement determine the standards by which the performance of such obligations is to be measured if such standards are not manifestly unreasonable.

(4) The presence in certain provisions of this Act of the word "unless otherwise agreed" or words of similar import does not imply that the effect of other provisions may not be varied by agreement under subsection (3).

(5) In this Act unless the context otherwise requires
  (a) words in the singular number include the plural, and in the plural include the singular;
  (b) words of the masculine gender include the feminine and the neuter, and when the sense so indicates words of the neuter gender may refer to any gender.

Section 1-103. Supplementary General Principles of Law Applicable
Unless displaced by the particular provisions of this Act, the principles of law and equity, including the law merchant and the law relative to capacity to contract, principal and agent, estoppel, fraud, misrepresentation, duress, coercion, mistake, bankruptcy, or other validating or invalidating cause shall supplement its provisions.

Section 1-104. Construction Against Implicit Repeal
This Act being a general act intended as a unified coverage of its subject matter, no part of it shall be deemed to be impliedly repealed by subsequent legislation if such construction can reasonably be avoided.

Section 1-105. Territorial Application of the Act; Parties' Power to Choose Applicable Law
(1) Except as provided hereafter in this section, when a transaction bears a reasonable relation to this state and also to another state or nation the parties may agree that the law either of this state or of such other state or nation shall govern their rights and duties. Failing such agreement this Act applies to transactions bearing an appropriate relation to this state.

(2) Where one of the following provisions of this Act specifies the applicable law, that provision governs and a contrary agreement is effective only to the extent permitted by the law (including the conflict of laws rules) so specified:

> Rights of creditors against sold goods. Section 2-402.
>
> Applicability of the Article on Bank Deposits and Collections. Section 4-102.
>
> Bulk transfers subject to the Article on Bulk Transfers. Section 6-102.
>
> Applicability of the Article on Investment Securities. Section 8-106.
>
> Perfection provisions of the Article on Secured Transactions. Section 9-103.

Section 1-106. Remedies to Be Liberally Administered
(1) The remedies provided by this Act shall be liberally administered to the end that the aggrieved party may be put in as good a position as if the other party had fully performed but neither consequential or special nor penal damages may be had except as specifically provided in this Act or by other rule of law.

(2) Any right or obligation declared by this Act is enforceable by action unless the provision declaring it specifies a different and limited effect.

Section 1-107. Waiver or Renunciation of Claim or Right After Breach
Any claim or right arising out of an alleged breach can be discharged in whole or in part without consideration by a written waiver or renunciation signed and delivered by the aggrieved party.

Section 1-108. Severability
If any provision or clause of this Act or application thereof to any person or circumstances is held invalid, such invalidity shall not

affect other provisions or applications of the Act which can be given effect without the invalid provision or application, and to this end the provisions of this Act are declared to be severable.

Section 1-109. Section Captions
Section captions are parts of this Act.

Part 2 General Definitions and Principles of Interpretation

Section 1-201. General Definitions
Subject to additional definitions contained in the subsequent Articles of this Act which are applicable to specific Articles or Parts thereof, and unless the context otherwise requires, in this Act:

(1) "Action" in the sense of a judicial proceeding includes recoupment, counterclaim, set-off, suit in equity and any other proceedings in which rights are determined.

(2) "Aggrieved party" means a party entitled to resort to a remedy.

(3) "Agreement" means the bargain of the parties in fact as found in their language or by implication from other circumstances including course of dealing or usage of trade or course of performance as provided in this Act (Sections 1-205 and 2-208). Whether an agreement has legal consequences is determined by the provisions of this Act, if applicable; otherwise by the law of contracts (Section 1-103). (Compare "Contract".)

(4) "Bank" means any person engaged in the business of banking.

(5) "Bearer" means the person in possession of an instrument, document of title, or certificated security payable to bearer or indorsed in blank.

(6) "Bill of lading" means a document evidencing the receipt of goods for shipment issued by a person engaged in the business of transporting or forwarding goods, and includes an airbill. "Airbill" means a document serving for air transportation as a bill of lading does for marine or rail transportation, and includes an air consignment note or air waybill.

(7) "Branch" includes a separately incorporated foreign branch of a bank.

(8) "Burden of establishing" a fact means the burden of persuading the triers of fact that the existence of the fact is more probable than its non-existence.

(9) "Buyer in ordinary course of business" means a person who in good faith and without knowledge that the sale to him is in violation of the ownership rights or security interest of a third party in the goods buys in ordinary course from a person in the business of selling goods of that kind but does not include a pawnbroker. All persons who sell minerals or the like (including oil and gas) at wellhead or minehead shall be deemed to be persons in the business of selling goods of that kind. "Buying" may be for cash or by exchange of other property or on secured or unsecured credit and includes receiving goods or documents of title under a pre-existing contract for sale but does not include a transfer in bulk or as security for or in total or partial satisfaction of a money debt.

(10) "Conspicuous": A term or clause is conspicuous when it is so written that a reasonable person against whom it is to operate ought to have noticed it. A printed heading in capitals (as: NON-NEGOTIABLE BILL OF LADING) is conspicuous. Language in the body of a form is "conspicuous" if it is in larger or other contrasting type or color. But in a telegram any stated term is "conspicuous." Whether a term or clause is "conspicuous" or not is for decision by the court.

(11) "Contract" means the total legal obligation which results from the parties' agreement as affected by this Act and any other applicable rules of law. (Compare "Agreement.")

(12) "Creditor" includes a general creditor, a secured creditor, a lien creditor and any representative of creditors, including an assignee for the benefit of creditors, a trustee in bankruptcy, a receiver in equity and an executor or administrator of an insolvent debtor's or assignor's estate.

(13) "Defendant" includes a person in the position of defendant in a cross-action or counterclaim.

(14) "Delivery" with respect to instruments, documents of title, chattel paper, or certificated securities means voluntary transfer of possession.

(15) "Document of title" includes bill of lading, dock warrant, dock receipt, warehouse receipt or order for the delivery of goods, and also any other document which in the regular course of business or financing is treated as adequately evidencing that the person in possession of it is entitled to receive, hold and dispose of the document and the goods it covers. To be a document of title a document must purport to be issued by or addressed to a bailee and purport to cover goods in the bailee's possession which are either identified or are fungible portions of an identified mass.

(16) "Fault" means wrongful act, omission or breach.

(17) "Fungible" with respect to goods or securities means goods or securities of which any unit is, by nature or usage of trade, the equivalent of any other like unit. Goods which are not fungible shall be deemed fungible for the purposes of this Act to the extent that under a particular agreement or document unlike units are treated as equivalents.

(18) "Genuine" means free of forgery or counterfeiting.

(19) "Good faith" means honesty in fact in the conduct or transaction concerned.

(20) "Holder" means a person who is in possession of a document of title or an instrument or a certificated investment security drawn, issued, or indorsed to him or his order or to bearer or in blank.

(21) To "honor" is to pay or to accept and pay, or where a credit so engages to purchase or discount a draft complying with the terms of the credit.

(22) "Insolvency proceedings" includes any assignment for the benefit of creditors or other proceedings intended to liquidate or rehabilitate the estate of the person involved.

(23) A person is "insolvent" who either has ceased to pay his debts in the ordinary course of business or cannot pay his debts as they become due or is insolvent within the meaning of the federal bankruptcy law.

(24) "Money" means a medium of exchange authorized or adopted by a domestic or foreign government as a part of its currency.

(25) A person has "notice" of a fact when

    (a) he has actual knowledge of it; or

    (b) he has received a notice or notification of it; or

    (c) from all the facts and circumstances known to him at the time in question he has reason to know that it exists.

A person "knows" or has "knowledge" of a fact when he has actual knowledge of it. "Discover" or "learn" or a word or phrase of similar import refers to knowledge rather than to reason to know. The time and circumstances under which a notice or notification may cease to be effective are not determined by this Act.

(26) A person "notifies" or "gives" a notice or notification to another by taking such steps as may be reasonably required to inform the other in ordinary course whether or not such other actually comes to know of it. A person "receives" a notice or notification when

    (a) it comes to his attention; or

    (b) it is duly delivered at the place of business through which the contract was made or at any other place held out by him as the place for receipt of such communications.

(27) Notice, knowledge or a notice or notification received by an organization is effective for a particular transaction from the time when it is brought to the attention of the individual conducting that transaction, and in any event from the time when it would have been brought to his attention if the organization had exercised due diligence. An organization exercises due diligence if it maintains reasonable routines for communicating significant information to

the person conducting the transaction and there is reasonable compliance with the routines. Due diligence does not require an individual acting for the organization to communicate information unless such communication is part of his regular duties or unless he has reason to know of the transaction and that the transaction would be materially affected by the information.

(28) "Organization" includes a corporation, government or governmental subdivision or agency, business trust, estate, trust, partnership or association, two or more persons having a joint or common interest, or any other legal or commercial entity.

(29) "Party," as distinct from "third party," means a person who has engaged in a transaction or made an agreement within this Act.

(30) "Person" includes an individual or an organization (See Section 1–102).

(31) "Presumption" or "presumed" means that the trier of fact must find the existence of the fact presumed unless and until evidence is introduced which would support a finding of its non-existence.

(32) "Purchase" includes taking by sale, discount, negotiation, mortgage, pledge, lien, issue or re-issue, gift or any other voluntary transaction creating an interest in property.

(33) "Purchaser" means a person who takes by purchase.

(34) "Remedy" means any remedial right to which an aggrieved party is entitled with or without resort to a tribunal.

(35) "Representative" includes an agent, an officer of a corporation or association, and a trustee, executor or administrator of an estate, or any other person empowered to act for another.

(36) "Rights" includes remedies.

(37) "Security interest" means an interest in personal property or fixtures which secures payment or performance of an obligation. The retention or reservation of title by a seller of goods notwithstanding shipment or delivery to the buyer (Section 2–401) is limited in effect to a reservation of a "security interest." The term also includes any interest of a buyer of accounts or chattel paper which is subject to Article 9. The special property interest of a buyer of goods on identification of such goods to a contract for sale under Section 2–401 is not a "security interest," but a buyer may also acquire a "security interest" by complying with Article 9. Unless a lease or consignment is intended as security, reservation of title thereunder is not a "security interest" but a consignment is in any event subject to the provisions on consignment sales (Section 2–326). Whether a lease is intended as security is to be determined by the facts of each case; however, (a) the inclusion of an option to purchase does not of itself make the lease one intended for security, and (b) an agreement that upon compliance with the terms of the lease the lessee shall become or has the option to become the owner of the property for no additional consideration or for a nominal consideration does make the lease one intended for security.

(38) "Send" in connection with any writing or notice means to deposit in the mail or deliver for transmission by any other usual means of communication with postage or cost of transmission provided for and properly addressed and in the case of an instrument to an address specified thereon or otherwise agreed, or if there be none to any address reasonable under the circumstances. The receipt of any writing or notice within the time at which it would have arrived if properly sent has the effect of a proper sending.

(39) "Signed" includes any symbol executed or adopted by a party with present intention to authenticate a writing.

(40) "Surety" includes guarantor.

(41) "Telegram" includes a message transmitted by radio, teletype, cable, any mechanical method of transmission, or the like.

(42) "Term" means that portion of an agreement which relates to a particular matter.

(43) "Unauthorized" signature or indorsement means one made without actual, implied or apparent authority and includes a forgery.

(44) "Value." Except as otherwise provided with respect to negotiable instruments and bank collections (Sections 3–303, 4–208 and 4–209) a person gives "value" for rights if he acquires them

(a) in return for a binding commitment to extend credit or for the extension of immediately available credit whether or not drawn upon and whether or not a chargeback is provided for in the event of difficulties in collection; or

(b) as security for or in total or partial satisfaction of a pre-existing claim; or

(c) by accepting delivery pursuant to a pre-existing contract for purchase; or

(d) generally, in return for any consideration sufficient to support a simple contract.

(45) "Warehouse receipt" means a receipt issued by a person engaged in the business of storing goods for hire.

(46) "Written" or "writing" includes printing, typewriting or any other intentional reduction to tangible form.

Section 1–202. Prima Facie Evidence by Third Party Documents

A document in due form purporting to be a bill of lading, policy or certificate of insurance, official weigher's or inspector's certificate, consular invoice, or any other document authorized or required by the contract to be issued by a third party shall be prima facie evidence of its own authenticity and genuineness and of the facts stated in the document by the third party.

Section 1–203. Obligation of Good Faith

Every contract or duty within this Act imposes an obligation of good faith in its performance or enforcement.

Section 1–204. Time; Reasonable Time; "Seasonably"

(1) Whenever this Act requires any action to be taken within a reasonable time, any time which is not manifestly unreasonable may be fixed by agreement.

(2) What is a reasonable time for taking any action depends on the nature, purpose and circumstances of such action.

(3) An action is taken "seasonably" when it is taken at or within the time agreed or if no time is agreed at or within a reasonable time.

Section 1–205. Course of Dealing and Usage of Trade

(1) A course of dealing is a sequence of previous conduct between the parties to a particular transaction which is fairly to be regarded as establishing a common basis of understanding for interpreting their expressions and other conduct.

(2) A usage of trade is any practice or method of dealing having such regularity of observance in a place, vocation or trade as to justify an expectation that it will be observed with respect to the transaction in question. The existence and scope of such a usage are to be proved as facts. If it is established that such a usage is embodied in a written trade code or similar writing the interpretation of the writing is for the court.

(3) A course of dealing between parties and any usage of trade in the vocation or trade in which they are engaged or of which they are or should be aware give particular meaning to and supplement or qualify terms of an agreement.

(4) The express terms of an agreement and an applicable course of dealing or usage of trade shall be construed wherever reasonable as consistent with each other; but when such construction is unreasonable express terms control both course of dealing and usage of trade and course of dealing controls usage of trade.

(5) An applicable usage of trade in the place where any part of performance is to occur shall be used in interpreting the agreement as to that part of the performance.

(6) Evidence of a relevant usage of trade offered by one party is not admissible unless and until he has given the other party such notice as the court finds sufficient to prevent unfair surprise to the latter.

Section 1-206. Statute of Frauds for Kinds of Personal Property Not Otherwise Covered

(1) Except in the cases described in subsection (2) of this section a contract for the sale of personal property is not enforceable by way of action or defense beyond five thousand dollars in amount or value of remedy unless there is some writing which indicates that a contract for sale has been made between the parties at a defined or stated price, reasonably identifies the subject matter, and is signed by the party against whom enforcement is sought or by his authorized agent.

(2) Subsection (1) of this section does not apply to contracts for the sale of goods (Section 2-201) nor of securities (Section 8-319) nor to security agreements (Section 9-203).

Section 1-207. Performance or Acceptance Under Reservation of Rights

A party who with explicit reservation of rights performs or promises performance or assents to performance in a manner demanded or offered by the other party does not thereby prejudice the rights reserved. Such words as "without prejudice," "under protest" or the like are sufficient.

Section 1-208. Option to Accelerate at Will

A term providing that one party or his successor in interest may accelerate payment or performance or require collateral or additional collateral "at will" or "when he deems himself insecure" or in words of similar import shall be construed to mean that he shall have power to do so only if he in good faith believes that the prospect of payment or performance is impaired. The burden of establishing lack of good faith is on the party against whom the power has been exercised.

Section 1-209. Subordinated Obligations

An obligation may be issued as subordinated to payment of another obligation of the person obligated, or a creditor may subordinate his right to payment of an obligation by agreement with either the person obligated or another creditor of the person obligated. Such a subordination does not create a security interest as against either the common debtor or a subordinated creditor. This section shall be construed as declaring the law as it existed prior to the enactment of this section and not as modifying it.

Note: *This new section is proposed as an optional provision to make it clear that a subordination agreement does not create a security interest unless so intended.*

Article 2 Sales

Part 1 Short Title, General Construction and Subject Matter

Section 2—101. Short Title

This Article shall be known and may be cited as Uniform Commercial Code—Sales.

Section 2—102. Scope; Certain Security and Other Transactions Excluded From This Article

Unless the context otherwise requires, this Article applies to transactions in goods; it does not apply to any transaction which although in the form of an unconditional contract to sell or present sale is intended to operate only as a security transaction nor does this Article impair or repeal any statute regulating sales to consumers, farmers or other specified classes of buyers.

Section 2—103. Definitions and Index of Definitions

(1) In this Article unless the context otherwise requires

(a) "Buyer" means a person who buys or contracts to buy goods.

(b) "Good faith" in the case of a merchant means honesty in fact and the observance of reasonable commercial standards of fair dealing in the trade.

(c) "Receipt" of goods means taking physical possession of them.

(d) "Seller" means a person who sells or contracts to sell goods.

(2) Other definitions applying to this Article or to specified Parts thereof, and the sections in which they appear are:

"Acceptance." Section 2—606.
"Banker's credit." Section 2—325.
"Between merchants." Section 2—104.
"Cancellation." Section 2—106(4).
"Commercial unit." Section 2—105.
"Confirmed credit." Section 2—325.
"Conforming to contract." Section 2—106.
"Contract for sale." Section 2—106.
"Cover." Section 2—712.
"Entrusting." Section 2—403.
"Financing agency." Section 2—104.
"Future goods." Section 2—105.
"Goods." Section 2—105.
"Identification." Section 2—501.
"Installment contract." Section 2—612.
"Letter of Credit." Section 2—325.
"Lot." Section 2—105.
"Merchant." Section 2—104.
"Overseas." Section 2—323.
"Person in position of seller." Section 2—707.
"Present sale." Section 2—106.
"Sale." Section 2—106.
"Sale on approval." Section 2—326.
"Sale or return." Section 2—326.
"Termination." Section 2—106.

(3) The following definitions in other Articles apply to this Article:

"Check." Section 3—104.
"Consignee." Section 7—102.
"Consignor." Section 7—102.
"Consumer goods." Section 9—109.
"Dishonor." Section 3—507.
"Draft." Section 3—104.

(4) In addition Article 1 contains general definitions and principles of construction and interpretation applicable throughout this Article.

Section 2—104. Definitions: "Merchant"; "Between Merchants"; "Financing Agency"

(1) "Merchant" means a person who deals in goods of the kind or otherwise by his occupation holds himself out as having knowledge or skill peculiar to the practices or goods involved in the transaction or to whom such knowledge or skill may be attributed by his employment of an agent or broker or other intermediary who by his occupation holds himself out as having such knowledge or skill.

(2) "Financing agency" means a bank, finance company or other person who in the ordinary course of business makes advances against goods or documents of title or who by arrangement with either the seller or the buyer intervenes in ordinary course to make or collect payment due or claimed under the contract for sale, as by purchasing or paying the seller's draft or making advances against it or by merely taking it for collection whether or not documents

of title accompany the draft. "Financing agency" includes also a bank or other person who similarly intervenes between persons who are in the position of seller and buyer in respect to the goods (Section 2—707).

(3) "Between merchants" means in any transaction with respect to which both parties are chargeable with the knowledge or skill of merchants.

Section 2—105. Definitions: Transferability; "Goods"; "Future" Goods; "Lot"; "Commercial Unit"

(1) "Goods" means all things (including specially manufactured goods) which are movable at the time of identification to the contract for sale other than the money in which the price is to be paid, investment securities (Article 8) and things in action. "Goods" also includes the unborn young of animals and growing crops and other identified things attached to realty as described in the section on goods to be severed from realty (Section 2—107).

(2) Goods must be both existing and identified before any interest in them can pass. Goods which are not both existing and identified are "future" goods. A purported present sale of future goods or of any interest therein operates as a contract to sell.

(3) There may be a sale of a part interest in existing identified goods.

(4) An undivided share in an identified bulk of fungible goods is sufficiently identified to be sold although the quantity of the bulk is not determined. Any agreed proportion of such a bulk or any quantity thereof agreed upon by number, weight or other measure may to the extent of the seller's interest in the bulk be sold to the buyer who then becomes an owner in common.

(5) "Lot" means a parcel or a single article which is the subject matter of a separate sale or delivery, whether or not it is sufficient to perform the contract.

(6) "Commercial unit" means such a unit of goods as by commercial usage is a single whole for purposes of sale and division of which materially impairs its character or value on the market or in use. A commercial unit may be a single article (as a machine) or a set of articles (as a suite of furniture or an assortment of sizes) or a quantity (as a bale, gross, or carload) or any other unit treated in use or in the relevant market as a single whole.

Section 2—106. Definitions: "Contract"; "Agreement"; "Contract for Sale"; "Sale"; "Present Sale"; "Conforming" to Contract; "Termination"; "Cancellation"

(1) In this Article unless the context otherwise requires "contract" and "agreement" are limited to those relating to the present or future sale of goods. "Contract for sale" includes both a present sale of goods and a contract to sell goods at a future time. A "sale" consists in the passing of title from the seller to the buyer for a price (Section 2—401). A "present sale" means a sale which is accomplished by the making of the contract.

(2) Goods or conduct including any part of a performance are "conforming" or conform to the contract when they are in accordance with the obligations under the contract.

(3) "Termination" occurs when either party pursuant to a power created by agreement or law puts an end to the contract otherwise than for its breach. On "termination" all obligations which are still executory on both sides are discharged but any right based on prior breach or performance survives.

(4) "Cancellation" occurs when either party puts an end to the contract for breach by the other and its effect is the same as that of "termination" except that the cancelling party also retains any remedy for breach of the whole contract or any unperformed balance.

Section 2—107. Goods to Be Severed From Realty: Recording

(1) A contract for the sale of minerals or the like (including oil and gas) or a structure or its materials to be removed from realty is a contract for the sale of goods within this Article if they are to be severed by the seller but until severance a purported present sale thereof which is not effective as a transfer of an interest in land is effective only as a contract to sell.

(2) A contract for the sale apart from the land of growing crops or other things attached to realty and capable of severance without material harm thereto but not described in subsection (1) or of timber to be cut is a contract for the sale of goods within this Article whether the subject matter is to be severed by the buyer or by the seller even though it forms part of the realty at the time of contracting, and the parties can by identification effect a present sale before severance.

(3) The provisions of this section are subject to any third party rights provided by the law relating to realty records, and the contract for sale may be executed and recorded as a document transferring an interest in land and shall then constitute notice to third parties of the buyer's rights under the contract for sale.

Part 2 Form, Formation and Readjustment of Contract

Section 2—201. Formal Requirements; Statute of Frauds

(1) Except as otherwise provided in this section a contract for the sale of goods for the price of $500 or more is not enforceable by way of action or defense unless there is some writing sufficient to indicate that a contract for sale has been made between the parties and signed by the party against whom enforcement is sought or by his authorized agent or broker. A writing is not insufficient because it omits or incorrectly states a term agreed upon but the contract is not enforceable under this paragraph beyond the quantity of goods shown in such writing.

(2) Between merchants if within a reasonable time a writing in confirmation of the contract and sufficient against the sender is received and the party receiving it has reason to know its contents, it satisfies the requirements of subsection (1) against such party unless written notice of objection to its contents is given within 10 days after it is received.

(3) A contract which does not satisfy the requirements of subsection (1) but which is valid in other respects is enforceable

    (a) if the goods are to be specially manufactured for the buyer and are not suitable for sale to others in the ordinary course of the seller's business and the seller, before notice of repudiation is received and under circumstances which reasonably indicate that the goods are for the buyer, has made either a substantial beginning of their manufacture or commitments for their procurement; or

    (b) if the party against whom enforcement is sought admits in his pleading, testimony or otherwise in court that a contract for sale was made, but the contract is not enforceable under this provision beyond the quantity of goods admitted; or

    (c) with respect to goods for which payment has been made and accepted or which have been received and accepted (Sec. 2—606).

Section 2—202. Final Written Expression: Parol or Extrinsic Evidence

Terms with respect to which the confirmatory memoranda of the parties agree or which are otherwise set forth in a writing intended by the parties as a final expression of their agreement with respect to such terms as are included therein may not be contradicted by evidence of any prior agreement or of a contemporaneous oral agreement but may be explained or supplemented

  (a) by course of dealing or usage of trade (Section 1—205) or by course of performance (Section 2—208); and
  (b) by evidence of consistent additional terms unless the court finds the writing to have been intended also as a complete and exclusive statement of the terms of the agreement.

Section 2—203. Seals Inoperative

The affixing of a seal to a writing evidencing a contract for sale or an offer to buy or sell goods does not constitute the writing a sealed instrument and the law with respect to sealed instruments does not apply to such a contract or offer.

Section 2—204. Formation in General

(1) A contract for sale of goods may be made in any manner sufficient to show agreement, including conduct by both parties which recognizes the existence of such a contract.

(2) An agreement sufficient to constitute a contract for sale may be found even though the moment of its making is undetermined.

(3) Even though one or more terms are left open a contract for sale does not fail for indefiniteness if the parties have intended to make a contract and there is a reasonably certain basis for giving an appropriate remedy.

Section 2—205. Firm Offers

An offer by a merchant to buy or sell goods in a signed writing which by its terms give assurance that it will be held open is not revocable, for lack of consideration, during the time stated or if no time is stated for a reasonable time, but in no event may such period of irrevocability exceed three months; but any such term of assurance on a form supplied by the offeree must be separately signed by the offeror.

Section 2—206. Offer and Acceptance in Formation of Contract

(1) Unless otherwise unambiguously indicated by the language or circumstances

  (a) an offer to make a contract shall be construed as inviting acceptance in any manner and by any medium reasonable in the circumstances;
  (b) an order or other offer to buy goods for prompt or current shipment shall be construed as inviting acceptance either by a prompt promise to ship or by the prompt or current shipment of conforming or non-conforming goods, but such a shipment of non-conforming goods does not constitute an acceptance if the seller seasonably notifies the buyer that the shipment is offered only as an accommodation to the buyer.

(2) Where the beginning of a requested performance is a reasonable mode of acceptance an offeror who is not notified of acceptance within a reasonable time may treat the offer as having lapsed before acceptance.

Section 2—207. Additional Terms in Acceptance or Confirmation

(1) A definite and seasonable expression of acceptance or a written confirmation which is sent within a reasonable time operates as an acceptance even though it states terms additional to or different from those offered or agreed upon, unless acceptance is expressly made conditional on assent to the additional or different terms.

(2) The additional terms are to be construed as proposals for addition to the contract. Between merchants such terms become part of the contract unless:

  (a) the offer expressly limits acceptance to the terms of the offer;
  (b) they materially alter it; or
  (c) notification of objection to them has already been given or is given within a reasonable time after notice of them is received.

(3) Conduct by both parties which recognizes the existence of a contract is sufficient to establish a contract for sale although the writings of the parties do not otherwise establish a contract. In such case the terms of the particular contract consist of those terms on which the writings of the parties agree, together with any supplementary terms incorporated under any other provisions of this Act.

Section 2—208. Course of Performance or Practical Construction

(1) Where the contract for sale involves repeated occasions for performance by either party with knowledge of the nature of the performance and opportunity for objection to it by the other, any course of performance accepted or acquiesced in without objection shall be relevant to determine the meaning of the agreement.

(2) The express terms of the agreement and any such course of performance, as well as any course of dealing and usage of trade, shall be construed whenever reasonable as consistent with each other; but when such construction is unreasonable, express terms shall control course of performance and course of performance shall control both course of dealing and usage of trade (Section 1—205).

(3) Subject to the provisions of the next section on modification and waiver, such course of performance shall be relevant to show a waiver or modification of any term inconsistent with such course of performance.

Section 2—209. Modification, Rescission and Waiver

(1) An agreement modifying a contract within this Article needs no consideration to be binding.

(2) A signed agreement which excludes modification or rescission except by a signed writing cannot be otherwise modified or rescinded, but except as between merchants such a requirement on a form supplied by the merchant must be separately signed by the other party.

(3) The requirements of the statute of frauds section of this Article (Section 2—201) must be satisfied if the contract as modified is within its provisions.

(4) Although an attempt at modification or rescission does not satisfy the requirements of subsection (2) or (3) it can operate as a waiver.

(5) A party who has made a waiver affecting an executory portion of the contract may retract the waiver by reasonable notification received by the other party that strict performance will be required of any term waived, unless the retraction would be unjust in view of a material change of position in reliance on the waiver.

Section 2—210. Delegation of Performance; Assignment of Rights

(1) A party may perform his duty through a delegate unless otherwise agreed or unless the other party has a substantial interest in having his original promisor perform or control the acts required by the contract. No delegation of performance relieves the party delegating of any duty to perform or any liability for breach.

(2) Unless otherwise agreed all rights of either seller or buyer can be assigned except where the assignment would materially change the duty of the other party, or increase materially the burden or risk imposed on him by his contract, or impair materially his chance of obtaining return performance. A right to damages for breach of the whole contract or a right arising out of the assignor's due performance of his entire obligation can be assigned despite agreement otherwise.

(3) Unless the circumstances indicate the contrary a prohibition of assignment of "the contract" is to be construed as barring only the delegation to the assignee of the assignor's performance.

(4) An assignment of "the contract" or of "all my rights under the contract" or an assignment in similar general terms is an assignment of rights and unless the language or the circumstances (as in an assignment for security) indicate the contrary, it is a delegation of performance of the duties of the assignor and its acceptance by the assignee constitutes a promise by him to perform those duties. This promise is enforceable by either the assignor or the other party to the original contract.

(5) The other party may treat any assignment which delegates performance as creating reasonable grounds for insecurity and may without prejudice to his rights against the assignor demand assurances from the assignee (Section 2—609).

Part 3   General Obligation and Construction of Contract

Section 2—301.   General Obligations of Parties
The obligation of the seller is to transfer and deliver and that of the buyer is to accept and pay in accordance with the contract.

Section 2—302.   Unconscionable Contract or Clause
(1) If the court as a matter of law finds the contract or any clause of the contract to have been unconscionable at the time it was made the court may refuse to enforce the contract, or it may enforce the remainder of the contract without the unconscionable clause, or it may so limit the application of any unconscionable clause as to avoid any unconscionable result.

(2) When it is claimed or appears to the court that the contract or any clause thereof may be unconscionable the parties shall be afforded a reasonable opportunity to present evidence as to its commercial setting, purpose and effect to aid the court in making the determination.

Section 2—303.   Allocation or Division of Risks
Where this Article allocates a risk or a burden as between the parties "unless otherwise agreed," the agreement may not only shift the allocation but may also divide the risk or burden.

Section 2—304.   Price Payable in Money, Goods, Realty, or Otherwise
(1) The price can be made payable in money or otherwise. If it is payable in whole or in part in goods each party is a seller of the goods which he is to transfer.

(2) Even though all or part of the price is payable in an interest in realty the transfer of the goods and the seller's obligations with reference to them are subject to this Article, but not the transfer of the interest in realty or the transferor's obligations in connection therewith.

Section 2—305.   Open Price Term
(1) The parties if they so intend can conclude a contract for sale even though the price is not settled. In such a case the price is a reasonable price at the time for delivery if
  (a) nothing is said as to price; or
  (b) the price is left to be agreed by the parties and they fail to agree; or
  (c) the price is to be fixed in terms of some agreed market or other standard as set or recorded by a third person or agency and it is not so set or recorded.

(2) A price to be fixed by the seller or by the buyer means a price for him to fix in good faith.

(3) When a price left to be fixed otherwise than by agreement of the parties fails to be fixed through fault of one party the other may at his option treat the contract as cancelled or himself fix a reasonable price.

(4) Where, however, the parties intend not to be bound unless the price be fixed or agreed and it is not fixed or agreed there is no contract. In such a case the buyer must return any goods already received or if unable so to do must pay their reasonable value at the time of delivery and the seller must return any portion of the price paid on account.

Section 2—306.   Output, Requirements and Exclusive Dealings
(1) A term which measures the quantity by the output of the seller or the requirements of the buyer means such actual output or requirements as may occur in good faith, except that no quantity unreasonably disproportionate to any stated estimate or in the absence of a stated estimate to any normal or otherwise comparable prior output or requirements may be tendered or demanded.

(2) A lawful agreement by either the seller or the buyer for exclusive dealing in the kind of goods concerned imposes unless otherwise agreed an obligation by the seller to use best efforts to supply the goods and by the buyer to use best efforts to promote their sale.

Section 2—307.   Delivery in Single Lot or Several Lots
Unless otherwise agreed all goods called for by a contract for sale must be tendered in a single delivery and payment is due only on such tender but where the circumstances give either party the right to make or demand delivery in lots the price if it can be apportioned may be demanded for each lot.

Section 2—308.   Absence of Specified Place for Delivery
Unless otherwise agreed
  (a) the place for delivery of goods is the seller's place of business or if he has none his residence; but
  (b) in a contract for sale of identified goods which to the knowledge of the parties at the time of contracting are in some other place, that place is the place for their delivery; and
  (c) documents of title may be delivered through customary banking channels.

Section 2—309.   Absence of Specific Time Provisions; Notice of Termination
(1) The time for shipment or delivery or any other action under a contract if not provided in this Article or agreed upon shall be a reasonable time.

(2) Where the contract provides for successive performances but is indefinite in duration it is valid for a reasonable time but unless otherwise agreed may be terminated at any time by either party.

(3) Termination of a contract by one party except on the happening of an agreed event requires that reasonable notification be received by the other party and an agreement dispensing with notification is invalid if its operation would be unconscionable.

Section 2—310.   Open Time for Payment or Running of Credit; Authority to Ship Under Reservation
Unless otherwise agreed
  (a) payment is due at the time and place at which the buyer is to receive the goods even though the place of shipment is the place of delivery; and
  (b) if the seller is authorized to send the goods he may ship them under reservation, and may tender the documents of title, but the buyer may inspect the goods after their arrival before payment is due unless such inspection is inconsistent with the terms of the contract (Section 2—513); and
  (c) if delivery is authorized and made by way of documents of title otherwise than by subsection (b) then payment is due at the time and place at which the buyer is to receive the documents regardless of where the goods are to be received; and

(d) where the seller is required or authorized to ship the goods on credit the credit period runs from the time of shipment but post-dating the invoice or delaying its dispatch will correspondingly delay the starting of the credit period.

Section 2—311. Options and Cooperation Respecting Performance

(1) An agreement for sale which is otherwise sufficiently definite (subsection (3) of Section 2—204) to be a contract is not made invalid by the fact that it leaves particulars of performance to be specified by one of the parties. Any such specification must be made in good faith and within limits set by commercial reasonableness.

(2) Unless otherwise agreed specifications relating to assortment of the goods are at the buyer's option and except as otherwise provided in subsections (1) (c) and (3) of Section 2—319 specifications or arrangements relating to shipment are at the seller's option.

(3) Where such specification would materially affect the other party's performance but is not seasonably made or where one party's cooperation is necessary to the agreed performance of the other but is not seasonably forthcoming, the other party in addition to all other remedies

(a) is excused for any resulting delay in his own performance; and

(b) may also either proceed to perform in any reasonable manner or after the time for a material part of his own performance treat the failure to specify or to cooperate as a breach by failure to deliver or accept the goods.

Section 2—312. Warranty of Title and Against Infringement; Buyer's Obligation Against Infringement

(1) Subject to subsection (2) there is in a contract for sale a warranty by the seller that

(a) the title conveyed shall be good, and its transfer rightful; and

(b) the goods shall be delivered free from any security interest or other lien or encumbrance of which the buyer at the time of contracting has no knowledge.

(2) A warranty under subsection (1) will be excluded or modified only by specific language or by circumstances which give the buyer reason to know that the person selling does not claim title in himself or that he is purporting to sell only such right or title as he or a third person may have.

(3) Unless otherwise agreed a seller who is a merchant regularly dealing in goods of the kind warrants that the goods shall be delivered free of the rightful claim of any third person by way of infringement or the like but a buyer who furnishes specifications to the seller must hold the seller harmless against any such claim which arises out of compliance with the specifications.

Section 2—313. Express Warranties by Affirmation, Promise, Description, Sample

(1) Express warranties by the seller are created as follows:

(a) Any affirmation of fact or promise made by the seller to the buyer which relates to the goods and becomes part of the basis of the bargain creates an express warranty that the goods shall conform to the affirmation or promise.

(b) Any description of the goods which is made part of the basis of the bargain creates an express warranty that the goods shall conform to the description.

(c) Any sample or model which is made part of the basis of the bargain creates an express warranty that the whole of the goods shall conform to the sample or model.

(2) It is not necessary to the creation of an express warranty that the seller use formal words such as "warrant" or "guarantee" or that he have a specific intention to make a warranty, but an affirmation merely of the value of the goods or a statement purporting to be merely the seller's opinion or commendation of the goods does not create a warranty.

Section 2—314. Implied Warranty: Merchantability; Usage of Trade

(1) Unless excluded or modified (Section 2—316), a warranty that the goods shall be merchantable is implied in a contract for their sale if the seller is a merchant with respect to goods of that kind. Under this section the serving for value of food or drink to be consumed either on the premises or elsewhere is a sale.

(2) Goods to be merchantable must be at least such as

(a) pass without objection in the trade under the contract description; and

(b) in the case of fungible goods, are of fair average quality within the description; and

(c) are fit for the ordinary purposes for which such goods are used; and

(d) run, within the variations permitted by the agreement, of even kind, quality and quantity within each unit and among all units involved; and

(e) are adequately contained, packaged, and labeled as the agreement may require; and

(f) conform to the promises or affirmations of fact made on the container or label if any.

(3) Unless excluded or modified (Section 2—316) other implied warranties may arise from course of dealing or usage of trade.

Section 2—315. Implied Warranty: Fitness for Particular Purpose

Where the seller at the time of contracting has reason to know any particular purpose for which the goods are required and that the buyer is relying on the seller's skill or judgment to select or furnish suitable goods, there is unless excluded or modified under the next section an implied warranty that the goods shall be fit for such purpose.

Section 2—316. Exclusion or Modification of Warranties

(1) Words or conduct relevant to the creation of an express warranty and words or conduct tending to negate or limit warranty shall be construed wherever reasonable as consistent with each other; but subject to the provisions of this Article on parol or extrinsic evidence (Section 2—202) negation or limitation is inoperative to the extent that such construction is unreasonable.

(2) Subject to subsection (3), to exclude or modify the implied warranty or merchantability or any part of it the language must mention merchantability and in case of a writing must be conspicuous, and to exclude or modify any implied warranty of fitness the exclusion must be by a writing and conspicuous. Language to exclude all implied warranties of fitness is sufficient if it states, for example, that "There are no warranties which extend beyond the description on the face hereof."

(3) Notwithstanding subsection (2)

(a) unless the circumstances indicate otherwise, all implied warranties are excluded by expressions like "as is," "with all faults" or other languages which in common understanding calls the buyer's attention to the exclusion of warranties and makes plain that there is no implied warranty; and

(b) when the buyer before entering into the contract has examined the goods or the sample or model as fully as he desired or has refused to examine the goods there is no implied warranty with regard to defects which an examination ought in the circumstances to have revealed to him; and

(c) an implied warranty can also be excluded or modified by course of dealing or course of performance or usage of trade.

(4) Remedies for breach of warranty can be limited in accordance with the provisions of this Article on liquidation or limitation of damages and on contractual modification of remedy (Sections 2—718 and 2—719).

Section 2—317. Cumulation and Conflict of Warranties Express or Implied

Warranties whether express or implied shall be construed as consistent with each other and as cumulative, but if such construction is unreasonable the intention of the parties shall determine which warranty is dominant. In ascertaining that intention the following rules apply:

(a) Exact or technical specifications displace an inconsistent sample or model or general language of description.

(b) A sample from an existing bulk displaces inconsistent general language of description.

(c) Express warranties displace inconsistent implied warranties other than an implied warranty of fitness for a particular purpose.

Section 2—318. Third Party Beneficiaries of Warranties Express or Implied

Note: If this Act is introduced in the Congress of the United States this section should be omitted. (States to select one alternative.)

Alternative A

A seller's warranty whether express or implied extends to any natural person who is in the family or household of his buyer or who is a guest in his home if it is reasonable to expect that such person may use, consume or be affected by the goods and who is injured in person by breach of the warranty. A seller may not exclude or limit the operation of this section.

Alternative B

A seller's warranty whether express or implied extends to any natural person who may reasonably be expected to use, consume or be affected by the goods and who is injured in person by breach of the warranty. A seller may not exclude or limit the operation of this section.

Alternative C

A seller's warranty whether express or implied extends to any person who may reasonably be expected to use, consume or be affected by the goods and who is injured by breach of the warranty. A seller may not exclude or limit the operation of this section with respect to injury to the person of an individual to whom the warranty extends.

Section 2—319. F.O.B. and F.A.S. Terms

(1) Unless otherwise agreed the term F.O.B. (which means "free on board") at a named place, even though used only in connection with the stated price, is a delivery term under which

(a) when the term is F.O.B. the place of shipment, the seller must at that place ship the goods in the manner provided in this Article (Section 2—504) and bear the expense and risk of putting them into the possession of the carrier; or

(b) when the term is F.O.B. the place of destination, the seller must at his own expense and risk transport the goods to that place and there tender delivery of them in the manner provided in this Article (Section 2—503);

(c) when under either (a) or (b) the term is also F.O.B. vessel, car or other vehicle, the seller must in addition at his own expense and risk load the goods on board. If the term is F.O.B. vessel the buyer must name the vessel and in an appropriate case the seller must comply with the provisions of this Article on the form of bill of lading (Section 2—323).

(2) Unless otherwise agreed the term F.A.S. vessel (which means "free alongside") at a named port, even though used only in connection with the stated price, is a delivery term under which the seller must

(a) at his own expense and risk deliver the goods alongside the vessel in the manner usual in that port or on a dock designated and provided by the buyer; and

(b) obtain and tender a receipt for the goods in exchange for which the carrier is under a duty to issue a bill of lading.

(3) Unless otherwise agreed in any case falling within subsection (1) (a) or (c) or subsection (2) the buyer must seasonably give any needed instructions for making delivery, including when the term is F.A.S. or F.O.B. the loading berth of the vessel and in an appropriate case its name and sailing date. The seller may treat the failure of needed instructions as a failure of cooperation under this Article (Section 2—311). He may also at his option move the goods in any reasonable manner preparatory to delivery or shipment.

(4) Under the term F.O.B. vessel or F.A.S. unless otherwise agreed the buyer must make payment against tender of the required documents and the seller may not tender nor the buyer demand delivery of the goods in substitution for the documents.

Section 2—320. C.I.F. and C. & F. Terms

(1) The term C.I.F. means that the price includes in a lump sum the cost of the goods and the insurance and freight to the named destination. The term C. & F. or C.F. means that the price so includes cost and freight to the named destination.

(2) Unless otherwise agreed and even though used only in connection with the stated price and destination, the term C.I.F. destination or its equivalent requires the seller at his own expense and risk to

(a) put the goods into the possession of a carrier at the port for shipment and obtain a negotiable bill or bills of lading covering the entire transportation to the named destination; and

(b) load the goods and obtain a receipt from the carrier (which may be contained in the bill of lading) showing that the freight has been paid or provided for; and

(c) obtain a policy or certificate of insurance, including any war risk insurance, of a kind and on terms then current at the port of shipment in the usual amount, in the currency of the contract, shown to cover the same goods covered by the bill of lading and providing for payment of loss to the order of the buyer or for the account of whom it may concern; but the seller may add to the price the amount of the premium for any such war risk insurance; and

(d) prepare an invoice of the goods and procure any other documents required to effect shipment or to comply with the contract; and

(e) forward and tender with commercial promptness all the documents in due form and with any indorsement necessary to perfect the buyer's rights.

(3) Unless otherwise agreed the term C. & F. or its equivalent has the same effect and imposes upon the seller the same obligations and risks as a C.I.F. term except the obligation as to insurance.

(4) Under the term C.I.F. or C. & F. unless otherwise agreed the buyer must make payment against tender of the required documents and the seller may not tender nor the buyer demand delivery of the goods in substitution for the documents.

Section 2—321. C.I.F. or C. & F.: "Net Landed Weights"; "Payment on Arrival"; Warranty of Condition on Arrival

Under a contract containing a term C.I.F. or C. & F.

(1) Where the price is based on or is to be adjusted according to "net landed weights," "delivered weights," "out turn" quantity or quality or the like, unless otherwise agreed the seller must reasonably estimate the price. The payment due on tender of the documents called for by the contract is the amount so estimated, but after final adjustment of the price a settlement must be made with commercial promptness.

(2) An agreement described in subsection (1) or any warranty of quality or condition of the goods on arrival places upon the seller the risk of ordinary deterioration, shrinkage and the like in transportation but has no effect on the place or time of identification to the contract for sale or delivery or on the passing of the risk of loss.

(3) Unless otherwise agreed where the contract provides for payment on or after arrival of the goods the seller must before payment allow such preliminary inspection as is feasible; but if the goods are lost delivery of the documents and payment are due when the goods should have arrived.

Section 2—322. Delivery "Ex-Ship"

(1) Unless otherwise agreed a term for delivery of goods "ex-ship" (which means from the carrying vessel) or in equivalent language is not restricted to a particular ship and requires delivery from a ship which has reached a place at the named port of destination where goods of the kind are usually discharged.

(2) Under such a term unless otherwise agreed

  (a) the seller must discharge all liens arising out of the carriage and furnish the buyer with a direction which puts the carrier under a duty to deliver the goods; and

  (b) the risk of loss does not pass to the buyer until the goods leave the ship's tackle or are otherwise properly unloaded.

Section 2—323. Form of Bill of Lading Required in Overseas Shipment; "Overseas"

(1) Where the contract contemplates overseas shipment and contains a term C.I.F. or C. & F. or F.O.B. vessel, the seller unless otherwise agreed must obtain a negotiable bill of lading stating that the goods have been loaded on board or, in the case of a term C.I.F. or C. & F., received for shipment.

(2) Where in a case within subsection (1) a bill of lading has been issued in a set of parts, unless otherwise agreed if the documents are not to be sent from abroad the buyer may demand tender of the full set; otherwise only one part of the bill of lading need be tendered. Even if the agreement expressly requires a full set

  (a) due tender of a single part is acceptable within the provisions of this Article on cure of improper delivery (subsection (1) of Section 2—508); and

  (b) even though the full set is demanded, if the documents are sent from abroad the person tendering an incomplete set may nevertheless require payment upon furnishing an indemnity which the buyer in good faith deems adequate.

(3) A shipment by water or by air or a contract contemplating such shipment is "overseas" insofar as by usage of trade or agreement it is subject to the commercial, financing or shipping practices characteristic of international deep water commerce.

Section 2—324. "No Arrival, No Sale" Term

Under a term "no arrival, no sale" or terms of like meaning, unless otherwise agreed,

  (a) the seller must properly ship conforming goods and if they arrive by any means he must tender them on arrival but he assumes no obligation that the goods will arrive unless he has caused the non-arrival; and

  (b) where without fault of the seller the goods are in part lost or have so deteriorated as no longer to conform to the contract or arrive after the contract time, the buyer may proceed as if there had been casualty to identified goods (Section 2—613).

Section 2—325. "Letter of Credit" Term; "Confirmed Credit"

(1) Failure of the buyer seasonably to furnish an agreed letter of credit is a breach of the contract for sale.

(2) The delivery to seller of a proper letter of credit suspends the buyer's obligation to pay. If the letter of credit is dishonored, the seller may on seasonable notification to the buyer require payment directly from him.

(3) Unless otherwise agreed the term "letter of credit" or "banker's credit" in a contract for sale means an irrevocable credit issued by a financing agency of good repute and, where the shipment is overseas, of good international repute. The term "confirmed credit" means that the credit must also carry the direct obligation of such an agency which does business in the seller's financial market.

Section 2—326. Sale on Approval and Sale or Return; Consignment Sales and Rights of Creditors

(1) Unless otherwise agreed, if delivered goods may be returned by the buyer even though they conform to the contract, the transaction is

  (a) a "sale on approval" if the goods are delivered primarily for use, and

  (b) a "sale or return" if the goods are delivered primarily for resale.

(2) Except as provided in subsection (3), goods held on approval are not subject to the claims of the buyer's creditors until acceptance; goods held on sale or return are subject to such claims while in the buyer's possession.

(3) Where goods are delivered to a person for sale and such person maintains a place of business at which he deals in goods of the kind involved, under a name other than the name of the person making delivery, then with respect to claims of creditors of the person conducting the business the goods are deemed to be on sale or return. The provisions of this subsection are applicable even though an agreement purports to reserve title to the person making delivery until payment or resale or uses such words as "on consignment" or "on memorandum." However, this subsection is not applicable if the person making delivery

  (a) complies with an applicable law providing for a consignor's interest or the like to be evidenced by a sign, or

  (b) establishes that the person conducting the business is generally known by his creditors to be substantially engaged in selling the goods of others, or

  (c) complies with the filing provisions of the Article on Secured Transactions (Article 9).

(4) Any "or return" term of a contract for sale is to be treated as a separate contract for sale within the statute of frauds section of this Article (Section 2—201) and as contradicting the sale aspect of the contract within the provisions of this Article on parol or extrinsic evidence (Section 2—202).

Section 2—327. Special Incidents of Sale on Approval and Sale or Return
(1) Under a sale on approval unless otherwise agreed

    (a) although the goods are identified to the contract the risk of loss and the title do not pass to the buyer until acceptance; and

    (b) use of the goods consistent with the purpose of trial is not acceptance but failure seasonably to notify the seller of election to return the goods is acceptance, and if the goods conform to the contract acceptance of any part is acceptance of the whole; and

    (c) after due notification of election to return, the return is at the seller's risk and expense but a merchant buyer must follow any reasonable instructions.

(2) Under a sale or return unless otherwise agreed

    (a) the option to return extends to the whole or any commercial unit of the goods while in substantially their original condition, but must be exercised seasonably; and

    (b) the return is at the buyer's risk and expense.

Section 2—328. Sale by Auction
(1) In a sale by auction if goods are put up in lots each lot is the subject of a separate sale.

(2) A sale by auction is complete when the auctioneer so announces by the fall of the hammer or in other customary manner. Where a bid is made while the hammer is falling in acceptance of a prior bid the auctioneer may in his discretion reopen the bidding or declare the goods sold under the bid on which the hammer was falling.

(3) Such a sale is with reserve unless the goods are in explicit terms put up without reserve. In an auction with reserve the auctioneer may withdraw the goods at any time until he announces completion of the sale. In an auction without reserve, after the auctioneer calls for bids on an article or lot, that article or lot cannot be withdrawn unless no bid is made within a reasonable time. In either case a bidder may retract his bid until the auctioneer's announcement of completion of the sale, but a bidder's retraction does not revive any previous bid.

(4) If the auctioneer knowingly receives a bid on the seller's behalf or the seller makes or procures such a bid, and notice has not been given that liberty for such bidding is reserved, the buyer may at his option avoid the sale or take the goods at the price of the last good faith bid prior to the completion of the sale. This subsection shall not apply to any bid at a forced sale.

Part 4 Title, Creditors and Good Faith Purchasers

Section 2—401. Passing of Title; Reservation for Security; Limited Application of This Section
Each provision of this Article with regard to the rights, obligations and remedies of the seller, the buyer, purchasers or other third parties applies irrespective of title to the goods except where the provision refers to such title. Insofar as situations are not covered by the other provisions of this Article and matters concerning title become material the following rules apply:

(1) Title to goods cannot pass under a contract for sale prior to their identification to the contract (Section 2—501), and unless otherwise explicitly agreed the buyer acquires by their identification a special property as limited by this Act. Any retention or reservation by the seller of the title (property) in goods shipped or delivered to the buyer is limited in effect to a reservation of a security interest. Subject to these provisions and to the provisions of the Article on Secured Transactions (Article 9), title to goods passes from the seller to the buyer in any manner and on any conditions explicitly agreed on by the parties.

(2) Unless otherwise explicitly agreed title passes to the buyer at the time and place at which the seller completes his performance with reference to the physical delivery of the goods, despite any reservation of a security interest and even though a document of title is to be delivered at a different time or place; and in particular and despite any reservation of a security interest by the bill of lading

    (a) if the contract requires or authorizes the seller to send the goods to the buyer but does not require him to deliver them at destination, title passes to the buyer at the time and place of shipment; but

    (b) if the contract requires delivery at destination, title passes on tender there.

(3) Unless otherwise explicitly agreed where delivery is to be made without moving the goods,

    (a) if the seller is to deliver a document of title, title passes at the time when and the place where he delivers such documents; or

    (b) if the goods are at the time of contracting already identified and no documents are to be delivered, title passes at the time and place of contracting.

(4) A rejection or other refusal by the buyer to receive or retain the goods, whether or not justified, or a justified revocation of acceptance revests title to the goods in the seller. Such revesting occurs by operation of law and is not a "sale."

Section 2—402. Rights of Seller's Creditors Against Sold Goods
(1) Except as provided in subsections (2) and (3), rights of unsecured creditors of the seller with respect to goods which have been identified to a contract for sale are subject to the buyer's rights to recover the goods under this Article (Sections 2—502 and 2—716).

(2) A creditor of the seller may treat a sale or an identification of goods to a contract for sale as void if as against him a retention of possession by the seller is fraudulent under any rule of law of the state where the goods are situated, except that retention of possession in good faith and current course of trade by a merchant-seller for a commercially reasonable time after a sale or identification is not fraudulent.

(3) Nothing in this Article shall be deemed to impair the rights of creditors of the seller

    (a) under the provisions of the Article on Secured Transactions (Article 9); or

    (b) where identification to the contract or delivery is made not in current course of trade but in satisfaction of or as security for a pre-existing claim for money, security or the like and is made under circumstances which under any rule of law of the state where the goods are situated would apart from this Article constitute the transaction a fraudulent transfer or voidable preference.

Section 2—403. Power to Transfer; Good Faith Purchase of Goods; "Entrusting"
(1) A purchaser of goods acquires all title which his transferor had or had power to transfer except that a purchaser of a limited interest acquires rights only to the extent of the interest purchased. A person with voidable title has power to transfer a good title to a good faith purchaser for value. When goods have been delivered under a transaction of purchase the purchaser has such power even though

    (a) the transferor was deceived as to the identity of the purchaser, or

    (b) the delivery was in exchange for a check which is later dishonored, or

    (c) it was agreed that the transaction was to be a "cash sale," or

    (d) the delivery was procured through fraud punishable as larcenous under the criminal law.

(2) Any entrusting of possession of goods to a merchant who deals in goods of that kind gives him power to transfer all rights of the entruster to a buyer in ordinary course of business.

(3) "Entrusting" includes any delivery and any acquiescence in retention of possession regardless of any condition expressed between the parties to the delivery or acquiescence and regardless of whether the procurement of the entrusting or the possessor's disposition of the goods have been such as to be larcenous under the criminal law.

(4) The rights of other purchasers of goods and of lien creditors are governed by the Articles on Secured Transactions (Article 9), Bulk Transfers (Article 6) and Documents of Title (Article 7).

Part 5 Performance

Section 2—501. Insurable Interest in Goods; Manner of Identification of Goods

(1) The buyer obtains a special property and an insurable interest in goods by identification of existing goods as goods to which the contract refers even though the goods so identified are nonconforming and he has an option to return or reject them. Such identification can be made at any time and in any manner explicitly agreed to by the parties. In the absence of explicit agreement identification occurs.

    (a) when the contract is made if it is for the sale of goods already existing and identified;

    (b) if the contract is for the sale of future goods other than those described in paragraph (c), when goods are shipped, marked or otherwise designated by the seller as goods to which the contract refers;

    (c) when the crops are planted or otherwise become growing crops or the young are conceived if the contract is for the sale of unborn young to be born within twelve months after contracting or for the sale of crops to be harvested within twelve months or the next normal harvest season after contracting whichever is longer.

(2) The seller retains an insurable interest in goods so long as title to or any security interest in the goods remains in him and where the identification is by the seller alone he may until default or insolvency or notification to the buyer that the identification is final substitute other goods for those identified.

(3) Nothing in this section impairs any insurable interest recognized under any other statute or rule of law.

Section 2—502. Buyer's Right to Goods on Seller's Insolvency

(1) Subject to subsection (2) and even though the goods have not been shipped a buyer who has paid a part or all of the price of goods in which he has a special property under the provisions of the immediately preceding section may on making and keeping good a tender of any unpaid portion of their price recover them from the seller if the seller becomes insolvent within ten days after receipt of the first installment on their price.

(2) If the identification creating his special property has been made by the buyer he acquires the right to recover the goods only if they conform to the contract for sale.

Section 2—503. Manner of Seller's Tender of Delivery

(1) Tender of delivery requires that the seller put and hold conforming goods at the buyer's disposition and give the buyer any notification reasonably necessary to enable him to take delivery. The manner, time and place for tender are determined by the agreement and this Article, and in particular

    (a) tender must be at a reasonable hour, and if it is of goods they must be kept available for the period reasonably necessary to enable the buyer to take possession; but

    (b) unless otherwise agreed the buyer must furnish facilities reasonably suited to the receipt of the goods.

(2) Where the case is within the next section respecting shipment tender requires that the seller comply with its provisions.

(3) Where the seller is required to deliver at a particular destination tender requires that he comply with subsection (1) and also in any appropriate case tender documents as described in subsections (4) and (5) of this section.

(4) Where goods are in the possession of a bailee and are to be delivered without being moved

    (a) tender requires that the seller either tender a negotiable document of title covering such goods or procure acknowledgment by the bailee of the buyer's right to possession of the goods; but

    (b) tender to the buyer of a non-negotiable document of title or of a written direction to the bailee to deliver is sufficient tender unless the buyer seasonably objects, and receipt by the bailee of notification of the buyer's rights fixes those rights as against the bailee and all third persons; but risk of loss of the goods and of any failure by the bailee to honor the non-negotiable document of title or to obey the direction remains on the seller until the buyer has had a reasonable time to present the document or direction, and a refusal by the bailee to honor the document or to obey the direction defeats the tender.

(5) Where the contract requires the seller to deliver documents

    (a) he must tender all such documents in correct form, except as provided in this Article with respect to bills of lading in a set (subsection (2) of Section 2—323); and

    (b) tender through customary banking channels is sufficient and dishonor of a draft accompanying the documents constitutes non-acceptance or rejection.

Section 2—504. Shipment by Seller

Where the seller is required or authorized to send the goods to the buyer and the contract does not require him to deliver them at a particular destination, then unless otherwise agreed he must

    (a) put the goods in the possession of such a carrier and make such a contract for their transportation as may be reasonable having regard to the nature of the goods and other circumstances of the case; and

    (b) obtain and promptly deliver or tender in due form any document necessary to enable the buyer to obtain possession of the goods or otherwise required by the agreement or by usage of trade; and

    (c) promptly notify the buyer of the shipment.

Failure to notify the buyer under paragraph (c) or to make a proper contract under paragraph (a) is a ground for rejection only if material delay or loss ensues.

Section 2—505. Seller's Shipment Under Reservation

(1) Where the seller has identified goods to the contract by or before shipment:

    (a) his procurement of a negotiable bill of lading to his own order or otherwise reserves in him a security interest in the goods. His procurement of the bill to the order of a financing agency or of the buyer indicates in addition only the seller's expectation of transferring that interest to the person named.

    (b) a non-negotiable bill of lading to himself or his nominee reserves possession of the goods as security but except in a case of conditional delivery (subsection (2) of Section 2—507) a non-negotiable bill of lading naming the buyer as consignee reserves no security interest even though the seller retains possession of the bill of lading.

(2) When shipment by the seller with reservation of a security interest is in violation of the contract for sale it constitutes an improper contract for transportation within the preceding section but impairs neither the rights given to the buyer by shipment and identification of the goods to the contract nor the seller's powers as a holder of a negotiable document.

Section 2—506. Rights of Financing Agency

(1) A financing agency by paying or purchasing for value a draft which relates to a shipment of goods acquires to the extent of the payment or purchase and in addition to its own rights under the draft and any document of title securing it any rights of the shipper in the goods including the right to stop delivery and the shipper's right to have the draft honored by the buyer.

(2) The right to reimbursement of a financing agency which has in good faith honored or purchased the draft under commitment to or authority from the buyer is not impaired by subsequent discovery of defects with reference to any relevant document which was apparently regular on its face.

Section 2—507. Effect of Seller's Tender; Delivery on Condition

(1) Tender of delivery is a condition to the buyer's duty to accept the goods and, unless otherwise agreed, to his duty to pay for them. Tender entitles the seller to acceptance of the goods and to payment according to the contract.

(2) Where payment is due and demanded on the delivery to the buyer of goods or documents of title, his right as against the seller to retain or dispose of them is conditional upon his making the payment due.

Section 2—508. Cure by Seller of Improper Tender or Delivery; Replacement

(1) Where any tender or delivery by the seller is rejected because non-conforming and the time for performance has not yet expired, the seller may seasonably notify the buyer of his intention to cure and may then within the contract time make a conforming delivery.

(2) Where the buyer rejects a non-conforming tender which the seller had reasonable grounds to believe would be acceptable with or without money allowance the seller may if he seasonably notifies the buyer have a further reasonable time to substitute a conforming tender.

Section 2—509. Risk of Loss in the Absence of Breach

(1) Where the contract requires or authorizes the seller to ship the goods by carrier

    (a) if it does not require him to deliver them at a particular destination, the risk of loss passes to the buyer when the goods are duly delivered to the carrier even though the shipment is under reservation (Section 2—505); but

    (b) if it does require him to deliver them at a particular destination and the goods are there duly tendered while in the possession of the carrier, the risk of loss passes to the buyer when the goods are there duly so tendered as to enable the buyer to take delivery.

(2) Where the goods are held by a bailee to be delivered without being moved, the risk of loss passes to the buyer

    (a) on his receipt of a negotiable document of title covering the goods; or

    (b) on acknowledgment by the bailee of the buyer's right to possession of the goods; or

    (c) after his receipt of a non-negotiable document of title or other written direction to deliver, as provided in subsection (4) (b) of Section 2—503.

(3) In any case not within subsection (1) or (2), the risk of loss passes to the buyer on his receipt of the goods if the seller is a merchant; otherwise the risk passes to the buyer on tender of delivery.

(4) The provisions of this section are subject to contrary agreement of the parties and to the provisions of this Article on sale on approval (Section 2—327) and on effect of breach on risk of loss (Section 2—510).

Section 2—510. Effect of Breach on Risk of Loss

(1) Where a tender or delivery of goods so fails to conform to the contract as to give a right of rejection the risk of their loss remains on the seller until cure or acceptance.

(2) Where the buyer rightfully revokes acceptance he may to the extent of any deficiency in his effective insurance coverage treat the risk of loss as having rested on the seller from the beginning.

(3) Where the buyer as to conforming goods already identified to the contract for sale repudiates or is otherwise in breach before risk of their loss has passed to him, the seller may to the extent of any deficiency in his effective insurance coverage treat the risk of loss as resting on the buyer for a commercially reasonable time.

Section 2—511. Tender of Payment by Buyer; Payment by Check

(1) Unless otherwise agreed tender of payment is a condition to the seller's duty to tender and complete any delivery.

(2) Tender of payment is sufficient when made by any means or in any manner current in the ordinary course of business unless the seller demands payment in legal tender and gives any extension of time reasonably necessary to procure it.

(3) Subject to the provisions of this Act on the effect of an instrument on an obligation (Section 3—802), payment by check is conditional and is defeated as between the parties by dishonor of the check on due presentment.

Section 2—512. Payment by Buyer Before Inspection

(1) Where the contract requires payment before inspection non-conformity of the goods does not excuse the buyer from so making payment unless

    (a) the non-conformity appears without inspection; or

    (b) despite tender of the required documents the circumstances would justify injunction against honor under the provisions of this Act (Section 5—114).

(2) Payment pursuant to subsection (1) does not constitute an acceptance of goods or impair the buyer's right to inspect or any of his remedies.

Section 2—513. Buyer's Right to Inspection of Goods

(1) Unless otherwise agreed and subject to subsection (3), where goods are tendered or delivered or identified to the contract for sale, the buyer has a right before payment or acceptance to inspect them at any reasonable place and time and in any reasonable manner. When the seller is required or authorized to send the goods to the buyer, the inspection may be after their arrival.

(2) Expenses of inspection must be borne by the buyer but may be recovered from the seller if the goods do not conform and are rejected.

(3) Unless otherwise agreed and subject to the provisions of this Article on C.I.F. contracts (subsection (3) of Section 2—321), the buyer is not entitled to inspect the goods before payment of the price when the contract provides

    (a) for delivery "C.O.D." or on other like terms; or

    (b) for payment against documents of title, except where such payment is due only after the goods are to become available for inspection.

(4) A place or method of inspection fixed by the parties is presumed to be exclusive but unless otherwise expressly agreed it does not postpone identification or shift the place for delivery or for passing the risk of loss. If compliance becomes impossible, inspection shall be as provided in this section unless the place or method fixed was clearly intended as an indispensable condition failure of which avoids the contract.

Section 2—514. When Documents Deliverable on Acceptance; When on Payment

Unless otherwise agreed documents against which a draft is drawn are to be delivered to the drawee on acceptance of the draft if it is payable more than three days after presentment; otherwise, only on payment.

Section 2—515. Preserving Evidence of Goods in Dispute

In furtherance of the adjustment of any claim or dispute

(a) either party on reasonable notification to the other and for the purpose of ascertaining the facts and preserving evidence has the right to inspect, test and sample the goods including such of them as may be in the possession or control of the other; and

(b) the parties may agree to a third party inspection or survey to determine the conformity or condition of the goods and may agree that the findings shall be binding upon them in any subsequent litigation or adjustment.

Part 6 Breach, Repudiation and Excuse

Section 2—601. Buyer's Rights on Improper Delivery

Subject to the provisions of this Article on breach in installment contracts (Section 2—612) and unless otherwise agreed under the sections on contractual limitations of remedy (Sections 2—718 and 2—719), if the goods or the tender of delivery fail in any respect to conform to the contract, the buyer may

(a) reject the whole; or

(b) accept the whole; or

(c) accept any commercial unit or units and reject the rest.

Section 2—602. Manner and Effect of Rightful Rejection

(1) Rejection of goods must be within a reasonable time after their delivery or tender. It is ineffective unless the buyer seasonably notifies the seller.

(2) Subject to the provisions of the two following sections on rejected goods (Sections 2—603 and 2—604),

(a) after rejection any exercise of ownership by the buyer with respect to any commercial unit is wrongful as against the seller; and

(b) if the buyer has before rejection taken physical possession of goods in which he does not have a security interest under the provisions of this Article (subsection (3) of Section 2—711), he is under a duty after rejection to hold them with reasonable care at the seller's disposition for a time sufficient to permit the seller to remove them; but

(c) the buyer has no further obligations with regard to goods rightfully rejected.

(3) The seller's rights with respect to goods wrongfully rejected are governed by the provisions of this Article on Seller's remedies in general (Section 2—703).

Section 2—603. Merchant Buyer's Duties as to Rightfully Rejected Goods

(1) Subject to any security interest in the buyer (subsection (3) of Section 2—711), when the seller has no agent or place of business at the market of rejection a merchant buyer is under a duty after rejection of goods in his possession or control to follow any reasonable instructions received from the seller with respect to the goods and in the absence of such instructions to make reasonable efforts to sell them for the seller's account if they are perishable or threaten to decline in value speedily. Instructions are not reasonable if on demand indemnity for expenses is not forthcoming.

(2) When the buyer sells goods under subsection (1), he is entitled to reimbursement from the seller or out of the proceeds for reasonable expenses of caring for and selling them, and if the expenses include no selling commission then to such commission as is usual in the trade or if there is none to a reasonable sum not exceeding ten per cent on the gross proceeds.

(3) In complying with this section the buyer is held only to good faith and good faith conduct hereunder is neither acceptance nor conversion nor the basis of an action for damages.

Section 2—604. Buyer's Options as to Salvage of Rightfully Rejected Goods

Subject to the provisions of the immediately preceding section on perishables if the seller gives no instructions within a reasonable time after notification of rejection the buyer may store the rejected goods for the seller's account or reship them to him or resell them for the seller's account with reimbursement as provided in the preceding section. Such action is not acceptance or conversion.

Section 2—605. Waiver of Buyer's Objections by Failure to Particularize

(1) The buyer's failure to state in connection with rejection a particular defect which is ascertainable by reasonable inspection precludes him from relying on the unstated defect to justify rejection or to establish breach

(a) where the seller could have cured it if stated seasonably; or

(b) between merchants when the seller has after rejection made a request in writing for a full and final written statement of all defects on which the buyer proposes to rely.

(2) Payment against documents made without reservation of rights precludes recovery of the payment for defects apparent on the face of the documents.

Section 2—606. What Constitutes Acceptance of Goods

(1) Acceptance of goods occurs when the buyer

(a) after a reasonable opportunity to inspect the goods signifies to the seller that the goods are conforming or that he will take or retain them in spite of their non-conformity; or

(b) fails to make an effective rejection (subsection (1) of Section 2—602), but such acceptance does not occur until the buyer has had a reasonable opportunity to inspect them; or

(c) does any act inconsistent with the seller's ownership; but if such act is wrongful as against the seller it is an acceptance only if ratified by him.

(2) Acceptance of a part of any commercial unit is acceptance of that entire unit.

Section 2—607. Effect of Acceptance; Notice of Breach; Burden of Establishing Breach After Acceptance; Notice of Claim or Litigation to Person Answerable Over

(1) The buyer must pay at the contract rate for any goods accepted.

(2) Acceptance of goods by the buyer precludes rejection of the goods accepted and if made with knowledge of a non-conformity cannot be revoked because of it unless the acceptance was on the reasonable assumption that the non-conformity would be seasonably cured but acceptance does not of itself impair any other remedy provided by this Article for non-conformity.

(3) Where a tender has been accepted

(a) the buyer must within a reasonable time after he discovers or should have discovered any breach notify the seller of breach or be barred from any remedy; and

(b) if the claim is one for infringement or the like (subsection (3) of Section 2—312) and the buyer is sued as a result of such a breach he must so notify the seller within a reasonable time after he receives notice of the litigation or be barred from any remedy over for liability established by the litigation.

(4) The burden is on the buyer to establish any breach with respect to the goods accepted.

(5) Where the buyer is sued for breach of a warranty or other obligation for which his seller is answerable over

(a) he may give his seller written notice of the litigation. If the notice states that the seller may come in and defend and that if the seller does not do so he will be bound in any action against him by his buyer by any determination of fact common to the two litigations, then unless the seller after seasonable receipt of the notice does come in and defend he is so bound.

(b) if the claim is one for infringement or the like (subsection (3) of Section 2—312) the original seller may demand in writing that his buyer turn over to him control of the litigation including settlement or else be barred from any remedy over and if he also agrees to bear all expense and to satisfy any adverse judgment, then unless the buyer after seasonable receipt of the demand does turn over control the buyer is so barred.

(6) The provisions of subsections (3), (4) and (5) apply to any obligation of a buyer to hold the seller harmless against infringement or the like (subsection (3) of Section 2—312).

Section 2—608. Revocation of Acceptance in Whole or in Part

(1) The buyer may revoke his acceptance of a lot or commercial unit whose non-conformity substantially impairs its value to him if he has accepted it

(a) on the reasonable assumption that its non-conformity would be cured and it has not been seasonably cured; or

(b) without discovery of such non-conformity if his acceptance was reasonably induced either by the difficulty of discovery before acceptance or by the seller's assurances.

(2) Revocation of acceptance must occur within a reasonable time after the buyer discovers or should have discovered the ground for it and before any substantial change in condition of the goods which is not caused by their own defects. It is not effective until the buyer notifies the seller of it

(3) A buyer who so revokes has the same rights and duties with regard to the goods involved as if he had rejected them.

Section 2—609. Right to Adequate Assurance of Performance

(1) A contract for sale imposes an obligation on each party that the other's expectation of receiving due performance will not be impaired. When reasonable grounds for insecurity arise with respect to the performance of either party the other may in writing demand adequate assurance of due performance and until he receives such assurance may if commercially reasonable suspend any performance for which he has not already received the agreed return.

(2) Between merchants the reasonableness of grounds for insecurity and the adequacy of any assurance offered shall be determined according to commercial standards.

(3) Acceptance of any improper delivery or payment does not prejudice the aggrieved party's right to demand adequate assurance of future performance.

(4) After receipt of a justified demand failure to provide within a reasonable time not exceeding thirty days such assurance of due performance as is adequate under the circumstances of the particular case is a repudiation of the contract.

Section 2—610. Anticipatory Repudiation

When either party repudiates the contract with respect to a performance not yet due the loss of which will substantially impair the value of the contract to the other, the aggrieved party may

(a) for a commercially reasonable time await performance by the repudiating party; or

(b) resort to any remedy for breach (Section 2—703 or Section 2—711), even though he has notified the repudiating party that he would await the latter's performance and has urged retraction; and

(c) in either case suspend his own performance or proceed in accordance with the provisions of this Article on the seller's right to identify goods to the contract notwithstanding breach or to salvage unfinished goods (Section 2—704).

Section 2—611. Retraction of Anticipatory Repudiation

(1) Until the repudiating party's next performance is due he can retract his repudiation unless the aggrieved party has since the repudiation cancelled or materially changed his position or otherwise indicated that he considers the repudiation final.

(2) Retraction may be by any method which clearly indicates to the aggrieved party that the repudiating party intends to perform, but must include any assurance justifiably demanded under the provisions of this Article (Section 2—609).

(3) Retraction reinstates the repudiating party's rights under the contract with due excuse and allowance to the aggrieved party for any delay occasioned by the repudiation.

Section 2—612. "Installment Contract"; Breach

(1) An "installment contract" is one which requires or authorizes the delivery of goods in separate lots to be separately accepted, even though the contract contains a clause "each delivery is a separate contract" or its equivalent.

(2) The buyer may reject any installment which is non-conforming if the non-conformity substantially impairs the value of that installment and cannot be cured or if the non-conformity is a defect in the required documents; but if the non-conformity does not fall within subsection (3) and the seller gives adequate assurance of its cure the buyer must accept that installment.

(3) Whenever non-conformity or default with respect to one or more installments substantially impairs the value of the whole contract there is a breach of the whole. But the aggrieved party reinstates the contract if he accepts a non-conforming installment without seasonably notifying of cancellation or if he brings an action with respect only to past installments or demands performance as to future installments.

Section 2—613. Casualty to Identified Goods

Where the contract requires for its performance goods identified when the contract is made, and the goods suffer casualty without fault of either party before the risk of loss passes to the buyer, or in a proper case under a "no arrival, no sale" term (Section 2—324) then

(a) if the loss is total the contract is avoided; and

(b) if the loss is partial or the goods have so deteriorated as no longer to conform to the contract the buyer may nevertheless demand inspection and at his option either treat the contract as avoided or accept the goods with due allowance from the contract price for the deterioration or the deficiency in quantity but without further right against the seller.

Section 2—614. Substituted Performance

(1) Where without fault of either party the agreed berthing, loading, or unloading facilities fail or an agreed type of carrier becomes unavailable or the agreed manner of delivery otherwise becomes commercially impracticable but a commercially reasonable substitute is available, such substitute performance must be tendered and accepted.

(2) If the agreed means or manner of payment fails because of domestic or foreign governmental regulation, the seller may withhold or stop delivery unless the buyer provides a means or manner of payment which is commercially a substantial equivalent. If delivery has already been taken, payment by the means or in the manner provided by the regulation discharges the buyer's obligation unless the regulation is discriminatory, oppressive or predatory.

Section 2—615. Excuse by Failure of Presupposed Conditions

Except so far as a seller may have assumed a greater obligation and subject to the preceding section on substituted performance:

(a) Delay in delivery or non-delivery in whole or in part by a seller who complies with paragraphs (b) and (c) is not a breach of his duty under a contract for sale if performance as agreed has been made impracticable by the occurrence of a contingency the non-occurrence of which was a basic assumption on which the contract was made or by compliance in good faith with any applicable foreign or domestic governmental regulation or order whether or not it later proves to be invalid.

(b) Where the causes mentioned in paragraph (a) affect only a part of the seller's capacity to perform, he must allocate production and deliveries among his customers but may at his option include regular customers not then under contract as well as his own requirements for further manufacture. He may so allocate in any manner which is fair and reasonable.

(c) The seller must notify the buyer seasonably that there will be delay or non-delivery and, when allocation is required under paragraph (b), of the estimated quota thus made available for the buyer.

Section 2—616. Procedure on Notice Claiming Excuse

(1) Where the buyer receives notification of a material or indefinite delay or an allocation justified under the preceding section he may by written notification to the seller as to any delivery concerned, and where the prospective deficiency substantially impairs the value of the whole contract under the provisions of this Article relating to breach of installment contracts (Section 2—612), then also as to the whole,

(a) terminate and thereby discharge any unexecuted portion of the contract; or

(b) modify the contract by agreeing to take his available quota in substitution.

(2) If after receipt of such notification from the seller the buyer fails so to modify the contract within a reasonable time not exceeding thirty days the contract lapses with respect to any deliveries affected.

(3) The provisions of this section may not be negated by agreement except in so far as the seller has assumed a greater obligation under the preceding section.

Part 7 Remedies

Section 2—701. Remedies for Breach of Collateral Contracts Not Impaired

Remedies for breach of any obligation or promise collateral or ancillary to a contract for sale are not impaired by the provisions of this Article.

Section 2—702. Seller's Remedies on Discovery of Buyer's Insolvency

(1) Where the seller discovers the buyer to be insolvent he may refuse delivery except for cash including payment for all goods theretofore delivered under the contract, and stop delivery under this Article (Section 2—705).

(2) Where the seller discovers that the buyer has received goods on credit while insolvent he may reclaim the goods upon demand made within ten days after the receipt, but if misrepresentation of solvency has been made to the particular seller in writing within three months before delivery the ten day limitation does not apply. Except as provided in this subsection the seller may not base a right to reclaim goods on the buyer's fraudulent or innocent misrepresentation of solvency or of intent to pay.

(3) The seller's right to reclaim under subsection (2) is subject to the rights of a buyer in ordinary course or other good faith purchaser under this Article (Section 2—403). Successful reclamation of goods excludes all other remedies with respect to them.

Section 2—703. Seller's Remedies in General

Where the buyer wrongfully rejects or revokes acceptance of goods or fails to make a payment due on or before delivery or repudiates with respect to a part or the whole, then with respect to any goods directly affected and, if the breach is of the whole contract (Section 2—612), then also with respect to the whole undelivered balance, the aggrieved seller may

(a) withhold delivery of such goods;

(b) stop delivery by any bailee as hereafter provided (Section 2—705);

(c) proceed under the next section respecting goods still unidentified to the contract;

(d) resell and recover damages as hereafter provided (Section 2—706);

(e) recover damages for non-acceptance (Section 2—708) or in a proper case the price (Section 2—709);

(f) cancel.

Section 2—704. Seller's Right to Identify Goods to the Contract Notwithstanding Breach or to Salvage Unfinished Goods

(1) An aggrieved seller under the preceding section may

(a) identify to the contract conforming goods not already identified if at the time he learned of the breach they are in his possession or control;

(b) treat as the subject of resale goods which have demonstrably been intended for the particular contract even though those goods are unfinished.

(2) Where the goods are unfinished an aggrieved seller may in the exercise of reasonable commercial judgment for the purposes of avoiding loss and of effective realization either complete the manufacture and wholly identify the goods to the contract or cease manufacture and resell for scrap or salvage value or proceed in any other reasonable manner.

Section 2—705. Seller's Stoppage of Delivery in Transit or Otherwise

(1) The seller may stop delivery of goods in the possession of a carrier or other bailee when he discovers the buyer to be insolvent (Section 2—702) and may stop delivery of carload, truckload, planeload or larger shipments of express or freight when the buyer repudiates or fails to make a payment due before delivery or if for any other reason the seller has a right to withhold or reclaim the goods.

(2) As against such buyer the seller may stop delivery until
   (a) receipt of the goods by the buyer; or
   (b) acknowledgment to the buyer by any bailee of the goods except a carrier that the bailee holds the goods for the buyer; or
   (c) such acknowledgment to the buyer by a carrier by reshipment or as warehouseman; or
   (d) negotiation to the buyer of any negotiable document of title covering the goods.

(3) (a) To stop delivery the seller must so notify as to enable the bailee by reasonable diligence to prevent delivery of the goods.
   (b) After such notification the bailee must hold and deliver the goods according to the directions of the seller but the seller is liable to the bailee for any ensuing charges or damages.
   (c) If a negotiable document of title has been issued for goods the bailee is not obliged to obey a notification to stop until surrender of the document.
   (d) A carrier who has issued a non-negotiable bill of lading is not obliged to obey a notification to stop received from a person other than the consignor.

Section 2—706. Seller's Resale Including Contract for Resale

(1) Under the conditions stated in Section 2—703 on seller's remedies, the seller may resell the goods concerned or the undelivered balance thereof. Where the resale is made in good faith and in a commercially reasonable manner the seller may recover the difference between the resale price and the contract price together with any incidental damages allowed under the provisions of this Article (Section 2—710), but less expenses saved in consequence of the buyer's breach.

(2) Except as otherwise provided in subsection (3) or unless otherwise agreed resale may be at public or private sale including sale by way of one or more contracts to sell or of identification to an existing contract of the seller. Sale may be as a unit or in parcels and at any time and place and on any terms but every aspect of the sale including the method, manner, time, place and terms must be commercially reasonable. The resale must be reasonably identified as referring to the broken contract, but it is not necessary that the goods be in existence or that any or all of them have been identified to the contract before the breach.

(3) Where the resale is at private sale the seller must give the buyer reasonable notification of his intention to resell.

(4) Where the resale is at public sale
   (a) only identified goods can be sold except where there is a recognized market for a public sale of futures in goods of the kind; and
   (b) it must be made at a usual place or market for public sale if one is reasonably available and except in the case of goods which are perishable or threaten to decline in value speedily the seller must give the buyer reasonable notice of the time and place of the resale; and
   (c) if the goods are not to be within the view of those attending the sale the notification of sale must state the place where the goods are located and provide for their reasonable inspection by prospective bidders; and
   (d) the seller may buy.

(5) A purchaser who buys in good faith at a resale takes the goods free of any rights of the original buyer even though the seller fails to comply with one or more of the requirements of this section.

(6) The seller is not accountable to the buyer for any profit made on any resale. A person in the position of a seller (Section 2—707) or a buyer who has rightfully rejected or justifiably revoked acceptance must account for any excess over the amount of his security interest, as hereinafter defined (subsection (3) of Section 2—711).

Section 2—707. "Person in the Position of a Seller"

(1) A "person in the position of a seller" includes as against a principal an agent who has paid or become responsible for the price of goods on behalf of his principal or anyone who otherwise holds a security interest or other right in goods similar to that of a seller.

(2) A person in the position of a seller may as provided in this Article withhold or stop delivery (Section 2—705) and resell (Section 2—706) and recover incidental damages (Section 2—710).

Section 2—708. Seller's Damages for Non-acceptance or Repudiation

(1) Subject to subsection (2) and to the provisions of this Article with respect to proof of market price (Section 2—723), the measure of damages for non-acceptance or repudiation by the buyer is the difference between the market price at the time and place for tender and the unpaid contract price together with any incidental damages provided in this Article (Section 2—710), but less expenses saved in consequence of the buyer's breach.

(2) If the measure of damages provided in subsection (1) is inadequate to put the seller in as good a position as performance would have done then the measure of damages is the profit (including reasonable overhead) which the seller would have made from full performance by the buyer, together with any incidental damages provided in this Article (Section 2—710), due allowance for costs reasonably incurred and due credit for payments or proceeds of resale.

Section 2—709. Action for the Price

(1) When the buyer fails to pay the price as it becomes due the seller may recover, together with any incidental damages under the next section, the price
   (a) of goods accepted or of conforming goods lost or damaged within a commercially reasonable time after risk of their loss has passed to the buyer; and
   (b) of goods identified to the contract if the seller is unable after reasonable effort to resell them at a reasonable price or the circumstances reasonably indicate that such effort will be unavailing.

(2) Where the seller sues for the price he must hold for the buyer any goods which have been identified to the contract and are still in his control except that if resale becomes possible he may resell them at any time prior to the collection of the judgment. The net proceeds of any such resale must be credited to the buyer and payment of the judgment entitles him to any goods not resold.

(3) After the buyer has wrongfully rejected or revoked acceptance of the goods or has failed to make a payment due or has repudiated (Section 2—610), a seller who is held not entitled to the price under this section shall nevertheless be awarded damages for non-acceptance under the preceding section.

Section 2—710. Seller's Incidental Damages

Incidental damages to an aggrieved seller include any commercially reasonable charges, expenses or commissions incurred in stopping delivery, in the transportation, care and custody of goods after the buyer's breach, in connection with return or resale of the goods or otherwise resulting from the breach.

Section 2—711. Buyer's Remedies in General; Buyer's Security Interest in Rejected Goods

(1) Where the seller fails to make delivery or repudiates or the buyer rightfully rejects or justifiably revokes acceptance then with respect to any goods involved, and with respect to the whole if the breach goes to the whole contract (Section 2—612), the buyer may cancel and whether or not he has done so may in addition to recovering so much of the price as has been paid

   (a) "cover" and have damages under the next section as to all the goods affected whether or not they have been identified to the contract; or

   (b) recover damages for non-delivery as provided in this Article (Section 2—713).

(2) Where the seller fails to deliver or repudiates the buyer may also

   (a) if the goods have been identified recover them as provided in this Article (Section 2—502); or

   (b) in a proper case obtain specific performance or replevy the goods as provided in this Article (Section 2—716).

(3) On rightful rejection or justifiable revocation of acceptance a buyer has a security interest in goods in his possession or control for any payments made on their price and any expenses reasonably incurred in their inspection, receipt, transportation, care and custody and may hold such goods and resell them in like manner as an aggrieved seller (Section 2—706).

Section 2—712. "Cover"; Buyer's Procurement of Substitute Goods

(1) After a breach within the preceding section the buyer may "cover" by making in good faith and without unreasonable delay any reasonable purchase of or contract to purchase goods in substitution for those due from the seller.

(2) The buyer may recover from the seller as damages the difference between the cost of cover and the contract price together with any incidental or consequential damages as hereinafter defined (Section 2—715), but less expenses saved in consequence of the seller's breach.

(3) Failure of the buyer to effect cover within this section does not bar him from any other remedy.

Section 2—713. Buyer's Damages for Non-Delivery or Repudiation

(1) Subject to the provisions of this Article with respect to proof of market price (Section 2—723), the measure of damages for non-delivery or repudiation by the seller is the difference between the market price at the time when the buyer learned of the breach and the contract price together with any incidental and consequential damages provided in this Article (Section 2—715), but less expenses saved in consequence of the seller's breach.

(2) Market price is to be determined as of the place for tender or, in cases of rejection after arrival or revocation of acceptance, as of the place of arrival.

Section 2—714. Buyer's Damages for Breach in Regard to Accepted Goods

(1) Where the buyer has accepted goods and given notification (subsection (3) of Section 2—607) he may recover as damages for any non-conformity of tender the loss resulting in the ordinary course of events from the seller's breach as determined in any manner which is reasonable.

(2) The measure of damages for breach of warranty is the difference at the time and place of acceptance between the value of the goods accepted and the value they would have had if they had been as warranted, unless special circumstances show proximate damages of a different amount.

(3) In a proper case any incidental and consequential damages under the next section may also be recovered.

Section 2—715. Buyer's Incidental and Consequential Damages

(1) Incidental damages resulting from the seller's breach include expenses reasonably incurred in inspection, receipt, transportation and care and custody of goods rightfully rejected, any commercially reasonable charges, expenses or commissions in connection with effecting cover and any other reasonable expense incident to the delay or other breach.

(2) Consequential damages resulting from the seller's breach include

   (a) any loss resulting from general or particular requirements and needs of which the seller at the time of contracting had reason to know and which could not reasonably be prevented by cover or otherwise; and

   (b) injury to person or property proximately resulting from any breach of warranty.

Section 2—716. Buyer's Right to Specific Performance or Replevin

(1) Specific performance may be decreed where the goods are unique or in other proper circumstances.

(2) The decree for specific performance may include such terms and conditions as to payment of the price, damages, or other relief as the court may deem just.

(3) The buyer has a right of replevin for goods identified to the contract if after reasonable effort he is unable to effect cover for such goods or the circumstances reasonably indicate that such effort will be unavailing or if the goods have been shipped under reservation and satisfaction of the security interest in them has been made or tendered.

Section 2—717. Deduction of Damages From the Price

The buyer on notifying the seller of his intention to do so may deduct all or any part of the damages resulting from any breach of the contract from any part of the price still due under the same contract.

Section 2—718. Liquidation or Limitation of Damages; Deposits

(1) Damages for breach by either party may be liquidated in the agreement but only at an amount which is reasonable in the light of the anticipated or actual harm caused by the breach, the difficulties of proof of loss, and the inconvenience or nonfeasibility of otherwise obtaining an adequate remedy. A term fixing unreasonably large liquidated damages is void as a penalty.

(2) Where the seller justifiably withholds delivery of goods because of the buyer's breach, the buyer is entitled to restitution of any amount by which the sum of his payments exceeds

   (a) the amount to which the seller is entitled by virtue of terms liquidating the seller's damages in accordance with subsection (1), or

   (b) in the absence of such terms, twenty per cent of the value of the total performance for which the buyer is obligated under the contract or $500, whichever is smaller.

(3) The buyer's right to restitution under subsection (2) is subject to offset to the extent that the seller establishes

   (a) a right to recover damages under the provisions of this Article other than subsection (1), and

   (b) the amount or value of any benefits received by the buyer directly or indirectly by reason of the contract.

(4) Where a seller has received payment in goods their reasonable value or the proceeds of their resale shall be treated as payments for the purposes of subsection (2); but if the seller has notice of the buyer's breach before reselling goods received in part performance, his resale is subject to the conditions laid down in this Article on resale by an aggrieved seller (Section 2—706).

Section 2—719. Contractual Modification or Limitation of Remedy

(1) Subject to the provisions of subsections (2) and (3) of this section and of the preceding section on liquidation and limitation of damages,

    (a) the agreement may provide for remedies in addition to or in substitution for those provided in this Article and may limit or alter the measure of damages recoverable under this Article, as by limiting the buyer's remedies to return of the goods and repayment of the price or to repair and replacement of non-conforming goods or parts; and

    (b) resort to a remedy as provided is optional unless the remedy is expressly agreed to be exclusive, in which case it is the sole remedy.

(2) Where circumstances cause an exclusive or limited remedy to fail of its essential purpose, remedy may be had as provided in this Act.

(3) Consequential damages may be limited or excluded unless the limitation or exclusion is unconscionable. Limitation of consequential damages for injury to the person in the case of consumer goods is prima facie unconscionable but limitation of damages where the loss is commercial is not.

Section 2—720. Effect of "Cancellation" or "Rescission" on Claims for Antecedent Breach

Unless the contrary intention clearly appears, expressions of "cancellation" or "rescission" of the contract or the like shall not be construed as a renunciation or discharge of any claim in damages for an antecedent breach.

Section 2—721. Remedies for Fraud

Remedies for material misrepresentation or fraud include all remedies available under this Article for non-fraudulent breach. Neither rescission or a claim for rescission of the contract for sale nor rejection or return of the goods shall bar or be deemed inconsistent with a claim for damages or other remedy.

Section 2—722. Who Can Sue Third Parties for Injury to Goods

Where a third party so deals with goods which have been identified to a contract for sale as to cause actionable injury to a party to that contract

    (a) a right of action against the third party is in either party to the contract for sale who has title to or a security interest or a special property or an insurable interest in the goods; and if the goods have been destroyed or converted a right of action is also in the party who either bore the risk of loss under the contract for sale or has since the injury assumed that risk as against the other;

    (b) if at the time of the injury the party plaintiff did not bear the risk of loss as against the other party to the contract for sale and there is no arrangement between them for disposition of the recovery, his suit or settlement is, subject to his own interest, as a fiduciary for the other party to the contract;

    (c) either party may with the consent of the other sue for the benefit of whom it may concern.

Section 2—723. Proof of Market Price: Time and Place

(1) If an action based on anticipatory repudiation comes to trial before the time for performance with respect to some or all of the goods, any damages based on market price (Section 2—708 or Section 2—713) shall be determined according to the price of such goods prevailing at the time when the aggrieved party learned of the repudiation.

(2) If evidence of a price prevailing at the times or places described in this Article is not readily available the price prevailing within any reasonable time before or after the time described or at any other place which in commercial judgment or under usage of trade would serve as a reasonable substitute for the one described may be used, making any proper allowance for the cost of transporting the goods to or from such other place.

(3) Evidence of a relevant price prevailing at a time or place other than the one described in this Article offered by one party is not admissible unless and until he has given the other party such notice as the court finds sufficient to prevent unfair surprise.

Section 2—724. Admissibility of Market Quotations

Whenever the prevailing price or value of any goods regularly bought and sold in any established commodity market is in issue, reports in official publications or trade journals or in newspapers or periodicals of general circulation published as the reports of such market shall be admissible in evidence. The circumstances of the preparation of such a report may be shown to affect its weight but not its admissibility.

Section 2—725. Statute of Limitations in Contracts for Sale

(1) An action for breach of any contract for sale must be commenced within four years after the cause of action has accrued. By the original agreement the parties may reduce the period of limitation to not less than one year but may not extend it.

(2) A cause of action accrues when the breach occurs, regardless of the aggrieved party's lack of knowledge of the breach. A breach of warranty occurs when tender of delivery is made, except that where a warranty explicitly extends to future performance of the goods and discovery of the breach must await the time of such performance the cause of action accrues when the breach is or should have been discovered.

(3) Where an action commenced within the time limited by subsection (1) is so terminated as to leave available a remedy by another action for the same breach such other action may be commenced after the expiration of the time limited and within six months after the termination of the first action unless the termination resulted from voluntary discontinuance or from dismissal for failure or neglect to prosecute.

(4) This section does not alter the law on tolling of the statute of limitations nor does it apply to causes of action which have accrued before this Act becomes effective.

Article 3   Commercial Paper

Part 1   Short Title, Form and Interpretation

Section 3—101. Short Title

This Article shall be known and may be cited as Uniform Commercial Code—Commercial Paper.

Section 3—102. Definitions and Index of Definitions

(1) In this Article unless the context otherwise requires

    (a) "Issue" means the first delivery of an instrument to a holder or a remitter.

    (b) An "order" is a direction to pay and must be more than an authorization or request. It must identify the person to pay with reasonable certainty. It may be addressed to one or more such persons jointly or in the alternative but not in succession.

    (c) A "promise" is an undertaking to pay and must be more than an acknowledgment of an obligation.

    (d) "Secondary party" means a drawer or indorser.

    (e) "Instrument" means a negotiable instrument.

(2) Other definitions applying to this Article and the sections in which they appear are:

"Acceptance." Section 3—410.
"Accommodation party." Section 3—415.
"Alteration." Section 3—407.
"Certificate of deposit." Section 3—104.
"Certification." Section 3—411.
"Check." Section 3—104.
"Definite time." Section 3—109.
"Dishonor." Section 3—507.
"Draft." Section 3—104.
"Holder in due course." Section 3—302.
"Negotiation." Section 3—202.
"Note." Section 3—104.
"Notice of dishonor." Section 3—508.
"On demand." Section 3—108.
"Presentment." Section 3—504.
"Protest." Section 3—509.
"Restrictive Indorsement." Section 3—205.
"Signature." Section 3—401.

(3) The following definitions in other Articles apply to this Article:

"Account." Section 4—104.
"Banking Day." Section 4—104.
"Clearing house." Section 4—104.
"Collecting bank." Section 4—105.
"Customer." Section 4—104.
"Depositary Bank." Section 4—105.
"Documentary Draft." Section 4—104.
"Intermediary Bank." Section 4—105.
"Item." Section 4—104.
"Midnight deadline." Section 4—104.
"Payor bank." Section 4—105.

(4) In addition Article 1 contains general definitions and principles of construction and interpretation applicable throughout this Article.

Section 3—103. Limitations on Scope of Article

(1) This Article does not apply to money, documents of title or investment securities.

(2) The provisions of this Article are subject to the provisions of the Article on Bank Deposits and Collections (Article 4) and Secured Transactions (Article 9).

Section 3—104. Form of Negotiable Instruments; "Draft"; "Check"; "Certificate of Deposit"; "Note"

(1) Any writing to be a negotiable instrument within this Article must

(a) be signed by the maker or drawer; and
(b) contain an unconditional promise or order to pay a sum certain in money and no other promise, order, obligation or power given by the maker or drawer except as authorized by this Article; and
(c) be payable on demand or at a definite time; and
(d) be payable to order or to bearer.

(2) A writing which complies with the requirements of this section is

(a) a "draft" ("bill of exchange") if it is an order;
(b) a "check" if it is a draft drawn on a bank and payable on demand;
(c) a "certificate of deposit" if it is an acknowledgment by a bank of receipt of money with an engagement to repay it;
(d) a "note" if it is a promise other than a certificate of deposit.

(3) As used in other Articles of this Act, and as the context may require, the terms "draft," "check," "certificate of deposit" and "note" may refer to instruments which are not negotiable within this Article as well as to instruments which are so negotiable.

Section 3—105. When Promise or Order Unconditional

(1) A promise or order otherwise unconditional is not made conditional by the fact that the instrument

(a) is subject to implied or constructive conditions; or
(b) states its consideration, whether performed or promised, or the transaction which gave rise to the instrument, or that the promise or order is made or the instrument matures in accordance with or "as per" such transaction; or
(c) refers to or states that it arises out of a separate agreement or refers to a separate agreement for rights as to prepayment or acceleration; or
(d) states that it is drawn under a letter of credit; or
(e) states that it is secured, whether by mortgage, reservation of title or otherwise; or
(f) indicates a particular account to be debited or any other fund or source from which reimbursement is expected; or
(g) is limited to payment out of a particular fund or the proceeds of a particular source, if the instrument is issued by a government or governmental agency or unit; or
(h) is limited to payment out of the entire assets of a partnership, unincorporated association, trust or estate by or on behalf of which the instrument is issued.

(2) A promise or order is not unconditional if the instrument

(a) states that it is subject to or governed by any other agreement; or
(b) states that it is to be paid only out of a particular fund or source except as provided in this section. As amended 1962.

Section 3—106. Sum Certain

(1) The sum payable is a sum certain even though it is to be paid

(a) with stated interest or by stated installments; or
(b) with stated different rates of interest before and after default or a specified date; or
(c) with a stated discount or addition if paid before or after the date fixed for payment; or
(d) with exchange or less exchange, whether at a fixed rate or at the current rate; or
(e) with costs of collection or an attorney's fee or both upon default.

(2) Nothing in this section shall validate any term which is otherwise illegal.

Section 3—107. Money

(1) An instrument is payable in money if the medium of exchange in which it is payable is money at the time the instrument is made. An instrument payable in "currency" or "current funds" is payable in money.

(2) A promise or order to pay a sum stated in a foreign currency is for a sum certain in money and, unless a different medium of payment is specified in the instrument, may be satisfied by payment of that number of dollars which the stated foreign currency will purchase at the buying sight rate for that currency on the day on which the instrument is payable or, if payable on demand, on the day of demand. If such an instrument specifies a foreign currency as the medium of payment the instrument is payable in that currency.

Section 3—108. Payable on Demand
Instruments payable on demand include those payable at sight or on presentation and those in which no time for payment is stated.

Section 3—109. Definite Time
(1) An instrument is payable at a definite time if by its terms it is payable

    (a) on or before a stated date or at a fixed period after a stated date; or

    (b) at a fixed period after sight; or

    (c) at a definite time subject to any acceleration; or

    (d) at a definite time subject to extension at the option of the holder, or to extension to a further definite time at the option of the maker or acceptor or automatically upon or after a specified act or event.

(2) An instrument which by its terms is otherwise payable only upon an act or event uncertain as to time of occurrence is not payable at a definite time even though the act or event has occurred.

Section 3—110. Payable to Order
(1) An instrument is payable to order when by its terms it is payable to the order or assigns of any person therein specified with reasonable certainty, or to him or his order, or when it is conspicuously designated on its face as "exchange" or the like and names a payee. It may be payable to the order of

    (a) the maker or drawer; or

    (b) the drawee; or

    (c) a payee who is not maker, drawer or drawee; or

    (d) two or more payees together or in the alternative; or

    (e) an estate, trust or fund, in which case it is payable to the order of the representative of such estate, trust or fund or his successors; or

    (f) an office, or an officer by his title as such in which case it is payable to the principal but the incumbent of the office or his successors may act as if he or they were the holder; or

    (g) a partnership or unincorporated association, in which case it is payable to the partnership or association and may be indorsed or transferred by any person thereto authorized.

(2) An instrument not payable to order is not made so payable by such words as "payable upon return of this instrument properly indorsed."

(3) An instrument made payable both to order and to bearer is payable to order unless the bearer words are handwritten or typewritten.

Section 3—111. Payable to Bearer
An instrument is payable to bearer when by its terms it is payable to

    (a) bearer or the order of bearer; or

    (b) a specified person or bearer; or

    (c) "cash" or the order of "cash," or any other indication which does not purport to designate a specific payee.

Section 3—112. Terms and Omissions Not Affecting Negotiability
(1) The negotiability of an instrument is not affected by

    (a) the omission of a statement of any consideration or of the place where the instrument is drawn or payable; or

    (b) a statement that collateral has been given to secure obligations either on the instrument or otherwise of an obligor on the instrument or that in case of default on those obligations the holder may realize on or dispose of the collateral; or

    (c) a promise or power to maintain or protect collateral or to give additional collateral; or

    (d) a term authorizing a confession of judgment on the instrument if it is not paid when due; or

    (e) a term purporting to waive the benefit of any law intended for the advantage or protection of any obligor; or

    (f) a term in a draft providing that the payee by indorsing or cashing it acknowledges full satisfaction of an obligation of the drawer; or

    (g) A statement in a draft drawn in a set of parts (Section 3—801) to the effect that the order is effective only if no other part has been honored.

(2) Nothing in this section shall validate any term which is otherwise illegal.

Section 3—113. Seal
An instrument otherwise negotiable is within this Article even though it is under a seal.

Section 3—114. Date, Antedating, Postdating
(1) The negotiability of an instrument is not affected by the fact that it is undated, antedated or postdated.

(2) Where an instrument is antedated or postdated the time when it is payable is determined by the stated date if the instrument is payable on demand or at a fixed period after date.

(3) Where the instrument or any signature thereon is dated, the date is presumed to be correct.

Section 3—115. Incomplete Instruments
(1) When a paper whose contents at the time of signing show that it is intended to become an instrument is signed while still incomplete in any necessary respect it cannot be enforced until completed, but when it is completed in accordance with authority given it is effective as completed.

(2) If the completion is unauthorized the rules as to material alteration apply (Section 3—407), even though the paper was not delivered by the maker or drawer; but the burden of establishing that any completion is unauthorized is on the party so asserting.

Section 3—116. Instruments Payable to Two or More Persons
An instrument payable to the order of two or more persons

    (a) if in the alternative is payable to any one of them and may be negotiated, discharged or enforced by any of them who has possession of it;

    (b) if not in the alternative is payable to all of them and may be negotiated, discharged or enforced only by all of them.

Section 3—117. Instruments Payable With Words of Description
An instrument made payable to a named person with the addition of words describing him

    (a) as agent or officer of a specified person is payable to his principal but the agent or officer may act as if he were the holder;

    (b) as any other fiduciary for a specified person or purpose is payable to the payee and may be negotiated, discharged or enforced by him;

    (c) in any other manner is payable to the payee unconditionally and the additional words are without effect on subsequent parties.

Section 3—118. Ambiguous Terms and Rules of Construction

The following rules apply to every instrument:

(a) Where there is doubt whether the instrument is a draft or a note the holder may treat it as either. A draft drawn on the drawer is effective as a note.

(b) Handwritten terms control typewritten and printed terms, and typewritten control printed.

(c) Words control figures except that if the words are ambiguous figures control.

(d) Unless otherwise specified a provision for interest means interest at the judgment rate at the place of payment from the date of the instrument, or if it is undated from the date of issue.

(e) Unless the instrument otherwise specifies two or more persons who sign as maker, acceptor or drawer or indorser and as a part of the same transaction are jointly and severally liable even though the instrument contains such words as "I promise to pay."

(f) Unless otherwise specified consent to extension authorizes a single extension for not longer than the original period. A consent to extension, expressed in the instrument, is binding on secondary parties and accommodation makers. A holder may not exercise his option to extend an instrument over the objection of a maker or acceptor or other party who in accordance with Section 3—604 tenders full payment when the instrument is due.

Section 3—119. Other Writings Affecting Instrument

(1) As between the obligor and his immediate obligee or any transferee the terms of an instrument may be modified or affected by any other written agreement executed as a part of the same transaction, except that a holder in due course is not affected by any limitation of his rights arising out of the separate written agreement if he had no notice of the limitation when he took the instrument.

(2) A separate agreement does not affect the negotiability of an instrument.

Section 3—120. Instruments "Payable Through" Bank

An instrument which states that it is "payable through" a bank or the like designates that bank as a collecting bank to make presentment but does not of itself authorize the bank to pay the instrument.

Section 3—121. Instruments Payable at Bank

Note: *If this Act is introduced in the Congress of the United States this section should be omitted. (States to select either alternative)*

Alternative A

A note or acceptance which states that it is payable at a bank is the equivalent of a draft drawn on the bank payable when it falls due out of any funds of the maker or acceptor in current account or otherwise available for such payment.

Alternative B

A note or acceptance which states that it is payable at a bank is not of itself an order or authorization to the bank to pay it.

Section 3—122. Accrual of Cause of Action

(1) A cause of action against a maker or an acceptor accrues

(a) in the case of a time instrument on the day after maturity;

(b) in the case of a demand instrument upon its date or, if no date is stated, on the date of issue.

(2) A cause of action against the obligor of a demand or time certificate of deposit accrues upon demand, but demand on a time certificate may not be made until on or after the date of maturity.

(3) A cause of action against a drawer of a draft or an indorser of any instrument accrues upon demand following dishonor of the instrument. Notice of dishonor is a demand.

(4) Unless an instrument provides otherwise, interest runs at the rate provided by law for a judgment

(a) in the case of a maker, acceptor or other primary obligor of a demand instrument, from the date of demand;

(b) in all other cases from the date of accrual of the cause of action.

Part 2   Transfer and Negotiation

Section 3—201. Transfer: Right to Indorsement

(1) Transfer of an instrument vests in the transferee such rights as the transferor has therein, except that a transferee who has himself been a party to any fraud or illegality affecting the instrument or who as a prior holder had notice of a defense or claim against it cannot improve his position by taking from a later holder in due course.

(2) A transfer of a security interest in an instrument vests the foregoing rights in the transferee to the extent of the interest transferred.

(3) Unless otherwise agreed any transfer for value of an instrument not then payable to bearer gives the transferee the specifically enforceable right to have the unqualified indorsement of the transferor. Negotiation takes effect only when the indorsement is made and until that time there is no presumption that the transferee is the owner.

Section 3—202. Negotiation

(1) Negotiation is the transfer of an instrument in such form that the transferee becomes a holder. If the instrument is payable to order it is negotiated by delivery with any necessary indorsement; if payable to bearer it is negotiated by delivery.

(2) An indorsement must be written by or on behalf of the holder and on the instrument or on a paper so firmly affixed thereto as to become a part thereof.

(3) An indorsement is effective for negotiation only when it conveys the entire instrument or any unpaid residue. If it purports to be of less it operates only as a partial assignment.

(4) Words of assignment, condition, waiver, guaranty, limitation or disclaimer of liability and the like accompanying an indorsement do not affect its character as an indorsement.

Section 3—203. Wrong or Misspelled Name

Where an instrument is made payable to a person under a misspelled name or one other than his own he may indorse in that name or his own or both; but signature in both names may be required by a person paying or giving value for the instrument.

Section 3—204. Special Indorsement; Blank Indorsement

(1) A special indorsement specifies the person to whom or to whose order it makes the instrument payable. Any instrument specially indorsed becomes payable to the order of the special indorsee and may be further negotiated only by his indorsement.

(2) An indorsement in blank specifies no particular indorsee and may consist of a mere signature. An instrument payable to order and indorsed in blank becomes payable to bearer and may be negotiated by delivery alone until specially indorsed.

(3) The holder may convert a blank indorsement into a special indorsement by writing over the signature of the indorser in blank any contract consistent with the character of the indorsement.

Section 3—205. Restrictive Indorsements
An indorsement is restrictive which either

    (a) is conditional; or

    (b) purports to prohibit further transfer of the instrument; or

    (c) includes the words "for collection," "for deposit," "pay any bank," or like terms signifying a purpose of deposit or collection; or

    (d) otherwise states that it is for the benefit or use of the indorser or of another person.

Section 3—206. Effect of Restrictive Indorsement
(1) No restrictive indorsement prevents further transfer or negotiation of the instrument.

(2) An intermediary bank, or a payor bank which is not the depositary bank, is neither given notice nor otherwise affected by a restrictive indorsement of any person except the bank's immediate transferor or the person presenting for payment.

(3) Except for an intermediary bank, any transferee under an indorsement which is conditional or includes the words "for collection," "for deposit," "pay any bank," or like terms (subparagraphs (a) and (c) of Section 3—205) must pay or apply any value given by him for or on the security of the instrument consistently with the indorsement and to the extent that he does so he becomes a holder for value. In addition such transferee is a holder in due course if he otherwise complies with the requirements of Section 3—302 on what constitutes a holder in due course.

(4) The first taker under an indorsement for the benefit of the indorser or another person (subparagraph (d) of Section 3—205) must pay or apply any value given by him for or on the security of the instrument consistently with the indorsement and to the extent that he does so he becomes a holder for value. In addition such taker is a holder in due course if he otherwise complies with the requirements of Section 3—302 on what constitutes a holder in due course. A later holder for value is neither given notice nor otherwise affected by such restrictive indorsement unless he has knowledge that a fiduciary or other person has negotiated the instrument in any transaction for his own benefit or otherwise in breach of duty (subsection (2) of Section 3—304).

Section 3—207. Negotiation Effective Although It May Be Rescinded
(1) Negotiation is effective to transfer the instrument although the negotiation is

    (a) made by an infant, a corporation exceeding its powers, or any other person without capacity; or

    (b) obtained by fraud, duress or mistake of any kind; or

    (c) part of an illegal transaction; or

    (d) made in breach of duty.

(2) Except as against a subsequent holder in due course such negotiation is in an appropriate case subject to rescission, the declaration of a constructive trust or any other remedy permitted by law.

Section 3—208. Reacquisition
Where an instrument is returned to or reacquired by a prior party he may cancel any indorsement which is not necessary to his title and reissue or further negotiate the instrument, but any intervening party is discharged as against the reacquiring party and subsequent holders not in due course and if his indorsement has been cancelled is discharged as against subsequent holders in due course as well.

Part 3   Rights of a Holder

Section 3—301. Rights of a Holder
The holder of an instrument whether or not he is the owner may transfer or negotiate it and, except as otherwise provided in Section 3—603 on payment or satisfaction, discharge it or enforce payment in his own name.

Section 3—302. Holder in Due Course
(1) A holder in due course is a holder who takes the instrument

    (a) for value, and

    (b) in good faith; and

    (c) without notice that it is overdue or has been dishonored or of any defense against or claim to it on the part of any person.

(2) A payee may be a holder in due course.

(3) A holder does not become a holder in due course of an instrument:

    (a) by purchase of it at judicial sale or by taking it under legal process; or

    (b) by acquiring it in taking over an estate; or

    (c) by purchasing it as part of a bulk transaction not in regular course of business of the transferor.

(4) A purchaser of a limited interest can be a holder in due course only to the extent of the interest purchased.

Section 3—303. Taking for Value
A holder takes the instrument for value

    (a) to the extent that the agreed consideration has been performed or that he acquires a security interest in or a lien on the instrument otherwise than by legal process; or

    (b) when he takes the instrument in payment of or as security for an antecedent claim against any person whether or not the claim is due; or

    (c) when he gives a negotiable instrument for it or makes an irrevocable commitment to a third person.

Section 3—304. Notice to Purchaser
(1) The purchaser has notice of a claim or defense if

    (a) the instrument is so incomplete, bears such visible evidence of forgery or alteration, or is otherwise so irregular as to call into question its validity, terms or ownership or to create an ambiguity as to the party to pay; or

    (b) the purchaser has notice that the obligation of any party is voidable in whole or in part, or that all parties have been discharged.

(2) The purchaser has notice of a claim against the instrument when he has knowledge that a fiduciary has negotiated the instrument in payment of or as security for his own debt or in any transaction for his own benefit or otherwise in breach of duty.

(3) The purchaser has notice that an instrument is overdue if he has reason to know

    (a) that any part of the principal amount is overdue or that there is an uncured default in payment of another instrument of the same series; or

    (b) that acceleration of the instrument has been made; or

    (c) that he is taking a demand instrument after demand has been made or more than a reasonable length of time after its issue. A reasonable time for a check drawn and payable within the states and territories of the United States and the District of Columbia is presumed to be thirty days.

(4) Knowledge of the following facts does not of itself give the purchaser notice of a defense or claim

  (a) that the instrument is antedated or postdated;
  (b) that it was issued or negotiated in return for an executory promise or accompanied by a separate agreement, unless the purchaser has notice that a defense or claim has arisen from the terms thereof;
  (c) that any party has signed for accommodation;
  (d) that an incomplete instrument has been completed, unless the purchaser has notice of any improper completion;
  (e) that any person negotiating the instrument is or was a fiduciary;
  (f) that there has been default in payment of interest on the instrument or in payment of any other instrument, except one of the same series.

(5) The filing or recording of a document does not of itself constitute notice within the provisions of this Article to a person who would otherwise be a holder in due course.

(6) To be effective notice must be received at such time and in such manner as to give a reasonable opportunity to act on it.

Section 3—305. Rights of a Holder in Due Course

To the extent that a holder is a holder in due course he takes the instrument free from

(1) all claims to it on the part of any person; and

(2) all defenses of any party to the instrument with whom the holder has not dealt except

  (a) infancy, to the extent that it is a defense to a simple contract; and
  (b) such other incapacity, or duress, or illegality of the transaction, as renders the obligation of the party a nullity; and
  (c) such misrepresentation as has induced the party to sign the instrument with neither knowledge nor reasonable opportunity to obtain knowledge of its character or its essential terms; and
  (d) discharge in insolvency proceedings; and
  (e) any other discharge of which the holder has notice when he takes the instrument.

Section 3—306. Rights of One Not Holder in Due Course

Unless he has the rights of a holder in due course any person takes the instrument subject to

  (a) all valid claims to it on the part of any person; and
  (b) all defenses of any party which would be available in an action on a simple contract; and
  (c) the defenses of want or failure of consideration, non-performance of any condition precedent, non-delivery, or delivery for a special purpose (Section 3—408); and
  (d) the defense that he or a person through whom he holds the instrument acquired it by theft, or that payment or satisfaction to such holder would be inconsistent with the terms of a restrictive indorsement. The claim of any third person to the instrument is not otherwise available as a defense to any party liable thereon unless the third person himself defends the action for such party.

Section 3—307. Burden of Establishing Signatures, Defenses and Due Course

(1) Unless specifically denied in the pleadings each signature on an instrument is admitted. When the effectiveness of a signature is put in issue

  (a) the burden of establishing it is on the party claiming under the signature; but
  (b) the signature is presumed to be genuine or authorized except where the action is to enforce the obligation of a purported signer who has died or become incompetent before proof is required.

(2) When signatures are admitted or established, production of the instrument entitles a holder to recover on it unless the defendant establishes a defense.

(3) After it is shown that a defense exists a person claiming the rights of a holder in due course has the burden of establishing that he or some person under whom he claims is in all respects a holder in due course.

Part 4 Liability of Parties

Section 3—401. Signature

(1) No person is liable on an instrument unless his signature appears thereon.

(2) A signature is made by use of any name, including any trade or assumed name, upon an instrument, or by any word or mark used in lieu of a written signature.

Section 3—402. Signature in Ambiguous Capacity

Unless the instrument clearly indicates that a signature is made in some other capacity it is an indorsement.

Section 3—403. Signature by Authorized Representative

(1) A signature may be made by an agent or other representative, and his authority to make it may be established as in other cases of representation. No particular form of appointment is necessary to establish such authority.

(2) An authorized representative who signs his own name to an instrument

  (a) is personally obligated if the instrument neither names the person represented nor shows that the representative signed in a representative capacity;
  (b) except as otherwise established between the immediate parties, is personally obligated if the instrument names the person represented but does not show that the representative signed in a representative capacity, or if the instrument does not name the person represented but does show that the representative signed in a representative capacity.

(3) Except as otherwise established the name of an organization preceded or followed by the name and office of an authorized individual is a signature made in a representative capacity.

Section 3—404. Unauthorized Signatures

(1) Any unauthorized signature is wholly inoperative as that of the person whose name is signed unless he ratifies it or is precluded from denying it; but it operates as the signature of the unauthorized signer in favor of any person who in good faith pays the instrument or takes it for value.

(2) Any unauthorized signature may be ratified for all purposes of this Article. Such ratification does not of itself affect any rights of the person ratifying against the actual signer.

Section 3—405. Impostors; Signature in Name of Payee

(1) An indorsement by any person in the name of a named payee is effective if

  (a) an impostor by use of the mails or otherwise has induced the maker or drawer to issue the instrument to him or his confederate in the name of the payee; or

  (b) a person signing as or on behalf of a maker or drawer intends the payee to have no interest in the instrument; or

  (c) an agent or employee of the maker or drawer has supplied him with the name of the payee intending the latter to have no such interest.

(2) Nothing in this section shall affect the criminal or civil liability of the person so indorsing.

Section 3—406. Negligence Contributing to Alteration or Unauthorized Signature

Any person who by his negligence substantially contributes to a material alteration of the instrument or to the making of an unauthorized signature is precluded from asserting the alteration or lack of authority against a holder in due course or against a drawee or other payor who pays the instrument in good faith and in accordance with the reasonable commercial standards of the drawee's or payor's business.

Section 3—407. Alteration

(1) Any alteration of an instrument is material which changes the contract of any party thereto in any respect, including any such change in

  (a) the number or relations of the parties; or

  (b) an incomplete instrument, by completing it otherwise than as authorized; or

  (c) the writing as signed, by adding to it or by removing any part of it.

(2) As against any person other than a subsequent holder in due course.

  (a) alteration by the holder which is both fraudulent and material discharges any party whose contract is thereby changed unless that party assents or is precluded from asserting the defense;

  (b) no other alteration discharges any party and the instrument may be enforced according to its original tenor, or as to incomplete instruments according to the authority given.

(3) A subsequent holder in due course may in all cases enforce the instrument according to its original tenor, and when an incomplete instrument has been completed, he may enforce it as completed.

Section 3—408. Consideration

Want or failure of consideration is a defense as against any person not having the rights of a holder in due course (Section 3—305), except that no consideration is necessary for an instrument or obligation thereon given in payment of or as security for an antecedent obligation of any kind. Nothing in this section shall be taken to displace any statute outside this Act under which a promise is enforceable notwithstanding lack or failure of consideration. Partial failure of consideration is a defense pro tanto whether or not the failure is in an ascertained or liquidated amount.

Section 3—409. Draft Not an Assignment

(1) A check or other draft does not of itself operate as an assignment of any funds in the hands of the drawee available for its payment, and the drawee is not liable on the instrument until he accepts it.

(2) Nothing in this section shall affect any liability in contract, tort or otherwise arising from any letter of credit or other obligation or representation which is not an acceptance.

Section 3—410. Definition and Operation of Acceptance

(1) Acceptance is the drawee's signed engagement to honor the draft as presented. It must be written on the draft, and may consist of his signature alone. It becomes operative when completed by delivery or notification.

(2) A draft may be accepted although it has not been signed by the drawer or is otherwise incomplete or is overdue or has been dishonored.

(3) Where the draft is payable at a fixed period after sight and the acceptor fails to date his acceptance the holder may complete it by supplying a date in good faith.

Section 3—411. Certification of a Check

(1) Certification of a check is acceptance. Where a holder procures certification the drawer and all prior indorsers are discharged.

(2) Unless otherwise agreed a bank has no obligation to certify a check.

(3) A bank may certify a check before returning it for lack of proper indorsement. If it does so the drawer is discharged.

Section 3—412. Acceptance Varying Draft

(1) Where the drawee's proffered acceptance in any manner varies the draft as presented the holder may refuse the acceptance and treat the draft as dishonored in which case the drawee is entitled to have his acceptance cancelled.

(2) The terms of the draft are not varied by an acceptance to pay at any particular bank or place in the United States, unless the acceptance states that the draft is to be paid only at such bank or place.

(3) Where the holder assents to an acceptance varying the terms of the draft each drawer and indorser who does not affirmatively assent is discharged.

Section 3—413. Contract of Maker, Drawer and Acceptor

(1) The maker or acceptor engages that he will pay the instrument according to its tenor at the time of his engagement or as completed pursuant to Section 3—115 on incomplete instruments.

(2) The drawer engages that upon dishonor of the draft and any necessary notice of dishonor or protest he will pay the amount of the draft to the holder or to any indorser who takes it up. The drawer may disclaim this liability by drawing without recourse.

(3) By making, drawing or accepting the party admits as against all subsequent parties including the drawee the existence of the payee and his then capacity to indorse.

Section 3—414. Contract of Indorser; Order of Liability

(1) Unless the indorsement otherwise specifies (as by such words as "without recourse") every indorser engages that upon dishonor and any necessary notice of dishonor and protest he will pay the instrument according to its tenor at the time of his indorsement to the holder or to any subsequent indorser who takes it up, even though the indorser who takes it up was not obligated to do so.

(2) Unless they otherwise agree indorsers are liable to one another in the order in which they indorse, which is presumed to be the order in which their signatures appear on the instrument.

Section 3—415. Contract of Accommodation Party

(1) An accommodation party is one who signs the instrument in any capacity for the purpose of lending his name to another party to it.

(2) When the instrument has been taken for value before it is due the accommodation party is liable in the capacity in which he has signed even though the taker knows of the accommodation.

(3) As against a holder in due course and without notice of the accommodation oral proof of the accommodation is not admissible to give the accommodation party the benefit of discharges dependent on his character as such. In other cases the accommodation character may be shown by oral proof.

(4) An indorsement which shows that it is not in the chain of title is notice of its accommodation character.

(5) An accommodation party is not liable to the party accommodated, and if he pays the instrument has a right of recourse on the instrument against such party.

Section 3—416. Contract of Guarantor

(1) "Payment guaranteed" or equivalent words added to a signature mean that the signer engages that if the instrument is not paid when due he will pay it according to its tenor without resort by the holder to any other party.

(2) "Collection guaranteed" or equivalent words added to a signature mean that the signer engages that if the instrument is not paid when due he will pay it according to its tenor, but only after the holder has reduced his claim against the maker or acceptor to judgment and execution has been returned unsatisfied, or after the maker or acceptor has become insolvent or it is otherwise apparent that it is useless to proceed against him.

(3) Words of guaranty which do not otherwise specify guarantee payment.

(4) No words of guaranty added to the signature of a sole maker or acceptor affect his liability on the instrument. Such words added to the signature of one of two or more makers or acceptors create a presumption that the signature is for the accommodation of the others.

(5) When words of guaranty are used presentment, notice of dishonor and protest are not necessary to charge the user.

(6) Any guaranty written on the instrument is enforcible notwithstanding any statute of frauds.

Section 3—417. Warranties on Presentment and Transfer

(1) Any person who obtains payment or acceptance and any prior transferor warrants to a person who in good faith pays or accepts that

   (a) he has a good title to the instrument or is authorized to obtain payment or acceptance on behalf of one who has a good title; and

   (b) he has no knowledge that the signature of the maker or drawer is unauthorized, except that this warranty is not given by a holder in due course acting in good faith

      (i) to a maker with respect to the maker's own signature; or

      (ii) to a drawer with respect to the drawer's own signature, whether or not the drawer is also the drawee; or

      (iii) to an acceptor of a draft if the holder in due course took the draft after the acceptance or obtained the acceptance without knowledge that the drawer's signature was unauthorized; and

   (c) the instrument has not been materially altered, except that this warranty is not given by a holder in due course acting in good faith

      (i) to the maker of a note; or

      (ii) to the drawer of a draft whether or not the drawer is also the drawee; or

      (iii) to the acceptor of a draft with respect to an alteration made prior to the acceptance if the holder in due course took the draft after the acceptance, even though the acceptance provided "payable as originally drawn" or equivalent terms; or

      (iv) to the acceptor of a draft with respect to an alteration made after the acceptance.

(2) Any person who transfers an instrument and receives consideration warrants to his transferee and if the transfer is by indorsement to any subsequent holder who takes the instrument in good faith that

   (a) he has a good title to the instrument or is authorized to obtain payment or acceptance on behalf of one who has a good title and the transfer is otherwise rightful; and

   (b) all signatures are genuine or authorized; and

   (c) the instrument has not been materially altered; and

   (d) no defense of any party is good against him; and

   (e) he has no knowledge of any insolvency proceeding instituted with respect to the maker or acceptor or the drawer of an unaccepted instrument.

(3) By transferring "without recourse" the transferor limits the obligation stated in subsection (2) (d) to a warranty that he has no knowledge of such a defense.

(4) A selling agent or broker who does not disclose the fact that he is acting only as such gives the warranties provided in this section, but if he makes such disclosure warrants only his good faith and authority.

Section 3—418. Finality of Payment or Acceptance

Except for recovery of bank payments as provided in the Article on Bank Deposits and Collections (Article 4) and except for liability for breach of warranty on presentment under the preceding section, payment or acceptance of any instrument is final in favor of a holder in due course, or a person who has in good faith changed his position in reliance on the payment.

Section 3—419. Conversion of Instrument; Innocent Representative

(1) An instrument is converted when

   (a) a drawee to whom it is delivered for acceptance refuses to return it on demand; or

   (b) any person to whom it is delivered for payment refuses on demand either to pay or to return it; or

   (c) it is paid on a forged indorsement.

(2) In an action against a drawee under subsection (1) the measure of the drawee's liability is the face amount of the instrument. In any other action under subsection (1) the measure of liability is presumed to be the face amount of the instrument.

(3) Subject to the provisions of this Act concerning restrictive indorsements a representative, including a depositary or collecting bank, who has in good faith and in accordance with the reasonable commercial standards applicable to the business of such representative dealt with an instrument or its proceeds on behalf of one who was not the true owner is not liable in conversion or otherwise to the true owner beyond the amount of any proceeds remaining in his hands.

(4) An intermediary bank or payor bank which is not a depositary bank is not liable in conversion solely by reason of the fact that proceeds of an item indorsed restrictively (Sections 3—205 and 3—206) are not paid or applied consistently with the restrictive indorsement of an indorser other than its immediate transferor.

Part 5 Presentment, Notice of Dishonor and Protest

Section 3—501. When Presentment, Notice of Dishonor, and Protest Necessary or Permissible

(1) Unless excused (Section 3—511) presentment is necessary to charge secondary parties as follows:

(a) presentment for acceptance is necessary to charge the drawer and indorsers of a draft where the draft so provides, or is payable elsewhere than at the residence or place of business of the drawee, or its date of payment depends upon such presentment. The holder may at his option present for acceptance any other draft payable at a stated date;

(b) presentment for payment is necessary to charge any indorser;

(c) in the case of any drawer, the acceptor of a draft payable at a bank or the maker of a note payable at a bank, presentment for payment is necessary, but failure to make presentment discharges such drawer, acceptor or maker only as stated in Section 3—502(1) (b).

(2) Unless excused (Section 3—511)

(a) notice of any dishonor is necessary to charge any indorser;

(b) in the case of any drawer, the acceptor of a draft payable at a bank or the maker of a note payable at a bank, notice of any dishonor is necessary, but failure to give such notice discharges such drawer, acceptor or maker only as stated in Section 3—502(1) (b)

(3) Unless excused (Section 3—511) protest of any dishonor is necessary to charge the drawer and indorsers of any draft which on its face appears to be drawn or payable outside of the states, territories, dependencies and possessions of the United States, the District of Columbia and the Commonwealth of Puerto Rico. The holder may at his option make protest of any dishonor of any other instrument and in the case of a foreign draft may on insolvency of the acceptor before maturity make protest for better security.

(4) Notwithstanding any provision of this section, neither presentment nor notice of dishonor nor protest is necessary to charge an indorser who has indorsed an instrument after maturity.

Section 3—502. Unexcused Delay; Discharge

(1) Where without excuse any necessary presentment or notice of dishonor is delayed beyond the time when it is due

(a) any indorser is discharged; and

(b) any drawer or the acceptor of a draft payable at a bank or the maker of a note payable at a bank who because the drawee or payor bank becomes insolvent during the delay is deprived of funds maintained with the drawee or payor bank to cover the instrument may discharge his liability by written assignment to the holder of his rights against the drawee or payor bank in respect of such funds, but such drawer, acceptor or maker is not otherwise discharged.

(2) Where without excuse a necessary protest is delayed beyond the time when it is due any drawer or indorser is discharged.

Section 3—503. Time of Presentment

(1) Unless a different time is expressed in the instrument the time for any presentment is determined as follows:

(a) where an instrument is payable at or a fixed period after a stated date any presentment for acceptance must be made on or before the date it is payable;

(b) where an instrument is payable after sight it must either be presented for acceptance or negotiated within a reasonable time after date or issue whichever is later;

(c) where an instrument shows the date on which it is payable presentment for payment is due on that date;

(d) where an instrument is accelerated presentment for payment is due within a reasonable time after the acceleration;

(e) with respect to the liability of any secondary party presentment for acceptance or payment of any other instrument is due within a reasonable time after such party becomes liable thereon.

(2) A reasonable time for presentment is determined by the nature of the instrument, any usage of banking or trade and the facts of the particular case. In the case of an uncertified check which is drawn and payable within the United States and which is not a draft drawn by a bank the following are presumed to be reasonable periods within which to present for payment or to initiate bank collection:

(a) with respect to the liability of the drawer, thirty days after date or issue whichever is later; and

(b) with respect to the liability of an indorser, seven days after his indorsement.

(3) Where any presentment is due on a day which is not a full business day for either the person making presentment or the party to pay or accept, presentment is due on the next following day which is a full business day for both parties.

(4) Presentment to be sufficient must be made at a reasonable hour, and if at a bank during its banking day.

Section 3—504. How Presentment Made

(1) Presentment is a demand for acceptance or payment made upon the maker, acceptor, drawee or other payor by or on behalf of the holder.

(2) Presentment may be made

(a) by mail, in which event the time of presentment is determined by the time of receipt of the mail; or

(b) through a clearing house; or

(c) at the place of acceptance or payment specified in the instrument or if there be none at the place of business or residence of the party to accept or pay. If neither the party to accept or pay nor anyone authorized to act for him is present or accessible at such place presentment is excused.

(3) It may be made

(a) to any one of two or more makers, acceptors, drawees or other payors; or

(b) to any person who has authority to make or refuse the acceptance or payment.

(4) A draft accepted or a note made payable at a bank in the United States must be presented at such bank.

(5) In the cases described in Section 4—210 presentment may be made in the manner and with the result stated in that section.

Section 3—505. Rights of Party to Whom Presentment Is Made

(1) The party to whom presentment is made may without dishonor require

(a) exhibition of the instrument; and

(b) reasonable identification of the person making presentment and evidence of his authority to make it if made for another; and

(c) that the instrument be produced for acceptance or payment at a place specified in it, or if there be none at any place reasonable in the circumstances; and

(d) a signed receipt on the instrument for any partial or full payment and its surrender upon full payment.

(2) Failure to comply with any such requirement invalidates the presentment but the person presenting has a reasonable time in which to comply and the time for acceptance or payment runs from the time of compliance.

Section 3—506. Time Allowed for Acceptance or Payment

(1) Acceptance may be deferred without dishonor until the close of the next business day following presentment. The holder may also in a good faith effort to obtain acceptance and without either dishonor of the instrument or discharge of secondary parties allow postponement of acceptance for an additional business day.

(2) Except as a longer time is allowed in the case of documentary drafts drawn under a letter of credit, and unless an earlier time is agreed to by the party to pay, payment of an instrument may be deferred without dishonor pending reasonable examination to determine whether it is properly payable, but payment must be made in any event before the close of business on the day of presentment.

Section 3—507. Dishonor; Holder's Right of Recourse; Term Allowing Re-Presentment

(1) An instrument is dishonored when

  (a) a necessary or optional presentment is duly made and due acceptance or payment is refused or cannot be obtained within the prescribed time or in case of bank collections the instrument is seasonably returned by the midnight deadline (Section 4—301); or

  (b) presentment is excused and the instrument is not duly accepted or paid.

(2) Subject to any necessary notice of dishonor and protest, the holder has upon dishonor an immediate right of recourse against the drawers and indorsers.

(3) Return of an instrument for lack of proper indorsement is not dishonor.

(4) A term in a draft or an indorsement thereof allowing a stated time for re-presentment in the event of any dishonor of the draft by nonacceptance if a time draft or by nonpayment if a sight draft gives the holder as against any secondary party bound by the term an option to waive the dishonor without affecting the liability of the secondary party and he may present again up to the end of the stated time.

Section 3—508. Notice of Dishonor

(1) Notice of dishonor may be given to any person who may be liable on the instrument by or on behalf of the holder or any party who has himself received notice, or any other party who can be compelled to pay the instrument. In addition an agent or bank in whose hands the instrument is dishonored may give notice to his principal or customer or to another agent or bank from which the instrument was received.

(2) Any necessary notice must be given by a bank before its midnight deadline and by any other person before midnight of the third business day after dishonor or receipt of notice of dishonor.

(3) Notice may be given in any reasonable manner. It may be oral or written and in any terms which identify the instrument and state that it has been dishonored. A misdescription which does not mislead the party notified does not vitiate the notice. Sending the instrument bearing a stamp, ticket or writing stating that acceptance or payment has been refused or sending a notice of debit with respect to the instrument is sufficient.

(4) Written notice is given when sent although it is not received.

(5) Notice to one partner is notice to each although the firm has been dissolved.

(6) When any party is in insolvency proceedings instituted after the issue of the instrument notice may be given either to the party or to the representative of his estate.

(7) When any party is dead or incompetent notice may be sent to his last known address or given to his personal representative.

(8) Notice operates for the benefit of all parties who have rights on the instrument against the party notified.

Section 3—509. Protest; Noting for Protest

(1) A protest is a certificate of dishonor made under the hand and seal of a United States consul or vice consul or a notary public or other person authorized to certify dishonor by the law of the place where dishonor occurs. It may be made upon information satisfactory to such person.

(2) The protest must identify the instrument and certify either that due presentment has been made or the reason why it is excused and that the instrument has been dishonored by nonacceptance or nonpayment.

(3) The protest may also certify that notice of dishonor has been given to all parties or to specified parties.

(4) Subject to subsection (5) any necessary protest is due by the time that notice of dishonor is due.

(5) If, before protest is due, an instrument has been noted for protest by the officer to make protest, the protest may be made at any time thereafter as of the date of the noting.

Section 3—510. Evidence of Dishonor and Notice of Dishonor

The following are admissible as evidence and create a presumption of dishonor and of any notice of dishonor therein shown:

  (a) a document regular in form as provided in the preceding section which purports to be a protest;

  (b) the purported stamp or writing of the drawee, payor bank or presenting bank on the instrument or accompanying it stating that acceptance or payment has been refused for reasons consistent with dishonor;

  (c) any book or record of the drawee, payor bank, or any collecting bank kept in the usual course of business which shows dishonor, even though there is no evidence of who made the entry.

Section 3—511. Waived or Excused Presentment, Protest or Notice of Dishonor or Delay Therein

(1) Delay in presentment, protest or notice of dishonor is excused when the party is without notice that it is due or when the delay is caused by circumstances beyond his control and he exercises reasonable diligence after the cause of the delay ceases to operate.

(2) Presentment or notice or protest as the case may be is entirely excused when

  (a) the party to be charged has waived it expressly or by implication either before or after it is due; or

  (b) such party has himself dishonored the instrument or has countermanded payment or otherwise has no reason to expect or right to require that the instrument be accepted or paid; or

  (c) by reasonable diligence the presentment or protest cannot be made or the notice given.

(3) Presentment is also entirely excused when

  (a) the maker, acceptor, or drawee of any instrument except a documentary draft is dead or in insolvency proceedings instituted after the issue of the instrument; or

  (b) acceptance or payment is refused but not for want of proper presentment.

(4) Where a draft has been dishonored by nonacceptance a later presentment for payment and any notice of dishonor and protest for nonpayment are excused unless in the meantime the instrument has been accepted.

(5) A waiver of protest is also a waiver of presentment and of notice of dishonor even though protest is not required.

(6) Where a waiver of presentment or notice or protest is embodied in the instrument itself it is binding upon all parties; but where it is written above the signature of an indorser it binds him only.

Part 6 Discharge

Section 3—601. Discharge of Parties

(1) The extent of the discharge of any party from liability on an instrument is governed by the sections on

  (a) payment or satisfaction (Section 3—603); or
  (b) tender of payment (Section 3—604); or
  (c) cancellation or renunciation (Section 3—605); or
  (d) impairment of right of recourse or of collateral (Section 3—606); or
  (e) reacquisition of the instrument by a prior party (Section 3—208); or
  (f) fraudulent and material alteration (Section 3—407); or
  (g) certification of a check (Section 3—411); or
  (h) acceptance varying a draft (Section 3—412); or
  (i) unexcused delay in presentment or notice of dishonor or protest (Section 3—502).

(2) Any party is also discharged from his liability on an instrument to another party by any other act or agreement with such party which would discharge his simple contract for the payment of money.

(3) The liability of all parties is discharged when any party who has himself no right of action or recourse on the instrument

  (a) reacquires the instrument in his own right; or
  (b) is discharged under any provision of this Article, except as otherwise provided with respect to discharge for impairment of recourse or of collateral (Section 3—606).

Section 3—602. Effect of Discharge Against Holder in Due Course

No discharge of any party provided by this Article is effective against a subsequent holder in due course unless he has notice thereof when he takes the instrument.

Section 3—603. Payment or Satisfaction

(1) The liability of any party is discharged to the extent of his payment or satisfaction to the holder even though it is made with knowledge of a claim of another person to the instrument unless prior to such payment or satisfaction the person making the claim either supplies indemnity deemed adequate by the party seeking the discharge or enjoins payment or satisfaction by order of a court of competent jurisdiction in an action in which the adverse claimant and the holder are parties. This subsection does not, however, result in the discharge of the liability

  (a) of a party who in bad faith pays or satisfies a holder who acquired the instrument by theft or who (unless having the rights of a holder in due course) holds through one who so acquired it; or
  (b) of a party (other than an intermediary bank or a payor bank which is not a depositary bank) who pays or satisfies the holder of an instrument which has been restrictively indorsed in a manner not consistent with the terms of such restrictive indorsement.

(2) Payment or satisfaction may be made with the consent of the holder by any person including a stranger to the instrument. Surrender of the instrument to such a person gives him the rights of a transferee (Section 3—201).

Section 3—604. Tender of Payment

(1) Any party making tender of full payment to a holder when or after it is due is discharged to the extent of all subsequent liability for interest, costs and attorney's fees.

(2) The holder's refusal of such tender wholly discharges any party who has a right of recourse against the party making the tender.

(3) Where the maker or acceptor of an instrument payable otherwise than on demand is able and ready to pay at every place of payment specified in the instrument when it is due, it is equivalent to tender.

Section 3—605. Cancellation and Renunciation

(1) The holder of an instrument may even without consideration discharge any party

  (a) in any manner apparent on the face of the instrument or the indorsement, as by intentionally cancelling the instrument or the party's signature by destruction or mutilation, or by striking out the party's signature; or
  (b) by renouncing his rights by a writing signed and delivered or by surrender of the instrument to the party to be discharged.

(2) Neither cancellation nor renunciation without surrender of the instrument affects the title thereto.

Section 3—606. Impairment of Recourse or of Collateral

(1) The holder discharges any party to the instrument to the extent that without such party's consent the holder

  (a) without express reservation of rights releases or agrees not to sue any person against whom the party has to the knowledge of the holder a right of recourse or agrees to suspend the right to enforce against such person the instrument or collateral or otherwise discharges such person, except that failure or delay in effecting any required presentment, protest or notice of dishonor with respect to any such person does not discharge any party as to whom presentment, protest or notice of dishonor is effective or unnecessary; or
  (b) unjustifiably impairs any collateral for the instrument given by or on behalf of the party or any person against whom he has a right of recourse.

(2) By express reservation of rights against a party with a right of recourse the holder preserves

  (a) all his rights against such party as of the time when the instrument was originally due; and
  (b) the right of the party to pay the instrument as of that time; and
  (c) all rights of such party to recourse against others.

Part 7 Advice of International Sight Draft

Section 3—701. Letter of Advice of International Sight Draft

(1) A "letter of advice" is a drawer's communication to the drawee that a described draft has been drawn.

(2) Unless otherwise agreed when a bank receives from another bank a letter of advice of an international sight draft the drawee bank may immediately debit the drawer's account and stop the running of interest pro tanto. Such a debit and any resulting credit to any account covering outstanding drafts leaves in the drawer full power to stop payment or otherwise dispose of the amount and creates no trust or interest in favor of the holder.

(3) Unless otherwise agreed and except where a draft is drawn under a credit issued by the drawee, the drawee of an international sight draft owes the drawer no duty to pay an unadvised draft but if it does so and the draft is genuine, may appropriately debit the drawer's account.

Part 8 Miscellaneous

Section 3—801. Drafts in a Set

(1) Where a draft is drawn in a set of parts, each of which is numbered and expressed to be an order only if no other part has been honored, the whole of the parts constitutes one draft but a taker of any part may become a holder in due course of the draft.

(2) Any person who negotiates, indorses or accepts a single part of a draft drawn in a set thereby becomes liable to any holder in due course of that part as if it were the whole set, but as between different holders in due course to whom different parts have been negotiated the holder whose title first accrues has all rights to the draft and its proceeds.

(3) As against the drawee the first presented part of a draft drawn in a set is the part entitled to payment, or if a time draft to acceptance and payment. Acceptance of any subsequently presented part renders the drawee liable thereon under subsection (2). With respect both to a holder and to the drawer payment of a subsequently presented part of a draft payable at sight has the same effect as payment of a check notwithstanding an effective stop order (Section 4—407).

(4) Except as otherwise provided in this section, where any part of a draft in a set is discharged by payment or otherwise the whole draft is discharged.

Section 3—802. Effect of Instrument on Obligation for Which It Is Given

(1) Unless otherwise agreed where an instrument is taken for an underlying obligation

    (a) the obligation is pro tanto discharged if a bank is drawer, maker or acceptor of the instrument and there is no recourse on the instrument against the underlying obligor; and

    (b) in any other case the obligation is suspended pro tanto until the instrument is due or if it is payable on demand until its presentment. If the instrument is dishonored action may be maintained on either the instrument or the obligation; discharge of the underlying obligor on the instrument also discharges him on the obligation.

(2) The taking in good faith of a check which is not postdated does not of itself so extend the time on the original obligation as to discharge a surety.

Section 3—803. Notice to Third Party

Where a defendant is sued for breach of an obligation for which a third person is answerable over under this Article he may give the third person written notice of the litigation, and the person notified may then give similar notice to any other person who is answerable over to him under this Article. If the notice states that the person notified may come in and defend and that if the person notified does not do so he will in any action against him by the person giving the notice be bound by any determination of fact common to the two litigations, then unless after seasonable receipt of the notice the person notified does come in and defend he is so bound.

Section 3—804. Lost, Destroyed or Stolen Instruments

The owner of an instrument which is lost, whether by destruction, theft or otherwise, may maintain an action in his own name and recover from any party liable thereon upon due proof of his ownership, the facts which prevent his production of the instrument and its terms. The court may require security indemnifying the defendant against loss by reason of further claims on the instrument.

Section 3—805. Instruments Not Payable to Order or to Bearer

This Article applies to any instrument whose terms do not preclude transfer and which is otherwise negotiable within this Article but which is not payable to order or to bearer, except that there can be no holder in due course of such an instrument.

Article 4 Bank Deposits and Collections

Part 1 General Provisions and Definitions

Section 4—101. Short Title

This Article shall be known and may be cited as Uniform Commercial Code—Bank Deposits and Collections.

Section 4—102. Applicability

(1) To the extent that items within this Article are also within the scope of Articles 3 and 8, they are subject to the provisions of those Articles. In the event of conflict the provisions of this Article govern those of Article 3 but the provisions of Article 8 govern those of this Article.

(2) The liability of a bank for action or non-action with respect to any item handled by it for purposes of presentment, payment or collection is governed by the law of the place where the bank is located. In the case of action or non-action by or at a branch or separate office of a bank, its liability is governed by the law of the place where the branch or separate office is located.

Section 4—103. Variation by Agreement; Measure of Damages; Certain Action Constituting Ordinary Care

(1) The effect of the provisions of this Article may be varied by agreement except that no agreement can disclaim a bank's responsibility for its own lack of good faith or failure to exercise ordinary care or can limit the measure of damages for such lack or failure; but the parties may by agreement determine the standards by which such responsibility is to be measured if such standards are not manifestly unreasonable.

(2) Federal Reserve regulations and operating letters, clearing house rules, and the like, have the effect of agreements under subsection (1), whether or not specifically assented to by all parties interested in items handled.

(3) Action or non-action approved by this Article or pursuant to Federal Reserve regulations or operating letters constitutes the exercise of ordinary care and, in the absence of special instructions, action or non-action consistent with clearing house rules and the like or with a general banking usage not disapproved by this Article, prima facie constitutes the exercise of ordinary care.

(4) The specification or approval of certain procedures by this Article does not constitute disapproval of other procedures which may be reasonable under the circumstances.

(5) The measure of damages for failure to exercise ordinary care in handling an item is the amount of the item reduced by an amount which could not have been realized by the use of ordinary care, and where there is bad faith it includes other damages, if any, suffered by the party as a proximate consequence.

Section 4—104. Definitions and Index of Definitions

(1) In this Article unless the context otherwise requires

    (a) "Account" means any account with a bank and includes a checking, time, interest or savings account;

    (b) "Afternoon" means the period of a day between noon and midnight;

    (c) "Banking day" means that part of any day on which a bank is open to the public for carrying on substantially all of its banking functions;

    (d) "Clearing house" means any association of banks or other payors regularly clearing items;

    (e) "Customer" means any person having an account with a bank or for whom a bank has agreed to collect items and includes a bank carrying an account with another bank;

    (f) "Documentary draft" means any negotiable or non-negotiable draft with accompanying documents, securities or other papers to be delivered against honor of the draft;

(g) "Item" means any instrument for the payment of money even though it is not negotiable but does not include money;

(h) "Midnight deadline" with respect to a bank is midnight on its next banking day following the banking day on which it receives the relevant item or notice or from which the time for taking action commences to run, whichever is later;

(i) "Properly payable" includes the availability of funds for payment at the time of decision to pay or dishonor;

(j) "Settle" means to pay in cash, by clearing house settlement, in a charge or credit or by remittance, or otherwise as instructed. A settlement may be either provisional or final;

(k) "Suspends payments" with respect to a bank means that it has been closed by order of the supervisory authorities, that a public officer has been appointed to take it over or that it ceases or refuses to make payments in the ordinary course of business.

(2) Other definitions applying to this Article and the sections in which they appear are:

"Collecting bank." Section 4—105.
"Depositary bank." Section 4—105.
"Intermediary bank." Section 4—105.
"Payor bank." Section 4—105.
"Presenting bank." Section 4—105.
"Remitting bank." Section 4—105.

(3) The following definitions in other Articles apply to this Article:

"Acceptance." Section 3—410.
"Certificate of deposit." Section 3—104.
"Certification." Section 3—411.
"Check." Section 3—104.
"Draft." Section 3—104.
"Holder in due course." Section 3—302.
"Notice of dishonor." Section 3—508.
"Presentment." Section 3—504.
"Protest." Section 3—509.
"Secondary party." Section 3—102.

(4) In addition Article 1 contains general definitions and principles of construction and interpretation applicable throughout this Article.

Section 4—105. "Depositary Bank"; "Intermediary Bank"; "Collecting Bank"; "Payor Bank"; "Presenting Bank"; "Remitting Bank"

In this Article unless the context otherwise requires:

(a) "Depositary bank" means the first bank to which an item is transferred for collection even though it is also the payor bank;

(b) "Payor bank" means a bank by which an item is payable as drawn or accepted;

(c) "Intermediary bank" means any bank to which an item is transferred in course of collection except the depositary or payor bank;

(d) "Collecting bank" means any bank handling the item for collection except the payor bank;

(e) "Presenting bank" means any bank presenting an item except a payor bank;

(f) "Remitting bank" means any payor or intermediary bank remitting for an item.

Section 4—106. Separate Office of a Bank

A branch or separate office of a bank [maintaining its own deposit ledgers] is a separate bank for the purpose of computing the time within which and determining the place at or to which action may be taken or notices or orders shall be given under this Article and under Article 3.

Note: *The brackets are to make it optional with the several states whether to require a branch to maintain its own deposit ledgers in order to be considered to be a separate bank for certain purposes under Article 4. In some states "maintaining its own deposit ledgers" is a satisfactory test. In others branch banking practices are such that this test would not be suitable.*

Section 4—107. Time of Receipt of Items

(1) For the purpose of allowing time to process items, prove balances and make the necessary entries on its books to determine its position for the day, a bank may fix an afternoon hour of 2 P.M. or later as a cut-off hour for the handling of money and items and the making of entries on its books.

(2) Any item or deposit of money received on any day after a cut-off hour so fixed or after the close of the banking day may be treated as being received at the opening of the next banking day.

Section 4—108. Delays

(1) Unless otherwise instructed, a collecting bank in a good faith effort to secure payment may, in the case of specific items and with or without the approval of any person involved, waive, modify or extend time limits imposed or permitted by this Act for a period not in excess of an additional banking day without discharge of secondary parties and without liability to its transferor or any prior party.

(2) Delay by a collecting bank or payor bank beyond time limits prescribed or permitted by this Act or by instructions is excused if caused by interruption of communication facilities, suspension of payments by another bank, war, emergency conditions or other circumstances beyond the control of the bank provided it exercises such diligence as the circumstances require.

Section 4—109. Process of Posting

The "process of posting" means the usual procedure followed by a payor bank in determining to pay an item and in recording the payment including one or more of the following or other steps as determined by the bank:

(a) verification of any signature;

(b) ascertaining that sufficient funds are available;

(c) affixing a "paid" or other stamp;

(d) entering a charge or entry to a customer's account;

(e) correcting or reversing an entry or erroneous action with respect to the item.

Part 2 Collection of Items: Depositary and Collecting Banks

Section 4—201. Presumption and Duration of Agency Status of Collecting Banks and Provisional Status of Credits; Applicability of Article; Item Indorsed "Pay Any Bank"

(1) Unless a contrary intent clearly appears and prior to the time that a settlement given by a collecting bank for an item is or becomes final (subsection (3) of Section 4—211 and Sections 4—212 and 4—213) the bank is an agent or sub-agent of the owner of the item and any settlement given for the item is provisional. This provision applies regardless of the form of indorsement or lack of indorsement and even though credit given for the item is subject to immediate withdrawal as of right or is in fact withdrawn; but the continuance of ownership of an item by its owner and any rights of the owner to proceeds of the item are subject to rights of a collecting bank such as those resulting from outstanding advances on the item and valid rights of set-off. When an item is handled by

banks for purposes of presentment, payment and collection, the relevant provisions of this Article apply even though action of parties clearly establishes that a particular bank has purchased the item and is the owner of it.

(2) After an item has been indorsed with the words "pay any bank" or the like, only a bank may acquire the rights of a holder

- (a) until the item has been returned to the customer initiating collection; or
- (b) until the item has been specially indorsed by a bank to a person who is not a bank.

Section 4—202. Responsibility for Collection; When Action Seasonable

(1) A collecting bank must use ordinary care in

- (a) presenting an item or sending it for presentment; and
- (b) sending notice of dishonor or non-payment or returning an item other than a documentary draft to the bank's transferor [or directly to the depositary bank under subsection (2) of Section 4—212] (*see note to Section 4—212*) after learning that the item has not been paid or accepted, as the case may be; and
- (c) settling for an item when the bank receives final settlement; and
- (d) making or providing for any necessary protest; and
- (e) notifying its transferor of any loss or delay in transit within a reasonable time after discovery thereof.

(2) A collecting bank taking proper action before its midnight deadline following receipt of an item, notice or payment acts seasonably; taking proper action within a reasonably longer time may be seasonable but the bank has the burden of so establishing.

(3) Subject to subsection (1) (a), a bank is not liable for the insolvency, neglect, misconduct, mistake or default of another bank or person or for loss or destruction of an item in transit or in the possession of others.

Section 4—203. Effect of Instructions

Subject to the provisions of Article 3 concerning conversion of instruments (Section 3—419) and the provisions of both Article 3 and this Article concerning restrictive indorsements only a collecting bank's transferor can give instructions which affect the bank or constitute notice to it and a collecting bank is not liable to prior parties for any action taken pursuant to such instructions or in accordance with any agreement with its transferor.

Section 4—204. Methods of Sending and Presenting; Sending Direct to Payor Bank

(1) A collecting bank must send items by reasonably prompt method taking into consideration any relevant instructions, the nature of the item, the number of such items on hand, and the cost of collection involved and the method generally used by it or others to present such items.

(2) A collecting bank may send

- (a) any item direct to the payor bank;
- (b) any item to any non-bank payor if authorized by its transferor; and
- (c) any item other than documentary drafts to any non-bank payor, if authorized by Federal Reserve regulation or operating letter, clearing house rule or the like.

(3) Presentment may be made by a presenting bank at a place where the payor bank has requested that presentment be made.

Section 4—205. Supplying Missing Indorsement; No Notice from Prior Indorsement

(1) A depositary bank which has taken an item for collection may supply any indorsement of the customer which is necessary to title unless the item contains the words "payee's indorsement required"

or the like. In the absence of such a requirement a statement placed on the item by the depositary bank to the effect that the item was deposited by a customer or credited to his account is effective as the customer's indorsement.

(2) An intermediary bank, or payor bank which is not a depositary bank, is neither given notice nor otherwise affected by a restrictive indorsement of any person except the bank's immediate transferor.

Section 4—206. Transfer Between Banks

Any agreed method which identifies the transferor bank is sufficient for the item's further transfer to another bank.

Section 4—207. Warranties of Customer and Collecting Bank on Transfer or Presentment of Items; Time for Claims

(1) Each customer or collecting bank who obtains payment or acceptance of an item and each prior customer and collecting bank warrants to the payor bank or other payor who in good faith pays or accepts the item that

- (a) he has a good title to the item or is authorized to obtain payment or acceptance on behalf of one who has a good title; and
- (b) he has no knowledge that the signature of the maker or drawer is unauthorized, except that this warranty is not given by any customer or collecting bank that is a holder in due course and acts in good faith
    - (i) to a maker with respect to the maker's own signature; or
    - (ii) to a drawer with respect to the drawer's own signature, whether or not the drawer is also the drawee; or
    - (iii) to an acceptor of an item if the holder in due course took the item after the acceptance or obtained the acceptance without knowledge that the drawer's signature was unauthorized; and
- (c) the item has not been materially altered, except that this warranty is not given by any customer or collecting bank that is a holder in due course and acts in good faith
    - (i) to the maker of a note; or
    - (ii) to the drawer of a draft whether or not the drawer is also the drawee; or
    - (iii) to the acceptor of an item with respect to an alteration made prior to the acceptance if the holder in due course took the item after the acceptance, even though the acceptance provided "payable as originally drawn" or equivalent terms; or
    - (iv) to the acceptor of an item with respect to an alteration made after the acceptance.

(2) Each customer and collecting bank who transfers an item and receives a settlement or other consideration for it warrants to his transferee and to any subsequent collecting bank who takes the item in good faith that

- (a) he has a good title to the item or is authorized to obtain payment or acceptance on behalf of one who has a good title and the transfer is otherwise rightful; and
- (b) all signatures are genuine or authorized; and
- (c) the item has not been materially altered; and
- (d) no defense of any party is good against him; and
- (e) he has no knowledge of any insolvency proceeding instituted with respect to the maker or acceptor or the drawer of an unaccepted item.

In addition each customer and collecting bank so transferring an item and receiving a settlement or other consideration engages that upon dishonor and any necessary notice of dishonor and protest he will take up the item.

(3) The warranties and the engagement to honor set forth in the two preceding subsections arise notwithstanding the absence of indorsement or words of guaranty or warranty in the transfer or presentment and a collecting bank remains liable for their breach despite remittance to its transferor. Damages for breach of such warranties or engagement to honor shall not exceed the consideration received by the customer or collecting bank responsible plus finance charges and expenses related to the item, if any.

(4) Unless a claim for breach of warranty under this section is made within a reasonable time after the person claiming learns of the breach, the person liable is discharged to the extent of any loss caused by the delay in making claim.

Section 4—208. Security Interest of Collecting Bank in Items, Accompanying Documents and Proceeds

(1) A bank has a security interest in an item and any accompanying documents or the proceeds of either

(a) in case of an item deposited in an account to the extent to which credit given for the item has been withdrawn or applied;

(b) in case of an item for which it has given credit available for withdrawal as of right, to the extent of the credit given whether or not the credit is drawn upon and whether or not there is a right of charge-back; or

(c) if it makes an advance on or against the item.

(2) When credit which has been given for several items received at one time or pursuant to a single agreement is withdrawn or applied in part the security interest remains upon all the items, any accompanying documents or the proceeds of either. For the purpose of this section, credits first given are first withdrawn.

(3) Receipt by a collecting bank of a final settlement for an item is a realization on its security interest in the item, accompanying documents and proceeds. To the extent and so long as the bank does not receive final settlement for the item or give up possession of the item or accompanying documents for purposes other than collection, the security interest continues and is subject to the provisions of Article 9 except that

(a) no security agreement is necessary to make the security interest enforceable (subsection (1) (a) of Section 9—203); and

(b) no filing is required to perfect the security interest; and

(c) the security interest has priority over conflicting perfected security interests in the item, accompanying documents or proceeds.

Section 4—209. When Bank Gives Value for Purposes of Holder in Due Course

For purposes of determining its status as a holder in due course, the bank has given value to the extent that it has a security interest in an item provided that the bank otherwise complies with the requirements of Section 3—302 on what constitutes a holder in due course.

Section 4—210. Presentment by Notice of Item Not Payable by, Through or at a Bank; Liability of Secondary Parties

(1) Unless otherwise instructed, a collecting bank may present an item not payable by, through or at a bank by sending to the party to accept or pay a written notice that the bank holds the item for acceptance or payment. The notice must be sent in time to be received on or before the day when presentment is due and the bank must meet any requirement of the party to accept or pay under Section 3—505 by the close of the bank's next banking day after it knows of the requirement.

(2) Where presentment is made by notice and neither honor nor request for compliance with a requirement under Section 3—505 is received by the close of business on the day after maturity or in the case of demand items by the close of business on the third banking day after notice was sent, the presenting bank may treat the item as dishonored and charge any secondary party by sending him notice of the facts.

Section 4—211. Media of Remittance; Provisional and Final Settlement in Remittance Cases

(1) A collecting bank may take in settlement of an item

(a) a check of the remitting bank or of another bank on any bank except the remitting bank; or

(b) a cashier's check or similar primary obligation of a remitting bank which is a member of or clears through a member of the same clearing house or group as the collecting bank; or

(c) appropriate authority to charge an account of the remitting bank or of another bank with the collecting bank; or

(d) if the item is drawn upon or payable by a person other than a bank, a cashier's check, certified check or other bank check or obligation.

(2) If before its midnight deadline the collecting bank properly dishonors a remittance check or authorization to charge on itself or presents or forwards for collection a remittance instrument of or on another bank which is of a kind approved by subsection (1) or has not been authorized by it, the collecting bank is not liable to prior parties in the event of the dishonor of such check, instrument or authorization.

(3) A settlement for an item by means of a remittance instrument or authorization to charge is or becomes a final settlement as to both the person making and the person receiving the settlement

(a) if the remittance instrument or authorization to charge is of a kind approved by subsection (1) or has not been authorized by the person receiving the settlement and in either case the person receiving the settlement acts seasonably before its midnight deadline in presenting, forwarding for collection or paying the instrument or authorization,—at the time the remittance instrument or authorization is finally paid by the payor by which it is payable;

(b) if the person receiving the settlement has authorized remittance by a non-bank check or obligation or by a cashier's check or similar primary obligation of or a check upon the payor or other remitting bank which is not of a kind approved by subsection (1) (b),—at the time of the receipt of such remittance check or obligation; or

(c) if in a case not covered by sub-paragraphs (a) or (b) the person receiving the settlement fails to seasonably present, forward for collection, pay or return a remittance instrument or authorization to it to charge before its midnight deadline,—at such midnight deadline.

Section 4—212. Right of Charge-Back or Refund

(1) If a collecting bank has made provisional settlement with its customer for an item and itself fails by reason of dishonor, suspension of payments by a bank or otherwise to receive a settlement for the item which is or becomes final, the bank may revoke the settlement given by it, charge-back the amount of any credit given for the item to its customers' account or obtain refund from its customer whether or not it is able to return the items if by its midnight deadline or within a longer reasonable time after it learns the facts it returns the item or sends notification of the facts. These rights to revoke, charge-back and obtain refund terminate if and when a settlement for the item received by the bank is or becomes final (subsection (3) of Section 4—211 and subsections (2) and (3) of Section 4—213).

[(2) Within the time and manner prescribed by this section and Section 4—301, an intermediary or payor bank, as the case may be, may return an unpaid item directly to the depositary bank and may send for collection a draft on the depositary bank and obtain reimbursement. In such case, if the depositary bank has received provisional settlement for the item, it must reimburse the bank drawing the draft and any provisional credits for the item between banks shall become and remain final.]

Note: *Direct returns is recognized as an innovation that is not yet established bank practice, and therefore, Paragraph 2 has been bracketed. Some lawyers have doubts whether it should be included in legislation or left to development by agreement.*

(3) A depositary bank which is also the payor may charge-back the amount of an item to its customer's account or obtain refund in accordance with the section governing return of an item received by a payor bank for credit on its books (Section 4—301).

(4) The right to charge-back is not affected by

   (a) prior use of the credit given for the item; or

   (b) failure by any bank to exercise ordinary care with respect to the item but any bank so failing remains liable.

(5) A failure to charge-back or claim refund does not affect other rights of the bank against the customer or any other party.

(6) If credit is given in dollars as the equivalent of the value of an item payable in a foreign currency the dollar amount of any charge-back or refund shall be calculated on the basis of the buying sight rate for the foreign currency prevailing on the day when the person entitled to the charge-back or refund learns that it will not receive payment in ordinary course.

Section 4—213. Final Payment of Item by Payor Bank; When Provisional Debits and Credits Become Final; When Certain Credits Become Available for Withdrawal

(1) An item is finally paid by a payor bank when the bank has done any of the following, whichever happens first:

   (a) paid the item in cash; or

   (b) settled for the item without reserving a right to revoke the settlement and without having such right under statute, clearing house rule or agreement; or

   (c) completed the process of posting the item to the indicated account of the drawer, maker or other person to be charged therewith; or

   (d) made a provisional settlement for the item and failed to revoke the settlement in the time and manner permitted by statute, clearing house rule or agreement.

Upon a final payment under subparagraphs (b), (c) or (d) the payor bank shall be accountable for the amount of the item.

(2) If provisional settlement for an item between the presenting and payor banks is made through a clearing house or by debits or credits in an account between them, then to the extent that provisional debits or credits for the item are entered in accounts between the presenting and payor banks or between the presenting and successive prior collecting banks seriatim, they become final upon final payment of the item by the payor bank.

(3) If a collecting bank receives a settlement for an item which is or becomes final (subsection (3) of Section 4—211, subsection (2) of Section 4—213) the bank is accountable to its customer for the amount of the item and any provisional credit given for the item in an account with its customer becomes final.

(4) Subject to any right of the bank to apply the credit to an obligation of the customer, credit given by a bank for an item in an account with its customer becomes available for withdrawal as of right

   (a) in any case where the bank has received a provisional settlement for the item,—when such settlement becomes final and the bank has had a reasonable time to learn that the settlement is final;

   (b) in any case where the bank is both a depositary bank and a payor bank and the item is finally paid,—at the opening of the bank's second banking day following receipt of the item.

(5) A deposit of money in a bank is final when made but, subject to any right of the bank to apply the deposit to an obligation of the customer, the deposit becomes available for withdrawal as of right at the opening of the bank's next banking day following receipt of the deposit.

Section 4—214. Insolvency and Preference

(1) Any item in or coming into the possession of a payor or collecting bank which suspends payment and which item is not finally paid shall be returned by the receiver, trustee or agent in charge of the closed bank to the presenting bank or the closed bank's customer.

(2) If a payor bank finally pays an item and suspends payments without making a settlement for the item with its customer or the presenting bank which settlement is or becomes final, the owner of the item has a preferred claim against the payor bank.

(3) If a payor bank gives or a collecting bank gives or receives a provisional settlement for an item and thereafter suspends payments, the suspension does not prevent or interfere with the settlement becoming final if such finality occurs automatically upon the lapse of certain time or the happening of certain events (subsection (3) of Section 4—211, subsections (1) (d), (2) and (3) of Section 4—213).

(4) If a collecting bank receives from subsequent parties settlement for an item which settlement is or becomes final and suspends payments without making a settlement for the item with its customer which is or becomes final, the owner of the item has a preferred claim against such collecting bank.

Part 3   Collection of Items; Payor Banks

Section 4—301. Deferred Posting; Recovery of Payment by Return of Items; Time of Dishonor

(1) Where an authorized settlement for a demand item (other than a documentary draft) received by a payor bank otherwise than for immediate payment over the counter has been made before midnight of the banking day of receipt the payor bank may revoke the settlement and recover any payment if before it has made final payment (subsection (1) of Section 4—213) and before its midnight deadline it

   (a) returns the item; or

   (b) sends written notice of dishonor or nonpayment if the item is held for protest or is otherwise unavailable for return.

(2) If a demand item is received by a payor bank for credit on its books it may return such item or send notice of dishonor and may revoke any credit given or recover the amount thereof withdrawn by its customer, if it acts within the time limit and in the manner specified in the preceding subsection.

(3) Unless previous notice of dishonor has been sent an item is dishonored at the time when for purposes of dishonor it is returned or notice sent in accordance with this section.

(4) An item is returned:

   (a) as to an item received through a clearing house, when it is delivered to the presenting or last collecting bank or to the clearing house or is sent or delivered in accordance with its rules; or

   (b) in all other cases, when it is sent or delivered to the bank's customer or transferor or pursuant to his instructions.

Section 4—302. Payor Bank's Responsibility for Late Return of Item

In the absence of a valid defense such as breach of a presentment warranty (subsection (1) of Section 4—207), settlement effected or the like, if an item is presented on and received by a payor bank the bank is accountable for the amount of

(a) a demand item other than a documentary draft whether properly payable or not if the bank, in any case where it is not also the depositary bank, retains the item beyond midnight of the banking day of receipt without settling for it or, regardless of whether it is also the depositary bank, does not pay or return the item or send notice of dishonor until after its midnight deadline; or

(b) any other properly payable item unless within the time allowed for acceptance or payment of that item the bank either accepts or pays the item or returns it and accompanying documents.

Section 4—303. When Items Subject to Notice, Stop-Order, Legal Process or Setoff; Order in Which Items May Be Charged or Certified

(1) Any knowledge, notice or stop-order received by, legal process served upon or setoff exercised by a payor bank, whether or not effective under other rules of law to terminate, suspend or modify the bank's right or duty to pay an item or to charge its customer's account for the item, comes too late to so terminate, suspend or modify such right or duty if the knowledge, notice, stop-order or legal process is received or served and a reasonable time for the bank to act thereon expires or the setoff is exercised after the bank has done any of the following:

(a) accepted or certified the item;

(b) paid the item in cash;

(c) settled for the item without reserving a right to revoke the settlement and without having such right under statute, clearing house rule or agreement;

(d) completed the process of posting the item to the indicated account of the drawer, maker or other person to be charged therewith or otherwise has evidenced by examination of such indicated account and by action its decision to pay the item; or

(e) become accountable for the amount of the item under subsection (1) (d) of Section 4—213 and Section 4—302 dealing with the payor bank's responsibility for late return of items.

(2) Subject to the provisions of subsection (1) items may be accepted, paid, certified or charged to the indicated account of its customer in any order convenient to the bank.

Part 4 Relationship Between Payor Bank and Its Customer

Section 4—401. When Bank May Charge Customer's Account

(1) As against its customer, a bank may charge against his account any item which is otherwise properly payable from that account even though the charge creates an overdraft.

(2) A bank which in good faith makes payment to a holder may charge the indicated account of its customer according to

(a) the original tenor of his altered item; or

(b) the tenor of his completed item, even though the bank knows the item has been completed unless the bank has notice that the completion was improper.

Section 4—402. Bank's Liability to Customer for Wrongful Dishonor

A payor bank is liable to its customer for damages proximately caused by the wrongful dishonor of an item. When the dishonor occurs through mistake liability is limited to actual damages proved. If so proximately caused and proved damages may include damages for an arrest or prosecution of the customer or other consequential damages. Whether any consequential damages are proximately caused by the wrongful dishonor is a question of fact to be determined in each case.

Section 4—403. Customer's Right to Stop Payment; Burden of Proof of Loss

(1) A customer may by order to his bank stop payment of any item payable for his account but the order must be received at such time and in such manner as to afford the bank a reasonable opportunity to act on it prior to any action by the bank with respect to the item described in Section 4—303.

(2) An oral order is binding upon the bank only for fourteen calendar days unless confirmed in writing within that period. A written order is effective for only six months unless renewed in writing.

(3) The burden of establishing the fact and amount of loss resulting from the payment of an item contrary to a binding stop payment order is on the customer.

Section 4—404. Bank Not Obligated to Pay Check More Than Six Months Old

A bank is under no obligation to a customer having a checking account to pay a check, other than a certified check, which is presented more than six months after its date, but it may charge its customer's account for a payment made thereafter in good faith.

Section 4—405. Death or Incompetence of Customer

(1) A payor or collecting bank's authority to accept, pay or collect an item or to account for proceeds of its collection if otherwise effective is not rendered ineffective by incompetence of a customer of either bank existing at the time the item is issued or its collection is undertaken if the bank does not know of an adjudication of incompetence. Neither death nor incompetence of a customer revokes such authority to accept, pay, collect or account until the bank knows of the fact of death or of an adjudication of incompetence and has reasonable opportunity to act on it.

(2) Even with knowledge a bank may for 10 days after the date of death pay or certify checks drawn on or prior to that date unless ordered to stop payment by a person claiming an interest in the account.

Section 4—406. Customer's Duty to Discover and Report Unauthorized Signature or Alteration

(1) When a bank sends to its customer a statement of account accompanied by items paid in good faith in support of the debit entries or holds the statement and items pursuant to a request or instructions of its customer or otherwise in a reasonable manner makes the statement and items available to the customer, the customer must exercise reasonable care and promptness to examine the statement and items to discover his unauthorized signature or any alteration on an item and must notify the bank promptly after discovery thereof.

(2) If the bank establishes that the customer failed with respect to an item to comply with the duties imposed on the customer by subsection (1) the customer is precluded from asserting against the bank

(a) his unauthorized signature or any alteration on the item if the bank also establishes that it suffered a loss by reason of such failure; and

(b) an unauthorized signature or alteration by the same wrongdoer on any other item paid in good faith by the bank after the first item and statement was available to the customer for a reasonable period not exceeding fourteen calendar days and before the bank receives notification from the customer of any such unauthorized signature or alteration.

(3) The preclusion under subsection (2) does not apply if the customer establishes lack of ordinary care on the part of the bank in paying the item(s).

(4) Without regard to care or lack of care of either the customer or the bank a customer who does not within one year from the time the statement and items are made available to the customer (subsection (1)) discover and report his unauthorized signature or any alteration on the face or back of the item or does not within 3 years from that time discover and report any unauthorized indorsement is precluded from asserting against the bank such unauthorized signature or indorsement or such alteration.

(5) If under this section a payor bank has a valid defense against a claim of a customer upon or resulting from payment of an item and waives or fails upon request to assert the defense the bank may not assert against any collecting bank or other prior party presenting or transferring the item a claim based upon the unauthorized signature or alteration giving rise to the customer's claim.

Section 4—407. Payor Bank's Right to Subrogation on Improper Payment

If a payor bank has paid an item over the stop payment order of the drawer or maker or otherwise under circumstances giving a basis for objection by the drawer or maker, to prevent unjust enrichment and only to the extent necessary to prevent loss to the bank by reason of its payment of the item, the payor bank shall be subrogated to the rights

(a) of any holder in due course on the item against the drawer or maker; and

(b) of the payee or any other holder of the item against the drawer or maker either on the item or under the transaction out of which the item arose; and

(c) of the drawer or maker against the payee or any other holder of the item with respect to the transaction out of which the item arose.

Part 5 Collection of Documentary Drafts

Section 4—501. Handling of Documentary Drafts; Duty to Send for Presentment and to Notify Customer of Dishonor

A bank which takes a documentary draft for collection must present or send the draft and accompanying documents for presentment and upon learning that the draft has not been paid or accepted in due course must seasonably notify its customer of such fact even though it may have discounted or bought the draft or extended credit available for withdrawal as of right.

Section 4—502. Presentment of "On Arrival" Drafts

When a draft or the relevant instructions require presentment "on arrival," "when goods arrive" or the like, the collecting bank need not present until in its judgment a reasonable time for arrival of the goods has expired. Refusal to pay or accept because the goods have not arrived is not dishonor; the bank must notify its transferor of such refusal but need not present the draft again until it is instructed to do so or learns of the arrival of the goods.

Section 4—503. Responsibility of Presenting Bank for Documents and Goods; Report of Reasons for Dishonor; Referee in Case of Need

Unless otherwise instructed and except as provided in Article 5 a bank presenting a documentary draft

(a) must deliver the documents to the drawee on acceptance of the draft if it is payable more than three days after presentment; otherwise, only on payment; and

(b) upon dishonor, either in the case of presentment for acceptance or presentment for payment, may seek and follow instructions from any referee in case of need designated in the draft or if the presenting bank does not choose to utilize his services it must use diligence and good faith to ascertain the reason for dishonor, must notify its transferor of the dishonor and of the results of its effort to ascertain the reasons therefor and must request instructions.

But the presenting bank is under no obligation with respect to goods represented by the documents except to follow any reasonable instructions seasonably received; it has a right to reimbursement for any expense incurred in following instructions and to prepayment of or indemnity for such expenses.

Section 4—504. Privilege of Presenting Bank to Deal With Goods; Security Interest for Expenses

(1) A presenting bank which, following the dishonor of a documentary draft, has seasonably requested instructions but does not receive them within a reasonable time may store, sell, or otherwise deal with the goods in any reasonable manner.

(2) For its reasonable expenses incurred by action under subsection (1) the presenting bank has a lien upon the goods or their proceeds, which may be foreclosed in the same manner as an unpaid seller's lien.

Article 5 Letters of Credit

Section 5—101. Short Title

This Article shall be known and may be cited as Uniform Commercial Code—Letters of Credit.

Section 5—102. Scope

(1) This Article applies

(a) to a credit issued by a bank if the credit requires a documentary draft or a documentary demand for payment; and

(b) to a credit issued by a person other than a bank if the credit requires that the draft or demand for payment be accompanied by a document of title; and

(c) to a credit issued by a bank or other person if the credit is not within subparagraphs (a) or (b) but conspicuously states that it is a letter of credit or is conspicuously so entitled.

(2) Unless the engagement meets the requirements of subsection (1), this Article does not apply to engagements to make advances or to honor drafts or demands for payment, to authorities to pay or purchase, to guarantees or to general agreements.

(3) This Article deals with some but not all of the rules and concepts of letters of credit as such rules or concepts have developed prior to this act or may hereafter develop. The fact that this Article states a rule does not by itself require, imply or negate application of the same or a converse rule to a situation not provided for or to a person not specified by this Article.

Section 5—103. Definitions

(1) In this Article unless the context otherwise requires

(a) "Credit" or "letter of credit" means an engagement by a bank or other person made at the request of a customer and of a kind within the scope of this Article (Section 5—102) that the issuer will honor drafts or other demands for payment upon compliance with the conditions specified in the credit. A credit may be either revocable or irrevocable. The engagement may be either an agreement to honor or a statement that the bank or other person is authorized to honor.

(b) A "documentary draft" or a "documentary demand for payment" is one honor of which is conditioned upon the presentation of a document or documents. "Document" means any paper including document of title, security, invoice, certificate, notice of default and the like.

(c) An "issuer" is a bank or other person issuing a credit.

(d) A "beneficiary" of a credit is a person who is entitled under its terms to draw or demand payment.

(e) An "advising bank" is a bank which gives notification of the issuance of a credit by another bank.

(f) A "confirming bank" is a bank which engages either that it will itself honor a credit already issued by another bank or that such a credit will be honored by the issuer or a third bank.

(g) A "customer" is a buyer or other person who causes an issuer to issue a credit. The term also includes a bank which procures issuance or confirmation on behalf of that bank's customer.

(2) Other definitions applying to this Article and the sections in which they appear are:

"Notation of Credit." Section 5—108.
"Presenter." Section 5—112(3).

(3) Definitions in other Articles applying to this Article and the sections in which they appear are:

"Accept" or "Acceptance." Section 3—410.
"Contract for sale." Section 2—106.
"Draft." Section 3—104.
"Holder in due course." Section 3—302.
"Midnight deadline." Section 4—104.
"Security." Section 8—102.

(4) In addition, Article 1 contains general definitions and principles of construction and interpretation applicable throughout this Article.

Section 5—104. Formal Requirements; Signing

(1) Except as otherwise required in subsection (1) (c) of Section 5—102 on scope, no particular form of phrasing is required for a credit. A credit must be in writing and signed by the issuer and a confirmation must be in writing and signed by the confirming bank. A modification of the terms of a credit or confirmation must be signed by the issuer or confirming bank.

(2) A telegram may be a sufficient signed writing if it identifies its sender by an authorized authentication. The authentication may be in code and the authorized naming of the issuer in an advice of credit is a sufficient signing.

Section 5—105. Consideration

No consideration is necessary to establish a credit or to enlarge or otherwise modify its terms.

Section 5—106. Time and Effect of Establishment of Credit

(1) Unless otherwise agreed a credit is established

(a) as regards the customer as soon as a letter of credit is sent to him or the letter of credit or an authorized written advice of its issuance is sent to the beneficiary; and

(b) as regards the beneficiary when he receives a letter of credit or an authorized written advice of its issuance.

(2) Unless otherwise agreed once an irrevocable credit is established as regards the customer it can be modified or revoked only with the consent of the customer and once it is established as regards the beneficiary it can be modified or revoked only with his consent.

(3) Unless otherwise agreed after a revocable credit is established it may be modified or revoked by the issuer without notice to or consent from the customer or beneficiary.

(4) Notwithstanding any modification or revocation of a revocable credit any person authorized to honor or negotiate under the terms of the original credit is entitled to reimbursement for or honor of any draft or demand for payment duly honored or negotiated before receipt of notice of the modification or revocation and the issuer in turn is entitled to reimbursement from its customer.

Section 5—107. Advice of Credit; Confirmation; Error in Statement of Terms

(1) Unless otherwise specified an advising bank by advising a credit issued by another bank does not assume any obligation to honor drafts drawn or demands for payment made under the credit but it does assume obligation for the accuracy of its own statement.

(2) A confirming bank by confirming a credit becomes directly obligated on the credit to the extent of its confirmation as though it were its issuer and acquires the rights of an issuer.

(3) Even though an advising bank incorrectly advises the terms of a credit it has been authorized to advise the credit is established as against the issuer to the extent of its original terms.

(4) Unless otherwise specified the customer bears as against the issuer all risks of transmission and reasonable translation or interpretation of any message relating to a credit.

Section 5—108. "Notation Credit"; Exhaustion of Credit

(1) A credit which specifies that any person purchasing or paying drafts drawn or demands for payment made under it must note the amount of the draft or demand on the letter or advice of credit is a "notation credit."

(2) Under a notation credit

(a) a person paying the beneficiary or purchasing a draft or demand for payment from him acquires a right to honor only if the appropriate notation is made and by transferring or forwarding for honor the documents under the credit such a person warrants to the issuer that the notation has been made; and

(b) unless the credit or a signed statement that an appropriate notation has been made accompanies the draft or demand for payment the issuer may delay honor until evidence of notation has been procured which is satisfactory to it but its obligation and that of its customer continue for a reasonable time not exceeding thirty days to obtain such evidence.

(3) If the credit is not a notation credit

(a) the issuer may honor complying drafts or demands for payment presented to it in the order in which they are presented and is discharged pro tanto by honor of any such draft or demand;

(b) as between competing good faith purchasers of complying drafts or demands the person first purchasing has priority over a subsequent purchaser even though the later purchased draft or demand has been first honored.

Section 5—109. Issuer's Obligation to Its Customer

(1) An issuer's obligation to its customer includes good faith and observance of any general banking usage but unless otherwise agreed does not include liability or responsibility

(a) for performance of the underlying contract for sale or other transaction between the customer and the beneficiary; or

(b) for any act or omission of any person other than itself or its own branch or for loss or destruction of a draft, demand or document in transit or in the possession of others; or

(c) based on knowledge or lack of knowledge of any usage of any particular trade.

(2) An issuer must examine documents with care so as to ascertain that on their face they appear to comply with the terms of the credit but unless otherwise agreed assumes no liability of responsibility for the genuineness, falsification or effect of any document which appears on such examination to be regular on its face.

(3) A non-bank issuer is not bound by any banking usage of which it has no knowledge.

Section 5—110. Availability of Credit in Portions; Presenter's Reservation of Lien or Claim

(1) Unless otherwise specified a credit may be used in portions in the discretion of the beneficiary.

(2) Unless otherwise specified a person by presenting a documentary draft or demand for payment under a credit relinquishes upon its honor all claims to the documents and a person by transferring such draft or demand or causing such presentment authorizes such relinquishment. An explicit reservation of claim makes the draft or demand non-complying.

Section 5—111. Warranties on Transfer and Presentment

(1) Unless otherwise agreed the beneficiary by transferring or presenting a documentary draft or demand for payment warrants to all interested parties that the necessary conditions of the credit have been complied with. This is in addition to any warranties arising under Articles 3, 4, 7 and 8.

(2) Unless otherwise agreed a negotiating, advising, confirming, collecting or issuing bank presenting or transferring a draft or demand for payment under a credit warrants only the matters warranted by a collecting bank under Article 4 and any such bank transferring a document warrants only the matters warranted by an intermediary under Articles 7 and 8.

Section 5—112. Time Allowed for Honor or Rejection; Withholding Honor or Rejection by Consent; "Presenter"

(1) A bank to which a documentary draft or demand for payment is presented under a credit may without dishonor of the draft, demand or credit

  (a) defer honor until the close of the third banking day following receipt of the documents; and

  (b) further defer honor if the presenter has expressly or impliedly consented thereto.

Failure to honor within the time here specified constitutes dishonor of the draft or demand and of the credit [except as otherwise provided in subsection (4) of Section 5—114 on conditional payment].

Note: *The bracketed language in the last sentence of subsection (1) should be included only if the optional provisions of Section 5—114(4) and (5) are included.*

(2) Upon dishonor the bank may unless otherwise instructed fulfill its duty to return the draft or demand and the documents by holding them at the disposal of the presenter and sending him an advice to that effect.

(3) "Presenter" means any person presenting a draft or demand for payment for honor under a credit even though that person is a confirming bank or other correspondent which is acting under an issuer's authorization.

Section 5—113. Indemnities

(1) A bank seeking to obtain (whether for itself or another) honor, negotiation or reimbursement under a credit may give an indemnity to induce such honor, negotiation or reimbursement.

(2) An indemnity agreement inducing honor, negotiation or reimbursement

  (a) unless otherwise explicitly agreed applies to defects in the documents but not in the goods; and

  (b) unless a longer time is explicitly agreed expires at the end of ten business days following receipt of the documents by the ultimate customer unless notice of objection is sent before such expiration date. The ultimate customer may send notice of objection to the person from whom he received the documents and any bank receiving such notice is under a duty to send notice to its transferor before its midnight deadline.

Section 5—114. Issuer's Duty and Privilege to Honor; Right to Reimbursement

(1) An issuer must honor a draft or demand for payment which complies with the terms of the relevant credit regardless of whether the goods or documents conform to the underlying contract for sale or other contract between the customer and the beneficiary. The issuer is not excused from honor of such a draft or demand by reason of an additional general term that all documents must be satisfactory to the issuer, but an issuer may require that specified documents must be satisfactory to it.

(2) Unless otherwise agreed when documents appear on their face to comply with the terms of a credit but a required document does not in fact conform to the warranties made on negotiation or transfer of a document of title (Section 7—507) or of a certificated security (Section 8—306) or is forged or fraudulent or there is fraud in the transaction:

  (a) the issuer must honor the draft or demand for payment if honor is demanded by a negotiating bank or other holder of the draft or demand which has taken the draft or demand under the credit and under circumstances which would make it a holder in due course (Section 3—302) and in an appropriate case would make it a person to whom a document of title has been duly negotiated (Section 7—502) or a bona fide purchaser of a certificated security (Section 8—302); and

  (b) in all other cases as against its customer, an issuer acting in good faith may honor the draft or demand for payment despite notification from the customer of fraud, forgery or other defect not apparent on the face of the documents but a court of appropriate jurisdiction may enjoin such honor.

(3) Unless otherwise agreed an issuer which has duly honored a draft or demand for payment is entitled to immediate reimbursement of any payment made under the credit and to be put in effectively available funds not later than the day before maturity of any acceptance made under the credit.

[(4) When a credit provides for payment by the issuer on receipt of notice that the required documents are in the possession of a correspondent or other agent of the issuer

  (a) any payment made on receipt of such notice is conditional; and

  (b) the issuer may reject documents which do not comply with the credit if it does so within three banking days following its receipt of the documents; and

  (c) in the event of such rejection, the issuer is entitled by charge back or otherwise to return of the payment made.]

[(5) In the case covered by subsection (4) failure to reject documents within the time specified in sub-paragraph (b) constitutes acceptance of the documents and makes the payment final in favor of the beneficiary.]

Note: *Subsections (4) and (5) are bracketed as optional. If they are included the bracketed language in the last sentence of Section 5—112(1) should also be included.*

Section 5—115. Remedy for Improper Dishonor or Anticipatory Repudiation

(1) When an issuer wrongfully dishonors a draft or demand for payment presented under a credit the person entitled to honor has with respect to any documents the rights of a person in the position of a seller (Section 2—707) and may recover from the issuer the face amount of the draft or demand together with incidental damages under Section 2—710 on seller's incidental damages and interest but less any amount realized by resale or other use or disposition of the subject matter of the transaction. In the event no resale or other utilization is made the documents, goods or other subject matter involved in the transaction must be turned over to the issuer on payment of judgment.

(2) When an issuer wrongfully cancels or otherwise repudiates a credit before presentment of a draft or demand for payment drawn under it the beneficiary has the rights of a seller after anticipatory repudiation by the buyer under Section 2—610 if he learns of the repudiation in time reasonably to avoid procurement of the required documents. Otherwise the beneficiary has an immediate right of action for wrongful dishonor.

Section 5—116. Transfer and Assignment

(1) The right to draw under a credit can be transferred or assigned only when the credit is expressly designated as transferable or assignable.

(2) Even though the credit specifically states that it is nontransferable or nonassignable the beneficiary may before performance of the conditions of the credit assign his right to proceeds. Such an assignment is an assignment of an account under Article 9 on Secured Transactions and is governed by that Article except that

(a) the assignment is ineffective until the letter of credit or advice of credit is delivered to the assignee which delivery constitutes perfection of the security interest under Article 9; and

(b) the issuer may honor drafts or demands for payment drawn under the credit until it receives a notification of the assignment signed by the beneficiary which reasonably identifies the credit involved in the assignment and contains a request to pay the assignee; and

(c) after what reasonably appears to be such a notification has been received the issuer may without dishonor refuse to accept or pay even to a person otherwise entitled to honor until the letter of credit or advice of credit is exhibited to the issuer.

(3) Except where the beneficiary has effectively assigned his right to draw or his right to proceeds, nothing in this section limits his right to transfer or negotiate drafts or demands drawn under the credit.

Section 5—117. Insolvency of Bank Holding Funds for Documentary Credit

(1) Where an issuer or an advising or confirming bank or a bank which has for a customer procured issuance of a credit by another bank becomes insolvent before final payment under the credit and the credit is one to which this Article is made applicable by paragraphs (a) or (b) of Section 5—102(1) on scope, the receipt or allocation of funds or collateral to secure or meet obligations under the credit shall have the following results:

(a) to the extent of any funds or collateral turned over after or before the insolvency as indemnity against or specifically for the purpose of payment of drafts or demands for payment drawn under the designated credit, the drafts or demands are entitled to payment in preference over depositors or other general creditors of the issuer or bank; and

(b) on expiration of the credit or surrender of the beneficiary's rights under it unused any person who has given such funds or collateral is similarly entitled to return thereof; and

(c) a charge to a general or current account with a bank if specifically consented to for the purpose of indemnity against or payment of drafts or demands for payment drawn under the designated credit falls under the same rules as if the funds had been drawn out in cash and then turned over with specific instructions.

(2) After honor or reimbursement under this section the customer or other person for whose account the insolvent bank has acted is entitled to receive the documents involved.

Article 6 Bulk Transfers

Section 6—101. Short Title

This Article shall be known and may be cited as Uniform Commercial Code—Bulk Transfers.

Section 6—102. "Bulk Transfers"; Transfers of Equipment; Enterprises Subject to This Article; Bulk Transfers Subject to This Article

(1) A "bulk transfer" is any transfer in bulk and not in the ordinary course of the transferor's business of a major part of the materials, supplies, merchandise or other inventory (Section 9—109) of an enterprise subject to this Article.

(2) A transfer of a substantial part of the equipment (Section 9—109) of such an enterprise is a bulk transfer if it is made in connection with a bulk transfer of inventory, but not otherwise.

(3) The enterprises subject to this Article are all those whose principal business is the sale of merchandise from stock, including those who manufacture what they sell.

(4) Except as limited by the following section all bulk transfers of goods located within this state are subject to this Article.

Section 6—103. Transfers Excepted From This Article

The following transfers are not subject to this Article:

(1) Those made to give security for the performance of an obligation;

(2) General assignments for the benefit of all the creditors of the transferor, and subsequent transfers by the assignee thereunder;

(3) Transfers in settlement or realization of a lien or other security interests;

(4) Sales by executors, administrators, receivers, trustees in bankruptcy, or any public officer under judicial process;

(5) Sales made in the course of judicial or administrative proceedings for the dissolution or reorganization of a corporation and of which notice is sent to the creditors of the corporation pursuant to order of the court or administrative agency;

(6) Transfers to a person maintaining a known place of business in this State who becomes bound to pay the debts of the transferor in full and gives public notice of that fact, and who is solvent after becoming so bound;

(7) A transfer to a new business enterprise organized to take over and continue the business, if public notice of the transaction is given and the new enterprise assumes the debts of the transferor and he receives nothing from the transaction except an interest in the new enterprise junior to the claims of creditors;

(8) Transfers of property which is exempt from execution.

Public notice under subsection (6) or subsection (7) may be given by publishing once a week for two consecutive weeks in a newspaper of general circulation where the transferor had its principal place of business in this state an advertisement including the names and addresses of the transferor and transferee and the effective date of the transfer.

Section 6—104. Schedule of Property, List of Creditors

(1) Except as provided with respect to auction sales (Section 6—108), a bulk transfer subject to this Article is ineffective against any creditor of the transferor unless:

    (a) The transferee requires the transferor to furnish a list of his existing creditors prepared as stated in this section; and

    (b) The parties prepare a schedule of the property transferred sufficient to identify it; and

    (c) The transferee preserves the list and schedule for six months next following the transfer and permits inspection of either or both and copying therefrom at all reasonable hours by any creditor of the transferor, or files the list and schedule in (a public office to be here identified).

(2) The list of creditors must be signed and sworn to or affirmed by the transferor or his agent. It must contain the names and business addresses of all creditors of the transferor, with the amounts when known, and also the names of all persons who are known to the transferor to assert claims against him even though such claims are disputed. If the transferor is the obligor of an outstanding issue of bonds, debentures or the like as to which there is an indenture trustee, the list of creditors need include only the name and address of the indenture trustee and the aggregate outstanding principal amount of the issue.

(3) Responsibility for the completeness and accuracy of the list of creditors rests on the transferor, and the transfer is not rendered ineffective by errors or omissions therein unless the transferee is shown to have had knowledge.

Section 6—105. Notice to Creditors

In addition to the requirements of the preceding section, any bulk transfer subject to this Article except one made by auction sale (Section 6—108) is ineffective against any creditor of the transferor unless at least ten days before he takes possession of the goods or pays for them, whichever happens first, the transferee gives notice of the transfer in the manner and to the persons hereafter provided (Section 6—107).

[Section 6—106. Application of the Proceeds

In addition to the requirements of the two preceding sections:

(1) Upon every bulk transfer subject to this Article for which new consideration becomes payable except those made by sale at auction it is the duty of the transferee to assure that such consideration is applied so far as necessary to pay those debts of the transferor which are either shown on the list furnished by the transferor (Section 6—104) or filed in writing in the place stated in the notice (Section 6—107) within thirty days after the mailing of such notice. This duty of the transferee runs to all the holders of such debts, and may be enforced by any of them for the benefit of all.

(2) If any of said debts are in dispute the necessary sum may be withheld from distribution until the dispute is settled or adjudicated.

(3) If the consideration payable is not enough to pay all of the said debts in full distribution shall be made pro rata.]

Note: *This section is bracketed to indicate division of opinion as to whether or not it is a wise provision, and to suggest that this is a point on which State enactments may differ without serious damage to the principle of uniformity.*

In any State where this section is omitted, the following parts of sections, also bracketed in the text, should also be omitted, namely:

    Section 6—107(2) (e).
              6—108(3) (c).
              6—109(2).

In any State where this section is enacted, these other provisions should be also.

Optional Subsection (4)

[(4) The transferee may within ten days after he takes possession of the goods pay the consideration into the (specify court) in the county where the transferor had its principal place of business in this state and thereafter may discharge his duty under this section by giving notice by registered or certified mail to all the persons to whom the duty runs that the consideration has been paid into that court and that they should file their claims there. On motion of any interested party, the court may order the distribution of the consideration to the persons entitled to it.]

Note: *Optional subsection (4) is recommended for those states which do not have a general statute providing for payment of money into court.*

Section 6—107. The Notice

(1) The notice to creditors (Section 6—105) shall state:

    (a) that a bulk transfer is about to be made; and

    (b) the names and business addresses of the transferor and transferee, and all other business names and addresses used by the transferor within three years last past so far as known to the transferee; and

    (c) whether or not all the debts of the transferor are to be paid in full as they fall due as a result of the transaction, and if so, the address to which creditors should send their bills.

(2) If the debts of the transferor are not to be paid in full as they fall due or if the transferee is in doubt on that point then the notice shall state further:

    (a) the location and general description of the property to be transferred and the estimated total of the transferor's debts;

    (b) the address where the schedule of property and list of creditors (Section 6—104) may be inspected;

    (c) whether the transfer is to pay existing debts and if so the amount of such debts and to whom owing;

    (d) whether the transfer is for new consideration and if so the amount of such consideration and the time and place of payment; [and]

    [(e) if for new consideration the time and place where creditors of the transferor are to file their claims.]

(3) The notice in any case shall be delivered personally or sent by registered or certified mail to all the persons shown on the list of creditors furnished by the transferor (Section 6—104) and to all other persons who are known to the transferee to hold or assert claims against the transferor.

Note: *The words in brackets are optional. See Note under § 6—106.*

Section 6—108. Auction Sales; "Auctioneer"

(1) A bulk transfer is subject to this Article even though it is by sale at auction, but only in the manner and with the results stated in this section.

(2) The transferor shall furnish a list of his creditors and assist in the preparation of a schedule of the property to be sold, both prepared as before stated (Section 6—104).

(3) The person or persons other than the transferor who direct, control or are responsible for the auction are collectively called the "auctioneer." The auctioneer shall:

    (a) receive and retain the list of creditors and prepare and retain the schedule of property for the period stated in this Article (Section 6—104);

(b) give notice of the auction personally or by registered or certified mail at least ten days before it occurs to all persons shown on the list of creditors and to all other persons who are known to him to hold or assert claims against the transferor; [and]

[(c) assure that the net proceeds of the auction are applied as provided in this Article (Section 6—106).]

(4) Failure of the auctioneer to perform any of these duties does not affect the validity of the sale or the title of the purchasers, but if the auctioneer knows that the auction constitutes a bulk transfer such failure renders the auctioneer liable to the creditors of the transferor as a class for the sums owing to them from the transferor up to but not exceeding the net proceeds of the auction. If the auctioneer consists of several persons their liability is joint and several.

Note: *The words in brackets are optional. See Note under § 6—106.*

Section 6—109. What Creditors Protected; [Credit for Payment to Particular Creditors]

(1) The creditors of the transferor mentioned in this Article are those holding claims based on transactions or events occurring before the bulk transfer, but creditors who become such after notice to creditors is given (Sections 6—105 and 6—107) are not entitled to notice.

[(2) Against the aggregate obligation imposed by the provisions of this Article concerning the application of the proceeds (Section 6—106 and subsection (3) (c) of 6—108) the transferee or auctioneer is entitled to credit for sums paid to particular creditors of the transferor, not exceeding the sums believed in good faith at the time of the payment to be properly payable to such creditors.]

Note: *The words in brackets are optional. See Note under § 6—106.*

Section 6—110. Subsequent Transfers

When the title of a transferee to property is subject to a defect by reason of his non-compliance with the requirements of this Article, then:

(1) A purchaser of any of such property from such transferee who pays no value or who takes with notice of such non-compliance takes subject to such defect, but

(2) A purchaser for value in good faith and without such notice takes free of such defect.

Section 6—111. Limitation of Actions and Levies

No action under this Article shall be brought nor levy made more than six months after the date on which the transferee took possession of the goods unless the transfer has been concealed. If the transfer has been concealed, actions may be brought or levies made within six months after its discovery.

Note to Article 6: *Section 6—106 is bracketed to indicate division of opinion as to whether or not it is a wise provision, and to suggest that this is a point on which State enactments may differ without serious damage to the principle of uniformity.*

In any State where Section 6—106 is not enacted, the following parts of sections, also bracketed in the text, should also be omitted, namely:

   Sec. 6—107(2) (e).
   6—108(3) (c).
   6—109(2).

In any State where Section 6—106 is enacted, these other provisions should be also.

Article 7 Warehouse Receipts, Bills of Lading and Other Documents of Title

Part 1 General

Section 7—101. Short Title

This Article shall be known and may be cited as Uniform Commercial Code—Documents of Title.

Section 7—102. Definitions and Index of Definitions

(1) In this Article, unless the context otherwise requires:

(a) "Bailee" means the person who by a warehouse receipt, bill of lading or other document of title acknowledges possession of goods and contracts to deliver them.

(b) "Consignee" means the person named in a bill to whom or to whose order the bill promises delivery.

(c) "Consignor" means the person named in a bill as the person from whom the goods have been received for shipment.

(d) "Delivery order" means a written order to deliver goods directed to a warehouseman, carrier or other person who in the ordinary course of business issues warehouse receipts or bills of lading.

(e) "Document" means document of title as defined in the general definitions in Article 1 (Section 1—201).

(f) "Goods" means all things which are treated as movable for the purposes of a contract of storage or transportation.

(g) "Issuer" means a bailee who issues a document except that in relation to an unaccepted delivery order it means the person who orders the possessor of goods to deliver. Issuer includes any person for whom an agent or employee purports to act in issuing a document if the agent or employee has real or apparent authority to issue documents, notwithstanding that the issuer received no goods or that the goods were misdescribed or that in any other respect the agent or employee violated his instructions.

(h) "Warehouseman" is a person engaged in the business of storing goods for hire.

(2) Other definitions applying to this Article or to specified Parts thereof, and the sections in which they appear are:

   "Duly negotiate." Section 7—501.
   "Person entitled under the document." Section 7—403(4).

(3) Definitions in other Articles applying to this Article and the sections in which they appear are:

   "Contract for sale." Section 2—106.
   "Overseas." Section 2—323.
   "Receipt" of goods. Section 2—103.

(4) In addition Article 1 contains general definitions and principles of construction and interpretation applicable throughout this Article.

Section 7—103. Relation of Article to Treaty, Statute, Tariff, Classification or Regulation

To the extent that any treaty or statute of the United States, regulatory statute of this State or tariff, classification or regulation filed or issued pursuant thereto is applicable, the provisions of this Article are subject thereto.

Section 7—104. Negotiable and Non-Negotiable Warehouse Receipt, Bill of Lading or Other Document of Title

(1) A warehouse receipt, bill of lading or other document of title is negotiable

(a) if by its terms the goods are to be delivered to bearer or to the order of a named person; or

(b) where recognized in overseas trade, if it runs to a named person or assigns.

(2) Any other document is non-negotiable. A bill of lading in which it is stated that the goods are consigned to a named person is not made negotiable by a provision that the goods are to be delivered only against a written order signed by the same or another named person.

Section 7—105. Construction Against Negative Implication

The omission from either Part 2 or Part 3 of this Article of a provision corresponding to a provision made in the other Part does not imply that a corresponding rule of law is not applicable.

Part 2   Warehouse Receipts: Special Provisions

Section 7—201.   Who May Issue a Warehouse Receipt; Storage Under Government Bond

(1) A warehouse receipt may be issued by any warehouseman.

(2) Where goods including distilled spirits and agricultural commodities are stored under a statute requiring a bond against withdrawal or a license for the issuance of receipts in the nature of warehouse receipts, a receipt issued for the goods has like effect as a warehouse receipt even though issued by a person who is the owner of the goods and is not a warehouseman.

Section 7—202.   Form of Warehouse Receipt; Essential Terms; Optional Terms

(1) A warehouse receipt need not be in any particular form.

(2) Unless a warehouse receipt embodies within its written or printed terms each of the following, the warehouseman is liable for damages caused by the omission to a person injured thereby:

(a) the location of the warehouse where the goods are stored;

(b) the date of issue of the receipt;

(c) the consecutive number of the receipt;

(d) a statement whether the goods received will be delivered to the bearer, to a specified person, or to a specified person or his order;

(e) the rate of storage and handling charges, except that where goods are stored under a field warehousing arrangement a statement of that fact is sufficient on a non-negotiable receipt;

(f) a description of the goods or of the packages containing them;

(g) the signature of the warehouseman, which may be made by his authorized agent;

(h) if the receipt is issued for goods of which the warehouseman is owner, either solely or jointly or in common with others, the fact of such ownership; and

(i) a statement of the amount of advances made and of liabilities incurred for which the warehouseman claims a lien or security interest (Section 7—209). If the precise amount of such advances made or of such liabilities incurred is, at the time of the issue of the receipt, unknown to the warehouseman or to his agent who issues it, a statement of the fact that advances have been made or liabilities incurred and the purpose thereof is sufficient.

(3) A warehouseman may insert in his receipt any other terms which are not contrary to the provisions of this Act and do not impair his obligation of delivery (Section 7—403) or his duty of care (Section 7—204). Any contrary provisions shall be ineffective.

Section 7—203.   Liability for Non-Receipt or Misdescription

A party to or purchaser for value in good faith of a document of title other than a bill of lading relying in either case upon the description therein of the goods may recover from the issuer damages caused by the non-receipt or misdescription of the goods, except to the extent that the document conspicuously indicates that the issuer does not know whether any part or all of the goods in fact were received or conform to the description, as where the description is in terms of marks or labels or kind, quantity or condition, or the receipt or description is qualified by "contents, condition and quality unknown," "said to contain" or the like, if such indication be true, or the party or purchaser otherwise has notice.

Section 7—204.   Duty of Care; Contractual Limitation of Warehouseman's Liability

(1) A warehouseman is liable for damages for loss of or injury to the goods caused by his failure to exercise such care in regard to them as a reasonably careful man would exercise under like circumstances but unless otherwise agreed he is not liable for damages which could not have been avoided by the exercise of such care.

(2) Damages may be limited by a term in the warehouse receipt or storage agreement limiting the amount of liability in case of loss or damage, and setting forth a specific liability per article or item, or value per unit of weight, beyond which the warehouseman shall not be liable; provided, however, that such liability may on written request of the bailor at the time of signing such storage agreement or within a reasonable time after receipt of the warehouse receipt be increased on part or all of the goods thereunder, in which event increased rates may be charged based on such increased valuation, but that no such increase shall be permitted contrary to a lawful limitation of liability contained in the warehouseman's tariff, if any. No such limitation is effective with respect to the warehouseman's liability for conversion to his own use.

(3) Reasonable provisions as to the time and manner of presenting claims and instituting actions based on the bailment may be included in the warehouse receipt or tariff.

(4) This section does not impair or repeal . . .

Note: *Insert in subsection (4) a reference to any statute which imposes a higher responsibility upon the warehouseman or invalidates contractual limitations which would be permissible under this Article.*

Section 7—205.   Title Under Warehouse Receipt Defeated in Certain Cases

A buyer in the ordinary course of business of fungible goods sold and delivered by a warehouseman who is also in the business of buying and selling such goods takes free of any claim under a warehouse receipt even though it has been duly negotiated.

Section 7—206.   Termination of Storage at Warehouseman's Option

(1) A warehouseman may on notifying the person on whose account the goods are held and any other person known to claim an interest in the goods require payment of any charges and removal of the goods from the warehouse at the termination of the period of storage fixed by the document, or, if no period is fixed, within a stated period not less than thirty days after the notification. If the goods are not removed before the date specified in the notification, the warehouseman may sell them in accordance with the provisions of the section on enforcement of a warehouseman's lien (Section 7—210).

(2) If a warehouseman in good faith believes that the goods are about to deteriorate or decline in value to less than the amount of his lien within the time prescribed in subsection (1) for notification, advertisement and sale, the warehouseman may specify in the notification any reasonable shorter time for removal of the goods and in case the goods are not removed, may sell them at public sale held not less than one week after a single advertisement or posting.

(3) If as a result of a quality or condition of the goods of which the warehouseman had no notice at the time of deposit the goods are a hazard to other property or to the warehouse or to persons, the warehouseman may sell the goods at public or private sale without advertisement on reasonable notification to all persons known to claim an interest in the goods. If the warehouseman after a reasonable effort is unable to sell the goods he may dispose of them in any lawful manner and shall incur no liability by reason of such disposition.

(4) The warehouseman must deliver the goods to any person entitled to them under this Article upon due demand made at any time prior to sale or other disposition under this section.

(5) The warehouseman may satisfy his lien from the proceeds of any sale or disposition under this section but must hold the balance for delivery on the demand of any person to whom he would have been bound to deliver the goods.

Section 7—207. Goods Must Be Kept Separate; Fungible Goods

(1) Unless the warehouse receipt otherwise provides, a warehouseman must keep separate the goods covered by each receipt so as to permit at all times identification and delivery of those goods except that different lots of fungible goods may be commingled.

(2) Fungible goods so commingled are owned in common by the persons entitled thereto and the warehouseman is severally liable to each owner for that owner's share. Where because of overissue a mass of fungible goods is insufficient to meet all the receipts which the warehouseman has issued against it, the persons entitled include all holders to whom overissued receipts have been duly negotiated.

Section 7—208. Altered Warehouse Receipts

Where a blank in a negotiable warehouse receipt has been filled in without authority, a purchaser for value and without notice of the want of authority may treat the insertion as authorized. Any other unauthorized alteration leaves any receipt enforceable against the issuer according to its original tenor.

Section 7—209. Lien of Warehouseman

(1) A warehouseman has a lien against the bailor on the goods covered by a warehouse receipt or on the proceeds thereof in his possession for charges for storage or transportation (including demurrage and terminal charges), insurance, labor, or charges present or future in relation to the goods, and for expenses necessary for preservation of the goods or reasonably incurred in their sale pursuant to law. If the person on whose account the goods are held is liable for like charges or expenses in relation to other goods whenever deposited and it is stated in the receipt that a lien is claimed for charges and expenses in relation to other goods, the warehouseman also has a lien against him for such charges and expenses whether or not the other goods have been delivered by the warehouseman. But against a person to whom a negotiable warehouse receipt is duly negotiated a warehouseman's lien is limited to charges in an amount or at a rate specified on the receipt or if no charges are so specified then to a reasonable charge for storage of the goods covered by the receipt subsequent to the date of the receipt.

(2) The warehouseman may also reserve a security interest against the bailor for a maximum amount specified on the receipt for charges other than those specified in subsection (1), such as for money advanced and interest. Such a security interest is governed by the Article on Secured Transactions (Article 9).

   (3) (a) A warehouseman's lien for charges and expenses under subsection (1) or a security interest under subsection (2) is also effective against any person who so entrusted the bailor with possession of the goods that a pledge of them by him to a good faith purchaser for value would have been valid but is not effective against a person as to whom the document confers no right in the goods covered by it under Section 7—503.

   (b) A warehouseman's lien on household goods for charges and expenses in relation to the goods under subsection (1) is also effective against all persons if the depositor was the legal possessor of the goods at the time of deposit. "Household goods" means furniture, furnishings, and personal effects used by the depositor in a dwelling.

(4) A warehouseman loses his lien on any goods which he voluntarily delivers or which he unjustifiably refuses to deliver.

Section 7—210. Enforcement of Warehouseman's Lien

(1) Except as provided in subsection (2), a warehouseman's lien may be enforced by public or private sale of the goods in block or in parcels, at any time or place and on any terms which are commercially reasonable, after notifying all persons known to claim an interest in the goods. Such notification must include a statement of the amount due, the nature of the proposed sale and the time and place of any public sale. The fact that a better price could have been obtained by a sale at a different time or in a different method from that selected by the warehouseman is not of itself sufficient to establish that the sale was not made in a commercially reasonable manner. If the warehouseman either sells the goods in the usual manner in any recognized market therefor, or if he sells at the price current in such market at the time of his sale, or if he has otherwise sold in conformity with commercially reasonable practices among dealers in the type of goods sold, he has sold in a commercially reasonable manner. A sale of more goods than apparently necessary to be offered to insure satisfaction of the obligation is not commercially reasonable except in cases covered by the preceding sentence.

(2) A warehouseman's lien on goods other than goods stored by a merchant in the course of his business may be enforced only as follows:

   (a) All persons known to claim an interest in the goods must be notified.

   (b) The notification must be delivered in person or sent by registered or certified letter to the last known address of any person to be notified.

   (c) The notification must include an itemized statement of the claim, a description of the goods subject to the lien, a demand for payment within a specified time not less than ten days after receipt of the notification, and a conspicuous statement that unless the claim is paid within that time the goods will be advertised for sale and sold by auction at a specified time and place.

   (d) The sale must conform to the terms of the notification.

   (e) The sale must be held at the nearest suitable place to that where the goods are held or stored.

   (f) After the expiration of the time given in the notification, an advertisement of the sale must be published once a week for two weeks consecutively in a newspaper of general circulation where the sale is to be held. The advertisement must include a description of the goods, the name of the person on whose account they are being held, and the time and place of the sale. The sale must take place at least fifteen days after the first publication. If there is no newspaper of general circulation where the sale is to be held, the advertisement must be posted at least ten days before the sale in not less than six conspicuous places in the neighborhood of the proposed sale.

(3) Before any sale pursuant to this section any person claiming a right in the goods may pay the amount necessary to satisfy the lien and the reasonable expenses incurred under this section. In that event the goods must not be sold, but must be retained by the warehouseman subject to the terms of the receipt and this Article.

(4) The warehouseman may buy at any public sale pursuant to this section.

(5) A purchaser in good faith of goods sold to enforce a warehouseman's lien takes the goods free of any rights of persons against whom the lien was valid, despite noncompliance by the warehouseman with the requirements of this section.

(6) The warehouseman may satisfy his lien from the proceeds of any sale pursuant to this section but must hold the balance, if any, for delivery on demand to any person to whom he would have been bound to deliver the goods.

(7) The rights provided by this section shall be in addition to all other rights allowed by law to a creditor against his debtor.

(8) Where a lien is on goods stored by a merchant in the course of his business the lien may be enforced in accordance with either subsection (1) or (2).

(9) The warehouseman is liable for damages caused by failure to comply with the requirements for sale under this section and in case of willful violation is liable for conversion.

Part 3 Bills of Lading: Special Provisions

Section 7—301. Liability for Non-Receipt or Misdescription; "Said to Contain"; "Shipper's Load and Count"; Improper Handling

(1) A consignee of a non-negotiable bill who has given value in good faith or a holder to whom a negotiable bill has been duly negotiated relying in either case upon the description therein of the goods, or upon the date therein shown, may recover from the issuer damages caused by the misdating of the bill or the non-receipt or misdescription of the goods, except to the extent that the document indicates that the issuer does not know whether any part or all of the goods in fact were received or conform to the description, as where the description is in terms of marks or labels or kind, quantity, or condition or the receipt or description is qualified by "contents or condition of contents of packages unknown," "said to contain," "shipper's weight, load and count" or the like, if such indication be true.

(2) When goods are loaded by an issuer who is a common carrier, the issuer must count the packages of goods if package freight and ascertain the kind and quantity if bulk freight. In such cases "shipper's weight, load and count" or other words indicating that the description was made by the shipper are ineffective except as to freight concealed by packages.

(3) When bulk freight is loaded by a shipper who makes available to the issuer adequate facilities for weighing such freight, an issuer who is a common carrier must ascertain the kind and quantity within a reasonable time after receiving the written request of the shipper to do so. In such cases "shipper's weight" or other words of like purport are ineffective.

(4) The issuer may by inserting in the bill the words "shipper's weight, load and count" or other words of like purport indicate that the goods were loaded by the shipper; and if such statement be true the issuer shall not be liable for damages caused by the improper loading. But their omission does not imply liability for such damages.

(5) The shipper shall be deemed to have guaranteed to the issuer the accuracy at the time of shipment of the description, marks, labels, number, kind, quantity, condition and weight, as furnished by him; and the shipper shall indemnify the issuer against damage caused by inaccuracies in such particulars. The right of the issuer to such indemnity shall in no way limit his responsibility and liability under the contract of carriage to any person other than the shipper.

Section 7—302. Through Bills of Lading and Similar Documents

(1) The issuer of a through bill of lading or other document embodying an undertaking to be performed in part by persons acting as its agents or by connecting carriers is liable to anyone entitled to recover on the document for any breach by such other persons or by a connecting carrier of its obligation under the document but to the extent that the bill covers an undertaking to be performed overseas or in territory not contiguous to the continental United States or an undertaking including matters other than transportation this liability may be varied by agreement of the parties.

(2) Where goods covered by a through bill of lading or other document embodying an undertaking to be performed in part by persons other than the issuer are received by any such person, he is subject with respect to his own performance while the goods are in his possession to the obligation of the issuer. His obligation is discharged by delivery of the goods to another such person pursuant to the document, and does not include liability for breach by any other such persons or by the issuer.

(3) The issuer of such through bill of lading or other document shall be entitled to recover from the connecting carrier or such other person in possession of the goods when the breach of the obligation under the document occurred, the amount it may be required to pay to anyone entitled to recover on the document therefor, as may be evidenced by any receipt, judgment, or transcript thereof, and the amount of any expense reasonably incurred by it in defending any action brought by anyone entitled to recover on the document therefor.

Section 7—303. Diversion; Reconsignment; Change of Instructions

(1) Unless the bill of lading otherwise provides, the carrier may deliver the goods to a person or destination other than that stated in the bill or may otherwise dispose of the goods on instructions from

(a) the holder of a negotiable bill; or

(b) the consignor on a non-negotiable bill notwithstanding contrary instructions from the consignee; or

(c) the consignee on a non-negotiable bill in the absence of contrary instructions from the consignor, if the goods have arrived at the billed destination or if the consignee is in possession of the bill; or

(d) the consignee on a non-negotiable bill if he is entitled as against the consignor to dispose of them.

(2) Unless such instructions are noted on a negotiable bill of lading, a person to whom the bill is duly negotiated can hold the bailee according to the original terms.

Section 7—304. Bills of Lading in a Set

(1) Except where customary in overseas transportation, a bill of lading must not be issued in a set of parts. The issuer is liable for damages caused by violation of this subsection.

(2) Where a bill of lading is lawfully drawn in a set of parts, each of which is numbered and expressed to be valid only if the goods have not been delivered against any other part, the whole of the parts constitute one bill.

(3) Where a bill of lading is lawfully issued in a set of parts and different parts are negotiated to different persons, the title of the holder to whom the first due negotiation is made prevails as to both the document and the goods even though any later holder may have received the goods from the carrier in good faith and discharged the carrier's obligation by surrender of his part.

(4) Any person who negotiates or transfers a single part of a bill of lading drawn in a set is liable to holders of that part as if it were the whole set.

(5) The bailee is obliged to deliver in accordance with Part 4 of this Article against the first presented part of a bill of lading lawfully drawn in a set. Such delivery discharges the bailee's obligation on the whole bill.

Section 7—305. Destination Bills

(1) Instead of issuing a bill of lading to the consignor at the place of shipment a carrier may at the request of the consignor procure the bill to be issued at destination or at any other place designated in the request.

(2) Upon request of anyone entitled as against the carrier to control the goods while in transit and on surrender of any outstanding bill of lading or other receipt covering such goods, the issuer may procure a substitute bill to be issued at any place designated in the request.

Section 7—306. Altered Bills of Lading
An unauthorized alteration or filling in of a blank in a bill of lading leaves the bill enforceable according to its original tenor.

Section 7—307. Lien of Carrier
(1) A carrier has a lien on the goods covered by a bill of lading for charges subsequent to the date of its receipt of the goods for storage or transporation (including demurrage and terminal charges) and for expenses necessary for preservation of the goods incident to their transportation or reasonably incurred in their sale pursuant to law. But against a purchaser for value of a negotiable bill of lading a carrier's lien is limited to charges stated in the bill or the applicable tariffs, or if no charges are stated then to a reasonable charge.

(2) A lien for charges and expenses under subsection (1) on goods which the carrier was required by law to receive for transportation is effective against the consignor or any person entitled to the goods unless the carrier had notice that the consignor lacked authority to subject the goods to such charges and expenses. Any other lien under subsection (1) is effective against the consignor and any person who permitted the bailor to have control or possession of the goods unless the carrier had notice that the bailor lacked such authority.

(3) A carrier loses his lien on any goods which he voluntarily delivers or which he unjustifiably refuses to deliver.

Section 7—308. Enforcement of Carrier's Lien
(1) A carrier's lien may be enforced by public or private sale of the goods, in block or in parcels, at any time or place and on any terms which are commercially reasonable, after notifying all persons known to claim an interest in the goods. Such notification must include a statement of the amount due, the nature of the proposed sale and the time and place of any public sale. The fact that a better price could have been obtained by a sale at a different time or in a different method from that selected by the carrier is not of itself sufficient to establish that the sale was not made in a commercially reasonable manner. If the carrier either sells the goods in the usual manner in any recognized market therefor or if he sells at the price current in such market at the time of his sale or if he has otherwise sold in conformity with commercially reasonable practices among dealers in the type of goods sold he has sold in a commercially reasonable manner. A sale of more goods than apparently necessary to be offered to ensure satisfaction of the obligation is not commercially reasonable except in cases covered by the preceding sentence.

(2) Before any sale pursuant to this section any person claiming a right in the goods may pay the amount necessary to satisfy the lien and the reasonable expenses incurred under this section. In that event the goods must not be sold, but must be retained by the carrier subject to the terms of the bill and this Article.

(3) The carrier may buy at any public sale pursuant to this section.

(4) A purchaser in good faith of goods sold to enforce a carrier's lien takes the goods free of any rights of persons against whom the lien was valid, despite noncompliance by the carrier with the requirements of this section.

(5) The carrier may satisfy his lien from the proceeds of any sale pursuant to this section but must hold the balance, if any, for delivery on demand to any person to whom he would have been bound to deliver the goods.

(6) The rights provided by this section shall be in addition to all other rights allowed by law to a creditor against his debtor.

(7) A carrier's lien may be enforced in accordance with either subsection (1) or the procedure set forth in subsection (2) of Section 7—210.

(8) The carrier is liable for damages caused by failure to comply with the requirements for sale under this section and in case of willful violation is liable for conversion.

Section 7—309. Duty of Care; Contractual Limitation of Carrier's Liability
(1) A carrier who issues a bill of lading whether negotiable or non-negotiable must exercise the degree of care in relation to the goods which a reasonably careful man would exercise under like circumstances. This subsection does not repeal or change any law or rule of law which imposes liability upon a common carrier for damages not caused by its negligence.

(2) Damages may be limited by a provision that the carrier's liability shall not exceed a value stated in the document if the carrier's rates are dependent upon value and the consignor by the carrier's tariff is afforded an opportunity to declare a higher value or a value as lawfully provided in the tariff, or where no tariff is filed he is otherwise advised of such opportunity; but no such limitation is effective with respect to the carrier's liability for conversion to its own use.

(3) Reasonable provisions as to the time and manner of presenting claims and instituting actions based on the shipment may be included in a bill of lading or tariff.

Part 4 Warehouse Receipts and Bills of Lading: General Obligations

Section 7—401. Irregularities in Issue of Receipt or Bill or Conduct of Issuer
The obligations imposed by this Article on an issuer apply to a document of title regardless of the fact that

(a) the document may not comply with the requirements of this Article or of any other law or regulation regarding its issue, form or content; or

(b) the issuer may have violated laws regulating the conduct of his business; or

(c) the goods covered by the document were owned by the bailee at the time the document was issued; or

(d) the person issuing the document does not come within the definition of warehouseman if it purports to be a warehouse receipt.

Section 7—402. Duplicate Receipt or Bill; Overissue
Neither a duplicate nor any other document of title purporting to cover goods already represented by an outstanding document of the same issuer confers any right in the goods, except as provided in the case of bills in a set, overissue of documents for fungible goods and substitutes for lost, stolen or destroyed documents. But the issuer is liable for damages caused by his overissue or failure to identify a duplicate document as such by conspicuous notation on its face.

Section 7—403. Obligation of Warehouseman or Carrier to Deliver; Excuse
(1) The bailee must deliver the goods to a person entitled under the document who complies with subsections (2) and (3), unless and to the extent that the bailee establishes any of the following:

(a) delivery of the goods to a person whose receipt was rightful as against the claimant;

(b) damage to or delay, loss or destruction of the goods for which the bailee is not liable [, but the burden of establishing negligence in such cases is on the person entitled under the document];

Note: *The brackets in (1) (b) indicate that State enactments may differ on this point without serious damage to the principle of uniformity.*

(c) previous sale or other disposition of the goods in lawful enforcement of a lien or on warehouseman's lawful termination of storage;

(d) the exercise by a seller of his right to stop delivery pursuant to the provisions of the Article on Sales (Section 2—705);

(e) a diversion, reconsignment or other disposition pursuant to the provisions of this Article (Section 7—303) or tariff regulating such right;

(f) release, satisfaction or any other fact affording a personal defense against the claimant;

(g) any other lawful excuse.

(2) A person claiming goods covered by a document of title must satisfy the bailee's lien where the bailee so requests or where the bailee is prohibted by law from delivering the goods until the charges are paid.

(3) Unless the person claiming is one against whom the document confers no right under Sec. 7—503(1), he must surrender for cancellation or notation of partial deliveries any outstanding negotiable document covering the goods, and the bailee must cancel the document or conspicuously note the partial delivery thereon or be liable to any person to whom the document is duly negotiated.

(4) "Person entitled under the document" means holder in the case of a negotiable document, or the person to whom delivery is to be made by the terms of or pursuant to written instructions under a non-negotiable document.

Section 7—404. No Liability for Good Faith Delivery Pursuant to Receipt or Bill

A bailee who in good faith including observance of reasonable commercial standards has received goods and delivered or otherwise disposed of them according to the terms of the document of title or pursuant to this Article is not liable therefor. This rule applies even though the person from whom he received the goods had no authority to procure the document or to dispose of the goods and even though the person to whom he delivered the goods had no authority to receive them.

Part 5 Warehouse Receipts and Bills of Lading: Negotiation and Transfer

Section 7—501. Form of Negotiation and Requirements of "Due Negotiation"

(1) A negotiable document of title running to the order of a named person is negotiated by his indorsement and delivery. After his indorsement in blank or to bearer any person can negotiate it by delivery alone.

(2) (a) A negotiable document of title is also negotiated by delivery alone when by its original terms it runs to bearer.

(b) When a document running to the order of a named person is delivered to him the effect is the same as if the document had been negotiated.

(3) Negotiation of a negotiable document of title after it has been indorsed to a specified person requires indorsement by the special indorse? as well as delivery.

(4) A negotiable document of title is "duly negotiated" when it is negotiated in the manner stated in this section to a holder who purchases it in good faith without notice of any defense against or claim to it on the part of any person and for value, unless it is established that the negotiation is not in the regular course of business or financing or involves receiving the document in settlement or payment of a money obligation.

(5) Indorsement of a non-negotiable document neither makes it negotiable nor adds to the transferee's rights.

(6) The naming in a negotiable bill of a person to be notified of the arrival of the goods does not limit the negotiability of the bill nor constitute notice to a purchaser thereof of any interest of such person in the goods.

Section 7—502. Rights Acquired by Due Negotiation

(1) Subject to the following section and to the provisions of Section 7—205 on fungible goods, a holder to whom a negotiable document of title has been duly negotiated acquires thereby:

(a) title to the document;

(b) title to the goods;

(c) all rights accruing under the law of agency or estoppel, including rights to goods delivered to the bailee after the document was issued; and

(d) the direct obligation of the issuer to hold or deliver the goods according to the terms of the document free of any defense or claim by him except those arising under the terms of the document or under this Article. In the case of a delivery order the bailee's obligation accrues only upon acceptance and the obligation acquired by the holder is that the issuer and any indorser will procure the acceptance of the bailee.

(2) Subject to the following section, title and rights so acquired are not defeated by any stoppage of the goods represented by the document or by surrender of such goods by the bailee, and are not impaired even though the negotiation or any prior negotiation constituted a breach of duty or even though any person has been deprived of possession of the document by misrepresentation, fraud, accident, mistake, duress, loss, theft or conversion, or even though a previous sale or other transfer of the goods or document has been made to a third person.

Section 7—503. Document of Title to Goods Defeated in Certain Cases

(1) A document of title confers no right in goods against a person who before issuance of the document had a legal interest or a perfected security interest in them and who neither

(a) delivered or entrusted them or any document of title covering them to the bailor or his nominee with actual or apparent authority to ship, store or sell or with power to obtain delivery under this Article (Section 7—403) or with power of disposition under this Act (Sections 2—403 and 9—307) or other statute or rule of law; nor

(b) acquiesced in the procurement by the bailor or his nominee of any document of title.

(2) Title to goods based upon an unaccepted delivery order is subject to the rights of anyone to whom a negotiable warehouse receipt or bill of lading covering the goods has been duly negotiated. Such a title may be defeated under the next section to the same extent as the rights of the issuer or a transferee from the issuer.

(3) Title to goods based upon a bill of lading issued to a freight forwarder is subject to the rights of anyone to whom a bill issued by the freight forwarder is duly negotiated; but delivery by the carrier in accordance with Part 4 of this Article pursuant to its own bill of lading discharges the carrier's obligation to deliver.

Section 7—504. Rights Acquired in the Absence of Due Negotiation; Effect of Diversion; Seller's Stoppage of Delivery

(1) A transferee of a document, whether negotiable or non-negotiable, to whom the document has been delivered but not duly negotiated, acquires the title and rights which his transferor had or had actual authority to convey.

(2) In the case of a non-negotiable document, until but not after the bailee receives notification of the transfer, the rights of the transferee may be defeated

   (a) by those creditors of the transferor who could treat the sale as void under Section 2—402; or
   (b) by a buyer from the transferor in ordinary course of business if the bailee has delivered the goods to the buyer or received notification of his rights; or
   (c) as against the bailee by good faith dealings of the bailee with the transferor.

(3) A diversion or other change of shipping instructions by the consignor in a non-negotiable bill of lading which causes the bailee not to deliver to the consignee defeats the consignee's title to the goods if they have been delivered to a buyer in ordinary course of business and in any event defeats the consignee's rights against the bailee.

(4) Delivery pursuant to a non-negotiable document may be stopped by a seller under Section 2—705, and subject to the requirement of due notification there provided. A bailee honoring the seller's instructions is entitled to be indemnified by the seller against any resulting loss or expense.

Section 7—505. Indorser Not a Guarantor for Other Parties

The indorsement of a document of title issued by a bailee does not make the indorser liable for any default by the bailee or by previous indorsers.

Section 7—506. Delivery Without Indorsement: Right to Compel Indorsement

The transferee of a negotiable document of title has a specifically enforceable right to have his transferor supply any necessary indorsement but the transfer becomes a negotiation only as of the time the indorsement is supplied.

Section 7—507. Warranties on Negotiation or Transfer of Receipt or Bill

Where a person negotiates or transfers a document of title for value otherwise than as a mere intermediary under the next following section, then unless otherwise agreed he warrants to his immediate purchaser only in addition to any warranty made in selling the goods

   (a) that the document is genuine; and
   (b) that he has no knowledge of any fact which would impair its validity or worth; and
   (c) that his negotiation or transfer is rightful and fully effective with respect to the title to the document and the goods it represents.

Section 7—508. Warranties of Collecting Bank as to Documents

A collecting bank or other intermediary known to be entrusted with documents on behalf of another or with collection of a draft or other claim against delivery of documents warrants by such delivery of the documents only its own good faith and authority. This rule applies even though the intermediary has purchased or made advances against the claim or draft to be collected.

Part 6 Warehouse Receipts and Bills of Lading: Miscellaneous Provisions

Section 7—601. Lost and Missing Documents

(1) If a document has been lost, stolen or destroyed, a court may order delivery of the goods or issuance of a substitute document and the bailee may without liability to any person comply with such order. If the document was negotiable the claimant must post security approved by the court to indemnify any person who may suffer loss as a result of non-surrender of the document. If the document was not negotiable, such security may be required at the discretion of the court. The court may also in its discretion order payment of the bailee's reasonable costs and counsel fees.

(2) A bailee who without court order delivers goods to a person claiming under a missing negotiable document is liable to any person injured thereby, and if the delivery is not in good faith becomes liable for conversion. Delivery in good faith is not conversion if made in accordance with a filed classification or tariff or, where no classification or tariff is filed, if the claimant posts security with the bailee in an amount at least double the value of the goods at the time of posting to indemnify any person injured by the delivery who files a notice of claim within one year after the delivery.

Section 7—602. Attachment of Goods Covered by a Negotiable Document

Except where the document was originally issued upon delivery of the goods by a person who had no power to dispose of them, no lien attaches by virtue of any judicial process to goods in the possession of a bailee for which a negotiable document of title is outstanding unless the document be first surrendered to the bailee or its negotiation enjoined, and the bailee shall not be compelled to deliver the goods pursuant to process until the document is surrendered to him or impounded by the court. One who purchases the document for value without notice of the process or injunction takes free of the lien imposed by judicial process.

Section 7—603. Conflicting Claims; Interpleader

If more than one person claims title or possession of the goods, the bailee is excused from delivery until he has had a reasonable time to ascertain the validity of the adverse claims or to bring an action to compel all claimants to interplead and may compel such interpleader, either in defending an action for non-delivery of the goods, or by original action, whichever is appropriate.

Article 8 Investment Securities

Part 1 Short Title and General Matters

Section 8—101. Short Title

This Article shall be known and may be cited as Uniform Commercial Code—Investment Securities.

Section 8—102. Definitions and Index of Definitions

(1) In this Article, unless the context otherwise requires:

   (a) A "certificated security" is a share, participation, or other interest in property of or an enterprise of the issuer or an obligation of the issuer which is
      (i) represented by an instrument issued in bearer or registered form;
      (ii) of a type commonly dealt in on securities exchanges or markets or commonly recognized in any area in which it is issued or dealt in as a medium for investment; and
      (iii) either one of a class or series or by its terms divisible into a class or series of shares, participations, interests, or obligations.
   (b) An "uncertificated security" is a share, participation, or other interest in property or an enterprise of the issuer or an obligation of the issuer which is
      (i) not represented by an instrument and the transfer of which is registered upon books maintained for that purpose by or on behalf of the issuer;
      (ii) of a type commonly dealt in on securities exchanges or markets; and
      (iii) either one of a class or series or by its terms divisible into a class or series of shares, participations, interests, or obligations.

(c) A "security" is either a certificated or an uncertificated security. If a security is certificated, the terms "security" and "certificated security" may mean either the intangible interest, the instrument representing that interest, or both, as the context requires. A writing that is a certificated security is governed by this Article and not by Article 3, even though it also meets the requirements of that Article. This Article does not apply to money. If a certificated security has been retained by or surrendered to the issuer or its transfer agent for reasons other than registration of transfer, other temporary purpose, payment, exchange, or acquisition by the issuer, that security shall be treated as an uncertificated security for purposes of this Article.

(d) A certificated security is in "registered form" if

  (i) it specifies a person entitled to the security or the rights it represents; and

  (ii) its transfer may be registered upon books maintained for that purpose by or on behalf of the issuer, or the security so states.

(e) A certificated security is in "bearer form" if it runs to bearer according to its terms and not by reason of any indorsement.

(2) A "subsequent purchaser" is a person who takes other than by original issue.

(3) A "clearing corporation" is a corporation registered as a "clearing agency" under the federal securities laws or a corporation:

  (a) at least 90 percent of whose capital stock is held by or for one or more organizations, none of which, other than a national securities exchange or association, holds in excess of 20 percent of the capital stock of the corporation, and each of which is

    (i) subject to supervision or regulation pursuant to the provisions of federal or state banking laws or state insurance laws,

    (ii) a broker or dealer or investment company registered under the federal securities laws, or

    (iii) a national securities exchange or association registered under the federal securities laws; and

  (b) any remaining capital stock of which is held by individuals who have purchased it at or prior to the time of their taking office as directors of the corporation and who have purchased only so much of the capital stock as is necessary to permit them to qualify as directors.

(4) A "custodian bank" is a bank or trust company that is supervised and examined by state or federal authority having supervision over banks and is acting as custodian for a clearing corporation.

(5) Other definitions applying to this Article or to specified Parts thereof and the sections in which they appear are:

"Adverse claim." Section 8—302.
"Bona fide purchaser." Section 8—302.
"Broker." Section 8—303.
"Debtor." Section 9—105.
"Financial intermediary." Section 8—313.
"Guarantee of the signature." Section 8—402.
"Initial transaction statement." Section 8—408.
"Instruction." Section 8—308.
"Intermediary bank." Section 4—105.
"Issuer." Section 8—201.
"Overissue." Section 8—104.
"Secured Party." Section 9—105.
"Security Agreement." Section 9—105.

(6) In addition, Article 1 contains general definitions and principles of construction and interpretation applicable throughout this Article.

Section 8—103. Issuer's Lien

A lien upon a security in favor of an issuer thereof is valid against a purchaser only if:

(a) the security is certificated and the right of the issuer to the lien is noted conspicuously thereon; or

(b) the security is uncertificated and a notation of the right of the issuer to the lien is contained in the initial transaction statement sent to the purchaser or, if his interest is transferred to him other than by registration of transfer, pledge, or release, the initial transaction statement sent to the registered owner or the registered pledgee.

Section 8—104. Effect of Overissue; "Overissue"

(1) The provisions of this Article which validate a security or compel its issue or reissue do not apply to the extent that validation, issue, or reissue would result in overissue; but if:

(a) an identical security which does not constitute an overissue is reasonably available for purchase, the person entitled to issue or validation may compel the issuer to purchase the security for him and either to deliver a certificated security or to register the transfer of an uncertificated security to him, against surrender of any certificated security he holds; or

(b) a security is not so available for purchase, the person entitled to issue or validation may recover from the issuer the price he or the last purchaser for value paid for it with interest from the date of his demand.

(2) "Overissue" means the issue of securities in excess of the amount the issuer has corporate power to issue.

Section 8—105. Certificated Securities Negotiable; Statements and Instructions Not Negotiable; Presumptions

(1) Certificated securities governed by this Article are negotiable instruments.

(2) Statements (Section 8—408), notices, or the like, sent by the issuer of uncertificated securities and instructions (Section 8—308) are neither negotiable instruments nor certificated securities.

(3) In any action on a security:

(a) unless specifically denied in the pleadings, each signature on a certificated security, in a necessary indorsement, on an initial transaction statement, or on an instruction, is admitted;

(b) if the effectiveness of a signature is put in issue, the burden of establishing it is on the party claiming under the signature, but the signature is presumed to be genuine or authorized;

(c) if signatures on a certificated security are admitted or established, production of the security entitles a holder to recover on it unless the defendant establishes a defense or a defect going to the validity of the security;

(d) if signatures on an initial transaction statement are admitted or established, the facts stated in the statement are presumed to be true as of the time of its issuance; and

(e) after it is shown that a defense or defect exists, the plaintiff has the burden of establishing that he or some person under whom he claims is a person against whom the defense or defect is ineffective (Section 8—202).

Section 8—106. Applicability

The law (including the conflict of laws rules) of the jurisdiction of organization of the issuer governs the validity of a security, the effectiveness of registration by the issuer, and the rights and duties of the issuer with respect to:

(a) registration of transfer of a certificated security;

(b) registration of transfer, pledge, or release of an uncertificated security; and

(c) sending of statements of uncertificated securities.

Section 8—107. Securities Transferable; Action for Price

(1) Unless otherwise agreed and subject to any applicable law or regulation respecting short sales, a person obligated to transfer securities may transfer any certificated security of the specified issue in bearer form or registered in the name of the transferee, or indorsed to him or in blank, or he may transfer an equivalent uncertificated security to the transferee or a person designated by the transferee.

(2) If the buyer fails to pay the price as it comes due under a contract of sale, the seller may recover the price of:

(a) certificated securities accepted by the buyer;

(b) uncertificated securities that have been transferred to the buyer or a person designated by the buyer; and

(c) other securities if efforts at their resale would be unduly burdensome or if there is no readily available market for their resale.

Section 8—108. Registration of Pledge and Release of Uncertificated Securities

A security interest in an uncertificated security may be evidenced by the registration of pledge to the secured party or a person designated by him. There can be no more than one registered pledge of an uncertificated security at any time. The registered owner of an uncertificated security is the person in whose name the security is registered, even if the security is subject to a registered pledge. The rights of a registered pledgee of an uncertificated security under this Article are terminated by the registration of release.

Part 2 Issue—Issuer

Section 8—201. "Issuer"

(1) With respect to obligations on or defenses to a security, "issuer" includes a person who:

(a) places or authorizes the placing of his name on a certificated security (otherwise than as authenticating trustee, registrar, transfer agent, or the like) to evidence that it represents a share, participation, or other interest in his property or in an enterprise, or to evidence his duty to perform an obligation represented by the certificated security;

(b) creates shares, participations, or other interests in his property or in an enterprise or undertakes obligations, which shares, participations, interests, or obligations are uncertificated securities;

(c) directly or indirectly creates fractional interests in his rights or property, which fractional interests are represented by certificated securities; or

(d) becomes responsibile for or in place of any other person described as an issuer in this section.

(2) With respect to obligations on or defenses to a security, a guarantor is an issuer to the extent of his guaranty, whether or not his obligation is noted on a certificated security or on statements of uncertificated securities sent pursuant to Section 8—408.

(3) With respect to registration of transfer, pledge, or release (Part 4 of this Article), "issuer" means a person on whose behalf transfer books are maintained.

Section 8—202. Issuer's Responsibility and Defenses; Notice of Defect or Defense

(1) Even against a purchaser for value and without notice, the terms of a security include:

(a) if the security is certificated, those stated on the security;

(b) if the security is uncertificated, those contained in the initial transaction statement sent to such purchaser, or, if his interest is transferred to him other than by registration of transfer, pledge, or release, the initial transaction statement sent to the registered owner or registered pledgee; and

(c) those made part of the security by reference, on the certificated security or in the initial transaction statement, to another instrument, indenture, or document or to a constitution, statute, ordinance, rule, regulation, order or the like, to the extent that the terms referred to do not conflict with the terms stated on the certificated security or contained in the statement. A reference under this paragraph does not of itself charge a purchaser for value with notice of a defect going to the validity of the security, even though the certificated security or statement expressly states that a person accepting it admits notice.

(2) A certificated security in the hands of a purchaser for value or an uncertificated security as to which an initial transaction statement has been sent to a purchaser for value, other than a security issued by a government or governmental agency or unit, even though issued with a defect going to its validity, is valid with respect to the purchaser if he is without notice of the particular defect unless the defect involves a violation of constitutional provisions, in which case the security is valid with respect to a subsequent purchaser for value and without notice of the defect. This subsection applies to an issuer that is a government or governmental agency or unit only if either there has been substantial compliance with the legal requirements governing the issue or the issuer has received a substantial consideration for the issue as a whole or for the particular security and a stated purpose of the issue is one for which the issuer has power to borrow money or issue the security.

(3) Except as provided in the case of certain unauthorized signatures (Section 8—205), lack of genuineness of a certificated security or an initial transaction statement is a complete defense, even against a purchaser for value and without notice.

(4) All other defenses of the issuer of a certificated or uncertificated security, including nondelivery and conditional delivery of a certificated security, are ineffective against a purchaser for value who has taken without notice of the particular defense.

(5) Nothing in this section shall be construed to affect the right of a party to a "when, as and if issued" or a "when distributed" contract to cancel the contract in the event of a material change in the character of the security that is the subject of the contract or in the plan or arrangement pursuant to which the security is to be issued or distributed.

Section 8—203. Staleness as Notice of Defects or Defenses

(1) After an act or event creating a right to immediate performance of the principal obligation represented by a certificated security or that sets a date on or after which the security is to be presented or surrendered for redemption or exchange, a purchaser is charged with notice of any defect in its issue or defense of the issuer if:

(a) the act or event is one requiring the payment of money, the delivery of certificated securities, the registration of transfer of uncertificated securities, or any of these on presentation or surrender of the certificated security, the funds or securities are available on the date set for payment or exchange, and he takes the security more than one year after that date; and

(b) the act or event is not covered by paragraph (a) and he takes the security more than 2 years after the date set for surrender or presentation or the date on which performance became due.

(2) A call that has been revoked is not within subsection (1).

Section 8—204. Effect of Issuer's Restrictions on Transfer

A restriction on transfer of a security imposed by the issuer, even if otherwise lawful, is ineffective against any person without actual knowledge of it unless:

(a) the security is certificated and the restriction is noted conspicuously thereon; or

(b) the security is uncertificated and a notation of the restriction is contained in the initial transaction statement sent to the person or, if his interest is transferred to him other than by registration of transfer, pledge, or release, the initial transaction statement sent to the registered owner or the registered pledgee.

Section 8—205. Effect of Unauthorized Signature on Certificated Security or Initial Transaction Statement

An unauthorized signature placed on a certificated security prior to or in the course of issue or placed on an initial transaction statement is ineffective, but the signature is effective in favor of a purchaser for value of the certificated security or a purchaser for value of an uncertificated security to whom the initial transaction statement has been sent, if the purchaser is without notice of the lack of authority and the signing has been done by:

(a) an authenticating trustee, registrar, transfer agent, or other person entrusted by the issuer with the signing of the security, of similar securities, or of initial transaction statements or the immediate preparation for signing of any of them; or

(b) an employee of the issuer, or of any of the foregoing, entrusted with responsible handling of the security or initial transaction statement.

Section 8—206. Completion or Alteration of Certificated Security or Initial Transaction Statement

(1) If a certificated security contains the signatures necessary to its issue or transfer but is incomplete in any other respect:

(a) any person may complete it by filling in the blanks as authorized; and

(b) even though the blanks are incorrectly filled in, the security as completed is enforceable by a purchaser who took it for value and without notice of the incorrectness.

(2) A complete certificated security that has been improperly altered, even though fraudulently, remains enforceable, but only according to its original terms.

(3) If an initial transaction statement contains the signatures necessary to its validity, but is incomplete in any other respect:

(a) any person may complete it by filling in the blanks as authorized; and

(b) even though the blanks are incorrectly filled in, the statement as completed is effective in favor of the person to whom it is sent if he purchased the security referred to therein for value and without notice of the incorrectness.

(4) A complete initial transaction statement that has been improperly altered, even though fraudulently, is effective in favor of a purchaser to whom it has been sent, but only according to its original terms.

Section 8—207. Rights and Duties of Issuer With Respect to Registered Owners and Registered Pledgees

(1) Prior to due presentment for registration of transfer of a certificated security in registered form, the issuer or indenture trustee may treat the registered owner as the person exclusively entitled to vote, to receive notifications, and otherwise to exercise all rights and powers of an owner.

(2) Subject to the provisions of subsections (3), (4), and (6), the issuer or indenture trustee may treat the registered owner of an uncertificated security as the person exclusively entitled to vote, to receive notifications, and otherwise to exercise all the rights and powers of an owner.

(3) The registered owner of an uncertificated security that is subject to a registered pledge is not entitled to registration of transfer prior to the due presentment to the issuer of a release instruction. The exercise of conversion rights with respect to a convertible uncertificated security is a transfer within the meaning of this section.

(4) Upon due presentment of a transfer instruction from the registered pledgee of an uncertificated security, the issuer shall:

(a) register the transfer of the security to the new owner free of pledge, if the instruction specifies a new owner (who may be the registered pledgee) and does not specify a pledgee;

(b) register the transfer of the security to the new owner subject to the interest of the existing pledgee, if the instruction specifies a new owner and the existing pledgee; or

(c) register the release of the security from the existing pledge and register the pledge of the security to the other pledgee, if the instruction specifies the existing owner and another pledgee.

(5) Continuity of perfection of a security interest is not broken by registration of transfer under subsection (4)(b) or by registration of release and pledge under subsection (4)(c), if the security interest is assigned.

(6) If an uncertificated security is subject to a registered pledge:

(a) any uncertificated securities issued in exchange for or distributed with respect to the pledged security shall be registered subject to the pledge;

(b) any certificated securities issued in exchange for or distributed with respect to the pledged security shall be delivered to the registered pledgee; and

(c) any money paid in exchange for or in redemption of part or all of the security shall be paid to the registered pledgee.

(7) Nothing in this Article shall be construed to affect the liability of the registered owner of a security for calls, assessments, or the like.

Section 8—208. Effect of Signature of Authenticating Trustee, Registrar, or Transfer Agent

(1) A person placing his signature upon a certificated security or an initial transaction statement as authenticating trustee, registrar, transfer agent, or the like, warrants to a purchaser for value of the certificated security or a purchaser for value of an uncertificated security to whom the initial transaction statement has been sent, if the purchaser is without notice of the particular defect, that:

(a) the certificated security or initial transaction statement is genuine;

(b) his own participation in the issue or registration of the transfer, pledge, or release of the security is within his capacity and within the scope of the authority received by him from the issuer; and

(c) he has reasonable grounds to believe the security is in the form and within the amount the issuer is authorized to issue.

(2) Unless otherwise agreed, a person by so placing his signature does not assume responsibility for the validity of the security in other respects.

Part 3 Transfer

Section 8—301. Rights Acquired by Purchaser

(1) Upon transfer of a security to a purchaser (Section 8—313), the purchaser acquires the rights in the security which his transferor had or had actual authority to convey unless the purchaser's rights are limited by Section 8—302(4).

(2) A transferee of a limited interest acquires rights only to the extent of the interest transferred. The creation or release of a security interest in a security is the transfer of a limited interest in that security.

Section 8—302. "Bona Fide Purchaser"; "Adverse Claim"; Title Acquired by Bona Fide Purchaser

(1) A "bona fide purchaser" is a purchaser for value in good faith and without notice of any adverse claim:

(a) who takes delivery of a certificated security in bearer form or in registered form, issued or indorsed to him or in blank;

(b) to whom the transfer, pledge, or release of an uncertificated security is registered on the books of the issuer; or

(c) to whom a security is transferred under the provisions of paragraph (c), (d), (i), or (g) of Section 8—313(1).

(2) "Adverse claim" includes a claim that a transfer was or would be wrongful or that a particular adverse person is the owner of or has an interest in the security.

(3) A bona fide purchaser in addition to acquiring the rights of a purchaser (Section 8—301) also acquires his interest in the security free of any adverse claim.

(4) Notwithstanding Section 8—301(1), the transferee of a particular certificated security who has been a party to any fraud or illegality affecting the security, or who as a prior holder of that certificated security had notice of an adverse claim, cannot improve his position by taking from a bona fide purchaser.

Section 8—303. "Broker"

"Broker" means a person engaged for all or part of his time in the business of buying and selling securities, who in the transaction concerned acts for, buys a security from, or sells a security to, a customer. Nothing in this Article determines the capacity in which a person acts for purposes of any other statute or rule to which the person is subject.

Section 8—304. Notice to Purchaser of Adverse Claims

(1) A purchaser (including a broker for the seller or buyer, but excluding an intermediary bank) of a certificated security is charged with notice of adverse claims if:

(a) the security, whether in bearer or registered form, has been indorsed "for collection" or "for surrender" or for some other purpose not involving transfer; or

(b) the security is in bearer form and has on it an unambiguous statement that it is the property of a person other than the transferor. The mere writing of a name on a security is not such a statement.

(2) A purchaser (including a broker for the seller or buyer, but excluding an intermediary bank) to whom the transfer, pledge, or release of an uncertificated security is registered is charged with notice of adverse claims as to which the issuer has a duty under Section 8—403(4) at the time of registration and which are noted in the initial transaction statement sent to the purchaser or, if his interest is transferred to him other than by registration of transfer, pledge, or release, the initial transaction statement sent to the registered owner or the registered pledgee.

(3) The fact that the purchaser (including a broker for the seller or buyer) of a certificated or uncertificated security has notice that the security is held for a third person or is registered in the name of or indorsed by a fiduciary does not create a duty of inquiry into the rightfulness of the transfer or constitute constructive notice of adverse claims. However, if the purchaser (excluding an intermediary bank) has knowledge that the proceeds are being used or that the transaction is for the individual benefit of the fiduciary or otherwise in breach of duty, the purchaser is charged with notice of adverse claims.

Section 8—305. Staleness as Notice of Adverse Claims

An act or event that creates a right to immediate performance of the principal obligation represented by a certificated security or sets a date on or after which a certificated security is to be presented or surrendered for redemption or exchange does not itself constitute any notice of adverse claims except in the case of a transfer:

(a) after one year from any date set for presentment or surrender for redemption or exchange; or

(b) after 6 months from any date set for payment of money against presentation or surrender of the security if funds are available for payment on that date.

Section 8—306. Warranties on Presentment and Transfer of Certificated Securities; Warranties of Originators of Instructions

(1) A person who presents a certificated security for registration of transfer or for payment or exchange warrants to the issuer that he is entitled to the registration, payment, or exchange. But, a purchaser for value and without notice of adverse claims who receives a new, reissued, or re-registered certificated security on registration of transfer or receives an initial transaction statement confirming the registration of transfer of an equivalent uncertificated security to him warrants only that he has no knowledge of any unauthorized signature (Section 8—311) in a necessary indorsement.

(2) A person by transferring a certificated security to a purchaser for value warrants only that:

(a) his transfer is effective and rightful;

(b) the security is genuine and has not been materially altered; and

(c) he knows of no fact which might impair the validity of the security.

(3) If a certificated security is delivered by an intermediary known to be entrusted with delivery of the security on behalf of another or with collection of a draft or other claim against delivery, the intermediary by delivery warrants only his own good faith and authority, even though he has purchased or made advances against the claim to be collected against the delivery.

(4) A pledgee or other holder for security who redelivers a certificated security received, or after payment and on order of the debtor delivers that security to a third person, makes only the warranties of an intermediary under subsection (3).

(5) A person who originates an instruction warrants to the issuer that:

(a) he is an appropriate person to originate the instruction; and

(b) at the time the instruction is presented to the issuer he will be entitled to the registration of transfer, pledge, or release.

(6) A person who originates an instruction warrants to any person specially guaranteeing his signature (subsection 8—312(3)) that:

(a) he is an appropriate person to originate the instruction; and

(b) at the time the instruction is presented to the issuer

  (i) he will be entitled to the registration of transfer, pledge, or release; and

  (ii) the transfer, pledge, or release requested in the instruction will be registered by the issuer free from all liens, security interests, restrictions, and claims other than those specified in the instruction.

(7) A person who originates an instruction warrants to a purchaser for value and to any person guaranteeing the instruction (Section 8—312(6)) that:
- (a) he is an appropriate person to originate the instruction;
- (b) the uncertificated security referred to therein is valid; and
- (c) at the time the instruction is presented to the issuer
  - (i) the transferor will be entitled to the registration of transfer, pledge, or release;
  - (ii) the transfer, pledge, or release requested in the instruction will be registered by the issuer free from all liens, security interests, restrictions, and claims other than those specified in the instruction; and
  - (iii) the requested transfer, pledge, or release will be rightful.

(8) If a secured party is the registered pledgee or the registered owner of an uncertificated security, a person who originates an instruction of release or transfer to the debtor or, after payment and on order of the debtor, a transfer instruction to a third person, warrants to the debtor or the third person only that he is an appropriate person to originate the instruction and, at the time the instruction is presented to the issuer, the transferor will be entitled to the registration of release or transfer. If a transfer instruction to a third person who is a purchaser for value is originated on order of the debtor, the debtor makes to the purchaser the warranties of paragraphs (b), (c)(ii) and (c)(iii) of subsection (7).

(9) A person who transfers an uncertificated security to a purchaser for value and does not originate an instruction in connection with the transfer warrants only that:
- (a) his transfer is effective and rightful; and
- (b) the uncertificated security is valid.

(10) A broker gives to his customer and to the issuer and a purchaser the applicable warranties provided in this section and has the rights and privileges of a purchaser under this section. The warranties of and in favor of the broker, acting as an agent are in addition to applicable warranties given by and in favor of his customer.

Section 8—307. Effect of Delivery Without Indorsement; Right to Compel Indorsement

If a certificated security in registered form has been delivered to a purchaser without a necessary indorsement he may become a bona fide purchaser only as of the time the indorsement is supplied; but against the transferor, the transfer is complete upon delivery and the purchaser has a specifically enforceable right to have any necessary indorsement supplied.

Section 8—308. Indorsements; Instructions

(1) An indorsement of a certificated security in registered form is made when an appropriate person signs on it or on a separate document an assignment or transfer of the security or a power to assign or transfer it or his signature is written without more upon the back of the security.

(2) An indorsement may be in blank or special. An indorsement in blank includes an indorsement to bearer. A special indorsement specifies to whom the security is to be transferred, or who has power to transfer it. A holder may convert a blank indorsement into a special indorsement.

(3) An indorsement purporting to be only of part of a certificated security representing units intended by the issuer to be separately transferable is effective to the extent of the indorsement.

(4) An "instruction" is an order to the issuer of an uncertificated security requesting that the transfer, pledge, or release from pledge of the uncertificated security specified therein be registered.

(5) An instruction originated by an appropriate person is:
- (a) a writing signed by an appropriate person; or
- (b) a communication to the issuer in any form agreed upon in a writing signed by the issuer and an appropriate person.

If an instruction has been originated by an appropriate person but is incomplete in any other respect, any person may complete it as authorized and the issuer may rely on it as completed even though it has been completed incorrectly.

(6) "An appropriate person" in subsection (1) means the person specified by the certificated security or by special indorsement to be entitled to the security.

(7) "An appropriate person" in subsection (5) means:
- (a) for an instruction to transfer or pledge an uncertificated security which is then not subject to a registered pledge, the registered owner; or
- (b) for an instruction to transfer or release an uncertificated security which is then subject to a registered pledge, the registered pledgee.

(8) In addition to the persons designated in subsections (6) and (7), "an appropriate person" in subsections (1) and (5) includes:
- (a) if the person designated is described as a fiduciary but is no longer serving in the described capacity, either that person or his successor;
- (b) if the persons designated are described as more than one person as fiduciaries and one or more are no longer serving in the described capacity, the remaining fiduciary or fiduciaries, whether or not a successor has been appointed or qualified;
- (c) if the person designated is an individual and is without capacity to act by virtue of death, incompetence, infancy, or otherwise, his executor, administrator, guardian, or like fiduciary;
- (d) if the persons designated are described as more than one person as tenants by the entirety or with right of survivorship and by reason of death all cannot sign, the survivor or survivors;
- (e) a person having power to sign under applicable law or controlling instrument; and
- (f) to the extent that the person designated or any of the foregoing persons may act through an agent, his authorized agent.

(9) Unless otherwise agreed, the indorser of a certificated security by his indorsement or the originator of an instruction by his origination assumes no obligation that the security will be honored by the issuer but only the obligations provided in Section 8—306.

(10) Whether the person signing is appropriate is determined as of the date of signing and an indorsement made by or an instruction originated by him does not become unauthorized for the purposes of this Article by virtue of any subsequent change of circumstances.

(11) Failure of a fiduciary to comply with a controlling instrument or with the law of the state having jurisdiction of the fiduciary relationship, including any law requiring the fiduciary to obtain court approval of the transfer, pledge, or release, does not render his indorsement or an instruction originated by him unauthorized for the purposes of this Article.

Section 8—309. Effect of Indorsement Without Delivery

An indorsement of a certificated security, whether special or in blank, does not constitute a transfer until delivery of the certificated security on which it appears or, if the indorsement is on a separate document, until delivery of both the document and the certificated security.

Section 8—310. Indorsement of Certificated Security in Bearer Form

An indorsement of a certificated security in bearer form may give notice of adverse claims (Section 8—304) but does not otherwise affect any right to registration the holder possesses.

Section 8—311. Effect of Unauthorized Indorsement or Instruction

Unless the owner or pledgee has ratified an unauthorized indorsement or instruction or is otherwise precluded from asserting its ineffectiveness:

   (a) he may assert its ineffectiveness against the issuer or any purchaser, other than a purchaser for value and without notice of adverse claims, who has in good faith received a new, reissued, or re-registered certificated security on registration of transfer or received an initial transaction statement confirming the registration of transfer, pledge, or release of an equivalent uncertificated security to him; and

   (b) an issuer who registers the transfer of a certificated security upon the unauthorized indorsement or who registers the transfer, pledge, or release of an uncertificated security upon the unauthorized instruction is subject to liability for improper registration (Section 8—404).

Section 8—312. Effect of Guaranteeing Signature, Indorsement or Instruction

(1) Any person guaranteeing a signature of an indorser of a certificated security warrants that at the time of signing:

   (a) the signature was genuine;

   (b) the signer was an appropriate person to indorse (Section 8—308); and

   (c) the signer had legal capacity to sign.

(2) Any person guaranteeing a signature of the originator of an instruction warrants that at the time of signing:

   (a) the signature was genuine;

   (b) the signer was an appropriate person to originate the instruction (Section 8—308) if the person specified in the instruction as the registered owner or registered pledgee of the uncertificated security was, in fact, the registered owner or registered pledgee of the security, as to which fact the signature guarantor makes no warranty;

   (c) the signer had legal capacity to sign; and

   (d) the taxpayer identification number, if any, appearing on the instruction as that of the registered owner or registered pledgee was the taxpayer identification number of the signer or of the owner or pledgee for whom the signer was acting.

(3) Any person specially guaranteeing the signature of the originator of an instruction makes not only the warranties of a signature guarantor (subsection (2)) but also warrants that at the time the instruction is presented to the issuer:

   (a) the person specified in the instruction as the registered owner or registered pledgee of the uncertificated security will be the registered owner or registered pledgee; and

   (b) the transfer, pledge, or release of the uncertificated security requested in the instruction will be registered by the issuer free from all liens, security interests, restrictions, and claims other than those specified in the instruction.

(4) The guarantor under subsections (1) and (2) or the special guarantor under subsection (3) does not otherwise warrant the rightfulness of the particular transfer, pledge, or release.

(5) Any person guaranteeing an indorsement of a certificated security makes not only the warranties of a signature guarantor under subsection (1) but also warrants the rightfulness of the particular transfer in all respects.

(6) Any person guaranteeing an instruction requesting the transfer, pledge, or release of an uncertificated security makes not only the warranties of a special signature guarantor under subsection (3) but also warrants the rightfulness of the particular transfer, pledge, or release in all respects.

(7) No issuer may require a special guarantee of signature (subsection (3)), a guarantee of indorsement (subsection (5)), or a guarantee of instruction (subsection (6)) as a condition to registration of transfer, pledge, or release.

(8) The foregoing warranties are made to any person taking or dealing with the security in reliance on the guarantee, and the guarantor is liable to the person for any loss resulting from breach of the warranties.

Section 8—313. When Transfer to Purchaser Occurs; Financial Intermediary as Bona Fide Purchaser; "Financial Intermediary"

(1) Transfer of a security or a limited interest (including a security interest) therein to a purchaser occurs only:

   (a) at the time he or a person designated by him acquires possession of a certificated security;

   (b) at the time the transfer, pledge, or release of an uncertificated security is registered to him or a person designated by him;

   (c) at the time his financial intermediary acquires possession of a certificated security specially indorsed to or issued in the name of the purchaser;

   (d) at the time a financial intermediary, not a clearing corporation, sends him confirmation of the purchase and also by book entry or otherwise identifies as belonging to the purchaser

      (i) a specific certificated security in the financial intermediary's possession;

      (ii) a quantity of securities that constitute or are part of a fungible bulk of certificated securities in the financial intermediary's possession or of uncertificated securities registered in the name of the financial intermediary; or

      (iii) a quantity of securities that constitute or are part of a fungible bulk of securities shown on the account of the financial intermediary on the books of another financial intermediary;

   (e) with respect to an identified certificated security to be delivered while still in the possession of a third person, not a financial intermediary, at the time that person acknowledges that he holds for the purchaser;

   (f) with respect to a specific uncertificated security the pledge or transfer of which has been registered to a third person, not a financial intermediary, at the time that person acknowledges that he holds for the purchaser;

   (g) at the time appropriate entries to the account of the purchaser or a person designated by him on the books of a clearing corporation are made under Section 8—320;

   (h) with respect to the transfer of a security interest where the debtor has signed a security agreement containing a description of the security, at the time a written notification, which, in the case of the creation of the security interest, is signed by the debtor (which may be a copy of the security agreement) or which, in the case of the release or assignment of the security interest created pursuant to this paragraph, is signed by the secured party, is received by

(i) a financial intermediary on whose books the interest of the transferor in the security appears;

(ii) a third person, not a financial intermediary, in possession of the security, if it is certificated;

(iii) a third person, not a financial intermediary, who is the registered owner of the security, if it is uncertificated and not subject to a registered pledge; or

(iv) a third person, not a financial intermediary, who is the registered pledgee of the security, if it is uncertificated and subject to a registered pledge;

(i) with respect to the transfer of a security interest where the transferor has signed a security agreement containing a description of the security, at the time new value is given by the secured party; or

(j) with respect to the transfer of a security interest where the secured party is a financial intermediary and the security has already been transferred to the financial intermediary under paragraphs (a), (b), (c), (d), or (g), at the time the transferor has signed a security agreement containing a description of the security and value is given by the secured party.

(2) The purchaser is the owner of a security held for him by a financial intermediary, but cannot be a bona fide purchaser of a security so held except in the circumstances specified in paragraphs (c), (d)(i), and (g) of subsection (1). If a security so held is part of a fungible bulk, as in the circumstances specified in paragraphs (d)(ii) and (d)(iii) of subsection (1), the purchaser is the owner of a proportionate property interest in the fungible bulk.

(3) Notice of an adverse claim received by the financial intermediary or by the purchaser after the financial intermediary takes delivery of a certificated security as a holder for value or after the transfer, pledge, or release of an uncertificated security has been registered free of the claim to a financial intermediary who has given value is not effective either as to the financial intermediary or as to the purchaser. However, as between the financial intermediary and the purchaser the purchaser may demand transfer of an equivalent security as to which no notice of adverse claim has been received.

(4) A "financial intermediary" is a bank, broker, clearing corporation, or other person (or the nominee of any of them) which in the ordinary course of its business maintains security accounts for its customers and is acting in that capacity. A financial intermediary may have a security interest in securities held in account for its customer.

Section 8—314. Duty to Transfer, When Completed

(1) Unless otherwise agreed, if a sale of a security is made on an exchange or otherwise through brokers:

(a) the selling customer fulfills his duty to transfer at the time he:

(i) places a certificated security in the possession of the selling broker or a person designated by the broker;

(ii) causes an uncertificated security to be registered in the name of the selling broker or a person designated by the broker;

(iii) if requested, causes an acknowledgment to be made to the selling broker that a certificated or uncertificated security is held for the broker; or

(iv) places in the possession of the selling broker or of a person designated by the broker a transfer instruction for an uncertificated security, providing the issuer does not refuse to register the requested transfer if the instruction is presented to the issuer for registration within 30 days thereafter; and

(b) the selling broker, including a correspondent broker acting for a selling customer, fulfills his duty to transfer at the time he:

(i) places a certificated security in the possession of the buying broker or a person designated by the buying broker;

(ii) causes an uncertificated security to be registered in the name of the buying broker or a person designated by the buying broker;

(iii) places in the possession of the buying broker or of a person designated by the buying broker a transfer instruction for an uncertificated security, providing the issuer does not refuse to register the requested transfer if the instruction is presented to the issuer for registration within 30 days thereafter; or

(iv) effects clearance of the sale in accordance with the rules of the exchange on which the transaction took place.

(2) Except as provided in this section or unless otherwise agreed, a transferor's duty to transfer a security under a contract of purchase is not fulfilled until he:

(a) places a certificated security in form to be negotiated by the purchaser in the possession of the purchaser or of a person designated by the purchaser;

(b) causes an uncertificated security to be registered in the name of the purchaser or a person designated by the purchaser; or

(c) if the purchaser requests, causes an acknowledgment to be made to the purchaser that a certificated or uncertificated security is held for the purchaser.

(3) Unless made on an exchange, a sale to a broker purchasing for his own account is within subsection (2) and not within subsection (1).

Section 8—315. Action Against Transferee Based Upon Wrongful Transfer

(1) Any person against whom the transfer of a security is wrongful for any reason, including his incapacity, as against anyone except a bona fide purchaser, may:

(a) reclaim possession of the certificated security wrongfully transferred;

(b) obtain possession of any new certificated security representing all or part of the same rights;

(c) compel the origination of an instruction to transfer to him or a person designated by him an uncertificated security constituting all or part of the same rights; or

(d) have damages.

(2) If the transfer is wrongful because of an unauthorized indorsement of a certificated security, the owner may also reclaim or obtain possession of the security or a new certificated security, even from a bona fide purchaser, if the ineffectiveness of the purported indorsement can be asserted against him under the provisions of this Article on unauthorized indorsements (Section 8—311).

(3) The right to obtain or reclaim possession of a certificated security or to compel the origination of a transfer instruction may be specifically enforced and the transfer of a certificated or uncertificated security enjoined and a certificated security impounded pending the litigation.

Section 8—316. Purchaser's Right to Requisites for Registration of Transfer, Pledge, or Release on Books

Unless otherwise agreed, the transferor of a certificated security or the transferor, pledgor, or pledgee of an uncertificated security on due demand must supply his purchaser with any proof of his authority to transfer, pledge, or release or with any other requisite necessary to obtain registration of the transfer, pledge, or release of the security; but if the transfer, pledge, or release is not for value, a transferor, pledgor, or pledgee need not do so unless the purchaser furnishes the necessary expenses. Failure within a reasonable time to comply with a demand made gives the purchaser the right to reject or rescind the transfer, pledge, or release.

Section 8—317. Creditors' Rights

(1) Subject to the exceptions in subsections (3) and (4), no attachment or levy upon a certificated security or any share or other interest represented thereby which is outstanding is valid until the security is actually seized by the officer making the attachment or levy, but a certificated security which has been surrendered to the issuer may be reached by a creditor by legal process at the issuer's chief executive office in the United States.

(2) An uncertificated security registered in the name of the debtor may not be reached by a creditor except by legal process at the issuer's chief executive office in the United States.

(3) The interest of a debtor in a certificated security that is in the possession of a secured party not a financial intermediary or in an uncertificated security registered in the name of a secured party not a financial intermediary (or in the name of a nominee of the secured party) may be reached by a creditor by legal process upon the secured party.

(4) The interest of a debtor in a certificated security that is in the possession of or registered in the name of a financial intermediary or in an uncertificated security registered in the name of a financial intermediary may be reached by a creditor by legal process upon the financial intermediary on whose books the interest of the debtor appears.

(5) Unless otherwise provided by law, a creditor's lien upon the interest of a debtor in a security obtained pursuant to subsection (3) or (4) is not a restraint on the transfer of the security, free of the lien, to a third party for new value; but in the event of a transfer, the lien applies to the proceeds of the transfer in the hands of the secured party or financial intermediary, subject to any claims having priority.

(6) A creditor whose debtor is the owner of a security is entitled to aid from courts of appropriate jurisdiction, by injunction or otherwise, in reaching the security or in satisfying the claim by means allowed at law or in equity in regard to property that cannot readily be reached by ordinary legal process.

Section 8—318. No Conversion by Good Faith Conduct

An agent or bailee who in good faith (including observance of reasonable commercial standards if he is in the business of buying, selling, or otherwise dealing with securities) has received certificated securities and sold, pledged, or delivered them or has sold or caused the transfer or pledge of uncertificated securities over which he had control according to the instructions of his principal, is not liable for conversion or for participation in breach of fiduciary duty although the principal had no right so to deal with the securities.

Section 8—319. Statute of Frauds

A contract for the sale of securities is not enforceable by way of action or defense unless:

    (a) there is some writing signed by the party against whom enforcement is sought or by his authorized agent or broker, sufficient to indicate that a contract has been made for sale of a stated quantity of described securities at a defined or stated price;

    (b) delivery of a certificated security or transfer instruction has been accepted, or transfer of an uncertificated security has been registered and the transferee has failed to send written objection to the issuer within 10 days after receipt of the initial transaction statement confirming the registration, or payment has been made, but the contract is enforceable under this provision only to the extent of the delivery, registration, or payment;

    (c) within a reasonable time a writing in confirmation of the sale or purchase and sufficient against the sender under paragraph (a) has been received by the party against whom enforcement is sought and he has failed to send written objection to its contents within 10 days after its receipt; or

    (d) the party against whom enforcement is sought admits in his pleading, testimony, or otherwise in court that a contract was made for the sale of a stated quantity of described securities at a defined or stated price.

Section 8—320. Transfer or Pledge Within Central Depository System

(1) In addition to other methods, a transfer, pledge, or release of a security or any interest therein may be effected by the making of appropriate entries on the books of a clearing corporation reducing the account of the transferor, pledgor, or pledgee and increasing the account of the transferee, pledgee, or pledgor by the amount of the obligation or the number of shares or rights transferred, pledged, or released, if the security is shown on the account of a transferor, pledgor, or pledgee on the books of the clearing corporation; is subject to the control of the clearing corporation; and

    (a) if certificated,

        (i) is in the custody of the clearing corporation, another clearing corporation, a custodian bank, or a nominee of any of them; and

        (ii) is in bearer form or indorsed in blank by an appropriate person or registered in the name of the clearing corporation, a custodian bank, or a nominee of any of them; or

    (b) if uncertificated, is registered in the name of the clearing corporation, another clearing corporation, a custodian bank, or a nominee of any of them.

(2) Under this section entries may be made with respect to like securities or interests therein as a part of a fungible bulk and may refer merely to a quantity of a particular security without reference to the name of the registered owner, certificate or bond number, or the like, and, in appropriate cases, may be on a net basis taking into account other transfers, pledges, or releases of the same security.

(3) A transfer under this section is effective (Section 8—313) and the purchaser acquires the rights of the transferor (Section 8—301). A pledge or release under this section is the transfer of a limited interest. If a pledge or the creation of a security interest is intended, the security interest is perfected at the time when both value is given by the pledgee and the appropriate entries are made (Section 8—321). A transferee or pledgee under this section may be a bona fide purchaser (Section 8—302).

(4) A transfer or pledge under this section is not a registration of transfer under Part 4.

(5) That entries made on the books of the clearing corporation as provided in subsection (1) are not appropriate does not affect the validity or effect of the entries or the liabilities or obligations of the clearing corporation to any person adversely affected thereby.

Section 8—321. Enforceability, Attachment, Perfection and Termination of Security Interests

(1) A security interest in a security is enforceable and can attach only if it is transferred to the secured party or a person designated by him pursuant to a provision of Section 8—313(1).

(2) A security interest so transferred pursuant to agreement by a transferor who has rights in the security to a transferee who has given value is a perfected security interest, but a security interest that has been transferred solely under paragraph (i) of Section 8—313(1) becomes unperfected after 21 days unless, within that time, the requirements for transfer under any other provision of Section 8—313(1) are satisfied.

(3) A security interest in a security is subject to the provisions of Article 9, but:

    (a) no filing is required to perfect the security interest; and

    (b) no written security agreement signed by the debtor is necessary to make the security interest enforceable, except as provided in paragraph (h), (i), or (j) of Section 8—313(1). The secured party has the rights and duties provided under Section 9—207, to the extent they are applicable, whether or not the security is certificated, and, if certificated, whether or not it is in his possession.

(4) Unless otherwise agreed, a security interest in a security is terminated by transfer to the debtor or a person designated by him pursuant to a provision of Section 8—313(1). If a security is thus transferred, the security interest, if not terminated, becomes unperfected unless the security is certificated and is delivered to the debtor for the purpose of ultimate sale or exchange or presentation, collection, renewal, or registration of transfer. In that case, the security interest becomes unperfected after 21 days unless, within that time, the security (or securities for which it has been exchanged) is transferred to the secured party or a person designated by him pursuant to a provision of Section 8—313(1).

Part 4   Registration

Section 8—401. Duty of Issuer to Register Transfer, Pledge, or Release

(1) If a certificated security in registered form is presented to the issuer with a request to register transfer or an instruction is presented to the issuer with a request to register transfer, pledge, or release, the issuer shall register the transfer, pledge, or release as requested if:

    (a) the security is indorsed or the instruction was originated by the appropriate person or persons (Section 8—308);

    (b) reasonable assurance is given that those indorsements or instructions are genuine and effective (Section 8—402);

    (c) the issuer has no duty as to adverse claims or has discharged the duty (Section 8—403);

    (d) any applicable law relating to the collection of taxes has been complied with; and

    (e) the transfer, pledge, or release is in fact rightful or is to a bona fide purchaser.

(2) If an issuer is under a duty to register a transfer, pledge, or release of a security, the issuer is also liable to the person presenting a certificated security or an instruction for registration or his principal for loss resulting from any unreasonable delay in registration or from failure or refusal to register the transfer, pledge, or release.

Section 8—402. Assurance that Indorsements and Instructions Are Effective

(1) The issuer may require the following assurance that each necessary indorsement of a certificated security or each instruction (Section 8—308) is genuine and effective:

    (a) in all cases, a guarantee of the signature (Section 8—312(1) or (2)) of the person indorsing a certificated security or originating an instruction including, in the case of an instruction, a warranty of the taxpayer identification number or, in the absence thereof, other reasonable assurance of identity;

    (b) if the indorsement is made or the instruction is originated by an agent, appropriate assurance of authority to sign;

    (c) if the indorsement is made or the instruction is originated by a fiduciary, appropriate evidence of appointment or incumbency;

    (d) if there is more than one fiduciary, reasonable assurance that all who are required to sign have done so; and

    (e) if the indorsement is made or the instruction is originated by a person not covered by any of the foregoing, assurance appropriate to the case corresponding as nearly as may be to the foregoing.

(2) A "guarantee of the signature" in subsection (1) means a guarantee signed by or on behalf of a person reasonably believed by the issuer to be responsible. The issuer may adopt standards with respect to responsibility if they are not manifestly unreasonable.

(3) "Appropriate evidence of appointment or incumbency" in subsection (1) means:

    (a) in the case of a fiduciary appointed or qualified by a court, a certificate issued by or under the direction or supervision of that court or an officer thereof and dated within 60 days before the date of presentation for transfer, pledge, or release; or

    (b) in any other case, a copy of a document showing the appointment or a certificate issued by or on behalf of a person reasonably believed by the issuer to be responsible or, in the absence of that document or certificate, other evidence reasonably deemed by the issuer to be appropriate. The issuer may adopt standards with respect to the evidence if they are not manifestly unreasonable. The issuer is not charged with notice of the contents of any document obtained pursuant to this paragraph (b) except to the extent that the contents relate directly to the appointment or incumbency.

(4) The issuer may elect to require reasonable assurance beyond that specified in this section, but if it does so and, for a purpose other than that specified in subsection (3)(b), both requires and obtains a copy of a will, trust, indenture, articles of co-partnership, by-laws, or other controlling instrument, it is charged with notice of all matters contained therein affecting the transfer, pledge, or release.

Section 8—403. Issuer's Duty as to Adverse Claims

(1) An issuer to whom a certificated security is presented for registration shall inquire into adverse claims if:

    (a) a written notification of an adverse claim is received at a time and in a manner affording the issuer a reasonable opportunity to act on it prior to the issuance of a new, reissued, or re-registered certificated security, and the notification identifies the claimant, the registered owner, and the issue of which the security is a part, and provides an address for communications directed to the claimant; or

    (b) the issuer is charged with notice of an adverse claim from a controlling instrument it has elected to require under Section 8—402(4).

(2) The issuer may discharge any duty of inquiry by any reasonable means, including notifying an adverse claimant by registered or certified mail at the address furnished by him or, if there be no such address, at his residence or regular place of business that the certificated security has been presented for registration of transfer by a named person, and that the transfer will be registered unless within 30 days from the date of mailing the notification, either:

    (a) an appropriate restraining order, injunction, or other process issues from a court of competent jurisdiction; or

    (b) there is filed with the issuer an idemnity bond, sufficient in the issuer's judgment to protect the issuer and any transfer agent, registrar, or other agent of the issuer involved from any loss it or they may suffer by complying with the adverse claim.

(3) Unless an issuer is charged with notice of an adverse claim from a controlling instrument which it has elected to require under Section 8—402(4) or receives notification of an adverse claim under subsection (1), if a certificated security presented for registration is indorsed by the appropriate person or persons the issuer is under no duty to inquire into adverse claims. In particular:

(a) an issuer registering a certificated security in the name of a person who is a fiduciary or who is described as a fiduciary is not bound to inquire into the existence, extent, or correct description of the fiduciary relationship; and thereafter the issuer may assume without inquiry that the newly registered owner continues to be the fiduciary until the issuer receives written notice that the fiduciary is no longer acting as such with respect to the particular security;

(b) an issuer registering transfer on an indorsement by a fiduciary is not bound to inquire whether the transfer is made in compliance with a controlling instrument or with the law of the state having jurisdiction of the fiduciary relationship, including any law requiring the fiduciary to obtain court approval of the transfer; and

(c) the issuer is not charged with notice of the contents of any court record or file or other recorded or unrecorded document even though the document is in its possession and even though the transfer is made on the indorsement of a fiduciary to the fiduciary himself or to his nominee.

(4) An issuer is under no duty as to adverse claims with respect to an uncertificated security except:

(a) claims embodied in a restraining order, injunction, or other legal process served upon the issuer if the process was served at a time and in a manner affording the issuer a reasonable opportunity to act on it in accordance with the requirements of subsection (5);

(b) claims of which the issuer has received a written notification from the registered owner or the registered pledgee if the notification was received at a time and in a manner affording the issuer a reasonable opportunity to act on it in accordance with the requirements of subsection (5);

(c) claims (including restrictions on transfer not imposed by the issuer) to which the registration of transfer to the present registered owner was subject and were so noted in the initial transaction statement sent to him; and

(d) claims as to which an issuer is charged with notice from a controlling instrument it has elected to require under Section 8—402(4).

(5) If the issuer of an uncertificated security is under a duty as to an adverse claim, he discharges that duty by:

(a) including a notation of the claim in any statements sent with respect to the security under Sections 8—408 (3), (6), and (7); and

(b) refusing to register the transfer or pledge of the security unless the nature of the claim does not preclude transfer or pledge subject thereto.

(6) If the transfer or pledge of the security is registered subject to an adverse claim, a notation of the claim must be included in the initial transaction statement and all subsequent statements sent to the transferee and pledgee under Section 8—408.

(7) Notwithstanding subsections (4) and (5), if an uncertificated security was subject to a registered pledge at the time the issuer first came under a duty as to a particular adverse claim, the issuer has no duty as to that claim if transfer of the security is requested by the registered pledgee or an appropriate person acting for the registered pledgee unless:

(a) the claim was embodied in legal process which expressly provides otherwise;

(b) the claim was asserted in a written notification from the registered pledgee;

(c) the claim was one as to which the issuer was charged with notice from a controlling instrument it required under Section 8—402(4) in connection with the pledgee's request for transfer; or

(d) the transfer requested is to the registered owner.

Section 8—404. Liability and Non-Liability for Registration

(1) Except as provided in any law relating to the collection of taxes, the issuer is not liable to the owner, pledgee, or any other person suffering loss as a result of the registration of a transfer, pledge, or release of a security if:

(a) there were on or with a certificated security the necessary indorsements or the issuer had received an instruction originated by an appropriate person (Section 8—308); and

(b) the issuer had no duty as to adverse claims or has discharged the duty (Section 8—403).

(2) If an issuer has registered a transfer of a certificated security to a person not entitled to it, the issuer on demand shall deliver a like security to the true owner unless:

(a) the registration was pursuant to subsection (1);

(b) the owner is precluded from asserting any claim for registering the transfer under Section 8—405(1); or

(c) the delivery would result in overissue, in which case the issuer's liability is governed by Section 8—104.

(3) If an issuer has improperly registered a transfer, pledge, or release of an uncertificated security, the issuer on demand from the injured party shall restore the records as to the injured party to the condition that would have obtained if the improper registration had not been made unless:

(a) the registration was pursuant to subsection (1); or

(b) the registration would result in overissue, in which case the issuer's liability is governed by Section 8—104.

Section 8—405. Lost, Destroyed, and Stolen Certificated Securities

(1) If a certificated security has been lost, apparently destroyed, or wrongfully taken, and the owner fails to notify the issuer of that fact within a reasonable time after he has notice of it and the issuer registers a transfer of the security before receiving notification, the owner is precluded from asserting against the issuer any claim for registering the transfer under Section 8—404 or any claim to a new security under this section.

(2) If the owner of a certificated security claims that the security has been lost, destroyed, or wrongfully taken, the issuer shall issue a new certificated security or, at the option of the issuer, an equivalent uncertificated security in place of the original security if the owner:

(a) so requests before the issuer has notice that the security has been acquired by a bona fide purchaser;

(b) files with the issuer a sufficient indemnity bond; and

(c) satisfies any other reasonable requirements imposed by the issuer.

(3) If, after the issue of a new certificated or uncertificated security, a bona fide purchaser of the original certificated security presents it for registration of transfer, the issuer shall register the transfer unless registration would result in overissue, in which event the issuer's liability is governed by Section 8—104. In addition to any rights on the indemnity bond, the issuer may recover the new certificated security from the person to whom it was issued or any person taking under him except a bona fide purchaser or may cancel the uncertificated security unless a bona fide purchaser or any person taking under a bona fide purchaser is then the registered owner or registered pledgee thereof.

Section 8—406. Duty of Authenticating Trustee, Transfer Agent, or Registrar

(1) If a person acts as authenticating trustee, transfer agent, registrar, or other agent for an issuer in the registration of transfers of its certificated securities or in the registration of transfers, pledges, and releases of its uncertificated securities, in the issue of new securities, or in the cancellation of surrendered securities:

(a) he is under a duty to the issuer to exercise good faith and due diligence in performing his functions; and

(b) with regard to the particular functions he performs, he has the same obligation to the holder or owner of a certificated security or to the owner or pledgee of an uncertificated security and has the same rights and privileges as the issuer has in regard to those functions.

(2) Notice to an authenticating trustee, transfer agent, registrar or other agent is notice to the issuer with respect to the functions performed by the agent.

Section 8—407. Exchangeability of Securities

(1) No issuer is subject to the requirements of this section unless it regularly maintains a system for issuing the class of securities involved under which both certificated and uncertificated securities are regularly issued to the category of owners, which includes the person in whose name the new security is to be registered.

(2) Upon surrender of a certificated security with all necessary indorsements and presentation of a written request by the person surrendering the security, the issuer, if he has no duty as to adverse claims or has discharged the duty (Section 8—403), shall issue to the person or a person designated by him an equivalent uncertificated security subject to all liens, restrictions, and claims that were noted on the certificated security.

(3) Upon receipt of a transfer instruction originated by an appropriate person who so requests, the issuer of an uncertificated security shall cancel the uncertificated security and issue an equivalent certificated security on which must be noted conspicuously any liens and restrictions of the issuer and any adverse claims (as to which the issuer has a duty under Section 8—403(4)) to which the uncertificated security was subject. The certificated security shall be registered in the name of and delivered to:

(a) the registered owner, if the uncertificated security was not subject to a registered pledge; or

(b) the registered pledgee, if the uncertificated security was subject to a registered pledge.

Section 8—408. Statements of Uncertificated Securities

(1) Within 2 business days after the transfer of an uncertificated security has been registered, the issuer shall send to the new registered owner and, if the security has been transferred subject to a registered pledge, to the registered pledgee a written statement containing:

(a) a description of the issue of which the uncertificated security is a part;

(b) the number of shares or units transferred;

(c) the name and address and any taxpayer identification number of the new registered owner and, if the security has been transferred subject to a registered pledge, the name and address and any taxpayer identification number of the registered pledgee;

(d) a notation of any liens and restrictions of the issuer and any adverse claims (as to which the issuer has a duty under Section 8—403(4)) to which the uncertificated security is or may be subject at the time of registration or a statement that there are none of those liens, restrictions, or adverse claims; and

(e) the date the transfer was registered.

(2) Within 2 business days after the pledge of an uncertificated security has been registered, the issuer shall send to the registered owner and the registered pledgee a written statement containing:

(a) a description of the issue of which the uncertificated security is a part;

(b) the number of shares or units pledged;

(c) the name and address and any taxpayer identification number of the registered owner and the registered pledgee;

(d) a notation of any liens and restrictions of the issuer and any adverse claims (as to which the issuer has a duty under Section 8—403(4)) to which the uncertificated security is or may be subject at the time of registration or a statement that there are none of those liens, restrictions, or adverse claims; and

(e) the date the pledge was registered.

(3) Within 2 business days after the release from pledge of an uncertificated security has been registered, the issuer shall send to the registered owner and the pledgee whose interest was released a written statement containing:

(a) a description of the issue of which the uncertificated security is a part;

(b) the number of shares or units released from pledge;

(c) the name and address and any taxpayer identification number of the registered owner and the pledgee whose interest was released;

(d) a notation of any liens and restrictions of the issuer and any adverse claims (as to which the issuer has a duty under Section 8—403(4)) to which the uncertificated security is or may be subject at the time of registration or a statement that there are none of those liens, restrictions, or adverse claims; and

(e) the date the release was registered.

(4) An "initial transaction statement" is the statement sent to:

(a) the new registered owner and, if applicable, to the registered pledgee pursuant to subsection (1);

(b) the registered pledgee pursuant to subsection (2); or

(c) the registered owner pursuant to subsection (3).

Each initial transaction statement shall be signed by or on behalf of the issuer and must be identified as "Initial Transaction Statement."

(5) Within 2 business days after the transfer of an uncertificated security has been registered, the issuer shall send to the former registered owner and the former registered pledgee, if any, a written statement containing:

(a) a description of the issue of which the uncertificated security is a part;

(b) the number of shares or units transferred;

(c) the name and address and any taxpayer identification number of the former registered owner and of any former registered pledgee; and

(d) the date the transfer was registered.

(6) At periodic intervals no less frequent than annually and at any time upon the reasonable written request of the registered owner, the issuer shall send to the registered owner of each uncertificated security a dated written statement containing:

(a) a description of the issue of which the uncertificated security is a part;

(b) the name and address and any taxpayer identification number of the registered owner;

(c) the number of shares or units of the uncertificated security registered in the name of the registered owner on the date of the statement;

(d) the name and address and any taxpayer identification number of any registered pledgee and the number of shares of units subject to the pledge; and

(e) a notation of any liens and restrictions of the issuer and any adverse claims (as to which the issuer has a duty under Section 8—403(4)) to which the uncertificated security is or may be subject or a statement that there are none of those liens, restrictions, or adverse claims.

(7) At periodic intervals no less frequent than annually and at any time upon the reasonable written request of the registered pledgee, the issuer shall send to the registered pledgee of each uncertificated security a dated written statement containing:

(a) a description of the issue of which the uncertificated security is a part;

(b) the name and address and any taxpayer identification number of the registered owner;

(c) the name and address and any taxpayer identification number of the registered pledgee;

(d) the number of shares or units subject to the pledge; and

(e) a notation of any liens and restrictions of the issuer and any adverse claims (as to which the issuer has a duty under Section 8—403(4)) to which the uncertificated security is or may be subject or a statement that there are none of those liens, restrictions, or adverse claims.

(8) If the issuer sends the statements described in subsections (6) and (7) at periodic intervals no less frequent than quarterly, the issuer is not obliged to send additional statements upon request unless the owner or pledgee requesting them pays to the issuer the reasonable cost of furnishing them.

(9) Each statement sent pursuant to this section must bear a conspicuous legend reading substantially as follows: "This statement is merely a record of the rights of the addressee as of the time of its issuance. Delivery of this statement, of itself, confers no rights on the recipient. This statement is neither a negotiable instrument nor a security."

Article 9 Secured Transactions; Sales of Accounts and Chattel Paper

Part 1 Short Title, Applicability and Definitions

Section 9—101. Short Title
This Article shall be known and may be cited as Uniform Commercial Code—Secured Transactions.

Section 9—102. Policy and Subject Matter of Article
(1) Except as otherwise provided in Section 9—104 on excluded transactions, this Article applies

(a) to any transaction (regardless of its form) which is intended to create a security interest in personal property or fixtures including goods, documents, instruments, general intangibles, chattel paper or accounts; and also

(b) to any sale of accounts or chattel paper.

(2) This Article applies to security interests created by contract including pledge, assignment, chattel mortgage, chattel trust, trust deed, factor's lien, equipment trust, conditional sale, trust receipt, other lien or title retention contract and lease or consignment intended as security. This Article does not apply to statutory liens except as provided in Section 9—310.

(3) The application of this Article to a security interest in a secured obligation is not affected by the fact that the obligation is itself secured by a transaction or interest to which this Article does not apply.

Note: *The adoption of this Article should be accompanied by the repeal of existing statutes dealing with conditional sales, trust receipts, factor's liens where the factor is given a non-possessory lien, chattel mortgages, crop mortgages, mortgages on railroad equipment, assignment of accounts and generally statutes regulating security interests in personal property.*

Where the state has a retail installment selling act or small loan act, that legislation should be carefully examined to determine what changes in those acts are needed to conform them to this Article. This Article primarily sets out rules defining rights of a secured party against persons dealing with the debtor; it does not prescribe regulations and controls which may be necessary to curb abuses arising in the small loan business or in the financing of consumer purchases on credit. Accordingly there is no intention to repeal existing regulatory acts in those fields by enactment or re-enactment of Article 9. See Section 9—203(4) and the Note thereto.

Section 9—103. Perfection of Security Interest in Multiple State Transactions

(1) Documents, instruments and ordinary goods.

(a) This subsection applies to documents and instruments and to goods other than those covered by a certificate of title described in subsection (2), mobile goods described in subsection (3), and minerals described in subsection (5).

(b) Except as otherwise provided in this subsection, perfection and the effect of perfection or non-perfection of a security interest in collateral are governed by the law of the jurisdiction where the collateral is when the last event occurs on which is based the assertion that the security interest is perfected or unperfected.

(c) If the parties to a transaction creating a purchase money security interest in goods in one jurisdiction understand at the time that the security interest attaches that the goods will be kept in another jurisdiction, then the law of the other jurisdiction governs the perfection and the effect of perfection or non-perfection of the security interest from the time it attaches until thirty days after the debtor receives possession of the goods and thereafter if the goods are taken to the other jurisdiction before the end of the thirty-day period.

(d) When collateral is brought into and kept in this state while subject to a security interest perfected under the law of the jurisdiction from which the collateral was removed, the security interest remains perfected, but if action is required by Part 3 of this Article to perfect the security interest,

(i) if the action is not taken before the expiration of the period of perfection in the other jurisdiction or the end of four months after the collateral is brought into this state, whichever period first expires, the security interest becomes unperfected at the end of that period and is thereafter deemed to have been unperfected as against a person who became a purchaser after removal;

(ii) if the action is taken before the expiration of the period specified in subparagraph (i), the security interest continues perfected thereafter;

(iii) for the purpose of priority over a buyer of consumer goods (subsection (2) of Section 9—307), the period of the effectiveness of a filing in the jurisdiction from which the collateral is removed is governed by the rules with respect to perfection in subparagraphs (i) and (ii).

(2) Certificate of title.
- (a) This subsection applies to goods covered by a certificate of title issued under a statute of this state or of another jurisdiction under the law of which indication of a security interest on the certificate is required as a condition of perfection.
- (b) Except as otherwise provided in this subsection, perfection and the effect of perfection or non-perfection of the security interest are governed by the law (including the conflict of laws rules) of the jurisdiction issuing the certificate until four months after the goods are removed from that jurisdiction and thereafter until the goods are registered in another jurisdiction, but in any event not beyond surrender of the certificate. After the expiration of that period, the goods are not covered by the certificate of title within the meaning of this section.
- (c) Except with respect to the rights of a buyer described in the next paragraph, a security interest, perfected in another jurisdiction otherwise than by notation on a certificate of title, in goods brought into this state and thereafter covered by a certificate of title issued by this state is subject to the rules stated in paragraph (d) of subsection (1).
- (d) If goods are brought into this state while a security interest therein is perfected in any manner under the law of the jurisdiction from which the goods are removed and a certificate of title is issued by this state and the certificate does not show that the goods are subject to the security interest or that they may be subject to security interests not shown on the certificate, the security interest is subordinate to the rights of a buyer of the goods who is not in the business of selling goods of that kind to the extent that he gives value and receives delivery of the goods after issuance of the certificate and without knowledge of the security interest.

(3) Accounts, general intangibles and mobile goods.
- (a) This subsection applies to accounts (other than an account described in subsection (5) on minerals) and general intangibles (other than uncertificated securities) and to goods which are mobile and which are of a type normally used in more than one jurisdiction, such as motor vehicles, trailers, rolling stock, airplanes, shipping containers, road building and construction machinery and commercial harvesting machinery and the like, if the goods are equipment or are inventory leased or held for lease by the debtor to others, and are not covered by a certificate of title described in subsection (2).
- (b) The law (including the conflict of laws rules) of the jurisdiction in which the debtor is located governs the perfection and the effect of perfection or non-perfection of the security interest.
- (c) If, however, the debtor is located in a jurisdiction which is not a part of the United States, and which does not provide for perfection of the security interest by filing or recording in that jurisdiction, the law of the jurisdiction in the United States in which the debtor has its major executive office governs the perfection and the effect of perfection or non-perfection of the security interest through filing. In the alternative, if the debtor is located in a jurisdiction which is not a part of the United States or Canada and the collateral is accounts or general intangibles for money due or to become due, the security interest may be perfected by notification to the account debtor. As used in this paragraph, "United States" includes its territories and possessions and the Commonwealth of Puerto Rico.
- (d) A debtor shall be deemed located at his place of business if he has one, at his chief executive office if he has more than one place of business, otherwise at his residence. If, however, the debtor is a foreign air carrier under the Federal Aviation Act of 1958, as amended, it shall be deemed located at the designated office of the agent upon whom service of process may be made on behalf of the foreign air carrier.
- (e) A security interest perfected under the law of the jurisdiction of the location of the debtor is perfected until the expiration of four months after a change of the debtor's location to another jurisdiction, or until perfection would have ceased by the law of the first jurisdiction, whichever period first expires. Unless perfected in the new jurisdiction before the end of that period, it becomes unperfected thereafter and is deemed to have been unperfected as against a person who became a purchaser after the change.

(4) Chattel paper. The rules stated for goods in subsection (1) apply to a possessory security interest in chattel paper. The rules stated for accounts in subsection (3) apply to a non-possessory security interest in chattel paper, but the security interest may not be perfected by notification to the account debtor.

(5) Minerals. Perfection and the effect of perfection or non-perfection of a security interest which is created by a debtor who has an interest in minerals or the like (including oil and gas) before extraction and which attaches thereto as extracted, or which attaches to an account resulting from the sale thereof at the wellhead or minehead are governed by the law (including the conflict of laws rules) of the jurisdiction wherein the wellhead or minehead is located.

(6) Uncertificated securities. The law (including the conflict of laws rules) of the jurisdiction of organization of the issuer governs the perfection and the effect of perfection or non-perfection of a security interest in uncertificated securities.

Section 9—104. Transactions Excluded From Article
This Article does not apply
- (a) to a security interest subject to any statute of the United States, to the extent that such statute governs the rights of parties to and third parties affected by transactions in particular types of property; or
- (b) to a landlord's lien; or
- (c) to a lien given by statute or other rule of law for services or materials except as provided in Section 9—310 on priority of such liens; or
- (d) to a transfer of a claim for wages, salary or other compensation of an employee; or
- (e) to a transfer by a government or governmental subdivision or agency; or
- (f) to a sale of accounts or chattel paper as part of a sale of the business out of which they arose, or an assignment of accounts or chattel paper which is for the purpose of collection only, or a transfer of a right to payment under a contract to an assignee who is also to do the performance under the contract or a transfer of a single account to an assignee in whole or partial satisfaction of a preexisting indebtedness; or
- (g) to a transfer of an interest in or claim in or under any policy of insurance, except as provided with respect to proceeds (Section 9—306) and priorities in proceeds (Section 9—312); or
- (h) to a right represented by a judgment (other than a judgment taken on a right to payment which was collateral); or

(i) to any right of set-off; or

(j) except to the extent that provision is made for fixtures in Section 9—313, to the creation or transfer of an interest in or lien on real estate, including a lease or rents thereunder;

(k) to a transfer in whole or in part of any claim arising out of tort; or

(l) to a transfer of an interest in any deposit account (subsection (1) of Section 9—105), except as provided with respect to proceeds (Section 9—306) and priorities in proceeds (Section 9—312).

Section 9—105. Definitions and Index of Definitions

(1) In this Article unless the context otherwise requires:

(a) "Account debtor" means the person who is obligated on an account, chattel paper or general intangible;

(b) "Chattel paper" means a writing or writings which evidence both a monetary obligation and a security interest in or a lease of specific goods, but a charter or other contract involving the use or hire of a vessel is not chattel paper. When a transaction is evidenced both by such a security agreement or a lease and by an instrument or a series of instruments, the group of writings taken together constitutes chattel paper;

(c) "Collateral" means the property subject to a security interest, and includes accounts and chattel paper which have been sold;

(d) "Debtor" means the person who owes payment or other performance of the obligation secured, whether or not he owns or has rights in the collateral, and includes the seller of accounts or chattel paper. Where the debtor and the owner of the collateral are not the same person, the term "debtor" means the owner of the collateral in any provision of the Article dealing with the collateral, the obligor in any provision dealing with the obligation, and may include both where the context so requires;

(e) "Deposit account" means a demand, time, savings, passbook or like account maintained with a bank, savings and loan association, credit union or like organization, other than an account evidenced by a certificate of deposit;

(f) "Document" means document of title as defined in the general definitions of Article 1 (Section 1—201), and a receipt of the kind described in subsection (2) of Section 7—201;

(g) "Encumbrance" includes real estate mortgages and other liens on real estate and all other rights in real estate that are not ownership interests;

(h) "Goods" includes all things which are movable at the time the security interest attaches or which are fixtures (Section 9—313), but does not include money, documents, instruments, accounts, chattel paper, general intangibles, or minerals or the like (including oil and gas) before extraction. "Goods" also includes standing timber which is to be cut and removed under a conveyance or contract for sale, the unborn young of animals, and growing crops;

(i) "Instrument" means a negotiable instrument (defined in Section 3—104), or a certificated security (defined in Section 8—102) or any other writing which evidences a right to the payment of money and is not itself a security agreement or lease and is of a type which is in ordinary course of business transferred by delivery with any necessary indorsement or assignment;

(j) "Mortgage" means a consensual interest created by a real estate mortgage, a trust deed on real estate, or the like;

(k) An advance is made "pursuant to commitment" if the secured party has bound himself to make it, whether or not a subsequent event of default or other event not within his control has relieved or may relieve him from his obligation;

(l) "Security agreement" means an agreement which creates or provides for a security interest;

(m) "Secured party" means a lender, seller or other person in whose favor there is a security interest, including a person to whom accounts or chattel paper have been sold. When the holders of obligations issued under an indenture of trust, equipment trust agreement or the like are represented by a trustee or other person, the representative is the secured party;

(n) "Transmitting utility" means any person primarily engaged in the railroad, street railway or trolley bus business, the electric or electronics communications transmission business, the transmission of goods by pipeline, or the transmission or the production and transmission of electricity, steam, gas or water, or the provision of sewer service.

(2) Other definitions applying to this Article and the sections in which they appear are:

"Account." Section 9—106.
"Attach." Section 9—203.
"Construction mortgage." Section 9—313 (1).
"Consumer goods." Section 9—109 (1).
"Equipment." Section 9—109 (2).
"Farm products." Section 9—109 (3).
"Fixture." Section 9—313 (1).
"Fixture filing." Section 9—313 (1).
"General intangibles." Section 9—106.
"Inventory." Section 9—109 (4).
"Lien creditor." Section 9—301 (3).
"Proceeds." Section 9—306 (1).
"Purchase money security interest." Section 9—107.
"United States." Section 9—103.

(3) The following definitions in other Articles apply to this Article:

"Check." Section 3—104.
"Contract for sale." Section 2—106.
"Holder in due course." Section 3—302.
"Note." Section 3—104.
"Sale." Section 2—106.

(4) In addition Article 1 contains general definitions and principles of construction and interpretation applicable throughout this Article.

Section 9—106. Definitions: "Account"; "General Intangibles"

"Account" means any right to payment for goods sold or leased or for services rendered which is not evidenced by an instrument or chattel paper, whether or not it has been earned by performance. "General intangibles" means any personal property (including things in action) other than goods, accounts, chattel paper, documents, instruments, and money. All rights to payment earned or unearned under a charter or other contract involving the use or hire of a vessel and all rights incident to the chart or contract are accounts.

Section 9—107. Definitions: "Purchase Money Security Interest"

A security interest is a "purchase money security interest" to the extent that it is

(a) taken or retained by the seller of the collateral to secure all or part of its price; or

(b) taken by a person who by making advances or incurring an obligation gives value to enable the debtor to acquire rights in or the use of collateral if such value is in fact so used.

Section 9—108. When After-Acquired Collateral Not Security for Antecedent Debt

Where a secured party makes an advance, incurs an obligation, releases a perfected security interest, or otherwise gives new value which is to be secured in whole or in part by after-acquired property his security interest in the after-acquired collateral shall be deemed to be taken for new value and not as security for an antecedent debt if the debtor acquires his rights in such collateral either in the ordinary course of his business or under a contract of purchase made pursuant to the security agreement within a reasonable time after new value is given.

Section 9—109. Classification of Goods; "Consumer Goods"; "Equipment"; "Farm Products"; "Inventory"

Goods are

(1) "consumer goods" if they are used or bought for use primarily for personal, family or household purposes;

(2) "equipment" if they are used or bought for use primarily in business (including farming or a profession) or by a debtor who is a non-profit organization or a governmental subdivision or agency or if the goods are not included in the definitions of inventory, farm products or consumer goods;

(3) "farm products" if they are crops or livestock or supplies used or produced in farming operations or if they are products of crops or livestock in their unmanufactured states (such as ginned cotton, wool-clip, maple syrup, milk and eggs), and if they are in the possession of a debtor engaged in raising, fattening, grazing or other farming operations. If goods are farm products they are neither equipment nor inventory;

(4) "inventory" if they are held by a person who holds them for sale or lease or to be furnished under contracts of service or if he has so furnished them, or if they are raw materials, work in process or materials used or consumed in a business. Inventory of a person is not to be classified as his equipment.

Section 9—110. Sufficiency of Description

For the purposes of this Article any description of personal property or real estate is sufficient whether or not it is specific if it reasonably identifies what is described.

Section 9—111. Applicability of Bulk Transfer Laws

The creation of a security interest is not a bulk transfer under Article 6 (see Section 6—103).

Section 9—112. Where Collateral Is Not Owned by Debtor

Unless otherwise agreed, when a secured party knows that collateral is owned by a person who is not the debtor, the owner of the collateral is entitled to receive from the secured party any surplus under Section 9—502(2) or under Section 9—504(1), and is not liable for the debt or for any deficiency after resale, and he has the same right as the debtor

 (a) to receive statements under Section 9—208;

 (b) to receive notice of and to object to a secured party's proposal to retain the collateral in satisfaction of the indebtedness under Section 9—505;

 (c) to redeem the collateral under Section 9—506;

 (d) to obtain injunctive or other relief under Section 9—507(1); and

 (e) to recover losses caused to him under Section 9—208(2).

Section 9—113. Security Interests Arising Under Article on Sales

A security interest arising solely under the Article on Sales (Article 2) is subject to the provisions of this Article except that to the extent that and so long as the debtor does not have or does not lawfully obtain possession of the goods

 (a) no security agreement is necessary to make the security interest enforceable; and

 (b) no filing is required to perfect the security interest; and

 (c) the rights of the secured party on default by the debtor are governed by the Article on Sales (Article 2).

Section 9—114. Consignment

(1) A person who delivers goods under a consignment which is not a security interest and who would be required to file under this Article by paragraph (3) (c) of Section 2—326 has priority over a secured party who is or becomes a creditor of the consignee and who would have a perfected security interest in the goods if they were the property of the consignee, and also has priority with respect to identifiable cash proceeds received on or before delivery of the goods to a buyer, if

 (a) the consignor complies with the filing provision of the Article on Sales with respect to consignments (paragraph (3) (c) of Section 2—326) before the consignee receives possession of the goods; and

 (b) the consignor gives notification in writing to the holder of the security interest if the holder has filed a financing statement covering the same types of goods before the date of the filing made by the consignor; and

 (c) the holder of the security interest receives the notification within five years before the consignee receives possession of the goods; and

 (d) the notification states that the consignor expects to deliver goods on consignment to the consignee, describing the goods by item or type.

(2) In the case of a consignment which is not a security interest and in which the requirements of the preceding subsection have not been met, a person who delivers goods to another is subordinate to a person who would have a perfected security interest in the goods if they were the property of the debtor.

Part 2 Validity of Security Agreement and Rights of Parties Thereto

Section 9—201. General Validity of Security Agreement

Except as otherwise provided by this Act a security agreement is effective according to its terms between the parties, against purchasers of the collateral and against creditors. Nothing in this Article validates any charge or practice illegal under any statute or regulation thereunder governing usury, small loans, retail installment sales, or the like, or extends the application of any such statute or regulation to any transaction not otherwise subject thereto.

Section 9—202. Title to Collateral Immaterial

Each provision of this Article with regard to rights, obligations and remedies applies whether title to collateral is in the secured party or in the debtor.

Section 9—203. Attachment and Enforceability of Security Interest; Proceeds; Formal Requisites

(1) Subject to the provisions of Section 4—208 on the security interest of a collecting bank, Section 8—321 on security interests in securities and Section 9—113 on a security interest arising under the Article on Sales, a security interest is not enforceable against the debtor or third parties with respect to the collateral and does not attach unless:

 (a) the collateral is in the possession of the secured party pursuant to agreement, or the debtor has signed a security agreement which contains a description of the collateral and in addition, when the security interest covers crops growing or to be grown or timber to be cut, a description of the land concerned;

 (b) value has been given; and

 (c) the debtor has rights in the collateral.

(2) A security interest attaches when it becomes enforceable against the debtor with respect to the collateral. Attachment occurs as soon as all of the events specified in subsection (1) have taken place unless explicit agreement postpones the time of attaching.

(3) Unless otherwise agreed a security agreement gives the secured party the rights to proceeds provided by Section 9—306.

(4) A transaction, although subject to this Article, is also subject to . . . . *, and in the case of conflict between the provisions of this Article and any such statute, the provisions of such statute control. Failure to comply with any applicable statute has only the effect which is specified therein.

> *Note: At * in subsection (4) insert reference to any local statute regulating small loans, retail installment sales and the like.*
>
> *The foregoing subsection (4) is designed to make it clear that certain transactions, although subject to this Article, must also comply with other applicable legislation.*
>
> *This Article is designed to regulate all the "security" aspects of transactions within its scope. There is, however, much regulatory legislation, particularly in the consumer field, which supplements this Article and should not be repealed by its enactment. Examples are small loan acts, retail installment selling acts and the like. Such acts may provide for licensing and rate regulation and may prescribe particular forms of contract. Such provisions should remain in force despite the enactment of this Article. On the other hand if a retail installment selling act contains provisions on filing, rights on default, etc., such provisions should be repealed as inconsistent with this Article except that inconsistent provisions as to deficiencies, penalties, etc., in the Uniform Consumer Credit Code and other recent related legislation should remain because those statutes were drafted after the substantial enactment of the Article and with the intention of modifying certain provisions of this Article as to consumer credit.*

Section 9—204. After-Acquired Property; Future Advances

(1) Except as provided in subsection (2), a security agreement may provide that any or all obligations covered by the security agreement are to be secured by after-acquired collateral.

(2) No security interest attaches under an after-acquired property clause to consumer goods other than accessions (Section 9—314) when given as additional security unless the debtor acquires rights in them within ten days after the secured party gives value.

(3) Obligations covered by a security agreement may include future advances or other value whether or not the advances or value are given pursuant to commitment (subsection (1) of Section 9—105).

Section 9—205. Use or Disposition of Collateral Without Accounting Permissible

A security interest is not invalid or fraudulent against creditors by reason of liberty in the debtor to use, commingle or dispose of all or part of the collateral (including returned or repossessed goods) or to collect or compromise accounts or chattel paper, or to accept the return of goods or make repossessions, or to use, commingle or dispose of proceeds, or by reason of the failure of the secured party to require the debtor to account for proceeds or replace collateral. This section does not relax the requirements of possession where perfection of a security interest depends upon possession of the collateral by the secured party or by a bailee.

Section 9—206. Agreement Not to Assert Defenses Against Assignee; Modification of Sales Warranties Where Security Agreement Exists

(1) Subject to any statute or decision which establishes a different rule for buyers or lessees of consumer goods, an agreement by a buyer or lessee that he will not assert against an assignee any claim or defense which he may have against the seller or lessor is enforceable by an assignee who takes his assignment for value, in good faith and without notice of a claim or defense, except as to defenses of a type which may be asserted against a holder in due course of a negotiable instrument under the Article on Commercial Paper (Article 3). A buyer who as part of one transaction signs both a negotiable instrument and a security agreement makes such an agreement.

(2) When a seller retains a purchase money security interest in goods the Article on Sales (Article 2) governs the sale and any disclaimer, limitation or modification of the seller's warranties.

Section 9—207. Rights and Duties When Collateral is in Secured Party's Possession

(1) A secured party must use reasonable care in the custody and preservation of collateral in his possession. In the case of an instrument or chattel paper reasonable care includes taking necessary steps to preserve rights against prior parties unless otherwise agreed.

(2) Unless otherwise agreed, when collateral is in the secured party's possession

(a) reasonable expenses (including the cost of any insurance and payment of taxes or other charges) incurred in the custody, preservation, use or operation of the collateral are chargeable to the debtor and are secured by the collateral;

(b) the risk of accidental loss or damage is on the debtor to the extent of any deficiency in any effective insurance coverage;

(c) the secured party may hold as additional security any increase or profits (except money) received from the collateral, but money so received, unless remitted to the debtor, shall be applied in reduction of the secured obligation;

(d) the secured party must keep the collateral identifiable but fungible collateral may be commingled;

(e) the secured party may repledge the collateral upon terms which do not impair the debtor's right to redeem it.

(3) A secured party is liable for any loss caused by his failure to meet any obligation imposed by the preceding subsections but does not lose his security interest.

(4) A secured party may use or operate the collateral for the purpose of preserving the collateral or its value or pursuant to the order of a court of appropriate jurisdiction or, except in the case of consumer goods, in the manner and to the extent provided in the security agreement.

Section 9—208. Request for Statement of Account or List of Collateral

(1) A debtor may sign a statement indicating what he believes to be the aggregate amount of unpaid indebtedness as of a specified date and may send it to the secured party with a request that the statement be approved or corrected and returned to the debtor. When the security agreement or any other record kept by the secured party identifies the collateral a debtor may similarly request the secured party to approve or correct a list of the collateral.

(2) The secured party must comply with such a request within two weeks after receipt by sending a written correction or approval. If the secured party claims a security interest in all of a particular type of collateral owned by the debtor he may indicate that fact in his reply and need not approve or correct an itemized list of such collateral. If the secured party without reasonable excuse fails to comply he is liable for any loss caused to the debtor thereby; and if the debtor has properly included in his request a good faith statement of the obligation or a list of the collateral or both the secured party may claim a security interest only as shown in the statement against persons misled by his failure to comply. If he no longer has an interest in the obligation or collateral at the time the request is

received he must disclose the name and address of any successor in interest known to him and he is liable for any loss caused to the debtor as a result of failure to disclose. A successor in interest is not subject to this section until a request is received by him.

(3) A debtor is entitled to such a statement once every six months without charge. The secured party may require payment of a charge not exceeding $10 for each additional statement furnished.

Part 3 Rights of Third Parties; Perfected and Unperfected Security Interests; Rules of Priority

Section 9—301. Persons Who Take Priority Over Unperfected Security Interests; Rights of "Lien Creditor"

(1) Except as otherwise provided in subsection (2), an unperfected security interest is subordinate to the rights of

    (a) persons entitled to priority under Section 9—312;

    (b) a person who becomes a lien creditor before the security interest is perfected;

    (c) in the case of goods, instruments, documents, and chattel paper, a person who is not a secured party and who is a transferee in bulk or other buyer not in ordinary course of business or is a buyer of farm products in ordinary course of business, to the extent that he gives value and receives delivery of the collateral without knowledge of the security interest and before it is perfected;

    (d) in the case of accounts and general intangibles, a person who is not a secured party and who is a transferee to the extent that he gives value without knowledge of the security interest and before it is perfected.

(2) If the secured party files with respect to a purchase money security interest before or within ten days after the debtor receives possession of the collateral, he takes priority over the rights of a transferee in bulk or of a lien creditor which arise between the time the security interest attaches and the time of filing.

(3) A "lien creditor" means a creditor who has acquired a lien on the property involved by attachment, levy or the like and includes an assignee for benefit of creditors from the time of assignment, and a trustee in bankruptcy from the date of the filing of the petition or a receiver in equity from the time of appointment.

(4) A person who becomes a lien creditor while a security interest is perfected takes subject to the security interest only to the extent that it secures advances made before he becomes a lien creditor or within 45 days thereafter or made without knowledge of the lien or pursuant to a commitment entered into without knowledge of the lien.

Section 9—302. When Filing Is Required to Perfect Security Interest; Security Interests to Which Filing Provisions of This Article Do Not Apply

(1) A financing statement must be filed to perfect all security interests except the following:

    (a) a security interest in collateral in possession of the secured party under Section 9—305;

    (b) a security interest temporarily perfected in instruments or documents without delivery under Section 9—304 or in proceeds for a 10 day period under Section 9—306;

    (c) a security interest created by an assignment of a beneficial interest in a trust or a decedent's estate;

    (d) a purchase money security interest in consumer goods; but filing is required for a motor vehicle required to be registered; and fixture filing is required for priority over conflicting interests in fixtures to the extent provided in Section 9—313;

    (e) an assignment of accounts which does not alone or in conjunction with other assignments to the same assignee transfer a significant part of the outstanding accounts of the assignor;

    (f) a security interest of a collecting bank (Section 4—208) or in securities (Section 8—321) or arising under the Article on Sales (see Section 9—113) or covered in subsection (3) of this section;

    (g) an assignment for the benefit of all the creditors of the transferor, and subsequent transfers by the assignee thereunder.

(2) If a secured party assigns a perfected security interest, no filing under this Article is required in order to continue the perfected status of the security interest against creditors of and transferees from the original debtor.

(3) The filing of a financing statement otherwise required by this Article is not necessary or effective to perfect a security interest in property subject to

    (a) a statute or treaty of the United States which provides for a national or international registration or a national or international certificate of title or which specifies a place of filing different from that specified in this Article for filing of the security interest; or

    (b) the following statutes of this state; [list any certificate of title statute covering automobiles, trailers, mobile homes, boats, farm tractors, or the like, and any central filing statute*.]; but during any period in which collateral is inventory held for sale by a person who is in the business of selling goods of that kind, the filing provisions of this Article (Part 4) apply to a security interest in that collateral created by him as debtor; or

    (c) a certificate of title statute of another jurisdiction under the law of which indication of a security interest on the certificate is required as a condition of perfection (subsection (2) of Section 9—103).

(4) Compliance with a statute or treaty described in subsection (3) is equivalent to the filing of a financing statement under this Article, and a security interest in property subject to the statute or treaty can be perfected only by compliance therewith except as provided in Section 9—103 on multiple state transactions. Duration and renewal of perfection of a security interest perfected by compliance with the statute or treaty are governed by the provisions of the statute or treaty; in other respects the security interest is subject to this Article.

*Note: *It is recommended that the provisions of certificate of title acts for perfection of security interests by notation on the certificates should be amended to exclude coverage of inventory held for sale.*

Section 9—303. When Security Interest Is Perfected; Continuity of Perfection

(1) A security interest is perfected when it has attached and when all of the applicable steps required for perfection have been taken. Such steps are specified in Sections 9—302, 9—304, 9—305 and 9—306. If such steps are taken before the security interest attaches, it is perfected at the time when it attaches.

(2) If a security interest is originally perfected in any way permitted under this Article and is subsequently perfected in some other way under this Article, without an intermediate period when it was unperfected, the security interest shall be deemed to be perfected continuously for the purposes of this Article.

Section 9—304. Perfection of Security Interest in Instruments, Documents, and Goods Covered by Documents; Perfection by Permissive Filing; Temporary Perfection Without Filing or Transfer of Possession

(1) A security interest in chattel paper or negotiable documents may be perfected by filing. A security interest in money or instruments (other than certificated securities or instruments which constitute part of chattel paper) can be perfected only by the secured

party's taking possession, except as provided in subsections (4) and (5) of this section and subsections (2) and (3) of Section 9—306 on proceeds.

(2) During the period that goods are in the possession of the issuer of a negotiable document therefor, a security interest in the goods is perfected by perfecting a security interest in the document, and any security interest in the goods otherwise perfected during such period is subject thereto.

(3) A security interest in goods in the possession of a bailee other than one who has issued a negotiable document therefor is perfected by issuance of a document in the name of the secured party or by the bailee's receipt of notification of the secured party's interest or by filing as to the goods.

(4) A security interest in instruments (other than certificated securities) or negotiable documents is perfected without filing or the taking of possession for a period of 21 days from the time it attaches to the extent that it arises for new value given under a written security agreement.

(5) A security interest remains perfected for a period of 21 days without filing where a secured party having a perfected security interest in an instrument (other than a certificated security), a negotiable document or goods in possession of a bailee other than one who has issued a negotiable document therefor

> (a) makes available to the debtor the goods or documents representing the goods for the purpose of ultimate sale or exchange or for the purpose of loading, unloading, storing, shipping, transshipping, manufacturing, processing or otherwise dealing with them in a manner preliminary to their sale or exchange, but priority between conflicting security interests in the goods is subject to subsection (3) of Section 9—312; or
>
> (b) delivers the instrument to the debtor for the purpose of ultimate sale or exchange or of presentation, collection, renewal or registration of transfer.

(6) After the 21 day period in subsections (4) and (5) perfection depends upon compliance with applicable provisions of this Article.

Section 9—305. When Possession by Secured Party Perfects Security Interest Without Filing

A security interest in letters of credit and advices of credit (subsection (2) (a) of Section 5—116), goods, instruments (other than certificated securities), money, negotiable documents, or chattel paper may be perfected by the secured party's taking possession of the collateral. If such collateral other than goods covered by a negotiable document is held by a bailee, the secured party is deemed to have possession from the time the bailee receives notification of the secured party's interest. A security interest is perfected by possession from the time possession is taken without a relation back and continues only so long as possession is retained, unless otherwise specified in this Article. The security interest may be otherwise perfected as provided in this Article before or after the period of possession by the secured party.

Section 9—306. "Proceeds"; Secured Party's Rights on Disposition of Collateral

(1) "Proceeds" includes whatever is received upon the sale, exchange, collection or other disposition of collateral or proceeds. Insurance payable by reason of loss or damage to the collateral is proceeds, except to the extent that it is payable to a person other than a party to the security agreement. Money, checks, deposit accounts, and the like are "cash proceeds." All other proceeds are "non-cash proceeds."

(2) Except where this Article otherwise provides, a security interest continues in collateral notwithstanding sale, exchange or other disposition thereof unless the disposition was authorized by the secured party in the security agreement or otherwise, and also continues in any identifiable proceeds including collections received by the debtor.

(3) The security interest in proceeds is a continuously perfected security interest if the interest in the original collateral was perfected but it ceases to be a perfected security interest and becomes unperfected ten days after receipt of the proceeds by the debtor unless

> (a) a filed financing statement covers the original collateral and the proceeds are collateral in which a security interest may be perfected by filing in the office or offices where the financing statement has been filed and, if the proceeds are acquired with cash proceeds, the description of collateral in the financing statement indicates the types of property constituting the proceeds; or
>
> (b) a filed financing statement covers the original collateral and the proceeds are identifiable cash proceeds; or
>
> (c) the security interest in the proceeds is perfected before the expiration of the ten day period.

Except as provided in this section, a security interest in proceeds can be perfected only by the methods or under the circumstances permitted in this Article for original collateral of the same type.

(4) In the event of insolvency proceedings instituted by or against a debtor, a secured party with a perfected security interest in proceeds has a perfected security interest only in the following proceeds:

> (a) in identifiable non-cash proceeds and in separate deposit accounts containing only proceeds;
>
> (b) in identifiable cash proceeds in the form of money which is neither commingled with other money nor deposited in a deposit account prior to the insolvency proceedings;
>
> (c) in identifiable cash proceeds in the form of checks and the like which are not deposited in a deposit account prior to the insolvency proceedings; and
>
> (d) in all cash and deposit accounts of the debtor in which proceeds have been commingled with other funds, but the perfected security interest under this paragraph (d) is
>
>> (i) subject to any right to set-off; and
>>
>> (ii) limited to an amount not greater than the amount of any cash proceeds received by the debtor within ten days before the institution of the insolvency proceedings less the sum of (I) the payments to the secured party on account of cash proceeds received by the debtor during such period and (II) the cash proceeds received by the debtor during such period to which the secured party is entitled under paragraphs (a) through (c) of this subsection (4).

(5) If a sale of goods results in an account or chattel paper which is transferred by the seller to a secured party, and if the goods are returned to or are repossessed by the seller or the secured party, the following rules determine priorities:

> (a) If the goods were collateral at the time of sale, for an indebtedness of the seller which is still unpaid, the original security interest attaches again to the goods and continues as a perfected security interest if it was perfected at the time when the goods were sold. If the security interest was originally perfected by a filing which is still effective, nothing further is required to continue the perfected status; in any other case, the secured party must take possession of the returned or repossessed goods or must file.
>
> (b) An unpaid transferee of the chattel paper has a security interest in the goods against the transferor. Such security interest is prior to a security interest asserted under paragraph (a) to the extent that the transferee of the chattel paper was entitled to priority under Section 9—308.

(c) An unpaid transferee of the account has a security interest in the goods against the transferor. Such security interest is subordinate to a security interest asserted under paragraph (a).

(d) A security interest of an unpaid transferee asserted under paragraph (b) or (c) must be perfected for protection against creditors of the transferor and purchasers of the returned or repossessed goods.

Section 9—307. Protection of Buyers of Goods

(1) A buyer in ordinary course of business (subsection (9) of Section 1—201) other than a person buying farm products from a person engaged in farming operations takes free of a security interest created by his seller even though the security interest is perfected and even though the buyer knows of its existence.

(2) In the case of consumer goods, a buyer takes free of a security interest even though perfected if he buys without knowledge of the security interest, for value and for his own personal, family or household purposes unless prior to the purchase the secured party has filed a financing statement covering such goods.

(3) A buyer other than a buyer in ordinary course of business (subsection (1) of this section) takes free of a security interest to the extent that it secures future advances made after the secured party acquires knowledge of the purchase, or more than 45 days after the purchase, whichever first occurs, unless made pursuant to a commitment entered into without knowledge of the purchase and before the expiration of the 45 day period.

Section 9—308. Purchase of Chattel Paper and Instruments

A purchaser of chattel paper or an instrument who gives new value and takes possession of it in the ordinary course of his business has priority over a security interest in the chattel paper or instrument

(a) which is perfected under Section 9—304 (permissive filing and temporary perfection) or under Section 9—306 (perfection as to proceeds) if he acts without knowledge that the specific paper or instrument is subject to a security interest; or

(b) which is claimed merely as proceeds of inventory subject to a security interest (Section 9—306) even though he knows that the specific paper or instrument is subject to the security interest.

Section 9—309. Protection of Purchasers of Instruments, Documents and Securities

Nothing in this Article limits the rights of a holder in due course of a negotiable instrument (Section 3—302) or a holder to whom a negotiable document of title has been duly negotiated (Section 7—501) or a bona fide purchaser of a security (Section 8—302) and the holders or purchasers take priority over an earlier security interest even though perfected. Filing under this Article does not constitute notice of the security interest to such holders or purchasers.

Section 9—310. Priority of Certain Liens Arising by Operation of Law

When a person in the ordinary course of his business furnishes services or materials with respect to goods subject to a security interest, a lien upon goods in the possession of such person given by statute or rule of law for such materials or services takes priority over a perfected security interest unless the lien is statutory and the statute expressly provides otherwise.

Section 9—311. Alienability of Debtor's Rights: Judicial Process

The debtor's rights in collateral may be voluntarily or involuntarily transferred (by way of sale, creation of a security interest, attachment, levy, garnishment or other judicial process) notwithstanding a provision in the security agreement prohibiting any transfer or making the transfer constitute a default.

Section 9—312. Priorities Among Conflicting Security Interests in the Same Collateral

(1) The rules of priority stated in other sections of this Part and in the following sections shall govern when applicable: Section 4—208 with respect to the security interests of collecting banks in items being collected, accompanying documents and proceeds; Section 9—103 on security interests related to other jurisdictions; Section 9—114 on consignments.

(2) A perfected security interest in crops for new value given to enable the debtor to produce the crops during the production season and given not more than three months before the crops become growing crops by planting or otherwise takes priority over an earlier perfected security interest to the extent that such earlier interest secures obligations due more than six months before the crops become growing crops by planting or otherwise, even though the person giving new value had knowledge of the earlier security interest.

(3) A perfected purchase money security interest in inventory has priority over a conflicting security interest in the same inventory and also has priority in identifiable cash proceeds received on or before the delivery of the inventory to a buyer if

(a) the purchase money security interest is perfected at the time the debtor receives possession of the inventory; and

(b) the purchase money secured party gives notification in writing to the holder of the conflicting security interest if the holder had filed a financing statement covering the same types of inventory (i) before the date of the filing made by the purchase money secured party, or (ii) before the beginning of the 21 day period where the purchase money security interest is temporarily perfected without filing or possession (subsection (5) of Section 9—304); and

(c) the holder of the conflicting security interest receives the notification within five years before the debtor receives possession of the inventory; and

(d) the notification states that the person giving the notice has or expects to acquire a purchase money security interest in inventory of the debtor, describing such inventory by item or type.

(4) A purchase money security interest in collateral other than inventory has priority over a conflicting security interest in the same collateral or its proceeds if the purchase money security interest is perfected at the time the debtor receives possession of the collateral or within ten days thereafter.

(5) In all cases not governed by other rules stated in this section (including cases of purchase money security interests which do not qualify for the special priorities set forth in subsections (3) and (4) of this section), priority between conflicting security interests in the same collateral shall be determined according to the following rules:

(a) Conflicting security interests rank according to priority in time of filing or perfection. Priority dates from the time a filing is first made covering the collateral or the time the security interest is first perfected, whichever is earlier, provided that there is no period thereafter when there is neither filing nor perfection.

(b) So long as conflicting security interests are unperfected, the first to attach has priority.

(6) For the purposes of subsection (5) a date of filing or perfection as to collateral is also a date of filing or perfection as to proceeds.

(7) If future advances are made while a security interest is perfected by filing, the taking of possession, or under Section 8—321 on securities, the security interest has the same priority for the purposes of subsection (5) with respect to the future advances as it does with respect to the first advance. If a commitment is made before or while the security interest is so perfected, the security interest has the same priority with respect to advances made pursuant thereto. In other cases a perfected security interest has priority from the date the advance is made.

Section 9—313. Priority of Security Interests in Fixtures

(1) In this section and in the provisions of Part 4 of this Article referring to fixture filing, unless the context otherwise requires

   (a) goods are "fixtures" when they become so related to particular real estate that an interest in them arises under real estate law

   (b) a "fixture filing" is the filing in the office where a mortgage on the real estate would be filed or recorded of a financing statement covering goods which are or are to become fixtures and conforming to the requirements of subsection (5) of Section 9—402

   (c) a mortgage is a "construction mortgage" to the extent that it secures an obligation incurred for the construction of an improvement on land including the acquisition cost of the land, if the recorded writing so indicates.

(2) A security interest under this Article may be created in goods which are fixtures or may continue in goods which become fixtures, but no security interest exists under this Article in ordinary building materials incorporated into an improvement on land.

(3) This Article does not prevent creation of an encumbrance upon fixtures pursuant to real estate law.

(4) A perfected security interest in fixtures has priority over the conflicting interest of an encumbrancer or owner of the real estate where

   (a) the security interest is a purchase money security interest, the interest of the encumbrancer or owner arises before the goods become fixtures, the security interest is perfected by a fixture filing before the goods become fixtures or within ten days thereafter, and the debtor has an interest of record in the real estate or is in possession of the real estate; or

   (b) the security interest is perfected by a fixture filing before the interest of the encumbrancer or owner is of record, the security interest has priority over any conflicting interest of a predecessor in title of the encumbrancer or owner, and the debtor has an interest of record in the real estate or is in possession of the real estate; or

   (c) the fixtures are readily removable factory or office machines or readily removable replacements of domestic appliances which are consumer goods, and before the goods become fixtures the security interest is perfected by any method permitted by this Article; or

   (d) the conflicting interest is a lien on the real estate obtained by legal or equitable proceedings after the security interest was perfected by any method permitted by this Article.

(5) A security interest in fixtures, whether or not perfected, has priority over the conflicting interest of an encumbrancer or owner of the real estate where

   (a) the encumbrancer or owner has consented in writing to the security interest or has disclaimed an interest in the goods as fixtures; or

   (b) the debtor has a right to remove the goods as against the encumbrancer or owner. If the debtor's right terminates, the priority of the security interest continues for a reasonable time.

(6) Notwithstanding paragraph (a) of subsection (4) but otherwise subject to subsections (4) and (5), a security interest in fixtures is subordinate to a construction mortgage recorded before the goods become fixtures if the goods become fixtures before the completion of the construction. To the extent that it is given to refinance a construction mortgage, a mortgage has this priority to the same extent as the construction mortgage.

(7) In cases not within the preceding subsections, a security interest in fixtures is subordinate to the conflicting interest of an encumbrancer or owner of the related real estate who is not the debtor.

(8) When the secured party has priority over all owners and encumbrancers of the real estate, he may, on default, subject to the provisions of Part 5, remove his collateral from the real estate but he must reimburse any encumbrancer or owner of the real estate who is not the debtor and who has not otherwise agreed for the cost of repair of any physical injury, but not for any diminution in value of the real estate caused by the absence of the goods removed or by any necessity of replacing them. A person entitled to reimbursement may refuse permission to remove until the secured party gives adequate security for the performance of this obligation.

Section 9—314. Accessions

(1) A security interest in goods which attaches before they are installed in or affixed to other goods takes priority as to the goods installed or affixed (called in this section "accessions") over the claims of all persons to the whole except as stated in subsection (3) and subject to Section 9—315(1).

(2) A security interest which attaches to goods after they become part of a whole is valid against all persons subsequently acquiring interests in the whole except as stated in subsection (3) but is invalid against any person with an interest in the whole at the time the security interest attaches to the goods who has not in writing consented to the security interest or disclaimed an interest in the goods as part of the whole.

(3) The security interests described in subsections (1) and (2) do not take priority over

   (a) a subsequent purchaser for value of any interest in the whole; or

   (b) a creditor with a lien on the whole subsequently obtained by judicial proceedings; or

   (c) a creditor with a prior perfected security interest in the whole to the extent that he makes subsequent advances

if the subsequent purchase is made, the lien by judicial proceedings obtained or the subsequent advance under the prior perfected security interest is made or contracted for without knowledge of the security interest and before it is perfected. A purchaser of the whole at a foreclosure sale other than the holder of a perfected security interest purchasing at his own foreclosure sale is a subsequent purchaser within this section.

(4) When under subsections (1) or (2) and (3) a secured party has an interest in accessions which has priority over the claims of all persons who have interests in the whole, he may on default subject to the provisions of Part 5 remove his collateral from the whole but he must reimburse any encumbrancer or owner of the whole who is not the debtor and who has not otherwise agreed for the cost of repair of any physical injury but not for any diminution in value of the whole caused by the absence of the goods removed or by any necessity for replacing them. A person entitled to reimbursement may refuse permission to remove until the secured party gives adequate security for the performance of this obligation.

Section 9—315. Priority When Goods Are Commingled or Processed

(1) If a security interest in goods was perfected and subsequently the goods or a part thereof have become part of a product or mass, the security interest continues in the product or mass if

   (a) the goods are so manufactured, processed, assembled or commingled that their identity is lost in the product or mass; or

   (b) a financing statement covering the original goods also covers the product into which the goods have been manufactured, processed or assembled.

In a case to which paragraph (b) applies, no separate security interest in that part of the original goods which have been manufactured, processed or assembled into the product may be claimed under Section 9—314.

(2) When under subsection (1) more than one security interest attaches to the product or mass, they rank equally according to the ratio that the cost of the goods to which each interest originally attached bears to the cost of the total product or mass.

Section 9—316. Priority Subject to Subordination

Nothing in this Article prevents subordination by agreement by any person entitled to priority.

Section 9—317. Secured Party Not Obligated on Contract of Debtor

The mere existence of a security interest or authority given to the debtor to dispose of or use collateral does not impose contract or tort liability upon the secured party for the debtor's acts or omissions.

Section 9—318. Defenses Against Assignee; Modification of Contract After Notification of Assignment; Term Prohibiting Assignment Ineffective; Identification and Proof of Assignment

(1) Unless an account debtor has made an enforceable agreement not to assert defenses or claims arising out of a sale as provided in Section 9—206 the rights of an assignee are subject to

(a) all the terms of the contract between the account debtor and assignor and any defense or claim arising therefrom; and

(b) any other defense or claim of the account debtor against the assignor which accrues before the account debtor receives notification of the assignment.

(2) So far as the right to payment or a part thereof under an assigned contract has not been fully earned by performance, and notwithstanding notification of the assignment, any modification of or substitution for the contract made in good faith and in accordance with reasonable commercial standards is effective against an assignee unless the account debtor has otherwise agreed but the assignee acquires corresponding rights under the modified or substituted contract. The assignment may provide that such modification or substitution is a breach by the assignor.

(3) The account debtor is authorized to pay the assignor until the account debtor receives notification that the amount due or to become due has been assigned and that payment is to be made to the assignee. A notification which does not reasonably identify the rights assigned is ineffective. If requested by the account debtor, the assignee must seasonably furnish reasonable proof that the assignment has been made and unless he does so the account debtor may pay the assignor.

(4) A term in any contract between an account debtor and an assignor is ineffective if it prohibits assignment of an account or prohibits creation of a security interest in a general intangible for money due or to become due or requires the account debtor's consent to such assignment or security interest.

Part 4 Filing

Section 9—401. Place of Filing; Erroneous Filing; Removal of Collateral

First Alternative Subsection (1)

(1) The proper place to file in order to perfect a security interest is as follows:

(a) when the collateral is timber to be cut or is minerals or the like (including oil and gas) or accounts subject to subsection (5) of Section 9—103, or when the financing statement is filed as a fixture filing (Section 9—313) and the collateral is goods which are or are to become fixtures, then in the office where a mortgage on the real estate would be filed or recorded;

(b) in all other cases, in the office of the [Secretary of State].

Second Alternative Subsection (1)

(1) The proper place to file in order to perfect a security interest is as follows:

(a) when the collateral is equipment used in farming operations, or farm products, or accounts or general intangibles arising from or relating to the sale of farm products by a farmer, or consumer goods, then in the office of the . . . . in the county of the debtor's residence or if the debtor is not a resident of this state then in the office of the . . . . in the county where the goods are kept, and in addition when the collateral is crops growing or to be grown in the office of the . . . . in the county where the land is located;

(b) when the collateral is timber to be cut or is minerals or the like (including oil and gas) or accounts subject to subsection (5) of Section 9—103, or when the financing statement is filed as a fixture filing (Section 9—313) and the collateral is goods which are or are to become fixtures, then in the office where a mortgage on the real estate would be filed or recorded;

(c) in all other cases, in the office of the [Secretary of State].

Third Alternative Subsection (1)

(1) The proper place to file in order to perfect a security interest is as follows:

(a) when the collateral is equipment used in farming operations, or farm products, or accounts or general intangibles arising from or relating to the sale of farm products by a farmer, or consumer goods, then in the office of the . . . . in the county of the debtor's residence or if the debtor is not a resident of this state then in the office of the . . . . in the county where the goods are kept, and in addition when the collateral is crops growing or to be grown in the office of the . . . . . . in the county where the land is located;

(b) when the collateral is timber to be cut or is minerals or the like (including oil and gas) or accounts subject to subsection (5) of Section 9—103, or when the financing statement is filed as a fixture filing (Section 9—313) and the collateral is goods which are or are to become fixtures, then in the office where a mortgage on the real estate would be filed or recorded;

(c) in all other cases, in the office of the [Secretary of State] and in addition, if the debtor has a place of business in only one county of this state, also in the office of . . . . . . of such county, or, if the debtor has no place of business in this state, but resides in the state, also in the office of . . . . . . of the county in which he resides.

Note: *One of the three alternatives should be selected as subsection (1).*

(2) A filing which is made in good faith in an improper place or not in all of the places required by this section is nevertheless effective with regard to any collateral as to which the filing complied with the requirements of this Article and is also effective with regard to collateral covered by the financing statement against any person who has knowledge of the contents of such financing statement.

(3) A filing which is made in the proper place in this state continues effective even though the debtor's residence or place of business or the location of the collateral or its use, whichever controlled the original filing, is thereafter changed.

Alternative Subsection (3)

[(3) A filing which is made in the proper county continues effective for four months after a change to another county of the debtor's residence or place of business or the location of the collateral, whichever controlled the original filing. It becomes ineffective thereafter unless a copy of the financing statement signed by the secured party is filed in the new county within said period. The security interest may also be perfected in the new county after the expiration of the four-month period; in such case perfection dates from the time of perfection in the new county. A change in the use of the collateral does not impair the effectiveness of the original filing.]

(4) The rules stated in Section 9—103 determine whether filing is necessary in this state.

(5) Notwithstanding the preceding subsections, and subject to subsection (3) of Section 9—302, the proper place to file in order to perfect a security interest in collateral, including fixtures, of a transmitting utility is the office of the [Secretary of State]. This filing constitutes a fixture filing (Section 9—313) as to the collateral described therein which is or is to become fixtures.

(6) For the purposes of this section, the residence of an organization is its place of business if it has one or its chief executive office if it has more than one place of business.

Note: *Subsection (6) should be used only if the state chooses the Second or Third Alternative Subsection (1).*

Section 9—402. Formal Requisites of Financing Statement; Amendments; Mortgage as Financing Statement

(1) A financing statement is sufficient if it gives the names of the debtor and the secured party, is signed by the debtor, gives an address of the secured party from which information concerning the security interest may be obtained, gives a mailing address of the debtor and contains a statement indicating the types, or describing the items, of collateral. A financing statement may be filed before a security agreement is made or a security interest otherwise attaches. When the financing statement covers crops growing or to be grown, the statement must also contain a description of the real estate concerned. When the financing statement covers timber to be cut or covers minerals or the like (including oil and gas) or accounts subject to subsection (5) of Section 9—103, or when the financing statement is filed as a fixture filing (Section 9—313) and the collateral is goods which are or are to become fixtures, the statement must also comply with subsection (5). A copy of the security agreement is sufficient as a financing statement if it contains the above information and is signed by the debtor. A carbon, photographic or other reproduction of a security agreement or a financing statement is sufficient as a financing statement if the security agreement so provides or if the original has been filed in this state.

(2) A financing statement which otherwise complies with subsection (1) is sufficient when it is signed by the secured party instead of the debtor if it is filed to perfect a security interest in

  (a) collateral already subject to a security interest in another jurisdiction when it is brought into this state, or when the debtor's location is changed to this state. Such a financing statement must state that the collateral was brought into this state or that the debtor's location was changed to this state under such circumstances; or

  (b) proceeds under Section 9—306 if the security interest in the original collateral was perfected. Such a financing statement must describe the original collateral; or

  (c) collateral as to which the filing has lapsed; or

  (d) collateral acquired after a change of name, identity or corporate structure of the debtor (subsection (7)).

(3) A form substantially as follows is sufficient to comply with subsection (1):

Name of debtor (or assignor) ....
Address ....
Name of secured party (or assignee) ....
Address ....

  1. This financing statement covers the following types (or items) of property:

     (Describe) ....

  2. (If collateral is crops) The above described crops are growing or are to be grown on:

     (Describe Real Estate) ....

  3. (If applicable) The above goods are to become fixtures on*

     (Describe Real Estate) ....
     and this financing statement is to be filed [for record] in the real estate records. (If the debtor does not have an interest of record) The name of a record owner is ....

  4. (If products of collateral are claimed) Products of the collateral are also covered.

     (use whichever is applicable)

....
Signature of Debtor (or Assignor)

....
Signature of Secured Party (or Assignee)

(4) A financing statement may be amended by filing a writing signed by both the debtor and the secured party. An amendment does not extend the period of effectiveness of a financing statement. If any amendment adds collateral, it is effective as to the added collateral only from the filing date of the amendment. In this Article, unless the context otherwise requires, the term "financing statement" means the original financing statement and any amendments.

(5) A financing statement covering timber to be cut or covering minerals or the like (including oil and gas) or accounts subject to subsection (5) of Section 9—103, or a financing statement filed as a fixture filing (Section 9—313) where the debtor is not a transmitting utility, must show that it covers this type of collateral, must recite that it is to be filed [for record] in the real estate records, and the financing statement must contain a description of the real estate [sufficient if it were contained in a mortgage of the real estate to give constructive notice of the mortgage under the law of this state]. If the debtor does not have an interest of record in the real estate, the financing statement must show the name of a record owner.

(6) A mortgage is effective as a financing statement filed as a fixture filing from the date of its recording if

  (a) the goods are described in the mortgage by item or type; and

  (b) the goods are or are to become fixtures related to the real estate described in the mortgage; and

  (c) the mortgage complies with the requirements for a financing statement in this section other than a recital that it is to be filed in the real estate records; and

  (d) the mortgage is duly recorded.

No fee with reference to the financing statement is required other than the regular recording and satisfaction fees with respect to the mortgage.

(7) A financing statement sufficiently shows the name of the debtor if it gives the individual, partnership or corporate name of the debtor, whether or not it adds other trade names or names of partners. Where the debtor so changes his name or in the case of an organization its name, identity or corporate structure that a filed financing statement becomes seriously misleading, the filing is not

effective to perfect a security interest in collateral acquired by the debtor more than four months after the change, unless a new appropriate financing statement is filed before the expiration of that time. A filed financing statement remains effective with respect to collateral transferred by the debtor even though the secured party knows of or consents to the transfer.

(8) A financing statement substantially complying with the requirements of this section is effective even though it contains minor errors which are not seriously misleading.

Note: *Language in brackets is optional.*

Note: *Where the state has any special recording system for real estate other than the usual grantor-grantee index (as, for instance, a tract system or a title registration or Torrens system) local adaptations of subsection (5) and Section 9—403(7) may be necessary. See Mass. Gen. Laws Chapter 106, Section 9—409.*

*Where appropriate substitute either "The above timber is standing on . . . ." or "The above minerals or the like (including oil and gas) or accounts will be financed at the wellhead or minehead of the well or mine located on . . . ."

Section 9—403. What Constitutes Filing; Duration of Filing; Effect of Lapsed Filing; Duties of Filing Officer

(1) Presentation for filing of a financing statement and tender of the filing fee or acceptance of the statement by the filing officer constitutes filing under this Article.

(2) Except as provided in subsection (6) a filed financing statement is effective for a period of five years from the date of filing. The effectiveness of a filed financing statement lapses on the expiration of the five year period unless a continuation statement is filed prior to the lapse. If a security interest perfected by filing exists at the time insolvency proceedings are commenced by or against the debtor, the security interest remains perfected until termination of the insolvency proceedings and thereafter for a period of sixty days or until expiration of the five year period, whichever occurs later. Upon lapse the security interest becomes unperfected, unless it is perfected without filing. If the security interest becomes unperfected upon lapse, it is deemed to have been unperfected as against a person who became a purchaser or lien creditor before lapse.

(3) A continuation statement may be filed by the secured party within six months prior to the expiration of the five year period specified in subsection (2). Any such continuation statement must be signed by the secured party, identify the original statement by file number and state that the original statement is still effective. A continuation statement signed by a person other than the secured party of record must be accompanied by a separate written statement of assignment signed by the secured party of record and complying with subsection (2) of Section 9—405, including payment of the required fee. Upon timely filing of the continuation statement, the effectiveness of the original statement is continued for five years after the last date to which the filing was effective whereupon it lapses in the same manner as provided in subsection (2) unless another continuation statement is filed prior to such lapse. Succeeding continuation statements may be filed in the same manner to continue the effectiveness of the original statement. Unless a statute on disposition of public records provides otherwise, the filing officer may remove a lapsed statement from the files and destroy it immediately if he has retained a microfilm or other photographic record, or in other cases after one year after the lapse. The filing officer shall so arrange matters by physical annexation of financing statements to continuation statements or other related filings, or by other means, that if he physically destroys the financing statements of a period more than five years past, those which have been continued by a continuation statement or which are still effective under subsection (6) shall be retained.

(4) Except as provided in subsection (7) a filing officer shall mark each statement with a file number and with the date and hour of filing and shall hold the statement or a microfilm or other photographic copy thereof for public inspection. In addition the filing officer shall index the statement according to the name of the debtor and shall note in the index the file number and the address of the debtor given in the statement.

(5) The uniform fee for filing and indexing and for stamping a copy furnished by the secured party to show the date and place of filing for an original financing statement or for a continuation statement shall be $. . . . . if the statement is in the standard form prescribed by the [Secretary of State] and otherwise shall be $. . . . ., plus in each case, if the financing statement is subject to subsection (5) of Section 9—402, $. . . . . . The uniform fee for each name more than one required to be indexed shall be $. . . . . The secured party may at his option show a trade name for any person and an extra uniform indexing fee of $. . . . . shall be paid with respect thereto.

(6) If the debtor is a transmitting utility (subsection (5) of Section 9—401) and a filed financing statement so states, it is effective until a termination statement is filed. A real estate mortgage which is effective as a fixture filing under subsection (6) of Section 9—402 remains effective as a fixture filing until the mortgage is released or satisfied of record or its effectiveness otherwise terminates as to the real estate.

(7) When a financing statement covers timber to be cut or covers minerals or the like (including oil and gas) or accounts subject to subsection (5) of Section 9—103, or is filed as a fixture filing, [it shall be filed for record and] the filing officer shall index it under the names of the debtor and any owner of record shown on the financing statement in the same fashion as if they were the mortgagors in a mortgage of the real estate described, and, to the extent that the law of this state provides for indexing of mortgages under the name of the mortgagee, under the name of the secured party as if he were the mortgagee thereunder, or where indexing is by description in the same fashion as if the financing statement were a mortgage of the real estate described.

Note: *In states in which writings will not appear in the real estate records and indices unless actually recorded the bracketed language in subsection (7) should be used.*

Section 9—404. Termination Statement

(1) If a financing statement covering consumer goods is filed on or after . . . ., then within one month or within ten days following written demand by the debtor after there is no outstanding secured obligation and no commitment to make advances, incur obligations or otherwise give value, the secured party must file with each filing officer with whom the financing statement was filed, a termination statement to the effect that he no longer claims a security interest under the financing statement, which shall be identified by file number. In other cases whenever there is no outstanding secured obligation and no commitment to make advances, incur obligations or otherwise give value, the secured party must on written demand by the debtor send the debtor, for each filing officer with whom the financing statement was filed, a termination statement to the effect that he no longer claims a security interest under the financing statement, which shall be identified by file number. A termination statement signed by a person other than the secured party of record must be accompanied by a separate written statement of assignment signed by the secured party of record complying with subsection (2) of Section 9—405, including payment of the required fee. If the affected secured party fails to file such a termination statement as required by this subsection, or to send such a termination statement within ten days after proper demand therefor, he shall be liable to the debtor for one hundred dollars, and in addition for any loss caused to the debtor by such failure.

(2) On presentation to the filing officer of such a termination statement he must note it in the index. If he has received the termination statement in duplicate, he shall return one copy of the termination statement to the secured party stamped to show the time of receipt thereof. If the filing officer has a microfilm or other photographic record of the financing statement, and of any related continuation statement, statement of assignment and statement of release, he may remove the originals from the files at any time after receipt of the termination statement, or if he has no such record, he may remove them from the files at any time after one year after receipt of the termination statement.

(3) If the termination statement is in the standard form prescribed by the [Secretary of State], the uniform fee for filing and indexing the termination statement shall be $. . . . ., and otherwise shall be $. . . . ., plus in each case an additional fee of $. . . . . for each name more than one against which the termination statement is required to be indexed.

Note: *The date to be inserted should be the effective date of the revised Article 9.*

Section 9—405. Assignment of Security Interest; Duties of Filing Officer; Fees

(1) A financing statement may disclose an assignment of a security interest in the collateral described in the financing statement by indication in the financing statement of the name and address of the assignee or by an assignment itself or a copy thereof on the face or back of the statement. On presentation to the filing officer of such a financing statement the filing officer shall mark the same as provided in Section 9—403(4). The uniform fee for filing, indexing and furnishing filing data for a financing statement so indicating an assignment shall be $. . . . . if the statement is in the standard form prescribed by the [Secretary of State] and otherwise shall be $. . . . ., plus in each case an additional fee of $. . . . . for each name more than one against which the financing statement is required to be indexed.

(2) A secured party may assign of record all or part of his rights under a financing statement by the filing in the place where the original financing statement was filed of a separate written statement of assignment signed by the secured party of record and setting forth the name of the secured party of record and the debtor, the file number and the date of filing of the financing statement and the name and address of the assignee and containing a description of the collateral assigned. A copy of the assignment is sufficient as a separate statement if it complies with the preceding sentence. On presentation to the filing officer of such a separate statement, the filing officer shall mark such separate statement with the date and hour of the filing. He shall note the assignment on the index of the financing statement, or in the case of a fixture filing, or a filing covering timber to be cut, or covering minerals or the like (including oil and gas) or accounts subject to subsection (5) of Section 9—103, he shall index the assignment under the name of the assignor as grantor and, to the extent that the law of this state provides for indexing the assignment of a mortgage under the name of the assignee, he shall index the assignment of the financing statement under the name of the assignee. The uniform fee for filing, indexing and furnishing filing data about such a separate statement of assignment shall be $. . . . . if the statement is in the standard form prescribed by the [Secretary of State] and otherwise shall be $. . . . ., plus in each case an additional fee of $. . . . . for each name more than one against which the statement of assignment is required to be indexed. Notwithstanding the provisions of this subsection, an assignment of record of a security interest in a fixture contained in a mortgage effective as a fixture filing.(subsection (6) of Section 9—402) may be made only by an assignment of the mortgage in the manner provided by the law of this state other than this Act.

(3) After the disclosure or filing of an assignment under this section, the assignee is the secured party of record.

Section 9—406. Release of Collateral; Duties of Filing Officer; Fees

A secured party of record may by his signed statement release all or a part of any collateral described in a filed financing statement. The statement of release is sufficient if it contains a description of the collateral being released, the name and address of the debtor, the name and address of the secured party, and the file number of the financing statement. A statement of release signed by a person other than the secured party of record must be accompanied by a separate written statement of assignment signed by the secured party of record and complying with subsection (2) of Section 9—405, including payment of the required fee. Upon presentation of such a statement of release to the filing officer he shall mark the statement with the hour and date of filing and shall note the same upon the margin of the index of the filing of the financing statement. The uniform fee for filing and noting such a statement of release shall be $. . . . . if the statement is in the standard form prescribed by the [Secretary of State] and otherwise shall be $. . . . ., plus in each case an additional fee of $. . . . . for each name more than one against which the statement of release is required to be indexed.

[Section 9—407. Information From Filing Officer]

[(1) If the person filing any financing statement, termination statement, statement of assignment, or statement of release, furnishes the filing officer a copy thereof, the filing officer shall upon request note upon the copy the file number and date and hour of the filing of the original and deliver or send the copy to such person.]

[(2) Upon request of any person, the filing officer shall issue his certificate showing whether there is on file on the date and hour stated therein, any presently effective financing statement naming a particular debtor and any statement of assignment thereof and if there is, giving the date and hour of filing of each such statement and the names and addresses of each secured party therein. The uniform fee for such a certificate shall be $. . . . . if the request for the certificate is in the standard form prescribed by the [Secretary of State] and otherwise shall be $. . . . . Upon request the filing officer shall furnish a copy of any filed financing statement or statement of assignment for a uniform fee of $. . . . . per page.]

Note: *This section is proposed as an optional provision to require filing officers to furnish certificates. Local law and practices should be consulted with regard to the advisability of adoption.*

Section 9—408. Financing Statements Covering Consigned or Leased Goods

A consignor or lessor of goods may file a financing statement using the terms "consignor," "consignee," "lessor," "lessee" or the like instead of the terms specified in Section 9—402. The provisions of this Part shall apply as appropriate to such a financing statement but its filing shall not of itself be a factor in determining whether or not the consignment or lease is intended as security (Section 1—201(37)). However, if it is determined for other reasons that the consignment or lease is so intended, a security interest of the consignor or lessor which attaches to the consigned or leased goods is perfected by such filing.

Part 5 Default

Section 9—501. Default; Procedure When Security Agreement Covers Both Real and Personal Property

(1) When a debtor is in default under a security agreement, a secured party has the rights and remedies provided in this Part and except as limited by subsection (3) those provided in the security agreement. He may reduce his claim to judgment, foreclose or otherwise enforce the security interest by any available judicial procedure. If the collateral is documents the secured party may proceed either as to the documents or as to the goods covered thereby. A

secured party in possession has the rights, remedies and duties provided in Section 9—207. The rights and remedies referred to in this subsection are cumulative.

(2) After default, the debtor has the rights and remedies provided in this Part, those provided in the security agreement and those provided in Section 9—207.

(3) To the extent that they give rights to the debtor and impose duties on the secured party, the rules stated in the subsections referred to below may not be waived or varied except as provided with respect to compulsory disposition of collateral (subsection (3) of Section 9—504 and Section 9—505) and with respect to redemption of collateral (Section 9—506) but the parties may by agreement determine the standards by which the fulfillment of these rights and duties is to be measured if such standards are not manifestly unreasonable:

(a) subsection (2) of Section 9—502 and subsection (2) of Section 9—504 insofar as they require accounting for surplus proceeds of collateral;

(b) subsection (3) of Section 9—504 and subsection (1) of Section 9—505 which deal with disposition of collateral;

(c) subsection (2) of Section 9—505 which deals with acceptance of collateral as discharge of obligation;

(d) Section 9—506 which deals with redemption of collateral; and

(e) subsection (1) of Section 9—507 which deals with the secured party's liability for failure to comply with this Part.

(4) If the security agreement covers both real and personal property, the secured party may proceed under this Part as to the personal property or he may proceed as to both the real and the personal property in accordance with his rights and remedies in respect of the real property in which case the provisions of this Part do not apply.

(5) When a secured party has reduced his claim to judgment the lien of any levy which may be made upon his collateral by virtue of any execution based upon the judgment shall relate back to the date of the perfection of the security interest in such collateral. A judicial sale, pursuant to such execution, is a foreclosure of the security interest by judicial procedure within the meaning of this section, and the secured party may purchase at the sale and thereafter hold the collateral free of any other requirements of this Article.

Section 9—502. Collection Rights of Secured Party

(1) When so agreed and in any event on default the secured party is entitled to notify an account debtor or the obligor on an instrument to make payment to him whether or not the assignor was theretofore making collections on the collateral, and also to take control of any proceeds to which he is entitled under Section 9—306.

(2) A secured party who by agreement is entitled to charge back uncollected collateral or otherwise to full or limited recourse against the debtor and who undertakes to collect from the account debtors or obligors must proceed in a commercially reasonable manner and may deduct his reasonable expenses of realization from the collections. If the security agreement secures an indebtedness, the secured party must account to the debtor for any surplus, and unless otherwise agreed, the debtor is liable for any deficiency. But, if the underlying transaction was a sale of accounts or chattel paper, the debtor is entitled to any surplus or is liable for any deficiency only if the security agreement so provides.

Section 9—503. Secured Party's Right to Take Possession After Default

Unless otherwise agreed a secured party has on default the right to take possession of the collateral. In taking possession a secured party may proceed without judicial process if this can be done without breach of the peace or may proceed by action. If the security agreement so provides the secured party may require the debtor to assemble the collateral and make it available to the secured party at a place to be designated by the secured party which is reasonably convenient to both parties. Without removal a secured party may render equipment unusable, and may dispose of collateral on the debtor's premises under Section 9—504.

Section 9—504. Secured Party's Right to Dispose of Collateral After Default; Effect of Disposition

(1) A secured party after default may sell, lease or otherwise dispose of any or all of the collateral in its then condition or following any commercially reasonable preparation or processing. Any sale of goods is subject to the Article on Sales (Article 2). The proceeds of disposition shall be applied in the order following to

(a) the reasonable expenses of retaking, holding, preparing for sale or lease, selling, leasing and the like and, to the extent provided for in the agreement and not prohibited by law, the reasonable attorneys' fees and legal expenses incurred by the secured party;

(b) the satisfaction of indebtedness secured by the security interest under which the disposition is made;

(c) the satisfaction of indebtedness secured by any subordinate security interest in the collateral if written notification of demand therefor is received before distribution of the proceeds is completed. If requested by the secured party, the holder of a subordinate security interest must seasonably furnish reasonable proof of his interest, and unless he does so, the secured party need not comply with his demand.

(2) If the security interest secures an indebtedness, the secured party must account to the debtor for any surplus, and, unless otherwise agreed, the debtor is liable for any deficiency. But if the underlying transaction was a sale of accounts or chattel paper, the debtor is entitled to any surplus or is liable for any deficiency only if the security agreement so provides.

(3) Disposition of the collateral may be by public or private proceedings and may be made by way of one or more contracts. Sale or other disposition may be as a unit or in parcels and at any time and place and on any terms but every aspect of the disposition including the method, manner, time, place and terms must be commercially reasonable. Unless collateral is perishable or threatens to decline speedily in value or is of a type customarily sold on a recognized market, reasonable notification of the time and place of any public sale or reasonable notification of the time after which any private sale or other intended disposition is to be made shall be sent by the secured party to the debtor, if he has not signed after default a statement renouncing or modifying his right to notification of sale. In the case of consumer goods no other notification need be sent. In other cases notification shall be sent to any other secured party from whom the secured party has received (before sending his notification to the debtor or before the debtor's renunciation of his rights) written notice of a claim of an interest in the collateral. The secured party may buy at any public sale and if the collateral is of a type customarily sold in a recognized market or is of a type which is the subject of widely distributed standard price quotations he may buy at private sale.

(4) When collateral is disposed of by a secured party after default, the disposition transfers to a purchaser for value all of the debtor's rights therein, discharges the security interest under which it is made and any security interest or lien subordinate thereto. The purchaser takes free of all such rights and interests even though the secured party fails to comply with the requirements of this Part or of any judicial proceedings

(a) in the case of a public sale, if the purchaser has no knowledge of any defects in the sale and if he does not buy in collusion with the secured party, other bidders or the person conducting the sale; or

(b) in any other case, if the purchaser acts in good faith.

(5) A person who is liable to a secured party under a guaranty, indorsement, repurchase agreement or the like and who receives a transfer of collateral from the secured party or is subrogated to his rights has thereafter the rights and duties of the secured party. Such a transfer of collateral is not a sale or disposition of the collateral under this Article.

Section 9—505. Compulsory Disposition of Collateral; Acceptance of the Collateral as Discharge of Obligation

(1) If the debtor has paid sixty per cent of the cash price in the case of a purchase money security interest in consumer goods or sixty per cent of the loan in the case of another security interest in consumer goods, and has not signed after default a statement renouncing or modifying his rights under this Part a secured party who has taken possession of collateral must dispose of it under Section 9—504 and if he fails to do so within ninety days after he takes possession the debtor at his option may recover in conversion or under Section 9—507(1) on secured party's liability.

(2) In any other case involving consumer goods or any other collateral a secured party in possession may, after default, propose to retain the collateral in satisfaction of the obligation. Written notice of such proposal shall be sent to the debtor if he has not signed after default a statement renouncing or modifying his rights under this subsection. In the case of consumer goods no other notice need be given. In other cases notice shall be sent to any other secured party from whom the secured party has received (before sending his notice to the debtor or before the debtor's renunciation of his rights) written notice of a claim of an interest in the collateral. If the secured party receives objection in writing from a person entitled to receive notification within twenty-one days after the notice was sent, the secured party must dispose of the collateral under Section 9—504. In the absence of such written objection the secured party may retain the collateral in satisfaction of the debtor's obligation.

Section 9—506. Debtor's Right to Redeem Collateral

At any time before the secured party has disposed of collateral or entered into a contract for its disposition under Section 9—504 or before the obligation has been discharged under Section 9—505(2) the debtor or any other secured party may unless otherwise agreed in writing after default redeem the collateral by tendering fulfillment of all obligations secured by the collateral as well as the expenses reasonably incurred by the secured party in retaking, holding and preparing the collateral for disposition, in arranging for the sale, and to the extent provided in the agreement and not prohibited by law, his reasonable attorneys' fees and legal expenses.

Section 9—507. Secured Party's Liability for Failure to Comply With This Part

(1) If it is established that the secured party is not proceeding in accordance with the provisions of this Part disposition may be ordered or restrained on appropriate terms and conditions. If the disposition has occurred the debtor or any person entitled to notification or whose security interest has been made known to the secured party prior to the disposition has a right to recover from the secured party any loss caused by a failure to comply with the provisions of this Part. If the collateral is consumer goods, the debtor has a right to recover in any event an amount not less than the credit service charge plus ten per cent of the principal amount of the debt or the time price differential plus 10 per cent of the cash price.

(2) The fact that a better price could have been obtained by a sale at a different time or in a different method from that selected by the secured party is not of itself sufficient to establish that the sale was not made in a commercially reasonable manner. If the secured party either sells the collateral in the usual manner in any recognized market therefor or if he sells at the price current in such market at the time of his sale or if he has otherwise sold in conformity with reasonable commercial practices among dealers in the type of property sold he has sold in a commercially reasonable manner. The principles stated in the two preceding sentences with respect to sales also apply as may be appropriate to other types of disposition. A disposition which has been approved in any judicial proceeding or by any bona fide creditors' committee or representative of creditors shall conclusively be deemed to be commercially reasonable, but this sentence does not indicate that any such approval must be obtained in any case nor does it indicate that any disposition not so approved is not commercially reasonable.

[Articles 10 and 11 are omitted as unnecessary.]

Appendix F
Excerpts from the United States Constitution, As Amended

Article I

Section 1.
All legislative Powers herein granted shall be vested in a Congress of the United States, which shall consist of a Senate and House of Representatives.

Section 8.
The Congress shall have Power: . . .

To borrow money on the credit of the United States;

To regulate Commerce with foreign Nations, and among the several States, and with the Indian Tribes;

To establish an uniform Rule of Naturalization, and uniform Laws on the subject of Bankruptcies throughout the United States;

To coin Money, regulate the Value thereof, and of foreign Coin, and fix the Standard of Weights and Measures;

To provide for the Punishment of counterfeiting the Securities and current Coin of the United States;

To establish Post Offices and post Roads;

To promote the Progress of Science and useful Arts, by securing for limited Times to Authors and Inventors the exclusive Right to their respective Writings and Discoveries;

To constitute Tribunals inferior to the supreme Court; . . .

To make all Laws which shall be necessary and proper for carrying into Execution the foregoing Powers, and all other Powers vested by this Constitution in the Government of the United States, or in any Department or Officer therof.

Article II

Section 1.
The executive Power shall be vested in a President of the United States of America. . . .

Article III

Section 1.
The judicial Power of the United States, shall be vested in one supreme Court, and in such inferior Courts as the Congress may from time to time ordain and establish. . . .

Section 2.
The judicial Power shall extend to all Cases, in Law and Equity, arising under this Constitution, the Laws of the United States, and Treaties made, or which shall be made, under their Authority;—to all Cases affecting Ambassadors, other public Ministers and Consuls;—to all Cases of admiralty and maritime Jurisdiction;—to Controversies to which the United States shall be a Party;—to Controversies between two or more States;—between a State and Citizens of another State;—between Citizens of different States;—between Citizens of the same State claiming Lands under Grants of different States, and between a State, or the Citizens thereof, and foreign States, Citizens or Subjects.

In all Cases affecting Ambassadors, other public Ministers and Consuls, and those in which a State shall be Party, the supreme Court shall have original Jurisdiction. In all the other Cases before mentioned, the supreme Court shall have appellate Jurisdiction, both as to Law and Fact, with such Exceptions, and under such Regulations as the Congress shall make.

The trial of all Crimes, except in Cases of Impeachment, shall be by Jury; and such Trial shall be held in the State where the said Crimes shall have been committed; but when not committed within any State, the Trial shall be at such Place or Places as the Congress may by Law have directed.

Article IV

Section 1.
Full Faith and Credit shall be given in each State to the public Acts, Records, and judicial Proceedings of every other State. . . .

Section 2.
The Citizens of each State shall be entitled to all Privileges and Immunities of Citizens of the several States. . . .

Amendments

(The first 10 Amendments, ratified December 15, 1791, are known as the "Bill of Rights.")

I. Congress shall make no law respecting an establishment of religion, or prohibiting the free exercise thereof; or abridging the freedom of speech, or of the press; or the right of the people peaceably to assemble, and to petition the Government for a redress of grievances.

IV. The right of the people to be secure in their persons, houses, papers, and effects, against unreasonable searches and seizures, shall not be violated, and no Warrants shall issue, but upon probable cause, supported by Oath or affirmation, and particularly describing the place to be searched, and the persons or things to be seized.

V. No person shall be held to answer for a capital, or otherwise infamous crime, unless on a presentment or indictment of a Grand Jury, except in cases arising in the land or naval forces, or in the Militia, when in actual service in time of War or public danger; nor shall any person be subject for the same offense to be twice put in jeopardy of life or limb; nor shall be compelled in any criminal case to be a witness against himself, nor be deprived of life, liberty, or property, without due process of law; nor shall private property be taken for public use, without just compensation.

VI. In all criminal prosecutions, the accused shall enjoy the right to a speedy and public trial, by an impartial jury of the State and district wherein the crime shall have been committed, which district shall have been previously ascertained by law, and to be informed of the nature and cause of the accusation; to be confronted with the witnesses against him; to have compulsory process for obtaining witnesses in his favor, and to have the Assistance of Counsel for his defence.

VIII. Excessive bail shall not be required, nor excessive fines imposed, nor cruel and unusual punishments inflicted.

X. The powers not delegated to the United States by the Constitution, nor prohibited by it to the States, are reserved to the States respectively, or to the people.

XIV. (Ratified July 9, 1868.)

Section 1.

All persons born or naturalized in the United States, and subject to the jurisdiction thereof, are citizens of the United States and of the State wherein they reside. No State shall make or enforce any law which shall abridge the privileges or immunities of citizens of the United States; nor shall any State deprive any person of life, liberty, or property, without due process of law; nor deny to any person within its jurisdiction the equal protection of the laws.

XVI. (Ratified February 3, 1913.)

The Congress shall have power to lay and collect taxes on incomes, from whatever source derived, without apportionment among the several States, and without regard to any census or enumeration.

Table of Cases

a

A & M Records, Inc. v. David L. Heilman, 838
ACLI International Commodity Services, Inc. v. Lindwall, 143
AFA Corporation v. Phoenix Closures, Inc., 310
Abramowitz v. Barnett Bank of West Orlando, 149
Accent Service Company, Inc. v. Ebsen, 102
Action Engineering v. Martin Marietta Aluminum, 170
Adams v. Lindsell, 257
Admiral Plastics Corp. v. Trueblood, Inc., 256
In re Adoption of Brousal, 147, 150
Aero Drapery of Ky., Inc. v. Engdahl, 689
Agricultural Insurance Co. v. Constantine, 223
Air Power, Inc. v. Omega Equipment Corp., 179
Air Products & Chemicals, Inc. v. Fairbanks Morse, Inc., 260
In re Albert A. Berges, 836
Aleci v. Virgie E. Tinsley's Enterprises, Inc., 127
Alfalfa Electric Co-op, Inc. v. The First National Bank & Trust Co. of Oklahoma City, 661
In re the Estate of Alfred v. Sipe, deceased, 211
Allen v. Houserman, 223
Allen v. Nicole, Inc., 321
Allen v. Southern Pacific Co., 233
George S. Allen d/b/a Allen's Garage v. Genevieve Small, 425
Allred v. Biegel, 222
Allway Taxi, Inc. v. The City of New York, 749
Alonso v. State of California, 137
Altman v. Altman, 606
Aluminum Co. of America v. Essex Group, Inc., 113
American Air Filter Company, Inc. v. McNichol, 197
American Card Co. v. H.M.H. Co., 446
American Financial Corporation v. Computer Sciences Corporation, 188
American Heritage Investment Corporation v. The Illinois National Bank of Springfield, *et al.*, 660
American Legal Aid, Inc. v. Legal Aid Services, Inc., 660
American Trust Co. v. Dixon, *et al.*, 822
In re Amex-Protein Development Corporation, 449, 451
Anderson v. Barnes, 79
Angelus v. Government Personnel Life Ins. Co., 487
Anglo-American Clothing Corporation v. Marjorie's of Tiburon, Inc. d/b/a Rebel Jeans, 527
Applestein v. United Board & Carton Corp., 645
Arizona v. Maricopa County Medical Society, *et al.*, 705
Arizona Governing Committee for Tax Deferred Annuity & Deferred Compensation Plans v. Natalie Norris, 553
Armory v. Delamire, 221
Arrow Builders Supply Corp. v. Royal National Bank, 419
In re Estate of Artha Mehus, 505
Atherton v. Anderson, 688
Augusta Bank & Trust v. Broomfield, 153
Aune, Becker, *et al.* v. United States, 13
Automotive Finance Co. v. Kesk, Inc., 509

b

Baarslag, Jr., *et al.* v. Hawkins, *et al.*, 816
Baehr v. Penn-O-Tex Oil Corporation, 124, 127
Baer v. Slater, 223
Bailes v. Bailes, 593
Bailey v. Kruithoff, 781
Bailey Employment Systems, Inc. v. Clifford Hahn, *et al.*, 622
Bank of Cabot v. Bledsoe, 178
Bankers Trust Company, *et al.* v. Chicago Title & Trust Company, 636
Bankers Trust Company of Western New York v. Robert F. Zecher, *et al*, 650
J. Baranello & Sons v. Hausman Industries, Inc., 270
Barboza, *et al.* v. Liberty Contractors Co., Inc., 156
Barnes v. Treece, 91
Baron & Company, Inc. v. The Bank of New Jersey, 148
Barr v. Wackman, 692
Barrett v. Freed, 223
Batson v. Kentucky, 24, A4
Baxter's Asphalt & Concrete Inc. v. Liberty County etc., 121
Beach Associates, Inc. v. Fauser, *et al.*, 147
Bennett Dairy v. Putney, 538
Bergen Pines County Hospital v. N.J. Dept. of Human Services, 721
In re Albert A. Berges, 836
In re Berry's Estate, 545
Beshada, *et al.* v. Johns-Manville Products Corporation, 55, 57, 64, 329
Bethlehem Steel Corporation v. Litton Industries, Inc., 271
Betz Laboratories, Inc. v. Hines, 157
Bicknell, Inc. v. John J. Havlin, 513
Bishop v. Allied Van Lines, Inc., 224
Bishop v. Ellsworth, 222, 224, 237
Richard Black aka Del Black and Mallot v. Frank Dahl, 522
Blaustein v. Burton, 89
Blockburger v. United States, 38
Bohonus v. Amerco, *et al.*, 586
Bole v. Lyle, *et al.*, 597
Bonebrake v. Cox, 243
Bonitz v. Travelers Insurance Company, 493
In the Matter of Borden, Inc., 712
Borders v. Roseburg, 787
Boroughs, *et al.* v. Leo Joiner, 540
Boulevard National Bank of Miami v. Air Metal Industries, Inc., 197
Bovy v. Graham, Cohen & Wampold, 611
Bowman v. American Home Assurance Company, 271
Bradley v. Fox, 214, 215
Roland and Ernesteen Bradley v. John M. Brabham Agency, Inc., 514
The Bremen v. Zapata Off-Shore Co., 854
Brennan v. Occupational Safety and Health Review Commission, 570
Briarcliff Communications Group, Inc. v. Associated Press, 636
Brinson v. Mill Supply Co., 653
In the Matter of Bristol-Myers Company, *et al.*, 712
Broida v. Hayashi, 793
Brooks, *et al.* v. Angelo's Cleaners, 91
Brousal, *In re* Adoption of, 147, 148, 150
Brown v. Board of Education, 12
Bruno v. Bruno, *et al.*, 114
In re Bubble Up Delaware, Inc., 198
Buckman v. Goldblatt, 593
Bukacek v. Pell City Farms, Inc., 643
Bunn v. Offutt, 766
Burk v. Emmick, 306
Burne v. Franklin Life Ins. Co., 149
Burns v. The State of Georgia, 40
Butterfield v. Forester, 51

T 1

c

Caban v. Mohammed, *et ux.*, 148
Cady v. Pitts, 109
Calvert Cliffs' Coordinating Committee, Inc. v. AEC, 747, 749
Cameron v. Terrell & Garrett, Inc., 539
Campbell v. Van Roekel, 56
Campbell v. Yokel, 249, 252
Edward A. Cantor v. Sunshine Greenery, Inc., 651
Capital Mortgage Corporation v. Michigan Basic Property Insurance Assoc., 484
Car Carrier's, Inc., *et al.* v. Ford, 711
Carlisle v. Fawcett Publications, Inc., 45
Carter v. United States, 35
Carver v. Gilbert, 763
Cassedy v. Connecticut Gen. Life Ins. Co., 504
Catania v. Brown, 311
Cenco Incorporated v. Seidman & Seidman, 536
Central Invest. Corp. of Denver v. Container Advertising Co., 103
Chanute Production Credit Ass'n. v. Wier Grain & Supply, Inc., 450
Charles Melbourne & Sons, Inc. v. Jesset, 138
Charles of the Ritz Distrib. Corp. v. FTC, 716
Chemical Bank v. Miller Yacht Sales, 455
Cherberg v. Peoples National Bank of Washington, 791, 794
Cherno v. Bank of Babylon, 456
Chevron Oil Company v. Sutton, 525, 527
Chicago Title Insurance Co. v. Renaissance Homes, Ltd., 150
Childs v. RIC Group, Inc., 149
Chrismer v. Chrismer, 370
Christensen v. McAtee, 432
Cicci v. Lincoln National Bank and Trust Co., 420
Cidis v. White, 132
Cintrone v. Hertz Truck Leasing & Rental Service, 242
Citizens National Bank of Quitman v. Carolyn Brazil, 407
Citizens State Bank v. Beermann Brothers, 431
Citizens State Bank v. Hewitt, 463
Citizens State Bank v. Timm, Schmidt & Co. and General Casualty Company of Wisconsin, 535
City of Los Angeles Department of Water and Power, *et al.* v. Manhart, *et al.*, 553
Clackamas County v. Holmes, 771
Clark v. DeLaval Separator Corp., 321
Clayton v. Communications Capital Corporation, 85, 178
Clinger v. Continental National Bank, *et al.*, 392
Clinkenbeard v. Central Southwest Oil Corporation, 549
In the Matter of The Coca-Cola Company, 712
Cohen v. Sabin, 127
Cole v. First National Bank of Gillette, 391
Colgate-Palmolive Co. v. FTC, 13
Colin v. Altman, 636

Collomb v. Wyatt, 473
Commercial Nursery Co. v. Ivey, 544
Commonwealth v. Doucette, 40
Commonwealth v. Hunt, 725
Commonwealth v. Robinson, 37
Commonwealth v. Yourawski, 41
Commonwealth Capital Investment Corporation v. McElmurry, 586
In re Conard, Debtor, 472, 496
Cone Oil Co. v. Green, 79
In re Conn, Debtor, 467
Connelly v. Uniroyal, Inc., *et al.*, 868
Consiglio v. Carey, 770
Consolidated Freightways v. The Industrial Commission, 431
Continental Bank v. Blethen, 198
Continental Bank & Trust Company v. Country Club Mobile Estates, Ltd., 505
Continental Ore Co. v. Union Carbide & Carbon Corp., 857
Conway v. Samet, 643
Cook v. Loftus, *et al.*, 816
Copperweld Steel Company v. DeMag-Mannesmann-Bohler, *et al.*, 869
Corbin Deposit Bank v. King, 463
E. A. Coronis Assocs. v. M. Gordon Constr. Co., 123
Countryside Casualty Co. v. Orr, 481
Courtney v. Bishop, 137
Cox v. Kelley, 782
Cramer v. General Telephone & Electronics Corporation, 688
Crosby v. Paul Hardeman, Inc., 84
Cross v. The Midtown Club, Inc., *et al.*, 660

d

Dalton v. Bundy, as Guardian, 133, 202
D'Andrea v. Feinberg, 371
Danning v. Daylin, Inc., 281
In re Darrell Elmer Gentry, Deceased, 815
Darsakilis, *et al.* v. Schildt, *et al.*, 164
Darvin v. Belmont Industries, Inc., 685
David v. Lose, 223
David Crystal, Inc., v. Ehrlich-Newmark Trucking Co., 227
Davis v. McDougall, 771
De Los Santos v. Great Western Sugar Co., 126
In re Dean Milk Company, 708, 754
In re Debs, 726
Delaney v. Fidelity Lease Limited, 622
Delmaro Associates v. New Jersey Engineering & Supply Co., 682
Demeri v. Morris, 56
Department of Transportation Federal Highway Administration v. Interstate Commerce Commission, 29
D'Ercole v. D'Ercole, 215
DeRosa v. Remington Arms Co., Inc., 337
DeVoe v. Cheatham, *et al.*, 145
Dewey v. A. R. Klaveness & Co., 50
Dillon v. Legg, 7

Dioguardi v. Durning, 28, 30
Dirks v. Securities and Exchange Commission, 678
Diversacon Industries, Inc. v. National Bank of Commerce of Mississippi, 638
Dodge v. Ford Motor Co., 667
Dolan v. New Orleans Public Service, Inc., 233
Donald J. Richardson, *et al.* v. Arizona Fuels Corporation, *et al.*, 672
Donoghue v. Stevenson, 10
Dorkin v. American Express Company, 534
Dorothy Simmons v. Parsons College, *et al.*, 831
Dorsey Bros., Inc. v. H. Anderson, 244
Dorton & Castle, d/b/a The Carpet Mart v. Collins & Aikman Corp., 269, 272
Dothard, Director, Department of Public Safety of Alabama v. Rawlinson, *et al.*, 554, 566
In re Drane, 450
Dunham v. Vaughan & Bushnell Mfg. Co., 327
J. C. Durick Insurance v. Andrus, 96

e

E. A. Coronis Assocs. v. M. Gordon Constr. Co., 123
Eastern Air Lines, Inc. v. Gulf Oil Corporation, 304, 307
Edward A. Cantor v. Sunshine Greenery, Inc., 651
Edward L. Mangan v. Joseph J. Mangan, Jr., *et al*, 804, 805
Eisenburg v. The Flying Tiger Line, Inc., 673
Eldredge v. Jensen, 793
Elias Saka v. Sahara-Nevada Corporation, 402
Elizabeth Kiljan, *et al.* v. Norman F. Hoover, 837
Elmergreen v. Horn, 54
Emerald Christmas Tree Company v. Bedortha, 186
In re Emma C. Lindberg, Deceased, 818
Emmenegger Construction Co., Inc. v. Frank King, *et al.*, 518
Empire Star Mines Co., Limited v. Butler, 760
Engbrecht v. Dairy Queen Co. of Mexico, Missouri, 711
English v. Dhane, 504
Environmental Defense Fund, Inc. v. Corps of Engineers of U.S. Army, 737
Equilease Corporation v. State Federal Savings and Loan Association, 183
Erie Railroad v. Tompkins, 29
Escola v. Coca Cola Bottling Co., 325, 327
Etterle v. Excelsior Insurance Company of New York, 483
In re Eugene Kraus, Deceased, 817
Everglades Sugar Refinery Inc. v. Raymond J. Donovan, Secretary of Labor, and Occupational Safety and Health Review Commission, 560
In re Excel Stores, Inc., 450
The Executive Council of the Protestant Episcopal Church in the Diocese of Delaware, Inc. v. Robert A. Moss, *et al.*, 836
Exxon Chemical Americas v. Kennedy, 463

f

F.H.T. Inc., v. James S. Bailey, et al., 683

FJS Electronics, Inc. v. The Fidelity Bank, 411

Falls Church Bank v. Wesley Heights Realty, Inc., 407

Famous Music Corp., et al. v. Bay State Harness Horse Racing and Breeding Association, Inc., 514

Faraca v. Clements, 143

Fargo Machine & Tool Co. v. Kearney & Trecker Corp., 293

Farmers Mutual Ins. Co. v. New Holland Turnpike Road Co., 480

Feather v. Mine Workers, 732

Fedders Corp. v. Federal Trade Commission, 331

Federal Insurance Co. v. Waldorf-Astoria Hotel, 232, 233

Federal Trade Commission v. Colgate-Palmolive Co., 707

Feingold v. Davis, 602

Feldman Construction Co., v. Union Bank, 392

Fenus v. Scheweiker, Secy. of Health & Human Services, 722

Ferguson v. Jeanes, 114

In re Fibre Glass Boat Corporation, 450

Fidelity Financial Services, Inc. v. McCoy, 137

Fiege v. Boehm, 117

Fielding Home for Funerals, as Assignee for the Life Insurance Policy of Debra Green, v. Public Savings Life Insurance Company, 514

Fireman's Fund Insurance Company v. Security Pacific National Bank, 410

Fireside Chrysler-Plymouth, Mazda, Inc. v. Edgar, Secretary of State, 149

1st American Systems, Inc. v. Rezatto, 149

First National Bank of Gwinnett v. Gerald Barrett, 414

First National Bank of Ottawa v. Larkins, 149

Fitzsimmons v. State Bar of California, 17

Harold Floyd, The Aetna Casualty & Surety Company v. Jay County Rural Electric Membership Corporation, 513

Flynn v. Reaves, 607

Fontainebleau Hotel Corp. v. Forty-Five Twenty-Five, Inc., 749

Ford v. Wisconsin Real Estate Examining Board, 527

Fort Smith Gas Co. v. Cloud, 48

Fortugno v. Hudson Manure Company, 599

Fortune Furn. Mfg. Co., Inc. v. Mid-South Plastic Fabric Co., 159

Fox v. Morris, 371

Framingham Savings Bank v. Joseph Szabo, Trustee, 648, 651

Francis v. Bartlett, 549

Francis, et al., v. United Jersey Bank, 691, 694, 699

Frank A. Principe, et al. v. McDonald's Corporation, 620, 623

Franklin Life Insurance Company v. Winney, 97

In re Frank's Will, 837

Fraver v. North Carolina Farm Bureau Mutual Insurance Company, 80

Frazier v. Northeast Mississippi Shopping Center, Inc., 170

Free For All Missionary Baptist Church, Inc. v. Southeastern Beverage & Ice Equipment Company, Inc., 657

Freeland C. Thorson v. Carl Bellamy, 622

Friend v. Childs Dining Hall Co., 56

Frost v. Mohawk National Bank, 462

g

Galleon Industries, Inc. v. Lewyn Machinery Co., Inc., 463

Garcia v. Freeland Realty, Inc., 793

Gaskin v. Stumm Handel Gmbh, 869

Gastonia Personnel Corporation v. Rogers, 136, 138

Gates Rubber Company v. USM Corporation, 302

George E. Failing Co. v. Cardwell Investment Co., 463

George S. Allen d/b/a Allen's Garage v. Genevieve Small, 425

Gerald Resnik v. Anderson and Miles, 503

Gerald T. Olivet, et al. v. Frederick Frischling, et al., 608

Gillespie v. Papale, 146

In re Estate of Gilliland, 137

Gillis v. Whitley's Discount Auto Sales, Inc., 137

Gimbel v. Signal Companies, Inc. 693

Glander v. Glander, 781

Glover v. National Bank of Commerce of Pine Bluff, 432

Warren Golden v. Oahe Enterprises, Inc., 649

Goldenberg v. Bartell Broadcasting Corporation, 658, 661

Gordon Supply Co. v. South Sea Apts., Inc., 371

In re Graham, Debtor, 495

Granite Equipment Leasing Corp. v. Hempstead Bank, 419

Ex parte Granite State Insurance Company v. Lowe, 484

Graulich Caterer, Inc. v. Hans Holterbosch, Inc., 278

Great American Music Machine, Inc. v. Mid-South Record Pressing Company, 296

Green v. American Tobacco Company, 318, 321

Gregory J. Walsh v. Ellingson Agency and Four Seasons Motor Inn, 593

Griggs et al. v. Duke Power Co., 569

Groh v. Shelton, 509

Gross Valentino Printing Co. v. Clarke, 251

Guaranty State Bank of St. Paul v. Lindquist, 182

Guest v. Stone, 215

Gulf Coast State Bank v. Nelms, 456

Gulf Towing Co., Inc. v. Steam Tanker, Amoco, et al., N.Y., 118

Gus N. Jebeles v. Gus V. Costellos *and* Gus V. Costellos v. Gus N. Jebeles, 594

h

H. C. Blackwell Company, Inc. v. Kenworth Truck Company, 621

Hadley v. Baxendale, 296

Halbman, Jr. v. Lemke, 138

Hancock v. Rand, 233

Harold Floyd, The Aetna Casualty & Surety Company v. Jay County Rural Electric Membership Corporation, 513

Harris v. Stephens Wholesale Bldg. Supply Co., Inc., 651

Harris by Harris v. Easton Publishing Co., 56

Hartford Accident and Indemnity Company v. Connecticut Bank and Trust Company, 381

Hastoupis v. Gargas, Executor, 192

Hatleigh Corporation v. Lane Bryant, Inc., 668

Hawkins v. Anderson, 30

Head & Seemann, Inc. v. Gregg, 195

Healy v. New York Cent. & H. R. R., 223

J. Lake Hellams v. Pauline Ross, 813, 818, 842

Henningsen v. Bloomfield Motors, Inc. and Chrysler Corporation, 315

Henry George & Sons, Inc. v. Cooper-George, Inc., et al., 644

Hensley v. Government Employees Insurance Company, 490

Hertz v. Ficus, 78

Hewitt, et al. v. Hewitt, 81

Hewlett v. Schadel, 49

Hilgendorf v. Mervin and Joan Hague, 527

Hill v. Oland, 172

Hill v. Thomas, 164

Hinojosa v. Castellow Chevrolet Oldsmobile, Inc. and G.M.A.C., 186

Hodge v. Garrett, Voeller, et al., 601

Hodgson v. Cactus Craft of Arizona, 569

Holcomb State Bank v. Adamson, 428

In the Matter of Horton, Bankrupt, 473

Horton, Davis & McCaleb v. Richard Howe, Ex'r of the Estate of Earl E. Howe, 593

Husky Industries, Inc. v. Craig Industries, Inc. and D. C. Craig, 530

i

Industrial National Bank of R.I. v. Leo's Used Car Exchange, Inc., 396

International Salt Co., Inc. v. United States, 706

IOTA Alumnae, Inc. v. Cornell University, 137

Isaacs M. D. v. Huntington Memorial Hospital, 56

ITT World Communications, Inc., et al., v. Western Union Telegraph Company, 857

Ivey's Plumbing & Electric Company, Inc. v. Petrochem Maintenance, Inc., 102

j

J. Baranello & Sons v. Hausman Industries, Inc., 270

J. C. Durick Insurance v. Andrus, 96

J. C. Schwartzman, *et al.* v. Schwartzman Packing Company, 669
J. Lake Hellams v. Pauline Ross, 813, 818, 842
Jackson v. Goodman, 525
Jackson v. Steinberg, 223
Nathan Jacobson v. Martin Stern, Jr., 650
Jadallah v. District of Columbia Dept. of Employment, 721
James Arvel Ralls, *et al.* v. Martin Mittlesteadt, *et al.,* 538
James Clark, d/b/a Jim's Service Center v. Mobil Oil Corporation, 618
Gus N. Jebeles v. Gus V. Costellos *and* Gus V. Costellos v. Gus N. Jebeles, 594
Jenkins v. Ray E. Friedman & Company, 474
Jessee v. Smith, 125
Jett v. Doe, 493
Joc Oil U.S.A., Inc. v. Consolidated Edison of New York, 286
John A. Pierson v. Gail Jones, 632
John F. Tills, Sr, *et al.*, v. United Parts, Inc., *et al.,* 682
John Massey, Thomas J. Downey, *et al.* v. Tube Art Display, Inc., 539
John W. Whittlesey v. Union Carbide Corporation, 556
Johnson v. Mobil Oil Corporation, 83, 86, 114
Jones v. Dressel, 133
Jones v. Star Credit Corporation, 75
In re Joseph McCready, Deceased, 816

k

K & K Manufacturing, Ind. and Knight v. Union Bank, 417, 420, 436
In re K. L. Smith Enterprises, Ltd., Debtor, 451
Kahn v. American Cone & Pretzel Co., 673
Karell v. West and Shobert, 779, 798
Katamay v. Chicago Transit Authority, 231
In re Katherine Jane Wiest McCrea, Deceased, 811
Kaufman v. Penn. R.R., 229
Keiswetter v. Rubenstein, 616
In re Kelley's Estate, 817
Kelly v. General Motors Corp., 337
Kelly v. United States Steel Corporation and The Thew Shovel Company, 509
Kelsey-Seybold Clinic v. Maclay, 610, 612
Kemp Motor Sales, Inc. v. Statham, 406
Kendrick v. Davis, 781
Kennedy Electric Co. v. Moore-Handley, Inc., 84
Kenneth J. Nelson and Homer Sharpe v. Mary Kring, 837
Kett v. Graeser, 152
Keyes v. Dyer, 463
Khabbaz v. Swartz, 197
Kiely v. St. Germain, 162, 165
Elizabeth Kiljan, *et al.* v. Norman F. Hoover, 837
Kinney v. Ewing, 215

Klor's Inc. v. Broadway-Hale Stores, Inc., 705
Knack v. Industrial Commission of Arizona, 84
Knudson v. Weeks, 504
Koenig v. Huber, 611
Kraaz v. La Quinta Motor Inns, Inc., 233
In re Eugene Kraus, Deceased, 817

l

Laclede Gas Company v. Amoco Oil Company, 126
Lamb v. Goring, 849
Matter of Landmark at Plaza Park Limited, 474
Larry R. Williams v. Natkin & Company, *et al.,* 533
Larsen v. General Motors Corporation, 325
Laval v. Leopold, 218
Leahy v. McManus, 370
Leeson v. Etchison, 85
Lefkowitz v. Great Minneapolis Surplus Store, Inc., 102
In re Leichter, 447
Lemay, *et al.* v. Rouse, *et al.,* 179
Lemle v. Breeden, 792
Lennis K. Rentz and Danny Rentz v. Myrtis R. Polk, 836
Estate of Leo G. Saathoff, 215
Leo Womack, Administrator, v. First National Bank of San Augustine, Texas, 600, 602
Leone v. Precision Plumbing and Heating of Southern Arizona, 125
Lewittes Furniture Enterprises, Inc. v. Bankers Trust of Suffolk, 391
Libertarian Party of Indiana v. Packard, 27
Liebe v. Battmann, 215
Limouze v. M. M. & P. Maritime Advancement, Training, Education and Safety Program, 616
Lincoln Income Life Ins. Co. v. Parker, 493
In re Emma C. Lindberg, Deceased, 818
Linton & Company, Inc. v. Robert Reid Engineers, Inc., 637
Lipin v. Salkin, 836
Lipschutz v. Gordon Jewelry Corp., 251
Local 12, International Union of Operating Engineers, AFL-CIO and Cal Tram Rebuilders, Inc., 733
Lockard v. City of Los Angeles, 769
Logan County Bank v. Taylor, 131
Loizeaux Builders Supply Co. v. Donald B. Ludwig Co., 261
Mary Long, Executrix v. Andrea C. Schull, *et al.,* 544
Loomis Land & Cattle Company v. Diversified Mortgage Investors, 623
Lopez v. Winchell's Donut House, 45
Loretto v. Teleprompter Manhattan CATV Corp., *et al.,* 767, 798
Louisville Gas and Electric Company v. Employer's Mutual Liability Insurance Co., 493
Lucas v. Constantini, 85

Lula Nannie Ella Reed and Fannie Reed Simmons v. Mary Shipp, *et al.,* 805, 842
Lynch Business Machines Inc. v. A. B. Dick Company, 711

mc

McBrearty v. United States Taxpayers Union, 141
McBride v. City of McCook, 158, 202
McDonald v. Verble, 100, 103
McDonnell Douglas Corp. v. Islamic Republic of Iran, 171
McIntosh v. Magna Systems, Inc., 193
McLaughlin v. Chicken Delight, Inc., 512, 515
McNeill v. Maryland Insurance Guaranty Association, 493
MacPherson v. Buick Motor Company, 6, 54, 323

m

M. A. Sherrill, Trustee of the William W. Sherrill Trust v. Bruce Advertising, Inc., *et al.,* 539
M.I.F. Securities Company v. R. C. Stamm & Co., 623
Maas v. Scoboda, 277
Mackowiak v. University Nuclear Systems, Inc., 720, 722
Maddox v. Maddox, 164
Madison National Bank v. Newrath, 611
Mahrenholz v. County Board of School Trustees of Lawrence County, 770
Malin v. Nuss, 179
Manasquan Savings and Loan Assn. v. Mayer, 134
The Manes Organization, Inc. v. Standing Dyeing and Finishing Co., 250
Manning v. Metal Stamping Corporation, 163
Marbury v. Madison, 29
Marguerite J. Witmer, *et al.* v. Jane A. Blair, 826
Marine Midland Trust Co. of Rochester v. Blackburn, 407
Marshall v. Marshall, 773
Marshall v. Sam Dell's Dodge Corp., 569
Marsili v. Pacific Gas & Electric Company, 660
Marvil Properties v. Fripp Island Development Corp., 594
Marvin v. Marvin, 78
Mary Long, Executrix v. Andrea C. Schull, *et al.,* 544
Maryland Supreme Corporation v. Blake Co., 99
Massachusetts Mutual Life Insurance Company v. Tate, 482
John Massey, Thomas J. Downey, *et al.* v. Tube Art Display, Inc., 539
Maszewski v. Piskadlo, 126
Matherson, *et al.* v. Marchello, *et al.,* 13
Matsushita Electric Industrial Co. Ltd., *et al.,* v. Zenith Radio Corporation, *et al.,* 709

Matthews v. Aluminum Acceptance Corp., 405, 407
In re Mazzola, Debtors, 469
In re Estate of Artha Mehus, 505
Charles Melbourne & Sons, Inc. v. Jesset, 138
Melton v. Mire, 511
In re Meyers, 833, 838
Michigan National Bank, Lansing v. City of Lansing, 761
Miller v. City Bank and Trust Company, 593
Miller v. Dictaphone Corporation, 93
Minonk State Bank v. Grassman, 213
Minton v. Cavaney, 633
Miotk v. Rudy, 519
Missouri v. Hunter, 38
Missouri Pacific R.R. v. Elmore & Stahl, 227
Mitchell v. Shepherd Mall State Bank, 450
Mitchell-Huntley Cotton Co., Inc. v. Waldrep, 297
Monroe v. Funeral Directors and Embalmers Examining Board, 722
Montgomery, *et al.*, v. Blankenship, *et al.*, 816
Montreal Trading Ltd. v. Amex, Inc., *et al.*, 869
Moon Over the Mountain Ltd. v. Marine Midland Bank, 353
Moore v. Clines, 371
Morales v. Lee, 56
Morin Building Products, Co., Inc. v. Volk Construction, Inc., 287
Moschelle v. Hulse, 113
Mott Grain Company v. First National Bank & Trust Co. of Bismark, 397
Mubi v. Broomfield, 550
Mullaney v. Wilbur, 15
Munchak Corporation v. Cunningham, 196, 198
Mund v. English, 164
Murphy v. Hanlon, 688
Murray v. Montgomery Ward Life Insurance Company, 484
Myerberg, Sawyer & Rue, P. A., *et al.* v. Agee, 198

n

Nader v. General Motors Corporation, 46
Nakhleh v. Chemical Construction Corporation, *et al.*, 869
Nathan Jacobson v. Martin Stern, Jr., 650
National Acceptance Company of America v. Pintura Corporation, *et al.*, 693
National Bank of Canada v. Interbank Card Association, 858
National Bank of Rochester v. Meadowbrook Heights, Inc., 137
National Cable Television Ass'n, Inc. v. United States, 721
National Cash Register Company v. Firestone & Co., Inc., 444
National Compressor Corporation v. Carrow and McGee, 263
National Heater Company, Inc. v. Corrigan Company Mechanical Contractors, Inc., 286, 288

National Organization for Women, Essex County Chapter v. Little League Baseball, Inc., 660
National Shawmut Bank of Boston v. Jones, 463
The Natural Kitchen, Inc. v. American Transworld Corporation, 160
Neal-Cooper Grain Co. v. Texas Gulf Sulphur Co., 288
Neel v. Indiana University Board of Trustees, 8
Neely Enterprises, Inc. v. American National Bank of Huntsville, 389, 392
Kenneth J. Nelson and Homer Sharpe v. Mary Kring, 837
Nevada State Bank v. Fischer, 432
New House Products, Inc. v. Commercial Plastics and Supply Corp., 431
New Jersey Mortgage and Investment Corp. v. Andrew and Anna Berenyi, 406
New York Life Insurance Co. v. Baum, 483
New York Telephone Company and Communication Workers, Local 1108, AFL-CIO, 732, 733
Newell v. High Lawn Memorial Park Co., 119
In re Newman, Debtor, 474
Newport News Shipbuilding and Drydock Company v. EEOC, 553
In re Nicolosi, 448
Nikki Cordet v. Robert Christopher Company, 513
Nix v. Tooele County, 781
NLRB v. Allis-Chalmers Mfg. Co., 733
NLRB v. Cities Service Oil Co., 718
NLRB v. General Electric Company, 729
NLRB v. International Rice Milling Co., 728
NLRB v. Jones & Laughlin Steel Corp., 727
NLRB v. Yeshiva University, 731, 733
North River Insurance Company v. Poos, 493
Northern Pipeline Construction Company v. Marathon Pipe Line Company, 465
Northshore Bank v. Palmer, 419
Nusbaum v. Saffell, 163

o

Oceanic Exploration Company v. Jack J. Grynberg, *et al.*, 666
Ochoa v. Rogers, 210
Gerald T. Olivet, *et al.* v. Frederick Frischling, *et al.*, 608
The Omaha National Bank v. Goddard Realty, Inc., 126
Oregon State Bar v. Gilchrist, 17
Orr v. New Orleans Public Service, Inc., 233
Oswald v. Leckey, 601
Owens v. Clow Corporation, 295

p

Pacific Photocopy v. Canon U.S.A., Inc., 103
Palsgraf v. Long Island R. Co., 12
Pan American World Airways, Inc. v. Continental National Bank of Miami, 385, 387
Panama Refining Co. v. Ryan, 716

Parker v. Arthur Murray, Inc., 178
Parker v. Lamb, 780, 782
Parkin v. Fitzgerald, 793
Parliament Industries Inc. v. William H. Vaughan & Co., 167
Parrish v. Richards, 769, 771
Paskvan v. Mesich, 130
Pastimes Publishing Co. v. Advertising Displays, 282
Patient Care Services, S.C. v. Segal, 693
Vance Payne v. J. T. Payne, Jr., 808
Pena v. Salinas, 493
People of the State of Illinois v. General Electric Company, 739
People of the State of New York v. Babits, 40
People of the State of New York v. Butler, 40
Perkins v. Stein, *et al.*, 44
Perry v. West, 371
Pestana v. Karinol Corporation, *et al.*, 264
Peterson v. Platt, 794
Philipp Brothers, Division of Englehard Minerals & Chemicals Corp. v. El Salto, S.A., 248, 341
Phoenix Savings and Loan, Inc. v. Aetna Casualty & Surety Co., 501
Phyllis Ann Thropp v. Bache Halsey Stuart Shields, Incorporated, 510
Picture Lake Campground, Inc. v. Holiday Inns, Inc., 618
John A. Pierson v. Gail Jones, 632
Pirkey v. Hospital Corporation of America, 853, 874
Plymouth Rock Fuel Corp. v. Leucadia, Inc., 164
Polikoff v. Levy, 621
Prah v. Maretti, 744
Premier Electrical Constr. Co. v. Miller-Davis Company, 86
The Premonstratensian Fathers v. Badger Mutual Insurance Co., 215
Frank A. Principe, *et al.* v. McDonald's Corporation, 620, 623
Pritchard v. Wilson, *et al.*, 49
Pritsker, *et al.* v. Brudnoy, *et al.*, 12
The Proctor & Gamble Company v. City of Chicago, 740
Public Administration of the County of New York v. Royal Bank of Canada and Royal Bank of Canada (France), 868
Pulprint Inc. v. Louisiana-Pacific Corporation, 103
Purex Corp. v. Teamsters Local 733

q

Quintel Corporation v. Citibank, N.A., 520

r

R.A.S., Inc. v. Crowley, 84
R. R. Waites Co., Inc. v. E. H. Thrift Air Conditioning, Inc., 299
Raffles v. Wichelhaus, 113

James Arvel Ralls, *et al.* v. Martin Mittlesteadt, *et al.,* 538

Ramirez v. Autosport, 176

In the Matter of Sam Ramos, Debtor, 474

Ranieri, *et al.* v. Terzano, *et al.,* 364

Rappaport v. International Playtex Corporation, 526

Rederscheid v. Comprecare, Inc., 56

Reed v. Bunger, 511

Reese v. Gas Engineering and Construction Company, 570

Regents of the University of California v. Alan Bakke, 12

Regina v. Dudley and Stephens, 11, 13

Reifsnyder v. Pittsburgh Outdoor Advertising Co., 673

Reiman v. Moore, 793

Reisman v. Martori, Meyer, Hendricks & Victor, an Arizona Professional Association, 629

Lennis K. Rentz and Danny Rentz v. Myrtis R. Polk, 836

Gerald Resnik v. Anderson and Miles, 503

Rex v. Esop, 12

Rice v. Jackson, 596

Richard Black aka Del Black and Mallot v. Frank Dahl, 522

Richardson v. Clarke, 623

Donald J. Richardson, *et al.* v. Arizona Fuels Corporation, *et al.,* 672

Rio Grande City Ry. Co. v. Guerra, 233

Riviello v. Waldron and Raybele Tavern, Inc., 537, 540

Roberts v. Buske, 103

Rock Island Auction Sales, Inc. v. Empire Packing Co., Inc., 420

Roland and Ernesteen Bradley v. John M. Brabham Agency, Inc., 514

Roto-Lith Ltd. v. F. P. Bartlett & Co., 271

In re Rowe, Debtor, 471

Royal Business Machines, Inc. v. Lorraine Corp., 310

Rumple v. Bloomington Hospital, 114

Rusch Factors, Inc. v. Levin, 535

Rushing, King and Kenney v. Garrett, Jr., 526

Rylands v. Fletcher, 52

s

S. & L. Painting Contractors, Inc. v. J.D. Victors, *et al.,* 637

In the Estate of Leo G. Saathoff, 215

Sabates M.D. v. International Medical Centers, Inc., 29

Elias Saka v. Sahara-Nevada Corporation, 402

Salinas Lettuce Farmers Cooperative v. Larry Ober Co. Inc., 291

In the Matter of Sam Ramos, Debtor, 474

Sambo's Restaurants, Inc. v. City of Ann Arbor, 114

Santa Fe, P. & P. Ry. Co. v. Grant Bros. Const. Co., 233

Sarokhan v. Fair Lawn Memorial Hospital, Inc., 548, 550

Schaneman v. Schaneman, 110

Schemel v. General Motors Corporation, 337

Schlenz v. John Deere Company, 319

Scholl v. Tallman, 426

J. C. Schwartzman, *et al.* v. Schwartzman Packing Company, 669

Scott v. The University of Delaware, 569

Seattle–First National Bank as Executor v. Burt W. Marshall, *et al.,* 589

Secor v. Pioneer Foundry Co., Inc., 480

Securities and Exchange Commission v. Glenn W. Turner Enterprises, Inc., 680, 683

Security Pacific National Bank v. Associated Motor Sales, 432

Security State Bank of Aitken v. Morlock, 184

Sedmak III v. Charlie's Chevrolet, Inc., 159

Sellers v. West-Ark Construction Co., 163

In the Matter of Sheldon Silverberg, and Ruben Schwartz, 611

Sherman County Bank v. Kallhoff, 463

M. A. Sherrill, Trustee of the William W. Sherrill Trust v. Bruce Advertising, Inc., *et al.,* 539

Shick v. United States, 32

Shields v. Gross, 131

Siegel v. Chicken Delight, Inc., 710, 712

Sierra Club v. Ruckelshaus, 748

Sierra Pacific Industries v. Joseph H. Carter, 514

Dorothy Simmons v. Parsons College, *et al.,* 831

Singer Company v. Stoda Corporation, 224

In re the Estate of Alfred V. Sipe, Deceased, 211

Skoglund v. Ormand Industries, Inc., 683

Sligo Furnace Co. v. Hobart-Lee Tie Co., 215

Smalich v. Westfall, 503

Smith v. County of Washington, 767

Smith v. Kelley, 584

Smith v. Morgan, 650

Snedeker v. Warring, 208

Snyder v. Freeman, 190

Snyder Electric Co. v. Robert J. Fleming, 692

Sommer v. Kridel, 786

Songbird Jet Ltd., Inc., v. Amax, Inc., 251

South County Sand & Gravel Co. v. Bituminous Pavers Co., 450

South Terminal Corp. v. EPA, 743

Southeast Consultants, Inc. v. McCrary Engineering Corp., 694

Southeast First National Bank of Satellite Beach v. Atlantic Telec, Inc., 419

Southland Mower Co. v. Consumer Product Safety Commission, 335, 338

Spray-Rite Service Corp. v. Monsanto Co., 711

St. Germain v. Boshouwers, 165

Stacks v. F. & S. Petroleum Co., Inc., 95

Standard Oil Co. v. FTC, 709

Standard Oil Company of New Jersey v. United States, 29

Stanley Smith & Sons v. Limestone College, 75

Star Provision Company v. Sears, Roebuck & Company, 406

Starr v. International Reality Ltd., 612

State of Iowa v. Clark, 33

State of Maryland v. Strickland, 85

State of Missouri v. Baker, 12

State of Missouri v. Walker, 41

State of Nevada v. Boueri, 38

State of Nevada v. Taylor, 719

State of South Dakota v. DeWall, 40

State of Tennessee v. Freeman, 8

Matter of Estate of Steffes, 148

Stein, Hinkle, Dawe & Associates, Inc., 106

Steward v. Torrey, 215

Stewart v. Board of Education of Ritenour Consolidated School District, 193

Strain v. Green, 215

Strawn Furniture Company, Inc. v. L. K. Austin, 142

Stroh v. Blackhawk Holding Corp., 681

Strother v. Morrison Cafeteria, *et al.,* 558, 573

Sullivan v. Economic Research Properties, 92

Sun Valley Express Moving and Storage, Inc. v. Arizona Department of Economic Security, 721

Sunshine v. Manos, 543

Susser v. Carvel Corporation, 617

t

T.L.C. Lines, Inc. and Machinists District No. 9, AFL-CIO, 733

T. M. Cobb Co., Inc. v. Superior Court of Marin County, 102

T.S.J. v. State of Florida, 40

Taca International Airlines v. Rolls-Royce of England, Ltd., 850

Taft v. Sweeney, 492, 493

Tankersley v. Albright, 673

Tappan Motors, Inc. v. Volvo of America Corporation, *et al.,* 621

Tate v. Rice, *et al.,* 56

Tatum v. Richter, 198

Taylor & Martin, Inc. v. Hiland Dairy, Inc., 189

Temple v. Velcro USA, Inc., 338

Temple Lumber Co. v. Miller, 656

Tepper v. Citizens Federal Savings and Loan Association, 355, 368, 371

Terry v. Atlantic Richfield Co., 175

Terry v. Puget Sound National Bank, 392

Textron, Inc. v. Froelich, 102

Thomas v. Anderson, 771

Thomas E. Waldrop and Sharlyn Waldrop v. George W. Holland, Sr., 611

Thompson v. Beth, 604

Freeland C. Thorson v. Carl Bellamy, 622

Phyllis Ann Thropp v. Bache Halsey Stuart Shields, Incorporated, 510

Thurber v. Jack Reilly's Inc., 143

Tidwell v. Critz, 105

John E. Tills, Sr., *et al.* v. United Parts, Inc., *et al.,* 682

Title & Trust Company of Florida v. Barrows, 484

In the Matter of Tobin, Jr., Bankrupt, 473

Tonka Corp. v. Commissioner of Taxation, 502

Total Automation, Inc. v. Illinois National Bank & Trust Co. of Rockford, 657

Town & Country Bank of Springfield v. Country Mutual Insurance Co., 197

Tracy v. Vinton Motors, Inc., 251

Transatlantic Financing Corp. v. United States, 171, 177, 179

Travelers Insurance Co. v. Delta Air Lines, Inc., 232

Travelodge International Inc. v. Eastern Inns, Inc., 113

Trustees of Dartmouth College v. Woodward, 501

Tucker d/b/a Consolidation Sales Co. v. Colorado Indoor Trap Shoot, Inc., 650

Turntables, Inc. v. Gestetner, 281

Tusso v. Security National Bank, 419

u

United Brands Co. and United Brands Continental B.V., Applicants v. Commission of the European Communities, Defendant, 870

United States v. Bridgeman, 125

United States v. Causby, 759

United States v. Eastman Kodak Co., *et al.,* 870

United States v. Giovengo, 36

United States v. Gorham, 113

United States v. Hemmen, 474

United States v. McBride, 119

United States v. Park, 39, 41

United States v. Unum, Inc., 430, 432

United States v. Wegematic Corporation, 284

United States of America v. Healthwin-Midtown Convalescent Hospital and Rehabilitation Center, Inc. and Israel Zide, 635, 638

United States of America v. Mercedes-Benz of North America, Inc., 706, 864, 870

United States Trust Company of New York v. McSweeney III, 179

United Steel Workers of America, Local No. 1330, *et al.* v. U.S. Steel Corp., 96

United Steelworkers of America, *et al.,* v. Weber, *et al.,* 555

Upton v. Hall, 132

In re U.S. Rubber Co., *et al.,* 712

v

Valley Bank & Trust Company v. Zions First National Bank, 386

Vance Payne v. J. T. Payne, Jr., 808

Vaughn v. American National Insurance Company, 483, 484

Vernon v. Provident Life & Accident Ins. Co., 486

Vierra v. Fifth Avenue Rental Service, 52

Vigil v. Lamm, A1

Village of Belle Terre v. Boraas, 743

The Village Press, Inc., v. Stephen Edward Company, Inc., *et al.,* 636

Vincenzi, *et al.* v. Cerro, *et al.,* 178

The Vista Fund v. Gordon O. Garis, *et al.,* 682

Vogel v. American Warranty Home Service Corp., 121

Vokes v. Arthur Murray, Inc., and J. P. Davenport, 81

Volvo of America Corp. v. Wells, 109

w

Wagner v. Hall, 539

R. R. Waites Co., Inc. v. E. H. Thrift Air Conditioning, Inc., 299

Thomas E. Waldrop and Sharlyn Waldrop v. George W. Holland, Sr., 611

Walker Bank and Trust Co. v. Burrows, 462

Gregory J. Walsh v. Ellingson Agency and Four Seasons Motor Inn, 593

Want v. Century Supply Company, 543

Ward v. American Mutual Liability Insurance Co., 179

Warren Golden v. Oahe Enterprises, Inc., 649

Waters v. Glasheen, 169

Watertown Federal Savings & Loan Association v. Spanks, 391

Weaver v. American Oil Company, 144

Weaver v. J.C. Penney Company, 90

Weeser v. Provident Mutual Life Ins. Co., 484

Weiss Medical Complex, Ltd. v. Sun C. Kim, M.D., *et al.,* 687

In re Wells' Will, 591, 594

West Bros. Inc. v. Resource Management Serv. Inc., 233

Westerly Hospital v. Higgins, 391

Western States Mutual Insurance Company v. Verucchi, 493

Westervelt v. Gateway Financial Services, *et. al.,* 399

Whipp v. Iverson, 108

White v. General Motors Corporation, 197

John W. Whittlesey v. Union Carbide Corporation, 556

Estate of Wilhelmina Friedman, 550

Wilkes v. Springside Nursing Home, Inc., 682

Willard Van Dyke Productions v. Eastman Kodak Co., 220

Wille v. Southwestern Bell Telephone Company, 112, 114

Willet v. Miller, 782

William Inglis & Sons Baking Co., 709

Williams v. Montana National Bank of Bozeman, 407

Larry R. Williams v. Natkin & Company, *et al.,* 533

Williams v. Walker-Thomas Furniture Company, 320

Willig v. Rapaport, *et al.,* 110

Marguerite J. Witmer, *et al.,* v. Jane A. Blair, 826

Leo Womack v. First National Bank of San Augustine, 600, 602

Wood v. Holiday Inns, Inc., 526

y

Yacht Club v. Utah Liquor Control Commission, 722

Youse v. Employers Fire Ins. Co., Boston, Mass., 489

z

Zagoria v. DuBose Enterprises, Inc., 631

Zaid v. Island House Condominium Association, 141

Zimmerman Ford, Inc. v. Cheney, 117

Glossary of Legal Terms and Definitions

a

ab initio from the beginning

abandoned property discarded goods in which the owner has voluntarily relinquished all interest

abstract of title a record of the history of the title to land as found in official records

abuse of civil legal process to make excessive and improper use of the right to sue in an attempt to exhaust someone into submission

acceptance the offeree's expressed assent to the offer in reliance on and in compliance with the offer

acceptor the drawee on a draft who has assented in writing on the draft to pay it

accession the increase in property by what it produces or by the addition of other property to it

accommodation party a person who signs commercial paper as an accommodation to another person whose signature is on the instrument for the purpose of assisting the latter to obtain credit

accord a new contract which provides that, on its performance, a previous contract as well as the new contract are discharged

accord and satisfaction a new contract (accord) which discharges a party from a previous contractual obligation; the old contract is discharged (satisfied)

account "any right to payment for goods sold or leased or for services rendered which is not evidenced by an instrument or chattel paper, whether or not it has been earned by performance" UCC 9–106

account stated an account which has been settled and the matured items and balance expressly or impliedly agreed to by the parties

accretion a method of obtaining title to another's land caused by gradual changes in the natural boundaries of such land

acknowledgement the formal written declaration, admission, or confirmation made by a person to a proper public official (usually a notary public) that he executed a particular legal instrument

act of God an unexpected force of nature

action a judicial proceeding concerning legal interests

actual authority express and implied authority

ad litem during the action

adhesion contract a standard form contract in which the weaker party has no realistic choice or opportunity to bargain

adjudicate to determine by judicial authority

administrative law rules and regulations created by an administrative agency, thereby becoming law

administrator (administratrix) a court-appointed man (woman) as an intestate's personal representative

administrator (administratrix) with the will annexed a court-appointed man (woman), who was not designated in a decedent's will, as the decedent's personal representative

adverse possession a method of acquiring title to land by actual, exclusive, and continuous possession of land under color of title adverse or hostile to the true owner in an open and notorious manner for a statutory period of time

affidavit the formal written statement of a person voluntarily confirmed by oath or affirmation before a public official with authority to administer oaths or affirmations (usually a notary public)

after-acquired property (in security) property acquired after the security agreement is made

agency a legal relationship between two persons who agree that one is to act on behalf of the other, subject to the other's control

agent a person authorized to act on behalf of another and subject to the other's control

agreement a manifestation of mutual assent between parties by offer and acceptance

air space, right to ownership of the air space above the surface of land

amicus curaie friend of the court

annuity an insurance policy that pays the insured a designated amount periodically, beginning at a date set in the policy

anticipatory breach a party's material breach of contract made by his repudiation before his performance is due

anticipatory repudiation a party's manifestation of an intent not to perform his contractual obligation, made before his performance is due; *see* **repudiation**

antitrust laws laws that limit monopolies, combinations, and unfair restraints to help prevent the undue concentration of economic power

apparent authority the power of a person (A) to act as though he were an agent, created by another's (P's) manifestation to a third person (T) that A is P's agent

appellant a party who appeals a case decision against him

appellee (respondent) a party against whom an appeal is taken

apprentice a student learning a particular craft

arbitration a method for deciding disputes outside of court by persons called arbitrators, appointed by the disputing parties

arson the willful and malicious burning of the dwelling house of another (at common law); today, by statute, arson includes one's own insured house and the buildings of another

articles of incorporation the written application to the state for permission to incorporate

artisan's lien a person's possessory lien on goods owned by another and improved at the owner's request

assault an unprivileged act by a person intentionally causing another to apprehend an immediate harmful or offensive bodily contact to the other

assignee the person to whom a contract right is transferred; (in realty) the person to whom *all* the remaining term of a lease is transferred

assignment the transfer of a contract right; (in realty) a transfer by the lessee of *all* the remaining term of the lease

assignor the transferor of a contract right; (in realty) one who transfers *all* the remaining term of the lease

assumption of risk voluntarily assuming a known risk of harm

G 1

attachment the seizure of tangible property by a proper public officer (usually a sheriff) pursuant to a writ of attachment pending an action

attempt (in criminal law) a preparatory crime

attest to witness

attractive nuisance a dangerous and attractive condition of realty which may lure children into trespassing

auction a public sale of property by public outcry to the highest bidder

auctioneer a person licensed by law to sell property of another at a public sale

authority an agent's power to act for the principal in accordance with the principal's manifestation of consent to the agent; *see* **actual authority, apparent authority, customary authority, express authority, implied authority, incidental authority**

avoid to void, annul

b

bad faith dishonesty in fact in the conduct or transaction concerned

bailee the person to whom goods are bailed

bailee's lien the bailee's legal right to retain possession of the bailed goods as security for the obligation owing to the bailee, usually payment for the bailee's services and for materials supplied to the bailed goods

bailment a delivery of goods by a bailor to a bailee which are to be returned to the bailor or as the bailor directs in accordance with the bailment agreement

bailor the person who bails goods

bankruptcy a federal procedure whereby a debtor's nonexempt assets are gathered together and used to discharge the debtor from most of his debts

bargaining unit a group of employees appropriately joined together for the purpose of collective bargaining

battery an act by a person intentionally causing harmful or offensive bodily contact with another

bearer the person in possession of an instrument, document of title, or certificated security payable or deliverable to bearer or indorsed in blank (a signature without additional words)

beneficiary a person who is to receive a benefit; (in insurance) the person designated in a life insurance policy to receive the death benefit

bid an offer; unless otherwise specifically indicated an auction is "with reserve," the auctioneer reserving the right to accept or reject any bid and a bid is an *offer;* while in an auction "without reserve" the auctioneer does not reserve such right and a bid is an *acceptance* of the auctioneer's offer to sell—in both auctions a bid may be withdrawn until the auctioneer announces completion of the sale

bilateral contract a contract in which the consideration is mutual promises

bill of lading a document issued to the shipper by a carrier of goods

bill of sale a formal document used to transfer title to personal property

binder an insurance company's memorandum of an oral contract of insurance pending the issuance of a formal policy

blank indorsement an indorsement which does not specify any particular indorsee; *see* **indorsement**

blue-sky laws state laws regulating the sale and transfer of securities

bona fide in good faith

bona fide purchaser a purchaser for value in good faith and without notice of any adverse claim or defense with respect to what is being purchased; (in corporations) a purchaser for value in good faith and without notice of any adverse claim, and who is either a holder of a certificated security or registered on the corporate books as the owner

boycott the act of a combination of persons to cause business harm to another by refraining from doing business with that other and inducing others to do likewise; *see* **group boycott**

breach of contract wrongful nonperformance of a contractual promise

breach of the peace a disturbance of public order by an act of violence, or by an act likely to produce violence, or which, by causing consternation and alarm, disturbs the peace and quiet of the community

breach of trust a trustee's violation of a trust duty

broker a person authorized to represent another and negotiate for him with others

bulk transfer "any transfer in bulk and not in the ordinary course of the transferor's business of a major part of the materials, supplies, merchandise or other inventory of an enterprise subject to Article 6" UCC 6–102(1)

burglary the breaking and entering in the night of the structure (e.g., building) of another with the intent to commit a felony therein

buyer in ordinary course of business "a person who, in good faith and without knowledge that the sale to him is in violation of the ownership rights or security interest of a third party in the goods, buys in ordinary course from a person in the business of selling goods of that kind but does not include a pawnbroker;" buying does not include a transfer for a past debt UCC 1–201(9)

bylaws (in corporations) rules and regulations of a corporation for its internal management and operation

c

C. & F. cost plus freight

C.I.F. cost, insurance, freight

C.O.D. collect on delivery

cancellation the nullification of a contractual obligation

capital corporate net assets

capital stock *see* **stated capital**

cartel a combination of private enterprises or States to control production, price, or distribution of like commodities or services

case law the law that comes from decided cases

cashier's check a check drawn by a bank on itself and payable to the order of a payee

caveat emptor let the buyer beware

caveat venditor let the seller beware

certificate of deposit a written "acknowledgement by a bank of receipt of money with an engagement to repay it," and which is in compliance with the UCC as being a negotiable instrument UCC 3–104(2)(c)

certiorari, writ of an appellate court's certification to an inferior court that a case will be reviewed by the appellate court

cestui que trust the beneficiary of a trust

charitable trust a trust for a charitable purpose

charter articles of incorporation approved by the state

chattel a tangible, movable thing

check a negotiable "draft drawn on a bank payable on demand" UCC 3–104(2)(b)

chose in action intangible personal property, such as an account receivable

closed container rule a bailee is not responsible for the contents of a closed container unless the bailee knows or should know the contents

closed shop an employer who, by agreement with a union, will employ only union members

code a comprehensive, systematic collection of statutes in a particular legal area

codicil a writing executed with the same formality as a will, expressly referring to a prior will, by its terms either partially revoking or adding to the prior will by making changes or additions to the will and thereby becoming a supplemental part of the will to the extent of such changes or additions, or entirely revoking the prior will

collateral property subject to a security interest

collecting bank "any bank handling the item for collection except the payor bank" UCC 4–105(d)

commercial frustration an excuse offered by a party to a contract justifying nonperformance of an obligation, usually because performance has been made impossible in fact

commercial unit "such a unit of goods as by commercial usage is a single whole for purposes of sale and division of which materially impairs its character or value on the market or in use" UCC 2–105(6)

common carrier a carrier which offers its services to the general public for a fee

common law principles of nonstatutory law reflecting the customs and usages of society and found in judicial decisions

common stock corporate stock with the ordinary rights of participation in a corporation; *see* **share of stock**

community property a form of ownership by husband and wife of property acquired by their efforts during their marriage

compensatory damages the money judicially awarded to an injured party to compensate for damage caused by another's wrongful conduct; *see* **damages**

complaint the first pleading in a civil action

composition (outside of bankruptcy) an agreement among some or all of the creditors with their insolvent or financially embarrassed debtor, each to take something less than what is owed to him and, on the debtor's performance, the debtor is discharged fully as to those creditors who are parties to the agreement

compromise an agreement resolving a dispute outside of court reached through concessions offered by the aggrieved parties

condemnation forcing a property owner to transfer property to a government in exchange for just compensation

condition an uncertain event on the occurrence of which a contractual obligation is made contingent or dependent; *see* **condition concurrent, condition precedent,** and **condition subsequent**

condition concurrent a condition which must occur at the same time as another condition; *see* **condition**

condition precedent a condition which must occur or not occur before a dependent promise becomes performable; *see* **condition**

condition subsequent a condition, on the occurrence or nonoccurrence of which, after a promise becomes performable, excuses the duty of performance; *see* **condition**

conditional estate an estate where ownership is dependent upon some act or event

conditional receipt a receipt that provides an applicant for life insurance with temporary coverage until the application is approved by the company

conditional sale a sale in which the seller reserves title until the buyer completes payments; now called a secured transaction under Article 9 of the Uniform Commercial Code

confession of judgment a party's consent to jurisdiction and judgment of a court without a trial in a civil case

confirmation an assuring expression of understanding

confusion the mixing of chattels of like kind of different persons so that the chattels of one person cannot be distinguished from the chattels of the other persons

consent a person's approval of something, made with full capacity, freely, and without fraud or mistake; (in torts) such approval permitting what would otherwise be an intentional tort

consequential (special) damages the money judicially awarded to an injured party for loss which the breaching party reasonably could foresee would be a result of his breach; *see* **damages**

consideration the legal price bargained for a promise and inducing a party to enter into a contract

consignee one to whom goods are shipped

consignment the shipment of goods from one person to another

consignor one who ships goods to another

consolidation (in corporations) the combination of two or more corporations forming a new corporation

conspiracy (criminal) a combination of persons for the purpose of committing an unlawful act

constructive eviction a tenant's moving out of leased premises because the landlord caused the premises to become unfit for their intended use by the tenant

constructive notice knowledge of a fact presumed or imputed by law

consumer a person who buys goods for use primarily for personal, family, or household purposes

consumer goods goods which "are used or bought for use primarily for personal, family, or household purposes" UCC 9–109(1)

contingent claim a claim not certain of occurring, depending on a possible future event

contract a promise which the law recognizes as creating a legal obligation of performance; *see* **executed contract, executory contract, express contract, formal contract, implied contract,** and **simple contract**

contract to sell a contract to transfer title to goods in the future

contribution (in suretyship) the right of sureties who have paid the creditor to collect part of the payment from other sureties

contributory negligence plaintiff's conduct which falls below the standard to which he should conform for his own protection and which is a legally contributing cause with the defendant's negligence causing the plaintiff's harm; *see* **negligence**

conversion the tort of intentional interference with another's right to possession, control, and dominion of a chattel

conveyance the transfer of an interest in land

copyright a governmental grant of protection of original works in a tangible medium of expression

corporate express powers those powers specifically stated in the corporation's articles of incorporation and in the corporation statutes

corporate implied powers those powers reasonably necessary to carry out the express powers

corporation a legal entity created by statute authorizing an association of persons to carry on an enterprise

cost-plus contract a contract in which the price is the cost of production or performance (whatever it turns out to be) plus an agreed upon profit

costs (in litigation) allowable recoverable expense by a party in a legal proceeding

counterclaim a claim asserted by the defendant against the plaintiff's claim in a civil action

counteroffer an offer which rejects a previous offer

course of dealing "a sequence of previous conduct between the parties to a particular transaction which is fairly to be regarded as establishing a common basis of understanding for interpreting their expressions and other conduct" UCC 1–205(1)

Glossary of Legal Terms and Definitions G 3

course of performance "where the contract for sale involves repeated occasions for performance by either party with knowledge of the nature of the performance and opportunity for objection to it by the other, any course of performance accepted or acquiesed in without objection shall be relevant to determine the meaning of the agreement" UCC 2–208(1)

court a judicial tribunal

covenant a promise as a part of a contract

covenant running with the land the promise of an owner of land which binds future owners of the same land

cover to seek a substitute performance of a contract

creditor one to whom money is owed

creditors' committee (in bankruptcy) a committee elected by the creditors to advise the trustee in bankruptcy

crime an act, committed or omitted, in violation of a public law governing it; *see* **felony** and **misdemeanor**

cross-examination a party's initial examination of a witness other than his own in a trial

cumulative voting a method of voting whereby a shareholder has as many votes as he has shares of voting stock multiplied by the number of directors to be elected

cure a seller's correction of his failure to deliver conforming goods under a contract for sale before the due date has expired

custom *see* **usage of trade**

customary authority implied authority to do those acts that conform to the general custom or usage; *see* **authority**

cy pres an equitable trust doctrine applicable particularly in charitable trusts whereby, by court order, the general trust purpose will be carried out *as nearly as possible* in accordance with the settlor's intent when the particular trust purpose cannot be carried out

d

d/b/a/ doing business as

damage loss or harm

damages the money judicially awarded to an injured party for another's wrongful conduct; *see* **compensatory damages, consequential (special) damages, incidental damages, liquidated damages, nominal damages,** and **punitive (exemplary) damages**

de facto **corporation** a corporation which has not complied substantially with the mandatory requirements of a valid state incorporation statute but has made a colorable attempt to do so, in good faith, and has begun to operate as a corporation

de jure **corporation** a corporation which has completely or substantially complied with the mandatory requirements of a valid state incorporation statute

de novo anew; a trial de novo is a new trial

debtor one who owes money to another

decedent one who is dead

deceit the tort of knowingly misrepresenting a material fact, intending to mislead another person by inducing the other person to rely on the misrepresentation and to act in a particular business transaction, causing financial damage to the other person

deed a formal document used to transfer title to real estate

defamation a person's unprivileged, wrongful publication to a second person of a false and defamatory statement concerning a third person, harmful to the third person's reputation

default a failure to perform a legal duty

defendant the party against whom a civil suit (or criminal action) is brought

defined benefit plan a plan under which the employee contributes an annual payment to the plan based upon a benefit expected to be received upon retirement

defined contribution plan a plan under which the employer is required to contribute a specific amount annually to the plan for the employee's retirement

delegation the transfer of one's duty to another, the transferor still being responsible for the duty

delivery a voluntary transfer of possession; (in realty) the voluntary transfer of a deed with the intent thereby to transfer ownership of the realty

demise (in realty) to lease or rent; this word also may mean death

demurrer a pleading which states that a preceding pleading does not state a cause of action

dependent promise a promise the performance of which is dependent upon the occurrence of a condition

deposit rule an acceptance is effective when sent, though never received, if an authorized medium is used timely by the offeree

depositary bank "the first bank to which an item is transferred for collection even though it is also the payor bank" UCC 4–105(a)

deposition a written statement made by a person under oath or affirmation in a judicial proceeding where there is opportunity for cross-examination before trial

detriment the doing, or forbearing from doing, something by a party who had no previous obligation so to do or refrain from doing

devise a testamentary gift of real property

devisee the beneficiary of a testamentary gift of real property

dictum that portion of a judge's opinion in a case which is not necessary to the decision of the case

directed verdict a jury verdict as directed by the judge

disaffirm to nullify one's previous consent

discharge (in contracts) termination of a contractual duty to perform a promise; (under the UCC) cancellation and termination; (in bankruptcy) a court order releasing the individual debtor from his debts after the estate has been liquidated and distributed

disclaimer denial of an obligation or a claim

disclosed principal a person known, or who reasonably should be known, by a third party to be a principal for an agent

dishonor the refusal of the drawee to accept the draft, or of the drawee, acceptor, or maker to pay the draft or note

distributor an independent contractor who sells on his own account, independent of the seller of goods to him

dividend a portion of corporate net profits or surplus set aside for distribution to the shareholders

divisible contract a contract which provides that performance of less than all the obligations on one side will become due by performance of less than all the obligations on the other side

document of title a document evidencing that the person possessing it "is entitled to receive, hold and dispose of the document and the goods it covers" UCC 1–201(15)

documentary draft "any negotiable or non-negotiable draft with accompanying documents, securities or other papers to be delivered against honor of the draft" UCC 4–104(f)

domicile the state in which a person has his/her permanent home, not merely a residence

dominant tenement property which is benefited by an easement appurtenant in nearby land

donee the recipient of a gift

donor the person who makes a gift

dower (at common law but generally abolished by statute today) a widow's life estate in a portion of the land of her deceased husband

dowry traditionally, property that the wife brings to the marriage

draft a negotiable instrument containing an unconditional order—e.g., "pay"

drawee the person on whom a draft is drawn and ordered to pay

drawer the person who initially draws or creates and signs a draft

due negotiation delivery of a negotiable document of title to a holder who purchases it for value, in good faith, and without notice of any claim or defense to the document.

durable power of attorney a statutory written power of attorney that will not terminate upon the principal's incapacity

duress wrongful inducement to do that which a reasonable person would have been unable to resist

duty a legal obligation not to interfere with another person's interest

e

easement an irrevocable right to the limited use of another's land

eleemosynary charitable, benevolent

emancipated minor a minor whose parents have given up their rights to take care of the minor and to have custody of and to claim the minor's earnings

embezzlement depriving someone of his property through breach of a trust relationship

emblements what is sown and produced on the land

eminent domain government power to appropriate private land for public use on payment of just compensation without the owner's consent

encumbrance a person's right in another person's property

enforceable contract a contract which can be proved and enforced by the courts

enjoining an order from a court to desist from doing

equipment goods which "are used or bought for use primarily in business (including farming or a profession) . . ." UCC 9–109(2)

equitable estoppel a doctrine which operates to prevent a person from denying anything to the contrary of that which, by the person's own deeds, acts or representations, has been set forward as the truth

equity principles of justice and fairness which developed when the relief at common law was inadequate

escheat the transfer of property to the state when a person dies without heirs

escrow the conditional delivery of property to a person who is to deal with it on the occurrence of specified conditions

estate (in realty) a bundle of ownership rights in, or powers over, realty; (in bankruptcy) the debtor's legal or equitable interest in property on the date the case commences

estoppel a principle of law that when one person "holds out" (represents) a material fact to another person, who changes his position materially to his prejudice in reasonable reliance on the holding out, the first person is "estopped" (prohibited) to deny what he asserted previously

et al. abbreviation of a latin phrase meaning "and another" or "and others"

eviction the dispossession of a tenant from the leased premises

evidence a fact from which an inference may be drawn of another fact

exclusive dealing contract an agreement between a seller or lessor and a purchaser or lessee that the latter shall not use or deal in products of a competing seller or lessor

exculpatory clause a clause which relieves one from liability

executed contract a contract which has been performed by all the parties to it; *see* **contract**

executor (executrix) a court-appointed man (woman) designated in a decedent's will as the decedent's personal representative

executory contract a contract which has not been performed by all the parties to it; *see* **contract**

exemplary damages *see* **punitive damages**

exemption (in bankruptcy) a debtor's property that is not liquidated and not distributed to creditors in bankruptcy

express authority an agent's authority specifically expressed in the principal's manifestation to the agent; *see* **authority**

express contract a contract in which the promise or promises are expressly made; *see* **contract**

express trust a fiduciary relationship between persons in connection with property whereby one person called the "settlor" by his manifestation of intention causes property to be held by a person called the "trustee" for the benefit of a person called a "beneficiary" or "*cestui que trust,*" the trustee being under a duty so to deal with the property

express warranty a warranty expressed by a party; *see* **warranty**

expropriation the taking of an owner's property by the government

f

F.A.S. free alongside

F.O.B. free on board

factor a person in business for himself with authority to buy goods, or to sell goods in his possession, in his own name for another

false imprisonment (false arrest) an unprivileged act intentionally restraining the movement of another who is aware of such restraint

farm products "crops or livestock or supplies used or produced in farming operations . . . in the possession of a debtor engaged in . . . farming operations" UCC 9–109(3)

featherbedding make-work arrangements for employees when there is no work for them to perform or their services are not required

Federal District Court the *trial* level court of the federal legal system

Federal Trade Commission a government body that monitors unfair competition and commercial practices

fee simple absolute the greatest bundle of ownership rights in, and powers over, realty

felony a serious crime for which, usually, the punishment can be more than one year in prison; *see* **crime**

fiduciary a person with a duty to act primarily for the benefit of another

financing statement a document which is filed by the secured party to give public notice of the security interest in personal property

firm offer (UCC) a merchant's signed irrevocable offer to buy or sell goods, giving assurance that it will be kept open; consideration is not required, and its maximum time is three months

fixture a chattel which, under real estate law, has become permanently attached to realty and thus ceases to be a chattel and becomes part of the realty; it still can be used as collateral for a security interest

fixture filing filing a financing statement in the office where mortgages are recorded

floating lien a security device which covers after-acquired property and future advances

foreclosure the cutting off of an owner's interest in realty by sale pursuant to court decree

forfeiture to lose a legal right as a penalty

forgery the unauthorized act of imitating or altering a writing with the intent to defraud and impose liability

formal contract a contract which must be in a certain form; *see* **contract**

franchise a business relationship between a franchisor, who markets goods or services through a franchisee, who has the right to use the franchisor's trade name, trademark, and methods of operation

fraud (in contracts) a misrepresentation of fact, known to be false, intentionally made to induce another person to make or to refrain from making a contract, and reasonably relied on by the other person

freehold "an interest in land for a period of time the termination of which cannot be measured or computed exactly in terms of years, months, and days, and which is not terminable at the will of the transferor" Restatement of Property, sec. 8

fungible goods every unit of goods is the equivalent of any other like unit, either actually or by contract

future goods "goods which are not both existing and identified" to the contract UCC 2–105(2)

g

garnishee the person against whom a writ of garnishment is issued

garnishment a statutory proceeding begun by a judgment creditor to reach the intangible assets of the judgment debtor by writ of garnishment

general agent (universal agent) an agent authorized to conduct a series of transactions involving a continuity of service

general intangibles a catch-all category covering a variety of personal property

general lien a lien on property other than the property on which services were rendered; *see* **lien**

general partnership *see* **partnership**

genuineness of assent reality of consent to an offer or acceptance

gift a voluntary transfer of real or personal property by someone who is not to receive anything in return

gift causa mortis a conditional, revocable gift by someone facing imminent death from a present illness or impending peril

good faith "honesty in fact in the conduct or transaction concerned" UCC 1–201(19)

goods tangible, movable things

grand jury a group of people selected to decide whether to recommend criminal prosecution of specified persons for the commission of crimes

grant (in realty) a conveyance by deed

group boycott a concerted effort by a number of firms to avoid doing business with a particular individual or firm; *see* **boycott**

guarantee (noun) the person to whom a guaranty is made; (verb) to make a guaranty

guarantor a type of surety

guaranty a type of suretyship

guardian a person legally entrusted with the custody and/or the property of another

guardian ad litem guardian for the legal action, appointed by a court

h

habendum that portion of a deed which indicates the encumbrances burdening the estate

harm *see* **damage**

hearsay matter not personally known but heard from others

heirs persons who, by statute, are entitled to property not disposed of by a decedent's will

holder "a person who is in possession of a document of title or an instrument or a certificated investment security drawn, issued, or indorsed to him or his order or to bearer or in blank" UCC 1–201(20)

holder in due course the holder of a negotiable instrument who takes it for value, in good faith, and without notice that the instrument is overdue or has been dishonored or of any defense against, or claim to, the instrument by any person

holographic will a will which is entirely in the testator's handwriting

horizontal merger a merger of competing firms

hot cargo agreement an agreement between an employer and a union that the employer is not to handle or otherwise deal with goods of another employer

i

illegal contrary to law

immunity exemption from liability

implied authority an agent's authority which the agent reasonably can understand he has from his principal's manifestation to him, but not expressed therein; *see* **authority**

implied contract a contract in which the promise or promises are implied from conduct; *see* **contract**

implied warranty a warranty imposed by law; *see* **warranty**

impossibility performance cannot factually be done

impostor (**impersonator**) a person who misrepresents himself (herself) as another person

in personam against the person

in re in the matter of

in rem against the thing

incidental authority implied authority to do what is incidental in carrying out the express authority; *see* **authority**

incidental damages the money judicially awarded to a non-breaching party for expenses reasonably incurred by the non-breaching party on the other party's breach; *see* **damages**

incontestability clause a clause in a life insurance policy providing that the company may not contest coverage after the policy has been in effect for a stated time period

incorporators the persons who sign the articles of incorporation

indemnity an absolute obligation to pay for another's loss

independent contractor a person who contracts independently for himself to render a result, and who is not acting on behalf of another nor subject to another's control

independent promise a promise the performance of which is not dependent upon the occurrence of a condition

indorsee the person named by an indorser on an instrument to whom it is to be paid

indorsement the indorser's signature on an instrument (or on a paper attached to it); *see* **blank indorsement, qualified indorsement, restrictive indorsement, special indorsement**

indorser the person who signs on an instrument (or on a paper attached to it) other than as a maker, drawer, or acceptor

injunction a court order requiring a person to do or not to do something

injury the wrongful invasion of another person's interest

innkeeper operator of an establishment engaged in making lodging accommodations available to transients

insolvency (in bankruptcy) when the debtor's assets are less than his liabilities; when the debtor "either has ceased to pay his debts in the ordinary course of business or cannot pay his debts as they become due or is insolvent within the meaning of the federal bankruptcy law" UCC 1–201(23) and Restatement (Second) of Contracts, sec. 252(2)

installment contract "one which requires or authorizes the delivery of goods in separate lots to be separately accepted" UCC 2–612(1)

instrument a writing which evidences a right to payment of money, including negotiable instruments and also certificated securities

insurable interest (in insurance) an interest the insured has in the risk covered by the insurance contract; (in sales) a person's interest in goods which can be insured against loss

insurance a contract in which the insurer agrees to pay the insured for losses affecting the insured's interests

insured the person whose risk has been assumed by another (in the insurance contract)

insurer the person who assumes another's risk (in the insurance contract)

inter alia among other things or matters

inter vivos among living persons

interest a person's desire which has been legally recognized as dominant over a similar desire of another person

interlocutory order an intermediate court order pending a final decision

intermediary bank "any bank to which an item is transferred in course of collection except the depositary or payor bank" UCC 4–105(c)

interpleader an equitable remedy of a person who has some thing but does not claim any interest in it, requesting the court to decide who, as between two or more claimants, is entitled to the thing

interrogatory a written question

intestate (noun) a person who died without a will; (adjective) property not disposed of by a will

inventory goods which are held for sale or lease

ipso facto by the fact itself

j

joint liability (in contracts) occurs when parties together obligate themselves to perform the same promise

joint tenancy a form of ownership of property by more than one person with the right of survivorship

joint venture an association of two or more persons as co-owners to engage in a limited business transaction for a profit

journeyman a skilled craftsman

judge the government officer who presides over a court

judgment the final decision of a case by a court

jurisdiction the power of a court to hear and decide a case involving a person or subject matter properly brought before the court

juristic by law

jury (**trial**) a group of people selected to decide the facts in a trial; (**grand**) a group of people selected to decide whether to recommend criminal prosecution of specified persons for the commission of crimes

k

Keogh plan a pension plan for self-employed individuals

l

laissez-faire government's policy of not interfering with business

land a tangible, immovable thing

larceny the taking and carrying away of the personal property of another without the right to do so

lateral support the physical support for the land surface

law norms established by the official leaders of society; also those interests recognized and secured by society

law-government continuum a method of showing the numerous ways of constructing legal systems

law merchant a body of law which developed by the customs and usages of merchants and which later became part of the common law

lawyer a person who is licensed to practice law by advising and representing clients in legal matters

lease (of goods) a form of contract giving one person, the lessee, the exclusive right to use or possess the goods of another, the lessor, for a stated period; (of realty) a form of contract giving one person, the tenant (or lessee), the exclusive right to occupy for a period the realty of another, the landlord (or lessor)

leasehold estate the estate in realty owned by tenants

legacy a testamentary gift of personal property

legal in compliance with the law

legatee the beneficiary of a testamentary gift of personal property

lessee a person who contracts with the owner of property to pay rent for the right to use, possess, or occupy the property

lessor an owner of property who contracts with another giving the other the right to use, possess, or occupy the property in exchange for rent

letter of credit "an engagement by a bank or other person made at the request of a customer and of a kind within the scope of UCC 5–102 that the issuer will honor drafts or other demands for payment upon compliance with the conditions specified in the" letter of credit UCC 5–103(1)(a)

libel a defamatory publication in written or other permanent form

license permission to do something; (real property) a temporary, revocable right (privilege) to some limited use of another's land

lien a legal right in another's property as security for the performance of an obligation; *see* **general lien, possessory lien,** and **specific lien**

lien creditor a creditor with a judicial lien or a writ of execution

life estate an estate that lasts only for the length of a particular person's life

limited partnership a partnership of one or more general partners and one or more limited partners formed in compliance with the Uniform Limited Partnership Act; *see* **partnership**

liquidated claim a claim for an amount which is either certain, or ascertainable by mathematical calculation, or by operation of law

liquidated damages the money judicially awarded in the amount as agreed to by the parties in their contract at the time it was made as reasonable compensation for damage which may be caused by the wrongful conduct of one of the parties in the future; *see* **damages**

lis pendens a pending suit

listing an agency contract between a broker and a seller of realty

livery of seisin an ancient ceremony used to transfer ownership of land

locus in quo the place in which

lost property goods in a place where they were not put by the owner who does not know where they are

m

majority (in contracts) the legal age at which a minor becomes an adult; also, in voting, one more than half

maker the person who initially makes and signs a promissory note

marshaling of assets an equitable doctrine that, when there are two classes of creditors, one class having recourse to more than one asset while the other class has recourse to only some but not all of those assets, creditors of the first class are to resort first to those assets not available to other creditors and then to the other assets available to the other creditors

master a principal who has the right to control, or controls, the physical conduct of his servant agent

material alteration "any alteration of an instrument is material which changes the contract of any party thereto in any respect" UCC 3–407(1)

mechanic's lien a statutory lien on real property given to a person who, pursuant to contract, has rendered labor or services, or supplied materials for the improvement of the property and who has not been paid

mediation the process of using a third party to bring disputants closer to resolution of their differences

medium an agency, instrument, means, or channel

mens rea the mental element required for a crime

merchant "a person who deals in goods of the kind or otherwise by his occupation holds himself out as having knowledge or skill peculiar to the practices or goods involved in the transaction or to whom such knowledge or skill may be attributed by his employment of an agent or broker or other intermediary who by his occupation holds himself out as having such knowledge or skill" UCC 2–104(1)

merger (in corporations) the absorption of one corporation by another corporation

mineral right right to dig or mine the earth

minor a person who is under the age of full legal capacity

misdemeanor a crime for which the punishment is less than one year in prison and the possibility of a fine; *see* **crime**

misfeasance misdoing

mislaid property goods which the owner has voluntarily laid down and forgotten where they were laid

misrepresentation an assertion of what is not true

mistake believing a fact to exist when it does not exist, or believing a fact not to exist when it does exist

mortgage a security interest in realty; also the instrument which gives lenders the power to sell the mortgaged realty, to repay the debt, when the borrower defaults on the payments

mortgagee the person to whom a mortgage has been given

mortgagor the person who has given a mortgage

motion a procedural device asking the court to take some action

n

natural law an ideal or cosmic law

navigable water a body of water which can support commerce between states

negligence (conduct) failure to use the degree of care demanded by the circumstances; (the tort) negligent conduct proximately causing injury to another person's interest; *see* **contributory negligence**

negotiable document a document of title which states that the goods covered by the document are to be delivered to bearer or to the order of someone

negotiable instrument a writing signed by the maker or drawer containing an unconditional promise or order to pay a sum certain in money payable on demand or at a definite time to order or to bearer

negotiable promissory note a written unconditional promise to pay a sum certain in money, payable on demand or at a definite time, payable to order or to bearer, and signed by the maker

negotiate to deliver a negotiable instrument, or document, or a certificated security to a holder

negotiation the delivery of negotiable paper to a person who thereby becomes a holder

no arrival, no sale a term used by a seller when it is shipping goods and does not want to be liable if the goods do not arrive at their destination

nolo contendere no contest

nominal damages the money judicially awarded to an injured party when no damage has occurred from another's wrongful conduct; *see* **damages**

nonfeasance not doing

nonperformance no performance

nonsuit termination of a lawsuit without a finding on the merits of the case

nontrading partnership a partnership in the business of selling only services; *see* **partnership**

no-par stock corporate stock which is issued without any stated nominal price; *see* **share of stock**

norm a group's standard of behavior

notarize verification by a proper public official of the authenticity of a signature

notary public a public officer with the authority to administer oaths and affirmations and to attest and certify documents

novation a new contract in which one of the parties was not a party to the old contract and which immediately discharges the old contract

NOW account a negotiable order of withdrawal

nuisance a tort concerned with a person's conduct which is a wrongful interference with the interest of other persons in their private and public use and enjoyment of land

null/nullity of no legal effect

nuncupative will an oral will as permitted by statute

o

obligee the person to whom a legal obligation is owed

obligor the person who owes a legal obligation

offer a promise proposed in exchange for another's act, forbearance, or return promise

offeree the promisee to whom an offer is made

offeror the promisor making an offer

option the irrevocable offer in an option contract

ordinance municipal legislation

p

par value stock corporate stock which is issued for a stated certain minimum nominal price; *see* **share of stock**

paralegal an individual trained to assist lawyers in their practice

pari delicto equal in legal fault or guilt

parol oral

parol evidence oral testimony

parol evidence rule a rule of law which provides that, when there is a written contract, it cannot be contradicted (added to or varied) by any prior or contemporaneous oral agreement, or by a prior written agreement

parol lease a lease not reduced to writing

partial performance incomplete performance which is insufficient to accomplish, or which defeats, the main purpose of a contract

partially disclosed principal a person whose identity is not disclosed to a third person who knows, or reasonably should know, that an agent is, or may be acting as, an agent for that principal whoever it may be

partition a division of property between joint owners

partnership (general partnership) "an association of two or more persons to carry on as co-owners a business for profit" U.P.A. sec. 6; *see* **limited partnership, nontrading partnership,** and **trading partnership**

patent a governmental grant of protection of an invention

payee the person to whose order the instrument is originally written

payor bank "a bank by which an item is payable as drawn or accepted" UCC 4–105(b)

per capita "by heads"; all persons who stand in the same degree of relationship to the intestate share equally in the estate without consideration of any right of representation

per curiam by the court, all the judges

per se in and of itself

per stirpes "by stocks, or by roots"; the survivors of their parent represent their parent and take the parent's share in an intestate's estate by such representation for division among themselves

perfection of a security interest when the creditor complies with Article 9 of the Uniform Commercial Code's requirements for perfection

performance the fulfillment of a contractual obligation

perjury knowingly falsely swearing under oath, or affirming, in a judicial or quasi-judicial proceeding

perpetuities, rule against *see* **rule against perpetuities**

personal covenant a promise in a lease which does not touch and concern the realty

personal or **limited defense** (in negotiable instruments) a defense which is not to *contractual* liability on an instrument but, rather, is to *avoid* liability on an instrument; any defense which is not a real defense

personal property (personalty) a movable thing, along with interests and rights in the thing

personal representative a court-appointed person to represent a decedent and administer his/her estate

plaintiff the party who initiates a civil suit by filing a complaint in the proper court

pleadings the formal documents filed with a court that usually include the complaint, answer, and motions regarding them

pledge the possessory security interest in bailed goods acquired by the bailee when there is a bailment for the purpose of security

police power the power of a state or federal government to legislate reasonably for the general public welfare

possessory lien a lien which includes the right to possession of the property which is subject to the lien

power of attorney written authority by a principal to an agent

pre-emptive right a shareholder's right to subscribe to a newly authorized issue of stock proportionate to his holdings in the corporation

preference (in bankruptcy) a debtor's transfer of his property, made when insolvent and within ninety days before a petition in bankruptcy was filed, which gives a creditor preferential treatment

preferred stock corporate stock with a preference over the common stock; *see* **share of stock**

prescription (in real property) a method of obtaining the right to use of another's land as an easement by open and continuous possession and use of the land under a claim of right to such use for a statutory period of time

present sale a contract causing the immediate transfer of the title to goods for a price at the time the contract is made

presenting bank "any bank presenting an item except a payor bank" UCC 4–105(e)

presentment "a demand for acceptance or payment made upon the maker, acceptor, drawee or other payor by or on behalf of the holder" UCC 3–504(1)

price discrimination the practice of offering the same product to different competing customers at different prices

prima facie at first sight

primary parties parties (maker and acceptor) on a negotiable instrument who are absolutely liable for its payment according to the terms at the time they sign

principal (in agency) a person who has authorized an agent to act on his behalf and subject to his control; (in money) the capital sum of a money debt; (in suretyship) the debtor in a suretyship arrangement

priorities (in bankruptcy) claims that are paid first after the estate has been liquidated; (in realty) the order in which claims against realty are satisfied

private carrier a carrier which does not offer its services to the general public

privilege that which exempts a person from liability for his or her conduct which, but for the exemption, would subject the person to liability for such conduct

privileged communication a communication between certain persons which, because of their relationship, is inadmissible in evidence without a waiver of the privilege

privity a mutuality of relationship between persons or between persons and a particular transaction

privity of contract a legal relationship between two or more parties created by their contract

privity of estate a legal relationship between two or more parties flowing from their ownership or possession of the same realty

probate the procedure of proving to a proper court that an instrument is the will of a decedent

probate court a court which has jurisdiction over the estate of a deceased person

professional agent a professional, independent contractor employed as a special agent

promise an assurance or undertaking that something shall or shall not happen

promisee the person to whom a promise is made

promisor the person who makes a promise

promissory estoppel an equitable principle of preventing injustice by enforcing a gratuitous promise as a contract, without consideration and agreement, the promisor reasonably expecting that his promise would be justifiably relied upon substantially by the promisee

promissory note *see* **negotiable promissory note**

promoter a person who organizes and brings a corporation into existence

proof of claim (in bankruptcy) the claim filed by a creditor in a bankruptcy case

property a thing; also an interest or right in a thing; (in trusts) an interest or right in a thing; not the thing itself

property interest a legally recognized and protected right in property

proscribe to prohibit

protest (in negotiable instruments) a formal certificate, issued by a properly authorized person, certifying that a foreign or international draft was duly presented for acceptance or payment and that it was dishonored

proximate cause the cause of an injury without which the injury would not have occurred

proxy a shareholder's written authorization to another person to vote his shares at a corporate meeting; also the person with such authority

public policy the concept of law under which the freedom to act is limited for the good of the community

punitive (exemplary) damages the money judicially awarded to an injured party in excess of compensatory damages to punish for malicious, wanton, or intentional wrongful conduct; *see* **damages**

pure competition a market in which many firms compete and no one firm has very much power

pure monopoly a market in which there is a single firm with no competitors

q

qualified indorsement an indorsement which disclaims or qualifies the liability of the indorser on the instrument; *see* **indorsement**

quantum meruit an action for services rendered based on an implied promise to pay plaintiff as much as plaintiff reasonably deserved to have for the plaintiff's services

quasi as if

quasi contract as if a contract; a contract implied in law

question of fact a dispute over what happened

question of law a dispute over the legal effect of what happened

quiet title, action to a legal proceeding initiated by a claimant to title in land affording any adverse parties opportunity to prove a claim to interest in the land or thereafter be barred from doing so

quitclaim deed a document used in transferring the grantor's interest in realty, if any, without any warranties

quorum (in corporation) the number of persons necessary to be present, or shares necessary to be represented, at a meeting in order to transact business

r

ratification (in contracts) a person's waiver of his power of avoidance; (in agency) a person's manifested consent to be bound by another's previously unauthorized act made in his name and not binding on him

real or **universal defense** (in negotiable instruments) a defense to *contractual* liability on an instrument

real property (realty) land and immovable things attached to land, along with interests and rights in the land; also a freehold interest in land

receiver a person appointed by a court to receive, preserve, and manage property which is involved in litigation

recognizance an obligation acknowledged by a person in a court to do something (e.g., to appear in court at a later time), i.e., personal bond

recourse a right to resort to some one or thing

redemption the reclaiming of a foreclosed ownership interest in realty

reformation an action to correct a writing so as to reflect correctly the intentions of the parties which mistakenly were not properly expressed in the writing

reimbursement one person's right against another to be repaid money paid on the other's behalf for which the latter was responsible; (in suretyship) the surety's right to recover from the principal

rejection (in contracts) the offeree's expression refusing the offer; (in sales) the buyer's refusal to accept goods provided by the seller under a contract for sale

remainder that remaining part of an estate in land which, on the termination of a preceding estate, passes to someone other than the grantor

remainderman a person who was not a grantor of an estate in land but who will acquire the remainder of an estate after a preceding estate has terminated

remedy the means by which a right is enforced or protected

renunciation the abandonment of a right by a person

replevin a common law form of action to regain possession of specific chattels

representation (in insurance) a statement of fact made by the insured which is not a part of the insurance contract but, during negotiation, is made to induce formation of the contract

repudiation a party's manifestation of an intent not to perform his obligation; *see* **anticipatory repudiation**

res ipsa loquitur the thing speaks for itself

res judicata the thing has been adjudicated; the principle of law that, once a matter has been litigated and finally adjudicated, it should not be the subject of litigation again between the same parties

rescind cancel, annul

rescission cancellation

respondeat superior let the master (superior) be responsible for the torts of his servant committed while acting within the scope of his employment

respondent (appellee) a party against whom an appeal is taken

restitution a legal remedy restoring one to his original position prior to the particular transaction

restrictive indorsement an indorsement which determines the type of interest in the instrument being transferred; *see* **indorsement**

reversion a future interest which will, or may, be returned to the grantor. In contrast, a remainder goes to one other than the grantor.

revocation (in contracts) the offeror's recalling of the offeree's power to accept as contained in the offer

right a legal claim by the owner of an interest that others shall not interfere with his interest

right of survivorship a relationship among co-owners where death of one owner causes the decedent's interest to be transferred to the remaining owners

riparian relating to land abutting a body of water

robbery the taking of money or goods of value from the person of another or in his presence, against his will, by force or fear

rule against perpetuities the beneficiary of a trust, or a contingent future interest in realty, must be identifiable at the time the trust or contingent future interest is created or, in most states, within a period for the life of a person or persons in existence at the time the trust or contingent future interest is created and twenty-one years after the death of such person or persons

s

sale the transfer "of title from seller to purchaser for a price" UCC 2–106(1)

sanction a group's technique for controlling its members

satisfaction the discharge of an obligation by paying what is due

seal a symbol attached to a writing attesting that it is a legal document

secondary boycott the bringing of pressure by a union on a neutral party who will then pressure the employer with whom the union has a dispute

secondary parties (in negotiable instruments) parties on a negotiable instrument who are liable on the instrument only if certain conditions occur

secured party a creditor with a security interest

secured transaction a transaction used to create a security interest

security (in secured transactions) a creditor's interest in specific property, or in the obligation of a third person, as assurance for the performance of the debtor's obligation

security agreement an agreement which creates or provides for a security interest

security interest "an interest in personal property or fixtures which secures payment or performance of an obligation" UCC 1–201(37)

servant an agent whose physical conduct his master (principal) has the right to control or controls

service usually labor rendered by one person for another

servient tenement property in which someone has an easement appurtenant

settlor the person who has created an express trust

several liability (in contracts) occurs when the same performance is separately promised by each party

shareholder (stockholder) the owner of a unit of interest in a corporation

share of stock (stock) a unit of interest in a corporation; *see* **common stock, no-par stock, par value stock, preferred stock,** and **treasury stock**

shipper-carrier a legal relationship between the shipper and the common carrier when goods have been delivered to the carrier for immediate shipment

shop right an employer's free, nonexclusive, irrevocable, nonassignable license to use the invention or discovery of an employee who has used his employment time or the employer's facilities in connection with such invention or discovery

signed "includes any symbol executed or adopted by a party with the present intention to authenticate a writing" UCC 1–201(39)

simple contract a contract which need not be in any particular form; *see* **contract**

slander a defamatory publication by spoken words, gestures, or other nonpermanent form

social engineering using the law to bring about societal change

sole proprietorship a business owned and operated by one person

special agent "an agent authorized to conduct a single transaction or a series of transactions not involving continuity of service" Restatement (Second) of Agency, sec. 3

special damages see **consequential damages**

special indorsement an indorsement which specifies a particular indorsee; see **indorsement**

specific lien a lien on the specific property on which services were rendered; see **lien**

specific performance the exact performance of a contract by a party as ordered by a court

standard an established measure

stare decisis a principle of law which says that earlier cases which are similar should, if possible, be followed to decide current issues before the court

stated capital (capital stock) generally, the money received by a corporation from the issuance of its shares exclusive of what has been allocated to capital surplus

status quo the state of things at any given time

statute law created by a legislative body and approved by the executive

statute of frauds a statute requiring that certain kinds of contract be proved only by a proper writing

statute of limitations a statute limiting the time in which a claim may be asserted in court; expiration bars enforcement of the claim

statutory law bills passed by the legislature and signed into law by the president or governor

stay (noun) a halt

stock see **share of stock**

straight bill a non-negotiable bill of lading

strict liability absolute liability irrespective of the absence of negligence or fault

strict surety a co-debtor with the principal for the same obligation owing to the creditor

subagent the person appointed by an agent and as to whom the appointing agent is a principal

sublet a transfer by the lessee of a *part* of the remaining term of the lease

subpoena an order to appear before a judicial or proper administrative body for the purpose of giving testimony

subrogation the substitution of one person for another with reference to a claim or a right; (in suretyship) the surety succeeds to the creditor's rights against the principal

subsidiary corporation a corporation owned by another corporation

substantial performance incomplete performance which is sufficient to accomplish, and does not defeat, the main purpose of a contract

substantive law that part of the law which creates, defines, and regulates rights

summary judgment a judgment rendered on a motion by a party in a civil action that, solely on the basis of the pleadings, with affidavits, if any, there is no genuine issue as to any material fact and the moving party is entitled to judgment as a matter of law without the necessity of a trial on the facts

summons a writ or process served on the defendant in a civil action notifying him of the action and summoning him to appear and plead

surety a person who promises the creditor to pay the principal's debt or to perform his obligation on the principal's nonperformance

surety bond a promise by a professional surety to pay if the principal defaults or commits a wrongful act

suretyship a legal relationship in which one person (surety) and another person (principal, the debtor) are obligated to perform the same obligation to a third person (creditor) who is entitled to only one performance, and as between the surety and the principal the latter is to perform the obligation and is ultimately liable therefor

surface right the right to occupy the surface of a piece of land

survivorship, right of a relationship among co-owners where death of one owner causes his interest to be transferred to the remaining owners

t

technology a particular kind of property concerned with material things

tenancy a form of nonfreehold ownership in realty

tenancy by entirety a form of co-ownership between husband and wife with the right of survivorship

tenancy in common a form of ownership of property by more than one person without survivorship

tenant see **lease**

tender (verb) proffer, make available

tenor what is stated as meant

testamentary trust a trust created by the will of a decedent

testator (testatrix) a man (woman) who executes a will

title insurance insurance that covers the title to real estate

tort a civil (private) noncontractual wrong for which a court will give a remedy

tortfeasor a person who has committed a tort

trade fixture a chattel attached to leased realty by a business tenant; it is usually treated as personal property

trademark an identifying designation differentiating one's goods from those of another; "any word, name, symbol, or device, or any combination thereof, adopted and used by manufacturer or merchant to identify his goods and distinguish them from those manufactured by others" Lanham Act, sec. 5

trading partnership a partnership in the business of buying and selling property; see **partnership**

transfer (noun) a delivery of some thing

transferee one to whom another has transferred some thing

transferor one who has transferred some thing to another

treason a felony specifically defined by the U.S. Constitution

treasure trove found buried treasure

treasury stock corporate stock reacquired by the issuing corporation; see **share of stock**

trespass (verb) to wrongfully interfere with another's possession of land or chattels

trust a legal device whereby legal title to property is held by one person (a trustee) for the benefit of a beneficiary

trust deed a deed given to a trustee, in trust, with the power to sell the land on default of the secured obligation

trust property the property held in trust, sometimes called the "trust res"

trustee a person who holds title to property in trust for the benefit of someone; (in bankruptcy) the officer responsible for administering the debtor's estate; (in realty) the one who holds the trust deed for the benefit of the lender

tying arrangement an agreement between a seller or lessor and a purchaser or lessee that a sale or lease of a product to the latter is contingent upon the latter's purchase or lease of another product of the seller or lessor

u

ultra vires beyond the powers

unconscionable offends the conscience; immoderate, too one-sided

unconscionable contract a contract in which one of the parties is in too unequal or one-sided a bargaining position at the time the contract is made

undisclosed principal a person not known, or who is not reasonably known, to be a principal for an agent by a third party

undue influence unfair persuasion by one who, because of his relationship with another, dominates the other

unenforceable contract a contract which the courts will not enforce

unfair labor practices tactics by an employer or a union which are legally prohibited as unfair

Uniform Commercial Code a body of statutory law governing commercial transactions concerning personal property (movable things)

unilateral contract a contract in which the consideration for a promise is an act or a forbearance

union shop a shop or place of employment where the employer may hire non-union employees but after a short period of time, usually thirty days, the new employees must become members of the union or be discharged

universal agent *see* **general agent**

unjust enrichment a legal doctrine that prevents persons from profiting or enriching themselves inequitably at the expense of others

usage of trade "any practice or method of dealing having such regularity of observance in a place, vocation or trade as to justify an expectation that it will be observed with respect to the transaction in question" UCC 1–205(2); used synonymously with "custom"

usury charging a rate of interest on a loan higher than that permitted by statute

v

value (UCC) any consideration sufficient to support a contract, a commitment to extend credit, or a past debt

verdict a jury's finding of fact

vertical merger a merger between a firm and one of its major suppliers or customers

void of no legal effect

voidable contract a contract which can be avoided by one or more of the parties

voir dire the examination before trial of a prospective juror or witness in which he or she is to answer the questions truthfully

voting trust a trust created by an agreement between the shareholders to transfer legal title to their voting stock to a party (trustee) who is authorized to vote the stock as a unit

w

warehouse receipt a document issued to the bailor by a warehouseman

warehouseman a person in the business of storing goods for a fee

warranty an express or implied assurance that certain facts exist; (in insurance) a statement of fact or a promise made by the insured which is part of the insurance contract and which must be true if the insurer is to be liable on the contract; (in sales of goods) generally, an affirmation of fact or an express promise made by a seller or manufacturer of goods, or a promise implied in a sales transaction by law, that the goods sold are of a certain quality or will perform in a certain manner; *see* **express warranty** and **implied warranty**

warranty deed a deed conveying title and giving warranties to the grantee

water right a right to control of the water on the surface or under the ground

watered stock corporate stock reduced in value by the issuance of par value shares for less than their par value

will a formal document which governs the transfer of property at death

writ a court order

writ of execution a court order authorizing a sheriff or other proper legal officer to seize tangible property to satisfy a court judgment

writ of garnishment *see* **garnishment**

wrong the illegal invasion of another person's interest

y

yellow dog contract an agreement between an employer and employee that the employee will not be, nor continue to be, a member of a union

Index

Part titles are in boldface type for greater convenience in searching for subtitles.

a

Acceptance
    additional terms, 99
    banker's, 352
    communication of, 97–98
    confirmation as
        contracts, law of, 99
        UCC 2–207, 99
    in contracts, 95–97
    defined, 95
    deposit rule, 98, 257
    of goods, 292, 471
    between merchants, 99
    revocation of, 464–65
    silence as, 96
    trade, 351
    UCC 2–207, 258–61
    use as, 96
Acceptor
    defined, 351
    of a draft, 351
Accession, 209
Accommodation party, 357
Accord, 173
Accord and satisfaction
    defined, 120, 173
    discharge of contract by, 173
Account
    defined, 442
    receivable, 442
    stated, 120, 173
Accountant, status and liability, 534–5
Act of God, 226
Adequate assurance of performance, 280, 290, 298
Adhesion contract, 853
Administrative agencies. *See* Administrative Law
Administrative Law
    Administrative Procedures Act, 714
    agencies, administrative
        Federal Trade Commission, 403–4, 632, 707, 715–17, 859
        judicial review of decisions by, 718–19
        need for, 714–16
        powers of, 719
        procedures, 716–18
        as tribunals, 20
    defined, 25
    source of, 715
Administrator, 153, 810
Administratix, 810
Adverse possession, 779
Advertisement, 89
After-acquired property, 443, 454
Age Discrimination In Employment Act, 555

Agency
    agent
        auditor liability, 535
        authority to sign commercial paper, 360
        bankruptcy of, 545
        contractual capacity, 508
        death, 544
        defined, 92, 501
        duties to principal, 521–23
        as fiduciary, 502
        foreign, 848
        general, 509
        insanity, 544–45
        liability in contract, 529–30
        professional, 504, 630–31
        public accountant, 534–35
        registered, 642
        servant, 502–3, 532–33
        special, 509
        subagent, 520–21
        termination, 542–43
    authority, 360, 517
        apparent
            defined, 518
            termination, 546–47
        coupled with an interest, 546
        defined, 266, 517
        delegation, 520–21
        duty to determine by third party, 519
        express, 517, 596
        implied
            customary, 517, 585
            defined, 517
            incidental, 517
        irrevocable, 546
        limitation on, 519
        termination, 542–44
    corporation, 501
    creation, 509–11
    defined, 502, 503
    employment, 532
    independent contractor, 503, 849
    irrevocable, 546
    liability under, 532
    master/servant relationship, 502–3, 532–33
    nature, 501
    partnership, 502
    power of attorney, 505–8
    principal
        bankruptcy, 545
        business organizations as, 501
        contractual capacity, 508
        death, 544
        defined, 501
        disclosed, 531
        duties to agent, 523
        insanity, 544
        liability to agent in contract, 530–31
        liability to third persons
            in contract, 530–31
            in tort, 532–33
        master, 532

        partially disclosed, 530–31
        proof, burden of, 511
        ratification, 509–10
        renunciation, 543
        respondeat superior, 525, 533
        revocation, 542–43
        sole proprietor, 502
        termination
            by acts of the parties, 542–43
            notice of, 546–47
            by operation of law, 544–46
        undisclosed, 530–31
Agent. *See* Agency
Agreement
    defined, 73
    genuineness of assent, 105
    unconscionable, 82
    unenforceable, 81
    void, 80
    voidable, 81
Air space, 759
American Federation of Labor, 725
Anticipatory repudiation, 192
Antitrust Law
    cartel, 858
    Clayton Act, 705–7
        exclusive-dealing contracts, 706
        stock acquisitions, 706
        tying arrangements, 616, 706, 851, 865–67
    defined, 704
    European Common Market, 859–62
    Federal Trade Commission Act, 707
        as administrative judge, 20
        the Commission, 707–8
        definition, 707
        holder in due course doctrine, ruling on, 403–4
        powers of, 707, 719
        procedure, 707, 716–18
        purpose of, 707
    free competition vs. fair competition, 703–4
    laissez-faire, 703
    mergers, 645, 647, 706–7
    pure competition, 704
    pure monopoly, 704
    restraint of trade, 144–5, 705
    Robinson Patman Act, 708
    Sherman Antitrust Act, 704
        boycott, by a group, 705, 847n.4
        inapplicable to export trade, 850
        text, partial, 655, 705
        transnational business, 857
        violation, penalty, for, 705
Appellant, A6
Appellee, A6
Arbitration, 16, 174, 855
Arson, 35–36
Articles
    of incorporation, 641–42
    of partnership, 581

I 1

Assault, 44–45, 47
Assignment
  of accounts, 442
  assignee
    defined, 182
    priorities among successive assignees, 185
    rights, 182
  assignor, 182, 789
  of contract rights, 182, 183
  defined, 182
  of lease, 789
  negotiation distinguished, 347
  notice of, 183
  for purpose of security, 184
  UCC, 186
Assumption
  of risk, 51, 80
Attempt, as crime, 38
Auction, 90
Auctioneer, 504
Avoidance, power of, 130–32

b

Bailment
  bailee
    defined, 217
    disclaimer by, 220
    duties, 219–20
    involuntary, 221
  bailor
    defined, 217
  cloakroom, 217
  closed container rule, 218
  common carrier
    goods, 226
    passengers, 230–31
  defined, 217
  documents of title, 229–30
  innkeepers, 231
  parking lot, 218
  safe deposit box, 218
Bankruptcy
  Bankruptcy Reform Act of 1978, 123, 465–71
    administrative framework, 465–66
  claims, 467
  commencing the case
    involuntary, 466
    voluntary, 466
  courts, 465
  creditors' committee, 467
  defined, 123
  discharge
    in bankruptcy, 469
    of contracts, 174
    reaffirmation, 470
  estate
    content, 467
    distribution, 469
    exemptions, 468
  insolvency, 467
  law, source of, 465
  plans
    reorganization, 471
    unions and Chapter 11, 471
    wage earner, 470
  preference, 467
  receiver, 585, 589
  stay, 466
  trustee, 465
Banks
  banking process, 358–59
  certificate of deposit, 349–50
  charging a customer's account, 410–11
  customer, relationship with, 409
  customer's duty, 412–13
  death or incompetence of customer, 412
  indorsement for customer, 414

kinds, 358–59
  midnite deadline, 409, 422, 424
  stale checks, 412
  stop-payment order, 411–12
  subrogation, 411
  warranties in collection process, 384–87, 410–11
  wrongful dishonor of checks, 410
Bargain
  defined, 254
  theory in contracts, 47
  UCC 2-207, 258–61
Bargaining unit, 727
Battery, 44, 47
Bearer, 357
Beneficiary, 187, 806, 820, 824–25
Bid, 90
Bill of lading
  defined, 229
  form, 230
  negotiable, 229
  negotiation, 229, 230
Bill of sale, 208, 209
Blue-sky laws, 673
Boulwarism, 729
Boycott
  by group, 705
  secondary, 728
Breach of contract. *See* Contracts; Sales
Breach of the peace, 956
Bribery, commercial, 38
Broker, 504
Bulk sales transfer, 281–82
Burglary, 38
Business trust, 616
Buyer in the ordinary course of business, 267

c

C. & F., 275
C.I.F., 275
C.O.D., 266
Carriers
  common
    defined, 217
    liability
      for goods, 226–27
      for passengers, 230–31
    private, 226
Cartel, 858
Caveat emptor, 82, 323
Caveat venditor, 82, 323
Certified check, 413
Charter, corporate, 642
Chattel, 46
Chattel paper, 443
Check. *See* Commercial Paper
Civil Rights Act, 553
Civil trial process
  appeal, A6–7
  introduction to, A1
  pre-trial, A2–4
  trial, A5–6
Clayton Act, 705–7
Clean Air Act, 737–9
Clean Water Act, 739–40
Closed container rule, 218
Codicil, 808
Collateral. *See* Security
Collective bargaining, 557
Commercial Paper
  acceleration clauses, 365
  acceptor
    defined, 351
    primary party, 353
  accommodation party, 357
  alteration, 401–2
  banker's acceptance, 352
  banks. *See* Banks
  bearer, defined, 357
  to bearer, 357, 366, 373

cancellation, 395, 428
check
  bad, crime 37
  cashier's, 353
  certified, 413
  defined, 75, 348, 409
  deposit stamp, form, 349
  flow chart, 349
  form, 349
  formal contract, 75, 409
conversion of, 387
defenses
  personal, 403
  real, 398½01, 403–4
destroyed, 414
discharge, 402, 425
dishonor, 355, 425
  wrongful, 410
drafts, 348, 351
drawee
  as acceptor, 351
  defined, 348
drawer
  defined, 348
  secondary party, 355
extension clauses, 365–66
finality of payment or acceptance, 387
forgery, 381–83, 401–2
form required, 359–67
fraud, 400–401
guarantor, 357
holder, 356, 394
holder in due course
  concept, 347, 394
  defenses against
    personal, 402
    real, 398–401, 403–4
  defined, 347, 394
  Federal Trade Commission rule, 403–4
  requisites, 394–98
  rights, 398
  shelter concept, 379–80
impostor, 383
indorsement
  by bank for customer, 414
  blank, 375, 376
  defined, 356
  forged, 381–83, 397, 401–2
  by impostor, 383, 401
  indorsee, 356
  indorser, 355
  for lesser amount, 379
  qualified, 377, 378
  restrictive, 348n.7, 376–77, 414, 427
  special, 348n.7, 356, 375
  transfer without, 379
  without recourse, 377
letter of credit, 353, 354
lost, 414–15
maker
  defined, 350
  primary party, 353
material alteration, 401–2
negotiable instrument
  defined, 347
  kinds, 349–53
  requisites, 359–67
negotiation
  assignment compared, 347
  defined, 373
notice of
  claim or defense, 396–98
  dishonor, 424–25
  overdue or dishonor, 397–98
NOW accounts, 415
to order, 361–63, 366–67, 373
parties, 353–58
payable
  at a definite time, 364–65
  on demand, 364
  sum certain in money, 363–64

payee, 348, 356
presentment, 355, 422–24, 425
primary parties, 353, 355
promissory note, 75, 350, 351
protest, 424–25
reacquisition, 380, 429
secondary parties, 355
signed writing, 360–61
stolen, 414–15
stop-payment order, 353, 411
subrogation, 411
trade acceptance, 351
traveller's check, 353
unconditional promise or order, 361–63
value, 394–5
warranties
  by banks, in collection process, 384–87, 410–11
  on presentment, 386–87, 410–11
  on transfer, 384–87
Common carrier. *See* Carriers
Common law
  defined, 33
  supplements the UCC, 245
Community property, 213–14
Competition
  Clayton Act, 705
  mergers, 706–7, 645, 647
  pure, 704
  pure monopoly, 704
  stock acquisitions, 706
  tying arrangements, 617, 706, 851
Complaint, form, 21, 22
Composition (outside bankruptcy), 120
Compromise, 16
Computer crimes, 36
Concealment (in contracts), 109 (in insurance), 481
Condemnation, 767, 779
Conditions
  defined, 171, 274
  failure of, 283
  kinds, 172
  in lease, 786–89
Confession of judgment, effect on negotiability, 364
Confirmation (of offer)
  as acceptance, 99, 246, 261
  between merchants, 246
  defined, 246
  statute of frauds, 246–47
Confirmation hearing (in bankruptcy), 471
Confusion, 210
Congress of Industrial Organizations, 725
Consent (in torts), 47
Consignee, 228
Consignment, 227
Consignor, 227
Consolidation (in corporations), 646, 647
Conspiracy, 34
Constitutional law
  Amendments, 27
  Bill of Rights, 27
  executive branch, 26
  judicial branch, 27
  legislative branch, 26
Consumer Credit Protection Act, 333
Consumer goods, 442
Consumer Law
  caveat emptor, 323
  consumer, 309
    credit transactions, 333
    products, 330
  introduction, 309
  privity rule, 316–17
  product safety, 330
  products liability
    defenses, 328
    introduction, 323
    privity, 316–17, 323

res ipsa loquitur, 325
strict liability, 52, 326–28
torts
  basis for liability, 324
  negligence, 324–26
  strict liability, 52, 326–28
unconscionable clause or contract, 315–16
warranties, 310–14
protection legislation, 82, 314, 333–34
Consumer Product Safety Act, 330
Continuation statement, 961
Contracts
  acceptance. *See* Acceptance
  accord and satisfaction, 120, 173
  account stated, 120, 173
  adhesion contract, 853
  agreement, 73
  alteration, material, 174
  assignment, 182, 183–85, 186
  auctions, 90
  avoidance, 130, 131–2
  bids, 90
  bilateral, 77
  breach
    anticipatory, 169
    defined, 167
    nonperformance, 169
    remedies
      damages
        defined, 192
        kinds, 192–3
        mitigation, 193
      defined, 191
      election, 194
      restitution, 194
      specific performance, 194
  of sales contract, *See* Sales
  cancellation, 176
  capacity to make, 129
  certainty of terms, 89–90
  classification, 80–82
  commerical frustration, 63, 171
  concealment, 109
  concept, 73–82
  conditions, 171–2
  confirmation. *See* Confirmation
  consideration
    adequacy, 118
    bargain theory, 117
    compositions (outside bankruptcy), 120
    defined, 116
    detriment, 116–17
    disputed claim, 120
    liquidated debt, 120
    moral obligation, 122
    past, 119
    reaffirmation (bankruptcy), 470
    UCC, 123
    unliquidated debt, 120
  cost-plus, 90
  cover, 169
  damages, *See* Damages
  defined, 74
  delegation, 183, 185
  discharge
    defined, 95, 167
    methods, 173–74, 175
  discrimination, 142–43, 148n.5
  disputed claim, 120
  divisible, 146
  duress, 109–10
  elements, 76
  enforceable, 152
  executed, 81
  executory, 101, 161
  formal, 75
  formation, 87–103
  fraud, 108, 152
  goods advertised as specials, 89

illegality, 141–47
implied, 78
impossibility of performance, 171
insanity, 129, 132
insolvency, 120
intention test, 90
joint, 78, 181
live-in agreements, 80
mail box rule, 257n.5
minors, 129, 131, 132, 133–34
misrepresentation, 108, 134
mistake, 106–7
mutual assent, 105
necessaries, 132–3
novation, 188–9
offer
  advertisement, 89
  bid, 90
  communication, 91
  counteroffer, 92, 93
  defined, 88
  duration, 91–92
  expiration, 91
  firm offer, 93–94
  irrevocable, 93–94
  rejection, 92
  revocation, 92
  UCC, 94, 256–61
offeree, 88
offeror, 88
option, 93
parol evidence rule, 156–57
parties, 181
performance, 161, 167–71, 282–84
personal satisfaction, 169
privity of, 181
promise, 77–79
promissory estoppel, 121–22
quantum meruit, 78
quasi contact, 78, 160
ratification, 133
reformation, 106, 194
rescission, 105, 173
restraint of trade, 144–45
sale of goods, compared, 256–57
several, 78
simple, 76, 181
specific performance, 159, 194
statute of frauds, 152–61
statute of limitations, 122, 174
third party beneficiaries, 187–88, 190
ticket terms, 220
unconscionable, 75, 82, 111
undue influence, 110
unenforceable, 81
unilateral, 77
voidable, 81, 129
Conversion, 46, 212, 267, 387
Copyright, 310, 856
Corporations
  articles of incorporation, 641–42
  authority, 685
  bona fide purchaser, 670–71
  business judgment rule, 688
  bylaws, 642
  certificated securities, 670
  certificate of stock, 664
  charter, 642
  classification, 628–32
  close, 630
  consolidation, 646, 647
  creation, 640–43
  de facto, 642–43
  defined, 627
  de jure, 642
  derivative suit, 672
  directors
    authority, 686
    liability, 687–89
    meetings, 687

Index   I 3

dissolution, 644
dividends, 664, 667–68
domestic, 629
by estoppel, 643
foreign corporation
   defined, 629
   doing business, 629, 632
Foreign Corrupt Practices Act, 678–79
historical background, 627–28
incorporator, 641
Insider Trading Sanctions Act of 1984, 677
insider transactions, 677
inspection of corporate books, 668–69
legal entity
   concept, 627, 632
   disregard of, 632–33
merger, 645, 647
nature, 627
nonprofit, 632
novation, 640
officers, 641–42, 689–90
powers, 653–56
pre-emptive rights, 670
private, 628–29
professional, 630–31
promoter, 640
proxy, 666, 668
public, 628
registered agent, 642
securities regulations, 674–77
shareholder (stockholder)
   defined, 627
   liabilities, 673
   meetings, 685–86
   remedies against directors, 671
   rights, 665–71
share of stock (stock)
   classes, 663–64
   defined, 627
   transfer
      bona fide purchaser, 670–71
      restrictions, 671
      statute of frauds, 671
subchapter (S), 630
subsidiary, 633–34, 850
termination, 644–45
ultra vires acts, 656–57
uncertificated securities, 670
watered stock, 673
Counterclaim, 21, A2
Counteroffer, 93
Course of dealing, 96, 157, 261
Course of performance, 28, 261
Courts
   administrative tribunals distinguished, 20
   criminal, 15
   defined, 17
   federal, 19–20
   state, 17–19
Covenant. *See* Real Property
Cover, 169, 294
Creditor benificiary, 187
Crime
   business crimes, 35–38
   categories, 33
   computer, 36
   by corporations, 35
   defenses, 34–35
   defined, 32
   promise to commit, 140
   requisites, 33–34
Crops, 243
Cure, 264, 277
Cy pres doctrine, 830

d

Damage, 192, 290, 295, 468–71
Damages
   defined, 43, 192, 45
   kinds, 192–93
   mitigation, 193
Decedents' estates. *See* Wills
Deceit (as a tort), 46, 193
Deed. *See* Real Property
De facto corporation, 642–43
Defamation, 54
Defendant, 21, A2
De jure corporation, 642
Delegation
   of agent's authority, 520–21
   of contract duties, 183, 185
   defined, 183
Deposition, A3
Deposit rule, 98
Detriment, 116–17
Disaffirmance, 130–32
Discharge, 95, 167, 173–74, 175
Disclaimer, 109, 220
Discrimination, 142, 148n.5, 552–56, 708
Distributor, 849
Dividend, 664, 667–68
Documents of title, 229–30, 443, 848
Domicile, 803
Duress, 35, 109–10, 399

e

Easement
   defined, 765
   kinds, 765–66
Embezzlement, 37
Eminent domain, 779
Employment
   at will, 552
   child labor, 557
   discrimination, 142, 552–56
   employee, defined, 552
   employer, defined, 552
   employer use of detection devices, 563–64
   ERISA, 563
   fair labor standards, 556–57
   Federal Insurance Contributions Act, 561–62
   Federal Unemployment Tax Act, 563
   health and safety laws, 559–60
   medicare, 563
   social security, 561
   unemployment insurance, 563
   unions and collective bargaining, 557
   women's rights, 564–65
   workmen's compensation laws, 557–59
Endangered Species Act, 742–43
Environmental Law
   Clean Air Act, 737–39
   Clean Water Act, 739–40
   ecosphere, 735
   Endangered Species Act, 742–43
   environment, 735
   Environmental Protection Agency
      powers, 739
      purpose, 735
   land use, 743–45
   National Environmental Policy Act
      courts and, 737
      environmental impact statements, 736–37
      pesticide regulation, 742
      Resource Conservation and Recovery Act, 741
   Superfund, 742
   Toxic Substances Control Act, 740–41
   zoning, 744–45, 766–67

Equal Credit Opportunity Act, 334
Equal Employment Opportunity Act, 552–55
Equipment, 442, 454
Escheat, 209, 779
Estate
   (in bankruptcy) *See* Bankruptcy
   (in realty) *See* Real Property
Estoppel, 212, 267
Ethics
   Agency and Employment, 571–74
   Business Organizations, 695–99
   Commercial Paper, 433–36
   Concepts, 58–69
   Contracts, 99–202
   Government Regulation of Business, 750–54
   International Marketplace, 871–75
   Personal Property and Bailments, 234–37
   Real Property, 795–99
   Sales and Consumer Law, 339–42
   Secured Transactions, Insurance and Bankruptcy, 494–97
   Will and Decedents' Estates, Trust, 839–42
European Economic Community, 859
Evidence, 24, 718
Exculpatory clause, 144, 146, 788

f

F.A.S., 272, 275
F.O.B., 266, 274, 275
Factor, 504
Fair Credit Reporting Act, 46, 334
Fair Labor Standards Act, 556–57
False imprisonment, 45
Farm products, 442
Federal Trade Commission, 403–4, 632, 707, 716–17
Fee simple absolute, 764
Felony, 33
Fiduciary, 110, 502, 608
Financing statement. *See* Security
Finder, 221
Firm offer, 93–94, 257
Fixture
   defined, 207
   filing, 454
   in leases, 761
   tests, 207–8
   trade, 761
Floating lien, 443–44
Foreclosure, 777
Foreign Corrupt Practices Act, 678–79, 849
Forgery, 37, 381–83, 401–2
Franchising, 616–18
Fraud, 108, 400–401

g

Garnishment, 466
Genuineness of assent, 105, 157
Gift, 210–11, 242
Good faith, 244, 395–96
   purchaser, 266
Goods
   conforming, 278–79
   consumer, 442
   defined, 241
   existing and identified, 263, 265
   fungible, 329
   future, 243, 266
   insurable interest in, 263
Government regulation of business
   administrative law, 713–21
   antitrust law, 702–12
   environmental law, 734–49
   labor law, 723–33
Guarantor
   commercial paper, 359
   suretyship, 458
Guaranty. *See* Suretyship

h

Hazardous wastes, 741
Health and Safety Laws, 559–60
Heir, 762, 810
Holder, 356, 394
Holder in due course. *See* Commercial Paper
Hot cargo agreement, 729

i

Illegality, 141–47
Impossibility, 80, 171
Impostor, 383
Indemnity, 427, 523, 605
Independent contractor, 503, 534–35
Indorsee, 356
Indorsement. *See* Commercial Paper
Indorser, 356
Infant. *See* Minors
Injunction, 191, 726, 730
Injury, 192, 309
Innkeeper, 231
Insanity, 34, 129, 132, 398–99
Insolvency
    bankruptcy, 467
    contracts, 120
    UCC, 280, 356
Instrument, 347, 443
Insurance
    automobile, 477, 489–94
    concealment, 481
    defined, 478
    fire, 488
    homeowner's, 488
    insurable interest, 263, 479–80
    insured, 478
    insurer, 478
    life
        beneficiaries, 487
        conditional receipt, 486
        incontestability, 487
        suicide, 487
        types, 486
    no-fault, 490–91
    representations, 481
    social security, 561
    trends, 491
    types, 476–78
    warranties, 481
Interest, legal rate, 142
International business law, *See* Transnational Business
Inventory, 442, 455
Invitee, 768

j

Joint liability, 78
Joint tenancy, 212–13, 763
Joint venture, 615–16, 850
Judgment, 24, 174
Jury, 24, A4
Jus tertii, 427

l

Labor Law
    AFL-CIO, 725
    American Federation of Labor, 725
    bargaining unit, 727
    collective bargaining, 557, 727
    criminal conspiracy, 725
    featherbedding, 728
    government employees, 729–30
    hot cargo agreement, 729
    industrial unions, 725
    injunction, 726
    Landrum-Griffin Act, 727–28, 729
    National Labor Relations Board, 727–28
    Norris-La Guardia Act, 726
    secondary boycott, 728
    strikes, 730
    Taft-Hartley Act, 727–29
    unfair labor practices
        by employers, 727
        by unions, 728
    unions, 725–26
    Wagner Act, 726
Laissez-faire doctrine
    defined, 703
Landlord-tenant relationship, 784
Landrum-Griffin Act, 729
Larceny, 37
Law
    administrative, 25
    case, 26, 847
    common, 725, 847
    constitutional, 26–27
    criminal, 31–41
    defined, 9
    importance, 5–6
    merchant, 617
    natural, 5
    as a norm, 9
    statutory, 25
Lease
    defined, 784
    real property. *See* Real Property
    space, 217
Legacy, 807
Legal system
    defined, 9
    federal, 19–20
    kinds, 5
    state, 17–19
Letter of credit, 353, 354, 848
License,
    export, 851
    realty, 765
    revenue and regulatory, 141
Lien
    artisan's 456
    bailee's, 456
    defined, 765
    floating, 443–44
    mechanic's, 765, 778
Limited partnership, 614–15
Liquidated
    damages, 193, 301, 789
    debt, 120
Lock-out, 730
Locus in quo, 221
Lost personal property, 221

m

Magnuson-Moss Warranty—Trade Commission Improvement Act, 314
Mail box rule, 257n.5
Malicious prosecution, 46
Marshaling of assets, 590
Master and servant
    relationship, 502–3, 532
    tort liability, 532
Material alteration, 259, 401–2, 412
Mediation, 16
Medicare, 477, 563
Mens rea, 34
Merchant, 94, 244, 259, 309
Merger
    antitrust, 706–7
    corporations, 645, 647
Minors
    contracts, 129, 131–34
    crime, 35
    partners, 583
Misdemeanor, 33
Misfeasance, 532
Mislaid personal property, 221
Misrepresentation, 108, 134
Mistake, 106–7, 285
Monopoly, 704
Mortgage. *See* Real Property

n

National Environmental Policy Act, 737
National Labor Relations Board, 727–28
Necessaries, 132–3
Negligence
    conduct, 48–52
    contractual limitation of liability for, 146
    defenses, 50–52
    products liability, 53, 324–28
    tort, 48–49
Nonfeasance, 532
Norm, 7, 9
Norris-LaGuardia Act, 557, 726
Notice
    agency, 546–47
    constructive, 790–91
    UC, 396–97
Novation, 188–89, 640
NOW account, 415
Nuisance, 46, 768

o

Obligee, 77
Obligor, 77
Occupational Safety and Health Act, 559–60
Offer, 88–95
Option
    defined, 93
    firm offer distinguished, 94, 257
Ownership of property, kinds, 212–14

p

Paralegal, 21
Parol evidence rule
    contracts, 156–57
    defined, 156, 248
    UCC, 248
Partition, 213
Partnerships
    agreement form, 582
    Articles, 581
    assets
        contributions of partners, 604
        property, 584
    business for profit, 583
    carrying on, 583
    charging order, 584
    co-owners, 583
    creation, 580–84
    creditors, 584, 589–90
    defined, 579
    dissolution
        causes, 587
        defined, 586
        notice of, 588
    distribution of assets, 589–90
    by estoppel, 584
    historical background, 579
    liability
        contracts, 606
        torts, 607
    limited, 614–15
    majority voting, 599
    management, 598, 604
    marshaling of assets, 590
    nature, 579
    nontrading, 580

partners
   agents, 244, 596
   apparent authority, 585, 598
   authority
      express, 596
      implied, 596
      limitation of, 597
   charging order, 584
   duties, 668–9
   fiduciary, 608
   indemnity, right of, 605
   kinds, 580
   liability
      contracts, 606
      torts, 607
   persons, 583
   reimbursement right of, 605
   rights, 604, 606
   property
      defined, 579, 584
      tenancy in partnership, 585
      title, 585
      transfer, 585
   termination, 586
   trading, 580
   winding up, 589–90
Passenger, 230–31
Past debt, 267, 394
Patent, 310, 851, 856
Payee, 348, 356
Pension plans, 563
Perfection of security interest. *See* Security
Perjury, 642
Perpetuities, rule against, 824
Personal representative, 810–11
Plaintiff, 21, A2
Pleadings, 21, 22, A3
Pledge
   defined, 429, 445, 665
   as security, 447
   of stock, 665
Police power, 767
Pollution
   air, 737–38
   water, 739–40
Power of attorney, 505–8
Pre-emptive right, 670
Preference (in bankruptcy), 467
Prescription (realty), 780
Price discrimination, 708
Price fixing, 709
Privacy, invasion of, 45
Privilege, 47
Privity, 10, 316–17
Probate, 809
Products liability
   consumer protection legislation. *See* Consumer Law
   defenses, 328
   introduction, 309, 328
   liability without causation, 329
   negligence, 324–26
   privity, 316–17, 323
   res ipsa loquitor, 325
   responsibility for, 6, 53
   statute of limitations, 317
   strict liability, 326–28
   tort liability, 324
   unconscionable contract or clause, 315
   warranties, 310–14
Promissory estoppel, 121–22
Promoter, 640
Property
   after-acquired, 443
   community, 213–14
   defined, 207
   interest, 262
   ownership, kinds, 212–14

personal
   abandoned, 221
   defined, 207
   lost, 221
   mislaid, 221
   real. *See* Real Property
Protest (commercial paper), 424–25
Proximate cause, 50, 328
Proxy, 666, 677
Public Accountant, 534–35
Public policy, 140
Pure competition, 704
Pure monopoly, 704

q

Quorum, 686

r

Ratification, 133, 509–10
Reaffirmation (in bankruptcy), 470
Real Property
   adverse possession, 779
   air space, right to, 759
   annexation, 760
   attractive nuisance, 768
   condemnation, 767, 779
   conveyance, 775
   co-ownership
      community property, 213, 763
      joint tenancy, 212, 763
      severalty, distinguished, 762
      tenancy by entirety, 213, 763
      tenancy in common, 213, 762
   covenants, 768
   deeding process, 773–76
   defined, 760
   dominant tenement, 766
   easement, 65–66
   emblement, 788
   eminent domain, 779
   encumbrance, 775
   estates
      freehold, 764, 784
      nonfreehold, 764, 784
   eviction, 786, 787, 790
   financing, 776
   fixture, 761
   foreclosure, 777
   grantor, 763, 775
   habendum, 773
   invitee, 768
   land sale contract, 777–78
   lateral support, 760
   lease
      assignment, 789
      covenants, 786–89
      defined, 784
      eviction, 786, 787, 790
      leasehold estates, 784, 785–86
      statute of frauds, 785
      subletting, 789
      termination, 790–91
      transfer of lessor's interest, 789–90
   leasehold estates, 784, 786–89
   license, 765
   licensee, 768
   liquidated damages, 789
   mineral rights, 759
   mortgage, 777
   prescription, 780
   quitclaim deed, 775–76
   recording realty documents, 778
   redemption, 777
   remainder, 764
   renting, 785–89
   reversion, 764

   a "taking" of, 766–67, 779
   tenant (lessee)
      defined, 784
      duties, 787
      holdover, 786
   transfer of ownership
      by deed, 773–76
      nonsale, 778–80
      trust deed, 777
   Uniform Residential Landlord-Tenant Act, 791
   water rights, 760
   zoning, 766–67
Recognizance, 75
Reformation, 106, 194
Reimbursement, 460, 523, 605
Remainder, 764
Repudiation, anticipatory, 192
Res ipsa loquitur, 49, 325
Respondeat superior, 525, 533
Restitution, 134, 194, 294
Restraint of trade, 144–45, 703, 704
Reversion, 764
Revolving charge account, 142n.1
Right to work, 728
Robbery, 38
Robinson Patman Act, 708
Roman law, 627

s

Safe deposit box, 218
Sales (of goods)
   acceptance, 256, 258, 261, 279, 280
      revocation of, 292
   adequate assurance of performance
      buyer's right to, 280, 290
      explained, 280
      seller's right to, 298
   bargain, 254, 259
   breach by buyer
      seller's remedies
         adequate assurance of buyer's performance, 280, 298
         cash, obtain on buyer's insolvency, 280, 298
         damages, 300
         limitations, 301–2
         monetary recovery, 299
         recover the goods, 301
         resale, 300
         stop goods in transit, 298–99
         withhold the goods, 298
   breach by seller
      buyer's remedies
         accept the goods, 292, 297
         adequate assurance of seller's performance, 290
         cover, 294
         damages, 295–97
         limitations, 301–2
         monetary recovery, 293, 295–97
         notice to seller, 293
         recover the goods, 297
         reject the goods, 290–91
         restitution, 293–94
         revoke the acceptance, 292
   bulk sales transfer, 281–82
   buyer in ordinary course of business, 267
   C. & F., 275
   C.I.F., 275
   C.O.D., 266
   casualty to identified goods, 283
   caveat emptor, 310, 323
   commercial unit, 277, 290
   confirmation of offer, 246, 258, 261
   consideration, 257
   consumer law. *See* Consumer Law
   contract for, 256–58

course of dealing, 261
course of performance, 261
cover, 294
cure, 264, 277
delivery, 266, 275, 283
documentary draft, 276
entrusting goods to merchant dealer, 267
estoppel, 267
F.A.S., 274, 275
F.O.B., 266, 274, 275
failure
    manner of delivery, 283
    means or manner of payment, 283
    presupposed conditions, 283–84
firm offer, 257
by foreign agent, 848
forms, battle of, 258–61
good faith, 244, 266
goods. *See* Goods
impracticability of performance, 283–84
insolvency, 280, 298, 301
inspection of buyer, 279
installment contract, 278
insurable interest, 263
interpretation of contract
    course of dealing and performance, 261
    modification, 262
    parol evidence rule, 427–28
    usage of trade, 261
limitations on relief for breach, 301–2
liquidated damages, 301–2
mail box rule, 257
merchant, 244
offer, 256
option, 257
parol evidence rule, 247–48
performance
    by buyer, 279–80, 283–84
    excused, 282–83
    by seller, 274–79
products liability. *See* Products liability
property interest, 262
risk of loss, 263–64, 284
sale, 242
sale on approval, 266
sale or return, 266
specific performance, 297
statute of frauds, 245–47
statute of limitations on breach, 302
stoppage in transit, 298–99
tender, 274, 277, 279
transferee/transferor rule
    defined, 266
    entrusting goods to merchant, 266
    estoppel, 266
    voidable title transfer, 266
transfer of title to goods, 265–67
unconscionable clause or contract, 242, 315–16
usage of trade, 261
value, 267
voidable title, 267
Scope of employment, 533
Secondary boycott, 728
Secured party. *See* Security
Secured transactions, 441
Securities, 673, 674–77
Securities and Exchange Commission, 675, 677
Security
    account, 442
    after-acquired property, 443, 454
    agreement, 301, 444
    assignment, 442
    buyer in ordinary course of business, 455
    chattel paper, 443
    collateral
        defined, 441
        movement, 448
        release of, 429

        repossession by seller on debtor's default, 447, 456–57
        secured party's right to retain, 456
        types, 442–44
    conditional sale, 443
    defined, 441
    filing
        financing statement, 445, 453
        fixture, 454
        place, 445
    financing statement
        defined, 445
        filing, 445–47
        form, 446
    floating lien, 443
    general intangibles, 443
    goods
        consumer goods, 442
        defined, 442
        equipment, 442
        farm products, 442
        inventory, 442
    interest
        attachment to collateral, 445
        creation, 444
        defined, 441
        enforcement, 453
        in fixtures, 454
        perfection, 445–48, 453–54
        in personal property, 207–8
        priorities, 453–54
        purchase money, 441, 447, 973
    pledge, 445, 447
    secured party
        defined, 441
        rights on debtor's default, 456–57
    secured transaction, 441
    value, 445
Servant, 502–3, 532–33
Shareholder (stockholder). *See* Corporations
Shelter concept, 379–80
Sherman Antitrust Act, 704
Social Security, 561
Solar zoning, 744–45
Stare decisis, 26
Statute of frauds, 152–61, 245–47, 458–59
Statute of limitations, 122, 174, 302, 317, 501
Stop-payment order, 353, 411
Strict liability, 53, 326–28
Sublet, 789
Subpoena, 717
Subrogation, 260, 411, 482
Summons, 21, 23, A2
Suretyship
    contract, 459
    defined, 457
    guaranty
        absolute, 458
        of collection, 357, 460
        conditional, 458
    principal (debtor), 458
    statute of frauds, 458–59
    surety
        bond, 458
        co-surety, 459, 460
        defenses to liability, 459–60
        defined, 129, 458
        guarantor, 458
        rights
            contribution, 460
            exoneration, 460
            reimbursement, 460
            subrogation, 260
        strict, 459
Survivorship, right of, 763

t

Taft-Hartley Act, 727–29
Tenancy, 764
Tender, 168, 274, 275–76, 279
Testator (testatrix), 803
Third party beneficiary contracts, 187–88, 190
Tort
    crime distinguished, 32
    defined, 32
    intentional, 44–48
    negligence, 48–52, 325
    products liability, 53, 324
    strict liability, 52, 326–28
Toxic Substances Act, 740–41
Trade acceptance, 351
Trade fixture, 761
Trademark, 617
Trade secrets, 37
Trade usage, 423
Transnational Business
    anti-boycott regulations, 847n.4
    antitrust
        cartel, 858
        European Common Market, 859
        export trade certificate of review, 859
        Export Trading Company Act of 1982, 858
        when inapplicable to export trade, 859
        tying arrangements, 851, 865–67
        United States, 703–9, 856–57
    contracts
        adhesion, 853
        arbitration clause, 855
        choice-of-forum clause, 852–54
        choice-of-law clause, 852–53
        currency clause, 852
        force majeune, 852
        language, 852
    Domestic International Sales Corporation, 847n.5
    effect and single enterprise theories, 862
    European Common Market
        antitrust law, 859
        Article 85, 860–61
        Article 86, 861
        Commission of the European Communities, 859–60
        European Court of Justice, 860
        negative clearance, 862
        Treaty of Rome, 859
    expropriation, foreign, 856
    Federal Trade Commission
        when inapplicable to export trade, 859
    gift giving and social courtesies, 863
    International Convention for the Protection of Industrial Property, 856
    Overseas Private Investment Corporation, 856
    sales
        direct export, 848
        document of title, 848
        foreign agent, 848
        Foreign Corrupt Practices Act, 678–79, 849
        foreign distributor, 849
        independent contractor, 849
        joint venture, 850
        letter of credit, 848
        turn-key operation, 850
    technology
        copyright, 856
        Export Administration Act, 851
        export license, 851
        export regulations, 851
        patents, 851, 856
Traveller's check, 853
Treason, 33
Treasure trove, 222

Trespass, 46, 768
Trial. *See* Civil trial process
Trust, 154, 249, 352, 820
Trust deed, 777
Trusts
  beneficiary
    charitable trust, 829–31
    express trust, 820, 824–25
  cestui que trust, 824
  charitable trust, 829–31
    beneficiary, 830
    creation, 821, 830
    cy pres, 830
    defined, 829
    purposes, 829–30
  constructive trust, 832
  cy pres, 830
  defined, 820
  distinguished, 820
  expres trust
    acceptance by beneficiary/trustee, 824
    administration, 825
    beneficiary, 820, 824
    breach of trust, 828
    creation, 821
    defined, 821
    illegality, 823
    manifestation of intent, form of, 822–23
    modification, 828–29
    notice to beneficiary/trustee, 824
    property, transfer of, 824
    purposes, 823
    settlor, 249, 821–23
    spendthrift trust, 829
    statute of frauds, 823
    termination, 829
    trustee
      defined, 820
      duties, 825–27
      exculpatory clause, 828
      liability, 828
      powers, 827–28
      qualifications, 824
    trust property, 820, 824
  property (in trusts), 820
  resulting trust, 831–32
  rule against perpetuities, 824–25
  settlor, 821–23
  testamentary trust
    defined, 823
    requisites, 823
  trust property
    allocation to principal/income, 826–27
    defined, 820
    transfer to create a trust, 824
    wasting, 826

Truth-In-Lending Act, 333
Tying arrangements
  Clayton Act, 705–7
  defined, 706, 851, 865
  in franchising, 617
  in transnational business, 851, 865

u

Ultra vires, 656–57
Unconscionable, 75, 82, 242, 315
Undue influence, 110
Unemployment insurance, 563
Unfair labor practices, 727, 728
Uniform Probate Code, 803
Uninsured motorist, 490
Unions, 725–26
Unliquidated debt, 120
Usage of trade, 157, 261, 423
Usury, 142, 333, 399

v

Value
  contract law, 116–17, 394–95
  UCC, 267
Verdict, 24

w

Wage-hour law, 556–57
Wages, 557
Wagner Act, 726
Warehouseman, 228
Warehouse receipt, 229, 265
Warranty, 184, 481, 530
Watered stock, 673
Wills and Decedents' Estates
  administration
    administrator (administratrix), 810
    executor (executrix), 810
    personal representative, 810–11
  beneficiary
    attesting witness, 806, 807
    defined, 807
    devisee, 807
    legatee, 807
    renunciation, 807
    simultaneous death, 807
  codicil, 808
  contest, 809
  decedent, 803, 807, 809
  devise, 807
  domicile, 803
  executor (executrix), 153, 810
  fraud, 805
  gift causa mortis, 211
  heir, 810
  holographic, 806
  incorporation by reference, 806, 823
  intestacy, 810
  legacy, 807
  legatee, 807
  nuncupative, 806
  per capita, 810
  personal representative, 810–11
  per stirpes, 810
  probate, 809
  requisites
    attestation, 806
    capacity, 804
    intent, 804–5
    law applicable, 803
    signature, 806
    writing, 806
  revocation
    act of the testator, 807–8
    act to the instrument, 808
    codicil, 808
    divorce, annulment, 809
    later-born child, 809
    marriage, 809
    by operation of law, 808–9
    taxes, 812
  testamentary trust, 803, 807
  testate, 809
  testator (testatrix), 803
  undue influence, 804–5
  Uniform Probate Code, 803
  will, defined, 803
Women's rights, 564–65
Workmen's compensation, 53, 557–59
Writ
  certiorari, 20
  of execution, 227
  of garnishment, 446
Wrong, 43–44

y

Yellow dog contract, 726

z

Zoning
  ordinance, 766–67
  solar, 744–45